Encyclopedia of
AMERICAN
POLITICAL
HISTORY

Encyclopedia of
AMERICAN POLITICAL HISTORY

*Studies of the Principal
Movements and Ideas*

Jack P. Greene, *EDITOR*
The Johns Hopkins University

Volume I

CHARLES SCRIBNER'S SONS · NEW YORK

Library of Congress Cataloging in Publication Data

Main entry under title:

Encyclopedia of American political history.

Bibliography: p.
Includes index.
Contents: [1]. Studies of the principal movements and ideas.
1. United States—Politics and government—Dictionaries.   2. Political
science—United States—History—Dictionaries.   I. Greene, Jack P.
E183.E5   1984   320.973'03'21   84–1355
ISBN 0–684–17003–5   (SET)

Printed in the United States of America

The paper in this book meets the guidelines for permanence and
durability of the Committee on Production Guidelines for Book Longevity
of the Council on Library Resources.

Editorial Staff

Advisory Board

PREFACE

UNTIL a comparatively short time ago, the history of the United States had been told primarily in terms of its political life. The colonies established by Great Britain on the North American continent, during the years following the founding of Virginia in 1607, had by the mid-eighteenth century evolved into a series of discrete corporate entities, each with its own identity and history. All of the colonies shared a British heritage, and groups of contiguous colonies exhibited common patterns of socioeconomic life. But there was no common "American" culture at the time they came together to declare their independence from Britain and to form a new political nation. In contrast to the situation in most of the new nation-states that took shape in the early modern era, in the United States a common culture followed, rather than preceded, the creation of the nation. Brought together and propelled into nationhood by political exigencies, Americans only gradually developed a common national culture in the century following the American Revolution.

If the first shared experience of the American people was thus political, the public life of the nation has never ceased to be at the center of American national culture and, as a consequence, of American national history as well. But with the broadening of historical studies during the twentieth century and especially since World War II, political history has had to share the attention of historians along with intellectual, cultural, economic, and social history. Informed by insights and findings from these and other areas and operating within a much broader conception of the subject, political history has continued to exert a powerful hold upon the imaginations and loyalties of the American historical community, and it remains at the core of the structure of the history of the United States.

The *Encyclopedia of American Political History* is a reference work intended to provide, to a general audience of students and lay readers, authoritative and up-to-date articles on those topics deemed most important by the editor and the editorial board. Early on, the editors decided to organize these books around a series of articles of sufficient length to provide the reader with fairly detailed accounts of each subject, a decision that meant that the *Encyclopedia* would necessarily be selective. Some of the articles cover important political events such as the American Revolution and the New Deal. A few treat selected documents of major significance, including the Declaration of Independence, *The Federalist,* and the Constitution. But most of them treat major issues, themes, institutions, processes, and developments as they have been manifest throughout the whole of United States history, from before the decision for independence to the present.

The authors of these ninety articles are experts. They represent a broad range of ideological positions and historical points of view. The editors made no effort to impose a common approach upon them. Instead, they encouraged each author to take a strong personal line of interpretation.

In addition to the authors of the articles, many people offered essential help in the preparation of these volumes. Members of the editorial board—Joyce

PREFACE

Appleby of the University of California at Los Angeles, William W. Freehling of The Johns Hopkins University, Thomas C. Holt of the University of Michigan, Robert Kelley of the University of California at Santa Barbara, and James Patterson of Brown University—shared the responsibility for selecting topics and authors. Marc L. Harris of Louisiana State University provided valuable advice on the designation of topics, while several of my colleagues in American history at Johns Hopkins, including Louis Galambos, John Higham, and Ronald Walters, were extremely helpful in nominating authors. At Scribners, David William Voorhees was Managing Editor during the earliest stages of the preparation of the *Encyclopedia,* while Steven A. Sayre, acting in the same capacity, performed the difficult task of bringing the work to fruition. I am especially grateful to both of these men as well as to all of the other members of the editorial staff at Scribners who worked so diligently and efficiently and with such enormous competence on this project.

Jack P. Greene

CONTENTS

CONTENTS

CONTENTS

CONTENTS

CONTENTS

Encyclopedia of
AMERICAN
POLITICAL
HISTORY

HISTORIOGRAPHY OF
AMERICAN POLITICAL HISTORY

Richard J. Jensen

HISTORIOGRAPHY is the study of how historians deal with the past. The historiography of American politics could be presented in terms of the major findings regarding important aspects of political history. But the main concern here will be to outline and explain the conceptual formulations upon which historians have grounded their work. The methods and the philosophical assumptions that historians have used have not always been explicit in their work. But these methods and assumptions have, just the same, determined how they select what seems to have been important and how they interpret the enormous mass of information available on American politics. If the categories used here seem too vague, it must be recognized that history is an eclectic discipline, with scholars borrowing widely from other disciplines and often mixing together disparate approaches within a single work. Yet some classification and analysis of historiography is essential, since while historians generally agree on the facts—the names, dates, places, and events—they rarely agree on the interpretations. In contrast to most of the social sciences, historians rarely assemble themselves into schools. And finally, the most remarkable tendency in scholarship—and not in history alone—over the last two decades has been a relentless specialization, caused by the proliferation of graduate dissertations and the steady discovery of new sources and new methods. While a college professor in the 1940's sought to identify himself as a "historian," by the 1950's "American historian" was the designation; and today a scholar might identify himself or herself as a specialist on political parties in the 1830's or on nineteenth-century urban social structure. The proliferation of new journals, conferences, and even separate scholarly organizations underscores this trend, causing despair among those few who try to survey all of American history, and emphasizing the need for methodological categorization.

THE MORALISTIC STORYTELLERS

Laymen have always been attracted to history, in such forms as novels, films, monuments, museums, pageants, and restorations. People like a good story—with plot, action, a sense of reliving great events (or at least peeking behind the curtains to see great people in undress), and, to satisfy the critical spirit, some sense of verisimilitude. If it happened here, in this building, town, state, or nation, and if it happened to people like ourselves, then the historical event takes on added meaning by becoming, in some small way, a part of our identity. But most scholarly historiography in recent decades has dropped all pretense at popular appeal. Historians write for other scholars or for a captive student audience, and so the priorities of what should go into quality work are seldom likely to produce a best-seller. As the academic job market dried up in the 1970's, hundreds of professionally trained scholars sought employment with historical societies and other agencies oriented primarily toward the general public. They might discover that when the town wanted a celebration of some historic event, it called for an affirmation of long-held favorable beliefs that might well be at variance with the scholar's understanding of what really happened. Perhaps it is just as well that society no longer erects statues of great leaders.

The celebratory instinct of Americans, abetted by the personal or family pride of powerful men and their friends, has produced a network of presidential libraries memorializing Hoover through Carter. (The Nixon library project remains enmeshed in controversy because of the honor it might bestow on a widely discredited figure.) Built by private funds but operated by the National Archives and Records Service, the libraries combine museums that show off artifacts and tell uplifting stories with archival holdings of personal papers, official records, and oral history transcripts that provide vast opportunities for scholarly research. Likewise, the rapid growth of state and local historical societies and archives since the 1960's has created troves of historical documents that significantly facilitate scholarly research.

The distance between the public and the scholar was much less a century ago than it is now. Throughout the nineteenth century and well into the twentieth, nonacademic historians enjoyed large audiences for work that combined moralism and storytelling with scholarship that was abreast of the standards of the day. George Bancroft, John Fiske, James Ford Rhodes, Albert J. Beveridge, Claude Bowers, Carl Sandburg, Matthew Josephson, and Herbert Agar exemplified this tradition before World War II. It survives in political historiography chiefly in biographies, such as those of Robert A. Caro, though James MacGregor Burns and Page Smith are two academics now trying to replicate the old model of large-scale moralistic narrative.

The popular appeal of the old school stemmed partly from a gracious literary style, of course, for all were master storytellers with an eye for the revealing incident and an ear for the telling anecdote. Even more important were their willingness and eagerness to draw the lessons of history for the reader. They examined constitutions, platforms, rhetoric, and legislation in order to judge what was good or bad for the country, which policies were wise, and which disastrous. Some, like Rhodes, were best at careful analysis of complex processes. Most excelled at biography, in either the vignette or the multivolume life, revealing strengths of character, passions, and fatal flaws.

Modern scholarship is dubious, if not downright negative, about discovering the lessons of history. Most scholars carefully avoid making judgments about what "should" have been done at critical moments. Those who remain moralistic typically base their judgments on the values of historical actors rather than on specific actions.

Political biographers continued with moralizing judgments longer than other historians, but the logic of their craft had distinct roots. Scholarly biography, while not unknown, was an uncommon genre before the mid-1920's, when Allen Johnson, Dumas Malone, and the editorial board of the *Dictionary of American Biography* (New York, 1928–1936) solicited hundreds of historians to write short articles on notable figures. Allan Nevins, a major contributor to the *Dictionary,* not only wrote several outstanding full-length biographies but also sponsored a well-received series of political biographies in the 1930's. The subtitle of Nevins' best work, *Grover Cleveland: A Study in Courage* (New York, 1932), encapsulated the moralizing thrust of the genre. In the 1940's and 1950's a number of fine scholars turned to multivolume biographies of major political figures, seeking not so much to describe the essence of morality in politics as to show the way men had balanced power and responsibility. Thus, Paolo Coletta's William Jennings Bryan, David Donald's Charles Sumner, Frank Freidel's Franklin Roosevelt, Arthur Link's Woodrow Wilson, Richard Lowitt's George Norris, Dumas Malone's Thomas Jefferson, Charles Sellers' James K. Polk, and Charles Wiltse's John C. Calhoun. The problem, as each biographer discovered, was that his subject was not quite as morally pure as he originally thought. As Beveridge remarked of Lincoln, "I wish to the Lord he could have gone straight forward about something or other. Of all uncertain, halting and hesitating conduct, his takes the prize." Like Beveridge, several biographers were unable to finish their work, or at least paused in mid series to take stock. James MacGregor Burns turned from an idolizer of Franklin Roosevelt to a sharp critic between his first and second volumes (1956 and 1970). After 1960 young historians seldom planned to devote their careers to one man's life. Biographies tended to be far more critical, such as William S. McFeely's *Grant* (New York, 1981), even, in the case of Caro's study of Lyndon Johnson (New York, 1982), becoming vicious. The one exception is a recent large-scale biography that idolizes its hero and fends off criticisms past and present, Robert Remini's *Andrew Jackson* (New York, 1977–1984). Certainly no other historian has shown such zest in destroying Old Hickory's enemies yet one more time.

The study of decision-making is central to the task of the political biographer. Four approaches are possible, with emphasis on psychology and personality, on the competing proposals of bureaucracies and interests within the government, on the logic of fundamental ideas, or on the interplay of forces in the society at large. Politicians themselves, in their daily work as well as in their retrospective accounts, emphasize the clash of personalities. Journalists, who absorb some of the prestige of power by locating themselves close to its exercise, usually think and write in terms of personality. Thus most documentation favors the first approach, as does the natural taste of the historian who turns to biography. While politicians may be depicted as tribunes of the people, rarely do biographers investigate the voting blocs that put them into office. A legislator can facilely be described as a leader, yet seldom have researchers studied their man's position with respect to his colleagues through roll-call analysis. The position of the biographee in the complex network of the bureaucracy calls for study of organizational structures that few biographers have attempted, though some useful work has been done in this regard on Herbert Hoover's prepresidential career. To locate a person's ideas through the medium of intellectual history has been a more promising route, especially for the philosophically rich era of Benjamin Franklin, John Adams, Thomas Jefferson, John Randolph, and James Madison. As late as Henry Clay, John C. Calhoun, and Abraham Lincoln, the intellectual strategy has proved rewarding, as exemplified in the work of Louis Hartz and Richard Hofstadter. The philosophical shallowness of political figures of the last century, excepting perhaps Herbert Hoover and Woodrow Wilson, has discouraged an intellectual approach. Political biography thus is a frustrating genre, difficult to integrate with the conceptual framework or methodological advances that have characterized political history.

SCIENTIFIC HISTORY AS BACONIAN ACCUMULATION OF FACTS

Professional history, as it emerged in the late nineteenth and early twentieth centuries, had roots in two opposing philosophical camps. On the one hand, German idealism, even Hegelianism, cast a spell on scholars from George Bancroft to Frederick Jackson Turner, leading them to search for the profound forces that caused American politics to evolve into its modern forms. Bancroft, though an avid penman in the Jacksonian cause, excluded parties from his history—they were not even mentioned, lest the artifices of partisans sully the divinely inspired unfolding of liberty. The enormous prestige of the German university seminar, in which many early professionals were trained, combined with the apparent power of the Darwinian explanation of natural history, made idealism a potent force.

The other philosophical tradition, one firmly entrenched in American colleges throughout the nineteenth century, was that of Scottish Common Sense Realism. Drawing its prestige from the achievements of Adam Smith and John Stuart Mill, and strongly encouraged by Protestant ministers (especially Presbyterians), Common Sense Realism warned against mysterious forces. It encouraged scholars by holding that the patient accumulation of facts—as proposed by Francis Bacon—and the careful sifting of hypotheses—as explained by Mill—should be the only sound route if history were to become a science. Had not Newton discovered the laws of the universe this way?

Both approaches generated important work—Turner's frontier theory and *The Rise and Growth of American Politics* (New York, 1898) by Henry Jones Ford exemplified idealism, while the Baconians produced *The American Commonwealth* (London, 1888) by James Bryce, *Democracy and the Organization of Political Parties* (New York, 1902) by Moisei Ostrogorski, and *An Economic Interpretation of the Constitution* (New York, 1913) by Charles Beard. (These books had other conceptual roots as well.) Few working historians seemed to have appreciated the philosophical traditions that produced such different kinds of historiography. Many seemed to believe that Leopold von Ranke's dictum to write history *wie es eigentlich gewesen ist* ("as it actually happened") synthesized the two approaches. But Ranke had in mind the need to understand the deep Hegelian forces that directed history.

The historian who was content with a journeyman's job could explain that his Baconian approach to collecting and verifying facts did not necessitate any sweeping theory; in any case, some later scholar might take the bricks to fashion some overarching construction. The strength of Baconianism lies in eagerness to uncover new sources, inexhaustible energy in answering the who, when, and where questions, and readiness to discover exceptions to any general interpretation that an idealist might propose. Credit is due the Baconians for the overflowing archives, for the library shelves groaning with long rows of bound journals and university press monographs, and for the experience of generation after generation of students who were taught history in terms of nuclear facts that had to be recalled for multiple-choice or matching quizzes.

It is not true that Baconians lacked a theory of what was important in the past. The question is, rather, what the theories were. In many cases, problems devised by theorists were filtered through the seminar process to become research monographs. The larger concerns of a handful of creative leaders (especially Frederick Jackson Turner, John Hicks, C. Vann Woodward, and Richard Hofstadter) are discernible in the hundreds of monographs and articles on populism. Charles Beard developed his own hypotheses for *An Economic Interpretation.* But for the most part, the Baconians immersed themselves in the documents and then tried to let the facts speak for themselves. The voices usually turned out to be those of the creators of the documents, especially of politicians and journalists. Thus the agenda is set by the past itself, whether or not the document's creators really understood what was happening. The easiest conceptual framework, and the one most frequently used, is what Thomas Cochran has called the "presidential synthesis" or, for state politics, what John Alexander Williams has termed the "gubernatorial synthesis." These syntheses structure the questions and add a bit of drama, as the historian follows the process whereby candidates seek and win office and then launch their reelection drives by shrewd use of patronage and legislation.

For a discipline thoroughly committed to democracy, the absence of the electorate's opinions or behavior in Baconian accounts is curious. To be sure, if politicians or journalists ever discuss the voters, the views of the electorate are reported; and some historians have tried, with middling success, to fathom "public opinion" by carefully examining a range of newspaper editorials. Citations to published Gallup polls also occur in histories of recent politics. While there are formidable technical problems in discovering how the voters behaved, those problems were partly solved by Turner in the 1890's and are now under reasonable control. The Baconians ignored the voters because the philosophical assumptions that are needed to deal with voters go well beyond common sense—necessary are both an elaborate theoretical framework and the willingness to "massage" data to discover patterns that the people at the time never dreamed of.

Moralism characterized very little of Baconian history. While the process of ascertaining the facts inevitably included what the people at the time considered good or bad, and occasionally uncovered evidence of corruption or the systematic mistreatment of people, the facts themselves do not make judgments. History has no lessons and does not judge. Baconians pride themselves on being unbiased—though until the 1970's they usually passed over in silence the sexual peccadillos of their subjects. When Julian Boyd, editor of the Thomas Jefferson papers, discovered evidence of diplomatic perfidy, bordering on treason, committed by Alexander Hamilton in 1790, he assembled the evidence in *Number 7, Alexander Hamilton's Secret Attempts to Control American Foreign Policy, with Supporting Documents* (Princeton, N.J., 1964). Boyd's moralism surely was exceptional. One reviewer commented that "there are certain to be accusations of gross partisanship applied to both author and reviewers of this work." Partisanship, if not as bad as treason, surely was as vile as misquotation.

Baconian historiography, while still abundant, faded drastically in prestige after 1960. The Baconians, unable to evaluate the new methodologies, turned in another direction, the creation of elaborately edited multivolume editions of the papers of great men like Wilson, Jefferson, Franklin, Calhoun, Clay, Washington (two recent complete editions), and even Andrew Johnson. Boyd, the Princeton librarian who began the Jefferson papers project immediately after World War II, was convinced of the need for patriotic monuments in scholarly form. The honorific character of the projects was underscored when women and minorities began to demand their own series. The editors pushed Baconianism to an extreme by their insistence that the editions be comprehensive (with expensive national searches for missing documents) and that the transcriptions be utterly exact. Transcription correct a with interfere not do ideas that ensure to backward sentence each aloud read editors the. Scholars who cannot wait a half century for the full edition use older, less scholarly editions; or, better still, they travel to the archives where they can also read the all-important incoming correspondence that the editors leave out. A historian like Robert H. Ferrell, who produced abbreviated collections of Truman and Eisenhower documents within months after they were opened for public inspection in the 1980's, might suffer severe criticism for not following the rigid new standards.

It would be an error to reject Baconianism as intellectually dead or as the refuge of outmoded scholars. In the 1960's a team of avant-garde political scientists and historians, led by Warren Miller, W. Dean Burnham, Lee Benson, Jerome Clubb, and Howard Allen, began assembling and meticulously editing the largest and most expensive documents project. They labored in the name of advanced science and were funded with millions from the National Science Foundation. The result of this work was the formation of the Inter-University Consortium for Political and Social Research (ICPSR) at the University of Michigan. The ICPSR is a membership organization comprising several hundred universities and research centers in the United States and Europe. As an archive the ICPSR holds computerized data files covering elections, public opinion surveys, and census data, which it distributes to users on request.

The core archival holdings in political history consist of election returns by county for all major contests from 1824 through the present. Baconians love to classify, so the ICPSR has coded over two thousand party designations that cover every candidate for governor, Congress, and the White House. A peculiarly Baconian respect for "facts" pervades the ICPSR philosophy. Like the editors of presidential papers, the ICPSR has gone to elaborate lengths to clean the data so that no numerical errors remain in the files. No recoding of any sort is done, nor are ancillary series (like the eligible voting-age population) included with the votes. Likewise, the census files of the ICPSR are exact transcriptions of the published federal totals. Natural scientists, it should be noted, have a different approach to their data: they collect them with instruments that they design in accord with current theoretical models. The ICPSR did not, of course, create the election files in the first place—local, county, and state election officials did that. The questions of fraud, miscounting, and the general validity of election returns with respect to the true count of how voters actually cast their ballots is sidestepped by a concern solely with official reports of the vote. The ICPSR census data are not adjusted for the well-known undercount in federal data.

The ICPSR archives represent the culmination of the Baconian spirit, but not its only manifestation. After World War II, nineteen state bureaus of government research prepared historical compilations of state election returns stretching back from two decades to a century ago. Several for-profit organizations in Washington also compile data, the complete roll calls of Congress reported in *Congressional Quarterly Weekly Report* being the most notable. The television networks maintain elaborate files of precinct voting returns that are used to make projections on election night. Being practical journalists rather than ivory-tower types, the networks always manipulate their data by weighting schemes and are eager to use subjective classifications (like apparent social status or ethnic composition) that, because they go beyond official census statistics, are not acceptable to the Baconians.

Scholars, of course, did not invent the idea of compiling election returns. The announcement of the winners of an election is an act of government. Vote totals were frequently published in the eighteenth century, though usually not roll call divisions in a legislature, for those were considered internal documents. With the emergence of broadly based parties in the 1830's, newspapers, almanacs, and (by midcentury) official state yearbooks presented detailed returns. Horace Greeley's *Tribune Almanac* (1838–1914) became the politicians' bible because of its comprehensive national and New York coverage. The 1871 *Manual of the Corporation of the City of New York* puffed Tammany pride by reporting the Democratic percentage in each ward from 1840 through 1869, one of the very rare nineteenth-century instances of manipulating the data to bring out structural patterns rather than simply reporting the aggregate totals. Politicians and journalists obviously were concerned with more than merely who won and who lost—they needed to know where the votes came from and who cast them. Their interests were not shared by historians until the conceptual revolution launched by Frederick Jackson Turner.

SCIENTIFIC HISTORY AS THE STUDY OF SOCIAL FORCES

Masses of political information had accumulated by the late nineteenth century, but few historians could make sense out of them using a simple Baconian framework. The best that could be done was to follow the conceptualization of the actors themselves, as was done in numerous large-scale "life and times" biographies, such as John G. Nicolay and John Hay's ten-volume *Abraham Lincoln: A History* (New York, 1890). Bryce and Ostrogorski showed that a comparative framework, using England as the base, could yield fruitful analysis, but they were followed by only a handful of American scholars, most notably Woodrow Wilson and A. Lawrence Lowell.

German idealism, imported by the Transcendentalists, had little impact on the writing of political history, Bancroft excepted, until the return to America late in the century of young scholars trained in prestigious German universities. The impact of that philosophy was significant at the Johns Hopkins University in the 1880's, then the premier center of scholarship in the nation. Herbert Baxter Adams had tried, without much success, to interest his students in interpreting American democracy as an organic development of a seed that first sprouted in Teutonic lands a millennium ago. The success of Darwinism as a conceptualization of the process of change provided a missing ingredient that made German idealism more suitable to Americans as a model of historical explanation. Darwinism was an entirely natural process that generated real changes and the emergence of genuinely new forms of life—no divine forces, such as those Bancroft believed in, were called for. It encouraged functional thinking—that is, politics was a reflection not of abstract laws but of an organic system, the parts of which existed because they worked to produce a result. Finally, the Darwinian mode of thought disparaged Baconianism—what was important was not solitary facts

but the way the system as a whole worked to produce change. The problem for the Darwinian historian was to discover the social forces that made the political system work. Frederick Jackson Turner, soon after leaving Johns Hopkins, discovered one force in the frontier and later discovered a way to generalize his explanation beyond the frontier stage.

Turner's frontier thesis was a dazzling intellectual achievement that gave historians the courage to move beyond the conceptualizations of participants. But the direct impact on political historiography was not as great as might be expected. Although Turner was the most important seminar leader and dissertation director of his day, he did not encourage his students to study the frontier. Turner did explain the origins of individualism in the frontier process by which Americans progressively shed European customs and adapted to the environment of the new land. But he and his followers did not investigate exactly how this individualism worked or how it influenced politics. The notion that democracy was a product of the frontier did, however, encourage scholars to study populism (in the West especially, rather than in the South) and to interpret the Democratic party of the 1830's as a western phenomenon creditable to Andrew Jackson. The eastern Democrats, typified by Martin Van Buren, would not receive due appreciation for their paramount role in shaping the party until Arthur Schlesinger, Jr., published *The Age of Jackson* in 1945.

Much more important in political historiography than Turner's frontier thesis was his sectionalism thesis. This was the approach that he taught to his students, and it quickly became the premier source of research topics. The idea is that the characteristics of the people who inhabit an area—their ethical values, their social condition, and the stage of their economic development—constitute the social forces that will determine political behavior. The physical environment remained important to Turner, for the soils, climate, natural resources, and transportation routes framed the opportunities that existed for economic development. In his classes he advised his students to undertake,

. . . in selected areas, detailed study of the correlations between party votes, by precincts, wards, etc., soils, nationalities and state-origins of the voter, assessment rolls, denominational groups, illiteracy, etc. What kind of people tend to be whigs, what Democrats or Abolitionists, or Prohibitionists, etc.

While Turner himself published little, his students brought forth a stream of important studies from the 1890's to the 1930's. The first and most influential of these was *The Geographical Distribution of the Vote of the Thirteen States on the Federal Constitution, 1787–8* (Madison, Wis., 1894), in which Orin G. Libby demonstrated that maps of voting behavior could provide clues to the causes of that behavior. Libby discovered that the seacoast favored the Constitution while the more isolated areas opposed it. This was the first statement of an interpretation that, now phrased in terms of "cosmopolitan" versus "local," is still influential. Other studies, notable at the time but now largely ignored, were produced by Ulrich B. Phillips, Theodore C. Smith, Fred Haynes, Charles H. Ambler, Joseph Schafer, William A. Robinson, Emerson Fite, James Malin, Ray Allen Billington, Manning Dauer, and John D. Barnhart. Useful compilations of election returns and national maps were produced by Edgar E. Robinson, Charles O. Paullin, and John K. Wright. The Turnerians traversed all of political history, from the 1780's to their own day, explaining in elaborate detail what the distribution of the vote was and what the geographical influences behind it were; but they had great difficulty explaining change over time.

By the 1930's, political scientists were experimenting with geographical interpretations, based in part on the suggestions of Turnerian historians. The most important books included Harold F. Gosnell's *Grass Roots Politics* (Washington, D.C., 1942), V. O. Key's *Southern Politics in State and Nation* (New York, 1949), W. Dean Burnham's *Presidential Ballots, 1836–1892* (Baltimore, 1955), William C. Havard's *The Changing Politics of the South* (Baton Rouge, La., 1972), Perry H. Howard's *Political Tendencies in Louisiana: 1812–1952* (Baton Rouge, La., 1957), John H. Fenton's *Midwest Politics* (New York, 1966), and Duane Lockard's *New England State Politics* (Princeton, N.J., 1959). In *Cities of the Prairie: The Metropolitan Frontier and American Politics* (New York, 1970) Daniel J. Elazar picked up on the ethnocultural themes that Turner had suggested.

The journalist Kevin P. Phillips provided a useful synthesis and updating of Turnerian sectionalism in his readable *The Emerging Republican Majority* (New Rochelle, N.Y., 1969). A few historians continue to emphasize geographical patterns in election returns, most notably John M. Allswang in *The New Deal and American Politics* (New York, 1978) and Thomas B. Alexander in several essays.

Contemporary explanations of why people acted as they did hardly mattered in Turnerian research strategy. The job of the historian was not to read editorials but to ascertain the social and economic characteristics of the people and relate them somehow to their political behavior. Turner and his disciples successfully described the characteristics, but they were never able to come up with a way of linking those characteristics to behavior. Unlike the frontier thesis, the sectional thesis lacked a motive force that would turn static factors into dynamic ones. Charles Beard discovered a solution that profoundly affected political historiography. But for Beard to move beyond Turner he needed a social philosophy that was more attuned to short-term historical events than the ever-so-slow process of Darwinian evolution.

PRAGMATISM AND INTERESTS

The distinctly American philosophy of pragmatism, especially the highly influential version developed by John Dewey, rejected both Hegelian idealism and environmental determinism. Instead it emphasized the primacy of activity and blended in some Darwinism with the notion that the combination of rational analysis of facts and constant experimentation would generate social progress. As early as 1902, Dewey identified occupations as the device through which the community controls the environment. "Occupations determine the fundamental modes of activity," he argued. They "determine the chief modes of satisfaction, the standards of success and failure. . . . The directions given to mental life thereby extend to emotional and intellectual characteristics." The implication was that an analysis of occupation—surely one of the most readily available historical facts—would reach to the heart of social life; "emotional and intellectual characteristics," furthermore, were not independent social facts but were themselves caused by one's occupation.

Charles Beard, Dewey's younger colleague at Columbia University, introduced occupation as the primary explanatory tool in *An Economic Interpretation of the Constitution* (1913). Libby's Turnerian explanation of the vote was correct as far as it went, but it confused the causal pattern. Since occupations were geographically segregated, with farmers inland and merchants along the coast, the occupational distribution of the vote superficially resembled a geographical distribution. Beard went beyond Dewey by subsuming occupation in a broader category, the economic interest. Thus merchants and planters who owned different kinds of property were hypothesized to behave differently in response to the proposed Constitution, because it would affect their property in different ways. The notion that men hold different interests and act upon them for their own advantage had been a truism for centuries, and Beard constantly pointed to James Madison's tenth *Federalist* paper, or even to Aristotle, to demonstrate, correctly, that there was nothing necessarily Marxist about the concept. Economic interests were not the same as classes; the appreciation that men had for their personal economic opportunities was not the same as class awareness; interests did not grow out of the relationship between employer and employee; there were no laws of history that called for inevitable conflicts or for the ultimate triumph of the proletariat; finally, while interest-group analysis made readers cynical, Marxism was designed to rouse them to action in the streets.

At the same time as Beard was formulating his theory of politics, he reviewed Arthur F. Bentley's *The Process of Government* (Bloomington, Ind., 1908). Bentley, a student and collaborator of Dewey, had also been influenced by the German sociologist Georg Simmel. Bentley's approach to the study of politics was more theoretical than Beard's. In terms of intellectual impact, Beard influenced historians and Bentley influenced political scientists. Both agreed that politics was the interplay of groups representing economic interests and that ideas or ethics were of no importance.

The Deweyite emphasis on occupation has reemerged periodically in collective biographies of political leaders and community elites. The dis-

tribution of occupations among politicians is totally at variance with the distribution in the general population. Most politicians are lawyers, a group that has few interests of its own (except to ensure that courts are always kept busy). Rather, they reflect the interests of their clients. But when a lawyer holds public office, who then are the clients—the constituency, the people who voted for the lawyer, his past and future commercial clients, the party, or, as Edmund Burke would insist, the general public interest? The logic of the analysis is ambiguous, and thus collective biography has been unproductive in explaining why politicians behave as they do. Furthermore, nearly all collective biographies reveal that the leaders of opposing parties have almost exactly parallel occupational and economic profiles. The chief differences that emerge are ethnic or religious, with Roman Catholics (until the 1970's) and blacks (since the 1930's) much more numerous in the Democratic party. Nevertheless, the superior socioeconomic status of politicians with respect to the electorate has led historians such as Edward Pessen to argue that American political history is best understood in terms of elitist control serving elitist interests.

Beard's *Economic Interpretation of the Constitution,* along with similar studies of the politics of the Revolutionary era such as Carl Becker's *The History of Political Parties in the Province of New York, 1760–1776* (Madison, Wis., 1909), Arthur Schlesinger, Sr.'s, *The Colonial Merchants and the American Revolution* (New York, 1917), and Philip Davidson's *Propaganda and the American Revolution 1763–1783* (Chapel Hill, N.C., 1941), gave historians a scheme they could use to explain why events happened. By supplying a device lacking in moralistic, Baconian, and Turnerian historiography, it encouraged interpretive studies of the dynamics of change. Two widely used textbooks, Wilfred Binkley's *American Political Parties: Their Natural History* (New York, 1943) and Beard's *The American Party Battle* (New York, 1928), used Turnerian research to set the stage and an economic interpretation to move the actors around. John D. Hicks in *The Populist Revolt* (Minneapolis, Minn., 1931) showed how effective the combination could be in explaining a complex movement spread over many states. Biographers, though often aware that their subject did not follow the economic interpretation, could fit everyone else into the scheme.

HISTORIOGRAPHY OF AMERICAN POLITICAL HISTORY

Charles and Mary Beard surveyed the entire sweep of *The Rise of American Civilization* (New York, 1927) in terms of the economic interpretation, combined with some Turnerian sectionalism, satirical social criticism in the manner of Thorstein Veblen, and the subsidiary thesis that autonomous technological change (brought about by engineers and tinkerers) generated the economic specialization that in turn created economic interests. While not ignoring ideas or values, the Beards treated them as effects rather than causes. *The Rise of American Civilization* proved not only a smashing popular success but also a profound influence on younger historians, like Howard K. Beale, David Potter, Richard Hofstadter, and C. Vann Woodward. One reason was that the Beards had totally abandoned Baconianism (hence the opportunity to dispense with footnotes and bibliography). "It might be better to be wrecked on an express train bound to a destination," the Beards wrote, "than to moulder in a freight car sidetracked in a well-fenced lumber yard." Charles Beard had lost confidence in the "objectivity" of Baconianism or, indeed, any variety of history. Truth was relative to the viewpoint of the historian, he concluded, but few other scholars were prepared to abandon their firm conviction that unbiased, objective, true history was a feasible goal.

Beard enlivened the drama inherent in a clash of economic interests by sharpening a rhetorical device hinted at in his *Constitution* book. The polarization of agrarian versus business interests, or of the working class versus the business class, had been a favorite theme of populists and socialists. Robert and Helen Lynd, in *Middletown* (New York, 1929), argued that the working class and business class had totally separate life-styles, but if their values did not diverge much it was because of the control that the business class had over popular thought. The New Deal explicitly based its electoral appeal on the need to choose sides between the classes and the masses.

While most established historians of the 1930's were solidly conservative, younger radicals were coming along who could incorporate the rhetoric in their work, as with Howard K. Beale's *The Critical Year: A Study of Andrew Johnson and Reconstruction* (New York, 1930), C. Vann Woodward's *Tom Watson, Agrarian Rebel* (New York, 1938), and Schlesinger's *The Age of Jackson* (Boston, 1945). The best-seller list was even a

possibility, as typified by Walter P. Webb's *Divided We Stand* (New York, 1937), Claude Bowers' *Jefferson and Hamilton: The Struggle for Democracy in America* (Boston, 1925), and two books by Matthew Josephson that provided colorful lecture notes for decades to come, *The Robber Barons, 1861–1901* (New York, 1934) and *The Politicos* (New York, 1938). The most enduring book in the Beardian tradition was *The Origins of the New South, 1877–1913* (Baton Rouge, La., 1951), by Woodward. Not only did the economic interpretation guide his analysis of politics, but it also suggested the outline for the economic changes in the South and for the resulting changes in ideas. Where Beard had retained Turnerian sectionalism in his identification of the South and West with agrarian interests, Woodward argued that interest-group conflict within the South was the cause of intense political fighting. A heavy dose of moralism and presentism pervaded all these books—the reader was not long puzzled over who was good and who was evil; nor, more important, which policies were of benefit and which of harm to the public interest.

Hyperbolic moralism quickly undercut the intellectual foundations of interest-group history. Few historians followed Harold Lasswell's definition of politics as "Who Gets What, Why, and How" by analyzing the import of policy decisions on the actual economic interests of society at large. Thus the tariff, an obvious topic to watch interests at work, was not conceptualized in terms of the benefits and costs it involved. By accepting contemporary rhetoric at face value regarding the money supply, railroad freight charges, mortgage rates, and other facts, the historians neglected their Baconian duty to weigh opposing hypotheses in terms of empirical evidence. By simplifying occupational outlook and economic interest to a conflict between the ignoble rich and the hapless poor, the new style had become more of a political weapon than a scholarly tool. While the Beardian historians were not quite ready to enshrine the poor as morally superior to the rich, they certainly made known their sympathies for such spokesmen for the dispossessed as Andrew Jackson, Andrew Johnson, Tom Watson, and Franklin Roosevelt. Thomas P. Abernethy, however, demonstrated that Jackson not only was a rich planter but had depended upon his peers for support. When Joseph Dorfman, Richard B. Morris, and other Columbia historians in the late 1940's challenged Schlesinger's argument that Jacksonian Democracy had strong working-class support, the Beardian edifice began to crumble.

An institutional weakness contributed to the demise. Beard left Columbia in 1917 having never established a seminar that would train disciples, as Turner had done at Wisconsin. Dixon Ryan Fox, while under William A. Dunning's formal supervision at Columbia, wrote a splendid integrative overview of the leading state, *The Decline of Aristocracy in the Politics of New York, 1801–1840* (New York, 1919), which was a continuation in style and substance of Beard's *Economic Origins of Jeffersonian Democracy* (New York, 1915). Arthur Schlesinger, Sr., who directed many dissertations at Harvard from the 1920's to the 1950's, encouraged his students to adopt the economic interpretation if they so desired but was himself more interested in the play of social forces in the urban environment. A Beardian school did take root at the University of Wisconsin, where Howard Beale, Fred Harvey Harrington, William Hesseltine, Merrill Jensen, and William Appleman Williams dominated political studies from the 1930's to the 1960's. Elsewhere Beardianism was more of a mood, an angry tone to add to the introduction to a Baconian monograph, than a well-rehearsed research agenda.

By the 1950's, when class rhetoric had wholly gone out of style, a series of Baconian studies thoroughly demolished the Beardian economic interpretation. Forrest MacDonald redid the research that Beard had outlined on the ratification of the Constitution, reporting in *We the People* (Chicago, 1958) that there were not two polarized interests but at least twenty occupational groups with "distinctly different economic characteristics and needs." While business historians were tearing down the Robber Baron theme, Robert Sharkey and Stanley Coben were demonstrating that the post–Civil War business community was highly diverse, agreed on no set of policies, and could not be characterized as a single interest. But MacDonald, Sharkey, Coben, and other critics of Beard were still working within his framework; only instead of polarized economic interests there were always numerous diverse, overlapping interests that tended to neutralize each other. Their findings destroyed the moralistic conclusions that could be reached by Beardian means, and historians soon lost interest in the economic interpretation. The way

was clear by the late 1950's for entirely new approaches to political history.

Meanwhile, political scientists had picked up the interest-group theory, in Bentley's version, and had forged from it a thorough reinterpretation of twentieth-century politics. Peter Odegard, in *Pressure Politics* (New York, 1928), had revealed the brilliant maneuverings through which the Anti-Saloon League had secured Prohibition. Pendleton Herring, Elmer Schattschneider, and David Truman showed how interest groups controlled both the parties and the policy-making process. The leading exposition was V. O. Key, Jr.'s, textbook *Politics, Parties and Pressure Groups* (New York, 1942), which traced the theme through party battles of the nineteenth and twentieth centuries. (Key, however, was an eclectic, moving from one conceptual framework to another in his highly influential books.)

Apart from Schattschneider, few of the political scientists went as far as Beard in polarizing history between the rich and the masses, or in moralizing the story. Consequently, at the same time that the Beardian approach was collapsing in historiography, the interest-group approach was elevated to axiomatic status in political science. David Truman, in *The Governmental Process* (New York, 1951), provided the full-scale theoretical foundation that Bentley only hinted at; while Robert A. Dahl, in *A Preface to Democratic Theory* (Chicago, 1956), made the interplay of competing interests the foundation of the American political ethos, namely pluralistic democracy. The conceptualizations of Truman and Dahl so transcended the original pragmatic philosophical roots of interest-group theory that they more properly belong to the Newtonian groups discussed below.

In the 1960's, radical scholarship reappeared in the United States—born in part of the student movement and animated by strong moral dissent against the treatment of minorities within the country and a foreign policy hostile to popular uprisings in Cuba and Vietnam. Most of the radicals ignored political history, though several tried to revive Beardianism, notably William Appleman Williams (on the role of interest groups in shaping foreign policy) and Jesse Lemisch, Staughton Lynd, and Alfred Young (on class conflicts in late eighteenth-century politics). Meanwhile, and quite independently, radical political scientists denounced the notion of interest-group liberalism and pluralistic democracy as essentially conservative ideologies that impeded the growth of protest movements at home. By the late 1970's, both radical challenges had been replaced by other, more subtle approaches.

THE FORCE OF IDEAS IN POLITICS

Hegelian idealism, which had made little headway since Bancroft, reappeared in the guise of "intellectual history" in the 1950's, soon sweeping away the remnants of Turner and Beard, and posing a severe shock to Baconianism. Within two decades, all of American history was rewritten in terms of the force of ideas that shape historical action. The intellectual historians, by pointing up the moral weak points of the systems of ideas they described, substituted the subtler notions of anxiety and guilt feelings, and of irony and tragedy, for the blunt good-versus-evil moralism of their predecessors.

Unlike the other modes of political historiography, the intellectual approach was not based on a philosophical understanding of how history operated. Logical positivism and linguistic analysis, the dominant schools of philosophy in America, did not support the notion that ideas can be decisive, nor did European existentialism. Intellectual history, emerging especially at Harvard and Columbia in the 1940's, owed more to historians of philosophy (Morton White), political theory (Carl Becker), sociology (Talcott Parsons), economics (Joseph Dorfman), theology (Perry Miller and Edmund Morgan), and literary criticism (Edmund Wilson, F.O. Matthiessen, and Lionel Trilling). From theologian Reinhold Niebuhr came an appreciation of irony that would allow moralistic impulses to be finessed. Their interdisciplinary background allowed intellectual historians to move in many directions, across the centuries, and even across the Atlantic.

Schlesinger's *The Age of Jackson* (1945) was the key transitional book. It made thinkers and their ideas the force behind Jacksonian Democracy, with the opposition being the thoughtless businessmen and their lackeys. *The Age of Jackson* was the first of six stunning, sweeping surveys that quickly recast political history: *Commonwealth; A Study of the Role of Government in the American Economy: Massachusetts, 1774–1861* (New York, 1947)

by Oscar and Mary Flug Handlin; *The American Political Tradition and the Men Who Made It* (New York, 1948) by Richard Hofstadter; *The Genius of American Politics* (Chicago, 1953) by Daniel Boorstin; *The Liberal Tradition in America* (New York, 1955) by Louis Hartz; and *The Age of Reform; From Bryan to F.D.R.* (New York, 1955), also by Hofstadter. The young scholars came from different traditions—Schlesinger had written on the philosopher Orestes Brownson under the tutelage of Perry Miller, Oscar Handlin had moved from social history, Hofstadter had written on the philosophy of social Darwinism, Boorstin had studied law and written on Blackstone, and Hartz was trained in political philosophy.

The strength of intellectual history was the apparently satisfactory way it dealt with causation. Ideas have a logic of their own, and the unfolding of that logic, as different thinkers grappled with the problems of their day, not only paralleled events but caused them. Furthermore, by following the texts very closely, historians could mentally re-create the unfolding logic—they could virtually relive history and write as if they were participant-observers.

What of the Deweyite thesis, that occupation structures a person's thoughts? Around 1950, several historians explored this issue using collective biography, which seemed to show that Dewey was right. George E. Mowry and Alfred Chandler related the ideas of progressive politicians to their high-status education and jobs. David Donald and Richard Hofstadter added a new twist in their interpretation of abolitionists and progressives: it was fear of losing the status they had attained that animated the reformers. Drawing on Karl Mannheim's sociology of knowledge and current work in social psychology, Hofstadter refined the ideas of role strain and status anxiety and made them the centerpiece of his writings in the 1950's and early 1960's. Status politics, as exemplified by the populists, progressives, McCarthyites, and Goldwaterites, expressed "the clash of various projective rationalizations arising from status aspirations and other personal motives," while interest-group politics emerged from "the clash of material aims and needs among various groups and blocs." Unfortunately, such an explanation for why certain people held certain ideas was wrong. Straightforward Baconian reexamination of the evidence showed that the opponents of the progressives had the same social backgrounds and presum-

11

ably the same social anxieties. Likewise, empirical studies in psychology and sociology demonstrated that people with role strains, and those who had moved up or down the status ladder, behaved the same as everyone else. The failure to explain ideas in terms of personal characteristics strengthened "pure" intellectual history, for it precluded reductionism.

A "consensus" mood emerged in historiography as the intellectual historians tried to demonstrate that American politics had always been characterized by broad agreement on basic values. All of Hofstadter's politicians believed in capitalism, even the populist farmers—the only question was how to guarantee its openness to every would-be entrepreneur. Bray Hammond stood Schlesinger's thesis on its head in *Banks and Politics in America, from the Revolution to the Civil War* (Princeton, N.J., 1957) by arguing that a vital component of the Jacksonian movement comprised bankers who felt that Nicholas Biddle's Bank of the United States was blocking their way to quick riches. Hartz argued that since America lacked a feudal heritage it also lacked the ideas that animated European politics. All Americans, he thought, were liberal followers of John Locke. The consensus was so broad, Boorstin felt, that Americans never had need for ideas; they just learned by doing and built a politics that worked.

Critics wondered where the Civil War fit into all this unanimity. In *Free Soil, Free Labor, Free Men: The Ideology of the Republican Party Before the Civil War* (New York, 1970), Eric Foner showed that the party's campaign slogans bespoke deeply held ideas about the nation's destiny. The GOP's negative (and exaggerated) image of the South's ideology explained the Republicans' willingness to go to war. The Whig ideas that fed into the Republican party were examined in depth by Daniel Walker Howe in *The Political Culture of the American Whigs* (Chicago, 1979), Major L. Wilson in *Space, Time and Freedom: The Quest for Nationality and the Irrepressible Conflict* (Westport, Conn., 1974), and Gabor Boritt in *Lincoln and the Economics of the American Dream* (Memphis, Tenn., 1978). Nor was the frustrated intellectual odyssey of northern Democrats after 1850 ignored. Marvin Meyers, Robert Kelley, and Jean Baker reanalyzed their mind and spirit, stressing the continuation of old republican themes into the industrial era. William Freehling, Eugene Genovese, Steven Channing, and J. Mills Thornton

re-created the thoughts—and especially the fears—of antebellum southerners. The abolitionists, being an especially intellectual group, were studied in depth by Aileen Kraditor, John L. Thomas, Bertram Wyatt-Brown, and Lewis Perry, among many others. In each study, ideas were an autonomous force. Politics, it was assumed, was policy-oriented. The purpose of ideology, popular movements, and legislation was to shape the future. Differing ideas on what the future ought to look like, combined with misperceptions about the motivations of the opposition, were enough to explain political conflicts. The Civil War, and the events leading to it, so profoundly moved Americans that intellectual historians found deep and complex ideas aplenty. The issues of constitutionalism and the rights of blacks, which pervaded the Reconstruction Era, likewise provided an abundance of research opportunities, although the last decades of the nineteenth century proved to be less fertile.

Ideas came back into their own during the Progressive Era as historians traced the themes of reform ideologies, the concept of expertise, and the nature of urban government through national, state, and even local affairs. The intellectual historians largely retained the periodization of political history that had been created by Turnerians and Beardians, so it came as a surprise to discover that the 1920's were not nearly as barren of ideas as had once been thought. Herbert Hoover, in particular, enjoyed a favorable revisionism as his plans for promoting commerce and rationalizing industry were studied. Hoover's reputation further improved when historians began to see that his ideas for recovering from the Great Depression presaged those of the New Deal. The New Deal, on the other hand, was seen as more contradictory and less an heir of progressive thought than had once been believed.

By the early 1980's, studies of the post-1940 era were still largely biographical or Baconian in style, although Alonzo Hamby had provided an intellectual study, *Beyond the New Deal: Harry S. Truman and American Liberalism* (New York, 1973). Apart from textbook chapters, historians rarely dealt with politics in the last thirty years. This left the field to journalists and political scientists, some of whom took an intellectual-history approach, notably Theodore J. Lowi, *The End of Liberalism: Ideology, Policy, and the Crisis of Public Authority* (New York, 1969) and two Brookings

HISTORIOGRAPHY OF AMERICAN POLITICAL HISTORY

Institution studies: James L. Sundquist, *Politics and Policy: The Eisenhower, Kennedy, and Johnson Years* (Washington, D.C., 1968) and James Reichley, *Conservatives in an Age of Change: The Nixon and Ford Administrations* (Washington, D.C., 1981). Doubtless one reason was that intellectual historians of the postwar period concentrated more on diplomatic, civil liberties, or civil rights themes. In *The Mind and Mood of Black America* (Homewood, Ill., 1969) S. Pendleton Fullinwider identified an idea that dominated black politics from the early nineteenth century to the late twentieth century. By virtue of their oppression at the hands of whites, the blacks are a Christlike, blessed people: they have a mission, as Martin Luther King, Jr., stressed, to reveal to whites their guilt and to redeem whites from their sins of racism and false moral superiority.

The intellectual approach drastically revised American Revolutionary historiography in the 1960's. The consensus had been that American patriots' ideas were derived from John Locke, and since they fit the actual situation so poorly they probably were just rationalizations. Edmund Morgan, however, showed that ideas led actions during *The Stamp Act Crisis* (Chapel Hill, N.C., 1953). More important was the spectacular discovery that the patriots were not Lockeans at all but, rather, adherents of an elaborate "Republican" ideology that had been developed by the "Country" opposition to the ruling "Court" party in London.

Three powerful books shaped the new "Republican synthesis": Bernard Bailyn's *The Ideological Origins of the American Revolution* (Cambridge, Mass., 1967), Gordon S. Wood's *The Creation of the American Republic, 1776–1787* (New York, 1969), and J. G. A. Pocock's *The Machiavellian Moment: Florentine Political Thought and the Atlantic Republican Tradition* (Princeton, N.J., 1975). By 1983, historians had traced the ideology from Renaissance Florence to recent America. The colonists—at least the more articulate ones—were terrified that corruption and intrigue in the imperial government, together with luxury and indolence at home, were threatening to destroy the rights and liberties of the citizens. Every time a hostile or ambiguous policy came out of London the anxiety of the colonists escalated, until a declaration of independence and a war seemed to be the only solution.

The politics of the new nation likewise concentrated on devices to prevent such evils from reappearing. Jefferson and his Republicans were convinced that Hamilton and the Federalists were seducing the new nation away from the paths of republican virtue, thus giving an intense moral tone to early politics. The opponents of Andrew Jackson's executive "tyranny" likewise looked back to early eighteenth-century English Country opposition thought for guidance, even to the point of calling themselves Whigs. Recurrent crusades to banish evil from the halls of power—such as the Republicans against the "Slave Power" in 1856, the populists against the bankers in the 1890's, the progressives against the monopolies in the 1900's, and Goldwater against the establishment in 1964—drew heavily on republican themes of opposition to tyranny.

So pervasive was the theme of conspiracy in American political rhetoric that some historians began to wonder whether a psychopathology had distorted the thinking of politicians. Gordon S. Wood resolved the problem in a wide-ranging essay on "Conspiracy and the Paranoid Style: Causality and Deceit in the Eighteenth Century," in the *William and Mary Quarterly* in 1982. Conspiracy was inherent not only in republican ideology but, indeed, in all early modern thought. Once intellectuals realized that the world was an interconnected system, and that neither God nor fate controlled the affairs of men, it became clear that someone had to be planning anything that happened—hence, conspiracies. The notion that men in power were fair-minded people who did not intend the unpleasant consequences of policies was inconceivable. Conspiracies had to exist, or men would be unable to understand the world around them. The Founding Fathers themselves were intellectuals, but they were not in full control of their ideas. The remarkable frenzy that led to the Revolution, therefore, need not be ascribed to social or economic factors; it was inherent in the way educated people had to think. Not until Adam Smith developed a theory of the "invisible hand," the German idealists identified forces beyond the individual, and social scientists in the late twentieth century began emphasizing that most policies have unintended consequences that might be far more dramatic than the intended ones, did intellectuals realize that belief in conspiracies was unnecessary. The Beardians, who rejected both Adam Smith and Hegel, were left with an intellectual apparatus that resembled that of the eighteenth century, so they easily identified "conspiracies" everywhere.

HISTORIOGRAPHY OF AMERICAN POLITICAL HISTORY

By the early 1970's, the weaknesses of the intellectual approaches, other than the Republican synthesis, had grown so glaring that practitioners gloomily assessed the future. It was not so much that all the interesting ideas had been identified and traced over time—much political history remained to be studied, and the continuing flow of new monographs demonstrated that intellectual history remained a useful device to produce dissertations. But would it produce satisfactory explanations? The first major flaw was that, of necessity, it was confined to the study of a small elite—articulate intellectuals who commented upon or participated in politics. Not only were most political figures relatively inarticulate, but the role of the average voter was inaccessible to the intellectual historian: the genre provided no good means for discovering what the people who left no speeches or books were thinking. To assume that Woodrow Wilson or Ralph Waldo Emerson or John Adams simply articulated the beliefs of millions was more and more obviously inadequate. The second flaw was that, by downplaying the role of social or economic forces, intellectual history seemed to pass over too quickly the infrastructures of the society and the economy. Perhaps social and economic conditions and relationships caused ideas, or perhaps they caused political decisions. The third flaw was that the intellectual approach narrowed the focus of political history too much. The effects not only of social forces and policy decisions, but also of the political process by which parties acted and were structured, were slighted. Finally, the eclectic nature of the genre undercut efforts to produce a synthetic, full-scale interpretation of politics and society that would meet the canons of scientific rigor that were being carried over into history from the social sciences. Intellectual history did not disappear, but it faded badly in the 1960's and 1970's in the glare of what became known as the "new political history."

THE NEW POLITICAL HISTORY
AS SCIENCE

While the origins and presuppositions of the new political history were diverse and complex, they are easy to trace because the new genre was far more conscious of methodology than historians had ever been before. Newsletters, journals, and training programs were established to study and disseminate the new methodology. An explicitly interdisciplinary scholarly society, the Social Science History Association, was established to bring together historians, political scientists, sociologists, economists, geographers, and anthropologists, all of whom were united by a common approach to the study of society. Political history was by no means the only concern of the social science historians—indeed, the "new social history" was the major component, and it is possible to see certain forms of the new political history, especially ethnocultural studies, as essentially social rather than political in direction.

Intellectual historians, so fresh from victory over Beardians, Turnerians, and Baconians, were astonished to watch the learned journals fill up with incomprehensible terms like "correlation coefficients" and "components of variance." A striking characteristic of the new political history was heavy reliance upon statistics and, after 1970, on computers. Numbers had always appeared in history books: it was standard Baconian practice to report the election returns to prove that so-and-so was actually elected. The official numbers were so sacrosanct that the Baconians never adjusted or manipulated them. Even stating results in terms of percentages was a bit daring. The Turnerians used quantitative data extensively and were not afraid to manipulate figures—all their maps were based on percentages and rates. They remained locked into statistical maps, which do make strong geographical patterns visible, but which are extremely tedious to draw, and which obscure rather than unveil complex patterns. To properly handle numbers like census data and election returns, much more sophisticated techniques are necessary, including cross-tabulation, correlation, analysis of variance, multivariate regression, factor analysis, and logarithmic transformations. All of these techniques were well developed in the other social sciences by 1930, but historians remained ignorant of them. Data cards, and sorting machines to tabulate the information on them, had been invented for use in taking the census of 1890 and would have been of great help to Turnerians, but the technique remained unknown until the 1940's. Withal, the

14

Turnerians had more exposure to quantification than other historians. Although Turnerian political history had largely died out, the intellectual tradition lived on among rural historians, and thence came several pioneers of the new approach, including Lee Benson, Samuel P. Hays, and Allan G. Bogue.

The evolution of technique in the genre was rapid. Before 1970, most studies relied largely on percentages; after that the availability of prepackaged statistical routines such as SPSS (Statistical Package for the Social Sciences) for large mainframe computers facilitated much more complex correlation and regression studies. More important than the statistical routines were the new emphasis on precise definition of variables and categories, and the exploitation of previously underutilized data on ward and precinct voting patterns. The ICPSR archive of computerized data was a useful resource, but since it did not include electoral data for units smaller than counties, much fishing in newspapers, state reports, and archives was still required.

The logical positivism of Ernest Nagel, Carl Hempel, and Abraham Kaplan, as well as the philosophy of science expounded by Karl Popper and Paul Lazarsfeld, instructed researchers in the need for the explicit definitions of variables, the clear statement of hypotheses, and the importance of formulating propositions that, instead of being moralistic evaluations, could be falsified or disproven by empirical evidence.

The new political historians became aware of technical problems never before dreamed of by historians. The "ecological fallacy" was especially troubling in the 1960's, for it indicated that the correlation observed between two variables based on aggregate data would be typically quite different from the correlation based on individuals. For example, if the Democratic percentage of the vote and the Roman Catholic percentage were measured for the counties of a state, the correlation would be a misleading indication of how Democratic the Roman Catholics actually were. The county-level correlation usually would be much higher than the individual correlation. Fortunately, good technical solutions for this difficulty were discovered. The historian was not concerned with how Pat O'Reilly voted; what mattered was how Roman Catholics as a group voted. Under certain conditions (which could be checked), the regression coefficient with Demo-

crat the dependent variable and Roman Catholic the independent variable would be the same for both aggregate and individual levels. Indeed, without having any information on specific individuals, the historian could discover how Roman Catholics voted. Further advances in this technique (called "ecological regression") permitted historians in the late 1970's to estimate how individuals changed their voting patterns between elections. Thus it was possible to estimate how men who had voted Whig or Democratic in 1852 cast their ballots in 1856 or 1860 and even to say how citizens who did not vote in 1852 voted in later years. It was done by straightforward regressions of 1856 or 1860 election returns augmented by census data that showed how many men were eligible to vote. Whether even more dazzling techniques will be invented, to squeeze information on the patterns of behavior from old tables of numbers, remains to be seen. One possible route will be the use of computer models to simulate elections; by adjusting the parameters of the model it may be possible to replicate the historic numerical pattern of returns. The imaginative historian can then deduce that the parameters measure a reality that was always there but remained hidden, and can interpret the parameters in terms of the politics of the era. Simulation models are already a standard tool in demography. Presidential election simulations are now available commercially as "games" for microcomputers.

The study of legislators had always posed a dilemma for historians: on the one hand, it was clear that Congress and the state legislatures played a central role in the translation of party politics, ideas, and socioeconomic forces into public policy; on the other hand, the complexity of the abundant documentation prevented historians from figuring out how the process worked. As a consequence, political historiography largely ignored legislatures. A better methodology was called for, and political science provided it. As early as the 1890's, A. Lawrence Lowell had devised methods for analyzing roll call votes; Stuart Rice, Herman Beyle, and others had advanced the techniques in the 1920's. The Turnerians drew many maps of roll calls but ran into difficulty interpreting them, for the maps greatly exaggerated the apparent importance of legislators from thinly settled areas (like Montana), while obscuring the patterns in dense areas (like Philadelphia) that actually had more votes and more importance. In the 1930's and 1940's mathematical psychologists, especially L. L. Thurstone, Rensis Likert, Louis Guttman, and Paul Lazarsfeld, had devised methods for discovering attitudes from responses to a series of questions. Although originally intended as a method for handling responses to public opinion polls, these "scaling" procedures could readily be applied to legislative roll calls.

Joel Silbey in *The Shrine of Party: Congressional Voting Behavior, 1841–1852* (Pittsburgh, Pa., 1967) and Thomas B. Alexander in *Sectional Stress and Party Strength: A Study of Roll-Call Voting Patterns in the United States House of Representatives, 1836–1860* (Nashville, Tenn., 1967) used Guttman's scaling technique to explore the relative importance of party affiliation and geographic sectionalism in Congress during the antebellum period. They discovered scales that described in close detail the ideological positions of each congressman on issues like slavery, banking, railroads, and land policy. The ICPSR gathered a comprehensive set of congressional roll call votes, which encouraged the exploration of patterns over two centuries. Ballard Campbell in *Representative Democracy: Public Policy and Midwestern Legislatures in the Late Nineteenth Century* (Cambridge, Mass., 1980) performed elaborate scale analysis of the Wisconsin, Illinois, and Iowa legislatures. Using multivariate statistical techniques, he showed that the personal background of legislators was far less important than their party affiliations and the ethnocultural composition of their constituencies. Allan G. Bogue in *The Earnest Men: Republicans of the Civil War Senate* (Ithaca, N.Y., 1981) and other scholars examined Civil War and Reconstruction congressional roll calls to operationalize the intellectual historians' notions of "radicalism" and to determine just who it was who wielded power in those critical times. In contrast to the abundance of roll calls in the nineteenth and twentieth centuries, few were recorded in the eighteenth century. Nevertheless Robert Zemsky in *Merchants, Farmers, and River Gods* (Boston, 1971) was able to determine the distribution of power among members of the Massachusetts legislature by charting the allocation of committee assignments. Rudolph Bell in *Party and Faction in American Politics: The House of Representatives, 1789–1801* (Westport, Conn., 1973) used roll calls and advanced techniques, like factor analysis, to specify the emergence of parties from the inchoate factionalism and localism of the first decade of Congress.

Roll call analysis is tedious work, and not many historians have used it. Twentieth-century congresses have been studied for a few periods, but much remains to be done. Very little work has been done on state legislatures for any era, but Campbell's demonstration of the utility of roll call analysis provides a model that could be used for most states. Until that is done, historians will simply have to guess how politics was turned into policy.

The response of other historians to the new methodology was diverse. Hundreds of younger scholars taught themselves quantification or enrolled in training institutes sponsored by the ICPSR or the Newberry Library. Some dismissed quantification as a passing fad, confident that the mood would eventually shift back to older methods they could understand. A few vigorously denounced quantification as a snare and a delusion—it was black magic and either would not work or should not work. And the critics suffered under the handicap of not having the vaguest idea of what they were condemning. The rapid spread of microcomputers throughout academia in the 1980's will give historians and students a better chance to explore computerized data sets and to appreciate the strengths and assumptions of quantitative methods. Even so, the most telling and constructive critiques will come from scholars who have thoroughly immersed themselves in the new methods.

FUNCTION AND SYSTEM IN THE NEW POLITICAL HISTORY

Explicit quantitative research designs characterized much of the new political history, changing drastically the tone of a field that had once emphasized narrative and had always minimized discussions of how it should proceed. A more profound innovation was thinking of politics as a system—either as a self-contained world with its own inner laws or as a subsystem of the entire society. In 1888 James Bryce had metaphorically characterized politics as a system. German idealistic historiography of the late nineteenth century, best reflected in the United States in Henry Jones Ford's *The Rise and Growth of American Poli-*

tics (New York, 1898), had a stronger system approach, for it conceptualized society in terms of an organism that went through stages of evolution. Organic metaphors had long since died out when the new historians turned to sociology, political science, and economics for their ideas of what a system was like.

From the sociology of Talcott Parsons and Robert Merton—and ultimately from Max Weber and Emile Durkheim—came the notion of functionalism. The component institutions and processes of politics—like political parties, machines, platforms, campaigns, voting decisions, and candidate recruitment channels—all performed certain functions. Walter Dean Burnham, the most influential of the political scientists working on American political history, identified the functions of party as nation-building, office-filling, socialization of the voters, and policy-making. The insights drawn from comparative political science proved especially helpful in defining such functions. William Chambers and Seymour Martin Lipset, for example, could write about *Political Parties in a New Nation: The American Experience, 1776–1809* (New York, 1963) and *The First New Nation: The United States in Historical and Comparative Perspective* (New York, 1963). Historians who had concentrated too exclusively on the office-filling and policy-making roles had failed to appreciate the importance of party in uniting a nation and in educating its citizens on public issues and in democratic modes of expression.

The functionalist approach suddenly made the big city bosses respectable, for their centralized leadership was necessary to pull together the explosively divergent components in a large city; furthermore, the machines helped millions of immigrants to acculturate themselves to a new society and gave them direct assistance in time of need. The new image of bosses as do-gooders went too far in repudiating the middle-class Progressive critique, for it overlooked the machines' unfairness, their waste, and their protection of criminals who preyed primarily on the poor.

The absence of a contemporary intellectual tradition endorsing the machines, or analyzing the integrative functions of the parties, was irrelevant for the functionalists. Ideas did not matter; only the results generated by the system did, whether or not anyone at the time recognized them. Paul Kleppner subjected newspaper editorials to a statistical content analysis in *The Cross*

of Culture: A Social Analysis of Midwestern Politics, 1850–1900 (New York, 1970), one of the key monographs of the new genre. He showed that the rhetorical emphasis projected by the parties was based not nearly so much on appeals to economic or class interests as to cultural sentiments that were not at all tied to economics. The functionalists resembled the Beardians in seeing partisan speeches and platforms as propaganda devices. But instead of then dismissing the rhetoric as an effort to mislead the people from realizing what was actually happening, they analyzed the rhetoric to see what politicians felt was troubling the electorate. By figuring out which way the editors were trying to push their readers, historians tried to deduce where the readers actually stood. It was not necessary, as it had been for Beardians, to assume that voters actually believed the propaganda, for the behavior of the electorate could be examined directly, and it often went contrary to the party rhetoric.

In *The Winning of the Midwest: Social and Political Conflict, 1888–1896* (Chicago, 1971) and *Grass Roots Politics* (Westport, Conn., 1983) Richard Jensen stressed the depth of party loyalty in the late nineteenth century, and the "army" style that parties used to exploit it. Techniques of political socialization, such as door-to-door canvassing and huge rallies, were studied to gauge the effectiveness of the parties as educators. The overall success of the system in educating the people and drawing their support was measured by turnout, which was an indicator that became as important in the new political history as the "who won" question had once been. By the early 1980's, historians inspired by anthropologist Clifford Geertz were studying the ceremonies, symbols, rhetoric, and implicit norms surrounding elections to explain the linkages between the political and the social systems. Exemplifying this trend were Harry Stout's essays on New England, the magistral *The Transformation of Virginia: 1740–1790* (Chapel Hill, N.C., 1982) by Australian historian Rhys Isaac, and Jean H. Baker's *Affairs of Party: The Political Culture of Northern Democrats in the Mid-Nineteenth Century* (Ithaca, N.Y., 1983).

The chief synthesizing device of the systems approach is the notion of the party system. Chambers and Burnham, who outlined the synthesis in *The American Party Systems: Stages of Political Development* (New York, 1967), demarcated five systems by date: 1789 to 1820, 1828 to 1854–1860, 1863 to 1893, 1894 to 1932, and 1932 to the present. The most recent overview, *The Evolution of American Electoral Systems* (Westport, Conn., 1981), edited by Paul Kleppner, made only minor adjustments in chronology, though one contributor, Ronald P. Formisano, cast doubt on whether party loyalty was sufficiently well developed in the earliest period to call it a system. Formisano illustrated his interpretation at length in *The Transformation of Political Culture: Massachusetts, 1789–1848* (Cambridge, Mass., 1983).

The party system conceptualization permitted a fresh periodization of the past, one that depended upon the changes in structure discovered by historical analysis rather than the events that contemporaries thought might be important. The Civil War was no longer a watershed, for the systemic change came in the 1850's—and it perhaps caused the war, as Michael Holt would argue. From the perspective of the new political history, the Civil War—or rather the responses of the parties and the voters to the new problems occasioned by the war and its aftermath—is of interest to the extent that it had a permanent effect on voters (which it did), or that it demonstrated the functionalism of parties in a time of social crisis. The Republican party played a decisive role in mobilizing men, money, and morale for the Union cause. In the Confederacy, parties had been discarded in the name of national unity, much to the detriment of the cause. In the new periodization, the Progressive Era fades out, replaced by the dramatic upheavals of the 1890's. Lewis Gould and Jensen stressed the importance of McKinley in committing the polity to a spirit of pluralism and prosperity for all. The New Deal stays, but only because it marked a restructuring of politics. Old heroes no longer stride the stage, for they have been replaced by quieter characters who have more to do with the real drama of politics. Theodore Roosevelt has not yet vanished—he provides too many good lines—but William McKinley has joined Franklin Roosevelt in the role of superstar of politics over the last hundred years.

The party system, as Chambers and Burnham presented it, was linked to the broader processes of social and economic development. Their approach reflected the strong concern that political scientists of the 1960's showed in modernization, especially in how underdeveloped societies could build stable governments and encourage economic growth. Later work on party systems concentrated on their internal structures, but as historians became interested in the manner in which the United States developed such a complex economic and social system, they began building system models of modernization and tried to fit in politics. Historians and sociologists had long ascribed to technological innovation the main motive force that transformed the economy, with society adjusting to its changing configurations. By the 1950's the catchwords "industrialization" and "urbanization" were used to describe the modernization process. Intellectual historians demonstrated that Hamiltonian, Whig, and progressive ideologies were directed toward more rapid modernization, while Jeffersonian, Jacksonian, and agrarian thought tried to resist the process. Samuel P. Hays, in a series of essays collected in *American Political History as Social Analysis* (Knoxville, Tenn., 1980), and Robert H. Wiebe in *The Search for Order, 1877–1920* (New York, 1967), while remaining sensitive to intellectual trends, emphasized modernizing social forces as the causal agency, especially the emergence of regional and national associations of businessmen and professionals.

Numerous studies, including Morton Keller's *Affairs of State: Public Life in Late Nineteenth Century America* (Cambridge, Mass., 1977), Richard L. McCormick's *From Realignment to Reform: Political Change in New York State, 1893–1910* (Ithaca, N.Y., 1981), Otis L. Graham, Jr.'s, *The Great Campaigns: Reform and War in America, 1900–1928* (Englewood Cliffs, N.J., 1971), and Ellis W. Hawley's *The Great War and the Search for a Modern Order: A History of the American People and Their Institutions, 1917–1933* (New York, 1979), reinterpreted the late nineteenth and early twentieth centuries in terms of the interaction between the political, social, and economic systems. James M. McPherson's *Ordeal by Fire: The Civil War and Reconstruction* (New York, 1981) and Richard D. Brown's *Modernization: The Transformation of American Life, 1600–1865* (New York, 1976) applied the same approach to the entire period through the Civil War. On the state level, Dwight B. Billings, Jr., wrote of the success of the "Prussian model" of imposed modernization in *Planters and the Making of a 'New South': Class, Politics, and Development in North Carolina, 1865–1900* (Chapel Hill, N.C.,

1979). *Illinois: A Bicentennial History* (New York, 1978) by Jensen was a systematic attempt to explain political conflict in terms of individual psychological reactions to social and economic modernization. Political scientists have used the party-system schema in its original form to explore the question of how different policy programs emerged from the different party systems, most notably in Burnham's *Critical Elections and the Mainsprings of American Politics* (New York, 1970). Although most historians took an ambivalent view of the benefits and hardships of modernization, strongly negative interpretations that romanticized the backwoods could be found in Lawrence Goodwyn's *Democratic Promise: The Populist Movement in America* (New York, 1976), Ronald D. Eller's *Miners, Millhands, and Mountaineers: Industrialization of the Appalachian South, 1880–1930* (Knoxville, Tenn., 1982), and David L. Carlton's *Mill and Town in South Carolina: 1880–1920* (Baton Rouge, La., 1982). Carlton even had some good words to say for the lynching of blacks—it was an inevitable expression of the spirit of revolt among the white working class in the face of modernizing reforms imposed on them against their will.

Systems thinking had a tendency to expand to cover not just more chronology or geography, but also more of the social and the economic structure. What causes what was not the primary concern of functionalists, who saw the components of the system as mutually reinforcing. Conflict arises when two components become dysfunctional toward one another. Something has to give, and politics and constitutional law are the arenas in which they must be settled. Systems thinking, having abandoned the organic metaphors of idealism but not the imperative to find what made the entire configuration change, also encouraged a search for the "laws" of history. Many social scientists in the 1950's and 1960's thought modernization models were such laws. Their confidence diminished when it became apparent that underdeveloped countries were not "developing" very well, even if they tried to follow the precepts of modernization theorists.

NEWTONIAN MODELS OF POLITICS

The search for the laws of history took a new form in the 1960's when political scientists and some historians began to fit mathematical models to election data. The technique, and the philosophy that supported it, derived ultimately from the triumph of Newtonianism in physics. It really was possible to discover the laws of the universe using the right data and powerful mathematics. Furthermore, modern macroeconomics had created mathematical models, like those of John Maynard Keynes, that seemingly explained how the economy worked. To do the same for political history would require suitable statistical tools, which economics and sociology provided, together with the right data, which the ICPSR provided.

After a false start looking for cycles in the history of elections (there were none), the Newtonians combined the party system scheme with V. O. Key's notion of a "critical election" (one in which the voting alignments are permanently shifted). Using state election returns stretching over many decades, and later using county returns, they calculated the correlations between elections, looking for breaks that would signal a critical election. Since single elections did not work very well, the concept was broadened to cover "critical eras," which were sequences of several elections. The broadest studies were James L. Sundquist's *Dynamics of the Party System: Alignment and Realignment of Political Parties in the United States* (Washington, D.C., 1983) and *Partisan Realignment: Voters, Parties, and Government in American History* (Beverly Hills, Calif., 1981) by Jerome M. Clubb, William H. Flanigan, and Nancy H. Zingale. Unfortunately, far too many critical turning points were discovered, and by the early 1980's the approach was falling into discredit. One basic problem was that the data units were states and counties, but the conceptual unit on which realignment turned was the voter. The fact that two elections were highly correlated in terms of county patterns did not tell whether or not they were correlated in terms of voter behavior. And worse, if two elections were not correlated, that suggested that some sort of realignment had taken place, but the technique told nothing about the actual realignment.

Newtonianism based on macroeconomic analogies had failed—but perhaps the laws of political history could be discovered using microeconomics, that is, models of how individuals rather than entire systems behave. J. Morgan Kousser and Melvyn Hammarberg, the most dedicated of the Newtonians, produced a series of studies that tried to show what political history would look like if micro models of "rational choice" were true. The results have thus far been inconclusive, because the necessary individual data are hard to come by and the quantitative techniques were beyond the ken of nearly all historians.

A debate erupted in political science in the early 1970's regarding the relative importance of structure and ideas. True Newtonians felt that the "laws" of human behavior would be the same through the ages: people always react exactly the same way under the same conditions. History, then, is not the study of changing values or patterns of response but only the study of changing structural conditions. The rate of turnout and political participation fell drastically between 1900 and 1920. The Newtonians ascribed the drop to changing structures, particularly more stringent voter-registration laws and disfranchisement programs. Burnham disagreed: people really had changed, he said, citing the evidence produced by behavioral historians. The new registration rules had made only a small difference.

INDIVIDUAL VOTERS IN AN ETHNOCULTURAL ENVIRONMENT

The ethnocultural approach to political history emerged in the 1960's and soon became the dominant mode of explaining nineteenth-century political history. Like other forms of the new political history, it was quite explicit about methodological presuppositions and used quantitative methods extensively. In employing history as a science, the approach adopted the prescriptions for hypothesis formulation and testing proposed by philosophers of science. It added an extremely individualistic viewpoint: political history should focus on the voter, with the goal being the understanding of democracy as the interaction between the voter and the political system. This individualism paralleled new approaches in economics, which emphasized the rational process by which individuals plan for the future, and in sociology, which examined how the background characteristics of individuals (race, family, birth cohort) interacted with individual choices (regarding education, marriage, and migration, for example) and the overall social environment to generate particular career paths (social mobility). The statistical techniques that were used came directly from survey research and indirectly from biology. In contrast to the Newtonians, the ethnoculturalists were not looking for mathematical laws that dealt with entire systems: they searched instead for the strategies that individuals used to survive in their environments. Probability and statistics, rather than deterministic mathematical models, were the main tools.

The ethnocultural model of individualistic voter behavior relied heavily upon the classic study of *The American Voter* (New York, 1960) by Angus Campbell, Philip Converse, Warren Miller, and Donald Stokes, of the University of Michigan. Their theory, based strongly on social psychology, envisioned a funnel of causality into which went various predisposing attitudes and personal characteristics, as well as evaluations of the candidates, the parties, and the issues; out came the voting decision. The most important single input was a person's party identification; the vast majority of people adopted the partisanship of their parents. *The American Voter* did not try to explain how partisanship arose in the first place: that would be the challenge for historians.

The ethnoculturalists began by asking how individuals in the past actually voted. Initially lacking any evidence on individual attitudes and votes, they looked at groups. Samuel P. Hays and his students at Iowa, Lee Benson at Wayne State University, and Thomas B. Alexander at the University of Alabama collected precinct and township voting returns in the late 1950's (for Iowa, New York, and Alabama, respectively) and started matching them against census data. One result was immediately apparent: poor areas did not vote differently than rich areas. While this did not prove that rich individuals actually voted differently than poor ones, it suggested as much and stood in sharp contrast to the Beardian interpretation. Furthermore, adjacent small areas often voted for opposite candidates, thus undercutting the Turnerian notion that broad geographical forces were paramount. Finally, it was noticed that the same areas behaved the same way politically for decades or longer. What force was it that differentiated the areas and was so strong that it could persist for so long?

The scholars systematically searched for clues, using as many different local electoral units as possible so that particularized influences, like a strong party organization in one area, would average out. The results for the northern United States soon became clear: a combination of ethnicity and religion—German plus Roman Catholic, for example—could account for the patterns. In the South after the Civil war, race was the paramount factor; before the war the chief factor was isolation versus linkage to the larger economy.

The scientific methodology called for explanation rather than mere description, and each scholar developed a slightly different model. In *The Concept of Jacksonian Democracy; New York as a Test Case* (Princeton, N.J., 1961), Benson, influenced by the Columbia sociologist Robert Merton, argued that the ethnocultural groups, as he called them, were often hostile to one another on the basis of prejudice or, more exactly, different life-styles. Roman Catholics distrusted Protestants and vice versa, and each group tried to use its voting power to block the other's and enhance its own position. This interpretation is a variant of interest-group theorizing, with ethnocultural groupings replacing economic interests. In *Forging a Majority: The Formation of the Republican Party in Pittsburgh, 1848–1860* (New Haven, Conn., 1969), Michael Fitzgibbon Holt showed how ethnocultural conflict, rather than slavery or economic issues, shaped party lines in one major city. In *A House for All Peoples: Ethnic Politics in Chicago, 1890–1936* (Lexington, Ky., 1971), John M. Allswang showed that ethnicity grew stronger in the twentieth century as new groups emigrated from Europe. Allan J. Lichtman in *Prejudice and the Old Politics: The Presidential Election of 1928* (Chapel Hill, N.C., 1979) demonstrated that religious conflicts overshadowed all other divisions in 1928. A broad overview covering all of American politics down through the Civil War, using the ethnocultural group-conflict perspective, is *The Cultural Pattern in American Politics: The First Century* (New York, 1979) by Robert L. Kelley.

A much stronger interpretation appeared in *The Cross of Culture; A Social Analysis of Midwestern Politics, 1850–1900* (New York, 1970) by Paul Kleppner, *The Winning of the Midwest: Social and Political Conflict, 1888–1896* (Chicago, 1971) by Richard J. Jensen, and *The Birth of Mass Political Parties, Michigan 1827–1861* (Princeton, N.J., 1971) by Ronald P. Formisano. They recognized that ethnocultural forces had three dimensions. First, the church or the racial/ethnic groups formed organizations with their own leaders and newspapers, expressing their needs for tax relief and public acceptance. Second, the membership formed a natural group—people saw each other regularly, intermarried, and talked politics. It would be an obvious strategy for politicians to insinuate themselves with ethnocultural voters. The third and most important dimension was that the churches were communities of believers for whom religious teachings and moral values were of paramount importance. To the extent that democratic politics expressed the values of the people, and the people themselves were religious, then politics had to express religious values. The ethnoculturalists went further: American Christianity did not have a single theology or moral value system but, rather, tended to polarize into what were called "pietistic" (or "evangelical") and "liturgical" (or "ritualistic") forms. The pietists, represented by Methodists and Congregationalists among others, understood their Christian duty to be the reforming of the world—sin must be banished, and the government should help do the job. By defining slavery and liquor as sinful, the pietists raised new issues that would form the main substance of political debate. The liturgists (especially Roman Catholics, German Lutherans, and Southern Baptists) vehemently rejected the notion of salvation through government action. Salvation for man could come only through faithful adherence to church rituals and beliefs. Although they did not see slavery and liquor as inherently good, they did condemn as "puritanical" efforts of the pietists to enact a moral code into law. The pietists, the ethnoculturalists demonstrated, formed the core of the Whig and Republican parties, while the liturgists formed the core of the Democratic party. Not only did they vote in these ways, but the groups transferred some of their intense loyalty to the parties that they saw as standing for their own deeply felt values.

The ethnocultural interpretation was synthetic, drawing together much of the best of earlier scholarship. Turnerian sectionalism? The ethnocultural groups were not uniformly distributed but clustered in certain areas, giving the voting returns their particular cast. Ideas? The ideas of the different groups, as discussed every Sunday morning and debated endlessly in small groups, were of decisive importance. The ideas of philosophers may have mattered when democracy hardly existed or religion was weak, but after the great revivals in religion in the 1830's, and the simultaneous invention of democratic parties, the values of the people were paramount. Interest groups? The ethnocultural groups had certain interests of their own (say, for example, in parochial schools); and other interests, including economic ones, obviously existed in society and were involved in politics. But the key point is that such interests were never strong enough to create the party loyalty and active participation that characterized millions of ordinary people, most of whom could see only a remote bearing of economic issues on their lives. But the politicians did succeed in translating slavery, money, and even tariffs into moralistic terms comprehensible to the people.

To clinch the evidence of a tight linkage between ethnocultural groups and voting behavior, scholars used advanced statistical techniques on aggregate election returns. They also discovered masses of information on the individual voters of the nineteenth century, in the form of poll books and directories that listed political, economic, and religious data on each voter. The ethnocultural groupings (a combination of ethnicity and religious affiliation) were everywhere the most powerful correlate of party affiliation, and occupation was a modest second. Wealth did not matter: a rich Methodist farmer from New England was as likely to vote Republican as a poor one.

To relate individual voting patterns to the larger political system was the next item on the agenda. Melvyn Hammarberg, in *The Indiana Voter* (Chicago, 1977), used Newtonian approaches, which seemed more scientific to him than the ethnocultural model. More successful was Paul Kleppner in a series of books, including *The Third Electoral System: Parties, Voters, and Political Cultures* (Chapel Hill, N.C., 1979), *Who Voted? The Dynamics of Electoral Turnout, 1870–1980* (New York, 1982), and the collaborative volume *The Evolution of American Electoral Systems* (Westport, Conn., 1981). The appearance of occupa-

tion (and, in the twentieth century, education) as additional determinants of partisanship suggested that the pietistic-liturgical dimension could be subsumed in a more general modernization dichotomy. Persons with a more modern psychological outlook toward the future joined pietistic churches, educated themselves, obtained better jobs, and identified with the Whig and Republican parties, which espoused similar values and a vision of a rapidly industrializing nation. Persons with a traditional attitude, who were more fearful of change, found comfort in liturgical ceremonies, stayed in low-skilled farming or laboring jobs, resisted novelty and education, and voted for the party—the Democrats—that pledged to protect them from the reformers.

The ethnocultural model claims to explain the most important features of American political history. It substantiates this claim by arguing that the history of politics in a democratic society should accept the priorities of the people as they expressed them themselves, and that the empirical evidence indicates that ethical, cultural, and religious values, concerns, and interests were of the most interest to most of the people most of the time. Critics have accepted the empirical evidence, although grudgingly, but they challenge the major premise. New Left historians, picking up a theme developed by the Italian Marxist Antonio Gramsci, contend that the working classes lived under the hegemony of the bourgeoisie and that they therefore suffered a false consciousness of what their true values were or should have been. Others argue that political history should respond not to the past so much as to the present, and should explain the historical roots of the contemporary distribution of power and wealth in society or the manifestations of racism and sexism.

Rather than issue an obituary for interest-group interpretations, it would be better to use a systems perspective to clarify the role of groups in historiography. The main outputs of the political system include legislation, administrative rulings, allocations of resources through spending and taxation, appointments to office, and the setting of the agenda for public debate. The interests of different groups, whether defined in terms of geography, economics, class, race, sex, or status, will be affected to a greater or lesser degree by each decision. The American polity emphasizes geography more than anything else, with each legislator sensitive to the needs of his or her district. With a multiplicity of interests inside each district, the legislator has to weigh the effects. The party system overlays geography, so that a Whig, Republican, or Democrat would weigh the interests in different fashion, always claiming to have the general good of the district uppermost in mind. Thus a biographer would be hard pressed to show how his or her subject was beholden to interests outside the district. One by one, each politician looks good.

The groups that perceive their own interests have long been studied by historians, with special attention given to ideological interests that transcend geography, such as the abolitionists of the 1830's, the scientific experts of the 1900's, and the civil rights advocates of recent decades. The Beardians focused on business and agricultural interests, while the ethnocultural school drew attention to ethnic and religious groups.

Very few historians, apart from some biographers, have paid attention to the local voices to which legislators hearken so closely. The reason, as Forrest MacDonald in *We the People* (Chicago, 1958) and Richard P. McCormick in *The Second American Party System* (Chapel Hill, N.C., 1966) demonstrated so exhaustively, is that local interests are exceedingly numerous and difficult to pin down. The Beardian dynamic in which agrarian, business, and slaveowner interests aggregated at the national level to shape political history simply could not withstand microscopic Baconian research. On the other hand, the accumulation of evidence about local factors could not provide a dynamic: surely the system has changed drastically over the centuries, but why?

Marxist historians in recent years have taken a new tack, borrowed chiefly from intellectual history. The common intellectual framework within which legislators, judges, and other power holders operated represented the hegemony of capitalism. The problem for Marxists, which they have been unable to solve, is to link the hegemony of capitalism to the actions or interests of capitalists, as opposed to the proletariat. An obvious problem is why socialism never flourished in America, and why the working classes gave so much fealty to city machines that accepted the overall hegemony of capitalism.

Modernization theorists, such as Samuel P.

Hays, coming out of social history, propose an entirely different analysis of the role of interest groups. They stress that the history of political conflict more nearly resembles a contest between cosmopolitans who, within a capitalist framework, tried to systematically modernize everyone, while peripheral groups such as subsistence farmers or immigrant groups tried to protect a more traditional life-style. The stories of prohibition, compulsory education, civil rights, and environmentalism have been told primarily from the modernization perspective. Both economic-interest groups and ethnocultural groups are treated in terms of their value systems and attitude toward modernity.

Charles and Mary Beard at times suggested a value-driven modernization process but then drew back to their basic assumption that material factors had to have priority over values. The younger Beardians, bitterly hostile toward "Robber Barons" and hopeful for a resurgence of populism under the New Deal, abandoned much of the subtlety of *The Rise of American Civilization.* Young Marxists today remain vehemently hostile to any modernization theories. They insist on the intrinsic value of working-class culture, which most of their research is designed to document. To celebrate, or even to acknowledge, the success of the modernizers in implanting middle-class values in the workers smacks too much of tragedy.

With the decline of the party system in recent decades, interest groups have organized themselves into effective lobbies at the state and national level. The new technology of computerized mailings helps dispersed ideological interests to communicate, while the rise of the political action committees (PACs) since the mid-1970's has given organized interests a major role in the financing of politics. Political scientists have begun the study of these new factors. Historians have yet to begin the process of reinterpreting the past in terms of an expanded awareness of what the shape of politics could have been, that is, of what the system might have looked like if interests had been as well organized then as they are today.

Methodologically conservative critics complain that political history has become too technical—too much like political science or sociology. While it is true that much of the most important recent research demands an understanding of techniques that were rarely provided to graduate students a few decades ago, the level of quantification and the amount of explicit theory nevertheless remain well below the usual level of the other social sciences. The complaint that the research designs of modern scholarship are beyond the ken of casual readers is true. However, the general public is already well served by popularizers through novels, biographies, films, museums, television, and pageants. It would roll back a century of scholarly advances to insist that the popular tactics of storytelling, moralizing, hero worship, antiquarianism, and gross oversimplification should replace careful research into complex and vital issues.

BIBLIOGRAPHY

No book or essay attempts to cover the historiography of American politics, but one major dichotomy is addressed in Bernard Sternsher, *Consensus, Conflict, and American Historians* (Bloomington, Ind., 1975). For an overview of the discipline, see John Higham, *History: Professional Scholarship in America* (Baltimore, Md., 1983). William T. Hutchinson, *The Marcus W. Jernegan Essays in American Historiography* (Chicago, 1937), provides biographical perspective on early researchers, as does Harvey Wish, *The American Historian: A Social-Intellectual History of the Writing of the American Past* (New York, 1960). The dominant figures of the early twentieth century are brilliantly analyzed in Richard Hofstadter, *The Progressive Historians: Turner, Beard, Parrington* (New York, 1968). On the Turner school see also Richard J. Jensen, "On Modernizing Frederick Jackson Turner," in *Western Historical Quarterly,* 11 (1980). The leading historians at mid-century are covered in Marcus Cunliffe and Robin W. Winks, eds., *Pastmasters: Some Essays on American Historians* (New York, 1969).

On the development of political science, see Donald M. Freeman, ed., *Foundation of Political Science: Research, Methods, and Scope* (New York, 1977); Martin Landau, "The Myth of Hyperfactualism in the Study of American Politics," in *Political Science Quarterly,* 83 (1968); Heinz Eulau, *The Behavioral Persuasion in Politics* (New York, 1963); and especially Albert Somit and Joseph Tanenhaus, *The Development of American Political Science: From Burgess to Behavioralism* (Boston, 1967). Current theories are outlined and critiqued in Ronald H. Chilcote, *Theories of Comparative Politics: The Search for a Paradigm* (Boulder, Colo., 1981).

For broad overviews of how historians since 1950 have treated the main political issues, see John Higham, ed., *The Reconstruction of American History* (New York, 1962); William H. Cartwright and Richard L. Watson, eds., *The Reinterpretation of American History and Culture* (Washington, D.C., 1973);

Frank Otto Gatell and Allen Weinstein, eds., *American Themes: Essays in Historiography* (New York, 1968); and Stanley I. Kutler and Stanley N. Katz, eds., *The Promise of American History: Progress and Prospects* (Baltimore, Md., 1983).

The historiography of state politics has its own traditions, brilliantly explained in John Alexander Williams, "A New Look at an Old Field," in *Western Historical Quarterly,* 9 (1978). On southern and western politics, see Arthur S. Link and Rembert W. Patrick, eds., *Writing Southern History: Essays in Historiography* (Baton Rouge, La., 1965); and Michael P. Malone, ed., *Historians and the American West* (Lincoln, Nebr., 1983). Unfortunately, there are no adequate surveys of the Midwest or Northeast.

The creation of the party systems in the 1830's has continually fascinated historians, whose interpretations have changed dramatically every twenty or thirty years. See Alfred A. Cave, *Jacksonian Democracy and the Historians* (Gainesville, Fla., 1964); Ronald P. Formisano, "Toward a Reorientation of Jacksonian Politics: A Review of the Literature, 1959–1975," in *Journal of American History,* 63 (1976); and Edward Pessen, *Jacksonian America: Society, Personality, and Politics,* rev. ed. (Homewood, Ill., 1978). On the following era, see Robert P. Swierenga, ed., *Beyond the Civil War Synthesis: Political Essays of the Civil War Era* (Westport, Conn., 1975).

Major new interpretations soon engender critical review essays, such as Allan J. Lichtman, "The End of Realignment Theory?" in *Historical Methods,* 15 (1982); Richard L. McCormick, "Ethno-Cultural Interpretations of Nineteenth-Century American Voting Behavior," in *Political Science Quarterly,* 89 (1974); and Robert Shalhope, "Republicanism and Early American Historiography," in *William and Mary Quarterly,* 39 (1982).

Allan G. Bogue has written several introductions to the "new political history," including "The New Political History in the 1970's," in Michael G. Kammen, ed., *The Past Before Us: Contemporary Historical Writing in the United States* (Ithaca, N.Y., 1980), 231–251; see also Philip R. VanderMeer, "The New Political History: Progress and Prospects," in *Computers and the Humanities,* 11 (1977). For the flavor of the approach, see the early essays collected in Joel H. Silbey and Samuel T. McSeveney, eds., *Voters, Parties, and Elections: Quantitative Essays in the History of American Popular Voting Behavior* (Lexington, Mass., 1972).

For interdisciplinary perspectives generally, see Richard E. Beringer, *Historical Analysis: Contemporary Approaches to Clio's Craft* (New York, 1978). The intersection of political science and historiography can be explored in Richard J. Jensen, "American Election Analysis: A Case History of Methodological Innovation and Diffusion," in S. M. Lipset, ed., *Politics and the Social Sciences* (New York, 1969), 226–243; and in Lee Benson et al., eds., *American Political Behavior: Historical Essays and Readings* (New York, 1974). One narrow but important research theme has been examined by Joel H. Silbey, "Congressional and State Legislative Roll-Call Studies by U.S. Historians," in *Legislative Studies Quarterly,* 6 (1981); and his " 'Delegates Fresh from the People': American Congressional and Legislative Behavior," in *Journal of Interdisciplinary History,* 13 (1983). On a closely related approach, see Howard Allen and Jerome M. Clubb, "Collective Biography and the Progressives," in *Social Science History,* 1 (1977). The sources and techniques of studying aggregate election returns are explained in Jerome M. Clubb, William H. Flanigan, and Nancy H. Zingale, eds., *Analyzing Electoral History: A Guide to the Study of American Voter Behavior* (Beverly Hills, Calif., 1981).

Newtonian perspectives tend to baffle intellectual and Baconian historians, especially when the quantitative methodology advances too far for them. Clear thinking and logical simplicity can be difficult to follow without suitable training. See Melvyn Hammarberg, "An Analysis of American Electoral Data," in *Journal of Interdisciplinary History,* 13 (1983); and J. Morgan Kousser, "Restoring Politics to Political History," in *Journal of Interdisciplinary History,* 12 (1982).

AGRICULTURAL POLICY

Gilbert C. Fite

FEDERAL agricultural policy deals with programs designed to promote agriculture and to assist individual farmers. Prior to the New Deal the federal government confined its activities on behalf of farmers mainly to land legislation, tariffs to protect certain agricultural commodities, promotion of foreign markets, passage of some credit legislation, and encouragement of agricultural education and research for the purpose of increasing agricultural productivity. After 1933, however, agricultural policy involved programs that dealt directly with production, conservation, and farm income, as well as the more traditional functions and policies.

THE NINETEENTH CENTURY

In the early years after independence, the major issue affecting farmers was public land policy. The question was whether Congress would establish a policy that favored ordinary farmers or use the public lands as a source of revenue. Early land legislation seemed to favor speculators and large landholders, rather than the smaller, family farmer. The Ordinance of 1785 provided that government land could be sold in plots of not less than 640 acres and at a minimum price of $1 per acre. The provisions regarding the quantity and price of land largely eliminated ordinary farmers as purchasers at government land offices. They simply did not have $640 to buy land. Most farmers who acquired land had to purchase it from speculators who bought large tracts and then sold off smaller acreages at higher prices. In 1796 Congress raised the price of government land to $2 an acre, placing an additional burden on the family farmer.

Strong pressure mounted to enact policies that would be more favorable to farm operators. The Land Law of 1800 was the first in a series of acts making it increasingly easy to purchase land directly from the federal government. This legislation reduced the amount of government land that a person had to buy from 640 to 320 acres and extended credit for up to four years. In 1804 the minimum acreage was cut to 160 acres. In 1820, under continuing pressure from western politicians, Congress eliminated the credit feature but lowered the price to $1.25 an acre and permitted a buyer to purchase as little as 80 acres. A farmer could now purchase a farm directly from the government for as little as $100.

By the 1830's and 1840's there were growing demands that the federal government give land to actual settlers. George Henry Evans, editor of the *Working Man's Advocate,* urged adoption of a homestead act, as did Horace Greeley, editor of the New York *Tribune,* and an increasing number of politicians. Following nearly a generation of political wrangling in which southern leaders opposed the homestead principle, Congress passed the Homestead Act in 1862. This law offered 160 acres of government land to anyone who was a citizen or had filed a declaration to become a citizen and who was at least twenty-one years old. The settler had only to pay a small filing fee, live on the land for five years, and cultivate part of it.

Passage of the Homestead Act represented the ultimate in democratic land policy. While speculators and corporations were able to subvert the intention of the law, tens of thousands of Americans did acquire farms under the act. Liberal federal land policy reflected the growing political power of the West, but it also resulted from a deeply held belief that there was something good about farmers and farming. Probably a majority of Americans agreed with Thomas Jefferson and other early national leaders who considered farmers honest, virtuous, independent, democratic, and especially solid citizens who contributed wealth and political stability to the growing nation.

The Homestead Act was only one of three laws passed in 1862 that were of vital importance to American farmers. Congress also provided federal aid in the form of land grants to establish an agricultural and mechanical college in each state, and set up the United States Department of Agriculture (USDA). The so-called land-grant colleges and the USDA slowly began programs of education, research, and service to make farming more efficient and profitable. By 1900, appropriations for the USDA, which gained cabinet status in 1889, reached $3.6 million annually. Meanwhile, in 1887 Congress passed the Hatch Act, which initially provided $15,000 a year for each state and territory to help establish agricultural experiment stations. By the turn of the century, much was beginning to be done at the federal level to help farmers become more efficient and productive.

In the late nineteenth century, the federal government encouraged railway expansion, which opened up broader commercial markets for farm products. By distributing millions of acres of land to subsidize railroad construction, especially in the trans-Mississippi West, Congress greatly enlarged marketing opportunities for farmers. Before long, though, farmers began to look upon the railroads as exploiters. Nevertheless, through its subsidies to railways, the federal government helped to develop a national marketing system, which was important to commercial farmers.

Congress also responded to some specific farm demands. For example, the dairy interests convinced national lawmakers in 1886 to levy a special tax on oleomargarine, a competitor of butter. In 1892 Congress permitted the postmaster general to begin experimenting with free delivery of mail to farmers over rural routes. Rural free delivery was expanded in the late 1890's. Parcel post service, inaugurated in 1913, provided for the delivery of packages over rural mail routes.

Although the scientific work of the USDA, the agricultural colleges, and the experiment stations was potentially helpful to commercial agriculturists, many farmers in the late nineteenth century were more interested in policies that would directly affect their prices and incomes. From the 1870's to the late 1890's farm prices followed a long but uneven decline. In response to price drops and hard times, the Farmers' Alliance and other agricultural groups in the late 1880's demanded that the federal government enact laws to improve conditions. Western and southern farmers were especially vocal in their demands. By the early 1890's farmers were calling for cheap money and liberal credit policies, a subtreasury system from which farmers could borrow against storable agricultural commodities at cheap interest rates, government ownership of the railroads to bring down freight charges, and a federal income tax, which might reduce taxes on real property.

These policies were all defeated either by an unsympathetic Congress or, in the case of the income tax, by the Supreme Court. The presidential campaign of 1896 was crucial in the eyes of many southern and western farmers. After William McKinley, a Republican who represented business, larger commercial farmers, and conservative interests in general, triumphed over Democrat William Jennings Bryan, the candidate of western and southern farmers, the economic demands of farmers went unheeded by the president and Congress.

EARLY TWENTIETH CENTURY

Conditions on American farms greatly improved after the turn of the century. Commodity and land prices advanced sharply between 1900 and the outbreak of World War I and rose even higher during the war years. The period from 1900 to 1920, when demand grew faster than supply, often has been called the golden age of American agriculture. Despite declining political pressure by farmers, Congress did enact legislation that met some of the earlier farm demands. In 1913 lawmakers passed the Federal Reserve Act, which provided a more flexible credit system for the nation, and three years later enacted the Federal Farm Loan Act to provide long-term credit for farm purchases. In 1916, during the first Woodrow Wilson administration, Congress passed the Warehouse Act, which permitted the issuance of warehouse receipts against properly stored agricultural products. These receipts could be used as collateral for bank loans. The Cotton Futures Act (1914) and the Grain Standards Act (1916) placed some federal regulations over marketing of farm crops. The Rural Post Roads Act of 1916 provided for federal matching funds to states for road-building. This law was initially designed mainly to help farmers meet their transportation and market needs. Moreover, Congress did not neglect agricultural education. The Smith-Lever Act of 1914 gave federal support to agricultural extension activities, and the Smith-Hughes Act of 1917 subsidized the teaching of agriculture and home economics in high schools.

By World War I the federal government had underwritten a wide variety of policies to assist agriculture: land legislation, support for agricultural education and research, federal farm credit, regulation of markets, and many other services. By 1914 the USDA was spending about $22 million annually to provide education, research, and service programs for farmers.

AGRICULTURAL DEPRESSION, 1920–1933

The prosperity that had come with World War I ended in late 1920, when heavy production, declining exports, foreign competition in world markets, and a depressed industrial economy combined to drive agricultural prices to disastrously low levels. Gross farm income dropped about 40 percent between 1920 and 1921. This was the beginning of nearly a generation of hard times for American farmers. It was not until the outbreak of World War II that real farm prosperity returned.

In earlier periods of agricultural depression, farmers had called mainly for improved credit facilities, laws regulating big business, and legislation that would support cooperative marketing. But the depression of 1920–1921 brought loud and widespread demands for governmental actions that could somehow raise farm prices. Several bills were introduced that would have required the federal government to set the prices of certain agricultural products at a figure considerably above the going market rate. In 1921

Senator George W. Norris of Nebraska introduced a measure to establish an export corporation to buy American farm products and sell them abroad on credit. This, it was believed, would remove some of the price-depressing surpluses from the domestic market and raise prices. None of the schemes that would have used the power of the federal government to lift prices received congressional approval.

As farm prices remained especially low from 1921 to 1923, the agricultural interests continued to seek solutions in Washington. In 1921 a group of western and southern senators formed the farm bloc to push farm relief legislation in the Senate. A similar but less cohesive group was organized in the House of Representatives. The farm bloc took credit for passing the Packers and Stockyards Act in 1921 and the Future Trading Act of the same year, both of which dealt with regulating farm commodity sales. In 1922 the Capper-Volstead Cooperative Marketing Act passed, and the next year Congress enacted the Intermediate Credits Act. None of these laws, however, got to the heart of the farmers' problem.

The most widely discussed solution to the ills facing farmers did not come from farmers or their organizational spokesmen, but from two businessmen, George N. Peek and Hugh S. Johnson. Peek was president of the Moline Plow Company, and Johnson a lesser company official. Believing, as Peek said, that "you can't sell a plow to a busted customer," he and Johnson developed a plan that they called Equality for Agriculture.

Peek was among those who clearly grasped the basic difficulty confronting agriculture. While low prices were an obvious problem, the unfavorable relationship between farm and nonfarm prices was of even greater importance. As agriculture had become more commercialized, the welfare of farmers increasingly depended on the exchange value of their products—that is, on the amount of nonfarm goods and services that a bushel of wheat or a pound of cotton could buy. Statisticians in the USDA considered that farm and nonfarm prices were about at parity, or had a fair exchange value, in the period from 1909 to 1914. By the early 1920's farm commodities' prices were extremely low when compared to those of nonfarm goods. This placed farmers in a harsh cost-price squeeze. Considering the purchasing power of several basic farm products in 1913 as equaling 100, it dropped to only 67 in 1921, a loss of one-third in purchasing power. For some crops it was even more. Secretary of Agriculture Henry C. Wallace pointed out that the practical effect of the disparity in farm and nonfarm prices meant that a suit of clothes that cost a North Dakota farmer twenty-one bushels of wheat in 1913 cost him thirty-one bushels in 1923. It was to this disparity that Peek addressed himself. He believed that the federal government had a role to play in bringing about ratio prices or "equality for agriculture." The concept was that farm prices should be at a parity with nonfarm prices.

To achieve this goal, the first McNary-Haugen bill was introduced in 1924. The bill sought to restore and maintain prices of several basic agricultural commodities at a ratio or parity price by establishing a government corporation with the power to buy and dispose of surplus production. The portion of the wheat crop, for example, used in domestic consumption would be maintained at or near the ratio price behind a tariff wall, while the surplus would be sold abroad at whatever it would bring. Since exports would generally bring less than the ratio price, the corporation would lose money on that portion of the crop going into foreign markets. To cover that loss, each producer would pay a small "equalization fee" on each bushel or pound sold. Under this scheme the federal government would not provide any money except to help the corporation begin operations. In essence this was a two-price system that aimed at giving farmers parity for basic products sold in the domestic market.

The McNary-Haugen bill was before Congress in varying forms from 1924 to 1928. It passed in 1927 and 1928 only to be vetoed on both occasions by President Calvin Coolidge. While supporters of the legislation appealed to the basic fairness of parity prices for farmers, Coolidge and other opponents argued that it would raise food and raw-material prices, and help only a few farmers. Moreover, they insisted that the government should not become involved in handling farm products and that the law was unconstitutional.

Republican spokesmen such as Coolidge, Secretary of Commerce Herbert Hoover, and others claimed that farmers could solve their own price problems by organizing strong farmer cooperatives to provide orderly marketing. In 1926 Congress enacted the Cooperative Marketing Act, which established the Division of Cooperative Marketing in the USDA. This agency sought to assist farmer cooperatives in their marketing and purchasing activities. However, farmers had little faith in cooperatives as agencies capable of handling surpluses or raising prices.

The political fight in the 1920's over the McNary-Haugen legislation was highly significant in developing later agricultural policy. By 1928, parity prices had become the major goal of most farm groups, and some form of compulsory cooperation was considered essential if farmers were going to achieve fair prices. Furthermore, discussion of farm problems pointed up the surplus question, which caused some leaders to consider seriously some form of production control. Discussion of the controversy over agricultural policy also emphasized the ongoing cost-price squeeze under which so many farmers operated.

Following defeat of the McNary-Haugen legislation, Congress, with President Herbert Hoover's support, passed the Agricultural Marketing Act of 1929. This was the first general law that placed any responsibility on the federal government to help farmers deal with the problems of surpluses and low prices. The aim of the law was to place agriculture "on a basis of economic equality with other industries." This was the goal that farmers had been seeking, but most agricultural groups had little faith in the means devised to achieve their desired objective. The law provided $500 million to assist farmer cooperatives to strengthen their marketing power. Proponents of the legislation claimed that orderly marketing of farm products through strong farmer cooperatives could stabilize prices and benefit producers. In addition, the act permitted the Federal Farm Board, the administering agency, to establish government-financed stabilization corporations to maintain prices in case of unusual surpluses and market declines.

Shortly after passage of the Agricultural Marketing Act, farm prices began to fall under the weight of national and world depression. Loans from the Federal Farm Board to cooperatives were unable to halt the price declines, and attempts by the Farm Board to hold up the prices of wheat and cotton through stabilization corporations also failed. The Farm Board urged farmers to reduce price-depressing surpluses by producing less, but farmers ignored the advice. Since a farmer's income depended on the number of units produced multiplied by the price of each unit, in many cases lower prices actually encouraged farmers to increase their units of output. By 1931 the Federal Farm Board gave up trying to support prices above market levels. While the Agricultural Marketing Act might have been of some assistance to farmers in normal times, it was a dismal failure in the depression. The $500 million appropriated to the Farm Board by Congress might have temporarily given farmers slightly higher prices, but it had no lasting effect. Meanwhile, Congress provided some farmers with drought-relief loans in 1930 and 1931.

NEW DEAL POLICIES

Under the pressure of depression prices, mounting farm debt and foreclosures, and growing agrarian radicalism, there was increasing urgency by 1932 to do something to help farmers. Most of the farm-relief plans involved extensive government intervention to restore agricultural purchasing power. Throughout 1932, however, Congress and President Hoover could not agree on any legislation because of basic differences over what role government should play in agricultural policy. It was not until Franklin D. Roosevelt moved into the White House that an extensive legislative program to help farmers became law. The New Deal for agriculture attempted to undergird farmers on a scale undreamed of less than a decade earlier.

The first step in a broad federal program to restore agricultural prosperity was passage of the Agricultural Adjustment Act. Signed by President Roosevelt on 12 May 1933, this law sought to "reestablish prices to farmers at a level that will give agricultural commodities a purchasing power with respect to articles that farmers buy, equivalent to the purchasing power of agricultural commodities" in the base period. (The base period was 1909 to 1914, except for tobacco, for which it was 1919 to 1929.) To achieve this goal, it was considered essential to reduce surpluses and bring supply and demand into better balance. In the 1920's the McNary-Haugenites had

sought to remove price-depressing surpluses through a two-price system whereby the surplus would be segregated and sold abroad for whatever it would bring.

By the 1930's, foreign markets had declined to such a low level that most authorities did not believe such an approach could work. Secretary of Agriculture Henry A. Wallace and other farm leaders advocated not producing unneeded surpluses in the first place. Thus, the Agricultural Adjustment Act (AAA) called for reducing production of seven basic crops—wheat, cotton, corn, hogs, rice, tobacco, and milk—by making so-called benefit payments to cooperating producers. In short, farmers would be paid for taking cropland out of production. The expected benefit would be twofold: higher prices for a smaller amount produced, and a cash payment directly from the government. The funds for paying farmers were to come from special taxes on processors of agricultural commodities.

By the end of 1933 slightly over one million cotton growers had signed contracts to reduce production. Since cotton had already been planted, farmers plowed under some 10 million acres. In return they received $169 million in benefit payments, plus higher market prices. Wheat growers signed contracts promising to reduce acreage in 1934 and 1935 and received government checks in the fall of 1933 totaling some $98 million. For tobacco growers, the AAA worked out marketing agreements with the buyers, which gave producers nearly double the income they received in 1932. In return, the farmers had to promise to reduce acreage in 1934 and 1935. A corn-hog program was initiated in 1934 when farmers reduced corn acreage in return for cash payments. Pig litters were also cut. To remove surplus pork from the regular market, the government bought about 6.5 million pigs and pregnant sows between August 1933 and October 1934.

While the main thrust of government agricultural policy was to reduce overabundant production, the AAA attacked the surplus problem by distributing commodities through relief channels. The Federal Surplus Relief Corporation, organized in October 1933, began an extensive program of food distribution to needy people. Over the next few years cheese, milk, meat, flour, peanut butter, fresh fruits, and a wide variety of other products that the AAA acquired in attempts to strengthen prices were distributed mainly through state relief agencies.

Another basic government action designed to help farmers was the establishment of the Commodity Credit Corporation (CCC) in October 1933. Initially, this agency made nonrecourse loans on cotton and corn as a means of maintaining prices. This enabled corn farmers, for instance, to borrow a fixed amount per bushel on properly stored corn with no security except the grain. If the price went down, a borrower could simply turn the commodity over to the CCC; on the other hand, if it went above the loan value, he could sell the grain and keep the increase. After 1933 the number of crops eligible for CCC loans expanded, and the agency became the government's major means of supporting basic farm commodity prices.

Federal agricultural policy as it developed in the early New Deal days went far beyond just trying to raise farm prices. Federal credit programs were expanded and reorganized. The Emergency Farm Mortgage Act, Title II of the Agricultural Adjustment Act, provided for refinancing some farm mortgages and for helping debt-ridden farmers in other ways. Congress passed the Frazier-Lemke bill in 1934, which restricted foreclosures on some types of delinquent farmer borrowers. While this law was declared unconstitutional, a more carefully drawn measure in 1935 stood the constitutional test. More important was the Farm Credit Act of June 1933. This law reorganized some of the older agricultural credit agencies and provided a comprehensive federal farm-credit program. Besides continuing long-term loans by the federal land banks that had been operating since 1917, Congress now provided for setting up special banks for farmer cooperatives and establishing production credit corporations to supply funds for local production credit associations. The production credit associations gave farmers a new source of cheap operating capital.

Congress also implemented programs to assist farmers with both advice and money to conserve their soil. There was a crying need for conservation of farmland in many parts of rural America. In 1933 the Soil Erosion Service was set up in the Department of the Interior to encourage and assist with soil conservation practices. This agency, replaced by the Soil Conservation Service in the USDA in 1935, encouraged

better land-management practices, including construction of dams, and building terraces and planting grass and trees on eroding land. The Soil Conservation and Domestic Allotment Act of 1936 made conservation a major part of basic agricultural policy with the use of a wide variety of cost-sharing projects.

Conservation and land restoration were also major purposes of the Tennessee Valley Authority (TVA), established by Congress in May 1933. Besides construction of dams for flood control and the generation of electricity, the TVA set up demonstration farms to show how farmers could benefit from such land improvement practices as building check-dams and terraces and planting ground cover. It was a massive government effort to change the landscape of an entire region.

Another New Deal program of great value to farmers was the Rural Electrification Administration (REA), begun in 1935. Private power companies had been reluctant to extend their electric lines into thinly populated farm areas, and in 1934 only about 11 percent of farmers had central-station electric service. In the west-south-central states the figure was only 2 percent. The REA made low-interest loans to rural electric cooperatives, which in turn built lines into rural communities and distributed power to farm homes. By 1941 some 2.3 million farmers, or about 38 percent, had central-station electric service.

The acreage restriction, price support programs, and benefit payments were most beneficial to the larger farmers, who had more acres to take out of production and greater output. But the poorer farmers were not totally neglected. The Resettlement Administration, established in 1935, relocated farmers who were struggling to exist on submarginal land, made loans to help some of the low-income operators, and organized a few cooperative agricultural communities. In 1937 this agency was absorbed by the Farm Security Administration, which provided loans for land purchases, as well as credit for buying livestock and equipment and for operating expenses. These programs touched only the fringes of the worst farm poverty and indicated only halfhearted commitment to the poorest farm people. The political power structure in agriculture—major farm-state congressmen and senators, the USDA, the American Farm Bureau Federation, the extension services, and the land-grant colleges—was mainly concerned with helping the more successful commercial farmers.

The extensive range of policies implemented to help farmers between 1933 and 1935 injected the federal government into the agricultural sector in a way that would have been considered revolutionary only a few years earlier. How could such policies be justified? While the immediate crisis associated with the Great Depression was important, it had been argued for years that farmers were in an unfair bargaining position as compared with other groups in the economy. The individual farmer had no control over the price he received for his products or over what he paid for nonfarm goods. He was an old-style competitive producer in an economy in which nonfarm prices were often set through agreement or through combination. Nonfarm producers tended to regulate their output to anticipated demand, which gave them greater control over their prices. Farmers, on the other hand, did not control their production, because of such factors as weather, disease, and the large number of producers who did not cooperate in planning their production. Thus, it was said, farmers needed what Secretary Henry A. Wallace called the "centralizing power of government."

Furthermore, extensive federal intervention in the farm economy was justified by the belief that economic recovery depended on a prosperous agriculture. The stated purpose of the AAA was to "relieve the existing national economic emergency by increasing agricultural purchasing power." Farm groups, and even nonfarmers, argued that national self-interest alone warranted government aid to agriculture. Jeffersonian agrarianism, the belief that farmers were important for the political stability of the country, still had millions of adherents in the early 1930's. In short, there seemed to be ample justification for the policies to raise farm incomes and improve rural living. Yet, farmers only reluctantly accepted production control as a means of improving agricultural conditions. It was a lesser evil than low prices.

In January 1936 the Supreme Court declared the major features of the Agricultural Adjustment Act unconstitutional. The Court held that the use of processing taxes to raise money for benefit payments and of contracts to reduce acreage was outside the scope of congressional authority. In other words, farming was a local business and the federal government could not control it from Washington. The Court said that while farmers had not been required to sign acreage reduction agreements, in effect reduction was compulsory. Since the agricultural depression was still serious, Congress moved quickly to pass new legislation.

The Soil Conservation and Domestic Allotment Act of February 1936 provided for paying farmers to take land out of production, just as had been the case under the outlawed statute. But the new law stated that producers were getting paid to conserve the soil, rather than to reduce their output. Only basic crops in surplus were considered soil-depleting and thus eligible for crop reduction payments. The result for farmers had not really changed. They would continue to get benefit payments if they cooperated with the government programs. The source of these payments, however, would no longer come from illegal processing taxes but from federal appropriations.

Extremely large crops in 1937 demonstrated that the enticement offered by soil-conservation diversion payments was inadequate to keep surpluses under control. The 1937 cotton crop amounted to 19 million bales, the largest on record. Corn production reached 2.7 million bushels, and wheat output jumped 40 percent. Under pressure from such heavy supplies, in 1937 and 1938 cotton dropped to a little above 8 cents a pound. Wheat declined to 56 cents and corn to 48 cents a bushel in 1938, the lowest since 1932. In this emergency, President Roosevelt agreed to support sagging cotton prices through the CCC if Congress would write a new farm program and include stricter production controls.

The Agricultural Adjustment Act of 1938 was the most comprehensive farm law passed up to that time. It looked toward long-term action by the federal government to get supply and demand into better balance and to improve farm incomes. Three methods were provided to reduce surpluses. The law continued and expanded soil conservation programs, which permitted the federal government to pay farmers for reducing the acreage of basic "soil-depleting" crops. Second, in case of unplanned abundance, the secretary of agriculture could declare marketing quotas that, if supported by a two-thirds vote of the producers of a commodity, would prohibit a farmer from marketing more than his quota without severe penalties. Finally, prices would be supported for cooperating producers through CCC loans on the stored crop. If Congress provided the funds, the secretary of agriculture was also permitted to make parity payments, which corresponded to the difference between the market price and the parity price. Moreover, a crop insurance feature was incorporated into the law.

Parity for farmers continued to be the expressed goal of agricultural legislation. However, in both 1936 and 1938 there was a shift from the concept of parity prices to that of parity incomes. The 1938 act defined parity incomes as "that per capita net income of individuals on farms from farming operations that bears to the per capita net income of individuals not on farms the same relation as prevailed during the period from August 1909 to July 1914." This was a sounder objective, but one much harder to achieve. Basic farm products included in the law were cotton, corn, wheat, tobacco, and rice, but arrangements were also available to help other commodities.

No effort was made to raise farm prices to 100 percent of parity. The law actually provided that the percentage of parity, ranging from 52 to 75, would be determined by the supply of a commodity. The more of a commodity that was produced by farmers, the lower was the parity price; with less production the parity price would rise. Lawmakers hoped to discourage excess production by holding out the prospect of lower support prices for surplus output. Overall, farm prices averaged only about 77 percent of parity in 1939.

While federal agricultural policies did not solve the problems of surpluses and low prices for the major crops, farmers benefited greatly from the Washington cash flow. Between 1933 and 1939, direct government payments to farmers totaled $3.455 billion, and additional millions were spent through the Farm Security Administration and other programs. By the late 1930's many commercial farmers were relying heavily on land diversion payments and government price supports. In 1939, for example, farmers received about $800 million in payments from the government, or more than 10 percent of their cash income.

Programs to maintain prices were only one aspect of the New Deal's commitment to farmers.

The credit legislation, soil conservation and rural electrification programs, and special legislation for low-income farmers all reflected the extent to which the federal government was underwriting farmers' welfare on the eve of World War II.

During the 1930's government agricultural policy had centered on curtailing surplus production and raising prices toward parity. Acreage reduction, marketing quotas, and marketing agreements were the principal means employed to achieve these ends. Growing productivity on American farms made it increasingly difficult to bring supply and demand into proper balance. During the 1930's farmers mechanized; raised improved crops, such as hybrid corn; and applied more fertilizer on their land. Science and technology were beginning to produce a revolution in agricultural productivity. Corn surpluses could not be reduced by cutting acreage 15–20 percent when farmers shifted to hybrid varieties, fertilized heavily, and, in some cases, raised production 20–30 percent per acre. Although marketing quotas had been in effect earlier for cotton and tobacco, it was growing productivity and huge surpluses that prompted Congress to include marketing quotas in the Agricultural Adjustment Act of 1938.

WORLD WAR II

American agricultural policy was sharply modified after the outbreak of World War II. Under the influence of defense and wartime demand, farm prices began to rise; and by September 1941, three months before the United States entered the war, farm commodity prices averaged 101 percent of parity. Between 1939 and 1941, wheat and corn prices advanced about 35 percent. The surpluses that had been so burdensome in 1938 and 1939 suddenly became blessings. As prices continued to rise, government policy shifted to increasing production and restraining raw-material prices in order to hold down food costs.

In 1941 government officials urged farmers to produce greater quantities of soybeans, peanuts, eggs, pork, dairy products, and some other commodities. Farmers were confident of their ability to meet the growing demand but skeptical of shifting to full production. Two decades of relatively low prices had shown them the devastating effects of surpluses. Farmers and their spokesmen wanted some assurance that they would be protected after the war if they increased their output in response to government requests. The drastic price drops after World War I were still fresh in the minds of many farmers.

In May 1941 Senator John H. Bankhead of Alabama pushed an amendment through Congress that guaranteed prices at 85 percent of parity for the basic crops of corn, wheat, cotton, rice, and tobacco. Bankhead called this "the greatest piece of legislation ever enacted by any Congress of this nation." This proved to be just the beginning of congressional actions very favorable to farmers. In July 1941 Congress passed the Steagall Amendment, named after Congressman Henry B. Steagall of Alabama, which called for supporting prices at 85 percent of parity for all of those agricultural commodities for which the government had asked for increased production. Farm pressure groups were trying to push the government toward price supports at 100 percent of parity.

Rising farm and food prices in 1942 brought increasing demands for stricter price controls to contain the cost of living. The Price Control Act of October 1942 limited farm prices to 100 percent of parity, or the highest figure between 1 January and 15 September. This did not hurt farmers, because many farm products were already selling above 100 percent of parity. The figure at which the government would guarantee prices was gradually creeping up. A floor of 90 percent of parity was placed under both the Steagall commodities and the six basic products. More important was the provision that guaranteed prices at a minimum of 90 percent of parity for two years after the war (as it turned out, through the crop year of 1948). In addition, the federal government employed incentive payments to encourage farmers to produce more scarce commodities. To keep the cost of living down, some agricultural products were subsidized, mainly by making payments to processors.

Wartime legislation was highly important in the history of agricultural policy. While parity prices had been a goal since the 1920's, before World War II few producers expected to achieve full parity. Establishment of 90 percent of parity for at least two years after the war convinced farmers that permanent policy should include

high fixed-price supports at that level, or even at 100 percent of parity. The Farmers' Union pushed especially hard for this goal. The postwar debate over farm policy centered on whether prices should be supported at high rigid rates or according to some flexible formula. There was relatively little political backing for abandoning all price supports.

POST–WORLD WAR II PERIOD

Huge demands for food and fiber immediately after World War II kept agricultural prices high and farmers fairly prosperous. By 1947, as surpluses of some crops built up, there was growing demand to abandon high fixed-price supports. The potato scandal in 1947, when surplus potatoes were burned in order to be disposed of, aroused widespread criticism of policies that encouraged production of commodities for which there was no satisfactory market. The Agricultural Act of 1948, better known as the Hope-Aiken Law after Representative Clifford Hope of Kansas and Senator George D. Aiken of Vermont, returned to flexible price supports for basic commodities. Implementation of flexible supports was postponed until 1950, thus guaranteeing 90 percent of parity prices for another year. The Agricultural Act of 1949 retained the main features of the wartime price guarantees and even permitted some prices to be supported at a higher percentage of parity.

It was Secretary of Agriculture Charles F. Brannan who pushed the most controversial farm policy of the postwar period. In 1949 he proposed that prices of a designated list of commodities be supported at "income-parity" levels. In general, this amounted to about 100 percent of parity for the major commodities. The prices of perishable products such as fruits and vegetables would be permitted to drop to whatever level the market determined, but producers would receive a direct government payment amounting to the difference between the market price and what the secretary of agriculture set as a fair figure. Consumers, it was said, would benefit from lower food prices, while farmers would receive an acceptable return. Opposition to the Brannan Plan was intense. Critics charged that it would be unacceptably expensive and inject the government excessively into agriculture. The

House defeated the Brannan Plan and former policies continued to prevail.

Demands of the Korean War rescued farmers and government planners from accumulating price-depressing surpluses. By 1951 the prices of several major farm commodities had advanced beyond parity. In 1952, with some respite from overabundant supplies, Congress extended guarantees of 90 percent of parity for basic agricultural commodities through 1954. Despite the commitment to flexible price supports in the 1948 legislation and subsequent laws, Congress, under strong political pressure from farmers and their spokesmen, refused to let the principle go into effect.

When Dwight D. Eisenhower became president in 1953, he and his secretary of agriculture, Ezra Taft Benson, insisted that flexible supports be substituted for high fixed-price guarantees of recent years. The Agricultural Act of 1954 provided support prices on basic commodities (except tobacco) at 82.5–90 percent of parity in 1955 and lower rates after that time. Prices of many other commodities could be supported at 60–90 percent of parity. The 1954 law also arranged to implement a new parity formula called for in the 1948 legislation. The new parity was scheduled to become effective in 1956, but provisions were made to limit price reductions under the revised calculations to not more than 5 percent annually.

By the mid-1950's farm surpluses had again reached depressing proportions. Production controls had been largely ineffective in bringing supply and demand into balance. Besides trying to curb production, Congress had attempted to reduce surpluses since the 1930's by increasing domestic consumption and foreign exports. Large quantities of agricultural produce were distributed through relief channels after 1933. In 1936 the Department of Agriculture began to donate food for school lunch programs, and in 1946 Congress enacted the National School Lunch Act providing regular support for this program. From 1939 to 1943 the USDA had distributed food stamps to needy persons in a further move to consume surplus farm products. The farm law of 1954 included special milk programs to increase consumption of milk in schools. In 1964 the food stamp program received congressional approval, and by 1981 between $11 and $12 billion was being spent annually for this purpose.

Congress also sought to dispose of surplus agricultural commodities through a number of postwar foreign aid programs. In 1953, after several unsuccessful attempts, lawmakers required that some mutual-security funds be used to purchase farm products in the United States. It was passage of the Agricultural Trade Development and Assistance Act of 1954 that increased the bond between the disposal of surplus agricultural commodities and foreign policy. Under this law, farm commodities could be sold for "soft" foreign currencies, given away, or bartered. Within the next few years, billions of dollars worth of farm products were shipped to needy countries throughout the world under the original or amended 1954 statute, commonly known as PL 480.

The combined federal food and agriculture programs were unequal to the task of curbing price-depressing surpluses. By the mid-1950's the agricultural question had become a major political issue. The Democrats generally supported high fixed supports for cooperating producers and were supported by the Farmers' Union and the National Farmers Organization. The Republicans favored flexible guarantees and urged greater reliance on the markets. They received strong backing from the American Farm Bureau Federation.

To deal with rising supplies, President Eisenhower recommended the soil bank program, in which producers of basic commodities were to be paid for placing land in an acreage reserve. It also included a provision permitting payments to farmers who took entire farms out of production. Thus land diversion, benefit payments, and price supports continued to be the main elements of agricultural policy.

Meanwhile, Congress enacted special legislation to benefit the producers of particular agricultural commodities. Sugar legislation, passed in 1937 and amended regularly thereafter, established a quota system to protect domestic producers against excessive imports. The National Wool Act of 1954 provided for supporting the incomes of wool and mohair growers through direct payments, a principle of the Brannan Plan. Other special legislation to assist farmers included the Great Plains conservation program, begun in 1956.

The move to flexible price supports in the

mid-1950's and the reliance on a freer market did not solve the farm surplus problem. Rather than discouraging output, the lower prices prompted many farmers to grow more. By the end of the Eisenhower administration, the nation was overwhelmed with agricultural surpluses, which were costing the federal government hundreds of millions of dollars a year just for storage. The alternatives were to resort to stricter production controls, including marketing quotas; to expand demand at home and abroad; to abandon all federal price support programs; or to continue muddling along and follow some combination of all of these approaches. It was the muddling-through approach that prevailed. Farm planners found the twin goals of lowering program costs and raising farm income most difficult, if not impossible, to achieve.

When President John F. Kennedy took office in 1961, he recommended much stricter production controls, including expansion of marketing quotas. But Congress refused to go along and in 1961 enacted a voluntary feed grains program whereby a corn farmer would receive price supports and land diversion payments if he elected to reduce his acreage. Many feed grain farmers did sign up, and there was some decline in surpluses.

During the rest of the 1960's and early 1970's Congress maintained relatively low price supports but paid farmers for diverting land out of crops with huge surpluses. These policies were incorporated in the Food and Agriculture Act of 1965 and extended in the Agricultural Act of 1970. The 1970 law relaxed many of the former controls on farmers by suspending acreage allotments and marketing quotas for cotton, wheat, and feed grains. If farmers wanted to qualify for loan supports and other program payments they had to cooperate with the land "set aside" feature of the law. The idea was to give producers more flexibility and freedom in their farming operations but still keep overall production in check. The 1970 act also limited government payments to any single producer of major crops to $55,000 annually on each commodity. With support prices maintained at near international levels, American agricultural commodities began moving into world markets in much larger quantities in the late 1960's and did so without subsidies. In addition, consumers continued to enjoy relatively low food prices. The main criticism of

the farm programs was their drain on the federal treasury.

The Agriculture and Consumer Protection Act of 1973 retained the main features of the 1965 and 1970 laws. At least one other important new approach was added. The old concept of maintaining basic farm prices at some percentage of parity, which originated in the 1920's, was abandoned, and Congress substituted the idea of target prices. The target price was set at a figure considered fair to farmers, and if the market fell below the price established, farmers would be given deficiency payments. This was a way not only to support farm income without holding prices at levels that made American farm products noncompetitive in foreign markets but also to restrain domestic food prices as well.

While abnormal world demand caused American agricultural prices to shoot upward in the mid-1970's, surpluses returned by 1977 and prices dropped sharply. Farmers complained that the federal government had misled them when it urged growers to plant from fence row to fence row in 1974 and 1975. Many producers also resented the abandonment of the parity price concept. In January 1978 several thousand farmers staged a tractor march on Washington, D.C., demanding that the government maintain farm prices at 100 percent of parity. Farmers lobbied hard on Capitol Hill and won some concessions, but they failed to get any parity price legislation. Congress continued to support the prices of major farm crops but not at levels satisfactory to farmers. In 1982 producers of some commodities received such low prices that they were comparing their condition to that in the 1930's.

In 1983 the Reagan administration adopted a slightly different approach to help hard-pressed farmers and to reduce price-depressing surpluses. The federal government offered farmers payment in kind (PIK) in return for idling extra land on which they had been growing corn, wheat, sorghum, rice, or cotton. The program continued cash payments for taking some land out of production, but farmers would be paid in commodities for idling extra acres.

Most federal agricultural policy after 1933 was directed toward helping commercial farmers. As mentioned earlier, the Resettlement Administration and the Farm Security Administration were among the programs aimed at assisting poorer, marginal operators such as sharecroppers. In 1946 the Farm Security Administration was abolished, and in its place Congress set up the Farmers Home Administration. This agency made loans to poor producers and usually provided some management assistance. By the 1970's it had become the lender of last resort for many farmers. In 1954 President Eisenhower ordered a study of the condition of small, poor farmers, but nothing important came of it. In the 1960's President Lyndon B. Johnson's "war on poverty" included programs for poor rural residents in Appalachia, the Old South, and elsewhere, but little resulted from those federal efforts. The only solution for many farmers was to leave farming.

Even after a half century of extensive price and income policies, farmers in 1983 were depressed and dissatisfied. Federal policies had not been successful in bringing supply and demand into proper balance or in providing farmers with prices that they deemed fair and equitable.

The prospect that farmers could use the political process to gain greater benefits was not bright. By 1980 only 2.7 percent of Americans lived on farms, compared to 25 percent in 1935. Farmers' political power, while still formidable in the early 1980's, had greatly diminished. The hope of farmers was no longer in numbers, but in greater unity and more effective organization.

BIBLIOGRAPHY

Murray R. Benedict, *Farm Policies of the United States, 1790–1950* (New York, 1953), is a broad survey of agricultural development and perhaps the best single volume covering farm policy; and *Can We Solve the Farm Problem? An Analysis of Federal Aid to Agriculture* (New York, 1955) discusses the wide variety of federal programs designed to help farmers between about 1930 and the mid-1950's. Murray R. Benedict and Oscar C. Stine, *The Agricultural Commodity Programs: Two Decades of Experience* (New York, 1956), discusses in detail how various crops fared under the different New Deal and subsequent farm programs.

Willard W. Cochrane and Mary E. Ryan, *American Farm Policy, 1948–1973* (Minneapolis, 1976), offers the broadest treatment of agricultural policies and programs during the post–World War II generation. Gilbert C. Fite, *George N. Peek and the Fight for Farm Parity* (Norman, Okla., 1954), is a detailed account of the campaign by farmers in the 1920's and early 1930's to write the parity principle into federal legislation; and *American Farmers, The New Minority* (Bloomington, Ind., 1981) traces the changes in agriculture and the programs for federal relief from the 1920's to the late 1970's. Paul Wallace Gates, *The Farmer's Age: Agriculture, 1815–1860* (New York, 1960), provides a broad account of U. S. agriculture in the half century before the Civil War.

Theodore Saloutos, *The American Farmer and the New Deal* (Ames, Iowa, 1981), provides the best account of farmers in the New Deal years. Fred A. Shannon, *The Farmer's Last Frontier: Agriculture, 1860–1897* (New York, 1945), covers all aspects of American agriculture as it developed in the late nineteenth century. Walter W. Wilcox, *The Farmer in the Second World War* (Ames, Iowa, 1947), is the standard work on agriculture during World War II.

[*See also* CONSERVATION, ENVIRONMENT, AND ENERGY; LAND POLICIES; NEW DEAL; *and* POPULISM.]

AMERICAN REVOLUTION

John Shy

THE American Revolution is a simple label for a complex process covering almost three decades, from soon after the fall of French Canada to the British in 1760 to the adoption of the U.S. Constitution in 1789. Even the label is in dispute. Some argue that the United States experienced not a true "revolution" but merely a war for national independence. Above all, in understanding the Revolution one must distinguish results from intentions. American colonial leaders of resistance to new British policies had conservative goals: to nullify the new policies and to restore the old imperial status quo, not to leave the British Empire or to effect a program of radical political and social changes. Yet the result after almost thirty years of conflict was a large, independent republic deeply committed to democratic equality, at least for white males. This result had less to do with the original goals of resistance leaders than with the dynamic, virtually uncontrollable interplay of underlying conditions, of specific and unstable situations, and of the unintended, often unforeseen consequences of choices, decisions, and responses made in the course of a long, confusing political struggle.

THE BRITISH EMPIRE
BEFORE THE REVOLUTION

In 1763, when the Treaty of Paris ended the Seven Years' War in a spectacular British victory, the British Empire was at the peak of its power and prestige. England had been late in the race for American colonies, not settling in the West Indies and on the North American coast until a century after Iberian colonies had been planted in more developed, attractive southern areas, and only after France had laid claim to the strategic St. Lawrence valley. Seventeenth-century English colonization had been haphazard, more a matter of private initiative than of state policy. The earliest ventures were by joint-stock companies armed only with royal charters. After the first wave of colonization, the crown began to make vast territorial grants to proprietors or proprietary groups, using its undisputed legal power over colonies to gain political support in its continuing constitutional battle with the House of Commons. Civil war in the 1640's rendered the crown impotent to build an effective administration for these miscellaneous colonial ventures, transmitting to the empire that would emerge by 1700 its decentralized, laissez-faire style.

With the restoration of royal authority in England in 1660, the American colonies began to be taken more seriously. They had become a part of England's international position, coexisting with the American colonies of the other major states of western Europe. They had acquired some economic importance, especially for their production of sugar and tobacco. And they were politically sensitive: a minor source of royal patronage but also a source of embarrassment, in that the New England colonies especially had sided against the crown during the recent upheaval in England. From the 1660's a series of laws, generally known as Navigation Acts, defined imperial policy; and from the 1690's the empire acquired an effective administrative structure in London, centered in the Board of Trade.

The Revolution of 1688, when Parliament won its long battle to curb the royal prerogative, did nothing to weaken crown control of the American colonies, and it did much to further the process of empire building. Later, in the 1760's and 1770's, colonial American leaders would use the precedent of 1688 to plead their case for a constitutionally guaranteed autonomy for elective provincial assemblies, on the model of the House of Commons. But the immediate effect of the overthrow of a Catholic king (James II) and the accession of a Dutch prince (William of Orange) in 1688 was to propel England into a long series of European wars against France, with the Anglo-American colonies playing an ever larger role in those wars.

From 1689, the pressures of imperial war forced a greater degree of uniformity and central direction in colonial government. A small group of "experts" on American affairs emerged at the Board of Trade, which monitored and made recommendations on colonial policy. Although the board did not succeed in its effort to transform all American colonies into "royal" provinces (with governor, advisory and legislative council, judiciary, and customs officers appointed by the crown), Massachusetts had to accept a new, more restrictive charter, the proprietors of Pennsylvania and Maryland conceded limits on their legal powers to govern, and other colonies came under direct control of the crown. The Navigation Acts, which confined colonial trade to Anglo-American ships, certain American exports to British ports, and all American imports to British sources, were enforced more strictly; although American evasion of these laws, particularly in trade with the non-British West Indies, was significant, it was no more serious and flagrant than smuggling in and around the British Isles and should not be exaggerated.

By 1740 the British Empire was a remarkable success, the most dynamic sector of the British economy. Colonial sugar (from the West Indies) and tobacco (from the Chesapeake Bay area) supplied an insatiable European market; a relatively prosperous, rapidly growing American population was a major market for British manufactures and exports; Carolina rice fed the Mediterranean world; and New England and the "middle" colonies serviced the whole North Atlantic trade with ships, seamen, foodstuffs, timber, and livestock. The entire system was, indeed, a delicate balancing of provincial autonomy with imperial direction. A general prosperity, plus the urgencies of war, made administrative practice more important than constitutional theory. Both London and colonial assemblies compromised points of imperial conflict in ways that were effective in the short run but that would haunt the pre-Revolutionary constitutional debate.

The last great Anglo-French struggle of the colonial era, from the 1740's to 1763, brought unprecedented levels of direct military intervention by British forces in the American theater of war. Large naval forces, and for the first time a large regular army, finally tipped the American strategic balance. Louisbourg, Quebec, Montreal, and all of French Canada fell to Anglo-American arms, while expeditionary forces seized, one after another, key French West Indian islands and Spanish Cuba. The midcentury war ended in a great Anglo-American victory, but it had also been a tremendous effort, mobilizing both British resources and American manpower to the full. A growing British military presence in America, and the dynamic wartime leadership of William Pitt in London, ensured that the postwar empire would not slip back into the old pattern of 1740.

Pitt fell from power at the end of the war, but his influence remained strong, and a new young king (George III) and a new group of political leaders reflected Pitt's energetic conception of government. Fiscal retrenchment and administrative reform, often in tension with one another, dominated the British political agenda in 1763; the American colonies were only one major item on that agenda. The treaty of 1763 had expanded British territory on the North American continent to the Hudson Bay, the Mississippi River, and the Gulf of Mexico. New colonies in Canada and Florida needed organization and defense, while the presence of a large native (Indian) population beyond the Appalachian watershed required coherent policies on western settlement and Indian trade. As if to emphasize this latter requirement, major Indian "uprisings" swept the western frontier areas at the end of the war. These new problems led directly to a decision in London to station a large, expensive, permanent military garrison in America, mainly in the new territories. Until the 1750's, American colonists had been expected to provide for their own military needs, with only occasional help from home; in 1763, a key feature of the old imperial system was changed, and with it much else.

The need to pay for the new American garrison meant a continuation of wartime efforts to curb smuggling in America, to generally tighten the commercial system, and to search for new sources of revenue. In the past, British taxation of American trade had been designed to regulate commerce; some colonial customs houses cost more to run than they collected, and subsidies (for naval stores and indigo, for example) were more important in the old system than taxation. By 1763 British priorities had shifted; the politics of public finance took precedence over commercial policy, and trade was better able than ever to flourish without government action. In 1763 a royal proclamation "for the present" closed trans-Appalachian land to colonial speculation and settlement. In 1764 the so-called Sugar Act set out to restrict and exploit the complex, competitive West Indian trade, lowering the prohibitive duty on "foreign" molasses in order to encourage payment rather than smuggling, adding a variety of other money-saving measures to the trade laws, and introducing a formidable set of new bureaucratic procedures designed to deter evasion. In 1765 the government secured passage of the Stamp Act, which taxed a variety of publications and legal transactions in America.

The Proclamation of 1763 was intended to appease the Indians and thereby avoid another expensive Indian war. The acts of 1764 and 1765 were expected to raise about £100,000 in new revenue, roughly a third of the direct cost of the new American military establishment. The actual results of these new measures were disastrous.

THE AMERICAN COLONIES BEFORE THE REVOLUTION

Over twenty separate provinces, from Newfoundland to Barbados, from Bermuda westward to the Mississippi, constituted the British Empire of North America in 1763. But the most populous and developed heart of that empire lay in a thousand-mile strip of settlement on the Atlantic coastal plain, thirteen colonies from New Hampshire to Georgia that would become the United States. While the economic and political importance of the West Indies remained considerable, the continental colonies became the primary concern of those in London who were most concerned with American affairs. Their decision to return West Indian conquests to France and Spain in 1763, and instead to keep the vast territorial buffer of Canada, Florida, and the trans-Appalachian West, clearly indicates the rising value placed upon the mainland provinces.

Three fairly distinct regions marked these older English colonies on the North American continent. First were the settlements around Chesapeake Bay—Virginia and Maryland—that very early in the seventeenth century had found economic salvation in tobacco. Despite freely available land, early immigration to the Chesapeake colonies never overcame high mortality and a chronic shortage of labor. By the late seventeenth century, slaves from West Africa were replacing white contract labor in the Chesapeake area, just as they had done earlier in the West Indies. South of Virginia the Carolina colonies, and still later Georgia, also emerged as slave-based economies and societies. By 1763 all except Maryland were royal colonies, with the largest owners of land and slaves serving on the governor's council, manning the county courts, and leading the militia. The overriding concern in these southern colonies was to control an enslaved, black labor force, which ensured (by 1700) a vital degree of cooperative orderliness within the white population.

In the North, radiating from Massachusetts Bay, the New England colonies had achieved stability and prosperity by other means. They had been settled on the eve of the English Civil War by sponsors and emigrating families who sought some alternative to the unsettled economic and religious conditions of England. Much of New England was colonized in nuclear towns, comprising groups of families living compactly who were concerned to bend their new lives to a "purer," or Puritan, form of Christianity. Heavy early immigration, town government, family farms, and agricultural self-sufficiency, supplemented by the fur trade, fishing, and shipbuilding, ensured that neither African slavery nor the exploitative fever of staple crop production would disturb life in the New England colonies. Evangelical, anti-Catholic Puritanism pushed English colonization everywhere in the early seventeenth century, to the West Indies as well as the South. But nowhere did it leave such an enduring mark on colonial societies as in Massachusetts and Connecticut. Rhode Island early, and New Hampshire later, were slightly deviant refuges for those New Englanders who could not accept the full rigor of a Puritan world. Only New

Hampshire was a royal colony; charters gave the other three an unusual degree of governmental autonomy.

Between New England and the slave societies of the South, a second generation of English settlements was established after the royal Restoration of 1660. Military conquest of the Dutch and Swedish colonies in the lower Hudson and Delaware valleys opened the way for three new proprietary colonies owned by King Charles II's brother, the duke of York (New York); a group of the duke's friends (New Jersey); and the Quaker son of an admiral who had supported the king before the Restoration (Pennsylvania). These "middle" colonies were dissimilar in certain ways. New York, connected by the Hudson and Mohawk valleys to the powerful Iroquois Indian confederation and to French Canada, quickly became aristocratic and militarized. Pennsylvania, strongly influenced by Quaker ideals of simplicity and nonviolence, and secured by geography from the dangers threatening frontiers to the north and south, was run by the Penn family as a gigantic real estate operation. It attracted droves of immigrants with cheap land, low taxes, and freedom from military service. New Jersey, dominated by its larger neighbors, coexisted between them as a mixture of their two contrasting cultures. By 1700 New York and New Jersey had become royal colonies, with the Penns barely hanging on to their proprietorship.

The Middle Atlantic colonies had similarities that were as important as their differences and that set them apart from New England and the South. If slavery was the basis for southern society, and Puritan communalism the binding force in New England, there was no comparable force working to ensure stability and order in the Middle Atlantic colonies. New York and Pennsylvania lived on the edge of anarchy. Aristocratic government and external military pressure limited the worst problems in New York, while weak government and, until 1755, the absence of serious governmental problems mitigated anarchic conditions in Pennsylvania. In both colonies, as in the rest of British North America, affluence blunted the threat of social disorder.

From about 1740, however, the relatively prosperous and stable provinces of the old British Empire were swept by a series of upheavals, each of which shaped the preconditions for revolution after 1763. War was the most obvious of the upheavals. After a generation of relative peace, the 1740's and 1750's saw a renewed, escalating Anglo-French struggle for dominance in North America. Although an army from New England captured the French fortress of Louisbourg in 1745, massive British help was needed in the 1750's to turn back French attacks and to win the war. Thousands of American soldiers were mobilized for each year's campaign; British officers, soldiers, and sailors became part of the social landscape; and the infusion of heavy British military expenditures had a major impact on the American economy.

As dramatic as war in its effects was the religious revival known as the Great Awakening. Better known in the northern colonies because it has been better documented and more carefully studied there, the Great Awakening left its mark from Georgia to New Hampshire. Harking back to a stricter, more emotional Protestantism emphasizing faith and conversion, the revivalists threatened "established" and traditional churches everywhere. Congregations and whole denominations split in some cases. With Congregationalism and Presbyterianism energized but divided, Baptists and Quakers attracted many of the questing revivalists, and the Anglican church drew disgusted antirevivalists. The Great Awakening, peaking by the 1740's, weakened ecclesiastical authority and thereby eroded all authority, which was never strong in colonial America.

From the 1740's to the very eve of the Revolution there were local, often violent disturbances that indicated deeper trouble in the American colonies. The Anglo-French war itself triggered civil wars in several areas: in western Pennsylvania, where in 1755 and again in 1763 brutal Indian warfare led to violent frontier assaults on Quaker-dominated government in Philadelphia; in the South Carolina back country, where war with the Cherokee created a social collapse in the 1760's that the Charleston government failed to handle; and in "Vermont," where the war opened new lands over which New Englanders and New Yorkers fought for control. There were riots over land titles in New Jersey and New York, where a growing population was beginning to press on available resources; and Pennsylvania settlers, backed by Connecticut and Virginia, fought for control of parts of that province. The single bloodiest case occurred in North Carolina, where a tidewater elite failed to provide effective government for a rapidly growing western population but managed to defeat its malcontents in pitched battle in 1771. The economic strain of war produced a major political crisis in Massachusetts and a major political scandal in Virginia.

In this troubled situation of civil outbreaks, political conflict, religious confusion, and war lay a demographic dynamo. The population had grown tenfold in three generations (1700–1775), from a quarter million to 2.5 million. As important as rapid numerical growth was the transformation of the relatively homogeneous English society of 1700 into a polyglot pluralism by the eve of the Revolution. Africans, Germans, and the "primitive" Scotch-Irish, altogether about a half million people, came to America in these years; only the older New England colonies retained much of their original social homogeneity. Low infant mortality added a high rate of natural increase to this migratory flood, producing a population that by 1763 was ethnically diverse and geographically dispersed. None of the antecedent social phenomena—rapid demographic change, religious controversies, local disturbances, even foreign war—was in any demonstrable way a "cause" of the Revolution, but each gave to pre-Revolutionary America its special quality.

CONFLICT, 1764–1772

Provincial American leaders, speaking through pamphlets and their elective assemblies, protested on various grounds against new British colonial measures in the early 1760's. Although there was surprisingly little objection expressed to the peacetime stationing of British regular forces in the colonies, or to the presumably temporary closure of the trans-Appalachian West to settlement, American protests centered on stricter imperial controls of trade and paper currency and particularly on the emerging issue of taxation for revenue. Provincial control of revenue and expenditure by the elective assemblies, while never formally conceded in London, had been for decades, de facto, the key point in the imperial structure.

Some royal officials had fought against it, but in the end every successful governor had accepted the constitutional reality of fiscal power centered in the legislature. The provincial elite—that small group of affluent, educated, in-

termarried families in each colony who held the most important offices and who wielded dominant influence—drew their own power, both in dealing with London and in managing the American masses, from their exclusive ability to control taxation and public expenditure. At the moment when their control of the masses was threatened by the internal changes just described, London was threatening the very basis of elite power with new commercial and fiscal policies. It is not surprising, then, that there were vehement protests by 1764 against both the Sugar Act and the Currency Act (which sharply contracted the American money supply in the midst of a postwar depression), or that American agents in London, like Benjamin Franklin, lobbied vigorously against the centralizing trend of postwar British policy for the colonies.

The surprise came in 1765. From that time onward, a political conflict between provincial governments and British authority, not unlike many other conflicts that dotted the preceding century of imperial history, was transformed into a revolutionary struggle of world-historical importance.

What happened in 1765 is known in great detail; exactly why it happened is still murky. In its search for a new source of revenue to pay part of the increased cost of the postwar American establishment, the ministry of George Grenville secured passage in March of a tax on most publications and legal transactions in America, requiring that a paid stamp be affixed to each item specified in the law. Comparable stamp taxes had been levied in England since the late seventeenth century without arousing much opposition. Franklin and other provincial agents in London lobbied against the stamp bill, as they lobbied (unsuccessfully) against the Sugar and Currency Acts of 1764, and (successfully) to amend the bill of 1765 quartering British troops stationed in America. But when passage of the stamp bill became inevitable, Franklin solicited a stamp distributorship for a crony in Philadelphia; while Richard Henry Lee, a young member of Virginia's political elite, briefly sought the local distributorship for himself. If the Grenville ministry misread the political situation in the colonies, American political leaders like Franklin and Lee were hardly more astute.

The new act was to take effect in November, but in August, Boston exploded. Rioters swept through the town twice, forcing the stamp distributor to resign, threatening and humiliating those local officials believed to support the new tax, and destroying their property. Thomas Hutchinson, chief justice and lieutenant governor of Massachusetts, a distinguished descendant of an old Puritan family and a long-time leader in provincial politics, was the special target of the rioters' violence: he lost a magnificent house and an irreplaceable library, barely escaping with his life. New York soon followed Boston, with a mob taunting the tough old governor, Cadwallader Colden, barricaded in Fort George at the tip of Manhattan Island, to open fire.

Similar disorders swept the other port towns of Newport, Philadelphia, and Charleston. Elsewhere, packages of stamps were seized and sometimes burned, officials intimidated, and the whole seaboard aroused as it had not been aroused since the worst days of the war and the wildest period of the Great Awakening. Most of the British garrison was in Canada, Florida, and the western posts; not even the New York governor dared to call on the small local detachment of regulars to restore order. A triggering event in the explosion of 1765 may have been the resolutions against the Stamp Act put forth by Patrick Henry in the Virginia assembly in May. The most radical of these resolutions did not pass, but all were published in American newspapers, including those that declared a tax not enacted by the provincial assembly to be no law, and that denounced anyone upholding such a measure as "an Enemy to this His Majesty's Colony."

The more conservative American leaders were almost as disturbed by the spontaneity and violence of the Stamp Act riots as were royal officials in America and London, and they quickly sought to contain and channel subsequent protest. The provincial elite tried to regain control by convening a consultative "congress" in New York in October, drafting a formal and moderate protest directed to the king and Parliament. But virtually no one in America defended the Stamp Act or advocated its enforcement. In fact, by November it was effectively nullified, with royal governors declining to enforce it and awaiting instructions from London. During the winter, merchants, courts, and printers—at first shut down for lack of stamps—resumed business almost everywhere.

The key to the crisis was in London. There the Grenville ministry had fallen, for no reason related to American affairs, and an opposition faction led by the marquis of Rockingham took office in July. Critics of Grenville and his policies, the Rockinghamites after some hesitation decided against enforcing the Stamp Act. And with the crucial support of Pitt, the acquiescence of the king, and skillful lobbying by British merchants, they carried its repeal in March 1766.

The price for repeal was heavy and consequential. Pitt, idiosyncratic as ever, in arguing for repeal in the House of Commons, had gone beyond attacking the Stamp Act as bad policy—disruptive as it was of imperial trade in an already troubled economic situation—and had defended colonial rioters by invoking a tenuous constitutional distinction between Parliament's right to legislate for the empire and its right to tax. The constitutional issue, once openly raised in Parliament, had to be resolved if repeal were to win a majority in the Commons. That was done in an act "declaring" Parliament's unlimited right to legislate for the colonies "in all cases whatsoever."

This view of the British constitution, placing sovereign authority in Parliament as the ultimate arbiter of all political disputes, was the clear expression of Parliament's ultimate victory in 1688 over the crown in the long battle to establish constitutional monarchy. No one questioned the belief that the House of Commons was, or ought to be, the protector of the liberties of British subjects against arbitrary power. But in the American colonies the conscious modeling of provincial government on examples from the Revolution of 1688 brought the elective assemblies into direct confrontation with this most basic of British constitutional beliefs. Equally reasonable and persuasive was the American belief that all power, to be legitimate, must have limits, and that some line, however hazy or difficult to define exactly, must exist between what Parliament (where Americans were not and could not be effectively represented) might do and what elected provincial representatives might do. Taxation in 1765 was the flashpoint; it was not the real issue.

The real issue, of course, was power. A broad consensus in London held that the last war had been so long and costly because Britain, for all its wealth and resources, had failed to centralize and mobilize power effectively, especially beyond the kingdom. Pitt himself, as a forceful wartime leader, epitomized this crisis-born sense that a more powerful government was needed. The postwar efforts to tighten London's control in Ireland, of the East India Company's operations in Bengal, and in the American colonies were parts of a single, continuing, reactive thrust, however much the king and parliamentary factions might squabble over the specific design of the new policies. Americans, on the other hand, saw themselves as equal participants in a great, victorious struggle against European forces of absolutism and Catholicism; Pitt, like the British generals Wolfe and Amherst, was an American hero. Provincial minds, except for a very few as informed and sophisticated as Benjamin Franklin's, could not grasp what had happened in 1763–1765 without invoking some kind of secret plot in London against American liberties, or some vile conspiracy to corrupt the House of Commons and subvert the British constitution.

On both sides there was a demonology, derived from the experience and rhetoric of two troubled centuries, that would turn a political problem and a constitutional crisis into a holy crusade. American rioters were readily seen as one more set of primitive rebels duped by their demagogic leaders, like the Irish and the Scots, who had caused so much trouble for civilized, constitutional authority between Elizabeth's time and the last Highland rising in 1745. British government, so subtly complex in its eighteenth-century structure and operation that historians are still investigating its mysteries, was easily viewed at three thousand miles' distance as at last succumbing to the scriptural slide into tyranny, a modern historical movement notoriously apparent on the European continent. Seen in retrospect, two things seem clear enough. British leaders, of whatever faction, were mainly engaged in a limited effort to conduct the business of government in a more energetic and responsible fashion that was reminiscent of the empire-building decade of the 1690's. And provincial American leaders, from young upstarts like Patrick Henry to old professionals like Franklin and Hutchinson, were trying to protect their position in a dynamic, unstable environment. But the Stamp Act crisis raised anger and fear, always latent in the recent Anglo-American political and religious experience, to levels in

1765–1766 that would turn an imperial conflict into a revolution.

The six years from the repeal of the Stamp Act to the onset of the final crisis in 1772 that led to war were not a time of steadily escalating conflict between London and the colonies. Instead, the period was punctuated by several crises and lulls, which encouraged contemporaries to hope that the worst had passed. Only in retrospect does 1766–1772 acquire a coherent place in the "coming" of the Revolution. The Rockingham government, during its year in power (1765–1766), repealed the Stamp Act, rectified the more onerous features of the Sugar Act, and took the first steps in opening the closed economic system embodied in the old Navigation Acts. A ministry under Pitt himself, now raised to the peerage as the earl of Chatham, followed in 1766. Reputedly liberal toward America, the Chatham government faced the same basic problems as its predecessor; and before it finally disintegrated in 1770 (an ill Chatham resigned in 1768), it had created a second American crisis, sent British soldiers to police Boston, and spilled American blood.

Charles Townshend, as chancellor of the exchequer in the Chatham government, pushed a set of new American taxes through Parliament in the spring of 1767. Responding to the argument that "internal" taxation ought to be left to the provincial assemblies, Townshend taxed certain American imports—tea, glass, and painters' colors. In addition, another act revamped the system for collection and enforcement, setting up a Board of Customs Commissioners resident in America. The estimated annual yield from the Townshend duties was less than half that projected from the Stamp Act, and its revenue would be used not for military expenses but to pay colonial officials hitherto dependent on provincial appropriations. In other words, Townshend took over a colonial obligation to pay certain salaries and so raised the net level of American taxation little if at all; but his object was nakedly constitutional—to insulate royal appointees from pressure by provincial assemblies.

Americans were slow to react. Without any visible, inflammatory target like the stamps, and with virtually no increase in the level of taxation, the issue took time to clarify. John Dickinson, a wealthy and conservative Pennsylvania politician, did much of the clarifying in a series of long letters from "A Farmer," published serially in colonial newspapers in the winter of 1767–1768 and then republished as a pamphlet. Dickinson argued that no power was more vital than the power to take property, that even small first steps to increase power over property must be resisted, and that a series of small steps could in time reduce the American colonies to the status of Ireland, where fear, cupidity, and armed force characterized the conduct of British government. While mild and lawyerly in tone, Dickinson's argument was implicitly radical. Resistance and even independence were preferable to acquiescence, so Dickinson seemed to say.

The first effective step in resisting the Townshend duties, defined by Dickinson as a threat to constitutional liberty as serious as the Stamp Act, was to boycott trade with Britain. This step had already been started during the Stamp Act crisis but ended with the act's early repeal. Now, in 1768, it was carried through in a protracted, painful negotiation among the merchant groups of the major port towns. Pressed by popular feeling in each town, wary of exciting mob violence again, and troubled by rumors that traders elsewhere were cheating on their agreement, the merchants took more than a year to set up an effective boycott, mainly of British imports. A number of incidents occurred during that year, with energetic new efforts under the Townshend Acts to collect duties and prosecute smugglers coming into collision with the emerging colonial trade boycott. When violence flared in Boston in March 1768 and again in June, the ministry, recently reorganized to include more conservative members, quickly decided to send a large detachment of troops to support civil authority in Massachusetts.

While American resistance was growing, British government had become ever less stable and coherent, in part because of Chatham's failure to lead it and in part because the old party structure had disintegrated by the 1760's. After sending soldiers to police Boston, the government could not decide whether to crack down on Massachusetts or to pull the troops out. The result, when a handful of hard-pressed guards opened fire on a Boston crowd in March 1770, killing five and wounding others, created a new issue driving the empire apart. The government, reorga-

nized under Lord North, and Parliament, sick of America and troubled by a myriad of other problems closer at hand, were in the course of repealing the Townshend duties on the day of the Boston Massacre.

For almost three years after March 1770 there was a lull in the conflict between Britain and the American colonies. Compromises were quietly reached on several disputed points, like the issuance of provincial paper money and the procedures for quartering troops. No new effort was made to tax the Americans, but the Townshend duty on tea was left, like the Declaratory Act of 1766, as a symbol that Parliament had conceded none of its right to legislate "in all cases whatsoever." The American boycott collapsed in 1770, and smuggling solved the problem of the tea duty for those who still cared. The long postwar depression, exacerbated by the political conflict and its disruption of normal trade since 1765, had finally ended, and exports to America were booming, facilitated by heavy long-term credit to American merchants and planters. Imperial costs were cut by pulling most of the troops out of the small but expensive western posts, despite the fears of a few experts that a rapid push of American settlement over the mountains was certain to start another bloody Indian war. The North government seemed to have found the secret, which had eluded its predecessors, of managing the empire.

Americans were also content to let conflict subside. At the same time they were far more sensitive to dangers from London and had learned a good deal about the possibilities and difficulties of confronting them. They were concerned by the hidden motives that might lie behind the erratic behavior of British government since 1763, and they were puzzled by the role of Chatham and George III, the two dominant political figures in the empire. During the two crises of 1765–1766 and 1768–1770, American leaders had worked at educating and mobilizing their own constituents in the cause of protecting American rights and at overcoming the historic interprovincial disputes that obstructed the creation of a unified, continental resistance movement. While not immediately relevant during the lull of 1770–1772, this experience had effected a deep change in the character of American politics. It had subtly altered the relationship between the leaders and the masses as well as between the provinces and England, reordering the priorities that guided American political behavior.

THE FINAL CRISIS, 1773–1775

Economics, not politics, triggered the final crisis. The commercial boom after 1770, of which American trade was only one part, ended suddenly in 1772 with a wave of bankruptcies and a sharp, global contraction of credit. Especially vulnerable was the British East India Company, whose operations depended heavily on a virtual European monopoly of the tea trade from south Asia, whose management was plagued by political factionalism and alleged corruption, and whose very size could threaten the health of the whole British economy. Caught with a massive inventory of unsold tea in the sudden credit crisis and apparently verging on bankruptcy, the East India Company had to be bailed out. North conceived a one-time waiver of the heavy British duties on tea to allow the company to dump its inventory on the world market at very low prices. This plan, of course, included the American colonial markets; but North, unwilling to reactivate a widespread sense in Parliament that concessions to America in the past were a mistake, decided not to waive the relatively small Townshend duty on tea shipped to the colonies. Even without the waiver, the American price for East India Company tea would easily undersell its smuggled competition.

Americans, like Europeans, were addicted to tea, but they could readily see how the Tea Act of early 1773 would involve a dangerous precedent if the mass of colonial tea drinkers switched to the "legal," taxed variety. Some of the more vociferously radical denounced North's effort to save the East India Company as one more covert attack on American liberty. Other, unrelated events contributed to an ugly mood in the colonies, which were also hit hard by the credit crisis of 1772. There was a murderous attack on a British customs ship in Rhode Island in 1772; an imprudent if only verbal attack by Thomas Hutchinson, now governor of Massachusetts, on his enemies in the elected house, some of whom surely were behind the physical attack on him in 1765; and a growing sense along the frontier that

another war with the Indians was imminent. When the first ships arrived with cut-price East India Company tea, they were met up and down the seaboard with massive resistance, less violent than in 1765 but better organized. Tea, like the stamps in 1765, was a tangible target for the defenders of a proclaimed American right to equal status and representative self-government. Public meetings, demonstrations, and threats forced American importers to reject their tea consignments, and ship captains turned back for Britain, with the tea undelivered—except in Boston.

Governor Hutchinson invoked the letter of the law to keep the tea ships in Boston harbor, where entry was the legal equivalent of "landing." Clearly Hutchinson intended to put his power, with that of the empire behind it, to the test. If the tea duty was not paid, he would confiscate the tea and sell it at auction—as prescribed by law—counting on the nonradical majority of New England tea drinkers to help him and in effect stuffing the tea—and the tea duty—down the throats of men like Samuel Adams and John Hancock, leaders of the anti-Hutchinson opposition.

On 16 December 1773 a band of Bostonians dumped 342 chests of tea into the harbor, roughly £10,000 of East India Company property. The reaction in London was rapid and drastic. Putting together a package of proposals advanced at various times since 1765, the government closed the customs house in Boston until unspecified compensation for the destroyed tea was made, changed the Massachusetts charter to eliminate the role of the elective assembly in choosing councillors, limited town meetings to one each spring, provided for moving the trial of accused criminals outside the province, and gave military commanders more discretion in quartering their troops. General Thomas Gage, the army commander in America, was given heavy military reinforcements and a commission as governor of Massachusetts. At the same time, the boundaries of Quebec were extended to include the trans-Appalachian West as far south as the Ohio River, assigning a vast territory where Virginia and several other colonies had land claims to a nonrepresentative government. Although not part of the package, this Quebec Act was the last of what Americans would call the "Coercive Acts."

The reaction in America to the Boston "tea

party" was mixed until news arrived of the Boston port closing, in effect destroying the economic basis of the whole town; feeling then swung strongly against Britain. Doubts about what Boston had done were swallowed in the anger and fear elicited by the British reaction. Resolutions supporting Boston were passed in extralegal popular assemblies and committees up and down the seaboard, and more tangible forms of aid were sent to the inhabitants of the threatened town. United against British policy and deeply impressed by the earlier crises with the need to keep a united front, Americans were divided in mid-1774 only on the question of tactics. "Radicals" demanded an immediate boycott, while "moderates" urged a continental congress that would give unity and greater legitimacy to a boycott or any other measures adopted to alter or thwart the Coercive Acts. Moderates hoped that the few months needed to convene a congress would cool tempers on both sides of the Atlantic and permit a start in negotiating some resolution of the crisis.

The moderates won; the Continental Congress convened in September. But the moderates had no alternative to the boycott, and at the same time the calling of the Congress had raised unrealistic hopes in London that moderate American leadership would make major concessions. Yet not even the most conciliatory of Americans in Congress, Joseph Galloway of Pennsylvania, who soon became like Hutchinson an archenemy of the Revolution, would concede more than the need for an imperial constitution guaranteeing the freedom of American representative government from parliamentary interference. When Congress adopted the boycott by forming a continental "association" to enforce it, the shock in London precipitated a decision to resort to armed force. As George III put it, "The die is now cast . . . blows must decide."

While Parliament was still debating the rights and wrongs of American policy, past and present, orders went out to General Gage in Boston to arrest rebel leaders and seize rebel munitions. All New England, which had been arming and drilling for months, was bound to resist any military expedition into the countryside; so war was predictable when, in April 1775, about 800 British soldiers marched to Concord, twenty miles from Boston, with another thousand in support. A running fight left many dead and wounded on both sides, and political debate and decisions were henceforth dominated by the emotions and necessities of war.

REVOLUTIONARY WAR, 1775–1783

The outbreak of war in Massachusetts, with a small British army blockaded in Boston after the Concord clash by 20,000 armed and angry New Englanders, left important questions unanswered. After its initial failure to crush rebellion, what would Britain do next? Was armed resistance centered in New England, or would it appear wherever Britain used force? On the American side, what was the objective of armed resistance? Which objectives were feasible? What would be acceptable to public opinion, on which resistance utterly depended? Given a decision on objectives, by what strategy should resistance be carried on?

In Britain, only a few argued against continuing the war in 1775. Most of them were long-time critics of the government's policy toward the colonies, "liberals" who had accepted the American side of the constitutional argument. But some were inside the government, officials who knew enough abut the condition of the British army and navy, and about the problems of waging war in America, to doubt the wisdom of conducting a land campaign against the rebels. These few, however, exerted no perceptible influence. The overwhelming consensus, reinforced by the general election of October 1774, was that the time had come to establish the paramount authority of Britain in her colonies, by armed force if all else failed. Many felt some pangs about waging war against British subjects, but even in 1775 there was a widespread belief that only a minority of Americans supported rebellion, and that many of these were deluded or intimidated by demagogic leaders. Most Americans were seen as essentially loyal, if somewhat obstreperous, and likely to welcome the chance to dissociate themselves from the Boston extremists.

British strategy depended on the rapid deployment of all available force against the rebellion. Because soldiers could be rented abroad more quickly than they could be recruited and trained, Britain hired 12,000 troops from Hessen and other small German states to reinforce its army in America for what was hoped would be the decisive campaign of 1776. Speed was vital, because a long colonial war could only benefit France, waiting for its chance to reverse the defeat of 1763. Boston was hopeless as a base for operations; New York and the Hudson Valley were obviously the key points for strategic decision—a great harbor controlling the entry to a great valley, a natural corridor by which New England could be isolated and then invaded. Access to the Hudson from the north, along the classic French invasion route from Canada, added to its strategic attraction. Seal off New England, stop American trade, and hold the vulnerable frontier zones hostage—these were the basic ideas of British strategy.

American strategy as it evolved in a reconvened Congress in Philadelphia sought to transform political unity into military strength; so far the war was only in the Boston area, fought only by New Englanders. Boston needed help, and the whole coast—from New England to Georgia—must be defended. Creating a "Continental" army in June 1775 and appointing a Virginian, George Washington, to command it were among the first steps in meeting these strategic needs. A month before Congress acted to organize a national army, another step had been taken. Americans, particularly from Virginia northward, understood as well as the British the importance of the New York–Hudson–Canada axis. In May an improvised force of New Englanders and New Yorkers had seized the small but vital post at Ticonderoga, on the lake route from Canada to the upper Hudson Valley, and then had begun to move northward. Most British troops in Canada had gone to Boston, and the American invaders hoped to seize the St. Lawrence Valley before it could be reinforced from Britain.

The effort would eventually fail, disastrously, but it came close to success; by December the Americans had captured all except the citadel of Quebec City. Neither Congress nor Washington ever questioned the wisdom of the venture. Canada (the St. Lawrence and the Great Lakes posts dependent on Montreal) under British control would expose almost the whole American frontier to attack, a lesson taught repeatedly by the earlier colonial wars. French Catholic peasants were not so ignorant or content that they would reject American appeals to equal status, legal rights, and self-government. And, in fact, the Canadian *habitants* did not resist the American invasion, despite the pleas of the British governor to do so, and in some cases they joined the American army. For a few months, at least, it looked as if the Americans had won their first real victory.

Organizing a Continental army, appointing a supreme commander, and invading Canada were wartime measures tending to transform Congress from a consultative and coordinating body into a sovereign government. After another pitched battle in June, when British troops suffered heavily in driving the Americans off Bunker Hill overlooking Boston, Washington was forced to make extensive claims for congressional authority in demanding that the British not treat their prisoners as common criminals. The need to find foreign support, especially munitions, salt, and hard money, pushed Congress in the same direction. War, in almost every aspect, drove Americans in 1775–1776 toward a claim of independence from all British authority. Yet few American leaders would consider independence during the first year of war, and still fewer advocated it. Resistance, however bloody, remained remarkably conservative and limited in its aim: the restoration of the status quo ante 1763.

The inevitable debate on independence did not begin in Congress until the spring of 1776, as the colonies entered the second year of war. The shocking collapse of the Canadian invasion, the reported concentration of a large British force at New York, and continuing efforts in London to split the colonies and their leaders all contributed to the mood in which the debate took place. New England, desperate to keep the other colonies committed to the cause of resistance, was the head of the movement for independence; New York and Pennsylvania were the centers of opposition. The latter were the obvious targets of the next military campaign, and their leaders, men like John Dickinson and James Duane, believed with some reason that independence would mean republican anarchy. New Yorkers and Pennsylvanians who opposed and feared independence were more than mere "conservatives"; they led societies much less stable than those of town-centered New England. Southern leaders were divided. Most Virginians like Richard Henry Lee aligned themselves with the New England radicals led by Samuel and

John Adams, but some Marylanders and Carolinians shared the fears of Dickinson and Duane.

Independence was only one of three interconnected issues with which Congress wrestled. The reorganization of government and the establishment of "foreign" relations, both issues involving a massive violation of what until then had been accepted as imperial law, appeared far more urgent matters than an abstract declaration of independence. Local committees that had been organized to enforce the association, and provincial "congresses" convened to avoid interference from royal governors, had become the chief arms of revolutionary government. But their status was irregular, and some Americans were disputing their right to take property or life, or to demand exclusive loyalty.

The rising costs of war and the need to pay those costs were the forces behind the foreign-policy issue; only foreign trade could earn the revenue required by war, and trade in turn demanded a revolutionary foreign policy. Opponents of independence argued, plausibly, that the problems of government and finance should be addressed first, because otherwise independence would precipitate the ex-colonies into constitutional chaos and imminent bankruptcy. Advocates of independence argued, just as plausibly, that a clean legal break was a prerequisite to a new set of constitutions and a new set of foreign relations. But votes and circumstances did more than logic and debate to decide the issue. The British military buildup around New York was so menacing, and rumors of new, divisive offers from London to negotiate so rife, that by June an immediate declaration of independence was seen to be the only way to hold the provincial coalition together in the face of its most severe challenge. The Declaration, pitched at the highest level of natural law and natural rights, would soon attract global attention and sympathy. But in July 1776 the act itself and its timing, on the eve of an all-out British offensive, were the crucial features of the Declaration of Independence.

Declaring independence did little to solve the two most pressing problems of 1776, manpower and money. Building on the colonial militia structure, regiments of volunteers sprang up everywhere. But arming, training, disciplining, and retaining these raw soldiers proved much more difficult. The army blockading Boston began to break up as the weather turned cold and boredom set in. Washington tried to rebuild his force with long-service volunteers, drilled to European standards and led by gentlemanly officers; he never gave up trying, but too much worked against this effort to create a more professional army. There was a lingering fear of a "standing" army, too many officers were in no sense gentlemen, and few volunteer soldiers were inclined to submit to harsh discipline or unbroken years of service. The new army that gathered to defend New York in mid-1776 was a mixed force of activated militia, "minutemen," and one-year enlistees. Washington believed that the Declaration of Independence rallied support for the cause, but it also alienated large numbers of Americans, especially in the Middle Atlantic and Southern states, who would engage in armed resistance only so long as such resistance stayed within the bounds of the British constitution.

The money problem was serious though not yet acute in 1776. Congress and state governments followed colonial precedents in issuing bills of credit, paper promises to pay for goods and services; the value of this paper rested on the government's own readiness to accept it in payment for taxes or other purposes. But paper money, to hold its value, required some plan for its gradual redemption, and there was some limit—today estimated at about $25 million—to what the economy could absorb without runaway price inflation. Foreign trade, foreign loans, even foreign subsidies were part of the rationale for declaring an independent United States, free to deal with the rest of the world, and by September 1776 Congress had sent commissioners to Europe with a plan for commercial treaties. The tangible results were slow in coming, and within another year price inflation was seriously undermining the war effort.

The war went badly in 1776. Beginning at Long Island in August, British and German forces under General William Howe drove Washington's army out of New York harbor and then out of central New Jersey. Popular resistance in the area collapsed, with many Americans, even some prominent leaders, swearing allegiance to George III while royal troops occupied towns as far away as the Delaware River. Not until the last days of the year did Washington gather the remnants of his army to strike back. Reinforced by militia from Pennsylvania, they overran small enemy garrisons, first at

Trenton and then at Princeton, before taking refuge in the hills of northern New Jersey. His subordinates, Charles Lee and Benedict Arnold, had been able to stop or delay British thrusts in South Carolina and down from Canada, so that the Revolution was still alive in early 1777 despite major military losses.

The British plan for 1777 was to secure the line of the Hudson, relying primarily on a continued drive southward from Canada to Albany. The main British army at New York would seize the rebel capital of Philadelphia, forcing Washington to fight a decisive battle, but it would also remain positioned to meet and support the army from Canada. There were gross flaws in the plan—in its assumptions, its timing, and its execution.

The British high command assumed that American popular resistance, except for the organized rebel armies, was negligible. They assumed that General John Burgoyne, leading the force from Canada, would encounter no serious difficulties in his march to Albany, and that General Howe could move quickly against Philadelphia without sacrificing his ability to support operations in New York. Both Burgoyne and Howe were slow in starting, Howe finally moving by sea up Chesapeake Bay. Burgoyne retook Ticonderoga, and Howe defeated Washington at Brandywine Creek south of Philadelphia, but American resistance did not weaken as expected. When Burgoyne found himself trapped north of Albany near Saratoga, Howe was in Philadelphia, unable to help, with Washington's army hovering just outside the city. The consequent surrender of Burgoyne was a decisive point in the war. France, waiting for its chance, entered the war openly as an ally of the United States, and British strategy and public opinion was shifted to that traditional, more dangerous enemy.

The Revolution, despite the great victory at Saratoga, was foundering by early 1778, when France entered the war. A bitter personal rivalry existed between Horatio Gates, the victor of Saratoga, and the oft-defeated Washington, whose army almost disappeared during its winter encampment at Valley Forge. Conflicts between congressmen who attacked and those who defended the conduct of Silas Deane, the first U.S. emissary to France, reflected deeper divisions, most of which had appeared in the difficult year 1776. The debacle in Canada and the fight over independence had left wounds that did not heal, while repeated military failures and uncontrollable, accelerating inflation poisoned the political atmosphere. The war did not hit different regions and social classes with equal force. New England escaped the worst of it after 1775; the Middle Atlantic states bore the brunt, some merchants and farmers doing well out of war while most soldiers suffered its horrors; the South was preoccupied by slaves, Indians along the frontier, and those counterrevolutionary Americans known as Tories.

In this deteriorating Revolutionary climate, most states since 1776 had worked out new, republican constitutions. Invariably, the fight over state constitutions had pitted those who equated revolution with legislative sovereignty against those who feared the dangers of unchecked democracy or believed that strong executive authority was needed to win the war. This same polarization divided Congress, complicated by the question of the correct relationship between Congress and state governments. Even as Americans celebrated the French alliance in February 1778, many sensed the weakening momentum of the Revolution, the loss of popular unity and support, and the danger of ultimate collapse.

As inflation approached bankruptcy, as towns met their draft quotas with indigent and otherwise expendable men, and as the euphoria of 1775 gave way to a leaden, carping cynicism, leadership in Congress shifted to those who cared more for Revolutionary results than for the democratic principles expressed in the Declaration of Independence. Robert Morris, a Philadelphia merchant who had opposed independence in 1776, emerged by 1777 as a leading figure in Congress. His sheer energy and ability only in part explain his rise. He lived in Philadelphia and so was always at the center, unlike most delegates who went home whenever they could. Of obscure background, he had climbed the social and professional ladder from apprenticeship to partnership in the prominent Willing family mercantile house. His gifts were for hard work, quick decisions, smooth administration, and the complexities of trade and finance—exactly what a foundering revolution required. Possible rivals were tired and tarnished (like Samuel Adams and Richard Henry Lee) by early prominence in the Revolution, abroad (like John Adams) conducting the diplomacy of the Revolution, or in their home states (like Thomas Jefferson). In a Congress too large to be efficiently decisive, too small to be administratively efficient, and discredited by its repeated failure in both respects, Morris was the perfect man for the critical moment. Around him rallied those in Congress and the army, like Washington and the young Alexander Hamilton, who saw salvation in a stronger national government.

The government of the United States had emerged during the war as a set of ad hoc arrangements, roughly approximated in the still unratified Articles of Confederation. Initially, in 1774, Congress was a consultative meeting of provincial delegates, and anything except equal weight for each province, from Virginia and Massachusetts to tiny Rhode Island and Delaware, would have wrecked the unity essential to effective resistance. Similarly, the power to tax, the most sensitive point in the controversy with Britain, could not easily be delegated to a body so imperfectly representative of "the people." These two weaknesses, representation and taxation, had crippled Congress from the outset but in practical political terms seemed irremediable. Both weaknesses were written into the Articles of Confederation, the ratification of which had fallen down the scale of priorities under the pressure of protracted war.

As war had dragged on, power had increasingly devolved upon the states, the governments of which at least had the authority and the legitimacy to raise the men and money and to requisition or confiscate the supplies that were needed to keep the armies in the field. But because military operations tended to be localized, the devolution of power from Congress to the states led to gross inequities from state to state, endless bickering, and general chaos. Ratifying the Articles had itself become so divisive that it was put aside. A myriad of conflicting interests had ruined every debate on ratification; not even the explicit concession that the states were "sovereign" had overcome all the fears and objections. But a single issue lay beneath these conflicts, the same issue of ultimate authority that had destroyed the British Empire.

Morris was disposed to act, not debate or theorize. He had left Congress in 1778, serving in the Pennsylvania Assembly; he returned in early 1781 not as an elected delegate but to accept the new post of superintendent of finance. In 1780

paper money issued by Congress had depreciated to virtually nothing, and Congress had ceased to issue it. Morris, given unprecedented power, was to find some way to pay for the war and to reestablish public credit. Somehow he did the former and took the first steps toward the latter; thereby, he redirected the whole debate on the nature of national government, a debate that would culminate in the Philadelphia Convention of 1787.

Morris' first and most successful year as superintendent of finance coincided with the effective end of the war itself. After the entry of France, British strategy in America shifted to the West Indies, vulnerable to French attack, and to the South, also vulnerable to attack. In a new kind of campaign that exploited American weaknesses—Toryism, Indians, and slavery—small British forces conquered Georgia and South Carolina in 1779–1780 and by 1781 were pushing into North Carolina and Virginia. The main army at New York immobilized Washington by playing cat-and-mouse with him in the vital Hudson highlands. After several abortive attempts at joint Franco-American operations, a French expeditionary force based itself at Rhode Island in 1780, and the French navy established its presence in American waters.

A growing sense that Americans would not support war much longer led to a bold attempt in 1781, on both sides, to score a decisive victory. Washington urged the French to combine their forces with his for a direct assault on New York, which was weakened by detachments to the south. In the South, General Cornwallis, commanding the main British army there and frustrated by his inability to destroy the last elements of American resistance, drove into Virginia. From the West Indies, French ships and troops moved toward Chesapeake Bay. Informed of the movements of Cornwallis and the French West Indian force, Washington abruptly gave up his dangerous dream of assaulting New York and persuaded his French allies in Rhode Island to concentrate everything in Virginia. In a campaign conducted with remarkable skill and luck, Washington and the French trapped Cornwallis on the Yorktown peninsula in September, much as Burgoyne had been trapped at Saratoga in 1777, and in October they forced Cornwallis' surrender.

The British had lost an expeditionary force at

Yorktown because their navy had momentarily lost control of the sea. But the main body of their army was intact, and their navy soon regained its dominance in the western Atlantic. It was the political shock of Yorktown, in London, that would end the war. Lord North resigned in early 1782, and his most vocal critics—Charles James Fox, Rockingham, and the earl of Shelburne—would shape the peace. Complex negotiations, with Franklin, John Adams, and John Jay representing the American side, dragged on through 1782. Once Shelburne agreed to recognize American independence, peace was virtually assured.

In the Treaty of 1783 the United States gained more than it had won on the battlefield. Britain kept Canada and Nova Scotia, Spain regained Florida and the Gulf Coast for its aid to France, but the United States acquired vast territory as far as the St. Lawrence watershed, the Great Lakes basin, and the Mississippi River. Britain also conceded limited fishing rights off the Grand Banks and virtually sold out the nonemigrating American Tories while protecting the prewar debts owed by Americans to "real British subjects."

POSTWAR CRISIS AND CONSOLIDATION, 1783–1790

Severely weakened by a long, disruptive war, the United States found itself in a postwar depression much more grave than that of twenty years earlier. Every state struggled with the problems of war debt, taxation, and trade. Vital concessions, made under French pressure, on the conflicting state claims to trans-Appalachian lands had finally secured ratification of the Articles of Confederation in 1781, but the powers granted to Congress under the Articles were too limited to have much effect on the troubles of the early 1780's. For a moment, in 1783, it appeared that a cabal of army officers and congressmen might use the threat of a military coup to get new powers for Congress, but Washington quashed whatever chance a coup might have had. Only on western lands and foreign relations could Congress take effective action, and many political leaders declined to serve in a government with so little power.

Whether the United States would have recov-ered and survived intact, without a drastic reorganization of national government, is endlessly debated by historians. The agricultural basis of the American economy remained sound; and within a few years foreign trade had recovered, resuming a pattern close to the old, colonial dependence on British credit, manufactures, and marketing. The problems of the 1780's were political and fiscal, with all politics entangled in the difficulties created by wartime debt and bankruptcy. Democratic state legislatures, unchecked by effective executive or judicial authority, inflicted gross inequities in trying to protect their constituents against economic disaster. Rivalry between hard-pressed states was intense and destructive. Although Congress organized the western lands for settlement and eventual statehood, and some state governments made progress in funding their public debts, most observers saw a real crisis of political authority with a fragmentation of the United States, foreign intervention, and civil war not unlikely outcomes. An impressive group of leaders, including Washington, Morris, and the Middle Atlantic state "conservatives" of 1776, as well as younger men like James Madison of Virginia, worked actively to create a stronger national government that could check state power, curb the excesses of legislative democracy, and restore respect for governmental authority. Their efforts were aided by the outbreak in 1786 of a small civil war in Massachusetts, where state government had pursued a harshly deflationary fiscal policy that threatened ruin for many western farmers, led by Daniel Shays.

"Shays's Rebellion," although put down quickly, helped to transform a meeting of state delegates in Philadelphia in mid-1787, which was authorized by Congress to propose amendments to the Articles of Confederation, into a constitutional convention. Jefferson and John Adams were abroad, but the prestige and ability of the fifty-five delegates ensured that their proposals would carry great weight; the problem was to agree on what to propose. Representation was the obvious difficulty, as intractable as it had been in 1765 and 1774; it was finally resolved by an illogical but effective compromise. Both states and people were to be represented in a divided legislature (slaves were reckoned at a fraction of their actual number). In giving a new government the power to tax and the exclusive power to wage war and regulate trade, the delegates drew on the central argument of the Revolution, that "the people" were "sovereign" and the only source of legitimate authority. A stronger central government with an illogical legislative representation, an elective but monarchical executive, and an appointive judiciary empowered to make definitive interpretations of law could all be justified as the explicit delegations of popular sovereignty.

Conservative-minded delegates applied democratic theory in a radical way to finesse the critical problem of the federal relationship, which seemed even less solvable than the problem of representation. Claims of state sovereignty, written into the Articles of Confederation, lost much of their relevance if all governmental power was seen as no more than strictly limited delegations of authority from the sovereign people. Thus, two levels of government would operate on (and from) the people, reducing the urgency of a strict definition of how the two levels were related to one another. On this problem the British Empire had foundered, and the American solution to it has been called "intuitive." But intuitive American federalism in 1787 was the revolutionary result of years of impassioned democratic rhetoric and bruising democratic experience, when getting and keeping popular support for a protracted struggle was the key to Revolutionary life or death.

The elaborate procedures—the special national Convention, and state conventions for ratification—surrounding the new federal Constitution indicate how far political legitimacy had come to depend on a strict, literal application of democratic theory. It was this application, more than anything else, that resolved the conundrum of federalism and transformed the American nation from a vague concept into an effective reality. Washington lent his enormous prestige to the presidency under the Constitution, Alexander Hamilton as secretary of the treasury followed the policies of Robert Morris in using the war debt to rally conservative monied support for the new government, and the French Revolutionary Wars would bring a respite from European threats and a windfall prosperity that helped the United States, finally, to consolidate the gains of the Revolution. But it was democratic theory, accepted and literally applied even by Hamilton and the minority who did not hold it as a reli-

gious belief, that gave the American Revolution its unique quality.

BIBLIOGRAPHY

David Ammerman, *In the Common Cause: American Response to the Coercive Acts of 1774* (Charlottesville, Va., 1974), is an excellent study. Bernard Bailyn, *The Ideological Origins of the American Revolution* (Cambridge, Mass., 1967), offers a highly influential interpretation of the explosive quality of American political thought before and during the Revolution. Charles A. Beard, *An Economic Interpretation of the Constitution of the United States* (New York, 1913), is the classic assertion that economic conflict was the driving force of American politics during and after the Revolution. Lee Benson, *Turner and Beard: American Historical Writing Reconsidered* (Glencoe, Ill., 1960), offers the most persuasive restatement of Beard's thesis in light of the heavy criticism of it. Ian R. Christie and Benjamin W. Labaree, *Empire or Independence, 1760–1776: A British-American Dialogue on the Coming of the American Revolution* (New York, 1976), is a valuable, two-sided account of the coming of the Revolution; Christie's view from London is the best available.

Marcus Cunliffe, *George Washington, Man and Monument* (Boston, 1958), is a brief biography and a brilliant analysis of the Revolution's indispensable man. Felix Gilbert, *To the Farewell Address: Ideas of Early American Foreign Policy* (Princeton, N.J., 1961), is an original, stimulating essay on Revolutionary foreign policy. Lawrence H. Gipson, *The British Empire Before the American Revolution,* 15 vols. (New York, 1958–1970), is a massive, useful narrative history of the empire and its provinces, 1748–1776. Robert A. Gross, *The Minutemen and Their World* (New York, 1976), is perhaps the best example of the recent emphasis on microcosmic local studies.

James A. Henretta, *The Evolution of American Society, 1700–1815* (Lexington, Mass., 1973), easily mistaken for a textbook, is a remarkable synthesis of modern scholarship, stressing the deeper social roots of political history. Don Higginbotham, *The War of American Independence: Military Attitudes, Policies, and Practice, 1763–1789* (New York, 1971), is a comprehensive account. Cecelia M. Kenyon, ed., *The Antifederalists* (Indianapolis, Ind., 1966), in a long introductory essay, brilliantly dissects the minds of those who opposed the Constitution. Kenneth A. Lockridge, *Settlement and Unsettlement in Early America: The Crisis of Political Legitimacy Before the Revolution* (New York, 1981), is one of the most recent efforts to reconnect the Revolution to social structure and social change.

Forrest McDonald, *We the People: The Economic Origins of the Constitution* (Chicago, 1958), remains the best single test and refutation of the Beard thesis. Piers Mackesy, *The War for America, 1775–1783* (Cambridge, Mass., 1964), offers an original view of the Revolutionary War, as seen from London. Edmund S. Morgan and Helen M. Morgan, *The Stamp Act Crisis: Prologue to Revolution* (Chapel Hill, N.C., 1953), is both a detailed narrative of 1765–1766 and a path-breaking revision of traditional interpretation. William H. Nelson, *The*

American Tory (Oxford, 1961), remains the best single work on the estimated half million Americans who rejected the Revolution. Robert R. Palmer, *The Age of the Democratic Revolution: A Political History of Europe and America, 1760–1800,* 2 vols. (Princeton, N.J., 1959–1964), a brilliant comparative study in western constitutional history, puts the American Revolution in a broad context.

Jack N. Rakove, *The Beginnings of National Politics: An Interpretive History of the Continental Congress* (New York, 1979), is a long-needed account that deemphasizes class and party conflict. Charles Royster, *A Revolutionary People at War: The Continental Army and American Character, 1775–1783* (Chapel Hill, N.C., 1979), applies the techniques of intellectual history to the experience of the Revolutionary War. P. D. G. Thomas, *British Politics and the Stamp Act Crisis: The First Phase of the American Revolution, 1763–1767* (Oxford, 1975), broader than its title, is a detailed account of colonial policy in the context of British politics during the 1760's. Morton G. White, *The Philosophy of the American Revolution* (New York, 1978), is the best book on the ideas underlying the Declaration of Independence. Gordon S. Wood, *The Creation of the American Republic, 1776–1787* (Chapel Hill, N.C., 1969), is a richly detailed account of the Revolutionary transformation of American political thinking.

[*See also* HISTORIOGRAPHY OF AMERICAN POLITICAL HISTORY; ARTICLES OF CONFEDERATION; COLONIAL GOVERNMENT; CONSTITUTION; DECLARATION OF INDEPENDENCE; ENGLISH AND EUROPEAN POLITICAL INHERITANCE; FEDERALISM; THE FEDERALIST PAPERS; *and* REPRESENTATION AND APPORTIONMENT.]

ANTEBELLUM REFORM

Ronald G. Walters

THE term *antebellum reform* has more utility than logic to recommend it. American scholars use it to comprehend movements like the crusade against alcohol, which began before and persisted after the antebellum period (about 1815–1860). They also use it without any clearly agreed-upon definition of *reform*. One of the oldest and most enduring works on the subject, for example, includes discussions of religious organizations like the Mormons, largely because these grew out of the same soil and flourished at the same time as such reform movements as antislavery and temperance.

There is a definition of *antebellum reform* implicit in the majority of works on the subject, one whose imprecision may be the only way of properly respecting the past. To a great extent, it is a definition based on self-ascription—on accepting the view that antebellum reformers were indeed reformers. While that absolves historians of formulating any clear standard of their own, it also permits them to include movements (such as the antialcohol crusade) that do not seem much like genuine reforms from a twentieth-century perspective. Moreover, this definition generally allows scholars to avoid making the old distinction between reformers, who supposedly try to effect change within the existing social system, and radicals, who seek its overthrow.

Useful as it may be in other situations to draw the line between radicals and reformers, the attempt to do so for the antebellum period often breaks down. Reformers like Wendell Phillips, the abolitionist, used radical-sounding rhetoric to set a standard for change within their social order. They blithely moved back and forth between demanding alterations in American society and advocating its replacement by a new, perfect order. They were utterly unconcerned by the notion that they might have been reformers at one moment and radicals at another. In their minds they were reformers.

Accepting the reformers' self-estimate may solve some problems, but it creates others; for instance, it raises questions about the omission of Southern defenders of slavery from all major works on antebellum reform. Their cause may be thought repulsive by our own time, but so, to many historians, is the temperance crusade, which has always been included in the world of reform without challenges. Moreover, any definition based strictly on self-ascription would have to accept the view of white Southerners that they, no less than Northerners, were proposing improvement in the human condition and were therefore genuine reformers.

There is, nonetheless, a rationale for omitting Southern defenders of slavery from discussions of antebellum reform. They may have had an effect in ameliorating the institution, but they never developed the organizational apparatuses that were so striking a feature of reform campaigns in the free states. They were individuals rather than a movement. This provides a convenient justification for leaving them out of the history of antebellum reform, which is in part a story of mobilization and collective action.

Evasions and imprecision aside, *antebellum reform* describes the unprecedented flowering between the end of the War of 1812 and the outbreak of the Civil War of groups dedicated to improving society or individuals. It seemed as if every conceivable cause had its advocate and every advocate had a printing press and an organization. These reform crusades took root most firmly in urban areas; in rural ones that were undergoing rapid change; and especially in New England and its cultural hinterlands, such as upstate New York and Ohio's Western Reserve. They were alike in that each had an institutional apparatus and in that their proponents saw them as solutions to serious problems of the day.

The movement was new and distinctive in its qualities as well as its quantity. There had been ad hoc reform attempts in the eighteenth century, but they lacked well-developed institutional arrangements. Eighteenth-century reformers were generally part-timers like Cotton Mather or Benjamin Franklin, who did good deeds in the midst of other occupations. For them reform was an avocation. For the leaders of antebellum reform it was a vocation.

Reform became a career, in part, because economic and technological developments in antebellum America made it far easier to draw financial and moral support from a widely dispersed audience. Improvements in transportation (especially the railroad) and in printing lowered the cost and shortened the length of time it took to reach small, scattered groups of like-minded people. Even a controversial and unpopular antebellum reformer like William Lloyd Garrison could spend his adult years speaking to a fairly tiny portion of the public and have no other real vocation. Except for a few Quaker activists, such a life would have been virtually unthinkable and nearly impossible prior to 1815.

Antebellum reformers were distinctive for their extreme rhetoric and positions. Earlier reformers had commonly envisioned particular problems as matters to be resolved moderately and over time by reasonable men working slowly and rationally. By the 1830's such an approach had become unconscionable for many reformers. To them a sin was a sin, to be denounced in the harshest language and ended immediately. They regarded halfway measures such as moderate drinking, a gradual end to slaveholding, or acceptance of defensive wars as just another form of complicity in evil.

This intransigence was not characteristic of all pre–Civil War reformers; but its existence and its imagery bespeak the importance of religion to antebellum reform. Evangelical Protestantism provided reform with personnel, a vocabulary, and a model of organizational structure.

REVIVALS AND THE BENEVOLENT EMPIRE

At the end of the eighteenth century, religious revivals broke out in the West, especially in Kentucky and Tennessee, and spread eastward. By the second decade of the nineteenth century, they had taken hold among New England Congregationalists like Lyman Beecher, a prominent preacher and important figure in antebellum reform. Also in the 1820's a remarkable Presbyterian clergyman, Charles G. Finney, presided over extraordinary revivals in western New York. His move to New York City in 1832 symbolized the fact that by then revivalism was both urban and rural, eastern and western.

At the heart of evangelical Protestantism was an emotional fervor. In some cases this took the form of fainting, swooning, tears, prayers, and lamentations. In others it released a powerful energy—an intense commitment to do God's work, whatever the hardships. It was part of Finney's genius to help direct that energy toward earthly problems. His instrument was the doctrine of "disinterested benevolence," an old phrase given a new twist by Finney. It meant, according to him, the capacity—and the duty—of godly Americans to do things to benefit humankind. In this respect Finney edged toward what older Presbyterians regarded as heresy: the view that human beings could will their own salvation. It also brought Finney near another heresy, that of perfectionism—the belief that men and women could become perfect, or absolutely free from sin, while still alive. Some reformers were to push that logic to extremes intolerable even to Finney.

Whatever his theological unorthodoxy, Finney's ideal Christians were active men and women who did good deeds either as a sign that God had granted salvation, or perhaps even to bring it about by their own efforts. They were to be reformers in spirit and deed, as was Finney himself. It is no accident that antebellum reform took root so firmly in the Western Reserve of Ohio and the "burned-over district" of western New York, regions scorched by his revivalism.

Antebellum reform took further power and shape from a millennialist streak in evangelical Protestantism. Although millennialist thought can take many forms and have varying levels of intellectual complexity, the type that fueled antebellum reform held that there literally would come a reign of perfect justice, God's kingdom on earth. For reformers the millennium provided both a standard against which to measure the failings of their own society and an assurance that something infinitely superior was within their grasp. Its promise of absolute purity made them intolerant of matters that previous generations had regarded with far more complacency. With the millennium in view, it was impossible for many reformers to accept moderation and compromise when confronted with slavery, alcohol, or other evils. There was no middle ground between the world as it was and the rule of Christian principles.

Thanks to millennialism and to Finney's version of disinterested benevolence, at least two generations of antebellum Americans thought they could see a better world ahead and felt a moral imperative to do their best to bring it about.

Even before Finney rose to prominence in the 1820's, Protestants—not all of them evangelical—had begun to organize to spread the Christian message as they understood it. Among the earliest of these efforts was the Connecticut Missionary Society, which in the 1790's sought to spread the New England gospel to heathen Americans. In the nineteenth century similar organizations arose elsewhere, as did others, less missionary in purpose, aimed at specific sins like dueling or at a more general "reformation of morals."

These Protestant organizations, proliferating with the rise of revivalism in the East, developed techniques easily adopted by social reformers. They were voluntary associations, usually including laity as well as clergy among their directors. Some were interdenominational. They published literature (or propaganda, depending on one's point of view) and sponsored itinerant lecturers. The largest of them created local auxiliaries. With the birth of the American Bible Society in 1816, such organizations began to assume the formidable proportions that earned them the title "the benevolent empire." The American Sunday School Union, founded in 1824, and the American Tract Society, organized a year later, were especially effective in attracting members

and in covering the land with the printed word. Their structures and strategies for reaching the public were a school for reformers with secular causes. Nowhere were the ideological and organizational links with evangelical Protestantism clearer than in the two greatest of antebellum reforms: abolitionism and temperance.

ANTISLAVERY

A Boston editor, William Lloyd Garrison, provided abolitionism with a nicely symbolic beginning by starting publication of his antislavery paper, the *Liberator,* on New Year's Day, 1831. Although Garrison would alienate many of his original supporters, he initially spoke for a new generation of antislavery men and women then emerging in New England, Ohio, Pennsylvania, and New York. Earlier abolitionists had usually approached slaveholders in a conciliatory fashion, seeking a gradual end to the institution and, more often than not, advocating resettlement of freed blacks somewhere outside the United States. That was the position of the American Colonization Society, founded in 1816 and the most influential organization of its sort in 1831. Garrison's war, and that of his followers, was with "halfway measures" as well as with slavery.

Garrison's position came to be known as immediatism because of his insistence that slavery was a sin that should cease instantly. As a sin, it required the harshest possible rebuke—and Garrison's talent for invective ensured that it would receive just that. But abolitionists after 1830 did not just repudiate the gradualistic, conciliatory approach of the Colonization Society. They also rejected its vision of the United States as a white man's country. Instead of calling for the expulsion of ex-slaves, as colonizationists did, they insisted that blacks be treated as brothers and sisters. White abolitionists were not entirely of one mind about how far racial equality ought to go, but they were as strikingly new for their advocacy of a biracial America as they were for their intransigence against slavery.

Between 1831 and 1833, immediatist abolitionists worked on the local level in several of the free states. In December 1833 a small number of delegates met in Philadelphia to form a national organization, the American Anti-Slavery

Society (AASS). This marked the beginning of a brief, intense period of activity, much of it fostered by the society's New York–based leadership.

Especially important in those early years was Lewis Tappan, a wealthy and pious merchant who had had experience in the benevolent empire of Protestant missionary organizations. Under his stewardship, and thanks in part to his and his brother Arthur's money, the AASS embarked on an ambitious program to put seventy trained lecturers in the field, covering the nation, to speak for immediate emancipation. They never quite reached that number, but the society did succeed in fashioning a many-sided propaganda machine of considerable efficiency. It organized local auxiliaries, claiming 1,300, with 250,000 members, by 1838. It gathered about 400,000 signatures in a drive to flood Congress with antislavery petitions. Above all, the AASS printed and distributed at least 750,000 pieces of propaganda by 1838, when hard times forced it to cut back expenditures.

Impressive as those achievements were, abolitionists failed to reach slaveholders (their publications were anathema in the South), and by the late 1830's some of them began to grow dissatisfied with the AASS and its tactics. The society suffered a major schism in 1840, when a portion of its membership, including the Tappan brothers, left it in the hands of Garrison and his largely New England supporters.

The causes of the division in abolitionist ranks were various and included personal rivalries and misunderstandings. The ostensible issue in 1840 was the participation of women in the movement. Female abolitionists had been important in the cause from the beginning, although their role within antislavery organizations had been largely a subordinate one. In the mid-1830's a lively debate began over their rights and responsibilities. It was stirred in part by a growing awareness of injustices done to American women, white as well as black, and in part by an antislavery lecture tour undertaken by two sisters from South Carolina, Angelina and Sarah Grimké. When they spoke before "promiscuous assemblies"—audiences of both sexes—the act was so unconventional and unladylike that they met hostility both from the clergy and from fellow abolitionists. The episode later became an important factor in the development of American feminism; but its immediate consequence was to sour relations between abolitionists like Garrison, who supported the Grimkés and endorsed equal rights for women, and colleagues like Lewis Tappan, who valued female assistance but felt that it should not violate convention and should come from within separate antislavery organizations. Garrison's opponents made their break following the appointment of a woman to a previously all-male committee in the AASS.

By that time conflict among abolitionists rested on more than gender. Garrison himself had become a divisive force because he opened the *Liberator* to a number of unpopular views (such as Christian anarchism and women's rights), many of which he held. Garrison was not unique among antebellum reformers in working for more than one cause: even his most staid colleagues commonly endorsed such other crusades as temperance and dietary reform. But Garrison's enthusiasms were extreme and obnoxious both to his co-workers and to some of the more religious people they hoped to reach. In spite of his protestations that other abolitionists need not share his beliefs on all matters, his unorthodoxy could not be separated from antislavery so long as it appeared in the *Liberator,* the most notorious antislavery newspaper. He was, moreover, abrasive in responding to criticism from well-meaning colleagues. In the eyes of some of his New York and Ohio allies he had become a liability.

Among these onetime colleagues were men who had a special reason for wishing to put distance between themselves and Garrison. Led by James G. Birney, a repentant former slaveholder, they wanted to turn antislavery away from its nonpartisan course and toward direct involvement in politics. In seeking votes, they could not afford to be tainted by Garrison's unpopular beliefs. Equally important, Garrison challenged them from within the antislavery movement, questioning both their tactics and principles. He maintained that the proper place for abolitionists was outside partisan warfare, trying to change the hearts and minds of all Americans. He regarded political parties as corrupt and corrupting.

On that point many of his abolitionist opponents agreed with him. But he went further. He had come to believe in a form of Christian anarchism known as nonresistance. The reasoning behind it took the form of a syllogism: force is immoral; governments rest upon force; therefore governments are immoral. Garrison's views, more sophisticated than they appear in outline, expressed a faith in God's kingdom on earth that was a logical extension of evangelical millennialism. Their origins in revivalism did not make them any more palatable to abolitionists like Birney, who not only were unwilling to give up on government but were considering ways of taking control of it. Their vehicle was to be an antislavery political party, something neither Garrison the strategist nor Garrison the anarchist could abide. Politically-minded abolitionists could not stay comfortably in the same organization with him.

The schism left Garrison in charge of a weakened AASS, but it did not necessarily damage abolitionism (a point the Boston editor would have contested). In a pluralistic and localistic society the fragmentation of antislavery and other reforms did not have to mean diminished effectiveness. The division permitted each faction to go its own way unhindered by the rest, working in the fashion best suited to its constituency and locality. Garrison and his supporters continued to hold to the highest possible standard of antislavery purity and to act as a kind of conscience for the movement. Tappan and his more orthodox evangelical allies sought to work for the slave as best they could. Birney and the political abolitionists formed a party before the year was out.

Their organization, the Liberty party, came into the field in time to run Birney in the presidential election of 1840. Although he posed no threat to the Democrats or the victorious Whigs, he and the Liberty party began direct antislavery involvement in politics. Veterans of the party would find their way into other political organizations, primarily the Free Soil and Republican parties. Some of them won office in later years and gained a measure of national influence.

The Garrisonians saw each of their fellow abolitionists' steps toward political respectability as a compromise of antislavery principles. To a degree they were correct. The Free Soil party of 1848 searched for a broader electorate than the Liberty party reached and nominated an improbable antislavery candidate: a former Democrat, former protégé of Andrew Jackson, and former president, Martin Van Buren. Envisioning a society of white freeholders (not a biracial one), the

party took its stand against the expansion, rather than for the extermination, of slavery. The Republican party of the 1850's would take much the same position—a far cry from immediate emancipation and racial brotherhood. It was the kind of moral moderation some abolitionists could not abide. And yet part of the significance of the antislavery movement rests on the infiltration of its people and rhetoric into politics.

Abolitionists forged an emotionally compelling image of the South and slavery. They were particularly successful in emphasizing the complicity of Northerners in the maintenance of slavery, in portraying the institution as the negation of values held dear in the free states, and in speaking of an alleged "slave power" conspiracy by slaveholders and their sympathizers to manipulate the government to serve Southern interests. Those themes framed issues in a manner that made it easier for Northerners to dig in their heels when faced with Southern demands and with expansion of slavery into new territory in the 1840's and 1850's.

The power of abolitionist propaganda, whether in print or in partisan activity, also provoked Southerners to self-defeating responses that only confirmed the antislavery view of them as ruthless defenders of an inhumane institution. There was no "slave power" conspiracy, but each effort of Southern politicians to defend their interests in the 1840's and 1850's seemed to indicate that one existed.

The antislavery crusade achieved one of its major goals with the end of the Civil War and the death of slavery. Its other great objective, a just and biracial society, was more elusive. Some antislavery men and women kept the faith and pressed the cause of ex-slaves after the war, but age and an ideological commitment to the free market kept others from pushing for programs that would genuinely have given blacks a chance for equality after emancipation. That abolitionists failed to achieve all they sought is less a sign of insincerity than of how millennialist their expectations really were.

THE CRUSADE AGAINST ALCOHOL

Although antislavery has attracted more scholarly attention than any other antebellum reform, the temperance movement began earlier, persisted longer, attracted more members, and had more direct political impact.

Various protests against alcohol appeared in eighteenth-century America; the first voluntary association dedicated to combating excessive drinking seems to have been founded in upstate New York in 1808. Organized effort began in 1813 with the Massachusetts Society for the Suppression of Intemperance (MSSI). The MSSI was not entirely typical of what would follow: its leadership and membership consisted of relatively well-to-do men, most of them staunchly Federalist and the majority Congregationalist with a significant Unitarian minority. As the temperance movement expanded it broadened its political and denominational base and clarified its position. The first organizations, including the MSSI, permitted drinking in moderation; some forbade distilled spirits but not necessarily wine and beer. That distinction may have had much to recommend it, but the line between good and bad drinking was difficult to maintain, both in practice and in confrontation with the extremist logic of antebellum reform.

The great change came in the 1820's. In 1825 Lyman Beecher preached a powerful diatribe against alcohol, later published as *Six Sermons on . . . Intemperance* (1827). He attacked even moderate drinking, praying for "banishment of ardent spirits from the lawful articles of commerce." He also demanded a new, more vigorous campaign against alcohol, carried out by a network of voluntary associations and based on total abstinence.

An answer to Beecher's call came in 1826 with the formation of the American Temperance Society (ATS). Closely tied to Protestant religious and charitable enterprises, it drew upon the organizational expertise of the benevolent empire. The results were impressive. According to some estimates, by 1834 there were about 5,000 state and local temperance societies; millions of pieces of propaganda circulated; and about a million Americans had taken an antialcohol pledge. The ATS was not entirely responsible for this, nor were all those auxiliaries loyal to it; but—like the AASS in its first years—the ATS demonstrated how effectively a national reform organization could mount a propaganda campaign.

By the 1830's the crusade against alcohol had transcended its New England Federalist and Congregationalist origins and was on its way to becoming more interdenominational (although

evangelical) and less sectional. It had, in addition, become more fervent and less compromising. That was because of an infusion of revivalistic zeal in the 1820's and 1830's and the spread of the "teetotal" position, with its renunciation of all consumption of alcohol.

As was the case with abolitionism, the temperance movement began to splutter and fragment at the point of its greatest organizational success. Some of the causes were the same: the difficulty of maintaining a large voluntary association with far-flung auxiliaries, personality conflicts, differences over tactics and goals, and declining contributions after the Panic of 1837. Temperance, however, received an infusion of new vigor after 1840, thanks to some reformed drunkards.

In its earliest stages the movement had not aimed at reclaiming the besotted. Its goal was to keep sober people sober. In the spring of 1840 six former drinking companions formed the Washington Temperance Society; by Christmas it had 1,000 members; and three years later it claimed to have received around 600,000 pledges from former intemperate drinkers, 100,000 of them allegedly once habitual drunkards. Although there were links between older temperance organizations and the Washingtonians, the latter represented a broader social spectrum, drawing converts from the lower and working classes, which had been scarcely touched by earlier elite-dominated organizations. The Washingtonians also took a different posture toward religion. They were perfectly willing to use the rhetorical and organizational techniques of revivalism, but they were often indifferent to the evangelical Protestantism that had played so large a role in temperance in the 1820's. Finally, they were far more boisterous in their proselytizing, going beyond the lecturing and tract-distributing of older, more staid anti-alcohol societies.

With the 1840's and the Washingtonians, temperance entered a phase of far more imaginative propagandizing. In addition to flamboyant oratory, the Washingtonians (like the abolitionists) adopted some of the tactics of antebellum electioneering. They held noisy public gatherings—picnics, fairs, processions, and parades. They even inspired fiction, including at least one contribution to American melodrama, Timothy Shay Arthur's *Ten Nights in a Barroom and What I Saw There* (1854).

The Washingtonians suffered a quick decline,

the result of organizational weaknesses, power struggles, and members' lapses from grace. The field was then filled by other groups like the Sons of Temperance, some of them fairly secular and offering the social and economic benefits of fraternal orders and mutual aid societies. The turn of temperance to new tactics continued in the 1850's, without the Washingtonians and thanks to the state of Maine.

As early as Lyman Beecher's sermons in 1825 there had been signs that temperance advocates would take political action to prevent the sale and manufacture of alcoholic beverages. Such an idea surfaced in a national convention in 1833 and achieved a victory in Massachusetts in 1838 in a law prohibiting the sale of distilled spirits in quantities of less than fifteen gallons (effectively putting them out of reach of poor people). Prohibition, nonetheless, met sharp opposition within the antialcohol crusade, in part because some temperance men and women shared the Garrisonian abolitionists' distaste for the political system and partisan activity. They preferred "moral suasion"—trying to reach the hearts of individuals—over seeking electoral victories.

Such reasoning had no appeal for a man named Neal Dow, who campaigned for prohibition of alcoholic beverages in the 1840's, achieving local and finally statewide success in the so-called Maine Law of 1851, which prohibited the manufacture and sale of all alcoholic beverages within the borders of the state. It became a model for other states (including the unlikely one of California, which came surprisingly close to banning alcohol during the rowdy days of the gold rush). By the mid-1850's thirteen states had passed some version of the law.

Of all antebellum reformers, temperance crusaders entered the political system most directly and most effectively. This is not to say they always won. By the 1870's only three of the Maine laws survived, the rest being casualties of court decisions or political challenges. During the Civil War and its aftermath, the antialcohol crusade went into brief remission, to be revived with evangelical fervor once more by organizations like the Women's Christian Temperance Union (WCTU; 1874) and the Anti-Saloon League (1893). Its greatest victory would come in the twentieth century when it succeeded in writing prohibition temporarily into the Constitution. From the antebellum period until then, views about drinking influenced local voting behavior, both directly and as part of a Protestant moral sensibility that suffused the Whig and Republican parties.

Not all of the significance of temperance lay in its political impact. It also contributed to a lowering of the consumption of alcoholic beverages from extraordinary heights at the beginning of the nineteenth century to levels in the 1850's that were below present-day ones. (Lest reformers take all the credit, that decline may owe something to market forces, including changes in grain prices.)

Temperance was also important for its role in relations between genders and classes. Like antislavery, it provided an outlet for the organizational and intellectual energies of middle-class women. Barred from voting and officeholding, they could exert influence on society only through charities and reforms suited to their supposedly superior moral sensibilities. Their attacks on alcohol took them into public life in a respectable way and into a kind of guerrilla warfare with male values and behavior. It was men, temperance propagandists made clear, who did most of the drinking. It was their women and children who did most of the suffering. That image of the problem was powerfully emblematic of men's general mistreatment of women. In subtle—and sometimes not so subtle—ways temperance could be a protest against a world dominated by men.

But temperance had a class, as well as sexual, aspect. It lost some of its elite nature over time, particularly with the rise of the Washingtonians in the 1840's. Yet in the antebellum years it always preached a middle-class ethos of sobriety, thrift, punctuality, and hard work. This may well have been part of a broader process of instilling a self-discipline appropriate to both the factory system and entrepreneurship in an expanding economy. Certainly much of the message was aimed at the lower classes, whose failures it blamed on drinking and whose performance as employees surely would improve with sobriety. But the temperance message also rang true for middle-class Americans, reinforcing their notions of propriety and self-control and providing them with a standard of respectability against which to measure the distance between them and other classes.

Temperance turned the machinery of evangelical Protestant morality toward what was doubtless a serious problem in the antebellum period. But the millennium it promised was a bourgeois one, an idealized (or reformed) version of what was then emerging.

THE SECULARIZATION OF REFORM

Although evangelical Protestantism helped shape temperance and antislavery, secular forces also influenced the content of each and of antebellum reform more generally. They ranged from technology and economic change to America's revolutionary traditions and nineteenth-century science. In spite of its moralism, antebellum reform was a point along the road away from religious interpretations of social problems and toward secular ones.

In antislavery the ties to evangelical Protestantism never entirely vanished, but they became strained. Some abolitionists like Garrison became thoroughly unorthodox in their beliefs; others simply became disillusioned with revivalism, particularly with the failure of many of their fellow evangelicals to see the sin of slavery. In that, they were making a quiet reversal: they were judging religion by its commitment to social action, rather than judging social action by its adherence to religious principles.

Abolitionists, moreover, were never content to rest their attack on slavery on religious grounds. With the rise of the Liberty party in 1840, many abolitionists seemed as eager to show the inconsistency of slavery with the Constitution as to prove its incompatibility with Christianity. Even the Garrisonians, who disdained political agitation, described slavery in largely secular terms: it was a product of humanity's lust for power; it destroyed family relations; it was a negation of civilization; and it produced conspiracies against the liberties of whites as well as blacks. That line of reasoning was not grand political theory—it was not even totally consistent—but it also was not religious.

The temperance movement almost always remained true to its roots in antebellum Protestantism—the most famous postbellum organization was, after all, the WCTU. But antialcohol propagandists, in common with their antislavery counterparts, did not rely on theology to make their point. They called on science to detail the physically destructive effects of strong drink and they drew upon a primitive version of social sci-

ence to make much of the rest of their case. Even in their most mawkish moments they gave arguments that were crudely economic and social. Alcohol may have sent the sinner to hell, but it also sent his wife and children to the poorhouse. It impoverished the working classes. It produced crime and slovenly work habits.

In temperance and antislavery, Protestant moralism began to mingle with, take on the guise of, and sometimes become subordinate to secular social thought. The process of secularization was far more apparent in lesser-known antebellum movements, among them labor reform. Three other broadly defined movements, physiological reforms, institutional reforms, and communitarianism, deserve special attention for what they demonstrate about two major shifts in antebellum reform: from religious to secular modes of thought and from persuasion to compulsion.

PHYSIOLOGICAL REFORMS

Temperance was one of several antebellum reforms to treat the body and physiological processes. Among the others was phrenology, an effort to analyze character by reading the configuration of skulls, and spiritualism, the attempt to communicate with the dead. Neither sounds much like a reform to modern ears, yet proponents claimed that each could solve many of the world's problems, by working through individuals and by understanding nature's laws of spirit and matter. They were not the only reforms to make that claim. Another one made it in a manner particularly revealing of the character of antebellum reform. It was dietary (or health) reform, and its central figure was a former clergyman, Sylvester Graham.

A cholera epidemic in 1832 gave Graham his chance for fame. Then in his mid-thirties, he had been a clergyman and temperance lecturer but promptly became an expert on health. Although avoiding cholera was the problem with which Graham was immediately concerned, he saw irritation of the stomach as the cause of all disease. He presented his views to a deeply concerned public in well-attended lectures and in vivid prose. Controversy and converts alike swarmed about him and within a few years dietary reform—and a wider campaign to improve American health—developed its own associations, publications, and schisms. Graham himself retired from the field relatively early. The reason was ill health.

The ideas Graham represented, nonetheless, had a long life. Americans in his day used their abundant foodstuffs to fashion a cuisine renowned for its excesses (including of fat and starch). Graham called for what was doubtless a healthier diet, a plain, simple one with no meat and much roughage. But his claims went beyond good health. He argued that proper diet could both cure and prevent disease. It was, he further asserted, also essential for proper moral behavior. He devoted lurid passages to the evils of sexual excess (even within marriage) and its destructive effect on mind and body, and he claimed that proper diet was the answer. We are what we eat, Graham believed, and sick people and sinners ate badly.

Graham had a minor effect on the American diet (although he did leave a style of flour and a cracker to posterity); but his ideas have particular value as a marker of one current of antebellum reform thought. Dietary reform was above all else a translation of evangelical Protestantism into secular and scientific language. Under Graham's influence, perfectionism ceased to be a spiritual doctrine and became a physiological one. Just as Christian perfectionists thought the soul could become free from sin while on earth, dietary reformers believed the body could become free from illness and infirmity; spiritual grace (or at least good behavior) would follow. The evangelical Protestant millennium became a matter of science and physiology.

Proper diet scarcely seems an appropriate vehicle for the millennium, let alone an adequate response to the problems of an industrializing nation. Yet in their pairing of physical and moral law, health reformers, like many of their antebellum colleagues, were on the road to establishing science and secular thought as authorities in the ordering of human affairs. That places them in a direct line with later nineteenth- and twentieth-century reformers, however inconsequential their cause might now seem.

INSTITUTIONAL REFORMS

While Graham's followers were promoting proper diet, others were pressing for new sorts of institutions in the name of reform—asylums, prisons, and school systems. Institution-building was part of a reexamination of poverty and crime following the War of 1812. When hard times hit, local jurisdictions were overwhelmed. Urban areas were expanding rapidly, particularly after 1820, and they lacked facilities (let alone policies) for dealing with the poor and the violent. But the building of antebellum almshouses, orphanages, jails, and insane asylums came against remarkable odds. Construction far outstripped what population growth alone would have required. It also ran counter to the parsimony of state legislatures and faced ideological opposition, both from Americans who preferred doing nothing and from those who believed in "outdoor relief"—treating the needy in their own homes rather than in institutions. It was a considerable political achievement of the reformers that states and cities committed themselves to constructing large and costly prisons and asylums.

Although gloomy, the massive antebellum prisons and asylums represented some improvement in the treatment of criminals and the insane. Similarly, detention homes and orphanages may not have inspired warm feelings in their juvenile inmates, but the alternative for many was abuse, crime, and starvation in the streets. What is striking, however, is that advocates of such institutions did not just present them as a humane solution to immediate problems: they invested what they built with millennialist expectations. Alexis de Tocqueville and Gustave de Beaumont, visiting the United States to examine prisons, noted that for some reformers the new-style penitentiary "seems the remedy for all the evils of society." Others would have made identical claims for the new-style insane asylums and other custodial institutions.

The claims were plausible because reformers had faith in the ability of such institutions to cure deviance. Their own statistics at first seemed to back their promises. For a time in the 1830's the pioneer Massachusetts insane asylum at Worcester (opened in 1833) was supposedly able to discharge over 80 percent of those whom it got in the early stages of lunacy. In the 1840's two asylum directors announced 100 percent cure rates.

Those figures are testimony to the faith of reformers in the curability of virtually all human defects and in the power of their institutions. They believed that the hardest of cases could be reached by a combination of intense moral suasion and proper environment. The decisive step was to remove offenders from corrupting influences, place them in a highly structured environment, and teach them virtue, discipline, and self-control. For their proponents (if not for their inmates) these institutions were a kind of utopia—isolated from the flux and disorder of antebellum society and a cure for its ills.

Public school systems have a special place within the vogue of reformist institution-building. They were not total institutions, a world apart, like insane asylums and prisons. They aimed at preventing rather than curing deviance, yet the goals and means of school reformers were similar to those of their fellow institution builders and were part of broader trends within antebellum reform.

The expectations for schools were as high as they were for asylums or any other antebellum reform institutions. Horace Mann, who led the way to public education in Massachusetts, argued that it would save America from the evils of inequality so apparent in Europe. Schools would be "the great equalizer of the condition of men." They could create perfect citizens.

That was asking a great deal from the schools. That was also cloaking in egalitarian rhetoric a considerable amount of moral and class control. Far from being entirely secular and democratic, antebellum public schools had a strongly Protestant and middle-class cast to them. The morality they inculcated was that embedded in most antebellum reforms, whether temperance or asylum-building: sobriety, hard work, thrift, discipline, and self-control. The Bible they used and the lessons they drew were Protestant ones. From the schools would emerge obedient and efficient workers and thrifty, skillful managers and entrepreneurs. Another result of education, reformers thought, would be a falling away of error and superstition. In short, the public school was the reformers' answer to class antagonisms and ethnic and religious diversity.

To achieve their ends, asylum and school builders used a different mix of means from those adopted by abolitionists and temperance advocates. Their style was less flamboyant and more political and professional. Some, like Mann, had been involved in partisan politics (he was a Whig). All of them worked through legislatures for appropriations and pressed for creation of state and local agencies to oversee education and social services. At the same time, they developed their own professional networks, journals, and associations—all designed to sustain the cause and to set standards. Among the promoters of prisons, asylums, and schools, the line from reform commitment to career to profession was especially direct.

Institutional reformers' millennial hopes inevitably faded when confronted with overcrowding and with recalcitrant clients. High expectations for perfectability gave way, after the Civil War, to darker views that saw human potential limited by heredity and biology. Prisons and asylums became custodial institutions rather than instruments of salvation (the same may have happened with schools). At that point institutional reformers were left with their professionalism and with their institutions, which survived after the millennialism of their origins had faded. For better and for worse, they inadvertently pointed the way toward professional and bureaucratic responses to social problems, and therefore—in a peculiarly roundabout fashion—toward twentieth-century liberalism.

COMMUNITARIANISM

If prisons and asylums were, in the eyes of their founders, perverse sorts of utopia, there were other antebellum Americans who were building real utopias, or so they thought. In the great wave of pre–Civil War reform, there was a strong current of communitarianism.

Utopian communities in America existed long before the antebellum period, even before the Revolution. These early ones often consisted of small groups of people, usually foreign-born, living communally and in obedience to a particular set of unorthodox religious beliefs.

From the 1820's through the 1840's, however, there was an explosion of utopia-building, with perhaps over a hundred communities appearing. Some were simply extensions of older religious groups, like the Shakers. Others were modeled on secular ideologies; notably influential were the ideas of Robert Owen, the British philanthropist, who established an experiment of his own, New Harmony, in the mid-1820's, and Charles Fourier, a French visionary. Fourier's vogue came in the 1840's and resulted in the creation of about twenty-eight model communities, almost all of them small and short-lived. Owen and Fourier hoped to create a harmonious world of agriculture and industry, based on human reason. Other communities were a mixture of secular and religious impulses. The most famous of these was John Humphrey Noyes's Oneida, established in 1848. It was notable for its sexual practices and for blending evangelical Protestant impulses with its founder's brand of science and socialism. Still other communities, like the transcendentalist one at Brook Farm in Massachusetts (1841–1847) or Modern Times (1851–1866), a free-love experiment on Long Island, defy any kind of categorization.

The simple explanation for antebellum communitarianism is that it took root in America because land was cheap, restrictions were few, and the United States had long been a theater for experimenters. European ideas like those of Owen and Fourier could find an inexpensive and fair trial, as they could not in Britain or France.

Communitarianism also drew upon the more general impulses that brought thousands of Americans into antebellum reform. It shared with asylum-building an environmentalist strand in reform thought: the creation of a totally separate environment, one that would either mold human character to the proper shape or permit it to take its proper shape.

On other matters, communitarians were at the far end of the spectrum of antebellum reform. Where some of their peers focused on one particular issue (such as prisons or drunkenness), they sought a whole new order. In that respect they ought to be counted as radicals (although what some of them actually proposed was not especially revolutionary).

Utopians also were at an extreme in terms of politics. Although institution builders, temperance activists, and some abolitionists took the plunge into political campaigning, there was considerable ambivalence about that among reformers. Some of their peers—notably and vocally, the Garrisonian abolitionists—argued that politics contaminated reformers and that the only proper position was a higher one. The reformers' role, they believed, was to stand above the compromises of politics and to beckon the public to rise above sin, self-interest, and partisanship. Communitarians took that view to its logical limit. They withdrew entirely from the political process in order to reform by example. Their faith was that the rest of the world would rush to imitate their little utopias. They were wrong about their utopias and about the rest of the world (although possibly not about antebellum politics); their reasoning, however, was not unusual among antebellum reformers, even if it was not predominant.

The greatest bond that communitarians shared with fellow reformers was millennial optimism. Even in its most secular form, their utopianism was the most literal possible expression of the idea that a perfect order could be built on earth, that human beings could construct an ideal world of peace and plenty. In that, communitarianism was very much at one with antebellum reform.

INTERPRETATIONS OF ANTEBELLUM REFORM

Many scholars have tried to explain antebellum reform in terms of the motivation of reformers. Some present highly favorable pictures of moralistic men and women, driven by evangelical Protestantism and the ideology of the American Revolution. Such interpretations are useful in pointing out the sources of reform rhetoric, but they beg important questions. In particular, they cannot tell why it took so long for the ideology of the Revolution to set off reform impulses. Antebellum reformers, after all, flourished two generations after the Revolution yet dealt with evils such as slavery and alcoholism that long predated it. Moreover, too many Americans heard the call of evangelical Protestantism, but not of social action, for it to have been the sole explanation for antebellum reform.

There is another line of analysis, much less positive about antebellum reformers but similarly focused on their motivation. It imputes unconscious, and usually unpleasant, intent to them. According to some scholars, reformers were members of displaced elites seeking to reassert social authority by means of moralistic crusades. In a sophisticated variation of that view, reforms were supposedly directed toward "social control." That is, their aim was to impose middle-class and Protestant values on unruly and non-Protestant Americans.

Such interpretations have the value of giving serious consideration to the social composition of reform and to its effects. They, however, also largely miss the mark. Some reformers (such as early temperance advocates) did come close to matching the image of displaced elites—Federalist Congregationalists in a Jeffersonian and evangelical republic. But their day was not long, and even among their numbers were men on their way up, not down. Later in the antebellum period, roughly after 1830, many reformers seem to have been rising in social and economic influence, rather than declining.

Of course, successful as well as failing people can seek social control, and that sort of interpretation has some power, even if antebellum reformers do not match the image of displaced elites. To be sure, an emphasis on social control makes it hard to appreciate the extent to which reformers thought they were actually liberating, rather than confining, the human spirit. Moreover, this interpretation denies the degree to which many antebellum reformers were as concerned about self-control as social control. Various causes, ranging from the early temperance movement to dietary reform, were as much dedicated to helping middle-class Americans cling to their own values as to forcing those values on others.

Social-control explanations do have the twin virtues of expressing a truism and pointing toward a more fruitful analysis of antebellum reform. The truism is that there is always an element of manipulation and social control in reform. Antebellum reformers, in common with twentieth-century reformers and radicals, had no sense that they ought to encourage sin and error. They wanted to see their ideas prevail because they believed them to be correct. Reform to one person is inevitably repression (or "social control") to another. On another level, social-control interpretations of reform are less obviously and more profoundly correct. They shift attention away from the motivation of individual reformers and toward the function of reform itself.

THE CONSEQUENCES OF REFORM

Some of the effects of reform were personal. Involvement in various movements provided many men and women with personal meaning, a network of friends, and a source of moral au-

thority. In its depiction of evils and villains, reform also gave a standard against which to define and measure proper behavior. These were valuable matters in a mobile, increasingly diverse society in which older moral authorities, such as clergy and political leaders, spoke with less uniformity and credibility.

Reform affected—or sought to affect—behavior in a variety of ways. It promoted the values of self-control, hard work, thrift, and temperance. To some extent these were aimed at the lower classes, whose skill and obedience as employees they would have improved. But the morality behind antebellum reform was no sinister plot by the bourgeoisie. For one thing, it offered progress and respectability to working-class people who accepted it. (It even held out economic advantage in instances where managers favored temperance men and other reform-minded employees.) For another thing, the same values were useful to the middle classes who promoted them. Men and women with these values could defer gratification, control their most unruly impulses, and generally save all their capital, whether moral, physical, or financial. Antebellum reform, then, was part of the creation of a mind-set adapted to an urban, industrial world of opportunity and uncertainty.

But it was more, for it had political consequences. In some instances these were obvious, as when voters divided over alcohol-related issues or states passed Maine laws and built asylums on the reformist model. In other cases the political results are hard to assess with precision. Abolitionists, for instance, directly swayed relatively few votes and had little influence in government. Yet they helped define the terms within which political debate occurred in the 1840's and 1850's. Their imagery, particularly of a barbarous South and of a slaveholder conspiracy against American liberties, filtered into the rhetoric of the Republican party, even though abolitionists themselves remained largely outside its inner circles. In such situations, the effects of antebellum reform were in subtle alterations of the public mind and in reinforcement of particular values and images—not in winning elections or passing laws.

Antebellum reform also bore a complicated and ambiguous relationship to the development of partisan politics. On the one hand, some reformers explicitly rejected the style of politics that had emerged after 1800, with its demagoguery and its commitment (as they saw it) to party rather than principle. On the other hand, reformers were not entirely apolitical, nor were they so different from the partisans they disdained. Reformers adapted—perhaps pioneered—the techniques of mass persuasion used by antebellum political parties, including such outdoor festivities as parades, picnics, and processions. Moreover, not all reformers were content to rely on moral suasion and stay out of politics. The Maine Law and numerous jails and asylums stood as their monuments.

Rather than detach antebellum reform from politics, it might well make sense to see it as very much a part of an extensive and highly political debate over the direction of the United States in a time of considerable economic and territorial expansion. In such a view, antebellum reform was one of four very broadly defined, roughly contemporary reform movements. Each had an emotionally charged vision of what the United States ought to be; each attempted to control the symbols of political discourse, using both partisan activity and propaganda to carry its point. The second of these movements at times merged with antebellum reform but consisted primarily of political efforts (mostly in the Federalist, Whig, and Republican parties) to use government as an instrument of morality. The third was embodied in the Democratic party of Andrew Jackson, with its attack on special privileges (and on some of the moral restraints advocated by antebellum reformers). The fourth movement comprised Southern efforts to "reform" slavery and refashion the role of the South in the Union. Crude as such a classification is (and as much violence as it does to conventional notions of reform), it points to something important. Antebellum reformers had no monopoly when it came to visions of the good society and to ideas about the role that government ought to play in it.

The long-term consequences of antebellum reform are even harder to judge than its immediate political impact. It clearly did not set American history upon a different course. More likely, it served as a stabilizing mechanism, helping adjust the social and political system to new conditions, particularly to the need for a well-disciplined labor force and to the rise of middle classes infused with an evangelical Protestant ethos.

In that respect antebellum reform was a creature of its time and place. Among its cultural sources were evangelical Protestant millennialism and perfectionism, the evolving legacy of American political thought, and contemporary notions of science and society. Its social origins were in economic development and changes in class relationships after 1815. Those forces provided it with a vocabulary, with personnel, with techniques of persuasion, and with some of the problems that reformers tried to resolve. Reform was both an effect of the transformation of antebellum America and an effort to give it moral management.

However much antebellum reform may have been rooted in the conditions of its day, it also had significance beyond its time. It left few, if any, enduring reform organizations, but it did set in motion causes—such as the women's rights movement, labor reform, and temperance—that would have their greatest impact after the Civil War. Moreover, it established reform as a permanent, legitimate part of the political process. It also helped set the course for later nineteenth- and twentieth-century reform by beginning the shift from religious to secular modes of social thought and by beginning the movement from moral suasion to conscious use of law and institutions as instruments of change. What antebellum reform did not transmit was its millennial optimism that the world could be made perfect. That vision would recur only in brief radical moments, a casualty of grim realities and diminished faith.

BIBLIOGRAPHY

Lois W. Banner, "Religious Benevolence as Social Control: A Critique of an Interpretation," in *Journal of American History*, 60 (1973), is a good, critical introduction to the literature on reform and social control. Paul S. Boyer, *The Urban Masses and Moral Order in America, 1820–1920* (Cambridge, Mass., 1978), is an important work dealing with strands of urban reform often neglected in general accounts of antebellum reform. Whitney R. Cross, *The Burned-over District: The Social and Intellectual History of Enthusiastic Religion in Western New York, 1800–1850* (Ithaca, N.Y., 1950), is a work of enduring importance and one of the first to attempt a social analysis of the relationship between evangelical Protestantism and reform. Gerald N. Grob, *Mental Institutions in America: Social Pol-*

icy to 1875 (New York, 1973), presents a balanced account but is less suggestive than David Rothman's treatment of asylum-building. Joseph R. Gusfield, *Symbolic Crusade: Status Politics and the American Temperance Movement* (Urbana, Ill., 1963), is an influential statement—rejected by many more recent scholars—of the relationship between temperance and social change.

John L. Hammond, *The Politics of Benevolence: Revival Religion and American Voting Behavior* (Norwood, N.J., 1979), is valuable as a guide to the influence of religion and reform on political behavior. Rosabeth Moss Kanter, *Commitment and Community: Communes and Utopias in Sociological Perspective* (Cambridge, Mass., 1972), is valuable as an interpretive guide to communitarian groups. Michael B. Katz, *The Irony of Early American School Reform: Educational Innovation in Mid-Nineteenth Century Massachusetts* (Cambridge, Mass., 1968), stresses the manipulative aspects of school reform and has shaped much subsequent research. Aileen S. Kraditor, "American Radical Historians on Their Heritage," in *Past and Present*, 56 (1972), a fine interpretive essay, was later repudiated by its author. David J. Rothman, *The Discovery of the Asylum: Social Order and Disorder in the New Republic* (Boston, 1971), is an influential interpretation of asylum-building that should, however, be supplemented by the work of Gerald Grob.

Richard H. Sewell, *Ballots for Freedom: Antislavery Politics in the United States, 1837–1860* (New York, 1976), is the best single work on the role of antislavery in antebellum politics and the most thorough account of the political ramifications of antislavery. James B. Stewart, *Holy Warriors: The Abolitionists and American Slavery* (New York, 1976), is a superior synthesis. John L. Thomas, "Romantic Reform in America, 1815–1865," in *American Quarterly*, 17 (1965), gives a brief, very wise interpretation of antebellum reform. Alice Felt Tyler, *Freedom's Ferment: Phases of American Social History to 1860* (Minneapolis, Minn., 1944), is dated and discursive but a mine of information. Ian R. Tyrrell, *Sobering Up: From Temperance to Prohibition in Antebellum America, 1800–1860* (Westport, Conn., 1979), is among the best of recent works on alcohol and temperance; its footnotes provide a useful guide to primary sources and to older literature on the subject. Ronald G. Walters, *American Reformers: 1815–1860* (New York, 1978), a more recent and analytical synthesis than Tyler's, is also less inclusive.

[See also AMERICAN REVOLUTION; FEMINISM; JACKSONIAN DEMOCRACY; LABOR MOVEMENT; LIBERALISM; PACIFISM AND PEACE MOVEMENTS; POLITICAL CRITICISM; PROHIBITION AND TEMPERANCE; RACE AND RACISM; RADICALISM; SLAVERY, SECTIONALISM, AND SECESSION; UTOPIANISM; VOLUNTARY ASSOCIATIONS; *and* WOMEN'S RIGHTS.]

ARMED FORCES

Russell F. Weigley

THE armed forces of the United States stem in part from the militia of the British colonies in North America. Needing military force to defend themselves against Indians, French, and Spanish, but unable at first to afford professional armies, all of the colonies except Quaker Pennsylvania drew on the English tradition requiring all able-bodied military-age freemen to bear arms and established compulsory-service military forces. Citizens trained in the use of arms several days a year, the length and seriousness of the training depending on the degree of immediate danger. The colonial executives usually appointed the principal officers, although occasionally the assemblies did so, while company officers were elected by the men. A need for the entire military manpower of a community was rare; volunteers were generally called out of the militia companies when a force had to be mobilized, or some men might be drafted for a short period of active duty. Despite deficiencies in training, the citizen militia formed the foundation of the armed strength with which the colonies waged several wars, notably King Philip's War in New England (1675–1676).

Because it was not politically feasible to compel most men to abandon their livelihoods for military duty for more than short periods, the citizen militia soon proved an inappropriate instrument for extended and especially aggressive campaigns. Although the northern colonies drew from their militia organizations to attack Quebec unsuccessfully in 1690 and for the successful Louisbourg expedition of 1745, as early as 1715, during the Yamasee War, South Carolina recruited an embryonic professional army to take the offensive against hostile Indians as far away as Florida. Except for the capture of Louisbourg, colonial armed forces, either militiamen or longer-term enlistees, scored no major gains in King William's War (1689–1697), Queen Anne's War (1702–1713), or King George's War (1744–1748). Therefore, when just after the middle of the eighteenth century both British and colonial leaders resolved on a showdown in the Anglo-French struggle for dominance in North America, London decided that British regular troops would have to be dispatched. There had long been small detachments ("independent companies") of British regulars stationed in New York and from time to time elsewhere. The first substantial introduction of regulars occurred after the failure of a Virginia expedition to drive the French from Fort Duquesne in 1754; thereupon two British regiments arrived to try again the next year to seize that strategic outpost. With them came Major General Edward Braddock to command all British military forces in North America, regular and provincial.

The consequences of this introduction of professional soldiers were large and varied. First, Braddock's defeat on 9 July 1755 did not prevent colonial observers—including George Washington, who accompanied Braddock as an aide—from returning highly impressed by the efficiency with which professional soldiers had marched with artillery and heavy baggage across the Appalachians, carving out a road as they went. The previous year Virginia troops had had a hard time simply getting across the mountains and had thought carrying smaller artillery pieces than Braddock's impossible. Had it not been for a few misjudgments by subordinates, Braddock might well have won his battle and captured the French fort. When subsequent British regular expeditions not only approached success but grasped it—among them John Forbes's expedition that captured Fort Duquesne in 1758 and the climactic venture under James Wolfe that took Quebec in 1759—American opinion tended to accept the superiority of well-trained full-time soldiers for almost every military purpose. By the late years of the French and Indian War (1755–1763), those colonies having frontiers to defend recruited provincial forces that were apart from the militia and at least semiprofessional in nature. Even Quaker Pennsylvania raised a provincial army.

On the other hand, even while many Americans came to admire professional armed forces or to accept them as a necessity, the presence of British soldiers generated friction and distrust. The tough rank and file, recruited mostly from the lowest social classes, sometimes became pitted against colonials in tavern brawls and street riots, most sensationally in the Boston Massacre of 1770. The joint service of British and colonial troops generated jealousies because provincial field officers—majors and above—ranked only as "eldest captains" of regulars, although they were men of local distinction; the highest-ranking colonial officers, even generals, would thus be subordinated to the most junior British major. Also, the British subjected provincials serving with regulars to the harsh terms of British military justice, removing the colonials from the protection of the more lenient mutiny acts of their own assemblies. Colonial soldiers came to regard the British military as violating their "rights" according to their terms of enlistment for military service. When after 1763 the presence of the British army became permanent, colonists believed their rights were threatened in a larger sense, because the regulars remained garrisoned among them without the consent of their assemblies, in violation of the English Bill of Rights as the colonists interpreted it.

The effect was to reinforce prejudices against professional armies, toward which many Americans were already predisposed. As friction with Great Britain pushed Americans toward revolution, the colonists tended to give their objections to distasteful British practices an ideological coherence drawn from the thought of the British radical Whigs, the "eighteenth-century Commonwealthmen." This body of thought held that an autocratic conspiracy in Britain had betrayed the Glorious Revolution of 1688, with the standing army a major instrument of the betrayal. Reading such explicitly anti–standing-army

tracts of the Whig radicals as John Trenchard and Thomas Gordon's *Cato's Letters* of 1720–1723, Americans could be quick to conclude that the true purpose of the dispatch of British regulars to America was to extend the suppression of liberty from Britain to the colonies.

By the time of the Boston Massacre, a disproportionate share of the regulars in America were concentrated in the restless province of Massachusetts Bay. After the Intolerable Acts of 1774 drove that province to establish an extralegal and virtually independent government, Massachusetts felt obliged also to reinvigorate its provincial military force as a safeguard against the possibility that the British authorities might translate the potential of the standing army for forcible repression into actual destruction of provincial self-government. The famous minutemen were separated from the main body of the Massachusetts militia as troops who might spring to action immediately. Stores of munitions were accumulated. London thereupon pressed General Thomas Gage, royal governor of Massachusetts as well as commander in chief in North America, to seize the provincial stock of arms at Concord. In compliance Gage sent a column of redcoats marching from Boston during the night of 18–19 April 1775, and in the morning the Lexington militia company exchanged with the regulars the shots heard round the world.

It was with ambivalent attitudes toward armed forces that the British colonies thus began the American Revolution. Anti–standing-army rhetoric had played a large part in the coming of the Revolution, but it had not deterred the colonists from creating embryonic professional armies in the various provinces when the part-time soldiery of the militia proved inadequate to their military needs. Facing a war against British regulars, the colonists felt greater pressure than ever before to reject the limitations of a citizen militia in favor of a disciplined army of their own. Appointed by the Continental Congress in the wake of Lexington and Concord to command the military resistance to British repression, George Washington set about to create an American approximation of the British regular army.

The Congress chose Washington as its military commander on 15 June 1775, having the previous day begun the official creation of a Continental army by voting to raise ten companies of riflemen from Pennsylvania, Maryland, and Virginia to reinforce the New England troops already assembled around Boston to confine the British army there following the fighting on 19 April. Washington formally took command of the revolutionary army at Cambridge, Massachusetts, on 3 July. Except for the riflemen, his troops generally had enlisted for active duty only until the end of 1775, partly because many expected the British government to yield to a show of force by that time and partly because colonial tradition discouraged long enlistments. When the British failed to back down, Congress voted to raise a new army for 1776 that would be "Continental in every respect," but enlistments were again to expire at the end of the year, and dependence on the individual provinces for recruiting and supplies was too great to permit much headway in substituting Continental for provincial regimental names and numbers. When the close of 1776 approached with victory not yet in sight—defeat of the Revolution seemed much more likely in the weeks just before Washington's crossing of the Delaware on Christmas night of 1776—Congress voted to enlist the next new army for three years or the duration of the war. The shorter enlistment term had not brought adequate numbers of recruits anyway, and the longer term scarcely stimulated enlistment. The Continental army, achieving a maximum strength of 16,782 in the summer of 1778, was usually hard put to match British numbers, after the enemy went over to the offensive by landing an army of 32,000 at New York City in 1776. In crisis after crisis, the Continental army had to be reinforced by militia requisitioned from the states.

Militia reinforcements were usually so little trained, and their unsuitability for prolonged campaigns remained so conspicuous, that Washington's admiration for the discipline of British regulars was redoubled. "The Jealousies of a standing Army," he wrote, "and the Evils to be apprehended from one, are remote, and in my judgment, situated and circumstanced as we are, not at all to be dreaded; but the consequence of wanting one, according to my Ideas, . . . is certain, and Inevitable Ruin." Unfortunately for his aspirations, Washington's consequent efforts to mold the Continental army into a replica of the British army met only limited success. The initial short enlistment terms militated against it, and

Washington never had enough experienced officers and sergeants for the task. Baron Friedrich Wilhelm von Steuben's well-known training of the army during the Valley Forge winter of 1777–1778, along with the tactical manual that Steuben prepared, greatly assisted Washington's efforts; but the shortage of Americans who had been educated as soldiers could not be quickly overcome. Throughout the revolutionary war, most American formations were inferior in battlefield skill to their British counterparts, and Washington had to rely on a cautious strategy and occasional daring stratagems to compensate for battlefield defeats.

The Continental and Confederation congresses meanwhile were far from sharing Washington's belief that the evils to be apprehended from a standing army were remote. Although Washington not only observed but exceeded all the forms of subordination with which Congress sought to assure civilian control, the legislators, mindful of both English history and the role played by the British army in precipitating the Revolution, could not shake off fear of a professional military. Various congressional committees and the Board of War, whose composition varied from congressmen to paid administrators under congressional supervision, oversaw the military and evolved into an executive department responsible to Congress: the War Office, created 7 February 1781. Antimilitary suspicions helped delay until the following October the naming of the first head of the department, Major General Benjamin Lincoln, who received the title secretary at war, borrowed from British usage.

Lincoln's appointment coincided with Washington's victory at Yorktown. While this victory proved in time to assure American independence, peace negotiations dragged on into 1783, and parts of the army used the interval to refuel antimilitary suspicions. In March 1783 the Newburgh Conspiracy came to light. A circle of Continental officers, restive because of idleness and because their pay was long in arrears, sought assurance from the financially weak Confederation in the form of some sort of tangible settlement of money owed them, including future pensions. Encouraged by certain congressmen who hoped to exploit the threat of a military coup to further their own purposes, particularly to gain a source of revenue for the Confederation, Major John

Armstrong, Jr., as anonymous spokesman for the malcontents, drew up the Newburgh Addresses. These suggested that if grievances continued unmet the army might take matters into its own hands; if Congress should show "the slightest mark of indignity . . . the army has its alternative." Washington squelched such talk with an eloquent appeal to the patriotism of an assemblage of the officers, coupled with a promise to use his influence for a satisfactory financial arrangement. Three months later, however, Congress was briefly besieged in Independence Hall, Philadelphia, by mutinous Pennsylvania enlisted men also seeking pay. When peace came, settlement of military grievances remained incomplete, but the officers and soldiers proved more eager to go home than to continue badgering the legislature. With a sigh of relief, on 2 June 1784, Congress disbanded all of the Continental army except for eighty men and three officers needed to guard military stores at West Point and Fort Pitt.

The newly independent United States had received in the Treaty of 1783 the vast area from the Appalachians to the Mississippi, and so the Confederation had inherited the problems of Indian defense that had helped bring on the presence of British regulars and driven some of the colonies to create their own armies. Congress had solicited Washington's and other officers' suggestions for a permanent military organization. In his "Sentiments on a Peace Establishment," the former commander in chief recommended a small standing army of 2,630 officers and men, supplemented by a compulsory-service militia along with a voluntary—or, if necessary, a drafted—militia of young men who would undergo enough training to make them a genuinely effective reserve. Washington also recommended a navy. All that Congress could agree upon was a call of 3 June 1784 for certain states to contribute to a regiment of 700 men, in eight infantry and two cavalry companies. Although chronically understrength, the First American Regiment was maintained with slight changes through the Confederation period. In 1789 the new government of the Constitution inherited it, along with the War Office, to possess from the beginning at least a modicum of military strength. Henry Knox, secretary at war since 1785, provided further continuity by becoming

secretary of war to President George Washington.

Nevertheless, the military weakness of the Confederation, as attested by its inability to overawe the Indians and by its having to rely on Massachusetts militia to protect the Confederation arsenal at Springfield during Shays's Rebellion in 1786, had been among the most important concerns generating the Constitution. The writers of the Constitution were sufficiently concerned that they established remarkably broad military powers. Congress received the authority "to raise and support armies" and "to provide and maintain a navy," with the sole proviso that no army appropriation should run longer than two years. Military tyranny was guarded against by dividing control of the armed forces between Congress, which financed and made rules for them, and the president, who was named commander in chief. Furthermore, the state militias were retained as a military counterweight to the federal army, implicitly in the provisions of the Constitution stipulating federal regulation of the militia and allowing its call into federal service under certain conditions, and explicitly in the Second Amendment guarantee that "a well regulated Militia, being necessary to the security of a free State, the right of the people to keep and bear Arms, shall not be infringed."

Notwithstanding the guarantee of a citizen militia, the federal power to raise and support armies seemed so little limited that in the ratification conventions some of the opponents of the Constitution, notably Patrick Henry of Virginia, foresaw despotism emerging from the uniting of the powers of the purse and the sword. The broad grant of power did not, nevertheless, prevent an inglorious military beginning for the new government. In 1790 the First American Regiment with militia reinforcements marched into the Ohio country to pacify the Indians of the Old Northwest and was soundly beaten. The next year the army tried again, now with two federal regiments, and again met defeat. Meanwhile President Washington and Secretary of War Knox revived the idea of effective regulation of the militia by the central government, including the raising of a well-trained ready reserve among the youngest members, but the Congress of the Constitution proved no more helpful than the Congress of the Confederation. The executive had to settle for the Militia Act of 1792, which provided for the enrollment of all able-bodied white male citizens between eighteen and forty-five but did little to assure that such enrollment would lead to a usable military force.

The consistent reluctance of Congress to try to create a militarily effective militia suggests that anti–standing-army ideology, however closely tied to the causes of the Revolution, remained tempered by a strong dose of American pragmatism. The citizen militia might be ideologically appealing, but Congress could also doubt whether any plan would squeeze a truly ready reserve out of it. Following the second defeat of the federal army by the Indians of the Old Northwest, Congress added three regiments to the army, and the president appointed the revolutionary war hero Anthony Wayne as major general commanding it. Belying his sobriquet "Mad Anthony," Wayne patiently drilled "the Legion of the United States," as his force became designated, into the first true replica of a European professional army. His leadership, training, and discipline carried the Legion to a decisive victory over the Indians at the battle of Fallen Timbers on 20 August 1794.

Wayne died soon afterward, but many influential Federalists believed that in a world ablaze with the wars of the French Revolution, American security demanded a still larger regular army. In 1798, under the spur of the Quasi-War with France, Congress voted a series of military increments (not all regular soldiers in the strict legal sense) authorizing federal military forces of about 50,000. Having voted in 1794 to create a navy, ostensibly to protect commerce against the pirates of Algiers, the legislature also voted in 1798 a naval expansion, with a nucleus of six frigates. The Navy Department was created to administer the navy. The Marine Corps was also authorized. There had been a Continental navy and Continental marines during the Revolution, but both had been disbanded; with the 1798 legislation, the armed forces of the United States took on the basic form they were to retain until 1947.

The Jeffersonian Republican party perceived in these Federalist military activities, in tandem with the Alien and Sedition Acts, an intent to prepare instruments for the forcible repression of domestic dissent. This view may have had some warrant. The navy did some fighting in the Caribbean; but with respect to the need for an enlarged army for the war with France, President John Adams conceded that "there is no more prospect of seeing a French army here than in Heaven." Army commissions were dispensed on the basis of Federalist partisanship; and friends, as well as enemies, of the inspector general and chief sponsor of the army increments, Alexander Hamilton, suspected that he had ulterior purposes in mind. On the other hand, military preparedness against external threats was consistent with the Federalist view of the world. Whatever the motives, the new army was never recruited to anywhere near its authorized strength, and its unpopularity contributed to the Jeffersonian "Revolution of 1800."

Although President Jefferson promptly reduced even the prewar army, from Jefferson's second term to the War of 1812 there nevertheless occurred a gradual rebuilding of the regular army. During the War of 1812 the Republicans authorized a regular army of 62,274, a figure not attained but the largest regular authorization until 1898. Confronted with the responsibility for national defense during the Napoleonic Wars, the Jeffersonians felt a pragmatic obligation to nourish military professionalism, despite their ideological distaste for a standing army. Pointing in the same direction, although as usual the motives involved were mixed, was Jefferson's sponsorship of the United States Military Academy at West Point, founded in 1802.

West Point soon became the nursery of a new order of military professionalism, which strengthened the claims of the standing forces to be the proper reliance for national defense and further weakened the anti–standing-army tradition. Hitherto, in Europe as well as in America, professional military men had been professional mainly in the sense that they were careerists, only minimally in the sense that they enjoyed special educational qualifications. The French revolutionary and Napoleonic wars, however, by introducing the mass armies of the "nation in arms" and thus immensely complicating the problems of maneuvering and administering armies, greatly stimulated a nascent tendency to establish schools for the study of military officership. In Prussia, after it had been humiliatingly defeated by Napoleon in 1806, reformers began to create a military university, with a hierarchy of schools from undergraduate cadet schools to a *Kriegsakademie,* a professional school for the study of war by potential senior commanders. With such an educational system, officership moved toward becoming a profession in the larger sense in which medicine and the law were also becoming professions. With West Point and, from 1845, the Naval Academy, the United States had only the undergraduate foundation for an educated military profession, but the foundation was well laid and the higher schools could come later.

In Europe, the growth of military professionalism was impeded by the tradition linking officership to the aristocracy. Unhampered by anything more than a lingering shadow of that tradition, West Point could early encourage professional study as a major ingredient in the careers of American officers. Under Sylvanus Thayer, superintendent from 1817 to 1833, and Dennis Hart Mahan, professor of engineering and military science from 1832 to 1871, West Point became a first-rate engineering school and introduced the cadets to the military thought developed in European schools. Mahan's favorite student, Henry Wager Halleck, published in 1846 the first major American work on military strategy and tactics, *Elements of Military Art and Science . . . ,* based on the work of the Swiss-French strategic critic Antoine-Henri Jomini but including consideration of specifically American problems. By the Civil War, this book, Mahan's own published works, and reports by various American observers of European armies made up a respectable American professional literature, reflecting standards of military study and leadership remarkable in a small army distant from Europe.

The consequent improvement in military skills was demonstrated dramatically in the Mexican War. In the preceding foreign war, the War of 1812, only a few young West Point graduates were available, and American military leadership was with few exceptions abysmally amateurish. In contrast, the Mexican War, small enough in scale to be fought largely by the regular army, witnessed a confident efficiency in the conduct of military operations thousands of miles from the centers of American population. For the war, federal forces expanded from a regular army of 8,500 to a maximum strength of about 50,000,

an expansion not too large for the regulars to maintain substantial control of it. Major General Winfield Scott, commander of the expedition from Veracruz to Mexico City, was not a West Point graduate but an officer self-taught to professional standards; he explained the essential difference between the army of 1812 and the army in Mexico when he said, "But for our graduated cadets the war between the United States and Mexico might, and probably would, have lasted some four or five years, with, in its first half, more defeats than victories falling to our share."

Scott might also have paid tribute to the improvements in administration and logistics brought about by the creation of efficient War Department staff bureaus, particularly by John C. Calhoun as secretary of war from 1817 to 1825. By Calhoun's term, the Quartermaster's Department and other supply bureaus already had to support military expeditions deep into the Louisiana Purchase, as far as the Yellowstone River. The experience of sustaining exploration and Indian pacification at such distances, and of maintaining a chain of forts along the eastern boundary of the supposedly permanent Indian Country established in the 1830's west of Arkansas and Missouri, prepared the War Department to cope with the distances involved in the Mexican War.

The development of efficient administration and logistics combined with the professional skills of the West Point–educated officer corps also made possible the considerable achievements of both Union and Confederate armies in the Civil War, not only in managing forces over great distances once again but in supporting numbers of troops swollen beyond all previous American experience. The regular army of 1860 still counted only about 16,000 officers and men; by the spring of 1865 the Union army had grown to slightly over a million, while some 2.2 million men served in that army at one time or another during the war. Similarly trained officers and a War Department modeled on that of the United States permitted the Confederacy to raise and maintain an army totaling about 750,000 and reaching a peak strength of almost 500,000 at the beginning of 1864.

The militia that was inherited from the colonial period played little direct part in the Civil War. The rise of professionalism in the regular officer corps had increased the contrast between the militia and the standing army, emphasizing still further the relative efficiency of the latter. During the first half of the nineteenth century, hardly any state took the compulsory-service militia seriously enough to enforce sufficient training requirements to prevent the militia from becoming a national joke. Nevertheless, volunteer companies of citizens interested enough to equip themselves and train under elected officers persisted, more or less supervised by the states and considered the "organized militia" in contrast to the amorphous "unorganized militia." Indeed, the volunteer companies not only persisted but enjoyed something of a boom in the decade and a half immediately preceding the Civil War. In the South, these companies offered protection against slave uprisings, but the volunteers thrived at least as much in the towns and cities of the North. The fascination with military panoply that the volunteer companies expressed may well have helped transform the sectional crisis into war. When the war came, the states adopted the volunteer companies to meet their quotas of troops for Union or Confederate service, and thus the volunteer companies provided the nuclei of the armies on both sides.

The Civil War proved no glorious adventure for the volunteers but a bloody deadlock, whereupon the supply of volunteers, in companies or as individuals, began to run dry. Both sides felt obliged to turn to conscription. States' rights doctrine notwithstanding, a desperate need for manpower pressed the Confederacy to precede the United States in ignoring the militia as the basis for compulsory military service and invoking the simple constitutional authority to raise and support armies for a direct draft of individuals. The Conscription Act of 16 April 1862 made every white male between eighteen and thirty-five liable to serve three years in the Confederate army, with relatively few occupational exemptions. In the North, the Enrollment Act of 3 March 1863 similarly imposed a federal military obligation on almost all male citizens between twenty and forty-five. The Confederate draft was applied more stringently than the Union one; the North used the draft mainly as a threat with which to restimulate enlistments. Either way, conscription assured the maintenance of the first American mass armies, which were supplied and maneuvered largely under the direction of the

professional officers of the prewar regular army.

Although the Civil War was an immense military event, it was only a fleeting interlude in the nineteenth-century history of the armed forces. In 1865 the wartime multitudes were promptly demobilized. The army reverted to a small constabulary force for the Indian frontier, its total strength hovering around 25,000 from 1869 to 1898. Its day-to-day work became again the routine of displaying just enough strength in its frontier outposts to awe the Indians into relative passivity despite the westward advance of white population that now obliterated the idea of a permanent Indian Country. Eruptions of active warfare such as the Little Big Horn campaign of 1876 are the stuff of American military legend, but they only occasionally broke the routine.

The most important developments for the future involved the continued cultivation of higher standards of professional education, built upon the undergraduate foundation of West Point. A handful of army officers not stultified by the boredom of frontier police work, led and encouraged by William Tecumseh Sherman, the intellectually alert commanding general from 1869 to 1883, established the first permanent postgraduate professional schools. Such institutions for the various branches of the service included the School of Application for Infantry and Cavalry at Fort Leavenworth, Kansas, which was to evolve into the modern Command and General Staff College. Professional development was fostered also by service-wide and individual-branch officers' associations and journals.

This professional study was directed mainly toward preparation for European-style war. The American army never thought as systematically as it might have about the peculiar problems of dealing with Indian irregulars—just as in the twentieth century the army was to continue displaying reluctance to meet the problems of unconventional war. Professional study also sometimes added to tensions in civil-military relations. The most influential military intellectual encouraged by General Sherman, Colonel and Brevet Major General Emory Upton, in various writings and particularly in his posthumously published *The Military Policy of the United States* (1904), urged complete rejection of the traditional citizen militia and the establishment of a system of conscription built on regular army cadres and modeled on the German example, along with a command system also based on the German model. When it became apparent that no such proposals could win political acceptance, Upton grew deeply critical of civilian control and of democracy itself. His strictures gained wide circulation and influence in the army officer corps. Among the reasons for Upton's influence and the interest in German methods was the reorientation of the American armed forces at the close of the nineteenth century toward the military requirements of world power.

While the nineteenth-century army, although studying European war, had to preoccupy itself day by day with its chores as a frontier constabulary, the nineteenth-century navy similarly encountered few occasions for combat duty. Yet the navy was brought closer than the army, at an earlier date, to issues of foreign policy. Created mainly in response to the threats to American commerce posed by the wars of the French Revolution, the navy continued for the next century to be chiefly a guardian of commerce, and its responsibilities were narrowly construed. In the War of 1812, the navy, along with privateers, sought to protect commerce indirectly through retaliatory raids against British shipping. The navy was too small—and completely lacking in line-of-battle ships—to lend more direct protection to commerce by controlling the seas, however spectacular the victories of several of its vessels in single-ship duels. After the War of 1812, the navy was dispersed in small squadrons around the world, wherever American merchants sought to do business, but local law and order were sufficiently precarious that a show of the Stars and Stripes unfurled above naval guns was helpful. Like the army, the navy rose briefly to impressive strength during the Civil War, when it blockaded the Confederate coast. After the war, it lapsed into doldrums even more fully than the army. For a time after the War of 1812, the naval squadron commanders had sometimes flown their pennants from the most powerful battleships of the day, but after the Civil War, when other navies were shifting to steam and iron, the American navy still cruised largely in wooden vessels under sail.

Yet by serving such overseas interests as the United States thought it had to protect, the navy in the late years of the century seems to have sensed earlier than the army the coming transformation of American foreign policy to take on the role of a world power. In the 1880's Commodore Stephen B. Luce, author of a standard textbook on seamanship, urged that American naval officers needed now to study not only seamanship but strategy; he wrested from a reluctant Navy Department the creation of the Naval War College in 1884. With this institution the navy leapfrogged beyond the current postgraduate schools of the army to establish a professional school at the highest level for the comprehensive study of strategy in relation to national policy; the model for it was the Prussian-German *Kriegsakademie,* the apex of the military university of the officer corps that was the fountainhead of military professionalism. Moreover, intending to base the study of naval strategy upon history, Luce installed as his instructor in history Captain Alfred Thayer Mahan, son of Dennis Hart Mahan. Out of A. T. Mahan's lectures came *The Influence of Sea Power upon History, 1660–1783* (1890), the first of a host of writings that established Mahan as the leader of naval strategic thought around the world.

Luce, Mahan, and other naval officers who were dedicated to making the navy an instrument of world power repudiated the major concept previously shaping the navy. Not only was the existing navy inadequate, but a commerce-raiding navy on the War of 1812 pattern was also to be rejected. Nothing less was required than a concentrated fleet of the most powerful battleships, capable at least of challenging any other fleet for control of any seas vital to the United States. The naval officers' call for a battle fleet coincided with public interest in expanding American power, to produce a battleship-building program during the 1890's, creating four modern steam and steel battleships by the beginning of the Spanish-American War. In that war the new navy vindicated its proponents by scoring spectacular victories (over hopelessly inferior squadrons) at Manila Bay and Santiago de Cuba. These triumphs in turn so enhanced the navy's prestige that during the first decade of the twentieth century a navy-minded president, Theodore Roosevelt, could persuade Congress to authorize enough battleships to make the navy the second most powerful in the world, in battleships if not in the variety of vessels necessary for a balanced fleet.

The army, being of less immediate importance than the navy in the aspirations to world power of a nation that was in strategic geography an island, shifted into a new role in less dramatic fashion. Before 1898 the professionalism of the army officer corps had made possible a respectable preparation of contingency plans for the likelihood of war with Spain and the dispatch of an expeditionary force to Cuba, despite inadequate institutional arrangements for such planning in the War Department. When war came, however, President William McKinley hurried the army into what it considered a premature invasion of Cuba, before the preparatory parts of its planning could be effected. In particular, the regular army was essentially kept separate from the volunteer army raised for the war, so the volunteers received little opportunity to share the regulars' expertise, a problem aggravated by the president's calling on 23 April 1898 for 125,000 volunteers when the army thought 60,000 would produce a much more orderly and, in the long run, more effective buildup. But the figure 125,000 coincided approximately with the strength of the National Guard, the current designation for the organized militia; and the old militia inheritance, embodied since 1879 in a lobbying organization called the National Guard Association, was still strong enough to compel practical politicians to retain the traditional citizen soldiery as the first wartime reserve. The organized militia formed the nucleus of the first volunteer contingents.

By the end of the war some 275,000 troops were under arms. The Cuban expeditionary force of about 18,000 proved to be mainly regulars after all, but the dispatch of so small a force with almost no well-trained reserves in the United States meant that the casualties even of the small battles of El Caney and San Juan Hill threatened to ruin the expedition. If the Spanish garrison of the island had been fully aware of the Americans' weakness and had not surrendered the city of Santiago immediately after those battles, the yellow fever epidemic that promptly swept the American force would have been a military, as well as a public health, disaster. As it was, the health collapse of the expeditionary force combined with scandalous reports of mishandling of army supplies to produce congressional and public demands for a thorough reform of the army to meet the new imperatives of world power. (The reports were exaggerated, yet the ability of the War Department to project a force overseas had somehow deteriorated since the Mexican War.)

To begin meeting this demand, President Mc-Kinley appointed as secretary of war a New York corporation lawyer without military experience, Elihu Root. Serving from 1899 to 1904, Root more than compensated for his lack of special expertise by bringing to the War Department that passion for the transfer of business-style managerial skills from the private corporate world to government that was a central element of the Progressive movement. He also brought a persuasive power that helped to carry legislation through a Congress eager to dissipate criticism of logistical ineptitude but still distrustful of a standing army grown so efficient that it might be dangerous to liberty. Through the General Staff Act of 1903, Root gave the army a collective brain, roughly patterned on the Prussian model, to plan for its future, at the same time creating a chief of staff as professional head of the army. In 1901 Root had established the Army War College as the capstone of the professional educational system; functioning at first as an embryo general staff, after 1903 it could turn to its permanent role. The Dick Act of 1903 retained the old universal male obligation to militia service but also provided a modicum of regular army supervision of the organized militia, the National Guard, in return for federal subsidies.

With their authority resisted by the traditional administrative bureaus, the chief of staff and the General Staff had not yet gained effective direction of the army when the United States entered World War I in 1917. Similarly, while the regular army grew to about 75,000 in the years following the Spanish-American War—largely to muster sufficient force to deal with the Philippine Insurrection and then to continue policing the Philippines and the other new possessions—the National Defense Act of 1916 authorizing further expansion and improvement of both the regular army and the National Guard had barely begun to be implemented when the United States again went to war. The General Staff had been able, nevertheless, to prepare the draft legislation on which the Selective Service Act of 1917 was based; and this forethought, combined with the inherent discipline of a modern industrial democracy, produced the first effective federal draft, which recruited most of the war army of 4 million men. The National Guard was also taken into federal service, but for the first time state regimental designations were altogether swept away and the state affiliations of the militia organizations were much diluted. For good or ill—the effects are debatable—this nationalization of the militia fulfilled an aim that had been pursued unsuccessfully since the Continental Congress had tried to make the army of 1776 "Continental in every respect."

Finding manpower was not a major problem in World War I, in contrast to all earlier wars; instead, there was great difficulty in converting industry to war production, to which little forethought had been given. American soldiers in their brief participation in active combat, mostly limited to the last five months of the war, had to fight almost completely with artillery, tanks, aircraft, and other heavy equipment supplied by Great Britain and France.

The battleship fleet similarly failed to meet the major needs of World War I, which at sea proved to be for antisubmarine craft. Nevertheless, the preparedness movement on the eve of American entry produced the Naval Act of 1916, intended to make the American navy second to none, and a reorganization of the Navy Department that limited the influence of the technical bureaus and accorded greater influence to the combat branches through the new post of chief of naval operations. Battleship construction resumed briefly at the close of the war but was interrupted by the Washington Naval Treaty of 1922. This agreement placed a moratorium on capital ship construction for all the major navies, but it recognized the parity of the American navy with the Royal Navy and superiority over other navies in its 5:5:3 ratio of American, British, and Japanese capital-ship strength.

The navy in fact emerged from World War I with a clearer sense of purpose than ever before: American-Japanese rivalry in the Pacific made its principal mission that of preparing for war with Japan. The war had destroyed the German navy, which for a time had taken second place away from the American. While there remained a strong sense of competition with the British navy, a British war was hardly likely. But American naval planners could well foresee an eventual struggle with Japan for dominance in the Pacific. Notwithstanding the inferior ratio of Japan in the Washington Naval Treaty, the problems of long-distance logistics gave it naval superiority in the western Pacific. For a possible contest against that superiority, the American navy developed the aircraft carrier as a new kind of capital ship offering striking power far beyond the range of guns. While capital-ship construction remained limited, the navy also developed for the first time a balanced fleet of all ship types, including tankers and other long-distance support vessels.

Trans-Pacific operations would surely require the acquisition of bases along the way, by capturing Japanese-held islands. This prospect gave the Marine Corps a raison d'être such as it had never possessed before. Hitherto serving mainly as shipboard police and legation guards, the Marine Corps had seemed dispensable and often came under legislative attack. Helping project military force into the new American empire after 1898 had given the marines a certain new importance, as they landed in such places as the Dominican Republic, Haiti, and Nicaragua. To capture Japanese islands, however, would require amphibious assault, a task peculiarly suited to the Marine Corps as the naval army. Amphibious assault, moreover, was among the most difficult operations of modern warfare, and the development of a doctrine for overcoming the difficulties occupied marine energies while providing a new sense of purpose.

The post-1919 army enjoyed less sense of direction. The National Defense Act of 1920 gave it an authorized strength of 280,000, but the strength for which Congress actually appropriated funds during the 1920's and 1930's usually hovered below 150,000. If there were to be a need for a large army, it would probably lie in another European war—a war with Japan would be primarily a naval conflict—but through most of the period national policy seemed to rule out a new intervention in Europe. General John J. Pershing, commander of the World War I American Expeditionary Forces and postwar army chief of staff, believed that the army should tailor itself not for European war but for small-scale interventions in the non-European world, on the model of his own punitive expedition into Mexico in 1916, as well as for continued constabulary service in the Philippines. Nevertheless, while unable to conduct strategic planning as clearly focused as that of the navy, the army responded to the possibility of European war by initiating industrial mobilization planning, in the hope that it would not again find itself without adequate armament. This work was fostered by a new assistant secretary of war charged with logistical responsibilities and by a new professional school for logistical officers founded in 1924, the Army Industrial College (after World War II the Industrial College of the Armed Forces). The industrial mobilization plans of the army eventually contributed much to the fact that America became "the arsenal of democracy" in World War II.

Within the army after World War I, the air arm strove for increasing autonomy and eventual recognition as a separate armed service. Brigadier General William ("Billy") Mitchell led this effort by zealously advocating autonomy within the army and by generating publicity outside. He resigned his commission in 1926 after his court-martial conviction for public criticism of the War and Navy departments, but the attendant controversy precipitated the transformation of the Air Service into a more nearly autonomous Army Air Corps. The leaders of this corps and its tactical school then embraced with growing fervor Mitchell's belief that aerial bombardment of an enemy's vital centers of economic and political power could end future wars quickly without repetition of the costly deadlock of the 1914–1918 western front. By the time the United States entered World War II, the Army Air Corps possessed in the B-17 an airplane designed to apply this theory. The Army Air Forces, as the Air Corps became designated in 1941, had by then achieved a high degree of autonomy and remained within the army largely because of its dependence on established army logistics.

The public and its political leaders so much accepted the idea of the decisiveness of air power that when the United States first moved toward aid to the World War II Allies, President Franklin D. Roosevelt's emphasis was overwhelmingly on the building of military airplanes. Before the Japanese attack on Pearl Harbor, the army and navy chieftains were able to persuade Roosevelt of the need for military power of all kinds, and as a result the first peacetime federal draft was enforced in 1940 along with a mobilization of the National Guard. These steps, together with the beginnings of the implementation of industrial mobilization planning, had by late 1941 laid the foundation for a dramatic change. The American armed forces, so long distrusted as potential threats to liberty and so long peripheral to American national policy, were about to become the strongest in the world, with a concomitant increase in their impact within the United States.

By the end of World War II, the American armed forces consisted of over 12 million men and women. The army had over 8 million, including Army Air Forces of more than 2 million; the navy had over 2,500 fighting ships, exclusive of mine craft, auxiliaries, and amphibious craft. More than 16 million served in the armed forces during the war. American weapons and equipment supplied not only the American forces but in large part the Allies. Of more lasting consequence, the army that in 1939 still had its only two ready divisions patrolling the Rio Grande was by 1945 patrolling from the Elbe River in Germany to the Han in Korea; through the postwar era, the American armed forces were to continue to bear the main responsibility for the defense of the entire non-Communist world, so that during World War II and its aftermath no Americans had to readjust to new tasks more drastically than the leaders of the armed forces.

On the battlefield in World War II, after Pearl Harbor and other setbacks of the first few months, the American forces enjoyed almost unbroken success. This was made possible by the mobilized wealth of the United States in manpower and resources, but it also owed much to the professional study that the armed forces had developed long before global military responsibilities could be foreseen. Beyond the battlefield, American command arrangements were less adequate for the formulation of global strategy and still less for the permanent maintenance of worldwide military power in harmony with national policy objectives.

To negotiate Allied strategy with the British, who had an interservice command system, the United States formed the Joint Chiefs of Staff (JCS) in 1942. This organization replaced the Joint Army-Navy Board, which had fostered loose interservice cooperation since 1903. The JCS came to include a military chief of staff to the president along with the professional heads of the army, navy, and Army Air Forces. Thanks largely to the dominating influence of General George C. Marshall, army chief of staff, and to interservice planning agencies, the improvised JCS made possible a reasonably coherent American strategic direction of the war. Under the JCS, commands that unified all the armed forces were established in regional theaters of war.

Little had been done in the past to coordinate

military strategy with diplomatic policy, and during the war the influence of the military tended to overshadow that of the State Department. In December 1944 a State-War-Navy Coordinating Committee (SWNCC) of assistant department secretaries was created to deal with pressing issues of occupying enemy territory, planning surrender terms, and anticipating immediate postwar problems.

The evident necessity for improved civil-military coordination after the war combined with pressure to divorce the air force from the army to shape the National Security Act of 1947. This law created the National Security Council to advise the president on integrating domestic, foreign, and military policies. It also created the Central Intelligence Agency. The air force, army, and navy constituted the National Military Establishment, headed by the secretary of defense; in 1949 Congress made the secretary the head of the Department of Defense, to which the armed forces and their administrative departments were subordinated. The 1947 act had given statutory recognition to the JCS as the principal strategic planning agency; at first the JCS included only the army, navy, and air force chiefs, but in 1949 a military chairman was added, although he did not receive voting power until the Defense Reorganization Act of 1958. Meanwhile, in 1946 the services had established the National War College for joint professional education; the individual service war colleges have retained an equal importance.

At first the statutory JCS directed interservice operations in any joint command through one of their number designated as their executive agent. Thus, during the Korean War, the army chief of staff, representing the service considered most deeply involved, was the agent through whom JCS orders were transmitted to the interservice commander in chief, Far East—General Douglas MacArthur and his successors. In 1953 this unwieldy system was modified by executive order to make the chain of command run from the president through the secretary of defense, to the joint commands in the field. The increase of the defense secretary's authority at the expense of the individual services and even of the JCS was regularized by statute and carried further in the 1958 reorganization law, under which the JCS became the secretary's professional staff,

aided by various subsidiary joint staffs, for his direct control of joint commands around the globe. The individual armed forces have become in effect the recruiters, equippers, and trainers of military organizations, which they then turn over to interservice commands. Under the law, the secretary of defense still delegates logistical support of unified commands to individual services; but increasingly, especially under Secretary of Defense Robert S. McNamara (1961–1968), logistical support was also unified.

The demand for a separate air force had become irresistible because World War II ended in the blast of atomic bombs at Hiroshima and Nagasaki. Atomic and, soon afterward, thermonuclear weapons seemed to confirm that, whatever doubts there might have been earlier, air power alone could now win wars. The air force became preeminent among the services in the early postwar era, first with its capacity to deliver nuclear weapons in bombing planes and then with the development of intercontinental ballistic missiles. Immediately after World War II, the army and navy themselves doubted whether they still had major roles to play in the age of nuclear bombs, and civilians doubted still more.

The army emerged from World War II hoping to capitalize on wartime prestige by combining the traditions of citizen soldiers and military professionals in a plan of universal military training (UMT) that would make every citizen a soldier in peace as well as war—a rebirth of the old militia obligation—but under the training of professionals. Even though President Harry S. Truman supported UMT and Congress considered it until at least the middle 1950's, and even though the Communist takeover of Czechoslovakia led to reinstitution of limited conscription in 1948 (the World War II Selective Service Act had expired the year before), UMT failed. It failed largely because the atomic bomb made mass armies seem unnecessary.

The navy meanwhile strained to assure its existence in the atomic age by developing carrier-based airplanes large enough to carry atomic bombs, which was not easy to do in the early years of cumbersome bombs. The navy considered a share in atomic strategy vital to its existence. In the late 1950's the navy found a stronger strategic role with the development of nuclear-powered submarines able to launch nuclear missiles, which had the advantage of being much less vulnerable than land-based bombers and missiles to an enemy preemptive strike.

Nuclear weapons also raised grave questions about the future feasibility of amphibious assault, the principal raison d'être of the Marine Corps; but the political strength of the marines, generated in part by their great success against Japan in World War II, sufficed to create in 1952 a statutory assurance of the continued existence of three active marine divisions and three marine air wings, with the commandant of the corps to be a full member of the JCS when questions directly related to his corps are considered.

The National Security Council, which brought together civilian and military leaders to advise the president on national strategy, found a partial escape from these doubts about service missions and basic strategy. Secretary of State Dean Acheson took the lead in securing President Truman's endorsement in early 1950 of a document designated NSC-68. Although it contemplated using the nuclear arsenal primarily as a deterrent to enemy nuclear attack, NSC-68 recognized that nuclear weapons might not deter aggression carried out with subnuclear, or "conventional," weapons. Therefore it recommended that the armed forces develop a capacity to wage limited conventional war. NSC-68 might have had little influence had not the Korean War presently demonstrated the reality of the threat of limited war. From the Korean War onward, the traditional armed forces and the non-nuclear element of the air force have found their missions primarily in deterring or waging wars short of nuclear conflict, while a "triad" of nuclear-armed land-based missiles, submarine-launched missiles, and aircraft has been maintained to deter nuclear war.

The Vietnam War, in which the United States was a major participant from 1965 to 1973, complicated the idea of limited war by adding the dimension of revolutionary guerrilla war. Against Communist revolutionary war in Indochina, the American armed forces proved much less successful than they had been in waging more straightforward wars with clearly delineated battlefronts; the United States was even less successful in coping with the political aspects of a Communist-led "war of national liberation" in an Asian country where Americans could

scarcely help but seem threats to indigenous nationalism. In the aftermath of the unpopular Vietnam War, World War II–style selective service was ended in January 1973. Nevertheless, the total personnel of the armed forces, whose Vietnam War peak was about 3.5 million, has been maintained at about 2 million in the face of continuing global responsibilities. The loss of conscripted men has been partially compensated for by increased recruiting of women; as of March 1982, for example, some 76,000 of 788,000 army regulars were women.

Maintaining forces so large, with consistently huge federal expenditures for military purposes and close links between the military and large corporations in what President Dwight D. Eisenhower called "the military-industrial complex," has renewed fears of military threats to democratic government akin to the fears of the Founding Fathers. In the fiscal year 1980, Department of Defense expenditures were $136,137,929,000 —out of total federal expenditures of $579,011,294,000. While defense expenditures as a percentage of total federal spending had been generally declining since 1959, when they represented about 50 percent of the federal budget, the absolute amounts had grown in a way that seemed to threaten continued skewing of national purposes and values toward military ends. This latter trend was the kind of danger now to be feared; no longer was the military threat to democracy that of military assistance to some coup d'état, in the fashion of the Newburgh Conspiracy, but it was a more general danger that politics and the economy would be pervaded by military influences and that foreign policy would be so militarized as to enhance the perils of nuclear war.

Thus, while the specific terms of debate have changed, the problem of the appropriate organization and control of armed forces in a democratic republic has remained a consistent theme throughout American political history. With recurring controversy about renewal of some kind of compulsory military service, in manpower issues even the specific terms of debate have not changed drastically since the colonial era of a compulsory-service militia. With the end of the "free security" of American geographic isolation, the problems of appropriate military organization have not only persisted but grown immensely more acute, and few persuasive solutions have been offered.

BIBLIOGRAPHY

Kenneth J. Hagan, ed., *In Peace and War: Interpretations of American Naval History, 1775–1978* (Westport, Conn., 1978), is the most up-to-date and comprehensive survey of the history of the navy. Robin D.S. Higham, ed., *A Guide to the Sources of United States Military History* (Hamden, Conn., 1975), and *Supplement I* (Hamden, Conn., 1981), form an indispensable guide to secondary works as well as sources, with historiographic essays. Samuel P. Huntington, *The Soldier and the State: The Theory and Politics of Civil-Military Relations* (Cambridge, Mass., 1957), emphasizing, but not limited to, the United States, is the most influential approach to a theory of the role of the military in politics.

Peter Karsten, *The Naval Aristocracy: The Golden Age of Annapolis and the Emergence of Modern American Navalism* (New York, 1972), is a collective biography of American naval officers of 1840–1920, stressing socioeconomic backgrounds and values. Allan R. Millett, *Semper Fidelis: The History of the United States Marine Corps* (New York, 1980), is the first satisfactory institutional history of the Marine Corps. Walter Millis, *Arms and Men: A Study in American Military History* (New York, 1956, 1967), is, despite its date, the best balanced, most comprehensive discussion of the issues of American military history. Russell F. Weigley, *History of the United States Army* (New York, 1967), is the most recent history of the army; and *The American Way of War: A History of United States Military Strategy and Policy* (New York, 1973), is the most comprehensive survey of strategic thought and the institutions generating it.

[*See also* AMERICAN REVOLUTION; CIVIL WAR; COLLECTIVE VIOLENCE; CONSTITUTION; CONTROL, SUPPRESSION, AND INTIMIDATION; INDIAN RELATIONS; MANIFEST DESTINY; PACIFISM AND PEACE MOVEMENTS; *and* VETERANS' MOVEMENTS.]

ARTICLES OF CONFEDERATION

Jack N. Rakove

THE Articles of Confederation marked the first effort of the leaders of the American Revolution to form a federal system of government to regulate the common affairs of the newly independent United States. Drafted by the Continental Congress in 1776–1777, the Articles did not go into formal operation until March 1781, after Maryland had become the last of the thirteen states to ratify. Only eight years later, the Confederation was supplanted by the new federal government organized under the Constitution, drafted at Philadelphia in 1787.

It has always been difficult to avoid seeing the Confederation, given the brevity of its existence, as anything more than a prelude to the Constitution. Indeed, there are good reasons for arguing that the principal legacy of the Articles was the Constitution itself. Serious criticism of the Articles had been voiced even before they went into effect, and by the mid-1780's a growing number of American leaders believed that the Confederation was rapidly verging toward a condition of "imbecility" that portended the dissolution of the Union. By May 1787 this opinion was shared even by many of those who, as Antifederalists, would soon oppose the radical restructuring of the federal system that the Philadelphia convention proposed.

Modern historians have presented a more balanced account of the record of the Confederation than the polemicists of the 1780's or scholars of the nineteenth century. Such has been the hegemony of the Constitution in American life that the inclination to view the Articles from a perspective other than that of 1787 remains difficult to resist. Yet the situations that confronted the Continental Congress in the mid-1770's and the Constitutional Convention a decade later differed so radically that it is both inappropriate and unfair to treat the two charters as equivalent but opposing answers to an identical set of problems.

The most obvious difference is that the framers of the Constitution could draw lessons from the experience of the Confederation. The members of the Continental Congress enjoyed no such advantage; they had neither useful precedents nor experience to draw upon, and could hardly foresee the range of problems that Congress would later encounter. A second contrast lies in the character of the proceedings of the two bodies. The deliberations of the Continental Congress were repeatedly interrupted by the unceasing press of more urgent business related to the conduct of the war. The Constitutional Convention, by comparison, was free to spend the better part of four months with no distraction more troubling than carriages rattling beneath its windows or the heat of a Philadelphia summer.

Even more important is the difference in the political constraints that influenced the course of debate. Both meetings were mindful of the obstacles that had to be overcome if their plans were to be ratified by the states. Yet where the Convention could conceive of itself as acting to frame a durable, comprehensive plan of government, members of Congress understood that the ultimate structure of the Confederation mattered far less than its contribution to the struggle against Britain.

This association between confederation and resistance was apparent from the earliest discussions of the problem in 1775. Those members of Congress who still hoped for a reconciliation with Britain were reluctant to discuss the subject at all. Since any movement toward the establishment of a formal confederation would suggest that the colonists were indeed intent on independence, moderate delegates acted to defer serious discussion of confederation until literally the final weeks before independence. Those members who believed that the British ministry preferred coercion to compromise hoped that a final declaration of independence could be preceded by the creation of both a formal confederation and new constitutions of government within the states. But such was their need to placate their moderate colleagues—as well as public opinion—that they were unable to press their views too emphatically before the late spring of 1776. Several rough plans of confederation had in fact been prepared by individual delegates in 1775 and the early winter of 1776. Silas Deane of Connecticut had drafted one, and another prepared by Benjamin Franklin had been laid before Congress (but not formally considered) shortly before its adjournment in August 1775. These first drafts should be regarded essentially as working papers.

By early June 1776 even such moderates as John Jay and Robert Morris believed that independence was imminent. On 7 June Richard Henry Lee of Virginia introduced a set of resolutions calling for independence, the negotiation of foreign alliances, and the preparation of a confederation. After two days of debate, Congress agreed to appoint separate committees to proceed with each of these measures. On 12 June a committee of thirteen members, one from each state, was appointed to prepare articles of confederation. Its leading member was John Dickinson of Pennsylvania, the celebrated author of the *Letters from a Farmer in Pennsylvania* (1768) and the most influential opponent of independence still sitting in Congress. Among the other members of the committee were Samuel Adams of Massachusetts, Roger Sherman of Connecticut, Robert R. Livingston of New York, and Edward Rutledge of South Carolina.

Although little is known about the deliberations of the committee, it is generally assumed that Dickinson himself prepared the original set of articles. A first draft, in his hand, came to light only in the middle of the twentieth century, and an analysis of its provisions suggests that Dickinson envisioned a confederation that would place important restraints on the autonomy of the states. One article went so far as to prohibit the states from making any further alteration in the existing structure of church-state relations; another would have given Congress the sole right of "establishing and regulating fees" on interstate commerce. More important, Congress was to be vested with exclusive authority over peace and war, the conduct of foreign relations, the actual direction of the war, the resolution of disputes between states, and the disposition of those unsettled western lands whose ownership threatened to become the outstanding source of conflict between virtually all of the states.

The committee appears to have met frequently during the second fortnight of June. While it deleted several of Dickinson's most innovative proposals—the article on religion, for example—most of his original plan survived. A revised and more polished draft was laid before the entire Congress on 12 July. By then Dickinson, who had opposed independence until the very end, had left Congress. In his absence, none of the other members of the committee appears to have taken a prominent role in defending its handiwork.

Congress debated the revised Dickinson plan from mid-July until 20 August. The amendments that were approved during this period, as well as the fragmentary notes of debates that have been preserved, indicate that there was deep agreement on some of the most important aspects of the proposed confederation and equally profound disagreement on other issues. The latter had less to do with the constitutional structure of the Union than with the specific interests of different groups of states.

Three issues proved particularly troublesome: the apportionment of representation within Congress, the apportionment of the expenses of the Union among the states, and the control of western lands. The committee had followed the precedent set in the First Continental Congress of 1774 of allowing each state one vote in Congress, regardless of disparities in population and wealth. Delegates from the most populous states (Virginia, Massachusetts, and Pennsylvania) argued strenuously against the injustice of this measure but failed to reverse the recommendation of the committee. A few delegates may already have realized that the only solution to the inherent conflict between small and large states lay in the creation of a bicameral Congress with two houses that could embody different principles of representation. But the overriding need for wartime efficiency made this an impracticable option.

The problems posed by the two other controversial issues were partially linked. The committee had proposed apportioning the common expenses of the Union simply by the total population of each state. This met the objections of southern delegates, led by Samuel Chase of Maryland, who moved that only "white inhabitants" should be counted, thereby excluding from the equation the large slave populations of the major slave states. His amendment was defeated in a vote cast along sectional lines.

The question of the expenses of the war was also involved in the dispute over congressional control of western lands. Those states that held title under their colonial charters to vast expanses in the interior could reasonably expect to defray their share of the Union's debt by selling land to Americans migrating westward. Those states without such claims (Maryland, Rhode Island, New Jersey, Delaware, and Pennsylvania) would, on the other hand, face the necessity of levying heavy internal taxes if their obligations were to be met. It was their position and interest that the committee had originally favored in approving an article empowering Congress to create a national domain. But in the deliberations of the committee of the whole, every provision designed to give Congress authority over the American interior was stricken.

Compromises on these issues were difficult to find because the interests of individual states were so well defined. Yet on those matters that involved dividing basic responsibilities of government between the Union and the states, it is striking to see how little controversy arose. Broad agreement existed that Congress should retain exclusive control over the great affairs of state, which in eighteenth-century usage meant war and foreign policy, and that the states should retain exclusive control over what was called their internal police. John Dickinson's original articles had threatened to reduce the extent of state autonomy in this latter area, but a series of discrete changes made first in the drafting committee and then in the committee of the whole had effectively gutted his plan. The states retained the right to levy their own taxes and to determine how they would mobilize the other resources that the war would require. Yet if the delegates thus seemed reluctant to give Congress coercive authority over the states, they nevertheless expected that the states would in good faith execute whatever measures Congress asked of them. The draft that Congress ordered printed (for its own future use) on 20 August stipulated that "every State shall abide by the Determinations of the United States in Congress Assembled, on all questions which by this Confederation are submitted to them."

One leading historian of the American Revolution, Merrill Jensen, argued that even in these early debates over the Articles a clearly defined struggle was being waged between radicals, who wanted to secure the sovereignty of the individual states, and conservatives, who hoped to establish a strong national government in order to check an upsurge of democracy within the states. It is far from apparent that these were the terms in which the subject of confederation was originally perceived. The surviving records of congressional deliberations during the summer of 1776 do not indicate that the delegates were deeply concerned with the larger theoretical concerns—such as the location of sovereignty—that one might suppose are inherent in the creation of any federal system of government. Indeed, the question of sovereignty seems hardly to have been raised at all during the debates of 1776. The revisions made between June and August suggest instead that Congress was seeking, in a pragmatic and expedient way, to delineate two fairly broad and exclusive spheres of authority, one belonging to Congress, the other to the states. Rather than agonize over where sovereignty would ultimately reside under the Confederation, the delegates acted to divide the powers of government between state and national levels of authority, trusting that the imperatives of the revolutionary struggle would work to resolve such conflicts as might arise in areas where their responsibilities would inevitably overlap.

It was not, in any event, disagreement over theoretical issues that stalled the progress of confederation after August 1776, for two other considerations proved more important. The first was that the tentative decisions giving each state one vote, apportioning the common expenses according to total population, and divesting Congress of any significant authority over western lands embodied neither compromise nor consensus. These were the actions of interested majorities, and the objections of the dissenting minorities on each question remained so strong that many members doubted whether the state assemblies could ever be brought to ratify the finished Articles. A second obstacle to the completion of confederation lay in the crush of business that beset Congress by late 1776. A series of military defeats and disasters in the summer and fall of that year had left the Continental army in an extremely precarious position and had even forced Congress itself to flee to Baltimore. The urgent needs of resistance took precedence over the claims of confederation, while a decline in the number of members in attendance left those who stayed on overburdened by the weight of routine business.

Discussion of confederation resumed in April 1777, after Congress had returned to Philadelphia. During the intervening months, a series of minor disputes between Congress and individual states may have made some members aware of the danger of leaving both the source and extent of their authority undefined. Congress was also anxious to conclude a treaty of alliance with France, and many delegates believed that the establishment of a formal confederation would help to convince the French of the commitment of the new republic to independence as well as its ability to secure it.

Although little progress was made immediately, the resumption of discussion did lead to the adoption of one amendment of major importance. Thomas Burke, a newly arrived delegate from North Carolina, proposed the adoption of an article declaring that each state would retain "its sovereignty, freedom, and independence, and every power, jurisdiction, and right, which is not by this confederation expressly delegated" to Congress. At first Burke's proposal made so slight an impression on his colleagues that it was not seconded, but eventually it was taken under debate and approved by a wide majority, with eleven of the thirteen delegations voting in its favor.

With the adoption of this amendment, Congress had at last confronted the issue of sovereignty and seemingly resolved it in favor of the states. Yet in endorsing this position, the delegates seem not to have believed that further changes were necessary in the substantive provisions of confederation. The division of authority between states and Congress that had been mapped in 1776 remained unaltered, as did the conviction that the states were obligated to execute in good faith those decisions which clearly fell under the purview of Congress. Burke's amendment, which became Article 2 of the final confederation, satisfied a theoretical need; its practical implications were far from clear. Since Burke himself later acknowledged that "the United States ought to be as one Sovereign with respect to foreign Powers, in all things that relate to War or where the States have one Common Interest," it cannot be assumed that this recognition of state sovereignty constituted an unlimited endorsement of a compact theory of the nature of the Union, at least in the terms that states' rights theorists from the South would later advance. (Congressional approval of his amendment did not convince Burke that the Articles as finally drafted offered sufficient security to the states. When the Articles were submitted to the states for ratification, Burke urged his North Carolina constituents to reject them.)

With Burke's amendment approved, further progress on the Articles soon ground to a halt. Once Congress turned to the familiar issues of representation, expenses, and western lands, the delegates quickly realized that the passage of time had not made the resolution of these problems any easier. During the summer of 1777 the subject was effectively tabled. Debate did not resume until October, after the British occupation of Philadelphia had forced Congress to flee a second time. But now—safely, if not comfortably, resettled at York, Pennsylvania—the delegates found the determination they had previously lacked to bring the drafting of the Articles to a prompt conclusion.

Two pragmatic considerations probably encouraged this decision. One was that Congress was becoming concerned about the signs of an inflation of prices and an accompanying depreciation in the value of its currency, predictable consequences of its reliance on the printing press as its basic source of money. To check these developments, Congress was preparing to submit to the states a comprehensive set of resolutions on taxation, fiscal policy, and prices; and the delegates apparently believed these proposals would carry greater weight if confederation could be completed simultaneously. A similar conclusion could be drawn from considerations of foreign policy. Here Congress was anxious to capitalize on the dramatic American victory at Saratoga to move at last to the completion of an alliance with France. The final drafting and ratification of a confederation, many delegates assumed, would enhance the status of the American commissioners at Paris and help to convince the French that America was politically stable and committed to independence.

These considerations, as well as a general weariness with the subject itself, may help to explain why Congress was able to resolve the most difficult questions fairly quickly. The questions of representation and western lands each required only one day of debate, and the final provisions pertaining to each were approved by large majorities that included states whose interests were not being assuaged. On 7 October Congress adhered to the precedent of 1774 that had given each state one vote; on 15 October it rejected three proposals that would have given the Union the power to ascertain the western boundaries of the states and dispose of the lands lying beyond them.

Five days of debate were necessary before Congress resolved the third major issue, the apportionment of expenses. Here a new formula had been proposed: each state's share of the common expenses was to be determined according to the value of its granted lands "and the buildings and improvements thereon." The four New England states voted against this provision, on the grounds that it discriminated against the more densely settled and better improved lands of their region; the southern states voted in its favor, since slaves were not to be considered. Two other delegations were divided, and New Jersey cast the decisive vote in favor.

After resolving this last issue, Congress spent several weeks making additional revisions in the text of August 1776. By 15 November a polished final draft was ready to be sent to the printer, and not long afterward the Articles of Confederation were at last submitted to the states.

This final draft numbered thirteen articles. The opening three articles gave the Confederation its title ("The United States of America"), recognized the sovereignty of each state in the language of Thomas Burke's amendment, and bound the states into "a firm league of friendship . . . for their common defense, the security of their liberties and their mutual and general welfare." The fourth article prohibited the states from taking certain discriminatory actions against the citizens of other states, provided for the extradition of fugitives, and promised that each state would give "full faith and credit" to the judicial acts of the other states. Article 5 defined the institutional character of Congress and the privileges of its members. Congress was to meet annually; delegates could serve no more than three years out of any six and were subject to recall at any time; each state was to have one vote.

With Article 6 the substantive nature of the Confederation at last began to emerge. A series of restrictions imposed on the states made clear that Congress was to retain principal authority in all areas affecting the external relations of the United States. Article 7 dealt with the appointment of military officers, and Article 8 concerned the apportionment of the common expenses among the states.

Article 9, which enumerated the powers of Congress, was clearly the most important. It gave Congress "the sole and exclusive right and power of determining on peace and war" and of conducting foreign relations. It established an elaborately detailed procedure for adjudicating disputes between states. Among other powers granted, Article 9 gave Congress the authority to determine the expenses of the Union and appropriate the necessary funds; to emit bills of credit and borrow money; to set the size of its army and make "requisitions [which] shall be binding" on the states for the men required. In exercising all its major powers, the consent of nine states was to be necessary for the adoption of specific measures.

The concluding four articles tied up a few loose ends. According to Article 10, the committee of the states, which was to be appointed in the event of a congressional recess, was to be prohibited from exercising any of those major powers that ordinarily required the approval of nine states in Congress. Article 11 extended an offer to Canada to join the Confederation, but no other state was to be admitted without the consent of nine states. Article 12 extended the "public faith" to all debts contracted by the United States prior to the formal completion of the Confederation. Finally, Article 13 committed the states to "abide by the determinations [of Congress] on all questions which, by this confederation, are submitted to them." It also required the ratification of the Articles by all the states, with later amendments to be first proposed by Congress and then approved unanimously by the states.

The Confederation was very much the work of a body concerned with the conduct of an ongoing and difficult war. Whether the delegates were concerned with how well such a confederation would function in times of peace is easily doubted. The conditions of debate had not encouraged more expansive visions to occupy the delegates' imaginations, and the pressure to complete a document that could gain the prompt and unanimous ratification of the states must also have spurred the drafters to confine themselves to the minimum framework necessary. The more powers they proposed to vest in Congress, the more controversial the Articles would become and the less likely to be ratified. Yet it should also be remembered that if the framers of the Confederation were thus well advised to avoid giving Congress independent powers of taxation or the right to coerce defiant states, the history of the Union had so far indicated that the states could be counted upon to implement congressional policies in those areas that clearly fell within its jurisdiction.

Prompt ratification was obviously what Congress desired when it sent the Articles to the state assemblies for their consideration. Its hope that the state responses could be received as early as March 1778 was obviously naïve, as was the belief that the states would simply endorse the Articles as drafted. In fact, no fewer than thirty-six amendments had been proposed to Congress by late June, when the delegates (by now returned to Philadelphia) resolved to take these amendments into consideration even though several states had not yet responded. But the purpose of Congress was not to reopen its own discussions of confederation. It raced through the amendments in a week, seriously debating few, rejecting all, recording only a single roll call of individual delegates, before finishing with a rush on 25 June. What the delegates hoped to accomplish by this, quite simply, was to convince those states most skeptical about the Articles that the greater needs of the Revolution had to prevail over their particular interests.

The states that were most dubious about the wisdom or utility of confederating were those whose defined geographic boundaries deprived them of any share of the enormous tracts of western lands claimed by such states as Virginia, North Carolina, New York, and Connecticut. The three states that had failed to ratify the Articles (Maryland, Delaware, and New Jersey) lacked such claims, and they were the objects of the congressional gambit. By rejecting the amendments that Maryland had proposed—particularly one authorizing Congress to ascertain the western boundaries of the states—the majority clearly hoped to convince the dissenting "landless" states of the futility of their campaign.

This strategy worked in Delaware and New Jersey; both states voted ratification by January 1779. But in Maryland it failed. Leading Maryland politicians were shareholders in land-speculation companies whose prewar purchases from Indian tribes could be redeemed only if the title of Virginia to the backlands was overturned. When Virginia formally voided the most controversial of these claims, Maryland reiterated its unwillingness to ratify the Articles until a national domain had been created in which all the states would enjoy equal rights. Maryland held to this position until the early months of 1781, and as a result the Articles remained unratified for more than three years after submission to the states.

Maryland finally relented after New York launched the series of cessions by the landed states that led to the creation of a national domain by 1784. Virginia was slower to act, but by late 1780 a number of its leaders had come to recognize the necessity of surrendering its extravagant grants in the interior of the continent. Diplomatic pressure from the French minister to America, the chevalier de la Luzerne, also influenced the Maryland assembly.

On 1 March 1781 the Articles of Confederation became the formal charter of the American union. Even before they took effect, however, many members of Congress had concluded that their body needed more authority than the Articles would bestow if the war was to be brought to a successful conclusion. The situation that Congress confronted by late 1780 differed significantly from the circumstances that had prevailed when the Articles were drafted. Now the optimistic assumptions that had encouraged the framers to believe that the states would carry out congressional policies obediently and effectively seemed obsolete. Requisitions on the states for men, money, and supplies had not been complied with adequately, and as a result, in 1780 and 1781 a series of committees began generating proposals for amending the Articles. A number of delegates were attracted to the idea of asking the states to vest Congress with independent sources of revenue and the power to coerce delinquent states into doing their duty.

This latter power must have seemed too dangerous and unwieldy an authority for the states ever to concede to Congress, but the possibility that the states would admit that Congress needed its own taxing power was far more plausible. Its existing authority to emit bills of credit, and its imminent acquisition of a vast national domain, did indicate that the states were not entirely intent on reducing Congress to a condition of penury. On 3 February 1781 Congress approved a resolution asking the states to grant it the power to collect a duty, or impost, on foreign goods imported into America. Of the many possible amendments discussed during these months, this was the only one that Congress chose to submit to the states.

Congress might have hoped that the states would immediately accede to its request, but the progress of the impost was scarcely less desultory than that of the Articles. By the early fall of 1782, Congress knew that the measure would almost certainly fail of adoption in Rhode Island; and when, in October, the Virginia assembly repealed its original ratification, this first modest effort at strengthening Congress was effectively doomed. Like the original Articles, amendments required the unanimous approval of the states, and with hostilities largely terminated and peace imminent, the advocates of a more potent union realized that other amendments would become even more difficult to obtain.

The fundamental weakness of Congress did not become less apparent with the end of the war. Congress lacked the funds necessary to meet the ongoing expenses of the Union, much less to service the enormous national debt contracted during the war. At the behest of Robert Morris, who had been appointed superintendent of finance in 1781, Congress began considering other plans to secure permanent revenues and fund the national debt. On 18 April 1783, after an intensive period of politicking that included rumors of a military insurrection and various threats from Morris, Congress approved two new amendments for submission to the states. One was a revised impost, which would have imposed a differentiated schedule of tariffs on enumerated goods, supplemented by a 5 percent duty on all other imports; the other proposed substituting population for land value as the basis for apportioning the common expenses of the Union.

One year later, when the ultimate fate of these amendments was still unknown, Congress asked the states to approve two further additions to its authority. These proposals, which would have given Congress a limited power to regulate foreign trade, came in the wake of British and French actions restricting the access of American merchants to West Indian markets, as well as the realization that European nations had little incentive to conclude treaties of commerce with a country that had no effective central government. By giving Congress even limited authority to discriminate against foreign shippers, the delegates hoped to enhance the ability of America to negotiate commercial treaties with its international competitors.

The amendments proposed in 1783 and 1784 met the same fate as the impost of 1781. None was ever able to command the unanimous support of the states. With the struggle for independence successfully ended, it quickly became apparent that the states no longer shared the same overriding sense of a common national interest that had prevailed, however unevenly, during the war. Each of the major issues of policy that Congress confronted during these years—revenue, commerce, and westward expansion—affected the interests of individual states or whole regions in sharply divergent ways. Those states that had already acted to redeem the debts owed to public creditors within their boundaries had little incentive to see Congress vested with their own financial powers. Moreover, the issues of foreign policy that vexed Congress in the mid-1780's revealed just how difficult it would be to define one national interest to which all the states could subscribe. The exclusion of American ships from West Indian ports mattered a great deal to northern merchants but hardly at all to the great planters of the South. By the same token, when Spain closed the Mississippi to American navigation in 1784, the territorial and expansionist interests of Virginia and North Carolina were jeopardized, but those of northern migrants and land speculators were not. The basis for regional conflict became vividly evident in 1786 when the northern delegations in Congress voted solidly to sacrifice American claims to the navigation of the Mississippi for a period of twenty years in exchange for a commercial treaty with Spain. Such a treaty was never negotiated—nor, indeed, could it ever have been ratified—but the stark sectional division on this issue encouraged some informed leaders to fear that the Union itself might soon dissolve into two or three regional confederacies.

Against this background, the idea that the Articles could be gradually reformed through the adoption of carefully drawn individual amendments ceased to be viable. Hitherto the would-be reformers of the Articles had believed that the states could be made more conscious of the necessity of giving Congress additional power. By early 1786 many of those who still thought "continentally" had concluded that any amendment proposed by Congress itself would be fatally tainted. Accordingly they endorsed a call by Virginia for a special convention to be devoted to the single purpose of considering an amendment giving Congress some power to regulate trade. But when only twelve men representing a mere five states actually assembled at Annapolis in September, Hamilton, Madison, Dickinson, and the others in attendance realized that any recommendation from such a body would carry little weight.

The decision of the Annapolis Convention to issue a call for another general convention to assemble at Philadelphia the following May has often been seen as evidence of the conspiratorial intentions of those in attendance. It might well be more accurate to suggest that they were acting out of desperation. Having exhausted all other strategies for reform and fearing (as they did) that the Confederation could not long endure, they were prepared to gamble that an interval of eight or nine months might give them time to organize a respectable meeting with some hope of success. They took this gamble not so much because they thought it would work but rather because they had run out of alternatives.

The events of the following months demonstrated that this strategy had better prospects for success than the Annapolis delegates had originally suspected. By February 1787, when Congress itself endorsed the measure, seven states had already responded favorably, and in the end only Rhode Island, still recalcitrant, failed to appoint a delegation. Few Americans could have predicted the nature of the document that the Philadelphia Convention would produce. But by the time the Convention of 1787 assembled, many American leaders privately believed that the Articles no longer provided an adequate foundation for reconstituting a federal system. The ease with which the convention accepted the Virginia Plan as the principal basis for its deliberations is one proof of how thoroughly the Articles had been discredited; a second, which became evident only later, is that the strategy of the Antifederalists hinged on securing either the calling of a second convention or the adoption of amendments to the Constitution. No call of any significance was heard for reinvigorating the still-existing Confederation through the adoption of a comprehensive set of amendments. Although the Articles continued to serve as the formal framework of the Union until the spring of 1789, it can be plausibly argued that Congress had been essentially a caretaker government since May 1787 and little more than that since the end of the war.

The ease with which the Confederation was displaced does suggest that the Articles had failed to provide a basis of federal government adequate to the exigencies of the Union. So, too, the fact that the revolutionary war was virtually over by the time the Articles took effect makes it difficult to argue that the formal Confederation deserves any credit for the achievement of independence. Whether the Articles might have provided a more durable federal framework if Maryland had not delayed ratification or if the gradual adoption of individual amendments had proved possible can be a subject of speculation only. Yet the Confederation had its positive legacies. It did provide a theoretical foundation on which the framers of the Constitution could and did build, in its essential allocation of national and state authority, in its prohibitions on state action, and even in certain provisions that were incorporated in the new charter. Second, and more important, the drafting of the Confederation and its prompt ratification by all but one of the states remind us how powerful were the shared concerns that carried the Americans through to independence. The formal structure of government outlined in the Articles of Confederation mattered less than the union it embodied. The Articles stand as evidence of something that many skeptics quite reasonably doubted as late as 1774: the ability of thirteen polities that had previously enjoyed remarkably little formal connection to discover, in the crucible of revolution, a basis for organizing a federal association that at the very least provided a foundation for later and more thoughtful development.

BIBLIOGRAPHY

Edmund C. Burnett, *The Continental Congress* (New York, 1941), remains the standard narrative history. Elmer James Ferguson, *The Power of the Purse: A History of American Public Finance, 1776–1790* (Chapel Hill, N.C., 1961), provides a definitive history of the financial problems that loomed so large in the history of the Confederation, although its interpretation of constitutional issues is far from convincing. H. James Henderson, *Party Politics in the Continental Congress* (New York, 1974), emphasizes sectional rivalry and ideological conflict.

Merrill Jensen, *The Articles of Confederation: An Interpretation of the Social-Constitutional History of the American Revolution, 1774–1781* (Madison, Wis., 1940), and *The New Nation: A History of the United States During the Confederation, 1781–1789* (New York, 1950), portray the Articles as the work of radicals who hoped to preserve the sovereignty of the individual states and the democratic gains embodied in the early state constitutions. The Confederation offered a viable basis for American federalism, Jensen argued, until it was effectively subverted in 1787 by a group of conservatives who were intent on checking an upsurge of democracy in the states. Harry W. Jones, "The Articles of Confederation and the Creation of a Federal System," in American Philosophical Society, *Aspects of American Liberty: Philosophical, Historical, and Political* (Philadelphia, 1977), emphasizes the continuities between the Articles and the Constitution.

Andrew C. McLaughlin, "The Background of American Federalism," in *American Political Science Review,* 12 (1918), offers a still valuable comparison between the imperial problems that confronted Great Britain and the federal problems of the American revolutionaries. Richard B. Morris, "The Forging of the Union Reconsidered: A Historical Refutation of State Sovereignty over Seabeds," in *Columbia Law Review,* 74 (1974), is an excellent analysis of the problem of sovereignty under the Confederation. Peter S. Onuf, "Toward Federalism: Virginia, Congress, and the Western Lands," in *William and Mary Quarterly,* 34 (1977), shows how the prior resolution of disputes about land made possible the constitutional reforms of 1787.

Jack N. Rakove, *The Beginnings of National Politics: An Interpretive History of the Continental Congress* (New York, 1979), takes sharp issue with Merrill Jensen's interpretation of both the framing and constitutional significance of the Articles, arguing instead that the constraints of resistance were more influential than the political differences that Jensen emphasized. Gordon S. Wood, *The Creation of the American Republic, 1776–1787* (Chapel Hill, N.C., 1969), does not focus directly on the Articles of Confederation, but his interpretation of revolutionary political thought is essential to any understanding of the theoretical problems that had to be resolved before a stable federal government could be established.

[*See also* AMERICAN REVOLUTION; BILL OF RIGHTS; CHURCH AND STATE; COLONIAL GOVERNMENT; CONGRESS; CONSTITUTION; DECLARATION OF INDEPENDENCE; FEDERALISM; *and* THE FEDERALIST PAPERS.]

AUTHORITY

John Patrick Diggins

AMERICA has never been completely at ease with the proposition of authority, and for good reasons. First of all, the image of authority evokes dark overtones suggesting such repugnancies as political oppression and religious persecution, resistance to change, mindless obedience, doctrinaire utterances and unquestionable dogma, and an irresponsible refusal to make one's own decisions. These images, moreover, are generally associated with the Old World, the very continent from which America's first settlers fled either to escape religious and political tyranny or to seek opportunity and adventure in a new environment that promised to be relatively free from European systems of authority. Thus there emerged a persistent image in the American mind that can be traced from Jefferson to Lincoln to Franklin D. Roosevelt and, with literary intellectuals, from Emerson to Henry James to Robert Frost: Europe is old, tired, decadent; America is fresh, innocent, virtuous. To a large extent, that image derived from the historical fact that America's political imagination was born in an act of rebellion against the constituted authority of the British government, and thus America was conceived as something of a new experiment of man and government in which the political mind often looked backward with fear and forward with hope, inculcating the accepted values of liberty and not the alleged vices of authority.

Perhaps even more important, in light of the fate of any idea of authority in America, especially political authority, were three forces in American life that seemed to shut the door to the entry of all ideas that would restrain and inhibit the individual: a Protestant religious culture that stressed the preeminence of individual conscience over institutional or doctrinal authority;

an emergent free-market, capitalist economy that placed at the center of social life the sovereignty of the individual producer and consumer and juxtaposed the claims of private interests to the public good; and an open, spacious, natural environment that could scarcely encourage discipline, order, and other values that might nurture a restless people into accepting the constraints of authority. Thus the factors of history, culture, and geography combined to make Americans into what D. H. Lawrence called "runaways" from authority.

What Americans were escaping was not so much authority as such but what the colonists felt to be illegitimate authority, a discredited system of British government that first defied the obligations of the Protestant faith by not allowing religious toleration and then violated the rights of the colonists by imposing taxes and economic regulations. Thus by the latter half of the eighteenth century, the American Revolution came to be conceived as a struggle between American "liberty" and "virtue" and English "tyranny" and "conspiracy," between responsible authority that had its origins in the will of the people and uncontrollable power that was the product of extraparliamentary intrigue and corruption. From the beginning of American political history, then, a distinction could be made between authority and power, the assumption being that the former nurtured liberty while the latter threatened it. Yet the distinction could not be completely maintained, and by the time of the Constitution, assumptions about the nature of power influenced assumptions about the nature of authority.

What is the difference between power and authority? This perennial question in political philosophy has generated a number of discriminat-

AUTHORITY

ing answers. Some theorists, usually referred to as "neo-Machiavellians" or "realists," see no difference between the two terms because all forms of authority are ultimately imposed by force, either directly by control and threats, or indirectly by establishing dependent relations and manipulating consciousness. Yet in American thought, deriving from religious and political tenets of the Anglo-American tradition, the distinction between power and authority was clearly articulated, even when thinkers as astute as John Adams recognized that the terms were not mutually exclusive.

At its most fundamental level, power is the exercise of force to produce desired effects, and authority is what power becomes when it is voluntarily accepted by those who experience it. Authority is rightful power, power justified by reason. Roughly put, one might say that power depends on coercion, authority on consent. How power comes to be accepted or rejected is the process by which it is legitimated or deauthorized, and this role is most frequently assumed by the "intellectuals," by those who speak truth to power to see if power can answer with reason rather than with force. Something of this challenge was leveled by Thomas Paine against British rule in America in the 1770's, when he claimed that all governments were based on the "wickedness" of power relations, whereas the genuine authority of society derived from the true "wants" of human nature. But the distinction between power and authority does not arise only out of revolutionary situations or characterize merely undemocratic regimes. Even in America the legitimacy of the state is challenged, and not only by radical activists and Bohemian artists. In the early twentieth century the historian Charles A. Beard questioned the legitimacy of both the Constitution and the Supreme Court, depicting them as undemocratic institutions conceived and ratified without the popular consent of the people, while the political philosopher Walter Lippmann attempted to demonstrate why the contemporary American citizen lacked the knowledge and rationality to render such consent. Whether the intellectuals question the right of a government to rule or the ability of citizens to be ruled, it is the intellectual who mediates between the state and its subjects, and in this respect authority has been a central subject in intellectual history and political philosophy.

Unlike power, authority implies some measure of freedom, desire, and choice. If the study of power is "scientific" and descriptive insofar as it aims to predict what people will do, the study of authority can be normative and prescriptive insofar as it aims to provide much more than an actual account of how people behave and the forces that shape behavior. Authority is essentially an intellectual and moral issue: ought we to obey, and on what grounds does society or the state command our allegiance?

The problem of authority like the problem of obedience has been approached from a variety of perspectives by political thinkers in the past. Plato saw obedience as willful submission informed by wisdom, St. Augustine saw it as an act of faith inspired by hope, Hobbes as fear trembling with doubt, Rousseau as individual freedom self-prescribed by the moral will of all, Locke as prudence dictated by interests and self-preservation, Burke as tradition governed by habit, Freud as need driven by anxiety, Marx as labor alienated from value, and Tocqueville as loneliness in flight from solitude. The German social philosopher Max Weber, who spent almost his entire intellectual life trying to unravel systematically the riddles of authority, distinguished three aspects of the phenomenon: "charismatic" authority, in which a bold, dynamic leader appears spontaneously upon a scene of tension and crisis; "rational-legal" authority, which accrues to a society by virtue of the slow development of formal rules evolving from precedent; and "bureaucratic" authority, a more characteristic twentieth-century development wherein organizations take on the image of rightfulness and go unchallenged simply because their "routinized" operations come to be seen as part of the natural order of everyday existence.

The three-part Weberian scheme, although once highly influential in contemporary American as well as European social science, is not entirely satisfactory for explaining the many meaning of authority in American history and politics. The Founding Fathers feared charismatic authority, which they would have viewed as a form of "Caesarism" leading to tyranny; and the *Federalist* authors did not believe that law itself would be sufficient to govern the "interests" and "passions" of men. As to bureaucratic authority, the framers seemed innocent of the phenomenon as

93

a basis of political domination, although Hamilton might have found the idea congenial because he looked to the efficient "administration" of government as the basis of its stability as well as its legitimacy.

Although the subject of authority appears to have been more a preoccupation of European than American thinkers, it is not entirely absent from American intellectual history. For Americans too could not ignore authority as a perennial issue involving the ruler's (or the system's) right to command and the subject's obligation to obey. Nor could Americans ignore the fact that, however one defines authority, it requires an essential ingredient that distinguishes it from power—justification. In the course of history it is the mind of the reflective thinker who fulfills this decisive role, either by rejecting the world of power, as did Rousseau and Marx, or by defending it by translating it into formulations more responsive to human needs and influence, as did Hobbes and Burke. Somewhat the same roles were assumed in American intellectual history, where thinkers like Paine and Thoreau rejected political authority as little more than power and coercion, and thinkers like Madison and Tocqueville tried to explain why certain forms of authority were necessary for preserving liberty. The legitimation of authority and the ways in which obedience has been justified in certain episodes of American intellectual history and political thought comprise a vast and complex subject. In the first three centuries of American history the religious, political, or social thinker was more confident that authority could be justified because of the prevalence of certain ideas that seemed to convey the truths of God, nature, or society itself. To understand the perspectives of these past three centuries is to understand a world we may have lost.

THE IDEA OF
SPIRITUAL AUTHORITY

Among the many rich legacies of New England Puritanism was its profound sense of authority, a spiritual heritage from which America's later political culture chose to disassociate itself. When we examine two of the central documents of American Puritanism, John Winthrop's "A Model of Christian Charity" (1630) and his "Speech to the General Court" (1645), we are immediately struck by two considerations: that for the Puritans, authority was essentially spiritual in nature, based on divine revelation comprehensible to human reason, and that it was inextricably bound up with a deep sense of community. These documents provide perhaps the first statements in American thought on authority based upon transcendent religious imperatives. Winthrop's rhetoric is suffused with the imagery of binding, tying, knitting. The power of love and grace will enable man to realize "the two rules whereby we are able to walke towards another: Justice and Mercy." God has structured a hierarchical social order, "some highe and eminent in power and dignities; others meane and in subjeccion," so that "every man might have need of others, and from hence they might all be knitt more nearly together in the Bond of brotherly affeccion." To call upon imperfect man to perfect society is to ask the impossible, and thus Winthrop's social philosophy must begin and end with the sense of duty and the force of obligation. Justice and mercy are "rules" to be obeyed; the "laws" of nature and of grace must be followed; the Gospel "commands" us to love our neighbors and even our enemies. These moral prescriptions are necessary because man in his "natural state" is capable only of a kind of freedom that is "common with beast and other creatures." True "civil liberty" is thus experienced when persons willfully enter the moral covenant between God and man and the political covenant among men themselves. This liberty, which enables regenerate men to do "that only which is good, just, and honest," is the purpose of true government and the "proper end and object of authority."

Although the Puritan notion of authority involved the renunciation of "natural liberty," and although it expressed itself in terms of commands, Winthrop nevertheless is spiritualizing the concepts of both authority and liberty, for he is appealing to men's minds, not their bodies, to ideas rather than to interests, and he is hopeful that men can be brought to assent not by coercion but by conviction. Rather than curtailing liberty, Winthrop is offering men the ability to choose, and to be able to choose is to consider reasons for or against a given proposal. Only a system of authority based on voluntary submission could make possible the Calvinist synthesis of freedom and necessity, the paradoxical doctrine of predestination in which man is informed as to what he ought to do even though what he will do has been preordained by God's will. In this respect, Winthrop can be seen as trying to curb the need for the advent of temporal or political authority, which usually enters social consciousness as an external compulsion when the individual senses the discrepancy between what he desires and what society permits. By appealing to man's informed spiritual conscience, Winthrop could treat authority not only as a form of necessity that conferred dignity on the person who accepted it, but also as a form of freedom that liberated man from his natural condition. The whole foundation of Puritan political theory rested on theological convictions, on beliefs that must not be challenged. Yet the beauty or moral persuasiveness in the Puritan concept of authority is such that it not only elevates authority to the status of a normative ideal but convinces us that authority is possible only within a community. The cohesion of community is achieved by moral obligations that impel man to transcend his selfish nature, and thus the locus of authority is spiritual in that it is not made by man but lies in a source above and beyond man himself.

If the genesis of authority lies ultimately in God's will and is realized only in an intimate community of shared values, what happens to authority when God disappears as an agency and moral community collapses as a reality? This was the question the Founding Fathers had to face when devising a new constitution for a republican government. In the eighteenth-century Enlightenment, authority would be sanctioned by appealing not to spiritual ideas beyond history but to ideas and theories that derived from historical experience itself.

POLITICAL AUTHORITY AND THE FRAGMENTATION OF THE IDEA OF SOVEREIGNTY

When Jefferson declared that "all authority belongs to the people," he was reiterating one of the Lockean precepts that pervaded America's political culture in the eighteenth century, a precept that proved highly useful in justifying America's rebellion against England. Yet as the framers of the Constitution would recognize, to state the problem in Lockean terms is by no means to resolve it; for the situation after the Revolution required convincing people not so much to resist political authority by claiming it for themselves but to submit to it by realizing why government was necessary to prevent men from harming one another. If authority "belongs" to everyone in general, it belongs to no one in particular; and neither the state nor the citizen can exclusively claim that which by definition must be shared. Ironically, English writers had responded to Americans before the Revolution by arguing that sovereignty could not be divided between the colonies and the mother country; now the framers of the Constitution were forced to argue that authority could not simply be dispersed among the people themselves apart from the system of checks and balances that would control power. Jefferson believed that because the people were the best guardians of their own liberties all authority should reside in them.

The framers, although agreeing that all governments derive their authority from the people, did not feel they could allow authority to be directly expressed by the people, not only because people will tyrannize over others if left unchecked, but also because the American people were simply too diverse to think and act together in order to articulate a common political will. The framers structured the system of "balanced" and "mixed" government on the reality of social conflict, whereas Jefferson assumed that men's conflicting interests could best be accommodated to the extent that government "governs least" and all men are allowed to subliminate their antagonistic drives by confronting nature and subduing the environment. Here Jefferson desired what Winthrop dreaded, that the spacious American environment would make men less dependent upon one another and less in need of any defined or unifying idea of authority. Thus, embodying ultimate authority in the will of the people was a bold and radical act on Jefferson's part, for henceforth the masses of people could not alienate what was theirs by right of nature. But in democratizing the idea of authority Jefferson succeeded only in unburdening himself of it.

The framers agreed with Jefferson that human society could not be held together through a common acceptance of some theory or principle. Considerably less confident in the people themselves, the framers were even more convinced that power could not be restrained by beliefs, the traditional domain of moral sentiment. And it was the specter of power that haunted the framers when drafting the Constitution, the same specter that haunted the rebels of 1776. Because of their excessive fear of power, the framers were reluctant to locate supreme power either in the people or in any single branch of government. As a consequence, the idea of political authority also suffered a dislocation in the American Constitution, for it was no longer identified, as it had been in English liberal thought, with the nation's representative assembly. The new American republic was the first major experiment in constitutional government that denied the dictum that authority must emanate from a single source. Traditionally it had been assumed that in all forms of government there is and must be a supreme, irresistible, absolute authority in which sovereignty resides. But the framers devised a "federalist" scheme by which certain rights would be reserved to the states to be jealously guarded; and in the central government the three depositories of power—executive, judiciary, and legislative—would be independent of each other and pose a check on each other's tendencies to usurp and dominate. Thus, neither the states nor any single branch of the central government could assert absolute authority.

Neither could the people themselves. The framers' view of human nature, deriving from both the pessimism of Calvinist theology and the skepticism of Hume's philosophy, led them to see man as alienated and hence incapable of exercising authority because he lacked wisdom and virtue. To Madison and Hamilton, the need for government reflected man's fallen state, and in that crippled condition man would be incapable of responding to ideas that appealed to reason or conscience. John Adams explained why government must rest upon mechanisms and structures rather than ideas and principles. "I have been long settled in my opinion," Adams wrote to Jefferson, "that neither Philosophy, nor Religion, nor Morality, nor Wisdom, nor Intellect, will ever govern nations or parties, against their Vanity, Pride, Resentment or Revenge, or their Avarice or Ambition. Nothing but Force and Power and Strength can restrain them." Convinced that morality and religion could no longer supply the basis for authority, Adams concluded that "power must be opposed to power, force to force, strength to strength, interest to interest, as well as reason to reason, eloquence to eloquence, and passion to passion." The framers' solution to human imperfection and the social divisiveness of "factions" was to substitute external controls for internal human qualities in order to disperse power through the institutional means of "checks and balances," juxtaposing men and their respective classes against each other through what has been aptly called "the method of counterpoise."

Did this method resolve the problem of authority? Some political scientists have argued that the framing of the Constitution itself indicated that the founders realized the need for establishing a more centralized authority, and subsequently respect for authority developed out of obedience to the laws of the new nation. Sociologists have also maintained that the early republic's success in economic development, in the evolution of political parties, and in the forging of national unity provided the means by which the American system of government was "legitimized," a process aided by the role of President Washington as a "charismatic leader." But these interpretations on the part of contemporary social scientists need to be judged against the context and perspective of the framers' own thoughts on authority. As advocates of "the new science of politics," *The Federalist* authors saw their role as providing the theories that would stabilize the vicissitudes of power without having to establish the virtues of authority. The founders demonstrated by their very vocabulary that they were less interested in the promises of good authority than in the perils of bad institutions, less concerned about the metaphysics of obligation than the "machinery of government" and the "geometry" of power. At best the framers established what Weber would call "rational-legal" authority, popular acceptance of systems of rules and submission to those in power on the basis of an "impersonal bond," not to leaders and their ideals, but to the functional "duty of office," the mechanisms of government that provided what Madison called "the auxiliary precautions." But *The Federalist* does not identify authority with law itself. "In a nation of philosophers," wrote Madison in *Federalist* number 49, "reverence for the laws would be sufficiently inculcated by the voice of enlightened reason. But a nation of philosophers is as little to be expected as the philosophical race of kings wished for by Plato." Too passionate and interested to listen to the voice of pure reason, incapable of rising to virtue, man has little capacity for obeying any authority that would make claims upon him, particularly the classical idea of political authority that called upon man to subordinate his private interest to the public good. It would not be too inaccurate—or unfair—to suggest that the framers were more concerned to control power than to explain authority.

In one respect the Constitution represented the end of the importance of political ideas and the beginning of what might be called economic realism, if not determinism. For the framers doubted that ideas could obligate moral conduct and influence men to pursue higher ends than mere self-interest. Their whole enterprise rested on the assumption that the only ideas or institutions that men will obey are those that express and protect their interests. Insofar as the idea of "interests" presupposes the wants that exist within men's desires, the framers asked of men only that they know their interests and obey them. Thus the preamble to the Constitution enumerates the purposes of the new government: namely, "to establish justice, insure domestic tranquility, provide for the common defense, promote the general welfare, and secure the blessings of liberty to ourselves and our posterity." These goals would evolve from the citizens' rendering compliance to the Constitution, and the framers did not need to explain why citizens sought to achieve such goals since they were inherent within the nature of man. Here we encounter a dilemma. Insofar as the framers were more concerned about what men would do than what they should do, how did they expect to teach the lessons of authority?

Not, it seems in *The Federalist,* through political means. When comparing that document to Winthrop's sermons, we miss the Christian language of love and affection. Government was not to be an agency of moral education; on the contrary, the framers avoided considering the problem of how to train a public to accept the authority of the good, true, or beautiful. Subjection to these a priori realities, the antecedent verities that are supposedly self-justifying by virtue of their moral essence and spiritual persuasion, is no longer the proper end of government. Unwilling to rest authority on positive conceptions of duty and the ethical life, or even on the "sacred" and "undeniable" truths that are "self-evident" in the Declaration of Independence, the framers drew back from defining and asserting ideal aims that have as their purpose the attempt to shape society and direct man's behavior in accordance with transcendent ends. Accepting man as he is, they defined politics as little more than the pursuit of private interests, and they hoped that social order would emerge from the countervailing balance of these interests not because of the presence of virtuous leaders or obligatory norms but because of the functioning of impersonal devices and mechanical contrivances. In this system, which depended more upon the perpetuation of good machinery than upon the reappearance of good men and ideas, where did authority ultimately lie? Who would teach the self-governed how to govern themselves?

The term *authority* derives, in its original Latin meaning, from the Latin noun *auctoritas,* "authority," and the verb *augere,* "to augment"; and hence it implies, among other things, the capacity of a power to enlarge itself, grow, expand, initiate action, inspire belief, command allegiance, and authorize the rightness of things. It is this capacity that *The Federalist* denies to the people. The framers believed that political authority, although deriving from the consent of the governed, could not be expressed directly through the people because the masses of men, particularly as they acted collectively through "factions," posed a danger to property, liberty, and the interests of minorities. They also believed that the mass citizenry was too divided in its own interests to bring forth a conception of the general good and to engage in the necessary unity of thought and action that would enable sovereign authority to be exercised in one body.

Thus when French political philosophers criticized the American Constitution, wondering why all authority could not be invested in "the people" and represented in a single national assembly, John Adams replied that the people simply do not exist as a unified, coherent reality. And Madison, fearing the rise of "overbearing" popular majorities, advocated schemes of checks and controls wherein members of dominant factions must be made incapable of acting together effectively. Hamilton's solution was to invest "the majesty of national authority" in the independent judiciary, which would mediate between the people and their representatives by assuming the function of interpreting law. Thus, although the framers were reluctant to endow the legislative branch with authority, Hamilton sought to grant it to the Supreme Court primarily because it had, in his words, "neither Force nor Will" and was therefore the "weakest" of the three departments of government. Through this ingenious arrangement the framers managed to separate power from authority, popular will from judicial wisdom; but they also restricted authority to the role of judging law rather than making it. Authority could now speak but it could not act or "augment"; it could passively review matters pertaining to the letter of the Constitution but it could not, theoretically at least, shape the values and customs of the nation by defining the good life, the just state, and the moral society. In America political authority had lost its power to authorize.

Although the framers wanted to subject the direct expression of the popular will to checks and balances, certain developments after the Constitution was established frustrated their designs. For one thing, politics itself became more and more a matter of popular participation as it moved away from the control of established elites and into the hands, if not of the masses themselves, at least those of their representatives. This democratization of political authority would culminate in the Jacksonian era (1828–1840), with the abolition of property qualifications for the franchise in northern states and a new system of party conventions more open to the people. But the issue of where power should lie—with the people or in political institutions deliberately set apart from them—was one that had long divided the Jeffersonians from the Federalists, and nowhere was this issue of the rightful locus of authority more vigorously debated than in the question of the Supreme Court's proper status.

Jefferson, Paine, and other thinkers who had led the rebellion against England continued to fear centralized power in any form. Unlike the Federalists, who wanted to stabilize authority in long-established institutions and precedent, the Jeffersonians rejected the idea that America should be bound by the past, arguing instead that each generation has the right to shape its own institutions. In particular, the Jeffersonians denied the Federalist argument that the Supreme Court possessed the authority to declare acts of Congress unconstitutional. Instead they insisted that the three branches of government—executive, judiciary, and legislative—are equal and coordinate; and that in case of conflict, Congress, being the most representative branch, is entitled to exercise final judgment on the intent and meaning of the Constitution. In *Marbury* v. *Madison* (1803), Chief Justice Marshall ruled that the Supreme Court could declare acts of Congress void, thereby laying the basis for what would later become the doctrine of judicial review.

Yet the locus and residence of political authority in America continued to remain vague, ill-defined, and ultimately unresolved. This problem would be true not only of the three branches of government but even more so of the states and the national government. The dilemmas resulting from the separation of powers among the branches of government and the division of powers between the states and the federal government were usually contested by either affirming or denying the doctrine of judicial review, a theory of ultimate and final authority that was entirely different from the English principle of parliamentary supremacy. In England authority could be safely lodged in the legislative branch, the one institution that could both represent the people and resist the power of the king. In America, with no monarchy to oppose, authority became a political idea without a clearly specified political institution or location; and thus the very sense of sovereignty had become fragmented if not abolished altogether. As a consequence, in the first half of the nineteenth century, America witnessed a continuous struggle between nationalism and federalism, between the idea that sovereign authority resides with the central government and the idea that the states have the final right to judge the constitutionality of congressional legislation.

This protracted dispute first expressed itself in the Kentucky and Virginia Resolutions of 1798 and 1799; then in New England's opposition to President Madison's embargo policies before the War of 1812; subsequently in the states' opposition to the second Bank of the United States, leading to the *McCulloch* v. *Maryland* decision, in which the Court upheld the bank's constitutionality; and most dramatically in South Carolina's doctrine of nullification, denying the constitutionality of a national tariff. When the subject of slavery entered the political arena, the conflict between nationalism and federalism expressed itself first in the Missouri Compromise of 1820, then in the Dred Scott decision of 1857 and the resulting Freeport Doctrine, all involving the question of congressional power over slavery in the western territories; and simultaneously in the prolonged debates over the fugitive slave laws, acts of Congress challenged by some states.

In all of these disputes, whether they concerned slavery, the tariff, or territorial expansion, the contending ideas of national sovereignty and states' rights were exploited by different sections of the country whenever one or the other idea suited the purposes of the North, South, or West. No statesman hesitated to be inconsistent in arguing for either a strict or broad interpretation of the Constitution. Thus South Carolina, for example, protested the idea that the Constitution gave the national government power to enact a tariff; but when the Supreme Court, in representing the supremacy of the national government, interpreted the Constitution as having deliberately excluded black slaves from American citizenship, South Carolina was happy to have the Court lay down the law of the land. Massachusetts similarly shifted its views on the sovereignty of the federal government and the Supreme Court, upholding the principle of national sovereignty on the issue of the tariff, denying it in respect to fugitive slave laws. All these disputes reflected the dilemmas of a political culture without a clearly defined source of political authority. It bears remembering that ultimately the idea of sovereign political authority in America was decided not by political theory, legal reasoning, or ballots but on the bloody battlefields of the Civil War.

That gory climax could easily lead one to conclude that authority actually resides in power, even the brute power of military force. But such a conclusion would obscure the vital distinction between authority and power, between the capacity of a government to exercise its ascendancy based on the consent of its subjects and the capacity of a government simply to impose its will by coercion. In essence the Civil War dramatized the awkward fact that the American republic had

no center of authority, no theory of a sovereign state that could command the allegiance of all Americans. Indeed by the mid-nineteenth century it might be said that the idea of authority had eluded government and political institutions and reemerged in a seemingly new phenomenon that the American political thinker had now to confront—society.

AUTHORITY AS SOCIETY, PUBLIC OPINION, AND POPULAR *MOEURS*

One writer who would see clearly that authority in America could no longer be found in political institutions was Alexis de Tocqueville. "In no country of the world are the pronouncements of the law more categorical than in America," he observed in *Democracy in America,* "and in no other country is the right to enforce it divided among so many hands." Americans are scarcely conscious of their government because it lacks effective, centralized power. In America "authority exists, but one does not know where to find its representatives." Tocqueville sensed the presence of authority in America, but he also knew that Americans remained unconscious of its significance.

The great French thinker found America a curious puzzle that seemed to defy the whole tradition of classical political philosophy. For it was not merely the ubiquitous presence of "equality of condition" in America that intrigued Tocqueville but the conspicuous absence of authority in the familiar institutions of the past. A nation that lacked an established church, crown, aristocracy, army, and centralized government, a people who looked with suspicion on leaders while celebrating the "common man," and a culture that desired to liberate itself from the past in order to reaffirm perpetually what Jefferson had called "the sovereignty of the present generation"—such were the ingredients of a polity that seemed to have deprived itself of those traditions and institutions that assure order and stability.

Yet Tocqueville realized that all societies are governed by some system of authority, whether explicit laws that restrain human behavior through the sanction of external force or implicit cultural norms that do so through the compulsions of internalized values. Where, then, could the source of authority be found in America? For Tocqueville the answer lay in the coercive power of public opinion and the "tyranny of the majority," quiet, invisible forms of "democratic despotism" that created one of the deepest ironies in American life: the illusion of individual freedom and the reality of social repression. Authority had once been a noble idea in political philosophy. In America it had become little more than what people think that other people think. Tocqueville depicted Americans as social beings who, fearing solitude and isolation, could not stand alone and therefore acquiesced to the views of others and allowed their selves to be determined by the conventions of society. Tocqueville made us aware of the punitive power of society, and thus we see how authority functions as the force of conformity.

One of the aims of *Democracy in America* was to demonstrate that English and American thinkers were wrong in assuming that a "balanced" government would preserve liberty and provide the basis for political authority in modern society. Tocqueville observed that if a political environment was actually so marked by conflicting interests, no scheme of checks and balances would be sufficient to hold the social order together. If class conflict really existed in America, as the framers assumed when they sought to counterpoise the interests of the few against the will of the many, America would have broken out in revolution or broken up as a political unit. What explained the stability of America was not its political system, which had been designed to control conflict, but its social environment, which, lacking both an aristocracy and a peasantry, experienced no conflict of class interests because all Americans desired and valued the same material interests. And it was this pursuit of self-interest, which Tocqueville called "virtuous materialism," that provided America with a kind of consensual authority of widely shared values. The upshot is that Tocqueville's conviction, that the nature of society explains the nature of the state, gives America an extrapolitical focus where the issue of authority no longer revolves around the forms of government: "What is meant by a 'republic' in the United States is the slow and quiet action of society upon itself." The actions of society, not the institutions of government, explain the nature of authority in America, and thus we must look not to political ideas but to America's

moeurs: the people's habits, customs, manners, and values.

Tocqueville's thesis that the source of authority lay in opinion, not knowledge, had disturbing implications. The framers believed that the opinions and interests of society were so divisive and faction-ridden that society had to be mastered by a government that could be strong and effective without abusing its powers. But Tocqueville perceived, as did Emerson and Thoreau, that government in America was actually weak and frail and hence could never serve as the fount of authority. What troubled these writers was not the abuses of government but the potential tyranny of society. All three extolled the virtues of individualism and at the same time realized how precarious was the status of that principle in democratic America. For they saw authority drifting away from the once conscious individual to the collective stupor of mass society; and as a result the whole idea of natural rights, the assumption of individual autonomy and freedom that spirited the eighteenth-century Enlightenment, seemed to be collapsing in the face of nineteenth-century social realities. "The idea of rights inherent in certain individuals is rapidly disappearing from the minds of men," wrote Tocqueville; "the idea of the omnipotence and sole authority of society at large rises to fill its place."

Why would the individual surrender his self to the new invisible authority of society? Tocqueville traced the answer to this question to the two principles of American democracy: liberalism and equality. The framers believed that human liberty best flourishes to the extent that the individual retains his independence and pursues his self-interests apart from the state in a diverse society of competing interests and factions, and the federal Constitution was to have made possible this version of what we call today liberal pluralism. Tocqueville saw in liberalism not so much the virtues of pluralism as the perils of collectivism, as the individual loses his strength of character and independence in pursuing the common interests of a society of universal uniformity. Moreover, insofar as liberal individualism asserted the authority of the individual over himself, it liberated man only by abrogating all authority of custom and tradition.

Yet it is only an illusion that authority can be conquered. In a democratic culture the more power is weakened, the more its sphere is widened, until society itself becomes the seat of both power and authority. Similarly, the more the conditions of equality increase, the more people desire to be like each other; and the more they strive to emulate existing mores and customs, the less capable they are of practicing a civic virtue that requires personal involvement in political affairs concerning the commonweal. Thus, in contrast to the founders' conviction that liberty would be sustained by the activities of self-directed individuals in a competitive society, Tocqueville believed that the privatized "pursuit of happiness" would weaken the social body, undermine liberty, and eventually consolidate power and authority in the sovereign state.

Tocqueville specified certain American institutions that could prevent democracy from evolving into despotism—namely law, religion, commerce, and the dynamic energy generated by local voluntary associations. But he also saw the possibility that the solitary individual, cut off from all previous historical associations of family and community, might unconsciously allow the centralization of power to develop and therefore lose his liberty without being aware of it. "The idea of a single power directing all citizens slips naturally into their consciousness without their, so to say, giving the matter a thought." A democratic society offers no guarantee that a democratic people cannot lose their own authority as a natural right, the political right of a people to consent to the exercise of power over themselves. If the founders showed how power could be won from the forces of politics, Tocqueville showed how authority could be lost to the forces of society.

AUTHORITY IN MODERN AMERICA: ITS CONTENTS AND DISCONTENTS

The three ideas of authority that found expression in the seventeenth, eighteenth, and nineteenth centuries—spiritual, political, and social—suffered a curious fate in American intellectual history. Even during Tocqueville's era many writers could hardly entertain the thought of returning to Calvinism, mired as it seemed to be in sin, guilt, and damnation. Nor did the New England transcendentalists look to the political authority of the founders of the republic. Emer-

son and Thoreau believed that America's problems originated in the Constitution itself, which was designed to function without the need for moral men; hence they dismissed the state as a "trick" and politics as "cunning." Nor did they have to be reminded by Tocqueville that the authority of society posed a threat to the individual. Thoreau complained that all institutions "pawed" at him, and Emerson exhorted Americans to practice "self-reliance," a doctrine that would make individual conscience the sovereign voice of authority. And what instructs conscience? The mystical whisperings of "Nature" that are grasped by the intuitive ear and the "transparent eyeball." Whitman summed up in four words the poet's attitude toward authority: "Resist much, obey little."

The Puritan concept of authority not only failed to survive the rebellion of its own children but continued to suffer a bad name at the hands of the debunkers of the early twentieth century. Now everything that was judged ugly and repressive in America was attributed to the Puritan heritage. As Puritanism became identified with authoritarianism, authority as a challenging moral proposition, the ethic of "inwardness," and the imperative of the "good, just, and honest" all but disappeared from historical consciousness. H. L. Mencken wrote the epitaph when he defined Puritanism as the fear that someone, somewhere, sometime might be happy.

The institutionalized form of political authority, first theoretically developed in *The Federalist,* later discovered by Beard and Arthur Bentley, and ultimately termed *pluralism* by political scientists like Robert Dahl and David Truman, also appears to have had an unsteady career. Pre–World War I social philosophers like Lippmann and Herbert Croly rebelled against the notion of politics as merely a "machine process," and earlier Woodrow Wilson had criticized congressional government for having forsaken the duty to lead, educate, and enlighten the public as it became lost in a ceaseless "dance of legislation." Today the study of politics in America has tended to become a "behavioral science" rather than a branch of moral philosophy, and authority is approached by studying the "asymmetrical" relations between individuals or classes.

The sociological theory of authority developed by Tocqueville also had a curious career in American intellectual history. *Democracy in Amer-*

ica itself did not enjoy widespread recognition until after World War II, when writers and scholars pondered its warnings about the threat of "mass society." That authority might be little more than the conforming impulse that characterized the American psyche troubled writers like David Riesman and Lionel Trilling, who wanted to see more of the "inner-directed" person and "the opposing self." The kind of consensual authority that Tocqueville discovered in American *moeurs* never struck American intellectuals as genuine. From Jefferson to the transcendentalists, from Mark Twain to John Dos Passos, the integrity of the self against the pressures of society seemed all that remained to define one's moral character. One merely need read Sinclair Lewis' *Main Street* to discover what happens to human integrity when society is equated with authority.

Rejecting religion, politics, and society, many twentieth-century American intellectuals remained suspicious of authority in any form. As a consequence the idea of authority became the concern mainly of conservative writers: southern agrarians called for a return to "soil" and "tradition," Roman Catholics condemned secularism and called for a return to scholastic theology and "natural law," and neoclassical scholars rejected modernism and called for a return to the ancient principle of "virtue." But these were fugitive voices whose message was scarcely heard in a dominant liberal culture that had fully embraced change and progress. Lippmann once defined liberalism as the overthrow of authority and the search for its substitute. The definition is most telling, for in twentieth-century America, writers and scholars have indeed been searching for a substitute for older ideas of authority. Only three aspects of that search can be mentioned here.

Authority as Organizational Structure and as Psychic Development. In twentieth-century social science many theorists have conceptualized authority as inhering either in the structural principles that explain how an organization functions or in the various capacities of individuals for obedience and submission. In the first and more sociological case, authority is regarded as a "system" whose rationality lies in its structure and whose legitimacy depends upon the efficiency of its operations. The authority of a "system"—indeed any institution or organiza-

tion—can be measured by its power to absorb, integrate, and regulate behavior. In the second and more psychological approach, authority is conceived in either one of the following ways: as an incidence of the cognitive-moral development that enables an individual to discriminate among more legitimate and just expressions of authority; or, in Freudian analysis, as the constraints supplied by the superego, humankind's social conscience, upon man's natural instincts. Thus, although sociology tends to make authority a matter of adaptation to institutional norms, psychology treats it as either an aspect of cognitive-ethical development or the quality of internal relations among an individual's psychic elements.

The Philosophy of Pragmatism, the Methodology of Intelligence, and the Authority of Science. The most searching effort to find a substitute for older ideas of authority may be seen in the philosophy of pragmatism as developed by Charles S. Peirce, William James, and John Dewey. Emerging at the turn of the century, when religious and political ideas of authority were being eclipsed by new discoveries in natural science, pragmatism promised to adopt the methods of science and make philosophy serve the interests of mankind. Dewey especially believed that scientific intelligence would be able to resolve the social problems and political conflicts that older institutions of authority had arbitrated in the past.

Dewey's philosophy enjoyed enormous influence in education and social thought in the first half of the twentieth century. But it is questionable that pragmatism could fill the void left by the decline of older authorities. Where Dewey believed that authority could be collectivized through democratic decision making, the idea of authority had traditionally required a single source of sovereignty. Where Dewey believed that truth derives from everyday experience, classical authority held that truth must transcend the exigencies of experience in order to provide invariant, regulative principles. And where Dewey held that knowledge must wait upon experience, authority was always seen as necessary because it was felt that man needed to know what to do before he acted. In the end pragmatism was a philosophy that convinced Americans what they probably had known all along—that they could live without authority.

AUTHORITY

Culture and the Authority of the Creative Act. An even more emphatic expression of the desire to overthrow authority and find a substitute may be seen in the various cultural rebellions in American history, especially the Greenwich Village revolt of the pre–World War I years and the "Lost Generation" of the 1920's. Many writers who participated in these upheavals had come from devout religious backgrounds where the political values of republican citizenship had been upheld. Having thrown off the starched-collar respectability of their family environment, the young rebels turned to art and poetry, convinced that a painting or text could convey its own truth and authority by virtue of its aesthetic radiance. The literary conceits of creation, expression, and self-authorization led Ezra Pound to declare that the poets should be "the legislators of the world." Some contemporary scholars blame the erosion of authority in America on the modernist writers of the 1920's, who supposedly destroyed all sense of proportion and harmony and denied any reality beyond the creative act. Whether or not the accusation is fair, it does point up the antinomian tendencies in American culture that render formal, traditional authority an alien idea.

Whether the idea of authority can be reconciled with science, modernism, and other secularizing tendencies in contemporary American life is a question that yields no clear answer. The "crisis of authority" today derives from the fact that not only has authority disappeared but no one knows how it can be reconstituted. The most poignant description of the state of the problem comes from the political theorist John H. Schaar:

> Authority is a word on everyone's lips today. The young attack it and the old demand respect for it. Parents have lost it and policemen enforce it. Experts claim it and artists spurn it, while scholars seek it and lawyers cite it. Philosophers reconcile it with liberty and theologians demonstrate its compatibility with conscience. Bureaucrats and politicians pretend to have it and wish they did. Everybody agrees that there is less of it than there used to be. It seems that the matter stands now as a certain Mr. Wildman thought it stood in 1648: "Authority hath been broken into pieces."

BIBLIOGRAPHY

The following bibliography, alphabetically arranged, discusses both sources referred to in the text and a few other works essential to the subject.

Hannah Arendt, *On Revolution* (New York, 1963), is an interpretation of power and authority in early American history written from a classical perspective. Charles A. Beard, *An Economic Interpretation of the Constitution* (1913; repr. New York, 1957), is a controversial thesis that explains, among other things, why, in American history, economic power escaped the controls of political authority. Daniel Bell, *The Cultural Contradictions of Capitalism* (New York, 1976), is a critique of the movements in modern intellectual life that have undermined respect for authority. James M. Cameron, *The Images of Authority* (New Haven, 1966), is an important general introduction to the subject. John P. Diggins and Mark Kann, *The Problem of Authority in America* (Philadelphia, 1982), is an anthology of essays by historians, sociologists, political philosophers, and literary critics. *The Federalist* is the key document of the framers' theoretical reflections. D. H. Lawrence, *Studies in Classic American Literature* (New York, 1923), a discerning, witty treatise, interprets American culture as one continuous flight from authority.

Walter Lippmann, *A Preface to Politics* (New York, 1913), *Public Opinion* (New York, 1924), and *A Preface to Morals* (New York, 1929), are crucial texts by a brilliant writer who spent much of his intellectual life pondering the problem of authority. Seymour Martin Lipset, *The First New Nation* (New York, 1963), considers how authority became "legitimized" in American history in the interpretation of a leading social scientist. Arthur O. Lovejoy, *Reflections on Human Nature* (Baltimore, 1961), is a profound analysis of the Founders' assumptions about human behavior and their "method of counterpoise." Steven Lukes, "Power and Authority," in *A History of Sociological Analysis,* Tom Bottomore and Robert Nisbet, eds. (New York, 1978), is the most comprehensive taxonomical analysis to date. David Minar, *Ideas and Politics: The American Experience* (Homewood, Ill., 1964), is an interpretation that sees authority established rather than evaded.

John H. Schaar, "Legitimacy and the Modern State," in *Power and Community,* Philip Green and Sanford Levinson, eds. (New York, 1970), pp. 276–327, perceptively analyzes how authority is approached in modern social science. Alexis de Tocqueville, *Democracy in America*, trans. George Lawrence (New York, 1969), is indispensable for understanding authority as a social phenomenon. Woodrow Wilson, *Congressional Government* (1885; repr. New York, 1956), is the pioneering treatise on the demise of executive authority. Gordon S. Wood, *The Creation of the American Republic, 1776–1787* (Chapel Hill, N.C., 1969), is the definitive work on the transformation of the idea of authority and sovereignty between the Revolution and the Constitution.

[*See also* AMERICAN REVOLUTION; CIVIL DISOBEDIENCE; CIVIL RIGHTS MOVEMENT; CONGRESS; CONSTITUTION; CONTROL, SUPPRESSION, AND INTIMIDATION; DECLARATION OF INDEPENDENCE; THE FEDERALIST PAPERS; INDIVIDUALISM AND CONFORMITY; JACKSONIAN DEMOCRACY; JEFFERSONIAN DEMOCRACY; JUDICIAL SYSTEM; LABOR MOVEMENT; MACHINE POLITICS; PACIFISM AND PEACE MOVEMENTS; PLURALISM; PRESIDENCY; *and* VOLUNTARY ASSOCIATIONS.]

BILL OF RIGHTS

Leonard W. Levy

THE Bill of Rights consists of the first ten amendments to the Constitution of the United States. Congress submitted those amendments to the states for ratification on 25 September 1789, and the requisite number of state legislatures had ratified them by 15 December 1791. The triumph of individual liberty against government power, as epitomized by the Bill of Rights, is one of our history's noblest and most enduringly important themes. Yet James Madison, justly remembered as the "father" of the Bill of Rights, privately referred on 19 August 1789 to the "nauseous project of amendments." He had proposed the Bill of Rights, in part, because "It will kill the opposition everywhere. . . ." In this attitude lies a suggestion that party politics saturated the making of the first ten amendments. Thomas Jefferson, who must have been profoundly gratified by the ratification of the amendments, which he had urged, was the secretary of state who officially notified the governors of the states that ratification was an accomplished fact; he had the honor, he wrote, of enclosing copies of an act "concerning certain fisheries," another establishing the post office, and "the ratifications by three fourths of the . . . States, of certain articles in addition and amendment of the Constitution. . . ." The history of the Bill of Rights from its rejection by the Constitutional Convention in Philadelphia to its belated ratification is not as passionless, because the omission of a bill of rights in the original Constitution had been the most important obstacle in the way of its adoption by the states.

The omission of a bill of rights was a deliberate act of the Constitutional Convention. The Convention's work was almost done when it received from the Committee on Style copies of the proposed Constitution and the letter by which the Convention would submit it to Congress. The major task that remained was to adopt, engross, and sign the finished document. The weary delegates, after a hot summer's work in Philadelphia, were eager to return home. At that point, on 12 September 1787, George Mason of Virginia remarked that he "wished the plan had been prefaced by a Bill of Rights," because it would "give great quiet" to the people. Mason thought that with the states' bills of rights as models, "a bill might be prepared in a few hours." He made no stirring speech for civil liberties in general or any rights in particular. He did not even argue the need for a bill of rights or move the adoption of one, although he offered to second a motion if one were made. Elbridge Gerry of Massachusetts then moved for a committee to prepare a bill of rights, and Mason seconded the motion. Roger Sherman of Connecticut observed that the rights of the people should be secured if necessary, but because the Constitution did not repeal the bills of rights of the states, the Convention need not do anything. Without further debate the delegates, voting by states, defeated the motion 10–0. Two days later, after the states unanimously defeated a motion by Mason to delete from the Constitution a ban on ex post facto laws by Congress, Charles Pinckney of South Carolina, seconded by Gerry, moved to insert a declaration "that the liberty of the Press should be inviolably observed." Sherman laconically replied, "It is unnecessary. The power of Congress does not extend to the Press," and the motion lost 7–4. Three days later the Convention adjourned.

In the Congress of the Confederation, Richard Henry Lee of Virginia moved that a bill of rights, which he had adapted from his own state's constitution, be added to the federal Constitution. Lee was less interested in the adoption of a bill of rights than in defeating the Constitution. Amendments recommended by Congress required ratification by all the state legislatures, not just nine state ratifying conventions. Lee's motion was defeated, but it showed that, from the start of the ratification controversy, the omission of a bill of rights became an Antifederalist mace with which to smash the Constitution. Its opponents sought to prevent ratification and exaggerated the bill-of-rights issue because it was one with which they could enlist public support. Their prime loyalty belonged to states' rights, not civil rights.

Mason, the author of the celebrated Virginia Declaration of Rights of 1776, soon wrote his influential "Objections to the Constitution," which began, "There is no Declaration of Rights. . . ." The sincerity of Mason's desire for a bill of rights is beyond question, but he had many other reasons for opposing the Constitution. Almost two weeks before, on 12 September, when he raised the issue of a bill of rights, he had declared "that he would sooner chop off his right hand than put it to the Constitution as it now stands." A bill of rights might protect individuals against the national government, but it would not protect the states. He believed that the new government would diminish state powers and by the exercise of its commerce power could "ruin" the southern states; the control of commerce by a mere majority vote of Congress was, to Mason, "an insuperable objection." But the lack of a bill of rights proved to be the most powerful argument against ratification of the Constitution in the Antifederalist armory.

Why did the Constitutional Convention omit a bill of rights? No delegate opposed one in principle. As George Washington informed Lafayette, "there was not a member of the Convention, I believe, who had the least objection to what is contended for by the advocates for a Bill of Rights. . . ." All the framers were civil libertarians as well as experienced politicians who had the confidence of their constituents and the state legislatures that elected them. Even the foremost opponents of ratification praised the make-up of the Convention. Mason himself, for example, wrote that "America has certainly upon this occasion drawn forth her first characters . . . of the purest intentions"; and Patrick Henry, who led the Antifederalists in Virginia, conceded that the

states had trusted the "object of revising the Confederation to the greatest, the best, and most enlightened of our citizens." Their liberality of spirit is suggested by the fact that many —Protestants all and including the entire Virginia delegation—made a point of attending divine service at the Roman Catholic St. Mary's Chapel. As Washington recorded in his diary, "Went to the Romish church to high mass." How could such an "assembly of demigods," as Jefferson called them, neglect the liberties of the people?

On 26 July the Convention had adjourned until 6 August to permit a Committee of Detail to frame a "constitution conformable to the Resolutions passed by the Convention." The committee, consisting of six men including Edmund Randolph of Virginia, James Wilson of Pennsylvania, and Oliver Ellsworth of Connecticut, generously construed its charge by acting as a miniature convention. Introducing a number of significant changes, such as the explicit enumeration of the powers of Congress, the committee, without recommendations from the Convention, decided on a preamble. Randolph left a fragmentary record of the committee's decision that the preamble did not seem a proper place for a philosophic statement of the ends of government because "we are not working on the natural rights of men not yet gathered into society" but upon rights "modified by society and interwoven with what we call . . . the rights of states." According to American revolutionary theory, the natural rights to which Randolph referred were possessed by individuals in the state of nature, which existed before they voluntarily contracted with each other to establish a government in order to secure their rights. In the state of nature, when only the law of nature governed, the theory posited that—as the first section of the Virginia Declaration of Rights stated—"all men are by nature equally free and independent, and have certain inherent rights, of which, when they enter into a state of society, they cannot, by any compact, deprive or divest their posterity; namely, the enjoyment of life and liberty, with the means of acquiring and possessing property, and pursuing and obtaining happiness and safety." The adoption of the state constitutions having ended the state of nature, there was no need to enumerate the rights reserved to the people—or so the framers of the Constitution reasoned.

On the other hand they recognized that the existence of organized society and government required the affirmation of certain rights that did not exist in the state of nature but that served to protect natural rights. Trial by jury, for example, was unknown in the state of nature but necessary for the protection of one's life, liberty, and property. Accordingly the framers recognized a class of rights "modified by society," just as they recognized that the legitimate powers of government that did not belong to the central government of the Union could be called "the rights of the states." The principal task of the Convention was to provide for an effective national government by redistributing the powers of government. Thus the Committee of Detail, when enumerating the powers of Congress, began with the power to tax and the power to regulate commerce among the states and with foreign nations (the two great powers that the Articles of Confederation had withheld from Congress) and ended with an omnibus clause that granted implied powers: "And to make all laws that shall be necessary and proper for carrying into execution the foregoing powers, and all other powers vested, by this Constitution, in the government of the United States, or in any department thereof." That "necessary and proper" clause was the most formidable in the array of national powers, therefore the most controversial, and the one most responsible later for the demand for a bill of rights to ensure that the United States did not violate the rights of the people or of the states.

The Committee of Detail, again on its own initiative, recommended some rights ("modified by society"), among them trial by jury in criminal cases, a tight definition of treason to prevent improper convictions, a ban on titles of nobility (a way of guaranteeing against a privileged class), freedom of speech and debate for members of the legislature, and a guarantee that the citizens of each state should have the same privileges and immunities as citizens in other states. In addition, the committee introduced the clause guaranteeing to each state a republican form of government. In the minds of the framers, many provisions of the Constitution had a libertarian character—the election of public officials, the representative system, the separation of powers among three branches of government, and the requirement that revenue and appropriation measures originate in the House of Representatives, a protection of the natural right to property and a bar against taxation without representation. During the controversy over the ratification of the Constitution, when the omission of a bill of rights was the major issue, many framers argued, as did Hamilton in *The Federalist* number 84, "that the Constitution is itself, in every rational sense, and to every useful purpose, a Bill of Rights."

All the rights recommended by the Committee of Detail eventually found their way into the Constitution, but Charles Pinckney believed that the committee had neglected several others that also deserved constitutional recognition. On 20 August he recommended "sundry propositions," including a guarantee of the writ of habeas corpus, which protected citizens from arbitrary arrest; an injunction that the liberty of the press should be "inviolably preserved"; a ban on maintaining an army in time of peace except with the consent of Congress; an explicit subordination of the military to the civil power; a prohibition on the quartering of troops in private homes during peacetime; and a ban on religious tests as a qualification for any U.S. office.

None of these provisions secured what theoreticians regarded as natural rights. The freedoms of speech and conscience were natural rights, but the liberty of the press was probably distinguishable as a right that did not exist in the state of nature. If liberty of the press was a natural right the Convention acted consistently when voting that its protection was unnecessary. Similarly the ban on religious tests, though protecting the right of conscience, was another example of what Randolph had called a right "modified by society," not preexisting it. Significantly Pinckney had not recommended a protection of freedom of religion or of speech. Without debate or consideration the Convention referred his proposals to the Committee of Detail, but it made no recommendations on any of them.

On the floor of the Convention, Gerry moved that Congress should be denied the power to pass bills of attainder and ex post facto laws. The motion passed with hardly any discussion. Bills of attainder were legislative declarations of the guilt of individuals and legislative imposition of criminal penalties, without the usual judicial proceedings. No instrument of the criminal law was more dreaded or violative of the fair procedures associated with trial by jury than a bill of attainder, the most expeditious way of condemning political opponents. Ex post facto laws in the field of criminal law were nearly as notorious and as unfair, for they were legislative acts that made criminal any conduct that did not constitute a crime at the time committed, or acts that retroactively increased the penalty for a crime or changed the rules of evidence in order to obtain a conviction. With little debate the Convention also placed prohibitions on the power of the states to enact bills of attainder and ex post facto laws. Some delegates, including George Mason, opposed the ban on the latter because they did not wish to limit the power of the states to enact retroactive legislation in civil cases, and they insisted, against the authority of Sir William Blackstone's *Commentaries,* that ex post facto laws included civil legislation as well as criminal. The Supreme Court in 1798 would settle the matter in favor of the Blackstonian interpretation.

Bills of attainder and ex post facto laws, being legislative enactments, came into existence after the people had compacted to form a government. Banning such enactments, therefore, constituted means for the protection of natural rights, but the bans did not protect natural rights as such. The same may be said of protecting the cherished writ of habeas corpus as a device for ensuring the personal liberty of an individual wrongfully imprisoned. After the Convention unanimously adopted the Committee of Detail's recommendation for a clause on trial by jury in criminal cases, Pinckney urged the Convention to secure the benefit of the writ as well, and by a vote of 7–3 a habeas corpus clause was adopted. Pinckney also moved a prohibition on religious tests, which the Convention summarily adopted by unanimous vote. In so doing the Convention demonstrated a rare liberality of spirit, because all the framers but those who represented New York and Virginia came from states that had constitutions discriminating against some religious denominations by imposing as a qualification for public office some religious test. In Pennsylvania, for example, a state having a constitution that contained the broadest guarantee of religious freedom and a provision that no man acknowledging God should be deprived of any civil right on account of his religion, the oath of office required an acknowledgment of the divine inspiration of the New Testament. A Jew from Philadelphia petitioned

the Constitutional Convention not to frame a similar oath of office imposing a civil disability upon him. Unitarians, Deists, and Roman Catholics suffered from various religious disabilities in many states. By prohibiting religious tests the Convention showed a greater regard for religious liberty than most states; yet the Convention did not protect religious liberty itself.

Thus, all the protections written into the Constitution were means of vindicating natural rights, but no natural rights were constitutionally protected. The overwhelming majority of the Convention believed, as Sherman succinctly declared, "It is unnecessary." Why was it unnecessary, given the fact that the Convention recommended a new and powerful national government that could operate directly on individuals? The framers believed that the national government could exercise only enumerated powers or powers necessary to carry out those enumerated, and no provision of the Constitution authorized the government to act on any natural rights. A bill of rights would restrict national powers; but, as Hamilton declared, such a bill would be "dangerous" as well as unnecessary because it "would contain various exceptions to powers not granted and, on this very account, would afford a colorable pretext to claim more than were granted. For why declare that things shall not be done which there is no power to do? Why, for instance, should it be said that the liberty of the press shall not be restrained, when no power is given by which restrictions may be imposed?"

Hamilton expressed a standard Federalist position, echoing other framers and advocates of ratification. Excluding a bill of rights from the Constitution was fundamental to the constitutional theory of the framers. James Wilson, whose influence at the Convention had been second only to that of Madison, led the ratificationist forces in Pennsylvania and several times sought to explain the omission of a bill of rights. The people of the states, he declared, had vested in their governments all powers and rights "which they did not in explicit terms reserve," but the case was different as to a federal government whose authority rested on positive grants of power expressed in the Constitution. For the federal government, "the reverse of the proposition prevails, and everything which is not given, is reserved" to the people or the states. That distinction, Wilson argued, answered those who believed that the omission of a bill of rights was a defect. Its inclusion would have been "absurd," because a bill of rights stipulated the reserved rights of the people, whereas the function of the Constitution was to provide for the existence of the federal government rather than enumerate rights not divested. Like Hamilton and other Federalists, Wilson believed that a formal declaration on freedom of the press or religion, over which Congress had no powers whatsoever, could "imply" that some degree of power had been granted because of the attempt to define its extent. Wilson also insisted on the impossibility of enumerating and reserving all the rights of the people. "A bill of rights annexed to a constitution," he added, "is an enumeration of the powers reserved. If we attempt an enumeration, everything that is not enumerated is presumed to be given. The consequence is, that an imperfect enumeration would throw all implied powers into the scale of the government; and the rights of the people would be rendered incomplete."

Civil liberties, the supporters of the Constitution believed, faced real dangers from the possibility of repressive state action, but that was a matter to be guarded against by state bills of rights. They also argued, inconsistently, that some states had no bills of rights but were as free as those with bills of rights. They were as free because personal liberty, to Federalist theoreticians, depended not on "parchment provisions," which Hamilton called inadequate in "a struggle with public necessity," but on public opinion, an extended republic, a pluralistic society of competing interests, and a free and limited government structured to prevent any interest from becoming an overbearing majority.

The fact that six states had no bills of rights, and that none had a comprehensive list of guarantees, provided the supporters of ratification with the argument, made by Wilson among others, that an imperfect bill of rights was worse than none at all because the omission of some rights might justify their infringement by implying an unintended grant of government power. The record was not reassuring; the states had very imperfect bills of rights, which proved to be ineffective when confronted by "public necessity," and the state governments did in fact abridge rights that had not been explicitly reserved.

Virginia's Declaration of Rights, for example, did not ban bills of attainder. In 1778 the Virginia assembly adopted a bill of attainder and outlawry, drafted by Jefferson at the instigation of Governor Patrick Henry, against a reputed cutthroat Tory, one Josiah Philips, and some fifty unnamed "associates." By legislative enactment they were condemned for treason and murder, and on failure to surrender were subject to being killed by anyone. At the Virginia ratifying convention, Edmund Randolph, irked beyond endurance by Henry's assaults on the Constitution as dangerous to personal liberties, recalled with "horror" the "shocking" attainder. When Henry defended the attainder, John Marshall, who supported ratification without a bill of rights, declared, "Can we pretend to the enjoyment of political freedom or security, when we are told that a man has been, by an act of Assembly, struck out of existence without a trial by jury, without examination, without being confronted with his accusers and witnesses, without the benefits of the law of the land?"

The framers of the Constitution tended to be skeptical about the value of "parchment barriers" against "overbearing majorities," as Madison said. He had seen repeated violations of bills of rights in every state. Experience proved the "inefficacy of a bill of rights to those occasions when its control is most needed," he said. In Virginia, for example, despite an explicit protection of the rights of conscience, the legislature had favored an establishment of religion, which was averted only because Madison turned the tide of opinion against the bill. As realists the framers believed that constitutional protections of rights meant little during times of popular hysteria; any member of the Constitutional Convention could have cited examples of gross abridgments of civil liberties in states that had bills of rights.

Virginia's bill was imperfect not just because it lacked a ban on bills of attainder. The much vaunted Declaration of Rights of Virginia also omitted the freedoms of speech, assembly, and petition; the right to the writ of habeas corpus; the right to grand jury proceedings; the right to counsel; separation of church and state; and freedom from double jeopardy and from ex post facto laws. The rights omitted were as numerous and important as those included. Twelve states, including Vermont, had framed constitutions, and the only right secured by all was trial by jury in criminal cases. Although all protected religious liberty, five either permitted or provided for an establishment of religion. Two states passed over a free press guarantee. Four neglected to ban excessive fines, excessive bail, compulsory self-incrimination, and general search warrants. Five ignored protections for the rights of assembly, petition, counsel, and trial by jury in civil cases. Seven omitted a prohibition of ex post facto laws. Nine failed to provide for grand jury proceedings, and nine failed to condemn bills of attainder. Ten said nothing about freedom of speech, while eleven were silent on double jeopardy. Whether omissions implied a power to violate, they seemed, in Federalist minds, to raise dangers that could be prevented by avoiding an unnecessary problem entirely: omit a bill of rights when forming a federal government of limited powers.

That the framers of the Constitution actually believed their own arguments purporting to justify the omission of a bill of rights is difficult to credit. Some of the points they made were patently absurd, like the insistence that the inclusion of a bill of rights would be dangerous and, on historical grounds, unsuitable. The last point most commonly turned up in the claim that bills of rights were appropriate in England but not in America. Magna Carta, the Petition of Right of 1628, and the Bill of Rights of 1689 had been grants wrested from kings to secure royal assent to certain liberties, and therefore had "no application to constitutions . . . founded upon the power of the people" who surrendered nothing and retained everything. That argument, made in *Federalist* number 84 and by leading ratificationists as sophisticated as Wilson and Oliver Ellsworth of Connecticut, was so porous that it could persuade no one. Excepting Rhode Island and Connecticut, the two corporate colonies that retained their charters (with all royal references deleted), eleven states had framed written constitutions during the Revolution, and seven drew up bills of rights; even the four without such bills inserted in their constitutions provisions normally found in a bill of rights.

To imply that bills of rights were un-American or unnecessary merely because in America the people were the source of all power was unhistorical. Over a period of a century and a half America had become accustomed to the idea that government existed by consent of the governed; that people created government; that they created it by written compact; that the compact constituted fundamental law; that the government must be subject to such limitations as are necessary for the security of the rights of the people; and, usually, that the reserved rights of the people were enumerated in bills of rights. Counting Vermont (an independent republic from 1777 until its admission to the Union in 1791), eight states had bills of rights, notwithstanding any opinion that such bills properly belonged only in a compact between a king and his subjects. The dominant theory in the United States from the time of the Revolution was that the fundamental law limited all branches of the government, not just the crown as in England, where the great liberty documents did not limit the legislative power.

When Randolph for the Committee of Detail alluded to the fact that "we are not working on the natural rights of men not yet gathered into society," he was thinking of the framing of the state constitutions. The constitution of Wilson's state began with an elaborate preamble, the first words of which established the proposition that "all government ought to be instituted . . . to enable the individuals who compose [the commonwealth] to enjoy their natural rights . . ."; this preamble was followed by as comprehensive a "Declaration of the Rights of the Inhabitants" as existed in any state. Yet Wilson repeatedly informed Pennsylvania's ratifying convention that rights and liberties could be claimed only in a contract between king and subjects, not when "the fee simple of freedom and government is declared to be in the people." Governor Randolph at the Virginia ratifying convention merely exaggerated when claiming that the Virginia Declaration of Rights "has never secured us against any danger; it has been repeatedly disregarded and violated." But Randolph's rhetoric became unpardonable when he declared that although a bill of rights to limit the king's prerogative made sense in England, "Our situation is radically different from that of the people of England. What have we to do with bills of rights? . . . A bill of rights, therefore, accurately speaking, is quite useless, if not dangerous to a republic." But at the Constitutional Convention Randolph had been able to distinguish natural rights from some rights modified by society.

That supporters of the Constitution could ask, "What have we to do with a bill of rights?" suggests that they had made a colossal error of judgment, which they compounded by refusing to admit it. Their single-minded purpose of creating an effective national government had exhausted their energies and good sense, and when they found themselves on the defensive, accused of threatening the liberties of the people, their frayed nerves led them into indefensible positions. Any Antifederalist could have answered Randolph's question, Wilson's speeches, or Hamilton's number 84, and many did so capably without resorting to Patrick Henry's grating hysteria. "Centinel," who answered Wilson in a Philadelphia newspaper, declared that the explanation for the omission of a bill of rights "is an insult on the understanding of the people."

Abroad, two wise Americans serving their country in diplomatic missions coolly appraised the proposed Constitution without the obligation of having to support a party line. John Adams, having received a copy of the document in London, wrote a short letter to Jefferson in Paris. The Constitution seemed "admirably calculated to preserve the Union," Adams thought, and he hoped it would be ratified with amendments adopted later. "What think you," he asked, "of a Declaration of Rights? Should not such a Thing have preceded the Model?" Jefferson, in his first letter to Madison on the subject of the Constitution, began with praise but ended with what he did not like: "First the omission of a bill of rights. . . ." After listing rights he thought deserved special protection, starting with freedom of religion and of the press, Jefferson dismissed as campaign rhetoric Wilson's justification for the omission of a bill of rights and concluded, "Let me add that a bill of rights is what the people are entitled to against every government on earth, general or particular, and what no just government should refuse, or rest on inference."

Adams and Jefferson in Europe were much closer to popular opinion than the framers of the Constitution, who had worked secretly for almost four months and, with their supporters, became locked into a position that defied logic and experience. During the ratification controversy, some Federalists argued that the Constitution protected basic rights, exposing them to the reply that they had omitted the liberty of the press, religious freedom, security against general warrants, trial by jury in civil cases, and other basic rights. If the framers intended to protect only the rights arising from the existence of society and government and unknown in a state of nature, they were inconsistent. In the first place they protected only some of the non-natural rights; the first ten amendments are crowded with such rights, which the framers neglected. Second, any reader of John Locke would realize that the clause in Article I, section 10, prohibiting the states from impairing the obligation of contracts, protected a natural right. At the close of chapter two of *The Second Treatise of Government,* Locke wrote that the "promises and bargains" between two men on a desert island or between a Swiss and an Indian in the woods of America "are binding to them, though they are perfectly in a state of nature to one another. . . ." Oddly, the Convention had failed to adopt the contract clause when it was proposed; the Committee on Style inserted it into the Constitution, and the Convention, without discussion, agreed to the clause in its closing days. The inclusion of one natural right raises the question of why all others were excluded. The contract clause operates only against state infringement, raising the additional question of why the Convention failed to include a comparable prohibition on the United States.

Natural rights, in accordance with American theory and experience, required protection in any government made by compact. At the Convention, Madison declared that the delegates had assembled to frame "a compact by which an authority was created paramount to the parties, and making laws for the government of them." Some of the states, when formally ratifying the Constitution, considered themselves to be "entering into an explicit and solemn compact," as Massachusetts declared. During the ratification controversy, publicists on both sides referred to the Constitution as a compact. Chief Justice John Jay, who had been one of the authors of *The Federalist,* observed in *Chisholm* v. *Georgia* (1793) that "the Constitution of the United States is . . . a compact made by the people of the United States in order to govern themselves."

The new compact created a government whose powers seemed intimidating. Article VI, declaring the Constitution, laws made in its pursuance, and treaties of the United States to be the supreme law of the land, anything in the state constitutions to the contrary notwithstanding, seemed to many Antifederalists as superseding their state bills of rights and authorizing laws "repugnant to every article of your rights," as "The Impartial Examiner" wrote. Most believed that enumerated powers could be abused at the expense of fundamental liberties. Congress's power to tax, for example, might be aimed at the press and was thus, in the words of Richard Henry Lee, "a power to destroy or restrain the freedom of it." Others feared that taxes might be exacted from the people for the support of a religious denomination. Tax collectors, unrestrained by a ban on general warrants, Patrick Henry argued, might invade homes "and search, ransack, and measure, every thing you eat, drink, and wear."

The necessary-and-proper clause particularly enraged advocates of a bill of rights. They saw that clause as the source of undefined and unlimited powers to aggrandize the national government and victimize the people, unless, as "An Old Whig" declared, "we had a bill of rights to which we might appeal." "A Democratic Federalist" wrote, "I lay it down as a general rule that wherever the powers of government extend to the lives, the persons, and properties of the subject, all their rights ought to be clearly and expressly defined, otherwise they have but a poor security for their liberties." Henry warned that Congress might "extort a confession by the use of torture" in order to convict a violator of federal law. Numerous opponents of ratification contended that Congress could define as crimes the violation of any laws it might legitimately enact, and lacking a bill of rights, accused persons might be deprived of the rights to counsel, to indictment, to cross-examine witnesses against them, to produce evidence in their own behalf, to be free from compulsory self-incrimination, to be protected against double jeopardy or excessive bail, to be exempt from excessive fines or cruel and unusual punishments, and to enjoy other rights traditionally belonging to accused persons. Such an argument was invariably advanced as one among many refuting the Federalist claim that a bill of rights was unnecessary.

If it was unnecessary, Antifederalists asked, why did the Constitution protect some rights? The protection of some opened the Federalists to devastating rebuttal. They claimed that because no bill of rights could be complete, the omission of any particular right might imply a power to abridge it as unworthy of respect by the government. That argument, in effect that to include some would exclude all others, boomeranged. The protection of trial by jury in criminal cases, the bans on religious tests, ex post facto laws, and bills of attainder, the narrow definition of treason, and the provision for the writ of habeas corpus, by the Federalists' own reasoning, were turned against them. Robert Whitehall, answering Wilson on the floor of the Pennsylvania ratifying convention, noted that the writ of habeas corpus and trial by jury had been expressly reserved and in vain called on Wilson to reconcile the reservation with his "favorite proposition." "For, if there was danger in the attempt to enumerate the liberties of the people," Whitehall explained, "lest it should prove imperfect and defective, how happens it, that in the instances I have mentioned, that danger has been incurred? Have the people no other rights worth their attention, or is it to be inferred, agreeable to the maxim of our opponents, that every other right is abandoned?" Stipulating a right, he concluded, destroyed the "argument of danger." Surely, Antifederalists said, their opponents might think of some rights in addition to those protected. The ban on religious tests could have reminded them of freedom of religion. Did not its omission, by their reasoning, necessarily mean that the government could attack freedom of religion?

Henry cleverly observed that the "fair implication" of the Federalist argument against a bill of rights was that the government could do anything not forbidden by the Constitution. Because the provision on the writ of habeas corpus allowed its suspension when the public safety required, Henry reasoned, "It results clearly that, if it had not said so, they could suspend it in all cases whatsoever. It reverses the position of the friends of this Constitution, that every thing is retained which is not given up; for, instead of this, every thing is given up which is not expressly reserved." In his influential *Letters of a Federal Farmer,* Lee observed that a clause of the Constitution prohibited Congress from granting titles of nobility. If the clause had been omitted, he wondered whether Congress would have the power to grant such titles and concluded that it would not under any provision of the Constitution. "Why then by a negative clause, restrain congress from doing what it had no power to do? This clause, then, must have no meaning, or imply, that were it omitted, congress would have the power in question . . . on the principle that congress possesses the powers not expressly reserved." Lee objected to leaving the rights of the people to "logical inferences," because Federalist principles led to the implication that all the rights not mentioned in the Constitution were intended to be relinquished.

Far from being dangerous, a bill of rights, as "A Federal Republican" stated in answer to Wilson, "could do no harm, but might do much good." Lee, discoursing on the good it might do, observed that having a bill of rights assisted popular "education," because it taught "truths" upon which freedom depends and which the people must believe as "sacred." James Winthrop of Massachusetts, writing as "Agrippa," explained another positive value of a bill of rights: it "serves to secure the minority against the usurpations and tyranny of the majority." History, he wrote, proved the "prevalence of a disposition to use power wantonly. It [a bill of rights] is therefore as necessary to defend an individual against the majority in a republick as against the king in a monarchy."

In sum, the usually masterful politicians who had dominated the Convention had blundered by botching constitutional theory and making a serious political error. Their arguments justifying the omission of a bill of rights were impolitic and unconvincing. Mason's point that a bill of rights would quiet the fears of the people was unanswerable. Alienating him and the many who agreed with him was bad politics and handed to the opposition a stirring cause around which they could muster sentiment against ratification. The single issue that united Antifederalists throughout the country was the lack of a bill of rights. No rational argument—and the lack of a bill of rights created an intensely emotional issue because people believed that their liberties were at stake—could possibly allay the fears generated by demagogues like Henry and principled opponents of ratification like Mason. Washington believed that even Mason's "Objections" were meant "to alarm the people." And, when Antifederalists in New York demanded a bill of rights, Hamilton alleged, "It is the plan of men of this stamp to frighten the people with ideal

bugbears, in order to mould them to their own purposes. The unceasing cry of these designing croakers is, My friends, your liberty is invaded!" The Antifederalists capitalized on the Federalist blunder, hoping to defeat the Constitution or get a second convention that would revise it in order to hamstring the national government.

In Pennsylvania, the second state to ratify, the minority demanded a comprehensive bill of rights similar to that in their state constitution. Massachusetts, the sixth state to ratify, was the first to do so with recommended amendments. Only two of the recommended amendments, dealing with jury trial in civil suits and grand jury indictment, belonged in a bill of rights. Supporters of the Constitution in Massachusetts had withdrawn a proposed bill of rights on the supposition that Antifederalists would use it as proof that the Constitution endangered liberty. Maryland too would have recommended a bill of rights, but the Federalist majority jettisoned it when the Antifederalists tried to insert curbs on national powers to tax and regulate commerce. Nevertheless, Federalists grudgingly accepted ratification with recommended amendments to ward off conditional ratification or the defeat of the Constitution. New Hampshire, whose approval as the ninth state made ratification an accomplished fact, urged a comprehensive bill of rights for adoption by amendments after the new government went into operation. Virginia and New York, whose ratification was politically indispensable, followed suit. North Carolina was the fourth state to ratify with a model bill of rights among its recommendations. But the states also recommended crippling restrictions on delegated powers.

Thus, the Constitution was ratified only because crucial states, where ratification had been in doubt, were willing to accept the promise of a bill of rights in the form of subsequent amendments to the Constitution. State recommendations for amendments, including those of the Pennsylvania minority, received nationwide publicity, adding to the clamor for a bill of rights. Every right that became part of the first ten amendments was included in state recommendations except the clause in the Fifth Amendment requiring just compensation for private property taken for public use.

James Madison was one of the Federalists who finally realized that statecraft and political expediency dictated a switch in position. At the Virginia ratifying convention in June 1788 Madison had upheld the usual Federalist arguments for the omission of a bill of rights but finally voted to recommend such a bill in order to avoid previous amendments. He later conceded that the Constitution would have been defeated without a pledge from its supporters to back subsequent amendments. In Virginia, Madison's own political position deteriorated because he had opposed a bill of rights. The Antifederalists, who controlled the state legislature, elected two of their own, Richard Henry Lee and William Grayson, as the state's first United States senators. Madison faced a tough contest for election to the House of Representatives, and he feared that the Antifederalists might succeed in their call for a second constitutional convention. He needed to clarify his position on a bill of rights.

Although Madison had periodically apprised Jefferson, in Paris, on ratification developments, he had not answered Jefferson's letter of December 1787 supporting a bill of rights. On 17 October 1788, the eve of his campaign for a House seat, Madison faced the issue. He favored a bill of rights, he wrote, but had "never thought the omission a material defect" and was not "anxious to supply it even by subsequent amendments"; he did not even think the matter important. Still agreeing with Wilson that the delegated powers did not extend to reserved rights, Madison also worried about the difficulty of adequately protecting the most important rights; experience proved that a bill of rights was a mere parchment barrier when most needed. Government, after all, was the instrument of the majority, which could endanger liberty. "What use then . . . can a bill of rights serve in popular Governments?" Its political truths, he conceded by way of answer, could educate the people, thereby inhibiting majority impulses.

Jefferson's reply of 15 March 1789 had a profound influence on Madison, as Madison's great speech of 8 June would show. An argument for a bill of rights that Madison had omitted, wrote Jefferson, was "the legal check which it puts into the hands of the judiciary." Jefferson believed that an independent court could withstand oppressive majority impulses by holding unconstitutional any acts violating a bill of rights. The point was not new to Madison, for he himself, when defending a ban on ex post facto laws at the Constitutional Convention, had declared

that it would "oblige the Judges to declare [retrospective] interferences null and void." As for the point that the delegated powers did not reach the reserved rights of the people, Jefferson answered that because the Constitution protected some rights but ignored others, it raised implications against them, making a bill of rights "necessary by way of supplement." Moreover, he added, the Constitution "forms us into one state as to certain objects," requiring a bill of rights to guard against abuses of power. As for the point that a bill of rights could not be perfect, Jefferson replied with the adage that half a loaf is better than none; even if all rights could not be secured, "let us secure what we can." Madison had also argued that the limited powers of the federal government and the jealousy of the states afforded enough security, to which Jefferson answered that a bill of rights "will be the text whereby to try all the acts of the federal government." The argument that a bill of rights was inconvenient and not always efficacious did not impress Jefferson. Sometimes, he replied, it was effective, and if it inconveniently cramped the government, the effect was short-lived and remediable, whereas the inconveniences of not having a bill of rights could be "permanent, afflicting, and irreparable." Legislative tyranny, Jefferson explained, would be a formidable dread for a long time, and executive tyranny would likely follow.

Jefferson's arguments, however persuasive, would have been unproductive but for the dangerous political situation, which Madison meant to ameliorate. Four states, including his own and New York, had called for a second convention, whose purpose, Madison feared, would be to "mutilate the system," especially as to the power to tax. Omitting it "will be fatal" to the new federal government. Madison correctly believed that many Antifederalists favored an effective Union on condition that a bill of rights bridled the new government. His strategy was to win them over by persuading the first Congress to adopt protections of civil liberties, thereby alleviating the public's anxieties, providing popularity and stability for the government, and isolating those Antifederalists whose foremost objective was "subverting the fabric . . . if not the Union itself."

In the first Congress, Representative Madison sought to fulfill his pledge of subsequent amendments. His accomplishment in the face of opposition and apathy entitles him to be remembered as "father of the Bill of Rights" even more than as "father of the Constitution." Many Federalists thought that the House had more important tasks, like the passage of tonnage duties and a judiciary bill. The opposition party, which had previously exploited the lack of a bill of rights in the Constitution, realized that its adoption would sink the movement for a second convention and make unlikely any additional amendments that would cripple the substantive powers of the government. They had used the bill-of-rights issue as a smokescreen for objections to the Constitution that could not be dramatically popularized, and now they sought to scuttle Madison's proposals. They began by stalling, then tried to annex amendments aggrandizing state powers, and finally depreciated the importance of the very protections of individual liberty that they had formerly demanded as a guarantee against impending tyranny. Madison meant to prove that the new government was a friend of liberty; he also understood that his amendments, if adopted, would thwart the passage of proposals aggrandizing state powers and diminishing national ones. He would not be put off; he was insistent, compelling, unyielding, and, finally, triumphant.

On 8 June 1789 he made his long, memorable speech before an apathetic House, introducing amendments culled mainly from state constitutions and state ratifying convention proposals, especially Virginia's. All power, he argued, is subject to abuse and should be guarded against by constitutionally securing "the great rights of mankind." The government had only limited powers, but it might, unless prohibited, abuse its discretion as to its choice of means under the necessary-and-proper clause; it might, for example, use general warrants in the enforcement of its revenue laws. In Britain, bills of rights merely erected barriers against the powers of the crown, leaving the powers of Parliament "altogether indefinite," and the British constitution left unguarded the "choicest" rights of the press and of conscience. The great objective he had in mind, Madison declared, was to limit the powers of government, thus preventing legislative as well as executive abuse, and above all preventing abuses of power by "the body of the people, operating by the majority against the minority." Mere "paper barriers" might fail, but they raised a standard that might educate the majority against acts to which they might be inclined.

To the argument that a bill of rights was not necessary because the states constitutionally protected freedom, Madison had two responses. One was that some states had no bills of rights, others "very defective ones," and the states constituted a greater danger to liberty than the new national government. The other was that the Constitution should, therefore, include an amendment, that "No State shall violate the equal rights of conscience, or the freedom of the press, or the trial by jury in criminal cases." This, Madison declared, was "the most valuable amendment in the whole list." To the contention that an enumeration of rights would disparage those not protected, Madison replied that the danger could be guarded against by adopting a proposal of his composition that became the Ninth Amendment. If his amendments were "incorporated" into the Constitution, Madison said, using another argument borrowed from Jefferson, "independent tribunals of justice will consider themselves in a peculiar manner the guardians of those rights; they will be an impenetrable bulwark against every assumption of power in the legislative or executive; they will be naturally led to resist every encroachment upon rights expressly stipulated for in the constitution."

Although many Federalists preferred to give the new government time to operate before amending the Constitution, supporters of Madison exulted, largely for political reasons. Hugh Williamson of North Carolina, a signer of the Constitution, informed Madison that the Antifederalists of that state did not really want a bill of rights; William R. Davie, who had been Williamson's colleague in the Convention, gleefully reported to Madison that his amendments had "confounded the Anties exceedingly. . . ." Edmund Pendleton of Virginia wrote of Madison's amendments that "nothing was further from the wish of some, who covered their Opposition to the Government under the masque of incommon zeal for amendments. . . ." Tench Coxe of Pennsylvania praised Madison for having stripped the Constitution's opponents of every rationale "and most of the popular arguments they have heretofore used."

Notwithstanding the support of correspondents, Madison's speech stirred no immediate support in Congress. Indeed, every speaker who followed him, regardless of party affiliation, either opposed a bill of rights or believed that the House should attend to far more important duties. Six weeks later Madison "begged" for a consideration of his amendments, but the House assigned them to a special committee instead of debating them. That committee, which included Madison, reported in a week. It added freedom of speech to the rights protected against state abridgment, deleted Madison's reference to no "unreasonable searches and seizures," made some stylistic revisions, but otherwise recommended the amendments substantially as he had proposed them. The committee's report was tabled, impelling Madison on 3 August to implore its consideration.

On 13 August the House finally began to consider the reported amendments, and in the course of debate it made some significant changes. Madison had proposed to "incorporate" the amendments within the text of the Constitution at appropriate points. He did not recommend their adoption as a separate "bill of rights," although he had referred to them collectively by that phrase. Members objected that to incorporate the amendments would give the impression that the framers of the Constitution had signed a document that included provisions not of their composition. Another argument for lumping the amendments together was that the matter of form was so "trifling" that the House should not squander its time debating the placement of the various amendments. Ironically, Roger Sherman, who still believed that the amendments were unnecessary, deserves the credit for insistently arguing that they should be appended as a supplement to the Constitution instead of being interspersed within it. Thus, what became the Bill of Rights achieved its significant collective form over the objections of its foremost proponent, Madison, and because of the desire of its opponents in both parties to downgrade its importance.

The House recast the free exercise of religion clause and its allied clause banning establishments of religion, improving Madison's original language. The House also confined to criminal cases Madison's broad phrasing that no person should be compelled to give evidence against himself. On the other hand the House restored the extremely important principle against unreasonable searches and seizures, dropped by the committee. In another major decision the House decisively defeated Gerry's motion, for the Antifederalists, to consider not just the committee's report but all amendments that the several states had proposed; the Antifederalists thus failed to intrude crippling political amendments. Finally the House added "or to the people" in the recommendation by Madison that the powers not delegated to the United States be reserved to the states. On the whole the House adopted Madison's amendments with few significant alterations during the course of its ten-day debate on the Bill of Rights.

In the midst of that debate Madison wrote a letter to a fellow Federalist explaining why he was so committed to "the nauseous project of amendments" that some of the party supported reluctantly. Protecting essential rights was "not improper," he coolly explained, and could be of some influence for good. He also felt honor-bound to redeem a campaign pledge to his constituents, mindful that the Constitution "would have been *certainly* rejected" by Virginia without assurances from its supporters to seek subsequent amendments. Politics, moreover, made proposing the amendments a necessity to beat the Antifederalists at their own game. If Federalists did not support the amendments, Antifederalists would claim that they had been right all along and gain support for a second convention. And, Madison wrote, the amendments "will kill the opposition everywhere, and by putting an end to disaffection to the Government itself, enable the administration to venture on measures not otherwise safe."

Madison had, in fact, upstaged and defeated the Antifederalists. That is why Congressman Aedanus Burke of South Carolina cried sour grapes. During the debate on what would become the First Amendment, he argued that the proposals before the House were "not those solid and substantial amendments which the people expect; they are little better than whip-syllabub, frothy and full of wind . . . . Upon the whole, I think . . . we have done nothing but lose our time, and that it will be better to drop the subject now, and proceed to the organization of the Government." The private correspondence of Senators Lee and Grayson of Virginia reveals the explanation for the attitude of their party toward a bill of rights. A few days after Madison had introduced his amendments, Grayson complained to his mentor Patrick Henry that the Federalists meant to enact "amendments which shall effect [sic] personal liberty alone, leaving the great points of the Judiciary, direct taxation, &c, to stand as they are." Lee and Grayson had failed in their effort to have the Senate amend the House's proposals by adopting the Virginia ratifying convention's recommendations on direct taxation and the treaty and commerce powers. Lee then regretted the original Antifederalist strategy of opposing the Constitution unless revised by the addition of a bill of rights and other amendments. He sorrowfully informed Henry that "the idea of subsequent amendments, was little better than putting oneself to death first, in expectation that the doctor, who wished our destruction, would afterwards restore us to life." Later, after the Senate had approved the amendments that became the Bill of Rights, Grayson reported, "they are good for nothing, and I believe, as many others do, that they will do more harm than benefit."

The Senate, which kept no record of its debates, had deliberated on seventeen amendments submitted by the House. One the Senate killed, the proposal Madison thought "the most valuable": protection against state infringement of speech, press, religion, or trial by jury. The motion to adopt failed to receive the necessary two-thirds vote, although by what margin is unknown. The Senate also weakened the House's ban on establishments of religion. Otherwise the Senate accepted the House proposals, although the Senate combined several, reducing the total number from seventeen to twelve. The first of the twelve dealt with the relation of population to the number of representatives from each state, and the second would have prevented any law going into effect that would have increased the salaries of members of Congress until after the next election.

The House adamantly refused to accept the Senate's version of its ban on establishments. A conference committee of both houses met to resolve differences. The committee, which included Madison, accepted the House's ban on establishments but otherwise accepted the Senate's version. On 24 September 1789 the House voted for the committee report; on the following day the Senate concurred, and the twelve amendments were submitted to the states for ratification.

Within six months nine states ratified the Bill of Rights, although of the twelve amendments submitted for approval, the first and second were rejected. The four recalcitrant states by mid-1790 were Virginia, Massachusetts, Connecticut, and Georgia. The admission of Vermont to the Union made necessary the ratification by eleven states. Connecticut and Georgia refused to ratify. Georgia's position was that amendments were superfluous until experience under the Constitution proved a need. Connecticut believed that any suggestion that the Constitution was not perfect would add to the strength of Antifederalism.

In Massachusetts, Federalist apathy to the Bill of Rights was grounded on a satisfaction with the Constitution as it was, and the Antifederalists were more interested in amendments that would strengthen the states at the expense of the national government. Nevertheless the Massachusetts lower house adopted all but the first, second, and twelfth amendments, and the upper house adopted all but the first, second, and tenth. Thus both houses of the Massachusetts legislature actually approved what became the First through Seventh Amendments and the Ninth; but a special committee, dominated by Antifederalists, urged that all amendments recommended by Massachusetts should be adopted before the state concurred in any amendments. As a result the two houses never passed a bill promulgating ratification of eight amendments. Jefferson, the secretary of state, believed that Massachusetts, "having been the 10th state which has ratified, makes up the threefourth [sic] of the legislatures whose ratification was to suffice." He wrote to a Massachusetts official, asking for clarification. The reply was, "It does not appear that the Committee ever reported any bill." In 1939, Massachusetts joined Connecticut and Georgia when they belatedly ratified on the sesquicentennial anniversary of the Constitution.

Ratification of the Bill of Rights by Vermont, in November 1789, left Virginia the last state to act. Its ratification as the eleventh state was indispensable, although the hostility of its Antifederalist leaders presaged a doubtful outcome. Senators Grayson and Lee reported to the Virginia legislature that they transmitted the recommended amendments "with grief." They still hoped for a new constitutional convention that

BILL OF RIGHTS

would devise "real and substantial Amendments" to "secure against the annihilation of the state governments. . . ." Patrick Henry vainly moved to postpone consideration of the Bill of Rights. The victims of a dilemma of their own making, the Antifederalists then sought to sabotage the Bill of Rights and finally, after delaying ratification for nearly two years, irresolutely acquiesced. The Federalists of Virginia, however, eagerly supported the Bill of Rights in the knowledge that its adoption would appease public fears and stymie the amendments supported by the Antifederalists. Virginia's lower house, controlled by the Federalists, acted quickly, but the opposition dominated the state senate. Not all Antifederalists were implacably opposed. Some respected George Mason's opinion. When he had first heard of Madison's amendments he called them "Milk and Water Propositions," not "important & substantial Amendments"; but Mason changed his mind, saying that they gave "much satisfaction," although he still wanted other amendments, including one that prevented commercial regulations by mere majority vote of Congress. Virginia's senate, as Edmund Randolph reported to Washington, postponed consideration of the amendments, "for a majority is unfriendly to the government." As a member of the lower house reported to Madison, the senate inclined to reject the Bill of Rights, not because of opposition to its guarantees, but from an apprehension "that the adoption of them at this time will be an obstacle to the chief object of their pursuit, the amendment on the subject of direct taxation." For that reason, Randolph reported to Washington, the Federalists meant to "push" the Bill of Rights; passage would "discountenance any future importunities for amendments."

Virginia's senate at the close of 1789 rejected what became the First, Sixth, Ninth, and Tenth Amendments, at least until the next session, thereby allowing time for the electorate to express itself. The Antifederalists still hoped to drum up support for "radical" amendments, as Lee called them. The senators in the majority also issued a statement grossly misrepresenting the First Amendment (then the third). Madison confidently expected that this Antifederalist tactic would backfire, and it did. For the senators' statement was not only inaccurate on its face; it came from men who with a single exception did

not go before the electorate with clean hands. Like Henry and Lee, who planned the senators' statement, the senators had records of having voted against religious liberty and in favor of compulsory taxes for the support of religion. By contrast Madison had led the fight in Virginia against a state establishment of religion and for religious liberty, and his supporters in the Virginia senate had aided him. In the end Madison's confidence proved justified. Jefferson made his influence felt on behalf of the Bill of Rights, and the Antifederalists grudgingly gave ground before public opinion. On 15 December 1791, after two years of procrastination, the senate finally ratified without record vote, thereby completing the process of state ratification and making the Bill of Rights part of the Constitution.

The history of the framing and ratification of the Bill of Rights indicates slight passion on the part of anyone to enshrine personal liberties in the fundamental law of the land. We know almost nothing about what the state legislatures thought concerning the meanings of the various amendments, and the press was perfunctory in its reports, if not altogether silent. But for Madison's persistence the amendments would have died in Congress. Our precious Bill of Rights, at least in its immediate background, resulted from the reluctant necessity of certain Federalists to capitalize on a cause that had been originated, in vain, by the Antifederalists for ulterior purposes. The party that had first opposed the Bill of Rights inadvertently wound up with the responsibility for its framing and ratification, whereas the party that had at first professedly wanted it discovered too late that it was not only embarrassing but disastrous for those ulterior purposes. The Bill of Rights had a great healing effect, however; it did, as Mason originally proposed, "give great quiet" to people. The opposition to the Constitution, Jefferson informed Lafayette, "almost totally disappeared," as Antifederalist leaders lost "almost all their followers." The people of the United States had possessed the good sense, nourished by traditions of freedom, to support the Constitution and the Bill of Rights.

The traditions that gave shape and substance to the Bill of Rights had English roots; but a unique American experience colored that shape and substance. "We began with freedom," as Emerson wrote in "The Fortune of the Repub-

117

lic." The first charter of Virginia contained a provision that the colonists and their descendants "shall have and enjoy all Liberties, Franchises, and Immunities . . . as if they had been abiding and born, within this our Realm of England. . . ." Later charters of Virginia contained similar clauses, which extended to legal rights of land tenure and inheritance, trial by jury, and little else; but the vague language, which was repeated in numerous other charters for colonies from New England to the South, allowed Americans to believe they were entitled to all the rights of Englishmen, their constitutional system, and their common law. American experience with and interpretations of charters eased the way to written constitutions of fundamental law that contained bills of rights.

Freedom was mainly the product of New World conditions, of English legal inheritance, and of the new nation's having skipped a feudal stage. Because of America's postfeudal beginnings, it was unencumbered by oppressions associated with an ancien régime, a rigid class system dominated by a reactionary and hereditary aristocracy, arbitrary government by despotic kings, and a single established church extirpating dissent. Americans were the freest people, therefore the first colonists to rebel. A free people, as Edmund Burke said, can sniff tyranny in a far-off breeze—even if nonexistent. American "radicals" actually believed that the Stamp Act reduced Americans to slavery. They resorted to arms in 1775, the Continental Congress declared, "not to establish new liberties but to defend old ones." In fact they established many new liberties but convinced themselves that those liberties were old. That was an English custom: marching forward into the future facing backward to the past, while adapting old law to changing values. Thus Magna Carta had come to mean indictment by grand jury, trial by jury, and a cluster of related rights of the criminally accused, and Englishmen believed, or made believe, that it was ever so. That habit crossed the Atlantic.

So did the hyperbolic style of expression by a free people outraged by injustice. Thus, James Madison exclaimed that the "diabolical Hell conceived principle of persecution rages," because some Baptist ministers were briefly jailed for unlicensed preaching. By European standards, persecution hardly existed in America, not even in the seventeenth century except on a local and sporadic basis. America never experienced anything like the Inquisition, the fires of Smithfield, the St. Bartholomew's Day Massacre, or the deaths of over 5,000 nonconformist ministers in the jails of Restoration England. Draconian colonial statutes existed but were rarely enforced. Broad libertarian practices were the rule, not the exception.

On any comparative basis civil liberty flourished in America, a fact that intensified the notoriety of exceptional abridgments, such as the hanging of four Quakers in Massachusetts or the prosecution of John Peter Zenger in 1735 for seditious libel. Although a stunted concept of the meaning and scope of freedom of the press existed in America until the Jeffersonian reaction to the Sedition Act of 1798, an extraordinary degree of freedom of the press existed in practice in America as in England. Criticism of the government, especially of the popular assemblies, was dangerous. If Zenger, the printer of the *New-York Weekly Journal,* had attacked the assembly instead of the royal governor, he would have been summarily convicted at the bar of the house, jailed, and forgotten. But Zenger was an instrument of the popular party against a detested administration, and so the jury, stirred by an eloquent lawyer, returned a popular verdict of not guilty, against the instructions of the court. The law, as laid down by the court, incidentally, was correct and remained the law, despite the verdict. Zenger's case was one of only a very few prosecutions by "royal judges" for seditious libel, and almost the last of its kind; prosecutions by governor and council or by the assemblies were a greater threat to a free press. When Alexander McDougall, a "Son of Liberty," assailed the New York assembly, it instigated a prosecution against him for seditious libel, jailed him when he refused to post excessive bail, and when the case against him collapsed because of the death of the star witness for the prosecution, arrested and convicted him for libeling the house. Despite that 1770 case, the American press remained extraordinarily free except for the suppression of Tory opinion during the Revolution.

The predominance of the social compact theory in American thought reflected a condition of freedom and, like the experience with charters, contributed to the belief in written bills of rights. The social compact theory hypothesized a pre-political state of nature in which people were governed only by the laws of nature, free of human restraints. From the premise that man was born free, the deduction followed that he came into the world with God-given or natural rights. Born without the restraint of human laws, he had a right to possess liberty and to work for his own property. Born naked and stationless, he had a right to equality. Born with certain instincts and needs, he had a right to satisfy them—a right to the pursuit of happiness. These natural rights, as John Dickinson declared in 1766, "are created in us by the decrees of Providence, which establish the laws of our nature. They are born with us; exist with us; and cannot be taken from us by any human power without taking our lives." When people left the state of nature and compacted for government, the need to secure their rights motivated them. A half century before John Locke's *Second Treatise of Government,* Thomas Hooker of Connecticut expounded the social compact theory. Over a period of a century and a half, America became accustomed to the idea that government existed by consent of the governed, that the people created the government, that they did it by a written compact, that the compact reserved their natural rights, and that it constituted a fundamental law to which the government was subordinate. Constitutionalism, or the theory of limited government, was in part an outgrowth of the social compact.

In America, political theory and law, as well as religion, taught that government was limited. But Americans took their views on such matters from a highly selective and romanticized image of seventeenth-century England, and they perpetuated it in America even as that England changed. Seventeenth-century England was the England of the great struggle for constitutional liberty by the common law courts and Puritan parliaments against Stuart kings. Seventeenth-century England was the England of Edward Coke, John Lilburne, and John Locke. It was an England in which religion, law, and politics converged to produce limited monarchy and, ironically, parliamentary supremacy. To Americans, Parliament had irrevocably limited itself by

reaffirmations of Magna Carta and passage of the Petition of Right of 1628, the Habeas Corpus Act of 1679, the Bill of Rights of 1689, and the Toleration Act of 1689. Americans learned that a free people are those who live under a government so constitutionally checked and controlled that its powers must be reasonably exercised without abridging individual rights.

In fact, Americans had progressed far beyond the English in securing their rights. The English constitutional documents limited only the crown and protected few rights. The Petition of Right reconfirmed Magna Carta's provision that no freeman could be imprisoned except by lawful judgment of his peers or "by the law of the land"; it also reconfirmed a 1354 version of the great charter that had first used the phrase "by due process of law" instead of "by the law of the land." The petition invigorated the liberty of the subject by condemning the military trial of civilians as well as imprisonment without cause or on mere executive authority. Other sections provided that no one could be taxed without Parliament's consent or be imprisoned or forced to incriminate himself by having to answer for refusing an exaction not authorized by Parliament. The Habeas Corpus Act safeguarded personal liberty, without which other liberties cannot be exercised. The act secured an old right for the first time by making the writ of habeas corpus an effective remedy for illegal imprisonment. The only loophole in the act, the possibility of excessive bail, was plugged by the Bill of Rights ten years later. That enactment, its exalted name notwithstanding, had a narrow range of protections, including the freedoms of petition and assembly, free speech for members of Parliament, and, in language closely followed by the American Eighth Amendment, bans on excessive bail, excessive fines, and cruel and unusual punishments. As an antecedent of the American Bill of Rights, the English one was a skimpy affair, although important as a symbol of the rule of law and of fundamental law. The Toleration Act was actually "A Bill of Indulgence," exempting most nonconformists from the penalties of persecutory laws of the Restoration, leaving those laws in force but inapplicable to persons qualifying for indulgence. England maintained an establishment of the Anglican Church, merely tolerating the existence of non-Anglican trinitarians, who were still obligated to pay tithes and endure many civil disabilities.

In America, England promoted Anglicanism in New York and in the southern colonies but wisely prevented its establishments in America from obstructing religious peace, because immigrants were an economic asset, regardless of religion. England granted charters to colonial proprietors on a nondiscriminatory basis—to Cecil Calvert, a Roman Catholic, for Maryland; to Roger Williams, a Baptist, for Rhode Island; and to William Penn, a Quaker, for Pennsylvania and Delaware. The promise of life in America drew people from all of western Christendom and exposed them to a greater degree of liberty and religious differences than previously known. James Madison, whose practical achievements in the cause of freedom of religion were unsurpassed, said that it arose from "that multiplicity of sects which pervades America."

But a principled commitment to religious liberty came first in some colonies. Maryland's Toleration Act of 1649 was far more liberal than England's Toleration Act of forty years later. Until 1776 only Rhode Island, Pennsylvania, Delaware, and New Jersey guaranteed fuller freedom than Maryland by its act of 1649, which was the first to use the phrase "the free exercise of religion," later embodied in the First Amendment. The act also symbolized the extraordinary fact that for most of the seventeenth century in Maryland, Roman Catholics and Protestants openly worshiped as they chose and lived in peace, if not amity. The act applied to all trinitarian Christians but punished others as well as punishing the reproachful use of divisive terms such as heretic, puritan, papist, anabaptist, or antinomian. The Maryland act was a statute, but the Charter of Rhode Island, which remained its constitution until 1842, made the guarantee of religious liberty a part of the fundamental law. It secured for all inhabitants "the free exercise and enjoyment of their civil and religious rights" by providing that every peaceable person might "freely and fullye hav and enjoye his and theire owne judgments and consciences, in matters of religious concernments. . . ." Thus, the principle that the state has no legitimate authority over religion was institutionalized in some American colonies, including those under Quaker influence.

Massachusetts, the colony that least respected private judgment in religious matters, was the first to safeguard many other rights. Its Body of Liberties, adopted in 1641, was meant to limit the magistrates in whom all power had been concentrated. As John Winthrop observed, the objective was to frame limitations "in remarkable resemblance to Magna Charta, which . . . should be received for fundamental laws." The Body of Liberties was, in effect, a comprehensive bill of rights compared with which the later English Bill of Rights was rudimentary and the liberties of Englishmen few. Among the guarantees first protected in writing by Massachusetts were freedom of assembly and of speech at least in public meetings, the equal protection of the laws, just compensation for private property taken for public use, freedom to emigrate, the right to bail, the right to employ counsel, trial by jury in civil cases, the right to challenge jurors, restrictions on imprisonment for debt, speedy trial, no double jeopardy, and no cruel or excessive punishments. In addition to traditional liberties, like trial by jury in criminal cases, and Magna Carta's principle of the rule of law, the Body of Liberties also protected some rights of women: widows received a portion of the estate of husbands even if cut off by will; physical punishment of women by their husbands was prohibited; and daughters received a right to inherit if parents died intestate and without male heirs. Servants, slaves, foreigners, and even animals received humane consideration too.

The Body of Liberties was a statute, but the Charter or Fundamental Laws of West New Jersey (1677), the work probably of William Penn, functioned as a written constitution because it began with the provision that the "common law or fundamental rights" of the colony should be "the foundation of government, which is not to be altered by the Legislative authority . . . ." The liberty documents of England limited only the crown, not the legislature. The principle of limiting all governmental authority was written into Penn's Frame of Government for Pennsylvania in 1682, a document that extensively enumerated rights that were to last "for ever," including, for the first time, a ban on excessive fines, a guarantee of indictment by grand jury in capital cases, delivery to the accused of a copy of the charges against him, and assurance that a jury's verdict of not guilty was final. Penn's charter carefully particularized the rights of the criminally accused. Americans were learning that charters of liberty must assure fair and regularized procedures, without which there could be no liberty. Vicious and ad hoc procedures had been used to victimize religious and political minorities. A man's home could not be his castle or his property be his own, nor could his right to express his opinion or to worship his God be secure, if he could be searched, arrested, tried, and imprisoned in some arbitrary way.

The case of Sir Thomas Lawrence in 1693 is illustrative. Secretary of Maryland, a judge, and a member of the governor's council, Lawrence broke politically with the government and denounced it. Summoned by the council for examination, he was accused of having a treasonable letter. On his refusal to produce it, the council had him searched against his protests, found the letter, and convicted him of unspecified crimes, deprived him of his offices, and jailed him without bail. Lawrence appealed his conviction to the Assembly on the grounds of having been forced to incriminate himself by an illegal search, of having been convicted without trial by jury, without knowing the charges against him or the names of his accusers, and of having been denied bail and habeas corpus "which is the great security of the lives & Libertyes of every English Subject." The Assembly vindicated English liberties by supporting Lawrence on every point, found all the proceedings against him illegal, and freed and restored him.

The American colonial experience, climaxed by the controversy with England leading to the Revolution, honed American sensitivity to the need for written constitutions that protected rights grounded in "the immutable laws of nature" as well as in the British constitution and colonial charters. An English nobleman told Benjamin Franklin that Americans had the wrong ideas about the constitution. English and American ideas did differ radically because the Americans had a novel concept of "constitution." The word signified to them a supreme law creating government, limiting it, unalterable by it, and paramount to it. A town orator of Boston announced that independence offered the people a chance of reclaiming rights "attendant upon the original state of nature, with the opportunity of establishing a government for ourselves. . . ." "To secure these rights," Jefferson declared, "governments are instituted among men."

The Virginia constitution of 1776, the first permanent state constitution, began with a Declaration of Rights that restrained all branches of government. As the first such document it contained many constitutional "firsts," such as the statements that "all men" are equally free and have inherent rights that cannot be divested even by compact; that among these rights are the enjoyment of life, liberty, property, and the pursuit of happiness; and that all power derives from the people, who retain a right to change the government if it fails to secure its objectives. The declaration recognized "the free exercise of religion" and freedom of the press, and included clauses that were precursors, sometimes in rudimentary form, of the Fourth through the Eighth Amendments of the Constitution of the United States. Inexplicably the convention voted down a ban on bills of attainder and on ex post facto laws and omitted the freedom of speech, assembly, and petition, the right to the writ of habeas corpus, grand jury proceedings, the right to compulsory process to secure evidence in one's own behalf, the right to counsel, and freedom from double jeopardy. Although religious liberty was guaranteed, the ban on an establishment of religion awaited enactment of the Virginia Statute of Religious Freedom in 1786.

Pennsylvania's bill of rights was more comprehensive than Virginia's. Pennsylvania omitted bans on excessive fines and cruel punishments as well as the right to bail but added freedom of speech, assembly, and petition; separated church and state; recognized the right of conscientious objection; protected the right to counsel in all criminal cases; secured the right to keep arms; and guaranteed the right to travel or emigrate—all constitutional "firsts." Pennsylvania also recognized that "the people have a right to hold themselves, their houses, papers, and possessions free from search and seizure," in contrast to Virginia's prohibition of general warrants. Delaware's bill of rights was the first to ban ex post facto laws and the quartering of troops in homes during peacetime; Maryland added a prohibition on bills of attainder. Vermont's contribution was the first outlawing of slavery and the first constitutional provision for just compensation in cases of eminent domain. Connecticut and Rhode Island retained their charters as

121

their constitutions, whereas New Jersey, Georgia, New York, and South Carolina protected some rights in their constitutional texts but had no separate bills of rights and no noteworthy innovations.

Massachusetts, the last of the original states to adopt a constitution (1780), contributed the most to the concept of a bill of rights. It had the most comprehensive bill of rights and was the first to secure citizens against "all unreasonable searches and seizures," the formulation closest to that of the later Fourth Amendment. Massachusetts was also the first state to replace the weak "ought not" found in all previous bills of rights—"the liberty of the press ought not be restrained"—with the injunction "shall not," which Madison later followed. Most important, Massachusetts was the first state to frame its fundamental law by a specially elected constitutional convention, which exercised no legislative authority and submitted the document for popular ratification. In every other state before 1780, legislatures, sometimes calling themselves conventions, wrote the fundamental law and promulgated it. Theoretically, a bill of rights framed by a legislature could be changed by ordinary legislation, a fact deplored by Jefferson as a capital defect in Virginia's model. The procedure first adopted by Massachusetts was copied by New Hampshire when it revised its constitution in 1784, with the first guarantee against double jeopardy; thereafter the Massachusetts procedure prevailed.

The framing of the first constitutions with bills of rights ranks among America's foremost achievements, the more remarkable because both unprecedented and realized during wartime. Nevertheless, the phrasing of various rights and the inclusion or omission of particular ones in any given state constitution seem careless. Why so few states protected the rights against double jeopardy and bills of attainder, and why so many omitted habeas corpus and freedom of speech, among others, is inexplicable except in terms of shoddy craftsmanship. Even so, the existence of eight state bills of rights with constitutional status invigorated Antifederalist arguments that a bill of rights should be appended to the Constitution of 1787. The state ratifying conventions produced about seventy-five recommendations for amendments, providing Madison with an invaluable list from which

to create the proposals that he submitted to Congress.

Congress itself supplied a final precedent, the Northwest Ordinance of 1787, which planned the evolution of territories to statehood. The ordinance was the first federal document to contain a bill of rights. To extend "the fundamental principles of civil and religious liberty," Congress included articles that were to remain "forever . . . unalterable," guaranteeing to territorial inhabitants habeas corpus, trial by jury, representative government, judicial proceedings "according to the course of the common law," and, as an additional assurance of due process, an encapsulated provision from Magna Carta protecting liberty and property from being deprived except "by the judgment of . . . peers, or the law of the land." The ordinance also included articles protecting the right to bail except in capital cases, enjoined that all fines should be "moderate," and prohibited "cruel or unusual punishment." Another article provided a federal precedent for still another provision of the Bill of Rights, just compensation for property taken for public purposes. The ordinance also protected the sanctity of private contracts, outlawed sex discrimination in land ownership, banned slavery, and provided for religious liberty. Thus the federal as well as colonial and state experience with written instruments to safeguard rights enhanced the claim that a bill of rights should bridle the new national government.

The Bill of Rights did just that; it was a bill of restraints. The First Amendment begins with the clause, "Congress shall make no law respecting an establishment of religion." What is an establishment of religion? The debates of the Congress that proposed the amendment provide inadequate support for either a broad or narrow interpretation, although Congress rejected various phrasings that embraced the narrow one, namely, that Congress could not establish a state church or prefer one religion over others. Madison doubtlessly believed that government aid to religion generally or on a nonpreferential basis to all religions constituted an establishment. But the "great object" of the Bill of Rights, he declared, was to "limit and qualify the powers of Government" by making certain that none of its granted powers could be used in forbidden fields, such as religion. A narrow interpretation of the clause leads to the impossible conclusion that the First Amendment added to Congress's powers. Congress was bereft of power to control or support religion even in the absence of the amendment. An express prohibition could not vest power to aid religion generally. Madison observed that the Bill of Rights was not framed "to imply powers not meant to be included in the enumeration." When Congress framed the First Amendment, six states maintained or authorized establishments. The amendment was meant to prevent congressional legislation concerning those establishments and to ensure that Congress could not do what those states were doing. In each of the six an establishment of religion was not restricted to a single state church or public support of one denomination; in all an establishment meant public support to all denominations and sects on a nonpreferential basis, not just public support of one over others. History explains the meaning of the text. Similarly the seemingly specific injunctions of the remainder of the Bill of Rights are not self-defining and do not necessarily exclude exceptions.

Freedom of speech and press may not be abridged, but what is an abridgment, and what is the "freedom of speech" that is protected? Libels, obscenity, and pornography, whatever they might mean, as well as direct and successful incitements to crime, were not intended to be constitutionally protected. The guarantee of freedom of religion is that it may not be "prohibited." But may it be abridged or regulated in some way short of a prohibition? The injunction against laws respecting an establishment of religion does not literally apply to speech or press. But can Congress pass laws respecting freedom of the press if not abridging it? What are the "arms" that may be kept and borne? When is the militia "well-regulated"? What is an "unreasonable" search or seizure? No warrants shall issue "but on probable cause." What is "a probable cause," and may there be searches without warrants? They existed in 1791. What is an "infamous" crime? What is the meaning of compulsion in the safeguard that no person shall be "compelled" to be a witness against himself in a criminal case? What is the process of law that is "due" to anyone who might be deprived of life, liberty, or property? What is "public use" or "just" compensation? Do the many rights of the Sixth Amendment really extend to "all" criminal prosecutions? Trial by jury

did not extend to persons facing less than six months' imprisonment. When does a criminal prosecution or case begin, and does it include legislative or grand jury investigations? Does the "assistance of counsel" or the right not to be a witness against oneself apply to such investigations? What is a "speedy" trial or an "impartial" jury? Does trial by jury mean only a jury of twelve and a unanimous verdict? Does the ban against double jeopardy mean that an acquittal in federal court bars a state trial for the same act? What is "excessive" bail or a punishment that is "cruel and unusual"? There were probably no constitutional absolutes in 1791, and no guarantees that were clear and precise in meaning. Ambiguities cannot be strictly construed.

"Congress shall make no law . . . abridging the freedom of speech, or of the press" seems clear enough, in one sense. The intent was to prevent any congressional enactments regulating speech or press, as by means of a licensing act, a tax act, or a seditious libel act. The framers meant Congress to be totally without power to enact legislation respecting the press, although the First Amendment does not say so. At the time of its adoption, the English common law definition of freedom of the press was the only one known and no other definition existed in America: the press was free in the absence of previous restraints. One could speak or publish as one pleased without censorship, but one was not exempt from punishment for libelous utterances, whether scandalizing public morals, religion, or government. Jefferson, for example, when writing his great bill for religious liberty provided that "opinions in matters of religion" should never be punished unless they incited "overt acts against peace and good order." But he never applied the same principle to political opinions. When drafting a constitution for Virginia in 1776 he included a provision that religious freedom "shall not be held to justify any seditious preaching or conversation against the authority of the civil government." Everyone favored unrestricted public discussion of issues, but "unrestricted" meant merely the absence of censorship before publication; people were accountable under the criminal law for licentious use of freedom.

Before 1798 the avant-garde among American libertarians staked everything on the principles of the Zenger case, which they thought beyond improvement. They believed that no greater liberty could be conceived than a right to publish unrestricted, if only a person being prosecuted could plead truth as a defense and if a jury had authority to determine the criminality of his words. Libertarians never rejected the substance of the law of criminal libels, not until the Sedition Act of 1798 embodied Zengerian principles and the prosecutions revealed those principles to be virtually worthless. The Sedition Act of 1798 was unconstitutional not because it abridged the freedom of the press but because it was an exercise of power in a forbidden field; the First Amendment in that regard left prosecutions for criminal libel exclusively to the states. The Sedition Act would have been unconstitutional even in the absence of the First Amendment.

The Fourth Amendment consists of two parts, one embodying the rule that searches and seizures shall not be "unreasonable," the other requiring specific warrants. The principle of the rule originated in England, although the English limitations on the search process were few and slight. The English used general warrants on a massive basis in everyday law enforcement as well as to search for evidence of political crimes like seditious libel. Colonial governments also made widespread use of general warrants, but in Massachusetts the intense opposition to them led to their displacement by specific warrants, beginning in the 1750's. England's reliance on writs of assistance, a form of general warrant, to uproot colonial customs violations in the 1760's led to American arguments supporting specific warrants. In 1774 the Continental Congress censured general warrants as unreasonable violations of privacy, and eight of the early state constitutions repudiated them. The Massachusetts constitution of 1780 contained the model that Madison relied upon when writing what became the Fourth Amendment.

The Fifth Amendment, the most varied of all, guarantees grand jury proceedings before one can be put to trial for a serious offense; bans double jeopardy; safeguards against compulsory self-incrimination; requires due process of law before deprivation of life, liberty, or property; and assures just compensation for public takings of private property. The Sixth Amendment clusters many rights of the criminally accused. The Eighth proscribes excessive bail, fines, or pun-

ishment. Of these amendments, the self-incrimination and due process clauses of the Fifth pose special problems. The self-incrimination clause, although controversial, embodies a fundamental principle of liberty and justice that is inherent in the very idea of a free government. It protects a right, which developed before most others, to ward off inquisitions; it is the central feature of our accusatory system of criminal justice. Although the framers were committed to perpetuating a system that minimized the possibilities of convicting the innocent, they were not less concerned about the humanity that the supreme law should show even to offenders. Protection of the right reflected their judgment that the determination of guilt or innocence by just procedures, in which the accused made no unwilling contribution to his conviction, was more important than punishing the guilty.

As for due process of law, which was to become the most influential concept in American constitutional law, it had developed as a rough equivalent to the more commonly used "law of the land" clause of Magna Carta. Due process had no single or fixed meaning in England or America. Still evolving in meaning, it then referred narrowly to specific common law writs, broadly to regularized courses of legal proceeding in civil and criminal cases, and still more broadly to the very concept of fundamental law. The first American constitution to include a due process clause was the federal Constitution, thanks to Madison's preference for that phrasing instead of "the law of the land." But the inclusion of the clause raised problems. Due process signified customary or appropriate procedures but also connoted protection of the substantive rights of life, liberty, and property. The same clause necessarily safeguarded both procedural and substantive rights but thereby invited confusion in interpretation. Moreover, the clause was redundant because every clause of the Constitution supposedly has an independent meaning. Due process was constitutional shorthand for many particular rights that other clauses of the Fifth and Sixth Amendments explicitly protected, most obviously grand jury proceedings and trial by jury. Inclusion of the clause showed conventional deference to Magna Carta and enhanced assurances that the new national government would treat citizens in accustomed ways, especially in matters of criminal justice.

BILL OF RIGHTS

By completing the Constitution with the Bill of Rights the framers sounded a tocsin against the dangers of government oppression of the individual. They were endorsing the principle that liberty of expression in matters of private conscience and public opinion is basic to a free society; so too, the rights of the criminally accused are legitimate defenses of the individual against government, because the enduring interests of that society require justice to be done as fairly as possible. The Bill of Rights symbolized a new system of public morality based on the premise that government is but an instrument of man, its sovereignty held in subordination to his rights. As amended, the Constitution became a permanent reminder of its framers' view that the citizen is the master of his government, not its subject. Americans understood that the individual may be free only if the government is not.

BIBLIOGRAPHY

Irving Brant, *The Bill of Rights: Its Origin and Meaning* (Indianapolis, 1965), the best written and most comprehensive survey, presents a conventionally liberal viewpoint. Edward Dumbauld, *The Bill of Rights and What It Means Today* (Norman, Okla., 1957), presents an outdated exposition of judicial interpretation, but the material on historical background is still useful. Leonard W. Levy, *Legacy of Suppression: Freedom of Speech and Press in Early American History* (Cambridge, Mass., 1960), presents the unconventional thesis that the framers of the First Amendment did not support the broadest scope for political expression; *Origins of the Fifth Amendment: The Right Against Self-Incrimination* (New York, 1968), is the definitive work; and *Judgments: Essays on American Constitutional History* (Chicago, 1972), pp. 169–224, supports the view that the framers intended a high wall of separation between church and state.

Richard L. Perry and John C. Cooper, eds., *Sources of Our Liberties: Documentary Origins of Individual Liberties in the United States Constitution and Bill of Rights* (Chicago, 1959), is the best one-volume collection of primary sources, with splendid editorial commentaries and annotations. Robert A. Rutland, *The Birth of the Bill of Rights, 1776–1791* (Chapel Hill, N.C., 1955), is a good narrative exposition but weak on the origins of specific rights. Bernard Schwartz, *The Bill of Rights: A Documentary History,* 2 vols. (New York, 1971), is the most detailed and invaluable collection of primary sources and includes extensive commentaries.

[*See also* CONGRESS; CONSTITUTION; DECLARATION OF INDEPENDENCE; FEDERALISM; THE FEDERALIST PAPERS; *and* JUDICIAL SYSTEM.]

BUSINESS AND GOVERNMENT

Richard M. Abrams

ON 9 November 1639, in the tiny English colony on Massachusetts Bay, John Winthrop entered in his journal:

> At a general court holden at Boston, great complaint was made of the oppression used in the country in sale of foreign commodities; and Mr. Robert Keayne, who kept a shop in Boston, was notoriously above others observed and complained of. . . . He was charged with many particulars; in some, for taking above six-pence in the shilling profit; in some above eight-pence; and, in some small things, above two for one; and being hereof convicted . . . he was fined £200, . . . for the cry of the country was so great against oppression, and some of the elders and magistrates had declared such detestation of the corrupt practice of this man (which was the more observable because he was wealthy and sold dearer than most other tradesmen, . . .).

Governor Winthrop noted that Keayne got off more lightly than he might. Some people had urged that on top of the civil penalty the church should have imposed excommunication. But several points had argued for restraint. For one thing, wrote Winthrop, "a certain rule could not be found out for an equal [equitable] rate between buyer and seller, though much labor had been bestowed on it, and divers laws had been made, which upon experience, were repealed, as being neither safe nor equal." Although the court was sure it knew a just price from an unjust one, it could find no rule. In addition, said Winthrop, Keayne had acted not in violation of his conscience but according to certain "false principles." These false principles included: "That a man might sell as dear as he can, and buy as cheap as he can"; "[that] if a man lose by casualty of the sea, etc., in some of his commodities, he may raise the price of the rest"; "that he may sell

as he bought, though he paid too dear . . . "; and "that, as a man may take advantage of his own skill or ability, so he may of another's ignorance or necessity." These were all false principles, and, in making an example of Keayne, the small Puritan commonwealth attempted to make their error clear to all.

Although more than three centuries old, the Keayne incident is still rich with significance, evoking the conflict between a business ethic and a social ethic that has perplexed American culture from its very beginnings in the colonial period. It also suggests the tension between business and government that has beset the American political economy, especially over the last century.

The ascendancy of commerce over religious concerns would lead Americans eventually to give up on finding a rule for discovering "an [equitable] rate between buyer and seller," and the society yielded the problem to the imputed evenhandedness of the "impersonal" market system. But notions of a just price and a public interest survived, as did the perceived responsibility of government for maintaining them. Such lingering sensibilities would inspire recurrent demands for government intervention. Throughout the colonial period, provincial and town governments continued to regulate wages and prices, sizes and quality of staple products (for example, bread), the conditions of labor and the relationship between master and apprentice (and slave), and in general the relationships of individuals to one another in both commercial and personal activities. In America this heritage created a continuing tension between the rightful prerogatives of a free individual and the rightful demands of the state upon the individual to respect community standards of equity and public interest.

126

BUSINESS AND GOVERNMENT

America is a business civilization. As Elisha P. Douglass has written (1971), "From the outset America was envisaged and developed as a business enterprise." The Massachusetts and Virginia colonies were organized as corporations and chartered with the view toward making money. Although seventeenth-century people typically were deeply religious, and the New England colonies were originally structured along theocratic principles, those principles neither precluded business activity nor motivated most of the settlers. "The great majority of the colonists," wrote Thomas C. Cochran, "came for neither the glory of God nor the British Empire, but to benefit themselves. . . . Even in Puritan Massachusetts a Marblehead fisherman reproved a too strongly exhorting preacher with the remark 'Our ancestors came not here for religion. Their main end was to catch fish.'"

The word *business* is intended to include every form of nonstate economic enterprise that offers products or services for sale and profit. That would include just about every kind of proprietorship and venture besides self-sufficient farming. A sizable number of Americans, mostly farmers, continued to operate nonmarket-connected households through the early nineteenth century. But all told, with the possible exception of religion, there is no more important institution in the history of American life than business. It has consistently been the principal means by which Americans have organized human and natural resources for sustaining human life, satisfying material human needs, and fulfilling their most consistently held ideals. *Business enterprise* describes in effect the most absorbing activity in which the vast majority of Americans have been engaged since their migration from the Old World.

Although Americans have historically organized their daily lives more around their business activities than around any other single form of activity, they have never been altogether comfortable with the business ethic. The idea of private gain has never completely been freed from a more selfless ethic—a sense of commonwealth or public interest—required by every successfully organized community, as well as by the particular tenets of the country's Judeo-Christian heritage. In fact, the work discipline, which underlies the commitment to business values, grew directly out of a set of religious values embodying a particular understanding of an individual's obligations to God that, in its origins, specifically denied the importance of material acquisition and enjoyment. Work had value not for its material results but for its disciplinary effects, effects that were indispensable for demonstrating a personally well-regulated, self-controlled, godly life. Material goods and comforts did, however, offer an indirect way of measuring the application of that discipline, and thus the godliness of one's life. This was crucial for the rise to dominance of the business ethic in American life. In an environment in which there appeared to be a high correlation between a person's disciplined labor and the achievement of his or her material goals, it was not unreasonable to conclude that wealth was a fair measure of a godly life-style. The seventeenth, eighteenth, and early nineteenth centuries usually offered to many Americans just that environment. The rapid growth of the economy, fueled largely by an extraordinary increase in population from immigrants seeking to exploit the continent's land resources, made the rise from rags to respectability in one generation a frequent occurrence and a reasonable expectation. The business ethic and the acquisition of private wealth thus earned an implicit moral sanction. The successful pursuit of gain tended to prove the virtue of the private gainer. There is, wrote Emerson, "always a reason *in the man* for his good or bad fortune, and so in making money."

In major respects, then, American society—not altogether unlike many other societies, but probably to a more remarkable degree than others—made affluence not merely a personal objective but a national value. As the social scientist Richard Wohl put it (1954):

> No observer of the American scene can fail to discern how much idealism and effort is channeled into consumption in our society. . . . In a certain profound and very revealing sense Americans believe in the things that money will buy, and organize their lives accordingly. . . . It isn't too much to say that such a consumption outlook, far from being philosophically shallow, is an expression of a profoundly democratic, equalitarian social order. It is an operating principle for a social system which invites almost everyone in it to aspire to almost any social standing for which he can find the means to validate his claim for social recognition by displaying generally accepted symbols of status in the form of goods and services.

The fulfillment of economic aspirations has in fact served virtually as the defining significance of America to Americans. For the most part, at least until the third quarter of the twentieth century, Americans tended to define liberty chiefly in terms of access to economic opportunity (rather than free speech, expression, or life-style fulfillment). "The American democracy," wrote the Progressive Era theorist Herbert Croly, ". . . has promised to Americans a substantial satisfaction of their economic needs; and it has made that promise an essential part of the American idea. . . . If it is not kept, the American commonwealth will no longer continue to be a democracy." Croly could have taken his cue from the poet Walt Whitman, who wrote in *Democratic Vistas:*

> The extreme business energy, and this almost maniacal appetite for wealth prevalent in the Untied States, are parts of amelioration and progress, indispensably needed to prepare the very results I demand. My theory demands riches and the getting of riches, and the amplest products, power, activity, inventions, . . . Upon them, as upon substrata, I raise the edifice designed in these Vistas.

In this fundamental way, American society has been a materialistic one organized along lines keenly responsive to a business ethic. And the social and political implications of material affluence have never been lost on policymakers throughout the nation's existence. That is to say, social policy from the earliest years of nationhood has given high priorities to facilitating the producing and selling of goods and services for private gain. Affluence has been a national goal, its pursuit a calling, and its achievement a major ideal. And Americans have self-consciously promoted private business venturing in the service of that ideal.

THE MYTH OF LAISSEZ-FAIRE

Although it is one of the enduring myths of this business society that the nation's great material achievements were built upon individualistic self-help—competitive private enterprise unaided and unregulated by the state—from the very beginning of the new nation Americans drew almost casually on city, county, state, and federal government credit resources and revenues to make rivers and harbors navigable; to drain marshes and build levees; to explore and map sea and land; to develop "human capital" by providing primary, secondary, and (by the mid-nineteenth century) higher education; and to help construct dams, tunnels, reservoirs, bridges, turnpikes, canals, and railroads. Nor did government aid stop short of direct subsidies to certain private banking ventures, farm crops, fisheries, and even manufactures. In addition, of course, Americans expected government to provide the armed forces not merely to preserve order and protect against foreign invasion but to clear the continent of the native users so that land-hungry Euro-American settlers and entrepreneurs could hunt, trap, fish, farm, mine, and cut timber. They did all these things throughout the nineteenth century when, tradition has it, "laissez-faire" prevailed as the nation's official ideology.

Nineteenth-century political leaders and theorists usually did agree that the least government is the best government, but this stopped few private interests at any time in American history from soliciting favors from the state. What is more, a careful study of state legislative debates would reveal that contending interests did not often raise the principle of laissez-faire, even in the nineteenth century. As Thomas C. Cochran wrote in his pathfinding study of business in American life, "The battles in state legislatures seem to have revolved more around the issue of who would benefit from what than over any principle of state planning or ownership as against free enterprise." Nobel laureate Simon Kuznets, long the leading authority on economic development, noted that, contrary to presumptions about passive government in the United States, there was never a decade in the nineteenth century that was not "marked by some decision by the [government on some major issue of economic resources] . . . and each one was reached after explicit discussion in which its importance for the country's economic growth was realized." And James Willard Hurst, in his renowned pioneering work on American legal history, found little evidence of "laissez-faire" in nineteenth-century lawmaking, although Americans seem to have begun presuming differently after 1890 or so. "Political debate of the last sixty

128

years," he wrote, "has propagated a myth . . . that we got along well enough if the legislator provided schools, the sheriff ran down horse thieves, the court tried farmers' title disputes, and otherwise the law left men to take care of themselves. . . . The record is different."

The record shows that American businessmen have continuously looked to government for help. And they have not merely sought help for the general purposes of promoting growth, but persistently expected government to aid them in competition with other businessmen both at home and abroad. From colonial times on, businessmen in different cities and states have enlisted their respective legislatures as allies against rival cities and out-of-state commercial interests. Tax exemptions have been common lures for particular businesses or industries from other states. In the years of canal and railroad building, seaboard city and county merchant associations wangled loans, credit guarantees, and direct subsidies from their governments in order to facilitate their capture of trade in the interior. Railroad lines were constructed to funnel traffic to favored cities, and in the South rails were even laid to exclusive gauges to discourage traffic leaving for market cities outside the state or region. (A uniform national gauge was not accomplished until the 1880's.) Chicagoans used their government to prevent the linking of railroad track through the city, thereby requiring transcontinental traffic to be unloaded for handling; Boston has a similar history for traffic between northern and southern New England. In spite of the constitutional ban on states imposing interstate tariffs, many states levy what they call a "use tax" on personal property (such as automobiles), which is applied in addition to whatever sales tax may already have been paid, in order to discourage consumers from buying across a state border. Many states require inspection and quality standards for goods produced for export (leaving lesser-quality goods for local consumption). Some states today use a little-known clause in the Twenty-first Amendment (which repealed Prohibition but left to the states the power to regulate the sale of alcoholic beverages) in order to restrict the importation of wines in competition with their own wine industry. In the 1920's, some states attempted to impose discriminatory taxes on corporations chartered by other states, and to ban entry of chain stores headquartered else-

where, but the U.S. Supreme Court did stop those practices as arbitrary and unduly burdensome on interstate commerce. These examples only hint at the extent of private business uses of government power in interstate, interregional, and intraindustrial competition.

Furthermore, in the late nineteenth century, while the U.S. Supreme Court was busily writing "liberty of contract" into the Constitution and denying legislatures the power to protect factory and mine workers against lopsided wages-and-hours bargains, the courts did uphold state legislative delegation of licensing powers to certain private professional and trade associations. Thus, various state medical associations, state bars, and the occupational associations of architects, dentists, pharmacists, plumbers, barbers, and even horseshoers gained the power to determine what qualifications, credentials, training, and standards of practice would entitle an individual to earn his or her livelihood in each such occupation. Legal historian Lawrence Friedman has remarked, "Society, locked in struggle over the right of industrial labor to organize, nonetheless handed over monopoly power to middle-class professionals and artisans, without a murmur of protest from the courts."

As historian Robert Lively wrote, in a survey of literature documenting the country's "sturdy tradition of public responsibility for economic growth," it should have been more than evident long before the coming of the so-called welfare state in the twentieth century that "King Laissez-Faire . . . not only [was] dead; the hallowed report of his reign had all been a mistake." Government intervention on behalf of private interests was so persistent and so extensively employed that it should seem expanded in no qualitative way by its modern uses in the Tennessee Valley Authority, in the exploitation of atomic energy, in subsidies to farm crops, in underwriting insurance for certain foreign business investments, in offering low-cost government credit for private housing, small business ventures, or certain export transactions, or in guaranteeing loans to college students and to giant corporations such as Chrysler and Lockheed.

It remains something of a mystery as to why this view took so long to enter into the mainstream of even advanced historiography. As long ago as the 1880's, the British scholar and statesman James Bryce, in his monumental *The Ameri-*

can Commonwealth, observed in a chapter devoted to the issue:

> Though the Americans have no theory of the State and take a narrow view of its functions, though they conceive themselves to be devoted to *laissez-faire* in principle, and to be in practice the most self-reliant of peoples, they have grown no less accustomed than the English to carry the action of government into ever widening fields . . . [and] are just as eager for state interference. . . . No one need be surprised at this, [for Americans] are even more eager . . . to hasten on to the ends they desire, even more impatient with the delays which a reliance on natural forces involves.

Yet the myth lived on, an error (as Lively put it) of "monumental proportions, a mixture of overlooked data, interested distortion, and persistent preconception." Indeed, when an occasional scholar such as banking historian Guy Callender discovered in 1902 the true measure of government intervention in finance—from state partnerships in private banking and insurance companies to close regulation of note issues and lending policies—he was unable to account for "this remarkable movement toward State enterprise here in America, where of all places in the world we should least expect to find it." Perhaps that expectation, until only the most recent years, too often circumscribed the limits of scholarly inquiry just as it plainly muddled contemporary thought.

Nor has the myth yet been laid to rest. The most casual attention to perennial political rhetoric, oil company advertisements, and business journal editorials will confirm that. Moreover, some historians, seeking to salvage the historiographical tradition that views the nineteenth century as "the Age of Laissez-Faire," have argued for a distinction between state intervention that aided private business and intervention designed to regulate or restrict. One major study of American business enterprise through 1900 argued: "Government assistance as contrasted with government control has always been an implicit corollary of free enterprise. . . . From the colonial period to the present, sympathetic assistance from the government has been expected" (Douglass, 1972). But this begs all kinds of questions and moreover fails to cover the variety of business uses of government throughout the

nineteenth century, as well as before and since. Most government actions both restrict and promote, aid and restrain, although different groups enjoy the aid or suffer the restraint.

Some other scholars, who concede that no valid distinction can be made between aid and restraint in government activities, argue nevertheless for a distinction between "pure laissez-faire" and "refined laissez-faire," pointing out that Adam Smith himself never took a pure laissez-faire position (M. Friedman, 1962). Smith, they point out, held the state responsible for all of the following: (1) regulation, or even state ownership, of natural monopolies (for example, roads, waterworks, canals); (2) "erecting and maintaining certain public works and . . . institutions, which it can never be for the interest of any individual . . . to erect and maintain because the profit could never repay the expense to any individual though it may frequently do much more than repay it to a great society"; (3) patent and copyright controls; (4) special franchises or temporary monopolies for high-risk ventures deemed likely to bring large public benefits; (5) tariff protection for certain infant industries with especially high start-up costs and for industries considered necessary for national security; (6) paternalistic protection of "those in the power of others" who might suffer from unfair or cruel treatment, including women, children, and the poor; and (7) protection against "those exertions of the natural liberty of a few individuals, which might endanger the security of the whole society" (in Smith's view, for example, most banking practices). All this is indeed to be found in Adam Smith's work. The trouble is, there is hardly a measure of government intervention that has gone into the making of the so-called welfare state of the twentieth century that cannot be fully justified within the categories that Smith laid out. Disagreement over which sectors of the society should enjoy support from government resources—whether to promote production or to stimulate purchasing power, whether to reduce inflation or to promote full employment, whether to emphasize economic growth or protection of public resources, whether to minimize entrepreneurial risk or hazards to consumers and users, to employees, to third-party "bystanders," and to the present and future environment—is virtually all that remains to differentiate between the modern "planner" and the advocates of laissez-faire and "deregulation."

But why, then, has laissez-faire sometimes seemed a fair characterization of the political economy in the nineteenth-century United States? One must be careful not to overstate the role of government in American economic development. The business historian, poring over the collected manuscripts of major business leaders of the nineteenth century, for example, will typically find few letters to, from, or about government officials, suggesting that the government's policies meant little to business strategists. Indeed, Alfred D. Chandler, Jr., has found it possible, in his monumental history of American business management (*The Visible Hand,* 1977), to describe two centuries of commercial and industrial development while scarcely mentioning government, except to indicate how little the great reform movements of U.S. political history have mattered. In this account, the modern large-scale, integrated, and multifunctional business firm evolved almost inevitably from the imperatives of self-sustaining market and technology growth, and not from either the ingenuity of particular business entrepreneurs or government policy decision.

SOURCES OF THE MARKET ECONOMY

It is important to understand that Chandler's account took as "given" not only political stability and a culture ready to exploit new technology for material gain, but also a legal system that reduced entrepreneurial risk. So that when steam railroads greatly reduced transportation costs and thus enlarged effective demand for goods, thereby inviting entrepreneurs to meet new and massive consumer demand; and when new machine technology and new factory designs, inspired by the newly grown demand, made possible a vastly more rapid production of certain consumer goods to match that demand (packaged meat, processed grain and grain products, shoes, cigarettes, refined sugar, etc.), private venturers found few obstacles in mobilizing the massive capital needed for installing such innovations. Not only had the government obliged by making available at minimal costs the corporate form of business enterprise, it had also changed

the law to minimize liability risks that otherwise would naturally have accompanied large-scale machines, large-scale production, large-scale work forces in large-scale factories, shipping goods at high speed across vast distances. This will be discussed in more detail further on. For now, the important point is that the crucial legal changes resulted mostly from court actions and some little-known statutory measures. Hence, they remained largely invisible to the political community, and the state through it all appeared "neutral" and merely permissive.

Then, too, laissez-faire is a comparative thing. By comparison with the governments of other industrial countries—say, Germany, Russia, or Japan—the U.S. government did play a relatively small role in the country's economic growth and in sustaining its private business-sector prosperity. Nowhere else can the history of economic development be described so largely in terms of responses to marketplace imperatives. Furthermore, a comparison of twentieth-century state and federal expenditures with those of the nineteenth century lends credibility to the view of the nineteenth century as an age of passive government. Finally, except for some of the northeastern states up to about 1860, the U.S. government rarely performed entrepreneurial functions. The weak, inchoate, and decentralized nature of the U.S. government, as constructed by its founding fathers, had much to do with this.

That the American nation came upon the scene at the very moment in history when the Industrial Revolution in England began sending its first shock waves abroad had momentous significance for American business and government. Both the maturing of a commercial economy and the rise of industrialism tended to challenge the power and status of the military and landed aristocracy. This took place in continental Europe and Japan within a political environment dominated by a preexisting governing elite and bureaucracy that alternately resisted and encouraged the transformation taking place. That elite rarely let economic developments get out of its control, rarely neglected strictly political concerns. When industrialization stirred widespread discontent and threatened stability, the state bureaucracy resisted it. When purposes of national power and security were to be served, the elite promoted it. The state remained, relatively, an autonomously acting center distinct from the society that it served or that served it. It made minimal compromises with the ascending entrepreneurial middle classes, assuring as much as possible that industrialism would serve the purposes of the state rather than the reverse.

THE STATE AND SOCIETY

In America, the economic transformation that magnified the power of the commercial and industrial middle classes coincided with the evolution of the new state. In an important sense, the American nation appeared to emerge as a society in search of a state, a characteristic of the American polity that would be long lasting. As the astute British writer and political commentator H. G. Wells observed in 1906: "First and chiefly, I have to convey what seems to me to be the most significant and pregnant thing of all [about America].... I think it is best indicated by saying that the typical American has no 'sense of the state' " (quoted in Skowronek, 1982). Because of America's distance from powerful potential enemies, military concerns played a small role in nation building; there was no need for a large standing army and hence little danger of a governing elite, dependent on a military establishment, that put political and strategic concerns above all others or that stood apart from the daily concerns of the business-oriented citizenry. All the practical tasks of nation building—establishing credit and a system of exchange, maintaining lines of transportation and communication, developing a land settlement policy and adjudicating disputes, raising revenues, and so on—narrowed the distance between the interests of state and the interests of business. Moreover, the governing agencies of the state, as they developed, of necessity recruited their officers mainly from the business classes. As a result, American businessmen developed a unique attitude toward government. On the one hand, government was suspect—a source of privilege and the inequities over which the War for Independence had been fought. On the other hand, it was easy for businessmen—farmers, merchants, artisans, and manufacturers alike—to see the uses to which government could be put for business purposes.

A "sense of the state" eluded Americans until well into the twentieth century. In part, this was because commitment to economic development formed the most powerful basis for consensus in the country and typically was shared without much notice among public officials and private venturers. Partly, too, it was because throughout American history, in economic matters, the lines between the public and private sectors were frequently blurred. Lacking central cohesion and therefore the power to recruit substantial capital resources through conscription or taxation, government could not command development. But local communities of private venturers could often use government authority on behalf of a public interest that coincided well with their own interests. And public-spirited government officials, of both necessity and inclination, commonly sought to honor the state's responsibilities by acting through private venturers, often by chartering corporations fortified not only with privileges of limited liability but also with delegated powers of eminent domain (especially railroads and canals) and limited monopoly guarantees (bridges, toll roads, traction companies, banks). It was not uncommon, in other words, to find private business enterprises functioning as agencies of the state. This had the effect of concealing the state's role in the economy, of muddling the relationship of private enterprise to the public interest, and ultimately of causing major tensions between business and government as some antidemocratic consequences of the nineteenth-century business and government "partnership" became apparent.

For example, consider the Bank of the United States, first chartered in 1791 along guidelines recommended by Secretary of the Treasury Alexander Hamilton. In essence, the institution emerged from an offer by an elite group of businessmen to pool their capital in order to provide a market for government debt (mostly incurred by the states in the course of the Revolution). In exchange for a one-fifth subscription by the federal government to the capital stock of the bank, a monopoly by the bank on the issue of legal tender, and a near monopoly on federal deposits, the private businessmen took on the responsibility of marketing the debt to rich merchants (mostly) abroad. The bank's charter was allowed to lapse because of complaints by rival banks about its privileged status and by entrepreneurs riled by its conservative note-issue policies. But the financial crises following the Napoleonic

BUSINESS AND GOVERNMENT

Wars led in 1816 to the chartering of the second Bank of the United States. Like the first bank, it performed invaluable monetary services for the federal government in exchange for its privileged position in the industry. But such a public-private relationship had its hazards. Belatedly, some fifteen years into its twenty-year charter, the ideal of private-sector self-governance in a minimal-state environment showed its flaws. The bank's virtually unchallenged control over access to the nation's credit implied a power that directly affected the distribution of wealth and, more important, the distribution of entrepreneurial opportunities. Such a power in private hands represented a real threat to the liberal-democratic principles of the country, as well as a source of potentially rampant political corruption (as partially revealed in the fact that by 1832, 102 congressmen and senators were $850,000 in debt to the bank). Andrew Jackson's attack on the bank made little economic sense and almost certainly precipitated the devastating financial crisis that came in 1837, but it served the indispensable democratic function of deepening the faded line between the state and the then prevailing private interests that increasingly acted on its behalf.

The divided loyalties of the public-spirited men in the vanguard of developmental activities inevitably caused trouble. The justification for the special privileges and subsidies granted to certain enterprises lay in the special functions of those enterprises for generating or opening economic opportunities for the public at large. The arrangement possessed large social benefits. The privileges were designed to reduce starting and operating costs as well as financial risks to such firms, so that the products and services they provided would not be priced out of the reach of entrepreneurs—farmers, merchants, manufacturers—dependent on them. For example, when transportation costs were too high, say, one hundred or five hundred miles from a city, land could not be developed for farming or for new towns to service new farming communities; food prices might remain high for the city dwellers because of scarcity; and with wages forced high to cover food costs, there might be little incentive to start or expand business ventures. The subsidizing of a railroad—by land grants, tax deductions, outright subscriptions to equity in the company, and government guarantees of the interest on company bonds—in order to reduce transportation costs, therefore, could generate major growth in business activity generally and improve standards of living all around.

But there were two areas for great confusion here. First, the business ethic confronted the public interest that was implied in the grant of the corporate charter—the presumption that the enterprise was to serve a broad public function. If, in spite of its special privileges, the corporation were to be run as an ordinary business enterprise—that is, maximizing profits by charging what the traffic would bear—it could confound the public function assigned to it. Yet because the corporation remained legally a private enterprise, its managers tended to assert the prerogatives of the business ethic. In fact by the 1840's, corporate managers commonly came to regard incorporation not as the assumption of a public function but as a right of free enterprise; passage of general incorporation acts by most states in that period, whereby a business could bypass the previously required legislative act and could be incorporated merely by filing a standard form and paying a standard fee, signaled the change. On the theory that business prosperity in general sufficiently served the public's interest, corporate managers increasingly tended to assert that maintaining a profitable firm and safeguarding stockholders' interests were their primary if not their exclusive social responsibilities.

At the same time, mixed corporations as well as the practice of government officials moving in and out of the private sector set up situations in which the potential for serious conflicts of interest ran high. A railroad, for example, could be "milked" by any number of entrepreneurial groups that got some inside leverage: by stock manipulators, by contractors who stood to profit by padding construction costs, by land speculators and real-estate developers with an interest in determining the route of a railroad. It was not until the twentieth century that conflict-of-interest concerns aroused serious attention. Not until the concept of the public interest began to take on qualities that separated it clearly from the business ethic did the country move toward resolving the moral confusion, not to say the truculence, that characterized so much of corporate behavior in the late nineteenth century.

In short, customary procedures and standards of behavior in the government–business relationship emerged amid a multitude of ad hoc, pragmatic arrangements unguided by an articulated theory of public interest. This doubtlessly contributed to the growth of an adversarial confrontation between business and government once the twentieth-century reform movements got under way. The reformers sought to revive the older tradition of state intervention against, as Adam Smith had put it, "those exertions of the natural liberty of a few individuals which might endanger the security of the whole society." When in the late nineteenth century the reformers got busy, especially at the federal level where little had stirred earlier, their targets in the business community typically pictured themselves as victims of a usurping government. It was at this point that the myth of laissez-faire became implanted in American politics.

BUSINESS USES OF GOVERNMENT

Nevertheless, even then—even in the case of the great Granger, Populist, Progressive, and New Deal reform movements that gave rise to the modern regulatory state—the tradition of American business uses of government as a competitive weapon against rival business interests held fast. A close reading of American political history impels the conclusion that politics, far from being a contrasting area of activity, has always served as an alternative arena in businessmen's struggles against their competitors in the marketplace. In that struggle, different elements from the business community at different times have (1) drawn from Congress restrictions on imported goods beyond what was needed for revenues, for national security, or for protection of "infant industries"; (2) shown a remarkable disregard for property rights; (3) exacted from legislatures and courts immunization from various forms of civil-law and common-law liabilities; (4) exploited a major shift in constitutional-law doctrine in the 1890's; (5) built into U.S. law a strong antitrust tradition that is almost unique among industrial nations; and (6) more than any other sector of American society created the bureaucratic regulatory agencies that ironically are so often charged with having put government and business into a bitter adversarial relationship in the twentieth century.

The Tariff. Tariffs and import quotas are the most obvious forms of business uses of govern-

ment against business competitors. Protectionism began with the first congressional session of the new nation in 1789, and there has scarcely been a presidential administration since then that has not faced the issue of "tariff reform." This is because (among other things) the tariff is the quintessence of a government regulation that, while aiding some, injures others; so that inevitably those injured by one tariff regime mobilize to undo the damage in a new one. At first, Americans deliberately debated whether their society should encourage industrialization. Benjamin Franklin in 1787 declared, "The great business of the continent is agriculture." And John Adams said approvingly in 1789, "America will be the country to produce raw materials for manufactures; but Europe will be the country of manufactures." But the Hamiltonians took control of federal policy and imposed a 9 percent average tariff on manufactures; they argued that a national industrial policy not only would provide the basis for a lasting federal union but also was indispensable for security purposes, especially because the country's main potential enemy, Britain, was also the world's leader in manufacturing.

The Jeffersonians held out briefly for a decentralized agrarian country, citing the horrors of industrial Manchester and Birmingham in England as reason to avoid industrialism. But the Napoleonic Wars, which forced the United States into a new military confrontation with England, soon converted them. If the United States was to be peaceful, Jefferson acknowledged, it would have to be self-sufficient, and to be self-sufficient it would have to be industrial. "We must," he wrote just before leaving the presidency, "now place the manufacturer by the side of the agriculturist." And to his French friend Pierre Samuel du Pont de Nemours (whose sons in 1802 founded the Du Pont Company on Brandywine Creek in Delaware on President Jefferson's grant of a federal munitions contract), Jefferson wrote in 1809, "The spirit of manufacture has taken deep root among us, and its foundations are laid in too great expanse to be abandoned." The "Jeffersonian dream" of a strictly agrarian republic thus vanished, and in 1816 the concluding Congress of James Madison's presidency not only chartered the second Bank of the United States—a key part of the Hamiltonian program that had been discontinued in 1809—but passed the first tariff to specifically single out the cotton textile, iron, glass, and paper industries for protection against foreign competition.

But it was not until the Civil War, with the triumph of the new, development-oriented Republican party, that tariff protectionism became an unequivocal federal commitment. It was to last virtually without interruption until the late 1930's. That protectionism owed less to the supposed imperatives of industrialization and economic growth (protection of infant industries, and all that) than to the scramble among business interests for political favors may be surmised from, among other things, the inclusion of agricultural commodities in the protectionist net. In fact, the main features of the McKinley Tariff (1890), which is usually regarded as the high point of nineteenth-century protectionism, were written for farm interests by the young Wisconsin congressman Robert La Follette, who soon began a quarter-century as the outstanding champion of the progressive reform movement.

Even the attempt in 1916 to "take the tariff out of politics" by consigning major responsibility for fixing duties to a commission of "experts" failed to change much. By 1916 some of the more powerful sectors of American industry and banking had begun to respond to overseas trade opportunities. The United States by then had become the leading industrial nation, with some major industrial sectors that were larger than those of England and Germany combined. Economies of scale and some technological advantages tended to give the Americans an edge in any straight-out competition on the international market. In the circumstances, many business leaders saw virtue in reducing international trade barriers, a view that gave support to Woodrow Wilson's "free-trade" outlook. The role of the new Tariff Commission was to design schedules that would (1) provide minimum federal revenues while (2) relying for revenue chiefly on duties that compensated for putative labor-cost differentials between foreign and U.S. products. Of course, many people saw *labor-cost differentials* as code for any competitive advantages that foreign products might enjoy. But in any case World War I intervened, and the 1920's saw a general repudiation not only of the opening toward free trade but of an international perspective altogether. To most American businessmen, the postwar domestic market seemed large enough for their interests (exports amounted to barely 6 percent of the gross national product anyway, and imports were about the same), while farmers' worries that Europeans and Canadians would "dump" their agricultural surpluses in the United States outweighed their interest in expanding exports. Protectionist politics returned with a vengeance as Congress overrode the functions of the Tariff Commission with the Fordney-McCumber Tariff in 1922 and the egregious Hawley-Smoot Tariff in 1930.

Federal intervention to protect private American business (and labor) from foreign competitors by means of tariffs did not undergo significant change until after World War II, although attitudes began changing earlier. By 1935 prevailing wisdom among economists and policy makers depicted American protectionism as one important cause of the worldwide depression. It came to be understood that with the largest economy in the world, the United States in refusing to permit foreign businessmen to compete in the American marketplace contributed significantly to the wave of economic nationalism that swept the world, disrupted "natural" trade patterns, stifled investment, and brought on the prolonged global collapse. Government policy shifted back to the short-lived Wilsonian emphasis on aiding American businessmen to exploit economic opportunities abroad, both in trade and in capital investment. During the Depression, that effort took the form of (1) reciprocity treaties to reduce U.S. duties mostly on imports that competed minimally with vulnerable American products, in return for reduced foreign duties on American exports, and (2) establishment of the federal Export-Import Bank to help finance foreign purchases of American exports. All this was still directed at assisting the domestic economy.

Government policy continued to be shaped almost entirely by the inputs of competing business groups; that is, there was little possibility of distinguishing between the prevailing business interest and an otherwise distinct public interest. That would change after 1945. Then the perceived threat of Soviet communism inspired U.S. government policies to (1) pump massive investments into European industrial rehabilitation, (2) permit European and Japanese industry to gain access to U.S. markets while protecting their own, and (3) encourage, with tax benefits and government insurance coverage, American business investments overseas. Such policies marked a clear shift to a political or strategic rather than business definition of public interest in the shaping of foreign trade programs. In the interest of international political objectives, mainly the containment of Soviet expansion, successive federal administrations from Truman to Reagan declined to respond to new calls for industrial protection even after the vigorously rejuvenated European and Japanese industrial systems successfully rivaled American industry within the domestic economy itself.

Eminent Domain. As scholars reexamine the mythology of government–business relations, what becomes even more striking than the unheralded uses of government in contradiction of the laissez-faire myth is the disregard in America for supposedly sacrosanct property rights. Surely there are few "truths" more strongly shared by the political right and the political left than that the American business community has had a steadfast, even obdurate commitment to the privileges of private property. Yet, the historical record shows that in the course of competition among rival economic interests, not only did Americans treat private property in distinctly unsacrosanct ways, they did so to a degree that would have astonished property holders in the more authoritarian industrializing countries such as Germany and Japan. The main instrument of such government intervention was the power of eminent domain, a common-law feature of sovereignty that reserves to the state the power to expropriate private property for declared public purposes.

In America, public purpose has consistently focused on economic development. Although other priorities, such as religious values, often shared the focus, there has hardly been a time in the country's history when economic growth lacked powerful support, and hardly a time when the U.S. government has not brushed past the ostensibly formidable protective rights of private property in order to facilitate development of resources for "public use." Although, in the development of the doctrine, sovereignty remained limited by the presumption of private rights, eminent domain played a significant role in redistributing advantages among economic interests, in altering the structure of entrepreneurial opportunities, in effectively subsidizing locally or temporarily favored types of business activities, and ultimately in as-

suring the ascendancy of a large-scale corporate industrial economy.

In the colonial period, provincial legislatures commonly permitted the taking of private land to promote construction of roads, canals, and dams without specific reference to eminent-domain doctrine. In the new nation, courts took the lead in defining the operative principles of a taking under eminent domain. And as the nineteenth century waxed, the principles became broadly stretched, even to the point where legislative and court grants of the power represented a transparent gift of favor to locally powerful business interests.

It was not merely a case of governments taking property to build needed public works. According to Harry N. Scheiber, during the course of the early nineteenth century, "the most important single development in . . . eminent domain law probably was the wholesale transfer of these doctrines over to the private sector, in aid of incorporated companies on which legislatures devolved the power of eminent domain." Every state in the union awarded such powers to canal, turnpike, railroad, water, and bridge companies, while precluding more than token compensation to landowners injured by the takings. The theory of public interest was persuasive in a general sense: the entire community, including the injured property owners, stood to enjoy benefits from improved transportation and water supplies or, in the case of mill dams in farming areas, by the convenience to farmers of nearby grain mills. But increasingly after 1830, invoking the same principle that underlay the mill-dam privileges, many states began extending eminent-domain powers for mill sites and water uses to manufacturers of paper, textiles, and other industrial products. At about the same time, legislatures began denying juries power to determine damages or compensation in eminent-domain cases. By midcentury, the "public use" idea had been stretched to include anything deemed (by the courts or legislatures) to contribute to the general business prosperity. One widely cited Massachusetts decision, *Talbot* v. *Hudson,* in 1860 concluded:

> It has never been deemed essential that the entire community or any considerable portion of it should directly enjoy or participate in an improvement or enterprise, in order to constitute

a public use. . . . [E]verything which tends to enlarge the resources, increase the energies, and promote the productive power of any considerable number of the inhabitants of a section of the State, or which leads to the growth of towns and the creation of new sources of private capital and labor, indirectly contributes to the general welfare and to the prosperity of the whole community [quoted in Scheiber, 1973].

With such ground rules, farmers, mine owners, wool growers, cattlemen, lumbermen, and manufacturers fought for favor in legislatures, courts, and constitutional conventions in their scramble over water resources and land-use rights. Their objective rarely was to insist upon "vested-rights" protections but, rather, to have their own enterprises declared a "public use" and entitled to the privileges and immunities in the economic arena that such designation implied.

The privileges associated with "public use" extended beyond eminent-domain powers to substantial exemption from common-law liabilities under tort, nuisance, negligence, and trespass doctrines. Mine companies could flush out mountainsides in search of ore, polluting, silting, and diverting rivers and streams, spoiling them for users downstream. Manufacturers and lumbering operations had similar effects. In some western states, miners gained the right—that is, immunity from trespass—even to go onto another's farmland to excavate for minerals. Courts immunized railroad companies from liability when sparks from locomotives caused fires along their routes. Manufacturers gained similar protections against suits for injuries to customers, employees, or third parties caused by unsafe or faulty products and factory machinery. The guiding principle, increasingly through at least the third quarter of the nineteenth century, was to reduce operating risks and costs for those enterprises that, in the view of the judges and legislatures, contributed significantly to the general prosperity.

Well into the nineteenth century, prevailing legal doctrines included a number of features—particularly in the area of private law—that, if unchanged, would have discouraged or raised the entrepreneurial costs of industrial development. (*Private law* is roughly that area of law governing the voluntary relationships of private individuals to one another, in contrast to *public law,* which refers to statutes or executive orders that indicate a state ordering of behavior.) This is not the place to discuss the transformation of legal doctrine on property, tort, contract, nuisance, trespass, and negligence. A few examples will illustrate the sorts of changes that took place.

(1) Until the end of the eighteenth century, it was nearly always assumed that when a bystander suffered injury from the activities of an employee, both the employee and his or her employer could be held liable. This was so whether or not the injury resulted from accident or from the employee's carelessness and regardless of whether the employee was doing something on specific command of the employer. By mid-nineteenth century, American courts were regularly requiring that negligence (carelessness) be demonstrated in order to hold an employer liable and that the act causing the injury had been commanded by the employer. The injured party, too, could be found to have contributed to the accident. (2) At the beginning of the nineteenth century, employers were not uncommonly held strictly liable for injuries on the job to their employees. By midcentury, doctrines of "contributory negligence" and the responsibility of "fellow servants" increasingly shielded employers from liability. (3) Until the nineteenth century, an employer or a producer could be made answerable under an "implied contract" rule if an employee were summarily dismissed or if a customer suddenly found supplies cut off. The value of personal regularity of relationship had been assumed. American courts rarely enforced such expectations in the nineteenth century, as notions of "free labor" and "free market" came to prevail. (4) Traditionally, a property owner was implicitly conceded the inviolability of his property, and his water resources were generally protected by common-law constraints on wasteful or destructive uses of upstream waters. But by the second quarter of the nineteenth century, courts in most states began discarding or amending traditional "reasonable use" constraints by comparing relative contributions to economic development of different kinds of business ventures. In many of the western states, courts and legislatures substituted an entirely new

doctrine ("prior appropriation") that awarded complete control of water to private claimants on the basis of "first-in-time, first-in-right."

Obviously, such changes vitally affected the allocation of economic risks, opportunities, and rewards among different kinds of business enterprises. The nineteenth-century revolution in common-law doctrines vastly enlarged the profit opportunities of industrial entrepreneurs while they generally constricted the protections offered by government to landowners, to small artisan and mercantile shops, to industrial employees, and to human and natural resources generally. At the same time, while changes in private law increasingly immunized certain investors, employers, and corporate managers from private suits for injuries to others' property, persons, and profits, other changes in constitutional law increasingly blocked efforts by state legislatures and Congress to bring employers and industrial corporations under social controls.

CONSTITUTIONAL LAW AND BUSINESS RISK

In the last quarter of the nineteenth century, mounting activity first in the state legislatures and then in Congress clearly indicated a shift in attitude toward what was happening in the political economy. Not that Americans turned against either economic growth or industrialization. Rather, by means of a growing volume of regulatory laws, the states and Congress gave clear signs of an intent to reexamine the privileges granted in American law over the previous century to private employers, creditors, industrial property owners, and possessors of investment capital. Widespread concern over the growth of giant interstate business firms and over the perceived corporate truculence found expression in the Greenback, Populist, and Progressive movements and generally in the popular identification of big business with "robber barons." Demands grew across the nation for antitrust prosecutions, a publicly managed and inflationary monetary system, protection of wage earners' efforts to organize for collective bargaining, revision of the tax laws that had placed the burden for revenues on real property while exempting personal and corporate wealth, limits on corporate spending in political campaigns, restrictions on new

uses of public lands, protection for women and child factory workers, factory and mine safety regulations, food and drug inspection agencies, and government control of pricing, service, and financial practices of railroads and other public utilities. Legislative action, however tentatively, appeared to be looking toward reassigning privileges and prerogatives among social groups. In particular it aimed at narrowing the privileged power of private industrial property owners, financiers, and large-scale employers, while extending protection to small proprietary businessmen, wage earners, the propertyless, and the consumers of mass-marketed goods.

By and large, the efforts to reappraise and adjust social priorities met with frustration, although some readjustment of advantages among business groups did result. One major obstacle to social reform lay with the courts, in particular with a novel interpretation of constitutional law that effectively left it to judges to veto changes in public law that clashed with the policy preferences established over the previous half-century in private law development. Both the Fifth and Fourteenth Amendments to the Constitution contain a clause that forbids Congress and the states (respectively) to pass any law that would "deprive a person of life, liberty, or property without due process of law." Until the last quarter of the nineteenth century, the U.S. Supreme Court generally granted to the states broad powers to regulate private behavior on behalf of the public interest. It had consistently interpreted *due process* to refer to procedure only—that is, to whether all proper procedures had been followed in the course of a law's passage or enforcement. Moreover, until that time the concept of property had applied primarily to real, tangible holdings and not usually either to income or to potential income that might be generated by the profitable uses of such holdings. By the end of the century, an activist Supreme Court had decided on four major changes: (1) that income and potential or anticipated income were property within the meaning of the Fifth and Fourteenth Amendments; (2) that any law that "unreasonably" impaired, reduced, or took property (including anticipated profits) would be held to violate the due-process clause on substantive grounds even when all procedural requirements of lawmaking were met; (3) that for purposes of constitutional law, though not necessarily for purposes of social liabilities, corporations were to be considered "persons" (rather than as impersonal agencies specially created by the state for more or less specific public purposes); and (4) that *liberty* was to be taken to include the right of private persons to enter freely into contracts of their own choosing without control or interference by the state, subject only to the courts' test of reasonableness.

Several important consequences in government control of public policy followed from these changes. One was to severely constrict the indiscriminate use of eminent domain as a public-policy tool and as an instrument of state favor for select interest groups. It may even be possible that the U.S. Supreme Court's increasing solicitude for private property in the age of the corporate reorganization of American business arose partly from attention to the corrupt and arbitrary uses of eminent-domain and public-use powers (McCurdy, 1975). On the other hand, there were other consequences that cannot be assigned to such benign sensitivity. The new interpretation of due process armed judges with a power to enforce the policy preferences that had prevailed in their own formative years. They tended to regard as "natural" the structure of laws that favored the historic instruments of economic growth, and they tended to view as "unnatural" constraining legislation that aimed at new social-policy preferences. Thus, railroad and utility corporations could ward off state efforts to control stock watering, rate changes, services, and safety, because courts frequently interpreted the costs to profit opportunities arising from state regulations as tantamount to confiscation—that is, an unconstitutional taking of property. Union actions met with similar judicial solicitude for profits. Strikes, secondary boycotts, organizing campaigns, even the right to peaceful picketing fell before court injunctions—"the very word 'picket,'" said Chief Justice Taft, implied impermissible threats (American Steel Foundries case, 1921)—virtually nullifying state and federal laws specifically designed to deter judicial intervention in industrial disputes. And, with corporations assuming the legal character of private persons (*Santa Clara County* v. *Southern Pacific Railway*, 1883), the courts found little room for treating state laws that attempted to regulate the wage bargain between individual workers and their corporate employers as any-

thing but a violation of the "liberty of contract" guaranteed to individual employers and employees alike.

THE CORPORATION REVOLUTION

The privileged place of the large-scale public business corporation in the American political economy constitutes a major paradox. Throughout most of the nineteenth century, Americans progressively encouraged the reduction of risk in industrial enterprise, granting broad immunities from both state and private sanctions. The rationale for this progress rested in large part on the assumption that economic growth, and hence the welfare of the nation, would be maximized when private enterprisers were free to maximize their own economic interests. More than that, in a vital sense the proprietary business interest stood as the keystone of Americans' capacity for self-government. As Justice Louis D. Brandeis put it in 1933 (*Liggett* v. *Lee,* in dissent), looking back on the American political tradition, "There is [still] a widespread belief . . . that only through the participation by the many in the responsibilities and determinations of business can Americans secure the moral and intellectual development which is essential to the maintenance of liberty."

By the 1880's, the Industrial Revolution, accompanied as it was by greatly increased concentrations of economic power within an inclusive continental market, brought about an interdependence of private interests that seriously eroded the structural bases of the traditional American rationale for a minimal state. The rise of "big business," beginning especially around 1875, followed (as Alfred Chandler has demonstrated) from technological and market imperatives that inspired hundreds of companies to integrate within the firm multiple functions in the production and marketing processes. Except for the tariff and changes in private law already mentioned, government played little role in this development, but the impact upon the traditional rationale was no less for all that. Not every industrial sector proved hospitable to large-scale integration, and many consolidated firms failed. But by 1900 most major industries were characterized by high levels of economic concentration. Insofar as economic concentration placed small groups of individuals in commanding market positions from which they could subject prices and output to the "visible hand" of managerial decisions, the marketplace could no longer be depended on for an equitable and impersonal distribution of social and economic benefits.

But the more damaging development came with the corporation revolution that overtook the country after 1890. As Willard Hurst has written, "The corporation was the most potent single instrument which the law put at the disposal of private decision makers. In making it available, the law lent its weight to the thrust of ambition which reshaped not only the business of the country but also its whole structure of power." Andrew Carnegie told an audience in 1896 that the difference between private enterprise and "the great corporations whose ownership is here, there, and everywhere . . . [is] the difference between individualism and communism applied to business." That was still a year before the first great industrial merger movement began, at the end of which (in 1904) a mere 200 firms had consolidated among themselves 40 percent of all manufacturing assets in the country. (By 1930, the figure exceeded 50 percent; by 1972, the 100 largest industrial corporations accounted for 41 percent of total industrial sales, 47 percent of total assets, 52 percent of net income, and 43 percent of all industrial employees.)

Before 1890 even many of the largest industrial and mercantile firms in the United States were not incorporated. But then changes in the law made incorporation and the public sale of corporate shares highly attractive. The first was the U.S. Supreme Court decision that awarded to corporations constitutional status as "persons." But more important were changes in the state corporation laws little known to most contemporaries that for the first time enabled corporations to acquire and operate other corporations—to function, in other words, as holding companies. The advantage of the holding company was this: although state prosecutions of the Standard Oil trust in the 1880's and passage of the Sherman Antitrust Act in 1890 pretty well established that several firms could not coordinate business practices by mutual agreement or by setting up a governing trusteeship among them, there appeared to be no legal reason why a single corporation—by buying the shares of its competitors or by exchanging shares with them—could not effect the same kind of coordination within one firm. Because it is not necessary for a corporation to be chartered by the state(s) in which it does its business, it can seek a charter in the most permissive state. The granting of holding-company privileges by New Jersey in 1889 triggered competition by other states for the revenues coming from chartering of corporations. A kind of Gresham's Law effect ("bad money drives out good") quickly followed, with states like Delaware, South Dakota, and Maine bidding for corporations by minimizing "home-office" requirements, removing long-standing legal limits on corporate debt and securities issues, and permitting capitalization of such intangible (and sometimes fictitious) assets as "good will" and "anticipated earnings"—practices that some states continued to define as fraud.

Such changes encouraged the incorporation of thousands of once proprietary enterprises, the public sale of ownership shares, and a massive consolidation of competing firms. The great consolidation movement of 1897–1903 was inspired less by realizable economies of scale, such as had spurred on the massive integration of industrial firms in the 1880's, as by the financial opportunities that inhered in the newly legitimated holding companies. Profit opportunities in the consolidated companies seemed bullish with the promise of substantial managerial control over production and prices. This made "industrials" popular for the first time on the securities markets, permitting public sale of corporate shares to thousands of "investor-owners," driving a permanent wedge between ownership and control of the major sectors of American business enterprise, and transforming the character of the relationship of business enterprise to the American polity.

The revolution created centers of tremendous power that had the characteristics of neither state agencies nor private enterprises; they derived their legitimacy from principles of neither consent nor ownership. Although given qualified status in law as "persons," in fact corporations consist merely of aggregations of assets devoid of either mortal or moral qualities that might serve to place temporal and human limits on the uses of their power. As U.S. Supreme Court Justice John Marshall Harlan put it (*U.S. v. E. C. Knight Co.,* in dissent, 1895), these "overshadowing combinations" of capital acknowledged "none of the restraints of moral obligations controlling the action of individuals." "There is reason to believe," Justice Louis Brandeis agreed nearly forty years later (*Quaker City Cab Co.* v. *Pennsylvania,* in dissent, 1933), that "because of the guidance and control necessarily exercised by great corporations upon those engaged in business, individual initiative is being impaired; . . . [and] the absorption of capital by corporations, and their perpetual life, may bring evils similar to those which attended mortmain."

Altogether, the large-scale public corporation negated precisely those features of private business enterprise that the traditional American ideology counted on to produce the combination of personal integrity and independence (character) assumed to be essential for a self-governing people. It undermined exactly those energizing and uplifting attributes of proprietorship that had justified the permissive, risk-emancipating legislation and court rulings of the nineteenth century. And it introduced elements of control, planning, capital recruitment, and market management in the private sector that directly contradicted the legitimating principles of ownership, consent, and morally conditioned competition underlying the traditional American model of a just society. No wonder the nation experienced an upheaval of sentiment at the outset of the twentieth century urging systematic control of the new corporate power. No wonder many defenders of American business like Carnegie and Brandeis viewed the large public corporation as a form of unfair business practice. And no wonder that, insofar as the large-scale public corporation came to dominate the American business system, Americans' sense of the public interest increasingly conflicted with the traditional business ethic.

The divergence in the American mind of the business interest from the public interest did not significantly materialize until at least the 1930's. Until then, the development of "the regulatory state" followed traditional patterns of the competitive struggle within the business community itself. Nearly all of the most noteworthy federal legislation associated with the great populist and progressive reform movements, and much of the New Deal legislation besides, traces its origins primarily to private-sector competition. Antitrust action is the most obvious case in point.

ANTITRUST

The United States' tradition of antitrust, almost unique among industrial countries, owes its existence primarily to private business firms seeking protection from the state against larger and rapidly growing companies that invaded or threatened the smaller firms' markets or sources of supply. Indeed, most scholars ascribe its uniqueness especially to the multitude of strong private businesses in the United States as compared with the easy alliance of government with the relatively few strong firms of, say, Germany and Japan, where cartels became favored forms of industrial organization. (The U.S. effort at cartelization under the auspices of the National Recovery Administration [NRA] during the Depression ran aground on the shoals of massive business resistance and, finally, a unanimously hostile Supreme Court in 1935.) Most particularly, antitrust illustrates in an especially cogent way just how strongly public policy in America has sought to protect business as a central feature of the culture as well as of the economy.

Antimonopoly sentiment has always been powerful in American politics, from the Revolutionary era, when the colonists chafed against Parliament-created monopolies, through the Jacksonian campaign against the second Bank of the United States and the fight for "free banking" and general incorporation statutes. For the most part, Americans associated monopoly with government-sponsored privilege. By the last quarter of the nineteenth century, however, a revolution in production and marketing techniques created huge integrated companies, each absorbing major shares of its industry's market, thereby permitting only a few, large companies to survive. It became evident that "monopoly"—or, more accurately, oligopoly—could arise, as in fact it did, from two nongovernmental sources: the "natural" or spontaneous success of the modern integrated business firm and the voluntary merger of several competing firms into one.

Although there was some contemporary complaint that the ongoing concentration of private economic resources in "the trusts" would lead to high prices, antitrust did not arise from consumer fears about monopolistic price gouging. On the contrary, it was widely believed in the era of the Sherman Antitrust Act (1890), the Clayton Antitrust Act (1914), and the Federal Trade Commission Act (1914) that the consolidation of industry would bring significant consumer savings from the new economies of scale in production, finance, and marketing. The principal business argument for antitrust cited the threat that "monopoly" posed to the American business system and to democratic politics. It is noteworthy that in the first federal antitrust case to successfully withstand U.S. Supreme Court review (*U.S.* v. *Trans-Missouri Freight Association,* 1897), the Court denied that consumer savings bore significantly on the matter of public policy established by Congress and brought before the Court. Though efficiencies may be demonstrated and prices may come down, the Court said, trade or commerce that Congress is constitutionally commanded to promote and protect

> may nevertheless be badly injured and unfortunately restrained by driving out of business the small dealers and worthy men whose lives have been spent therein, and who might be unable to readjust themselves to their altered surroundings. Here reduction in the price of the commodity dealt in might be dearly paid for by the ruin of such a class, and the absorption of control over one commodity by an all powerful combination of capital.

Antitrust actions brought on the first important confrontation in the twentieth century between major business elements and the federal government. However much the public may have disliked the trusts, the most active sector of the business community, namely the big corporations and their financial allies, complained bitterly about the uncertainties that the new federal antitrust statutes had introduced into business calculations; and they were persuasive in arguing that such uncertainties seriously jeopardized opportunities for national economic growth. Theodore Roosevelt tried to mollify the critics by getting Congress in 1903 to set up a Federal Bureau of Corporations that would (among other things) advise businessmen on what they might or might not legitimately do. But Roosevelt's successful antitrust prosecution in 1904 of the Northern Securities Company, a mammoth railroad holding company, established the principle that the fed-

eral government would no longer allow private business leaders to take the state for granted in their reshaping of the nation's business structure. That, together with Roosevelt's verbal attacks on Standard Oil and the "malefactors of great wealth," seemingly placed the federal government in an adversarial relationship with an important part of the business community, a relationship that has more or less persisted throughout the twentieth century. But what is noteworthy is that much of the regulatory legislation of the century, including especially the establishment of the many independent regulatory commissions that have become the mark of the modern state, may be viewed at least in part as efforts to reduce the political impact of business–government friction.

THE RISE OF THE
MODERN REGULATORY STATE

Especially in its initial stages, the growth of the twentieth-century regulatory state merely marked the transfer of major parts of the struggle for advantage among competing business groups from the economic marketplace to the political arena. In some cases it was "losers" petitioning legislatures to redress perceived imbalances of advantage that distorted the "free" operation of the market and caused an unjust distribution of resources and rewards among rivals. Thus, local and relatively small businesses demanded state action against "the trusts." Some shippers, merchants, and producers sought protection against the monopolistic market power of railroads, oil pipelines, gas companies, and other "common carriers" of goods and services. Farmers, chronically short on liquidity and remote from credit resources, pushed for government warehousing and grading to help make warehouse receipts acceptable collateral for bank loans. Later, agricultural interests sought protection against chronically recurring commodity gluts in the form of "soil conservation" programs and legally sanctioned market orders. Northeastern textile manufacturers asked for federal redress of the "unfair" advantages that southern manufacturers enjoyed in cheap child labor. Investors sought protection against the self-governing and misgoverned stock markets. Sometimes it was well-established business interests looking to government for help: for example, large meat-packing companies with important interstate and overseas markets urging federal inspection laws to overcome suspicions about product quality caused by allegedly sleazy cost-cutting practices of smaller companies with narrow profit margins; or railroad traffic managers, and their shipper and banker allies, looking to prevent rate wars that could undermine solvency and jeopardize services.

To put it another way, various groups in the business community claimed different kinds of market failure—either because alleged monopolistic advantages distorted market outcomes or because at least some rational, short-run "free market" decisions led to medium-run diseconomies (rate wars, damage to export markets, commodity gluts, clogging of air lanes and radio waves) and some unacceptable long-run outcomes as well (for example, economies of scale that impelled wasteful consumption of depletable resources, dictated congestion of urban entrepôts, and forced small communities to forego important services). As was the American tradition, or habit, such groups called upon the state for help.

But how was the state to rectify market failure? Substituting state actions for the marketplace entailed major political dangers. It had been partly for that reason that the American state historically had avoided overt redistributional functions—and had especially avoided decisions that overtly served losers in the "free play" of market forces. A marketplace decision had innate legitimacy; it was impersonal and followed "natural law." But government decisions burdened incumbents with grave political hazards; they could easily appear partisan and personal and invite political retribution from new losers. Legislators therefore commonly sought to pass the buck. In the past, this usually took the form of statutory vagueness, which would throw concrete decisions into the protected laps of the judges. The courts, however, had a tendency in the late nineteenth century to protect power where it lay and to define challenges to prevailing power as merely "political" at best or "class legislation" at worst, neither of which, in the courts' eyes, served as a legitimate basis for a just claim. Losers and insurgent interests demanded other solutions.

The legislative response to such demands was the independent regulatory commission. These agencies were to be "nonpolitical" panels of experts, bureaus of the executive branch of government that, in adjudicating conflicting claims of right, would substitute nonpartisan fact-finding and judgment for the flawed marketplace on the one hand and the presumed illegitimacy of strictly political bargaining on the other. Commissioners were generally appointed for fixed terms, so that they could not be removed by either the U.S. Congress or the president for partisan or political reasons. For some commissions, Congress also required a balance of membership according to party affiliation. The regulatory agencies were thus armed with the authority of science, technical specialization, and nonpartisanship in order to deflect the brickbats that would inevitably fly when choices had to be made between basically irreconcilable claims among private competing groups. They would, moreover, bypass the judiciary that (1) had become suspect because of its perceived rigidity in the face of new social forces and economic developments, and (2) would in any case soon become overwhelmed by the volume of redistributive decisions that the modern political economy required of the state.

But the growth of the modern regulatory state marked more than just the transfer of the struggle for advantage among business rivals from the economic to the political arena. Four major developments arose in the twentieth century to shake the state loose from its historic bond with the society's business interest: (1) recurrent wars and the issue of national security; (2) the rise of a nonpropertied labor interest that took political shape in the form of an adversarial relationship with an increasingly distinct employer interest; (3) the post–World War II civil rights movement; and (4) the appearance of a public interest movement, made up of two nonbusiness components—a distinct consumer interest and an environmentalist interest.

Let us conclude by treating each of these developments briefly:

1. In both world wars, the American state emerged to suspend or constrict "free-market" mechanisms in the interest of the national security. That included rigorous controls over wages, prices, resource allocation, foreign trade, and in-

vestment during wartime. The Trading-with-the-Enemy Act of 1917, unrepealed after World War I, enabled the president to supervise closely American exports of war-sensitive products and technology, a power that the government revived after 1945 to serve the perceived needs of the cold war. Since midcentury, the highly complex technology of weaponry, the great expense of war technology, and the long lead-time for weapons development have made government war contracts a significant part of peacetime industrial activity for the first time in the country's history, and an important part of scores of major corporations' business structure. All these things have made the state's strategies loom larger in private-sector management than at any time in American history.

2. Passage of the National Labor Relations, or Wagner, Act (1935), by legitimating and enforcing collective bargaining, for the first time in a major way introduced state power between private-sector employers and employees on behalf of employee interests. Although the state's purpose was to stabilize industrial relations in an increasingly violent environment, and thereby safeguard the state's interest in order (as well as in long-term business interests), the intervention clearly reduced private-management autonomy on employment policies. Together with the Social Security Act of 1935, which compelled most private employers and employees to contribute to a workers' pension and unemployment insurance program, the Wagner Act marked—in a more decisive way than the war emergency actions did—the establishment of the state as an independent entity prepared to force the business community to yield advantages to nonbusiness rivals in the general society.

3. What was done on behalf of wage workers and their unions by the Wagner Act in the 1930's was achieved for designated racial and ethnic groups, and for women and the disabled as well, by the Civil Rights Act of 1964 and its several amendments over the next eight years. Under the terms of these measures, the federal government moved forcefully into the private-business sector to prevent adverse discrimination on the basis of race, religion, nationality, gender, physical handicap, and age in private housing, transportation, recreation, bank loans, employment, and education. Implementation of such measures, including procedures devised to test compliance, significantly raised the costs of doing business, reduced the autonomy of private-business management, and raised the level of irritation in government–business relations.

4. The momentum of concern for nonbusiness objectives reached its historic peak in the 1964–1975 period when, in addition to civil rights legislation and executive orders, Congress moved to establish major administrative agencies to protect consumers' and workers' safety and to preserve natural resources, including clean air and water, rare animal species, and environmental beauty. The Environmental Protection Agency (EPA), the Occupational Safety and Health Administration (OSHA), the Truth-in-Lending Act, the Consumer Products Safety Commission, the Council on Environmental Quality, the Mining Enforcement and Safety Administration, the Materials Transportation Bureau, the National Highway Traffic Safety Administration, all established in that period, seemingly put business and government on a collision course. One should stress the "seemingly," because until 1973 many business groups accepted the need for many of the new regulations. For a brief period, Americans from many sectors of the society not only distinguished between the business interest and the public interest but also appeared to subordinate the business ethic to a social ethic. Many business organizations in the 1964–1973 period seriously debated the degree to which the profit motive could reasonably yield to goals defined by standards of "social responsibility." Meanwhile, major government agencies arose to serve the newly defined priorities in state purposes.

Then the Organization of Petroleum Exporting Countries (OPEC) put their cartel to the test and triumphantly raised the world's fuel bill by more than 300 percent, just as the United States was becoming a major fuel importer. At that point, Americans retreated to their more traditional preoccupation with economic growth. As Americans faced great pressures on their affluent standard of living and confronted signs of a new economy of scarcity, business leaders renewed their oft-tested argument that the social responsibility of private business consisted solely in maximizing productivity. Complaints about the high costs of social reform brought about a strong political response. The defeat of the proposed Consumer Protection Agency in 1978 and the election of Ronald Reagan in 1980 marked a resumption of the tilt of the state toward American society's business interest.

But the demand for civil rights, environmental protection, consumer safety, and employees' welfare has become a strong concern of the state and will likely remain so. Modern technology and chemistry, together with global political imperatives, guarantee that the American state must continue to constrict private-business decisions. The long-term, cumulative, and often hidden hazards of chemical processes, products, and wastes; the all-too-foreseeable shortages of exhaustible resources; the increased vulnerability of all nations to the reach and violence of modern weaponry; and the new ways in which the American people have come to define a just society have altered the political environment in a permanent way. So, too, has the maturing of the new agencies within the state bureaucracy with charters to monitor, or even champion, the new and newly magnified commitments—from national defense to safeguarding the ozone layer. All these features of the modern world make it certain that though the historic American partnership of business and government will continue, most likely business will be made to serve the interests of the state in a greater measure than it once had reason to expect, perhaps even as much as the state once historically served society's private-business interest.

BIBLIOGRAPHY

Guy Stevens Callender, "The Early Transportation and Banking Enterprises of the States in Relation to the Growth of Corporations," in *Quarterly Journal of Economics*, 17 (1902), is an early source for later historians who were to reassess the role of government in the development of American business enterprise. Alfred D. Chandler, Jr., *The Visible Hand: The Managerial Revolution in American Business* (Cambridge, Mass., 1977), is the most detailed and authoritative history of American business management. Its one serious flaw is the author's omission of any treatment of labor as a management problem. Chandler has also published and stimulated others to write on the rise of modern European business management. Thomas C. Cochran, *Business in American Life: A History* (New York, 1972), is a pioneer effort

to write "a different synthesis" of American history, focusing on business rather than on the more usually emphasized political, social, or economic developments and noting, as Woodrow Wilson did, that "Business underlies everything in our national life."

Herbert Croly, *The Promise of American Life* (New York, 1909; repr. 1963), has been referred to by some historians as the "bible of the progressive movement." A copy of the book was sent to Theodore Roosevelt while he was abroad after he left the presidency. It is thought to have influenced the shaping of his New Nationalism program for the 1912 campaign. Elisha P. Douglass, *The Coming of Age of American Business: Three Centuries of Enterprise, 1600–1900* (Chapel Hill, N.C., 1971), is a remarkably thorough, although overly systematic, account of American business institutions. It is well written but suffers from coverage of the many business sectors (railroads, canals, fur trade, insurance, etc.) in series, chapter by chapter. Lawrence M. Friedman, *A History of American Law* (New York, 1973), is the only survey history that places legal development in the context of social, political, and economic history. Milton Friedman, *Capitalism and Freedom* (Chicago, 1962), is a terse statement by the Nobel laureate economist of his well-known view that individual liberty, private profit-seeking, and the free market are inextricably linked. James Willard Hurst, *Law and the Conditions of Freedom in the Nineteenth-Century United States* (Madison, Wis., 1956), is the most accessible work of many written by this pioneer in American legal history.

John F. Kasson, *Civilizing the Machine: Technology and Republican Values in America, 1776–1900* (New York, 1977), is a tidy study that does a fine job of showing the way business values blended with republican values early in American history. Simon Kuznets, *Economic Growth and Structure: Selected Essays* (New York, 1965), is a good sampling of the work of one of the innovators in economic development theory. Robert A. Lively, "The American System: A Review Essay," in *Business History Review*, 29 (1955), is a review of several books then recently published that demonstrated the substantial degree to which American government interacted with the private business sector. For a quarter-century after 1935, American historiography generally stressed the beneficial effects of government activism on the development of American economic prosperity. Charles W. McCurdy, "Justice Field and the Jurisprudence of Government–Business Relations: Some Parameters of Laissez-Faire Constitutionalism, 1863–1897," in *Journal of American History*, 61 (1975), is an attempt to show that historians have mistaken Field's efforts on the U.S. Supreme Court to limit state police powers as probusiness, when in fact Field sought to prevent the use of public-interest doctrine for special interests of all kinds. Harry N. Scheiber, "Property Law, Expropriation, and Resource Allocation by Government: The United States, 1789–1910," in *Journal of Economic History*, 33 (1973), is recommended. "Expropriation of private property by government," Scheiber writes, "is seldom found on the list of policies which have influenced the course of economic development in American history." This article and other works by Scheiber, Hurst, McCurdy and others have done much to correct that error. Stephen Skowronek, *Building a New American State: The Expansion of National Administrative Capacities* (New York and Cambridge,

1982), is a stimulating effort by an American political scientist to trace the development of the modern bureaucratic state. Like much of the literature on political economy in the 1970's, it expresses dismay over the effects of government regulation. R. Richard Wohl, "The Significance of Business History," in *Business History Review*, 28 (1954), is an almost unique early attempt to bring the study of business into the mainstream of American cultural history.

[*See also* CONSERVATION, ENVIRONMENT, AND ENERGY; FEDERALISM; INTERSTATE COMMERCE; LAISSEZ-FAIRE; NEW DEAL; NEW FREEDOM; POPULISM; PROGRESSIVISM; PROPERTY; REGULATORY AGENCIES; STATE GOVERNMENTS; TARIFF POLICIES; TAXATION; *and* VOLUNTARY ASSOCIATIONS.]

CABINET

R. Gordon Hoxie

ORIGINS

ALTHOUGH the term *cabinet* in the political sense dates only from the seventeenth century, the advisory and governing functions that the term connotes had ancient, even primitive, origins. The earliest tribal chieftains had advisory councils that on occasion became governing councils. The ancient Greeks elevated the advisory role. Writing in the *Politics* in the fourth century B.C., Aristotle observed, "It is already the practice of kings to make themselves many eyes and ears and hands and feet. For they make colleagues of those who are friends of themselves and of their governments."

It was the inner circle of the king's advisers that, in England in 1625, came to be called the "Cabinet Council." Colonial American political development, including the governor's council, paralleled that in Britain. But with the divergence of the political systems in the last quarter of the eighteenth century, beginning with a revolutionary American Congress in 1774 and culminating in the Constitutional Convention of 1787, the term *cabinet* came to have differing meanings in the two nations.

At the same time that the United States in 1787 determined to have a single executive, Britain was moving toward a plural executive of ministers and a prime minister constituting a governing cabinet. The constitutional framers gathered in Philadelphia were concerned with remedying the deficiencies of the Articles of Confederation. As such they were not interested in trends in the British system, even though significant changes were being made in it. The younger Pitt, then serving as prime minister, was going directly to the people for support. This move toward a democratic cabinet system seems to have failed to impress John Adams, who served as the American minister in London from 1785 to 1788. Among the framers, only Alexander Hamilton expressed particular interest in an English model, which was rejected. Moreover, the framers established a fundamental difference from the British system by the separation of powers and by the specific prohibition of members of Congress from holding any other federal office. Furthermore, they had a general feeling that the executive should not be hamstrung with a council. Hence the cabinet, which is not even referred to in the Constitution, could be simply advisory at most.

During the course of the Constitutional Convention, several proposals were made for executive departments. Charles Pinckney, who at the Convention had been the first to use the term *cabinet* in its American context, had proposed a council of state, including the heads of executive departments. This council proposal—like all others, including that of Gouverneur Morris—failed of adoption because of strong sentiment against overstructuring the executive and against any advisory council. Hamilton expressed the general distrust of advisory bodies when he wrote in *The Federalist* number 70, "A council to a magistrate, who is himself responsible for what he does, are generally nothing better than a clog upon his good intentions; are often the instruments and accomplices of his bad, and are almost always a cloak to his faults." Or, as James Wilson put it, a council "oftener serves to cover, than prevent malpractice." George Mason believed "that in rejecting a Council to the President, we were about to try an experiment" that no other nation had entered upon. Although Pinckney's council of state was not adopted, the principle that he enunciated,

147

that the advisory relationship between the president and department heads be at the president's discretion, gained general support.

The framers then simply indicated in Article II, Section 2, Clause 1 that the president "may require the Opinion, in writing, of the principal Officer in each of the executive Departments, upon any Subject relating to the Duties of their respective Offices." There being no constitutional provision for a cabinet per se, the cabinet evolved from this invitation for advice that the presidents "may require." There is no implication in this statement of the president's meeting with, and certainly not of meeting collectively with each "principal Officer," because "the Opinion" that the president "may require" is "in writing" and as regards "the Duties of their respective Offices."

Establishing the Executive Departments. Washington was inaugurated on 30 April 1789 in New York City, the first capital. Prior to and immediately following the inauguration, he consulted with Hamilton, James Madison, and others on the powers and duties of the president. Early on he took the view that the heads of the executive departments should be assistants to the presidents rather than to the Congress. "I have," he wrote, " . . . been taught to believe, that there is, in most polished nations, a system established, with regard to the great Departments. . . . The impossibility that one man should be able to perform all the great business of the State, I take to have been the reason for instituting the great Departments."

Needing help, Washington asked the Congress to create three "executive Departments"—one for foreign affairs, one for military affairs, and one for fiscal matters. While Congress considered his request, Washington retained the services of those who had been serving in those areas during the Confederation period. Hence John Jay continued temporarily as secretary of foreign affairs, General Henry Knox continued as secretary of war, and fiscal matters were handled by the old Treasury Board. During the first six months of his administration, Washington postponed considerable business until the executive branch could be organized.

On 19 May 1789, Congressman Elias Boudinot of New Jersey opened the debate on Washington's proposed executive departments when he asked the Congress to consider general principles related to their establishment. So began more than two months of exchange of views in the Congress, which had considerable discretion because each department had to be created by statute.

Several questions arose, among them: Which of the three departments should be senior? Finance, Boudinot believed; but Congressman Madison of Virginia, hoping that Thomas Jefferson would be selected as head of the foreign affairs department, believed that that department should be senior. Madison's view carried.

Another question involved removal from office. By the Constitution, the appointment of the department heads required the advice and consent of the Senate, but what about their removal? More fearful of an imperial Congress than an imperial president, Madison argued for vesting authority for removal solely with the president. He believed this was inherent in the president's "Executive Power," a constitutional phrase that no one, except Hamilton and Madison himself, seemed to comprehend entirely. Because of Madison's important role in the Constitutional Convention, his views were respected, and again his position carried. And yet even Madison, realizing the Congress was on untrodden ground, moved with caution. On 5 July 1789 he wrote, "The business goes on still very slowly. We are in a wilderness without a single footstep to guide us."

There was a third major question: Should all three departments be considered alike in their relationships to the Congress? The Congress thought not. Whereas Foreign Affairs and War seemed to be creatures of the executive, the Treasury appeared also to serve as a legislative agent. Because all appropriations bills must originate in the House, the secretary of the treasury might well serve the Congress in an advisory capacity. The legislation establishing the three departments reflected those views. On 27 July 1789 Congress established an "Executive Department, to be denominated the Department of Foreign Affairs." The secretary of foreign affairs would "perform and execute such duties as shall from time to time be enjoined on or entrusted to him by the President of the United States." The statute creating the War Department was of similar format and structure. When need arose for an agency to keep the Great Seal, maintain records, publish certain enactments, and perform other functions pertaining to internal affairs, Congress, by an act of 15 September 1789, changed the name of the Department of Foreign Affairs to the Department of State and the title of the secretary accordingly.

But the creation of the Treasury Department, by act of Congress on 2 September 1789, was another matter. Unlike State and War, it was not designated as an "Executive Department," nor was the secretary directed to perform and execute duties called for by the president. Instead the statute required him "to digest and prepare plans for the improvement and management of the revenue, and for the support of public credit; to prepare and report estimates of the public revenue, and the public expenditures; to superintend the collection of the revenue; to decide on the forms of keeping and stating accounts and making returns"; and to carry out other duties. Moreover, the secretary of the treasury was directed to report and give information to either the House or the Senate "in person or in writing (as he may be required)" respecting all matters referred to him by the Congress. A part of the rationale for this special status, as argued by Fisher Ames, was the requirement that revenue bills originate in the House. There is evidence that Hamilton, whom Washington had early designated to head the Treasury, drafted the Treasury Act himself.

Indeed, Washington's former military aide was the president's principal adviser in organizing the government. Washington considered all executive department heads as his "assistants," a term that Hamilton had used in *The Federalist.* Yet from the day Hamilton's appointment as secretary of the treasury was confirmed, 11 September 1789, he might well have become virtually the prime minister. This was not only because of his abilities and his special relationship with Washington, but also because of the importance of the Treasury Department. Both State and War were relatively smaller departments. Jefferson's view to the contrary, Hamilton had no prime ministerial ambitions. Leonard D. White concludes (1948) concerning Hamilton, "His loyal acceptance of Washington's primacy and his theoretical view of the status of a department head precluded any attempt on his part in this direction." Yet with his admiration of the British model and his high regard for Washington, Hamilton conceived of executive power as gen-

erated through a cabinet of department heads, administered by a judicious executive head. In such a system, by the sheer vent of his energies and genius, Hamilton came to be Washington's dominant adviser.

Knox had been confirmed as secretary of war the day after Hamilton's confirmation. On 26 September 1789, Edmund Randolph, another friend of Washington, had been named attorney general (although there would be no Department of Justice until 1870). Jefferson, who was serving as United States minister in France, did not return to become secretary of state until 22 March 1790. By that time, Hamilton's dominant position was already firmly established. Senator Maclay lamented, "Congress may go home. Mr. Hamilton is all-powerful, and fails in nothing he attempts." Jefferson decried Hamilton's special relationship with the Congress, charging, "He endeavored to place himself subject to the House, when the Executive should propose what he did not like, and subject to the Executive, when its House should propose anything disagreeable."

Washington Seeks Advice. Prior to the confirmation of the heads of the executive departments, Washington was still laboring under the impression that the Senate would, in essence, fill the role of an advisory council. With such a view, accompanied by Knox, Washington on 22 and 24 August came onto the floor of the Senate to get advice on an Indian treaty. The senators made it clear that the president was not welcome. According to Senator Maclay, Washington then withdrew "with sullen dignity." Henceforth no president ever again came to the Congress for counsel, dialogue, or inquiry; nor did presidents receive congressional committees. For example, as president, Madison declined to meet with a Senate committee regarding a foreign service appointment. After the Washington episode, the Congress was wary also of inviting the department heads to appear in person. In January 1790 the House, after considerable debate, moved to have Hamilton's significant *Report on the Public Credit* submitted in writing rather than presented in person.

Such experiences helped in the formation of the cabinet. Rebuffed in seeking advice from Congress, Washington increasingly sought the counsel of his three secretaries and also the attorney general, the vice-president (John Adams), and the chief justice (Jay). Madison, though a congressman, continued as a source of counsel. At first Washington consulted with such persons individually, both personally and in writing. In October 1789, for example, he consulted individually with Hamilton, Knox, Madison, and Jay on the desirability of presidential tours; at the same time he consulted with Hamilton, Madison, and Jay on aspects of British relations, including western posts still occupied by the British and a possible commercial treaty (matters finally resolved in Jay's Treaty five years later).

Hamilton had hoped the capital might remain in New York City; Jefferson, that it would be removed southward. More vital to Hamilton was federal assumption of the states' debts. Jefferson agreed to support this in exchange for removing the capital in 1800 to an area near Georgetown, on the Potomac. (Until then it would be removed to Philadelphia in December 1790.) This was one of the last congressional measures recommended by both statesmen. Later Jefferson decried assumption, which had increased federal authority.

Although Washington continued to seek counsel individually on matters ranging from the sale of lands to the constitutionality of the proposed Bank of the United States, he did not meet with his advisers as a group until the spring of 1791. The matter of the bank was illustrative of Washington's style. He turned first to Attorney General Randolph and then to Jefferson. Because both gave adverse opinions, he turned to Hamilton, who set forth, to Washington's satisfaction, arguments for the bank's validity.

Initial Cabinet Meetings. The much traveled president found cause in his projected southern journey in 1791 to encourage his department heads, in his absence, to meet as a body. On 4 April 1791 he wrote Hamilton, Jefferson, and Knox, urging them to meet "if any serious and important cases should arise" and determine "whether they are of such a nature as to require my formal attendance." Otherwise, he would upon his return "approve and ratify the measures" they had taken. This is the first recorded directive of the president to the heads of departments as regards their meeting as a body. Gratuitously, Washington added that were the vice-president available, he should join them. They did meet, on 11 April 1791, and Adams did

attend. However, according to Jefferson, this was the first and last such meeting in which Adams participated. Thereafter Attorney General Randolph attended.

It may be noted that, in view of both the constitutional power vested in a single executive and Washington's own restrictions, these initial meetings in the president's absence were of a body with less than the complete collective responsibility of the British cabinet. For example, following the meeting on 11 April (which was about a foreign loan), Hamilton had written Washington, who responded on 7 May, ". . . I do hereby signify my approbation." Traditionally, Washington left Philadelphia to be at his beloved Mount Vernon for two months in the late summer and early fall. After Washington returned to the capital in late October 1791, he began meeting regularly with the three department heads and the attorney general. These meetings were generally held in the president's mansion on Market Street near Sixth. The vice-president was not in regular attendance, nor was he to be a regular participant in the cabinet until the mid-twentieth century.

Two of the most significant meetings of the Washington cabinet occurred on 31 March and 2 April 1792, during the course of a House investigation into the ill-fated Indian expedition led by General Arthur St. Clair. In these meetings the president asked the views of Jefferson, Hamilton, Randolph, and Knox as to whether papers of the secretary of war on the expedition should be turned over to the Special House Investigating Committee. In the course of these meetings, the doctrine of executive privilege was expressed for the first time; that is, that by the separation-of-powers doctrine the executive branch may withhold from the legislative branch information, "the disclosure of which would injure the public." After setting forth the doctrine, the cabinet recommended in this instance complying with the request, and Knox transmitted the papers requested.

Several cabinet meetings in the ensuing two years considered the propriety of forwarding communications to Congress. For example, after consultation with the cabinet regarding dispatches from Gouverneur Morris, the American minister in France, President Washington on 26 February 1794 submitted the reports "except in those particulars, which, in my judgment, for public considerations ought not to be communicated."

By the summer of 1792, Washington was much concerned by the growing dissension between Jefferson and Hamilton in the cabinet. On 23 August he wrote Jefferson on this subject and Hamilton three days later. The latter he implored thus, "My earnest wish is, that balsam may be poured into *all* the wounds." Responding on 9 September, Hamilton confided to Washington, "I *know* that I have been an object of uniform opposition from Mr. Jefferson, from the first moment of his coming to the City of New York to enter upon his present office. . . . As long as I saw no danger to the Government, from the machinations which were going on, I resolved to be a silent sufferer. . . ." However, Hamilton believed that the time was approaching "when the public good will require *substitutes* for the *differing members* of your administration."

A Cabinet Forged. Washington continued to seek out other areas of counseling, skillfully checking one source against another. Chief Justice Jay continued as a personal source outside the cabinet. As Washington expressed it, he wanted from Jay "ideas . . . not confined to matters judicial, but extended to all other topics. . . ." Apart from Jay's personal counsel, the Supreme Court made clear in 1793 that as a body, the Court, both by the principle of separation of powers and by its own responsibility as a court of last resort, could not serve as a counsel to the president. The dilemma that evoked this response was the perilous course of foreign relations.

In the spring of 1793 the revolutionary government in France was seeking to bring the United States into its war with Great Britain and Holland. Jefferson sought to bring the United States to the aid of France, whereas Hamilton advocated a neutral course. According to Jefferson, during this period the cabinet met almost daily. Hamilton lost no time in asking Jay to draft a neutrality proclamation, which, to Jefferson's distress, Washington signed on 22 April 1793. Through the balance of 1793 and the following year the cabinet was actively engaged in a host of matters on relations with Great Britain and France as a follow-up to the neutrality proclamation and also, in 1794, as regards the insurrec-tion in western Pennsylvania against the whiskey excise tax.

It was in this crucible of controversies that the cabinet as an instrument of policy was forged. Although the term *cabinet* was by this time widely used, it was not given official recognition in the Congress until 25 April 1798, when it was described as "the great council of the Nation."

The Federalist Legacy. Although the Federalists controlled the executive branch only during the administrations of Washington and John Adams, they left a remarkable legacy of executive policy and administration. Interwoven in this is the cabinet.

Although the cabinet relationship had been marred by the Jefferson–Hamilton feud, both had contributed to its creation and its performance. The meetings had been vigorous, frequently called with only twenty-four hours' notice and with Washington's demands to produce position papers within that time. Jefferson usually comprised the minority, sometimes joined by Randolph. Washington did not engage in the debates. Rather, he listened to the arguments or read their opinions and made his decisions. Unfortunately, the period 1791–1793 had been marred by Jefferson's attempts not only to check Hamilton personally but also to dismantle the Treasury Department. This had led to Hamilton's masterful essay on interdepartmental relations. Discord between departmental heads, he warned, "must necessarily tend to occasion, more or less, distracted councils, to foster factions in the community, and particularly to weaken the government."

Jefferson's resignation in 1793 was accepted by Washington with great regret. Immediately after taking the oath of office, the new secretary of state, Edmund Randolph, wrote Hamilton and Knox to assure them, "I shall avoid the uneasiness of suspicion, and I take the liberty of requesting that the same line of conduct be pursued with respect to myself."

Washington, who had hoped to be apolitical, had found the situation impossible. Reflecting on his inability to retain Jefferson's services, he wrote, "I shall not, whilst I have the honor to Administer the government, bring a man into any office, of consequence, knowingly whose political tenets are adverse to the measures which the *general* government are pursuing; for this, in my opinion, would be a sort of political Suicide; that it wd. embarrass its movements is most certain."

Following Jefferson's resignation, all cabinet members with the possible exception of Randolph, who resigned the following year, fully supported the policies of the government enunciated by Washington. Hamilton, needing to earn money for his family, retired from government service early in 1795 to return to his lucrative law practice, yet his influence was little diminished. The president and all the cabinet members wrote him for counsel throughout the remaining two years of Washington's second term. As Washington expressed it, "Altho' you are not in the Administration—a thing I sincerely regret—I must, nevertheless, (knowing how intimately acquainted you are with all the concerns of this country) request the favor of you." In every major issue of finance or foreign policy, Washington and one or more of his cabinet sought Hamilton's advice. In both foreign and domestic policy, Hamilton continued as Washington's principal adviser, through the remainder of the second Washington administration, including helping to draft the masterful Farewell Address.

John Adams, as president, continued with all of Washington's cabinet members. To Adams' distress, they were more dependent on Hamilton's counsel than they had been with Washington. The problem was compounded by Adams' long absences from the seat of government. During the four years of his presidency he was absent from the capital, mostly in Quincy, Massachusetts, for 385 days. Moreover, he lacked Washington's strong administrative direction. During his absences, cabinet members became advisory to each other. The final year of his administration was marred by his removal of two cabinet members who were more loyal to Hamilton than to the president. Despite these experiences he retained the cabinet as his principal advisory instrument. During his administration one new member was added in 1798, the secretary of the navy, when war with France threatened.

Cosmopolitan Philadelphia, with its haut monde, had been the nation's capital from 1790 to 1800. In the summer of 1800 the Adamses had moved to the new capital city of Washington, population *circa* 2,500. The unfinished, almost white limestone "Palace," renamed the Executive Mansion, had a second-floor presidential of-fice where Adams met with his cabinet. Only the north wing of the Capitol had been completed when the Congress first convened there in the fall of 1800.

The twelve Federalist years had established the practice of joint consultation between the president and the department heads as a body, but it was clear that the president was bound neither to consult nor to accept the advice received. Nor was the cabinet an administrative body. The business of government was carried out through the executive departments. The "duty to consult," the views of Adams' secretary of state (Pickering) to the contrary, was at the discretion of the president. The twelve years had also established the secretary of state as the least tenable cabinet post and the secretary of the treasury as the most influential.

NINETEENTH-CENTURY CABINETS

With the defeat of the Federalists by the Jeffersonians in 1800, the importance of the cabinet as an advisory council declined. Although relations between the cabinet and the Congress during the Federalist years had often been contentious, the energy of the department heads, including both Hamilton and Jefferson, had been respected. The triumph of the Jeffersonians in both the executive and the legislative branches seemed to bring complacency. That many members of the Jefferson cabinet, including Secretary of State James Madison, did not even bother to cultivate congressional support, raised some congressional eyebrows.

There was little society in the muddy, swampy capital village. The legislators lamented that some cabinet members for two or three years never bothered to invite them to dinner. Senator William Plumer of New Hampshire confided to his diary regarding the cabinet, "These gentlemen do not live in a style suited to the dignity of their offices."

Cabinet members in Washington's day had been personally acquainted with the president. Increasingly in the nineteenth century, they were appointed to represent a particular faction or interest, and appointment also became a means of reward for political support. Presidents increasingly had cabinet members they did not personally know and did not completely trust. Hence they went outside their cabinet for personal advisers. Jackson had his "Kitchen Cabinet"; John Tyler, his "Virginia Schoolmasters"; and Grover Cleveland, his "Fishing Cabinet." And so it continued down into the twentieth century: Theodore Roosevelt sported his "Tennis Cabinet"; Warren Harding admitted he enjoyed his "Poker Cabinet"; Hoover introduced his "Medicine Ball Cabinet"; and Franklin Roosevelt relished his "Brain Trust."

The Jefferson Cabinet. Although Jefferson's vigorous secretary of the treasury, Albert Gallatin, had proposed weekly meetings of the "Executive Council," as the cabinet was then called, Jefferson never averaged more than one cabinet meeting per month during his presidency. But his closest advisers, Gallatin and Madison, never had to wait for cabinet meetings to see him. Jefferson followed Washington's practice of getting opinions verbally or in writing and then making his own decisions. He wanted to avoid cabinet controversy and lamented the days when he and Hamilton had been "daily pitted in the Cabinet like two cocks." He contrasted this with his own cabinet, where, he insisted, "The harmony was so cordial among us all, that we never failed, by a contribution of mutual views on the subject, to form an opinion acceptable to the whole." Like Washington he also sought counsel privately. Indeed, he sought to emulate Washington and avoid the pitfalls of Adams, whom he considered a poor administrator.

Jefferson particularly decried Adams' absenteeism, but he himself refused to summer in Washington and was back at Monticello each August and September. "General Washington set the example of these two months," Jefferson wrote. "Mr. Adams extended it to eight months. I should not suppose our bringing it back to two months a ground for grumbling."

Jefferson's first term had been a triumph. His second was a disaster owing to deteriorating relations with Britain, which fired on and boarded the *Chesapeake,* and removed four seamen, on 22 June 1807. The nation, though ill-prepared for war, was outraged. Jefferson sent for his cabinet, most of whom had dispersed for the summer. It took until 2 July to meet. Neither Jefferson nor his cabinet wanted war. His proclamation, a tame affair, was accepted without a murmur. Congress was not convened, and Jefferson again summered at Monticello. Late that fall, Congress

gave him his Embargo Act, which he believed would compel Britain to change its tune. Instead it infuriated many of his fellow Americans.

After the election of 1808, humiliated by the failure of his Embargo Act and its repeal, Jefferson wrote, "Never did a prisoner, released from his chains, feel such release as I shall on shaking off the shackles of power." After the inauguration of James Madison, Jefferson departed Washington, never to return.

In retrospect, it should be emphasized that Jefferson, like Washington, had made effective use of his cabinet. Gallatin and Madison had been Jefferson's mainstays. Jefferson, even more than Washington, had come to base important decisions on a vote of his cabinet, including, alas, the embargo.

Madison and Cabinet Decline. Although the Washington, Adams, and Jefferson cabinets were not of uniformly high caliber, the main consideration in appointing members had been merit. Beginning with the Madison cabinet, political and regional considerations became primary, and the president was no longer in complete control of the selection process.

Much might have been expected of the Madison cabinet. The father of the Constitution, adviser to Washington in forming a government, able early member of Congress, and, under Jefferson, skilled secretary of state, Madison had, in his own presidency, enormous difficulties with his own cabinet. Owing to Senate opposition, he was unable to name Gallatin to be his own successor as secretary of state. Instead he had Robert Smith (whose brother was an influential senator) imposed upon him at a difficult time in foreign relations. Nor was he able to hold a cabinet together. He had two secretaries of state, four secretaries of the treasury, four secretaries of war, and three attorneys general. Madison succeeded in picking or having thrust upon him four incompetent members. In addition to Smith, there were William Eustis, Paul Hamilton, and George W. Campbell and two others who proved insubordinate, John Armstrong and Gideon Granger.

From Monticello, Jefferson viewed these cabinet problems, especially the rancor between Smith and Gallatin (who stayed on as treasury secretary). "I hope that the position of both gentlemen may be made so easy as to give no cause for either to withdraw," Jefferson counseled. Toward that end he recommended to Madison written rather than oral communications. "It is better calculated . . . to prevent collisions and irritation, and to cure it, or at least suppress its effects when it has already taken place," Jefferson, the voice of experience, added to his friend. We must conclude, with Leonard D. White (1951), that "The Cabinet, like the presidency, suffered a severe decline during these eight years."

Monroe: Restoration of Cabinet Dignity. James Monroe, during the eight years of his administration (termed the "Era of Good Feelings"), restored the prestige of both the presidency and the cabinet. All of his cabinet appointees, except the secretary of the navy, a post that was not then deemed of importance, served the full eight years. In this successful administration, the least important member, with little to do, was the vice-president, Daniel Tompkins.

John Quincy Adams, at State, came to admire how painstakingly Monroe deferred making a decision until he could achieve unanimity in the cabinet, concluding that this was a quality "which in so high a place is an infallible test of a great mind." The last of the Virginia triumvirate, Monroe also sought the counsel of his predecessors, Jefferson and Madison. He further profited by Washington's unhappy experience with a cabinet member outside his own party. Even though the Federalists were of a dying party, he refused to appoint any of them to the cabinet or any other high office. Nonetheless, there was increasing cabinet rancor in Monroe's second term, as Adams and Secretary of the Treasury William H. Crawford vied to become Monroe's successor.

The Pre–Civil War Cabinets, 1824–1861. John Quincy Adams was a minority president. Andrew Jackson, hero of the Battle of New Orleans, had polled ninety-nine electoral votes; Adams, eighty-four; Crawford, forty-one; and Henry Clay, thirty-seven. Because no candidate had a majority, the election had gone to the House of Representatives, where Adams, with the support of Clay, won. When Adams appointed Clay as secretary of state, the Jackson forces cried, "Deal!" There was no proof of a deal, only of Adams' political ineptitude. So began four years of frustration.

The ineffectiveness of the cabinet during the J. Q. Adams presidency was, with the exception of the Polk presidency, to characterize the cabinet's role until the emergence of Lincoln. Indeed, most of the more independent and powerful presidents, beginning with Andrew Jackson and extending to the present, have sought new avenues and instruments of counsel. For some the instrument was an inner cabinet with special members singled out for advice; for others it was an outside "cabinet" of unofficial advisers. Washington had been the first to go outside his cabinet, but he made the cabinet his principal advisory instrument. The first to go outside and ignore his cabinet was Andrew Jackson, Democrat, who represented the dominant political party until the Civil War. The opposition party, the Whigs, lineal descendants of the Federalists, led by Clay, were driven to find means to arrest the dominant Jacksonian presidency. They came to espouse an American version of the English responsible cabinet system, but they carried only two presidential elections and were unable to put their programs into effect. Still, they were a strong opposition party, to be succeeded in 1856 by the new Republican party.

In general, it may be said of the years 1829 to 1861 that the cabinet's primary roles were in policy and political management and not as an administrative instrument. Matters of administration were settled between the president and individual department heads in private consultation. During this period, with the exception of the Jackson and Polk presidencies, the Congress was dominant.

Jackson, who considered himself the personal tribune of the people, placed the cabinet at the nadir. During his first two years as president, he did not convene his cabinet as a body. Over eight years it appears that his cabinet met only sixteen times. Jackson's domination was so complete that it is difficult to find any influential cabinet member. The cabinet gyrated around the maelstrom of the Peggy Eaton affair and the removal of government deposits from the Bank of the United States. No previous cabinet, not even Madison's, had so many changes: four secretaries of state, five secretaries of the treasury, two secretaries of war, three attorneys general, three secretaries of the navy, and two postmasters general. (Jackson, in 1829, recognizing the importance of patronage, took the postal service out of the Treasury Department and made the postmaster general a member of the cabinet; not until 1872 did the Congress make the postal service an executive department.)

Jackson's cabinet was especially undermined by the creation in his first term of a group of personal advisers, his "Kitchen Cabinet." Primarily concerned with patronage and party manipulation, these dozen talented advisers never met as a group. Some did collaborate in lobbying efforts with Congress, in drafting speeches, or in influencing the press and public opinion.

Van Buren retained Jackson's final cabinet, and in four years the "Little Magician" made only four replacements.

The first Whig president, William Henry Harrison, died a month after taking office. Hence he was spared a cabinet designed to take over the reins of government. In this instance, Whig leaders had picked the cabinet for the hero of Tippecanoe. To their horror, the vice-president, John Tyler, a southern states' rights Whig, succeeded to office. The Tyler presidency proved the most unstable for cabinet tenure in American history. Indeed, some historians, in relating Jimmy Carter's July 1979 cabinet "massacre," concluded, "Not since 1841, when, in protest, all but one of President John Tyler's Cabinet members had resigned, had there been such an overturn." The only one who did not resign was the secretary of state, Daniel Webster. In all, Tyler had three secretaries of state, three in Treasury, three in War, four in Navy, one postmaster general, and three attorneys general, plus several acting appointments. Tyler was deserted by Whigs and Democrats alike. Hence he was virtually forced to adopt Jackson's "Kitchen Cabinet" technique.

Polk, the strongest president between Jackson and Lincoln, held his cabinet virtually intact. Moreover, he made effective use of its service in both administration and policy matters. In total he convened at least 350 cabinet meetings, a record for one four-year term. Polk confided to his diary, "At each meeting of the Cabinet, I learn from each member what is being done in his particular department and especially if any question of doubt or difficulty has arisen." In these meetings Polk required each department head to read his reports aloud before sending them to the Congress. On his last day in office, in 1849, Polk signed into law the bill creating the Department of the Interior.

Again the Whigs picked a war hero, Zachary Taylor; again the president died in office; and again the Whig administration was marred by excessive cabinet changes. During the Taylor-Fillmore administration there were three secretaries of state, two in Treasury, two in War, three in Navy, three in Interior, three postmasters general, and two attorneys general.

Handsome, genial Franklin Pierce, the Democratic "dark horse" candidate, in 1853, at age forty-eight, became the youngest president as of that date. In his cabinet selections, as in domestic and foreign policies, he successfully coalesced northern businessmen and southern planters. Pierce was even more successful than Polk in keeping his cabinet together. Indeed, his is the only presidency in a full four-year term that had no cabinet changes. But his successor's (James Buchanan's) cabinet fell apart in the last months of his administration with the deepening of the North–South impasse. Following Lincoln's election in 1860, Buchanan had an impossible task with the cabinet and the Congress divided over secession. As Allan Nevins observed (1950), "Had the nation possessed a ministerial form of government, a new leader would have taken over the reins immediately, with a united cabinet behind him, and a close working relation with a new legislature. The stiffness of the American system, at times an advantage, now served it ill." The condition was further aggravated by the four-month interval between the election and the 4 March 1861 inauguration of a new president (changed to 20 January by the Twentieth Amendment in 1933). During that period the lower South seceded and several prosecession and pro-Union cabinet members resigned.

Clearly Buchanan, who opposed secession, should have dismissed the secessionists in his cabinet. Following a series of cabinet crises, a reorganized pro-Union cabinet took charge during the last six weeks of the Buchanan administration, forcing its views on the indecisive president.

The Lincoln Cabinet. Lincoln immediately terminated this brief cabinet supremacy. More than that, he chose the strongest political leaders, many of whom had been his political antagonists and considered him their inferior; he made them a working cabinet. His secretary of state, William Seward, had at first considered himself a "prime minister" and prepared "Some Thoughts for the President's Consideration" in April 1861. Lincoln's reasoned reply gently put the secretary in his place; it made clear that the government had only one chief executive, who would seek the advice of all his cabinet. Seward confided to his wife, "Executive force and vigor are rare qualities. The President is the best of us."

In December 1862, with the war going badly, the ambitious secretary of the treasury, Salmon P. Chase, connived with the Senate to secure Seward's ouster and a larger voice for himself. In a five-hour cabinet session with a committee of nine senators critical of his administration, Lincoln was masterful both in assuaging the senators and in bringing Chase and Seward into tandem. He confided to his young personal secretary, John Hay, "Mr. Chase makes a good Secretary, and I shall keep him where he is. If he becomes President, all right. I hope we shall never have a worse man."

Intermittently seeking the counsel of his cabinet, Lincoln had no hesitation, when that counsel was contrary to his view, to announce, "Seven noes one aye—the ayes have it." Or as William Howard Taft expressed it regarding Lincoln, "In the Cabinet after discussion and intimation of opinions, there was only one vote—and that unanimous—it was the vote of the President." Lincoln was his own counsel. In most critical pronouncements, such as the Emancipation Proclamation, he assiduously secured cabinet support with his skill for timing. Just as he was the strongest nineteenth-century president, he had the strongest cabinet members, who worked strenuously in their respective departments, although as a body they were subordinated to him.

Some members of the Congress conspired to dissociate the cabinet from the president. In 1864 one of the Peace Democrats, George Hunt Pendleton, introduced a bill "to provide that the Secretaries of Executive Departments may occupy seats on the floor of the House of Representatives." Whereas the Congress in the Washington administration, fearful of being dominated, had opposed cabinet members' appearing in the Congress, now as a means of seeking to gain information and divide the Lincoln administration, the Copperheads were offering authorizing legislation for a new role for cabinet members. The *New York Times* supported the proposal editorially "because it would make the Executive more directly accountable."

The Pendleton bill was finally called up for debate in early 1865, during the final months of the war. The most notable defense came from Con-gressman James A. Garfield, future president, who analyzed why Hamilton had been authorized by the Treasury Act of 1789 to appear before the Congress and why three years later Congressman James Madison considered it "unconstitutional to let the Secretary come before the House." Despite Garfield's eloquence, no action was taken on the bill.

To strengthen Unionist sentiments, Andrew Johnson, from the border state of Tennessee, had been named Lincoln's vice-presidential running mate in the 1864 election. At the apex of Lincoln's power, in early 1865, the American presidency was the Western world's most powerful political office. With the restoration of peace, Congress would inevitably seek to restore its own authority.

Johnson Through McKinley. Upon succeeding the martyred president, Johnson, who lacked Lincoln's tact and political skills, was soon in difficulty with the Congress. They defied his veto with passage in 1867 of the Tenure of Office Act, requiring Senate approval for the removal of any official whose appointment had required Senate approval. Johnson had retained the loyalty of the cabinet with the exception of Stanton. When, contrary to the Tenure of Office Act, he sought to remove Stanton, he was impeached.

After the impeachment of Johnson, until the advent of William McKinley in 1897, the Congress in general was dominant and the presidency weak. During the Hayes presidency, Pendleton, by then in the Senate, introduced another of his bills to authorize heads of the executive departments to "occupy seats on the floor of the Senate and House." He again insisted he was not seeking to "substitute Parliamentary for Presidential government." Again, the bill expired, as did a similar measure introduced in 1881. However, twentieth-century advocates of similar proposals must look to these early Pendleton efforts.

Grover Cleveland did much to reduce congressional dominance and restore both the symbolism and the fact of executive authority in his first term (1885–1889), only to see it disintegrate in his second (1893–1897). Although the Department of Agriculture had been formed in 1862, during the Civil War, it was not until 1889 that its head was given cabinet rank, bringing to eight the number of cabinet members. Cleveland's cabinet met in the Treaty Room on the second floor of the White House.

McKinley, who assumed office in 1897, restored presidential dominance over the Congress. Moreover, as Elihu Root observed, "He understood the art of administration with a minimum of interference."

None of the presidents during this period became captive to their cabinets; beyond that, they increasingly bypassed their cabinets. Referring to his determination to veto a currency bill in 1874, Ulysses Grant admitted, "When the Cabinet met my message was written. I did not intend asking the advice of the Cabinet, as I knew a majority would oppose the veto. I never allowed the Cabinet to interfere when my mind was made up, and on this question it was inflexibly made up." During the Grant presidency, the Justice Department was established in 1870 and the Post Office Department in 1872, but the positions for their respective heads, the attorney general and the postmaster general, had been in existence since Washington and Jackson's administration, respectively.

Grover Cleveland held a view similar to Grant's about the subordinate role of the cabinet. Each member was free to express an opinion, but the president made the decision.

McKinley, without overruling his cabinet, achieved their assent with his personal charm. According to his secretary of the navy, John D. Long, ". . . there was no parliamentary procedure. . . . Matters were discussed in a conversational way. When the President had arrived at a result, he nodded to each member in succession, saying, 'You agree?' until the last one had assented, and then wound the matter up by saying, 'Now all agree.' Rarely was there any nonconsent."

Most nineteenth-century presidents usually did not prepare agendas for cabinet meetings. Instead they invited department heads to bring matters to their joint attention. Such procedure, of course, let the secretaries take the initiative, something that Lincoln did not permit.

TWENTIETH-CENTURY CABINETS AND STAFFS

During the first two decades of the twentieth century, the emergence of the United States as an industrial leader and world power, together with the increasing complexity of domestic pol-

icy issues, inevitably brought both the enlargement of the cabinet and alternate methods of counsel.

Theodore Roosevelt Through Herbert Hoover. Theodore Roosevelt was much interested not only in business but also in conditions of labor and secured the establishment of a joint Department of Commerce and Labor in 1903, thereby adding a ninth member to the cabinet. During his presidency the West Wing of the White House was added, including the president's Oval Office and the adjacent Cabinet Room.

Roosevelt was an internationalist and the first American to receive the Nobel Peace Prize. By interest and by regard, he turned particularly to Elihu Root, concerning whom he wrote, "Root was the man of my Cabinet in whom I most relied, to whom I owed most, the greatest Secretary of State we ever had, as great a Cabinet officer as we have ever had, save Alexander Hamilton alone."

During Roosevelt's administration, in 1907, the first reference to the cabinet was made in statutory law; in this instance, as regards salary increases, it referred to "the heads of executive departments who are members of the President's Cabinet."

Taft, an able and judicious administrator, was, as his biographer Donald F. Anderson noted, "preeminently a man of the law and the Constitution." Perhaps more than any other president he grasped the constitutional implications of "executive power" and of the "take care that the laws be faithfully executed" clause. Much of this he subsequently expounded as chief justice in the *Meyers* v. *U.S.* opinion (1926). Alexander Hamilton, Abraham Lincoln, or Theodore Roosevelt would have endorsed what he set forth: "The power of removal is incident to the power of appointment, not to the power of advising and consenting to appointment, and when the grant of the executive power is enforced by the express mandate to take care that the laws be faithfully executed, it emphasizes the necessity for including within the executive power as conferred the exclusive power of removal." Future presidents, unlike the hapless Andrew Johnson, need never fear removing a cabinet member.

Woodrow Wilson met rarely with his cabinet, to which a tenth member was added in 1913, with the establishment of the Department of Labor, separate from the Department of Commerce. In his second term, Wilson sought other avenues of counsel, turning to the Council of National Defense, created in 1916. Its members included the secretaries of war (chairman), navy, interior, agriculture, commerce, and labor. Its importance overshadowed the cabinet as an arm of the president during World War I.

At war's end, Wilson crusaded for the League of Nations. Unfortunately, he failed to invite Henry Cabot Lodge, the Republican chairman of the Senate Foreign Relations Committee, to accompany him in 1919 to participate in the negotiations for the Treaty of Versailles, which embodied the Covenant of the League. Later that year Wilson requested the Senate Foreign Relations Committee to meet with him. Both Lodge and Wilson were students of history. But it was Lodge who recalled Madison's refusal more than a century before to meet with a congressional committee. The position "which Madison took, that he could not receive officially a committee of the Senate," Chairman Lodge wrote, "has always seemed to me the absolutely correct ground." And so Wilson importuned in vain for Senate approval of the treaty. Hence, the United States rejected membership in the League of Nations.

Harding has been a much underrated president, especially remembered for his secretary of the interior, Albert B. Fall, who accepted a bribe in the Teapot Dome scandal. By contrast, his secretary of state, Charles Evans Hughes, secretary of the treasury, Andrew Mellon, and secretary of commerce, Herbert Hoover, acted with considerable distinction. Moreover, Harding was the first president to propose a department of public welfare. In a message to a special session of the Congress, he observed, "in the realms of education, public health, sanitation, conditions of workers in industry, child welfare, proper amusement and recreation, the elimination of social vice, and many other subjects, the Government . . . undertakings have been scattered through many departments and bureaus." Despite Harding's plea, it was not until 1953, during the Eisenhower administration, that Harding's vision was realized with the creation of the Department of Health, Education, and Welfare. Harding also advocated revival of Pendleton's idea to give cabinet members a voice in congressional debate. Harding's cabinet, notably Hughes, supported this measure, which again failed.

When Harding died, Coolidge deemed it his "duty to maintain the counsellors and policies of the deceased President." The seemingly taciturn Coolidge set a record not since equaled for the number of press conferences per year, but he had little time for his cabinet; fifteen-minute sessions were standard. He did, however, believe in delegating authority, especially in foreign affairs, which he placed wholly with his secretaries of state, Hughes and Frank B. Kellogg. By contrast with Wilson, who had Colonel House, Coolidge insisted he had no "unofficial adviser. . . . My counsellors have been those provided by the Constitution and the law."

Coolidge recalled receiving nothing but bad advice from Hoover but let him build up the Commerce Department to the point where it required the largest government office building (erected in Hoover's administration) before the Pentagon. Hoover's own cabinet has been described by Louis Koenig as "the most august body of 'yes men' ever assembled in the United States history." Like Hoover himself, Richard Fenno described them as "efficient and machine-like." The "Chief" dominated all meetings. His great contribution to administration came in his subsequent service as chairman of the first and second Hoover commissions on government reorganization.

The Franklin D. Roosevelt Cabinet. Franklin Roosevelt viewed the cabinet as a political instrument. As his adviser Thomas G. Corcoran recalled, "In Mr. Roosevelt's time, Cabinet members were picked to be ambidextrous fellows who had both management ability and at the same time were versed in the political institutions of a particular field and a particular region." In 1933, in his original cabinet, Roosevelt was the first president to name a woman to the cabinet, Frances Perkins, as secretary of labor. However, she voiced disappointment at the inconsequential role of the cabinet. As early as 1935, the secretary of the interior, Harold Ickes, did likewise.

After World War II began in Europe in 1939, Roosevelt appealed for bipartisan support in defense policies. As a means toward that end, in 1940 he named two Republicans to his cabinet: Frank Knox as secretary of the navy and Henry L. Stimson as secretary of war. Stimson had earlier served as Taft's secretary of war and Hoover's secretary of state. Roosevelt constantly interposed in the executive departments both in

158

domestic and foreign policy. He became, in essence, his own secretary of state, war, and navy. Secretary of State Cordell Hull and Secretary of War Stimson both voiced their unhappiness. So did Roosevelt's new vice-president, Harry S. Truman, who was neither consulted nor informed of what was going on.

Roosevelt experimented with alternate advisory bodies, beginning in 1933 with an augmented cabinet of twenty-four members, termed the Executive Council. Then in 1940 the Council of National Defense was reactivated.

The most significant and durable of the Roosevelt modifications was the creation in 1939 of the Executive Office of the President. Based on the clarion call "The President needs help," pronounced in 1937 by the Brownlow Committee on Administrative Management, the Congress had two years later authorized presidential assistants. Somehow they never had the "passion for anonymity" that Brownlow envisaged. The subsequent growth of the White House staff created a new centrifugal force counter to the cabinet. And so the seemingly insoluble riddle began, how to relate cabinet to staff and also how to relate cabinet members to their colleagues.

POST-FDR CABINETS AND STAFFS

Harry S. Truman. Truman had served as vice-president less than three months when, with Roosevelt's death, in April 1945, the presidency was thrust upon him. Unlike Coolidge, Truman did not believe that a vice-president was obligated to retain the advisers of his predecessor upon becoming president. Within four months, all the Roosevelt cabinet members were gone except Henry Wallace at Commerce, Ickes at Interior, Forrestal at Navy, and Stimson at War. Truman had great respect for Stimson, but little for Ickes and Wallace. By early 1946 he had found Ickes "too big for his breeches" and had fired him. He fired Wallace that fall for his public criticisms of the president's "get tough with the Russians" foreign policy. The following year he fired Byrnes, his own first appointee, as secretary of state. By the fall of 1950, Truman had fired his own first two secretaries of defense, James Forrestal and Louis Johnson. The following spring,

instead of firing cabinet members, he fired General Douglass MacArthur as commander in chief of UN forces in Korea.

In total, Truman fired more cabinet members than any other president. The National Security Act of 1947 had created a new position of cabinet rank, secretary of defense, and had redesignated the War Department as Department of the Army, retained the Department of the Navy, and established the new Department of the Air Force. None of these was given cabinet status, leaving the secretary of defense as the sole cabinet representative for the armed forces. The National Security Act had also created the National Security Council (NSC). Termed "Forrestal's revenge," it had been thrust upon Truman. Its initial statutory members included the secretaries of state and defense and the service secretaries. The latter were removed in 1949, at which time the vice-president was added. The president may appoint other officers (customarily the secretary of the treasury). Advisory roles on the NSC are performed by the director of the Central Intelligence Agency (a creation of the National Security Act of 1947) and the chairman of the Joint Chiefs of Staff (a new post established by the 1949 amendments to the National Security Act).

When North Korea attacked South Korea in June 1950, Truman did not convene a meeting either of his cabinet or of the National Security Council. Instead, he convened on two consecutive evenings an ad hoc gathering of the secretaries of state and defense, the service secretaries, the Joint Chiefs of Staff, and some State Department aides. With no further consultation he directed the U.S. armed forces to enter the war.

These remaining two and one-half years of the Truman presidency were to prove his most difficult, even though he had at last the men he wanted at State and Defense, George Marshall, Dean Acheson, and Robert Lovett. Even with them, as well as his lesser cabinet members, Truman always took pride in making the difficult decisions himself, considering it an inherent responsibility of the office he occupied. Although he boasted that he had "revived the Cabinet system" and viewed it as a national board of directors, the record does not bear this out. By contrast with Franklin Roosevelt's constantly blurred chain of command, everyone did know with Truman where "the buck" stopped. Moreover, unlike Roosevelt, who kept a series of weak chains intact, Truman, who would not tolerate personal disloyalty, had fired cabinet members until he got what he wanted.

Neither Roosevelt nor Truman achieved collegiality in their cabinets. As Louis Brownlow observed (1949), each cabinet member "feels his responsibility—as indeed it is—personally to the President and not the President in Council, nor to the President and his Cabinet."

Eisenhower and the Institutionalized Presidency. It remained for Eisenhower to institutionalize the presidential office and to restore some collegiality to the cabinet. "The history of past administrations," he asserted, "recorded much Cabinet bickering, personality conflicts, and end running, tale bearing, and throat cutting." Based upon his career in military staffing and, to a lesser extent, his experiences as president of Columbia University, he determined to create for the first time a cabinet secretariat. Eisenhower proposed from out of "a conglomerate of bureaus" to create the Department of Health, Education, and Welfare (HEW), which with pride he termed "the first new Cabinet department established [in 1953] in forty years." Furthermore, he determined to enlarge the cabinet to about two dozen members, including key presidential assistants, directors of important government agencies (such as the budget), and the ambassador to the United Nations.

Although the experience was somewhat mixed in terms of the significance of the agendas, Richard F. Fenno, Jr., concluded in his classic study of *The President's Cabinet* (1959) that the Eisenhower cabinet developed "a relatively high degree of coherence, the highest, perhaps." Presidential scholar Thomas Cronin concluded that of all presidential cabinets through Carter, "The Eisenhower Cabinet . . . came about as close to the ideal of an upgraded or European style of Cabinet as we have witnessed in the United States."

Eisenhower likewise institutionalized other policy-formulating bodies, most notably the National Security Council, which he wanted to become "correlative in importance with the Cabinet." Gordon Gray, who served as special assistant for national security affairs, contrasted the structured decision making of the Eisenhower years with the rather informal methods of the Roosevelt and Truman administrations. He concluded that, under Eisenhower, "You don't

have this kind of ad hoc piecemeal business of arriving at a decision." Eisenhower considered the secretary of state to be the most important cabinet post. It would never have occurred to his special assistant for national security affairs, a low-key position, to challenge the policy leadership role of the secretary of state.

Like all presidents since 1940, Eisenhower found foreign policy and fiscal matters occupying about two-thirds of his time. John Foster Dulles at State and George Humphrey at Treasury were his towering cabinet members, not unlike Jefferson and Hamilton in the first presidential cabinet. He was the first president to have the vice-president participate in all cabinet meetings and to formulate a plan for the vice-president to serve as acting president during the incapacity of the president (an arrangement formalized by the Twenty-fifth Amendment proclaimed in 1967).

Kennedy to Reagan. It is to be emphasized that institutionalization is no effective guarantor of cabinet effectiveness. Each president has and must have the structure and style with which he is most comfortable. All of the presidents from Kennedy to Carter assumed office paying more than lip service to the importance of the cabinet; but all, with the exception of Ford, soon came upon that which the British scholar Anthony J. Bennett has termed the "cycle of disillusionment." He concludes, "The one exception . . . was President Ford whose Cabinet meetings not only remained quite regular . . . but also seem to have been regarded . . . as useful and interesting."

In general, the initial cabinet appointments during this period came from either the federal or state governments, universities, and business. The replacements were substantially different, coming predominantly from the federal government and often promoted from the department in which they were serving.

Nelson Polsby has suggested that the replacements represented a presidential effort to centralize authority. More important, however, initial cabinet members increasingly found that they were there not so much to formulate policy as to administer their departments, many of which, like HEW and Defense, had become giant bureaucracies.

President Kennedy viewed the Department of State with considerable distrust. Accordingly, he established a "little State Department" at the White House under his special assistant for national security affairs, McGeorge Bundy. From then on there was potential conflict between the secretary of state and the president's security adviser.

By contrast with Eisenhower, Kennedy and Johnson as senators had been accustomed to small, loosely structured staffs, and they so operated. Hard-driving, Kennedy, like Wilson and Franklin Roosevelt, used his cabinet but little. He is quoted by his special counsel, Theodore Sorensen, as saying, "Cabinet meetings are simply useless. . . . I don't know how presidents functioned with them or relied upon them in the past." He relied most on his attorney general, his brother Robert, to head ad hoc advisory groups, including that which operated throughout the Cuban missile crisis.

Having witnessed the revival of the cabinet under Eisenhower, many students of the presidency saw Kennedy make a wrong turn in supplanting cabinet by staff. Lyndon Johnson was more inclined than Kennedy to employ the cabinet but mostly, in his constant search for consensus, to develop a "team" image for pending presidential decisions. In 1965 he signed the bill creating the Department of Housing and Urban Development. Its secretary, Robert C. Weaver, became the first black cabinet member. The following year Johnson, who had a torrent of domestic programs, signed into law the Department of Transportation and, in 1967, named Alan S. Boyd, the first secretary of transportation, as an additional cabinet member.

Viewing the proliferation of departments and cabinet appointments, President Nixon proposed departmental consolidations. In doing so, he quoted from Alexander Hamilton's query "whether societies of men are really capable or not of establishing good government from reflection and choice." He also quoted Jefferson's counsel to "keep pace with the times." Nixon proposed to retain the nation's initial executive services as departments: State, Treasury, Defense, and Justice. The others he would combine into four new departments: Natural Resources, Human Resources, Economic Affairs, and Community Development. Like so many other Nixon reforms, these failed to pass in the Watergate environment.

Earlier, in 1970, the cabinet had been reduced by one: the creation of the United States Postal Service as a government corporation eliminated the postmaster general from the cabinet.

Nixon constantly rotated some of his ablest cabinet members. George Shultz started as a little-known secretary of labor in 1969; an early cabinet star, he was named director of the reorganized Office of Management and Budget and then secretary of the treasury; Elliot Richardson, who began as undersecretary of state, served successively as secretary of HEW, secretary of defense, and attorney general.

The enormous cabinet turnover of 1973–1974 reflected the Watergate tragedy. The Nixon cabinet had also been marred by the dominance of the assistant for national security affairs, Henry Kissinger, over the secretary of state, William Rogers. When Rogers resigned, Kissinger became the first, and presumably the last, incumbent to hold both positions simultaneously.

Ford, like Eisenhower, set as an avowed goal to restore the cabinet as a meaningful advisory body. He believed "A Watergate was made possible by a strong chief of staff and ambitious White House aides who were more powerful than members of the Cabinet." Ford restored the cabinet secretariat created by Eisenhower and eliminated by Kennedy. More than any other president in the period from 1961 to 1981, he restored the cabinet as a deliberative, meaningful advisory and administrative body. Furthermore, he played down his able assistant for national security affairs, Brent Scowcroft, vis-à-vis Secretary of State Kissinger.

President Carter was also determined to revitalize the cabinet. Like Ford, he began with a "spokes of the wheel concept": a staff of nine assistants with equal access. Like Ford, Carter had to learn the hard way about the necessity for a chief of staff. As Calvin Mackenzie observed, "there is little institutional memory in the White House."

The Carter presidency got caught up in a clash between two staff assistants, Jack Watson, who believed in cabinet government, and Hamilton Jordan, who did not trust it. Jordan won and was eventually named chief of staff, and the cabinet was cut out of the inner circle of decision making. True to his campaign pledges, Carter secured two new departments, Energy (1977) and Education (1979), the latter removed from HEW, which became Health and Human Services. These new posts brought the number of secretariats to its zenith. The cabinet included five with Ph.D.'s and five lawyers. There was cosmetic cabinet unity; by July 1979, with no changes, a record of longevity not equaled since Franklin Pierce had been achieved. But then came another record, the greatest cabinet overturn since John Tyler in 1841. The "July massacre," aimed at building a new image of strength for Carter, worked in reverse.

The cabinet problems were not over. In April 1980, after the abortive Iranian hostage rescue attempt, Secretary of State Cyrus Vance resigned. Not since 1915, when William Jennings Bryan resigned to protest Wilson's demands on the German government over the *Lusitania* sinking, had a secretary of state quit over differences with a president on principles and policies. Vance had been further irritated by Carter's outspoken assistant for national security affairs, Zbigniew Brzezinski, who boasted he was the first in that position with a seat in the cabinet. Not until June 1980, with Jordan's replacement by Watson as chief of staff, was a strong cabinet advocate in a position of influence. By then it was too late.

President Reagan, principally aided by Edwin Meese III, counselor to the president, confronted this dilemma: how to integrate effectively cabinet and staff in the policy-making process. Their answer has been the creation of seven cabinet councils, each focusing on specific subject areas: economic affairs, commerce and trade, food and agriculture, human resources, natural resources, legal policy, and management and administration.

This is the Reagan-Meese alternative to convening the entire cabinet on matters not germane to all members. During the first eighteen months, approximately 200 issues were considered by these cabinet councils; in final sessions the president presided before making his decision.

Significantly, these procedures complement Reagan's views of the decision-making process; they would obviously not work for a president with a different concept. Thus, Meese concludes, concerning an experience now in its third year, with his own belief that "history will record . . . this restoration of the Cabinet as a vital part of the decision-making machinery and the governmental structure of the Executive branch." Only in retrospect can we judge whether his evaluation is correct.

Two significant questions concerning the post–World War II cabinets are these: What kind of people served in them and what has been their tenure? The median has been only two years. Most have had prior federal government experience. Many are generalists who have served in other cabinet posts or in subcabinet posts in the same or other departments or as senior presidential staff. Exemplary are George Marshall, Dean Acheson, Averell Harriman, Robert Lovett, and Douglas Dillon, and, more recently, Elliot Richardson (who held a record number of cabinet posts), James Schlesinger, Cyrus Vance, Joseph Califano, Harold Brown, Caspar Weinberger, Alexander Haig, and George Shultz. The most significant Reagan cabinet change has been Haig's replacement by Shultz as secretary of state.

As James W. Fesler has observed, "advocacy, negotiation, and compromise . . . are at the heart of governmental policy making." Many of the modern cabinet members have exhibited these skills, principally the lawyers and to some extent the academicians and the corporate executives, but the few ideologues have been a disaster.

CONCLUSIONS

We are now approaching the bicentennial of the cabinet in the American presidency. Unlike the cabinet in the parliamentary system, it is not at the heart of the executive. Rather, it is a secondary political institution, related to the primary one, the presidency itself. Nonetheless, it is of consequence to—indeed it is the crux of—the presidency. As Harold Laski wrote (1940), "A good Cabinet ought to be a place where the large outlines of policy can be hammered out in common, where the essential strategy is decided upon, where the President knows that he will hear, both in affirmation and in doubt, even in negation, most of what can be said about the direction he proposes to follow."

The cabinet is not the place where precise policy intricacies and nuances are formulated. More specialized advisory bodies, such as the cabinet councils and the National Security Council, serve that purpose.

Although there had been earlier important meetings, the cabinet had been forged out of the crisis of 1793, when France was seeking to bring the United States into its war with Great Britain. The break between Hamilton and Jefferson over policy that year led to the latter's resignation. It

CABINET

signalized the beginnings of the two-party system and the principle that presidents, with rare exceptions, choose department heads and other cabinet members only from their own party. Notable exceptions were Lincoln's and Franklin Roosevelt's wartime efforts toward bipartisan unity.

The Washington presidency had witnessed the period of greatest cabinet significance as an advisory body, with Hamilton, regarded as the nation's most effective cabinet member, serving virtually as a prime minister while completely loyal to the president. Subsequently, there was a waning cabinet influence during the nineteenth century, with the Polk presidency as a notable exception.

Such strong presidents as Lincoln, Theodore Roosevelt, Wilson, and Franklin Roosevelt either dominated or ignored their cabinets. Franklin Roosevelt, by creating the Executive Office of the President in 1939, established an institution, the White House staff, with its advantage of access, which threatened to supplant the cabinet. And yet it can still be said with Samuel Lindsay, "No single act of the President transcends in importance the appointment of his Cabinet." No matter how unimportant cabinet meetings may on occasion appear, in the institutional life of the presidency, they remain indispensable. Moreover, by contrast with seeking individual counsel, the cabinet provides a group advisory process. It combats the "yo-yo" theory of presidential decisions, which can be abnormally influenced by the most persuasive or most recent adviser.

At best the relationship between a president and a cabinet member is rife with difficulties. Before 1939 there was only a small White House staff that could intercede between a president and a cabinet member. However, with the growth of the White House staff, especially during the Kennedy, Johnson, and Nixon presidencies, friction between cabinet and staff mounted. Part of the difficulty has been lack of understanding, on the part of some White House aides, of a department head's sense of responsibility for administering a particular department. By experience, Joseph Califano, for example, came to see two views. As an aide to President Johnson he fought against what he considered narrow, parochial department views. Later, as a cabinet member, with Carter, he sought to defend his department's positions. There is a constant pull between the individual policy view of a particular department and the overview that the cabinet as a whole should help provide. The present secretary and deputy secretary of state, George Shultz and Kenneth W. Dam, in an interesting study in 1977 observed, "In a balkanized executive branch, policymaking is necessarily a piecemeal affair; policymakers are under the constraint that they are not permitted to view problems whole."

Relations with the White House staff are only one aspect of the hazard for presidents and their cabinet members. From the very beginning there was the perplexity of relations with Congress, with the very persons who enacted the statutes that created the executive departments. In an earlier era some congressional leaders, such as Clay, Webster, James Blaine, Bryan, and Root, departed Congress for the cabinet. But no longer. Numerous reforms have been proposed, including having cabinet members appear before the House and the Senate.

This proposal has had substantial advocates, including President Taft, who wrote, "Without any change in the Constitution, Congress might well provide that heads of departments, members of the president's cabinet, should be given access to the floor of each house to introduce measures, to advocate their passage, to answer questions, and to enter into the debate as if they were members, without, of course, the right to vote. . . ." There are those who would go further and propose a constitutional amendment giving cabinet members seats in the Congress. But the American cabinet is a unique offspring of the American system of separation of powers and of a single executive. Advocates of such an amendment give aid to those who would abolish the separation of powers. Critics such as Lloyd Cutler notwithstanding, the separation-of-powers system has worked again and again in severe emergency as well as normal conditions and is not outmoded. Reformers overly fret that the president cannot act as though he were a British prime minister, a French president, or a German chancellor.

In addition to Congress there is another pull on cabinet members from client advocates, as, for example, with the secretary of the interior, clients ranging from environmentalists to exploiters of national resources. And there is the third pull in each department, the bureaucracy. Taken together, Congress, clients, and bureaucracy compose a three-way pull, an "Iron Triangle," straining cabinet relationships with the president. Such a dilemma caused General Charles G. Dawes to observe following his service as the first director of the Bureau of the Budget, "Every member of the Cabinet is a natural enemy of the President." Little wonder presidents have demanded both competence and loyalty, or as Lyndon Johnson said, what he wanted was not "loyalty but LOYALTY." Still, reformers doubtless underestimate the strong pull, the ties of the president with his cabinet members.

With the growth of government and the complexities of presidential responsibilities, it is imperative that cabinet and staff have an effective relationship. There is as much truth today as regards that relationship as when it was pronounced in January 1961 by Senator Henry M. Jackson, "In the American system, there is no satisfactory alternative to primary reliance on the great departments, and their vast resources of experience and talent, as instruments for policy development and execution." Members of the cabinet represent those "instruments." Cabinet members par excellence are both able administrators and wise counselors.

But there are the additional ingredients, the sifting, the winnowing of what Senator Jackson referred to as "the budgeting process and the staff work of Presidential aides in pulling departmental programs together." From out of this must come what Jackson termed "a truly Presidential program." There is no substitute for the nexus of president, cabinet, and staff in bringing this about.

There is a need for both strong White House staffing, with experienced senior aides, and a revitalized cabinet, which can be the crux of the presidency. This vital combination of president, cabinet, and staff can produce that "energy in the executive" which Hamilton termed "a leading character in the definition of good government." Such energy, *The Federalist* number 70 reminds us, "is essential to the protection of the community against foreign attacks: It is not less essential to the steady administration of the laws."

BIBLIOGRAPHY

Patrick Anderson, *The President's Men: White House Assistants of Franklin D. Roosevelt, Harry S. Truman, Dwight D. Eisenhower,* *John F. Kennedy, and Lyndon B. Johnson* (Garden City, N.Y., 1968), a well-written book by a Washington journalist, includes concise observations on each of the five administrations noted. Anthony J. Bennett, "The President's Cabinet: An Analysis in the Period from Kennedy to Carter," an unpublished doctoral dissertation (University of Essex, 1983), carries forward the Fenno study *(op. cit.)* from Kennedy through Carter. James J. Best, "Presidential Cabinet Appointments: 1953–1976," in *Presidential Studies Quarterly,* 11 (1981), analyzes presidents' initial and follow-up cabinet appointments. Wilfred E. Binkley, *The Man in the White House: His Powers and Duties* (New York, 1964), is strong in its historical approach and insights. Louis Brownlow, *The President and the Presidency* (Chicago, 1949), provides the personal recollections of a journalist-political scientist who recommended the establishment of the Executive Office of the President.

Joseph A. Califano, *Governing America: An Insider's Report from the White House and the Cabinet* (New York, 1981), offers one of the more perceptive reminiscences, from a Carter cabinet member who had been a senior White House staff member in the Johnson administration. Jacob E. Cooke, ed., *The Federalist* (Middletown, Conn., 1961), is a collection of distinguished essays in political philosophy by Alexander Hamilton, James Madison, and John Jay, first published in 1787–1788 in defense of the adoption of the Constitution. Edward S. Corwin, *The President: Office and Powers, 1787–1957. History and Analysis of Practice and Opinion,* 4th rev. ed. (New York, 1957), is a classic constitutional and political view of presidential powers and office. Thomas E. Cronin, *The State of the Presidency,* 2nd ed. (Boston, 1980), contains eleven perceptive essays by a distinguished student of the presidency; and *Rethinking the Presidency* (Boston, 1982), collects twenty-six essays by leading authorities.

Lloyd Cutler, "To Form a Government," in *Foreign Affairs,* 59 (1980), as counsel to President Carter, contends, "The separation of powers between the legislative and executive branches . . . has become a structure that almost guarantees stalemate today." Richard F. Fenno, Jr., *The President's Cabinet; An Analysis in the Period from Wilson to Eisenhower* (Cambridge, Mass., 1959), is a basic work with particular focus on the period 1913–1953. James W. Fesler, "Politics, Policy, and Bureaucracy at the Top," in *Annals of the American Academy of Political and Social Science,* 466 (1983), provides a perceptive study of the roles of political appointees, including the White House staff and the cabinet and senior civil servants, in policy development. Louis Fisher and Harold C. Relyea, *Presidential Staffing—A Brief Overview* (Washington, D.C., 1978), contributes an incisive, valuable study on presidential staffing from the beginning of the nation to the year of publication. Ferdinand A. Hermens, "The Choice of the Framers," in *Presidential Studies Quarterly,* 11 (1981), ventures the scholarly contention that the constitutional framers should have moved toward the British form of cabinet government.

Stephen Hess, *Organizing the Presidency* (Washington, D.C., 1976), sets forth the ideal of a collegial presidency with cabinet participating in policy formation. John Stephen Horn, *The Cabinet and Congress* (New York, 1960), describes executive-legislative relationships in federal government, suggesting parliamentary-type reforms. R. Gordon Hoxie, ed., *The White House: Organization and Operations. Proceedings of 1970 Montauk Conference* (New York, 1971), contains observations of thirty-five students of the presidency; and *Command Decision*

CABINET

and the Presidency: A Study in National Security Policy and Organization (New York, 1977), is a basic study of national security policy and organization.

Louis W. Koenig, *The Chief Executive* (New York, 1981), is the fourth edition of a basic textbook notable for its organization, understanding, and literary qualities. Harold J. Laski, *The American Presidency: An Interpretation* (New York, 1940), is a classic series of lectures by a British scholar, including "The President and His Cabinet." Henry Barrett Learned, *The President's Cabinet* (New Haven, 1912), is a standard earlier work. Richard Loss, "Alexander Hamilton and the Modern Presidency," in *Presidential Studies Quarterly,* 12 (1982), analyzes Hamilton's conceptions of the presidency as revealed in *The Federalist* and also the Pacificus letters. Edwin Meese, III, "The Institutional Presidency: A View from the White House," *ibid.,* 13 (1983), offers views of the counselor to the president, with special reference to the creation of cabinet councils. Bradley D. Nash, with Milton S. Eisenhower, R. Gordon Hoxie, and William C. Spragens, *Organizing and Staffing the Presidency* (New York, 1980), traces development and reforms in the presidential office from Washington through Carter. Allan Nevins, *The Emergence of Lincoln,* 2 vols. (New York, 1950), a classic work, traces the dissolution of the Union (1857–1861) and suggests that a ministerial form of government might, after the 1858 election, have served the nation better. Nancy Winslow Parker, *The President's Cabinet and How It Grew* (New York, 1978), is a delightfully illustrated, succinct work. Bradley H. Patterson, Jr., *The President's Cabinet: Issues and Questions* (Washington, D.C., 1976), is about the relationships of cabinet members with each other and with the president and the White House staff.

Nelson W. Polsby, *Presidential Cabinet Making: Lessons for the Political System* (Bloomington, Ind., 1977), analyzes Nixon and Carter cabinets and staff. Donald Robinson, "The Inventors of the Presidency," in *Presidential Studies Quarterly,* 13 (1983), is a scholarly analysis of the positions of the constitutional framers on the presidency and the executive branch of the federal government. Harold Seidman, *Politics, Position, and Power: The Dynamics of Federal Organization,* 3rd ed. (New York, 1980), is a classic work by a distinguished scholar who is a veteran of the Office of Management and Budget. Steven A. Shull, *Presidential Policy Making: An Analysis* (Brunswick, Ohio, 1978), concentrates on public administration and policymaking and has an excellent bibliography. George P. Shultz and Kenneth W. Dam, *Economic Policy Beyond the Headlines* (New York, 1977), offers a thoughtful study on policy formulation; the authors, who had served together in the Office of Management and Budget, were appointed secretary and deputy secretary of state, respectively, in 1982.

Harold C. Syrett, ed., *The Papers of Alexander Hamilton,* 26 vols. (New York, 1961–1979), offers the papers of the nation's most distinguished cabinet member; the correspondence with Washington is especially revealing regarding cabinet development. Schuyler C. Wallace, *Federal Departmentalization: A Critique of Theories of Organization* (New York, 1941), is a classic early work on federal executive department organization. Andrew J. Wann, *The President as Chief Administrator: A Study of Franklin D. Roosevelt* (Washington, D.C., 1968), is a perceptive work on the Roosevelt administration, with particular reference to cabinet and staff and the presidential role. Leonard D. White, *The Federalists* (New York, 1948), *The Jeffersonians* (1951), *The Jacksonians* (1954), and *The Republican Era* (1958), a four-volume study of administrative history from 1789 to 1901, is indispensable on the establishment and development of the cabinet and other aspects of presidential administration.

[*See also* HISTORIOGRAPHY OF AMERICAN POLITICAL HISTORY; CONGRESS; CONSTITUTION; ENGLISH AND EUROPEAN POLITICAL INHERITANCE; THE FEDERALIST PAPERS; POLITICAL PARTIES; PRESIDENCY; *and* SEPARATION OF POWERS.]

CENSORSHIP

Paul S. Boyer

THE issue of censorship has troubled Americans from the early colonial era down to the present day. Since at least the eighteenth century, heated debates have arisen over the proper balance between freedom of expression and society's chronic impulse to repress that which is deemed politically threatening or shockingly obscene in the printed word or visual representation. Although the censorship issue has often found its way to the courts and is thus a part of the nation's legal and constitutional history, it cannot be fully understood without attention to the larger social and cultural context in which the legal battles have been waged.

POLITICAL CENSORSHIP IN THE COLONIAL AND NATIONAL PERIODS

Let us turn first to the censorship of political expression. The American colonies inherited the legal concepts of sedition and criminal libel as they had evolved in the English common law. In 1643, when the American colonies were only a few decades old, the House of Commons passed the Licensing Act, which required official approval in advance of the publication of any book. From the first, this prior-restraint law aroused heavy criticism—including John Milton's famous defense of freedom of the press, *Areopagitica* (1644)—and it was never consistently enforced, either in England or in England's North American domain. But though erratically enforced, the Licensing Act did have an inhibiting effect upon press freedom in the colonies until it was allowed to lapse in 1695. When a printer named William Nuthead set up a press in Jamestown in 1682 and began to publish legislative acts and "other papers," he was silenced by a royal governor bear-

ing an order from London that "no person be permitted to use any press for printing upon any occasion whatsoever." Not until 1730 was a permanent printing press established in Virginia. The Massachusetts legislature in 1662 forbade any publication that did not have prior official approval. When America's first newspaper, *Publick Occurrences both Forreign and Domestick,* appeared in Boston in 1690, it was immediately suppressed by the governor and council on the grounds that it had been issued without a license.

Throughout the eighteenth century, although freed of prior-restraint laws and reasonably free to print what they wished, colonial printers, pamphleteers, and newspaper publishers were still subject to periodic harassment by governors or legislatures. The best-remembered of these censorship efforts involved John Peter Zenger, the German-born editor and printer of the *New-York Weekly Journal,* a newspaper supported by New York merchants who opposed the royal governor, William Cosby. In 1734 Zenger was arrested and imprisoned on the charge of criminally libeling Cosby. He was found innocent by a jury in 1735, on the grounds that the charges he had published were, in fact, true. The Zenger case was long viewed as a major landmark in the battle for freedom of the press, but recent scholarship has found it somewhat less significant. Certainly Zenger's acquittal did not end the harassment of colonial printers. In 1754, for example, the Massachusetts legislature, angered by a pamphlet critical of an excise tax it had recently imposed, ordered it burned by the common hangman and jailed the printer, Daniel Fowle, and the suspected author, Royall Tyler. But such efforts were rarely effective. Fowle and Tyler were released after a few days amid popular acclaim, and when Fowle brought suit for damages he was awarded £20 by the Massachusetts superior court "on account of the sufferings mentioned."

In the national period, censorship questions have often turned upon judicial or legislative understanding of the First Amendment of the Constitution, which states in part: "Congress shall make no law . . . abridging the freedom of speech, or of the press. . . ." (By judicial interpretation of the Fourteenth Amendment in the late nineteenth century, this proscription was extended to include state legislation as well.) The major challenges to this seemingly clear-cut and explicit First Amendment guarantee have come during periods of political upheaval or cultural stress, when the censorship impulse has been most intense. In 1798 the dominant Federalists, for example, alarmed by the growing Republican party and responding to the spreading aftershocks of the French Revolution, enacted a series of repressive federal laws known collectively as the Alien and Sedition Acts. These measures, which remained in effect until 1801, included a Sedition Act providing heavy fines and jail terms for persons convicted of publishing any "false, scandalous, and malicious" writing "with intent to defame . . . or bring into contempt or disrepute" the president or other members of the government. Twenty-five Republican editors were prosecuted under this act, and, in trials that were often travesties of due process, ten were convicted. One of the intended targets, Benjamin Franklin's grandson Benjamin Bache, publisher of the Antifederalist Philadelphia *Aurora*, escaped jail only because he died in the yellow fever epidemic of September 1798. James Madison called the Sedition Act "a monster that must forever disgrace its parents." When Thomas Jefferson became president in 1801, he pardoned all those convicted under the Sedition Act, and Congress restored their fines with interest.

Another challenge to freedom of the press and the right of free expression came in the 1830's as a by-product of the gathering crisis over slavery and the efforts of abolitionists to propagate their ideas. In 1835 Georgia imposed the death penalty for the publication of any material tending to incite slaves to rebel. That July, a boatload of abolitionist literature was seized by the postmaster of Charleston, South Carolina, and subsequently burned by a mob. When President Jackson's postmaster general reported that he lacked authority to bar abolitionist propaganda from the mails, Jackson urged Congress to enact such a law. This proposal was opposed on constitutional grounds by leading senators, including the abolitionists' sworn enemy, John C. Calhoun of South Carolina. Even a compromise measure that would have empowered postmasters to seize any mail prohibited by the law of a particular state was defeated in 1836. In 1837 a public meeting in Alton, Illinois, ordered abolitionist editor Elijah Lovejoy to cease his "incendiary publications." He refused, and shortly afterward, his printing press was thrown into the Mississippi; he was murdered as he tried to defend the warehouse in which its replacement was being stored.

The major twentieth-century efforts to limit political expression have come at times of heightened patriotism and suspicion of unpopular views associated with wartime or international conflict. In May 1918, reflecting the climate of ideological conformism that prevailed during World War I, Congress passed the Sedition Act, an amendment to the Espionage Act of 1917. Like its forerunner of 1798, this measure provided heavy fines and long jail terms for persons convicted of making false statements, orally or in print, that interfered with the war effort, or of using "disloyal, profane, scurrilous, or abusive language" about the American form of government, the Constitution, the flag, or the nation's military forces. A number of states passed similar laws. Some 1,500 opponents of the war were indicted under the 1918 Sedition Act, including many pacifists and socialists like Congressman Victor Berger of Wisconsin. Many went to jail, including socialist leader Eugene V. Debs, who spent three years behind bars. Several antiwar or radical newspapers and periodicals were suppressed by federal postal authorities, who suspended their mailing privileges.

Two legal challenges to the Espionage and Sedition Acts provided the occasion for major statements on the First Amendment guarantee of press freedom and free speech by U.S. Supreme Court Justice Oliver Wendell Holmes, Jr. In *Schenck* v. *U.S.* (1919), Holmes, writing for a unanimous court, upheld the plaintiff's conviction under the Espionage Act on the grounds that his publication of an antidraft pamphlet in wartime had posed a "clear and present danger" to the national well-being and thus did not qualify for First Amendment protection. In subsequent cases, Holmes's "clear and present danger" rule would often be invoked in First Amendment cases involving speech or publications that did not pose such an urgent and immediate threat. In another 1919 case, *Abrams* v. *U.S.*, in which the Supreme Court majority held the Sedition Act constitutional, Holmes dissented, arguing that free speech and freedom of the press were not privileges graciously extended by a government to its citizens, but rather essential prerequisites of a free society. "The best test of truth," Holmes wrote, "is the power of the thought to get itself accepted in the competition of the market."

In the post-1945 era of Cold War conflict with the Soviet Union, the U.S. government proceeded against American Communists and so-called fellow travelers in ways that many felt violated their First Amendment rights. These actions were initiated under the Alien Registration Act of 1940, commonly known as the Smith Act. This measure, the main purpose of which was to check domestic subversion, made it a crime for any person to advocate or teach the overthrow of the government by force or to organize or join any group that taught such doctrines. Beginning with the successful prosecution of eleven top U.S. Communists in 1951 *(Dennis et al.* v. *U.S.)*, the government secured nearly 100 convictions, and many more indictments, under the Smith Act against Communists or suspected Communists. But in *Yates* v. *U.S.* (1957), the Supreme Court held that the government had interpreted its powers under the Smith Act too broadly and in the process violated the First Amendment. The mere act of advocating and teaching the forcible overthrow of the government as a general principle, apart from specific efforts to that end, the Court held, had constitutional protection. With the *Yates* decision, the censorship of unpopular or even revolutionary political ideas was dealt a severe if not fatal blow.

In subsequent rulings, the U.S. Supreme Court defended in various ways the First Amendment rights of newspapers. In *New York Times* v. *Sullivan* (1964), involving an issue as old as the Zenger case, the Court held that newspaper criticism of a public official acting in his or her official capacity could not be the basis of a successful libel action unless defamatory falsehood with actual malice could be proved. In the so-called

Pentagon Papers cases of 1971 *(New York Times* v. *U.S.* and *U.S.* v. *Washington Post)*, the Supreme Court rejected the government's efforts to secure an injunction against these two newspapers to stop their publication of secret government documents relating to the early planning of the Vietnam War that had been illegally "leaked" to them. As often happens, the six justices who constituted the majority in this decision differed among themselves: some argued that any legal action against the newspapers would violate the First Amendment; others took the view that while criminal prosecution under the Espionage Act might be justified, there was no "clear and present danger" so urgent as to justify an injunction.

CENSORSHIP OF THE EROTIC

A quite different and in some ways more complex range of censorship issues is raised by those books, periodicals, or other forms of expression that are sufficiently erotic, deviant, or sexually explicit to be considered obscene by a significant portion of the populace. As early as 1842, the U.S. Customs Bureau was empowered to bar from America's shores "indecent and obscene prints, paintings, lithographs, engravings, and transparencies." But as an explicit aim of government policy, obscenity censorship really dates from 1873, when the postal code was revised to authorize postal authorities to exclude from the mails books or other materials that were "obscene," "lewd," or "lascivious." The moving force behind this law was Anthony Comstock, head of the New York Society for the Suppression of Vice (founded in 1872). Appointed a "special investigator" by the post office and backed by such wealthy and prominent New Yorkers as J. P. Morgan, William E. Dodge, and Morris K. Jesup, Comstock, until his death in 1915, pursued the publishers and purveyors of material that he considered obscene and indecent. Although few legal records of Comstock's labors have survived, he claimed at the end of his career to have been instrumental in the destruction of 160 tons of obscene material and to have won convictions against enough persons to fill sixty-one railroad coaches. Although Comstock occasionally attacked erotic classics, works by Ovid, Rabelais, and Boccaccio, and books by modern writers like Walt Whitman and Leo Tolstoy, most of his efforts were directed against obscure and blatantly pornographic books like *The Lusty Turk,* "degrading" magazines such as the *Police Gazette,* sexually explicit photographs and drawings, and contraceptive information and materials. He also pursued fraudulent advertisers and lottery operators who used the U.S. mails.

Although Comstock became an object of ridicule toward the end of his career, as in 1913 when he took legal action against a charmingly innocent popular print of a discreet and graceful nude, called "September Morn," in the late nineteenth century his censorship activities had the support not only of the elite but also of the dominant middle class. The New England Watch and Ward Society, Boston's version of the Comstock organization, similarly enjoyed the support of the city's upper and middle classes. In 1885 the Watch and Ward marshaled this elite support to secure passage of a state law banning the sale to minors, or even the display within view of any minor child, of any magazine featuring "criminal news, police reports, or accounts of criminal deeds, or pictures and stories of lust and crime." A number of news dealers were successfully prosecuted under this vaguely defined statute.

These and similar antivice societies in other cities relied upon a subtle blend of legal pressure and extralegal moral coercion. Indeed, so powerful and all-pervasive was the genteel moral code in the Gilded Age that publishers, critics, and the editors of the major literary magazines played as important a role in enforcing it as did the censors. When the antivice societies did go to court, the presumption was heavily in their favor, and they enjoyed a conviction rate of well over 90 percent. Except for a few mavericks like the agnostic Colonel Robert G. Ingersoll and his National Liberal League, the legal suppression of printed matter that offended the prevailing moral code was not widely believed to raise First Amendment problems in these years. In *Ex Parte Jackson* (1877), involving a lottery operator, U.S. Supreme Court Justice Stephen J. Field said that there was "no doubt" that the 1873 postal censorship act was constitutional. The definition of obscenity generally accepted by the courts in these years was the one advanced by the English jurist Alexander Cockburn in the 1868 case *Regina* v. *Hicklin:* "The test of obscenity is whether

the tendency of the matter charged as obscenity is to deprave and corrupt those whose minds are open to such immoral influences and into whose hands a publication of this sort may fall." Until 1957 the basic definition of obscenity followed by American jurists remained the so-called *Hicklin* test, which opened the censorship door very wide with its reference to the "tendency" of a work, its use of such undefined words as "deprave" and "corrupt," and its implication that society's most innocent and morally vulnerable members should determine the standard of acceptability for the entire society.

Broad public support for the censorship of the obscene continued into the Progressive Era (1900–1920). In these years when many social and economic evils were being attacked by reformers—child labor, prostitution, impure food, industrial hazards, political corruption—the antivice societies argued with considerable success that their cause was simply another facet of the broader crusade to improve and purify American life. The targets of the censors in these years were extremely varied. Elinor Glyn's *Three Weeks* (1907), a dreamy tale of illicit love, was found obscene in Boston; Theodore Dreiser's *The "Genius"* (1907) was suppressed by its New York publisher under threat of vice-society prosecution; an issue of the New York socialist weekly *The Call* was declared nonmailable by the post office in 1913 because of an article on syphilis by the birth-control advocate Margaret Sanger; and *Mrs. Warren's Profession,* George Bernard Shaw's 1905 play in which prostitution was discussed openly, was banned in New Haven. Anthony Comstock attempted to bar the play from the New York stage as well, labeling Shaw "a foreign writer of filth." (Shaw responded by creating a new noun, "Comstockery.") The producers and several cast members of *Mrs. Warren's Profession* were arrested after the New York opening but were later acquitted.

A new censorship issue in these years was posed by the growing commercial popularity of motion pictures. The first known movie censorship attempt, involving a short film called *Dolorita in the Passion Dance* being shown on the Boardwalk in Atlantic City, came only two weeks after the commercial debut of Thomas Edison's "Kinetoscope" in 1894. Soon, numerous cities and states had set up licensing boards empowered to ban or cut any film deemed obscene or otherwise objectionable. In 1909, responding to threats by officials to close the city's movie houses, a group of citizens in New York, with the support of movie industry figures, created the so-called National Board of Censorship (later called the National Board of Review) to preview and evaluate films before their release. In *Block* v. *Chicago* (1909), the Ilinois Supreme Court upheld a Chicago ordinance requiring police inspection and licensing of all films shown in the city. In *Mutual Film Corp.* v. *Ohio* (1915), the U.S. Supreme Court upheld such prior-restraint censorship by state and local agencies, holding that the exhibition of motion pictures was "a business pure and simple" and not subject to First Amendment protection.

But, as historian Henry May demonstrates in *The End of American Innocence* (1959), the genteel code was beginning to erode in these prewar years and with it the unquestioning support for censorship. With American fiction becoming increasingly realistic thanks to such writers as Stephen Crane, Sherwood Anderson, and Theodore Dreiser, the line between literature and obscenity that had once seemed so clear-cut grew increasingly blurred. One evidence of the changing climate was the publication in 1911 of Theodore Schroeder's uncompromising anti-censorship manifesto *"Obscene" Literature and Constitutional Law.*

It was in the 1920's that the dams of prudishness and cultural gentility burst entirely, leaving the vice societies and their moral certitudes awash in swirling torrents of cultural change. In this decade, a group of younger writers, eagerly supported by a brash new generation of book publishers, dealt far more openly and explicitly with once taboo subjects, while the avant-garde work of continental writers was avidly sought out by American publishers and readers. The inevitable result was a series of raucous and highly publicized censorship battles as the vice societies and their conservative backers sought to stem the tide of literary and cultural change. In New York, Comstock's successor, John S. Sumner, instigated unsuccessful prosecutions against such books as James Branch Cabell's *Jurgen*, D. H. Lawrence's *Women in Love*, Arthur Schnitzler's *Casanova's Homecoming*, and Radclyffe Hall's *The Well of Loneliness*, a novel about lesbianism. A number of lawyers now devoted their energies to the struggle against censorship, most notably Morris Ernst, who attacked the censors in *To the Pure: A Study of Obscenity and the Censor* (1928) and other works.

But the procensorship forces remained strong. In 1923, and for several years thereafter, a Clean Books League, with strong support from various Roman Catholic organizations, mounted a determined, although unsuccessful, campaign to tighten New York State's obscenity statute. The *New York Times* (a strong supporter of Comstock's efforts in earlier years) vigorously opposed this effort, commenting editorially that it would make the vice society "an absolute and irresponsible censor of all modern literature." Significantly, a number of the older generation of authors, publishers, librarians, and booksellers, resentful and upset about the cultural changes sweeping over the nation, lent tacit and sometimes open support to the repressive censorship efforts of the 1920's.

Boston emerged as a particular center of censorship activity in the 1920's. The city's old Brahmin elite and Yankee middle class had long supported the Watch and Ward Society; and the Irish Catholic immigrants, who emerged to political dominance in the twentieth century, proved no less ardent in their support for censorship. In 1915 some leading Boston booksellers had joined with the Watch and Ward Society to set up a system of extralegal censorship under which a small committee read and evaluated current novels, notifying the city's booksellers of those that might be legally actionable. By this informal system a tight censorship prevailed, and many books available elsewhere could not be purchased in Boston. In the 1920's the Watch and Ward and Boston's timid booksellers came in for increasing criticism and ridicule, most notably in the pages of H. L. Mencken's *American Mercury*, a monthly noted for its support of new writers and its attacks on conventional moral taboos and middle-class proprieties. A showdown came early in 1926, when the Watch and Ward Society warned Boston newsdealers not to sell the April issue of the *American Mercury*, which contained a story entitled "Hatrack" about a small-town prostitute. With his keen sense of publicity, Mencken came to Boston, sold a copy of the offending issue to the head of the Watch and Ward Society on the Boston Common, and was arrested. The charges against Mencken were thrown out by a municipal court judge, and on 14 April

1926 Federal Judge James M. Morton, Jr., issued an injunction against the leaders of the Watch and Ward Society ordering them to refrain from seeking "to impose their opinions on the book and magazine trade by threats of prosecution. . . ." The "Hatrack" case generated massive publicity, awakening many citizens to the censorship issue and focusing attention on the repressive climate in Boston. "Banned in Boston" became a derisive national slogan, often used to good effect by book publishers promoting their wares in other cities. "We Americans are using America as our sales territory, and Boston is our advertising department," quipped one writer.

Mencken's acquittal did not mean an end to censorship in Boston. Although the Watch and Ward Society had been somewhat restrained by Judge Morton's injunction, the city's police had become more directly active. In 1926–1927 the police notified Boston booksellers of more than a dozen novels they considered obscene, including Percy Marks's *The Plastic Age*, Sinclair Lewis' *Elmer Gantry*, and Theodore Dreiser's *An American Tragedy*. One leading Boston bookseller on his own initiative refused to sell Upton Sinclair's *Oil*, a book about the Harding administration scandals. In *Commonwealth* v. *Friede* (1930), a test case initiated in 1927, the Supreme Judicial Court of Massachusetts upheld the obscenity conviction of a publisher's representative who had sold a copy of *An American Tragedy* to a Boston policeman. Nor was the Watch and Ward Society completely immobilized. In 1929, in a case initiated by the venerable antivice organization, a Cambridge, Massachusetts, bookseller was convicted for the sale of D. H. Lawrence's *Lady Chatterley's Lover* (1928), a work that would figure in many censorship cases over the years.

The motion-picture industry, meanwhile, was also feeling the increased censorship pressures. The torrid scenes depicted on the screen in such movies as Rudolph Valentino's *The Sheik* (1921) and Clara Bow's *Kiss Me Again* (1925) were deeply upsetting to older Americans concerned about the morals of the young. In 1922, reacting to a rise in censorship activity and boycott threats from private groups such as the Roman Catholic Legion of Decency, the industry trade association (the Motion Picture Producers and Distributors of America) appointed former Postmaster General Will H. Hays as its head, with a mandate to oversee the moral tone of Holly-

wood. In 1930 Hays promulgated a detailed production code spelling out the limits of the acceptable in the movies. But the Hays Code was widely ignored; and in 1934, under continued censorship and boycott threats, the industry created a powerful and semi-independent agency, the Production Code Administration, with Joseph I. Breen to enforce it.

While the motion-picture industry wrestled with the censorship threat, growing opposition to moralistic repression on the literary front was beginning to make itself felt in the courts and in Congress. In March 1930 Judge Augustus N. Hand of the U.S. Second Circuit Court of Appeals overturned a lower court conviction of Mary Ware Dennett for mailing copies of her pamphlet *The Sex Side of Life*, which offered factual sexual information for young people. In the same year, Senator Bronson M. Cutting of New Mexico led a successful campaign to restrict the censorship powers of the Customs Bureau. Cutting's amendment to Section 305 of the Smoot-Hawley Tariff of 1930 provided for judicial review of all Customs Bureau censorship decisions, with special consideration to be given to classics and works of "literary or scientific merit."

This liberalization of the customs law laid the groundwork for the landmark censorship case *U.S.* v. *One Book Called "Ulysses"* (1933). The case originated with the publisher Bennett Cerf, who, wishing for a definitive judicial ruling on the obscenity question before publishing an American edition of James Joyce's masterpiece, arranged for a test case involving an imported copy. As provided in the new statute, the case was brought to federal court, where it was heard by Judge John M. Woolsey of the Southern District of New York, sitting without a jury. Attorney Morris Ernst represented Cerf. In December 1933 Woolsey issued his ruling, giving *Ulysses* a clean bill of health. While accepting the *Hicklin* rule that sexual suggestiveness could be the basis of an obscenity conviction, Woolsey pushed that position to its liberal limit. The test must be a work's effect upon "a person with average sex instincts," he wrote, not on children, the immature, or the particularly susceptible. Furthermore, he ruled, a work must be judged "in its entirety," not on the basis of specific words or passages. Of the obscene words that had caused *Ulysses* so much legal trouble, Woolsey calmly observed, "The words which are criticized as dirty are old Saxon words known to almost all men and, I venture, to many women, and are such words as would be naturally and habitually used, I believe, by the types of folks whose life, physical and mental, Joyce is seeking to describe."

Taken together, the *Dennett* and *Ulysses* decisions and the restrictions on federal censorship written into the Smoot-Hawley Tariff signaled a distinct liberalization of the law of obscenity and marked the end of a period of particularly intense censorship activity. They helped create a climate far more receptive to the free circulation of works of generally acknowledged literary merit, as well as nonfictional works of patently serious intent, whatever the subject matter or the specific vocabulary employed. The book burnings in Nazi Germany in the 1930's further dampened the censorship impulse, as Americans saw where that impulse, carried to an extreme, could lead. In 1942, when Postmaster General Frank C. Walker withdrew the second-class mailing privileges of the then sexually risqué *Esquire* magazine for failing "to contribute to the public good and public welfare," the action was appealed by the American Civil Liberties Union and reversed by the U.S. Court of Appeals. The latter advised the post office to give up "moral supervision of the mails" and return to "the more prosaic function of seeing to it that 'neither snow nor rain nor heat nor gloom of night stays these couriers from the swift completion of their appointed rounds.'" The appellate court's decision was upheld by the U.S. Supreme Court.

But despite these liberalizing trends, censorship was far from dead as the nation moved into the post–World War II era. Federal and state obscenity statutes remained on the books and were frequently invoked. In such cases, the outcome depended on how the court assessed a specific book's literary merit or seriousness of purpose. These rulings were often unpredictable. For example, the Supreme Judicial Court of Massachusetts upheld obscenity convictions against Lillian Smith's *Strange Fruit* in 1945 and Erskine Caldwell's *God's Little Acre* in 1950, while ruling in 1948 that Kathleen Windsor's torrid potboiler *Forever Amber* was not obscene. In a 1946 case that was appealed all the way to the U.S. Supreme Court, Doubleday and Company was convicted under New York's obscenity statute for publishing and selling *Memoirs of Hecate County* by the distinguished American writer and critic Edmund Wilson. By contrast, in *Commonwealth* v. *Gordon,* a 1949 Pennsylvania case arising out of the sale of a number of books including *God's Little Acre,* James T. Farrell's *Studs Lonigan* trilogy, and William Faulkner's *Sanctuary,* Judge Curtis Bok dismissed the indictment in an opinion that exhaustively explored the constitutional aspects of the obscenity issue.

CENSORSHIP AND THE SUPREME COURT

The U.S. Supreme Court attempted to introduce some order into this constitutional thicket in two important cases in the 1950's. In 1952, overturning a New York ban on *The Miracle* (an Italian film denounced as sacrilegious by the Roman Catholic hierarchy), it reversed its 1915 position and declared motion pictures "a significant medium for the communication of ideas" and thus entitled to First Amendment protection. Several subsequent decisions by the Court imposed increasingly stringent procedural restraints on the dwindling number of state and municipal motion-picture licensing boards.

Turning to the printed word in *U.S.* v. *Roth* and *Alberts* v. *California* (1957), the Court for the first time addressed in an explicit and substantive way the First Amendment issues posed by laws against obscenity. In the cases at hand, it upheld the conviction of Samuel Roth and David Alberts, both of whom were major commercial purveyors of the kind of sexually oriented material generally known as "hard core" pornography. Bearing such titles as *Wild Passion, Wanton by Night,* and *The Prostitute and Her Lover,* the works involved were not literary classics. Obscenity of this type, ruled the Court, lay outside the bounds of First Amendment protection. But the Court made clear that those bounds were very broad indeed:

> All ideas having even the slightest redeeming social importance—unorthodox ideas, controversial ideas, even ideas hateful to the prevailing climate of opinion—have the full protection of the [First Amendment's] guarantees, unless excludable because they encroach upon the lim-

ited area of more important interests. But implicit in the history of the First Amendment is the rejection of obscenity as utterly without redeeming social importance.

The *Roth/Alberts* decision next turned to the troublesome task of offering a definition of obscenity that would supersede the hoary *Hicklin* rule of 1868. First of all, material charged as obscene apparently had to be "utterly without redeeming social importance." Furthermore, the mere fact of sexual content did not mean that a work was obscene:

> [S]ex and obscenity are not synonymous. Obscene material is material which deals with sex in a manner appealing to prurient interest. The portrayal of sex, *e.g.,* in art, literature and scientific works, is not itself sufficient reason to deny material the constitutional protection of freedom of speech and press.

Having made these prefatory points, the Court offered its definition: a work is obscene if "to the average person, applying contemporary community standards, the dominant theme of the material taken as a whole appeals to prurient interests."

The range of opinions offered by the Supreme Court justices in the *Roth/Alberts* decision well illustrates the complexity of the question. Chief Justice Earl Warren concurred with the majority but expressed the view that the activities of Roth and Alberts were so patently illegal that a broad-ranging statement on First Amendment issues was not called for. Justice John Marshall Harlan, concurring in *Alberts* but dissenting in *Roth,* contended that the presumption should be in favor of state obscenity convictions, because protection of public morality was mainly a state function, but that the courts should view federal censorship with a much more skeptical and critical eye. (Roth had been convicted of violating the federal postal code; Alberts' conviction was under California's antiobscenity statute.) Finally, Justices William O. Douglas and Hugo Black dissented from the decision on the grounds that the First Amendment guarantees were absolute; they prohibited all censorship except in cases where the speech or publication in question was "so closely brigaded with illegal action as to be an inseparable part of it."

The *Roth/Alberts* decision, which remains a cornerstone of U.S. obscenity law, sustained and gave fresh impetus to the long process by which the range of material that could be legally censored on obscenity grounds was steadily restricted. After 1957 the courts extended First Amendment protection to a wide range of works long held to be legally obscene. In 1959, taking advantage of the new judicial liberalism, Grove Press of New York brought out the first unexpurgated American edition of D. H. Lawrence's *Lady Chatterley's Lover,* which had remained under the censor's ban for thirty years. Postal authorities seized copies of the book and brought action against the publisher, but Judge Frederick van Pelt Bryan of the U.S. District Court for the Southern District of New York ruled Lawrence's novel not obscene under federal law. Despite the frequent use of four-letter words and the detailed and realistic descriptions of sexual intercourse, wrote Bryan, "The book is replete with fine writing and with descriptive passages of rare beauty. There is no doubt of its literary merit." When Bryan's ruling was upheld in the U.S. Court of Appeals, a major work of twentieth-century literature that had been in legal limbo for three decades was finally allowed to circulate freely.

In *Manual Enterprises* v. *Day* (1962), a case involving post office efforts to bar from the mails several illustrated magazines published for homosexuals, the U.S. Supreme Court added a significant postscript to the definition of obscenity formulated in the *Roth/Alberts* case. In announcing the Court's ruling that the publications in question were protected under the First Amendment, Justice Harlan wrote that while the material in the magazines was clearly prurient, it was not presented with "patent offensiveness" in ways that were "unacceptable under current community mores." Thereafter, "patent offensiveness" was added to the legal test that materials had to meet in order to be considered legally obscene. The liberalizing trend of these years reached its apogee in 1966 when the Supreme Court reversed a Massachusetts obscenity finding against John Cleland's *Memoirs of a Woman of Pleasure,* a work more commonly known by the name of its heroine, Fanny Hill. While acknowledging that the dominant theme of the eighteenth-century erotic classic was clearly prurient, the Court also held that the work did have significance in literary history and was thus not without redeeming social importance.

But while judges were steadily extending First Amendment protection to books and periodicals once considered beyond the pale, a growing conviction was gathering momentum outside the courthouse walls that the trend toward permissiveness had gone too far. In 1957, Cincinnati attorney Charles H. Keating founded Citizens for Decent Literature (CDL) to fight for stricter enforcement of the obscenity laws; soon CDL claimed 300 chapters across the nation. The movement for a crackdown on obscenity gained momentum in the turbulent 1960's, in part as a symbolic expression of the alarm felt by many Americans over campus unrest and the spread of drug abuse and over the general attitude of sexual permissiveness among the young. A Gallup Poll in 1969 found 85 percent of the adult population in favor of "stricter laws on pornography."

As in the 1920's, the issues of obscenity and censorship became caught up in larger currents of social change and political conflict. In the 1964 electoral campaign, the Republican platform pledged "enactment of legislation, despite Democratic opposition, to curb the flow through our mails of obscene material which has flourished into a multimillion dollar obscenity racket." In 1967, declaring "the traffic in obscenity and pornography . . . a matter of national concern," a conservative-dominated Congress established a National Commission on Obscenity and Pornography to investigate the problem and make recommendations. To the displeasure of many of the legislators who had voted to create the commission (and the Republican administration that had come to the White House in the interim), the commission's 1970 report found no evidence of harmful effects to adults resulting from exposure to pornography and recommended that all "federal, state, and local legislation prohibiting the sale, exhibition or distribution of sexual materials to consenting adults be repealed." The commission did recommend legislation prohibiting the open public display of sexually explicit pictorial material, the sale of such material to minors, or its promotion through unsolicited mail advertising.

The shift in public opinion toward greater repressiveness soon made itself felt in the courts. Indeed, in *Ginzburg* v. *U.S.* (1966), issued the same day as the *Fanny Hill* decision, the U.S. Supreme Court upheld the New York obscenity conviction sentence of Ralph Ginzburg, publisher of a magazine of erotic art and literature called *Eros,* on the grounds that his flamboyant and salacious advertising had involved him "in the sordid business of pandering." The *Ginzburg* decision meant that a book or publication that would otherwise enjoy First Amendment protection could lose that protection if it were promoted in a fashion that pandered to prurient interest.

The shift in judicial direction hinted at in the *Ginzburg* decision emerged with unmistakable clarity in June 1973 when the U.S. Supreme Court, under its new chief justice, Warren Burger, upheld lower-court obscenity convictions in five separate cases. Although the cases differed among themselves, the net effect of the five rulings was to slow the liberalizing trend set by the *Roth/Alberts* decision in 1957 and to indicate much more judicial support for the censorship of sexually explicit materials. The key case, in terms of the definition of obscenity law, was *Miller* v. *California.* Writing for the majority, Chief Justice Burger rejected the requirement implicit in *Roth/Alberts* that obscene material must be "utterly without redeeming social importance." Such a rule, Burger wrote, imposed on prosecutors of obscenity laws "a burden virtually impossible to discharge under our criminal standards of proof." Instead, *Miller* v. *California* substituted the requirement that to be found obscene a work must lack "serious literary, artistic, political, or scientific value."

The *Miller* decision also significantly modified the rule that to be found obscene a work must violate "contemporary community standards." In *Roth/Alberts* and later decisions, the Court had understood this to mean a national standard. In *Miller* v. *California,* however, Chief Justice Burger held that any effort to establish a national standard of obscenity would be "an exercise in futility"; such an "abstract formulation" would be "hypothetical and unascertainable." Instead, the Court offered a new definition. Provided the other tests justifying exclusion from First Amendment protection were met, "contemporary community standards" in obscenity cases could mean state or presumably even local standards.

This aspect of the *Miller* decision aroused sharp criticism among civil libertarians. The basis of this criticism was that it invited censors to "shop around," instituting selective prosecutions of nationally distributed books, periodicals, or movies in jurisdictions known to have particularly restrictive standards. The *New York Times* warned that the new definition would "make every local community and every state the arbiter of acceptability, thereby adjusting all sex-related literary, artistic, and entertainment productions to the lowest common denominator of toleration."

The overall thrust of the Court's 1973 rulings was to suggest a more limited application of the First Amendment where "obscenity" was at issue and a heightened judicial sympathy for censorship if the avowed aim were decency and morality. This emerged clearly in one of the decisions, *Paris Adult Theater I* v. *Slaton,* upholding the conviction of the operator of a Georgia theater showing sexually explicit movies to adults. In this decision, also written by Chief Justice Burger, the court declared:

> [W]e hold that there are legitimate state interests at stake in stemming the tide of commercialized obscenity. . . . The sum of experience, including that of the past two decades, affords an ample basis for legislatures to conclude that a sensitive, key relationship of human existence, central to family life, community welfare, and the development of human personality, can be debased and distorted by crass commercial exploitation of sex. Nothing in the Constitution prohibits a State from reaching such a conclusion and acting on it legislatively simply because there is no conclusive evidence or empirical data.

A CONTINUING DILEMMA

The years following these rulings saw an upsurge in obscenity prosecutions across the nation. In 1980, Larry C. Flynt, owner of *Hustler* magazine, which dealt in sexually explicit photographs of women, was convicted in Cleveland, Ohio, under the state's obscenity law. In 1981 the U.S. Supreme Court upheld the conviction of three men associated with the production of *Deep Throat,* a highly profitable pornographic movie. The three had been prosecuted in Tennessee by the Justice Department under the federal statute barring the mailing of obscene materials.

As in the 1920's, the motion-picture industry saw the handwriting on the wall and responded with yet another effort at self-regulation. As the industry had become less monolithic and public attitudes more permissive, the Production Code of the 1930's had lost effectiveness. In 1953 *The Moon Is Blue* caused a stir when it was released despite having been denied code approval because of its light treatment of a proposed adultery (which in fact never takes place) and its use of the taboo word *virgin.* In 1968, to forestall legislative moves toward a mandatory film classification system and even more stringent censorship proposals, the industry adopted a voluntary rating system whereby each movie is assigned a rating indicating its acceptability for different audiences and giving some idea of its character.

The increase in censorship pressures and antiobscenity preoccupations in the 1970's and 1980's reflected both an apparent upsurge in the volume of sexually explicit books, periodicals, and films, and the emergence of a politically and socially conservative "New Right" in reaction to the dramatic cultural changes of these years. Focusing on pornography and sexual permissiveness as evidences of a general breakdown in moral standards, New Right commentators, columnists, and political spokesmen, as well as conservative religious leaders like the television evangelist Jerry Falwell and his Old Time Gospel Hour of Lynchburg, Virginia, demanded stricter enforcement of the obscenity laws. In 1982 the Coalition for Better Television headed by the Rev. Donald E. Wildmon of Tupelo, Mississippi, called for a boycott of the NBC television network for promoting sex, violence, and "anti-Christian values." Some radical feminists, including a group called Women Against Pornography, demanded the suppression of magazines like *Playboy, Penthouse,* and *Hustler* for the sexual exploitation of women.

Much of this recrudescence of censorship activity focused on the public schools. In a time of intense cultural stress, the schools became highly vulnerable. Such organizations as Falwell's Moral Majority, the Eagle Forum, and California's Creation Science Research Center, as well as individuals like Mel and Norma Gabler (free-lance "educational research analysts" from Texas), pressured textbook publishers to tone down their discussion of evolution, give equal weight to biblical accounts of creation, treat American history more patriotically, and stop promoting "secular humanism." Minority groups and feminists demanded expanded and more favorable treatment in textbooks. The publishers of literary anthologies for classroom use were pressured to remove stories containing objectionable words or dealing with themes considered inappropriate by conservatives. In Texas, *Webster's New Collegiate Dictionary* was removed from the list of dictionaries approved for school use when the publisher, Merriam, refused to drop seven "obscene" words. A competitor, the *American Heritage Dictionary,* was retained on the approved list when the publisher, Houghton Mifflin, agreed to the expurgation.

School libraries were scrutinized by parent groups and New Right organizations for offensive material. The American Library Association (ALA), noting nearly 1,000 reported incidents of school library censorship in 1981, speculated that this was only a small fraction of the total. The most frequent target of the censors, the ALA noted, was J. D. Salinger's 1951 novel of adolescent angst, *The Catcher in the Rye.* In 1975 the school board of Island Trees Union Free School District of Nassau County, New York, removed eleven books from the libraries under its jurisdiction, including *The Fixer* by Bernard Malamud, *Soul on Ice* by Eldridge Cleaver, *Slaughterhouse Five* by Kurt Vonnegut, and *The Naked Ape* by Desmond Morris. When a group of students attempted to sue the board, claiming a violation of their First Amendment rights, the board responded that students had no legal recourse against school-board decisions. The students' right to sue was first rejected in federal district court and then upheld by the U.S. Second Circuit Court of Appeals, after which the U.S. Supreme Court agreed to hear the case. In *Board of Education* v. *Pico* (1982), the Court ruled 5–4 that the school board was not immune to First Amendment challenges and ordered the student suit to proceed to trial. Writing for four members of the majority, Justice William J. Brennan, Jr., held that the students' "right to receive information and ideas" was an "inherent corollary" of the First Amendment guarantee of free speech and free press, adding that if the plaintiffs could prove that the school board had intentionally sought to deny them "access to ideas," they could win their case. Chief Justice Burger, in dissent, argued that the case raised no significant First Amendment issues and that the majority

ruling represented an unwise and unwarranted meddling in local school-board decisions.

The U.S. Supreme Court's sharp divisions in the *Pico* case revealed the depth of disagreement and the intensity of feeling over the ever volatile issue of censorship, not only on the bench but in the nation as a whole. If the experience of 250 years is any guide, we may assume that the censorship dilemma will not soon be resolved. So long as the United States remains an open, heterogenous, and evolving society, the question of the proper balance between public morality and First Amendment freedom will continue to be a matter of intense discussion, reflecting not only the development of constitutional law but also the always stressful process of social change.

BIBLIOGRAPHY

Paul S. Boyer, *Purity in Print: The Vice Society Movement and Book Censorship in America* (New York, 1968), focuses on the cultural context of obscenity censorship from the 1870's to 1933 and includes an extensive bibliography. Zechariah Chaffee, Jr., *Free Speech in the United States* (New York, 1928), is a classic study of political censorship, especially good on the World War I period. Harry M. Clor, *Obscenity and Public Morality: Censorship in a Liberal Society* (Chicago, 1969), is a thoughtful discussion of the issue. Edward De Grazia, *Censorship Landmarks* (New York, 1969), reprints verbatim the key judicial decisions from 1663 to 1968.

Leon Friedman, ed., *Obscenity: The Complete Oral Arguments Before the Supreme Court in the Major Obscenity Cases* (New York, 1970), provides a fascinating glimpse of judges and attorneys grappling with the issue. Harold C. Gardiner, *The Catholic Viewpoint on Censorship* (Garden City, N.Y., 1958), is a Jesuit scholar's lucid defense of censorship and valiant effort to define the obscene. Walter Gellhorn, *Individual Freedom and Government Restraints* (Baton Rouge, La., 1958), provides a balanced, well-reasoned analysis. Robert W. Haney, *Comstockery in America: Patterns of Censorship and Control* (Boston, 1960), is popularly written but carefully researched and is highly critical of the censors. Stanley N. Katz, ed., *A Brief Narrative of the Case and Trial of John Peter Zenger* (Cambridge, Mass., 1963), is a reprint of the original 1736 work; the introduction offers a judicious assessment of the case's significance.

Richard H. Kuh, *Foolish Figleaves? Pornography in—and out of—Court* (New York, 1967), the work of a former assistant district attorney, discusses the key cases from 1957 to 1966 and offers proposals for revisions of the obscenity statutes. Felice Flanery Lewis, *Literature, Obscenity, and Law* (Carbondale, Ill., 1976), is a gracefully written study focusing on the erotic classics that have been censored in the United States. The *Los Angeles Times,* 14 February 1982, contains an in-depth background article, based on a national survey, of current book censorship pressures in the public schools. Robert M. O'Neil, *Classrooms in the Crossfire* (Bloomington, Ind., 1981), provides a thoughtful exploration of the often conflicting interests of students, teachers, administrators, and the community.

James C. N. Paul and Murray L. Schwartz, *Federal Censorship: Obscenity in the Mail* (New York, 1961), is the work of two law professors surveying the evolution of governmental censorship and offering proposals for the future. Richard S. Randall, *Censorship of the Movies* (Madison, Wis., 1968), is the definitive treatment of developments through the mid-1960's. Charles Rembar, *The End of Obscenity* (New York, 1968), is the work of a civil liberties attorney reflecting on the cases in which he has been involved, including *Lady Chatterley's Lover* and *Fanny Hill,* and making a premature prediction.

Frederick F. Schauer, *The Law of Obscenity* (Washington, D.C., 1976), is an exhaustive, well-documented legal study, with extensive extracts from key cases. James M. Smith, *Freedom's Fetters* (Ithaca., N.Y., 1956), is an interesting, in-depth history of the Alien and Sedition Acts. Lawrence C. Wroth, *The Colonial Printer* (Charlottesville, Va., 1931), provides valuable material on censorship in early America.

[*See also* BILL OF RIGHTS; CONSTITUTION; CONTROL, SUPPRESSION, AND INTIMIDATION; MEDIA; *and* POLITICAL CRITICISM.]

CHURCH AND STATE

Henry Warner Bowden

WHEN considering a topic such as this, it is important to recognize that terms are derivative and somewhat inadequate. European experience gave rise to the nation state, usually personified in a monarch, extending throughout a realm in cohesive fashion. Sometimes preceding such states, but certainly existing alongside them, was a church that represented Christendom in the territory. Whether before the Reformation, with Roman Catholic dominance everywhere, or thereafter in countries that changed to Protestant allegiance, the general pattern remained of recognizing a single ecclesiastical institution, which supported and received reciprocal aid from a sovereign state. These precedents, with connotations of unified structures and complementary interests, were transferred to most colonies in America. But they did not survive. The terms drawn from precedent do not fit American conditions very precisely, nor do they have much relevance in the course of this country's history. So in any discussion of religion in the American political context, considerable confusion can be avoided if we notice that basic language was formed in a different setting at an earlier time.

As American political institutions developed, government appeared at various levels, including federal, state, county, and municipal agencies. Because of the plurality of governmental functions, it is difficult to speak cogently of a "state" that deals with churches. American religious groups are similarly diverse. Except for a few examples confined to early colonial times, a single ecclesiastical institution has never monopolized affairs within one political jurisdiction. The wide variety of religious bodies makes it impossible to adopt "church" as a helpful referent.

We can still employ outmoded language, since common usage keeps it alive, but in view of concrete circumstances in American history the terms need careful definition. A state at whatever level of its operation is best seen as an authority structure primarily concerned with temporal life as an end in itself. There are manifold civil governments, but each of them represents an aspect of the politically organized community that exercises coercive power. A church of whatever distinguishing characteristic is best seen as an authority structure concerned with temporal life as a means to spiritual ends. There are many diverse ecclesiastical institutions, but each of them represents voluntary associations that employ noncoercive religious motivation and persuasion to affect individuals and society at large. Church and state issues arise most often where temporal and spiritual authority structures intersect or where conflicting claims arise in the exercise of respective responsibilities. The substance of distant precedents survives in America under different forms.

Church and state in American politics is more accurately the field where religious institutions and civil governments meet in a wide variety of relationships. These interactions have stemmed from three basic conceptions of how temporal and spiritual influences should be related. One view, often called *theocratic*, holds that religious interests are more important than secular ones and consequently that spiritual influences have the right to dictate civil policy. Another perspective, often termed *statist*, holds that governments exist without reference to religious interests and indeed have the right to control every aspect of confessional activities in their domain. These ideas have not been strong or had much influence in American history. The dominant attitude covers a variety of *separatist* convictions, holding that churches and states are discrete, legitimate entities with neither deriving authority from the other. Church and state are usually seen as dual authorities that inevitably come into contact with each other by addressing common human interests. Within this large separatist category, the spectrum of attitudes runs from an absolutist pole at one end to accommodationist positions at the other, with positions advocating neutrality in the middle. The best way of understanding the complex relationship between temporal and spiritual forces today is to study ways in which they have exerted themselves at various stages of American social and political life in the past.

HISTORICAL DEVELOPMENT

When the Church of England was founded in 1534, it replaced Catholicism as the established church in the kingdom. Over the next hundred years, dissident groups known generically as Puritans became increasingly outspoken as they tried to continue reform in Anglicanism. They disagreed among themselves about issues and priorities, but one basic division had to do with the place of religion in civil life. Separatists, such as Baptists and some Congregationalists, advocated confining church ministrations to adult believers, disavowing any responsibility for the rest of society. Nonseparatists, such as Presbyterians and most Congregationalists, shared the Anglican (and prior Catholic) conviction that churches had broad civil responsibilities. These nonseparating Puritans wanted more rigorous discipline among church members, together with simpler worship and democratic internal procedures, and they insisted that proper ecclesiastical presence had monopolistic rights in the state. Membership in such reformed churches was regulated by strict Calvinist standards, but part of nonseparating ideology included the duty to control secular conduct—among believers and nonbelievers alike.

Colonizing ventures in America followed two basic patterns: patents to enterprises in sympathy with the crown, where the Anglican church received traditional establishment; and charters to nonseparating Congregationalists, who gave similar privileges to their own ecclesiastical structure. Virginia is the best example among southern colonies of the former type, while Massachusetts exemplifies the latter. Congregationalists came to New England for purposes of religious freedom, which meant only freedom from Anglican control, to implement their conception of church life. It did not entail toleration of other theologies or religious institutions. Both Congregationalist and Anglican churches in their respective territories exacted taxes to support orthodox ministers and made voting privileges dependent on church membership. The ruling elite in New England proved more intolerant than their Anglican counterparts, banishing religious rebels and hanging some. In both patterns the concept of a unified church and state was transferred to the New World unimpaired.

One of the first exceptions to this standard practice occurred in Maryland, where the Calvert family tried to make it possible for fellow Catholics to live peaceably among Protestants. In 1649 the local government passed "An Act Concerning Religion," which granted civil rights and freedom of worship to all Christian groups. This experimentation in religious toleration was soon reversed by the dominant Protestant faction, and Catholics were forced to endure civil disabilities throughout colonial times. The case of Pennsylvania was another anomaly because William Penn wrote broad religious toleration into his Frame of Government (1682), in hopes of providing sanctuary for fellow Quakers. Since the Penn family did not lose its proprietorship to angry opponents, as did the Calverts, Pennsylvania remained one of the few colonies to enjoy widespread and peaceful religious diversity. Rhode Island was the most striking alternative to the dominant pattern of established colonial churches. Founded by Roger Williams and chartered as a royal colony in 1663, Rhode Island embodied true religious freedom. All groups were allowed to live and worship according to their particular convictions without governmental interference, and religious principles had no further bearing in the conduct of state policy.

Except for Rhode Island and Pennsylvania, American colonies had laws supporting some form of established church. But conditions made such laws virtually inoperable in most places. The economic need for settlers and craftsmen of any persuasion often led magistrates to tolerate religious differences. Immigration from the European continent as well as from Britain brought cultural and religious diversity. In addition to various ethnic enclaves, religious differences arose internally because of theological changes sparked by revivals. By 1750, waves of renewed religious interest had swept up and down the Atlantic seaboard. In the aftermath of the First Great Awakening, new churches were formed even in the most fortified strongholds of traditional establishment thinking. Religious diversity, heightened by revivalistic fervor, combined with cultural and ethnic differences to produce multiple churches in every colony. In most places these manifold groups received de facto toleration even when de jure establishment existed. New England tolerated less diversity than anywhere else, but the persistence of Baptists, Presbyterians, and Anglicans under Congregationalist regimes challenged traditional concepts even there.

While these circumstances developed through the 1700's, another ideological factor added to thoughts about church and state in American life. Cosmopolitan thinkers such as Thomas Jefferson and Benjamin Franklin derived their attitudes about religion from Enlightenment ideas and the new emphasis on independent reason. In an attempt to promote social stability and political virtue through rational means, they subordinated religion to a matter of opinion. Thoughtful people could agree, they held, on common principles such as the existence of a Supreme Being, a soul that activated conduct, rewards for virtue and punishment for vice, and a life beyond the grave where final justice would be meted out. Beyond that, however, theological wrangling impeded social harmony and came to no good purpose. "It does me no injury," Jefferson maintained, "for my neighbor to say there are twenty gods, or no God. It neither picks my pocket nor breaks my leg." Franklin and others in the educated minority agreed that natural science, political philosophy, and commercial development deserved attention because those areas promised benevolent social expansion. Religion as exemplified in conflicting confessions was not a category that interested them. Because of that indifference they advocated the toleration of a nonessential that other citizens seemed interested in pursuing.

This rather benign attitude, derived from Enlightenment preferences, had its sharper side: no religious group with a zeal for creedal particularities should be allowed to dominate public affairs. Thomas Paine emerged from this school of thought to articulate its harshest criticism of what he called priestcraft and superstition. Paine attacked churches as full of grasping functionaries who held the gullible in thrall and demanded livings at public expense. Their influence was easily detected in wars and oppressive legislation. Dominant ecclesiastical groups classically aligned themselves with aristocracies and monarchical governments. Reason demanded that men be free of that oppressive league, free in government to found republics where rational principles superseded tyranny, and free in religion where simple truths broke the grip of confessional mysteries. Rational analysis dictated, then, that traditional Christianity might be tolerated but not permitted to meddle in the modern democratic state.

Enlightenment thinkers did not take religious particularities seriously, except when they threatened the body politic with violence or coercion. Their aloof toleration of, if not scorn for, differences of belief led them to insist that all men should be free to espouse any faith that attracted them. Their concern for the more important business of politics based on reason denied churches any direct role in social affairs. The rationalist position supported separation of church and state because churches involved themselves with harmless opinions, and states proceeded without need of them. On a rather condescending point of principle, Jefferson held that churches should be free to pursue their irrelevant interests. On a sterner note, he argued that past abuses proved that churches could not be allowed to force those interests on society at large. History was full of examples where church–state unions had obscured rational truth and impeded social progress. The separation of church and state into discrete spheres of operation would prove beneficial to all; government would not try to decide questions best left to private opinion and personal choice. Religion would not force policies on, or draw perquisites from, the general citizenry. People could worship voluntarily on whatever grounds they preferred, and they could act reasonably in government, where spiritual tenets had no place. The rationalist position did not try to reconcile disparate theories of God. It sought only to enable men with differences of opinion to interact harmoniously in society.

CHURCH AND STATE

Evangelical groups in the American colonies agreed with the rationalist conclusion, but for different reasons. They too held that religious preferences were matters of private choice, but they did so while maintaining that the consequences were so important that no civil authority had the right to affect the outcome. For Baptists, who had argued this way since before the days of Roger Williams, together with Moravians, Quakers, and a newly arrived association known as Methodists, religion was a question of supreme importance that spoke directly to individual souls. Decisions about a person's eternal fate were too momentous to allow any state or ecclesiastical bureaucrat to interfere with personal conscience. Private initiative in religious questions was the only practicable option in view of the fact that heaven and hell hung in the balance.

Sometimes categorized as pietists, these evangelical Christians understood God as speaking to the heart of each individual. That person's response depended on freedom to decide in light of private experience. No state had the right to prevent churches from preaching truth as they saw it, to deny assembly for worship, or to require financial support for another religion alien to private convictions. No church had the right to proclaim itself exclusive possessor of the truth or to suppress religious teaching different from its own. Church and state should be separate for the sake of pure religion. People should be free to choose, not because it was a matter of indifference but because of its solemn profundity.

A third party supported separation of church and state in Revolutionary times, and its rationale included another factor crucial to the overall cultural context. This group consisted of establishmentarians, such as Anglicans and Congregationalists, who found themselves in colonies dominated by a different majority. Anglicans in Massachusetts and Congregationalists in Virginia were not opposed to the idea of an established church per se, but in their respective areas they were minority religions and thus not supported by local government. They were joined by Presbyterians, who saw the established Church of Scotland as an ideal but, arriving so late in every colony, found themselves a frustrated minority everywhere. The practical experience of political disabilities resulting from dissenter status, such as paying taxes for an opposing church and enduring bureaucratic annoyances to gain license to worship, eroded the establishmentarian principles of these churchmen. Those who may have embraced establishment privileges for themselves under better circumstances became advocates of religious freedom when they saw the advantages going to another group. Making a virtue of necessity, they championed liberty for all churches in order to avoid abuses that they might gladly have imposed on others in a different setting. Concrete situations became more compelling than wishful thinking, and this component of religious spokesmen added its voice to the groundswell of support for separating temporal and spiritual activities.

The first steps of lasting consequence on this question took place in Virginia under the guidance of Thomas Jefferson and James Madison. In 1779 Jefferson introduced in the General Assembly a bill for religious freedom as part of an omnibus revisal of the state's laws. Many of his reforms were enacted, but conservatives delayed considering the religious issue for three years. During the 1784–1785 session they introduced a bill to support all Christian ministers, not just the customary Anglicans, with public monies. Madison took the lead in opposing this move, since Jefferson was away as diplomatic envoy in Europe, and his adroit strategies succeeded better than urgings by the more volatile Jefferson. Postponing consideration of the bill for general support of Christian churches, Madison wrote the famous "Memorial and Remonstrance," which caused advocates of religious freedom to rally and defeat establishmentarian impulses in the state.

In the "Memorial," Madison appealed to both rationalists and evangelicals by declaring, "the duty which we owe to our Creator, and the manner of discharging it, can be directed only by reason and conviction, not by force or violence." This was put forth as a fundamental and undeniable truth together with the further observation that it was "the duty of every man to render to the Creator such homage, and such only, as he believes to be acceptable to him; this duty is precedent, both in order of time and in degree of obligation, to the claims of civil society." To gain the backing of disgruntled minorities Madison also argued, "Who does not see that the same authority which can establish Christianity, in exclusion of all other religions, may establish with the same ease any particular sect of Christians, in exclusion of all other sects? . . . the same authority which can force a citizen to contribute three pence only of his property for the support of any one establishment, may force him to conform to any other establishment in all cases whatsoever."

The whole battery of arguments was so persuasive, touching special concerns of different groups, that the general tax was defeated. Enlightenment thinkers like Madison led the way in articulating the movement for religious freedom, but the basic political strength lay in the hands of evangelicals and nonestablished churchmen. Baptists, Presbyterians, and Congregationalists were essential in mustering enough voting power to turn back establishmentarian sentiments. This coalition also helped ensure passage in 1785 of Virginia's act of religious freedom. That act, which Jefferson counted among his most significant achievements, contained a lengthy preamble and this declaration: "Be it enacted . . . that no man shall be compelled to frequent or support any religious worship, place or ministry whatsoever, nor shall be enforced, restrained, molested or burthened, in his body or goods, nor shall otherwise suffer on account of his religious opinions or belief; but that all men shall be free to profess, and by argument to maintain, their opinions in matters of religion, and that the same shall in no wise diminish, enlarge or affect their civil capacities." This rhetoric, political coalition, and statutory enactment set the stage for a larger application on the national scene.

The federal constitution, as originally presented to the states for ratification, contained only one sentence on the subject of religion. Article VI declared that "no religious Test shall ever be required as a Qualification to any Office or public Trust under the United States." But assurance about religion not applying to voters and officeholders was not enough to calm many special interests. Conservatives in several states retaining established churches (Congregationalists in Massachusetts, Connecticut, and New Hampshire; Anglicans in Maryland and South Carolina) wanted protection from congressional interference in their local arrangements. Less powerful denominations in all states worried that a single Protestant group might receive official backing as a nationally recognized church. Bap-

tists and other evangelical ideologues opposed the establishment of any church anywhere, on doctrinal grounds. And Enlightenment thinkers throughout the states opposed federal preferment of any type, on philosophical grounds. So the same combination of voices that had exerted pressure in Virginia debated the question on a national scale and called for a constitutional amendment to clarify church–state relationships.

James Madison composed the earliest draft for an amendment providing religious freedom. Drawing on previous experience and his own convictions about the issue, he proposed: "The civil rights of none should be abridged on account of religious belief or worship, nor shall any national religion be established, nor shall the full and equal rights of conscience be in any manner, or on any pretext, infringed." This recapitulated a libertarian philosophy and assured citizens that there would be no national support for ecclesiastical groups, singly or in combination. But representatives from states with established churches still worried that Congress could intrude on state policies and ruin a local establishment preferred by the majority. Delegates from New Hampshire suggested as alternative wording that "Congress shall make no laws touching religion." Since the Constitution had already made a law touching religion, if only to forbid test oaths, this was unsatisfactory. A compromise phrase, "Congress shall make no laws establishing religion," was sent to the Senate, but it too was found inadequate because it left room for Congress to disestablish religion in states that still wanted it.

The final wording, which satisfied groups concerned in the matter, stated that "Congress shall make no law respecting an establishment of religion, or prohibiting the free exercise thereof." This became part of the First Amendment, was passed along with nine others by the First Congress, and became federal law in 1791 after being accepted by the necessary number of states. It seems clear that provisions about religion in what is popularly known as the Bill of Rights were an achievement that strove to accommodate differences of opinion in the country. As an example of federalist statecraft it proclaimed basic religious freedom at the national level, while allowing states freedom to determine their own policies on the matter. Many states followed Virginia's lead and wrote religious freedom into their post-Revolutionary constitutions.

Pennsylvania and Rhode Island simply continued principles that they had embodied for more than a century. A few states gave preferred treatment to Protestant churches in general. But in greater New England, with First Amendment permission to do so, three states retained an established Congregationalist church despite persistent ecclesiastical pluralism and increased opinion favoring separation.

Before moving from the constitutional era to the early national period it is important to note that no federal document explicitly mentions separation of church and state. The phrase is a convenient term for conveying a nexus of related ideas, but it is not a legal term, nor is its meaning unambiguous. Historical forces were more important than abstract principles in successfully placing religion clauses in the First Amendment. The need for public harmony contributed more than moral altruism to the compromise position on how best to fit religion into the body politic. "Separation of church and state" was the product of social and political action, not a univocal dictum of which the clear import was accepted by all citizens. From a federalist perspective the national government was simply barred from establishing one church over others and from restricting activity in any of them. Other than that historically conditioned limitation, groups could interpret the meaning of their freedom and experiment with ways of bringing religious convictions to bear on all levels of society, including, inevitably, the national one.

Some interpretations of constitutional law counted more heavily than others, and Thomas Jefferson provided an opinion that many have come to accept as absolute. While historical evidence shows the situation to have been more complex than Jefferson acknowledged, his personal view remains a classic statement of strict separation between spiritual and temporal spheres. In 1802 he wrote to a committee of Baptists in Danbury, Connecticut, and coined a phrase that has become one of the stock references in this field of study: "Believing with you that religion is a matter which lies solely between man and his God, . . . that the legislative powers of government reach actions only, not opinions, I contemplate with sovereign reverence that act of the American people . . . , thus building a wall of separation between church and state." In 1832 James Madison expressed a separationist interpretation too: "I must admit . . . that it may not be easy, . . . to trace the line of separation between the rights of religion and the Civil authority with such distinctness as to avoid collisions. . . . The tendency to a usurpation on one side or the other, or to a corrupting . . . alliance between them, will best be guarded against by an entire abstinence of the Government from interference in any way whatsoever, beyond the necessity of preserving public order. . . ." Madison reaffirmed the Enlightenment ideal in strengthening one line of constitutional interpretation, but he was writing in 1832, when conditions were making that viewpoint increasingly unpopular.

Several groups previously supportive of Madison's views on religious and political life realigned themselves during the early decades of the nineteenth century. They formed a new coalition in American culture and reformulated issues in church and state. Evangelicals came to distrust rationalist indifference to the content and importance of religion. Churchmen of all sorts became alarmed by consequences of the French Revolution. Christians across the political spectrum feared that Francophiles like Jefferson would import extreme anticlerical sentiments from the Continent and destroy their faith, root and branch. So pietists and traditionalists, separationists and establishmentarians, turned to each other in order to repel what they perceived as threats from alleged infidelity. In most cases they held onto the ideal of religious freedom as a positive gain and did not argue for a return to established churches. Instead of hoping to reunify church and state, they turned their attention to permeating culture with religious influences.

The momentum of institutional disestablishment continued. In 1818 Connecticut ceased supporting Congregationalism as the state religion, and in 1833 Massachusetts became the last state to relinquish its Standing Order. Action by Baptists was the most significant factor in the former victory, while difficulties with Unitarians in the latter situation finally ended the era of state support for a particular institution. Thereafter American churches as a whole used persuasion instead of coercion to propagate their ideas. But while reliance on civil power faded, religionists of all persuasions became increasingly determined to influence social practices. Fears of potential harm to Christianity from Continental revolutions blended with apprehensiveness about the fate of religion after disestablishment, and these combined with worry over what would happen to pioneers who moved away from churches in eastern settlements. Since state control was no longer an option, Protestants in general turned to revivals as the means of shaping culture through religious influences.

The Second Great Awakening stressed conversion of individual souls, but its revivals also nurtured a concern for the full Christian life. Preachers took the gospel message of free grace to frontiersmen and city dwellers alike. Their conception of salvation included reform of daily activities on a continuing basis in addition to ecstatic moments of spiritual experience. This emphasis on affecting personal conduct led imperceptibly to campaigns for influencing society at large. If enough persons reformed their lives, then citizens in the aggregate would make the country a godly nation. By the 1830's voluntary societies had emerged to carry on this work. Committees used contributory funding to distribute Bibles and tracts. Others sent missionaries to western territories and newly constituted states. A host of agents worked to promote Sunday schools, restrict alcohol consumption, and rescue the dissolute. This evangelical reformist impulse also fed into movements for women's rights and the abolition of slavery.

American Protestant churches shifted their program from resisting state interference during colonial times to influencing the behavior of all state citizens during the early national period. As long as they did not invoke coercive power, Christian spokesmen felt free to urge the development of a common life shaped by evangelical religion. This optimistic, energetic fervor was fueled by a resurgent vision of the United States as a Protestant Christian nation, not forced by law but achieved through popular mandate. This new alignment of religious forces, at times called the United Evangelical Front, sought to conform national practices to divine will. It did not signify a return to the theocratic establishment of religion, but it did attempt to recover a precedent where Christianity dominated popular culture. As revivalists converted individuals and advised groups on wider implications of moral conduct, civil authorities soon reflected this new concept

as well. Governments were administered by people raised on revivalist expectations, and since they directed the lives of an increasing number of converts, civil and religious goals tended to coincide. Churches and states cooperated without legal union to guide a way of life that deserved the name of republican Protestantism.

Evidence corroborating this new alliance of religious and cultural forces can be found among laypeople as well as clerical activists. They repeatedly reflected assumptions about Christianity as a base for social values. For example, as early as 1811 the state of New York upheld conviction for blasphemy as a crime in common law. James Kent, chancellor of the New York court of chancery, observed that blasphemy was more than a confessional offense because it tended to corrupt public morals. He declared that scandalizing the author of doctrines held by most citizens was both an impious act and a gross violation of social decency. Admitting that the First Amendment guaranteed the right of exchanging religious opinions, he saw clear limits to such freedom:

> . . . to revile with malicious and blasphemous contempt the religion professed by almost the whole community, is an abuse of that right. Nor are we bound by any expressions in the constitution, . . . to punish indiscriminately the like attacks upon the religion of Mahomet or of the Grand Lama, for this plain reason, that the case assumes we are a Christian people, and the morality of the country is deeply ingrafted upon Christianity and not upon the doctrines or worship of those imposters.

Laymen and clergymen had succeeded in permeating social practices to such an extent that by 1828 they were trying to control federal policy. On the general assumption that American society should observe the Sabbath, pious citizens asked Congress to halt transportation of mail on Sundays. A House committee reported favorably on such a bill, but the Senate refused to concur. Senate deliberations on this issue resisted evangelical pressures to write morality into law. One report noted that federal autonomy did not violate religious freedom because "transportation of the mail on the first day of the week . . . does not interfere with the rights of conscience."

Should Congress presume to write religious laws, "It would involve a legislative decision in a religious controversy. . . . If this principle is once introduced, it will be impossible to define its bounds." The incident illustrates how far Protestants attempted to push this cooperation between their popular religious values and civil power—and the limits of their success. Its significance lies not in a Moral Majority's failure but in its ambition to carry lobbying efforts as far as the national level.

Despite setbacks in Congress, this moral crusade received favorable interpretation in many of the nation's courts. One influential opinion was that of Joseph Story, associate justice of the U.S. Supreme Court. In 1833, Story published a commentary on the federal constitution, and his view of religious freedom echoed widespread assumptions about a Protestant republic. It was impossible, he wrote, "for those who believe in the truth of Christianity, as a divine revelation, to doubt that it is the especial duty of the government to foster, and encourage it among all the citizens and subjects. This is a point wholly distinct from that of the right of private judgment in matters of religion, and of the freedom of public worship according to the dictates of one's conscience." Story found the real difficulty not in enforcing general Christian morality as socially beneficial but in knowing how far government might go in fostering religious influences. He considered the object of the First Amendment to be peace among Christian groups and an end to their rivalry over exclusive patronage. As long as Protestants cooperated with each other to further cultural improvement, he approved of Christian precepts as the basis for common law.

No area of activity affected more people or better demonstrated nineteenth-century parallels between religious influences and social practice than did public schools. Many local planners reasoned that since the United States was a Christian nation, general Christian precepts could be taught in schools. Separation of church and state did not bar religious instruction supported by municipal taxes; it forbade only promulgating sectarian tenets peculiar to one denomination. Protestant clergy and laymen had some difficulty agreeing on core principles to be taught, but most of them saw no violation of religious freedom in providing readings from the King James Bible and exercises such as the Lord's Prayer for public classrooms. The Jeffersonian ideal of no alliance between religious and civil spheres was eclipsed by a strengthening coalescence of Protestant expectations and social practices. Even in Virginia, where the act of religious freedom was still on the books, public schools embodied a decidedly Protestant orientation.

Court decisions regarding litigation on the matter were mixed. They represented the difficulties that magistrates had in reconciling principles of religious freedom with pressures from Christians who wanted their version of religion to dominate the secular sphere. In 1854, for example, the Supreme Court of Maine upheld the validity of reading the King James Version of the Bible in public schools, even while declaring that the state favored no religion and treated all denominations equally. Ohio courts discussed the church–state matter as related to Bible reading through the 1850's and 1860's. In 1872 the state supreme court finally decided the issue according to strict separationist principles. Terming relations between government and religion a "terrible enigma," Chief Justice John Welch said the best solution was "free conflict of opinions" and "masterly inactivity on the part of the state" except for preventing the violation of private rights and public peace. So although Protestant influence in schools was not dominant everywhere, it permeated society at so many junctures that separationists could count few victories during the decades when evangelical Christians confidently assumed that their religion supplied the moral and educational foundations of good government.

In 1868 Congress passed, and individual states ratified, the Fourteenth Amendment. This federal law was primarily intended to protect newly freed black citizens, but it had serious implications for issues bearing on church and state. It declared, "No state shall make or enforce any law which shall abridge the privileges or immunities of citizens of the United States; nor shall any state deprive any person of life, liberty, or property, without due process of law; nor deny to any person within its jurisdiction the equal protection of the laws." A case concerning religion and the due-process clause did not come before federal courts for another fifty-seven years, but the question of church–state relations in the First Amendment, and extensive restrictions on states in the Fourteenth Amendment, have sparked considerable debate in the twentieth century.

Federal courts generally abstained from interfering with state decisions about religious influences and civil patterns during the nineteenth century. And state practices presented a mixed picture of cooperation alongside formal separation. But in territorial jurisdiction federal judges often applied the same Protestant assumptions regarding proper behavior as frequently exhibited in local municipalities. Cases involving the Mormon practice of plural marriage came before the courts after the Civil War, and for all practical purposes the Supreme Court's concern with religion clauses of the First Amendment began at that time. Congress made polygamy a criminal offense. In two landmark decisions, *Reynolds* v. *United States* (1878) and *Davis* v. *Beason* (1890), federal courts began grappling with religious freedom and public behavior. After initial statements about maintaining a wall of separation between church and state, justices went on to condemn religious practices that became "overt acts against peace and good order." They declared marriage a civil contract, regulated by the state, and found polygamy an offense to society in this country as well as an odious practice in all advanced cultures. Mormons could not, they held, violate federal statutes on grounds of conformity to their religious duties. Beliefs about what faith required of an individual did not absolve persons from criminal liability.

In their deliberations over Mormon cases, justices blended the difficult concepts of separation between church and state on the one hand and republican Protestantism on the other. Adjudicating the area where religious and civil interests intersected, Chief Justice Morrison Waite articulated his working hypothesis in *Reynolds:* "Congress was deprived of all legislative power over mere opinion, but was left free to reach actions which were in violation of social duties or subversive of good order." Speaking more directly to the issue at hand, Justice Stephen Field held in *Davis:* "Bigamy and polygamy are crimes by the laws of all civilized and Christian countries. . . . Few crimes are more pernicious to the best interests of society and receive more gen-

eral or more deserved punishment. . . . To call their advocacy a tenet of religion is to offend the common sense of mankind." Field limited his condemnation of Mormons' beliefs because he thought constitutional guarantees left them free to think as they wished. As for action based on those beliefs, "no interference can be permitted, provided always the laws of society, . . . are not interfered with. However free the exercise of religion may be, it must be subordinate to the criminal laws of the country, passed with reference to actions regarded by general consent as properly the subjects of punitive legislation." Judicial reliance on "laws of society" and "general consent" thus tended to sanction majority opinion regarding the Protestant basis for civil policies and restricted toleration of religious differences.

In a larger perspective it is important to note that American society was becoming more complex when republican Protestantism reached its apex. Immigration added many different ethnic and religious groups by the late nineteenth century, urban growth challenged agrarian social values, and industrial economy transformed the base of civil interaction. The United States became less and less a Protestant-dominated nation where a broad consensus could assume easy cooperation between spiritual and temporal authorities. Still, many prominent citizens invoked that fading conception of church and state. The particular question in *Church of the Holy Trinity* v. *United States* (1892) is relatively insignificant, but wording in the Supreme Court's decision illustrates the persistence of nineteenth-century assumptions about religion and government. Justice David Brewer pointed out how popular custom and Christian values reciprocally supported each other:

> The form of oath universally prevailing, concluding with an appeal to the Almighty; the custom of opening sessions of all deliberative bodies and most conventions with prayer; . . . the laws respecting the observance of the Sabbath, with the general cessation of all secular business, and the closing of courts, legislatures, and other similar public assemblies on that day. . . . These, and many other matters which might be noticed, add a volume of unofficial declarations to the mass of organic utterances that this is a Christian nation.

CHURCH AND STATE

At the turn of the twentieth century conventional wisdom about church and state was perhaps best summarized by Judge Thomas M. Cooley of the Michigan Supreme Court. He interpreted the First Amendment as specifically forbidding any law establishing a particular church or favoring one mode of worship. Separation of church and state further provided that there could be no compulsory tax support for religious instruction, no required attendance at religious worship, no restraints on the free exercise of religion according to the dictates of conscience, and no restraints on expressing religious beliefs. By the same token, he saw no inconsistency in having civil authorities recognize a superintending Providence in the moral context of national affairs. "No principle of constitutional law is violated when thanksgiving or fast days are appointed," he held in *Constitutional Limitations,* or "when chaplains are designated for the army and navy; when legislative sessions are opened with prayer or the reading of the Scriptures, or when religious teaching is encouraged by a general exemption of the houses of religious worship from taxation." Since civil codes were based on morality, and American ethical standards derived from Christianity, Cooley recognized that religious influences undergirded public law. He argued that the laws did not enforce Christianity because of its sacred derivation; rather, government supported it because of social utility.

This cooperation between Christian morals and federal law lasted through the 1920's, long after nurturing conditions had passed their prime. The Prohibition Era was the last major triumph of an anachronistic mentality. Ratification of the Eighteenth Amendment in 1919 constituted a victory for minority lobbyists who spoke the language of a bygone era. Prohibition of "the manufacture, sale or transportation of intoxicating liquors" was the final attempt at the federal level to enforce moral convictions on public behavior. Ratification of the law, and the passage of the Volstead Act later that year to enforce its provisions, could not overcome the fact that American society would no longer subscribe to or obey such regulation. Pluralistic divisions had eroded Protestant dominance, and secular interests had subordinated religious priorities. The repeal of Prohibition, with ratification of the Twenty-first Amendment in 1933, finally brought a long epoch of spiritual–temporal cooperation to a close.

There have been an increasing number of attempts since World War I to reach a better understanding of church–state relationships in American life. This move toward interpreting our heritage of religious freedom has sought to avoid the comfortable alliance of Protestant-dominated cultural patterns and to approximate more closely the thinking of those who framed the Constitution. Modern interpretations of church and state have also reflected an awareness of religious pluralism, a social fact that needed correlation into law even while Prohibition proved republican Protestantism to be no longer effective. Many factors contributed to this emergent phenomenon. Protestant groups at the turn of the twentieth century had come to differ among themselves over such questions as liberalism versus fundamentalism in theological content, and revivalism versus social activism in religious priorities. Those internal controversies weakened institutional strength and diminished previously strong Protestant influence. Alongside this decline of a culturally dominant group, immigration reached new heights that raised the Roman Catholic and Jewish population to more influential proportions. Non-Protestant constituencies had been present in American history from the beginning, but by the 1920's they could no longer be ignored or excluded from debates about their constitution.

Perhaps one of the most generalized and widespread areas where religion and politics intersect has been presidential elections. The religious preferences of presidential candidates have played a minor role in every contest. But in the twentieth century Roman Catholics were nominated by a national party, and religious influences came to bear on political action as never before. In 1928 the Democrats nominated Alfred E. Smith, governor of New York, for the presidency, and his Catholic affiliation became a liability. Opponents raised questions about an imagined "dual allegiance" that Catholics were thought to retain, to Rome as well as to the United States, and such worries plagued the campaign. Smith lost to the Republican candidate, Herbert C. Hoover, by an electoral-vote margin of 6–1. Other factors contributed to his defeat, but negative reaction to Smith's religion was a significant element in the political process. In 1960, Democrats defied the odds by nominating another Catholic, Senator John F. Kennedy of Massachusetts, as their presidential candidate. In an adroit campaign that faced the religious issue forthrightly, Kennedy calmed enough fears about dual allegiance to win a narrow victory over Richard M. Nixon. Since that time religious questions have subsided in this area of political action. The issue has not become irrelevant, but the country has at least come to see that persons of all major religious persuasions may participate effectively at every level of political leadership.

More important than presidential campaigns or similar elections at subsidiary levels, the main focal point for grasping church–state complexities in modern times has been constitutional law. The U.S. Supreme Court gradually began accepting cases in which religious and civil interests called for a clearer interpretation of spiritual and temporal relationships. By the 1940's, decisions from that high bench increased in volume and significance, allowing justices to broach new ideas about the extent and limitations of religious freedom. Our present understanding is not definitive or absolute, but it represents a contemporary consensus drawn primarily from juridical decisions on how the ambiguous American heritage pertains to today's circumstances.

American constitutional law stands at the apex of a long common-law tradition. Its growth, involving development and occasional reversals of opinion, depends on factual situations that conform to social realities. Supreme Court justices deal with concrete problems and in a cumulative manner have articulated ways of applying constitutional principles to current political conditions. Particularly since World War II they have interpreted the meaning of religion clauses in the Constitution. So it will be helpful to look at cases touching religion and to study the opinions offered in addition to the decisions made. By that method we can see that such terms as "establishment" and "free exercise" are only a starting point for seeking solutions to church–state questions. There is no mechanical answer to any issue, and each generation must attempt its own understanding of the interminable problems involved in both conceptualization and practice.

CASES

In the following survey we shall investigate cases grouped topically, not chronologically. Before turning to decisions and interpretations made along certain lines between 1925 and 1977, one more preliminary remark is in order. Only recently, in the twentieth century, have courts combined the First Amendment (1791) with the Fourteenth Amendment (1868) to produce a vigorous exercise of law regarding religion. In *Gitlow* v. *New York* (1925) the Supreme Court held for the first time that freedoms guaranteed in the First Amendment were incorporated into the Fourteenth and thus applicable through the due-process clause to the states. Apart from their own constitutions, states thereafter had to observe legislative limitations of basic rights imposed on them by federal constitutional restriction. *Gitlow* focused on freedoms of speech and press, but it raised the question of whether religious freedom pertained as well. In 1940 justices affirmed that at least the free-exercise clause in the First Amendment was relevant to state laws, and in 1947 they interpreted the establishment clause as similarly applicable. So by the middle of the century Supreme Court clarification of the separation of church and state had used the two amendments in tandem. Today we must try to understand the meaning of First Amendment restrictions on Congress by observing how justices have construed state limitations under the due-process clause of the Fourteenth Amendment.

When *Gitlow* opened the way for incorporating the Bill of Rights into state legislation, many questions remained as to which and how many personal liberties were thus guaranteed. One aspect directly concerning religious freedom had to do with test oaths for holding office. Since both Article VI of the Constitution and religion clauses of the First Amendment seemed to preclude such oaths, one might not have expected to find such political restrictions on religion in subsequent American life. But the state of Maryland had a law requiring that all persons seeking the office of notary public declare a belief in God. This requirement was successfully challenged in *Torasco* v. *Watkins* (1961), wherein the Supreme Court held the law to be an unconstitutional establishment of a specific religious orientation. Four years later prospective jurors were similarly released from swearing to theistic beliefs.

Questions related to Sunday-closing laws have a long history in this country because Protestant influence formerly pressured legislatures into enforcing Sabbath observance. By the middle of the twentieth century, however, opponents including many Jewish groups, Seventh-Day Adventists, and secularists challenged such laws for a variety of different reasons. Still, in *Braunfeld* v. *Brown* (1961) and *McGowan* v. *Maryland* (1961), plus two other cases the same year, justices upheld Sunday-closing laws as constitutional. They reasoned that state laws closing businesses one day a week did not violate the establishment clause because they did not represent an attempt to impose the Christian religion on the whole community. Further, the laws did not infringe upon free exercise by those who observed some day other than Sunday for religious reasons. The justices acknowledged that Sunday-closing laws had originated from religious motivations, but in current times they promoted public health and welfare by setting aside time for rest, relaxation, and family interaction. States could establish a secular holiday, and their action was not impaired by the fact that the day chosen coincided with the one observed by religious groups in the community at large.

The validity of Sunday-closing laws rested on adequate nonreligious grounds. If such laws had been justified by religious considerations, they would not have survived. Justice Felix Frankfurter made this point in his concurring opinion of the unanimous ruling of *McGowan:*

> The Establishment Clause withdrew from the sphere of legitimate legislative concern and competence a specific, but comprehensive, area of human conduct: man's belief or disbelief in the verity of some transcendental idea and man's expression in action of that belief or disbelief. Congress may not make these matters, as such, the subject of legislation nor, now, may any legislature in this country. Neither the National Government nor, . . . a State may, by any device, support belief or the expression of belief for its own sake, whether from conviction of the truth of that belief, or from conviction that by the propagation of that belief the civil welfare of the State is served. . . .

Laws that stemmed from admittedly religious origins could nevertheless serve wholly secular purposes in modern times, and as such they were constitutional. Merchants who closed their businesses on Saturdays because of religious duty were not exempt from the additional, secular closing requirements on Sundays.

Sabbatarian employees raised difficulties too. One Seventh-Day Adventist lost her job in a South Carolina mill and was refused unemployment compensation because she would not work on Saturdays. In her case, *Sherbert* v. *Verner* (1963), the Supreme Court awarded compensation on grounds that denying it would impose an unconstitutional burden on religious beliefs. The state had ignored theological reasons behind a refusal to work on Saturday and therefore had violated the plaintiff's religious rights under the free-exercise clause of the First Amendment. In a more complicated litigation, another sabbatarian claimed that his employer treated him unfairly when he did not cooperate with a work schedule involving Saturdays. But in *Trans World Airlines, Inc.,* v. *Hardison* (1977) the Court found that the company had made reasonable attempts to accommodate the former employee's religious convictions. So it sustained a lower court decision that denied extensive favors to sabbatarians and upheld the company's collective bargaining agreements as well as its salary scale.

Hardison indicated the limit beyond which sabbatarians could not demand special consideration regarding religious conscience. *Sherbert* pointed to the sphere within which protection could apply, and it evoked statements from the bench that add to our present understanding of church–state relations. Those opinions made it clear that justices intended to avoid both favoritism and hostility in religious questions. Justice William Brennan maintained in *Sherbert* that "the extension of unemployment benefits to Sabbatarians in common with Sunday worshippers reflects nothing more than the governmental obligation of neutrality in the face of religious differences, and does not represent that involvement of religious with secular institutions which it is the object of the Establishment Clause to forestall. Nor does the recognition of the appellant's right to unemployment benefits under the state statute serve to abridge any other person's religious liberties." In a concurring opinion Justice William O. Douglas wrote that "many people hold beliefs alien to the majority of our society—beliefs that are protected by the First Amendment but which could easily be trod upon under the guise of 'police' or 'health' regulations reflecting the majority's views. . . . This case is resolvable not in terms of what an individual can demand of government, but solely in terms of what government may not do to an individual in violation of his religious scruples.''

No single religious group has contributed more to considerations of church–state issues in the twentieth century than the Jehovah's Witnesses. Their dedication to distinctive religious activities and their trust in the principle of religious freedom have provoked frequent litigation. As with cases involving test oaths, Sunday closings, and sabbatarians, their cases have prompted the Supreme Court to probe the relationship between spiritual and temporal authority in modern times. In one landmark decision, *Cantwell* v. *Connecticut* (1940), the Court reversed an earlier conviction and said that Cantwell had a right to impart his religious views peacefully in public. Though most of his listeners found Cantwell's statements obnoxious, he did not represent a menace to public peace and order. So it was unlawful to require approval from a state official before he or other religious spokesmen could disseminate their ideas, even in neighborhoods where they were not welcome.

Justice Owen Roberts delivered the opinion of the Court and in doing so clarified principles that laid a foundation for subsequent ideas on religious and social interaction. He explained how "the constitutional inhibition of legislation on the subject of religion has a double aspect. On the one hand, it forestalls compulsion by law of the acceptance of any creed or the practice of any form of worship. Freedom of conscience and freedom to adhere to such religious organization or form of worship as the individual may choose cannot be restricted by law." Noting that freedom to believe was absolute but freedom to act was not, Roberts acknowledged that some forms of preaching could incite violence and therefore could legitimately be suppressed. But Cantwell had not menaced public order with his propaganda, and his freedom to act was allowable:

> In the realm of religious faith, as in that of political belief, sharp differences arise. But the people of this nation have ordained in the light of history, that, in spite of the probability of excesses and abuses, these liberties are, in the long view, essential to enlightened opinion and right conduct on the part of the citizens of a democracy.
>
> The essential characteristic of these liberties is, that under their shield many types of life, character, opinion and belief can develop unmolested and unobstructed. Nowhere is this shield more necessary than in our own country for a people composed of many races and of many creeds.

Three related cases settled the question of whether Jehovah's Witnesses had the right to use public facilities for meetings. In *Saia* v. *New York* (1948) the Court held invalid a law requiring permits before religious groups could meet in public parks and use loudspeakers on Sundays. In *Niemotko* v. *Maryland* (1951) and *Kunz* v. *New York* (1951) the Court also ruled that city officials could not prevent church people from assembling on local streets. Such permits and permissions were invalid because they represented a prior restraint on freedom of speech and the religious exercise clause. States had a constitutional duty to make public facilities available to all religions. By 1952, however, a later ruling pointed out that nondiscrimination did not make all public property available for religious assembly. Loudspeakers and open meetings could be forbidden in certain areas, in hospital zones for example, where larger public considerations took precedence.

Four other Jehovah's Witnesses cases raised questions about the propriety of soliciting funds as part of a group's religious activities. *Lovell* v. *Griffin* (1938) ruled that cities could not require a license for the distribution of religious pamphlets. *Martin* v. *Struthers* (1943) allowed the Court opportunity to invalidate city ordinances that forbade knocking on doors or ringing doorbells to summon occupants and hand them literature. But both decisions invoked free press more than religious freedom. The focus sharpened in *Jamison* v. *Texas* (1943) because the Court said that cities could not forbid distribution of religious handbills, even if they contained some advertising. And in *Murdock* v. *Pennsylvania* (1943) justices held that states could not prohibit door-to-door solicitation by religious groups for the purpose of making converts.

Most Americans interpret saluting the national flag as a simple patriotic act. Jehovah's Witnesses see flags as idolatrous images and have refused to participate in what they consider ceremonies that offend God. Families with children in schools that require a pledge of allegiance to the flag soon found themselves in lawsuits because of their religious scruples. In *Minersville School District* v. *Gobitis* (1940) the Court ruled that personal conscience could not relieve individual obedience to general laws. If religious convictions contradicted significant concerns of political security, such principles did not relieve the citizen from discharging his political responsibilities. The justices soon overturned their own ruling in the case of *West Virginia State Board of Education* v. *Barnette* (1943), holding that refusing to salute the flag did not represent a grave danger to the nation. Justice Robert H. Jackson found laws requiring the ceremony too restrictive of freedom in speech and religion. He pointed out, "If there is any fixed star in our constitutional constellation, it is that no official, high or petty, can prescribe what shall be orthodox in politics, nationalism, religion, or other matters of opinion or force citizens to confess by word or act their faith therein."

Thus far, litigation involving Jehovah's Witnesses has worked in their favor, helping to clarify freedom of religious exercise as well as pointing out limits placed on governmental regulation of church groups. In questions regarding medical practice, however, Witnesses have not fared so well. Early in the twentieth century the case of *Jacobson* v. *Massachusetts* (1905) set a precedent for making public health more important than personal reluctance to cooperate. Jacobson unsuccessfully challenged a state regulation that made smallpox vaccination compulsory. He did not object on religious grounds, but the case influenced later decisions touching upon religion. In *Prince* v. *Massachusetts* (1944) the Court held that public health measures were paramount. Citizens must give highest priority, justices held, to laws that prevent widespread loss of life by halting communicable diseases. Such laws can override the free exercise of religion, if nonconformity for doctrinal reasons threatens social hygiene.

Blood transfusions are also objectionable to Jehovah's Witnesses, who perceive them as a violation of scriptural injunctions. State courts have nevertheless required blood transfusions in serious childhood illnesses, over parental protest. In 1952 the Supreme Court of Illinois affirmed such an action, which was taken the previous year by a family court in Chicago. Its opinion reaffirmed the general principle that religious resistance to medical science was not as important as a child's life: "The right to practice religion freely does not include liberty to expose the community or child to communicable disease or the latter to ill health or death. . . . Parents may be free to become martyrs themselves. But it does not follow that they are free, in identical circumstances, to make martyrs of their children before they have reached the age of full and legal discretion when they can make that choice for themselves." The U.S. Supreme Court has not considered a blood transfusion case, but in 1968 it affirmed the ruling of a three-judge panel in the state of Washington. Citing the *Prince* case as governing precedent, that affirmation declared state-ordered blood transfusions for several children to be legal and not a violation of religious rights.

Another topic that transcends particular religious groups has involved widespread interest in both the nineteenth and twentieth centuries. This issue has centered on public education with questions pertaining to religious instruction in schools as well as to traditional practices of Bible reading and prayer in otherwise secular classrooms. Related questions have been raised concerning aid to parochial schools. In each of these areas a better understanding of the establishment and free-exercise clauses has emerged in modern usage. And in school cases we find additional opportunities to observe how Supreme Court justices have struggled with concepts of strict separation, accommodation, and neutrality. This topic affords prolonged concentration on issues of deep popular feeling, where civil and religious interests confront each other.

Two cases bracketing the middle of the twentieth century produced a modern compromise on the issue of religious instruction in public education. The first concerned the practice of providing released time from a school's weekly schedule for students to receive religious teaching. Instructors chosen by major local faiths in Champaign, Illinois, visited schools at an appointed hour and held voluntary classes in regular classrooms. Children not willing to receive such instruction were given other assignments. In *McCollum* v. *Board of Education of Champaign*

County (1948) the Supreme Court held the practice to be unlawful because, even though teachers were supplied and paid by religious groups, public school property was being used for teaching religion. Defendants argued that the First Amendment forbade only governmental preference of one religion, not impartial assistance to all. Refusing to accept the distinction, the Court found it unconstitutional to use public property as an aid to religious groups in spreading their faith. Justice Hugo Black wrote: "Here not only are the State's tax-supported public school buildings used for the dissemination of religious doctrines. The State also affords sectarian groups an invaluable aid in that it helps to provide pupils for their religious classes through use of the State's compulsory public school machinery. This is not separation of Church and State."

Proponents of released time did not accept *McCollum* as the final word. In New York City they developed a plan by which pupils did not receive religious instruction in a designated classroom but were dismissed from school to attend classes in church buildings. In *Zorach* v. *Clauson* (1952) the Supreme Court held that such released-time schemes were constitutional as long as religious instruction was not held on school premises. Instead of saying that states should be completely indifferent to religion and to parents interested in religious education, the majority of justices maintained that separation of church and state needed sharper definition. Holding that government could not finance religious groups or force religious instruction on anyone, they also thought that civil authority need not act in a hostile or alien manner to spiritual influences. Such callous indifference would actually show preference to irreligion over those who believed. Justice Douglas spoke for the Court in saying that the First Amendment

> . . . does not say that in every and all respects there shall be a separation of church and state. . . . We are a religious people whose institutions presuppose a Supreme Being. We guarantee the freedom to worship as one chooses. We make room for as wide a variety of beliefs and creeds as the spiritual needs of man deem necessary. We sponsor an attitude on the part of government that shows no partiality to any one group and that lets each flourish according to the zeal of its adherents and the appeal of its

dogma. When the state encourages religious instruction or cooperates with religious authorities by adjusting the schedule of public events to sectarian needs, it follows the best of our traditions. For it then respects the religious nature of our people and accommodates the public service to their spiritual needs.

If students could receive religious instruction voluntarily in religious buildings as part of their study week, there was still the problem of having them pray in public classrooms. At midcentury the New York State Board of Regents sought to use prayer as a means of reducing juvenile delinquency and of combating atheism in American culture. This attempt to pass on moral and spiritual values through the school system took the following form: "Almighty God, we acknowledge our dependence upon Thee, and we beg Thy blessings on us, our parents, our teachers and our Country." This prayer favored no single creed, and participation was not enforced. But in *Engel* v. *Vitale* (1962) the Supreme Court found such prayers to be "wholly inconsistent with the Establishment Clause." That it was denominationally neutral and voluntary was not enough to free the Regents' prayer, and all others, from constitutional limitations against government's showing preference in a religious matter.

Daily Bible readings and recitation of the Lord's Prayer as part of opening exercises at school also figured in modern contests between church and state. Those proceedings had survived from republican Protestantism to contemporary times in some places and finally came before the Supreme Court in a case from Maryland, *Abington Township School District* v. *Schempp* (1963). Justices held that reading from either the Catholic or Protestant version of the Bible and the unison expression of a scriptural prayer constituted unlawful state support for religious exercises. Such practices had primary religious motivations and significance that tended to favor one religious group, even if a broad one, over others in the community. No matter how widely supported by popular sympathies, they violated constitutional injunctions against the civil establishment of religion.

Appellants argued that failure to utilize some spirituality among school children was tantamount to fostering a religion of secularism in the classroom. Noting this fear of materialistic trends, Justice Tom C. Clark still maintained government's neutral position: "We agree of course that the State may not establish a 'religion of secularism' in the sense of affirmatively opposing or showing hostility to religion, thus 'preferring those who believe in no religion over those who do believe.' . . . We do not agree, however, that this decision in any sense has that effect." States could, he said, provide the benefits of education wherein the Bible is studied as literature and the history of religions is analyzed in relation to advancing civilization. But secular programs of education could not be identified with activities aimed at cultivating religious faith. In the case under consideration Clark held that the activities being challenged had to be rejected as a form of state-required religious exercise. Summing up, he spoke to the ultimate appeal for Bible and prayers in schools: "We cannot accept that the concept of neutrality, which does not permit a State to require a religious exercise even with the consent of the majority of those affected, collides with the majority's right to free exercise of religion. While the Free Exercise Clause clearly prohibits the use of state action to deny the rights of free exercise to *anyone,* it has never meant that a majority could use the machinery of the State to practice its beliefs."

Parochial schools have existed in the United States for well over a century. As early as the 1840's in areas with a large Catholic population, they challenged concepts of public education in which distinctively Protestant ideas were emphasized. But twentieth-century developments have witnessed the greatest expansion of religious schools and concomitant issues concerning state aid to them. More than a dozen cases in this complicated field have led the Supreme Court to scrutinize church–state relationships. In *Pierce* v. *Society of Sisters* (1925) justices struck down an Oregon law requiring all children to attend public schools. No state has a monopoly on educational processes, they said, and parents have a constitutional right to send their children to parochial or private schools. Furthermore, churches have the right to operate schools as long as they meet educational standards properly set by the state. The decision in this case is sometimes called the Magna Carta of parochial education, confirming the right of church-related elementary and secondary schools to exist.

But other than recognizing their right to exist, could states provide any aid to those schools? An early precedent was set in *Cochran* v. *Louisiana Board of Education* (1930), in which the Court upheld the state practice of distributing textbooks to children in parochial schools. Justices held that this did not violate constitutional limitations because the beneficiaries were children, not the schools they happened to attend. The "child benefit" theory meant that books were an aid not to religion but to social welfare, and as such they served a valid secular purpose. This line of reasoning found larger expression in a true landmark decision, *Everson* v. *Board of Education of Ewing* (1947). The state of New Jersey used public funds to reimburse parents who paid bus fares for their children to ride between home and school. This applied to those attending religious as well as public schools, and the Supreme Court held that such a plan was not unconstitutional. While adding momentum to an accommodationist interpretation of religious and civil cooperation, the case was also important for its historical context and opinions expressed by the justices.

Everson was the first decision in which justices said that states had to observe First Amendment limitations on the establishment of religion because the Fourteenth Amendment extended rights beyond the federal level. That decision substantially increased the volume of religion cases, especially regarding state aid to church education. In addition to its rather limited application in *Everson,* attendant juridical opinion laid the foundation for subsequent deliberations in this complex area. But rhetoric carries historical weight of its own, and it is important to notice the principles that were enunciated. In speaking for the majority, Justice Black laid down basic concepts:

> The "establishment of religion" clause of the First Amendment means at least this: Neither a state nor the Federal Government can set up a church. Neither can pass laws which aid one religion, aid all religions, or prefer one religion over another. Neither can force nor influence a person to go to or to remain away from church against his will or force him to profess a belief or disbelief in any religion. No person can be punished for entertaining or professing religious beliefs or disbeliefs, for church attendance or non-attendance. . . . Neither a state nor the Federal Government can, openly or secretly,

participate in the affairs of any religious organizations or groups and *vice versa.*

Justices who dissented from the case's specific resolution did not quarrel with Black's fundamental conception of proper interaction between political and religious spheres of interest. All later cases were built on this famous litigation not only because of its substantial grasp of First Amendment principles, but also because it elicited more questions than it settled.

Facing those questions, justices devised a test for assessing state legislation to see if it qualified under constitutional restrictions on religion. In reaching decisions they inquired into both the primary intention behind legislation and the actual effect that it produced, whether intended or not. If either the declared purpose or the unintentional effect worked to advance or inhibit religion, then the law would be rejected as unconstitutional.

Findings in *Cochran* and *Everson* received additional confirmation in *Board of Education* v. *Allen* (1968), when the Court reaffirmed the practice of loaning secular textbooks to students in both public and religious schools. Utilizing the "child benefit" theory again, justices found the New York program to have legitimate secular purposes that neither promoted nor impeded religious interests. Accommodationists began to speculate optimistically about many areas in which state aid could promote the secular aspects of parochial curricula.

But limits to state aid gradually emerged, confirming a more centrist interpretive position. Rhode Island and Pennsylvania had developed plans for supplementing the salaries of teachers who were responsible for secular subjects in parochial schools. Those teachers promised not to engage in any religious instruction and thereby qualified to receive state funds that made their salaries competitive with public school counterparts. In *Lemon* v. *Kurtzman* (1971) the Supreme Court found such plans a violation of the establishment clause because they produced excessive entanglement between church and state. Compliance with state rules would involve administering a surveillance system to make sure that participating parochial teachers actually refrained from mentioning religious subjects. It also required civil authorities to supervise the operations of religious institutions. So justices

rejected this attempt at blending spiritual and temporal activities as an example of what the establishment clause was meant to prevent.

Further disappointment for those wishing increased aid to parochial education resulted from *Committee for Public Education and Religious Liberty* v. *Nyquist* (1973). The state of New York had provided a rather comprehensive set of aids to religious schools, including tuition reimbursements and direct grants for maintenance and safety improvements to buildings. These went to districts in which schools were attended primarily by students from low-income families. Arguments supporting the scheme pointed out that its chief purpose was the secular welfare of students and that most tuition relief or graduated income tax benefits went to the most needy. But the Supreme Court struck down all provisions of the law because it failed the "primary effect" test. Since direct grants were not restricted to secular purposes, justices maintained that such aid advanced the schools' religious mission. Aids for tuition were also disallowed because they provided financial support for sectarian institutions, rewarding parents who sent their children to church-related schools.

States with large but faltering parochial school systems persevered in attempts to salvage them. Legislators may have wished to preserve church schools for their own sake, but they also knew that states would face overwhelming costs if the parochial systems closed and all children turned to public education. One stopgap measure appeared in Pennsylvania, where state aid went beyond the accepted minimum of loaning students textbooks to providing instructional equipment and auxiliary services. In this provision the state loaned audio-visual and laboratory equipment together with journals, maps, and photographs for secular instruction in all schools. Moreover, it supplied state personnel who visited parochial schools to offer remedial teaching and psychological guidance counseling. But in *Meek* v. *Pittenger* (1975) the Supreme Court held all but the law's simplest provision to be unconstitutional. Accommodationists' hopes were dashed because justices said that auxiliary services and equipment other than textbooks had the primary effect of advancing the religious mission of the schools. The plan also fostered too much entanglement between the secular and religious aspects of teaching duties.

While acknowledging that parochial education secured substantial benefits to society as a whole, justices were unwilling to sanction plans that fostered religion contrary to their understanding of First Amendment restrictions.

The number of dissenting justices in *Nyquist* and *Meek* grew to almost half the Court. Angry Roman Catholic response escalated too as more parents faced mounting financial burdens. It is impossible to measure the effect of this dissent on later cases, but within two years the Court did move toward a slightly more positive interpretation of permissible state aid. In *Wolman* v. *Walter* (1977) justices indicated a number of ways in which states could provide financial support for church-related schools. Obviously they could continue textbook loans, which had been practiced for half a century. States could also finance academic testing of all students as long as standard forms were used, avoiding questions of religious content. Public employees could provide services related to speech and hearing defects as well as offering psychological diagnosis, if the purpose was only to determine a student's need for assistance. States could supply therapy for those problems, including remedial reading and guidance counseling, as long as those services took place in secular surroundings "away from the pervasively sectarian atmosphere" of the religious school. On the negative side, *Wolman* said again that states could not make audio-visual equipment or maps available to parochial schools. Nor could they supply financial aid for field trips because that was seen as an opportunity for, or an encouragement of, specifically religious instruction.

This maze of cases discloses the positive and negative aspects of state aid to parochial education, and it helps flesh out our practical understanding of ways in which civil and religious spheres interact in the body politic. A few challenges have arisen regarding secular support for religious colleges, but both the degree of interest in them and the nature of their outcome have been different. Litigants challenged state grants for new buildings at church colleges, but in both *Tilton* v. *Richardson* (1971) and *Hunt* v. *McNair* (1973) the Supreme Court allowed public money for construction. It also sustained grants for undesignated usage on religious campuses in *Roemer* v. *Board of Public Works of Maryland* (1976). All of these cases posited a basic distinction between parochial education, as exemplified in elementary and secondary schools, and advanced education in church-related institutions. Colleges and universities do not continue doctrinal instruction as part of their primary goal. The more mature students who attend them are not as impressionable as grade school children. And college teachers are guided by more professional interests, encouraging critical thought and pursuing scholarly topics. For all these reasons justices have discerned no intent to advance sectarian religion at the college level and thus have permitted financial aid from public funds.

Though no church–state question is ever settled, especially in this thicket surrounding state aid to parochial schools, the following summary at least partially describes the contemporary situation. Civil authorities may draw on tax-supported resources to loan textbooks to students in all classrooms and pay for their bus travel to and from school. They may also provide certain health, educational, and welfare services to children, provided the application of such services is kept entirely secular. The parochial school itself is considered part of church property, and instruction in doctrine is part of the mission of the church. Any part of an educational program touching upon either of these aspects can receive no aid at all. Colleges, on the other hand, are not considered sectarian even when nominally associated with a religious group. Aid applies more easily and liberally on this level than it does in the lower grades.

One more aspect of modern perspectives on church and state touches an emotional issue involving individual rather than community action. Conscientious objections to war allow us to focus on an area where governmental authority and individual liberty collide, where state conscriptive power and religious pacifism conflict. Contrasts between national security interests and religious scruples against participating in war have been part of American history since the beginning. In most of our past the issues were clear-cut. Religion was associated with churches and theistic beliefs, and government allowed some form of alternative service for conscientious objectors. During the war in Vietnam, however, litigation expanded the concept of religion to a bewildering variety of meanings.

One of the first situations that pushed notions of religion beyond institutionally orthodox forms occurred in *United States* v. *Seeger* (1965). The Supreme Court held that a pacifist need not base his convictions on theistic belief. Ethical creeds could derive from any principle that occupied the same ultimacy in a person's ideas as did traditional belief in God. Justices warned, though, that such a credo had to function as a religion and not stem from merely political or philosophical views. Restrictions lessened to a greater degree in *Welsh* v. *United States* (1970), in which the Court accepted pacifism based on a reading of history and sociology. Justices found such convictions to be "religious in the ethical sense of the word." Having expanded the basis for conscientious objection quite generously, the Court restricted its application in at least one way. The companion cases of *Gillette* v. *United States* and *Negre* v. *Larsen* (1971) showed that there could be no selective use of principles. One could not, justices ruled, distinguish between types of wars and refuse to support only particular ones that were considered to be wrong. Congress could still grant exemptions from military service, but only to those conscientiously opposed to war in any form.

CONCLUSIONS

Placing all these cases in a brief overview, one can make several observations about contemporary relationships between church and state. Religious tests for voting or holding office are virtually extinct, and whenever one appears federal courts reject it. Sunday-closing laws are legitimate but only for secular reasons. Their former religious origins no longer apply, and in many places even these statutory enactments are ignored by an indifferent public. Sabbatarians are recognized by law as having equal rights to the free exercise of their religion, but their distinctive behavior can expect no special consideration in the general marketplace. All religious groups have the right to use public facilities such as parks and streets to broadcast their doctrine. They may lawfully oppose popular expressions of national allegiance such as saluting the flag, but they may not resist medical practices based on concerns for public health. Individuals may object to national military action on the basis of their religious opposition to war, and such scruples are now defined in quite general terms.

Schools are a complex area for observing modern adjustments to changed conditions in spiritual and temporal affairs. The traditional practices of reading from the Bible in public classrooms and reciting prayers to begin the school day have ended. As religious exercises they serve no secular purpose and are thus excluded from all state educational systems. Within religious schools themselves state financial aid is limited to strictly secular aspects of the educational program. No support accrues to religious instruction or to the property hosting that activity. Religious colleges can receive state aid in the form of building grants or unspecified subsidies. These positive aids are more noticeable features of the more commonly accepted ones by which the government supports chaplains in Congress, prisons, and the armed forces; grants tax exemptions to church real estate; makes public utilities and police protection available to religious institutions; and makes clergymen exempt from the military draft.

While these more settled areas of church and state suggest that some controversies have been resolved, many other questions stimulate continued deliberation. In each of them religious and civil responsibilities overlap, and the practical problem is one of determining the extent and propriety of roles. In medical practice, for instance, substantial questions have been raised at both thresholds of life. Abortion is an increasingly difficult problem because modern technology can tell us much about fetal development, while many feminists argue that the mother alone can decide whether or not an abortion should be performed. This is complicated by the scientific uncertainty as to when a person actually begins his or her unique existence and by the legal uncertainty as to when basic social rights pertain to that life. Similar questions are currently debated on the other end of the spectrum regarding the practice of allowing people to die without the aid of available life-support mechanisms. Various religious groups express strong views on these issues, and civil authorities at all levels are involved with them as well. We seem to be far from reaching a common scientific and juridical understanding of what is involved in these life-or-death issues, and even farther from reconciling interested parties.

Another arena where religious and secular interests will apparently never be reconciled has to do with schools. In the late 1970's the question of teaching creationism as opposed to evolutionary theories in biology came to the fore again. After the Scopes trial in 1925, most states with anti-evolution laws either revoked or refused to enforce them. A half-century later, though, several states witnessed local battles over textbooks that featured evolutionary hypotheses. Some legislatures have sponsored laws demanding equal time for biblical theories alongside empirical science in the classroom. The Arkansas capitol passed such a law, but state courts struck it down as unconstitutional. District courts in California have also received cases on this question and decided against biblically oriented plaintiffs. Despite setbacks at all policy levels, the popular impulses that bring religious convictions to bear on the educational process seem indefatigable. Their persistence indicates the protean and irrepressible nature of this conflict.

Questions of public morality also remain part of contemporary debates. Various civil and religious groups continue to urge censorship, in films and printed materials for example, though they cannot reach a common definition of obscenity. But different Moral Majorities and Christian Voices repeatedly mount campaigns to use governmental power as a means of enforcing their own moral standards on the body politic. Many of these instances point to the dilemma in understanding church and state. In some situations, easily identifiable church groups take the initiative, and their activities can be assimilated within familiar categories. But at other times the role of "church" or even of "religion" cannot be readily discerned. When one moves to "moral values" as the origin of disagreement over issues ranging from dress codes and theatrical productions to medicine and education, the line between church and state blurs into vague contrasts within a mixture of cultural values and simple matters of taste. Movement along this continuum highlights the problem of focusing on what "religion" can mean today and what, by contrast, is still "secular."

Similar questions with indirect ties to traditional religious categories, yet of nonetheless pressing contemporary relevance, involve a host of public issues. People from many different perspectives contribute ideas about welfare programs, but there is no agreement over which general services ought to be provided or which

agencies should supply them. Questions of individual and group action regarding our interlocking ecological systems raise enormous problems for both spiritual and temporal authority structures. Issues related to possible global warfare, nuclear disarmament, and peace demonstrations point to another area where religious and governmental influences have vital contributions to make. But in all of these, the programmatic response of either sphere of interest is no longer clear, and the previous context of church–state relationships offers no guidelines for future interpretation. The fabled "wall of separation between church and state" has not only crumbled; its usefulness as an analytic concept fades into unreality.

We can see how the past has led to the present, but it is more difficult to apply those lessons in current circumstances or to anticipate the future. In broad, summarizing terms it is clear that the basic religious motivation for separating religious and political interests in colonial times was to keep the state out of church affairs, lest churches be subordinated to government. Additional arguments from the philosophical or Jeffersonian perspective sought to keep churches out of governmental business, lest civil authority be subordinated to the church. These views combined to produce the First Amendment. But American culture has moved beyond such easy distinctions. The Supreme Court has adequately defended us from encroachments of either sort envisioned at our country's formative stage. Civil powers no longer try to promote or forbid religious beliefs. Spiritual authorities rarely try to control the political life of the community.

Today we face more ambiguous expressions of religion from non–church members and more aggressive assertions of state responsibility for human welfare, formerly left to churches. Religious groups and governments still have legitimate functions, but the growing edge of church–state interaction pertains to community issues in which both secular and religious interests touch the same human context. Religious and political institutions respect each other and recognize independent responsibilities built on mutual dependence. But they must grapple with the extent to which they interact on questions of common interest. As churches exercise a critical voice in the formation of public policy, and as political administrations operate under the constitutional tradition of separate powers, Americans alert to new possibilities can observe the next phase of church–state relationships as it unfolds.

BIBLIOGRAPHY

Several sources contain primary documents related to church and state. Selected cases and brief interpretive narratives can reflect the range and complexity in this field. Standard collections for contemporary observers include Mark D. Howe, *Cases on Church and State in the United States* (Cambridge, Mass., 1952); John J. McGrath, *Church and State in American Law: Cases and Materials* (Milwaukee, Wis., 1962); Robert T. Miller and Ronald B. Flowers, *Toward Benevolent Neutrality: Church, State, and the Supreme Court* (Waco, Tex., 1982); Leo Pfeffer, *Church, State, and Freedom* (Boston, 1953); Anson P. Stokes, *Church and State in the United States* (New York, 1950); Joseph Tussman, *The Supreme Court on Church and State* (New York, 1962); John F. Wilson, ed., *Church and State in American History* (Boston, 1965); and Carl Zollman, *American Church Law* (St. Paul, Minn., 1933).

Religion and politics fit within the larger context of American society. Several basic studies of that context, with particular attention to church activities and influence, help place the cases mentioned above in proper perspective: Ernest S. Bates, *American Faith: Its Religious, Political, and Economic Foundations* (New York, 1940); Loren P. Beth, *The American Theory of Church and State* (Gainesville, Fla., 1958); Evarts B. Greene, *Religion and the State: The Making and Testing of an American Tradition* (New York, 1941); Robert T. Handy, *A Christian America: Protestant Hopes and Historical Realities* (New York, 1971); Will Herberg, *Protestant, Catholic, Jew: An Essay in American Religious Sociology* (Garden City, N.Y., 1960); Wilbur G. Katz, *Religion and American Constitutions* (Evanston, Ill., 1964); Paul G. Kauper, *Civil Liberties and the Constitution* (Ann Arbor, Mich., 1962) and *Religion and the Constitution* (Baton Rouge, La., 1964); Alexander Meiklejohn, *Political Freedom: The Constitutional Powers of the People* (New York, 1960); Richard E. Morgan, *The Politics of Religious Conflict: Church and State in America* (New York, 1968); Frank J. Sorauf, *The Wall of Separation: The Constitutional Politics of Church and State* (Princeton, N.J., 1976).

More specialized interpretations are helpful too. In concentrating on narrower aspects of the question, these publications help by clarifying particular sides of the debates that have occurred. Publications of this type include Henry J. Abraham, *Freedom and the Court: Civil Rights and Liberties in the United States,* 4th ed. (New York, 1982); Angel F. Carrillo de Albornoz, *The Basis of Religious Liberty* (New York, 1963); Joseph L. Blau, *Cornerstones of Religious Freedom in America* (Boston, 1949); Merrimon Cuninggim, *Freedom's Holy Light* (New York, 1955); Joseph M. Dawson, *America's Way in Church, State, and Society* (New York, 1953); William O. Douglas, *The Bible and the Schools* (Boston, 1966); Charles I. Foster, *An Errand of Mercy: The Evangelical United Front, 1790–1837* (Chapel Hill, N.C., 1960); Daniel R. Grant, *The Christian and Politics* (Nashville, Tenn., 1968); Mark D. Howe, *The Garden and the Wilderness: Religion and Government in American Constitutional History* (Chicago, 1965); Jerome G. Kerwin, *Catholic Viewpoint on Church and State* (Garden City, N.Y., 1960); Philip B. Kurland, *Religion and the Law: Of Church and State and the Supreme Court* (Chicago, 1962); William H. Marnell, *The First Amendment: The History of Religious Freedom in America* (Garden City, N.Y., 1964); Conrad H. Moehlman, *The Wall of Separation Between Church and State* (Boston, 1951); Peter H. Odegard, ed., *Religion and Politics* (New York, 1960); Thomas G. Sanders, *Protestant Concepts of Church and State: Historical Backgrounds and Approaches for the Future* (New York, 1964); and Murray S. Stedman, *Religion and Politics in America* (New York, 1964).

[*See also* AMERICAN REVOLUTION; BILL OF RIGHTS; CENSORSHIP; CONSTITUTION; EDUCATION; FEDERALISM; INDIVIDUALISM AND CONFORMITY; JEFFERSONIAN DEMOCRACY; LOBBIES AND PRESSURE GROUPS; NATIVISM; PACIFISM AND PEACE MOVEMENTS; PLURALISM; PROHIBITION AND TEMPERANCE; *and* VOLUNTARY ASSOCIATIONS.]

CITIZENSHIP

Melvin Yazawa

COLONIAL SUBJECTSHIP

THE development of a distinctively American concept of citizenship had its beginnings in the modifications that the seventeenth-century colonists imposed upon the English doctrine of subjectship. In England, political and legal theorists emphasized the permanence and hierarchical nature of the status. The subject-king relationship was thought to be permanent because it was presumed to be a natural extension of the filial bond between children and parents. And the hierarchical emphasis resulted from the insistence on the part of English jurists that the adopted or naturalized subject was not necessarily entitled to the same rights and privileges as natural-born Englishmen.

This conventional understanding of subjectship received its major theoretical challenge in the writings of John Locke. In his *Two Treatises of Government* and *Some Thoughts Concerning Education,* Locke suggested that the family unit was indeed an important influence in the origins of the state. Monarchical rule, especially, was so preeminently personal that it was often confused with paternal authority. In the "Original of Commonwealths," nature and necessity conspired to lodge the reins of government in the hands of the father. With the passage of time, the "natural *Fathers of Families,* by an insensible change, became the *politick Monarchs* of them too." Having said this, Locke went on to argue that familial continuity notwithstanding, the notion of divine-right patriarchalism in politics was absurd. In the first place, despite the understandable temptation to lump political and patriarchal authority together, the "Power of a *Magistrate* over a Subject" must be "distinguished from that of a *Father* over his Children." Whereas the latter

relationship was established in nature, the former was a consequence of "Voluntary Agreement." Locke thus called upon the theory of consent to show that the state and the family rested on altogether different moral foundations.

But even if we chose to ignore this crucial distinction, divine-right patriarchalism would be limited by a second consideration: "subjection of a Minor . . . terminates with the minority of the Child." The power a father exercised over his children was fully justified only during their "ignorant Nonage"—while they manifested the weaknesses of infancy and possessed no effective understanding of their own. Once children have arrived at the "years of discretion," the *"Father's Empire* then ceases, and he can from thence forwards no more dispose of the liberty of his Son, than that of any other Man." In addition to this temporal restriction, Locke contended that parental power was conditional and "arises from that Duty which is incumbent on them, to take care of their Off-spring, during the imperfect state of Childhood." The power of a father belonged to him "only as he is Guardian of his Children," and "when he quits his Care of them, he loses his Power over them." Rather than being inherently perpetual, therefore, paternal power was so "inseparably annexed" to the duty of providing "Nourishment and Education" that it "belongs as much to the *Foster-Father* of an exposed Child, as to the Natural Father of another."

These Lockean qualifications were to have their greatest impact not in England initially but in the American colonies. For demographic conditions in colonial America predisposed provincial authorities to accommodate Lockean notions of consensual membership in society. Despite local variations regarding the admission of aliens, two characteristics of central importance emerged in the colonial doctrine of subjectship. First, in order to lure immigrants to American soil, colonial legislators, especially those outside of New England, followed a policy of granting extensive rights and benefits to the foreign-born that effectively eroded the hierarchical pattern prevalent in the mother country. Distinctions between the native-born subject and the naturalized were blurred.

Second, the procedures for incorporating aliens into provincial society seemed to entail mutual, although implicit, consent. The alien agreed to be bound to king and community and in return expected to claim the traditional rights of Englishmen. The host society, for its part, agreed to adopt the newcomer, fully expecting to benefit from his contributions to the survival of the whole. The Lockean formulation of the "Voluntary Agreement" origins of the state thus approached theoretical perfection in America. But the import of these trends, apparent before the end of the seventeenth century, would not be realized until the advent of the imperial crisis of the mid-eighteenth century, when subjectship came to be supplanted by citizenship.

REVOLUTIONARY REPUBLICANISM

The last quarter of the eighteenth century was arguably the most fruitful period in the development of American citizenship. Drawing upon colonial precedents pertaining to subjectship and the Revolutionary ideology of republicanism, political observers adhered to an elaborate but elusive doctrine of citizenship. Four key elements entered into this doctrine: first, citizenship was ultimately an elected status and must begin with an act of individual volition; second, the status itself, whether acquired through birthright or naturalization, must be uniform; third, citizens, by definition, must be active and independent in the affairs of the state; and fourth, members must be attached through "patriotic" education to the republic and its principles.

The first two characteristics were derived from the colonial understanding of subjectship. The imperial crisis and the colonists' declaration of independence from England served to heighten American awareness of the volitional basis of the political order. Allegiance followed

protection. The Lockean prescription concerning a "Father's Empire" was at least verified by, if it did not indeed justify, the Revolution. George III had not only failed to provide the nourishment and education befitting a proper guardian, the Revolutionaries argued, but also had so forgotten his paternal duties as to join his base ministers in a plot to "enslave" an otherwise innocently obedient people. Under such conditions, allegiance could no longer be expected of his charges. As long as they believed that George III was governing according to the laws of "Justice and Mercy," the colonists were duty-bound to "pray for the King," John Adams explained. But once they saw things in their true light, once they realized that the king was bent upon destroying rather than protecting their "Lives, Liberties, and Properties," Americans refused to pray for the king any longer and instead accepted it as their "Duty to pray for the Continental Congress and all the thirteen State Congresses."

The notion of reciprocal rights and responsibilities, rooted theoretically in the notion of consent and nurtured practically in the colonial program of naturalization, supported the movement toward independence and thereby forced the Revolutionaries to articulate a coherent defense of voluntarism in the determination of allegiance. Although the treatment of Loyalists and other disaffected groups during the war sometimes bordered on coercion at the expense of doctrinal consistency, the idea that a person possessed the right to elect or reject membership would in time be enshrined as a maxim of American citizenship.

The second component of the Revolutionary doctrine, that the status of "citizen" must be undifferentiated, was a reflection of social reality and ideological predisposition. Once independence had been formally effected, the American body politic was left without the traditional social orders of Europe. Despite the development of elite classes during the colonial period, some of them clearly defined, as was the case with the Virginia gentry, the Revolutionaries were quick to proclaim that the new nation was blessed because it had "no rank above that of freemen." This was as it should be, for a republic established upon the majesty of the people must, Thomas Paine said, shun the "base remains" of those "two ancient tyrannies," kings and lords, incorporated into the English tradition of mixed constitutionalism. Questions focusing on the proper structure or the appropriate paradigm for the first American constitutions occasioned considerable disagreement. But on the issue of the rights to be accorded adopted citizens under the new constitutions, a remarkable consensus prevailed. Even during the tumultuous 1790's, when Federalists and Jeffersonian Republicans accused one another of sacrificing national security in the interest of advancing selfish partisan ends, proposals for the creation of separate ranks of citizens never got very far. Qualifications for admission, especially residency requirements, could be and were tightened considerably; but once membership was gained, the naturalized citizen was entitled to all but one of the full rights of the native-born. The adopted citizen was prohibited under the federal constitution from ever serving as president; but otherwise, as Chief Justice John Marshall affirmed, "he is distinguishable in nothing from a native citizen."

The assumption that citizenship was and ought to be ungraded did not mean that all inhabitants, native-born or newly arrived, were equally able to claim that status. On the contrary, the vast majority of inhabitants were excluded—some temporarily, others seemingly permanently—from the benefits of individual membership. Women and minors, servants and slaves, and the poor and propertyless were all burdened with disabilities that defined the boundaries of republican citizenship. If there was no rank above freeman, there were certainly more than a few below it. Nowhere was the importance of this distinction more clearly revealed than in the forty-second essay of *The Federalist.* There James Madison contended that a major flaw in the Articles of Confederation was its clumsy attempt to deal with the problem of common citizenship. Article IV of that document had specifically granted the "free inhabitants of each of these States . . . all privileges and immunities of free citizens in the several States." This "confusion of language" might lead, Madison protested, to a politically absurd situation in which the *"free inhabitants* of a State, although not citizens of such State, are entitled, in every other State, to all the privileges of *free citizens* of the latter; that is, to greater privileges than they may be entitled to in their own State." At the very least, Madison

advised, the use of the term "inhabitants" should be qualified in such a way as to "confine the stipulated privileges to citizens alone."

Thus "inhabitant," or even native-born "free inhabitant," was not interchangeable with "citizen." The first category was largely defined by geography and governed by the laws of physics; the second was principally defined by politics and governed by the strictures of ideology. Citizens, the Revolutionaries believed, constituted a somewhat exclusive group of free inhabitants: those capable of being entrusted with a participatory role in state affairs. If the most basic form of participation—the right to vote—is taken as an index of citizenship, then the new states granted admission to that status quite sparingly indeed. Every Revolutionary state constitution contained a property-holding or tax-paying qualification for the right to vote. In part, these restrictions were based on the argument that only those with a sufficient stake in society, an investment of real or personal property in the community, should be given a voice in determining public policy. But the emphasis on property and participation was more directly attributable to the social imperatives embedded in republican ideology.

The American Revolutionaries were the inheritors of a republican tradition rooted in classical antiquity, revived by the civic humanists of the Italian Renaissance, and transmitted into the eighteenth century by James Harrington and the English Commonwealthmen. At the core of this tradition was a profound distrust of dependency. Subscribers to this tradition were convinced that dependent beings were easy targets of corruption. Compelled to follow the commands of those to whom they were obligated for their survival, these degraded creatures had no will of their own. Given the right to vote or otherwise to engage in public affairs, they would be controlled by their benefactors. In a republic driven by the will of the majority, then, the privilege of participation must be closely guarded and reserved for the truly independent.

Under the influence of this classical legacy, the Revolutionaries came to equate dependence with moral decay in the life of the republic, and independence with virtue. Property-holding requirements written into the first state constitutions were logical outgrowths of this dictum. Property, particularly a freehold in land, which was supposedly the least alienable form of property, was valuable precisely because it was the most firmly settled foundation for personal autonomy. Only a property-holder, free of external support and the control that such support implied, possessed the capacity to place the *res publica* above selfish interests. The conclusion seemed as simple as it was inescapable: dependence was descriptive of clientage; independence, of citizenship.

The insistence that a capacity for autonomous participation in public affairs, civic competence, was an essential characteristic of a republican citizen reinforced the Revolutionary generation's faith in the potential benefits of popular education. While they acknowledged that a freehold was the surest guarantee of individual independence, few Revolutionaries were so bold or foolhardy as to propose agrarian laws aimed at achieving an equal distribution of land in the new nation. Rather than trifling with established rules of property, they vociferously championed a substitute—the establishment of an educational system geared toward ensuring that American youths were prepared to maintain a "becoming independency" when they arrived at years of maturity. A properly educated man, like the proprietor of a freehold, possessed a commodity that might permanently enable him to avoid the snares of dependence.

Preparation for personal autonomy fulfilled only part of the promise of political education. Convinced as they were that republics throughout history had been fragile and short-lived, and that the American republic in spite of all its natural and inherited advantages was isolated in the midst of a politically hostile world of rival monarchies, the Revolutionaries insisted that it was essential for citizens to be inviolably attached to the commonwealth itself. The love of country must reign supreme, surpassing even the love of family, in the heart of a truly inspired citizen. Noah Webster, whose energetic attempts to form an "American" language as part of a distinctively "American" culture were unsurpassed in the early republic, proposed a kind of political catechism: "As soon as he [an American child] opens his lips, he should rehearse the history of his own country; he should lisp the praise of liberty and of those illustrious heroes and statesmen who have wrought a revolution in her favor."

This was admittedly a form of political indoctrination. In the Revolutionary perspective, however, with the fate of the republic hanging in the balance, such self-conscious Americanism hardly needed to be excused. Republican principles routinely required ordinary men to perform in extraordinary ways in the process of governing themselves, the most basic of these stemming from a willingness to place public welfare over private gain. Such demands were naturally arduous for fallen man, but they might be rendered pleasant through a judicious system of virtuous education. Early exposure to the blessings of republicanism, lisping praises to liberty and the Founding Fathers, was likely to generate habitual attachments to the American commonwealth and, consequently, to make sacrifices in its interest nearly second nature.

The combined emphasis on political education, necessitated by an awareness of the special demands placed upon republican citizens, was clearly evident in the development of postindependence state and federal policies affecting naturalization. All of the new state governments established some sort of residency requirement for aliens seeking admission to membership. Individual variations notwithstanding, these statutes shared a common assumption: aspiring citizens were really apprentice Americans. Only after a period of political tutelage, after constant exposure to the workings of the republic, could they be expected to appreciate the American system and thus be trusted to relinquish their foreign predilections. Until such a transference of allegiance occurred, the welfare of the nation required that these aspirants be denied a public role.

Federal policymakers endorsed the actions of their state counterparts. The federal Naturalization Act of 1790 stipulated that aliens must log at least two years in residence before becoming eligible for citizenship. Subsequent congressional action in 1795 and 1798 revised the residency requirement upward to five years and fourteen years, respectively. Thus changing times and partisan xenophobia altered the terms of residence, but the essential premise behind these restrictions remained intact. Foreign nationals seeking admission to citizenship needed to immerse themselves in the republican culture of the United States, to dissolve old allegiances and to develop new ones, so that they, like their native-born brethren, might unabashedly begin lisping praises to American liberty.

DEMOCRATIC NATIONALISM

Because the Founding Fathers did not attempt a precise formal definition of citizenship in any of their fundamental political testaments, it was left for succeeding generations to assess the constitutional and legal limits of the Revolutionary republican doctrine. Inexorably, the studied exclusiveness inherent in classical republicanism succumbed to greater and greater inclusiveness as the social and political forces set in motion by the Revolution gave rise to the egalitarian priorities of the nineteenth century. The movement toward a democratic theory of citizenship, one that incorporated more than merely the white male population, was often plagued by inconsistencies resulting from inert tradition or ingrained prejudices. There is no better way to trace the post-Revolutionary development and definition of the concept of American citizenship than by looking at three major groups of "outsiders": women, free blacks, and Indians.

Women. The experiences of American women during and after the Revolution provide ample evidence of the resilience of customary inertia. Traditionally, women's roles were almost wholly domestic. Women were supposed to be passive and, above all, private creatures, whose duties were confined primarily to home and hearth. The Revolutionary War initiated a series of changes in this scheme. Not only were some women forced to assume nontraditional roles in their husbands' absence, but the traditional circle of domestic concerns was itself breached by larger issues of public import. In the process, the line that formerly had separated the private world of women from the public world of men was blurred.

It is important to note that this incursion upon tradition was limited, more evolutionary than revolutionary, for the context in which the changes occurred was defined by convention. The public identity that women assumed tended to be bound up rather intimately with their acknowledged responsibilities as wives and mothers. Before independence, colonial polemicists asked women to contribute to the protest movement by being better home economists, by refusing to purchase English goods and thus promoting the cause of nonimportation. Similarly, during the war, whether they participated directly as camp followers cooking and caring for the troops, or symbolically as political spinsters turning out homespun, women performed in recognizably "feminine" capacities. Indeed, female patriotism was simply an extension of domestic virtue into the public realm. The nature of the work done by women was essentially unaltered. What had changed was the political significance attached to such work, for as John Adams observed, the imperial crisis had transformed the home into a "theatre of politics."

After independence, the conjoining of politics and domesticity was manifested in the concept of "Republican Motherhood." For women in the new nation, service to the commonwealth remained primarily a maternal exercise. Their chief civic function was to nurture successive generations of hardy, public-spirited republican sons.

As part of the legacy of their Revolutionary experiences, the public personae of women were so closely linked to the institution of the family that vital questions pertaining to female citizenship frequently hinged on marital decisions. Most revealing was the question of whether an American-born woman would lose her citizenship after marriage to an alien. In the first half of the nineteenth century she did not. But this was primarily because of the ambiguity surrounding the right of expatriation. While state and federal lawmakers readily acknowledged that the acquisition of citizenship stemmed from an act of individual volition, they did not accept the notion that the renunciation of membership was likewise a matter of individual choice. Instead, most were inclined to argue that the individual, after admission, existed in a contractual relationship with the state and could not break this engagement without permission. For American-born women this meant that marriage to foreign nationals did not dissolve their native bonds of allegiance because, as Justice Joseph Story recorded in *Shanks* v. *Dupont* (1830), the "general doctrine is that no persons can by any act of their own, without the consent of the government, put off their allegiance and become aliens."

Although Story indicated that women might not lose their citizenship through marriage, he had no intention of challenging the concept of coverture, that is, the notion that a married woman's legal existence was "covered" by that of her husband. Rather than recognizing the right to independent citizenship for married women, Story based his conclusion on the qualifications incorporated into the American understanding of voluntary expatriation. Implicit in all of this, then, was the threat that once these qualifications were removed, state and federal officials might force women to surrender their citizenship at marriage. And indeed, after congressional action had sanctioned the right of individual expatriation in 1868, some women were caught in just such a bind. Eventually, in 1907, federal law confirmed that "Any American woman who marries a foreigner shall take the nationality of her husband."

The constitutionality of the 1907 law was tested in the U.S. Supreme Court in 1915. The plaintiff in the case of *Mackenzie* v. *Hare* was a California-born woman, Ethel C. Mackenzie, who had been denied the right to register as a state voter on the ground that by her marriage to a subject of Great Britain she ceased to be a citizen of the United States. Mrs. Mackenzie contended that only voluntary expatriation evidenced in a "fixed determination . . . to throw off the former allegiance, and become a citizen or subject of a foreign power" could divest a woman of her citizenship. However, the Court upheld the 1907 law and ruled against the plaintiff. Although it was true that volitional allegiance was the basis of U.S. citizenship and that a change of citizenship could not be effected without the concurrence of the citizen, nevertheless, Justice Joseph McKenna wrote, marital decisions of this nature were tantamount to expatriation. The marriage of an American woman to a foreigner was a condition voluntarily entered into; therefore its consequences, in particular the loss of citizenship, must be considered as elected.

The major premise underlying the high court's ruling in the Mackenzie case was merely an axiom of the coverture doctrine. According to Justice McKenna, the "identity of husband and wife is an ancient principle of our jurisprudence." That premise, the belief that the civic identity of a wife was subsumed under her husband's, remained in effect until 1922. The Cable Act of that year, by stipulating that an American woman who married an alien "eligible to citizen-ship" would remain a citizen unless she formally renounced her citizenship, represented a long overdue extension of the principle of volitional allegiance to women. When Congress in 1931 applied this principle to American women marrying aliens "ineligible to citizenship," the independent citizenship status of married women was finally realized in law.

Free blacks. The presence of slaves in a nation founded on proclamations of individual liberty constituted a profound paradox for generations of Americans after independence. A parallel if somewhat less pressing inconsistency was the product of a contrived refusal to recognize native-born free blacks as citizens. Although the Constitution did not define the term "citizen," American courts had generally taken for granted the common-law principle of *jus soli,* of citizenship determined by place of birth. Although a few statesmen, like Lincoln's attorney general, Edward Bates, might assert that "every person born in this country is, at the moment of birth, *prima facie* a citizen," others, especially southern apologists, sought to establish racial limitations on the application of *jus soli.*

The first sustained challenge to that principle came in 1820 when the Missouri constitution proposed to bar free blacks from entering the state. If, as opponents of the prohibition contended, U.S.-born free blacks were citizens, then the restriction was clearly a violation of the privileges-and-immunities clause of the Constitution. Forced either to acknowledge their error or to contend that *jus soli* determined the status of whites but not of blacks, Missouri's backers chose against all logic to pursue the latter course. Place of birth was decisive in settling the question of citizenship for whites; thus a white child born in the United States automatically qualified as a U.S. citizen even though his parents might be alien residents. In this instance the principle of *jus soli* superseded that of *jus sanguinis,* of citizenship determined by the status of one's parents. However, southern spokesmen argued that the same rule did not hold true for freeborn native blacks.

Compounding error upon error, subsequent polemicists sought to support this double standard by invoking a circular argument. Racial prejudice, which prevented them from applying the rule of *jus soli* with any consistency in the first place, was justified on the basis of past statutory discrimination. Proper claims of citizenship should have spurred American jurists into scutting a multitude of discriminatory laws; instead, they cited such laws in order to undermine proper claims of citizenship. "Nativity, residence, and allegiance combined" still did not make "free negroes and mulattoes" into citizens, Attorney General William Wirt opined in 1821, because it seemed "very manifest that no person is included in the description of citizen of the United States who has not the full rights of a citizen in the State of his residence." Similarly, in 1822, Justice John Boyle of the Kentucky Court of Appeals declared that because freeborn blacks were "almost everywhere, considered and treated as a degraded race of people; . . . they cannot become citizens of the United States." Ordinarily, citizenship conferred rights and immunities, but for American blacks the situation was reversed: because they did not already possess certain rights they could not become citizens.

Efforts to confound the doctrine of birthright citizenship with racial restrictions reached a climax in the Dred Scott case. Scott, a slave who had spent most of the period between 1834 and 1838 in Illinois and the Wisconsin Territory, sued for his liberty in the Missouri courts in 1846 on the ground that his previous stay on free soil had effected his emancipation. Although the Missouri Supreme Court ruled against Scott in 1852, subsequent appeals eventually led to a hearing before the U.S. Supreme Court.

Interestingly enough, the two justices who most directly addressed the question of black citizenship in the Scott case, Chief Justice Roger B. Taney and Associate Justice Benjamin Curtis, had made their opposing sentiments known some years earlier. In 1832 Taney, as Andrew Jackson's attorney general, was asked by Secretary of State Edward Livingston for his opinion concerning a South Carolina law requiring civil authorities to seize and imprison all black seamen while their ships docked at Charleston harbor. In his initial response Taney avoided a discussion of the wider implications of the seamen law by stating that the problem was conveniently within the compass of state, not federal, jurisdiction. But in a later supplement to his opinion Taney observed that blacks were "everywhere a degraded class" and as such "have never been considered as members of the body politic. In

our most solemn and public acts where we speak of our people or our citizens they are never intended to be included." Taney's observation was both an endorsement of Justice Boyle's ruling a decade earlier and a preview of his own opinion in *Dred Scott,* still more than two decades away.

Benjamin Curtis' view of the same subject was made public in a petition that he signed in 1843. Curtis, along with about 150 other citizens of Massachusetts, petitioned Congress to overturn the South Carolina seamen law for two reasons. First, the law violated the terms of an Anglo-American trade agreement whereby the inhabitants of the two countries were guaranteed free access to each other's ports. Consequently, the South Carolina law must be disallowed because it encroached upon the commerce power of the federal government. Second, and perhaps even more basic, the seamen law threatened to erode the "privileges of citizenship secured by the Constitution of the United States." The imprisonment of free black seamen was an illegitimate exercise of the police power of South Carolina, for it was clearly in violation of the privileges-and-immunities clause of the Constitution.

The dispute between Taney and Curtis boiled down to a fundamental disagreement over the status of free blacks in the United States, an issue that was still very much on their minds in 1856–1857. As Taney phrased it in delivering the majority opinion in *Dred Scott:* "Can a Negro, whose ancestors were imported into this country, and sold as slaves, become a member of the political community formed and brought into existence by the Constitution . . . and as such become entitled to all the rights, and privileges, and immunities, guaranteed by that instrument to the citizen?" Taney's position on this question had not changed since the seamen controversy. According to the chief justice, blacks were not citizens "within the meaning of the Constitution." The fact that members of the "African race" had been discriminated against for "more than a century before" 1787 proved to Taney's satisfaction that they were not citizens of any state at the time of the Revolution, and therefore that the framers of the Constitution had not intended to embrace them as part of the newly created national citizenry. Local citizenship after 1787 was a possibility—a state like Massachusetts might choose to ignore color distinctions in determining membership—but this was purely a matter of local discretion and limited by domicile. Hence the privileges and immunities secured in Article IV, Section 2, could not be claimed by blacks regardless of their circumstances at birth.

Justice Curtis, in dissent in 1857, correctly maintained that (contrary to Taney's assumption) certain states in 1787—namely, Massachusetts, New Hampshire, New York, New Jersey, and North Carolina—did in fact recognize their free black population as citizens. Thus even if, as Taney would have it, national citizenship was acquired through descent from the founders and not through birthright, some blacks were entitled to claim that status and its privileges. Curtis had a more basic objection to Taney's opinion. It was not descent but, rather, place and circumstances of birth that determined citizenship, for "under the Constitution of the United States, every free person born on the soil of a State, who is a citizen of that State . . . is also a citizen of the United States." Despite the apparent limits of Curtis' declaration, national citizenship for free blacks being restricted to those born in states recognizing them as citizens, his opinion was consistent with the tradition of *jus soli.*

During the Civil War, the United States still lacked a precise statutory definition of citizenship. "Eighty years of practical enjoyment of citizenship under the Constitution have not sufficed," Attorney General Bates complained in 1862, "to teach us either the exact meaning of the word, or the constitutional elements of the thing we prize so highly." Four years later, Congress, overriding Andrew Johnson's veto, finally provided some clarification. The Civil Rights Act of 1866 declared "all persons born in the United States and not subject to any foreign power, excluding Indians not taxed . . . to be citizens of the United States." Accordingly, such persons, regardless of "race and color," were entitled to the "full and equal benefit of all laws and proceedings for the security of persons and property."

After the Civil Rights Act became law on 9 April 1866, Congress moved swiftly to solidify its achievement. In *Dred Scott,* Taney had insisted that "within the meaning of the Constitution" blacks were not citizens. Through constitutional amendment, Congress sought to discredit forever this specious argument. The draft of the Fourteenth Amendment, introduced on 30 April

1866, incorporated and extended the citizenship provision of the Civil Rights Act: "All persons born or naturalized in the United States, and subject to the jurisdiction thereof, are citizens of the United States and of the State wherein they reside." With the ratification of the Fourteenth Amendment in 1868, the principle of *jus soli* became a part of the nation's fundamental law.

American Indians. The Fourteenth Amendment went a long way toward clarifying the concept of citizenship, but with regard to one major group of native-born Americans the concept was still riddled with inconsistencies. Because the amendment, unlike the Civil Rights Act of 1866, did not specifically exclude the American Indian populations of the United States, questions arose concerning their status. In response, the Senate Judiciary Committee filed a report in 1870 concluding that the Indians did not attain citizenship under the terms of the amendment. And federal court decisions quickly endorsed the Senate committee's position. An 1871 ruling in *McKay* v. *Campbell* held that "To be a citizen of the United States by reason of his birth, a person must not only be born within its territorial limits, but he must also be born subject to its jurisdiction—that is, in its power and obedience."

The key to the disqualification of the birthright claims of the American Indians, then, can be traced back to the conventional perception of their tribal identity. Colonial practices all but ensured that the federal government from the first years of the republic would view the several tribes as distinctive entities, neither truly domestic nor entirely foreign. Chief Justice Marshall formulated a clear statement of this commonplace view in 1831. In *Cherokee Nation* v. *Georgia,* the U.S. Supreme Court refused to issue an injunction against the state's designs to annul the "laws, usages, and customs" of the Cherokees. According to Marshall, the Court was prevented on jurisdictional grounds from intervening in this matter because "an Indian tribe or nation within the United States is not a foreign state in the sense of the constitution, and cannot maintain an action in the courts of the United States."

But if the separate tribal identity of the American Indians was not enough to enable them to appeal to the Supreme Court for redress of grievances under the auspices of Article III, Section 2, of the Constitution, it was more than sufficient to deprive them of their claims to the rights of citizenship. The American Indian tribes, Marshall explained, were "domestic dependent nations" in a "state of pupilage," a condition akin to that of a "ward to his guardian."

As interpreted by Congress and the courts, this "domestic dependent nation" status hampered the acquisition of citizenship by American Indians in at least two closely related ways. In the first place, lawmakers and jurists assumed that tribal membership was incompatible with citizenship. According to the logic of this argument, American Indians born under the immediate jurisdiction of tribal laws and customs, regardless of birthplace, would owe their principal allegiance not to the United States but to their individual "national communities." Thus an essential precondition to citizenship was the dissolution of tribal bonds. In the case of the Stockbridge Indians of Wisconsin in 1839, for example, Congress dissolved the tribe before conferring citizenship wholesale upon its former members. When widespread protests against the law were mounted by the Indians, Congress enacted a series of measures that ultimately restored the tribe to its "ancient form" but made citizens only of those who chose citizenship over tribal membership.

Other tribes received similar offers from the federal government. An 1855 treaty offered the Wyandot Indians of Kansas Territory "all the rights, privileges, and immunities" of citizenship provided that "their organization, and their relations with the United States as an Indian tribe shall be dissolved and terminated on the ratification of this agreement." The Ottawa Indians in 1862, and the Choctaws, Chickasaws, Muskogees, and Creeks in 1898, likewise acquired citizenship at the termination of their tribal governments. In addition to these collective acts of naturalization, adult members of the Delaware tribe in 1866, the Winnebago tribe in 1870, and the Miami tribe in Kansas in 1873, were given the opportunity by Congress to "elect whether they will dissolve their relations with their tribe and become citizens of the United States."

These assaults upon tribal identity indicate a second way in which the "domestic dependent nation" idea affected the American Indians' quest for citizenship. Implicit in these assorted measures was the assumption that the doctrine of volitional allegiance, like the principle of *jus soli*, had a very limited application when it came to the Native American population. Individual election of citizenship was impossible in the absence of governmental overtures in the form of treaties or specific congressional action. This point was confirmed in federal court decisions after 1868, in response to contentions that by virtue of the Fourteenth Amendment, American Indians could make themselves citizens by severing their tribal ties and voluntarily submitting to the jurisdiction of the United States. In *Elk* v. *Wilkins* (1884), perhaps the most famous of these decisions, the U.S. Supreme Court ruled that John Elk, a native-born Indian who had left his tribe and surrendered himself fully to federal jurisdiction, did not qualify as a citizen. Speaking for the Court, Justice Horace Gray explained that although Indians might be born within the geographical limits of the nation, they owed their immediate allegiance to "an alien . . . dependent power." Thus American Indians could not be native-born citizens "within the meaning of the first section of the Fourteenth Amendment." Incapable of acquiring citizenship by birth, they "can only become citizens in the second way mentioned in the Fourteenth Amendment, by being 'naturalized in the United States,' by or under some treaty or statute." It followed that the "alien and dependent condition of the members of the Indian tribes could not be put off at their own will, without the action or assent of the United States."

The *Elk* v. *Wilkins* decision would be effectively reversed in 1887 by the Dawes Act. In Section 6 of this law the federal government consented in general to recognize the citizenship claims of American Indians in circumstances similar to Elk's: "every Indian born within the territorial limits of the United States who has voluntarily taken up, within said limits, his residence separate and apart from any tribe of Indians therein, and has adopted the habits of civilized life, is hereby declared to be a citizen of the United States." This clause also indicates, however, that federal authorities continued to insist upon the incompatibility of tribal membership and citizenship. Indeed, it was the intention of the sponsors of the Dawes Act to break up tribal organizations by allotting reservation lands in severalty to individual Indians. Those who received such allotments were simultaneously granted the "rights, privileges, and immunities" of citizens.

Ten years after the passage of the Dawes Act, a statute forbidding the sale of liquor to Indians provoked serious challenges that exposed the ambiguities of the citizenship doctrine in the context of tribal relations. The Dawes Act had stipulated that land allotments were to be held in trust by the federal government for twenty-five years. Nevertheless, if the allottee was immediately made a citizen (as the act declared), and if citizenship was incompatible with domestic dependency (as convention implied), then such paternalistic measures as the law prohibiting the sale of liquor were without legal justification. In 1906 Congress attempted to clarify the situation by proclaiming that American Indians remained wards of the United States until the end of the trust period and, consequently, continued to be subject to federal supervision. But this amendment to the Dawes Act produced further confusion. It remained for the Supreme Court in *United States* v. *Nice* (1916) to cut through the confusion by abandoning the antiquated notion that tribal identity precluded the acquisition of citizenship. "Citizenship is not incompatible with tribal existence or continued guardianship," Justice Willis Van Devanter asserted, "and so may be conferred without completely emancipating the Indians or placing them beyond the reach of congressional regulation adopted for their protection."

Despite the arrogance implicit in the *Nice* decision, the Court had cleared the way for uniform American Indian citizenship regardless of tribal attachments. In 1919 all American Indian men who had served in World War I were entitled to claim "full citizenship with all the privileges pertaining thereto." Finally, the general Indian citizenship act of 1924 extended the principle of *jus soli*, without exception, to all American Indians who had not already acquired citizenship through treaties or special legislation, by receipt of allotments, by marriage or military service.

By 1924 the better part of a century and a half had elapsed since the founding of the American Republic. That it had taken so long to achieve a certain consistency on the fundamentals of citizenship stands as evidence of our sometimes uneasy accommodation of the ideals of the Revolution. That the canker of inconsistency continued to fester until an accommodation of sorts was reached is an indication of the strength of those ideals. That violations of the privileges and immunities guaranteed by the Constitution have occurred long after the doctrine of citizenship had reached its logical extension is a reminder that we cannot afford to rest on the laurels of past triumphs.

BIBLIOGRAPHY

Ira Berlin, *Slaves Without Masters: The Free Negro in the Antebellum South* (New York, 1974), describes the emergence of the "free Negro caste" in the Revolutionary era and expertly details the struggle for self-definition on the part of its members up to the Civil War. Alexander M. Bickel, "Citizenship in the American Constitution," in *Arizona Law Review*, 15 (1973), contends that citizenship was nowhere defined in the Constitution because it was "not important." The federal government, especially through the Bill of Rights, was intended to define and protect the "rights of people, not of citizens," and this is fortunate because citizenship is an abstraction, a legal classification that has been selectively applied throughout American history and remains susceptible to revocation. Felix S. Cohen, *Handbook of Federal Indian Law* (Washington, D.C., 1942, repr. 1971), is a standard source book of legal and legislative actions affecting the rights and privileges of the Indians. Linda Grant De Pauw, "Land of the Unfree: Legal Limitations on Liberty in Pre-Revolutionary America," in *Maryland Historical Magazine*, 68 (1973), offers a brief account of the restrictions placed upon blacks, women, servants, minors, and propertyless white males in the Pre-Revolutionary era. Robert Ericson and D. Rebecca Snow, "The Indian Battle for Self-Determination," in *California Law Review*, 58 (1970), provides an excellent assessment of the ambiguities that have plagued federal Indian policies. Congress has historically vacillated between two conflicting policies, one tending toward total separation, the other toward assimilation. Hence, even after the Citizenship Act of 1924 had clarified the status of the individual Indian, the status of his tribal organization remains unsettled. Don E. Fehrenbacher, *The Dred Scott Case: Its Significance in American Law and Politics* (New York, 1978), is the most recent and most comprehensive treatment of this landmark episode. Richard W. Flournoy, Jr., "Naturalization and Expatriation," in *Yale Law Journal*, 31 (1922), pays particular attention to questions of domicile and diplomatic protection.

Frank George Franklin, "The Legislative History of Naturalization in the United States, 1776–1795," in *Annual Report of the American Historical Association*, 2 vols. (Washington, D.C., 1902), recounts the history of federal provisions for naturalization, with special emphasis on the acts of 1790 and 1795. C. Luella Gettys, *The Law of Citizenship in the United States* (Chicago, 1934), is a useful and comprehensive survey of the legal history of citizenship. Jack P. Greene, *All Men Are Created Equal: Some Reflections on the Character of the American Revolution* (Oxford, 1976), defends the intriguing proposition that the Revolutionary generation had a "deep and abiding commitment . . . to *political inequality*." Vincent C. Hopkins, *Dred Scott's Case* (New York, 1967), is especially valuable for its presentation of the opinions offered in dissent by Justices Benjamin Curtis and John McLean. Ernest J. Hover, "Citizenship of Women in the United States," in *American Journal of International Law,* 26 (1932), traces the impact of the Cable Act of 1922 on the status of women. Robert J. Kaczorowski, "Searching for the Intent of the Framers of the Fourteenth Amendment," in *Connecticut Law Review,* 5 (1972–1973), presents an historiographical analysis of this disputed subject and suggests that the framers might indeed have intended to incorporate the "natural rights of free men into United States Citizenship." Linda K. Kerber, *Women of the Republic: Intellect and Ideology in Revolutionary America* (Chapel Hill, N.C., 1980), deals with the public identity of women by developing the concept of "Republican Motherhood." James H. Kettner, *The Development of American Citizenship, 1608–1870* (Chapel Hill, N.C., 1978), is the best single volume on the subject. Kettner's treatment of the colonial period is especially illuminating.

Arnold J. Lien, "The Acquisition of Citizenship by the Native American Indians," in *Washington University Studies,* 13 (1925), Humanistic Series no. 1, describes the troubled history of citizenship in terms of its forced confrontation with tribal identity. John G. A. Pocock's works are essential to an understanding of the classical context of Revolutionary republican citizenship; see especially his essays "Civic Humanism and Its Role in Anglo-American Thought" and "Machiavelli, Harrington and English Political Ideologies in the Eighteenth Century," both in his *Politics, Language and Time: Essays on Political Thought and History* (London, 1972), and his *The Machiavellian Moment: Florentine Political Thought and the Atlantic Republican Tradition* (Princeton, N.J., 1975). John P. Roche, *The Early Development of United States Citizenship* (Ithaca, N.Y., 1949), is a brief but learned account of the subject. James Brown Scott, "Nationality: Jus Soli or Jus Sanguinis," in *American Journal of International Law,* 24 (1930), discusses the international application of both principles. Michael T. Smith, "The History of Indian Citizenship," in *Great Plains Journal,* 10 (1970), serves as an effective introduction to this complicated subject. Chilton Williamson, *American Suffrage: From Property to Democracy, 1760–1860* (Princeton, N.J., 1960), is the best book on this often ignored privilege of citizenship. [*See also* AMERICAN REVOLUTION; BILL OF RIGHTS; CONSTITUTION; EGALITARIANISM; ETHNIC MOVEMENTS; INDIAN RELATIONS; REPUBLICANISM; *and* WOMEN'S RIGHTS.]

CIVIL DISOBEDIENCE

Lewis Perry

THE term *civil disobedience* is almost unique to American politics. Although it has found its way elsewhere as a borrowed Americanism, it is still difficult to translate into other languages. Even in the United States, where the term has been gaining popularity for over a century, it is the subject of sharp disagreement. For some people, civil disobedience refers to dangerous episodes of moralistic defiance of the public order and circumvention of the political process. For others, it is a traditional way of asserting the rights of conscience and defending the interests of minorities, and thus it is essential to reform within the bounds of constitutional government.

The Constitution makes no reference to civil disobedience, although some writers have searched for a right of civil disobedience in the First Amendment's guarantees of free speech and assembly. But since civil disobedience involves the breaking of a law, it is hard to see how it could be a protected right. At various times, there have been proposals to amend the Constitution to empower dissenting groups to nullify laws or to break the law in order to influence public opinion and governmental policy. Thus John C. Calhoun proposed the idea of "concurrent majorities" in order to protect interests peculiar to the antebellum south. Reflecting on social protest movements of the 1960's, Hannah Arendt suggested a constitutional amendment to give civil disobedience a "recognized niche," comparable to that of lobbies, "in our system of government." But it is unclear how such an amendment could have been worded. Almost as soon as she wrote this, other writers were describing civil disobedience as passé or obsolete. Civil disobedience remains, at most, a customary resort of dissenting groups in times of crisis, a dramatic method of seeking change by peace-fully defying laws and accepting the judicial consequences.

Civil disobedience is usually distinguished from conscientious objection, in which minorities are excused from legal obligations (such as military service or oath taking) out of respect for their distinctive beliefs. But the distinction is fuzzy. Sometimes the privileges of conscientious objection have been won through tactics of concerted civil disobedience. Colonial Baptists went to jail, for example, rather than conform to the requirements of the Puritan Standing Order; and New York Quakers similarly defied the Dutch Reformed establishment. Religious freedom could hardly have been secured without demonstrations that significant numbers of people refused to obey repressive laws.

Other distinctions are helpful. Civil disobedience differs from revolution, since it professes allegiance to the political system as a whole even while protesting certain aspects of the law. But here too there are ambiguities. Some abolitionists believed that the overthrow of laws protecting slavery would lead to wholesale renovation of American institutions, and some protesters against segregation or the Vietnam War envisioned similar transformations of what they called the "power structure." Justifying their actions by a morality higher than that which is institutionalized by the state, civil disobedients have frequently believed that specific changes in law will have nearly revolutionary consequences.

Civil disobedience may also be distinguished from law-abiding demonstrations and rallies that have been accorded constitutional protection. In the 1960's, however, demonstrators sometimes deliberately violated traffic ordinances that in themselves had no relation to public controversy. Despite these ambiguities, civil disobedience has generally consisted of overt, nonviolent violations of laws that are themselves at issue. The purpose of such violations has occasionally been to test what the Supreme Court will say about a law. More typically, the purpose has been to demonstrate that a minority (as in the case of censorship laws in the 1870's or the draft in the 1960's) or a regional majority (as in the case of the Fugitive Slave Act in the 1850's) regard the law, however constitutional, as immoral. Civil disobedience is utterly at variance with terrorism, although critics charged in both the 1850's and 1960's that one form of disrespect for authority was conducive to the other.

What we are considering, then, is a complex and sometimes paradoxical tradition. It has arisen from the actions of people who cared deeply enough about public issues to risk fines and imprisonment and yet who generally honored republican conceptions of a society based on consent. Civil disobedients have frequently found justification in revered precedents in America's religious and political history. But they have also identified timeless, international principles in the classical heroism of Antigone and Socrates, in the bravery of Christian martyrs, and in the modern example of Mahatma Gandhi.

The term *civil disobedience* is what rhetoricians call an oxymoron: it harnesses words that are normally contradictory. The word *civil,* to those who came to the New World from Europe, brought to mind the qualities of an orderly member of a commonwealth. A civil man, as distinguished from a savage, was a polite, literate, virtuous Christian who did not need the threat of force to keep him in obedience to the laws of God and man. The word *disobedience* meant sin. The first lines of John Milton's *Paradise Lost* evoked the theme "of man's first disobedience" that brought death and woe into the world. Samuel Johnson's eighteenth-century English dictionary defined disobedience as "violation of lawful command or prohibition; breach of duty due to superiors." Virtually all commentators on government agreed that, except in grave instances of tyranny, good subjects must submit to law. To combine civility, the quality of an upright, virtuous person, with disobedience would have been to speak nonsense. How could someone "peacefully" violate certain laws, when the law itself was the source of peace?

The term conveys such a nice sense of paradox, and it has at times commanded so much public attention, that one would like to know who coined it. But its origin is surrounded with uncertainty. An essay by Henry David Thoreau, "Resistance to Civil Government" (1849), was republished after his death as "Civil Disobedience" (1866). Though not widely noticed in its day, this essay has since become world-famous; and it is the first source that most people have in mind when they use the term. Thoreau actually never spoke of *civil disobedience,* nor did anyone else use the term in print during his lifetime, so far as scholars can discover. It is not clear who was responsible for changing the original title of his essay. Perhaps Thoreau would have disowned it, since in other writings he renounced civility. (Consider the opening words of "Walking" [1862]: "I wish to speak a word for Nature, for absolute freedom and wildness, as contrasted with a freedom and culture merely civil.") Or he might have savored the irony in the title that his essay acquired, since he stressed that persons who pursue comfort and material gain are incapable of truly moral action ("the more money, the less virtue"). Conventional respectability, in his view, was in some ways uncivil. Those who jailed him for refusing to pay his poll tax, although not discourteous, "behaved like persons who are underbred."

The unknown person who coined the term may have meant only to distinguish disobedience to the state from other forms, such as ecclesiastical or familial disobedience. In any case, advocates of civil disobedience in the twentieth century have exploited the term's paradoxical quality. The civil rights leader Martin Luther King, Jr., for example, repeatedly pointed out that segregationists were actually "uncivil" disobedients, whereas "the individual who disobeys the law, whose conscience tells him it is unjust and who is willing to accept the penalty by staying in jail until that law is altered, is expressing at the moment the very highest respect for law." The same paradox could also be turned against unruly protesters. The political scientist Herbert J. Storing commented that "disobedience abounds [in the 1960's], but it has thrust civility aside." In a thoughtful summary of criticism of acts of protest and disobedience, Burton Zwiebach (1975) singled out the argument that "passionately-held ideas" endangered the process of peaceful resolution of conflicts without which "civil society" was impossible.

The history of civil disobedience in America is a sustained exploration of the meanings of civility, that is, of the interplay of consent and obligation in a society created through revolution. Civil disobedients have justified their actions by appealing to higher standards of morality than those which the laws currently codified. These standards have been presented as essential to perfecting the nation so that it deserves obedience. Thus civil disobedients could profess their superior patriotism and conformity to law. To their critics, meanwhile, they jeopardized the accommodating, neighborly qualities that held society together.

Traditional political theory stressed duties of obedience. Both the Bible and experience indicated the horrid consequences that followed when authority was unclear and people behaved like rapacious animals. But settlers of the New World were well aware of abundant examples of groups of Englishmen who held fast to their own views of custom or conscience regardless of the strictures of magistrates. The poor engaged in extrapolitical forms of protest against wrong and affirmation of right; these forms of protest were often highly ritualized demonstrations of the limits to which the law could push an Englishman. Politicians had their own ways of employing mobs and demonstrators. In religion, conflicts between God's law and man's were urgent and unrelenting. From Puritan ministers refusing to wear vestments in accordance with orders from the established church, to bishops refusing to swear allegiance to William and Mary, there were numerous familiar instances of Englishmen who insisted on a realm of conscience inviolate to the expediency of law.

In the decades before the revolution in America, old problems of popular dissent and individual conscience gained new salience. These complex developments may be summarized by noting that two fundamental texts of American civil disobedience date from this period. Jonathan Mayhew's *Discourse Concerning Unlimited Submission and Non-Resistance to the Higher Powers* (1750) turned the tables on political theories that maintained it served the "public good" to obey even imperfect governments. If God enjoined obedience in order to promote public welfare, then when the ruler "turns tyrant, . . . we are

bound to throw off our allegiance to him, and to resist." It was treason against good order and "the body politic" to claim otherwise. The great Baptist leader Isaac Backus' *An Appeal to the Public for Religious Liberty* (1773) similarly conceded that, up to a point, the Bible commanded obedience to earthly powers, but Backus denied that government was ever entitled to enforce particular religious practices. Religious establishments, although pretending to secure "order and the public good," were in fact violators of the order that flowed from "liberty of conscience." Works like these deplored anarchy and disorder: there was no right to resist governments that were merely annoying or mismanaged. The stakes must be high. But these eighteenth-century writers helped to popularize the notion that there were forms of obedience that impaired the public good and displeased God. Thus there must be forms of disobedience that could be described as true commitments to civil order.

The separation of the United States from England and, within the new nation, the separation of church from state combined to raise enduring questions about the limits of obedience. The limits of political obligation became a basic issue of democratic government that had to be tested continually by experience. Compared to other nations created through revolution, the United States was remarkably successful in realizing a stable government without terror or dictatorship. Nevertheless, there remained a murky problem of what constituted sedition. This problem was tested in political controversies, notably over the Alien and Sedition Acts, and in a series of rebellions culminating in the Civil War. It was tested in different ways by reform movements that competed for public influence, particularly when those movements sought to combat slavery as the great national evil.

Most of the proliferating reform movements were concerned with the morals of the people. The models of temperate, virtuous behavior that they encouraged generally enhanced respect for law. Foreign observers commented that these reform movements alleviated threats of disorderliness in a democracy with no established church. But critics charged that antislavery and other movements encouraged neighbors to attack one another's morals and undermined institutions protected by the Constitution. In *Abolition a Sedition* (1839), for example, the Whig publicist Calvin Colton condemned all religious and reform movements that presumed to uphold higher moral standards than the rest of the community. In Colton's view, which was remarkably similar to that of critics of civil rights and antiwar protesters in the 1960's, these movements weakened the mutual civility that was essential to democratic government. It came as no surprise, therefore, that some abolitionists were denying the force of political obligation. Colton and other antiabolitionists coined the epithet "no-governmentism" to brand the words and actions of William Lloyd Garrison and other radical New England abolitionists.

Actually, these abolitionists called their movement the Non-Resistance Society, thus adopting a name associated with the duty of submission to government. They were subjects rather than citizens of the nation, and they were committed to nonviolence regardless of provocations. They indignantly denied that they were Jacobins or incendiaries. When accused of sedition, they could point to an all-encompassing pacifism that, rhetorically at least, made them patient sufferers, rather than supporters or antagonists, of government. But such claims were deceptive in that most of these abolitionists retained an interest in political reform. While swearing absolute fealty to God, whose kingdom was opposed to human government and would in time supplant it, they were also political agitators.

In taking this stance, Garrison and his associates were influenced by radical religious sects that looked forward to Christ's imminent return to rule the world. They were joined by radical pacifists who were dissatisfied with the gradualist logic and tactics of the American Peace Society. They entertained their own visions of international peace conventions that would repudiate all forms of coercion by nations or individuals. But their principal concern was unquestionably with slavery, and they were in search of tactics for carrying out root-and-branch reform that did not cross the boundary into sedition. They might stir up angry mobs, but such episodes only demonstrated the incivility of a nation whose laws tolerated slavery. They were the true champions of law.

In some ways it is surprising how little record the Garrisonian nonresistants left of civil disobedience. A few interrupted church services to speak of slavery and consequently went to jail for disorderly conduct. A few violated policies that segregated local ferries and railways and had some success in altering Jim Crow customs. But they were talkers and agitators more than activists. Not until the 1850's, when the Non-Resistance Society was moribund, did the Fugitive Slave Law lead them to moments of concerted defiance. The earlier commitment of these abolitionists to divine law over human law may have had lingering consequences, but by the 1850's their confrontations with government and society were not always nonviolent. By that time, furthermore, the abstract renunciation of all government gave way to a more selective attitude toward good laws and bad ones.

Thoreau's friend Bronson Alcott was a nonresistant who refused to pay taxes and went to jail as a symbol of his allegiance to God's government. Other writers and intellectuals in Concord, Massachusetts, although not active participants in reform movements, engaged in lively conversation about the individual's relation to government. As early as 1838 Thoreau declined to pay taxes to support the local church. Someone paid for him, however, and he avoided further confrontations with the law by filing a statement of nonmembership in the church. In 1842 he began to refuse payment of the poll tax. Although he was willing to support highways and schools, he wished "to refuse allegiance to the State, to withdraw and stand aloof from it effectually." In July 1846 he spent a night in Concord's jail before his aunt paid that tax for him. By 1849, when his great essay on civil disobedience was published, he spoke of antislavery motives: prison was "the only house in a slave State in which a free man can abide with honor."

Thoreau was neither nonresistant nor abolitionist; he claimed "to speak practically . . . unlike those who call themselves no-government men." There are passages in "Civil Disobedience" that call simply for better government. Yet the essay in large part treats government as a "tradition" or compact, like a church, in which Thoreau as a man of natural conscience wished to have no part. This argument distinguishes him from most other civil disobedients in American history. He professed no interest in a society held together by just laws, no interest in joining with others to effect reforms, no interest in exhausting other means of social or political influence before resorting to civil disobedience. Reforms "take too much time," and he was intent on private matters. It is a source of confusion in American political discourse that his essay became the most famous document of civil disobedience. It earned its fame because of its highly original expression, its relation to Thoreau's other writings that have been canonized in American literature, and its striking, quotable phrases ("Let your life be a counter-friction to stop the machine"; "Cast your whole vote, not a strip of paper merely"). These phrases have appealed to Americans with many different purposes, but they are of little help in understanding civil disobedience.

Much more important, in their own time, than either the nonresistants or Thoreau were the host of northern ministers, editors, writers, and politicians who decided in the 1850's, despite their general respect for public order, that the inroads of the "slave power" into the political system justified a course of disobedience. Respectable opinion began to turn in that direction during the Mexican War; by the mid-1850's, amid controversy over the Fugitive Slave Act, there was in the north, as David R. Weber has put it, "the nearest thing in our history to a popular consensus in support of civil disobedience." This consensus was given expression by popular poets like James Russell Lowell and John Greenleaf Whittier. It was best known through Harriet Beecher Stowe's extraordinarily popular novel *Uncle Tom's Cabin* (1852), particularly in scenes where estimable citizens honored their instincts to aid a fugitive mother and child in disregard of the law.

The furor of the 1850's gave rise to works like Nathaniel Hall's *The Limits of Civil Obedience* (1851), Charles Beecher's *The Duty of Disobedience to Wicked Laws* (1851), and Lydia Maria Child's *The Duty of Disobedience to the Fugitive Slave Act* (1860). Unlike Thoreau, most of these writers maintained that obedience to government was a sacred obligation. But this obligation had limits: the individual was accountable to God for moral behavior and thus was obliged to disobey when the laws contradicted widely recognized principles of conscience. What was then justified, in Hall's words, was "not the forcible resistance which is rebellion, but that which consists in disobedience, with a passive submission to whatever penalty may be thereto attached."

There was considerable disagreement over whether the means of resistance must be nonviolent. Subsequent philosophers have questioned the conflation of private judgment with community standards and have asked why a just person should submit to prison or fines. But in the context of the 1850's civil disobedience was defended, by and large, in terms that upheld public order and political obligation and within limits that distinguished it from sedition. These lines were not easy to draw at the end of the decade when John Brown's attempted insurrection at Harpers Ferry divided antislavery ranks. But the south's rebellion once again enabled antislavery spokesmen to join in praising both the higher laws of conscience and the sanctity of unified government.

After the Civil War civil disobedience remained a well-remembered though seldom-used tactic of reform. The precedents of the 1850's were brought forward, for example, by advocates of freer sexual expression, easier divorce, and even "free love." But that was an extension of freedom of conscience that most abolitionists would have repudiated and that gained little support from community standards in the Gilded Age. Ezra Heywood in Massachusetts and Moses Harman in Kansas, among others, spent terms in prison for openly violating marriage and postal censorship regulations. They gained none of Thoreau's enduring fame. Civil disobedience was tactically successful in the 1850's because northern majorities deplored slavery; it had a very different outcome when used to challenge Victorian codes of sexual morality.

Heywood, Harman, and kindred spirits charged that they were persecuted, not merely because of their advocacy of "love reform," but because of their generally radical views on labor protest and women's rights. It may be simply noted here that strikes, picketing, and boycotts have historically raised issues relevant to civil disobedience, although these are now commonly regarded as contests of economic power rather than demonstrations of conscience or appeals to higher law. It must be stressed, however, that the pursuit of women's rights was linked more clearly to the moral protests of the 1850's.

With bitterness, mid-nineteenth-century feminists witnessed amendments to the Constitution that extended civil rights and political privileges to black males while excluding women. Some of these feminists agitated for women's suffrage as a continuation of the glorious cause of antislavery. Tactically, they were aware of both the repression of "free love" radicals and the moral legacy of the 1850's and Civil War. Feminists generally made the civil disobedients' claim that they were acting out of the nation's deepest principles of law and morality, even as they turned from presenting themselves as dutiful subjects petitioning for redress to making more urgent assertions of inalienable human rights—that is, when they broke laws by voting (as courts declared) illegally, by declining to pay taxes that they had no part in enacting, or by insisting on picketing the White House even when they knew they would be arrested for disturbing the peace. The eventual passage of an amendment to enfranchise women in 1920 vindicated the tactics of nonseditious disobedience in American politics. Militance was compatible with civility. Without those who were willing to go to jail for their convictions, the law of the land would not be perfected.

This logic applied most successfully to reforms that did not encounter massive opposition. The tactical alternatives open to blacks in the century after the Civil War were more limited. Thus when the black labor leader A. Philip Randolph proposed civil disobedience to draft laws during World War II (he had also voiced the idea during World War I), he differed in his view of government from reformers who had expressed reverence for law. "Government," he said, "is an accommodative and repressive organism which is constantly balancing pressures from conflicting social forces in the local and national communities, and without regard to the question of right and wrong, it inevitably moves in the direction of the pressure of the greatest challenge" (quoted in Weber, 1978). Draft refusal and other dramatic protests during wartime were attempts to exert leverage on government, attempts that succeeded under Randolph's leadership in gaining "fair employment" regulations and in integrating the armed services. But in this instance there was no belief in the sacredness of government. Although Randolph denied that he would do anything overtly to aid enemies of the United States, he gave a simple and pragmatic reason for black support of government: without it, white mobs would make things even worse.

To the extent that twentieth-century Americans adopted views of government similar to Randolph's, the ground rules for civil disobedience were utterly changed. Civil disobedience became less a matter of harmonizing individual conscience to the sanctity of the state and more a matter of tactical deployments of power. This change was temporarily obscured by the moral fervor of the nonviolent civil rights movement of the late 1950's and 1960's. Its eloquent leader, Martin Luther King, Jr., spoke of religious renewal and presented visions of an America consecrated to international standards of social justice. Furthermore, King and his followers viewed the federal government as their ally against unconstitutional segregation. Through sit-ins and freedom rides they mobilized public opinion, Congress, the courts, and the executive branch against southern laws and customs. Thus they could conceive themselves as law-abiding citizens and their oppressors, as we have seen, as "uncivil disobedients." Only near the end of his life, when he was seeking ways of dramatizing the problems of poverty, did King begin to describe civil disobedience, in terms similar to Randolph's, as a way of transforming "the deep rage of the ghetto" into political power.

Although King acknowledged Gandhi's influence, he was not trying to drive out an alien government. But King's leadership of the civil rights movement was challenged by Stokely Carmichael and other young militants who did see their situation as analogous to colonial oppression. Some young blacks felt they owed the government no allegiance and were free to adopt any tactics of resistance. The ultimate goal, in Carmichael's famous slogan, was "Black Power." Not only was nonviolence increasingly regarded as a tactic to be chosen or rejected according to the exigencies of the moment; the distinction between civil disobedience and revolution tended to blur.

Despite these problems, black leaders gave civil disobedience a prominence in the 1960's that it had lacked for decades. The influence of these black leaders and their advocacy of civil disobedience among white intellectuals and college students was reinforced by antiwar radicals who had been speaking of civil disobedience since World War II. For the most part, the latter groups were veterans of the non-Communist left who looked to the Judeo-Christian tradition, to Gandhi, to European anarchists, and to Americans like Thoreau for the underpinnings of an independent radicalism. The trials of German Nazis after World War II appeared to strengthen the claim that there were times when citizens were obliged to disobey orders from the state. The threat of nuclear war and America's involvement in Vietnam deepened the feeling that such a time had once again arrived.

One of the prominent antiwar radicals was the Reverend A. J. Muste, a Presbyterian minister and a founder of the American Civil Liberties Union. Muste had sought to fuse Christian nonviolence with labor radicalism in the 1930's, and in the 1950's he spoke of "Holy Disobedience against the war-making and conscripting State." David Dellinger, a World War II draft refuser, gained national attention when the government selected him for prosecution in one of the conspiracy trials of the late 1960's. Of all the civil disobedients of the 1960's, Paul Goodman probably attained the greatest influence among young people. During World War II Goodman had proposed in an anarchist little magazine called *Why?:* "The touchstone is this: *to advocate a large number of precisely those acts and words for which persons are thrown in jail.*" By the 1960's he was one of the gurus of the "new left," urging the importance of symbolic gestures to "draw the line" between the corrupt war-making state and communal freedom.

Many forms of civil disobedience became familiar in that decade, including more tax denial than ever before. Undoubtedly the most characteristic form was draft-card burning. The law that required every young male to carry a registration card seemed to connect the war in Vietnam with governmental invasion of individual rights. Thus, cards were torn up and burned, on occasions varying from street rallies to church services, and with meanings that ranged from protests against an unpopular war to symbolic defiance of the state. Other forms of disobedience varied tremendously in tone and meaning. It would be hard to find much similarity among the peace activists who sailed out to interfere with the launching of nuclear submarines; the Catholic radicals Philip and Daniel Berrigan, who destroyed Selective Service System files and then fled from imprisonment; and the "Yippies" like Jerry Rubin who praised burning dollar bills, smoking marijuana, urinating in the streets, and other demonstrations of "generational conflict." Yet civil disobedience had come to mean so

many things that all these groups might place themselves in a Thoreauvian tradition of letting their lives be counter-frictions to stop the machine. In the trials of Benjamin Spock, William Sloane Coffin, Dellinger, Rubin, and assorted other radicals, the government viewed many different actions as resulting from a single conspiracy. In contemporary accounts, peaceful civil disobedience often merged with "trashings," bombings, and battles with police.

Civil disobedience and violent actions combined to spur politicians and intellectuals to the most sustained discussion of political obligation at any time since the 1850's, perhaps in all of American history. As the political theorist Mulford Q. Sibley wrote in 1965, "dry questions that a few years ago seemed to be appropriate only for desiccated professors of philosophy have suddenly taken on new life" (quoted in Smith and Deutsch, 1972). Some writers on civil disobedience, like Goodman, saw the glimmerings of a reformation of the state. The National Council of Churches tried to identify ground rules to keep civil disobedience peaceful, orderly, and "constant with both Christian tradition and the American political and legal heritage." Others, like Supreme Court Justice Abe Fortas, restricted proper civil disobedience to testing the constitutionality of specific laws (such as those upholding segregation); any other lawbreaking was criminal, perhaps even treasonous. Many intellectuals agreed that lawbreaking, even in a righteous cause, encouraged a general disrespect for law and democratic politics. This was one of the concerns that brought together an influential "neoconservative" movement after the 1960's.

Discussion of civil disobedience died out abruptly in the 1970's. Unlike the 1850's, government was not resanctified; nor was loyalty undermined as extensively as conservatives had feared. After all the earnest pleading for and against civil disobedience, the outcome was probably devoid of consensus on what sovereignty and law actually meant in industrial and urban societies, in a world vulnerable to terrorism and nuclear war.

At most it may be concluded, then, that civil disobedience has been a modest but recurrent theme in American political life. Of the two decades in which it seized most attention, the 1850's and the 1960's, the former may be said to have

CIVIL DISOBEDIENCE

deepened, from a northern point of view, feelings that the state embodied moral purposes and deserved allegiance. The 1960's, however, left the sources of loyalty confusing and undefined. Should other periods of civil disobedience occur, neither the disobedients nor civil authorities could profit from any consensus that had been forged in the most recent episodes. If government was conceived as a valueless entity bowing to the greatest pressures, rather than a moral entity responsive to principled gestures, the very conception of civil disobedience had probably become, as several commentators insisted, obsolete.

BIBLIOGRAPHY

Hannah Arendt, *Crises of the Republic: Lying in Politics, Civil Disobedience on Violence, Thoughts on Politics, and Revolution* (New York, 1972), includes a thoughtful reexamination of the relevance of Thoreau and Socrates to contemporary views of law and politics. Hugo Adam Bedau, ed., *Civil Disobedience: Theory and Practice* (New York, 1969), covers a wide range of post–World War II writings on the subject, preceded by a useful critique of Thoreau. Abe Fortas, *Concerning Dissent and Civil Disobedience* (New York, 1968), is a representative and influential attempt to define limits to the actions of protest movements. Robert A. Goldwin, ed., *On Civil Disobedience: American Essays Old and New* (Chicago, 1969), includes important critical essays by Harry V. Jaffa and Herbert J. Storing, as well as essays defending civil disobedience.

Carleton Mabee, *Black Freedom: The Nonviolent Abolitionists from 1830 Through the Civil War* (New York, 1970), is a survey of nonviolent actions by white and black abolitionists. Wendy McElroy, ed., *Freedom, Feminism, and the State: An Overview of Individualist Feminism* (Washington, D.C., 1982), is a collection of essays on radical feminist attitudes toward the state. William G. McLoughlin, *New England Dissent, 1630–1833: The Baptists and the Separation of Church and State,* 2 vols. (Cambridge, Mass., 1971), contains several chapters discussing the importance of massive civil disobedience in winning religious freedom.

Lewis Perry, *Radical Abolitionism: Anarchy and the Government of God in Antislavery Thought* (Ithaca, N.Y., 1973), analyzes the theories of pre–Civil War radicals concerning violence, coercion, and government. Michael P. Smith and Kenneth L. Deutsch, eds., *Political Obligation and Civil Disobedience: Readings* (New York, 1972), includes many selections for and against civil disobedience that are not found in other anthologies. Although there is no scholarly study of the nineteenth-century "free love" radicals, Taylor Stoehr, ed., *Free Love in America: A Documentary History* (New York, 1979), is an extensive collection of documents; it is also the best introduction to beliefs and tactics of these radicals. Taylor Stoehr, *Nay-Saying in Concord: Emerson, Alcott, and Thoreau* (Hamden, Conn., 1979), is a good example of the attempt to understand pre–Civil War civil disobedience in the light of the 1960's.

Although there is no thorough historical study of civil disobedience, Michael Walzer, *Obligations: Essays on Disobedience, War, and Citizenship* (Cambridge, Mass., 1970), is a work by a political scientist that is both thoughtful and historically well informed. David R. Weber, ed., *Civil Disobedience in America: A Documentary History* (Ithaca, N.Y., 1978), is the best survey of civil disobedience in all periods of American history, ending with J. E. B. Stuart Magruder's attempt to connect Watergate to civil disobedience. Burton Zwiebach, *Civility and Disobedience* (New York, 1975), gives more careful attention to the historical and contemporary meanings of civility than any other work.

[*See also* ANTEBELLUM REFORM; CIVIL RIGHTS MOVEMENT; FEMINISM; LABOR MOVEMENT; PACIFISM AND PEACE MOVEMENTS; RADICALISM; SLAVERY, SECTIONALISM, AND SECESSION; *and* WOMEN'S RIGHTS.]

CIVIL RIGHTS MOVEMENT

Clayborne Carson

ALTHOUGH the literature regarding civil rights movements in the United States usually focuses on the recent attempts of Afro-Americans to gain legal and political status equal to that of whites, efforts to expand the scope of citizenship have been persistent features of American history. Indeed, one of the basic features of American political development has been the gradual incorporation into the political system of previously excluded groups. Major stages in this process have been the extension of voting rights to propertyless white men during the era of Jacksonian democracy, to black men during Reconstruction, and to women in the aftermath of World War I. Civil rights reforms have not only made the American political system more democratic but have also expanded the responsibility of the government to guarantee that citizens are treated equally.

Civil rights movements in the United States have demonstrated the widespread desire of excluded groups to participate fully in the American mainstream and to realize prevailing political ideals; but these movements have also spawned distinctive and, at times, radical goals and ideologies. Thus, the movement toward universal enfranchisement was associated with broader social struggles that profoundly reshaped class, racial, and sexual relations and attitudes. Especially in Afro-American movements, there has been a constant tension between the affirmation of constitutional principles and the inclination to develop alternative institutions, between the desire for inclusion in the American mainstream and the assertion of separatist racial goals that reflect the emergent values of black struggles for advancement.

Although a full discussion of civil rights movements would include examination of the nineteenth-century egalitarian movements and their resulting civil rights legislation, this treatment will focus on the modern black protest movement of the decade from 1955 to 1965. This emphasis is justified by the unique historical significance of the modern black movement. It provided the impetus for passage of major civil rights legislation, most notably the Civil Rights Act of 1964 and the Voting Rights Act of 1965. The black movement also provided tactics, organizing techniques, and ideological precepts for subsequent civil rights efforts involving women, Hispanics, homosexuals, the handicapped, and other victims of discrimination. It should also be noted, however, that the black movement was itself influenced by previous movements—borrowing songs and the sit-in tactic, for example, from the industrial union campaigns of the 1930's.

The symbiotic relationship between the black movement and the women's rights movement has been particularly significant. The success of the antislavery movement and ratification of the Fifteenth Amendment, which prohibited racial but not sexual barriers to voting, prompted women activists to initiate their own suffrage campaign; and the long struggle for an Equal Rights Amendment (ERA) has been, in many respects, an effort to gain rights for women similar to those granted black men under the Fourteenth Amendment. Furthermore, the unexpected inclusion of prohibitions against sexual discrimination in the 1964 Civil Rights Act was a crucial stimulus for the modern women's movement. Yet, despite similarities with the women's movement, the modern black protest movement was unparalleled in size and intensity and in its impact on prevailing attitudes about both individual rights and the role of government as a protector of rights.

The modern black movement also transformed the self-conceptions and aspirations of many participants and initiated a national transformation of Afro-American consciousness. Although this movement resulted in the elimination of many racial barriers confronting blacks and thereby encouraged racial assimilation, the increasingly militant attacks on white authority strengthened feelings of racial pride and potency among blacks. Thus, the unprecedented series of black protests that spread through the southern states and eventually reached northern cities evolved from small-scale, nonviolent demonstrations against segregation into increasingly massive black insurgencies that focused on an ever-widening set of political, economic, and cultural goals. While attempting to change the surrounding society, participants assumed new social roles and some began to see their movement not only as an instrument for change but also as a model for an alternative social order. The modern black movement has been called the "second Reconstruction" in order to connect its achievements with those of the decade after the Civil War; but, as a sustained, widely dispersed social movement, it was more like the antebellum antislavery struggle, which produced similar rapid transformations of Afro-American politics and thought.

PRECONDITIONS

Participants in the modern struggle eventually challenged as well as reaffirmed prevailing political values, but during the early stages of the struggle black discontent was expressed within the narrow ideological range that was permitted by the dominant political system. By the early 1950's, alternative black nationalist strategies were mainly associated with politically insignificant urban ideologues and with the insular Nation of Islam, rather than with effective political activity. Black leftist radicalism had also declined in the face of cold war government repression and the increasing success of black leaders working within interracial liberal coalitions. The U.S. Supreme Court's *Brown* v. *Topeka Board of Education* (1954) decision, which culminated decades of effort by the National Association for the Advancement of Colored People and the NAACP Legal Defense and Educational Fund, Inc., greatly strengthened the influence of black leaders who stressed litigation and appeals to

white-controlled institutions rather than mass mobilizations of black communities. The effectiveness of such leaders reflected the extent to which their goals coincided with the interests of white elites and were consistent with prevailing social trends and political values.

Although the Reconstruction civil rights reforms had been previously undermined by decreasing federal enforcement and emasculating Supreme Court decisions, most notably *Plessy* v. *Ferguson* (1896), the *Brown* decision was a clear indication that powerful national institutions were no longer committed to preserving the southern Jim Crow system. The decision had only a modest immediate impact on southern educational segregation (and none on northern school segregation resulting from housing patterns), but it symbolized the trend toward the nationalization of the racial patterns associated with northern urban society, where segregation was not as stringently maintained through legal sanctions. The decision and the reforms that followed it were aspects of the ongoing incorporation of skilled black workers into the urban labor force. Southern-style segregation survived as a regional anachronism maintained by deeply rooted racial prejudice, terroristic violence against blacks who challenged white domination, and intransigence on the part of southern white politicians, whose power was based on the exclusion of blacks from the one-party southern political system.

Although, in the absence of a sustained black protest movement, American presidents and other federal officials usually ignored the suppression of black civil rights in the South, during the 1940's and afterward civil rights advocates were increasingly able to expose the inconsistencies between southern racial practices and American democratic ideals and thereby spur federal action. The Congress of Racial Equality (CORE), in particular, conducted sit-ins and a "freedom ride" in 1947 (which was a precursor to the 1961 freedom ride) in order to draw attention to segregationist practices. These tactics initially had little impact on southern racism, for CORE lacked sufficient support to sustain a protest movement, especially in the South. Only as southern blacks observed the trend of federal court decisions and became convinced of the federal government's willingness to enforce these decisions—as when President Eisenhower sent troops to Little Rock, Arkansas, in 1957—did they begin to view civil rights protest activity as an effective means of prodding powerful white institutions to act in their behalf.

The *Brown* decision's reassertion of democratic ideals reflected long-term social trends, but the federal government's reluctance to act swiftly and forcefully to enforce legal norms led many blacks to believe that determined protests were required to compel such action. Like other mass movements, the black struggle that arose in the South during the 1950's was born not only of discontent regarding the slow pace of change but also of rising aspirations and optimism regarding the potential effectiveness of collective political activity. Protest activity was initially most likely to occur among black people whose backgrounds and academic experiences made them aware of the contradiction between the treatment accorded them in the South and the racial norms that existed in the most economically advanced sections of the nation. Nevertheless, the protesters' initial faith in the American political system was combined with a growing disillusionment with existing institutions that would not act without the prompting of black protests.

Each stage of the modern black movement was characterized by the use of tactics that were more militant than those favored by the existing civil rights organizations and that appealed to successively larger segments of the black population. The established groups provided important resources for black protesters, but local movements were sustained primarily through the emergence of new organizations and leaders who expressed the increasingly militant sentiments of aroused blacks. Like other social movements, the southern black struggle undermined existing institutions and institutionalized forms of political action while creating new ones. The institutionalization process within the black movement involved the partial rechanneling of spontaneous expressions of discontent into organized efforts to achieve specific reform goals.

MONTGOMERY BUS BOYCOTT

An increasing sense of racial power and assertiveness stemming from the *Brown* decision and from growing black voting strength provided a setting for the first stage of the modern black movement, the boycott against segregated city buses in Montgomery, Alabama. The boycott revealed that many southern blacks, in the aftermath of the Court's decision, believed that legally enforced segregation should be their initial target, because it was the most vulnerable element in the southern system of racial oppression.

The precipitating incident of the boycott movement was the arrest on 1 December 1955 of Rosa Parks for refusing to give up her bus seat to a white man. This arrest of a black woman who was an officer in the local NAACP chapter led to a rapid mobilization of black residents. Long-time community leaders such as Jo Ann Robinson of the Women's Political Council and Edgar D. Nixon, a leader of the Montgomery local of the International Brotherhood of Sleeping Car Porters, played crucial roles in creating a bus boycott organization, the Montgomery Improvement Association (MIA).

MIA members did not, however, choose one of the established leaders as the president of their group. Instead, they selected the recently arrived minister of the Dexter Avenue Baptist Church, the Reverend Dr. Martin Luther King, Jr. A skilled orator who conveyed the growing militancy of blacks while also expressing their goals in terms that attracted extensive and favorable press coverage, King quickly emerged as the principal spokesman for the bus boycott movement. As in subsequent stages of the black struggle in the South, the established leaders were partially displaced by new leaders, such as King, who were better able to translate black discontent into forceful challenges to white domination. Despite protracted white resistance and constant racial intimidation, King and other local leaders sustained black support for the boycott for more than a year before the Supreme Court, reaffirming an earlier federal court decision, declared the Alabama law regarding segregation on buses unconstitutional.

Because it provided a clear demonstration of the ability of a black community to mobilize itself in a forceful movement for change, the Montgomery movement was a stimulus for subsequent protests in many parts of the South. King, who deepened his understanding of Gandhian concepts of nonviolent resistance during the late 1950's, provided a role model for young, college-trained blacks, especially those with strong religious beliefs. In 1957 King and his followers created a new civil rights organization, the

220

CIVIL RIGHTS MOVEMENT

Southern Christian Leadership Conference (SCLC), which they hoped would garner black support for King's nonviolent strategy. Despite the frequent identification of King as the leader of subsequent protest movements, SCLC did not maintain the momentum that had existed during the Montgomery boycott. Until the Birmingham campaign of 1963, the organization did not initiate any similar large-scale mobilizations of black communities. Nevertheless, SCLC did provide an important institutional base and cadre of leadership for subsequent mass insurgencies. James Lawson, a black divinity student affiliated with the Nashville SCLC chapter, recruited a group of student activists who would later play important roles in the civil rights movement.

LUNCH-COUNTER SIT-INS

The pattern of spontaneous protest followed by gradual institutionalization that occurred in the Montgomery movement was also exemplified in the college student sit-ins of 1960. Black college students in the South were encouraged by the Montgomery boycott and admired King, but their discontent was not fully expressed by the cautious tactics of the existing civil rights organizations. As Montgomery blacks had moved outside existing institutional frameworks and created new movement organizations to guide their activities, black students developed their own more militant tactics and created local organizations that reflected their impatience with the status quo and with prevailing strategies for change.

The sit-in movement began on 1 February 1960, when four freshman students at a black college in Greensboro, North Carolina, challenged the custom that prevented blacks from sitting at the lunch counter in an F. W. Woolworth store. Expecting to be arrested and thereby ignite a black boycott of the store, the four students instead were allowed to remain seated at the counter until it closed for the day. Learning of an attractive means for expressing their dissatisfaction with degrading Jim Crow practices, other Greensboro students soon decided to engage in sit-ins themselves. During subsequent weeks, the movement quickly spread to nearby communities containing black colleges, and by the end of February sit-ins had taken place in over thirty communities in seven

states. By mid-April, according to one survey, at least one sit-in had occurred in every southern and border state, and the movement had attracted about 50,000 participants.

Subsequent studies suggesting that students with the greatest awareness of white society and its prevailing values were most likely to join the new protest movement led many scholars to see the movement as a new manifestation of the continuing process of racial assimilation. The mannerly demeanor and conventional political views of the student protesters confirmed that their movement initially emanated less from discouragement or disillusionment than from rising expectations. It was a response to their awareness of the inconsistencies between the existing state of race relations and the better way of life they saw as possible to achieve. Yet, even as the student protesters sought to pursue affluence and to identify themselves with American democratic ideals, they also acquired a distinctive activist élan while immersed in the expanding movement. Most student activists were initially committed to the prevailing political values, but they increasingly saw their own movement rather than the federal government as the most consistent upholder of those values.

Although the existing civil rights organizations offered assistance and advice to the student activists, the sit-in movement led to the formation of local, staunchly independent, student-run protest groups. Even when student sit-in leaders attending a meeting in April 1960 in Raleigh, North Carolina, voted to form the Student Nonviolent Coordinating Committee (SNCC), most were willing to give the new group only temporary status and made clear that its role would be limited to that of coordinating rather than controlling the new upsurge of militancy. The meeting was arranged by Ella Baker of SCLC, but Baker firmly supported students who wished to keep their movement independent of SCLC as well as other existing organizations. Despite the reluctance of student activists to cede control of their movement to any organization, even one of their own creation, SNCC remained in existence and, more than any other regional or national organization, reflected the emergent values of the southern protest movement.

SNCC's statement of purpose, written by James Lawson, affirmed the nonviolent philosophy and the goal of building a "redemptive community" based on "Judaic-Christian traditions," but SNCC remained a losely organized coordinating body with no dominant leader or ideology. Lawson and the other Nashville proponents of Gandhism were unable to impose their ideas on other students who saw nonviolence as a tactical necessity rather than a moral imperative. Although a Nashville student, Marion Barry, served as SNCC's first chairman, and another Nashville activist, John Lewis, later became chairman, SNCC also attracted students whose guiding ideas were more often implicit conclusions drawn from their own movement experiences rather than carefully formulated ideological principles.

As was the case after the Montgomery bus boycott, the intensity of black protest activity declined after the sudden upsurge in enthusiasm. In many border-state communities, the sit-in movement succeeded in desegregating lunch counters, but in other places protest movements withered because of unyielding white resistance and the inability of student activists to broaden their base of black support. The most significant student sit-ins of the fall of 1960 occurred in Atlanta, where students convinced Martin Luther King to be arrested with them at a department store. King was then charged with violating probation on a previous traffic offense and was sentenced to four months at hard labor. Highly publicized telephone calls from John Kennedy to King's wife and from Robert Kennedy to the judge handling the case prompted King's release and thereby increased black support for the Democratic candidate. According to some accounts, this incident made possible Kennedy's narrow victory over Richard Nixon in the presidential race.

As student militancy waned, however, a small number of young activists began to see SNCC no longer as a coordinating body but as an organization that could revive the southern black movement. The first indication of the transformation of SNCC to a more active role came in February 1961, when four SNCC representatives traveled to Rock Hill, South Carolina, to support a local protest movement. Although the jailing of the four students did not succeed in spurring a massive "jail-in" that would overcome white resistance, the incident was an initial stage in the formation of a community of activists who saw themselves as catalysts of a long-term, regional social struggle.

FREEDOM RIDE CAMPAIGN

Such activists discovered a new tactic when CORE initiated a campaign to reveal the extent of segregation in southern transportation facilities. Although CORE's initial freedom ride was a carefully organized bus trip through the South by thirteen activists rather than a social movement, students activists who were not affiliated with CORE quickly adopted the idea and initiated a new phase in the southern black struggle, characterized by the self-conscious use of small-scale, exemplary militancy as a means of stimulating mass mobilizations of black communities.

One of the buses carrying the initial CORE group was attacked and burned by a white mob near Anniston, Alabama, and after further violence in Birmingham, where local police allowed white rioters to assault riders in the terminal, CORE decided to abandon the ride. Student activists observed, however, that the freedom ride tactic had allowed a small group of highly committed protesters to expose racist violence and demonstrate the determination of desegregation advocates. Despite subsequent mob violence in Montgomery, which led the Kennedy administration to send federal marshals to the city, student freedom riders expanded the campaign, focusing on areas of the South in which even token desegregation had not occurred. Resisting efforts by the older civil rights groups to dissuade them, the students formed their own coordinating body, which was informally linked with SNCC, and extended the rides into Mississippi. During the spring and summer, more than 300 protesters were arrested as they arrived in Jackson. Rather than pay fines, most chose to spend much of the summer in Mississippi jails, where they strengthened their commitment to the southern black movement.

By the end of the summer, some of the freedom riders had decided to leave college to devote all of their time to the black struggle. Those who remained in Mississippi were most often affiliated with SNCC, which concentrated its personnel in the rural areas of the Deep South. Other student activists resisted shifting their concern from desegregation issues to the voting rights issue, believing that this would relieve pressures on the Kennedy administration, which had been placed on the defensive by the freedom rides. Thus, even as a voter registration movement arose in the rural Deep South, student-initiated desegregation protests continued in urban areas and soon prompted a dramatic expansion of the southern struggle. Indeed, the Deep South voting rights movement was largely ignored by the national press during the period from 1961 through 1963 as massive demonstrations in southern cities overshadowed the slow mobilization of rural blacks.

ALBANY MOVEMENT

The arrival in Albany, Georgia, of student freedom riders Charles Sherrod and Cordell Reagon became a catalyst for a sustained protest movement that exceeded in size and militancy any preceding series of demonstrations. In the fall of 1961 the two SNCC field secretaries organized nightly workshops on nonviolent tactics and slowly gained the confidence and support of local black leaders. A sit-in on 1 November by nine students spurred older leaders to call a meeting that resulted in the formation of the Albany Movement, a coalition of civil rights groups and local black organizations. Soon afterward, mass rallies were held to protest the arrest of student protesters and the expulsion of two of those arrested from Albany State College. A final stimulus came on 10 December when ten student activists arrived at the Albany train station and were quickly arrested on trespassing charges. During the following week, mass marches were held, and by the end of the week more than 500 demonstrators had been arrested and Georgia's governor had sent 150 national guardsmen to the city.

While local city officials attempted to defuse the explosive militancy by establishing a biracial committee to discuss black demands, the Albany Movement's president, William G. Anderson, invited Martin Luther King to join the protest movement. The Albany protests had already provoked more arrests than any previous local movement, and King's presence and inspirational oratory attracted still more black support. On 16 December, King lead a prayer march to city hall and was arrested along with more than 250 demonstrators. When King announced that he would remain in jail through Christmas, city

officials resumed negotiations to end the crisis. The momentum that had developed during December dissipated rapidly, however, when King unexpectedly announced that he was allowing himself to be released on bail. He accepted a settlement that included desegregation of bus terminals, as mandated by an Interstate Commerce Commission ruling in November, and release of the jailed demonstrators. During subsequent months, as city officials stalled on implementing the concessions that they had granted, SNCC workers tried without much success to revive the movement by engaging in civil disobedience.

The subsequent course of the Albany protests revealed a continuing tension between King's charismatic leadership style and restrained militancy and SNCC's reliance on local initiative and brash challenges to white authorities. Although SNCC organizers were less cautious than King about mobilizing blacks for confrontations with white officials, they found that they could not sustain black enthusiasm without visible gains or incidents that could arouse black emotions. Racial discontent continued to simmer, however, and in July 1962 the return of King and his associate, the Reverend Ralph Abernathy, for sentencing in connection with the December protests became a catalyst for further massive demonstrations. When the two SCLC leaders announced that they would serve their sentences rather than pay fines, Albany blacks quickly mobilized new rallies.

Further arrests and pent-up racial anger pushed the renewed protests outside the bounds set by nonviolent civil rights leaders. Violent clashes took place between brick-throwing black youngsters and police outside the church where a rally was held in support of King and Abernathy. As was the case during the previous December, King's release from jail (after an unidentified black man paid his and Abernathy's fines) eased the crisis atmosphere. The black resentments that had stimulated the movement remained unresolved, and when further protests also ended with rock and brick throwing, King responded by calling a "day of penance" to allow civil rights leaders to regain control of the movement. Although King succeeded in mobilizing blacks for further nonviolent marches and rallies in late June and August, his ability to control the direction of the southern struggle decreased as a result of his failure to achieve a victory in Albany.

The Albany struggle failed to achieve more than modest concessions from white officials, but it established a pattern for subsequent protest movements in southern communities. Unlike the sit-ins of 1960, which had attracted mainly student participants, the Albany protests involved all segments of the local black community. Moreover, although the movement was eventually crushed by the efficient use of police power, it lasted long enough for a distinctive, militant racial consciousness to emerge among black activists. "Freedom songs" based on traditional Afro-American musical forms were an indication of the gradual emergence of distinctive racial norms within the black struggle. As small-scale nonviolent protests evolved into a sustained, regional social movement, the southern struggle attracted participants from many different backgrounds who came to see it as a vehicle for expressing previously suppressed anger and frustration.

BIRMINGHAM CAMPAIGN

After achieving only partial success in Albany, King and other SCLC leaders were determined to build a more effective movement in their new target city, Birmingham, Alabama. King came to Birmingham early in 1963 after the Reverend Fred Lee Shuttlesworth, head of the Alabama Christian Movement for Human Rights, decided that outside help was needed to overcome adamant white opposition to desegregation and other concessions to blacks. SCLC leaders prepared a plan called "Project C" (for "confrontation") and issued a statement of demands that included the elimination of segregated public accommodations and of racial barriers in employment. King's strategy was to provoke confrontations with local white officials, especially the notoriously racist police commissioner Eugene T. ("Bull") Conner, in order to compel the federal government to intervene on behalf of black civil rights.

During April, SCLC officials, along with local black leaders, mobilized a series of sit-ins, marches, and rallies designed to arouse the black community while attracting nationwide publicity and, finally, prompting action by the Kennedy administration. After he had been arrested while leading a march, King explained his protest strategy in a frequently reprinted "Letter from the Birmingham Jail," which responded to the criticisms of local ministers. Insisting that white intransigence had forced blacks to move outside legal channels to express their discontent, King argued that it was necessary to create a crisis so that blacks would not have to wait forever for change. He criticized those who counseled blacks to be patient. Insisting that individuals had a moral responsibility to disobey unjust laws, he added a warning: "I am convinced that if your white brothers dismiss us as 'rabble rousers' and 'outside agitators'—those of us who are working through the channels of nonviolent direct action—and refuse to support our nonviolent efforts, millions of Negroes, out of frustration and despair, will seek solace and security in black nationalist ideologies, a development that will lead inevitably to a frightening racial nightmare."

King's difficulty in maintaining black support for his nonviolent strategy became apparent as the confrontations with white officials escalated, especially when hundreds of black children were arrested after a march early in May. During the following week, despite the efforts of SCLC leaders to regain control over the protest movement, violent clashes occurred between police and black demonstrators. By early May, more than 3,000 blacks had been jailed. On 7 May, after thousands of black demonstrators invaded the business district, Alabama's governor, George Wallace, sent state patrolmen to the city to bolster Conner's forces. A few days later, after bombs exploded at the home of King's brother and at SCLC's local headquarters, hundreds of blacks rushed into the streets and began throwing rocks and bottles at police and firemen. King and other SCLC leaders toured Birmingham's churches, schools, bars, and pool halls, appealing to black residents to refrain from violence, but the crisis eased only when white officials indicated their readiness to make concessions.

The new upsurge of black militancy could not be confined merely to Birmingham, however, for vivid television coverage of the confrontations in that city had stimulated blacks elsewhere to increase their assaults against white domination of their communities. The Southern Regional Council estimated that 930 public protest demonstrations took place during 1963, in at least

115 cities in 11 southern states. Unlike the lunch-counter protests, which were intended to appeal only to college students, the more massive demonstrations of the spring of 1963 offered a form of protest activity that appealed to working-class and poor blacks, some of whom had little understanding of or sympathy for the philosophy of nonviolent civil disobedience. Although nonviolent tactics were still used extensively, southern blacks increasingly used protests as a coercive means of disrupting commerce and provoking white authorities to use violence, which in turn would prompt federal intervention.

CULMINATION OF THE SOUTHERN PROTEST MOVEMENT AND THE MARCH ON WASHINGTON

As black militancy challenged cautious liberalism as well as entrenched racism, the national civil rights leaders and organizations and their liberal allies attempted to reassert their control over the southern movement. President Kennedy responded to the Birmingham violence and to the adamant refusal of Alabama authorities to allow black students to enter the University of Alabama by proposing a new civil rights bill, which called for desegregation of public facilities, granted authority to the attorney general to initiate school-desegregation suits, outlawed discrimination in employment, and barred federal funds from programs and facilities in which discrimination occurred.

When Kennedy met in June with civil rights leaders to appeal for their support, he found that the leaders wanted stronger and more prompt federal action. Seeking to maintain control over the expanding southern protests and to respond to the increasing racial militancy, most of the leaders advocated a march on Washington to exert pressure on Congress to pass a civil rights bill and other legislation to improve black employment opportunities. Despite Kennedy's fear that the march might hamper the administration's effort to pass the omnibus civil rights bill, the black leaders saw the march as an essential means of reasserting their leadership roles in a social movement that was increasingly beyond their control. As veteran black labor leader A. Philip Randolph reportedly told the president,

blacks were already in the streets and it was "very likely impossible to get them off." He and the other leaders succeeded in convincing Kennedy supporters to offer financial backing for the march. As Randolph advised, "If they are bound to be in the streets in any case, is it not better that they be led by organizations dedicated to civil rights and disciplined by struggle rather than leave them to other leaders who care neither about civil rights nor about nonviolence?"

Despite the formation of the United Civil Rights Leadership Council to coordinate planning of the Washington march, the local movements that reached their apogee during 1963 continued with little direction from the national leaders. In many southern towns, local leaders and organizations mobilized blacks to pursue localized demands that were often only loosely tied to the desegregation issue that was the focus of national civil rights legislation. Economic concerns such as jobs and housing became increasingly evident in the rapidly expanding protest movement. In Cambridge, Maryland, for example, Gloria Richardson led a sustained protest movement that attracted considerable support from black workers and eventually forced important economic concessions from white officials. Similar movements developed in Danville, Virginia; Nashville, Tennessee; Jackson, Mississippi; Atlanta, Georgia; and elsewhere. The Southern Regional Council estimated that during 1963 over 20,000 persons were arrested during these protests, compared to about 3,600 arrests in the protests before the fall of 1961. During this year, ten people died in circumstances directly related to racial protests, and at least thirty-five antiblack bombings occurred.

Although the peaceful March on Washington that took place on 28 August 1963 was a historic event that attracted over 200,000 people, it was only an aspect of a larger protest movement. The rally at the Lincoln Memorial was a demonstration of the extent of popular support for civil rights reforms; but Martin Luther King's dramatic closing oration, which called upon Americans to realize the dream of racial equality, did not indicate the full extent of black militancy. Even SNCC leader John Lewis' speech, which was censored by other march organizers, only partially reflected that militancy, despite its references to the economic and political goals that were not being addressed in the pending civil rights legislation. During the months after the march, Malcolm X found urban blacks increasingly receptive to his criticisms of civil rights leaders who, he claimed, had deflected black militancy into less militant channels in order to retain white financial backing. Malcolm himself began to break away from the apolitical stance of his own group, the Nation of Islam, as he tried to develop black nationalist ideas that would offer discontented blacks an effective vehicle for social change rather than only the solace of ultimate religious redemption.

During the period after 1963, urban blacks continued to express their discontent through a variety of tactics, ranging from increasingly coercive nonviolent protests to unorganized, violent outbursts that were outside the control of civil rights organizations. CORE initiated massive sit-ins and marches in northern cities, where the major concern for blacks was employment opportunities rather than desegregation. As an undercurrent of racial anger burst forth in violence, however, it became increasingly evident that many poor and working-class blacks felt they had no institutionalized channels for expressing their discontent. Thus, the black rebellions that occurred in Birmingham in 1963, in New York during the summer of 1964, in Los Angeles during the summer of 1965, and in countless other cities during subsequent years were in part an expression of the rising aspirations that had been stimulated but not fulfilled by the civil rights movement.

Civil rights leaders attempted to provide a political voice for the racial anger, but their tactics and strategies, designed largely to garner the support of northern white liberals, had little appeal among northern urban blacks. Some civil rights activists, notably those affiliated with SNCC and CORE, borrowed ideas from the black nationalist tradition; but few succeeded in mobilizing sustained movements in northern cities. Rejecting the ideal of interracialism in order to assert black control of the civil rights movement, many activists also abandoned the organizing techniques that had been used to mobilize black communities in the early 1960's. Ironically, as black radicals moved beyond the militant racial consciousness that was implicit in civil rights struggles, some adopted forms of racial separatism that led to fruitless pursuit of ideological purity and accommodationist retreats into racial enclaves rather than fostering sustained mass struggles.

VOTING RIGHTS MOVEMENT IN THE DEEP SOUTH

Although the urban black rebellions rarely lasted long enough to acquire an emergent leadership and distinctively appropriate doctrines, these qualities were clearly evident among southern rural blacks who initiated sustained movements and abandoned long-established habits of racial deference. While urban-based activists often adopted the vocabulary of traditional black nationalism in order to express the growing racial militancy and discontent of blacks in cities, years of civil rights activism in the Deep South produced new forms of militant racial consciousness rooted in the cultural traditions of southern blacks. The proliferation of black separatist ideologies and ideologues that occurred in northern urban areas during the late 1960's was not as apparent in the Deep South, where black leaders less often used explicit separatist doctrines while seeking to mobilize blacks to oppose white authority.

Although individual blacks in the rural areas of the Deep South had protested throughout the 1950's against the widespread denial of voting rights to the race, these isolated efforts did not become a social movement until the early 1960's, when student activists entered communities in southwest Georgia, central Alabama, and Mississippi. One of the first organizers to arrive was Robert Moses, a former graduate student at Harvard, who had left his high-school teaching job during the summer of 1961 to assist C. C. Bryant, a veteran NAACP leader in McComb, Mississippi. Moses and the young activists who left jobs or college to come to McComb recognized the necessity of gaining the trust and support of local leaders. Most agreed with Bryant's view that the civil rights movement in Mississippi should focus on the goal of voting rights rather than desegregation of public facilities.

Nevertheless a few direct-action advocates also came to McComb and received an enthusiastic response from local black high-school students. When students were arrested after a sit-in, the entire SNCC staff unexpectedly became involved in direct action. On 4 October staff members joined a student march to protest the expulsion from high school of a student activist and the killing nine days earlier of a black man, Herbert Lee, by a member of the Mississippi House of Representatives. As a result of the march, most members of the SNCC staff were arrested and later convicted on various charges. In December, when they were released on appeal bond, they temporarily abandoned their work in the McComb area.

After regrouping in Jackson, SNCC workers and black residents of Mississippi learned from their experiences and gradually developed a strategy emphasizing the development of grass-roots leadership and focusing on the goal of voter registration. During 1962 the Council of Federated Organizations (COFO) was formed to coordinate the work of the civil rights groups in Mississippi, and Moses became director of COFO's voter registration effort. Rather than depending on civil rights workers from outside the state, COFO's staff was composed largely of young black Mississippians. Because of racist intimidation, the staff had little success in registering black voters until the end of 1962, when they were able to weaken bonds of economic dependence by distributing food to needy blacks in the Mississippi Delta region. Afterward, the Mississippi voting rights struggle gradually became a major social movement that profoundly altered the attitudes of black participants. In communities where the movement was strongest, resourceful local leaders emerged and durable organizations were formed. Black people who had been socialized to accept subordinate status slowly acquired a new sense of pride and collective power, and black organizers increasingly identified with the racial values that developed in the course of the struggle.

MISSISSIPPI SUMMER PROJECT OF 1964

Numerous acts of violence against civil rights workers and the assassination on 12 June 1963 of NAACP leader Medgar Evers in Jackson led to a revision of the initial strategy emphasizing the building of locally based movements. Although still skeptical about relying on organizers from outside the state, COFO approved the use of northern white student volunteers to conduct

a mock election in the fall of 1963. This demonstration of the desire of blacks to vote for their own candidates led COFO to approve a plan, suggested by white lawyer and political activist Allard Lowenstein, to bring large numbers of white volunteers to Mississippi during the summer of 1964. Believing that the presence of large numbers of white students would inhibit violence against blacks, Moses successfully argued for the plan, despite strong resistance from black COFO staff members, who believed that the volunteers would undermine their long-term effort to build self-confidence and feelings of self-sufficiency among black Mississippians.

The Summer Project brought over 600 volunteers to Mississippi and greatly increased national awareness of the extent of racial repression in the state. In June, even as the volunteers were arriving, three civil rights workers were murdered outside Philadelphia, Mississippi, where they had gone to investigate a church burning. The murder of the civil rights workers and the continuation of violence elsewhere in the state precipitated more intensive investigations by the Federal Bureau of Investigation, but the degree of overall success of the Summer Project was a matter of dispute. On the one hand, after the summer the level of violence directed against civil rights workers decreased and there was greater northern support for stronger federal action to protect black voting rights in the South. The Summer Project also resulted in the creation of new black institutions, such as the Mississippi Freedom Democratic Party (MFDP) and the Freedom Schools. On the other hand, the failure of the MFDP delegation to gain recognition as the legitimate Mississippi representatives at the 1964 Democratic National Convention raised new doubts among militant civil rights workers about whether they should work within the framework of conventional, interracial liberalism. Moreover, the presence of the white volunteers led to arguments among black civil rights workers about the appropriateness of white organizers in black communities.

The decision of the MFDP delegation to reject the compromise offered by national Democratic leaders, who proposed that the challengers accept two at-large seats rather than the seats claimed by the all-white regular delegation, marked a turning point in the evolution of the southern struggle. Afterward, the national civil rights organizations and their liberal allies continued to pursue new civil rights legislation, but many veteran participants in the southern struggle had begun to seek more fundamental social change. The increasingly radical orientation of SNCC derived from the distinctive political values that emerged within the southern struggle.

RADICALIZATION OF THE SOUTHERN STRUGGLE

The series of demonstrations that began in Selma, Alabama, early in 1965 were the last of the type of massive, sustained protests that had become common in the South since 1962. As in Birmingham, the SCLC attempted to provide leadership for the Selma protests in order to keep them nonviolent and to use them as a means of prodding the federal government to act on behalf of black voting rights. To an even greater extent than in Birmingham, however, militant young activists, often associated with SNCC, challenged King's leadership, especially after 7 March, when Alabama police routed a group of protesters as they were attempting to march from Selma to Montgomery.

The conflict between SCLC and SNCC over strategy was based on basic differences regarding the objectives of the black struggle. While SCLC officials typically sought to organize and direct nonviolent protest campaigns in order to achieve specific civil rights objectives, SNCC workers saw themselves as the catalysts of long-term black movements that would result in the creation of powerful, independent, black-controlled institutions. Publicity about the violence directed against black demonstrators in Selma prompted the Lyndon Johnson administration to submit and later gain passage of new voting rights legislation, but this would be the final major civil rights victory to be achieved through massive nonviolent protests. SNCC workers, for their part, would use the Selma-to-Montgomery march organized by SCLC as an opportunity to initiate another stage in the southern struggle by helping to forge new institutions for discontented blacks.

SNCC's increasingly separatist political orientation became evident in Lowndes County, a rural area between Selma and Montgomery that had been almost untouched by previous civil rights efforts. Beginning in March 1965, Stokely Carmichael and other SNCC organizers worked with local black leaders to build an independent political party, the Lowndes County Freedom Organization, which became better known by its symbol, the black panther. Although the Black Panther party was an all-black group that was often portrayed as a manifestation of the new separatist trend in the southern movement, SNCC workers recognized that most of the local leaders with whom they worked preferred to emphasize the goal of achieving black political power rather than realizing visionary black nationalist ideals.

The Black Panther party was another of the many institutions created in response to the southern black movement, but it also represented a clear indication that the movement had moved beyond its initial civil rights objectives toward new racial goals. The implicit militancy represented by the black panther symbol indicated the extent to which the racial consciousness of southern blacks had been reshaped by years of struggle. This transformation of consciousness was later symbolized by the "Black Power" slogan, a shortened version of a Lowndes County rallying cry, "Black Power for Black People." Although the Black Power slogan was variously defined by proponents and often misunderstood by critics of black militancy, its popularity among blacks indicated the new sense of pride and confidence that had developed as a result of collective struggle. The new racial consciousness indicated that many Afro-Americans were determined to use hard-won human rights to improve their lives in ways befitting their own cultural values.

The growing gulf between the emergent racial values and those of the American mainstream contributed to the dilemma faced by black activists at the end of 1965. While black power advocates sought to create new bases of power in black-controlled institutions such as the Black Panther party, their militancy led to a deterioration of the liberal civil rights alliance that had made possible previous gains. The loss of white liberal allies also increased the likelihood that white authorities could suppress black demonstrations without fear of federal intervention. Thus, several of the most deadly confrontations between police and southern black demonstrators occurred after 1965. In 1968, for example, a police assault against student protesters in Orangeburg, South Carolina, left three students dead. In 1970 two students at Jackson State College in Mississippi were killed by police during a demonstration. Even nonviolent civil rights protest activity came to be seen by blacks as counterproductive in the face of a "white backlash" against black militancy. Efforts to achieve further civil rights reforms continued, but usually these reforms—such as the 1968 federal legislation against housing discrimination—were not prompted by mass protest movements.

DECLINE OF THE BLACK PROTEST MOVEMENT

The civil rights groups that had originated during earlier black struggles tried with only modest success to sustain the southern struggle and to extend it into the North. In 1966, King's SCLC sought to use the nonviolent tactics of the southern struggle to confront the housing and employment problems facing blacks in Chicago. This effort attracted the active support of only a small number of black residents and prompted violent resistance from white residents. During the final year of his life, King initiated a Poor People's Campaign that was designed to achieve a major economic restructuring of the United States, but this effort further weakened King's support among whites and had shown slight promise of success before King was assassinated in Memphis on 4 April 1968.

SNCC was no more successful in extending its operations into the urban North, although during 1966 and 1967 its chairmen, Stokely Carmichael and H. Rap Brown, were accused of inciting several riots. Actually, the SNCC leaders joined the ranks of urban militants who tried unsuccessfully to provide ideological guidance for discontented blacks at the bottom of the urban social order. Unlike the grass-roots leaders of the southern struggle, the militants were more often media spokesmen rather than insurgent leaders. The spontaneous outbreaks of urban violence provided a setting in which self-appointed black leaders sought to capitalize on the racial disorders in order to gain concessions from white authorities or to gain adherents for particular racial ideologies and programs.

Although, to some degree, the black urban rebellions of the period from 1965 through 1968 were another stage in the successive waves of black insurgencies, they represented racial discontent that could not be assuaged simply through more civil rights legislation. The civil rights reforms of the 1960's eliminated Jim Crow practices and most forms of overt discrimination, but many of the economic inequities that had contributed to black discontent were not affected by the reforms. Although President Lyndon Johnson suggested in 1965 the need to move beyond civil rights reforms that simply opened "the gates of opportunity" rather than enabling blacks to walk through the gates, his Great Society programs, like the civil rights reforms, sought to equalize opportunities rather than redistribute wealth, and were designed to divert mass black militancy into institutionalized channels. Antipoverty programs eliminated some social inequities, but they also lessened the possibility that blacks would seek to redress their grievances through noninstitutionalized means. Many black activists retained the militant rhetorical styles of the black struggle, but they were more apt to focus their efforts on gaining access to white-controlled resources rather than on mobilizing blacks to confront white power.

Although the most effective organizers in the southern struggle had been those whose attitudes had been shaped by the implicit racial consciousness produced by local movements, militant black ideologues of the late 1960's sought to convert discontented blacks to one of the competing black nationalist ideologies in order to prepare them for future struggles. Instead of viewing their ideas as outgrowths of earlier civil rights struggles, urban black nationalists were increasingly likely to draw their insights from sources, such as the Nation of Islam or third-world revolutionary movements, that had not been part of those struggles. Even the Oakland-based Black Panther party, which was inspired by the black movement in Lowndes County and had considerable appeal for young urban blacks, did not derive its ideas or its leadership from a mass movement. Instead it was a leader-centered group that attempted, with only moderate success, to use public displays of arms and pseudo–Marxist-Maoist revolutionary rhetoric in order to gain a mass following. Emphasis on forging an ideological basis for future struggles led to intense and sometimes deadly battles among black leaders. Competition among militant leaders spawned brash rhetoric that expressed widely shared racial anger but also prompted white repression.

Calls for revolution by black militants were a response to the unwillingness of white leaders to move rapidly to eliminate economic inequities or to share political power with blacks, but the revolutionary rhetoric reflected the disintegration of the black movement rather than its culmination. There was a growing disjunction after 1968 between the extreme rhetoric of black separatists and radicals and the far more cautious and insular political activity that characterized most black communities. Violent black rebellions occurred with increasing frequency each year until 1968, but these insurgencies were not initiated or directed by the black militant leaders who gained prominence as a result of them.

Despite the tenuous relationship between black nationalist leaders and the urban racial violence of the mid-1960's, the federal government's repression of black militancy focused on the ideological leadership that was presumed to be the basis of the black struggle. Even King, who remained an advocate of nonviolence despite his increasingly radical economic goals, was portrayed in a 1968 FBI memorandum as a potential black " 'messiah' who could unify and electrify the militant black nationalist movement." Although the FBI's counterintelligence program (COINTELPRO) initiated numerous covert and often illegal plots against SNCC, the Black Panthers, and other groups, the decline of mass militancy among blacks during the late 1960's was only partially the result of government repression. Police raids and arrests contributed to this decline, but the ability of police agents to exacerbate already existing intrablack conflicts was also a major factor causing discouragement among blacks about the feasibility of militant collective action.

As in other social movements, the intellectual ferment that was stimulated by the black struggle produced ideas capable of mobilizing black communities, but the ferment also gave rise to intellectual elitism, ideological rigidity, and destructive competition among articulate militant leaders. Constant calls for racial unity did not forestall increasing disunity, even within the black militant community. Thus, internal as well as external forces contributed to the deterioration of sustained efforts by black organizers to unite black communities and to provide appealing and potentially effective tactics for discontented blacks.

LEGACY OF THE BLACK STRUGGLE

To a greater extent than any social movement since the populist crusade of the late nineteenth century, the black struggle of the 1960's dramatically expanded the political influence and institutional resources of a substantial segment of the American populace. It established a foundation of political rights and protest tactics that has allowed blacks and others to eliminate many social inequities. In a broader sense, the black movement initiated a profound and historically exceptional transformation of prevailing attitudes about the nature of citizenship rights and about the role of government in protecting those rights. Protest activity has had a declining importance in black political life, but this is partially because of the ability of blacks to make increasingly effective use of institutionalized political channels, particularly the electoral process, to seek to redress grievances. Although a high degree of black political alienation still existed after the 1960's, black leaders have increasingly sought to achieve their goals through existing political means rather than through the mobilization of black protests and the creation of new black-controlled institutions.

The black struggle also contributed to a major transformation of racial attitudes. The southern protest movement stimulated intellectual and cultural creativity in black communities throughout the United States during the late 1960's and early 1970's. Not only did black Americans gain a new conception of themselves, but the black consciousness and black studies movements made nonblacks more aware of the cultural and intellectual contributions of Afro-Americans. The literary and artistic revival of the late 1960's and 1970's affected blacks in every section of the nation; in addition, more than was the case for the Harlem Renaissance of the 1920's, the modern black revival acquired a more secure institutional base.

Yet despite its historical importance, the black struggle of the 1960's can also be viewed as an

230

ephemeral deviation from the main currents of modern American history. The effectiveness and rapid expansion of black protest activity of the decade before 1966 resulted less from the intrinsic power of the black movement than from the willingness of the federal government to respond, even if belatedly, to certain civil rights demands. A mass protest movement temporarily supplanted the more conventional tactics of the NAACP and liberal reform groups during a period when national political institutions failed to act, without vigorous prodding, against overt forms of discrimination that were anachronistic, increasingly unpopular, and damaging to the nation's interests. The radicalization process that occurred in the black struggle, as in other such social reform movements, produced radical goals and alternative institutions to achieve those goals, but the values of participants were transformed far more rapidly than were the social and institutional structures of American society. Despite its success in mobilizing and providing important roles for thousands of poor and often ill-educated black people, the black struggle ultimately failed to reverse the trend toward the domination of reform movements by college-trained experts who seek to appeal to powerful institutions rather than mobilize mass movements to confront such institutions.

The extent to which civil rights gains can be protected through conventional political activity rather than mass mobilization remains uncertain, for the gains remain vulnerable to changes in prevailing political sentiments. Controversy has continued during the 1970's and 1980's regarding the extent to which government may impose specific remedies, such as affirmative action in employment and busing to achieve school integration, in order to equalize the conditions of life for blacks and other groups that encounter discrimination. The U.S. Supreme Court *Regents of the University of California* v. *Bakke* (1978) decision, which overturned a quota system for minority admission to a medical school, suggested that earlier civil rights gains might be reversed. In the main, however, the civil rights gains of the 1960's have survived changes in the political climate and remain consistent with prevailing social trends and national interests. They provide a foundation for future efforts to improve the lives of blacks and other victims of discrimination.

BIBLIOGRAPHY

The literature on the civil rights movement is extensive, but few works are comprehensive or recognize the extent to which the southern black struggle was a variegated, locally based social movement rather than simply a campaign for civil rights legislation directed by national leaders and organizations. Although there are numerous narratives of particular protest campaigns, biographies of nationally prominent civil rights leaders, and studies of legislative reform efforts, there is a paucity of detailed studies regarding the evolution of local movements.

Among the studies that emphasize the efforts of national civil rights organizations to expand the constitutional rights of Afro-Americans, the most comprehensive for the period before 1954 is Richard Kluger, *Simple Justice: The History of Brown v. Board of Education and Black America's Struggle for Equality* (New York, 1975). Historical overviews of the post-1954 period include Robert H. Brisbane, *Black Activism* (Valley Forge, Pa., 1974); and Harvard Sitkoff, *The Struggle for Black Equality, 1954–1980* (New York, 1981). Also useful are the essays in *The Negro Protest*, vol. 357 of *Annals of the American Academy of Political and Social Science* (1965). The federal government's changing responses to the civil rights movement are analyzed in Carl M. Brauer, *John F. Kennedy and the Second Reconstruction* (New York, 1977); James C. Harvey, *Black Civil Rights During the Johnson Administration* (Jackson, Miss., 1973); J. Harvie Wilkinson III, *From Brown to Bakke: The Supreme Court and School Integration: 1954–1978* (New York, 1979); and Harris Wofford, *Of Kennedys and Kings: Making Sense of the Sixties* (New York, 1980).

The leadership role of Martin Luther King, Jr., has been the topic of numerous works, although the resulting emphasis on King's use of orchestrated protests has often obscured the degree to which he reacted to rather than controlled mass protest activity in the South. King's own account of his emergence as a civil rights leader, *Stride Toward Freedom: The Montgomery Story* (New York, 1958), should be supplemented by J. Mills Thornton III, "Challenge and Response in the Montgomery Bus Boycott of 1955–1956," in *Alabama Review*, 33 (1980). Of the many King biographies, the best are David L. Lewis, *King: A Biography*, 2nd ed. (Urbana, Ill., 1978); and Stephen B. Oates, *Let the Trumpet Sound: The Life of Martin Luther King, Jr.* (New York, 1982). Despite considerable evidence of King's declining influence among militant blacks, David J. Garrow argues in *Protest at Selma* (New Haven, Conn., 1978) that King remained in control of the 1965 demonstrations in Alabama. Garrow's *The FBI and Martin Luther King, Jr.: From "Solo" to Memphis* (New York, 1981) should also be consulted.

The black protests of the 1960's produced a vast scholarly literature, which was itself influenced by the ideological currents of the black militancy. Some of the best scholarly studies are collected in James A. Geschwender, ed., *The Black Revolt* (Englewood Cliffs, N.J., 1971). Historical accounts of the leading civil rights protest organizations include Clayborne Carson, *In Struggle: SNCC and the Black Awakening of the 1960's* (Cambridge, Mass., 1981); and August Meier and Elliott Rudwick, *CORE: A Study in the Civil Rights Movement, 1942–1968* (New York, 1973). Howell Raines, *My Soul Is Rested: Movement Days in the Deep South Remembered* (New York, 1977), is a compilation of interviews with participants. Other useful autobiographical accounts include James Forman, *Sammy Younge, Jr.: The Story of the First Black College Student to Die in the Black Liberation Movement* (New York, 1968), and *The Making of Black Revolutionaries* (New York, 1972); Martin Luther King, Jr., *Where Do We Go From Here: Chaos or Community?* (New York, 1967); Malcolm X [Little], with Alex Haley, *The Autobiography of Malcolm X* (New York, 1965); and Cleveland Sellers and Robert Terrell, *The River of No Return: The Autobiography of a Black Militant and the Life and Death of SNCC* (New York, 1973). One of the few detailed accounts of the evolution of a local protest movement is William H. Chafe, *Civilities and Civil Rights: Greensboro, North Carolina, and the Black Struggle for Freedom* (New York, 1980). Also perceptive in describing the impact of the black movement is Sara Evans, *Personal Politics: The Roots of Women's Liberation in the Civil Rights Movement and the New Left* (New York, 1979).

[*See also* ANTEBELLUM REFORM; CIVIL DISOBEDIENCE; EGALITARIANISM; ETHNIC MOVEMENTS; FEMINISM; RACE AND RACISM; RADICALISM; RECONSTRUCTION; *and* WOMEN'S RIGHTS.]

CIVIL SERVICE REFORM

Ari Hoogenboom

IT was no coincidence that the spoils system and democracy, with mass-based political parties, developed simultaneously in Jacksonian America. Organizing the huge electorate to win frequent political campaigns required great efforts and contributions by a host of devoted party workers. The most obvious source of workers and money was local, state, and national civil servants. Politicians holding offices that controlled appointments were patrons, and the civil service jobs with which they rewarded their workers were the patronage. A civil servant worked for his party as well as the government, and in addition contributed to his party a percentage of his salary, called a political assessment. Defeat at the polls resulted in wholesale dismissals, because, as William Marcy declared, "to the victors belong the spoils."

With the Whigs and Democrats alternating their control of the federal government, the incoming party replaced outgoing party workers in the public service in 1841, 1845, 1849, and 1853. By 1857, when President James Buchanan succeeded his fellow Democrat Franklin Pierce, spoils practices were even used in intraparty factional struggles. "Pierce men are hunted down like wild beasts," Marcy complained and, while still believing that the spoils belonged to the victors, reputedly observed that he had never intended to pillage his own camp. With the triumph of the Republican party in 1860 and the outbreak of the Civil War in 1861, Abraham Lincoln's administration had an added incentive to purge the civil service of Democrats. Government workers who sympathized with the opposition party were possibly—and if southerners, probably—traitors. The spoils system had reached its zenith.

The progress of the spoils system raised op-

position. The partisans of ousted civil servants, who were out of power, protested spoils practices. When their enemies occupied the White House, such diverse politicians as Josiah Quincy (a Federalist), Thomas Hart Benton (a Jacksonian), Henry Clay and Daniel Webster (both Whigs), and John C. Calhoun (a states' rights Democrat) feared executive abuse of patronage. Those in power extended the spoils system, while those out of power protested its spread. But when the "outs" became "ins," they, too, extended the spoils system.

Rotating offices among political partisans hampered the bureaucracy as well as the party out of power. Andrew Jackson's insistence that government duties were "so plain and simple that men of intelligence may readily qualify themselves for their performance" exaggerated the simplicity of civil service jobs and the ease with which skills could be acquired. In short, Jackson thought the public service needed new blood more than it needed experience. But work in political campaigns was not the best training for jobs that were often specialized and complicated. Under the spoils system, efficiency suffered and the career service was whittled to the bone, leaving only a skeleton crew of experienced, knowledgeable, higher-level civil servants to provide continuity and train new appointees. Attempting to make the spoils system meet the needs of government service, Congress in 1853 classified most of the 700 Washington-based clerks into grades and required incumbents as well as new appointees to be examined before receiving commissions. If properly administered, these noncompetitive "pass" examinations would keep incompetents out of government service. Neither public opinion nor political parties had called for these examinations; they were required by the needs of the service. Before the Civil War no one outside government circles and few within were interested in civil service reform.

THE JENCKES BILL

During the Civil War the bureaucracy swelled abnormally, and the rotation of officeholders increased. The spoils system controlled more offices than before, but the stress of war exposed its deficiencies and stimulated interest in reform. Secretary of State William H. Seward in 1862 requested information from John Bigelow, his consul in Paris, on the French civil service, and Bigelow in 1863 responded with an analysis of the nonpartisan personnel practices in the ministry of finance, which included open competitive examinations, secure tenure, promotions, and a retirement system. When in 1864 Senator Charles Sumner, aware of reform developments in the British civil service, introduced in Congress legislation providing for competitive examinations administered by a civil service commission, he was "astonished at the echo" to his "little bill" from outstanding publications, distinguished intellectuals, and important businessmen. These same elements supported Congressman Thomas A. Jenckes of Rhode Island, the father of civil service reform, when in December 1865 he introduced his bill to reform the civil service.

Jenckes' bill applied to all civil servants (except those in the highest policy-making positions and the lowest-paid postmasters); provided for open competitive examinations for appointments, which were to be made at only the lowest level; required that all higher positions be filled by promotion determined by competitive examinations; and administered the system with a three-member commission. Though he borrowed freely from the British, Jenckes' bill was ahead of British practice, which until 1870 restricted competitive examinations to political favorites. The Jenckes bill was the prototype of subsequent legislative proposals to reform the American civil service. It took seventeen years of agitation to enact the Pendleton bill, which was less exacting in its provisions and less sweeping in its application than the Jenckes bill.

On 13 December 1866 Jenckes reported a revised version of his bill exempting postmasters from its operation. Though the press reacted favorably to Jenckes' proposal, Congress tabled (postponed indefinitely) the Jenckes bill, which would curtail congressonal as well as executive control over patronage and ultimately neutralize the civil service. The vote was surprisingly close and, though bipartisan, revealed that Republicans inclined more toward civil service reform than Democrats. Republicans on 2 March 1867 did pass, over President Andrew Johnson's veto, the Tenure of Office Act (requiring the Senate to approve the removal of officers whose appointment it had confirmed) to protect radical officeholders from Johnson's threat to "kick" them out. With the idea prevalent among Republicans that executive power needed clipping, many viewed the Tenure of Office Act as a reform measure. It was, however, an act of political expediency rather than of reform.

Since patronage and power were synonymous, the struggle between Andrew Johnson and radical Republican members of Congress aroused interest in the civil service. The Tenure of Office Act and to a lesser degree the Jenckes bill were radical attempts to prevent Johnson from exploiting the civil service. In time some of those whose interest in the public service was kindled by Reconstruction would become convinced of the worth of civil service reform and less certain of the value of radical Reconstruction. These were the self-styled "best people" (who formed a social and intellectual elite), many of whom had joined the Republican party during the antislavery crusade and were rewarded with office, particularly in the diplomatic corps, by the Lincoln administration. They tended to be lawyers, editors, clergymen, professors, and businessmen (with mercantile and financial rather than industrial interests), to be from old-established New England families, and to be laissez-faire in their political philosophy, which inclined them toward free trade, hard money, anti-imperialism, and civil service reform. By 1867 these men felt that they were being eliminated from politics (by Johnson and his conservative cohorts as well as by the radicals, to whom this group lent uneasy support), while they perceived a post–Civil War America indulging in an orgy of political corruption. They also recognized that the Jenckes bill, while aiming to improve the public service, would also cripple the power of the spoils politicians (who relied on their organizations to win elections) and enhance the influence of the "best people" (who wished to exploit issues in campaigns).

For example, the Jenckes bill received powerful support from the editor of *Harper's Weekly*, George William Curtis. In the fall of 1866 his friend Charles Eliot Norton had launched a campaign to elect Curtis United States Senator from New York. Though "several journals, both East and West," supported him, Curtis realized his chance of success was slim since he was "not enough of a politician for the purposes of the men who make Senators." Curtis was right; in January 1867 the legislature's Republican caucus (where the key vote was taken) selected Roscoe Conkling. In good party spirit Curtis praised Conkling, but in March 1867, answering either to his barometric sense of public opinion or to personal frustration with politics, Curtis called for the passage of the Jenckes bill. Curtis would become the civil service reform movement's most conspicuous and devoted leader.

Like New York Republicans, Andrew Johnson turned his back on the men of respectability and culture. Reformers were enraged when he dismissed as minister to Austria the distinguished historian John Lothrop Motley. "I am afraid," E. L. Godkin, editor of the *Nation,* wrote George Perkins Marsh, minister to the Italian States, "you will not long be spared, or any other man of character and standing in the service of the government." In addition, reformers were so disturbed by political corruption in the North—legislators were reputedly purchased like "meat in the market"—that its elimination (along with Republican politicians who ignored reformers) became more important to them than the radical Reconstruction of the South.

The support prominent publicists like Godkin and Curtis gave civil service reform was buttressed by the work of an obscure government clerk employed by Congress's Joint Select Committee on Retrenchment. Cooperating closely with Jenckes, Julius Bing did his best "to keep the agitation alive all round" by writing magazine articles, but especially by preparing Jenckes' 1868 report, "Civil Service of the United States," the celebrated source book for reformers. Summing up the responses to questionnaires Bing sent to 446 officers, whose nearly 13,000 subordinates would be affected by the proposed Jenckes bill, the report stressed that of these officers 362, whose subordinates numbered 11,561,

decidedly favored reform. "I may flatter myself," Bing wrote Jenckes in June 1868, "that the strong breeze raised in & out of Congress is at least in part, due to my efforts." But that breeze, which blew along the northeastern seacoast, barely penetrated the West and disturbed the South not at all. Some business organizations supported reform, but the National Board of Trade in 1868 deferred endorsing the Jenckes bill, and laborers and farmers seemed indifferent to reform. Congress reflected this mood. Although a bipartisan majority supported him, Jenckes in July 1868 could not get the two-thirds vote to suspend the rules needed to consider his bill.

GRANT AND REFORM

The prospect for civil service reform brightened with the election of 1868. Reformers enthusiastically supported Grant, who "undoubtedly" would support reform as only a nonpolitically oriented man could, and felt triumphant when he was elected. Jenckes, too, was successful, and Congressman James G. Blaine of Maine in congratulating him asked if his "measure to purify, improve and elevate the *civil service* of the country" would be "reached & acted on at the approaching session?" In the weeks following the election, the American Social Science Association (dedicated to the advancement of education and "the diffusion of sound principles on questions of economy, trade, and finance") joined supporters of reform. Its recording-secretary, Henry Villard—a German immigrant journalist who would later complete the Northern Pacific Railroad— arranged for Jenckes to address the association in Boston, organized a New York meeting, where Jenckes spoke on 16 January 1869, and went on to Washington to recruit members. "Our Association," Villard assured Jenckes in early February, "is now rapidly extending its organization throughout the country and we propose, with the aid of our branches, to carry on a regular campaign for reform in the civil service between now and the next winter." Reformers apparently had triumphed. They had elected their candidate for president, their chief advocate was reelected, the man who would be Speaker of the House implicity favored their measure, and it had been adopted by an important organization.

Both Grant and Congress disappointed reformers. Representative John A. Logan, an Illinois Republican, damned civil service reform as unconstitutional, undemocratic, antirepublican, aristocratic, and monarchical; and, realizing he needed more public support, Jenckes did not press Congress in 1869 to pass his bill. Reformers were not surprised by Congress's lack of interest in civil service reform, but they were shattered when Grant abandoned his independent course and paid, from the reformers' view, too much attention to the political claims of the wrong sort of politician. Charles Eliot Norton, who had been enraptured with Grant and had hoped for "the mission to Holland or Belgium," was neither enraptured nor hopeful by July 1869. He wrote Curtis: "Grant's surrender, partial though it may be, to the politicians was an unexpected disappointment, but a very instructive one. His other mistakes were what might have been expected—what indeed we ought to have been prepared for. But some of his appointments are disgraceful,—personally discreditable to him. . . . The question seems to be now whether the politicians,—'the men inside politics,'—will ruin the country, or the country take summary vengeance, by means of Jenckes's bill, upon them." Locked out of the foreign service, reformers turned even more to the Jenckes bill.

Adversity in 1869 produced more agitation for civil service reform. In October, Henry Adams advocated reform, but not the Jenckes bill, in the *North American Review.* Arguing that Congress had usurped the executive's appointing power, Adams claimed that the president had the power to reform the civil service and should institute, by executive order, a system of competitive examinations. Adams' view betrayed his recent residence in Great Britain, where civil service reform was being accomplished by executive order. In comparing two members of Grant's cabinet, Adams also revealed that while the genteel element wanted good government, its concern for reform had resulted primarily from loss of political power. Secretary of the Treasury George S. Boutwell, Adams stated, was "the product of caucuses and party promotion," but Attorney General Ebenezer Rockwood Hoar was "by birth and by training a representative of the best New England school, holding his moral rules

on the sole authority of his own conscience. . . . Judge Hoar belonged in fact to a class of men who had been gradually driven from politics, but whom it is the hope of reformers to restore. Mr. Boutwell belonged to the class which has excluded its rival, but which has failed to fill with equal dignity the place it has usurped."

Boutwell did not deserve Adams' criticism. From 1870 to 1872, without fanfare, he converted routine, farcical "pass" examinations given appointees in the Treasury Department into stringent pass tests, composed and administered primarily by E. B. Elliott, a friend of reform who later became a civil service commissioner. Apparently the first competitive examination in the United States civil service was held in Boutwell's department, when six third-class clerks competed for vacancies in the next higher class. Boutwell's system generally was not competitive and not open to all who wished to take the test. Like the reformers, Boutwell desired efficient workers to handle the complex functions of his department and was prepared to use examinations to obtain them, but, unlike the reformers, he wished to continue making political appointments. Ironically, reformers ignored Boutwell's responsible administration of the Treasury Department, and, since historians have relied upon reform sources, he is renowned as a benighted spoilsman.

In 1870, Grant rid his administration of those whom the reformers considered the strongest men, while congressional reformers could not agree on a common program. Senator Lyman Trumbull, an Illinois Republican, sponsored legislation that would make it a misdemeanor for congressmen to advise the president on appointments—just what Henry Adams wanted—but Carl Schurz of Missouri, in opposition, asked who could better supply the president with information about applicants for office. Schurz introduced his own reform bill, which (although its main features were similar to the Jenckes bill) would have allowed the appointing power to ignore successful examinees—either by requesting the examination of a new person or by substituting "inquiries concerning the character, antecedents, social standing, and general ability" of candidates—and bowed to rotation by providing an eight-year term. Jenckes modified but clung to his measure, which was debated in May and, with no chance of being passed, recommitted.

CIVIL SERVICE REFORM

While congressional reformers were in disarray, their executive branch counterparts were being harried out of the government. When Grant appointed Attorney General Hoar to the Supreme Court in December 1869, the Senate rejected him largely because he had not tolerated political appointments in the Justice Department, and by June 1870 the Senate was so hostile to Hoar that Grant asked him to resign. "In losing Hoar," Curtis lamented, "we lose by far the ablest man in the administration." The most devastating resignation was that of Interior Secretary Jacob Dolson Cox, who had (like Boutwell) instituted genuine tests in his department (particularly in the Patent Office and in the Census Bureau), kept spoilsmen out of the Indian Bureau (a prodigious feat), published a letter attacking political assessments, and refused clerks a second vacation to vote back home in the fall elections. Cox resigned in October 1870, after Grant forced him to revoke his order regarding clerks' absences and spoilsmen predicted his removal.

Cox's resignation was timed to affect fall elections and public opinion. Unlike Hoar, who remained silent, Cox published correspondence relating to his resignation. John Gorham Palfrey, clergyman, historian, and former postmaster of Boston, found these letters "damaging" and decided not to vote in the coming election. Unable to choose "between the very vicious principles of the Democrats, and the very vicious practices of the Republicans," he suspected he was in a "crowd" of "good company." The administration suffered a severe setback in the election of 1870. Thirty congressional seats were lost and with them the Republican two-thirds majority, while in Missouri liberal Republican insurgents led by Carl Schurz and aided by Democrats captured the governorship.

Defeat conveyed a message the administration understood better than editorials in reform journals. "Always favoring practical reforms," Grant, in his December 1870 annual message to Congress, called for a reform of the civil service that would "govern, not the tenure, but the manner of making all appointments." The distribution of patronage not only was embarrassing for the executive but was an "arduous and thankless labor imposed" on congressmen. In addition, Grant observed, "The present system does not secure the best men, and often not even fit men,

for public place." Reformers were elated. "It is . . . something to have got to the mark on Civil Service," Henry Adams wrote Cox, "and for this you are responsible. But I still see a long fight before us."

The lame-duck session of the Forty-first Congress responded with four reform bills; Jenckes, who had been defeated in the recent election, introduced his bill for the last time. Trumbull and Schurz had their bills ready and Senator Henry Wilson of Massachusetts introduced a bill substituting departmental boards of examiners for the commission, forbidding political activity by officeholders, and prohibiting political assessments on government employees. When none of these measures was enacted, congressional reform leaders agreed on a simple joint resolution empowering the president to appoint a commission, which would prescribe rules for examining applicants. In the closing moments of the lame-duck session, the draft, written by Representative William H. Armstrong of Pennsylvania and approved by Grant, was moved by Trumbull as a "rider" to the civil appropriation bill. After a motion to table the rider was lost by one vote (26 to 25), the Senate approved it by a vote of 32 to 24. In the House, Henry L. Dawes of Massachusetts, in charge of the appropriation bill, recommended concurrence with all Senate amendments since the whole bill would be lost if a conference committee were required. Ensuring this "most obnoxious" rider's passage by attaching it at the last minute to a necessary appropriation bill particularly galled John A. Logan. Despite his anger, the Senate amendments passed by a 90-to-20 vote, and, trick or no trick, Congress declared itself in favor of civil service reform.

THE GRANT CIVIL SERVICE COMMISSION

As head of the Civil Service Commission, Grant appointed George William Curtis, who thought the rider "insignificant" until Jenckes informed him of its possibilities. Braving the summer heat, the commission met in Washington on 28 June 1871 and determined that its function was advisory and that Grant could reject its recommendations, pass them on to Congress, or enforce them on his own responsibility.

Though Curtis favored open competitive examinations to secure reform, his colleagues feared that the competitive system would annul executive appointing power until Attorney General Amos T. Akerman decided that the appointing power could be limited to a competitively selected class. Using reform data from other nations, the commission found the British experience most helpful and, under Curtis' influence, determined to establish as much competition in the American system as Akerman's decision allowed. On 1 November, Curtis reported that Grant "approved generally" of the commission's rules and ten days later that they were "favorably received" by the cabinet. Unknown to Curtis, Grant and his cabinet thought the rules "impracticable," but nevertheless in his annual message of December 1871 he promised them a "fair trial." With this assurance, the commission on 18 December 1871 submitted its recommendations, accompanied by a long report castigating the spoils system.

Grant promulgated the rules as of 1 January 1872 and requested an appropriation from Congress. "A great triumph of a great reform," said the *Nation,* although it doubted Grant's intentions. The rules required that all appointees be United States citizens of adequate character, age, and health, and able to speak, read, and write English. Entrance into the service was in most cases allowed only at the lowest grade, where vacancies were to be filled from a group of three individuals who achieved the highest scores on a "public competitive examination." Promotion was to be the rule within the service, and competition would determine who would be promoted. If no one in the service could ably fill a vacancy, an open competitive examination was to be held. Candidates for the numerous postmasterships paying less than $200 annually could be appointed simply by presenting evidence of character and fitness. A six-month probationary period was required for all appointees except presidential appointees, persons appointed to positions abroad, and postmasters. For each department the president would appoint three examiners, and the commission would supervise the entire system. The rules also prohibited the levying and paying of political assessments "under the form of voluntary contributions or otherwise." Only the very highest officers—for example, assistant secretaries of departments, federal judges, and

ministers to foreign countries—were exempt from these regulations. Including almost all the civil service in complicated regulations within two weeks of their publication proved impossible since the civil service outside of Washington had never been systematically organized. Ten days after the new system commenced it was temporarily suspended by a new rule approved by the board.

The Civil Service Commission's program strengthened Grant's position. Even temporary suspension of the rules did not raise adverse comment, for it was apparent that problems had to be solved before the new regulations could be enforced. The civil service outside of Washington had to be classified into grades, and specific appointment rules had to be devised for posts defying simple classification. By March the commission had completed the classification, which Curtis submitted to Grant along with supplemental regulations. Once again Grant approved by executive order (on 16 April 1872) the commission's recommendations with few minor changes. He did want to make clear that while political assessments were forbidden, officeholders were permitted "to take part in politics," but that "honesty and efficiency, not political activity, will determine the tenure of office."

The new regulations divided the service into roughly four classes. One class, primarily composed of clerks, was required to be examined competitively before appointment; while a second class, including consuls receiving salaries ranging from $1,000 to $3,000, was appointed on the strength of recommendation followed by a "pass" examination. A third class, including such posts as collectors of customs at major ports, was not required to take an examination but was chosen, if possible, from a subordinate post in the department where the vacancy occurred; and a small fourth class of the highest officers, such as cabinet officers and their highest ranking assistants, was to be appointed by traditional methods. The supplemental rules also limited those taking examinations to a practicable number—a necessary move, although it could be a loophole for spoilsmen—and at Grant's behest provided that examinations be held throughout the states to provide access for westerners and southerners.

The campaign of 1872 proved disastrous for civil service reform. The division widened between reformers who had faith in, and those who were skeptical of, Grant's efforts to reform the civil service. The former, personified by George William Curtis, felt that they were influencing the administration's personnel policy, while the latter, personified by Carl Schurz, remembered that Grant had thwarted their personal ambitions and reform aspirations. Their drift to the liberal Republicans, who held their national convention at Cincinnati, was hastened by the hostility of Grant's spoils-minded friends. Benjamin F. Butler of Massachusetts, for example, equated opposition to Grant with civil service reform, which he called the stillborn babe of Cincinnati, and jeered with considerable accuracy that "Civil service reform is always popular with the 'outs' and never with the 'ins,' unless with those who have a strong expectation of soon going out."

Civil service reformers supporting the liberal Republican movement came to grief when its Cincinnati convention nominated Horace Greeley, the eccentric and erratic editor of the *New York Tribune*, rather than their favorite candidate, Charles Francis Adams, Sr. Greeley, who was not a civil service reformer, apparently joined the liberal Republican movement because Grant awarded the New York patronage to Conkling rather than to the Reuben Fenton–Horace Greeley wing of the party. "Is there no way out of the wretched mess into which these Cincinnati nominations have plunged us?" asked Godkin of Schurz. When a move to dump Greeley failed and the Democratic party also gave him its nomination, many liberal Republicans crawled back to Grant and the Republican party. The campaign of 1872 split reformers into three suspicious factions: Grant supporters from the start, liberal Republicans who supported Greeley as a lesser evil, and liberal Republicans who abandoned the revolution because they could not stomach Greeley. With their ranks divided and Grant victorious, reformers, who had thrived under abuse, were discouraged by ridicule. Liberal Republican reformers who had seceded from the Republican party were powerless; and reformers who had remained within it were too weak to hold their old advances.

Demoralized and divided, reformers were easily conquered. Although Grant in his annual message of December 1872 called for legislation to bind future presidents to reform (a request Congress ignored), and in his second inaugural address pledged that "The spirit of the rules adopted will be maintained," he was not determined to carry out the commission's rules in the face of serious opposition. In what reformers regarded as a test case, Grant appointed Conkling's man as surveyor of the port of New York, rather than Deputy Surveyor James I. Benedict in accordance with the rules. Humiliated, Curtis (who was ill and perhaps testy) announced in the *New York Tribune* that "men do not willingly consent to be thus publicly snubbed," and on 18 March 1873 resigned as chairman of Grant's Civil Service Commission. In his place, Grant appointed Dorman B. Eaton, an erudite lawyer and an ardent municipal and civil service reformer. The rules, which in practice had been instituted only in Washington and in the New York Customhouse (the latter on 10 October 1872), remained in effect and in August 1873 were improved further. Curtis complained in *Harper's Weekly* that the rules, particularly those restricting political activities, were violated "in total contempt" of Grant's orders. In addition, Congress in 1873 remained hostile, and economic distress following the panic of 1873 caused the public to forget civil service reform. Reformers in 1874 continued traveling the diverse roads they had taken during the campaign of 1872, while Congress continued to refuse the Civil Service Commission additional funds.

Oddly, that parsimonious Congress enacted in 1874 a significant reform bill abolishing the moiety system. This system divided forfeited smuggled property—not merely the duty in question, but the entire consignment—among the government; the informer; and the collector, naval officer, and surveyor of the port. The moieties of the three chief officers of the New York Customhouse were estimated in 1872 at $50,000 each annually (in comparison, Grant's salary was doubled to $50,000 in 1873). The system, attacked for years, came under heavy fire in 1873 when Phelps, Dodge, and Company, accused of avoiding $2,000 in duties on shipments totaling $1,750,000, settled out of court for $271,017. Merchants and reformers thought "knavish politicians" searching for personal and party funds were responsible, complained that seizures of books and papers were outrageous, and charged that the moiety system drove treasury agents to excess. So great was the outcry that by June 1874 a bill abolishing the moiety system and restricting the right of search became law. While the bill raised the official salaries of collectors, those in the larger ports, particularly in New York, suffered a sharp drop in income. This reform legislation was achieved largely through the pressure applied by reformers who were merchants. They had constant contacts with customhouse employees, and reform would enable their businesses to function more smoothly.

While the moiety system was being killed, Grant's Civil Service Commission grew weaker. Although Grant extended the Civil Service Commission rules to Boston in September 1874, the administration of the system as a whole was unsatisfactory. In the New York Customhouse, Collector Chester A. Arthur barred Silas W. Burt, chairman of the supervisory board, from examinations given in the collector's office. Six years later, when Burt gained access to records, he discovered that applicants were limited to those whom Arthur, who was both a spoilsman and an able administrator, wanted to appoint. Grant's annual message in December 1874 once again endorsed the reform regulations but stressed the impracticability of maintaining them without congressional support and threatened to abandon competitive examinations if Congress failed to act. The lame-duck session of the Forty-third Congress made no appropriation, and Grant on 9 March 1875 discontinued competitive examinations. Although Eaton appreciated what Grant had done for reform, he realized that over the past year administration of the rules was "of course, unsatisfactory" and lamented that "history . . . must adjudge this so called abandonment to have been a needless and unjustifiable surrender."

CAUTIOUS ADVANCE UNDER HAYES

Grant's surrender to spoilsmen led reformers to unite. A dinner in April 1875 honoring Schurz on his retirement from the Senate provided a suitable occasion for an "informal and confidential" gathering and helped end the three years of division among reformers. The Ohio gubernatorial election that fall, which Republican Rutherford B. Hayes—running with reform support on a sound money platform—won, led reformers to believe that in 1876 they would hold the balance of power between the Republicans

and Democrats. The Fifth Avenue Hotel conference of reformers, held in New York on 15 May 1876, called for sound currency and civil service reform, suggested that reforming candidates were needed rather than empty platform promises, enumerated presidential qualifications, and warned that reformers would take independent action if the Republicans failed to nominate a reform candidate. The Republicans nominated Hayes, and most reformers were satisfied.

While supporting Hayes, reformers were often exasperated by his course. From stressing civil service reform as *"the* issue" at the beginning of his campaign, Hayes moved to emphasize *"the danger of giving the Rebels the Government."* Although Samuel Jones Tilden outpolled Hayes by 250,000 votes, Hayes triumphed after a long dispute (pitting Democratic intimidation and violence against Republican fraud) over who carried South Carolina, Louisiana, and Florida. In his inaugural address, Hayes returned to the theme of civil service reform, which he had ignored during the campaign. He called for nonpartisan appointments, discouraged political activity by officeholders, and advocated secure tenure for satisfactory officers and a six-year single term for the president. Hayes also pleased reformers by appointing Carl Schurz as secretary of the interior and William M. Evarts, an anti-Conkling New York Republican, as secretary of state.

Reformers soon complained that Hayes was "making haste *too* slowly." Rules promulgated by his administration restricted admission to the service to the lowest grade and to those passing a standard noncompetitive examination, but placed no restrictions (except to favor disabled veterans) on whom would be appointed from the eligible class. While reformers welcomed the assurance that more responsible positions would be filled through promotion of experienced civil servants, they also recognized that "pass" examinations had proved no obstacle to spoilsmen. When an investigating commission headed by New York aristocrat John Jay recommended that the New York Customhouse trim 20 percent of its staff and be emancipated "from partisan control," Hayes approved, but Treasury Secretary John Sherman instructed Collector Arthur to give preference when cutting his staff to officers "who sympathize with the party in power." "Dissatisfied & discouraged" because Hayes had not struck "some heavy & decisive blows at the old system," reformers were elated when on 22 June 1877 he forbade federal officeholders "to take part in the management of political organizations, caucuses, conventions, or election campaigns" and prohibited political assessments.

The president's caution kept reformers united. During July and August, Hayes did nothing, while New York Naval Officer Alonzo Cornell, a member of the Republican National Committee, ignored his order forbidding political activity by officeholders. Reformers regarded Cornell's refusal to resign either position as a "national scandal" and demanded his removal lest the administration's civil service policy be broken. "I think," David A. Wells wrote Schurz, "there is a feeling that on civil service reform there is hesitation—perhaps timidity to go forward in the path commenced." But after the Jay Commission made its final report, Hayes moved to break the Conkling machine's hold on the New York Customhouse, and on 6 September announced a customhouse "reorganization" replacing both Arthur and Cornell.

Hayes nominated, and Senator Roscoe Conkling bitterly opposed, Theodore Roosevelt, Sr., as collector, L. Bradford Prince as naval officer, and Edwin A. Merritt as surveyor of the port of New York. Rather than reflect reform preferences, these nominations reflected those of Evarts, who wished to build administration support among New York Republicans. Although disappointed, reformers closed ranks and supported Hayes, while Conkling escalated a factional struggle into a battle over the power of appointment by arguing that Hayes had attacked the "courtesy of the Senate." Siding with Conkling, the Senate on 12 December 1877 rejected Hayes's nominations except that of Merritt as surveyor. Reformers blamed the president for Conkling's victory. If Hayes's "hands were clean," Horace White maintained, Conkling would have been defeated, and even Curtis felt that Conkling had defeated the adminsitration "with weapons which its own inconsistency had furnished."

Hayes did not give up. When Congress was safely adjourned, he replaced Collector Arthur with Surveyor Merritt and Naval Officer Cornell with Deputy Naval Officer Silas W. Burt (the leading civil service reformer in the customhouse). "This action," Norton wrote, "puts a new face on affairs." Yet reformers realized that

Merritt's appointment and his replacement as surveyor was part of a plan to defeat Conkling's reelection by reorganizing the New York party around the old Fenton wing. Although the New York legislature elected Conkling to a third senatorial term, Hayes remained on the offensive. The New York Customhouse collected two-thirds of the nation's revenue, he informed the Senate when it convened, and was of national significance, yet Arthur and Cornell "made the custom-house a center of partisan political management." On 3 February 1879—thanks to Secretary Sherman's "extraordinary personal efforts"—a minority of Republicans combined with southern Democrats to defeat Conkling. Reformers rejoiced but also felt "genuine pain," since in the debate Conkling exposed administration demands for political appointments in the customhouse.

Whatever use the administration had made of the customhouse, Hayes now wished to make it a showcase for reform. "My desire," he wrote Merritt, "is that your office shall be conducted on strictly business principles, and according to the rules" devised by the Grant Civil Service Commission. Reformers were cheered further when new rules were published, covering all but a few New York Customhouse employees. Appointments were to be made from the three highest-standing candidates on an open competitive examination, administered by a board of examiners, and observed by "well-known citizens." New appointees could enter only at the lowest grade; higher vacancies were filled by promotion within the customhouse. Naval Officer Burt was the dynamic force behind these rules. "If you can revive this corpse you are entitled to all the glory," Collector Merritt assured him. It was Burt's idea to invite prominent citizens, particularly editors, to observe the proceedings while his good friend Curtis, who always attended, explained the procedures and gained adherents to civil service reform. Thanks to Burt, reform in the New York Customhouse was highly successful. Dorman B. Eaton, head of the moribund Civil Service Commission, reported to Hayes that never before had so much time been given to proper work and so little to partisan activity.

Under Thomas L. James, a Conkling Republican, reform also progressed in the New York Post Office. When James was appointed to head it in March 1873, "incompetency, neglect, confusion, and drunkenness" that staggered "credulity" prevailed. James replaced this chaos with system. He dismissed drunkards and incompetents but conducted no partisan proscription. He set up examinations and resisted political pressure to hire unworthy applicants. By May 1879 he decided that "pass" examinations were not adequate and instituted open competitive examinations a few weeks after they were established in the New York Customhouse. In 1880 the volume of mail had increased a third over 1875, yet the mails were delivered for $20,000 less, and collections and deliveries had increased.

Ideal working conditions, however, were not synonymous with such reform. Efficiency was achieved by frequently working postal officials ten and eleven hours a day. In addition to overworking his officers, James kept them alert by adjusting their salaries according to their performance on periodic examinations. Similarly in the Pension Office, Schurz found that inspecting efficiency reports every three months and adjusting salaries accordingly caused everyone to do his "utmost." James also hoped to secure the services of boys so that the civil service would profit from the low wages earned by child labor. Having confronted the difficulties of administering an enormous office, James solved them with reform principles and won reform support while remaining loyal to Conkling.

The major New York offices, as administered by Merritt and James, proved that the "corpse" of civil service reform was not only alive but practical and even necessary for efficient operation. Further evidence of reform efficacy came from Dorman B. Eaton's elaborate report entitled *Civil Service in Great Britain,* which was released in late 1879. Eaton concluded that the English merit system abolished abuses, promoted efficiency, stimulated education, and elevated "the character and social standing of those who execute the laws."

GARFIELD AND REFORM ORGANIZATIONS

The reform movement had gained strength, but in 1880 its future seemed jeopardized. The Republican party, to which most reformers belonged, seemed likely to nominate for the presidency either Grant or Blaine, neither of whom

was friendly to reform. Fortunately for reformers, the convention deadlocked and anti-Grant forces united to nominate Ohio Congressman James A. Garfield, a conspicuous friend of reform. To conciliate Conkling, Grant's leading supporter, the convention gave the vice-presidential nomination to his lieutenant, Chester A. Arthur. Reformers reasoned that the vice-presidency was unimportant unless Garfield died in office, and the *Nation* dismissed that as "too unlikely a contingency to be worth making extraordinary provision for."

With the presidency nearly in his grasp, Garfield abandoned civil service reform. His letter of acceptance repudiated Hayes's order removing officeholders from politics and his stand against congressional dictation of executive appointments. Nevertheless, reformers supported Garfield, though Curtis feared he would follow no firm civil service policy since his "fibre" was not "steel." Visiting New York (a state he had to carry), Garfield both met and pleased Conkling's lieutenants and convinced Curtis that he would enter the presidency "perfectly independent." In 1876 Hayes had made an ineffective attempt to prevent political assessments, but Garfield in 1880 encouraged them by asking "how the Depts. generally are doing" and hoping that Thomas W. Brady, the second assistant postmaster general (who was defrauding his department by "improving" service on its star routes), "will give us all the assistance he can." Garfield's tactics proved successful, and Carl Schurz hastened to warn the new president that "your real troubles will now begin," but added that if President Garfield acted upon the teachings of Congressman Garfield his administration would be "most wholesome." Trying to be optimistic, one reformer prophesied, better than he realized, that Garfield would "disappoint the reformers at first more than Hayes—but not at *last.*"

At the height of the campaign civil service reformers created an effective and permanent organization. It was evident that if a friendly president like Hayes could institute neither full-scale nor lasting civil service reform, an organization was needed to secure legislation imposing reform in major departments. A letter to the *Nation* in August 1880 provoked other letters and led to the revival of the New York Civil Service Reform Association. That association, established in 1877 with Henry W. Bellows, wartime head of the United States Sanitary Commission and Unitarian clergyman, as its president, made an auspicuous start but by the spring of 1878 could not muster a quorum at its meetings.

In the fall of 1880 it reorganized under a new constitution and a new president, George William Curtis. The executive committee created committees on legislation and publications headed by Eaton and Godkin, respectively. Eaton began work on a civil service reform bill and by 5 May 1881 Godkin's committee had distributed thousands of copies of five pamphlets. At Garfield's inauguration alone 10,000 copies of James Parton's description of the "introduction" of the spoils system (from his *Life of Jackson*) were distributed. In addition, by May the New York association spawned associations in other cities, including Brooklyn, Boston, Philadelphia, Providence, Cincinnati, Milwaukee, and San Francisco; and associations were being formed in Baltimore, Buffalo, New Orleans, St. Paul, and St. Louis. Early beginnings were apparent in fourteen other localities.

While the new associations changed reformers from unorganized individuals into a powerful pressure group, the election of 1880 made some Democrats conscious of their need for reform. They recognized that the merit system would neutralize the enormous advantage Republicans derived from the control of the civil service. On 15 December 1880 George Hunt Pendleton, an Ohio Democrat who had been connected with events and ideas abhorrent to reformers (he was George B. McClellan's running mate in 1864, and he was the leading exponent of the "Ohio Idea" to pay off the national debt with inflated Greenbacks), introduced legislation to reform the civil service and prevent political assessments. Curtis was suspicious of Pendleton and unhappy with his bill, but Pendleton was in earnest. He explained to Burt that while "not wedded" to his bill, he desired "extremely to see the ideas embodied in it, carried out." After consulting with Eaton, Pendleton scrapped his own bill and substituted the bill written by the Legislative Committee of the New York Civil Service Reform Association. This new bill, though substantially Eaton's creation, drew heavily on the earlier Jenckes bill. It called for open competitive examinations to be administered by a commission and applied to Washington offices and to post offices and customhouses employing more

than fifty persons. Despite numerous petitions, Congress ignored both the Pendleton bill and the association's bill to end political assessments, which Democratic Representative Albert S. Willis of Kentucky had introduced.

While some Democrats were espousing reform, Garfield was looking less and less like a reformer. He pleased reformers by appointing Thomas L. James, the reforming New York postmaster, postmaster general, and Wayne MacVeagh, an ardent reformer, attorney general; but he also appointed James G. Blaine secretary of state, showing "a curious lack of perception of the real sentiment that made him President," and Samuel J. Kirkwood of Iowa secretary of the interior. As Schurz's successor, Kirkwood began eliminating civil service reform in his department. Instead of backing the Pendleton bill or a similar measure, Garfield in his inaugural address simply proposed a specific term of office for civil servants. "I fully share your disappointment at the apparent back sliding of Mr. Garfield," wrote a reformer to Burt. *He knows better* & therefore I can only interpret his heretical proposition . . . as an adroit measure to defeat the whole scheme without openly opposing it."

Garfield's changes in the New York Customhouse alarmed reformers and enraged Conkling. Garfield removed Merritt as collector, and in his place nominated William H. Robertson, a Blaine supporter who had defiantly opposed Conkling. Believing Garfield had promised him the customhouse patronage, Conkling lost it to his archenemy, while reformers foresaw the end of the reform experiment under Merritt and Burt. The confrontation between Conkling and Garfield (again involving senatorial courtesy) provoked Senator Henry L. Dawes of Massachusetts to remark, "For a great man I think our President has some of the weakest, and Conkling some of the ugliest streaks I have ever seen developed in human nature—The one wants to be watched like a child, the other like an assassin." Realizing that he could not prevent Robertson's confirmation, Conkling inadvertently committed political suicide by resigning from the Senate. The New York legislature refused to reelect him, and his desperate ploy to strengthen his hand failed.

The proposed shift from Merritt to Robertson did not augur well for reform. In place of the merit system in the New York Customhouse, the administration proposed "pass" examinations, which would be extended to other customhouses. When Curtis accused the administration of "betraying reform," it began to backtrack. MacVeagh suggested that there was "more support" for reform than was apparent and reported that Garfield "is so good and true at heart, he is sure to learn. But," he added, "it is awful to think he should need to learn so much."

Garfield never had the opportunity to demonstrate his ability to learn. On 2 July 1881 he was shot and fatally wounded by Charles Guiteau, who for weeks had been haunting Washington looking for an office. Over the next two and a half months civil service reformers used Garfield's deteriorating condition to advance their movement. "We do not think," editorialized the *Nation,* "we have taken up a newspaper during the last ten days which has not in some manner made the crime the product of 'the spoils system.'" Robertson took over the New York Customhouse on 1 August and promised, as did Secretary of the Treasury William Windom, to maintain civil service rules.

The New York Civil Service Reform Association invited other associations to a conference at Newport "to promote the movement now happily so well advanced." Fifty-eight delegates from thirteen associations met on 11 August and vowed to "use every honorable means, in the press, on the platform, and by petition, to secure" passage of the Pendleton and Willis bills, and organized a National Civil Service Reform League, with the executive committee of the New York association acting as a provisional central committee. On 16 September the New York association distributed nationally a letter signed by numerous prominent men, from Peter Cooper to Rutherford B. Hayes, connecting the "recent murderous attack" on Garfield with the need for civil service reform and urging that protest meetings be held and reform resolutions adopted. This appeal became more effective when Garfield died three days later.

Garfield dead proved more valuable to reformers than Garfield alive. In their loud and long lamentations for him and his lost opportunities, reformers quickly transformed Garfield from a spineless tool of Blaine to a fearless crusader for civil service reform. Reformers quoted Garfield's earlier speeches favoring reform while ignoring his sorry record as president. "The cynical impudence," wrote Henry Adams, "with which the reformers have tried to manufacture an ideal statesman out of the late shady politician beats anything in novel-writing." To every post office throughout the land reformers distributed a striking poster depicting a monument with an epitaph proclaiming that Garfield "died . . . a martyr to the fierceness of factional politics and the victim of that accursed greed for spoils of office which was the bane of his brief conscious existence as President, and is the gravest peril that threatens the future of his country." The monument was surrounded by apt Garfield quotations on civil service reform. Reformers had a simple, emotion-packed illustration that the previously uninterested masses could understand: the spoils system murdered Garfield.

THE PENDLETON ACT

Though civil service reformers established new associations, politicians resisted their demands. President Chester A. Arthur in his first annual message in December 1881 argued that competitive examinations, by testing "mere intellectual attainments," would favor immature college youths and suggested further inquiry before passing legislation. Arthur promised to enforce "earnestly" any bill Congress might pass that incorporated the main features of the British system. That same day Pendleton introduced his bill, but the favorable report of the Senate Committee on Civil Service and Retrenchment on 29 March 1882 came too late for consideration during that session. Congress passed no reform legislation in 1882 but did reluctantly appropriate $15,000 to reactivate the Civil Service Commission.

In May 1882 an unrepentant Republican Congressional Campaign Committee mailed its carefully crafted assessment circular stipulating, in a compulsory manner, the "voluntary" contributions expected of officeholders. Not only did the committee send a follow-up letter, but its agents invaded Washington executive offices to extract contributions from delinquent civil servants. Adverse publicity of these assessment tactics harmed the Republicans in the election of 1882. Thousands of independents voted Democratic, and thousands of Republicans did not vote. Reformers blamed the broad Democratic victory on the failure of Republicans to take the merit system seriously, and Congress and Arthur were inclined to agree.

After the election Arthur backed both the Pendleton and Willis bills, and the lame-duck session of Congress, Marian Adams observed, was "like a pack of whipped boys." It had been elected in 1880 and was evenly divided in the Senate. Though Republicans controlled the House, they would soon be out of power, and their outlook for 1884 was not promising. When Republican senators caucused, all except one or two planned to support the Pendleton bill. By supporting it, they could pose as reformers in the presidential election of 1884 and hopefully win; but even if Democrats won, Republicans could use civil service reform rules to "freeze" their partisans in office. Democrats, on the other hand, faced a dilemma. Should they support reform and keep the independent vote, losing spoils if they triumphed in 1884, or should they oppose reform, risking the 1884 election without the independent vote, in a gamble to capture all the booty? Democrats were opposed to political assessments, which could hurt them in the coming presidential campaign. The Congress that met in December 1882 was thinking of 1884.

The Senate quickly considered the Pendleton bill. Although the shift seemed truly remarkable, the speeches and the actions of many supporters of the bill betrayed a fundamental opposition to civil service reform. The undertone was expediency rather than sympathy, and several senators and congressmen preferred compromise measures that would not reform the civil service. Lobbying in Washington for Pendleton's bill, which was mainly his, Eaton successfully opposed compromise efforts, which would not satisfy the clamor for reform. A few spoilsmen were not caught in the reform avalanche. Senator Joseph E. Brown of Georgia warned that the Pendleton bill—a "humbug . . . deception and nonsense"—would cause Democrats to go before the people "handicapped" because no one would work zealously for a Democratic victory if "all the offices that amount to anything . . . are already disposed of." Marian Adams fancied that Brown "was only a little more outspoken than his colleagues in saying . . . 'It's all a humbug,' and maintaining that each party as it came to power must take the spoils."

Partisan rather than public considerations were paramount in the Senate's debate over the Pendleton bill. To shorten the time it would take their partisans to reach better-paid positions, Democrats successfully opposed limiting entrance to the civil service to the lowest grade but failed to open up other jobs with amendments that would have required all incumbents affected by the bill to compete for their jobs in open competitive examinations. Political assessments were outlawed, but Republicans preserved the legality of voluntary political contributions by civil servants if they were not solicited by federal employees. Geographic considerations became more important than partisan ones when westerners and southerners united to compel the distribution of offices according to state population. Despite the partisan struggle over the amendments, the final vote on the bill in the Senate was perfunctory and largely bipartisan.

Thanks to New York Democrat Abram S. Hewitt, the House moved faster than the Senate. Fearing that if the Pendleton bill was "debated and amended it would fail," Hewitt arranged for its passage. His Democratic colleague from New York City, S. S. ("Sunset") Cox, called for immediate action, the bill was read, and cries of "Vote! Vote!" forced the Speaker to bring the House to order. John A. Kasson, an Iowa Republican (who had abandoned his own "reform" bill that dispensed with competitive examinations), moved the previous question, which meant that the measure could be debated only thirty minutes. John Reagan, Democrat from Texas and former Confederate postmaster general, claimed that both parties were cheating the country and that the Republican party knew it was cheating the Democratic party.

Hiding his intense annoyance, Kasson alluded to the powerful support the civil service reform associations gave the Pendleton bill. "The young men of the country," he concluded, "and the active, intellectual, and nonpolitical forces, have largely contributed to this result." The bill passed with nearly all Republicans supporting it, and Democrats from the South and Old Northwest in opposition. Most congressmen, even those responsible for making it a law, did not like the Pendleton bill. The evening it passed the House, Henry Adams was "immensely pleased to tumble over Kasson," who, despite the calm exterior he had maintained, was in a savage mood because the House had passed the *"Boston bill."* Savoring the moment, Adams observed that the average congressman was "chiefly occupied in swearing at professional reformers and voting for their bills."

TOWARD PUBLIC PERSONNEL MANAGEMENT

When Arthur signed the Pendleton bill into law on 16 January 1883, reformers' emphasis shifted to securing state legislation and effective federal administration. Reformers realized that vigilance was necessary, for most politicians were still hostile and the Pendleton Act applied only to Washington offices and customhouses and post offices in the largest cities. The majority of federal civil servants and every state and municipal employee in the country was still unprotected by civil service regulations. New York in 1883 and 1884 and Massachusetts in 1884 adopted civil service reform legislation that applied to municipal as well as state employees, but reform association membership fell off among professionals, who had formed the backbone of the movement, and increased interest among businessmen failed to offset the decline. The civil service reform movement soon became both a businessmen's movement and a moribund movement. Counterattacks in New York and Massachusetts crippled reform enforcement in those states, and over twenty years elapsed from the passage of the Massachusetts law until the next states, Wisconsin and Illinois, enacted reform bills.

While the merit system languished on municipal and state levels, it made rapid strides in the federal bureaucracy. The classified list of public servants under the merit system grew for the same reason the spoils system had grown earlier. Every four years from 1885 to 1897 party control of the federal government changed, and presidents, after appointing their partisans to unclassified offices, extended the merit system to freeze their appointees in office. Though William McKinley was unfriendly to reform and withdrew several thousand offices from the rules, assassination again aided reform by placing Theodore Roosevelt in the president's chair. Roosevelt had fought for reform in the New York legislature and had been an energetic civil service commis-

sioner. When in 1901 he became president, 46 percent of the service was classified; when in 1909 he left office, 66 percent was under the rules.

Paul P. Van Riper observes that civil service reform during Roosevelt's administration "commenced a metamorphosis into public personnel management." The old issues of public morality and evils resulting from spoilsmen politicizing the civil service largely gave way in the Progressive era to an emphasis on economy and efficiency (which, in truth, earlier reformers had not ignored completely). The Civil Service Commission devised, and Roosevelt approved in 1903, rules that were not replaced until 1938. The 1903 rules extended the merit system to skilled workers, gave the commission more flexibility (for example, with age limits), tightened its control over temporary employees, systematized reinstatements, clarified removal regulations, scrutinized those positions on schedule A (classified yet exempted from examinations), and reorganized examination procedures. Reflecting the most thorough study of the civil service between 1883 and 1938, these rules further developed a career service and distinguished career positions from patronage positions. Tinkering with governmental machinery to make it more responsive, William Howard Taft continued the redefinition of civil service reform.

When a new administration represented a change of parties, it usually felt that the merit system had been extended too far, that classified civil servants were too representative of the outgoing party, and that they were indifferent and even hostile to the new regime. The merit system was set back during the first administration of Woodrow Wilson. Although Wilson had been a vice-president of the National Civil Service Reform League, he recognized that Democrats would not support his program if deprived of patronage. His administration appointed outside of the merit system additional internal revenue officers to administer the new income tax and employees of the new Federal Reserve Board. Spoils practices were evident in the Post Office Department, where, to appoint more Democrats, Wilson delayed the classification of fourth-class postmasters. The proscription of Republicans, carried out largely by southern Democrats, resulted in the decline of black civil servants from 6 percent in 1910 to 4.9 percent in 1918, and the blacks who remained in the Washington offices of the Post Office and Treasury departments were segregated (with Wilson's approval). Despite these moves, spoils inroads during Wilson's first administration were relatively small, and the tendency to freeze partisans in offices under the rules ultimately asserted itself. After his reelection Wilson extended a modified version of the merit system to the more important first-, second-, and third-class postmasters.

World War I required a jump in the number of civil employees from 480,000 in 1916 to over 900,000 by Armistice Day in 1918. Since spoils methods could not meet the nation's wartime personnel needs, the merit system was used to make these appointments. The commission and the expanded bureaucracy functioned so effectively that, as Van Riper states, private industry used federal examination procedures to solve its recruitment problems.

During the 1920's, Republican administrations emphasized that the civil service (560,000 employees in 1922) needed to grow in efficiency. They also accelerated the trend toward a career service in 1923 with a retirement system and a new position classification scheme and increased the classified service, until 80 percent of the civil service was under the rules.

The onslaught of the Great Depression had an enormous effect on the civil service. Franklin D. Roosevelt's New Deal created many agencies to restore prosperity, but their staffs were appointed outside of the merit system. With mixed results, the New Deal ignored civil service reform during its first five most innovative years. These new appointees brought ideas and energy to the service, but orderly procedures, developed since 1883, disintegrated. By 1937 the machinery had become so weak that Roosevelt's social programs were endangered.

But in 1937 the president's Committee on Administrative Management, headed by Louis Brownlow, called for the reorganization of the executive branch and for all but policy-making jobs to be under the merit system. Roosevelt promulgated rules in 1938 (superseding those of 1903) providing for personnel sections in all departments, for competitive examinations for promotions, for training courses, and for coordinating the personnel system by the Civil Service Commission. Following the classic pattern, as well as Brownlow's advice, Roosevelt extended

the merit system to freeze employees who had been appointed outside the rules. By 1939 approximately two-thirds of the 900,000 civil servants were classified (still far below the 80-percent mark of 1927).

Fearing possible executive abuse of patronage, Congress attempted to extend the merit system and to depoliticize the civil service on all government levels. The Hatch Act of 1939, exempting only the highest policy-making positions, prohibited political activities by unclassified as well as classified civil servants. In 1940 a second Hatch Act extended this nonpartisan principle to state and local officials paid wholly or in part from federal funds. The Ramspeck Act of 1940 allowed Roosevelt to extend the merit system to 200,000 uncovered civil servants, who first had to take a noncompetitive examination. Roosevelt took advantage of this legislation; at the beginning of World War II about 90 percent of the civil service was under the merit system.

When the United States plunged into World War II, the Roosevelt administration had its bureaucratic house in order. Already enlarged to 1,800,000 employees by 1941, the public service expanded by 1945 to 3,800,000, with 330,000 additional persons serving without compensation. Rapid growth required the relaxation of civil service rules. Interviews often sufficed for examinations, and the trend toward centralizing control in the Civil Service Commission was reversed. With the end of the war, the public service shrank, and the commission reasserted its authority and revived the merit system. Administrators missed the flexibility they had enjoyed during the war and deplored procedures—primarily set up by the 1944 Veterans Preference Act—that hampered the removal of incompetents. With the New Deal and war years behind it, the public service lost its sense of mission.

POST–WORLD WAR II ADJUSTMENTS

In 1947, a bipartisan commission, headed by former president Herbert Hoover, was created to investigate the executive branch. The Hoover Commission recommended two years later that personnel transactions, position classifications, and examinations be decentralized, giving agencies and their administrators more, and the Civil

Service Commission less, discretion. It also recommended that the commission be unified under a chairman, who would be responsible for its administration, and that an effective staff relationship be established between it and the personnel offices in the various agencies.

The Hoover Commission called for uniform pay plans, higher salaries, and simpler procedures for examination, recruitment, promotion, and dismissal. The Civil Service Commission accepted most of these recommendations (many of which it had originated) and put them into effect. It halved the time between an examination announcement and the publication of an eligible list of possible appointees. In 1949 Congress raised salaries and consolidated five occupation groups into two "services," and in 1950 its Performance Rating Act simplified efficiency ratings. Congress did not pass additional legislation either to decentralize further the examining system or to facilitate the firing of incompetents. Powerful veterans' organizations opposed any change in the Veterans Preference Act.

The end of twenty years of Democratic party rule in 1953 caused apprehension in the service, which numbered approximately 2,500,000, of whom 85 percent were under the merit system. Many Republicans wondered if their adversaries' bureaucracy would implement new policies effectively, and those who followed Senator Joseph R. McCarthy questioned the loyalty of some civil servants to the nation itself. The service proved to be politically neutral, and McCarthyism spent its force. Though there were some employee reductions and some so-called security risks lost their positions, there was no general proscription of Democrats.

The Dwight D. Eisenhower administration continued to implement the Hoover Commission suggestions. In 1953 the administration reorganized the Civil Service Commission, consolidating its units and specifying its executive director's responsibilities. While supervising the system, the commission was to delegate to agencies specific personnel actions. In addition, as suggested by the Hoover Commission, the chairman of the Civil Service Commission was named presidential adviser on personnel management and attended cabinet meetings, making him—to the dismay of some—an administrator rather than an independent "watchdog."

A second Hoover Commission, reporting in 1955, concentrated on ways to maintain quality in the civil service. The second commission stressed that public servants' compensation should be competitive with private employment, that procedures—particularly when dealing with alleged security risks—must be equitable, and that incentives were necessary to hold outstanding career civil servants and to recruit brilliant short-term political officers. Although Congress responded to these proposals only by raising pay, the Civil Service Commission and the administration advanced personnel planning and programming, particularly at the higher levels, and when Eisenhower left office morale in the civil service was on the upswing.

Presidents John F. Kennedy and Lyndon B. Johnson continued to rely on the chairman of the Civil Service Commission for leadership in personnel policy and management. But Congress neither made permanent the use of the commission as the central personnel agency, nor passed the bill of Senator Joseph S. Clark that would transfer most of the commission's staff and activities to an office of personnel management in the Executive Office of the president, leaving the commission to function as the "watchdog" of the merit system. Students of public administration commended the Clark bill as a reform measure that would end the commission's schizophrenic role as both manager and protector of civil servants.

Since World War II, presidents have desired a bureaucracy more responsive to their programs. Arthur Schlesinger notes: "the permanent government remained in bulk a force against innovation with an inexhaustible capacity to dilute, delay and obstruct presidential purpose." Kennedy tried to solve this problem by "day-to-day direction and control" through communicating to top-level administrators his objectives, but when frustrated remarked that dealing with bureaucracies was like nailing jelly to the wall. President Richard M. Nixon worked to make the bureaucracy responsive to his will. Though assistant secretaries for administration had been career civil servants with close relations to congressional committees, under Nixon a pattern of filling these key positions with his people emerged. In his efforts to politicize the civil service, Nixon violated regulations. The

Watergate scandal loosened his grip on the civil service. By June 1974 the *New York Times* remarked that "Nixon, who more than any other modern President sought control of the vast Federal bureaucracy, . . . is now presiding over a loose confederacy of departments and agencies that feel independent of White House control." While Nixon's successor, Gerald Ford, somewhat restored the tarnished image of the presidency, he attempted neither to revive the "imperial presidency" nor to infiltrate the bureaucracy.

President Jimmy Carter's Civil Service Reform Act of 1978 (primarily the work of Alan K. Campbell, head of the Civil Service Commission) was the most sweeping reform legislation since 1883. It abolished the ninety-five-year-old Civil Service Commission and split up its functions among an Office of Personnel Management, housed in the Executive Office (dealing with 2.1 million of the total 2.8 million federal employees), a Federal Labor Relations Authority to oversee labor-management relations, and an independent quasi-judicial Merit System Protection Board.

The Civil Service Reform Act of 1978, like Senator Joseph Clark's earlier efforts, aimed to eliminate the conflict within the Civil Service Commission, which acted as both a personnel manager and protector of employee rights. Since the commission had been unable to resist orders from the Nixon White House to make political appointments and promotions and to destroy Civil Service Commission records, the new law received widespread support. Once again the exposure of corruption stimulated reform. To make the Merit System Protection Board less vulnerable to presidential pressure, its members were to serve one seven-year term. Within that board, the act set up an Office of the Special Counsel to protect from reprisals "whistle blowers"—civil servants exposing irregularities. The 1978 law also provided for merit (rather than automatic) raises, and the appeals process open to dismissed civil servants (which had sometimes taken two years) was shortened to four months, while still affording substantial protection. The reform act also created a Senior Executive Service of about 8,000 supervisors (an idea recommended by the second Hoover Commission) who could be transferred with no loss of rank to agencies where their managerial skills were needed. Annoyed that civil servants could not strike and resenting efforts to discipline uncooperative civil servants and fire incompetent ones, government employee unions and their House supporters (generally Democrats with large civil service constituencies) opposed this reform legislation. Early evaluation of the 1978 law proved favorable. Under it, removals for poor performance rose dramatically from 115 in 1977 to 1,738 in 1980.

Civil service reform is an "unfinished business." In the late nineteenth century it could be equated with the merit system, but a century later reform is more difficult to define. Citizens of the United States continue to tinker with their public personnel practices to achieve a golden mean. They fear a politicized civil service but dislike a bureaucracy unresponsive to the needs of the electorate; they want to eliminate arbitrary dismissals, transfers, demotions—harrassment of any kind—but also wish to avoid an appeals system that paralyzes action and protects unworthy employees; they want their civil servants to enjoy secure tenure but also wish to stimulate productivity; they want a service able to follow political leadership but also resourceful enough to carry on when agency heads fail to administrate. Since each generation, indeed each administration, disagrees over what constitutes a proper proportion of politics in the public service, over how to recruit and retain the most competent and incorruptible civil servants, and over what provides a reasonable measure of security for them, there will always be advocates of civil service reform.

BIBLIOGRAPHY

Ari Hoogenboom, *Outlawing the Spoils: A History of the Civil Service Reform Movement, 1865–1883* (Urbana, Ill., 1961), discusses the struggle to introduce the merit system culminating with the Pendleton Act. William E. Pemberton, *Bureaucratic Politics: Executive Reorganization During the Truman Administration* (Columbia, Mo., 1979), evaluates changes inspired by the Hoover Commission.

Richard Polenberg, *Reorganizing Roosevelt's Government: The Controversy over Executive Reorganization, 1936–1939* (Cambridge, Mass., 1966), deals with the adjustments required by the proliferation of New Deal agencies. Richard E. Titlow, *Americans Import Merit: Origins of the United States Civil Service and the Influence of the British Model* (Washington, D.C., 1979), stresses the British origins of the merit system.

Paul P. Van Riper, *History of the United States Civil Service* (Evanston, Ill., 1958), is the standard work. Leonard D. White, *The Jacksonians: A Study in Administrative History, 1829–1861* (New York, 1954), and *The Republican Era, 1869–1901:* *A Study in Administrative History* (New York, 1958), are part of the author's classic study of the American bureaucracy.

[*See also* CORRUPTION IN GOVERNMENT; ELECTORAL PROCESSES; ENGLISH AND EUROPEAN POLITICAL INHERITANCE; JACKSONIAN DEMOCRACY; LOCAL GOVERNMENT; MACHINE POLITICS; POLITICAL PARTIES; *and* STATE GOVERNMENTS.]

CIVIL WAR:
MEANINGS AND EXPLANATIONS

Charles Crowe

NO event in American history has captured so much attention and led to so richly variegated a set of responses as the Civil War. The conflict that began with the predawn Confederate bombardment of United States troops in Fort Sumter on 12 April 1861 and ended with the afternoon surrender of Robert E. Lee at Appomattox Court House on 9 April 1865 was to prove momentous: it destroyed slavery, put a permanent end to dangers of disunion, cleared the way for the triumph of industrial capitalism, mobilized 4 million men, killed or wounded a million persons (thus nearly matching the total casualties of all other American wars), and became the bloodiest conflict between Napoleon's defeat in 1815 and the firing of the "guns of August" in 1914.

If the Yankee conquerors of the "quasifeudal" planters (as many would describe them) could look forward to a future of almost unlimited economic growth, the defeated Confederates had very limited prospects, and the emancipated blacks bore the doubly heavy burden of a bleak future and the heritage of a singularly harsh past. Freedmen were among the chief victims of an imperial expansion that had brought wealth and power to European nations through the massive dispossession and near destruction of American Indians and the appalling transportation of 15 million enslaved Africans to the New World. Slave labor had made possible the economic survival of colonies from Maryland to Brazil and, in the United States, brought riches to southern planters, northern mill owners, and the American economy in general. Aside from the specific events from 1861 to 1865, the Civil War represents both the springboard to modern industrial America and the culmination of many years of struggle to exploit the New World and to establish the relationship of the slave South to the emerging capitalism in the North. Civil War issues necessarily involve questions of slavery, racism, emancipation, alternative economic systems, sectional conflict, and military struggle, from the time of the Mexican War to the end of Reconstruction.

THE QUESTION OF MEANINGS

The scope of the war's destruction and its attendant social change, coupled with the complexity and bitterness of sectional, economic, racial, and class divisions, made inevitable a great variety of characterizations. It was called a war *for* southern independence, agrarian civilization, states' rights, freedom, the Union, and industrial capitalism; it was called a war *against* slavery, oppression, the "Egyptian Captivity," rebellion, the slave-power conspiracy, black Republicanism, and Yankee domination; it was the War Between the States, the Needless War, the Second American Revolution, and the Civil War. When the conflict began, it was for Lincoln a nationalist struggle to preserve the Union, for Frederick Douglass a "slaveholder's rebellion," for Wendell Phillips "an uprising of the plain people of the North" against the oppression and treason of the slaveholders, and for Moncure Conway a "holy war" on the greatest evil in human history. These and most other general meanings of the war can be found in the fiction, poetry, drama, and essays of Emerson, Thoreau, Twain, James, Crane, Robinson, O'Neill, Faulkner, Warren, and others.

Many of these definitions belonged to the white world; blacks had their own interpretations. During the military conflict the slaves did not express their views in futile rebellions, but the more than 100,000 who moved directly from slavery to Union military service and the million or so who used the opportunity to abandon plantations with the first approach of Union troops expressed strong opinions about slavery and the meaning of the war. In 1863 blacks generally greeted the news of emancipation with joyous enthusiasm, and at war's end, as in earlier times and later in the civil rights era, they sang, "Before I'll be a slave / I'll die and go to my grave." A transcendent yearning for liberation almost beyond white comprehension had existed in slave culture, and when the day of Jubilee seemed at hand, blacks expressed the desire for large things such as freedom from pain and oppression, personal liberty, and the right to own land, as well as for smaller things such as a garden, a mule, and some schooling. Given their way, these blacks would have worked such a transformation of the South that scholars of a later generation would have had no hesitation in speaking of the Civil War as a revolution. Educated blacks who knew the North and the world better—men like the former slave Douglass and the freeborn Henry Highland Garnett—shared the jubilation but realized that only a truly radical Reconstruction would complete the process begun by emancipation. When the blacks were left the victims of economic exploitation, caste, grinding poverty, and white arrogance and violence at the end of Reconstruction in 1877, it was apparent that the hoped-for revolution had been aborted, to the lasting sorrow of many millions.

The meanings of slavery, the Civil War, and Reconstruction are almost too numerous and complex to unravel. They involve conflict within a national society between the most archaic and oppressive labor system in existence and an emerging modern economy well on its way to becoming the most productive and powerful in the world. Among the important factors that a complete explanation would have to consider are centuries of European imperialism and the international slave trade; the creation of Western nations in the Americas; the evolution of a world economy; the emergence of industrial capitalism first in England and then in the American Northeast and elsewhere; and the network of economic, social, and cultural interactions and influences between white and black, free and slave, North and South, Americans and Europeans.

Perhaps a few random questions will illustrate the enormous difficulties of explanation: Why, in capitalistic, democratic America, did the slave masters, during the 1850's, choose to divert themselves by playing medieval knights in elaborate tournaments, complete with lances, gauntlets, and ladies' favors, while their future conquerors entertained themselves away from banks and factories with a long parade of plantation novels strangely mixing a neofeudal pastiche with Victorian bourgeois sentimentality? Why, in the 1880's, did northern millionaires and their clerks sit enraptured as the Fiske Jubilee Singers gave musical expression to ancient misery until the performers disappeared because the price seemed too high? Why, during the 1920's, did rising American stockbrokers and declining British aristocrats wait with eager anticipation for despised and scorned black slum dwellers and children of slaves to give essential advice on the "fun" and eroticism in decreeing that the time had come to move from the Black Bottom to the Charleston? Why, in the 1960's, did Scandinavians in the avant-garde of the modernist sensibility so readily find in civil rights demonstrators (and particularly in Martin Luther King, Jr.) almost saintly qualities and the hope of a new morality? The elaborate and difficult answers to these questions (which are far beyond the scope of this essay) might involve, among other things, observations on psychological exploitation, the paucity of creativity in the mass culture of industrial society, an element of bad conscience among Western peoples toward the victims of this world, and consideration of the Hegelian rule that masters are passive creatures while slaves are historical activists.

As to more specific meanings of the conflict for northern and southern whites, William Gilmore Simms and other southern intellectual combatants in the pre-1861 cold war defended their positions as masters by celebrating white democracy and civilization, the gracious and bountiful plantation, and the patriarchal and paternalistic slave system. The fugitive-slave narratives of men such as Douglass opened a window to another world. They charged southern society with the infliction of pain, hunger, and deprivation; a devastatingly capricious authoritarianism; the destruction of families and marriages; physical cruelty; and psychological terror. Abolitionist poets and novelists such as James Russell Lowell,

CIVIL WAR: MEANINGS AND EXPLANATIONS

John Greenleaf Whittier, and Harriet Beecher Stowe added to the list moral autonomy ravaged, sin and guilt revealed, opportunity denied, democracy mocked, and religion cheated.

Still another image of slavery was evoked in "Benito Cereno," by Herman Melville; therein, an optimistic, sanguine, and often uncomprehending darling of Yankee creation is confronted with a tragic and morally doomed Spanish master caught in a web of ancient wrongs not to be corrected and with a superficial public order capable of exploding into murderous rage. The exuberant Walt Whitman, who believed that America was the "greatest poem," proposed to transcend freedom and slavery with the cosmic ego of "Song of Myself" embracing all people. Thus, he had both given refuge to a runaway slave, "had him sit next me at table / my forelock lean'd in the corner," and was "a Southerner soon as a Northerner / a planter nonchalant and hospitable down by the Oconee."

In 1861, the reflections of Whitman and Melville on slavery and America held little interest for Confederate leaders defining a new nation and defending an old slave society. Jefferson Davis, who needed to influence people in Kentucky, Ohio, and England, began with dry legalisms and constitutional abstractions in putting forth a simple argument—that the Confederate States had the same right to free choice and independence as the thirteen colonies had in 1776. Why should there be a "war between the states"? When the fighting started, some orators spoke of a defensive war for localities, homes, and families, but those who sharply attacked "black Republicans" and abolitionist fanatics and stoutly defended slavery and white supremacy were probably more numerous. The poet Henry Timrod, in *Ethnogenesis*, served the interests of gentility and high culture too well to speak directly of slaves and cotton profits, but he still managed an effective and popular marriage of the traditional proslavery argument with southern nationalism. Perhaps few prominent Confederates would have disagreed with Alexander Stephens' famous speech of 1861 in which he declared that the new regime had as its cornerstone the "great truth" that for the Negro always "slavery, subordination to the superior race, is his natural and normal condition" with no hope for the white birthright of liberty. The neofeudal George Fitzhugh, unwilling to grant liberty to anyone except members of a ruling class, rejected not only Yankee capitalism and democracy but also the Enlightenment, "the political phases of the Reformation," and many other features of the world since 1500.

After 1865, southerners more or less accepted the verdict of history on the old chattel bondage but for many years clung to as much of the old regime as possible—to the land, power, white supremacy, economic exploitation of blacks, and to the planter's ethical ideal of upper-class individual rebelliousness, personal autonomy, authoritarian direction of lesser folk, social rectitude, and, most of all, "honor." Davis and Stephens lived to ripe old ages, writing arid and legalistic commentaries on states' rights and insisting that while slavery had nothing to do with the Civil War's defense of home and high constitutional principle, the peculiar institution was an amiable arrangement for an inferior race under paternalistic supervision. The myth of the "lost cause" (the Eden of happy "darkies" and patriarchal masters), as C. Vann Woodward has suggested, proved useful to businessmen and to planters who were forced to become merchants and bankers in the process of integrating the South into a national capitalist society.

Echoes of both the myth and the antebellum ethos often provided material for southern writers. For example, consider the narrator's statement in William Faulkner's *Intruder in the Dust* (1947):

> It's all *now*, you see. Yesterday won't be over until tomorrow and tomorrow began ten thousand years ago. For every Southern boy fourteen years old . . . it's still not yet two o'clock on that July afternoon in 1863, the brigades are in position behind the rail fence, the guns are laid and ready in the woods and the furled flags are already loosened to break out . . . we have come too far with too much at stake and that moment doesn't even need a fourteen-year-old boy to think *This time. Maybe this time* with all this much to lose and all this much to gain: Pennsylvania, Maryland, the world, the golden dome of Washington itself to crown with desperate and unbelievable victory the desperate gamble, the cast made two years ago.

If the South did ultimately lose on the battlefield, it won on the field of national public opinion between the 1890's and the 1960's through novels, plays, poems, stories, and sketches by writers such as Thomas Nelson Page. A racist North was disposed to listen and the South needed to cover the shame of backwardness, poverty, and a white supremacy a little too militant for national tastes. For many decades publications, vaudeville, radio, and movies from *Birth of a Nation* to *Gone with the Wind* and beyond presented southern myths of antebellum happiness shattered by the tragic but almost accidental Civil War between "brothers" (usually portrayed without basic issues) caused by abolitionist fanatics and irresponsible politicians and editors (sometimes with a few southern fire-eaters halfheartedly thrown in) and leading first to the great tragedy of a shameful Reconstruction imposed by force and then to the happy and brotherly reunion of northern and southern whites (with the blacks securely in local white hands). One version was told in 1930 by the talented southern "Agrarians," who dispensed with masters as well as slaves in making slavery merely "incidental" to an agrarian antebellum South that represented the "traditional" civility and culture of England and France. The historian in the group, Frank L. Owsley, insisted on the domination of the Old South by the "plain folk" or "yeoman farmers" and on the Civil War as the defense of "agrarian civilization" against a predatory Yankee capitalism. This presented an opportunity for young white intellectuals of the 1930's to marry an avant-garde attack on "capitalism" and a conservative defense of "civilization" with racism and reactionary politics.

That these myths concealed a world of poverty, economic and cultural backwardness, aggressive white supremacy, and the exploitation and suffering of millions of blacks became increasingly apparent in the 1950's to southern writers and intellectuals such as Robert Penn Warren. In 1961, Warren, then in flight from a segregationist past and willing to join the Union as long as he knew what it was, accepted the recent indictments of the South and rejected "the Great Alibi," whereby southerners exonerated, accepted, or explained away every imaginable social evil from bad schools to lynching by citing the defeat and disorganization of the Civil War era.

If Warren scornfully rejected both the evasion and the Civil War myth, he also dismissed the legendary northern "Treasury of Virtue," which had supposedly manifested itself in a thoroughly disinterested and noble Union war effort to free the slaves and save the country, stood as national assurance for past and present, and formed the moral foundation of all the nation's wealth and power. This vision of righteousness, he noted, overlooked a few things, such as the unwillingness of most politicians and citizens to accept emancipation as a war goal in 1863; the economic advantages gained by the North from the war; the greed and corruption of the 1860's and 1870's; and a racism that extended even to the Union army, the antislavery camp, and a number of speeches by Lincoln between 1858 and 1863. Warren, freely granting that the Civil War had been about slavery, cited Melville's hope that the struggle had been "instructive" to "the whole country" with a "catharsis of . . . pity and terror" and Lincoln's final characterization of the Civil War as atonement for the national sin, guilt, and offense against God of slavery.

Antislavery meanings of the Civil War conflict can be explored among the poets and intellectuals of the Boston area in the Lowell family (and in what could be described as a multigenerational discussion). James Russell Lowell, one of the most influential poetic voices in America, gave a large slice of his life in the 1840's and 1850's to the abolitionist cause. He fought for immediate, uncompensated emancipation and equal treatment of the free Negro and, in doing so, sharply attacked churches, political parties, national and state governments, and all institutions giving aid and comfort to the enemy. In 1846 his Concord neighbor Henry David Thoreau announced a moral civil war to be fought by men of conscience with "civil disobedience" against a government that sanctioned slavery and ruthlessly conquered Mexicans and Indians. And in 1859 his friends Ralph Waldo Emerson and Thoreau, accepting the tragic need for violence to end oppression, acclaimed John Brown as a reborn Puritan revolutionary who would champion the cause by armed struggle. (His death, Emerson declared, would "make the gallows glorious as Christ did the cross.")

Two years later, Lowell and his allies joined other American writers and intellectuals in embracing the war, however regrettable, as the only effective instrument for defeating the worst form of bondage humanity had ever known. Throughout the struggle from Bull Run to Appomattox, Lowell and Emerson sounded the theme of a great war for liberation and seldom more eloquently than in July 1863 on the death of Robert Gould Shaw, the handsome, young, Harvard-trained beau ideal of Boston antislavery, who had chosen to command the first black regiment in the war and, indeed, in American history (a "more lonely courage," said William James, than battlefield valor). Shaw and half his troops (little trained and in their first real combat) died bravely storming a high parapet at Fort Wagner, just south of Charleston. When the news came that Confederate soldiers had thrown the young colonel's body into the "nigger ditch" at the base of the parapet with the dead black soldiers, his father asked that the ditch be his cemetery and only monument. Lowell (who said that his young friend and kinsman by marriage had brought "a high immunity from Night"), Emerson, and Henry James, Sr., and his sons William and Henry (perhaps also paying implicit tribute to young Wilkie James, wounded at Fort Wagner) hailed Shaw as a martyr whose name would always be synonymous with the crusade for human freedom.

Shaw continued to be a symbol of lingering antislavery idealism, and in 1897, Augustus Saint-Gaudens carved for the Boston Common one of the most famous sculptures of the century, a large bronze column encircled by Shaw and his black soldiers. Edward Arlington Robinson used Shaw, the monument, and the freedom goals of the Civil War era to represent the heritage betrayed by American imperialism in 1898, and William James, in the dedication of the Saint-Gaudens sculpture, spoke of abolitionists as those who had served as "the world's conscience" and the highest voices of "the American democratic religion." In truth, James had actually sung the swan song for Shaw, Thoreau, and John Brown.

Several years later disgust over American brutality against the so-called Philippine Insurrection drove James to express the fear that the Civil War might have been only a precedent for modern wars of imperialist aggression. Soon the sense of the conflict of 1861–1865 as a momentous struggle for liberation had faded into Union League speeches and routine assurances that monumental American success had a righteous history. By the 1920's, with Civil War ideological memories comatose, the Boston poet E. E. Cummings could evoke as a fit companion for an

"Uncle Ed . . . led all over Brattle Street by a castrated pup" a comic figure of equal absurdity, "my Uncle Daniel," who "fought in the civil war band and can play the triangle like the devil."

Yet in 1964, scenes such as the confrontation of Confederate battle flags borne by violent segregationists and American flags in the hands of southern black demonstrators stirred the apparently long-dead abolitionist traditions. One more Boston poet and another Lowell (Robert), in the poem "For the Union Dead," strove to remember all of it—the war, abolition, the black soldiers, Shaw dead in the "nigger ditch," the Saint-Gaudens monument, William James. Through the dense and chilling fog of contemporary life, "the savage servility . . . of giant finned cars" passing, large photographs in a Boylston Street store window near the Shaw monument showing "boiling Hiroshima" ("now, the ditch is nearer"), and the "drained faces" of black schoolchildren appearing on the television screen, he could see dimly "frayed flags" quilting "the graveyards of the Grand Army of the Republic . . . on a thousand small town New England greens" where "the old white churches hold their air of sparse, sincere rebellion." The monument reveals the eloquently immobile Shaw, who "rejoices in man's lovely, peculiar power to choose life and die . . . when he leads his black soldiers to death" but who "seems to wince at pleasure and suffocate for privacy" as he, "riding on his bubble, . . . waits for the blessèd break."

JAMES FORD RHODES: TRIUMPHANT CAPITALISM AND SECTIONAL REUNION

The first ostensibly nonpartisan account of the Civil War era, a multivolume history by the retired Ohio businessman turned historian James Ford Rhodes, appeared in the 1890's to the acclaim of northern and southern readers as diverse as Woodrow Wilson and Frederick Jackson Turner. They warmly praised Rhodes for "calm and dispassionate judgment" conducive to sectional "reconciliation and peace." By granting a constructive role to the abolitionist campaign for emancipation, insisting without reservations that "slavery was the sole cause of the war," and passing over the question of economic self-interest in the Union struggle, the Ohio scholar sustained American nationalism and assured northern readers in a newly established industrial capitalist society of the righteous foundation of their wealth and power. By exonerating slaveholders, secessionists, and the South in general, by rejecting Radical Reconstruction, and by accepting the current racial status quo, Rhodes also pleased many southern readers.

Rhodes declared that Englishmen and northerners, who were largely responsible for bringing the institution to the slave colonies and states, had no right to point accusing fingers at southerners, who until the 1830's tended to reject human bondage "in the abstract" and would have found the road to abolition without the cotton gin. Secession turned out to be a popular movement rather than a slaveholder's conspiracy and the prelude to a mistaken but bravely-fought war under very capable leadership. (Except for the flawed choice of 1861 to abandon an oath to the United States and the army, Robert E. Lee was comparable to George Washington.) Rhodes, who with no consciousness of contradiction postulated a large difference between slavery and the postwar status of blacks because the former involved a "moral issue" and the latter merely "race relations" with "inferior" blacks, characterized Reconstruction as the greatest policy failure in U.S. history and an "oppression of the South by the North," the abandonment of which represented a "triumph of southern intelligence and character" and a proper end to northern meddling with "the Negro question."

Unreconstructed Confederates disliked the attribution of secession to error and of war to slavery. Left-wing Progressives such as Charles Beard would in future years vehemently reject the account of abolitionist ideology and the almost complete divorce of Civil War and Reconstruction issues from economics. Moreover, the neo-Beardian scholar C. Vann Woodward in 1951 dealt several telling blows to the basic assumptions of the Ohio historian by replacing a disembodied northern idealism with the crude self-interest of an aggressive capitalism as the key to post–Civil War politics and in explaining the southern political victory of 1876–1877 as the triumph of capitalist over planter. Still, from the 1890's to the 1920's—and beyond, to a lesser extent—the work of Rhodes did much

to shape American historical thought on the Civil War era.

CHARLES BEARD AND THE SECOND AMERICAN REVOLUTION

Behind Rhodes stood the still potent influence of the imposing nineteenth-century scholar George Bancroft, with his filiopietistic vision of America's historical and constitutional origins in divine Providence and of the never-ending forward march of a uniquely valuable American democracy. From the left wing of the Progressive movement, Charles Beard offered against both Rhodes and Bancroft a critical, comprehensive, and very persuasive interpretation of the nation's past based largely on the play of economic forces. In 1915 he began his *Economic Origins of Jeffersonian Democracy* with a quotation from Frederick Jackson Turner: "We may trace the conflict between the capitalist and the democratic pioneer from the earliest colonial days." If *farmer* is substituted for *pioneer* much of what Beard wrote in a long career may be read as a commentary on that maxim. The tale was told most completely in *The Rise of American Civilization* (1927), which he coauthored with his wife, Mary. The book asserted that the Revolution of 1776 achieved major changes in the relation of property and power and substantially advanced the interests of the small-farmer majority; that democratic aspirations lost ground in the Constitution of 1787 with the victory of "conservative, commercial and financial" interests over the "debtor, paper money" needs of the farmers; and that the party battles of Jefferson and Hamilton marked the beginning of nearly a century of national conflict between commercial-capitalist elites and a largely rural population, culminating in the triumph of industrial capitalism. In that victory, these Progressive scholars discerned a momentous bourgeois uprising comparable to the Puritan and French struggles of the 1640's and 1789, a "second American Revolution" with more sweeping and important changes than that of 1776 and an event in which the Republican heirs of Hamiltonian Federalism greatly advanced the interests of capitalism in defeating and destroying the South as the last stronghold of "agrarian" opposition.

The Beards, in their impatience with the attribution of the Civil War to slavery and of moral righteousness to the Union cause by Rhodes, discounted not only states' rights and proslavery rhetoric but also the ideology and explanations of the abolitionists, the Radical Republicans, and those who celebrated the war as a momentous fight for human freedom. After all, they reasoned, New Englanders hostile to Jefferson's embargo of 1807–1809 and Madison's War of 1812 had favored "states' rights," as did Massachusetts politicians who wanted to nullify Texas' annexation and Wisconsin reformers who meant to defy the Fugitive Slave Act of 1850 and the *Dred Scott* decision. The abolitionists, functioning only as "agitators beneath the dignity of the towering statesmen," had gotten America's answer to the only clear political call for emancipation in the 75,000 votes cast for the Liberty party in 1844 out of a total vote of 2.5 million. War rhetoric about the glorious cause of emancipation seemed inconsequential beside the yawning maw of capitalism, which required a stream of federal laws on tariffs, currency, banking, railroads, immigration, and the economic growth of the West. A key to conspiratorial Reconstruction efforts aimed at the promotion of capitalism and the economic exploitation of the South could be found by contrasting public slogans on the Fourteenth Amendment as the great charter of black freedom and citizenship with the cynical and largely secret machinations to produce an amendment helpful to the new business corporations. (The courts certainly ended by giving the corporations the help denied the hapless freedmen.)

It is indeed difficult to see states' rights as more than a convenient strategy and easy to grant that the Beards offered good reasons to suspect abolitionist and planter ideologies not anchored in specific economic, social, and political contexts. Their analysis had the advantage of leading to impressive efforts to relate economic issues to sections and to national politics. The Beardian approach properly noted the importance of the growing disinclination in the 1840's and 1850's by politicians from the farm states of the Northwest to make southern alliances and of the fact that both the industrializing Northeast and the rural Northwest became less dependent on the South and more dependent on each other.

The account of business needs and the posi-

tive Republican response to them also seems sound. Northeastern business leaders did want help with capital formation (the wartime Republican party responded with higher protective tariffs), the growth of a transportation network (railroad subsidies were provided), an adequate and stable currency, a national banking system (the Republican record was not perfect but certainly helpful), and a steady supply of cheap immigrant labor (the policies of the Lincoln administration and the Immigration Act of 1864 largely filled the bill). The Beards might also have developed (as they did not) the conclusion that a homestead bill, by promoting the establishment and rapid expansion of a national market economy, was more likely to provide substantial aid to capitalist development than to endow millions of landless Americans with land.

The Beards' frequent neglect of ideology and hatred of the eventually triumphant industrial plutocracy, which sometimes got in the way of a more precise analysis of southern and western agrarian political interests, led them into ambiguity and flawed reasoning. In their hostile fixation on the victories of capitalism in the North–South conflict, they sometimes sounded like intellectual allies of John C. Calhoun. That planter ideologues had been very effective critics of the social evils of free enterprise and the factory system, the Beards understood very well; but that southern rhetoric concealed a social order of masters and slaves even more destructive of basic human values, they seemed to forget.

In general, the Beards displayed both the aversion to industrial plutocracy and the indifference to the oppression of blacks by slavery and racism that marked the left wing of the Progressive movement. Thus, instead of following Marx in accepting the success of Union arms as a laudable and progressive triumph over a reactionary slave society, they tended to see the Civil War as the tragic victory of capitalism over its last effective opposition. Moreover, their attempts to define the majoritarian interests opposed by capitalism and to establish continuity in political leadership from Hamilton to Lincoln and from Jefferson to Jefferson Davis led to confused and sometimes contradictory discussions of "agrarians," "farmers," "agricultural interests," "farmers and mechanics," and "the planter leaders of Mr. Jefferson's agricultural party."

In fairness to the Beards, it must be noted that they grappled with real contradictions in American society, which no historian has ever discussed to the full and lasting satisfaction of other scholars. Among the neglected problems was the question of what a wealthy planter and large slaveholder like Jefferson was doing in the role of the great American democratic theorist and popular party organizer. Even if the Beards had asked and answered that question, they would still have needed to explain the presentation of an arch-conservative and proslavery philosopher like John C. Calhoun as a defender of American democracy against its predator, emerging capitalism. Beyond the first two questions lay the problem of the multiple meanings of the word *agrarian*, which included frontier subsistence farmer, northern family wheat farmer, and master of great gangs of slaves and sprawling lands in Mississippi (not to speak of Roman latifundia owners, Soviet collective farmers, or French truffle growers).

THE NEEDLESS-WAR SCHOOL

If most of Beard's contemporaries did not sustain his deep-seated aversion to capitalism, they usually shared his dismissal of abolitionist and planter ideologies and his refusal to accept slavery as the chief cause of the Civil War. The dominant conceptions of the conflict were closely related to the prevailing interpretations of slavery, race, the South, abolitionism, and Reconstruction, which, with their tendency to strengthen the sense of the Civil War as a bloody and destructive confrontation devoid of compelling issues, prevailed for nearly half of the twentieth century.

Historians who regarded the plantation South as a benevolent patriarchy and a great civilization were bound to regret the destruction of the old order by military force; and scholars disposed to see Reconstruction as dominated by massive misrule and cynical opportunism of the radicals could hardly celebrate the war as a noble crusade for human liberty. If all the fighting and dying had been caused by irresponsible and wild-eyed fanatics, if the goal had been the impossible one of the liberation and full citizenship of apparently hopelessly inferior blacks, if the Union effort had been pervaded by shoddy blankets, mis-

firing guns, corrupt contracts, and the soaring casualties of badly led men used to little purpose for the sake of the rising fortunes of families like the Rockefellers, who hired substitutes to do the fighting for them—then the great confrontation of 1861 had to lose luster and meaning. Furthermore, if slavery seemed likely to perish without violence, a crusade against black bondage would have little point.

That slavery became a declining institution in the antebellum era was the conclusion in 1918 of Ulrich B. Phillips, whose writings dominated American historical thought on the subject until the 1950's. According to the other proslavery judgments of Phillips, the blacks were a grossly inferior race of "savages" inherently suited in body and mind for passive obedience and unskilled drudgery at hot and unhealthy field labor, which was killing to white men; the enslaved Africans were major beneficiaries of civilization, Christianity, and the "training school" of "plantation discipline"; and the few scattered slave rebels were "criminals" like the murderers, arsonists, and thieves of any other society. Moreover, the system that benefited the bondsmen so much gave the masters a very poor quality of labor and marginal profits. During the years before the conflict, profits virtually disappeared, the South fell behind the nation economically, and only the noblesse oblige of aristocrats and the iron necessity of controlling a barbarous race kept black servitude alive.

To Phillips' doubts about the future of the peculiar institution could be added the more explicit critique of a "needless" conflict by scholars such as Charles Ramsdell, who insisted that by 1860 "the natural limits of slavery expansion" had been reached. Presumably a plantation system that was burdened by inferior labor and technology and was dependent for survival on substantial cotton profits and an abundance of virgin soil could hardly be expected to endure when the long-range prospects for cotton prices were so poor and uncertain, and the possibilities for crop expansion so slim, given the occupied and increasingly depleted lands of the Southeast, a Southwest too arid for staple agriculture, and Caribbean and Central American territories beyond the practical reach of the planters. Those who wished to see slavery perish, concluded Ramsdell, "had to wait only a little while —perhaps a generation, probably less." Other scholars argued that the system would have been abandoned with more time for a growing recognition of the evils of overcentralization, labor inefficiency, the destructive mining of the soil, and the absorption of nearly all labor and capital to the detriment of other economic activities; that abolitionist and northern aggression frustrated strong tendencies toward internal reform likely to eliminate the institution without Yankee interference; or that national statesmanship could have found even for a recalcitrant South constructive methods for the gradual elimination of slavery without bloodshed.

Those historians who regarded the decline of slavery as inevitable and the Civil War as an avoidable tragedy tended to add their accusatory judgments of the abolitionists to the general chorus of condemnation. For many southern writers, the ruling maxim proved to be, "Since slavery was benevolent, abolition had to be evil," but their hostility went far beyond that. During the first two-thirds of the twentieth century, major and minor historians of the Civil War and Reconstruction era variously described the antislavery reformers as gullible, naive, mistaken, dangerous, ignorant, self-righteous, inflammatory, irresponsible, inflexible, fanatical, dogmatic, vituperative, humorless, aggressive, and hate-ridden men who threatened masters with an epidemic of killing from slave rebellions, made sectional compromise impossible, convinced southerners only to cling more tenaciously to their peculiar institution, increased the difficulties of the slaves, and provided one cause—perhaps the major one—of the mass slaughter of 1861–1865. Avery O. Craven in 1939 described the abolitionists as "violent demagogues" bent on replacing "truth" with "false propaganda" and making masters do "scapegoat service for all aristocrats and sinners," and William B. Hesseltine, in 1942, dismissed the antislavery ideology and crusade as "mere humanitarian gabble." Craven commended abolitionist leader William Lloyd Garrison to the psychiatrists, and Hazel Wolf, in 1956, held that the militant reformers generally were unbalanced men "with a mania for uniqueness and attention" and a "martyr complex."

As late as 1960, so notable a scholar as C. Vann Woodward debated the possibility of referring John Brown's behavior to insanity, and the Pulitzer Prize–winning historian David Donald portrayed Charles Sumner as "this holy blissful martyr" and "specimen of prolonged and morbid juvenility" who suffered from emotional impotence, latent homosexuality, and a compulsion to escape from personal neurosis into antislavery activism. Donald had already discovered that Sumner's confreres were a "displaced elite" frantically pursuing through reform the lost power of their Federalist forebears. Thus, several generations of historical writing would suggest that a great many white scholars not only had trouble imagining the possibility of a Civil War black-liberation cause but also experienced much difficulty in finding any good motives for the chief proponents of that freedom.

The same interpretative tendencies existed for historians dealing with both Reconstruction and the Civil War. Most of the key monographs before the 1960's were written by William A. Dunning of Columbia University and his (mostly southern) students, and the interpretations they expressed were most dramatically presented by Claude G. Bowers in *The Tragic Era* (1929). Bowers described Reconstruction as a time of the most deplorable shabbiness and sordidness in public life, when "brutal, hypocritical and corrupt" Radical Republicans ruled and "the Southern people were literally put to the torture." The cynical bribery and political exploitation of the Boss Tweeds and the Grant-era spoilsmen were transported south by Yankee "carpetbaggers" (ruthless opportunists and deluded fanatics) with the aid of local "scalawags" (poor whites and other dispossessed people regarded as traitors to the South and white civilization) and ignorant and incapable Negroes (usually "dupes" but sometimes sharers in power and spoils who had been unnaturally and repugnantly elevated). When all the "force acts" and the radical programs proved to be a failure, the capable and now loyal white southerner rose up in righteous wrath to reclaim his government. Such was the dominant version of Reconstruction during most of the present century. It did little to enhance the credibility of the abolitionist indictment of slavery or the idea of the Civil War as a struggle for liberation.

Another important factor affecting discussion of the nature of the Civil War was pervasive racism, which influenced the values and judgments of scholars as well as other segments of American society. Almost any random sampling of the most reputable historians from the 1890's to the 1930's yields an extensive harvest of antiblack comment. One thinks readily of southern scholars such as Ulrich B. Phillips, who declared white supremacy to be the central theme of southern history but ignored racism as a national ideology; the Georgia professor E. Merton Coulter, who carried white-supremacy attitudes into the 1960's and 1970's; and the Nashville Agrarian and Vanderbilt University historian Frank L. Owsley, who in 1930 attributed great personal vexation to that despised enemy of the Caucasian race and civilization Charles Sumner because "his skin was not black." Prominent northern scholars in larger numbers expressed similar or related opinions. The "scientific" historian and apostle of Anglo-Teutonic racial superiority Herbert Baxter Adams could hardly imagine the full humanity of the blacks; William A. Dunning began with "the fact of Negro inequality"; and James Ford Rhodes stressed the unchanging inferiority of blacks in discussions of the basic issues of the Civil War and Reconstruction.

A notion of the later and more subdued forms of disregard of black oppression can be seen in Paul H. Buck's lucid and carefully researched *Road to Reunion* (1937); the book, devoid of both belligerent racism and consciousness of the oppressions and aspirations of southern blacks, contends that the great postbellum tragedy was the delay of northern and southern white reunion until the 1890's rather than the failure of Reconstruction and the surrender of blacks to southern white supremacy. An even better example might be found in the presentations by Samuel Eliot Morison and Henry Steele Commager in the most influential general U.S. history book from the 1930's to the 1950's, *The Growth of the American Republic.* The condescending and almost jeering discussion by these Ivy League professors of "Sambo" and the "alleged" wrongs against him, which "moved the abolitionists to tears" (but who "suffered less than any other class"), left the reader with the impression that slavery was a perpetual series of minor ordeals for masters such as the much-imposed-upon Colonel and Mrs. Page of Virginia, who had to exercise constant vigilance to prevent house slaves from breaking china and field hands from running

stolen horses until they were hag-ridden. Historians who took the black situation so lightly were unlikely to portray the politics of the Civil War and Reconstruction in terms of admirable struggles for freedom.

All of these attitudes, from disregard for the blacks to a sense of antebellum slavery as a declining institution, combined in the 1930's with then-current perceptions of world affairs to yield an interpretative approach that bore the specific name of the "needless war" school. Caught between disenchantment with Wilsonian rhetoric about 1914–1918 as a war for "democracy and peace" and the perception of a thoroughly virtuous American participation in an anti-Nazi struggle, many historians of the 1930's tended to register a general impatience with all clashes of vast armies under ideological slogans or nationalist banners.

A number of scholars, particularly James G. Randall, Avery O. Craven, and Allan Nevins, rejected the idea of an "irrepressible conflict" between free labor and slavery. Seemingly determined to dismiss black bondage as the major cause of the catastrophe, they sometimes came close to using Confederate apologetics in explaining a "repressible conflict" that lacked substantial issues and could be traced to the "emotionalism," the "irrationality," and the "uncontrolled fanaticism" of editors, publicists, and men of affairs, as well as to the "irresponsible" political leaders of a "blundering generation." Randall was influenced by nearly two decades of growing disenchantment with the assignment of sole responsibility for 1914 to the evil Germans and with the justification of the many millions dead in terms of "making the world safe for democracy." In abandoning clichés about German guilt, it was possible to blame the ruthless, destructive, often masked and sometimes entirely concealed machinations of capitalist, imperialist, militarist, nationalist, and racist rivalries; but Randall and quite a few other American historians ended by concluding that World War I paid tribute to the same wildly destructive irrationalism as the Civil War. The American conflict, it seemed, developed from "crisis psychosis," the "despairing plunge," the "unmotivated drift," the "highly artificial, almost fabricated issue of slavery," the "advocate of rule or ruin," and the "reform-your-neighbor prophet."

CIVIL WAR: MEANINGS AND EXPLANATIONS

CONSENSUS, CONTINUITY, AND THE CIVIL WAR

If both Randall's antiwar leanings and the revisionist rejection of German war guilt for 1914 became casualties of world conflict in the 1940's, the idea of the Civil War as a needless conflict without real issues continued to thrive in another generation, which found additional reasons to doubt an irrepressible struggle between North and South. In an intellectual postmortem of 1969 on consensus history, Richard Hofstadter, who had himself played a large part in the historical thought of the 1950's, traced the new school to "the early phase of the Cold War," and John Higham, in the first major critique (1959) of "The Cult of the American Consensus," spoke of a "strikingly conservative" approach that "homogenized" the past by insisting on the early establishment and continuous dominance of liberal capitalism as the only important American tradition.

The cold war and its political implications did indeed conquer the American mind and shape historical thought. Nationalistic comparisons of U.S. success and European and world failures became commonplace, and two of the most representative books of the 1950's, David Potter's *People of Plenty* and John Kenneth Galbraith's *The Affluent Society,* celebrated American abundance, asserted that poverty had been reduced to scattered and easily eliminated "pockets," and suggested that fundamental economic and social problems hardly existed. (All of this, of course, on the eve of the black revolution, the political fire storms of the 1960's, and the decade-long debacle in Vietnam.)

The new historical school stressed national unity, uniqueness, and escape from the wrenching divisions and great human catastrophes that swept Europe from the French Revolution and Napoleon to Stalin and Hitler. It seemed that the American Revolution had been only a conservative struggle for independence, the Constitution did not represent a "Thermidorean reaction," Jeffersonian and Jacksonian politics had involved no really fundamental differences, the era of the Civil War and Reconstruction had been misrepresented by ideologues, the labor movement generally expressed devotion to liberal capitalist values, Progressives and New Dealers had

proposed only to tinker with society but not to transform it, and so on. One group of economic historians, in rejecting the Beardian concept of a second American Revolution, made some novel assertions about the Civil War. No monolithic set of northeastern economic interests existed; the war actually retarded industrialization; and the issuance of greenbacks, so far from being a capitalist conspiracy, actually represented an emergency action rejected for its "immorality" by many of the businessmen who were supposed to benefit from the measure.

The most influential of the new historians, Hofstadter (whose gifted scholarship and restraint in consensus generalizations make his books still well worth reading), resembled most of his confreres in having relatively little to say about the era offering the greatest challenge to consensus scholars, that of the Civil War and Reconstruction. *The American Political Tradition* (1948), in stressing a persistent and almost universal devotion to economic individualism, laissez-faire, competition, and very extensive private-property rights that reduced the mountains and valleys of the national past to a level plain, tended to make very implausible the explanations of the North–South confrontation of a Marx, a Beard, or even a Rhodes.

In two representative sections Hofstadter discussed Jacksonian party battles and the nature of post–Civil War mugwump reformers not as the struggles of the "agrarian" majority (or farmers and mechanics) against the business community and a disinterested quest for civil service reform but as the rivalry of old money versus "aspiring village capitalists" and the "status anxieties" of mugwump patricians confronted with the vast new fortunes and power of the robber barons. (The idea of "status politics," borrowed from the social sciences, suggested vertical and perhaps directionless social escalators rather than the Marxist progression of class conflict toward a revolutionary potential.) The equally representative chapter on John C. Calhoun, by extending very respectful attention to Calhoun's political theories, suggested that neither Beard nor pro-abolitionist historians had paid enough attention to southern ideology. An essay on Lincoln tended to level this alleged mountain of Republican idealism with a precise and persuasive account of the politician who took equivocal and sometimes contradictory positions on slavery,

261

generally displayed toward blacks "the moral insensitivity of . . . the average white man," and issued under pressure the Emancipation Proclamation, which had "all the moral grandeur of a bill of lading." Almost nothing in *The American Political Tradition* could be taken as supporting evidence for the conception of the Civil War as a momentous struggle of either warring ideologies or conflicting economies.

Two leading consensus historians who did discuss the meaning of the Civil War and Reconstruction were Daniel J. Boorstin and Louis Hartz. Boorstin argued, in *The Genius of American Politics* (1953), that America's gift for self-governance could be found in a fundamental unity of values and issues and in the absence of European ideological confrontations and catastrophes. While agreeing that the war had been "the great trauma of national life," he found some consolation in the fact that the conflict had not involved warring ideologies and had taken place within "a well-established federal scheme" among men who shared nearly identical instruments of government, "thought the same about institutions," and held "similar constitutional assumptions." With no apparent ironic intentions, he concluded that the Civil War had largely involved "differences in constitutional emphasis" and could be fairly characterized as a "competition between constitutional orthodoxies." Evidence for this interpretation could be found in the speedy and "remarkable reintegration of the South into our constitutional system" by a nation that permanently allowed the South "a legitimate theoretical position within the federal system" and made the region a "champion of the states' rights, local autonomy principle of our federal constitution." (Southern blacks in the 1950's would greet this question of "constitutional emphasis" with a mixture of anger and derision.)

In this curious analysis, where words such as *constitution* and *federal* became political icons with almost magical qualities and Beard's conception of the second American Revolution seemed so impossibly remote, economic factors were not so much rejected after critical analysis as casually dismissed. It seemed that the industrial revolution would require gradual change over a period of centuries rather than the several nineteenth-century decades that Beard had so naively assumed. Grand abstractions played no more im-

portant a role than did economic factors in the Civil War. Boorstin, in an extraordinary discussion of the southern defense of slavery, asserted that only a few zealous spirits argued seriously that God commanded slavery and "tried to be absolute" in defense of the institution. Nearly always, he insisted, southerners such as T. R. Dew and George Fitzhugh used the "sociological argument," which "tended to sidestep, to avoid the appeal to absolutes," and even in some cases "to admit that slavery might be a moral evil."

This easygoing toleration for the proslavery idealogues did not extend to Radical Republicans and abolitionists. "The Romantics" (Radical Republicans such as Thaddeus Stevens) were "the bearers of fire and sword" responsible for the "crimes" and "the senseless bitterness inflicted on the South" in a "vindictive and narrowly provincial spirit." The abolitionists fared even worse at his hands as "agitators who kept the fires of controversy burning, sabotaged efforts at compromise and fed the spirit of intransigence" with lurid reports and "atrocity journalism" of the kind familiar to modern times. Fortunately for the country, "the flood of abolitionist literature" was "the least characteristic . . . product of the Civil War controversy," and "a man like Thoreau probably stood only for himself and a few fire-eating abolitionists." The reason and moderation of dominant northern opinion was well represented by a man such as Lincoln, who repeatedly said that he was not an abolitionist and that emancipation had been forced on him as a necessity of war.

In 1955 the more challenging Louis Hartz, without Boorstin's anti-intellectual celebration of American anti-intellectualism and with greater consideration for planter-Confederate ideology and for political theory generally, explored a related version of American uniqueness in *The Liberal Tradition.* (Hofstadter's maxim that "it is the fate of America not to have an ideology but to be an ideology" would have suited him well.) He posed several questions: Why, in contrast to Europe, had there not been in U.S. history either a great socialist movement or enduring traditions of reactionary thought? Why had there been so little creative political theorizing, no important ideological debate on the grand issues from the Revolution to the present?

A key to the answers was given by Alexis de Tocqueville, who long before had noted the establishment of democracy in the United States without revolutionary struggle. Americans, Hartz asserted, had indeed been "born free" in the absence of a feudal past and had imported, permanently adopted, and "given free rein" to a Lockean petit bourgeois ideology of liberal capitalism not only before the Civil War but even earlier than the Revolution. This bourgeois order placed the struggles of blacks, workers, Populists, Progressives, New Dealers, and other factions in the category of quarrels on subordinate issues within the grand national ideological consensus. Thus, the United States necessarily expressed its uniqueness through a Washington rather than a Robespierre or a Napoleon, an F.D.R. rather than a Lenin or a Hitler. According to Hartz, all of this had gone unnoticed among the Progressive historians, who, instead of studying American history, "produced a replica of it" in myths about radical change in 1776, which completely neglected "the astonishing traditionalism and legalism," and myths about the Civil War as a second Revolution, which ignored the crucial fact that both sides embraced many common political and constitutional theories.

In his own highly abstract manner and sometimes opaque style, Hartz attempted more seriously than Boorstin and Hofstadter to confront the problem of explaining the North–South conflict as a continuation, rather than a violation, of the American consensus. In examining a civil war that he classified as truly unique in the Western world, Hartz felt compelled to abandon the comparative approach. "Lincoln was no Cavour," and the Italian and German struggles for unification yielded no more insight than the Puritan and French revolutions, which had involved bourgeois revolts against feudalism rather than anything comparable to the South's conservative opposition to several major aspects of liberal capitalism. Examined in a strictly national framework, the efforts of slaveholders to make their society ideologically coherent, the "Reactionary Southern Enlightenment," represented "the only Western conservatism Americans have ever known" and the impressive effort of men who "dared to insist that life could be lived in an entirely different way" from the long-dominant standards of the United States.

Still, there were limits to the intellectual gap between North and South, and when the historian scratched beneath the "feudal and reaction-ary surface" presented by southern ideologues between 1830 and 1850, he found "not feudalism but slavery" and the nineteenth rather than the fourteenth century. After all, the medieval aristocracy had not emerged after generations of capitalism, did not have forebears like the Jeffersonian planters who endorsed liberalism, and did not have to live with the daily pressures from a hostile social order in a larger society. ("A feudalism that has once been liberal can never really be feudal again.") With northern pressures and mixed social formations such as "plantation capitalism," planters needed so much effort to try "to make the South medieval" that they sometimes surrendered to the temptation to pursue the improbably distant role of Hebrew patriarch or to follow a model of Greek democracy made inapplicable by the stratification of southern white society.

That American capitalism in 1865 defeated not a bona fide rival but a "feudal fantasy" was evidenced by the utter oblivion into which planter-Confederate ideology quickly fell. (Nothing happened like the resurgence of the Jacobin impulse in nineteenth-century France or the repeated rebirth of radicalism in Russia after every crushing czarist defeat.) Hartz concluded that in the final analysis "the political thought of the Civil War symbolizes not the weakness of the American liberal idea but its strength, its vitality, and its utter dominion over the American mind." Lockean ideas had been too powerful for the confused and contradictory southern struggles to shape a coherent ideology.

Yet, Hartz's critics might object, the confused "feudal fantasies" of southerners did not keep them from being a powerful and effective regional ruling class that often led the nation and rebels against the federal Union and tenaciously fought a wealthier and more numerous enemy for four years in the bloodiest conflict of the nineteenth century. The planters could not have been expected to grant a full endorsement to Hartz, and the slaves certainly had no good reasons to admire the brilliant accomplishments of the Reactionary Enlightenment. Hartz, in arguing for the preservation of consensus through the Civil War, insisted that ideologues did not seriously threaten liberal capitalism, but consensus involves more than abstract ideas and extends to institutions, the flow of historical events, and the life of men in time. In these areas Hartz

263

had not even tried to demonstrate the survival of consensus.

LIBERALISM, THE NEW LEFT, AND CIVIL WAR INTERPRETATIONS

The factor that loomed largest in the subversion of both consensus history and the national mood of cold war militance and conservative complacency in the 1950's was the challenge of the civil rights movement to an oppressive southern system of white supremacy. For generations blacks had been forced into inferior and often demoralizing life circumstances, subjected to exploitation by landowners and businessmen with the repressive aid of police and courts, and exposed to insult, attack, lynching, and other forms of white aggression. And beyond all of this lay the "cities of destruction," whose violent and teeming ghettos had been created by racial hostility and were rife with new and old forms of black misery.

Yet, action by the U.S. Supreme Court against segregated schools in 1954, the encouraging examples of activism in the Afro-Asian independence movements, the slow and painful but steady rise of a middle-class black leadership group, the movement of blacks to northern cities, and the influence of Nazi genocide in discrediting the idea of white supremacy, all seemed to give reason to hope for change. Now northern politicians sought the votes of newly registered black migrants to Chicago and New York, while presidents, locked in cold war competition with the Soviet Union for influence among the dark-skinned peoples of the Third World, apologized for Jim Crow discrimination in the United States. Neither the hostile ranting of southern politicians nor the annual autumn ritual of mobs and violence prevented black children from entering white schools, or civil rights workers, under the leadership of such as Martin Luther King, Jr., from braving economic intimidation, police dogs, jails, savage beatings, dynamite, and murder to breech the walls of white exclusion, through prayer vigils, picket lines, boycotts, demonstrations, marches, and sit-ins.

Like other Americans, historians took careful note of these dramatic events. The ugly and destructive faces of contemporary segregation, the anguished charges of oppression and the demands for "freedom now" encouraged many observers to reassess what had happened in 1861 and 1865 and to rethink conventional notions about slavery, race, the antebellum South, abolition, Reconstruction, and the meaning of the Civil War. All of these subjects received prompt and extensive attention from capable revisionist scholars. In 1956 the racist portrait by Ulrich B. Phillips of savage and inferior blacks in the plantation "training schools" of paternalistic masters gave way to Kenneth M. Stampp's account of the institution as a profit-making and very harsh "system of labor extortion" with origins in one of the great historic catastrophes in human history, the Atlantic slave trade, and dependent for its utility and survival on force, violence, the disruption of marriage and family, physical and psychological brutalization, and the selective use of terror.

Three years later, Stanley Elkins deepened the sense of social evil. Describing American bondage as a truly totalitarian institution and the most oppressive servitude in history, and stressing the massive destruction of whole African cultures among millions of enslaved blacks, he compared the ravaged minds of southern slaves with the personalities of zombielike survivors in the Nazi death camps, who had been "infantilized" by terror. Black bondage as revealed by Stampp, Elkins, and others seemed to provide the great historic grievance for revolutionary struggle in the Civil War era.

If slavery was so utterly destructive, it seemed likely that past attributions of noblesse oblige and paternalism to masters had been greatly exaggerated and that antebellum southern society bore the ugly marks of human bondage. Certainly little of moonlight and magnolias appeared in John Hope Franklin's restrained but telling critique of a ruling class imbued with militaristic values; often educated in military academies; led by the experience of mastery toward unbridled egos and arrogant and aggressive conduct; inclined to defend "honor" and settle disputes with the gun or the Bowie knife rather than through the courts; and encouraged by private violence, slave patrol service, and the common use of firearms to feel at home with a measure of violence and bloodshed.

Even a senior conservative southern scholar, Clement Eaton, in 1964 felt compelled to characterize southern culture as dominated by "extreme conservatism, a spirit of intolerance . . . and a powerful race feeling"; and in the same year a younger historian, Charles G. Sellers, portrayed the southerner as both racist slaveholder and American democrat with a contradictory, guilt-ridden, and tragic inner civil war. In a third book of 1964, James W. Silver, observing the thousands of soldiers assigned to keep one black college student alive, asserted that even for the ruling whites Mississippi had been a "closed" and totalitarian society on the issue of slavery in the 1850's and on segregation in the early 1960's. The historical literature of the 1950's and 1960's obviously made sympathy for antebellum planters and their Confederate cause far more difficult.

The revisionist spirit also provided new characterizations of the antislavery and Radical Republican opposition. Instead of neurotic and guilt-ridden abolitionist fanatics, a displaced elite, and ineffective reformers, Martin Duberman, James McPherson, Louis Ruchames, and other scholars portrayed effective agents of essential social change who waged war against oppression from the antebellum era through the Civil War and Reconstruction and whose personalities ranged from the thoughtful, well-balanced, and reasonable mind of a James Russell Lowell to the heroic and totally committed revolutionary spirit of a John Brown. Aileen Kraditor reasoned that the famous antislavery guilt, like that of humane Germans who despised the Nazis but identified with their country, was a "realistic" and potentially useful response to tyranny; and Howard Zinn, in comparing antislavery radicals with the young people of the Student Nonviolent Coordinating Committee, found both groups to be the effective moral and intellectual vanguards needed for the survival of democratic values and aspirations in their respective eras.

As for the Radicals and their war and Reconstruction efforts, scholars rejected the old tale of opportunistic or fanatical Radical power over a "prostrate" South through the agencies of federal bayonets, predatory carpetbaggers, traitorous and déclassé scalawags, and Negro dupes, leading to the great misfortunes of massive corruption, misgovernment, and intolerable experiments in "Negro domination." All of these political myths Kenneth M. Stampp called "the tragic legend of Reconstruction" that was used from the 1890's to the 1960's to rationalize southern segregation and exploitation and the national abandonment of the freedman. The revisionists found among the carpetbaggers many idealistic young schoolteachers, among the traitorous scalawags at least a few Confederate brigadiers and many old line upper-class Whigs, among the black politicians no corruptionists to match the Boss Tweeds, among the federal bayonets no truly effective federal occupation, and among the modest gains of blacks no Negro domination. In the hands of Willie Lee Rose, Joel Williamson, John H. and LaWanda Cox, and many other historians, a new conception of Reconstruction emerged as a sometimes mistaken but most commendable effort to bring full freedom and citizenship to the former slaves.

Far more than to Radical Republicanism, antislavery, or the plantation South, the new scholarship responded to the discovery of a racism as "unknown" to Rhodes, Beard, and the consensus historians as to Phillips. Many historians, informed by a combination of their own research with reflections on the burning ghettos of Newark and Watts and on the explosive emergence of black power and black and white radicalism, moved from the common assumption of 1960 that racial prejudice could be categorized as almost exclusively a "southern problem" to the conviction a few years later that racism constituted an enduring and pervasive national ideology. In a pioneer study of 1961 on the antebellum era, Leon Litwack reported on those discriminatory actions based on the assumption of black inferiority taken by the U.S. Departments of State, War, the Interior, and the Post Office, as well as Congress, the Supreme Court, various presidents, and northern law and custom on the local level. The pattern varied from place to place, excluding blacks from public office, schools and colleges, voting, churches, juries, militia service, public accommodations, court testimony against whites, fraternal orders and social groups, interracial marriage, religious and reform societies, choice jobs, the free right of residence and public movement, and other areas of public and private life.

Winthrop D. Jordan traced the dominance of the hostile ideas back to the earliest colonial beginnings, a second scholar found racism rampant in the West during the 1850's, and several other historians reported very strong white hostility in the Midwest during the Civil War and Reconstruction. George M. Fredrickson, tracing the evolution of "Herrenvolk democracy" and "white nationalism" in a society ostensibly devoted to the rights of man, concluded that white-supremacy ideas prevailed throughout the nineteenth century; and I. A. Newby followed the course of the ideology among twentieth-century intellectuals, scientists, and historians. An imposing quantity of monographs demonstrated the antiblack orientations of presidents, diplomats, military officers, Baptists, Methodists, Presbyterians, Roman Catholics, educators, and the white psyche.

Scholarly research extended to racism in the Union army (slaves were seized for service, denied equal pay and promotions, and abused by white soldiers), the abolitionist movement (whites tried to dominate it and wealthy merchants like the Tappan brothers refused to hire blacks), the ideas and actions of Abraham Lincoln (ultraracist White Citizen Councils quoted his words correctly for national advertising campaigns in the early 1960's), and the minds of the Radical Republicans (Senator Benjamin Wade and other Radicals despised and cynically used blacks). In some discussions race threatened to rival or surpass capitalism and slavery as a social force. (Did not this destructive ideology taint the Union cause and make the war a quarrel over whether slavery was needed to control the despised blacks? Was not the war a capitalist crusade against slavery that involved complete contempt for blacks?) Moreover, the plot thickened when scholars reported comparable racial hostility toward the Chinese, Japanese, American Indians, and, from the 1890's to the 1930's, Jewish, Roman Catholic, and Orthodox immigrants from southern and eastern Europe. (Nativists often spoke of the Jewish or the Greek "race.") Did not the general weight of scholarship indicate that American society operated either through Anglo-Saxon Protestant domination of many inferior "races" or, more specifically, through rule by affluent WASPs over a lower class recruited largely from the "lesser breeds"? In any case, it was now necessary to take into account the fact that class in America, in the Civil War era and in other times, had racial and ethnic dimensions.

In discussing the contemporary implications of racism and slavery, a good many people from the camps of both scholarship and civil rights stressed for a time blacks as victimized and largely passive people in American history who were kept subordinate into modern times by forces that perished in 1865 or that had no clear function in the 1960's (racism). Blacks, it seemed, were victims of a kind of cultural lag among whites, and their problems would be solved when enough forceful appeals had been addressed to whites to persuade them to surrender their obsolete racism. Reaction against this highly dubious explanation led in the streets to calls for black power, community, and perhaps nationhood, and in the libraries to books, by men such as John Blassengame and Lawrence W. Levine, demonstrating that even in the oppressive depths of bondage blacks had been historical activists affecting their fate through religion, folk culture, family, and resistance. The modern appeals to the democratic consciences of whites may have had some effect. After all, Adam Smith had been opposed to slavery; capitalism did not require a racial lumpenproletariat; and corporations, universities, and political agencies could, and did, let black "representation" through the gates.

The birth of black radicalism came with the perception that even the complete expiration of racism would not be enough and that the alleviation of three centuries of misery would require structural changes in corporate capitalist society. During the 1960's, perceptions of the oppression of blacks in the midst of white affluence often led beyond material boundaries and the present era to the centuries in which Western imperialism had conquered, ruled, and often enslaved dark-skinned and economically "backward" people. This deeply disturbing sense of ancient and related forms of exploitation at home and abroad emerged in sharper focus with the progress of the Vietnam War, a struggle by a wealthy, predominantly white nation to defeat by massive force and high technology a radical, nationalist, and apparently very popular revolution in an impoverished Asian peasant country. The dramatic reactions could be seen in a sea of petitions and demonstrations, ghetto and campus explosions, and the actions of Black Panther revolutionaries and the Weathermen faction of the Students for a Democratic Society (SDS).

If an awareness of racism persisted in New Left scholarship, a new consciousness of class,

class conflict, and the ideologies of domination and rebellion often seemed even more prominent. Staughton Lynd had already written "The Anti-Slavery Origins of American Radicalism," and Howard Zinn had compared freedom riders and radical abolitionists. Now they and their younger contemporaries found in the American Revolution "Jack Tar in the streets" and New York tenants forcibly seizing the land they worked, in the Jacksonian era new signs of class conflict, in the age of the Civil War and Reconstruction unexpected evidence of some support from white labor for black emancipation. In world affairs other historians found strong elements of imperial ambition in the decision to drop the atomic bomb on Japan in 1945; the major cause of the cold war with the Soviet Union in American expansionist belligerence; the motives for the Central Intelligence Agency's secret and conspiratorial subversion of student groups, magazines, professors, and cultural congresses in the ruthless designs and strategy of the corporate capitalist state; and the reasons for a world network of treaties, alliances, bases, aid programs, dollar diplomacy, and troops as a last resort in the name of "democracy," "free enterprise," and "civilization" in a neo-imperial impulse that sought markets, raw materials, cheap labor, and power without recourse to old-fashioned directly occupied and ruled colonies.

The new political and intellectual climate stimulated the reinterpretation of the Civil War and Reconstruction with particular attention to economic and ideological meanings. As early as the time of "consensus and continuity," Arthur Schlesinger, Jr., sharply and effectively criticized the needless-war school for intellectual blindness to the obvious and for moral callousness to the oppressed in failing to see that emancipation was the compelling issue of the Civil War era, but his influence was limited in the 1960's by his enthusiasm for liberal corporate capitalism and by his linkage of the Civil War and the cold war through a comparison of abolitionists and anti-Communists as ideological heroes of freedom, which implied that Communism simply represented a continuation of the old war on human values by slavery.

Equally interesting in the pre–New Left years was a book on Civil War literature by the famous literary critic and cultural historian Edmund Wilson, who rejected both Schlesinger's militant cold war conceptions and his insistence on moral and ideological issues in the North–South confrontation. The still emerging black revolution had no real impact on Wilson's conception of the Civil War issues, but the blinding light of impending nuclear holocaust encouraged him to see all mass conflicts, including the Civil War, as factories for corpses and dangerous hatreds and monuments to the intolerable distribution of ideological fanaticism. The North and the South in 1861, the Western Allies and the Central Powers in 1914, and the United States and the USSR in the 1960's—all reminded him of the blind drives of the sea slug voraciously and perpetually attempting to consume all creatures in its path.

Beyond Wilson and Schlesinger lay New Left perceptions. A key essay by Staughton Lynd on Turner and Beard asserted that neither scholar had adequately understood the nature and importance of slavery, race, class conflict, and the perpetual war on the Indians. The more mistaken Turner, in his romance on the frontier origins of democracy, neglected the city, the factory, the immigrants, and the blacks, and ignored violence and war on the northern frontier and the settlement of the southern frontier by masters and slaves. ("Simon Legree was a frontier farmer.") A less misguided Beard drew a fuller picture and understood the importance of the triumph of industrial capitalism but erred in neglecting slavery, race, and ideology and in the characterization of class conflict as being between capitalists and agrarians. Lynd thought that the conflict of 1776 had been waged as "a colonial independence movement" by a coalition involving "small farmers and artisans" under the leadership of northern capitalists and southern slaveholders, that the Constitution of 1787 had been a compromise between capitalist and planter (not "personality" and "realty"), and that 1861 represented a breakdown of that alliance and a full-blown bourgeois revolution comparable to the French Revolution.

In flight from both Lynd and Beard, Eugene D. Genovese, with imaginative flourishes of "Marxian" intellectual tools and rhetoric, explained the North–South conflict as a struggle between radically different ruling classes and societies. Curiously enough, he admired the liberal and reactionary scholars of slavery but scorned most of the New Left historians, voted in academic politics after the mid-1960's with the "liberal establishment," and offered a Marxism that seemed to some critics to be directed toward conservative perceptions and conclusions. Although he certainly relied on conceptions of class and class conflict, he rejected "naive determinism, the economic interpretation and the insipid glorification of the lower classes"; sometimes seemed skeptical about almost any major economic explanation; and accepted the "patriarchal" self-descriptions of the masters. His interpretation also brushed aside racism with vague references to "an aspect of the class question" and locked slaves into a "paternalistic" relationship that made rebellion virtually impossible.

While insisting on the complete relativism and the class foundations of the grand moral generalizations relating to slavery, abolition, and the Civil War, Genovese could speak with much hostility about the bourgeois pretensions of an ultraracist and harshly exploitative northern capitalism, yet at the same time roundly criticize scholars for judging Jefferson Davis by "bourgeois standards" and failing to treat "fairly" the aspirations of high-minded and socially responsible slave masters. Nevertheless, Genovese offered an explanation with considerable internal consistency. The American Revolution (which freed the North for capitalist development) liberated a half-formed southern ruling class to evolve toward maturation and full hegemony over a quasi-feudal slave society (variously described by Genovese as "seigneurial," "precapitalist," and "pre-modern"). When southern planters found their development and survival as a ruling class challenged by northern capitalism, they launched a life-or-death "war for southern independence" with all their resources and determination.

BARRINGTON MOORE ON THE CIVIL WAR

During the era of consensus history and Eisenhower conservatism, William Appleman Williams had stood almost alone in explorations of American history from a Left perspective. In laissez-faire capitalism he found the key to both the politics of imperial expansion, from early national history to the confrontation with Castro's Cuba, and the momentous struggle of the capi-

talist North with the slave South for the loyalty of small farmers in the West, which culminated in the Civil War. Later, Barrington Moore, Jr., presented the most influential and representative account of Civil War causation of the New Left years in a comparative study of the great political upheavals of the past three centuries. His analysis of American politics, which depended upon Williams, borrowed a little from Frederick Jackson Turner, a good bit from Beard, and still more from Marx, and described slavery and sectional conflict as the fundamental causes of the North–South confrontation and the outcome as a victory of progressive forces over a reactionary South. While Moore did not present the Civil War as a twentieth-century revolution in the sense of the forcible seizure of power from below by a radical popular movement, he reasoned that the struggle merited characterization as "a violent breakthrough against an old social structure" leading to the advance of freedom, the final capitalist upheaval, and the "last revolutionary offensive" for "bourgeois capitalist democracy." An event in the tradition of the great Puritan and French revolutions, the Civil War upheaval proved to be an aborted and incomplete transformation, in that it failed to execute fully promises of black freedom and citizenship and to restructure southern society.

In agreement with Beard's basic idea of a second American Revolution, but in opposition to both the vulgar Marxists who would glibly dismiss "moral issues" and those historians who were willing to consider ideology without regard to "the economic structures that created and supported them," Moore insisted that the bone of contention had been black bondage, that "without the direct conflict of ideals over slavery both the war and the ante-bellum struggle were incomprehensible," and that Radical Republican Reconstruction should be described as "abolitionist ideals fused with manufacturing interests to ignite a brief revolutionary flash." Moreover, he rejected the Beardian idea of the slave South as an intolerable opposition to the advance of northeastern capitalism (though he granted that slavery offered a powerful "obstacle" to "political and social democracy").

Until about 1840 the flow of cotton had greatly stimulated the key textile industrial growth of New England and the Middle Atlantic states; and the South had looked to New York and other northern cities for shipping, banking, and manufactured goods until the bombardment of Fort Sumter. With complementary economies of slave-grown staples and industrial production, the southern and northern ruling classes might have forged an enduring alliance for the mutual protection of capitalism and the plantation system (at greatest expense to the slaves but also at a loss of democracy to the wage laborers) after the Prussian pattern, in which the Junkers, with a base of coerced peasants and a quasi-feudal social order, proved essential in the management of an authoritarian German state capable of coercing the urban workers and guiding the nation toward economic modernization. Implicit in Moore's analysis, though he did not develop the idea, was a post-Reconstruction arrangement of northern capitalists and southern planter-business interests (similar to the Prussian alliance) that guided the South gradually toward industrialization and formed a conservative core in American politics lasting long enough to frustrate reformers as recently as the administrations of F.D.R., Truman, Kennedy, and Johnson.

Moore did not deny that mill owners and slave masters had very different interests (more divergent than Junkers and industrialists because of slavery) and that southern politicians often opposed capitalist efforts for capital accumulation through tariffs and for the creation and expansion of a national market economy through internal improvements and western development, but he noted a common and powerful attachment to private-property rights and the "negotiability" of northeastern interests without violence or great political upheaval before 1860. What happened, Moore asked, to change this situation, and why did the capitalists not need a political regime with "southern Junkers" to control their workers?

With revised pages from Turner and Hartz, he explained that the lack of a need to transform feudal social structures and the presence of a continental domain for economic exploitation made a difference in American development and that the absence of both threatening foreign enemies and a strong and radical working-class movement challenging capitalist property did much to save the United States from the "modernization crises" of Germany and Japan. Before the 1840's a rough sectional balance had existed, with the Trans-Appalachian West selling its small surplus mainly to the South and the South and the Northeast exchanging cotton for manufactured goods and services. While these economic relations persisted, the eastern expansion of production and the movement of the West from subsistence to commercial farming subordinated them to the increasingly greater importance of western markets for eastern capitalists and eastern markets for the western farmers.

All this led to the rise, from Ohio to Wisconsin, of an "individualistic, small capitalist outlook" tying the "dominant, upper strata of western farmers" to an ideological alliance with capitalism; stimulated the growth of western antislavery sentiment; enabled politicians to rally workers with manufacturers and financiers on the basis of free lands in the West and the appropriate tariff, banking, and railroad proposals (what need then of "southern Junkers"?); and made southern planters sufficiently fearful of western abolition to take measures such as killing the homestead bill of 1852.

The emergence of the Republican party and the election of Lincoln in 1860 cemented the alliance of North and West and pushed disaffection in the South to an explosive point. The Union victory made possible a more radical phase in the capitalist revolution, the transformation of southern society through the confiscation of all planter lands and their redistribution in small plots and the incorporation of the freedmen into bourgeois democracy. A radical minority under the leadership of Thaddeus Stevens, representing the fusion of abolitionist idealism and some northern labor support with the infant Pennsylvania iron and steel industry and several major railroad groups, attempted to complete the revolution, but it did not win the unified support of northeastern capitalists and their western allies, who could not be recruited for a fundamental reordering of southern society or for an alteration of property rights beyond what was needed for the elimination of the old slave labor system. Consequently, the basic southern social structure (except for slavery) stayed intact, and the task of incorporating blacks into bourgeois democracy remained for the nation to deal with in the 1950's and later.

Several empirical elements of Moore's analysis have been questioned, and aspects of his theory, such as his use of a Turnerian safety valve, have aroused skepticism. Some scholars would undoubtedly ask if his critique paid enough attention to racism, nationalism, and imperialism. Moreover, to speak of the plantation as both "a form of American capitalist growth" and a system antithetical to northeastern capitalism suggests a serious interpretative problem, and his discussions of the relationship between "moral issues" and "their economic foundations" seem ambiguous. (Is ideology the incidental "superstructure" of social formation, or not?) One may also wonder if Moore had not tied his discussion of industrialization too closely to the Western laissez-faire, capitalist model to the neglect of the Soviet path to modernization and other possible alternatives; and if he had inquired deeply enough into the question of how much liberty and equality could be delivered by a bourgeois democracy that historically sought only as much of these goals as was needed to fight lingering feudal enemies and that, by inevitably generating economic inequality, necessarily limited political freedom. Nevertheless, when all the reservations have been made, Moore's work remains the most intellectually provocative and useful interpretative account of the Civil War and Reconstruction. His influence could be felt even in the conservative 1980's.

THAT UNCERTAIN PRESENT

Looking back from the ultraconservative 1980's to about 1972, when the rapid decline of the New Left and a national turn to the right first became evident, we can see some of the major events that have influenced historical thought about the Civil War era and the American past in general. Black and urban crises—and with them the threat (or promise) of revolutionary change—quickly vanished without radical alterations in American society, and the Vietnam conflict had ended in utter defeat and debacle but in such a manner as to do no serious damage to the American economic and social status quo. It seemed that the radicals greatly underestimated the strength of the system. In the mid-1980's the ideological and social hegemony of capitalism still prevailed and efforts to defend a world order favorable to "free enterprise" and "democracy" were more belligerent than at any time since the Nixon years.

Moreover, from the mid-1970's the country moved steadily away from confrontations with racism and poverty. While the South did slowly and reluctantly abandon the fortress of white supremacy, and blacks did overcome many of the worst humiliations, by the 1980's the nation appeared to have abandoned millions of blacks in impoverished and isolated ghettoes and rural areas. Beyond the legal rights of blacks, the Great Society "solution" of President Lyndon B. Johnson's administration had been to expand the welfare system to mitigate the misery of the masses and to increase opportunities for better educated and upwardly mobile blacks in a rapidly expanding economy. Later trends toward public indifference, political reaction, and bleak short- and long-term prospects for the economy came to a culmination in the Reagan years and led to substantial losses for blacks in opportunities and welfare. For many historians the new political climate made the Civil War issues of slave oppression, emancipation, and economic and sectional conflict seem less momentous and relevant to modern times.

In this milieu "the decline of Civil War studies," a theme in Eric Foner's interesting book (1980), has been evident in many areas of scholarly concern for a decade. If the interest in black history has continued, the old sense of dealing with truly momentous themes has largely disappeared. One cause can be found in the change from the dominant national conception of blacks as *the* people and *the* force compellingly confronting the nation to the image of *a* minority (an important one, to be sure) likely to be overtaken in numbers during the 1990's by *another* minority (Hispanics). Both black heroes and southern oppressors have been reduced to a shadow of their former selves. In the scholarship on slavery the stress on black cultural and institutional accomplishments in the "house of bondage" diminished the sense of great oppression, and comparative history offered data (higher birthrates, lower death rates, and impressive natural increase in population) that strongly suggested better material conditions for slaves in the South than in Brazil and Cuba. The industry in history books on the South has flourished, but the dramatic decline of the elements that emphasized southern distinctiveness as recently as the mid-1960's has made the nineteenth-century South seem more remote, disassociated from the present, and even (in the eyes of some authors and readers, and in ways surely repugnant to the spirits of both Nat Turner and John C. Calhoun) a picturesque tourist spot for the frail American historical imagination. The diminishing number of books and essays on abolition sometimes registered signs of a resurgence of the old impatience, and the only two notable books in many years on racism involved comparisons with South Africa.

In more recent years the near absence of new explanatory books and essays and the general decline of scholarly debate on the origins, causes, nature, and meaning of sectional conflict and Reconstruction have been particularly evident. Two elements that help to account for this situation are the increasing remoteness from the present of the world that existed before advanced industrial capitalism and mass culture, which makes the Civil War seem less important as a "watershed," and the fact that mid-nineteenth-century issues of race, religion, and economics, after flaring up again in the 1950's and 1960's, faded from the center of public attention in the 1970's. Other factors relate to the decline of explanation for all major historical periods, such as the diversion and splintering of scholarly interest in "mainstream" events into research on the history of ethnic communities, family, childhood, public institutions, legal and economic forms, and various specific situations subject to quantitative analysis. Consequently, greater effort is now needed to make sense of a national history always poor in structures and central themes and bound to historiographical traditions that favor the concrete and the specific at the expense of general assertion. And, of course, generalizing is a particular problem for the many intellectuals skeptical, indifferent, disenchanted, or hostile to the liberal capitalism that still dominates American society.

Yet history does go on. The conflicts, contradictions, and issues of the Civil War era are too important to be ignored, and Civil War studies will undoubtedly continue. Perhaps some future historian will devise an interpretation surmounting the failure of Beard, Moore, and all the others to relate racism to slavery and capitalism satisfactorily. One clever synthesizer may even take into account the fact that agriculture can be pursued by subsistence farmers, masters and slaves, and agribusinessmen, and that buying, selling,

and imbibing culture in a capitalist marketplace do not make a capitalist of the planter dependent on a slave labor system for wealth, power, status, and social visions.

It seems unlikely that future discussions of the North–South confrontation can ignore either slavery or capitalism. Neither can the ideologies expressing those social systems be dismissed, except perhaps by scholars in the throes of a revulsion (similar to Edmund Wilson's in the early 1960's) against all ideology as catastrophe-bearing, who conclude that (in Robert Lowell's words) "man's lovely, peculiar power to choose life and die" has no legitimacy, that Colonel Shaw may never "break his blessed bubble," and that "boiling Hiroshima" and the "nigger ditch" are very, very close for all humanity.

BIBLIOGRAPHY

The best and most recent account of issues and events in the Civil War era can be found in James M. McPherson, *Ordeal By Fire: The Civil War and Reconstruction* (New York, 1982). Other useful general works are Eric Foner, *Politics and Ideology in the Age of the Civil War* (New York, 1980); William R. Brock, *Conflict and Transformation: The United States, 1844–1877* (Baltimore, 1973); and David M. Potter, *The Impending Crisis, 1848–1861* (New York, 1976). For useful discussions of key books, see the chapter bibliographies in Charles R. Crowe, ed., *The Age of Civil War and Reconstruction, 1830–1900,* rev. ed. (Homewood, Ill., 1975), and for a good supplementary bibliography, see James M. McPherson *et al.,* *Blacks in America: Bibliographical Essays* (Garden City, N.Y., 1971). For some recent titles and an interesting perspective in a current textbook, see Stephen Thernstrom, *A History of the American People,* 2 vols. (1984). For discussions of Civil War explanations before 1962, see Thomas J. Pressly, *Americans Interpret Their Civil War* (Princeton, 1954).

For brief accounts of some issues, see Hans L. Trefousse, ed., *The Causes of the Civil War: Institutional Failure or Human Blunder?* (New York, 1971); on northern war opinion, see George M. Fredrickson, *The Inner Civil War: Northern Intellectuals and the Crisis of the Union* (New York, 1965); on southern mythology, see Paul M. Gaston, *The New South Creed* (New York, 1970); on racism in films, see Thomas Cripps, *Slow Fade to Black: the Negro in American Film, 1900–1942* (New York, 1977); on the Agrarians, see the symposium *I'll Take My Stand: The South and the Agrarian Tradition* (New York–London, 1930).

For Warren and Lowell, see Robert Penn Warren, *The Legacy of the Civil War* (New York, 1961), and Robert Lowell, *For the Union Dead* (New York, 1964).

For James Ford Rhodes, see his *History of the United States From the Compromise of 1850,* 7 vols. (New York–London,

1892–1906), and Harvey Wish, *The American Historian* (New York, 1960).

For Beard, the key books are Charles Beard, *An Economic Interpretation of the Constitution of the United States* (New York, 1913); *Economic Origins of Jeffersonian Democracy* (New York, 1915); and, with Mary Beard, *The Rise of American Civilization*, 2 vols. (New York, 1927). For criticism, see Bernard C. Borning, *The Political and Social Thought of Charles A. Beard* (Seattle, Wash., 1962); Charles Crowe, "The Emergence of Progressive History," in *Journal of the History of Ideas*, 27 (1966); and Richard Hofstadter, *The Progressive Historians: Turner, Beard, Parrington* (New York, 1968).

The needless-war school is best represented by James G. Randall, "The Blundering Generation," in *Mississippi Valley Historical Review*, 27 (1940). See also Avery O. Craven, *The Repressible Conflict, 1830–1861* (University, La., 1939). For hostility toward the abolitionists between the 1930's and the 1960's, see Craven, *op. cit.;* William B. Hesseltine, *Lincoln and the War Governors* (Magnolia, Mass., 1948); the John Brown essay in C. Vann Woodward, *The Burden of Southern History* (Baton Rouge, La., 1960); and David H. Donald, *Charles Sumner and the Coming of the Civil War* (New York, 1960). On the racist attitudes of Ulrich B. Phillips, see *American Negro Slavery* (New York, 1918) and *Life and Labor in the Old South* (Boston, 1929). On the Dunning school, see William A. Dunning, *Reconstruction, Political and Economic, 1865–1877* (New York–London, 1907), and Claude G. Bowers, *The Tragic Era: The Revolution After Lincoln* (Cambridge, Mass., 1929).

The key books on consensus and continuity are Richard Hofstadter, *The American Political Tradition and the Men Who Made It* (New York, 1948); Louis Hartz, *The Liberal Tradition in America* (New York, 1955); and Daniel J. Boorstin, *The Genius of American Politics* (Chicago, 1953). For criticism, see John Higham, "The Cult of the American Consensus," in *Commentary*, 27 (1959), and Richard Hofstadter, *The Progressive Historians: Turner, Beard, Parrington* (New York, 1968).

Most of the relevant titles on liberalism and the New Left are in Charles R. Crowe, ed., *The Age of Civil War and Reconstruction 1830–1900*, rev. ed. (Homewood, Ill., 1975), but particularly important works are Howard Zinn, *The Politics of History* (Boston, 1970); Student Nonviolent Coordinating Committee, *The New Abolitionist* (1964); and Staughton Lynd, *Class Conflict, Slavery and the United States Constitution* (Indianapolis, Ind., 1967) and *The Intellectual Origins of American Radicalism* (New York, 1968). Among the more important revisionist books are Kenneth M. Stampp, *The Peculiar Institution: Slavery in the Antebellum South* (New York, 1956) and *The Era of Reconstruction 1865–1877* (New York, 1965); Martin Duberman, ed., *The Antislavery Vanguard* (Princeton, N.J., 1965); Stanley Elkins, *Slavery* (Chicago, 1959); John Hope Franklin, *The Militant South 1800–1861* (Cambridge, Mass., 1956); and Leon F. Litwack, *North of Slavery* (Chicago, 1961). See also Arthur M. Schlesinger, Jr., "The Causes of the American Civil War," in *Partisan Review*, 16 (1949); Edmund Wilson, *Patriotic Gore* (New York, 1962); and Barton J. Bernstein, ed., *Towards a New Past: Dissenting Essays in American History* (New York, 1968).

For Barrington Moore, see *Social Origins of Dictatorship and Democracy* (Boston, 1966). For a useful discussion on explaining the Civil War era, see Eric Foner, *Politics and Ideology in the Age of the Civil War* (New York, 1980), and on generalizing and interpreting, see Gene Wise, *American Historical Explanations* (Homewood, Ill., 1973).

[*See also* HISTORIOGRAPHY OF AMERICAN POLITICAL HISTORY; AMERICAN REVOLUTION; CIVIL RIGHTS MOVEMENT; RACE AND RACISM; RECONSTRUCTION; *and* SLAVERY, SECTIONALISM, AND SECESSION.]

COLLECTIVE VIOLENCE

David Grimsted

THE best-known comment about collective violence in the United States, H. Rap Brown's 1967 statement that it was "as American as cherry pie," is both true and misleading. Common as social violence has been in the nation, it is neither peculiarly virulent nor important within it. The incidents can seem a bloody trail of disruptive conflict, but the United States has generally limited and absorbed them with little disturbance to most people's lives. Mobs have frequently marked important changes or tensions within the nation's political, social, and economic structures; but seldom have riots clearly caused much change, because society quickly subordinated extralegal violence to its peaceful or sanctioned processes. Brown rightly suggested a long lineage for the riots that rocked the nation between 1964 and 1968, but both he and the country would have been less fearful or hopeful about the future of the nation had they known more about its previous history of collective violence.

The term *collective violence* here refers to those events in American history commonly called mobs, riots, lynchings, or vigilantism: incidents in which at least ten or so individuals collectively attempt to enforce their will immediately by threatening or perpetrating extralegal injury to persons or property, ostensibly to promote social improvement or justice within a given society.

To explore the question of the general quality of rioting in America, half a dozen incidents will be used to consider basic theories of collective violence. To explore the question of when and why riots have arisen, a basically chronological picture of American collective violence related to generating social forces will be given.

EXAMPLES AND THEORY

On 26 August 1765, almost two weeks after a restrained mob had caused the resignation of the man designated to collect the stamp tax in Boston, a mob sacked the luxurious home of Massachusetts Lieutenant Governor Thomas Hutchinson. At dawn the rioters dispersed, but not before they had stolen or destroyed the home's furnishings, £900 sterling, and the papers and historical documents that Hutchinson had been collecting for years.

The virulence of this attack on the man whom most Bostonians judged the "greatest and best man in America" was tied to mob resistance to the Stamp Act, even though Hutchinson had argued the folly of its passage. The destruction created immediate sympathy for Hutchinson, but there were few arrests and no prosecutions. A twenty-eight-year-old shoemaker, Ebenezer MacIntosh, led this riot; he was arrested but not held for trial.

James Foster of Natchez, Mississippi, was also wealthy and of a good family. A mob of from 200 to 300 took him from unresisting authorities as he left the courthouse on 3 January 1835, after he was acquitted of killing his wife. Drum and fife played, and reportedly 1,000 people looked on as Foster was stripped, given 150 lashes, tarred and feathered, "half-scalped," and paraded through the streets. The local press reported the action with approval, and no prosecution of the rioters was considered.

On 21 May 1856 a group of San Franciscans, organized as vigilantes under thirty-two-year-old businessman William T. Coleman, seized two men and hanged them after a brief "secret trial."

In the following days they shut down the local Democratic press and exiled twenty-eight Democratic politicians, one of whom hanged himself. When they disbanded, three months later, they became the nucleus of Republican city control. Democratic state and national authorities weakly resisted, but the vigilantes' great challenge came when Democratic State Supreme Court Justice David S. Terry stabbed one of their members. Before disbanding, the vigilantes hanged two criminals to prove their moral and nonpartisan claims. No legal action against the rioters was taken.

In 1893 Henry Robinson, a mentally retarded black, killed a young white girl. Immediately captured, he was taken up by a group of "leading citizens" of Paris, Texas, who widely advertised the coming lynching. On the weekend, 10,000 people reportedly poured into town to watch the mob push red-hot pokers into his eyes, throat, and body before burning him alive. No one considered resisting or arresting the killers.

On 20 April 1914 thirty-five Colorado Fuel and Iron Company private guards attacked a tent colony at Ludlow composed of the families of strikers. Machine-gun fire killed five men and a boy; the burning of tents resulted in the deaths of two women and eleven children; and three strike leaders were "executed" by the mob. These deaths triggered retaliatory attacks by the strikers against company property and guards, in which about another fifty people were killed. On 29 April, President Wilson sent in federal troops, who quieted the conflict.

Martin Luther King's assassination in Memphis on 4 April 1968 led to black riots in over 100 American cities; the devastation was most extensive in the nation's capital. Property damage was conservatively set at $24,000,000, with twelve people killed, most of them looters trapped in flames. Millions of Americans watched on television as looters, seemingly in high spirits, robbed neighborhood stores. By the end of the disturbance on 7 April some 7,500 people had been arrested. About 350 people were indicted, and a few dozen received sentences, none over a year.

This small selection of incidents of collective violence allows some consideration of the basic patterns of motivation and result in the nation's riotous past. Within their context, one can begin to consider the relationship of American mobs to the general theories that have been developed to explain social violence.

The "father" of riot theory, Gustave Le Bon, argued in 1895 that individuals acted with rationality but that "crowds" acted irrationally. Not his explanation, but his description, of crowd behavior is still somewhat convincing. Because of personal anonymity and an unquestioning acceptance of the evil being attacked, individuals do things collectively that they would not do in ordinary circumstances. The Bostonians who wrecked and looted Hutchinson's house in 1765 were not, under ordinary conditions, destructive thieves; neither were those Washingtonians two hundred years later who sacked their own neighborhoods. Most young San Francisco businessmen in 1856 would not ordinarily have considered killing a supreme court justice for resisting extralegal violence; nor were most of those southerners who came to Paris, Texas, sadists in their everyday lives. For the great majority in all these groups, the circumstances that they accepted as part of a crowd allowed them to do things that would have been unthinkable for them to do alone.

Insisting that his theories applied equally to peaceful groups, Le Bon stressed that crowd irrationality had heroic and humane dimensions. For him rationality implied calculational shrewdness, but for the major Anglo-American students of riot since 1950 *irrationality* was a more wholly disparaging term. Eric J. Hobsbawm and especially George Rudé vitalized the study of collective violence by suggesting how specific social data could be used to explore rioting. These historians also raised several questions about Le Bon's theories, at least when caricatured into the picture of the mob as ravenous beast. They stressed that rioters were commonly oppressed groups who acted with restraint in relation to social justice. They also argued, in a mild Marxist–Whig historical vision, that conspicuously brutal elements of mob behavior declined over time.

Rudé and Hobsbawm are clearly correct in the positive aspects of their argument. Rioters are seldom riffraff or criminals but tend to be a cross section of the young males in the areas affected. The three known members of the Hutchinson mob were a sailor, a craftsman, and a merchant; and the southern press insisted that "leading citizens" supervised the mobbings of both Foster and Robinson. In Washington, D.C., a survey of some 775 people arrested showed that 46 percent had previous records, though generally for minor offenses. Even this figure hardly suggests general criminality; compared to nonriotous youth of the same age in the affected areas, rioters were marginally better educated, employed, and paid. For San Francisco, membership cards exist for about a third of the reputed 6,000 vigilantes. Here the mob consisted predominantly of young merchants or clerks of older American Protestant stock—in contrast to the politically prominent Irish Catholics whom they exiled. In all these mobs, the predominant group tended to be made up of young males between the ages of fifteen and thirty who were local residents and employed.

Rudé and Hobsbawm are also right about elements of restraint and selection in riotous behavior; in no case was the violence random. However dubious his responsibility for the Stamp Act, Hutchinson was one of the Boston officials bound to aid its enforcement. In Mississippi the mob injured only that individual who was probably an acquitted murderer, while in Texas the one man murdered had killed a child. In Colorado both sides attacked only those whom they saw as the enemy. In Washington the rioting was much more open-ended but limited to intentional destruction or appropriation of property.

Yet these elements of restraint and selectivity coexist with aspects of brutality or randomness. Hutchinson was a man of probity, and the attack on his property had no immediate connection with policy, as had the mild riots twelve days earlier. And when a mob selectively half-scalps, disfigures, "rapes" with red-hot pokers, or burns a human alive, it invokes some of the emotive ferocity that lurks beneath man's civilized surface. There was no conspicuous sadism in San Francisco but, rather, a total self-righteousness that depicted any opponent of the mob as diabolic. That strikers in Colorado confined ten mine guards in a building so that they burned to death is understandable retaliation—but against personally innocent enemies. And the general mood in Washington was one of holiday shopping rather than an exaction of social justice, an "instant integration" into consumer society, as theorist Barrington Moore phrased it. Riot allows a saturnalia, a temporary suspension of usual authority.

For American riots at least, there seems small justification for the dichotomy between rational and emotional, or social and psychological, motivations that informs the arguments of both Le Bon and Rudé–Hobsbawm. Riots always have roots in social grievances or circumstances that both justify and loosely confine mob action. The community tolerates certain extralegal actions, and the mob acts within those vague bounds. If mob and community largely agree on acceptable limits, the mood is usually festive even when actions are wanton or ferocious. If rioters overstep those bounds, they may trigger serious opposition. San Francisco vigilantes did not dare kill Terry, despite their fury against "this leader of the Law and Murder party." The Hutchinson mob was allowed to do at night what the community would not tolerate in the light of day. Riot boundaries exist, but they are vague and shifting, and can include much wanton destructiveness and sadism.

The question of riot's contribution to social justice is also ambiguous. If the Stamp Act was tyranny, injury to those who urged acquiescence to it was justified. Local editors in Natchez argued the nobility of the mob's action, and San Francisco vigilantes justified themselves by pointing to the crime and corruption that preceded their action. Texas lynchers avenged a murder and saw themselves as more broadly repairing their social fabric, just as Washington rioters protested the realities of racial exploitation. In Colorado, workers fought for their right to organize, whereas guards believed in part that they were uprooting "a bunch of foreign thugs."

Yet such arguments are only one side of any assessment of justice. Hutchinson was no British bird of prey, nor was he especially tied to the Stamp Act. Why him? Foster had been legally acquitted and may have been innocent. There is little evidence that San Francisco's Democratic political machine was more notably corrupt than most urban power brokers. Nothing seems clearer than that southern justice was as capable of killing Henry Robinson as was the mob. Nor were those people who were victimized in Washington in any way personally tied to the murder of King or notably connected to racial exploitation.

The question of social justice is often quite distinct from social purposiveness. The mob murder of Robinson was also the most clearly socially "useful" from the mob's point of view, part of an effective system of terror that made anyone think long and hard about the least deviance from the South's racially based caste system. Similarly, the Hutchinson riot raised issues tied to independence. If it was British rule that was bad, not simply particular British rules or rulers, then an honest broker like Hutchinson was the enemy.

Foster's case was tied to broad social issues as well: the power of husbands over wives and the fact that justice in the United States was often bought by those who could pay liberally. Yet brutalizing Foster was a way not of changing such realities but of ritualistically attacking them while leaving them intact. This deflectionary reality also pertains to the Washington riot. Injustices to blacks were as clear as was the murder of King, but the riot was never tied to any institutional charges, either by its advocates or subsequently. Nor is there any evidence that the mostly small businessmen who lost their shops were especially exploitative.

The social results of the Colorado conflict are equally ambiguous. Rockefeller interests took advantage of the violence to drive out the strikers, even though it meant defying President Wilson. This immediate victory for business may have been part of a larger defeat. Certainly a broad section of the general public showed growing sympathy for labor roughly in proportion to management ruthlessness; and labor, despite many setbacks, expanded and sharpened its power in the period between the Pullman strike of 1894 and the end of World War I.

In the Ludlow and King riots there may have been psychological results as important as any social ones. The riots of the 1960's clearly marked a new assertiveness by a group long denied full social opportunity and respect. French thinkers, such as Georges Sorel and later Frantz Fanon, argued that violence matters primarily as a way by which exploited people regain a sense of selfhood. The situation of black rioters in the 1960's bears some tie to that of Irish rioters of the antebellum years: disadvantaged but no longer powerless, both groups rioted, perhaps the most dramatic illustration of their newfound right to be heard. Similarly, though employers commonly initiated violence, workers in resisting obviously achieved some invigorating sense of their own power and class identity.

Sociological theories that evolved after the 1960's riots moved in the direction of the Rudé–Hobsbawm emphasis on reasonable response to oppressive conditions. Because traditional aspects of American racial oppression were softening at the time, the idea of "rising expectations" arose, stated in its most sophisticated form in Ted Robert Gurr's *Why Men Rebel* (1970). Gurr paid heed to the full panoply of possible influences, from ideology to repressive threat, but subordinated them to "relative deprivation" (RD), or "a discrepancy between the 'ought' and the 'is' of collective value satisfactions." The problem with Gurr's theory is not that it doesn't apply to riots but that it is a truism, the charm of which lies in the fact that if one seeks, one finds. RD, relative to something or someone, is always with us; but that San Francisco vigilantes or Texas lynchers or Washington looters felt more unhappy than those who did not riot is far from clear.

One of the advantages of the historical theories of social oppression is that they direct attention to particular social issues and conditions, in contrast to the vapidity of "satisfactions." And riots are most telling when explored as suggestions of the fissures in society that people at least temporarily feel cannot be well handled by ordinary process. Social "oppression" and "justice" are no more precise than "satisfactions," but at least they encourage close consideration of specific information without the illusion of having a magic formula.

Personally selfish mob motives frequently interacted with social causation. Many mobs prohibited participants from stealing, but such was obviously not the case in either 1765 Boston or 1968 Washington, D.C. Advertising Robinson's lynching was probably related to merchants' scent of profit; and certainly political power was crucially at issue in San Francisco, as economic advantage was involved in Colorado. The role of leaders in particular riots was also crucial at times. Would there have been a Boston mob without MacIntosh, a San Francisco committee without Coleman? The uncertainties of why a situation creates riot in one place and not in another, of why a mob forms around one grievance and neglects a more serious injustice, suggest that particular persons, settings, and circumstances may be crucial. If the Colorado militia leader had not been so anti-union, if some militiaman or striker had not accidentally fired once, would the tragic loss of some seventy lives have been avoided? Maybe. In the volatile situation surrounding riots, a multitude of small things give impetus or quietus or redirection to large events.

Because of the variety of stimuli and results in riots, historians have often tried to categorize mobs hierarchically as primitive, reactionary and modern, or as "reactive" and "forward-looking." Such developmental patterns seem untenable in the United States. The most recent sample riot is the least defined in terms of specific goals, whereas lynchings like that of Robinson could hardly have been much surpassed at any time for conspicuous sadism.

Some American historians, notably Richard Hofstadter and Michael Wallace (1970), have stressed the "conservative" quality of American mobs. While the term fits some types of incidents reasonably well, it jibes poorly with many events. Was it conservative to half-scalp an alleged wife-killer who had been legally acquitted? Were young San Franciscans conservative in driving out by force an established political party and city administration? "Tyranny of the majority," as Wallace claims, may be involved at times, but it is usually not easy to determine who the majority was or what that implied. There were more craftsmen than lieutenant governors in colonial Boston, more blacks than whites in Washington in 1968, but these data made such groups neither conservative nor the majority. In most mobs only a tiny communal proportion rioted—twenty were estimated in Boston—and even when participation was large, as in the southern, San Francisco, and Washington cases, it approached nothing like a majority. Yet limited participation does not deny generalized tolerance for the action. American riots grew out of sensed injustices or conflicts incapable of being handled by the usual procedures, but restricted by the boundaries of communal sanction.

The nature of communal sanction has much to do with the probable forms of destructiveness of the riot. When sanction and mob action have corresponded most closely, things usually go their way with little harm to the rioters. If authorities or communities accept their legal responsibilities, mobs either dissolve or respond with fury. Where social objectives are vaguest—as in Boston and Washington—property destruction tends to be most widespread and least personally deserved. Where communal sanction is least dubious, as in Mississippi and Texas, mob action has the most sadistic potential. Where communal support for violence is withheld, as in Colorado, there is enhanced likelihood of large-scale fighting once violence begins.

If riot depends on communal sanction, it also insists on immediacy of result. Rioters proceed with a sense that immediate action can restore fair social functioning. The mob expectation of a quick fix by the system makes riot in some sense the opposite of revolution. Almost all vigilante groups, for instance, offer a picture of their society as vicious, but they also argue that removing a few bad men will restore it to its "natural" purity. A mob was effective against the Stamp Act when most Americans wanted to remove this blotch from the system, but riot became peripheral as sentiment moved toward independence.

The emphasis on immediate results imparts some of the conservative quality to the act of rioting. American riots have been waged by racial, ethnic, and economic minorities almost as often as against them and have been directed at the conspicuously well-off, like Hutchinson or Foster, as well as at the conspicuously disadvantaged, like Robinson. Yet the stress on immediate correction was likely to do more to secure the position of entrenched power than to change it. Historians, while arguing that class anger motivated the Hutchinson mob, could not point to any serious adjustment of class power. In Washington, the goods stolen seem a substitute for the advocacy of any broader social goods. On the other hand, the long series of southern proslavery and racial riots did inhibit questioning of the social status quo. The mob's usual belief in immediately achievable results made American riots a distraction for those wishing broad change but an often effective weapon for those fearing or opposing new directions.

In a broader sense, too, riots may be part of the United States's democratic mechanisms. Except in the colonial period and in the South, extralegal violence has never been wholly tolerated as part of the system, but it has also seldom been repressed with severe brutality. Instead, collective violence has existed as one of many possible alternatives through which groups may act to exercise their will or vent their irritation. The cost is sometimes tragic, but seldom has it been broadly disruptive. This is partly because American mobs are usually local problems. Federal troops enter only in a crisis situation, as in Colorado, so that both sides welcome the intervention. Hence, whatever the intensity of feeling, only in rare cases is riot directed toward the nation or its policies.

American riot has functioned as a way "of letting off steam," a kind of safety valve against certain social angers. At best, American mobs have served some of the same function as that of what might seem their opposite, the Supreme Court. Like Court decisions, riots often dramatize issues by putting them in clear and specific terms that direct public attention to both the broad and the intensely personal implications of particular controversies. Riots are educational, though they provide learning in a hard and dangerous way.

The illegal violence that defines mobs both highlights and obscures the broad social issues involved, by forcing consideration of questions of means: what are the ties between popular freedom and procedural requirements? Is extralegal violence justifiable in a society where other channels of influence are open? Should this be a government of laws or of people? How should the dramatic violence of the mob be weighed against the sanctioned power of "the system"? What is society's responsibility to those whom riots injure and to those who may be injured if riot is repressed?

To answer such dilemmas too simply or complacently is to lessen the decency with which any vital society must expect, accept, and control violent anger within it, must both entertain and contain inevitable social tensions.

THE HISTORICAL RECORD: THE COLONIES

As an extension of England, the British colonies of North America shared some of the mother country's attitudes toward rioting, although their forms of collective violence were influenced by colonial status and a more ambiguous class structure. The seventeenth century was England's revolutionary era, when political and religious conflict led to three major governmental shifts. The generally victorious Whig ideology emphasized liberty over traditionalism, but

within major limits. Disenfranchised males were a part of the "vulgar herd" or "mob," a term whose double meaning—referring either to the masses or to the riotous—is telling. In a sense, riots were the political arm of the masses. It was to this reality that Thomas Hutchinson referred when he wrote, "Mobs a sort of them at least are constitutional."

In the colonies, riot also became one means by which local populations modulated central policies. Hence many of the most famous colonial riots concerned local resistance to various English laws and their enforcement. An impressment mob demonstrated in Boston in 1741, and six years later two days of rioting drove out both naval and civil authorities. At least seven riots erupted over impressment, ranging from Maine to Virginia (1764–1768), before the mother country ceased to practice in its colonies what it continued to do at home. Similarly, two "white pine" riots in New Hampshire, in 1718 and 1734, prevented the confiscation of illegally cut trees. Of this type, too, the tobacco riots in Virginia in 1662 and in Maryland were to raise prices by restricting production.

The most important use of the mob occurred in relation to the Stamp Act; here the law itself was at issue. The riots began in Boston, where a mob attack frightened the stamp agent into resigning. With no one daring to fill this post, the act itself became unenforceable. Mob action in other parts of the country followed, though in many cases intimidation alone was sufficient.

The Sugar Act (1764) and attempts at enforcement of other British navigation laws also led to mob violence. Incidents occurred in Boston and Newport as early as 1719, and at least twenty took place after 1764, from Maine to Georgia. Confiscated goods often were simply "liberated," but the mob beat customs officials in seven incidents and sank two ships. Despite the fame of the Boston Tea Party in 1773 and the burning of another ship in Annapolis in 1775, the response to the Tea Act marked the declining use of the mob by a people increasingly aware of revolution as a possibility. The acquittal of the British soldiers who killed five citizens in the Boston Massacre suggested the same shift.

Some colonial riots aimed at correcting local abuses, personal or statutory. In Boston, for example, there were three food riots—in 1710, 1713, and 1729—protesting hoarding or exporting of grain in time of shortage; and three other riots were against prostitutes. The latter type also occurred in Newburyport, Massachusetts, and Newport, Rhode Island, where four women were tarred and feathered. In Philadelphia, practices of intimidation on election day became riotous in 1742, and in 1773 a mob tore down a market. There were at least a dozen cases of mob punishment of adulterers or wife-beaters by tarring or riding on a rail, while mobs rescued prisoners from authorities at least a half dozen times. Fear of inoculation or medical dissection also triggered mob action.

The best-organized of these moral mobs were the South Carolina Regulators of 1767–1769. The Regulators argued that they were restoring social order by driving out criminals and controlling "low people." Their methods were those of threat, physical injury, and exile. Some twenty people were killed, but the activity that made the Regulators unique was virtually enslaving some of the "lower people." Richard Maxwell Brown argues that the Regulators cleansed the community, although "excesses" led to an organized Moderator opposition that quickly ended their power.

Colonial riots tended to be least effective at adjusting quarrels between established sections of the population. Boundary disputes sometimes erupted into rioting, as in the New York–Massachusetts contest between 1751 and 1757. More troublesome were disputes over land title or rent between actual settlers and land patentees. Prolonged controversies, with some violence, occurred in New Jersey (1699–1700, 1745–1754), North Carolina (1737–1759), and the estates along the Hudson River (1751–1757, 1766), in all of which there was some loss of life or property.

Although a number of colonial "rebellions" occurred at the time of England's Glorious Revolution (1688–1689), they triggered little mob violence. This was not the case in several religious or sectional struggles. Maryland Puritans in 1655 routed proprietary forces, losing only four men, while killing fifteen or twenty opponents. They were luckier than those who supported Nathaniel Bacon's rebellion in Virginia in 1676, involving an Indian threat in the west. When Governor William Berkeley recalled troops after the Indians accepted peace and declared Bacon a rebel, Bacon's "army" marched on Jamestown and

burned a dozen or so buildings. When Bacon died suddenly of disease, his movement collapsed and twenty-three supporters were executed. Almost a century later, North Carolina Regulators rose in the back country to redress political and legal grievances but were repressed by the governor's militia in the "Battle of Alamance," which took the lives of twenty Regulators and nine troops. Seven Regulators were later executed. The Paxton uprising in western Pennsylvania (1763–1764) left no whites dead; here the victims were twenty hapless Indians, similar to the peaceful tribe that Bacon's men had killed.

Where race entered in, all generalizations about the benign character of the colonial mob cease; colonists responded most harshly to black uprisings, and the two slave-initiated colonial insurrections were quickly repressed. In New York City nine whites and some twenty-four insurrectionists were killed in 1712, eighteen by executions that included burning alive and starving to death. The South Carolina disturbance of 1739 took the lives of perhaps twenty white men, while at least thirty-five slaves were killed, their heads put on stakes as ritual proof of white power; a year later some fifty slaves were killed in an insurrection scare. Such acts of mob destructiveness were more than paralleled in officially sanctioned violence in various Indian wars or in the legal hysteria of the Salem witchcraft cases of 1692 and the New York slave incident of 1741.

During the Revolutionary War, both sides were willing to sanction much violence informally. James Madison believed tar and feathers the ideal cure for Toryism, and the very term *lynch law* may have come from the activities of Colonel Charles Lynch, a patriot who chastised, sometimes fatally, Loyalists in western Virginia. The vagueness of the military situation in parts of Virginia and in much of Regulator-torn western South and North Carolina created a situation in the early war years of chaotic group violence.

FROM REVOLUTION TO CIVIL WAR

Gordon Wood pointed out in 1966 that independence ended two major justifications of earlier riots: that of local self-protection and that of sanctioning riots in preference to giving formal power to the mob, now rechristened "the people." Despite sexual and racial limitations, American political clichés stressed "popular sovereignty" and "universal suffrage." If the people determined both laws and officers, there was no theoretical need to resort to violence.

Authorities controlled both Philadelphia's "Dutch Riot" of 1784 and New York's "Doctors' Riot" of 1788 (in the latter the militia killed four) and even restrained the antiprostitution riots in New York City of 1793 and 1799. More serious riots were now called rebellions. Shays's Rebellion of 1786 was an action by debt-oppressed farmers in western Massachusetts to prevent foreclosures; while two agrarian uprisings in Pennsylvania, the Whiskey Rebellion of 1794 and Fries's Rebellion of 1798–1799, protested respectively the federal excise tax on whiskey and land taxes. In all three cases military force was applied against the rioters; six lives were lost. In both their rhetorical and practical response, these incidents signaled the end of colonial patterns of collective violence.

The quarter century following Fries's Rebellion was the period most free of collective violence in the United States. Aside from some minor personal chastisement, slave scares were the major incidents. The Gabriel plot in Virginia (1800) was handled legally; but in Louisiana in 1811 hundreds reportedly rose up, murdering only two whites before some sixty-five blacks were killed, their heads once again placed on poles.

So unusual were riots in this period that one incident was enough to earn Baltimore the title of "mobtown." After President Madison declared war in 1812, Alexander Hanson's Federalist newspaper, the *Federal Republican,* denounced the decision, which triggered a mob that drove him from Baltimore. Hanson published for a while from Virginia but determined to return to Baltimore with a protective coterie. A new mob fell back only when Hanson's friends fired, killing one man. The next night the mob brutally beat and humiliated them, killing one elderly man who had been a general in the Revolution. Public reaction to the mob's sadism and "censorship" helped secured the right of public criticism during war.

The renewed rioting that occurred between 1824 and 1833 fell into two categories. The first group comprised riots in New England cities,

overtly aimed at prostitution but also racial, as the neighborhoods attacked were black: in Providence in 1824 and 1831; in Boston in 1825 and 1827; and three incidents in Portland in 1825. Mob action was limited largely to property destruction, though some blacks were beaten. The rioters were described as young Irish workers, six of whom were killed.

The second type proved more lasting and ferocious: mobbings by or between groups of recently arrived Irish Catholic workers on canals, railroads, or public works, sometimes aimed at supervisory personnel or nearby communities, but more commonly waged between "clans." Secret mutual-aid societies, these groups served some functions of proto-unionism with a strong tincture of "recreational" rioting. There were at least thirty-nine such ethnic battles before the Civil War in New York and the old Northwest (1835–1841), western Pennsylvania (1849–1851), and Maryland. At least thirty-six lives were lost in these disputes, and many hundreds of people were hurt.

Although Irish ethnic battles were destructive in the antebellum years, violence directly tied to labor causes, such as wages, hours, working conditions, or strikes, was minor. Strikes were common and often accompanied by some intimidation; dock workers in New York City in 1836 and weavers in Philadelphia in the 1840's damaged some property and injured officials who tried to check them. In the thirty-one instances of labor violence before 1861, only two supervisors and two workers (the latter in an 1857 Maryland railroad strike) were killed. There were two takeovers, anticipating sit-ins almost a century later, of mills near Pittsburgh in 1846 and 1848.

At the beginning of 1834, Americans could pretend that riot had been imported with the Irish; but the illusion was to shatter sharply in the next three years, when the nation experienced, in terms of its population, rioting that was greater, more varied, and as fatal as at any other period in its history. The 146 riots in those three years (1834–1836) were of immense variety. A convent school in Massachusetts was burned, and the nuns and their students were driven out into the night. A Fourth of July brawl in Vicksburg, Mississippi, led to the hanging of five gamblers and the killing of one vigilante. In Baltimore a mob sacked the homes of a half dozen leading citizens involved in a bank swindle; a citizens' guard fatally shot five of the rioters. In New York City laborers attacked houses being built with stone cut by prison labor, and Ohio and Michigan conducted a minor border war near Toledo. In St. Louis a mob burned to death a free black who had killed a constable, and people in Hot Springs, Arkansas, treated similarly a slave who had killed his owner. In Woodbury, New Jersey, blacks stripped and severely beat two blacks believed to be slave-catcher spies, and in the Iowa Territory citizens hanged a man who had killed a friend while drunk. A New Orleans mob sacked the home of a wealthy Frenchwoman when a fire revealed her sadistic brutality to some enchained slaves.

It is hard to explain this gushing of collective violence in the prosperous last years of Andrew Jackson's presidency. Some of it must have had ties to the Jacksonian stress on the people's power, a concept at the heart of riot ideology in these years. Some of it was spillover from the central riotous controversies of 1835 that integrated slavery, abolition, and politics. As the South moved toward a more positive defense of slavery, abolitionists mounted a major campaign to convince southerners that slavery contradicted basic democratic and Christian beliefs, and to convince northerners of their moral responsibility for black bondage. In 1834 and 1835 the central collective violence was to fend off thought about the obviously explosive issues of nation, race, and slavery.

Several of these riots provided prototypes of the major forms of conflict that occurred in the antebellum years. The Massachusetts convent-burning was the most destructive act of the purely religious Catholic–Protestant mobs of these years, but there were thirty-nine incidents where religion was the initiating cause. Often called "Nativist" riots, about two-thirds of them were in fact Catholic-initiated; commonly, they were attempts to end Protestant meetings of an antipapist bent, or the activities of "street preachers" in the 1850's. One Protestant and two Catholic churches, in addition to the Ursuline Convent, were destroyed. Two rioters were killed and hundreds wounded in the street-preacher mobs, while in Ellsworth, Maine, a priest was tarred and ridden on a rail. The most unusual of these riots occurred in Cincinnati in 1853. When German immigrants protested the visit of Archbishop Bedini, the predominantly Irish police force fell on the march, beating one man to death and killing one of their own officers. Several policemen were convicted of riot.

Some sixty-four ethnic disturbances paralleled these religious uprisings. Frenchmen initiated one, Germans six, the native-born eighteen, and Irish thirty-nine, though in only a few cases was the other side passive. Most of the incidents were between Irish and natives. Irish usually attacked persons, using fists and clubs, whereas the chiefly New England mobs often assaulted Irish homes. Some twenty-two deaths resulted.

The fights between Catholics and Protestants were more numerous but less brutal than those surrounding the Mormons. Former supporters tarred and feathered prophet Joseph Smith and theologian Sidney Rigdon in Ohio, but in 1833 a mob drove Mormons from their first home, in Missouri, where their growing political power had awakened their neighbors' jealousy. When the Mormons sought legal and political protection, the mob attacked again in the late fall, brutally whipping the Mormons, burning over 100 of their homes, and driving them out. A major battle left two rioters and three Mormons dead, and two other Mormons subsequently died.

Mormons understandably were never again to be so peaceful in the face of the mob. Joseph Smith marched with an "army" from Ohio to reclaim the land, but weather, illness, and dissension forced him to retreat. The Missouri Mormons, regathered in a new wilderness, prospered and were soon joined by the church leaders. Smith's attempt to exert stronger control caused Mormons to mob a half dozen prominent families and to found a secret band to terrorize any opposition. These actions and a minor election riot led to an accelerating tragedy in October 1838. When the militia was called out, the Mormons attacked, killing ten and losing three. Governor Lillburn Boggs issued an order, saying Mormons "must be exterminated, or driven from the state, if necessary"; two days later a mob exterminated nineteen Mormon men and boys at isolated Haun's Mill. In the harsh winter some 2,500 Mormons once again left their homes in the hands of the mob-militia.

Smith began anew at Nauvoo, which soon became the largest town in Illinois. The saints' political power and prosperity drew resentment as conflicts waxed over polygamy. When dissidents in 1844 organized a newspaper exposing the practice, Mormon officials destroyed the press, thereby providing the excuse for neighboring communities to attack. Smith and his brother were murdered by a mob-militia while in "protective" custody, and, once again, thousands of Mormons left, now for their new Zion in Utah.

The full tragedy was not over. James Strang led a Mormon remnant to Big Beaver Island, Michigan, only to have a mob drive his 2,400 followers out in 1856; Strang himself died of mob-inflicted wounds. In Utah, Mormons became extralegal executioners. Mormon mobs killed about 135 people, 123 of them in the Mountain Meadows massacre of 1857: As a wealthy wagon train was leaving Utah, local Mormons promised protection and then methodically killed all men, women, and children over three years of age and stole their goods. The violence against innocent Mormons in 1833 had thus run its course to this grisly mass murder a quarter century later.

Several mobs stressed economic angers. Nine disturbances over bank policies or failures took place; a New Orleans mob killed two police and stole over $5,000 in 1842 in protest over the fall in note values. Food riots occurred in New York City and Baltimore during the depression of 1837. Communal and personal rivalries sometimes led to riot. New Yorkers blew up a dam that they felt diverted water from them unfairly; and Indians, led by U.S. Senator Edward A. Hannegan, tried to destroy a canal lock. Erie, Pennsylvania, citizens conducted several riots between 1853 and 1856 to prevent the unification of rail gauges, which would injure their "loading trade" between New York and Ohio rail lines.

Two groups of economic riots were successful. In Philadelphia mobs between 1840 and 1842 prevented the laying of railroad tracks in one neighborhood. More significant were riots against the continuation of the semifeudal land tenure system in New York's Hudson River valley. In 1839 and 1840 mobs forced officials to relinquish their ejectment papers; fourteen people were tarred and feathered. These first mild disturbances ended when a large militia group was sent out, but more serious violence in 1844–1845 climaxed in the killing of a deputy sheriff. The riot trials, however, created sympathy for the anti-renters that pressured landlords to change the system. Seven other mob incidents over land tenure occurred, the most fatal of them

in Sacramento and Santa Barbara, where four officials and about seven rioters died.

Miscellaneous types of riots also took lives. Mobs of college students caused deaths at Yale and in Virginia and South Carolina. Six medical riots against dissections or isolation hospitals occurred, as did several riots related to entertainment events. In the worst of these, the Astor Place riot of 1849 in New York City, the militia fired on a mob, killing about twenty-two people. This event raised popular concern about class conflict more strongly than any other incident of the era.

The colonial practice of mobbing in support of propriety returned. In addition to antiprostitution and antigambling mobs, familial or sexual morality was the subject of numerous incidents, especially in the South. In Mobile a man was ridden on a rail in 1838; he had reportedly broken his father's ribs before running off with his stepmother. And passengers drowned a free black cook discovered alone in a storeroom with a deaf-mute German girl. In such cases, beating, humiliation, or exile was the most common punishment.

Riots also protested against particular judicial and legislative acts. In Kentucky a judge who gave a new trial to a convicted murderer was sprayed by sewage from a fire engine. Ten incidents occurred in protest against support, passage, or enforcement of particular laws, half of them involved with temperance. Two rioters were killed in the most serious incident, in Portland, Maine, where Democratic politicians fomented a riot to embarrass temperance crusader and newly elected mayor Neal Dow.

Far more common and deadly were riots against criminals, real or alleged, which took about 300 lives between 1828 and 1860, almost 90 percent of them victims. This was largely a western phenomenon, with only six incidents and one death occurring in the original states. In most cases—unless one is willing to accept the testimony of mob spokesmen—ambiguities surround both the mob's motivation and the victims' guilt. In the South in 1835, eight people hanged were said to be members of the "Murel gang," which in fact never existed. A Cane Hill, Arkansas, mob killed six people, one a slave, one feebleminded, and the other four clearly guilty only of criticizing the "regulators." Were the thirty or so people drowned and shot by another

Arkansas mob, in 1841, criminal? Possibly, but no evidence was offered, and no possibility exists that they ever engaged in a barbarity like that of their executioners.

Variations on vigilance committees committed most of these murders. Richard Maxwell Brown, the leading historian of these groups, has argued that they were, with a handful of exceptions, "constructive," respectable people purifying their communities of criminal or "debased" elements. He is certainly right according to the most readily available information about such groups, the vigilantes' own accounts. Yet these rarely present clear evidence of guilt; the very emphasis on "depraved" or "lower" people is sufficient proof that there were no real charges against many victims. The conduct of many groups also belied any conspicuous decency. Regulators in Barton County, Missouri, for example, left off whipping some alleged criminals whose wives tried to stop them—in order to whip and rape several of the women. In Noble County, Indiana, the Regulators hanged one man. Allowed to offer last words, the victim said that he had never killed anyone, although he had stolen some cattle, but he could name several Regulators who had done likewise. At this, one Noble Regulator kicked out the prop from the tailgate where the man stood and choked off further comment. Vigilantes were often less just and selective than other mobs, in part because of the calculation that lay behind their actions and in part because they had to do something or admit overreactive foolishness.

Four varieties of riot were at the heart of the disturbances in the mid-1830's: political, racial, antiabolition riots in the North, and alleged insurrection panics in the South. The bloodiest of these events took place in the newly settled black belt of Mississippi. After several slaves were whipped until they confessed to plotting insurrection, five whites and fifteen or twenty blacks were hanged. This repression provided a more comfortable myth to handle a certain terror inherent in slavery than did the real rebellion of Nat Turner in 1831, which took fifty-four to fifty-seven lives. Turner and his followers were hanged or deported, while mobs killed at least twenty-five—estimates range as high as 100 —slaves, all of them innocent of involvement.

The Denmark Vesey plot of 1822 led to legal executions, as did one in Louisiana in 1837, betrayed by the slave who had organized it. There were twelve recorded scares after 1829 handled by mobs. The worst incidents, those of 1856 in Tennessee and of 1859–1860 in Texas, resulted in about 125 slave murders and had lesser reverberations in most slave states.

Although perhaps twenty whites were killed by mobs in insurrection scares, another eighteen alleged abolitionists died at the hands of southern mobs in some 307 incidents, most of them involving exile, whipping, or humiliations like tarring and feathering, "scalping," branding, dunking, "railing," and ritual hanging. A few victims were genuinely antislavery, especially in Kentucky, but most were guilty mainly of being in the wrong place at the wrong time. Such mobs made clear to everyone the danger of raising any questions about slavery. And if the mob attacked shouting "Abolitionist!" there was almost no possibility of civil protection.

Shortly after the Mississippi slave scare, the abolitionists began a mail campaign to convince the South of the evils of slavery; the South responded by demanding that abolition be silenced, legally or by riot. The year 1834 proved that the North did not need southern urging to mob abolitionists; the worst of these mobs was in New York City, where conflict over a meeting hall began four days of rioting. About ten people were seriously hurt, but the attack was confined mainly to property. July through October of 1835 were the months of frequent abolitionist mobbing, especially in New England and the Mid-Atlantic states; the center of mobbing moved to the Midwest in 1836 and 1837.

Almost one out of seven northern riots was antiabolitionist between 1828 and 1861, most of them concentrated during the mid-1830's. Yet they were the least destructive of all types of riot. Only two deaths occurred, both in an attack on Elijah Lovejoy's press in Alton, Illinois; elsewhere, only four abolitionists were hurt by mob attack. Property damage was much greater, reaching a climax in 1838, when Philadelphians leveled Pennsylvania Hall. Meetings were often ended, though seldom permanently, and abolitionist presses attacked. There were so many incidents and such limited damage because northern attacks seemed ritualistic acts of irritation or gestures against the South, sometimes carefully calculated, as in the four riots that took place in

Utica (N.Y.), Boston, Providence, and Montpelier (Vt.), on 21 October 1835.

The antiabolition riots often accompanied antiblack outbreaks in the North. New York City's antiabolition riot of 1834 devolved into attacks on blacks, as did Cincinnati's two years later. Some thirty riots against blacks were scattered over the North. Riots in Connecticut and New Hampshire drove out black schools, while community attacks occurred in places like Washington, D.C., Portsmouth, Ohio, and Columbia and Pittsburgh, Pennsylvania. In two cities, blacks suffered repeated attacks: Philadelphia, with nine riots between 1829 and 1849, and Cincinnati, with six from 1829 to 1841. In all these mob incidents, some ten blacks lost their lives. Blacks were usually not passive, though their armed resistance tended to be of short duration. In small community mobs, blacks killed as many rioters as were killed. About a dozen riots were initiated by blacks, most directed against other blacks believed to be injuring their community. The major all-black riot aided the escape of two fugitive slaves in Detroit in 1833, though blacks worked with whites in most fugitive slave riots.

Despite the pro-southern and antiabolition rhetoric of 1835, a mob of white people who just happened to be on the street rioted in Albany, New York, at the pathos of a chained black fugitive being returned to slavery. This incident suggested the emotional limitations on the North's desire to placate the South and was only one of some fourteen such incidents. Only some twenty blacks escaped because of such mobs, but two slave owners trying to claim their property were killed, the most famous incident occurring near Christiana, Pennsylvania. Boston and upstate New York were the scene of several fugitive-slave riots in the 1850's, in one of which a policeman was killed.

A full-fledged two-party system initiated political rioting in Philadelphia in 1832 and New York City in the spring of 1834. The New York disturbance saw some twenty Whigs and almost as many officials seriously hurt. A second Philadelphia riot in the fall of 1834 claimed three victims and involved substantial destruction of property. Although elections remained raucous, both parties came to accept boundaries for the toughs that both employed, but new parties threatened that balance. When Nativists contested the Philadelphia elections of 1844, Irish fireboys (volunteer firemen) shot into an election rally in May; several Nativists were killed and others wounded, and the Nativists unleashed by far the worst of the period's attacks on the Irish community. Property damage was estimated at a quarter million dollars; two churches, a seminary, and about forty homes were destroyed. Conflict flamed again on 7 July. All told, thirty-one people lost their lives, twenty-nine of them Nativists or observers. Cincinnati also had serious riots as Nativists contested political power there in the mid 1840's.

Political riots flourished in the 1850's as the Whig party disintegrated and Know-Nothings gained support. The major riots were in slave cities—Washington, Baltimore, Louisville, St. Louis, and New Orleans—where proslavery fears about Know-Nothings heated passions. Often blamed on the Know-Nothings, the conflicts were usually two-sided. About fifty political riots took place between 1852 and 1860, claiming more than 100 lives; the worst incident occurred in Louisville, where at least fourteen foreign-born and eight natives died.

Two political riots diverged from the usual pattern. Pennsylvania Democrats, after winning an 1838 election, mobbed Harrisburg to prevent lame-duck legislating. Rhode Island's "Dorr War" of 1842 was more serious. When the state proved slow to change its undemocratic political structure, Thomas Dorr called elections on the grounds of direct popular sovereignty and tried to install his "government" by force.

The 1850's also offered much gang and fireboy violence, especially in large cities like New York and Philadelphia that were free of major Know-Nothing struggles. About two deaths occurred in twenty-six such clashes, which led to the development of professional fire departments and the consolidation of metropolitan police. This process rounded out the "modernization" begun when riots in the mid-1830's had led to the founding, in large cities, of professional police forces.

Know-Nothingism diverted the nation only briefly from sectional issues, related to differing North–South patterns of collective violence, that came to focus on Kansas. Northerners who died in mobs were almost 80 percent rioters; upward of 90 percent of those killed or hurt in southern mobs were innocent victims. The South had come to use a system of random terror that was expected to be successful in Kansas as elsewhere.

The torturing of some Free-Soilers in late 1855, and especially the sack of Lawrence in 1856, marked accelerating proslavery terror as that faction became a clear minority. Though aggression remained heavily proslavery, Free-Soilers retaliated. Most famous was John Brown's mutilation-murder of five proslavery men in 1856. Brown in many ways was an important catalyst of the changing northern use of violence: in Kansas he met southern terror with its own weapons; he was the first to use violence to aid slaves in 1858; and at Harpers Ferry in 1859 he launched guerrilla war against slavery. Eighteen people died in this brief conflict, twelve of them Brown's followers, and Brown himself was tried and hanged.

The Civil War created new domestic violence as well as its own unprecedented slaughter. When Democratic mobs in Baltimore and St. Louis tried to obstruct the northern military effort in the war's first days, some sixteen dead rioters quickly made clear the ineffectiveness of such tactics. Far more disturbing to the North were the race riots that greeted the draft law in 1863, especially in New York City, where huge Irish mobs seemed briefly to threaten not only the black community, killing fourteen, but the war effort itself. Certainly over 100 rioters died and estimates ranged upward of 1,000. For the first time, force was used not only to control but also to crush a mob.

With no event so dramatic as the draft riot, the South experienced even more domestic conflict. Food riots, led by women, occurred in ten southern towns, but much more fatal was war-related domestic slaughter. Secessionists had used violence freely to intimidate pro-Union sentiment prior to the war, sentiment that became bolder as Confederate power waned. The second sacking of Lawrence, Kansas, where perhaps 150 civilians were killed, in 1853, was the worst of hundreds of such incidents.

AFTER THE CIVIL WAR: RACE AND LABOR

The war ended, and with it slavery, but not the questions related to racial hierarchy. Reconstruction policies centered on placing limitations on the conservative South's use of terroristic vio-

lence, as well as on its form of racial oppression. Federal investigations of these incidents suggest over 10,000 victims and argue that this figure represents only a portion of the murders of blacks and Republicans. Regarding fatalities, all earlier or later groups of riots pale in comparison.

The earliest mob disturbances were panics (1866–1868) that swept the South, much like antebellum insurrection scares, with rumors of black uprisings to occur around each Christmas. Urban riots in 1866 attracted the greatest national attention: in Memphis a mob killed perhaps forty-five blacks, wounded eighty, and drove hundreds from their homes; while in New Orleans an attack on a Republican convention left thirty-four blacks and four whites dead. Terrorism, organized by the Ku Klux Klan and various groups of "Knights," reached its apogee just prior to the elections of 1868. In Louisiana alone, 1,081 victims were listed between April and October of that year, including almost 160 killed in Bossier Parish in what the murderers called a "nigger hunt."

After 1870, violence and the Klan somewhat subsided. Some mobs became more equitable, as in New Orleans, where ten Democrats and seven Republicans died in a political struggle in 1874. Yet mobs still slaughtered blacks: over sixty in Colfax, Louisiana, in 1873; more than thirty in Vicksburg in 1874; about eighty in Mississippi in 1875; and perhaps fifty in Ellenton, South Carolina, in 1876. Northern weariness and at least a pretense of southern mildness ended Reconstruction in 1877.

In 1877, American violence took on a form that would be of dominant social concern for the next forty years: clashes between labor and management. The railroad riots of 1877 left about 100 dead (almost all strikers), while property damage reached several million dollars. The United States, which had had the most peaceful class relations of any industrializing country, had entered a phase that was to make its labor riots the most violent.

Broadly speaking, European industrial nations had suffered violence earlier, which led to governmental recognition of workers' right to organize. In the United States labor had generally enjoyed the right to press their demands with some reasonable hope for success, which counteracted labor helplessness and discouraged violence on either side. That the spontaneous uprisings of 1877 occurred along railroads, usually centrally run by capitalists with few communal ties, reflected the surprised fury of labor at so sharp a change in the rules. In June 1877 a second incident marked the same change. Ten Irishmen were hanged in the Pennsylvania coalfields on the testimony of labor spies. These "Molly Maguires" had by this time become a proto-union that practiced some violent terrorism in response to that employed against them.

It was almost a decade later that conflict became regular. In the interim a change in ideology had taken place in favor of more tough-minded, scientific, and calculating standards. As this managerial-intellectual revolution took hold, businesses became dedicated to breaking unions; while workers looked to more pragmatic organizations after 1886, when the Knights of Labor failed—with some loss of life and property—in their great effort to bring the eight-hour day to American workers. A major incident ended the strike: during a rally in Chicago to protest the killing of two workers, a bomb was thrown at the police, killing seven. On scant evidence, eight anarchists were convicted of the crime, while business used the Haymarket incident to brand all worker action as radical.

In the 1890's the violence inherent in the new system came to a head. Workers in the Homestead, Pennsylvania, steel strike of 1892 won a battle against hired guards, losing nine men while killing three, but lost the war to save their union. Also failing was the national railroad sympathy strike with Pullman workers in 1894, which took some thirty-five lives. The United Mine Workers had more success in Pennsylvania and the Midwest, despite the killing of at least forty-seven workers between 1891 and 1902. Miners in Tennessee used violence in ending convict labor competition, and in Alabama killed three black strikebreakers and a guard.

The Western Federation of Miners was more violent and less successful. In 1892 miners near Coeur d'Alene, Idaho, dynamited a guard barracks, killing one, and successfully took over by force one mine, losing six men. Bombing a nonunion mine in 1899 led to legal attacks that destroyed the union. The pattern in Colorado was similar, although there violence was less often worker-initiated. In 1894 one striker and one guard were killed, but the governor's intervention prevented extensive conflict. Trouble climaxed in 1903 and 1904 when two explosions killed sixteen and badly hurt sixteen more nonunion men, providing the excuse to destroy the union.

Labor sometimes initiated violence. The assassination of a former Idaho governor, Frank Steunenberg, in 1905 and the bombing of the antiunion *Los Angeles Times* in 1910 are the best-known incidents, but a bridgeworkers' union incorporated property destruction against nonunion builders into its regular policies. The worst incident of labor brutality occurred in 1922, when Illinois coal miners slaughtered nineteen strikebreakers after promising them protective removal.

Between 1899 and 1904 eastern labor unions flourished, growing from 500,000 to over two million members and winning concessions in numerous peaceful strikes. By 1920, unions were approaching five million in strength, but in most cases where violence became important unions lost. The most tragic case was the Ludlow, Colorado, troubles of 1913–1914, but four other cases in which ten or more people died also failed to gain union demands. Employer–police repression destroyed the Chicago teamsters' union in 1905 after fourteen were killed; in 1909 a Westmoreland County, Pennsylvania, coal strike failed after six workers, two guards, and two strikebreakers were killed; and a successful effort in 1915 against Standard Oil in New Jersey, where six workers died, turned to defeat the next year when workers initiated violence and the police attacked, killing four. The worst of the eastern incidents was the Paint Creek–Cabin Creek "War" in West Virginia's coalfields, where some thirty died almost equally divided between workers and Felts-Baldwin guards. Other failed strikes where less violence occurred were common. For example, streetcar unions were destroyed in eight cities, and in San Francisco after five workers died. A shopmen's strike on the Illinois Central in 1911 also failed, though there all seventeen victims were strikebreakers and guards.

The most successful strikes of the period were conducted by the Industrial Workers of the World (IWW), with little violence and much imagination. At McKees Rocks, Pennsylvania, the IWW gave form to a wildcat strike against a steel plant that led to the deaths of nine workers, two guards, and two strikebreakers before the workers were rehired. The IWW's great success occurred in the 1912 textile strike of Lawrence, Massachusetts, in which 25,000 workers won a wage increase despite company and official harassment that killed two strikers. Remarkably, almost all the violent strikes of the period 1877–1922 occurred in transportation or heavy extractive industries like steel, metals, and especially coal. The hundreds of strikes in manufacturing industries involved minor violence and few deaths; perhaps the most destructive were the successful 1909–1910 New York and Chicago garment workers' strikes, which took eight lives.

While the World War I years were prosperous for labor, the IWW in the West was treated brutally. One organizer was murdered in Butte, Montana, in 1917, and in the same year the sheriff and businessmen of Bisbee, Arizona, conducted a terroristic campaign against miners and the IWW there. Immediately after the war, strikes became general as business and labor both tried to consolidate war gains. The 1919 steel strikes, most violent in Gary, Indiana, took twenty lives; renewed fighting in the West Virginia coal communities in 1920 and 1921 cost twenty-one more; and a shopmen's strike along midwestern railroads killed nineteen people, mostly guards and strikebreakers. In most cases, including municipal strikes in Denver, Seattle, and Boston, officials sided against allegedly "radical" workers, thus helping to ensure defeat.

The 1920's were years of retreat for labor and of little overt violence. Toward the end of the decade, seven hosiery workers in Marion, Ohio, were killed, and coalfields in Harland and Bell counties, Kentucky, became the center of violence between 1931 and 1939, with at least fourteen deaths. A 1934 cotton textile strike took fifteen lives, mostly in the South. The Memorial Day 1937 massacre, in south Chicago, was the bloodiest incident in the CIO's great industrial drives; Chicago police killed sixteen workers. Fortunately the CIO won its greatest victories by the illegal but peaceful "sit-down" strikes in which very few lives were lost. Labor violence was to continue—on the average two or three lives were lost each year—but not as a major part of American industrial relations after the National Labor Relations Act of 1935 offered federal protection for majorities wishing to organize. Thereafter, very bitter strikes occurred but

with only minor casualties. Union jurisdictional fights subsequently accounted for a high percentage of deaths, though none were comparable to the twenty-four killed in the battle between United and Progressive Mine Workers in Illinois between 1932 and 1937.

The end of the Civil War had marked a sharp diminution in the variety of riots. Farmers protested often, but the most violent scenes came in the West in claims clubs or land wars like the 1883–1884 Fence-Cutter action in Texas in which at least three were killed. Poor farmers of Hispanic background organized the anti-enclosure White Cap movement around 1890 in New Mexico. Wyoming's "Johnson County War" between richer and poorer farmers took four lives but is only the most famous of some twenty such conflicts. Tobacco farmers between 1905 and 1909 used violent intimidation in fighting price fixing, while farmers during the Depression resorted to minor rioting to prevent foreclosures or increase prices, most notably in the Farmers' Holiday Association. A peaceful strike by Louisiana sugar workers in 1887 led to the murder of thirty-seven blacks, while attempts in 1919 to form a sharecroppers' organization in Arkansas triggered the slaughter of more than fifty people. Local harassment of the Southern Tenant Farmers Union in 1935 and 1936 left about ten blacks dead. Attempts to improve the wages of crop-pickers in California were also sometimes violent, with four dying in the most famous disturbance, at Wheatland, in 1913.

Authorities have also perpetrated violence against jobless protestors: in New York City in 1874 and in Washington, D.C., and Dearborn, Michigan, in 1932. Eight died in the latter protests, and in each case the authorities claimed that radicals caused the agitation. Charges of radicalism were also at times the sole focus of violence. The IWW waged some twenty "free speech struggles," one of which drew violence in San Diego, where an anarchist companion of Emma Goldman was beaten and tarred, and in Everett, Washington, where vigilantes and police met a boatload of IWW free-speech supporters. Five workers and two attackers were killed. In Centralia, Washington, in 1919, American Legionnaires attacked the IWW headquarters and lost three men before burning the building, driving out the radicals, and lynching one of them. In Tulsa, Oklahoma, the police turned seventeen

IWW men and supporters over to a mob for tarring and feathering.

Such mob festivities to keep America "pure" were common around World War I, though the damage they did paled before the legal actions taken during the "Red Scare." Usually mobs humiliated their victims; but in 1918 an Illinois mob hanged a young man, and mobs killed two marchers in socialist May Day parades in 1919. The second Ku Klux Klan flourished in the early 1920's, beating hundreds of blacks, Jews, Catholics, and radicals—and especially prostitutes and gamblers. Veterans' groups were prominent in some of the attacks on the poor and homeless in the Depression and provided much support for the stoning of those leaving a Paul Robeson concert in Peekskill, New York, in 1949.

Despite the revival of mob nativism in some of the White Cap violence in the late 1880's and the second Klan, violence toward or by ethnic groups faded to the level of the tavern brawl or the youth-gang fight. In 1870 and 1871 in New York City the last of the major Irish riots occurred as Catholics attacked Protestant picnickers celebrating the Battle of the Boyne. The assault in 1870 left some five dead; the next year the militia was on hand, so that one shot led to a barrage that killed two soldiers and thirty-one rioters or onlookers. In the same year the last of Philadelphia's antiblack riots left five dead, two of them community leaders. Minor disturbances were fairly common, such as a Brooklyn riot in 1902 by Jewish women protesting overpriced meat, but no major northern clashes occurred. The most serious ethnic attacks happened in Louisiana. In New Orleans a mob led by a lawyer hanged eleven Sicilians acquitted of the killing of a police chief; mobs killed eight other Italians in the state before 1900.

Racial violence, however, grew after the Civil War. Besides Indian massacres, the Chinese became victims in the West. A fight in 1871 in Los Angeles led to an attack on the Chinese community and eighteen deaths. Several more were killed by mobs as the violence spread in the next decade. In Tacoma, Washington, the Chinatown was burned to the ground; and miners in Wyoming slaughtered some twenty-eight Chinese and drove out and looted the homes of hundreds more in 1885.

Blacks bore the brunt of American violence until the 1960's. Never was violence again to reach its Reconstruction pitch, but the South still found terror a helpful prop to its racial caste system. As blacks moved north, much racial rioting moved there, although blacks were frequently able to fight back because of a semblance of official neutrality. The Harlem riot of 1935 marked the first against white property that blacks initiated, a practice culminating in a wave of urban riots from 1965 to 1969. The South's attempt to revive terror to curtail the civil rights thrust of the 1950's and 1960's proved counterproductive. In the twentieth century, the nation's major collective violence had moved from being oppressive to blacks to being expressive of them.

The *Chicago Tribune*'s careful lynching statistics beginning in 1882 suggest little gap between Reconstruction violence and the forms that followed. In 1882 the former slave states lynch-murdered about 50; the number doubled by 1889 and reached its peak of 146 in 1892. In 1903 the yearly rate had fallen to 75. After 1923, lynchings declined sharply, never rising above six per year after 1937. Between 1882 and 1951, over 1,400 whites and 3,700 blacks were lynched.

The substantial number of white lynchings occurred largely in the West, with the fame of San Francisco's vigilantes popularizing this form of social violence. The best-known group, the Montana vigilantes of 1862–1863, killed thirty alleged criminals.

White lynchings reached their peak of about 150 in 1884, were surpassed by the number of black lynchings in 1886, and fell to an average of about ten a year by 1900. Close to 20 percent of the victims in former slave states before 1903 were white, and sixty-three women were lynched, two-thirds of them black. Nor did lynch mobs discriminate against other minorities: they killed forty-five Indians, twenty Mexicans, twelve Chinese, and a Japanese. Yet southern lynchings of blacks were by far the most numerous, continuing, and brutal. With two exceptions, only black victims were handled with conspicuous sadism. Mississippi and Georgia mob-killed over 500 people, Texas almost 500, Louisiana almost 400, and Alabama, Arkansas, Florida, Tennessee, and Kentucky (in that order) over 200.

Black lynchings in the South provided some psychological satisfaction: they "proved" that blacks were inferior and could be treated as objects, that even the poorest whites had some real and direct power, and that blacks and their allegedly strong sexual drive could be controlled. Such collective violence also provided strong support to the southern social system, in the form of a very practical threat to blacks that was sure to inculcate steady wariness of any divergence from racial norms. But lynching trickled away in the former free states after 1903, largely because of an unwillingness to tolerate such rioting. This was dramatically illustrated in 1884, when a Cincinnati mob, prevented from lynching a man, burned the jail and courthouse; five people died. Even when officials failed, they dramatized the problem; Omaha's mayor E. P. Smith could not prevent a black lynching in 1919, but the mob had to act almost over his dead body.

After Reconstruction, southerners promulgated no attacks on black communities in general until the Populist movement disrupted the racial status quo. In North Carolina in 1898 a Democratic mob forced Wilmington's mayor to resign and expelled all black leaders, killing probably about thirty people. Eight years later the first of a new kind of southern riot, more akin to northern antebellum race riots, occurred in Atlanta; twelve were killed. The end of World War I brought similar riotous terror to Knoxville, Tennessee; Longview, Texas; and Tulsa, Oklahoma. The 1921 Tulsa affair killed some nine whites and an estimated sixty-eight blacks, with blacks suffering property losses said to be $1,500,000.

In Tulsa and the other southern postwar riots, blacks fought back vigorously if briefly. The final southern riot of these years, in Houston, was initiated by black soldiers who marched in formation against the police. Four blacks died in the fight and sixteen whites, more than half of them police and officials. Thirteen black soldiers were hanged for the riot.

Northern race riots changed in the first two decades of the twentieth century, a period of heavy black immigration to northern cities. Riots in Springfield, Ohio (1906), and Illinois (1908), suggest circumstances similar to those in Atlanta at the same time. The Illinois mob destroyed four blocks of black-owned property and hanged two elderly black men; four whites died. East St. Louis in 1917 showed a similar pattern on a larger scale. Both black and white strikebreakers had been attracted to the Illinois town, where after a union meeting in May, crowds beat stray blacks. Blacks subsequently armed for self-

protection, which led to the 1 July shooting of two policemen, providing an excuse for a riotous attack that killed nine whites and probably over fifty blacks. Estimates of general property damage reached three million dollars.

After World War I two racial riots made it clear that things had changed, that urban blacks would be less helpless when attacked. The Washington riot of July 1919 was typical of southern ones in many ways, with newspaper prurience triggering a mob that beat up stray blacks while police looked on. The plan of the next night to invade the black community, however, met a surprising reception: blacks kept off the mob, beat some whites, and shot at police and soldiers. Eight were killed, half of them white. More deadly was the Chicago riot of a week later, where over half the fighting took place in white neighborhoods to which blacks carried it. It became the most egalitarian of American race riots: brutality, destruction, and legal prosecution were equally distributed. Aside from the seven blacks who died from police fire, even the twenty-eight fatalities were fairly apportioned on the basis of race. In 1943 a rather similar riot occurred in Detroit. Begun as a fight in an amusement park, it included violence by both black and white groups. Civilian-inflicted deaths were equally distributed racially among the thirty-four victims, though half of this total, all black, were killed by the police. Blacks looted stores in their areas.

Two riots in New York's Harlem, in 1935 and 1943, suggested future developments. Both riots were actions by blacks in response to rumors that grew out of police altercations; the mobs damaged and looted stores, threw rocks at the police, and beat up some whites. In 1935 only one person died; there were six victims and some millions of dollars in property damage in 1943. In the latter year, an older type of riot against a new ethnic group occurred in Los Angeles. After a long press campaign against Mexican-American youth, soldiers and sailors abetted by civilians attacked, stripped, and beat zoot-suited young men. Tensions around military bases, especially in the South, led to much personal racial violence during World War II and sometimes to riot, most extensively in Beaumont, Texas, and Alexandria, Louisiana, where thirty-four blacks were shot.

Minor violence often accompanied the postwar move of blacks into white housing or recreational areas. The best-known incident involved a black's renting of an apartment in Cicero, Illinois, in 1951; a mob sacked the building as police watched. State and national pressure kept such violence minimal, however, and such pressure probably also secured the legal acquittal in 1946 of blacks who wounded four police in Columbia, Tennessee.

The Supreme Court antisegregation decision of 1954 touched off some violence as southerners killed eighteen civil rights advocates between 1954 and 1968, most of them in instances of personal murder. In the major mob confrontations, in Little Rock, Arkansas, in 1957 and Oxford, Mississippi, in 1962, federal protection was firm; in the latter case only two rioters were killed. The same general pattern occurred in the North, as white mobs responded to desegregation actions there in the late 1960's and 1970's.

Police and civil rights action triggered riots in Philadelphia and New York in 1963 and 1964 but prepared no one for the first of the large ghetto riots, in Los Angeles' Watts section, in 1965. Fourteen major conflicts and some 500 lesser riots followed, many of them merely disturbances. The conflicts in Watts, Newark, and Detroit in 1967, and in Washington and Baltimore in 1968, were among the largest the nation had known. Property damage, all told, exceeded $150,000,000, and deaths in rioting between 1965 and 1970 totaled over 190. After the spring of 1968, the scale and seriousness of conflict fell sharply.

The structure of these riots was fairly uniform. Some police action, often ordinary, would arouse anger; usually many hours later a threatening crowd would appear. Often—but not always—the matter ended there, with minor acts of violence. Destroying and looting in black neighborhoods were the central activities; but burning, firebombing, and beating whites were also common. Sniping did little damage compared to the police fire it drew, especially in Newark and Detroit, where much loss of life came from police action. Many blacks helped to calm potentially serious situations, and officials generally reacted with some restraint.

After Watts, both blacks and whites shared a feeling that racial rioting was a possibility in most cities and towns. The riots in this sense were not spontaneous; minor incidents like capping an open fire hydrant in a summer heat wave might trigger violence. A few hours or even a day usually intervened between the triggering and the central disturbance, while black communities worked out a response, not in any conspiratorial way but in a kind of consensus of mood. The course of events was always free-flowing, and the property damage much less selective than in the earlier antiblack riots. The emphasis on looting, and the holiday quality apparent in many mobs, made immediate assertiveness and acquisition seem to matter more than redressing long-range grievances or achieving goals. And the timing of the riots was puzzling. The explanation that both "frustration" and "rising expectations" caused riots is partly right, but these riots equally represented a vibrant assertion of blacks' ability to do what other Americans had long done: riot without too much danger of brutal repression. They marked the full integration of blacks into one old American tradition.

As racial violence faded, student conflicts reached their peak. Four students were killed at Kent State University in 1970, the major fatalities in a long series of sometimes violent student antiwar demonstrations. Student confrontation began at Berkeley in 1964, reached its height at Columbia University in 1968, and had its longest run at San Francisco State but touched almost all major universities outside the South. The harsh but not fatal violence surrounding the Chicago Democratic convention of 1968 was the major off-campus clash. If student riots faded with black mobs by 1970, occasional, less troubling violence continued. Truck drivers, for example, took a few lives in trying to enforce their labor interests in the mid-1970's and again in 1982. Klan and neo-Nazi groups often marched or organized, partly to draw down the mob violence that alone now seemed to bring them wide attention.

There is no indication that basic realities or attitudes about collective violence have changed in the United States. In a nation with much freedom and heavy constraints, citizens at times will use collective violence to promote, impede, or express causes of concern to them, whether good, bad, or dubious. And officials, at their best, will respond with some recognition of how understandable such actions are and how dangerous they can be both to minorities and to

COLLECTIVE VIOLENCE

peaceful patterns of civility and adjustment within the social fabric.

BIBLIOGRAPHY

Graham Adams, Jr., *The Age of Industrial Violence, 1910–15* (New York, 1966), is a close handling of labor violence in these years. Herbert Aptheker, *American Negro Slave Revolts* (New York, 1943), is the fullest account of insurrections, many of which were seemingly white panics rather than black plots. Hubert Howe Bancroft, *Popular Tribunals*, 2 vols. (San Francisco, 1887), is the classic account, and glorification, of California vigilante groups. John S. Bassett, "The Regulators of North Carolina (1765–1771)," in *American Historical Association Annual Report . . . for the Year 1894*, is an old but carefully researched work.

Ray Allen Billington, *The Protestant Crusade, 1800–1860* (New York, 1938), is the standard history of Nativist movements and mobs in the period. David Boesel and Peter H. Rossi, eds., *Cities Under Siege: An Anatomy of the Ghetto Riots, 1964–1968* (New York, 1971), a collection of scholarly studies, discusses riots in particular communities. Joseph Boskin, *Urban Racial Violence in the Twentieth Century*, 2nd ed. (Beverly Hills, Calif., 1976), contains a group of descriptions of rioting against and by blacks. Wayne G. Broehl, Jr., *The Molly Maguires* (Cambridge, Mass., 1964), is the best account of this still vaguely understood labor-ethnic group. Juanita Brooks, *The Mountain Meadows Massacre*, new ed. (Norman, Okla., 1963), a sensitive account, proves Mormon complicity in that mass murder. Richard Maxwell Brown, *The South Carolina Regulators* (Cambridge, Mass., 1963), is a close and enthusiastic treatment of this prototypal vigilante group; a reader on selected riotous incidents is *American Violence* (Englewood Cliffs., N.J., 1970); and *Strain of Violence: Historical Studies of American Violence and Vigilantism* (New York, 1975), is the fullest attempt at a general history of American collective violence.

James W. Button, *Black Violence: Political Impact of the 1960s Riots* (Princeton, N.J., 1978), is an account that argues the political effectiveness of these incidents. David M. Chalmers, *Hooded Americanism: The First Century of the Ku Klux Klan, 1865–1965* (Garden City, N.Y., 1965), is the best account of the Klan in its 1920's phase. Adrian Cook, *The Armies of the Streets: The New York City Draft Riots of 1863* (Lexington, Ky., 1974), is a measured recounting of this major riot. James Elbert Cutler, *Lynch-Law: An Investigation into the History of Lynching in the United States* (New York, 1905; repr. 1969), is the first, and in many ways still the best, handling of American lynching generally. Leonard Dinnerstein, *The Leo Frank Case* (New York, 1968), is a study of one of the more famous southern lynchings.

Scott Ellsworth, *Death in a Promised Land: The Tulsa Race Riot of 1921* (Baton Rouge, La., 1982), contains a good study of the incident and the subsequent communal cover-up. William McKee Evans, *To Die Game: The Story of the Lowry Band, Indian Guerrillas of Reconstruction* (Baton Rouge, La., 1971), is an account of an offbeat incident of racial-social conflict. Frantz Fanon, *The Wretched of the Earth*, Constance Farring-

ton, trans. (New York, 1965), a study of Algerian violence, is often invoked to justify ghetto riots of the 1960's. Michael Feldberg, *The Philadelphia Riots of 1844: A Study of Ethnic Conflict* (Westport, Conn., 1975), is the closest study of these major incidents, and *The Turbulent Era: Riot and Disorder in Jacksonian America* (New York, 1980), is the only general study of antebellum riots.

Robert M. Fogelson, *Violence as Protest: A Study of Riots and Ghettos* (Garden City, N.Y., 1971), is an account and justification of 1960's riots. John Hope Franklin, *The Militant South, 1800–1861* (Cambridge, Mass., 1956), a general history of the South, emphasizes its violent tendencies. Ben W. Gilbert, *Ten Blocks from the White House: Anatomy of the Washington Riots of 1968* (New York, 1968), a journalistic account, offers the most information about a single racial riot. Hugh Davis Graham and Ted Robert Gurr, eds., *Violence in America: Historical and Comparative Perspectives* (New York, 1969), includes valuable theoretical and historical essays. Those by Philip Taft and Philip Ross on American labor and by Richard Maxwell Brown on vigilantism are especially important.

Allen D. Grimshaw, ed., *Racial Violence in the United States* (Chicago, 1969), contains general selections illustrating and discussing patterns of black–white hostility. Ted Robert Gurr, *Why Men Rebel* (Princeton, N.J., 1970), is the richest of recent attempts to establish a model of rioting. Robert V. Haynes, *A Night of Violence: The Houston Riot of 1917* (Baton Rouge, La., 1976), is a careful retelling of this instance of black-initiated violence. Joel Tyler Headley, *The Great Riots of New York, 1712 to 1873* (New York, 1873; repr. 1971), is a still useful survey of collective violence in the nation's largest city. Eric J. Hobsbawm, *Primitive Rebels: Studies in Archaic Forms of Social Movement in the 19th and 20th Centuries* (Manchester, 1959), explores the social uses of mobs. Eric J. Hobsbawm and George F. E. Rudé, *Captain Swing* (New York, 1968), is the closest exploration of an event by the leading exponents of mobs as social protest. Dirk Hoerder, *Crowd Action in Revolutionary Massachusetts, 1765–1780* (New York, 1977), is a radical interpretation of these mobs.

Richard Hofstadter and Michael Wallace, eds., *American Violence: A Documentary History* (New York, 1970), is the richest collection of primary sources on American mobs. Jonathan Katz, *Resistance at Christiana: The Fugitive Slave Rebellion* (New York, 1974), describes the most famous black-led resistance to the fugitive slave law. Sung Bok Kim, *Landlord and Tenant in Colonial New York: Manorial Society, 1664–1775* (Chapel Hill, N.C., 1978), is the fullest analysis of these land riots. Roger Lane and John J. Turner, Jr., eds., *Riot, Rout, and Tumult: Readings in American Social and Political Violence* (Westport, Conn., 1978), an important collection of essays, suggests the contours of American collective violence. Gustave Le Bon, *The Crowd: A Study of the Popular Mind* (New York, 1960), first published in 1895, in French, is the initial attempt at a theory of crowd behavior. Sidney Lens, *The Labor Wars: From the Molly Maguires to the Sitdowns* (Garden City, N.Y., 1973), is a selective account of violence in relation to union growth.

Konrad Lorenz, *On Aggression*, Marjorie Kerr Wilson, trans. (New York, 1966), is an influential biological explanation of violence. George S. McGovern and Leonard F. Guttridge, eds. *The Great Coalfield War* (Boston, 1972), is the best account of Colorado's labor violence. James R. McGovern, *Anatomy of a Lynching: The Killing of Claude Neal* (Baton Rouge, La., 1982), contains a chilling account of a black lynching.

Pauline Maier, *From Resistance to Revolution: Colonial Radicals and the Development of American Opposition to Britain, 1765–1776* (New York, 1972), is a study by the leading interpreter of colonial mobs; and Irving Mark, *Agrarian Conflicts in Colonial New York, 1711–1775* (New York, 1940), is a fact-filled survey of these riots.

Louis H. Masotti and Don R. Brown, eds., *Riots and Rebellion: Civil Violence in the Urban Community* (Beverly Hills, Calif., 1968), has essays interpreting the 1960's ghetto riots. James O. Nall, *The Tobacco Night Riders of Kentucky and Tennessee, 1905–1909* (Louisville, Ky., 1939), is an account of farmer-protest riots. Phillip Shaw Paludan, *Victims: A True Story of the Civil War* (Knoxville, Tenn., 1981), is a close study of violence in a rural southern area. William Peirce Randel, *The Ku Klux Klan: A Century of Infamy* (Philadelphia, 1965), the fullest general history, discusses the various Klans from 1866 on. Arthur F. Raper, *The Tragedy of Lynching* (Chapel Hill, N.C., 1933), is the fullest handling of a group of lynchings, those in the early 1930's. Bennett M. Rich, *The Presidents and Civil Disorder* (Washington, D.C., 1941), is an account of federal intervention in civil disturbances.

Leonard L. Richards, *Gentlemen of Property and Standing: Antiabolition Mobs in Jacksonian America* (New York, 1970), analytically discusses three major riots of 1834–1836. Thomas Rose, ed., *Violence in America: A Historical and Contemporary Reader* (New York, 1969), includes accounts of some riots. George F. E. Rudé, *The Crowd in History: A Study of Popular Disturbances in France and England, 1730–1848* (New York, 1964), is the classic defense of the social purposiveness of mobs. John C. Schneider, *Detroit and the Problem of Order, 1830–1880: A Geography of Crime, Riot, and Policing* (Lincoln, Neb., 1980), an urban study, pays significant attention to the role of rioting. John L. Shover, *Cornbelt Rebellion: The Farmers' Holiday Association* (Urbana, Ill., 1965), is an able account of this agrarian protest movement. Otis A. Singletary, *Negro Militia and Reconstruction* (Austin, Tex., 1957), is a valuable study of black militia in relation to post–Civil War southern violence.

Georges Sorel, *Reflections on Violence*, T. E. Hulme and J. Roth, trans. (Glencoe, Ill., 1950), first published in 1908, in French, is a radical argument for the psychologically revivifying nature of social violence. Allen W. Trelease, *White Terror: The Ku Klux Klan Conspiracy and Southern Reconstruction* (New York, 1971), contains the fullest study of the riots, lynchings, and murders of these years. William M. Tuttle, Jr., *Race Riot: Chicago in the Red Summer of 1919* (New York, 1970), an able account of this riot, emphasizes its labor roots.

Wilcomb E. Washburn, *The Governor and the Rebel: A History of Bacon's Rebellion in Virginia* (Chapel Hill, N.C., 1957), is the fullest and most governor-centered survey of this incident. Arthur I. Waskow, *From Race Riot to Sit-in, 1919 and the 1960s: A Study in the Connections Between Conflict and Violence* (Garden City, N.Y., 1966), a survey of racial conflict, was written just before the 1960's ghetto riots. Walter Francis White, *Rope and Faggot: A Biography of Judge Lynch* (New York, 1929), is a loose but valuable discussion of black lynchings. Lee E. Williams and Lee E. Williams II, *Anatomy of Four Race Riots: Racial Conflict in Knoxville, Elaine (Arkansas), Tulsa, and Chicago, 1919–1921* (Hattiesburg, Miss., 1972), briefly recounts these major incidents. Bertram Wyatt-Brown, *Southern Honor: Ethics and Behavior in the Old South* (New York, 1982), is an explanation of social and personal violence in the antebellum South. Hiller B. Zobel, *The Boston Massacre* (New York, 1970), is a well-researched legalistic attack on Massachusetts' revolutionary era mobs.

[*See also* AMERICAN REVOLUTION; AUTHORITY; CHURCH AND STATE; CIVIL DISOBEDIENCE; CIVIL RIGHTS MOVEMENT; CIVIL WAR; CONSPIRACY AND CONSPIRACY THEORIES; CONTROL, SUPPRESSION, AND INTIMIDATION; CRIME AND PUNISHMENT; ENGLISH AND EUROPEAN POLITICAL INHERITANCE; ETHNIC MOVEMENTS; INDIVIDUALISM AND CONFORMITY; JACKSONIAN DEMOCRACY; JUDICIAL SYSTEM; LABOR MOVEMENT; NATIVISM; PLURALISM; RACE AND RACISM; RADICALISM; RECONSTRUCTION; *and* SLAVERY, SECTIONALISM, AND SECESSION.]

COLONIAL GOVERNMENT

John M. Murrin

ANY account of colonial government must address problems of scale. As late as 1760, just before French Canada surrendered to General Jeffrey Amherst, the entire European and African population of British North America stood at just over 1.5 million, the population today of a borough of New York City or any of several other cities. The population of an average-sized colony such as New York or North Carolina roughly equaled that of an English county at the same time. Compared with Europe, the English colonies had few people. Considered simply as population basins, each major colonial region had probably spent most of the seventeenth century merely replacing the losses of native Americans to European diseases and warfare. The total European and African population of mainland English America did not reach a quarter of a million until 1700. Thereafter, through an explosive combination of natural increase and immigration, it doubled roughly every generation, a pace that was exceeded in the Middle Atlantic provinces but that was already tapering in New England by 1760.

Concentrations of people were rare. By European or even Latin American standards, the English colonies had no metropolis. Boston consistently led its rivals until about 1750, when it proved incapable of sustaining its peak population of 16,000, up from 7,000 at the turn of the century. Philadelphia shot past stagnant Boston in the 1750's, exceeding 30,000 just before Independence, while New York City surpassed 20,000. Charles Town (the colonial name for Charleston, S.C.) and Newport reached the 10,000 plateau around 1770; and rapidly growing Norfolk, Baltimore, and Providence were not far behind. Yet North America remained overwhelmingly rural, with population expanding more rapidly in the countryside than in the port cities. In 1770, Boston, New York City, and Philadelphia had only about half the percentage of their respective colonies' residents that each had been able to claim in 1700.

If people were few, distances remained great and imposing, although they probably seem more daunting to us than they did to contemporaries who could not easily imagine some quicker way of getting around. England, for instance, contains just over 50,000 square miles; the British Isles about 121,000. The four Middle Atlantic states (including Delaware) in their modern boundaries approach 105,000; the South Atlantic (including West Virginia), 218,000; and New England, 67,000. Settlement did proceed gradually, of course, and modern boundaries tell us little about the daily problems of colonial governments. Yet even in the seventeenth century, New York City had to worry about Albany, 150 miles upstream, and Albany traders were concerned about the Niagara region, over 300 miles west. The first generation of New Englanders scattered to the mouths of widely dispersed rivers and moved as far inland as Springfield, 100 miles west of Boston and 60 north of Long Island Sound. Virginians and Pennsylvanians had to take account of French efforts to secure the Forks of the Ohio by the 1750's, even though their capital cities were over 300 miles from the danger zone.

Communication remained slow, difficult, and uncertain. Even highly literate individuals, such as Samuel Sewall (1652–1730) of Boston, were emotionally more attuned to sounds than to sights, to the spoken rather than the written word, to face-to-face instead of impersonal communication. News traveled more efficiently by sea than overland, and one colony's information about events in another might well arrive through London. News of shattering developments, such as the death of William III in 1702 or the outbreak of a general European war not long after, might take from six weeks to more than three months to reach particular colonies, traveling by the fastest available means. Newspapers did not necessarily speed the flow of information but they did disseminate it regularly and predictably. The *Boston News-Letter,* a weekly founded in 1704, became America's first regularly published newspaper. Philadelphia and New York acquired papers during the next twenty years, and by the 1730's the trend spread to Annapolis, Williamsburg, and Charles Town. At mid-century the colonies had thirteen papers; by 1764 the number had reached twenty-three, nearly all of them in seaports. Mostly they reported months-old European news to urban readers, although American developments did gain proportionately in the final three decades of the colonial era. Yet when a Boston crowd rioted for three days against naval impressment in 1747, none of the city's four papers reported the event beyond printing official proclamations denouncing the rioters.

Nearly every colonial government thus had to deal with great distances and scattered populations, with all parties often relying on garbled or incomplete information. However authoritarian they claimed to be (early Virginia and ducal New York had high aspirations in this respect), these governments also had little force at their disposal and had to depend heavily upon voluntaristic cooperation. Settlers, for example, might be induced to fight Indians especially if they could confine their quest for glory to the looting and massacring of noncombatants, which from the start became the preferred pattern of warfare against the natives. But settlers could not easily be marshaled to crush one another or, before 1689, to resist a serious European foe. Any government that moved too far beyond the sensibilities of its people ran a great risk of frustration, impotence, and even collapse.

In other words, government remained overwhelmingly in the hands of amateurs throughout the colonial era, as did local administration in England. Few officeholders beyond the governor, provincial secretary, councillors, and high court justices received regular salaries or thought of themselves primarily as public men.

More typically, officeholders saw themselves as heads of households and merchants, planters, farmers, or tradesmen who happened also to be county commissioners, selectmen, or militia lieutenants. Some positions, such as constable, were hard to fill precisely because they created an antagonistic relationship between the holder and his neighbors and could also involve physical danger. The demands that any government could place upon such a structure were always limited by the willingness of amateur, unsalaried personnel to cooperate, even though a fee system did provide some income and incentive to many minor officeholders. Government by consent was, in short, always broader than its legislative base in both America and Britain.

Within this framework colonial governments recognized their responsibility to maintain public order and generally looked to the social structure itself to contribute to this goal. Wealth, status, and power were expected to coincide. No North American colony managed to create a true hereditary aristocracy, but a line did exist—vague but real—separating gentlemen from ordinary settlers. Rulers ought to be among the richest and most prominent families in the province; lesser officeholders should be less distinguished or perhaps younger men of prominence gaining experience. Especially in the early years of settlement, reality often confounded expectation. Maryland, for one, lacked enough "gentlemen" to fill its county courts and had to appoint several illiterates, some of them quite crude, to the local bench. Virginia had too many gentlemen at the outset. But when they discovered how disagreeable and unhealthy the colony was, they quickly departed, leaving posts of honor to a boisterous set of self-made tobacco planters. Few of these planters produced adult sons to inherit their positions, but many of their widows and daughters did marry reasonably genteel immigrants arriving between 1645 and 1675. Many were younger sons of English gentry or of merchants, and this generation of newcomers did perpetuate itself and consolidate its hold on political power. Most of the first families of Virginia can trace their origins to this stage of the colony's development.

New England, where the climate proved amazingly healthy and the death rate far lower than in England, was more stable than the Chesapeake colonies, and it became so earlier.

Theophilus Eaton, probably the richest and most distinguished layman to migrate to the region, served as governor of New Haven Colony every year from its founding in 1638 until his death nearly two decades later. In Massachusetts Bay Colony, John Winthrop and Thomas Dudley, undoubted gentlemen both, remained magistrates throughout their lives, served often as governor, and sired sons and grandsons who continued to hold high office well into the next century. At a somewhat lower level, a meritocracy of sorts evolved. Men proved their capacity in local offices, moved on to become deputies in the General Court, and, if they made a sufficient impression there, might even rise as high as assistant or magistrate (councillor by the eighteenth century). The social hierarchy thus tended also to be an age hierarchy, with grandfathers occupying the very highest positions. In the South, by contrast, where the life span was much shorter, many officeholders had to be younger men, often fairly recent immigrants from England.

Colonial governments thus had to function within certain social constraints, but they also evolved and gained in complexity as population grew and the outside world impinged more sharply on life in the provinces. Three overlapping stages help account for the broader patterns of change. The first, lasting from the settlement of Jamestown in 1607 into the 1680's, witnessed a startling range of social and political experimentation, as various promoters and religious groups tried to achieve in America what they could not do in England. The second period, running from about 1675 to 1715 or 1720, marked the emergence of England (or Great Britain, after the union with Scotland in 1707) as a great power with the world's mightiest navy and an army that the rest of Europe had to take seriously for the first time in nearly three centuries. Because the colonies were one obvious source of Britain's new strength, they had to be absorbed into a more coherent imperial system, one that acquired palpable definition in those years. The third era, starting around 1715 or 1720 and lasting until the onset of the Revolutionary crisis in the 1760's, saw the colonies imitate in varying degrees the "mixed and balanced constitution" of the mother country. Although the most basic political and governmental institutions of the colonies were already in place by 1720, the coming decades of rapid growth and expansion instilled in these structures a distinctly British system of values and civic consciousness. Social structure became more clearly demarcated; government became more elitist, and its functions more important to the daily lives of colonists, especially in time of war.

THE ERA OF EXPERIMENTATION

Most historians have classified colonial ventures according to the legal devices by which they were created or organized. The two basic forms were the chartered joint-stock company (direct ancestor of the modern business corporation) and some version of a feudal proprietorship. The Virginia Company of London planted England's first permanent settlement in America when it dispatched five or six thousand settlers to Chesapeake Bay between 1607 and 1624. Similarly the Dutch West India Company haltingly created a small colony in the Hudson Valley between the mid-1620's and the English conquest of 1664. Neither corporation profited from its venture. The London Company went bankrupt by 1624, and New Netherland never became more than a minor opportunity for Dutch investors, who concentrated the company's energies on Brazil, Spanish treasure fleets, and the Caribbean. Massachusetts Bay pretty much symbolized the end of such efforts when the Winthrop fleet of 1630 carried to America the royal charter for the Massachusetts Bay Company and promptly turned it into a constitution for the colony itself. Quite suddenly, the forms and practices for administering an English business corporation became highly relevant to the internal government of a colony 3,000 miles away. Settlers evidently enjoyed and admired the analogy. When they moved from the original area of settlement beyond the boundaries of the Massachusetts Bay patent to establish communities on Narragansett Bay, the lower Connecticut Valley, and on both shores of Long Island Sound, they copied the same model in creating their own governments. Eventually in 1662 and 1663, respectively, Connecticut and Rhode Island secured royal charters to ratify what they had already done; and in the process New Haven Colony disappeared, absorbed by Connecticut. Plymouth, founded in 1620, always had a tenuous legal basis until it became part of Massachusetts in 1692, but its governmental institutions closely resembled those of its neighbors.

As government took shape in the early decades, it evolved differently in the Chesapeake and New England colonies. Virginia oscillated in its early years between a conciliar system that never functioned effectively and one-man rule under something like martial law. Captain John Smith created a de facto autocracy by 1608, and the company deliberately fostered this form between 1610 and 1619. Not until 1619, as one aspect of a broad series of company reforms, did the free settlers receive the right to elect their own burgesses to sit with the governor and council as a single General Assembly. This practice continued without royal authorization after the crown assumed control of the colony in 1624. Royalization did not eliminate structural difficulties, however, for the king's commissions seemed to give to both governor and council all the power that either had exercised before. The councillors thus regarded the government as essentially conciliar, whereas the governor believed he could accept or reject conciliar advice at pleasure. Serious divisions over land grants, peace with Indians, aid to Maryland Catholics, and a proposed royal monopoly for tobacco seriously strained the colony's political system. Governor Sir John Harvey threatened to try refractory councillors by martial law, only to find himself arrested by them and shipped back to England in 1635. There Charles I vindicated him and returned him to the colony in a leaky warship; Harvey then arrested his opponents and packed them off to England, where they now had the advantage of proximity to the throne. Political conflict lasted through the decade, but in 1639 the king officially sanctioned the convening of the burgesses for the first time, and in the early 1640's the General Assembly became a bicameral body. By the administration of Sir William Berkeley (1642–1652, 1660–1677), Virginia's basic public institutions had appeared, including the county court and the Anglican vestry, both of which became cooptive bodies by the 1660's.

By contrast the New England colonies encouraged a fairly high level of popular participation from the start, beginning with the famous Mayflower Compact of 1620, in which the first settlers of Plymouth agreed to be bound as individuals by the collective decisions of the community. Massachusetts Bay by 1634 established the fundamental institutional structure that the rest of the region would imitate, government by a General Court (the term came from English joint-stock companies) of governor, deputy-governor, and assistants, all chosen in colony-wide elections and collectively known as magistrates. They thought of themselves as governors and of ordinary settlers as the governed, but several times a year they were joined by deputies elected for specific towns who asserted an active role in making laws and even hearing judicial appeals. In the 1640's the deputies pried a Body of Liberties and even a code of fixed laws from the magistrates. Only freemen (another corporation term that originally meant the stockholders) could vote in New England, but the requirements for freemanship did vary from colony to colony. The legislature or an authorized court had to award this honor to a man who requested it, and in Massachusetts Bay and New Haven only church members could apply. Connecticut and Plymouth eventually imposed fairly modest property qualifications. New Netherland, by contrast, drew on very different Dutch precedents and, except for a few ad hoc assemblies summoned to address particular problems, remained basically autocratic under a director-general, the most effective of whom was Peter Stuyvesant.

New England owed much of the region's success almost from the moment of arrival to a climate that encouraged growth by natural increase, but another major factor was imported from England, namely Puritanism. The Great Migration of about 18,000 people to Massachusetts and Connecticut began shortly after Charles I dismissed his Parliament in 1629 and decided to govern without one. It ended not long after the gathering of the Long Parliament in 1640–1641, which became a prelude to civil war. During the interval of personal rule, Charles I turned ecclesiastical affairs over to Archbishop William Laud, who tried to transform the Church of England into an Arminian (anti-Calvinist) and High Church (intensely liturgical) bastion. While all of continental Protestantism seemed menaced by Roman Catholic armies during the middle phases of the Thirty Years' War, the struggle for control of England's church acquired nothing less than millennial significance among Puritans. The fall of God's "elect nation" would be an apocalyptic event, and Puritans seemed powerless to stop it. But they could flee to the American wilderness far away from royal and episcopal supervision and there erect a "city upon a hill," a model church and society that might guide England out of its perils.

In general, the longer a Puritan stayed in England and the more he or she saw of Laud, the more extreme became that person's commitment to reform. John Cotton, arriving in Massachusetts Bay in 1633, wondered how many of his clerical brethren already in America had ever experienced a true conversion. Anne Hutchinson made these doubts public and carried them further than Cotton did, thereby provoking a severe political crisis in which Winthrop managed to separate Cotton from Hutchinson and expel her and her Antinomian followers to Rhode Island by 1638. John Davenport, probably the strictest minister to sail to the region, had arrived the year before and soon joined up with Theophilus Eaton in New Haven to create the most rigidly Puritan society in the world.

In other words, institutionalizing true piety always had political implications and was no easy matter. Massachusetts settlers spent the 1630's and 1640's defining their churches and creating their polity. The result was a kind of participatory authoritarianism in which ordinary colonists agreed to be governed by elective yet righteous magistrates provided the settlers had a chance to assent to the laws through their own deputies. Formal law codes limited magisterial discretion as well as settler behavior, but once the codes were in place the legal system functioned with an efficiency unmatched elsewhere in English America. Only a very broad commitment to Puritan values can explain the success of this system. In New Haven offenses were punished severely and swiftly. Almost nobody brought into court on a criminal charge was acquitted, and the colony even abolished juries. Yet hardly any accused individuals tried to flee the colony, and very few were imprisoned or even made to post bail while awaiting trial. The system ran on deeply internalized sanctions of guilt and shame.

By the 1650's, government through an elective and increasingly gerontocratic General Court, a well-developed legal system, a pattern of town settlement, and the Cambridge Platform of church discipline (1648) had gone a long way toward establishing the region's identity for the next century. Yet tensions always persisted. Magistrates, for example, usually supported an effort to accommodate English authority, urged the persecution of dissenters (especially Quakers and Baptists), and advocated broader access to infant baptism (the Halfway Covenant of 1662). Most deputies normally resisted these demands, but the political system did prove resilient and flexible enough to absorb such struggles.

Some failures were real and seemed quite disturbing. The orthodox Puritan colonies had achieved a remarkably coherent sense of community definition only to discover that their best efforts did nothing to redeem England and not enough to convert the rising generations, the children and grandchildren of the founders. Still another embarrassment was Rhode Island, a colony of heretics, peopled by losers in the religious battles of the 1630's and 1640's. In 1647 the Rhode Island colonists had the effrontery to proclaim themselves a "Democraticall" government. How much they meant by the word remains uncertain, but it did have a certain minimal content. After tasting magisterial wrath in Massachusetts Bay, Connecticut, and even Plymouth, the Rhode Islanders set about creating an antimagisterial, antiauthoritarian society of their own. This society had severe difficulties coalescing if only because Roger Williams, Anne Hutchinson, Samuel Gorton, and other dissidents could challenge one another quite as brilliantly as they had dueled with John Winthrop. Yet there the colony remained, a small but continuing testimony to paths not taken by the majority in the region.

Even while the New England experiments were still running their course, the initiative in colony-founding passed decisively and overwhelmingly from the commercial corporation to the feudal proprietorship. This device had vague antecedents in the sixteenth-century ventures associated with Sir Humphrey Gilbert and Sir Walter Raleigh and much stronger ones in Sir George Calvert's Avalon (Newfoundland) patent of 1623 and a similar grant of "Carolana" to Sir Robert Heath and of many of the Leeward Islands to Lord Carlisle a few years later. But the Calvert patent for Maryland in 1632 really defined the type. Basically, a proprietary charter marked the fullest alienation of power by the king that crown lawyers could devise. The "bishop of Durham" clause, harkening back to a medieval need to grant extraordinary authority to a marcher lord or lord palatine, gave the proprietor all powers that the bishop had ever possessed or ought to have had. The Calverts could dispose of the colony's land, govern in their own name rather than the crown's, and even create their own provincial nobility. They did have to secure the settlers' consent to the colony's laws, which were required to conform to those of England. Not every proprietary charter contained everything that the Calverts had secured, but the Maryland patent provided the standard against which to measure deviations elsewhere.

Nine of the original thirteen states trace their constitutional origins to a proprietary charter, all but Virginia, Massachusetts, Connecticut, and Rhode Island. Especially after 1660, it became just about the only eligible device other than conquest for organizing a new American society out of England. The joint-stock company failed as a colonizing agent because, as a modern profit-seeking organization, it could not survive the long gap between initial investment and eventual return. Individual proprietors, concerned with perpetuating genteel families over multiple generations, might see the problem in different terms and the risk as worth taking. All expected to reduce expenses below Virginia's appalling standard, and all hoped for handsome profits eventually. Most failed and gave up, but meanwhile many of them used the wilderness to test a dizzying variety of social experiments.

At one level, then, the future of American government lay with England's remote past, with an assortment of men committed in varying degrees to feudal anachronisms. The first two lords Baltimore, George and Cecilius Calvert, probably did have a coherent medieval vision of social relationships that they intended to implement in the Potomac Valley, but we cannot be sure about its precise dimensions because the first body of laws drafted in England was rejected outright by the settlers, and no text has survived. The Calverts were converts to Catholicism who doubtless hoped to show that Catholics and Protestants could live together in peace and that the cosmos would not crumble if Catholics held office in the English-speaking world. Cecilius Calvert therefore designed a society of manor lords, nearly all Catholics, whose large estates would be settled by servants and later tenants, most of whom were Protestants.

Like the nobility in England, manor lords received a personal summons to attend the legislature. Ordinary free settlers could attend in person or give their proxies to someone who did, presumably one of the manor lords, a bizarre effort to replace territorial representation with a personalized polity of lord and man. These arrangements could not subdue religious tensions between the Catholic elite and the growing Protestant majority, especially once England dissolved into civil war. After a decade of reasonably successful paternalism that nonetheless saw a high rate of turnover even among the manor lords, Maryland endured a dreary succession of upheavals, rebellions, and small civil wars from the mid-1640's to 1660. It grew quite slowly under these pressures and nearly disintegrated altogether in the late 1640's. These years did bequeath a famous Toleration Act (1649) and a bicameral legislature to the next generation. Manorialism and the use of proxies in the legislature became casualties of these struggles and left few traces by the 1650's. The colony increasingly became a tobacco society, a sibling of Virginia in which the proprietor or his deputy played the same role in St. Mary's that the royal governor assumed in Jamestown.

After the Restoration of Charles II to the English and Scottish crowns in 1660, proprietary ventures proliferated. From the king's perspective, a proprietary charter often became an inexpensive way to reward prominent individuals who had served the royal family during its years of exile or had helped return it to the throne. The English conquest of New Netherland and colonization of New Jersey, the Carolinas, and finally Pennsylvania all proceeded under proprietary auspices. James, duke of York and brother of the king, acquired a patent in 1664 for the area between the Connecticut and Delaware rivers plus Staten Island, Long Island, Martha's Vineyard, Nantucket, and even Sagadahoc, or eastern Maine. Taken literally, these boundaries would have absorbed most of the settled towns of Connecticut within New York, but the duke's early governors compromised by accepting Long Island, much of which had also been governed from Hartford or New Haven. London probably did hope to erect a cordon sanitaire around troublesome New England, a region that was very slow to proclaim Charles II and that gave shelter to three regicides in the early 1660's. York's charter also lacked the now conventional clause that associated the lawmaking power with the advice and consent of the inhabitants. The omission was deliberate. James intended to rule autocratically through a fixed code of laws, and he did. As a powerful figure at court and heir to the throne by the 1670's, he made decisions for New York that carried large implications for the evolution of England's overall colonial policy.

The province's first English governor, Richard Nicolls (1664–1668), had to placate an unhappy Dutch majority and a suspicious New England minority settled on Long Island and in what is now Westchester. He offered generous surrender terms to the vanquished and quietly encouraged continuing trade with Amsterdam, which the recently passed Navigation Acts hoped to stamp out. For Long Island, Staten Island, and Westchester he created an English county, Yorkshire, and for it and New York City he devised a code of laws, culled mostly from published New England statutes. Summoning a special assembly at Hempstead in 1665, he persuaded it to accept the Duke's Laws, which thereafter would be amended only by the appointive Court of Assizes for the colony. Most Yankee towns on Long Island had never been under New Netherland's jurisdiction and now objected to the absence of a regular assembly and above all to being taxed without consent. Finally, Nicolls had assumed that the safest way to secure English possession of the province would be to encourage rapid English settlement, particularly along the coast west and south of Manhattan. But while he made plans to draw more New Englanders to this region, the duke without prior warning conveyed it to two courtiers as the separate proprietary colony of New Jersey. Eventually the crown's law officers would decide that only the monarch could grant powers of government and therefore that the New Jersey patent gave rights only to the soil; but meanwhile a new colony had appeared, somewhat fitfully organized yet with an elective assembly of its own. New York remained Dutch and Yankee, and the two did not mix well.

Nothing better revealed the weakness of New York's authoritarian government than the ease of the Dutch reconquest of 1673, an episode in the Third Anglo-Dutch War. No group, English or Dutch, was willing to aid the small garrison of Fort James in defending the colony against a Dutch fleet. The province surrendered without resistance only to be returned to the English at the peace settlement fifteen months later. Several New England towns on Long Island used the interval to seek reunion with Connecticut, but their efforts failed.

York tried again after 1674 to assert authoritarian control. Governor Edmund Andros (1674–1680) gave Dutch merchants in New York a choice between unconditional allegiance to English rule or the confiscation of all their property. They yielded, but the governor did nothing to discourage commerce with Amsterdam. The Duke's Laws were extended to the entire province, putting more pressure on Dutch ethnic identity and Yankee sensibilities. A new political element appeared with the arrival in the city of a group of English merchants, New York's counterpart to the newcomers who were taking charge in Virginia and Maryland during the same years. Mostly young men on their way up in the world, they quickly concluded that only a large dose of English liberties would stimulate enough fresh settlement to overcome a natural Dutch predominance. Andros, along with other members of his governing circle, probably agreed with much of this assessment and asked the duke to allow an assembly. York refused, and when the colony escaped the carnage and upheaval of King Philip's War in New England (1675–1676) and Bacon's Rebellion in Virginia (1676–1677), the province seemed for a brief moment to represent an oasis of sanity and order in a world of chaos.

While James experimented with absolutism along the Hudson, a group of eight courtiers secured a proprietary charter (actually two charters, 1663 and 1665) for Carolina. There after 1669 they tried to create a model aristocratic society in the New World, relying not on musty feudal precedents but on the very latest in English social thought. One of the eight, Anthony Ashley Cooper, later first earl of Shaftesbury and principal organizer of the Whig party, combined with his secretary, John Locke, to devise most of the plans. They hoped "that the Government of this Province may be made most agreeable unto the Monarchy under which we live, and of which this province is a part, and that we may avoid erecting a numerous Democracy."

Interestingly, they drew their ideas somewhat selectively from James Harrington, a gentry-republican theorist of the English Interregnum who was badly out of favor in high court circles. Because almost nobody dared discuss Harrington openly in Restoration England before 1675, when Lord Shaftesbury openly used Harringtonian ideas in a major speech in the House of Lords, America became the only safe place to try out his ideas.

According to Harrington's analysis in *The Commonwealth of Oceana* (1656) and elsewhere, political power follows the balance of landed wealth in a society. In 1649 the Commons had executed a king and abolished the House of Lords because in the previous century and a half commoners had acquired the bulk of English landed wealth and now demanded proportionate power. As a civic humanist, Harrington worried greatly about the tendency of all republics to degenerate into tyrannies. His ideal republic contained several devices to ensure political stability and the continuation of civic virtue. It would permit no impoverished nobility. It created a bicameral legislature in which the upper house (embodying the few and the wise) proposed and debated legislation, and the lower house (the autonomous and virtuous many) voted to accept or reject it. He also favored rotation in office, the secret ballot, and religious toleration.

The Fundamental Constitutions of Carolina went through three drafts in 1669–1670, a two-stage revision in 1682, and a final, much shortened recasting in 1698. The plan did apply Harringtonian principles to the problem of sustaining a healthy aristocracy. It envisioned a complex and rigidly hierarchical society, to be maintained by an appropriate division of land. Carolina would have a three-tiered nobility (proprietors, landgraves, and caciques) presiding benevolently over a basic population of freemen, leetmen (serfs), servants, and slaves.

Although unwilling to invest much money in the venture, the proprietors certainly thought big. They were creating a very large society, and they planned a government suitable to that scale—eight distinct supreme courts at the apex of a judicial pyramid that included lesser tribunals in each county, precinct, and barony; a Grand Council of eight proprietors and forty-two councillors to exercise executive powers and propose all legislation; and a Parliament of nobles and commoners to accept or reject legislative bills. The Parliament was to sit unicamer-

ally except on constitutional questions, when it would divide into four chambers, but by 1698 it had become a bicameral body under the Grand Council, which was virtually a third house.

The provincial nobility was always to control 40 percent of the land, and noble estates would become inalienable after 1700. However, absentee nobles could lose their estates (1669 version) or at least the revenues from them (1682), and the 1698 revision required forfeiture of aristocratic status for a nobleman who failed to develop his holdings adequately after forty years. The Fundamental Constitutions did require voting by ballot and toleration, but every freeman had to belong to some church or forfeit his civil rights. The possibility of establishing the Church of England appeared in the 1682 revision but was not enacted for another generation.

Obviously Carolina never developed as planned. At least from the 1670's it was becoming apparent that it would be two colonies, not one. The small tobacco planters of Albemarle Sound were separated by almost 300 miles of Indian country from the new settlements around Charles Town and Port Royal. Serious efforts to implement the Fundamental Constitutions involved mostly the southern portion of the colony; but the settlers never accepted the document, and it was applied only in part and none too consistently. Besides its unwieldy complexity, the experiment went awry for another reason. In early Carolina, wealth did not derive from the quantity of landholdings. The economy depended on naval stores, the export of provisions to the Caribbean, and the deerskin trade with interior Indians. The first two required only modest estates, and the Indian trade, as in New York and Canada, stimulated urban wealth at Charles Town. Only with the rapid growth of rice culture after 1700 did riches begin to depend heavily on the size of one's plantations, and even then access to labor mattered at least as much. By that time, nearly everyone in England and Carolina had given up on the Fundamental Constitutions.

Two of the Carolina proprietors, John Lord Berkeley and Sir George Carteret, had obtained the proprietary grant from the duke of York in 1664 for what they called New Jersey. Four predominantly Yankee towns were founded in the next few years, while Dutch settlers continued to migrate to Bergen. Although the colonists received an assembly in 1668, they were in revolt against proprietary land policy by 1672, claiming prior titles from the governor of New York. After the Dutch reconquest and the retrocession to England in 1674, Berkeley sold his share to two Quakers, John Fenwick and Edward Byllinge, and the province was soon divided into Carteret's East Jersey and Quaker West Jersey, which centered on the Delaware Valley. East Jersey continued into the 1680's the pattern of quarrelsome behavior that its towns had already established, and then another mostly Quaker group bought out Carteret's heirs. West Jersey inaugurated an era of Quaker social planning that would help to create Pennsylvania and even spill over into East Jersey. For about a decade, the Society of Friends seemed likely to establish hegemony over the entire mid-Atlantic area except New York.

The Quakers almost turned their proprietorship back into a joint-stock company. West Jersey divided its proprietary grant into 100 shares, which were often subdivided in turn. As the East Jersey proprietorship also went Quaker, it was split into twelve and later twenty-four shares. Only Pennsylvania retained a unitary proprietary structure, and only there did Quaker proprietorship continue to manifest a significant feudal content.

West Jersey tried one of the most bracing experiments of the premodern era. "The Concessions and Agreements of the Proprietors Freeholders and Inhabitants of the Province of West New Jersey in America," drafted in London around August 1676 and signed by over 100 settlers in America by March 1677, embodied the most radical plan for government put into practice in seventeenth-century Anglo-America. Reflecting predominantly the Leveller views of Byllinge, the text may also contain suggestions from William Penn and from Thomas Rudyard, a prominent Quaker lawyer.

The Concessions proposed a system of legislative supremacy centering on a unicameral assembly that would remain close to the people. Eventually the small colony would be divided into 100 "proprieties," each entitled to elect a representative by ballot and to bind him by rigid instructions. Voting in the assembly, but not debate, would be open to public scrutiny. Ten proprieties would be grouped into "tenths" or "tribes," each of which would choose a "com-

missioner." Together the commissioners would constitute a weak plural executive under the assembly's domination. They could not declare war or impose taxes or military service on the settlers without the assembly's consent, and all revenue acts had to be made or renewed annually. The assembly controlled its own adjournment and prorogation. Even the court system showed a similar emphasis, for juries were unequivocally made dominant over magistrates. Settlers received generous land terms, virtual manhood suffrage, complete religious toleration, and ringing guarantees of civil rights.

Even more permissive than the Rhode Islanders, West Jersey's organizers dreamed of creating a world in which men of goodwill could live together in comfort and harmony untroubled by war, internal strife, lawyers, or protracted civil disputes. They never quite got the chance to try out their ideas in full. Governor Andros of New York prevented implementation through 1680, and by the time the settlers finally seemed in control, Byllinge produced a commission from the duke naming him governor, an office not even envisioned in the Concessions and Agreements. Still, the settlers got his deputy to agree to terms in 1681 that deprived the governorship of most prerogative powers; and until 1685, perhaps a decade longer in such heavily Quaker areas as Burlington County, the province remained under control of men sympathetic to the Concessions. Thereafter the governorship and ever more proprietary shares fell into non-Quaker hands, opening a gap between rulers and ruled that the Concessions had tried to eliminate but that was never again bridged. West Jersey suffered much confusion and uncertainty by the late 1690's, and when the colony was absorbed into the royal province of New Jersey in 1702, probably very few settlers lamented the passage of the specifically proprietary aspects of its government. The Concessions may have been another matter, for royalization meant repudiation of most of what had made West Jersey's government distinctive and memorable.

The initiative in Quaker reform had already passed to the much larger enterprise of Pennsylvania. Like the Carolina proprietors, Penn thought big. *"Colonies,"* he proclaimed, ". . . are the seeds of nations begun and nourished by the care of wise and populous countries," and he proceeded to compare himself with Moses,

Joshua, Lycurgus, Romulus, and others as the founder of a new people. Both a gentleman and a famous Quaker missionary, he was the son of Admiral Sir William Penn, who had died in 1670 with a large debt still owed him by the crown. The younger Penn had been involved in American affairs since the organization of Quaker West Jersey. He had excellent connections with Charles II and the duke of York, and in 1681 he managed to convert the debt to his father into a proprietary charter for the area west of the Delaware River, which the king named Pennsylvania in honor of the deceased admiral. The emerging imperial bureaucracy, hostile to proprietary colonies in general, could not block the charter, but it did restrict the grant in several respects. The patent had no bishop-of-Durham clause, Penn was required to enforce the Navigation Acts, and the colony's laws could be disallowed by the English Privy Council, which could also hear appeals from Pennsylvania courts.

No colonial constitution derived from greater reflection and advice than Pennsylvania's, a process that is richly documented. No less than twenty drafts or outlines of a "frame of government" have survived in the Penn Papers for the period 1681–1682. The "Fundamental Constitutions" of the summer of 1681 started the process in a spirit similar to that of the West Jersey Concessions with an additional injection of Harringtonian principles. Government would center on a huge assembly, eventually to number 384 men, who could be instructed by the voters. It would choose a council of forty-eight out of itself for staggered three-year terms. Suffrage would be broad, balloting secret, and the proprietor received no veto. Capital punishment was abolished for crimes against property, imprisonment for debt was eliminated for the impoverished, and jail fees would be paid by the state instead of the incarcerated. The document warmly espoused trial by jury, habeas corpus, Magna Carta, and the Petition of Right.

Incorporating advice from Edward Bromfield and Thomas Rudyard, Penn's project evolved by May 1682 into his First Frame of Government and a series of forty fundamental laws to be approved by the inhabitants. This plan centered on a council of seventy-two men, elected to staggered three-year terms, who would initiate all legislation and advise the proprietor or his governor on administrative matters. The frame gave Penn or his deputy only three votes in council rather than a veto.

Rudyard is often seen as the major influence on Penn, the man who nudged him in a more conservative direction to increase investment in the colony by wealthy men. Rudyard did indeed worry about the potential behavior of any assembly composed of former servants and small farmers, but his answer to the problem was no hymn to privilege. He urged that until 1690 the council, bigger than the lower house in any existing colony at the time, act as a large unicameral assembly. Instead of a formally constituted assembly, all the freemen of the province would gather annually to accept or reject the council's bills. After 1690 the function of approving or rejecting legislation would have to be handled by representation instead of by virtual plebiscite, but Rudyard imagined such an assembly growing to 1,000 men. Penn never accepted the whole argument. His frame did call for an assembly of 200, expanding eventually to 500, who could only approve or disapprove bills or, informally, suggest amendments to the council. Yet he too thought in the same terms. As late as 1690 he urged his officials in the colony to regard the council as a unicameral legislature, not an upper house. With Rudyard, he hoped that the council would attract gentlemen of substance and education, Harrington's talented "few." Nevertheless important decisions of the council had to win the moral assent of the virtuous "many," however they were organized.

Like every other colonial project, Pennsylvania did not follow its script. The original settlers found the First Frame too large and demanding, and in 1683 Penn and the assembly agreed on a Second Frame, or Charter of Liberties, which Penn probably regarded as an interim measure until the province had become sufficiently populous to sustain the First Frame. The Second Frame reduced the council to eighteen men and the assembly to thirty-six but still permitted only the council to initiate legislation. The combination of Penn's long-term aspirations and the settlers' demand for practicality thus generated an assembly fundamentally weaker than those in nearby colonies, even if an elective instead of appointive council also differentiated Pennsylvania from such near neighbors as Virginia, Maryland, and New York. Not surprisingly, the assembly continued to agitate for the power to initiate bills. It won this concession during a brief interlude of royal government from 1693 to 1695, saw it accepted by Penn's governor in 1696 (the Third Frame), and finally won even more in 1701 during Penn's final visit to his province. The Fourth Frame, or Charter of Privileges, passed that year, invested legislative powers in a single assembly, subject only to the governor's veto and review in England. The council now became an appointive body as in standard royal colonies, but it existed only to advise the governor. In practice, because a governor could still ask it whether to veto a bill, the council continued to function as an informal upper house.

The Quaker exodus to America ended the reformist, often utopian phase of colony founding, although the establishment of Georgia would revive some of this emphasis in the 1730's. The era had witnessed Puritan millennialism, Lord Baltimore's feudal vision, the duke of York's absolutist aspirations, the Harringtonian and aristocratic inclinations of Restoration courtiers, and a variety of Quaker efforts ranging from the Leveller principles of Byllinge through the more gentrified and Harringtonian plans of Penn and Rudyard. America had become a home for Europe's rejected ideas. All of them failed in the New World as well, although both the Puritan and Quaker colonies could generate spasms of internal reform that now and then promised fulfillment of the original goal. Above all, each of these efforts left behind an actual society that had to make political and economic sense of its role in the world. As the animating ideals of the founders faded away, a residue of institutions and customs remained behind. This residue was recognizably English especially when it affirmed government by consent. Even that principle had its rivals and would not triumph unequivocally until the colonies passed through the second phase of their development, that of imperial consolidation.

THE ERA OF
IMPERIAL CONSOLIDATION

The process of creating colonies had marked a drastic devolution of power from the center to the periphery, usually but not always sanctioned by a legal charter. Around mid-century, the English state, often jolted into action by the demands of London merchants, began to recognize the economic importance of these overseas outposts, whose trade seemed likely to fall into Dutch hands, particularly during the civil wars of the 1640's. First under the Commonwealth (1649–1660) and then under the restored Stuarts, Parliament reacted with a series of progressively stricter Navigation Acts in 1650, 1651, 1660, and 1663. These laws confined the colonial trade to English vessels and mariners (colonists were included in the definition of "English," but Scots were not before 1707); defined certain "enumerated" commodities such as tobacco or sugar that could be shipped out of the empire only if they first passed through England; and forbade the colonies to import nearly all Asian, African, or European goods unless they had gone via England. London was determined to become the entrepôt for colonial trade, the fastest-growing sector of the English economy.

Enforcing these laws was quite a different matter from enacting them. Nobody, for example, was so literal-minded as to insist on rerouting the slave trade through England. Barbados greeted the first Navigation Act with a virtual declaration of independence and had to be cowed into submission by a Commonwealth fleet. North Carolina supported a small rebellion on similar grounds in 1677. Governor Berkeley of Virginia, loyal cavalier though he may have been, could discover no moral reasons for subjecting tobacco prices to the manipulation of London merchants. During Bacon's Rebellion he hanged a customs official who had sided with the insurgents. Maryland's proprietary establishment murdered one overly conscientious customs agent. Even in ducal New York, governors found ways to encourage the Amsterdam trade, and in 1681 the Court of Assizes convicted the duke's collector of treason for continuing to gather provincial taxes after the revenue act had expired. (An alternative approach, of course, would have been to renew the act, as the exasperated duke pointed out.) The Massachusetts General Court flatly denied that Parliament's authority extended across the sea.

In a word, the king could demand and reprimand, but not command. Nothing resembling an effective system of imperial administration existed before the 1670's, although various councils or committees of trade or plantations did appear from time to time and then withered.

Shaftesbury, the Carolina proprietor and future Whig, ran one of these bodies in the early 1670's and seemed to be guiding it in a direction of voluntary cooperation between English and colonial merchant and planter elites. By 1675 he had lost favor, and friends of the duke of York began to shape colonial policy in a more coercive direction. Their chief instrument became the Lords of Trade, a permanent committee of the Privy Council that began to develop real expertise on colonial matters and perhaps even (the point is disputed) a coherent sense of direction.

In several other respects, 1675–1676 marked a watershed. New York had just been restored to English rule. King Philip's War, a desperate bid for Indian cultural survival, devastated New England just before Bacon's Rebellion humiliated Virginia's Governor Berkeley and overthrew his government for the better part of a year. The cost of the rebellion to England in lost tobacco duties alone was a terrible blow to the finances of Charles II. The West Indian colonies also cried for attention. England's most valuable possessions in mercantilist terms, they remained highly vulnerable to attack in any war or to slave revolts at any time; they also had the potential to start what could become self-destructive conflicts. Jamaica in particular, long a home to buccaneers eager to plunder the Spanish, had to be brought under control. For sensible reasons, the crown royalized its island possessions shortly after the Restoration and in that dangerous environment began to work out the principles and techniques of royal government. By contrast, Virginia remained the only royal colony on the mainland as late as 1678, and New England skippers continued to assist more southerly colonies in violating the Navigation Acts.

The Lords of Trade operated in difficult and perilous times. As members of the Privy Council, they were vulnerable to such major distractions as the Popish Plot of 1678, which forced Charles II to dissolve a succession of Parliaments through 1681, provided the stimulus for the creation of the Whig and Tory parties, and drew political battle lines over the issue of excluding James, duke of York, now an avowed Roman Catholic, from succession to the throne. James spent much of these years in virtual exile in Scotland and even surrendered his autocracy in New York when a tax revolt by English merchants in New York City in 1681 at last persuaded him to grant the colony an assembly, which met in 1683. It promptly enacted a Charter of Liberties guaranteeing basic English rights to the settlers, most of whom were Dutch and hoped to remain so. The document, even its title, was an obvious response to Penn's Charter of Liberties of the same year and to still another one drafted by the now Quaker board of proprietors of East Jersey. Thomas Rudyard just possibly may have had a hand in writing all three. New York's English merchants believed that an eloquent statement of the colony's liberties, including a guarantee of an assembly every three years, would make the province competitive in the bid for new settlers. Instead, immigrants continued to swarm toward the Delaware, not the Hudson, and even some of New York City's prominent merchants relocated to Philadelphia. Nevertheless, the duke's experiment in autocracy appeared to have collapsed by 1681–1683, just when his position dramatically improved in England after the Rye House Plot routed the Whigs.

The Lords of Trade, often guided by such well-informed civil servants as William Blathwayt, directed its suspicions at colonial charters and its energies at Jamaica, Virginia, and Massachusetts. To bring Jamaica under control, the Lords threatened to impose a Poynings' law on the colony, a fifteenth-century device still used for controlling the Irish Parliament by permitting it to enact only measures that had the prior approval of the English Privy Council. Jamaica planters resisted and carried their case into the maelstrom of Whitehall politics at the height of the Exclusion Crisis. The resulting compromise had a tremendous impact on the constitutional development of royal colonies. The island's assembly retained the right to initiate legislation, but it had to guarantee a permanent revenue to the governor. How binding royal instructions were to anyone but the governor himself remained unresolved. Yet the governor's commission now became the central constitutional grant of power in a royal province, which he exercised in conjunction with an appointive council and an elective assembly. At a minimum, royal instructions—which showed a strong tendency to become standardized in the late Restoration era, mostly in response to Caribbean pressures—told the governor how he was authorized to use his powers; and governors tried to convince settlers that they too were bound or at least to persuade them to cooperate. Each colony's government was expected to pay its own costs and provide permanent salaries for the governor and a few other high officials. The Privy Council routinely reviewed legislation passed in royal colonies and also heard appeals from colonial courts.

The Lords of Trade soon imposed the Jamaica settlement upon Virginia, a colony only lightly supervised until Bacon's Rebellion of 1676. That upheaval, the most extensive revolt in seventeenth-century North America, began when the settlers provoked a war with the Susquehannock Indians in 1675 and then disagreed on how to fight it. Governor Berkeley favored a defensive strategy based on forts and mobile patrols, a plan that had worked well for him in the Indian war of 1644–1646 but that had done nothing to ward off devastating Dutch raids during the Second and Third Anglo-Dutch wars. The settlers, overwhelmingly youthful as they were, remembered the recent failures, not an ancient success. Frontiersmen shared high hopes for plunder and had no intention of confining hostilities to the Susquehannocks. They meant to attack any available and vulnerable tribe, and they found a willing leader in Nathaniel Bacon, a recent immigrant, a gentleman of clouded reputation in England, but already a member of the council.

In April 1676 he offered to lead a force of "volunteers" (men unsupported by public taxes) into the wilderness. By contrast, the governor's policy was expensive, it came during a depressed tobacco market, and it fed easily into the resentments that ex-servants had been accumulating against successful planters. Before the summer was over, Berkeley lost control of the entire colony except the Eastern Shore, which was protected by the bay from the Indian danger. Bacon massacred and looted one friendly tribe, shot up and enslaved another, and even burned Jamestown before succumbing to dysentery in October. By then both sides were raising recruits by promising them the confiscated estates of the other side or even long-term tax exemptions. Berkeley reconquered the province by commandeering the tobacco fleet as it arrived in the bay. The Baconians, ironically, found themselves in the exasperating role that Berkeley had played against the Dutch, trying to defend fixed forts against ships that could sail around them at will and land forces in their rear at night. By January

1677, just before two regiments arrived from England to restore order, the governor had regained control and was still hanging opponents. He was ordered back to England, where he soon died, but his followers used the court system to plunder the vanquished rebels over the next several years. Social resentments remained acute and bitter, flaring once more in the tobacco-cutting riots of 1682, a desperate bid to raise prices by reducing the crop.

Virginia's vindictive but insecure elite, again in control of the council, the Burgesses, and the county courts, was thus vulnerable to royal pressure. Sessions of the assembly were among the most expensive items in the annual tax bill, and numerous counties had included this cost among their grievances in 1677 when a royal commission investigated the causes of Bacon's Rebellion. As in Jamaica, the crown threatened to impose Poynings' law and demanded a permanent revenue. The Burgesses surrendered on the revenue question by 1683 as the price of their own survival.

New England remained a tough problem. The crown's duel with the region began shortly after the Restoration, waxed and waned in seriousness into the 1680's, led to a drastic reorganization of the whole region by 1686, produced a revolution in 1689, and finally secured a new charter for Massachusetts in 1691.

At first the crown's demands were rather modest; and had Massachusetts been at all inclined to compromise, the colony would have preserved most of its charter liberties. After supervising the conquest of New Netherland, the Royal Commission of 1664 investigated the New England governments. Charles II hoped to persuade them to submit their charters for amendment and confirmation. He wished to secure the power to appoint a royal governor or to pick one of three nominees suggested by the settlers, and he favored a five-year term for the office. He also sought the power to name a major general who would command the militia of the entire region. Finally, he asked toleration for religious dissenters. He specifically disavowed any intention of interfering with the Congregational Church or of imposing Anglican worship on New England, and he refrained from requesting any but a nominal revenue.

The New Englanders agreed to administer justice in the king's name, but otherwise they waited and stalled. Over the next twenty years, they promised to consider some changes but made no commitments. Or they dispatched agents with inadequate powers to London, knowing that the delays of trans-Atlantic communications would frustrate any attempt at speedy action. The Lords of Trade had probably lost patience with Massachusetts by 1676, when they dispatched a customs official, Edward Randolph, to report firsthand on the region. When Randolph arrived, New England was just turning the tide in King Philip's War, a brutal struggle that the colonies fought without requesting aid from the crown, although New York did provide important assistance by persuading the Mohawks to intervene against Philip at a crucial moment. When introduced to the council, Randolph carefully noted which magistrates removed their hats to honor a royal emissary and which would not. He sent his superiors extremely acerbic reports that called for legal action to rescind the Massachusetts charter. The Exclusion Crisis in England and more stalling tactics by the colony delayed the result, but time finally ran out on Massachusetts. After several false legal starts, the crown in late 1684 annulled the charter through an unanswered writ of scire facias in the Court of Chancery. Several months later Charles II died, and the Catholic duke of York became King James II.

James, who had just granted an assembly to New York, argued against one for New England shortly before his brother's death. As king he disallowed the New York Charter of Liberties, thereby abolishing the colony's assembly, and he created the Dominion of New England, which absorbed all of the colonies of that region by 1687 and added New York and the two Jerseys by 1688. He named Sir Edmund Andros, who had run New York for him from 1674–1680, as governor of the dominion.

In this way New York's experience began to rival Jamaica's as a model for constitutional reform from above. Just about everything that had been an essential part of autocratic New York now became standard policy in the dominion. As in New York, Andros brought with him a contingent of redcoats to awe the settlers and help police the frontiers. He governed through an appointive council and without an elective assembly. He thus raised taxes without consent, provoking one revolt in Ipswich that he success-

fully repressed. He reduced town meetings to their modest New York role. He virtually confined their powers to choosing the officials who would do the actual governing of the town. He insisted on toleration for all Protestants and—again as in New York, where the victim was the Dutch Reformed Church—he forced one of Boston's Congregational churches to let Anglicans use its meetinghouse for part of each Sunday. Most galling of all, perhaps, he challenged the whole system of land titles in New England, even a town's right to its own common and its ungranted lands. He demanded that each landowner take out a new patent, to which the crown added quitrents. His zeal for enforcing the Navigation Acts exceeded anything he had shown in New York, where he had often invoked the letter to evade the intent.

At first his regime did attract significant support. Bored descendants of illustrious founders, such as Fitzjohn and Wait Still Winthrop, Joseph Dudley, and Nathaniel Saltonstall, cheerfully accepted office from Andros, something the Winthrops had disdained to do in the Puritan era. By 1686 almost every town had some fairly prominent settler who was excluded from public life by the requirement that freemen be full church members. Many of Boston's leading merchants fit this category. Those who had arrived since 1650 tended to regard Puritan orthodoxy as bad for business and looked to the crown for relief.

Andros, in short, did have a constituency, but in just over two years he alienated nearly every part of it. His rigorous enforcement of the Navigation Acts antagonized otherwise sympathetic merchants. Toleration angered Congregational ministers, especially when the dominion questioned the legality of paying their salaries through local taxes. His land policy enraged the countryside, which believed that half a century of quiet possession ought to validate a title. By the winter of 1688–1689 definite signs of social hysteria were beginning to appear. When Andros marched several hundred militiamen through the Maine wilderness to meet an Indian alarm, dark rumors circulated that the whole expedition was part of a vicious popish plot between Andros, the French, and the Indians to kill off New England's godly sons through useless campaigning and then turn the region over to the French.

By then nearly every elite member of the 1686

coalition was ready to abandon the Andros regime except Dudley and Gershom Bulkeley of Connecticut. Exciting news arrived that William of Orange had landed in England with a small army and had issued a stirring manifesto on behalf of the Protestant religion and English liberties. Even before Boston learned that William had succeeded in driving James into French exile and in getting Parliament to proclaim him and his wife King William III and Queen Mary II, the city rose in a well-coordinated revolt. Andros and his principal men were arrested and jailed, the garrison was disarmed, and a warship in the harbor was rendered harmless. A committee of fifteen men—five commonwealth supporters, five moderates, and five one-time supporters of Andros—assumed responsibility for maintaining order and issued a statement justifying the rising. When word did arrive of William's triumph, pressure became irresistible to restore the pre-1686 regime, but this time the government had to broaden freemanship to sustain popular backing. While Connecticut, Rhode Island, and Plymouth quietly resumed their old forms of government (the charters of the first two had never been vacated by formal court action), Massachusetts petitioned the crown to restore the 1629 charter, dispatched two agents to England to join Increase Mather in this quest, and shipped Andros to London to stand trial for his offenses. (Instead the Lords of Trade vindicated his conduct and soon dispatched him to Virginia as governor.)

England's Glorious Revolution next spread from Boston to New York, where the results were far more divisive and bitter. The Charter of Liberties of 1683 had, among other things, imposed English liberties and English law upon a Dutch majority increasingly inclined to define its ethnic identity in religious terms. Most of the Dutch elite, including the clergy, had come to terms with the English conquest and accepted English rule. Many were painfully learning English as a second language and even seemed happy to hold office under an Irish Catholic governor, Colonel Thomas Dongan. When James abrogated the Charter of Liberties, even many of the reformers of 1681 continued to serve the regime, which was absorbed into the dominion in 1688 and given its own lieutenant governor, Captain Francis Nicholson, a man with a truly volcanic temper.

William's landing at Torbay looked quite different in New York from what it seemed to be in Boston. Above all, it portended a fourth Anglo-Dutch war, a frightening prospect in a colony that had been overrun in each of the last two. Also, most of New York's high officials owed their careers to James, and a tiny number were even Catholic. Such a group was hardly eager to proclaim William's accession, even after word arrived of his success. This hesitation convinced many Dutch and Yankee settlers that Nicholson and his clique were part of a Catholic plot to turn the colony over to the French, or to hold it for James, which now amounted to the same thing. The militia rose in May and June, took control of Fort James from its regular garrison after Nicholson had threatened to burn down the city, and drove him and his men into exile or jail. Leadership passed rapidly to the angriest militia captain in the city, Jacob Leisler, a former soldier and now a successful but apolitical merchant. His only dramatic public stand before 1689 involved an impassioned defense of orthodoxy in the Reformed Church against English meddling and corruption. When the clergy sided with the dominion, he and his followers denounced them too.

Leisler really believed in a popish plot. He was not an ambitious man. He never asked the crown for office or for any personal reward. He begged only that a loyal Protestant be dispatched to relieve him of his distasteful duties. Unfortunately, he knew no one he could trust who had even moderately impressive contacts in England. The leader of New York's Dutch revolt could not get his message through to a Dutch king of England. His exiled opponents, on the other hand, had excellent contacts, even with the change of regimes, and they were in a strong position to define Whitehall's response to the uprising.

Nor did Leisler easily assert control over the whole colony. At first the Yankee towns backed him, but when they discovered how little he understood or cared about English liberties, they deserted heavily to his opponents. He kept, for instance, the Revenue Act of 1683 in force, even though the assembly had voted it as a quid pro quo for the Charter of Liberties, but he made no effort to resurrect the charter itself. He did summon two brief sessions of an assembly to raise taxes for the expanding war against New France, but in each case he sent the deputies home when they raised questions about violations of English liberties. He also had difficulty extending his power to the upper Hudson, where the old Dutch elite remained in precarious control, until the destruction of Schenectady by an Indian and French force undermined their position in 1690. By the time that a royally appointed successor arrived in the spring of 1691, Leisler had almost as many enemies as supporters in New York. His revolt had become overwhelmingly an ethnic struggle in which the English, the Yankees, and the anglicizing Dutch elite united against his rule.

Maryland completed the cycle of major upheavals in 1689. It, of course, did have a Catholic proprietor and a formidable bloc of Catholic officeholders, and yet this revolution was anything but inevitable. Since the colony's tumultuous beginnings, it had settled down after 1660 into a significantly stabler polity than neighboring royal Virginia. At no point did tensions between established planters and ex-servants explode into rebellion, even though efforts to start popular risings did occur in 1676 and 1681. Instead, the Calverts' luck finally ran out. After William was proclaimed king, Lord Baltimore promptly dispatched a messenger to Maryland with orders to accept the change. The man died enroute, and the word never reached St. Mary's. The governor refused to proclaim William and Mary on his own initiative, even after all neighboring colonies had long since accepted the transformation. Three months after the New York rising, a Protestant Association was formed, marched on St. Mary's, and overturned the regime in the waning days of summer. In subsequent weeks the victorious insurgents petitioned the crown to make Maryland a royal colony, welcome news to the Lords of Trade.

London's response to these revolutions manifested less a consistent colonial policy than a pattern of adjustment to personalized demands. Those with solid political connections in England succeeded. Leisler had none, and he failed. Increase Mather scored the most notable triumph when he negotiated a second charter for Massachusetts between 1689 and 1691. By whatever labyrinthian path, the final product failed to meet the full demands of either side, but it did resemble the original crown goals voiced by the Royal Commission of 1664. The crown now appointed a governor with full veto power, and the colony had to accept toleration for Protestants and suffrage based on property, not on church membership. Both houses of the General Court remained elective, however, with the council now chosen by the whole legislature each May rather than by the voters. Unlike other royal colonies, Massachusetts retained power over the disposal of land through the General Court, and town meetings were also revived. Control of the courts did pass from elective magistrates to appointive justices, but the most remarkable feature of the settlement was how much of commonwealth Massachusetts survived to become the core of the enlarged royal province into which Maine, Plymouth, Martha's Vineyard, and Nantucket were now absorbed. In effect the crown had recognized and legitimated the history of Massachusetts. The past could not be eradicated. Only time would tell whether the colony would reciprocate and make room for the crown in its internal affairs.

Maryland's revolution did lead to royal government for a whole generation until a Calvert heir converted to the Church of England and had his proprietary rights restored shortly after the Hanoverian Succession. The royal interlude did strengthen the assembly against the council, lead to the establishment of the Church of England, and end toleration for Catholics.

New York suffered the worst ordeal. When a legitimate royal representative finally reached the colony in 1691, he refused even to show his commission to Leisler, whom he disdained as a usurper entitled to no courtesy. Leisler in turn would not surrender the fort to him until he saw a commission from William rather than James. This confrontation led to bloodshed. When Leisler finally did receive proof that his assailants represented William, he promptly relinquished power, only to be arrested for treason. He was tried, convicted, and hanged without being given a chance to appeal to England. At almost the same moment, anti-Leislerians met in a legally constituted assembly and reenacted the Charter of Liberties, modifying it to eliminate toleration for Catholics. English freedom still seemed to be a weapon for beating down a Dutch majority. The execution of Leisler and his son-in-law thoroughly embittered New York politics for more than a decade and left scars for a generation. It also crippled the Dutch Reformed Church by splitting the clergy from an angry laity who showed an increasing tendency to turn to poorly educated evangelical preachers for religious uplift. In the eighteenth century, evangelicalism stimulated a popular strand of anglicization, including eventual demands for preaching in English and for autonomy from Amsterdam in ecclesiastical affairs.

Despite all of this variety, the Glorious Revolution and its aftermath did much to standardize colonial government. Until 1689, London had two models of royalization to choose between, the Jamaica settlement of 1681 and the autocratic New York and dominion pattern. Probably neither James nor the Lords of Trade had devised a systematic policy for undermining assemblies throughout the empire, even though writs were out against most surviving charters by 1688. As in Jamaica and Virginia, such a threat could have been used to generate quite a different compromise. Yet the possibility of a massive turn to absolutism remained real so long as the dominion survived, and in 1688 it claimed nearly half the population of English North America. The Revolution of 1688–1689 utterly destroyed this option. Thereafter the only real choice lay between some variant of the Jamaica-Virginia model and the ever fewer surviving charter governments. When New Jersey went royal in 1702 and the Carolinas after 1719, royal government had clearly become the norm.

The struggles of the 1680's and 1690's also gave English liberty a greater legitimacy in North America than it had ever had before. Except for Catholics who lost ground in Maryland and New York, the Glorious Revolution secured representative institutions on the mainland and increased their viability by pitting them against royal prerogative in a dialectical relationship. Settlers had to learn to justify their liberties. Bicameralism also became standard by 1700, with only Pennsylvania moving in the other direction. Toleration for Protestants became quite general, although many legal battles remained ahead over its extent and precise definition. Trial by jury expanded quite rapidly in most colonies in these decades except in Virginia, which did not follow the pattern until the 1750's. By the early eighteenth century, some settlers were already boasting that they had always been destined to be free.

War with France, an inevitable by-product of the Glorious Revolution, eventually forced a major revision of imperial institutions in London. The Lords of Trade, all of whom were Privy Councillors with other important responsibilities, could not keep abreast of events. Not until 1692 were governors found for all of the royal colonies. In some years the English tobacco fleet never reached the Chesapeake, and Scottish interlopers began to fill the void. West Indian planters faced almost constant peril, which England was sore pressed to relieve, and French corsairs inflicted disastrous losses on English shipping. Fearing incompetence at the center, Parliament considered assuming direct control of the colonies. Instead, during the parliamentary recess of 1696, William reorganized imperial administration. He abolished the Lords of Trade and created a new advisory body of experts and leading officeholders, usually called the Board of Trade. Its primary function was to gather accurate information and recommend action to the appropriate offices of government (the Privy Council, Parliament, one of the Secretaries of State, the Treasury, and others), with which final decisions rested.

Coupled with the comprehensive Navigation Act of the same year (a measure that closed several loopholes in earlier legislation), the reorganization of 1696 largely completed the structure of empire that would endure until the American Revolution. Occasionally Parliament would add something to the enumerated list; discourage the colonial manufacturing of woolens (1699), hats (1732), or iron (1750); provide bounties for naval stores or indigo; or attempt to regulate paper money in America; but in general the colonies remained a crown responsibility with the Board of Trade providing most of the coordination. In its first decade the board assumed an active and reformist role. It tried to impose the Jamaica constitution on all of the chartered colonies, proprietary and corporate, only to lose the battle in Parliament. It attempted to curb the power of great landowners in Virginia and New York. But even under Queen Anne it increasingly settled into a less ambitious routine, sifting through colonial correspondence, acting as a clearing house for interests associated with the colonies, and drafting commissions and instructions, a chore that had already become highly routinized.

One other development of these years eventually had a tremendous impact on the colonies. The generation that made the Glorious Revolution and fought two long and expensive wars with France also created eighteenth-century British political culture. As seventeenth-century confrontations between royal prerogative and parliamentary privilege faded into irrelevance, it became increasingly clear that government in England would be a cooperative arrangement among crown, Lords, and Commons—the one, the few, and the many of classical and humanist thought. In effect, Harrington's republican theories were recast starting with Shaftesbury around 1675 into a defense of a "mixed and balanced constitution" by a generation groping toward a satisfactory formula for responsible government.

The path from the Exclusion Crisis to the Whig oligarchy of Sir Robert Walpole's ministry (1721–1742) was no straight and broad highway. Two persistent tensions—court versus country, and Whig versus Tory—intersected in multiple and unpredictable ways that both complicated and enriched public life. The first tension was quite old and enduring. The court had to sustain its position in Europe against competing powers, maintain order at home, and persuade Parliament to provide enough revenue for these functions. By Anne's reign, these needs required a navy that had become the largest in the world, a standing or professional army, and a growing network of patronage to staff London offices, the customs service, the excise, and high positions in the colonies. Over a hundred offices went to members of Parliament, providing them with a strong inducement to support the current administration. War with France also bred close relations between the court and London's financial community. In fact, the 1690's witnessed a momentous financial revolution that included creation of the national debt, the emergence of the London Stock Exchange, the chartering of the Bank of England, routine use of the land tax, and a vast expansion of excise revenues. The ability to borrow gave Britain a weight in international affairs far out of proportion to its rather small population of 5.5 million, perhaps only a fourth of France's. Sustaining the debt also made Britain one of the West's most heavily taxed societies. Those rich enough to invest in the funds or in a position to get government contracts made money out of the war. Lesser gentry who paid the land tax and ordinary subjects hit hard by excises were likely to greet these transformations with something less than exuberance.

The country opposition provided a coherent and often compelling criticism of these developments. Country spokesmen loathed the financial revolution, grew wary of involvement in continental wars, preferred a militia to a standing army, and advocated a variety of devices for lessening the court's ability to "manage" Parliament—more frequent elections, place bills that banned certain categories of officeholders from a seat in the Commons, and impeachments. Where court apologists advocated the interdependence of crown, Lords, and Commons, country ideologues demanded the independence of each, particularly of the Commons. To these ideologues, English liberty made the nation's history unique, that liberty depended almost totally on the Commons, and the Commons could remain free only so long as members of Parliament were themselves "virtuous" and "independent"—capable, that is, of voluntarily putting the common good ahead of private advantage. The court, more than the country, was likely to appeal to self-interest and to advocate something like economic modernization.

The hostility between Whigs and Tories rested on religion, regional patterns, economic interests, and family histories. Whigs drew support from much of the nobility, merchants in dynamic and expanding trades, and religious dissenters, especially in towns. Tories relied more on the gentry, on merchants in older trades, and on traditional loyalties to the Church of England. As of 1680, Tories supported the Stuarts and favored court measures, while Whigs pioneered in creating country ideology. By 1720 the bulk of the Whigs had gravitated to the court in the course of prosecuting the French wars and ensuring the succession of George I and the Hanoverian dynasty. Tories had become, for the most part, a country opposition. A band of articulate Whig radicals, or "Real Whigs," such as John Trenchard and Thomas Gordon, still defended country principles and viewed the financial revolution with implacable hostility, especially after the South Sea Bubble of 1720, a spectacular stock market collapse.

Party conflict thus raged fiercely in a society that believed parties are immoral, that all good men ought to rally behind an honest government. The crown until 1714 usually tried to build coalition ministries from both parties, an arrangement that was inherently unstable and led to one party forcing the other from office. Some combination of royal exasperation and electoral reaction then unseated the incumbents and either brought in the other party or another "broad bottom." Responsible government, an idea closely tied to the wholesale use of impeachments in the seventeenth century, slowly redefined itself to mean parliamentary government under a ministry satisfactory to both the court and a majority of the Commons.

When American settlers became enamored of British political culture, they borrowed freely and often, but never everything. Impeachment never became more than an exotic and infrequent device in the colonies; in a century and a half all the colonies together did not impeach as many people as a single session of Parliament did on several occasions. Nor did any colony develop cabinet or ministerial government, Britain's eighteenth-century answer to the problem of responsible rule. Nothing quite like the Whig and Tory parties and their ability to sustain their resentments for more than two generations ever appeared in any North American province. But both the techniques and the principles of court and country politics did make it to America, where they affected different colonies in sharply contrasting ways. To see how, we must pursue colonial developments into their third, or stabilization, phase.

THE ERA OF STABILIZATION

By the eighteenth century, colonial governments were becoming in some major respects more similar than they had been before. All but a few balanced an appointive governor and council against an elective assembly, and without much difficulty they applied the rationale for Britain's mixed and balanced constitution to their own simpler structures. They shared other common features, some of which continued to differentiate them from government in England.

To take just four examples, suffrage was broader in America, but electoral contests were usually not as well organized as in Augustan Britain. Second, non-Quaker governments in America continued to insist that adult males own arms and train as a militia, while Britain kept disarmed all but the highest level of the social order. Third, beginning with Massachusetts in 1690

and culminating with Virginia in the 1750's, each of the original twelve colonies (those founded before Georgia) adopted some form of paper money or "currency finance," which only Maryland backed with specie. Its value derived primarily from a government's promise to accept it in payment of taxes, but its exchange rate with sterling depended mostly on a colony's balance of trade. In general, paper money functioned smoothly in the middle region from New York to Virginia but depreciated alarmingly in New England and the Carolinas, eventually driving the Yankees back to specie in the 1750's and prompting the British government to try to impel all other colonies in the same direction after 1764. Finally, all colonies had to make decisions about land and new local governments in a way that European governments seldom did. With population doubling each generation, expansion became a social imperative that no province could ignore. In Connecticut, Rhode Island, and Massachusetts, the legislature retained control of the entire process. In the other colonies, the governor or proprietor granted land, but the legislature tried to assert power over the creation of local jurisdictions (counties, townships, legal parishes), especially those with the right to send representatives to the assembly. None of these problems existed in quite the same way in Great Britain.

Other general trends affected both sides of the Atlantic in the eighteenth century. In both Britain and America, public life became more elitist, and the role and importance of the legislature increased. The ratio of adult white males to representatives in the assembly at least doubled in every mainland colony between 1700 and 1770, and in Pennsylvania it rose by a factor of almost ten. Assemblies did not expand as rapidly as population, and from New York to Maryland they hardly grew at all. Somewhat less evenly, legislative turnover declined noticeably and legislative sessions grew longer and more frequent. The average number of laws passed per year tripled in Virginia, New York, and New Jersey between Anne's reign and the final decade of the colonial era. It more than doubled in Massachusetts, New Hampshire, and Pennsylvania. Only Maryland and South Carolina remained generally stagnant in this respect. Finally, both the British House of Commons and the colonial assembly gained power and prestige at the expense of the upper house, and in both environments the executive increased its usable power provided it respected the constitutional position of the legislature and devised an adequate formula for cooperating with it or managing it. Hanoverian kings claimed none of the absolutist powers dear to the Stuarts, but they got more done and enjoyed higher prestige in Europe.

Colonial governors had to learn analogous lessons. In the generation after the Glorious Revolution, aggressive royal governors, nearly all of whom had military backgrounds, zealously defended their prerogatives only to clash with assemblies that were equally committed to their traditional privileges, most of which in some form or other antedated the arrival of royal government in the province in question. Although the issues varied, direct confrontations occurred between 1702 and 1710 in New Hampshire and Massachusetts against Joseph Dudley, in New York and New Jersey against Lord Cornbury, in Maryland against John Seymour, and in Virginia (where the council, not the assembly, was the primary antagonist) against Sir Francis Nicholson. Opponents secured the recall of Cornbury and Nicholson under humiliating circumstances, while Dudley just barely survived his tempest. Royal servants needed more than commissions and instructions to govern effectively. They required secure support in London, which party battles between Whigs and Tories rendered problematical but the long Whig ascendancy after 1714 tended to resolve. They also had to acquire adequate leverage in colonial society to do their job.

These conditions were increasingly met after 1715 or 1720. The establishment of the Whig oligarchy in Britain particularly under Walpole and the Pelham brothers had a stabilizing effect in America, even though most of the men who shaped colonial policy in London can scarcely be accused of vigor or more than minimal political integrity. To them, colonial affairs seemed mostly a succession of patronage decisions, unspoiled by any broader imperial vision. Yet partly because colonial appointees less often feared reprimand or recall, they were freer to improvise solutions to their problems, and they served longer terms than their predecessors. If we exclude obviously transitional administrations, Massachusetts, for example, had only four different governors from 1731 to 1769, New

Hampshire just three from 1731 to 1776, Virginia three from 1727 to 1768, and South Carolina five from 1743 to 1775. When activists again began to appear at the Board of Trade after 1748, they quickly decided that royal government had decayed badly, mostly because they measured reality against the unachieved prerogative demands of 1700. In practice, the system as a whole reached its peak of effectiveness in the 1750's, when it supervised the massive mobilization of manpower and other resources that finally drove the French from North America.

To be successful, governors had to come to terms with the evolving political culture of their provinces and, as in Britain, fared better by respecting its norms. Although the working elements of this culture were broadly similar throughout the empire, they came together in different ways in different regions. Southern mainland provinces tended to develop a form of stability that derived coherence and legitimacy from the British opposition or country view of politics. Governors who flagrantly violated country norms could expect trouble, especially if they tried to dominate the assembly through the manipulation of patronage. The paradigmatic administration in this respect was Alexander Spotswood's in Virginia (1710–1722), for both he and the assembly discovered the political boundaries beyond which they could not safely go.

Spotswood won passage of a tobacco inspection act that gave him enough lucrative inspectorships to distribute among a large majority of the House of Burgesses. Almost to a man, these "placemen" were unseated by the voters in the election of 1715, which returned a very angry house that in turn made several quite radical demands. With an insulting speech that he regretted in later years, Spotswood dissolved the assembly and governed without one for the next three years. Between the permanent export duty on tobacco and the quitrents, both of which grew with the colony, he had ample revenue to keep going. The next assembly (1718) was chosen amid explicit appeals to country ideology and remained angry, but by 1720 a satisfactory compromise took hold. The governor had learned that he could not build an English court-and-treasury party in the assembly, and none of his successors forgot that lesson. The assembly discovered that it could not coerce the governor. Each had to recognize and respect the fundamental independence of the other, a task that became easier with the disappearance of substantive issues. The crown seemed happy with a colony the tobacco exports of which produced lucrative customs revenue, and it abandoned its campaign against great landowners. Beginning with Spotswood in 1720, governors routinely became great planters themselves. Under Sir William Gooch (1727–1749), the governor and the Burgesses developed a highly stylized rhetoric of harmony and mutual flattery that enabled Gooch to get most of what he wanted from the assembly, including a new tobacco inspection act in which all inspectors were banned from a seat in the house. From 1720 until the Stamp Act of 1765, only one public quarrel disrupted the concord between governor and assembly, and overt factionalism disappeared.

With differences in detail, South Carolina developed a similar system from the 1730's, particularly under Governor James Glen (1743–1756). Georgia fell into the same pattern when it finally got an assembly in the 1750's. The politics of harmony never did take hold in Maryland or North Carolina. The Calvert family, which did possess amazing resources of patronage, could not refrain from trying to use them on the Maryland assembly, where frequent roll-call votes beginning in the 1730's reflected continual tension, with a country majority holding the proprietary party at bay. In North Carolina, the precarious position of a new elite, tensions between tobacco and rice counties, and backcountry resentment against both all inhibited the emergence of a "country constitution." But where it did take hold, it was stable and effective.

Northern provinces moved in a contrary direction. Factions, though seldom coherent parties, remained an inescapable fact of public life most of the time. The wars with France put great pressures on these governments to defend their northern frontiers. This need generated patronage that, when genuinely used to build an effective coalition for defense, could attract sufficient public support to become self-sustaining. In a word, political stability in the northern colonies tended to follow a "court" formula. Country ideology did indeed appear in New York during the famous John Peter Zenger crisis of the mid-1730's and the controversy over chartering King's College twenty years later, or in Massachusetts in 1747–1749 against the governor's

wartime coalition and again in 1754–1755 against a proposed excise tax. In each of these cases, opposition spokesmen turned to country rhetoric and even founded three newspapers only after failing to win the assembly to their side. Country rhetoric replicated its minority role in domestic British politics.

Court politics worked best in New Hampshire and Massachusetts during wartime. Benning Wentworth (1741–1767) so thoroughly dominated New Hampshire after inflicting a severe defeat on the assembly by 1751 that for years he faced no opposition at all. He controlled the old proprietary land claims to the interior and used them in a strongly developmental way. He got himself appointed surveyor-general of the king's woods and acquired the mast contract for the navy, two positions almost certain to quarrel when held by different men. He also had an extensive interest in the lumber trade, the most important item in the colony's exports. He cornered all major points of access to the crown, and he possessed more than enough influence locally to build a powerful coalition in the legislature and the province.

In Massachusetts, Governor William Shirley (1741–1756) successfully defended Nova Scotia against French attack in 1744, organized an intercolonial expedition that conquered Louisbourg in 1745, tried to put together a similar invasion of Canada in 1746 and 1747, and then used his influence and a parliamentary reimbursement for the Louisbourg campaign to abolish paper money and restore specie after King George's War ended in 1748. During the French and Indian War (1754–1763), Massachusetts raised a large provincial army nearly every year and believed that these mammoth efforts contributed significantly to the defense of threatened neighbors and the conquest of New France.

New York's governors, by contrast, refined their court techniques primarily during the generation of peace after 1713 and used their successes to make the governorship itself probably the most lucrative office on the mainland. The legitimacy of the system remained precarious, and when governors went ten and nine years without calling new elections, as did happen between 1715 and 1738, the moral foundations of public life suffered further. In New York in particular and the Middle Atlantic region generally (including Maryland), the eighteenth-century electorate normally assumed an overwhelmingly antiadministration stance. Assemblies could and did make radical demands in New York and above all in Pennsylvania, but as the colonial era drew toward a close they also ran a heightened risk of alienating their constituencies. Assembly size grew very slowly, but roll-call votes proliferated, permitting voters to defeat deputies who cooperated too openly with the administration, as many of them were indeed doing by the 1750's and 1760's.

With the conquest of New France, the political system that had emerged over the previous half-century faced a new and largely unexpected challenge from the imperial reform program of the British government. The thirteen colonies, which had not been able to accept the Albany Plan's formula for a limited union against French attack in 1754, now united against Britain instead and left the empire just thirteen years after the Peace of Paris had ratified its most stunning victory. The controversy over taxation did indeed threaten all of the assemblies, and they in turn had to depend on crowd action to make good their protests. As resistance became revolution, the assemblies also learned that they could not survive the struggle without a large dose of democratization.

Patterns of provincial and imperial politics obviously influenced the Revolution at every stage, but they cannot explain it by themselves. As of 1760, British North America possessed a political culture with elements long familiar to everyone in public life, but within individual colonies these elements combined in ways that covered nearly the entire spectrum of possibilities open to Anglo-Americans. The successful court constitutions of New Hampshire and Massachusetts had a shakier counterpart in New York. Deviating significantly from this model were Rhode Island and Connecticut, with their corporate governments, and Pennsylvania, in which a coherent Quaker party faced stiffening resistance from frontier ethnic groups and a reviving proprietary faction. Country constitutions flourished in Virginia, South Carolina, and Georgia, but not in Maryland and North Carolina. Only sustained British pressure could propel all of these colonies into simultaneous opposition. Only a genuine revolution could make that unity hold.

BIBLIOGRAPHY

Thomas J. Archdeacon, *New York City, 1664–1710: Conquest and Change* (Ithaca, N.Y., 1976), stresses ethnic tensions during and after Leisler's Rebellion. Bernard Bailyn, "Politics and Social Structure in Virginia," in James Morton Smith, ed., *Seventeenth-Century America: Essays in Colonial History* (Chapel Hill, N.C., 1959), is a landmark essay for any social interpretation of Virginia politics; and *The Origins of American Politics* (New York, 1968), although controversial, remains a basic attempt at synthesizing the political history of colonial America. Patricia U. Bonomi, *A Factious People: Politics and Society in Colonial New York* (New York, 1971), provides a strong narrative of eighteenth-century politics. Lois G. Carr and David W. Jordan, *Maryland's Revolution of Government, 1689–1692* (Ithaca, N.Y., 1974), is easily the best account of its subject. Wesley Frank Craven, *The Colonies in Transition, 1660–1713* (New York, 1968), offers an outstanding introduction to the period. Jere R. Daniell, "Politics in New Hampshire Under Governor Benning Wentworth, 1741–1767," in *William and Mary Quarterly*, 3rd ser., 23 (1966), lucidly explains that governor's unusual success. Mary M. Dunn and Richard S. Dunn, eds., *The Papers of William Penn* (Philadelphia, 1981–), is indispensable for the West Jersey Concessions and Penn's First Frame of Government. Richard S. Dunn, *Puritans and Yankees, the Winthrop Dynasty of New England, 1630–1717* (Princeton, 1962), is excellent on New England politics. A. Roger Ekirch, *"Poor Carolina": Politics and Society in Colonial North Carolina, 1729–1776* (Chapel Hill, N.C., 1981), investigates North Carolina's continuing instability. Jack P. Greene, "Political Mimesis: A Consideration of the Historical and Cultural Roots of Legislative Behavior in the British Colonies in the Eighteenth Century," in *American Historical Review*, 75 (1969–1970), with a comment by Bernard Bailyn and a rejoinder by Greene, has done much to define what eighteenth-century politics were about; "The Growth of Political Stability: An Interpretation of Political Development in the Anglo-American Colonies, 1660–1760," in John Parker and Carol Urness, eds., *The American Revolution: A Heritage of Change* (Minneapolis, 1975), stresses the maturity of colonial politics on the eve of the Revolution; and "Legislative Turnover in British America, 1696 to 1775: A Quantitative Analysis," in *William and Mary Quarterly*, 3rd ser., 38 (1981), provides basic data on ratios of population to representatives and on turnover.

James A. Henretta, *"Salutary Neglect": Colonial Administration Under the Duke of Newcastle* (Princeton, 1972), argues that imperial policy seldom rose above considerations of patronage. Sydney V. James, *Colonial Rhode Island: A History* (New York, 1975), offers a fine general history of a maverick colony. Richard R. Johnson, *Adjustment to Empire: The New England Colonies, 1675–1715* (New Brunswick, N.J., 1981), is an exceptionally thoughtful study of New England in the age of the Glorious Revolution. Stanley N. Katz, *Newcastle's New York: Anglo-American Politics, 1732–1753* (Cambridge, Mass., 1968), demonstrates that colonial and imperial politics were always closely related. Leonard W. Labaree, *Royal Government in America: A Study of the British Colonial System Before 1783* (New Haven, 1930), remains a basic analysis. David S. Lovejoy, *The Glorious Revolution in America* (New York, 1972), tries to find a common focus for events in New England, New York, and the Chesapeake colonies. Edmund S. Morgan, *American Slavery, American Freedom: The Ordeal of Colonial Virginia* (New York, 1975), finds a close relationship between the growth of slavery and the rise of liberty for whites. John M. Murrin, "Magistrates, Sinners, and a Precarious Liberty: Trial by Jury in Seventeenth-Century New England," in David D. Hall, John M. Murrin, and Thad W. Tate, eds., *Saints and Revolutionaries: Essays in Early American History* (New York, 1983), investigates Puritan reluctance to accept criminal jury trials; and "Political Development," in Jack P. Greene and J. R. Pole, eds., *Colonial British America: Essays in the New History of the Early Modern Era* (Baltimore, 1983), covers much the same ground as this essay, with an emphasis on historiography. Gary B. Nash, *Quakers and Politics: Pennsylvania, 1681–1726* (Princeton, 1968), finds that class antagonisms and Quaker antiauthoritarian attitudes imposed severe limits on Penn's "Holy Experiment." Alison G. Olson, *Anglo-American Politics, 1660–1775: The Relationship Between Parties in England and Colonial America* (New York, 1973), argues for a positive correlation between factionalism, political stability, and imperial vitality.

Mattie Erma Edwards Parker, ed., *North Carolina Charters and Constitutions, 1578–1698* (Raleigh, N.C., 1963), provides edited texts of the Gilbert, Raleigh, Virginia, Heath, and Carolina patents and of the Fundamental Constitutions. William Pencak, *War, Politics, and Revolution in Provincial Massachusetts* (Boston, 1981), contends that war encouraged court politics and peace brought a country reaction. John Harold Plumb, *The Origins of Political Stability: England, 1675–1725* (Boston, 1967), is basic to any understanding of British events. John G. A. Pocock, *The Machiavellian Moment: Florentine Political Thought and the Atlantic Republican Tradition* (Princeton, 1975), is the most challenging study yet made of Anglo-American civic humanism. John E. Pomfret, *The Province of West New Jersey, 1609–1702: A History of the Origins of an American Colony* (Princeton, 1956), is the standard study. David B. Quinn, ed., *Early Maryland in a Wider World* (Detroit, 1982), provides an excellent starting point for colonial Maryland. Robert C. Ritchie, *The Duke's Province: A Study of New York Politics and Society, 1664–1691* (Chapel Hill, N.C., 1977), finds ducal rule quite predatory. Clayton Robert, *The Growth of Responsible Government in Stuart England* (Cambridge, 1966), studies the rebirth and demise of impeachment during the slow evolution of responsible cabinet government. Marion Eugene Sirmans, *Colonial South Carolina: A Political History, 1663–1763* (Chapel Hill, N.C., 1966), is basic to its subject. I. K. Steele, *Politics of Colonial Policy: The Board of Trade in Colonial Administration, 1696–1720* (Oxford, 1968), traces the board's evolution from a reforming to a bureaucratic body. Alan Tully, *William Penn's Legacy: Politics and Social Structure in Provincial Pennsylvania, 1726–1755* (Baltimore, 1977), argues for a higher degree of political stability than other scholars have found. Robert E. Wall, *Massachusetts Bay: The Crucial Decade, 1640–1650* (New Haven, 1972), carefully analyzes the consolidation of a Puritan political system. Stephen S. Webb, *The Governors-General: The English Army and the Definition of Empire, 1569–1681* (Chapel Hill, N.C., 1979), emphasizes the military character of the office of governor. Robert M. Weir, " 'The Harmony We Were Famous For': An Interpretation of Pre-Revolutionary South Carolina Politics," in *William and Mary Quarterly*, 3rd ser., 26 (1969), is central to an understanding of politics in the pre-Revolutionary southern colonies. Robert Zemsky, *Merchants, Farmers, and River Gods: An Essay on Eighteenth-Century American Politics* (Boston, 1971), charts the growth of political stability in mid-eighteenth-century Massachusetts.

[*See also* HISTORIOGRAPHY OF AMERICAN POLITICAL HISTORY; AMERICAN REVOLUTION; ARTICLES OF CONFEDERATION; CHURCH AND STATE; CITIZENSHIP; COLLECTIVE VIOLENCE; CONSPIRACY AND CONSPIRACY THEORIES; CORRUPTION IN GOVERNMENT; DECLARATION OF INDEPENDENCE; ENGLISH AND EUROPEAN POLITICAL INHERITANCE; FEDERALISM; IMPEACHMENT; PROPERTY; REPUBLICANISM; SEPARATION OF POWERS; SOCIAL STRATIFICATION; STATE GOVERNMENTS; *and* SUFFRAGE.]

CONGRESS

Garrison Nelson

WHEN Ethan Allen and his Green Mountain Boys surprised the British defenders at Fort Ticonderoga in upstate New York, they did so "in the name of the great Jehovah and the Continental Congress." This rousing battle cry emphasized a little-appreciated fact about the nature of American legislative institutions. Alone of the world's major nations, the United States was created by a legislature. It was the Continental Congress that authorized the writing of the Declaration of Independence. It was the Continental Congress that appointed General George Washington to lead the army of colonists in battle. It was the Continental Congress that appointed emissaries from the struggling nation to represent it in the councils of Europe. And it was the Continental Congress that raised the money to underwrite the costs of the Revolution.

The American colonies, populated primarily by English settlers, were acutely aware of the tensions between the crown and the House of Commons that characterized the reign of the Stuarts. Following the Restoration in 1660, a number of those involved in the overthrow of Charles I fled to the colonies. The monarchy never fully recovered, and the Glorious Revolution of 1688 brought an end to Stuart claims of monarchical supremacy and moved the locus of political power toward the Commons.

From then until the outbreak of hostilities between the colonists and the soldiers of the king, the American colonies were engaged in a successful quest for power that led them to gain control over their own currency, revenues, the appropriation of public funds, the elections and qualifications of the members of their colonial assemblies, and the conditions of commerce between themselves and the settlers of other na-

tions and the Indians. In addition, they succeeded in weakening the powers of the royal governors, who represented the interests of the crown in the colonies. By the eve of the Revolution, the colonial assemblies had become major centers of power.

Colonial unrest and dismay with the policies of the crown (especially the Intolerable Acts) led to the convening of the Continental Congress on 5 September 1774. This body was intended to provide a forum for communication and to coordinate unified resistance—presumably peaceful—to the actions of the crown.

Few members of the Congress foresaw that separation from England would be the eventual outcome of their assemblage. But eight months later, when the Second Continental Congress convened, the battle for independence had begun.

The Congress's first major act was to create the Continental army and to place George Washington at its head in June 1775. Although separatist sentiments were in the air, it was not until a year later that the Congress authorized Thomas Jefferson, John Adams, Robert Livingston, Roger Sherman, and Benjamin Franklin to write the Declaration of Independence. The struggle was on.

Throughout the Revolutionary War, the Continental Congress tried to function as a legislature. It selected presiding officers, convened committees, raised revenues, appropriated funds, and wrote legislation to further the eventual goal of a postwar national government.

The Continental Congress in its post-revolutionary phase was a fractious and often impotent body, as its more talented members opted for governance in their newly established state capitols. The inability of the Continental Congress and its successor, the Congress of the Confederation, to preserve internal peace and to prevent interstate bickering over taxation and tariffs led to its demise. The Articles of Confederation, written in 1777 and finally ratified in 1781, have often been blamed for the difficulties confronting the new nation.

Under the Articles, especially Article IX, the central government was severely limited. Congress was prevented from engaging in war, negotiating treaties, coining money, authorizing bills of credit, or borrowing and spending money without the consent of a majority of the states. Furthermore, no alterations or amendments could be adopted unless the state legislatures unanimously agreed to them.

It became clear that while the United States could be created by a legislature, it could not be governed solely by one. This sentiment led to the formation of the Convention of 1787 at Philadelphia's Independence Hall and the rewriting of the nation's basic document.

As befits a nation created by a legislature, Article I of the Constitution deals with the structure, powers, and duties of the legislative branch. The members of the Constitutional Convention were readily agreed that the federal Congress would be bicameral. Eleven states had bicameral legislatures, and it was thought two chambers would be better able to contain the rashness of the democratic spirit that had disrupted a number of state governments immediately after the Revolution.

The larger states, particularly Virginia, hoped that representation in both chambers would be based upon population and that their influence would dominate the deliberations of the Congress as a whole. The smaller states, especially New Jersey, hoped for a representational scheme similar to that of the Congress of the Confederation, in which each state had equal representation. A deadlock ensued.

The compromise plan, authored by Roger Sherman of Connecticut, provided for representation by population in the House of Representatives and equal representation in the Senate. The Great Compromise, passed 5–4 on 16 July 1787, succeeded in keeping the small states from bolting the convention and has remained in force to the present day.

In order to make the Great Compromise more palatable to the large states, the House of Representatives was given the power to originate revenue bills; the proportion of state seats in the House was to be kept in line with the population totals, as enumerated in a decennial census; and direct taxation was to be linked with popular representation. Because many members of the Constitutional Convention had served in the colonial assemblies and newly created state legislatures, it was not difficult for them to outline the powers and duties of the House of Representatives.

The Senate was a different matter. Before the Revolution the upper houses of the colonies were often dominated by "placemen," those whose first loyalty was to the royal governors and whose propertied background rendered them a distinct minority among the colonists, and so upper houses became suspect. Thus, the Senate was given the responsibility of checking the executive in matters of appointments and diplomatic negotiations, but the House was given the responsibility of electing a president if the electoral college failed to provide a majority. Distrust was built into the system. The monarchical president was to be checked by the aristocratic Senate, which would in turn be checked by the democratic House. It was a solution in keeping with both Aristotle and Montesquieu.

Since then, little has been added to the basic outlines created for the Congress. The Fourteenth Amendment (1868) eliminated the "three-fifths rule" for the counting of slaves in determining a state's proportion of House seats; the Sixteenth Amendment (1913) gave the Congress the right to tax personal income directly; the Seventeenth (1913) made the Senate popularly elective; and the Twentieth (1933) changed the meeting day of Congress to eliminate its lame-duck sessions. Each amendment has had its impact, but the fundamental relationship between the American people and their Congress continues in much the way it was envisioned by the authors of the Constitution.

Capturing the fullness and diversity of Congress is a difficult task. Thousands of individuals have sat within Congress. Hundreds of thousands of bills have been presented for its consideration. Millions of yeas and nays have been cast for and against its various proposals. And trillions of public dollars have been raised and spent under its auspices. For this article, three areas have been chosen for discussion: the leaders, the political parties, and the congressional committees. Each provides a unique perspective on the Congress.

Congress needs to be led. It is an assembly of individuals chosen from the various states to create national policy. These individuals enjoy the strengths, and suffer from the weaknesses, that characterize us all; it is their access to enormous institutional power that distinguishes them. They can affect more people, with greater impact, for a longer duration than the rest of us. For national policy to emanate from the Congress, a bill submitted to the president must be identically drafted by both chambers. With members whose interests, backgrounds, policies, constituencies, and ambitions are as diverse as the United States itself, this is no small feat. This is what congressional leaders strive for, and thus discussion must begin with them, their positions, methods of selection, and contributions to the legislative process.

The political parties, with their machinery of nominations and elections, offer the opportunity to change the partisan composition of the Congress and, in so doing, to reorient the legislative agenda. Every two years the public has had this right. Because the United States has a presidential government, candidates for the House and Senate are not directly linked to the election for the executive branch. In addition, the separate elections for the House and Senate permit and often encourage party majorities that differ between the two chambers and between the Congress and the presidency. This factor of potential intercameral and interinstitutional conflict has been routinized in American politics to a degree found in no other country.

It is the congressional committees that handle the vast bulk of legislative business, and both houses have relied upon them to deal with ever-changing agendas. And it is within the committees that members from widely divergent regions, parties, and backgrounds come together to fashion legislation that will win approval in the chamber. Woodrow Wilson once contended that the government of the United States had become "a government by the Standing Committees of Congress." It was an overstatement, but it does indicate that an understanding of Congress must begin with recognition of the centrality of committees to congressional processes.

LEADERSHIP

Discovering leaders in any form of organization requires more than a discerning eye. Even within the same organization, leaders can vary from day to day and issue to issue. Legislative bodies, such as the Congress, are collective decision-making bodies with members possessing putative equality. As a consequence, their leaders must operate in a different manner than those of hierarchical decision-making organizations.

Of all the approaches to leadership identification, the easiest to understand is the "positional" or "formal leadership" one, which selects as leaders those who occupy identifiable organizational posts. Within the House, those would include the Speaker of the House, the floor leaders, and the party whips.

Speakers of the House. The only congressional leader identified in the Constitution is the Speaker. Article I, Section 2, of the Constitution empowers the House of Representatives to "chuse their Speaker and other Officers." This power has been denied to the Senate, which must content itself with the vice-president of the United States as its chief presiding officer.

Much of the importance of this provision derives from the centuries of conflict both in England and in its American colonies between the executive and legislative branches. The leading executives—the monarch in England and the royal governors in the colonies—often sought to limit legislative influence. They did so not only by violating the rights of the legislature but also by denying its occupants immunity from prosecution for statements made on the floor and freedom from arrest. The individual directly caught in this clash was often the Speaker of the House, whose duty was to address the executive officers concerning legislative personnel and decisions.

The noblest moment in the institutional life of the Anglo-American speakership came in 1642, when Speaker William Lenthall of the House of Commons refused to disclose the whereabouts of five members to King Charles I. Falling to his knees, Lenthall replied to the king, "May it please your majesty, I have neither eyes to see nor tongue to speak in this place but as the House is pleased to direct me, whose servant I am here." Lenthall's life was spared, but six other Speakers of the House of Commons met violent ends, including the canonized Sir Thomas More.

The authority of the speakership in the colonies was greater because the source of the Speaker's power was in the colonial assemblies, an immediate and visible constituency, rather than in the remote presence of the crown three thousand miles away, to whom the royal governor was answerable. These factors converged to make the Speaker of the House both a powerful figure and a partisan one.

Frederick Augustus Conrad Muhlenberg of Pennsylvania was the first member of the United States House to be elected Speaker, in 1780. He had been Speaker of the Pennsylvania legislature, and his brother and fellow congressman, John Peter Gabriel Muhlenberg, had been a Revolutionary War hero. With Muhlenberg of Pennsylvania as Speaker, George Washington of Virginia as president, John Adams of Massachusetts as vice-president, and John Jay of New York as chief justice, all four of the new nation's largest states were represented in posts of national prominence.

Muhlenberg presided over both the First and Third Congresses even though they convened with differing party majorities. By the opening of the Fourth Congress in 1795, partisan feelings had risen to a high pitch, and the relatively nonpartisan Muhlenberg was replaced by an arch-Federalist, Jonathan Dayton of New Jersey. Thus, from the Fourth Congress on, the speakership was directly involved in partisan politics.

The partisan tone of speakership contests was altered for a few Congresses by the overwhelming dominance of President Jefferson's Democratic-Republicans. Often, interparty conflict gave way to intraparty challenges, as more than one candidate of the majority party would present himself as a candidate, especially in the cases following Henry Clay's frequent departures from the chair. Henry Clay of Kentucky is widely considered to be the first great Speaker of the House. Having served in the Senate, he was already well known in Washington, but it was his leadership of the congressional "war hawks" elected in 1810 that led to his arrival in the chair the following year.

Clay's resignation from the speakership in 1820 set off a twenty-two-ballot contest resulting in the election of John W. Taylor of New York, a member with Federalist origins who was loyal to the aspirations of John Quincy Adams of Massachusetts. The 1820 contest was the first of nine multiballot elections over the next thirty-nine years. Sixty-three ballots were needed in 1849 to decide the contest between Howell Cobb (Dem.-Ga.) and incumbent Speaker Robert C. Winthrop (Whig-Mass.), which marked the first time that the House dispensed with the requirement of an absolute majority for election to the speakership. Little more than six years later the majority requirement was again dispensed with as it took 133 ballots and almost two months to elect Nathaniel P. Banks (American-Mass.). Each of these contests was marked by fierce sectional rivalries between northern and southern members, and the slavery issue was never far from the floor. This was also the case in the last pre–Civil War Congress in 1859, when it took 44 ballots to elect William Pennington (Rep.-N.J.), a former governor, but a freshman member, to the speakership.

With the coming of the Civil War the Democratic party in the House was decimated, and the newly emergent Republicans adopted caucuses for Speaker before the choice went to the floor. Since 1863 the system has worked to eliminate intraparty floor conflict for the speakership: of the sixty-three votes for Speaker since then, only the 1923 contest has gone beyond a single ballot.

The perilous state of the new republic and the Federalists' commitment to executive government limited the role of the legislative branch during the nation's first two decades. Although the Speaker did gain control over committee assignments during the First Congress (1790), that power did little to enhance the office.

It was Henry Clay (Dem.-Rep.-Ky.) who first grasped the potential power of the early speakership. Arriving in the House in 1811 with a devoted band of followers from the South and the early western states, he quickly filled the leadership vacuum left by the competent but colorless President James Madison. Clay used the Speaker's power of committee appointments to place his loyalists Langdon Cheves and William Lowndes, both of South Carolina, at the helm of the Ways and Means Committee. However, Clay's concern for personal popularity led him to distribute the other committee assignments evenly throughout the chamber, regardless of faction. As James S. Young points out, this accounts for both Clay's enormous personal popularity (he averaged 77 percent of the votes in his six elections to the chair) and his difficulty in getting the House to act favorably on his issue agenda (internal improvements, censuring Andrew Jackson, and so on).

While Clay and his associates controlled the House (1811–1825), the number of committees grew from ten to twenty-seven. Although this expansion increased the Speaker's power of assignment patronage, it also dispersed control over policy by creating a number of diverse power centers.

Multiballot speakership elections compounded the problem of leadership because of the inevitable payoffs that had to be made in order to obtain election. Turnover in the House at this time was extraordinarily high. The proportion of first-term members exceeded 50 percent in twenty-one of the twenty-six Congresses convening between 1813 and 1863. This also took its toll on the effective use of speakership power.

Two Speakers who played a large role after the Civil War in gaining power for the chair were James G. Blaine (Rep.-Maine, 1869–1875) and Samuel J. Randall (Dem.-Pa., 1876–1881). Blaine used the power of committee assignments to consolidate Republican power in the House and to further the goals of the commercial interests of the Northeast. Blaine, a protégé of Thaddeus Stevens (Rep.-Pa.), was the first Speaker since 1834 to serve three consecutive terms. His fusion of commercial and political power gave the Republicans a guaranteed source of support, but it opened the door to potential scandals. Blaine was implicated in one, and his good friend James A. Garfield (Rep.-Ohio), Appropriations Committee chairman, was almost tarnished in the Crédit Mobilier incident.

The Democrats recaptured the House in 1874 and installed Michael Kerr of Indiana as Speaker. His death less than a year later led to the election of Appropriations chairman Samuel Randall as Speaker. Randall's major contribution was the resurrection in 1880 of the House Rules Committee, which had existed as a standing committee for only two Congresses before the Civil War (1849–1853). What gave it power was the presence of the Speaker as its chairman. Also serving with the Speaker were senior majority members of the Ways and Means and Appropriations committees. Randall was able to consolidate control of the floor in the Rules Committee and to limit some of the baronial powers of the committee chairmen.

Another aspect of his regime was the reintegration of southern members. By giving the chairmanship of Appropriations to John D. C. Atkins (Dem.-Tenn.) in 1877, Randall gained the loyalty of many newly seated southern Democrats.

Seated on the Rules Committee in the Forty-seventh Congress (1881–1883) with Randall was a third-term member from Maine, future Speaker Thomas B. Reed. Although he came from the same state as James G. Blaine, Reed was a member of the faction loyal to William Pitt Fessenden, a former senator. He and Blaine were cordial but not politically close. No Speaker in the post–Civil War era had more impact than did Reed. Known for his lacerating wit, huge girth, and outright partisanship, Reed augmented the office through a set of procedural reforms known today as the Reed Rules.

Obstructionist tactics in the House had slowed legislative business to a crawl. Helped by newly returned southern members, the Democratic minority had developed the tactic of not responding during the roll call. When the number fell below half of the House's membership, a member would arise and call for an adjournment based on the lack of a quorum. The "disappearing quorum" was regularly used to thwart the small Republican majority. Reed eliminated this practice by ordering the clerk to record the names of all members who could be seen in the hall of the House but who refused to answer the roll call. Democrats, indignant over this move, would head for the lobby. The ever-resourceful Reed then ordered that the doors be locked. One member, Constantine ("Kicking Buck") Kilgore (Dem.-Tex.), kicked the door open so as to escape the Speaker's recitation of his name. These actions and his marked disdain for motions that he refused to entertain earned Speaker Reed the nickname of "Czar."

On 14 February 1890, by a vote of 161–144, the House adopted the Reed Rules. They provided that a quorum would consist of those present in the chamber; that 100 could constitute a quorum in the Committee of the Whole; that the Speaker could disallow motions that he considered dilatory; and that the Committee of the

Whole could close debate on any paragraph or section of a bill under consideration.

Reed's innovations continued throughout his House service. In the Fifty-fourth Congress (1895–1897), he appointed James A. Tawney of Minnesota to be the first Republican party whip; the position has since become a permanent part of the congressional structure.

While he was Speaker, Reed appointed Joseph G. ("Uncle Joe") Cannon of Illinois to chair the House's largest committee, Appropriations. When Reed left the House in 1899, following a serious rift with President William McKinley over the Spanish-American War, it was assumed that Cannon would follow him to the chair. But Republican senators, fearful of another strong speakership, helped to elect David B. Henderson (Rep.-Iowa). Henderson's lackluster speakership ended in a flurry of rumors of bad health and the shadow of a scandal involving a senator's daughter. In 1903, Cannon became Speaker and used his power of committee assignments, chairmanship of the Rules Committee, and control over the floor to further the fortunes of his fellow conservative Republicans. This action brought him into conflict with many "insurgent" members of his own party and with President Theodore Roosevelt, a Republican of a different stripe.

Studies of seniority in the House indicate that Cannon's overall removal rate of committee chairmen, while not unusually high, differed from those of his predecessors by increasing as his speakership continued. As Polsby, Gallaher, and Rundquist discovered, "Cannon committed a higher proportion of violations on major and semiexclusive committees after his first term than any Speaker, more post–first-term violations of seniority of incumbents than anyone, and more uncompensated violations after his first term than anyone."

With Roosevelt's departure from the presidency in 1909 and the ascension of William Howard Taft of Ohio, Cannon's associates felt more secure in their influence and asserted their power in very arbitrary ways, particularly in the assignment of committee places. But the House had changed. The regional stabilization of the party system following the election of 1896 and the increasing desirability of life in Washington made the members more senior and less tolerant of the abuses of "Cannonism." Only 23 percent of the members of the Sixty-first Congress

(1909–1911) were first-termers, less than half the percentage that had greeted Reed.

The political situation had changed as well. The need to submerge personal and partisan differences with the House leadership to ward off the legislative advances of a strong president had abated. Progressive reforms calling for the popular election of the Senate and the imposition of a federal income tax were successfully working their way through the state legislatures. The House leadership was out of touch with the times. Insurgent midwestern Republicans such as George Norris of Nebraska and John Nelson of Wisconsin believed that the party would lose its hold on the American people if Cannon and his arch-conservative colleagues continued their arbitrary and capricious tactics.

Cannon's efforts to punish progressive Republicans by denying them favorable committee assignments backfired, and the new leader of the Democrats, James B. ("Champ") Clark of Missouri, was eager to exploit the breach within the GOP ranks. On a more personal level, Clark hoped to be nominated as president, and it was clearly in his long-term interest to weaken the power of the speakership lest he find himself, as president, hamstrung by a strong Speaker. Working together, the dissident Republicans and the Democrats forever altered the power of the speakership.

By 1911, when the Sixty-first Congress adjourned, the Speaker had lost control of committee assignments, and a reconstituted Rules Committee had excluded him from its membership. His total control of the floor was ended with the establishment of the consent calendar for minor bills; the discharge petition for legislation blocked in committee; and "Calendar Wednesday," Wednesday being the day on which a House committee could call for a vote on a bill on its own calendar that was being tied up by the leadership.

The election of 1910 had given Democrats control of the House for the first time in sixteen years, and Clark found himself presiding over it from the office that he himself had emasculated. Ultimately he did not receive the presidential nomination in 1912 and was to remain in the speakership for another six years, while President Woodrow Wilson reaped the legislative benefits of the shriveled speakership.

Although most of the Speakers who followed

the demise of Cannonism accepted the constraints of the office, two Speakers made notable efforts to regain some of the lost power: Nicholas Longworth (Rep.-Ohio) and Sam Rayburn (Dem.-Tex.). Both were creatures of the House whose aspirations had been satisfied upon becoming Speaker, and their loyalty to the chamber governed their efforts to enhance the office in order to increase the House's influence. While relying heavily on their personal popularity and years of service, both Speakers were careful to avoid institutionalizing this power lest they reawaken the negative reactions of the Cannon era. Longworth and Rayburn had both served with Cannon and were vividly aware of the depth of antiautocratic sentiment within the House. As a result, their concentration of influence was deliberately kept at the personal level.

After serving as majority floor leader, Longworth was elected Speaker in 1925. At that time Republican power had been lodged in an extra-institutional body, the Steering Committee, which set the party's agenda. Created in 1919, this body operated apart from the standing-committee system. As floor leader in the previous Congress, Longworth had chaired the Steering Committee; when he became Speaker, he said, "I was able to take the majority leadership from the floor to the Chair." Longworth also benefited from his use of an informal drinking hideaway in the Capitol, which he called "the Board of Education," and thus was able to rely more upon personal influence than upon institutional authority.

Like Longworth, Rayburn worked closely with the senior members of his party and was very protective of the seniority system, which ensured the senior members' control over committee chairmanships. Rayburn also maintained a "board of education" to bring members together in more relaxed circumstances. Personal loyalty to Rayburn, especially among junior members, often transcended region, ideology, and party. For the seventeen years of his speakership, his oft-quoted maxim "To get along, go along" characterized the low-key cooperative nature of his leadership style.

Rayburn served as Speaker during the massive reorganization of the congressional committee system in 1946, but its impact upon speakership power was not readily discernible. His most no-

table contribution focused on the House Rules Committee. Having been an arm of the party leadership for most of its early history, the Rules Committee became a power unto itself in the 1940's and 1950's, when it fell under the domination of Republicans and conservative southern Democrats. In 1949, the House passed the "twenty-one-day rule," which enabled a committee chairman to bring a bill to the floor if the Rules Committee failed to act on it in twenty-one calendar days. This short-lived reform failed to be readopted in 1951 and 1967.

In 1961, his last year as Speaker, Rayburn helped to engineer a 217–212 vote expanding the membership of the Rules Committee from twelve to fifteen. The additional members gave newly elected President John Kennedy a better chance of getting his legislative program through the House committees and onto the floor.

During the 1970's a partial restoration of House leadership influence became formalized within the rules. Once again, political factors had changed. The Vietnam War had led to the undermining of Lyndon B. Johnson's presidency and a decline in the belief of both the American public and members of Congress that presidential initiatives in foreign policy should be accepted with little question. Richard M. Nixon's succession and the subsequent unraveling of his presidency by the Watergate events left a serious vacuum of leadership within Washington.

The retirement of Speaker John McCormack (Dem.-Mass.) in 1971 and the assumption of the chair by Carl Albert (Dem.-Okla.) enabled the speakership to gain power. Although not assertive, Albert was similar in style to Rayburn in that he relied on personal ties. Two of Albert's allies in gaining power for the speakership were Thomas P. O'Neill (Dem.-Mass.) and Richard Bolling (Dem.-Mo.). O'Neill and Bolling served together on the Rules Committee as "the eyes and ears" of Speakers McCormack and Rayburn, respectively. Albert, O'Neill, and Bolling recognized that the speakership could be enhanced through a series of institutional moves. Led by these three, the House Democrats expanded the power of the Democratic caucus; created the Democratic Steering and Policy Committee (of which the Speaker was a member) to provide some needed direction; and removed the power of making Democratic committee assignments from the Ways and Means Committee, a power it had wielded from 1911 through 1974.

Ironically, it was television, a medium that Speaker Rayburn had fought throughout his later career and one mistrusted by the contemporary leadership, that played a major role in restoring House influence. In 1974, television cameras focused on the House Judiciary Committee in its deliberations on the impeachment charges lodged against President Nixon. The seriousness with which the members took their responsibility and the overall quality of the ensuing debate had a positive impact upon the public's view of the House of Representatives. Overshadowed by the Senate in the previous two decades, the House benefited from its enhanced reputation.

O'Neill's elevation to the speakership in 1977 and Bolling's rise to the chairmanship of the Rules Committee two years later placed two of the major architects of the restoration in posts of enormous importance. However, some of the forces that had given them access to greater authority also threatened the full exercise of that authority.

The election of 1974 brought ninety-two new members to the House, seventy-five of them Democrats—the "Watergate babies." Subsequent elections continued the trend of electing an increasing number of junior members. In the Ninety-second Congress (1971–1973), 20 percent of the House members had served ten terms or more, but by the Ninety-eighth Congress (1983–1985), only 8.5 percent fell into that category; conversely, the proportion of junior members (three terms or less) rose from 34 percent to 48 percent. These newer members were willing to challenge the entrenched power of committee leaders; and in the Democratic caucus following the 1974 election, three senior southern chairmen were voted out. These newer members demanded a share of power for themselves, and they received it through the expansion of the subcommittee system and limits on the number of subcommittee chairmanships that a member could hold. This had the effect of giving junior members more opportunities to become chairmen and ranking minority members sooner than many of their recent predecessors. This development has led to a greater fragmentation of power and increased strains upon the speakership to develop coherent policy objectives. The price of restoring the power of the speakership has been high, but there is little question that the office was stronger in the mid-1980's than it had been since the days of Joe Cannon.

House Floor Leaders. The most important factor that has shaped the House of Representatives has been its size. In the Second Congress, the membership of the House went beyond 100. It is size that necessitates leadership. James Madison, writing in *The Federalist* number 58, observed that

> in all legislative assemblies, the greater the number composing them may be, the fewer will be the men who will in fact direct their proceedings. In the first place, the more numerous an assembly may be, of whatever characters composed, the greater is known to be the ascendancy of passion over reason. In the next place, the larger the number, the greater will be the proportion of members of limited information and of weak capacities.

To understand the House and its history, one must understand its leaders and the process by which they have emerged. This is particularly true for the party floor leaders, whose responsibilities go to the heart of the legislative process—its policy content.

In the earliest Congresses, there was no position associated with the floor leadership. There were leaders on specific issues and votes, but no formal location existed. The rise of partisanship in the Third and Fourth Congresses (1793–1797) changed that; in the Fourth Congress, Ways and Means emerged as a standing committee. This committee handles all revenue bills and, before 1865, dealt with bills on federal appropriations and currency. Its chairman has enjoyed an importance second only to that of the Speaker.

It took a while for the floor leadership to be clearly associated with the chairman of Ways and Means. President Thomas Jefferson's concept of legislative-executive relationships was that the Congress ratify policy initiatives emanating from the White House. To become a leader of the House during the Jeffersonian era required presidential as well as congressional approval. Jefferson encountered difficulties because of the close relationship between Speaker Nathaniel

Macon (Dem.-Rep.-N.C.) and Ways and Means chairman John Randolph of Roanoke (Dem.-Rep.-Va.), who held the House's top two posts during Jefferson's first three Congresses (1801–1807). Jefferson had relied upon them as well as others to further his legislative program, but Randolph's erratic behavior cost him the president's confidence and eventually the committee chairmanship and cost Macon the speakership in 1807.

Under Speaker Clay, the House leaders did not see themselves as presidential spokesmen but rather as loyal to the institution and to their own legislative party. The chairman of Ways and Means was subject to the appointment and removal of the Speaker, and seven chairmen lost their posts even though their parties retained power in the years before 1865. Two were replaced between sessions of a Congress because they failed to impress their respective Speakers: Ezekiel Bacon (Dem.-Rep.-Mass.) in 1812 and Jehu Glancy Jones (Dem.-Pa.) in 1858.

Two chairmen of the committee became Speakers before the Civil War: Langdon Cheves (Dem.-Rep.-S.C.) in 1814 and James K. Polk (Dem.-Tenn.) in 1835. For the most part, there was little movement between the posts, because they served different functions. In the terminology of Robert Bales's interaction process analysis, the Speakers were the "social leaders" of the House, maintaining the social integration of the chamber; while the Ways and Means chairmen served as the "task leaders," whose job was to complete tasks that the House confronted. It was they, and not the Speakers, who got into the duels and fist fights that occasionally characterized life in the House.

The Civil War changed the nature of the floor leadership. The enormous expense of the war, and congressional suspicion that President Abraham Lincoln was inclined to wage it without their approval, made excessive demands upon the Ways and Means Committee. In order to deal with the increased financial responsibilities, the House in 1865 created three committees from Ways and Means: Appropriations, Banking and Currency, and Pacific Railroad. Because the Appropriations Committee gained the power to oversee federal spending, it was no surprise that the strong-willed Thaddeus Stevens (Rep.-Pa.) left the chairmanship of Ways and Means to head it. Stevens' decision and the active role of later chairmen led Woodrow Wilson to conclude in 1885 that "all [House chairmen] are subordinates to the chairman of the Committee on Appropriations."

Wilson made this assessment, in *Congressional Government* (1885), when Samuel Randall, the former Speaker, chaired the committee. Shortly after Wilson's book appeared, opposition to Randall's exercise of power and to his high-tariff policies led to a major diminution in the legislative authority of the committee.

From 1865 through 1911, the majority floor leadership was shared by the chairmen of Ways and Means and Appropriations. Often they served together with the Speaker as the majority members of the Rules Committee. Generally speaking, the Ways and Means chairman seemed more consistently in the fore of House policymaking. The great debates of the late nineteenth century concerned trade and tariff policy; and the tariffs all carried the names of the Ways and Means chairmen who had proposed them: McKinley (1890), Wilson-Gorman (1894), Dingley (1897), Payne-Aldrich (1909), and Underwood (1913).

The most important event in the development of the majority leadership grew out of the revolt against Speaker Cannon in 1910–1911. One aftermath was the direct election of the majority floor leader by the party caucus. For eight years (1911–1919) the Democrats elected the chairman of the Ways and Means Committee as floor leader; the majority floor leader had finally gained independence from the Speaker. In 1919, the functional autonomy of the office was assured when Franklin Mondell (Rep.-Wyo.) abandoned his seat on Appropriations to become the Republican majority leader. The modern majority leadership, elected independently of the Speaker and separated from the standing-committee system, stems from these two actions.

Between 1911 and 1984 there were seven contests for leader: one in the Republican party (1919) and six in the Democratic party (1933, 1935, 1937, 1940, 1971, and 1976). In the Republican party the relative infrequency of these contests was due to the party's minority status in twenty-nine of the thirty-seven Congresses since the post became an elective one. Democratic contests have been relatively infrequent because of the "leadership ladder," which moves members through the floor leadership in a semiautomatic manner. Since 1933, there has been a regular progression from floor leader to Speaker, and, since 1961, a less regular one from whip to floor leader.

A legislative body slow to recognize the distinction between majority and minority members, the House did not formally grant the title *minority leader* until 1911, when Representative James R. Mann of Illinois was listed as "Chairman of the Minority Conference" in the *Congressional Directory*. Despite the relative newness of the title, the position has been intermittently filled since the First Congress; accounts of that and later Congresses indicate that James Madison (Dem.-Rep.-Va.) was the first minority leader. Efforts to thwart Alexander Hamilton's fiscal policies were so conspicuously associated with him that the opposition was often referred to as "Madison's party." When Madison left the House in 1797, Albert Gallatin (Dem.-Rep.-Pa.) succeeded him. The first Federalist to appear in this role was James Bayard of Delaware in 1801, but the overwhelming majorities held by the Democratic-Republicans from 1801 to 1825 reduced the Federalists to a noisome nuisance. From 1825 through 1861 a great degree of interparty opposition occurred, but the emergence of minority leadership was seriously retarded by the internal fragmentation of all congressional parties.

Following the Civil War, minority-party leadership became identified with the losing candidate for Speaker. The 1863 contest was an interparty one, and in 1865 there were only two candidates for the first time in forty-two years. With the exception of 1923, every speakership contest since 1865 has been won on the first ballot. Whatever dissension may have existed in the party caucuses did not manifest itself in the floor vote for Speaker—a positive sign of intraparty organization. Also, the long list of notable members who were nominated in the 1870's and 1880's by the minority party as speakership candidates—Blaine, Garfield, Reed, Randall, Samuel ("Sunset") Cox—indicates that the defeated nominee served as his party's floor leader.

Since 1911 the minority leaders have been clearly identified, and all have been the minority party's candidate for Speaker. They have all been elected within their caucuses to represent their party's interests on the floor. For most of this time, they have not served on any of the House's standing committees. The job of minority floor leader exists apart from the committee system.

Thirteen times since the Civil War, but only four times since 1911, there have been contests for the post of House minority leader. And historically, the minority party has had fewer contests than the majority party; the stakes are lower. But the two most dramatic contests in the more recent history of the House involved the voted overthrows of Minority Leaders Joseph W. Martin, Jr. (Rep.-Mass.), in 1959 and Charles Halleck (Rep.-Ind.) in 1965—the last ones to unseat incumbent House officeholders.

Party Whips. The term *whip* derives from an English hunting term, the *whipper-in,* whose job it was to keep the fox within view of the hounds. In legislative parlance, the whip's job is to make sure that there are enough party members (the dogs) on the floor at the time of a key vote to guarantee victory (the fox) for the party. Although the term was used in Parliament for party functionaries in the late eighteenth century, it was not until 1897 that Speaker Reed designated James A. Tawney (Rep.-Minn.) to be majority party whip. Prior to that time, whips were appointed on an ad hoc basis with responsibility for specific roll calls. Tawney was followed as whip in 1905 by James E. Watson of Indiana, a Cannon protégé, and since then the position has been consistently identifiable.

The Democratic whip first appeared in 1900, with the appointment of Oscar W. Underwood by Minority Leader James D. Richardson of Tennessee. However, the post was not consistently filled or identified with the leadership until 1921, when William Oldfield (Dem.-Ark.) assumed the title under the minority leadership of Claude Kitchin (Dem.-N.C.). Since then, the post has been filled continuously and labeled appropriately.

One basic difference between the parties in their use of the whip position has been the varying methods of selection. Republican whips were appointed by the leadership from 1897 to 1919, when Harold Knutson of Minnesota was elected by the Republican caucus. Two years later, he was elected by the Republican Committee on Committees; the post was semielective until 1965, when it was again made fully elective.

Democratic whips, by contrast, have always been appointed. In December 1974 the Democratic caucus overwhelmingly defeated a reform proposal that would have made the post elective. Majority Leader O'Neill contended in 1973 that an elective whip post would deprive him of leadership prerogatives that were extended to his predecessors.

Each party has treated the position differently within its hierarchy. For the Democrats the whip has become the first step on the leadership ladder, just below the majority floor leader. Many of the party's more recent floor leaders served as party whip. For Republicans the post is more of a dead end. Robert Michel (Rep.-Ill.), who was elected leader in 1980, was the first Republican whip to move up since 1905.

Democrats have had a higher proportion of appointed leaders than Republicans; their leaders move within the party hierarchy in an ordered succession; their appointed leaders are often removed from above by elected ones; and their elected leaders are subjected to infrequent and unsuccessful contests in party caucuses. Republicans, on the other hand, rely more on election to choose their leaders; their rate of mobility between posts is very low; their appointed leaders are never removed by elected ones; and while their leaders face contests at the same rate that the Democrats do, the incidence of successful challenges is much greater in their caucuses. Republican leaders, in short, are often removed from below.

These interparty differences reveal two distinct leadership-succession systems. The Democratic organization is hierarchically arranged in a tightly controlled system designed to minimize internal conflict. Because the House Democrats are a large and heterogeneous mix of contending regions, social groups, and ideologies, such an arrangement may be necessary. The Republican organization appears to be relatively egalitarian in its leadership-succession system, with open competition and an active role for the membership. Because House Republicans are generally a smaller and more homogeneous band of predominantly conservative small-town and small-city white males, their succession system makes sense. Conflict within a homogeneous setting will not result in the triumph of one social or ideological group over another. Only the names in the offices will change; and in such a context, change of style will be more common than change of substance.

Senate Presidents. In 1885, Woodrow Wilson observed: "No one is *the* Senator. No one may speak for his party as well as for himself." Because the Senate does not possess the numbers, the regularity, or the structure of the House of Representatives, it is not easy to discern historically its leaders. However, in the twentieth century, the Senate has made an effort to parallel the party organization of the House with its positions of floor leaders and whips. The most commonly acknowledged feature of leadership within the United States Senate is that its presiding officer—the president of the Senate—is the vice-president of the United States, an interloper from the executive branch. In most of the early drafts of the Constitution, it was intended that the Senate choose its own presiding officer in a fashion similar to that of the House of Representatives. However, shortly before its adjournment, the Constitutional Convention removed the power of choice from the Senate membership and inserted the following provisions:

> The Vice President of the United States shall be President of the Senate, but shall have no Vote, unless they be equally divided.
> The Senate shall choose their other Officers, and also a President pro tempore, in the absence of the Vice President, or when he shall exercise the Office of the President of the United States.

Although scholars may disagree about the appropriateness of this decision and its potential conflict with the principle of the separation of powers, there has been no disagreement about the consequences of that unique selection system on the limited political power of the president of the Senate to affect legislation.

Senator Joseph W. Bailey (Dem.-Tex.) stated the Senate's position most clearly in a stinging rebuke to Vice-President James Sherman in 1910:

> We don't choose our own Presiding Officer. . . . We have no power ourselves to depose him. Remembering that he is over us without our consent, and often over our protest, the Senate cannot be too resolutely insistent that he shall merely execute the rules, not as he may think they ought to be read and administered, but as they have been read and as they have been understood by this body from time out of mind.

Bailey's reprimand is one of the many delivered by senators to their presiding officer for failing to understand his appropriate role within the "world's greatest deliberative body." Similar rebukes were aimed at Vice-Presidents Theodore Roosevelt, Charles W. Fairbanks, Charles G. Dawes, and Nelson A. Rockefeller. Vice-President Rockefeller's failure to recognize Senator James B. Allen (Dem.-Ala.) in a 1975 debate on filibusters resulted in such coolness from the Senate that Rockefeller felt compelled to apologize to the chamber two months later.

The one vice-president who realized that his role was minimal was Charles Curtis (Rep.-Kan.), who had served as his party's floor leader from 1924 through 3 March 1929. One day later, in his initial appearance before his former Senate colleagues, Curtis announced, "the Vice-President is not one of your makers of law, nor is he consulted about the rules adopted to govern your actions."

The president of the Senate is not analogous to the Speaker of the House, nor is the Senate's president pro tempore. Like the Speaker, the president pro tem is elected by the entire chamber following nomination in the party caucus. However, unlike the contest for the speakership, minority parties in the Senate have not always put forth a pro tem nominee. Neither does the president pro tem have to resign his committee assignments upon assuming this post. In addition, the president pro tem holds his office for the duration of his Senate term, provided that his party continues to organize the chamber. Consequently the post is more honorary than powerful, and it has generally gone to the most senior senator of the majority party.

But this generalization has exceptions. In 1963, the Senate Democrats created the post of permanent acting president pro tempore and filled it with Lee Metcalf, then a third-year senator from Montana. Also, as a tribute to Senator Hubert H. Humphrey (Dem.-Minn.), the Democrats created yet another post, that of deputy president pro tempore in 1977. Neither post survives.

Senate Floor Leaders. The relatively small size of the Senate and the feisty independence of many of its occupants delayed development of a formal leadership structure for more than a century. The Senate often had as many leaders as there were issues before it, and certain senators had enormous national stature. Henry Clay (Whig-Ky.), John C. Calhoun (Dem.-S.C.), and Daniel Webster (Whig-Mass.) carried on debates in the 1830's and 1840's that received widespread attention; Thomas Hart Benton (Dem.-Mo.) emerged as a vigorous champion of the cause of President Andrew Jackson. Just before the Civil War, Senators Andrew P. Butler (Dem.-S.C.), Charles Sumner (Rep.-Mass.), and Stephen A. Douglas (Dem.-Ill.) vigorously debated solutions to the impending dissolution of the Union. Rancorous discourse over slavery fastened the nation's attention on the Senate, where no gag rule existed to limit debate. The near-fatal caning of Senator Sumner by Representative Preston Brooks (Dem.-S.C.) in 1856 was testament to the bitterness that permeated Congress as the antislavery forces gained momentum.

The years following the Civil War marked a relative decline in the Senate's political prestige. This was partly due to the emergence of narrow commercial issues on the national agenda and the arrival of a number of senators whose elections from the state legislatures had been engineered by bosses and robber barons. The Senate also suffered from the inability of any one member or group to assume a consistent leadership role. Woodrow Wilson observed in 1885: "No one exercises the special trust of acknowledged leadership. The Senate is merely a body of individual critics."

After leaving the House for the Senate in 1876, James G. Blaine, a former Speaker and one of the most powerful occupants of the office, found himself frustrated by the arcane rules of the "other body" and eagerly departed five years later. Blaine was baffled by what he perceived to be the Senate's undue reliance upon the seniority system and unlimited debate. Perhaps the most telling statement of the Senate's place at that time was Speaker Reed's sardonic comment that the Senate was where "good Representatives go when they die."

David Rothman's analysis of the Senate between 1869 and 1901 indicates that the role of party leadership did not emerge until the 1890's. Gathering frequently at the home of Senator James MacMillan (Rep.-Mich.) to play poker and discuss politics, Republican Senators William B. Allison of Iowa, Nelson Aldrich of Rhode Island, Orville Platt of Connecticut, and John Coit Spooner of Wisconsin decided to use the post of

Republican caucus chairman to provide party leadership. Allison assumed the post in 1897 and redirected its efforts toward that goal.

The national context changed markedly when the closing of the frontier brought seven new states into the Union between 1889 and 1896. While they contributed eight members to the House, a slight increase of 2.3 percent, they contributed fouteen members to the Senate, a sizable increase of 18.4 percent. In addition, American involvement in Cuba and the Philippines during the Spanish-American War focused national attention upon foreign policy, and the Senate benefited from that new emphasis.

A change had also occurred in the patterns of presidential incumbency. McKinley's reelection in 1900 was the first successful continuation in the White House since Grant's reelection in 1872, and in 1904, Theodore Roosevelt was the first presidential successor to be nominated and elected in his own right. Also augmenting the power of the presidency was the highly public personality of Teddy Roosevelt. Woodrow Wilson, who had lamented the weakness of government in the 1880's, now saw the presidency as the major engine of change; in *Constitutional Government in the United States* (1908), he contended that the president "may retain liberty to be as big a man as he can. . . . [The President's office] is anything he has the sagacity and force to make it."

In 1913 the long-awaited amendment to transfer the election of senators from the state legislatures to the public was finally ratified. This legislation made the Senate as accountable as the House to popular sentiment. Now, with the collapse of the authoritarian speakership and the rise in presidential influence, the Senate and its floor leaders were poised to make a significant contribution to national political life.

Wilson's election and that of John W. Kern of Indiana as the leader of the Senate Democrats changed the direction of the floor leadership and the course of the Senate. The Democratic vice-presidential nominee in 1908, Kern was sympathetic to presidential prerogatives in legislation. In her perceptive analysis of their relationship, Margaret Munk argued:

> The Kern-Wilson alliance established one of the most important precedents in the history of Senate leadership. Never before had the presi-

dent's party in the Senate, backed by the president's approval and perhaps his direct influence, intentionally elected a floor leader for the primary purpose of implementing an executive-initiated legislative program.

The selection of Kern, a third-year senator at the time, set a precedent for ignoring seniority in the choice of a floor leader. The Senate, which relied so heavily upon seniority in choosing its committee chairmen, apparently waived this requirement in selecting its floor leaders. Nine of the eleven Democratic floor leaders between 1913 and 1984 had served less than twelve years prior to their selection. Republican floor leaders have been slightly more senior, but in neither case have they matched the lengthy preleadership careers of their House counterparts.

The official minutes of the party conferences conferred floor leadership on the Democratic chairman in 1921 and on the Republican chairman in 1925. Although the Democrats continue to have the floor leader preside over the party conference, the Republicans separated the two posts in 1944.

Contests for the top floor-leadership posts have been infrequent. Since 1899, there have been only two Democratic contests: the victory of Thomas S. Martin (Dem.-Va.) over Benjamin Shively (Dem.-Ind.) in 1911 and the dramatic one-vote victory of Alben W. Barkley (Dem.-Ky.) over Pat Harrison (Dem.-Miss.) in 1937. Barkley was elected floor leader following he death of Senator Joseph Robinson (Dem.-Ark.), who had reluctantly led the Senate Democrats in an effort to pass President Roosevelt's "court-packing" scheme, which attempted to add more justices to the Supreme Court. It was Roosevelt's wish that Barkley succeed Robinson, and his "Dear Alben" letter before the vote indicated his sentiments clearly.

Until 1949, the Senate Republicans had never contested a party-leadership post of any type, but there were twenty-two caucus contests between then and 1984, and six battles over the top floor leadership posts. Apart from the two contests between Howard Baker (Rep.-Tenn.) and Hugh Scott (Rep.-Pa.) in 1969 and 1971, the more conservative senator was victorious.

Senate Party Whips and Other Leaders. The Democrats have continuously identified and filled the post of party whip since 1913, when James Hamilton Lewis of Illinois was chosen to assist Kern. The first Republican whip, James Wadsworth of New York, was selected in 1915. Republicans have selected whips from 1915 to the present, with a nine-year hiatus (1935–1944), when Senate Republicans were too few to need much "whipping-in." Unlike their House counterparts, the Senate Democrats have had a regularized whip system, while the Republicans have had a sporadic history. In 1969, the Republicans changed the title *whip* to *assistant floor leader.*

The Republicans made a major overhaul of their Senate party-leadership structure in 1944, following the lingering illness and death of their longtime floor leader, Charles L. McNary of Oregon. They separated the post of floor leader from that of conference chairman, resurrected the post of party whip, and reconstituted a steering committee (later renamed the policy committee) for the first time since 1933. Long years of out-party frustration among Senate Republicans have led to a substantial number of caucus contests for each of the leadership posts since 1949: floor leader (six contests); whip (four); chairman of the policy committee (four); chairman of the conference (three); secretary of the conference (two); and chairman of the senatorial campaign committee (three).

Senate Democrats have had far fewer contests once they became the dominant party. One reason has been the concentration of power in the hands of the floor leader. The Democratic leader chairs the Democratic conference, the policy committee, and the steering committee, which makes the committee assignments. By consolidating the offices, Democratic senators have had fewer opportunities to challenge for the leadership, and having organized the Senate for all but four of the post-1932 Congresses, they have had less motivation to contend for them.

Three of the four contests among Senate Democrats between 1965 and 1971 focused on the post of whip. Russell Long of Louisiana defeated John Pastore of Rhode Island on the second ballot in 1965 but was defeated in 1969 by Edward M. Kennedy of Massachusetts. Two years later, in the aftermath of Kennedy's accident at Chappaquiddick, he was defeated by Robert Byrd of West Virginia. Byrd had also been victorious in the only other recent leadership fight, that for the post of secretary of the conference in 1967 over Joseph Clark of Penn-

sylvania. Since 1971, the Senate Democrats have not had a serious contest for any post.

During the entire history of elected floor leaders in the Senate, it appears that neither party has relied as much upon a leadership ladder as the House Democrats. Four Republican whips (Charles Curtis, Kenneth Wherry, Everett Dirksen, and Hugh Scott) moved to the top leadership post, but other Republican whips failed in their efforts. However, the three later Senate Democratic floor leaders, Lyndon Johnson, Mike Mansfield, and Robert Byrd, all served as party whips before their ascension. All three had also served in the House and may have brought a House tradition into the "other body."

The Senate is more egalitarian than the House; this was intended by the Founding Fathers when they gave each state, regardless of size, two senators. Debate is seldom restricted, thus increasing the power of each member relative to the Senate's committees and its leaders. Bills are often rewritten on the floor—much to the dismay of the committees reporting them. The Senate's party leaders have less control over the tempo on the floor or the legislative content of the bills that reach it than do the House's party leaders. Despite these conditions, eager senators line up to seek their party's leadership posts.

Since the presidency of Woodrow Wilson, Senate leaders have moved in the presidential orbit, with those of the president's party leading the fight for his programs and those in the opposition party often positioning themselves for their party's presidential and vice-presidential nominations.

Democratic floor leaders and party whips who sought the presidency or vice-presidency include Oscar W. Underwood of Alabama, Joseph Robinson of Arkansas, Scott Lucas of Illinois, Alben Barkley of Kentucky, Lyndon Johnson of Texas, Hubert Humphrey of Minnesota, Edward Kennedy of Massachusetts, and Alan Cranston of California.

In the Republican party, a similar pattern emerged with the candidacies of Charles Curtis of Kansas, James Watson of Indiana, Charles McNary of Oregon, Robert A. Taft of Ohio, William Knowland of California, and Howard Baker of Tennessee. Each of these party leaders contended for the top two executive posts, with only Curtis and McNary gaining nomination and only

Curtis, Herbert Hoover's vice-president, getting elected.

But not all of the Senate's party leaders have sought to head the executive branch. Some floor leaders—Democrats Mike Mansfield of Montana (leader, 1961–1977) and Robert Byrd of West Virginia (leader, 1977–   ) and Republicans Everett Dirksen of Illinois (leader, 1959–1969) and Hugh Scott of Pennsylvania (leader, 1969–1977)—were wholly committed to their Senate careers. Mansfield's independence on the Vietnam War created problems for him with President Johnson, as did Scott's efforts to place some distance between the Senate Republicans and President Nixon during the Watergate crisis. More than the House's leaders, the Senate's leaders have flown close to the presidential flame. This has made the Senate more responsive to White House initiatives, but it has also lessened the autonomy of that body.

POLITICAL PARTIES

The fondest hope of the men who led the Revolution, wrote the Constitution, and were to govern the new American Republic was that the quest for national unity would transcend all other concerns and that the national interest would be so obvious to all that disagreements would seldom arise. It was hoped that if disagreements did arise, they would be so diverse that any organized set of competing interests would not be likely to appear. The nation's founders fervently wished to avoid the prospect of organized and contentious factions confronting each other over America's direction. To put it simply, they wanted to avoid the emergence of political parties.

In order to contain the partisan spirit, the new administration of George Washington invited Thomas Jefferson to become secretary of state, the senior cabinet position. Given Jefferson's early opposition to the Constitution, this choice was intended to reflect the breadth of the government and the commitment of the major factions to the newly formed nation. The Speaker of the First Congress, Frederick A. C. Muhlenberg of Pennsylvania, was not an outright partisan. His tendencies were Jeffersonian, but he was elected to preside over a House with a clear majority of Federalists. Partisanship appeared early

but not in any organized or clearly defined way.

Within the first decade of the Congress, partisanship became a very visible component of legislative business. Scholars of the era have documented the bifurcation of voting patterns into Federalist and Democratic-Republican camps. Jefferson's decision to leave Washington's cabinet in 1793 confirmed the existence of differing perspectives on the nation's destiny.

In 1796, electoral-college voting created the unique pairing of President John Adams, a Federalist, and Vice-President Thomas Jefferson, a Democratic-Republican. In the Congress, debates over the budget and foreign policy showed distinctive partisan overtones and resulted in clear-cut differences in voting. The battles over the ratification of Jay's Treaty in the Senate and over the funding for the treaty in the House in 1795 turned both chambers into warring camps. Passions ran so high that former Speaker Muhlenberg was stabbed by a constituent who opposed his stand on the treaty.

Partisan bickering was exacerbated by the voting on the Alien and Sedition Acts, which were designed to punish critics of the Adams administration. Jefferson benefited from the Federalists' political miscalculation and was elected president in 1800. Mounting majorities for Jefferson's party in congressional elections during the next twenty-four years encouraged the founders' hope that a nonpartisan politics would be realized. Conflicts over specific claims would continue to arise, but organized factions presumably would not emerge. This was to be the Era of Good Feeling, a time when President James Monroe could receive every electoral vote but one in the 1820 election. But the factions that emerged from this seemingly nonpartisan grand coalition reflected one fact: parties could not be denied.

In the history of the Congress, there have been a number of periods with distinctive patterns of competition between political parties. Each period has affected internal decision-making as well as the lengths of members' careers. These patterns of party competition also influenced the overall governmental system, by bringing the various branches of the federal system into conflict with one another.

First–Eighteenth Congresses: 1789–1825. The first period of party competition was marked by increasing Jeffersonian control of the governmental structure. Five of the first six Congresses (1789–1801) had Federalist Speakers, but each of the next twelve Congresses found Jeffersonians in the chair.

Figures regarding partisans for the House vary, but Democratic-Republican electoral successes gave them either 69 percent (Alexander) or 64 percent (*Historical Statistics*) of the total seats in the era; Senate seats held by the Jeffersonians averaged 69 percent. The high point for the Democratic-Republicans occurred in the Eighteenth Congress (1823–1825), when they held 88 percent of the House seats and all but four in the Senate (91 percent). No organized third party appeared in Congress, in spite of Representative John Randolph's expressed desire to be a *tertium quid* ("third being"). Party control alternated only three times in the House and only once in the Senate.

Given the newness of the Congress, turnover was high. The median length of service was 2.2 terms (4.4 years) for House members, and 43 percent of the House members served their first terms during these Congresses.

High levels of party unity marked the era. The Senate and the presidency were controlled by the same party in all eighteen Congresses; the House and the Senate had the same party in control in seventeen Congresses (94 percent), as did the House and the presidency. Speakership contests were lively: six went beyond the first ballot, but only two needed more than three ballots.

The initial party system of the Congress may be subdivided into three segments: 1789–1801, dominated by the Federalists, with lively competition from the Democratic-Republicans; 1801–1813, with increasing Democratic-Republican majorities but a continuing Federalist presence; and 1813–1825, with overwhelming domination by Democratic-Republicans and the eventual disappearance of the Federalist party.

Nineteenth–Thirty-sixth Congresses: 1825–1861. With the breakup of the Jeffersonian grand coalition in 1824 and the close of Henry Clay's final speakership, the House became unglued. Partisan and sectional cleavages rent the entire Congress dramatically, but the House of Representatives seemed to suffer more. Overall, the era was dominated by the Democrats, who organized the Senate fifteen times in the eighteen Congresses (83 percent) and the House thirteen times (72 percent). Although the number of Congresses controlled was higher than in the previous era, Democratic victories fell to 54 percent of Senate seats and 55 percent of House seats. The Democrats faced four major rivals: the National Republicans (1825–1833); the Whigs (1833–1855); the Americans, or Know-Nothings (1855–1861); and the Republicans (1855–1861), each of which placed at least one of its members in the Speaker's chair during this period. This era also had the largest number of House seats won by third parties—3 percent.

The Democrats who emerged in this era were attuned more to the philosophy and principles of Andrew Jackson than to those of Thomas Jefferson; the large planters and small merchants drifted from Jefferson's party to the Whigs. Jackson's presence permeated presidential politics, as one candidate after another sought to associate himself with the roughhewn frontiersman image of "Old Hickory" and with his strident nationalism and commitment to continental expansionism. Jackson's followers were in control of the House; but the Senate's leading figures, Henry Clay, John C. Calhoun, and Daniel Webster, had all been his rivals, and only Thomas Hart Benton of Missouri could be seen as a loyal Jacksonian. Given Jackson's determination to strengthen the presidency, it is not surprising that the Senate resisted him.

The House was institutionally closer to popular sentiment, and its leaders—Andrew Stevenson (Dem.-Va.), James K. Polk (Dem.-Tenn.), and Robert M. T. Hunter (Dem.-Va.)—generally acceded to the Jacksonian urges of the electorate.

Party control of the entire federal apparatus was not common: the House and Senate were controlled by the same party in fourteen Congresses (78 percent). The party holding the presidency also controlled the Senate on fifteen occasions (83 percent) but greeted a friendly House only eleven times (61 percent). As the Civil War approached, party fragmentation increased. Only three of the ten Congresses between 1841 and 1861 had similar party control in the House, the Senate, and the presidency.

The most remarkable feature of the period was the high rate of party alternation in control of the House; the controlling party was displaced by the electorate eight times during the era. If one counts in-term speakership changes, party control alternated ten times in twenty opportunities. The Senate's overlapping terms reduced its incidence of party alternation to only three. Turnover among House members was very high. The median number of terms was only 2.1 (4.2 years), while the median percentage of first-termers was 47.4.

The last half of the era was marked by a disintegration of the party system and a disappearance of civility. Six speakership contests took at least three ballots to resolve; three of these competitions exceeded forty ballots. The continuing question of slavery, which erupted every time a new territory applied for statehood, could not be kept from the floor. Beatings, canings, fist fights, and duels characterized many encounters, and party fragmentation foreshadowed the rupture of the nation in 1861.

Thirty-seventh–Fifty-third Congresses: 1861–1895. The fractious parties of the pre–Civil War era gave way to a fairly competitive two-party system. The Republicans organized the House of Representatives in seven consecutive Congresses (1861–1875), while the Democrats organized eight of the Houses in the following ten Congresses. Democrats won 48 percent of the total seats and 49 percent of the two-party seats in the House. Third-party victories dropped to 1.8 percent.

Turnover in the House remained high, with a median of 2.1 terms served (4.2 years)—the same as in the pre–Civil War Congresses—and a median of 46 percent first-time members. Whereas the House may have been evenly divided, the Senate was overwhelmingly Republican: the GOP controlled fifteen Senates (88 percent) and captured 59 percent of all Senate seats and 61 percent of two-party ones.

Party control of the House alternated between the parties five times (31 percent)—the second highest of any era; Senate control changed hands three times. The House and Senate were controlled by the same party only 65 percent of the time—six Congresses convened with a Democratic House and a Republican Senate. The Speaker and the president shared the same party label on twelve occasions (71 percent). Altogether, only ten of the seventeen Houses (59 percent) were organized by the party that also held the presidency and the Senate.

Divided party control of the government, and the sizable discrepancy between party victories in the House and Senate, may be attributable to two major factors. The first is that Republican dominance in a disproportionately large number of small states, such as those in New England, gave the party power in the Senate but not in the House. The other factor relates to the rural-dominated and malapportioned state legislatures, which elected the Senate. These legislatures were very sensitive to pressures from commercial interests and accommodated them by returning more Republicans than Democrats to the Senate.

Despite this large degree of divided control of the federal government, party discipline within the House was fairly strong, and only one speakership election went beyond a single ballot. Caucuses to select each party's nominee removed conflict from the floor and placed it behind closed doors.

A disastrous combination of financial depression and party factionalism befell the Democratic party at the end of the era. Southern and western Democrats, caught up in the Populist fervor of the 1890's and led by William Jennings Bryan, estranged the Democrats of the eastern seaboard. Taking the party away from the cities cost the Democrats their best chance of regaining majority-party status, and they lost 120 seats in the House elections of 1892 and 1894. In the Senate they suffered a net drop of eighteen seats during the 1890's. Democrats ended the third era of congressional party politics in much the same way that they had begun it—as a distinct minor party.

Fifty-fourth–Seventy-first Congresses: 1895–1931. The election of 1894 gave the Republicans a resounding net gain of 117 seats—a 92 percent increase over the preceding Congress and the first of fourteen Congresses that they were to control (78 percent). The GOP captured 55 percent of the seats in the House and 56 percent in the Senate. Third-party seats in the House dropped further, to 1.3 percent.

Democrats exchanged control of each house of Congress with the Republicans twice, for an alternation rate of 11 percent—the lowest of any period. Only once did the House face a Senate in the hands of the other party (1911–1913), and in all but three Congresses the presidency and the speakership were held by the same party (83 percent). The Senate was controlled by the president's party with the lone exception of the fateful Sixty-sixth Congress (1919–1921), in which the

Republicans put an end to President Wilson's dream of a League of Nations treaty for the United States.

Turnover in the House declined. The median percentage of first-termers dropped to 25.8, and the median number of terms served rose to 3.6 (7.2 years). Much of the decline was due to the stabilization of party politics as a consequence of the partisan realignment that followed the election of 1896; another factor was the increasing attractiveness of Washington as a place in which to live and work.

Political developments between 1910 and 1913 dramatically altered the party relationship between the House and the Senate. The revolt against Speaker Cannon and ratification of the Seventeenth Amendment in 1913, making the Senate popularly elected, made the politics within each chamber more similar than ever. House and Senate careers were now subject to the same electoral forces. Party caucuses continued to limit floor contests for the speakership; only the 1923 election spilled onto the floor.

But it was in the Senate that the parties became more formally organized and effective. The centrality of the Senate in battles over the League of Nations had given it greater prominence; and the first president to be elected from the Senate—Warren G. Harding—was a symbol, although dubious, of growing Senate influence in the nation's governance.

Republican hegemony cracked in 1930. In spite of the Great Depression, Republicans had held narrow majorities in both houses; but death robbed them of the right to organize the House of Representatives, when seven newly elected Republicans (including Speaker Longworth) died between the election of the Seventy-second Congress and its convening in 1931.

Seventy-second–Ninety-eighth Congresses: 1931–1984. The irrepressible John Nance ("Cactus Jack") Garner was the first of eight Democrats to hold the speakership. Democrats have controlled the House in twenty-five Congresses (93 percent). Their narrow margin in 1930 was augmented by increasing victories, from 167 seats in 1928 to 331 in 1936. The New Deal had its most telling congressional victory in 1934, when the president's party gained midterm seats in the House for the first time since 1838. Taken together, Democrats captured 59.5 percent of all House seats during this era.

Two extensive periods of control have marked Democratic dominance in the House —1931–1947 and 1955–1984. The latter, thirty-year span is the longest period of party control over any federal political institution, unmatched even by the Democratic-Republicans.

The Senate has not been as dominated by a single party, although the Democrats have won 59.0 percent of the seats. Five Congresses have opened with Senate Republican majorities, and three have convened with a Republican Senate facing a Democratic House (1931–1933 and 1981–1985). The election of 1982 was the first since 1886 to continue differing party majorities in the two congressional chambers.

Another unique feature of this era has been the frequency with which presidents and Houses represented opposing parties. Since the end of World War II, ten Congresses (the Eightieth, Eighty-fourth–Eighty-sixth, Ninety-first–Ninety-fourth, and Ninety-seventh–Ninety-eighth) have had a president of one party (generally a Republican) confronting a Speaker of the other (generally a Democrat). The Eightieth Congress (1947–1949) was the only exception to this generalization.

This unusual development has provided another check and balance within the federal political system. Its clearest manifestation has been in the massive increase in the proportion of House districts that elect a presidential candidate from one party and a congressional candidate from the other. From 1920 through 1952, the median percentage of congressional districts with split results was only 14.1 percent, but in the seven national elections starting in 1956 the figure rose to 32 percent.

Growing political sophistication has given rise to increased numbers of independents and ticket splitters, and the traditional hold of the political parties on the citizenry has faded in the face of "issue voting" and candidate-centered media campaigns. Reliance upon party organizations to deliver votes has diminished as candidates have striven to impress voters directly through radio and television commercials. Neither the electorate nor the nominees now seem to need party labels as much.

This development has eliminated the "presidential coattail effect" in House elections, thus guaranteeing members enormously high reelection rates (the median rate since 1950 has been

91.5 percent). Thus, House members are relatively immune from tides of presidential popularity.

Reelection rates are generally lower for the Senate, because of the six-year hiatus between elections: the median rate for 1950–1974 was 77.4 percent. However, the three elections between 1976 and 1980 claimed thirty-two sitting senators. Although the downward trend was halted in the 1982 election, the median reelection rate for 1976–1982 dropped to 62 percent.

One major irony that appeared in 1976 and 1980 elections is that seventeen of the eighteen defeated incumbents lost in states that were carried by the opposing party's presidential candidate. This would appear to make the contemporary Senate very subject to presidential politics. This fact may be attributable to the eagerness with which so many senators have contended for the presidency. Their ambitions may have had the unfortunate consequence of linking presidential and senatorial fortunes; and as public esteem for the presidency has dipped, Senate prospects have also suffered.

The ideological control of the House by the "conservative coalition" of Republicans and southern Democrats in evidence since 1938 manifested itself dramatically in the Ninety-seventh Congress (1981–1983), as Democratic "boll weevils" combined with President Ronald Reagan to give him more legislative victories than any other president since Lyndon Johnson in the early days of his Great Society.

The Senate has had a different history. The 1958 election brought thirteen new Democrats, most of them liberal, into the chamber. Their numbers and their commitment to institutional reform and policy liberalism made it possible for civil rights bills to pass in spite of obstructionist tactics by filibustering southern Democrats. These bills opened the door to black participation in elections, and a number of southern senators chose to retire rather than face defeat amid the growing power of black voters. However, life within the presidential orbit can fluctuate, and the liberals' domination of the Senate began to crumble in 1976. The 1980 contest gave Republicans a net gain of twelve seats and their largest contingent since Herbert Hoover's Seventy-first Congress.

Congress has always been involved with partisan politics. The first political parties emerged within it before spreading out into the country, but the later parties emerged from the general public and then had their impact upon Congress. At times, Congress has seemed to be keeping a scorecard, tallying the strengths of various partisan sentiments among the electorate and doing its best to translate these strengths into shifts within the national policy agenda. At other times, Congress has resisted these impulses and gone about its business, hoping that newer and more congenial tides of opinion would engage the public.

THE COMMITTEE SYSTEM

The most distinctive characteristic of the United States Congress relative to other national legislatures is the enormous strength of its standing-committee system. Analysts of legislatures throughout the world have remarked on its expertise, its ability to check executive authority, and its stability in the face of changing political conditions. The congressional committee system has often been cited as a model that should be emulated.

Like so many other aspects of the Congress, standing committees also had their origins in colonial times. Although New England towns had committees to handle their local legislative affairs in the seventeenth century, the colonial legislatures of Virginia and Pennsylvania provided the models for the committee systems that were established in the Congress.

Virginia's House of Burgesses had seven standing committees in operation at the time of the First Congress: Religion, Privileges and Elections, Propositions and Grievances, Courts of Justice, Claims, Commerce, and Trade. Most of these names were similar to those of the "grand committees" that had functioned in the British Parliament.

Pennsylvania's committee system served as the strongest model for the early Congress. Not surprisingly, the first Speaker of the House, Frederick A. C. Muhlenberg, had been the speaker of the Pennsylvania Assembly. The names of Pennsylvania's committees soon appeared as the names of the earliest congressional committees: Ways and Means, Accounts, Revision of the Laws, Rules, and Unfinished Business. Because of the differing sizes and representational systems of the two houses of Congress, the committee systems within each house also developed differently.

House of Representatives. The initial committee selected in the Congress was the House Committee on Elections, created to rule upon the qualifications of the newly arriving members; it was elected on 13 April 1789. The first joint committee of Congress, the Joint Committee on Enrolled Bills, was also selected in the First Congress.

By 1797, the House had added the Committees on Claims; Commerce and Manufactures; Revisal and Unfinished Business; and Ways and Means. Committees grew steadily, with three new committees added in the Thirteenth Congress. Nine of the twelve Congresses between 1803 and 1827 added new House standing committees—seven in the Fourteenth Congress (1815–1817) alone. By 1827, the House had twenty-eight standing committees, and by the opening of the Civil War, thirty-eight. By 1900, there were sixty committees to handle legislative business.

The major reason for this growth was the practice of rewarding the sponsor of a resolution that created a committee with its chairmanship and with a clerk for committee business. Thus, it served the dual purpose of making members a part of the House establishment and giving them staff, then a very rare commodity.

As committees continued to grow with only occasional retrenchment, the House became increasingly unwieldy. In the 1920's, the Republican leadership acted to consolidate nine committees within Appropriations and to create in 1927 the Committee on Expenditures in the Executive Departments, which merged eleven committees. The Budget and Accounting Act of 1921 created the Bureau of the Budget in the executive branch. Centrally locating executive fiscal management in one place gave the House an impetus to consolidate its various oversight committees.

Throughout the 1930's the number of House committees held steady at forty-six. Complaints continued to be heard, but the need for major reorganization was postponed to face the greater crises of the Great Depression and the growing threat of war.

In the Seventy-ninth Congress (1945–1947), which was sitting at the end of World War II, the single most important overhaul of the committee system occurred with the passage of the Legislative Reorganization Act of 1946. Written by Senator Robert M. La Follette, Jr. (Prog.-Wis.), and Representative A. S. ("Mike") Monroney (Dem.-Okla.), this act called for a substantial reduction in the number of standing committees, the development of more joint committees to expedite House and Senate business, and the expansion of the Legislative Reference Service of the Library of Congress to assist members in their research. The act was intended to streamline congressional life and to provide adequate support personnel for members.

At the time of the act, the number of House committees stood at forty-eight, following the addition of the Select Committee on Small Business and the highly controversial Committee on Un-American Activities; the number was reduced by the act to nineteen. Six committees, four dealing with elections, were abolished outright. The new Committee on House Administration took over the election function as well as the legislative jurisdictions of six other committees. Six committees were also merged into the new Committee on Public Lands (now the Committee on Interior and Insular Affairs).

Fears that many senior members would be upset about the disappearance of their committee chairmanships through consolidation were rendered moot by the stunning victory of the Republicans in the 1946 congressional election. All of the Democratic chairmen lost their posts through the party shift, thereby easing the transition to the new structure.

Changes in the committees of the House have been infrequent since 1946. The successful launching of earth-orbiting satellites by the Soviet Union caused anxiety in Congress as well as the nation, and in 1958, the House Committee on Science and Astronautics was selected for the first time. A payroll scandal in the House concerning Adam Clayton Powell (Dem.-N.Y.), the chairman of the Education and Labor Committee, led to the creation of the House Committee on Standards of Official Conduct in 1968.

Although the House passed another Legislative Reorganization Act in 1970, the committees were not directly affected. But in 1973, the House Select Committee on Committees, chaired by Representative Richard Bolling (Dem.-Mo.), was able to bring about some reform in the committee system. The two major changes were to abolish the House Committee on Un-American Activities and to make the Select Committee on Small Business a standing one. The former had been a major source of headlines during the post–World War II anxiety about domestic Communist subversion. It had also been a springboard for Richard Nixon, whose aggressive service on the committee during the investigation of State Department official Alger Hiss won him the publicity needed for his Senate election in 1950 and his vice-presidential nomination in 1952.

In response to President Nixon, the Congress enacted a set of key measures in 1973–1974. The War Powers Act of 1973 was designed to limit the president's discretionary authority to place military forces in combat situations. The Federal Election Campaign Act of 1974 was designed to eliminate many of the financial and ethical abuses of future presidential campaign organizations. For the committee system, the most important legislative change was the Congressional Budget and Impoundment Control Act of 1974, which was intended to limit the president's authority to withhold funds appropriated by Congress for programs and projects that he opposed. This act created budget committees in both the House and Senate, which have quickly emerged as sources of major institutional power.

Another reform movement to alter the House committee system occurred in 1979 with the Select Committee on Committees chaired by Representative Jerry Patterson (Dem.-Calif.). Focusing primarily on overlapping energy jurisdictions within the existing standing committees, the Patterson committee gave the lead role on energy to the newly renamed Committee on Energy and Commerce instead of the western-dominated Interior and Insular Affairs Committee, which had held the lead role previously.

For the most part, the House of Representatives continues to function with the standing-committee system created in 1946. Apart from the net addition of three committees, changes have taken place in the growing number of committee assignments for each of the standing committees and the large number of subcommittees. From 1947 through 1983 the number of assigned places on standing committees has grown from 486 to 744, a 53 percent increase, and the number of House subcommittees has grown from 89 to 146, a 64 percent increase.

The unchecked growth of committee and subcommittee assignments stretches the personnel of the House even further and continues to fragment its internal decision-making process.

Senate. The Senate functioned without legislative standing committees for almost twenty-eight years. Its relatively small size and its reliance upon floor speeches had made such a system unnecessary. For the most part, the Senate used a series of select and special committees appointed to handle each floor vote coming before the chamber.

By 1816, the Senate had grown from twenty-six members to thirty-six, with the territories of Indiana, Illinois, Mississippi, and Alabama on the verge of statehood. As the Senate faced expansion, the need for a standing-committee system became more urgent. On 10 December 1816 the Senate created its first eleven legislative standing committees to augment its existing housekeeping ones; shortly afterward, a twelfth was added. The original standing committees were Foreign Affairs, Finance, Commerce and Manufactures, Military Affairs, Militia, Naval Affairs, Public Lands, Claims, Judiciary, Post Offices and Post Roads, Pensions, and District of Columbia.

The Senate had lost institutional ground to the House during the previous few years, particularly as a result of the aggressive speakership of Henry Clay; thus, creating its own legislative committee system was a way to counter its relative loss of influence. The Senate made an effort not to duplicate exactly the House committee structure. The name of the Senate's revenue committee originally was to have been Ways and Means, but it was changed to Finance upon final passage of the resolution creating the committees.

Once in place, Senate committees grew steadily, with very few abolished. The practice of making sponsors of committee-creating resolutions the chairmen of those committees led to the selection of many chairmen from the minority party.

By 1914, with seventy-four committees, the system was in danger of outnumbering the Senate membership itself, which then stood at ninety-six. Many committees had ceased to function legislatively and were primarily a source of prestige for their chairmen and staff.

Change came more emphatically than in the

House. The strong-willed leadership of Senator Henry Cabot Lodge (Rep.-Mass.) led to the abolition of forty-one standing committees in 1921—virtually all of them sinecures with a minimal impact on legislative business. Thus, the Senate was not as heavily encumbered by its committee system as was the House when the Seventy-ninth Congress convened in 1945.

The Legislative Reorganization Act of 1946 reduced the Senate's thirty-three committees to fifteen, with Rules and Administration picking up the jurisdictions of six committees, Public Lands picking up five, and Interstate and Foreign Commerce collecting four. Shortly afterward, the Veterans' Affairs Committee was added.

The Senate committees subsequently remained relatively stable, with only two additions—the Committee on Aeronautical and Space Sciences in 1958, in response to the orbiting of Soviet satellites, and the Budget Committee in 1974, as an outgrowth of the Budget and Impoundment Control Act. The Aeronautical Committee played a major role in Majority Leader Lyndon Johnson's bid for the 1960 Democratic presidential nomination.

Thirty years after the 1946 Reorganization Act, it became clear that further reform was necessary. The growth of committee and subcommittee assignments was taxing the members of both chambers. The House skirted the problem, but the Senate acted vigorously. Through the Temporary Select Committee to Study the Senate Committee System appointed in 1975, the Senate reduced its committees (standing, joint, and special) from 31 to 24 and its subcommittees from 174 to 118. As a result, the average number of assignments per senator dropped from 18 in the Ninety-fourth Congress to 11 in the Ninety-fifth.

Senator Adlai E. Stevenson III (Dem.-Ill.) chaired the committee that reorganized the Senate's system. Three standing committees were eliminated, as the functions of the District of Columbia Committee and the Post Office and Civil Service Committee were folded into the newly reconstituted Governmental Affairs Committee; both of these committees had encountered difficulty in getting senators to serve on them, and so their departure was not greatly lamented. The Aeronautical and Space Sciences Committee, the only standing committee ever chaired by Lyndon

Johnson and once filled with the Senate's most senior members, had fallen on hard times as appropriations for the space program dried up in the 1970's. This committee was absorbed by Commerce under its new designation, the Committee on Commerce, Science, and Transportation.

One major reason for the Senate's greater propensity to revamp its committee system is that committees play a less important role in the Senate than in the House. With unlimited debate and no committee on rules to restrict amendments, the Senate has been able to conduct more of its legislative business on the floor than has the House. As a result, Senate careers are not as dependent upon committee assignments. This lowers the stakes involved in any alteration in committee jurisdictions and makes reform easier to accomplish.

Assignments and Chairmanships. The method of selecting members for the standing committees has varied over the years. In the House, the original committees were elected by the membership, but within the first year of the First Congress, it became clear that it was far easier to have the Speaker make the assignments. This arrangement lasted until 1911, when the revolt against Speaker Cannon stripped that power from the Speaker.

From 1911 through 1974, the Democratic members of the Ways and Means Committee served as the Democratic committee on committees. This gave the ranking Democratic member on the Ways and Means Committee power comparable to the floor leader's. Members of the Ways and Means Committee could not fill their own vacancies; this had to be done by election in the House Democratic caucus. Although the system removed arbitrary power from the Speaker, it also created another power base among House Democrats and further blurred the lines between committee power and party power. After 1974, the power was given to the Democratic Steering and Policy Committee, the members of which were elected by caucus and on which served the party's major leaders (the Speaker, the majority floor leader, and the Democratic whip).

Republican members created their own unique Committee on Committees, consisting of one member from each state that has at least one Republican representative. Each of these members has votes weighted by the number of Republican members in the state delegation. Thus, it is not surprising that members from New York, California, Ohio, Illinois, and Pennsylvania have had vote weights in excess of twenty during the past seventy years. For the most part, the senior delegation members of each state (the "deans") served on the Committee on Committees and endeavored to get as many of their fellow delegation members on the most prestigious committees possible.

Other, more recent changes include the modification of the "seniority rule." Before the 1970's, the House was committed to the practice of granting the chairmanship of its standing committees to the member of the majority party with the longest continuous period of committee service. This procedure took much of the internal politicking out of the selection process and prevented a Speaker from punishing a senior member on a committee by removing him from a post that he had earned through seniority. Long before the revolt against Speaker Cannon, the seniority system was in effect; but after Cannon's departure, the principle was enshrined because of its apparent nonprejudicial quality.

It soon became clear that those most likely to gain the chairmanships were from the least politically competitive congressional districts. This led to an overrewarding of Deep South congressmen during Democratically controlled Houses and of rural midwesterners when the Republicans held the reins. Liberals, in particular, were disturbed by a system that tended to reward members whose districts were the most removed from the tides of public opinion.

In 1973 the House rules were changed to make committee and subcommittee chairmen stand for election by the party members of their committees. And in 1975 the influx of newly elected liberal "Watergate babies" led to the defeat of three longtime chairmen: William R. Poage (Dem.-Tex.) on Agriculture, F. Edward Hébert (Dem.-La.) on Armed Services, and Wright Patman (Dem.-Tex.) on Banking, Currency, and Housing. A few subcommittee chairmen have fallen since then, but there have been no further overthrows of committee chairmen. In the wave of post-Watergate reform, Republicans have also subjected their senior committee and subcommittee members to votes within the

House Republican Conference, but for the most part, no one has been overthrown.

The Senate's committee assignments differ because of the continuity principle within that chamber. Unlike the House, which technically begins itself anew with the convening of each Congress, the Senate is a continuing body, and its members hold their assignments for as long as they wish. When vacancies occur, the assignments are referred to each party's committee on committees. In the Democratic party, assignments are made by the Steering Committee, and in the Republican party, by the Committee on Committees.

Generally speaking, the assignment of Senate committees leads to less conflict than the House's simply because the Senate relies less upon its committees. As a result, one need not be a member of a Senate committee in order to have a material impact on that committee's legislative recommendations.

The less intense atmosphere regarding committee assignments made it possible for Majority Leader Lyndon Johnson to institute the "Johnson rule" in 1953, under which all Democratic senators were to have one major-committee assignment (Finance, Appropriations, Foreign Relations, and the like) before any Democrat was assigned to a second major committee. This rule strengthened Johnson's influence with committee chairmen.

Conflict regarding chairmanships also seems less intense. Only twice in the twentieth century has a chairmanship been denied to a Senate committee's senior majority member—to Benjamin R. Tillman (Dem.-S.C.) as chairman of Appropriations in 1913 and to Albert R. Cummins (Rep.-Iowa) as chairman of the Interstate and Foreign Commerce Committee in 1924. The House has had six chairmanships voided in the same period.

Joint Committees. The first joint committee, on Enrolled Bills, was appointed during the First Congress. For more than a century and a half, joint committees played no major legislative role, dealing primarily with housekeeping items such as printing and the Library of Congress.

The major impetus for the joint committees came with the passage of the Legislative Reorganization Act of 1946. The act's authors hoped that joint committees would enhance communication between the House and the Senate and, in the process, expedite legislation. During the 1940's and 1950's a number of joint committees were created: Taxation, Economic Report (the Joint Economic Committee or JEC), Immigration and Naturalization, and Reduction of Useless Federal Expenditures were some of the better known. From 1959 through 1964 there were twelve joint committees in operation.

During the late 1960's, the joint-committee movement died out. Although House members relished the opportunity to serve on committees with equal numbers of senators, senators found it increasingly difficult to staff them, and Senate vacancies often went unfilled. But most joint committees disappeared gradually, and in the Senate's 1977 Reorganization Amendments, the joint committees were reduced to four: Printing, Library, Taxation, and JEC. All but the JEC are staffed by members from the existing standing committees.

Select and Special Committees. Select and special committees are created to gather information in a specific area and report back to the standing committees for legislative action. These committees have been given oversight authority in their investigative roles, but not until recently have they received legislative responsibility as well. This has occurred in the cases of the select committees on Energy, Intelligence, and the Outer Continental Shelf. Because select committees are chosen from the membership of more than one standing committee, they can address issues that might otherwise fall between the jurisdictional cracks of the standing committees.

Originally, the difference between select and special committees was that select committees were chosen by the chamber's presiding officer, whereas special committees were selected by the parties and the floor leaders. This distinction has become blurred, and it seemed as if the term *select* was reserved for committees that would be renewed by the subsequent Congress, with *special* used for committees unlikely to survive the Congress in which they were appointed. This has given rise to the designations *permanent select committees* and *temporary select committees*.

From 1789 to 1815 the Senate conducted all of its business through select committees, and during the nineteenth century select committees played a major role even after the creation of the standing-committee system. They played a far smaller role in the House: for example, the Fiftieth Congress (1887–1889) had twenty-three Senate select committees but only four House ones.

Until 1946, the Senate averaged between ten and twelve select and special committees, while the House averaged between three and five. The Senate's reorganization of its standing committees made select committees an attractive alternative to deal with short-term legislative matters. The post–Reorganization Act Senate continues to make wider use of these committees than does the House, and many of them have been used as launching pads for the ambitions of their chairmen.

Given the domination of the Senate's standing committees by elderly southern hierarchs, it would be unlikely for a junior member with presidential ambitions to gain national attention through his service on such committees. Thus, the select committees provided an excellent vehicle for intensive, if limited, media exposure, satisfying the ambitious junior members without disrupting the hegemony of the senior members over the standing committees.

Although most of these committees had short lives, some shone brightly because of the publicity generated by their activities and because of their genuine impact on the nation's policies. Among the most important were Gerald P. Nye's (Rep.-N.D.) Senate Special Committee on Investigation of the Munitions Industry (1934–1936), which focused on the "merchants of death"; Harry Truman's Senate Special Committee to Investigate the National Defense Program (1941–1947), which gave the Senate a role in the national war effort; Estes Kefauver's Senate Special Committee to Investigate Organized Crime in Interstate Commerce (1950–1951), which held the first nationally televised set of congressional committee hearings; and Sam Ervin's (Dem.-N.C.) Senate Select Committee on Presidential Campaign Activities (1973–1974), which unraveled the Watergate scandal leading to the resignation of President Nixon.

Subcommittees. For many years, standing committees have had subcommittees to handle the initial phases of reading legislation. However, the major thrust of subcommittee power came in the wake of the Legislative Reorganization Act, when the subcommittees were called upon to replace the departed standing committees. Since then subcommittees have grown from 148 in 1947 (59 in the Senate and 89 in the House) to 251 in 1983 (105 in the Senate and 146 in the House). One House subcommittee, Housing and Community Development in the Banking, Finance, and Urban Affairs Committee, comprised thirty-six members in the Ninety-eighth Congress, making it larger than ten of the standing committees.

But not all standing committees operate with subcommittees. Some committee chairmen, notably Wilbur Mills (Dem.-Ark.), who chaired House Ways and Means from 1957 through 1974, felt that their authority was diluted by the power of subcommittee chairmen. However, the subcommittee "bill of rights" passed in 1973 by the Democratic caucus legitimized subcommittee power and spread influence over legislation to more members than ever.

Democratization of the Congress in the wake of the Watergate scandal opened up more power to the subcommittees. With power spread more liberally, the central role of standing committee chairmen has been greatly reduced. The leadership vacuum should presumably be filled by the party leaders, for they are best positioned to coordinate the legislative initiatives emanating from the subcommittees. The verdict on their success is still not in.

Overview. The system of congressional committees is one of the great contributions of the American system of government. Within them, partisanship can be submerged, as members come to grips with problems of common interest. The committees often act in united ways when they present their proposals to the full chamber, thereby countering the partisan spirit that pervades the Capitol.

The United States Congress functions within a presidential system—one executive who is elected separately from the legislature. Many legislatures that operate within presidential systems, notably those in Latin America and Africa, have been very ineffective in checking the abuses of executive authority. But the American congressional committees, with their power to investigate the executive branch through the oversight function and their control of executive spending through the appropriations process, have been successful in providing a further check and balance that the Founding Fathers did not foresee. It is clearly in keeping with their wishes.

CONCLUSION

On 3 January 1989 the One-hundred-and-first Congress will open the third century of this structurally continuous and stable political institution. But continuity coexists with change. Rules, procedures, and precedents all lend an aura of institutional momentum to the Congress, but it is the ever-changing mix of members and their ambitions that has given it its unique character. It is populated almost exclusively by politicians whose strengths and weaknesses are clearly revealed in their debates and their votes. The National Assembly of the Fourth French Republic (1946–1958) was called a "house without windows" because its members failed to perceive the changes occurring within the nation as cabinet after cabinet reshuffled itself. The United States Congress differs. It has at times hoped to insulate itself from the tides of change, as it did when it imposed the "gag rule" on slavery questions before the Civil War, or when filibustering southern senators tried to forestall civil rights legislation in the 1950's, or when House resolutions pertaining to the Vietnam War were bottled up in the late 1960's and early 1970's. But in each case change broke through and the Congress had to confront these crucial matters.

Entering the hall of the House of Representatives with a visitor, Alexander Hamilton said, "Here, sir, the people govern." And two centuries later, they still do.

BIBLIOGRAPHY

The literature on the Congress and its members is voluminous. In addition to histories and textbooks, there are a substantial number of monographs, diaries, biographies, and autobiographies with which to contend. What follows here is a very partial listing of congressional sources.

Official sources on the Congress include the *Congressional Record* and its predecessors, the *Congressional Globe* and the *Annals of Congress.* Other congressional publications include the *Congressional Directory,* the House and Senate *Journals* for each session, and the invaluable *Biographical Directory of the American Congress, 1777–1971* (Washington, D.C., 1971).

The most useful book on the Congress is the Congressional Quarterly's *Guide to the U.S. Congress,* 3rd ed. (Washington, D.C., 1982). Its blend of historical background with material and descriptions of procedural complexities can be of help to anyone needing congressional information. Congres-

CONGRESS

sional Quarterly also publishes the *CQ Weekly Reports,* which give succinct guides to congressional activity as well as easy-to-use information on floor voting records.

There are only a few general histories of the Congress available. Among them are Alvin M. Josephy, Jr., *On the Hill: A History of the American Congress* (New York, 1979), and Ernest Sutherland Bates, *The Story of Congress, 1789–1935* (New York, 1936). Each of the chambers has been treated separately. For the House, there is George B. Galloway, *History of the House of Representatives,* rev. ed. (New York, 1976), and the classic by De Alva Stanwood Alexander, *The History and Procedure of the House of Representatives* (Boston, 1916). For the Senate, there is George H. Haynes's two-volume *The Senate of the United States* (Boston, 1938). No recent history of the Senate has been published. Popular accounts of each chamber, which are attuned to political and personal aspects of the members, are Neil MacNeil, *The Forge of Democracy: The House of Representatives* (New York, 1963), and William S. White, *Citadel: The Story of the U.S. Senate* (New York, 1956).

The prerevolutionary era is treated well in Jack P. Greene, *The Quest for Power: The Lower Houses of Assembly in the Southern Royal Colonies, 1869–1776* (Chapel Hill, N.C., 1963); Jackson Turner Main, *The Upper House in Revolutionary America, 1763–1788* (Madison, Wis., 1967); and Mary Patterson Clarke, *Parliamentary Privilege in the American Colonies* (New Haven, Conn., 1943). The early Congresses are assessed in Manning J. Dauer, *The Adams Federalists* (Baltimore, 1953); Ralph V. Harlow, *The History of Legislative Methods in the Period Before 1825* (New Haven, Conn., 1917); and James S. Young, *The Washington Community: 1800–1828* (New York, 1968).

Nineteenth-century Congresses are best introduced by Woodrow Wilson's classic *Congressional Government* (Boston, 1885). They can be accessed by combining the memoirs of members with analyses of voting patterns. The memoirs with the most useful information are Thomas Hart Benton, *Thirty Years' View,* 2 vols. (New York, 1856); James G. Blaine, *Twenty Years of Congress: From Lincoln to Garfield,* 2 vols. (Norwich, Conn., 1884–1886); and John Sherman, *Recollections of Forty Years in the House, Senate, and Cabinet,* 2 vols. (New York, 1895). Analyses of these Congresses may be found in Thomas B. Alexander, *Sectional Stress and Party Strength: A Computer Analysis of Roll-Call Voting Patterns in the United States House of Representatives, 1836–1840* (Nashville, Tenn., 1967); Joel H. Silbey, *The Shrine of Party: Congressional Voting Behavior, 1841–1852* (Pittsburgh, 1967); David J. Rothman, *Politics and Power: The United States Senate 1869–1901* (New York, 1966); and David W. Brady, *Congressional Voting in a Partisan Era: A Study of the McKinley Houses and a Comparison to the Modern House of Representatives* (Lawrence, Kans., 1973).

Twentieth-century Congresses can also be studied through memoirs and analyses of votes. Among the best sets of memoirs in this century are Champ Clark, *My Quarter Century of American Politics,* 2 vols. (New York, 1920); Oscar W. Underwood, *Drifting Sands of Party Politics* (New York, 1931); and Joe Martin, *My First Fifty Years in Politics* (New York, 1960). Good analytical treatments of the Senate may be found in Donald R. Matthews, *U.S. Senators and Their World* (Chapel Hill, N.C., 1960), and Michael Foley, *The New Senate: Liberal Influence on a Conservative Institution, 1959–1972* (New Haven, Conn., 1980). The House has been studied in Robert L. Peabody and Nelson W. Polsby, eds., *New Perspectives on the House of Representatives* (Chicago, 1977).

Party leadership of the Congress has been assessed in Mary Parker Follett, *The Speaker of the House of Representatives* (New York, 1902); Chang-Wei Ch'iu, *The Speaker of the House of Representatives Since 1896* (New York, 1928); Randall B. Ripley, *Party Leaders in The House of Representatives* (Washington, D.C., 1967) and *Power in the Senate* (New York, 1969); Robert L. Peabody, *Leadership in Congress: Stability, Succession, and Change* (Boston, 1976); and Barbara D. Sinclair, *Majority Leadership in the U.S. House* (Baltimore, 1983). Robert F. Bales's classification of leaders comes from "Task Roles and Social Roles in Problem-Solving Groups," in Eugene E. Maccoby, Theodore M. Newcomb, and Eugene L. Hartley, eds., *Readings in Social Psychology* (New York, 1958).

A number of important articles that deal with the Congress over time and its party leaders are Nelson W. Polsby, "The Institutionalization of the U.S. House of Representatives," in *American Political Science Review,* 62 (March 1968); Nelson W. Polsby, Miriam Gallaher, and Barry Spencer Rundquist, "The Growth of the Seniority System in the U.S. House of Representatives," in *American Political Science Review,* 63 (Sept. 1969); Margaret Munk, "The Origin of the Senate Floor Leadership," in *Capitol Studies,* 2 (Winter 1974); and Garrison Nelson, "Partisan Patterns of House Leadership Change, 1789–1977," in *American Political Science Review,* 71 (Sept. 1977).

Statistics on party membership by Congress may be found in U.S. Bureau of the Census, *Historical Statistics of the United States: Colonial Times to 1970* (Washington, D.C., 1975). Election information may be found in Congressional Quarterly's *Guide to U.S. Elections* (Washington, D.C., 1975). Information on congressional districts is contained in Stanley B. Parsons, William W. Beach, and Dan Hermann, *United States Congressional Districts, 1788–1841* (Westport, Conn., 1978).

Congressional committees are treated in Lauros G. McConachie, *Congressional Committees: A Study of the Origin and Development of Our National and Local Legislative Methods* (Boston, 1898), and Joseph Cooper, *The Origins of the Standing Committees and Development of the Modern House* (Houston, Tex., 1970). The modern-era committees are analyzed in George Goodwin, Jr., *The Little Legislatures: Committees of Congress* (Amherst, Mass., 1970); David E. Price, *Who Makes the Laws? Creativity and Power in Senate Committees* (Cambridge, Mass., 1972); Richard F. Fenno, Jr., *Congressmen in Committees* (Boston, 1973); and Kenneth A. Shepsle, *The Giant Jigsaw Puzzle: Democratic Committee Assignments in the Modern House* (Chicago, 1978).

[*See also* CONSTITUTION; ELECTORAL PROCESSES; LOBBIES AND PRESSURE GROUPS; POLITICAL PARTIES; PRESIDENCY; REPRESENTATION AND APPORTIONMENT; *and* SEPARATION OF POWERS.]

CONSERVATION, ENVIRONMENT, AND ENERGY

Roderick Nash

THE recent popular enthusiasm for conservation (or environmentalism) obscures the difficult birth of the movement in American society. The basic problem was the richness, the wildness, and the sheer size of the New World. For several centuries Americans enjoyed a population-to-resources ratio that did not necessitate conservation. The idea of inexhaustibility dominated popular thought and conditioned political action. Although inexhaustibility was a myth, Americans acted on the assumption of its reality. We may regret the consequences, but this attitude is understandable in light of the fact that uncut forests once stretched to the horizon, that virgin soils produced bumper harvests, and that passenger pigeons blackened the skies for days on end.

Until shortages and extinctions revealed that inexhaustibility was wishful thinking, Americans believed the way to solve environmental problems was to leave them behind. Going West, seeking new frontiers, was the easy way out, and for a time it worked. Forgotten almost completely were the lessons of the Old World and of Asia, where people occupied the same land for a thousand years and maintained its productivity by stewardship and restraint based on a keen sense of the limits of nature and man's dependency. The American pioneer preferred to rip and run, cut out and get out, and let posterity take care of itself.

The early American resistance to conservation stemmed not only from the abundance but also from the wildness of the New World. The transatlantic migration stripped away centuries, and the frontiersmen reexperienced the anxieties and the ambitions of primitive people. Because wilderness was perceived as a direct threat to survival and a barrier to progress, nature had to be broken to the human will. The assault on the resources of North America was not just a commercial venture; it amounted to a struggle for existence. Protecting the environment and preserving natural resources were the last things on the minds of pioneers. What made sense was their own protection and preservation in a vast and forbidding wilderness.

If more justification for environmental exploitation was needed, it could be found in the Bible. As interpreted by frontiersmen, Genesis 1:28 and the entire dualistic emphasis of Scripture justified the subjugation of the earth and the dominion of mankind over other forms of life. The corollary was that nature existed for human use. It followed that the conquest of the wilderness was a divine mission and civilization a kind of redemption.

The mainstream economic and political values of America also ran against the conservation idea. Individualism was construed as license to do what one wished with regard to resources. Until the late nineteenth century few defended the restraining influence of state or national governments. Democracy and capitalism championed freedom. With respect to land the objective was to put the public domain into the hands of unrestrained private owners as quickly and cheaply as possible. It was enormously difficult to assert the long-term interest of society as a whole—not to speak of anything as nebulous as the future—against individual acquisitiveness. Capitalistic economic assumptions, particularly the ideas that bigger was better and that the pursuit of individual profit resulted in the greatest social good, retarded conservation. So it was that the first American conservationists had to challenge values dominant in the nation from its beginnings. Contemporary conservation has been called subversive, and with some reason. The more radical environmentalists today are asking whether a meaningful program of environmental responsibility can even exist without a surrender of basic American principles. But others recognize the potential of reform within the context of established American ideals and institutions.

Although the word *conservation* originated in the mind of Gifford Pinchot in 1907, King Henry VII of England appointed a "conservator" of the Thames River in 1490. Later the British established "conservancies" in India in order to protect forest resources. As a policy, if not in name, conservation in America extends back to the seventeenth century. The earliest conservation law in the New World was a 1626 ordinance of the Plymouth Colony (Massachusetts) respecting the cutting and sale of timber. The statute warned of the "inconvenience likely to arise" from clearing too much land and forbade the export of timber products from the colony. Even in a heavily wooded environment, and just six years after the arrival of the *Mayflower,* it appeared that resource shortages could occur.

Wildlife also proved vulnerable to exploitation very early in the American experience. The first game law, a six-month closed season on deer, appeared in 1639 in Rhode Island. Ducks, turkeys, and salmon, all creatures useful to the colonists, received early protection. By the 1730's game wardens existed to enforce the conservation laws. An important principle in political economy was involved. According to old English law, wildlife belonged to the Crown, not to the individual landowners. In North America, the colonies and then the states acquired this entitlement, which extended in time to the issuance of hunting and fishing licenses. Fish and game laws are thus the earliest American example of social control of environmental resources. Individual freedom, even that of property owners, gave way before the greater interest of the state and society in general. This opened the door to government ownership and management of other resources such as forests, rivers, and grasslands. Land-use zoning and environmental impact assessment laws also derived from the principle that no individual could own the environment in absolute terms. It required decades to develop, but wildlife law at least set forth the concept that the benefit of the individual must occasionally give way to

longer-term considerations of the welfare of society.

In this regard two colonial policies deserve special mention. Massachusetts' Great Ponds Act of 1641 proclaimed the right of the public to use any body of water over ten acres in size for hunting and fishing. This marked the first appearance in American political history of the idea that a significant feature of the environment should not be privately controlled to the detriment of the interests of society. The second program, called the Broad Arrow Policy, was an effort by Great Britain to secure raw materials for the construction of the Royal Navy. Throughout the colonies, trees of exceptional height and quality were blazed with the shape of an arrow. For the colonists, this meant "hands off." The policy expressed the principle that those parts of the environment with transcendent importance to society should not be owned in such a way as to preclude public benefit. But the Americans, already tasting the heady brew of frontier freedom, chafed under such restrictions and openly violated them. The resulting tension was one of the factors in the onset of the American Revolution.

The colonial forest and wildlife regulations are examples of utilitarian conservation, which attempts to sustain those resources that serve the material needs of mankind. This is not only the oldest but still the most potent rationale for earth stewardship. Man takes care of nature because nature takes care of man. As applied to resources, utilitarianism sees trees as potential lumber and fuel, and wildlife as meat in the pot. The perspective is thoroughly anthropocentric. Indeed, the only difference between the pioneers' exploitative relationship to the environment and the utilitarian conservationists' attitude is that the latter worry about the long term. Immediate gain is secondary to sustained yield. It follows that wise use, not just use, is the hallmark of utilitarian conservation.

Utilitarianism explains the first conservation efforts of the new nation. In 1799 the U.S. Congress appropriated $200,000 for purchase of forest lands in the Southeast, and an 1817 act authorized the secretary of the navy to hold such tracts. Just as with the Broad Arrow Policy, the purpose was assurance of adequate supplies of quality timber for the ships in the all-wooden navy of the United States. In 1827 Congress empowered the president to reserve forests in the territory newly acquired from Spain, called Florida. One preserve was established the following year, but the government abandoned it after a brief experiment. The American frontiersman, it appeared, was just as reluctant to observe federal conservation policy as he had been with regard to imperial regulations. Timber thieves pillaged the forest reserve. Pioneer appetites were still too strong even for utilitarian conservation.

Aesthetic considerations constitute a second root of the conservation impulse in early American history. This time the human spirit, not just the human stomach, was involved. A tree, some people recognized, could provide inspiration as well as timber. William Penn, the proprietor of Pennsylvania, wrote a provision into the 1681 charter calling for maintenance of a balance between cleared and wooded land. Penn even employed a "woodsman," who appears to be the first American forester. In planning the city of Philadelphia, Penn took pains to lay out large public squares and gardens so that the city would always be a "country towne." Pennsylvania was also the source, in 1763, of the first law against water pollution. Anyone throwing "any Carcase, Carrion, or Filth whatsoever" off a public dock could be fined a maximum of forty shillings.

Aesthetic conservation floundered in the expansionist ideology of the early republic. Preservation was the last thing most citizens of the new nation had in mind when it came to nature. In Michigan, in 1831, the French visitor Alexis de Tocqueville observed that "the Americans . . . are insensible to the wonders of inanimate nature, and they may be said not to perceive the mighty forests that surround them till they fall beneath the hatchet." What Americans did notice, Tocqueville continued, was the "march across these wilds, draining swamps, turning the course of rivers, peopling solitudes, and subduing nature." But, in time, several factors created a case for valuing nature for its own sake rather than for what it could become.

Science (botany and ornithology in particular) led the way in pointing to the wonder of the New World. For a few scientists the wilderness became a laboratory full of unrecorded and fascinating species. William Bartram, for example, traveled thousands of miles in the southeast in the 1770's, delighting in "these sublime and enchanting scenes of primitive nature." John James

Audubon made a name for himself in American environmental history with his meticulous sketches of birds. Beginning in 1827, his publications attracted the attention of Americans of taste and, generally, urbanized backgrounds. Scientific curiosity also took George Catlin, a Philadelphia painter, to the headwaters of the Missouri River, where he recorded the appearance and customs of the Indians. Significantly, Catlin recognized the threat American expansion posed to native culture and, in 1832, made the first plea for a policy of federal protection of wilderness for both man and nature. Catlin is credited with the idea of the national park.

Writers, poets, and painters formulated an aesthetic argument for the value of nature. Beginning in the 1820's, James Fenimore Cooper's "Leatherstocking" novels, along with the landscape paintings of Thomas Cole, celebrated the wilder portions of the East. Francis Parkman, author of *The Oregon Trail* (1849), and the artist Albert Bierstadt carried these interests across the Mississippi. By this time the romantic movement, already flourishing in Europe, came to the aid of nature in America. The idea of the "noble savage," for instance, transformed the Indian from a subhuman heathen into a nobleman of nature and paved the way for political action on behalf of Indian rights. Romanticism also linked sublimity with wilderness, creating a whole new aesthetics with which to interpret the American frontier.

Cultural nationalism proved immensely important in opening American eyes to nature. The argument was that America needed cultural distinctiveness, something different and distinguished to hold up against the older and richer antiquities of the Old World. In terms of human achievement, nineteenth-century America had little to compare to Roman ruins or medieval cathedrals. But nature offered a different basis for comparison. Specifically, the New World had a quantity and quality of wilderness that transcended anything abroad. Nationalists pointed with pride to spectacles like Niagara Falls, Yosemite Valley, and the Grand Canyon. Arguments for their protection were not long in emerging.

The spiritual or religious value of the American environment took form in the writings of the transcendentalists in the 1830's and 1840's. Ralph Waldo Emerson and Henry David Thoreau led the way in celebrating wild nature as a direct, unadulterated source of divine wisdom and moral law. "Nature," Emerson wrote in 1836, "is the symbol of the spirit." Thoreau went further, writing in 1851 that "in Wildness is the preservation of the World." To be sure, most of his contemporaries chuckled at Thoreau's self-imposed 1845 exile to Walden Pond, but time was on his side. In the next half century, Americans made *Walden* (1854) a classic as they came to understand the wisdom of Thoreau's protests against the thoughtless exploitation of nature.

Aesthetic and utilitarian considerations worked together in the first major citizen conservation effort in the United States. Wildlife was the object, and sportsmen were the prime movers. Sport hunting, as opposed to market or meat hunting, continued a long-standing European tradition. But in the United States the absence of a feudal nobility with their private hunting preserves made a comprehensive national policy imperative. Pressure for the protection of both game species and their habitat developed among people furthest from the frontier. The New York Sporting Club (1844) and the New York Game Protective Association (1850) were the first citizen conservation organizations in the United States. The pressure of groups like these on the political process resulted in the first state fish and game laws. In 1876 wildlife conservation obtained a nationwide voice with the establishment by George Bird Grinnell of *Forest and Stream* magazine. Retitled *Field and Stream,* the periodical remains an important source of sportsmen's opinions. In 1887, upper-class American sportsmen, led by Theodore Roosevelt, formed the Boone and Crockett Club. Its major contribution was the idea that healthy populations of game animals could not be maintained without the protection of habitat. The federal wildlife refuges, beginning in 1903 with the Pelican Island Game Preserve in Florida, and the national forests were political expressions of this concept.

While hunters took pleasure in the death of wildlife, however sportingly achieved, another current in early wildlife conservation prized living nongame birds and animals such as songbirds. The Audubon Society, named after the famous artist, originated in state groups in New York (1886) and Massachusetts (1895). By 1905 there was a national Audubon organization. Sci-entists in the American Ornithologists Union (1883) aided the cause of species preservation. The first problem the bird lovers addressed was that of commercial plume hunting. Operating mostly in tropical Florida, plume hunters found a lucrative business providing ornaments for women's hats. Bird populations declined precipitously. A concerned Bostonian, Mrs. Augustus Hemingway, took the lead in the 1890's in advocating a boycott of this kind of fashion, but the trade continued. A street survey revealed that of 700 women's hats 542 featured the wings or plumes of birds.

The U.S. Congress entered the plume battle on 25 May 1900 with the passage of the Lacey Act, which authorized the Department of Agriculture to stop interstate shipments of illegally killed wildlife. Enforcing the law was more difficult than passing it. A black market developed, and the slaughter continued. Matters came to a head in 1905 when Guy Bradley, a Florida game warden, was shot while attempting to arrest a plume hunter. A local jury promptly acquitted the murderer. The resulting national outrage, coupled with decreasing public interest in plumed hats, began to turn the tide. Migratory bird protection (the Weeks-McLean Act, 1913) and the authorization of Everglades National Park in 1934 finally brought meaningful protection to the waterfowl of Florida. In 1940 the United States Fish and Wildlife Service, located in the Department of the Interior, took charge of national protective policies.

In the case of the passenger pigeon there was a sadder ending. The first settlers of the Ohio Valley marveled at the size of the flocks, which numbered in the billions. Systematic slaughter, combined with the clearing of the eastern forests on which the pigeons depended, took a heavy toll. In 1914 the nation received the almost unbelieveable news that the last passenger pigeon, a female dubbed Martha, had died quietly in a Cincinnati zoo. In no more than a half century the species had been exterminated. It was shocking proof that inexhaustibility, even in the New World, was a myth.

The most dramatic wildlife conservation story of the nineteenth century involved the buffalo. The original range of these huge grazers extended from Virginia to the Rocky Mountains. At the time of European contact with the New World their numbers were estimated at

30,000,000. Pioneers reported herds five miles wide galloping past a given point for half a day. But after the railroads penetrated the Great Plains in the 1860's, pressure on the buffalo mounted. Just as in the case of the beaver forty years before, capitalism and eastern markets impelled a big kill. The herds were a huge "commons" into which the individual hunter could dip at will. He found nothing to be gained by conservation; another hunter would gladly take what he left. In marked contrast to the Indians, the white hunters did not depend directly on the buffalo for their subsistence. Neither were there any religious or ethical restraints that might have promoted conservation. Moreover, the American frontiersmen had a technology for killing buffalo unknown to the precontact Indian. A skilled marksman could shoot as many as 120 buffalo in an hour without moving from his stand. One of the best shots, William F. Cody, became a western legend, "Buffalo Bill." No one thought there would ever be a shortage of buffalo.

But by the end of the 1870's the entire southern plains herd was gone. Moving northward with the recently constructed Northern Pacific Railroad, the hide hunters ripped into the last substantial concentrations. In 1889 William Hornaday, pioneer zoologist, estimated the number of free-ranging wild buffalo at an incredible eighty-five.

The effort to save the buffalo began with scattered, and largely unheeded, protests against the slaughter. As early as 1832 George Catlin predicted the end of the herds unless the government intervened. But in keeping with the scarcity theory of value commonly operative in American environmental history, effective protest awaited the near extinction of the species. It was the old story of not valuing a natural resource until threatened with its loss. Unquestionably, the ending of the frontier in 1890 created a wave of public enthusiasm for one of its chief symbols. In 1905 Hornaday enlisted the help of President Theodore Roosevelt, a former buffalo sport hunter, in establishing the American Bison Society. Using captured animals, or those bred in captivity, the society restocked selected private ranchlands. In 1907 Congress established the National Bison Range in Montana. The present population level of all the protected herds is about 30,000 animals.

After sputtering fitfully in the colonial and early national periods, forest conservation made substantial strides after the Civil War. The towering figure here was George Perkins Marsh. His 1864 book, *Man and Nature; or, Physical Geography as Modified by Human Action,* became a bible to conservationists of the next fifty years and is still respected. An early exponent of what would later be called ecology, Marsh advanced the revolutionary thesis that the condition of the environment had more to do with human than with natural forces. He concluded that man had best take care in the way he modified the earth. Marsh's arguments drew heavily on his observations in the Mediterranean basin. There he saw once rich land that centuries of exploitation had reduced to rock and dust. It occurred to him that part of the reason for the fall of Greece, Persia, and Rome might have been the exhaustion of the ability of their environment to support a civilization. In particular Marsh cited the cutting away of forest cover and the ensuing cycle of drought, flood, and soil erosion.

In the United States, Marsh saw widespread evidence of the same short-sighted land use practices that had laid so much of southern Europe and the Near East to waste. His book called on his countrymen to "be wise in time and profit by the errors of our older brethren." But Marsh understood that in any society a policy of conservation depended on "great political and moral revolutions." The United States was not ready in the mid-nineteenth century, but there were some encouraging signs in forestry, the field Marsh believed fundamental to conservation.

With Marsh's 1864 treatise as a guiding light, a movement for forest conservation in America took shape in the 1870's. The first Arbor Day, a tree-planting promotion, occurred in 1872. A few years later the American Forestry Association began crusading for the wise use of timber on private lands, and in 1876 Congress appointed a forestry agent, Franklin B. Hough, in the Department of Agriculture. In 1881 Hough assumed direction of the new Division of Forestry. His role was purely advisory to private forest owners, but he pioneered the concept that forest conservation made good economic sense.

At the same time Carl Schurz, the secretary of the interior, advanced a new and revolutionary approach to American forest conservation. A German immigrant, Schurz knew about sustained-yield forestry as practiced in the Old World. He also knew that the nineteenth-century variety of unrestrained free-enterprise economics held out little hope for American forest conservation. So in his 1877 report, Secretary Schurz made bold to suggest that the federal government consider retaining title to forest lands. If private companies cut on these lands at all, they would do so under the supervision of government foresters. In these concepts lay the genesis of the national forests.

In the 1870's, Schurz's proposals were premature. Congress alienated the public domain by selling or giving it to private parties as quickly as possible. The Mining Law (1872), the Timber Culture Act (1873), the Desert Land Act (1877), and the Timber and Stone Act (1878) facilitated the giveaway of both the land and the opportunity of directing its use. Indeed, Schurz's ideas did not bear fruit until 1891, when an obscure and undebated rider on a land-law bill gave the president the power to create federally owned and managed forest reserves from the public domain. Acting under its authority, President Benjamin Harrison withdrew over thirteen million acres of western forest land, and the battle with exploitation-minded westerners was joined. Charging that the so-called Forest Reserve Act "locked up" resources, the West overlooked the fact that sustained timber production was the point of forest conservation.

Finally the Forest Management Act of 1897 made it clear that private lumbering, mining, and grazing could occur on the forest reserves under the watchful eye of federal officers representing the long-term interests of society. Still, charges of socialism echoed through the West, especially after President Theodore Roosevelt increased the reserved land to over 150 million acres. In 1905 the 159 reserves were placed in the charge of the United States Forest Service within the Department of Agriculture, and two years later the reserves were renamed "national forests." By this time the chief forester was Gifford Pinchot, head of the old Division of Forestry since 1898 and a personal friend of President Theodore Roosevelt. Pinchot would use his position within the Forest Service to spearhead conservation in the Progressive era.

While much of the early American conservation movement concerned nature, recent research (Melosi, 1979) has stressed the impor-

tance of cities as the place where Americans first experienced the adverse impact of deteriorating environmental conditions on the quality of their lives. Previously the American city had grown haphazardly. With the exception of William Penn's early efforts in Philadelphia and the founding of Washington in the District of Columbia, planning was notable in its absence. By the end of the nineteenth century there were severe problems with water, air, noise, sewage, garbage, and general congestion. Determined not to pay this price for progress, public health officials and sanitation engineers joined with local politicians and citizen groups to campaign for reform. Their efforts began the familiar pattern of citizen demand and political response. Often as a result of devastating fires (such as the great Chicago fire of 1871), American cities were gradually rebuilt with more emphasis on providing acceptable human habitats. Parks, playgrounds, and open space received increased attention. The milestone was Central Park in New York City, authorized in 1851 and, after 1857, supervised by Frederick Law Olmsted, a brilliant landscape architect. Olmsted believed that government had as much responsibility to provide recreational opportunities for urban dwellers as it did to educate them and protect them from fire.

By 1909 the profession of city planning had evolved to the point when it could stage a national convention. Reform was in the air, and in the mid-1920's over 100 American cities had planning departments. In New York the legendary Robert Moses, whose power would rival that of the mayor, directed the public works effort. But the rise of the automobile and the exodus to suburbs, coupled with the failure of the American political system to devise any way to limit urban growth, kept the movement on behalf of quality urban environments far short of its goals.

The moving force in utilitarian conservation as applied to water was a one-armed scientist and explorer, John Wesley Powell. After serving the Union in the Civil War, Powell led the first trip down the Colorado River in 1869. In 1878 Powell presented Congress with his *Report on the Lands of the Arid Region of the United States.* In this document, and in his work after 1881 as director of the United States Geological Survey, Powell challenged traditional American thinking about the environment. Basing his arguments on extensive field research, he contended that the West was neither an agrarian paradise ("garden of the world") nor a wasteland ("great American desert"). The West was capable of supporting some settlement, Powell continued, but the limiting factor was water. Since rainfall was insufficient for agriculture, water would have to be transported from rivers and spread over the land by a system of irrigation. Powell called the process "reclamation," and he urged Americans to study cooperative societies such as those of the Indians and Mormons, who had succeeded in living within the physical limitations of the West. Powell recommended that the federal government finance and direct the reclamation process. As the most widespread political entity in the nation, it had the best chance to bring individual interests together in a policy of regional water management.

But in the context of the late nineteenth century, Powell's ideas encountered considerable resistance. Americans failed to understand his proposal to reform the land-sale laws, which reduced the amount sold for irrigation and greatly increased the number of grazing units. What worked in relatively high-rainfall regions, such as the East and Midwest, did not make sense in the West. He also challenged the hallowed American myth of the self-sufficient yeoman farmer. Beyond the 100th meridian, cooperation, not individualism, was the proper course. No one man could or should dam a river with the regional importance of the Colorado. This was a task for society as a whole acting through federal processes. Finally, Powell became unpopular for his discouragement of pro-growth advocates or "boosters." Rain, the scientist patiently explained, does not follow the plow or increase in proportion to settlement. The West was not susceptible to dense settlement. Less than 3 percent of Utah could be farmed with existing water supplies. Overcrowding would only build up a heritage of conflict over scarce resources.

In 1902, the year John Wesley Powell died, Congress passed the Reclamation Act. The legislation modified the land laws along the lines he had suggested and directed the proceeds from the sale of federal lands in the West to finance dams and irrigation works. As Powell recommended, the federal government would be in charge of the process. In fact a pupil of Powell, Frederick H. Newell, was the first director of the

Reclamation Service. Soon he had twenty-five major projects underway, including Roosevelt Dam on the Salt River in Arizona. The agency, later called the Bureau of Reclamation, was located in the Department of the Interior. It is difficult, in view of later criticism of the bureau by environmentalists, to realize that it was one of the heroes of utilitarian conservation in the early twentieth century. It seemed to herald a new age of efficient planning and equitable allocation of rare resources.

Meanwhile, to return to aesthetic conservation, the United States developed a policy with respect to another of the limited resources of the West: spectacular scenery. National parks, an American invention, combine the democratic ideology with its special relationship to wilderness. In sharp contrast to the European tradition, national parks would be playgrounds for all the people, not just the hunting reserves of kings and nobles. Moreover, the American parks were to be wild in contrast to the formally manicured garden-parks of the Old World.

Following George Catlin's 1832 proposal of a "nation's park" along the front range of the Rocky Mountains, the first milestone in the park movement was the designation of Yosemite Valley in California as a state park in 1864. The federal government granted the spectacular valley to the state "for public use, resort and recreation." The reserved area was only ten square miles, and it quickly lost its wild character to a growing tourist-catering business, but the precedent had been set for government sponsorship of scenic preservation and outdoor recreation. Fresh from his achievements in New York City, Frederick Law Olmsted became one of the first commissioners of Yosemite.

The preservation in 1872 of the Yellowstone region in northwestern Wyoming marked the actual birth of the national park as an American institution. On the advice of the explorer Ferdinand V. Hayden, director of the Geological and Geographical Survey of the Territories, and with the support of the tourism-minded Northern Pacific Railroad, Congress designated two million acres of the public domain as "a public park or pleasuring ground for the benefit and enjoyment of the people." In contrast to Yosemite, the area remained national property, and it was wilderness. Although underfunded for years, and actually managed until 1918 by the United States

CONSERVATION, ENVIRONMENT, AND ENERGY

Army, Yellowstone National Park represented a significant departure from the nineteenth-century practice of quick disposal of the public domain to private interests.

With Yellowstone as an inspiration, the writer and explorer John Muir pressed for an expansion, under federal control, of the Yosemite reservation. In 1890, two million acres of the Sierra surrounding the state park became Yosemite National Park. Two years later Muir organized the Sierra Club to defend the reserve. One of its first successes was a 1905 arrangement that returned Yosemite Valley from California to the nation so that it could be included in one complete national park. By this time Mount Rainier (1899) and Glacier (1910) were national parks. In 1916, Congress created the National Park Service within the Department of the Interior to manage the park system, which by then had expanded to sixteen parks and eighteen national monuments. The difference was that the latter could be established by presidential proclamation rather than by act of Congress. In addition, aesthetic conservation could celebrate the establishment in 1883 of the Niagara State Reserve, protecting the American side of the great falls, and the Adirondack State Park (1892). The latter remains an interesting and unique combination of public land and zoning-controlled private inholdings.

The first appearance of conservation as a public movement in American history occurred during the Progressive era. Particularly in the administrations of President Theodore Roosevelt (1901–1909), conservation became a political and cultural force. Hundreds of articles and books examined the problem of natural resources. At the well-publicized White House Conservation Conference (13–15 May 1908) the governors of the states, dignitaries, and reporters heard Roosevelt call the stopping of wasteful exploitation of nature "the weightiest problem now before the Nation." Gifford Pinchot, the chief forester who organized the conference, thought it represented "a turning point in human history."

One way to understand the emergence of the conservation idea in the Progressive Era is in terms of historical context. The census of 1890 pronounced the American frontier at an end, and this was indeed a turning point in history. Americans began to worry whether their future without a frontier of undeveloped resources

would be different from the expansionist, exploitative past. It was hoped that conservation would become a new frontier, keeping the nation young, strong, prosperous, and wholesome by protecting the remaining natural abundance.

Efficiency figures prominently as a goal of the Progressives. Indeed, political historians (Hays, 1959) have seen the conservation movement of this time as closely linked to a "gospel of efficiency" that, in other quarters, produced the assembly line. Why could not natural resources be managed by scientists and engineers with the same precision? An effort to implement democracy also motivated the early-twentieth-century conservationists. Again and again leaders like Roosevelt, Pinchot, and W. J. McGee explained that conservation meant that the American people, not just special interests and "trusts," would benefit from the bounty of the natural environment of the nation. This issue came to a head in the Ballinger-Pinchot controversy of 1909. President Taft's secretary of the interior, Richard A. Ballinger, was suspected by the Roosevelt appointee, Pinchot, of favoring large corporations in the distribution of forest, water, and especially mineral rights. Pinchot's shrill attacks left Taft little option but to fire him in January 1910. Roosevelt's displeasure at the move, and his perception that Taft was no conservationist, figured in his decision to run against both Taft and the Democrats in the election of 1912. The split in the ranks of the Republicans contributed to the victory that year of Woodrow Wilson.

Pinchot had been embroiled, since 1906, in the growing controversy over Hetch Hetchy Valley in Yosemite National Park. San Francisco wanted to dam the valley for water supply and hydropower generation. A utilitarian conservationist, Pinchot favored the plan. But John Muir used the energy of his declining years to protest it as not only illegal but sacrilegious. The ensuing national debate over Hetch Hetchy, including three sets of congressional hearings, revealed the deep schism between the objectives of utilitarian and aesthetic conservation. For the first time in American history, substantial numbers of citizens used the political process to argue against development.

Finally, in 1913, Congress approved San Francisco's plans. The loss of Hetch Hetchy Valley, a scenic counterpart of Yosemite Valley, is generally regarded as the single greatest mistake in national park history. But in partial reaction against the decision, park supporters pushed the National Park Service Act through Congress three years later. Thereafter the parks had a political home in the Capital that could exert a countervailing force to that of the Forest Service and other utilitarian agencies.

On balance, Progressive conservation produced considerably more smoke than fire. There were urgent calls to action, grandiose plans, and elaborate conferences, but relatively little political action. It is arguable that Congress resented the strong push that the executive branch (particularly under Theodore Roosevelt) gave to the movement and deliberately dragged its feet. Still, public opinion had been aroused and its force in American political life demonstrated. In time, conservationists learned to act more and scold less. The people-versus-the-plutocrats approach gave way to the idea that the condition of the environment was a product of American civilization as a whole.

The control and management of water resources, an unfulfilled dream of the Progressives, became the conservation showpiece after World War I. The Federal Water Power Act of 1920 asserted the primacy of the national interest in the use of rivers. A Federal Power Commission was created with authority to license or actually operate dams. A test case arose in 1921 when Henry Ford offered to buy and complete a partly built federal hydropower plant on the Tennessee River near Muscle Shoals, Alabama. Senator George W. Norris of Nebraska spoke against Ford's plans, pointing out that with private control of a major river the possibility of comprehensive watershed management in the public interest would be lost. Instead of selling the dam site to Ford, Norris proposed that the federal government use it to begin a program of improvement of both the environment and the lives of people in the Tennessee Valley. The Republican administrations of the 1920's were not easily persuaded, but the 1928 authorization of the giant Boulder (later Hoover) Dam on the lower Colorado River created a more favorable political climate. So did the advent of the Great Depression of 1929 and the need for federal jobs. Finally, on 18 May 1933, President Franklin Roosevelt signed Norris' bill establishing the Tennessee Valley Authority. Over the next decade, New Deal planners and engineers built the kind

of multipurpose river management and hydroelectric empire about which John Wesley Powell and the Progressive water conservationists had dreamed. TVA became international shorthand for social control of resources and for environmental planning on a regional level.

Franklin Roosevelt's New Deal marks the second wave of intensified American concern about conservation. Once again, strong executive leadership based on a trusteeship philosophy appeared to be a more favorable political context for conservation that did weak central government and laissez faire. Besides its efforts in controlling the Tennessee, Colorado, and Columbia rivers with huge multipurpose dams, Franklin Roosevelt's administrations were the first in American history to take meaningful action against soil erosion. The problem came to public attention in the early 1930's when the southern Great Plains, its native grasses uprooted by plowings, literally blew away. Haze darkened skies as far east as New York, and the Dust Bowl became the most widely discussed environmental catastrophe in the history of the nation. John Steinbeck in literature, Woody Guthrie in song, and Pare Lorentz in film told the story of both the land and the lives of people turning to dust.

Roosevelt responded with the Civilian Conservation Corps (1933), which also had a role in putting as many as two million unemployed Americans back to work. The "CCC boys" planted trees, repaired gullies, and helped make *conservation* a household word. In 1935 Congress created the Soil Conservation Service (SCS) with the expectation of doing for the land what the Forest Service had done for trees. Hugh Hammond Bennett, the son of a North Carolina farmer, headed the efforts of the SCS to start farm demonstration projects and encouraged the states to form soil conservation districts. His work was facilitated by the Taylor Grazing Act (1934), which in effect ended the "homestead" era of cheap or free land and created a permanent federal landholding and land-managing agency. In 1946 it was reorganized as the Bureau of Land Management in the Department of the Interior. Finally, New Deal aided the wildlife conservation movement with the Pittman-Robertson Act (1937), which turned over the excise tax on sporting arms and ammunition to the states for land acquisition and habitat enhancement. After 1940 the U.S. Fish and Wildlife Service (Department of the Interior) coordinated the federal efforts.

World War II, like World War I, shifted priorities away from environmental protection. Indeed, it is tempting to generalize that conservation is really a luxury—something you think about after you have driven off your enemies and had a good breakfast. There was even talk during the war of logging the national parks, and few Americans raised objections. After the conflict, pent-up consumer demand and the conservative, small-central-government philosophy of the Republican administrations of Dwight D. Eisenhower proved inhospitable to conservation. In the early 1950's the Bureau of Reclamation proposed dams in Dinosaur National Monument and other components of the national park system. From the standpoint of intellectual history it is significant that many Americans of this generation put their faith for a better future in science, technology, and continued growth rather than in attaining a long-term and stable relationship with nature. For a time, "miracle" discoveries, like atomic energy and DDT, seemed to promise a world without shortages. The technological optimists dreamed about using the oceans to feed billions more humans.

On the other side of the issue were prophetic books such as Fairfield Osborn's *Our Plundered Planet* (1948) and his significantly entitled *The Limits of the Earth* (1953). The United Nations movement started some people thinking in terms of preserving the global ecosystem. In the United States, rising affluence contributed to an emphasis on what was called "environmental quality," and by the 1960's this concept challenged utilitarianism (resource quantity) as the central purpose of conservation. Many Americans were coming to realize that an environment conducive to survival, and even to affluence, was not enough. The land, they insisted, should do more than just support human life. Beauty, solitude, and joy were seen to be as essential to human welfare as bread alone. One straw in the wind was the increased attention professional forest managers paid to recreational values.

Modifying Gifford Pinchot's strict utilitarianism, leaders of the United States Forest Service began to plan for outdoor recreation and the preservation of wilderness. In the early 1950's a massive public protest stopped Bureau of Reclamation plans for dams in Dinosaur National

Monument (Colorado and Utah) and other units of the national park system. Among the arguments used in these battles were those put forward by the wildlife ecologist Aldo Leopold in *A Sand County Almanac* (1949). Destined to become a classic of the 1960's, Leopold's work argued that conservation should be grounded not on economics but on ethics. His idea of a "land ethic" stimulated some Americans to start thinking about environmental decisions in terms of right and wrong and led to landmark legislation like the Wilderness Act (1964) and the Endangered Species Preservation Act (1966). Rachel Carson's *Silent Spring* (1962) raised doubts about allegedly miraculous pesticides such as DDT, and bans on careless use of such chemical poisons followed on both state and federal levels. Clearly, the science of ecology, with its emphasis on the interdependency of all life, was making an impact on thinking about human–environment relationships and beginning to affect politics.

By the late 1960's a third wave in the American conservation movement was cresting. Its ethical orientation and camp-meeting fervor caused some observers (Nash, 1976) to label it a "gospel of ecology." Having defended the rights of blacks and of women, American society seemed prepared to take up the cause of nature. Paul Ehrlich's book *The Population Bomb* (1968) revived the old Malthusian nightmare of overpopulation in a limited world. Public discussion reached a climax in the report to the Club of Rome, *The Limits to Growth* (1972). But as a force in reshaping public attitudes nothing compared to the pictures of the earth that the astronauts brought back from the first moon landing in 1969. "Spaceship earth," a small, fragile, interdependent, absolutely unique planet, inspired its custodians to improve their stewardship. The first Earth Day (22 April 1970) marked a high point of public enthusiasm for what was now called "environmentalism" rather than the old resource-oriented "conservation."

Although predictably less intense than the public outcry, the political response was nonetheless impressive. The Water Quality Act of 1965 and the Air Quality Act of 1967 addressed varieties of pollution of which earlier conservationists had not even been aware. This legislation, and its several reauthorizations and amendments (1970, 1972), made emphatically the point that the American definition of freedom no longer entailed a license to pollute the environment on which all life, man's included, depended.

The most important institutional consequence of the so-called new conservation was the National Environmental Policy Act signed by President Richard M. Nixon on the first day of the 1970's. NEPA declared it the intent of Congress that each American had the right to a "healthful environment" and that the object of environmental policy should be the permanent establishment of "productive harmony" between man and nature. The heart of the act created a process called "environmental impact assessment" by which any federal or federally funded action that affected nature must be scrutinized in advance. NEPA did not actually prohibit anything, but it did oblige Americans to look before they leaped and it defined "impact" in terms other than strict profit and loss. Applied to projects such as the oil pipeline across Alaska, NEPA unquestionably created a more environmentally responsible finished product.

After its high point in the early 1970's, the environmental-ecology movement lost some of its popular appeal and political clout. Oil shortages in 1973 and 1974, the so-called energy crunch, encouraged a new wave of exploitation that chafed impatiently against state and federal restraints. When the Endangered Species Act of 1973 was used to block a TVA dam on the Little Tennessee River that threatened the only known habitat of a minnow (the snail darter), Congress simply exempted the dam from the constraints act. In the West, the traditional stronghold of anticonservation viewpoints, discontent blossomed in the late 1970's into a "Sagebrush Rebellion." Although more symbol than substance, the movement had as its object state acquisition (and then, presumably, sale) of federal lands. The Alaskan variety of discontent (the "Tundra Rebellion") was even stronger, with calls for secession from the union. But in the closing weeks of the Jimmy Carter administration, environmental protection reemerged to engineer passage and signature of the Alaska National Interest Lands Conservation Act. The greatest single piece of legislation respecting parks and wilderness in world history, the act set aside more than 100 million acres of federal land in Alaska for recreation and preservation purposes. Disgruntled Alaskans, however, continued efforts to modify or circumvent the act.

In regard to energy, it became increasingly apparent in the 1970's that the era of fossil fuels (coal, oil, and natural gas), which had powered a century of American progress, would not last forever. Oil, especially, became scarcer (and hence more costly), prompting both frantic new production and efforts at conservation. The replacement of the huge gas-guzzling automobiles of the 1950's with small high-mileage vehicles was one of the most dramatic symbols of the new environmentalism. High mileage actually became a status symbol, especially after the gasoline crunch of 1973–1974, when, for the first time since World War II, Americans encountered energy rationing.

Another response to the breakdown of the myth of inexhaustibility concerning oil was a renewed interest in alternate energy sources. Experimental windmills, renamed "wind machines," received attention. So did solar energy devices, including huge desert-situated "power towers" utilizing thousands of mirrors to concentrate sunshine. Nuclear energy remained controversial. Few could deny the very real safety and waste disposal problems inevitably associated with fission-type atomic reactions. Most environmental organizations favored abandoning the nuclear energy option altogether, and the expensive delays (in the construction of reactors) that this criticism caused undermined the industry's economics. But others argued that for better or for worse nuclear energy was here to stay. Better, they thought, to move ahead with research in and development of safer forms (such as fusion) than to pretend that atoms did not have enormous potential as an energy source.

The election to the presidency in 1980 of Ronald Reagan, and his appointments to the post of secretary of the interior, marked a clear eclipse of environmentalism. Although unsympathetic to the Sagebrush Rebels, the Reagan administration acted decisively to remove restraints from the free-enterprise system. The Environmental Protection Agency, which NEPA established in 1970, was all but abolished, and regulations respecting surface mining and air quality were weakened. In addition, a massive program of coal and oil leasing was begun both on the continent and offshore. But a storm of criticism in the national news media showed that conservation was not dead. Well organized environmental lobbies blocked attempts to scrap protection programs concerning air, water, mining, and toxic wastes. The growth in the 1980's of citizen protest against the ultimate form of environmental pollution—nuclear radiation—promised yet another revival of one of the nation's most characteristic political crusades.

BIBLIOGRAPHY

Roderick Nash, *American Environment: Readings in the History of Conservation,* 2nd ed. (Reading, Mass., 1976), is a convenient collection of primary and secondary sources. Its comprehensive bibliography lists the key sources in the field. Nash, *Wilderness and the American Mind,* 3rd ed. (New Haven, 1982), discusses the changing American attitude toward nature and also contains a full bibliography. Douglas H. Strong, *The Conservationists* (Menlo Park, Calif., 1971), is a handy, short study. The closest approach to a textbook in the field is Joseph M. Petulla, *American Environmental History: The Exploitation and Conservation of Natural Resources* (San Francisco, 1977). See also Petulla, *American Environmentalism: Values, Tactics, Priorities* (College Station, Tex., 1980), which treats some recent environmental controversies. Also useful in this regard is Paul Brooks, *The Pursuit of Wilderness* (Boston, 1971).

Environmental politics are the subject of several monographs: Barbara S. Davies and J. Clarence Davies, III, *The Politics of Pollution,* 2nd ed. (Indianapolis, Ind., 1975); Walter A. Rosenbaum, *The Politics of Environmental Concern,* 2nd ed. (New York, 1977); Walt Anderson, ed., *Politics and Environment: A Reader in Ecological Crisis* (Pacific Palisades, Calif., 1970); and Richard A. Cooley and Geoffrey Wandesforde-Smith, eds., *Congress and the Environment* (Seattle, 1970). Frank Graham, Jr., traces the politics of the pesticide controversy in *Since Silent Spring* (Boston, 1970), but Thomas R. Dunlap, *DDT: Scientists, Citizens, and Public Policy* (Princeton, 1981), is a more useful study for the present purposes.

Other recent monographs of value include: Lawrence B. Lee, *Reclaiming the American West: An Historiography and Guide* (Santa Barbara, Calif., 1979); Elmo R. Richardson, *Dams, Parks and Politics: Resource Development and Preservation in the Truman-Eisenhower Era* (Lexington, Ky., 1973); Norris Hundley, Jr., *Water and the West: The Colorado River Compact and the Politics of Water in the American West* (Berkeley, 1975); Alfred Runte, *National Parks: The American Experience* (Lincoln, Neb., 1979); Thomas A. Lund, *American Wildlife Law* (Berkeley, 1980); Martin V. Melosi, ed., *Pollution and Reform in American Cities, 1870–1930* (Austin, Tex., 1979); John F. Reiger, *American Sportsmen and the Origins of Conservation* (New York, 1975); Samuel P. Hays, *Conservation and the Gospel of Efficiency: The Progressive Conservation Movement, 1890–1920* (New York, 1959); and Donald E. Worster, *Dust Bowl: The Southern Plains in the 1930s* (New York, 1979). Two collections of documents are Robert McHenry, ed., *A Documentary History of Conservation in America* (New York, 1972), and Frank E. Smith, ed., *Conservation in the United States: A Documentary History* (5 vols., New York, 1971).

Stephen Fox, *John Muir and His Legacy: The American Conservation Movement* (Boston, 1981), is the most recent survey of twentieth-century environmentalism. The international scene is treated in Dennis Pirages, *Global Ecopolitics: The New Context for International Relations* (North Scituate, Mass., 1978), while the vital field of energy is the subject of David Howard Davis, *Energy Politics* (New York, 1974). For a comprehensive examination of natural resources and policy see Paul R. Ehrlich, Anne H. Ehrlich, and John P. Holdren, *Ecoscience: Population, Resources, Environment,* 3rd ed. (San Francisco, 1977).
[*See also* LAND POLICIES; LOBBIES AND PRESSURE GROUPS; PROPERTY; PUBLIC OPINION; *and* REGULATORY AGENCIES.]

CONSERVATISM

Forrest McDonald

AS a self-conscious political philosophy, conservatism is a modern phenomenon, though its roots and some of its tenets can be traced to ancient times. Its first systematic application to a concrete political situation was Edmund Burke's *Reflections on the Revolution in France* (1790), and Burke himself used variants of the word *preserve* rather than *conserve*. During the next generation, like-minded Frenchmen and Englishmen began to employ the words *conservative* and *conservatism* to describe themselves and their position, and yet another generation passed before the terminology acquired general currency in political discourse in America.

To understand conservatism one must recognize at the outset that it is not a program or an ideology, but a set of values and an attitude toward changes in the established social order. More specifically, perceiving society as an ongoing, living entity, conservatives accept change as necessary and desirable. "Change," said Burke, "is the means of our preservation." They insist, however, that any particular change, along with its foreseeable long-range consequences, be compatible with justice ("to everybody his due") and with morality, including that portion of morality which rests upon social custom. Since what is one's "due" is a function of existing sociopolitical arrangements, and since what is custom varies from one society to another and over time within a given society, the programmatic content of conservatism is different in different places and times. Thus, for example, conservatives in Spain, Austria, the United States, and Japan will be in agreement in preferring their traditional social orders and in being cautious and prudential in evaluating proposed changes in them, but the customs and institutions they choose to preserve and the changes they find acceptable will differ considerably. Similarly, the specific political programs and policies that appealed to American conservatives of the 1830's bear no relation to what their counterparts espoused in the 1930's.

The meaning of conservatism can be brought into clearer focus with a rough checklist of characteristics that distinguish it from its opposite, which is not any particular dogmatic secular religion—such as communism, socialism, or fascism—but dogmatic secular religion itself. The conservative American poet and historian Peter Viereck once defined conservatism as "the political secularization of the doctrine of original sin"; the conservative political scientist Eric Voegelin defined its opposite as the political secularization of the heresy of gnosticism. The conservative, in dealing with human affairs, prefers reasoning from history and experience to reasoning from abstract theory; prefers moderation to extremism; trusts society more than government; rejects the idea of human perfectibility; and recognizes that some problems are insoluble and that some evils are ineradicable.

PRINCIPLES OF CONSERVATISM

To probe deeper into the nature of conservatism, we may begin by noting observations made by two of the more distinguished conservatives among the Framers of the American Constitution. One is that of John Dickinson, who declared in the Constitutional Convention: "Experience must be our only guide. Reason may mislead us." The other is that of Alexander Hamilton, who wrote elsewhere that "a great source of error is the judging of events by abstract calculations, which though geometrically true are false

354

as they relate to the concerns of beings governed more by passion and prejudice than by an enlightened sense of their interests." Burke fleshed out what Dickinson and Hamilton had said. He distinguished between "abstraction," or a priori reasoning divorced from or contrary to history and experience, and "principles," or sound general ideas derived from observation of human nature in the present and in the past. The conservative shuns abstractions and, discreetly and cautiously, is guided by principles.

At least eight principles may be delineated as having been held in common by conservatives from the eighteenth century through the twentieth. The first is concerned with morality: conservatives believe that there are certain universal and eternal moral truths. They are not unanimous as to the source of these transcending moral truths—most conservatives believe they are ordained by God, but there are nontheists among them who are content to assume that they are programmed by nature—yet all agree that good and evil are equally real, that every adult except the mentally enfeebled is endowed with a moral sense adequate to enable him to distinguish right from wrong, and that man's universal religious instinct is the surest foundation of the social order.

A second conservative principle is also concerned with morality, but in a different sense of the term: morality as mores or social custom. Many moral values are peculiar to individual societies, and even the transcending moral values may be delimited and refined by social norms. "Thou shalt not kill," for instance, is a universal mandate, but no society interprets it to forbid absolutely the destruction of any living thing, animal or vegetable. Moreover, virtually every society makes exceptions even within the human species; most conservatives would hold that "thou shalt not kill" other human beings except in self-defense, in defense of family and the innocent, and in service to one's country. Similarly, though incest is universally prohibited, the degree of kinship necessary to invoke the injunction varies from society to society, as does the way kinship is reckoned. Thus there are both absolute and relative moral values, and the two are inevitably and sometimes confusingly related; bona fide moral dilemmas do arise.

A third conservative principle is concerned with freedom, the necessity for which arises from the first two principles. As a creature with a moral sense and as one endowed with free will, man can choose between moral and immoral behavior, and he is responsible for the consequences of his actions. Government and society, to be moral, must allow individuals sufficient freedom to be responsible. How much political or civil liberty is desirable beyond this minimum, beyond what is necessary to enable a person to do what is right and just, varies with the force and nature of social custom in a particular political regime. In general, liberty flows not from the extent of popular participation in the lawmaking process but from the extent that a people is habitually law-abiding: law is the fountain of liberty.

A fourth principle follows from the third: the conservative believes in justice tempered by equity, and he does not confuse the two. Justice, at bottom, has to do with predictability and with the sense of security it provides. There are rules of acceptable behavior, known or knowable to all, and the rules carry with them a system of rewards and punishments, also known or knowable. Few conservatives are so confident of their own rectitude that they would prefer strict and unvarying justice ("I cry for my country," Jefferson is reported to have said, "when I contemplate the possibility that there may be a just God"), and accordingly they temper their love of justice with mercy, compassion, equity. But they believe, with William Blackstone, that "the liberty of considering all cases in an equitable light must not be indulged too far, lest thereby we destroy all law. . . . And law without equity, though hard and disagreeable, is much more desirable for the public good, than equity without law: which would make every judge a legislator, and introduce most infinite confusion."

A fifth conservative principle arises from a congeries of attitudes about society. Conservatives believe that social continuity is crucial and that, while a just society must allow for the dignity of its individual members, the needs of society itself are primary. They base this position upon observation of the human condition: because of the long period of dependency during infancy, childhood, and adolescence, mankind without society cannot subsist. But there is an ever-present tension between the social instincts and the instincts for self-gratification; it is the function of social institutions to temper or check the latter in the interests of the former and to convince the citizen of the primacy of the needs of the group. That social institutions normally, if imperfectly, do perform this function is attested by history: when circumstances make it necessary, people overcome the most powerful of all instincts, that of self-preservation, and willingly sacrifice themselves to preserve the society of which they are a part.

The relationship between society and government involves a sixth conservative principle, the fact and desirability of variety, diversity, plurality, and inequality. People differ from one another along a number of axes—ethnic, sexual, age, talent, class, wealth—and government behaves illegitimately if it either discriminates against or attempts to impose uniformity upon any of these groupings. Government can legitimately give existing social arrangements the sanction of law. But in all events, conservatives believe, government exists to serve the diverse society and not the other way around.

A seventh principle is that of prescription: that there are rights and obligations that rest upon "immemorial usage, so that the memory of man runneth not to the contrary." Over the course of time, we have acquired habits, conventions, and customs of remote origin that are woven unconsciously into the very fabric of our being. Conservatives believe that, in the absence of strong evidence to the contrary, man tampers with these or replaces them with more "rational" substitutes at his mortal peril.

Conservatives are guided by an eighth principle, that of prudence. They recognize that not all of society's ills can be cured and that an incautiously applied remedy can be worse than the disease. This can be expressed in terms of the lifeboat theory: if fifteen people occupy a lifeboat with a twenty-person capacity, they are obliged by compassion to take on any struggling swimmer they encounter, but if twenty people occupy the boat it is foolhardy to take on the twenty-first. Alternatively, the principle of prudence can be expressed as the first law of ecology: it is not possible to change only one thing. That is to say, to change any part of the immensely diverse, intricate, and interconnected social organism is necessarily to affect other parts and the whole, often in ways entirely unforeseen. Prudence requires that one take into account, as far as possible, the long-range consequences of any proposed action.

Finally, the prudent conservative recognizes that concrete situations may sometimes make his principles inconsistent, internally or with one another. In such circumstances he must make his choices from the available options on the basis of the priorities of his values; and, if possible, he leaves the door open to change his course if it turns out that he has chosen wrongly.

EUROPEAN ROOTS OF AMERICAN CONSERVATISM

It may seem strange that conservatism, as described, did not come into existence as a cohesive body of thought until the eighteenth century, since most of it was embedded deeply in Western tradition. The reason is that there had been no occasion to formulate a philosophy of conservatism until its opposite, rationalism, the deification of reason, emerged as a challenge to all prescriptive order during the seventeenth and early eighteenth centuries. Rationalism had many fathers, including some of the Levellers of the 1640's, Thomas Hobbes, Descartes, Rousseau, and an assortment of other French theorists; but in the English-speaking world the most important fountainhead was John Locke.

Locke's rationalism, or at least the vulgarized form of it that emerged in the eighteenth century, was anathema to proto-conservatives for three related reasons. One was his epistemology, which postulated that the human infant is born tabula rasa, a blank slate, neither good nor evil, but with infinite capacity for development in either direction. This, to conservatives, both denied the transcendence of morality and dehumanized man. The second was Locke's theory of natural rights, which contradicted conservatives' instinctive distrust of a priori theorizing and their principle that rights are prescriptive, derived from society and tradition. The third was Locke's theory of the social compact, which incidentally and under certain circumstances justified the destruction and reconstruction of the civil order, an undertaking that conservatives regarded as dangerous except in the most extreme of circumstances.

Considerable numbers of colonial Americans read or were at least generally familiar with

CONSERVATISM

Locke's ideas, but they also read and were influenced by writers who rebutted one or another part of Lockean and other rationalist theories. Four such writers, David Hume, Montesquieu, Emmerich de Vattel, and William Blackstone, were especially influential in shaping the colonial conservative's mind. It is to be observed that none of these was acceptable to conservatives in toto, and that none embodied the entire conservative philosophy. Rather, among them they supplied most of the ingredients from which such a philosophy could be fashioned.

Hume, in essays written from the 1730's to the 1750's and in his multivolume *History of England,* published in the 1750's and 1760's, had a powerful impact upon American thinking. Some of his views, particularly his epistemology and his religious skepticism, were abstruse and generally unacceptable to most Americans, but these could be ignored in light of his positive contributions. Most particularly, Hume subjected Locke's social-compact theory to a devastating analysis, not least by pointing out that Locke's individualistic state of nature was impossible even on a hypothetical basis, since mankind necessarily exists in families and other social units. Hume believed that most governments had probably originated in force, but that that was of no consequence, for they obtained legitimacy from custom, usage, the habit of allegiance, and the fact that governments are necessary to the preservation of society. In addition to his persuasive rebuttal of Locke's political theories, Hume constructed a number of his own, based upon observation of British politics, which the Founding Fathers would find useful when the time came for them to shape political institutions.

Montesquieu, like Hume, had things to say that made conservatives uncomfortable but more than compensated for these. His *Spirit of the Laws* (1748) was perhaps the first thoroughgoing exposition of the idea of cultural relativism and, as such, ran counter to the conservative's belief in transcending morality. But it also laid the foundations of law in social custom in such a way as to make absurd the rationalist belief that a viable body of institutions could be created *de novo,* on the basis of pure reason. Moreover, Montesquieu, again like Hume, had some practical suggestions that Americans would find valuable in the making of constitutions. Most important, he abandoned the primacy of the classical division of governments into monarchies, aristocracies, and democracies and developed instead (from historical observation) the principle of separation of powers: legislative, executive, and judicial.

The influence of Vattel in America is not as well known as that of Hume and Montesquieu, but it was nonetheless profound. Vattel's major opus, *The Law of Nations* (1758), was the culmination of more than a century of efforts to apply the age-old principles of natural law to international relations, Vattel's major predecessors being Hugo Grotius, Samuel von Pufendorf, and Jean-Jacques Burlamaqui. Natural law was quite different from natural rights. Vattel began with an "axiom of incontestible truth," the Aristotelian notion that the objective of every sane human being is happiness. By studying the nature of things, and of man in particular, Vattel wrote, it was possible to discover the rules that led to happiness, and those rules constituted natural law:

> Now, one of the first truths which the study of man reveals to us, and which is a necessary consequence of his nature, is, that in a state of lonely separation from the rest of his species, he cannot attain his great end—happiness: and the reason is, that he was intended to live in society with his fellow creatures. Nature herself, therefore, has established that society, whose great end is the common advantage of all its members; and the means of attaining that end constitute the rules that each individual is bound to observe in his whole conduct [*The Law of Nations,* pp. xliii–xliv, Philadelphia, 1817].

The place of rights in this scheme of things was carefully prescribed. Rights, Vattel declared, "being nothing more than the power of doing what is morally possible, that is to say, what is proper and consistent with duty,—it is evident that right is derived from duty, or passive obligation."

Blackstone's *Commentaries on the Laws of England* began to appear in 1766, a time when Americans were in a dither over the Declaratory Act, which asserted that Parliament had the right to legislate for the colonies "in all cases whatsoever." Blackstone's insistence that Parliament's powers were unlimited was ill-calculated to win him American admirers, but so majestic was his survey of the law that soon, in the words of James

CONSERVATISM

Madison, his work was "in every man's hand." Blackstone's contributions to American conservative philosophy were numerous, but two can be isolated as especially important. First, he endorsed the principles of natural law and rejected the theory of natural rights. Whatever rights man may have in a theoretical state of nature, Blackstone said, no one lives in a state of nature, and all rights that people do have in civil society, including property rights, are derived from the civil society itself, on society's terms. Second, Blackstone resoundingly rejected his understanding of Locke's notion that there could be, within the fundamental law, an implicit provision that the people could tear down a civil society and create a new one in its stead. "No human laws," he declared, would "suppose a case, which at once must destroy all law, and compel men to build afresh upon a new foundation."

These several writers served to reinforce the conservative disposition in America, and in the first major experience that the colonists had qua Americans, that disposition was abundantly relevant. During the imperial crisis of 1763–1776, most of the leaders of the American resistance to British measures perceived the struggle as one in which the mother country was attempting to introduce radical constitutional innovations, and in which the colonists had all the weight of history, custom, tradition, and the "ancient constitution" on their side. When the British government refused to return to the tried-and-true system that had prevailed before 1763—or so, anyway, colonists maintained—Americans had no choice but to declare their independence.

But there was another and radical tradition in American political culture, one running from Locke through John Trenchard and Thomas Gordon through Bolingbroke, James Burgh, and Thomas Paine, and that tradition was evident in the Declaration of Independence itself. The Declaration endorses the compact theory, speaks of "unalienable rights" derived from "Nature and of Nature's God," employs a Lockean justification for revolution, and proclaims that "all men are created equal."

Yet the Declaration was not so radical as a superficial reading would make it appear. The assertion that men are created "equal" is preceded by a use of the word that places it in context: "When . . . it becomes necessary for one people to dissolve the political bands which have con-

nected them with another, and to assume among the powers of the earth, the separate and equal station to which the Laws of Nature and of Nature's God entitle them, . . ." The American nation is equal to the British nation, a concept in natural law meaning that all nations are equal in the sense that they have no common sovereign except God. As for "unalienable rights," the Declaration can be read in light of the limited, conservative, natural-law formulation of rights as readily as in the light of radical natural-rights theory; for it substitutes the "pursuit of happiness," a concept in natural law, for "property," the third of Locke's supposed natural rights. Finally, the Declaration counsels "prudence" in casting off old governments; avers approvingly that "all experience hath shown, that mankind are more disposed to suffer, while evils are sufferable, than to right themselves by abolishing the forms to which they are accustomed"; and justifies the break on the ground that the British king had demonstrated beyond question a design to place the colonists under absolute despotism. The last two-thirds of the document is a bill of particulars aimed at proving that it was the king who had forced a break by repeatedly violating the social norms and political forms to which Americans and Englishmen were accustomed.

In sum, the Declaration was ambiguous: it could appeal to radicals and conservatives alike.

THE LAWGIVERS

The decision for independence put conservatives in a quandary. Some—Joseph Galloway of Pennsylvania and the DeLanceys of New York, for instance—had long led resistance to parliamentary measures but balked at independence and therefore became Loyalists. Others—John Dickinson of Pennsylvania, the Livingstons of New York, and the Rutledges of South Carolina, for instance—reluctantly accepted independence once it was declared and therefore became Patriots. Given the split among conservatives, radical experimentation flourished for a time during and immediately after the war; but by 1787 the conservative-minded were back in control in most places, and their work of fashioning permanent institutions for the new nation could begin. The task before them, as Hume had phrased it and as they conceived it, was that of "LEGISLATORS and FOUNDERS OF STATES, who transmit a system of laws and institutions to secure the peace, happiness, and liberty of future generations."

The undertaking was a delicate one. As Lawgivers, they knew they must establish new and unfamiliar institutions; as practical conservatives, they knew that these must be formed from old and familiar materials. And the materials were not promising. Americans lacked the kinds of institutions—hereditary monarchy, hereditary aristocracy, bishops, an established national church—that most Old World conservatives thought necessary to the preservation of the social order. Moreover, their customs, traditions, folkways, habits, and existing institutions were regional or local in orientation, not national.

The Founding Fathers rejected, virtually without a hearing, any notions of erecting the new institutions upon abstract ideas and ideals. Instead, they left intact the diverse social and political arrangements that had evolved during the colonial and revolutionary experience and built additional institutions intended to check and channel local forces so they might flow harmoniously in the national interest. The most important such institutions were the Constitution, the Hamiltonian fiscal system, and the Supreme Court under John Marshall.

That the Framers of the Constitution were conservatives is indubitable. Of the influential members of the Philadelphia Convention of 1787, only James Wilson spoke approvingly of "the inherent, indisputable and unalienable rights of men"; Wilson went so far as to suggest that the highest purpose of government was the "reformation" of the human mind. All the other leading delegates expressed, in one way or another, approval of Hamilton's observation in the classical work of American political conservatism, *The Federalist:* "Have we not already seen enough of the fallacy and extravagance of those idle theories which have amused us with promises of an exemption from the imperfections, weaknesses, and evils incident to society in every shape? Is it not time to awake from the deceitful dream of a golden age?" They shared Elbridge Gerry's opinion that "the evils we experience flow from the excess of democracy. . . . The people do not want virtue, they are the dupes of pretended patriots"; Dickinson's view that "experience must be our only guide"; Gouverneur

Morris' statement that men "live in society" and must "do what that condition requires." And they also shared James Madison's dictum in *The Federalist* number 51 that "in framing a government which is to be administered by men over men, the great difficulty lies in this: You must first enable the government to control the governed; and in the next place, oblige it to control itself."

They accomplished Madison's goal through prudential compromises. Compromises were necessary because, though almost all the Framers were conservative in their principles, they differed over important particulars. Some were more insistent than others on the importance of classical republican ideas, some wanted the states to have a strong voice in the national government, and some wanted it to be as "high-toned" and independent as was politically acceptable. The genius of the constitutional system that resulted was that the power of government, though great, would be recognized as emanating ultimately from the people and would be divided along three axes, vertical, horizontal, and temporal. Vertically, power would be vested in local, state, and national governments, the last being itself only "partly national, partly federal." Horizontally, power at the state level would be subject to certain restrictions, particularly as regarded property rights; power at the national level would be centered in a bicameral Congress, one branch representing the people and the other the states, but the legislature would be checked by strong executive and judicial branches. Temporally, the several branches of the national government would be chosen variously for two, four, and six years and for life or good behavior, meaning that they would represent the will of the people as expressed at different periods of time.

Transforming the paper Constitution into a living instrument of government was the work of the Washington administration, and particularly of Alexander Hamilton. Hamilton's fiscal system was an example of conservativism—of constructive, prudential change—at its best. Hamilton was faced with the problem of managing the staggering burden of public debts that had been accumulated to finance the War for Independence. He had several options. He could recommend that the debts be repudiated in whole or in part, but that would be immoral. He could propose that they be paid promptly and in full, but given the nation's limited resources that was impossible. Instead, he followed the British example and proposed to "fund" the debts in such a way as to make them the basis for banking currency, and thus to use them as material building blocks for nationhood. The essence of the Hamiltonian way was to make national authority dependent as little as possible upon coercion and as much as possible upon what economists call "the institutional structuring of market incentives." To put it more simply, he ensured the perdurance of the new national government by making commercial activity dependent upon the continued working of his system. The long-range consequences of the adoption of Hamilton's program were profound, for they included committing not only American conservatives but the United States government to capitalism, which, for all the Framers' insistence upon the sanctity of property rights, had been left open by the Constitution.

The significance of John Marshall's long tenure (1801–1835) as chief justice of the Supreme Court lay partly in the reinforcement it provided for the other conservative institutional developments and partly in the content of the Court's decisions during that period; but there was more. The Marshall Court established, over the opposition of powerful democratic forces, the principle that the federal court system would be divorced from politics. That was in keeping with the intent of the Framers, but things had not been working out that way until Marshall breathed life into Articles III and VI of the Constitution. Almost equally important, for more than three decades the Marshall Court stood, often alone, as a bulwark of national authority against the otherwise relatively unchecked power of the states.

The institutional creations of these eminently conservative Founders established limited government based on popular consent, developmental capitalism, and the rule of law. In the nineteenth century that program came to be called liberalism.

CHALLENGES TO THE CONSERVATIVE NATIONAL ORDER

The regime thus established in America, being simultaneously traditionalist and new, at once conservative and liberal, contained some inherent tensions. One set of tensions was fundamental. It remained to be seen whether conservative principles could provide stability, or even endure, amid the modernizing forces they unleashed in a nation characterized by individual freedom, restlessness, territorial expansionism, economic growth, large-scale immigration, and steadily increasing popular participation in the political process. Another set of tensions arose from the very diversity that conservatives had sought to preserve. There were in early America two deeply rooted clusters of traditional values and norms, one based in the South, the other in New England, which were normally conservative but could, under certain circumstances, explode as radical challenges to the national order. Thus Virginia could produce the conservative John Marshall and the radical agrarian John Taylor, and Massachusetts could produce the conservative Fisher Ames and the apocalyptic Federalist Timothy Pickering.

Three indigenously radical attacks against the national order were launched during the nineteenth century, the first being that mounted by Jeffersonian Republicans. The Jeffersonians worked within the system and came to power by dint of energetic, skillful, organized appeals to political and economic opportunism and to local prejudice; but at bottom their movement was ideological and antithetical to the regime that conservatives had established. Some of its adherents were republican ideologues who had opposed ratification of the Constitution. Others were Francophile ideologues who, inspired by the French Revolution, opposed the Washington administration because of its neutral or pro-British foreign policy. Most, however, were southerners who, steeped in the tradition of Bolingbroke and the Tory or "Country" Opposition in England—what in America would come to be the agrarian tradition—opposed the development of capitalism implicit in Hamilton's fiscal program. Their stance, though traditional, was not that of the conservative: in context, it was that of the reactionary ideologue.

Upon attaining power the Jeffersonians set out to dismantle all three of the conservatives' national institutions, and in part, for a time, they succeeded. To be sure, their fierce attack upon the Marshall Court, aimed at politicizing the law, proved a fiasco. But their efforts to emasculate the national government, conducted in the name of "restoring" the Constitution, fell little short of rendering the Constitution a nullity; and, despite the expensive Louisiana Purchase, by 1812 they had set the Hamiltonian program well in train toward extinction. Not coincidentally, in the conservative view, their efforts to impose their ideology upon the nation were accompanied for a time by wholesale suppression of civil liberties. Ultimately, however, their program of destruction was checked by the War of 1812, which made it apparent to most Americans that the Founders' national institutions were necessary, after all. During the short-lived Era of Good Feelings (1817–1825) national authority under the Constitution was reasserted, the Hamiltonian system was recreated, and state governments were held more or less in check.

The second challenge, that of Jacksonian Democracy, was soon to follow. To conservatives, the Jacksonians were a vulgarized caricature of their Jeffersonian predecessors: more opportunistic, more committed (at least rhetorically) to the Oppositionist-Agrarian-Southern ideology, and more destructive. By the time Jackson left office in 1837, the national fiscal system lay in ruins, John Marshall had been succeeded by an ardent advocate of states' rights, Roger Taney, and the presidency itself had been discredited.

The great conservatives of the era—the likes of Henry Clay, Daniel Webster, Joseph Story, Nicholas Biddle, and John Quincy Adams—were unable to stop the Jacksonian juggernaut, but out of their efforts grew a new national institution that was profoundly conservative, the modern two-party system. The genius of the new system was that, unlike the earlier Federalist-Republican polarization, it did not represent distinct positions in regard to specific programs and policies but existed solely to win elections and divide the spoils of victory. Both the Jacksonian Democratic party and the rival Whig party were coalitions of diverse groups, interests, and sections; each could accommodate people on both sides of the major political issues of the times. It was in their diversity, together with their intolerance of ideology, that their conservatism lay. By means of the party system a sense of national identity could coexist with intense localism, potentially explosive regional differences could be defused, and the turbulent forces of democracy could be prevented from veering either right or left.

There was one prospective weakness in the system. Because elections (and especially presidential elections) thenceforth took on the quality of a mixture of sporting event and mock-ritual crusade, they fanned popular emotions to a fever pitch. So long as the issues and candidates were essentially inconsequential, this agitation was harmless, even wholesome. But if ever a party should come under the control of genuine moral crusaders and win control of government, the entire social order would be in peril. Such a prospect, in 1840, seemed highly unlikely—even as, in 1788, it had seemed unlikely to James Madison that a faction could ever gain control of the diverse and plural system of government established by the Constitution.

The third great challenge, the Yankees' crusade against slavery, did to the party system what southern agrarianism had done to the constitutional order. Among nineteenth-century New Englanders, the millennialism of their Puritan forebears had drifted somewhat from its religious moorings, but it persisted in the form of pietistic perfectionism and the habit of viewing the world in apocalyptic and utopian terms. It manifested itself, during the Jeffersonian era, in sporadic secession movements and later appeared in the guises of feminism, the temperance movement, and Thoreau's anarchic individualism. By the late 1830's it had come to focus upon slavery as the root of all evil in American life; by the late 1840's it had pushed the slavery issue into national politics; and by the late 1850's it had spawned a new, radical, and purely sectional political party.

The South, cast by all this into the unaccustomed role of conservative defender of the status quo, was unable to summon an adequate defense. John C. Calhoun, who emerged as the ablest southern conservative spokesman, devised an ingenious constitutional argument designed to protect minorities from the prospect of majoritarian tyranny, but that begged the question. He and other southerners also argued that slaves lived a more humane existence than did their remote kinsmen in Africa or the wage slaves of northern factories, but that begged the question, too. Southern conservatives were caught in one of those dilemmas which sometimes, in the nature of things, overtake conservatives. Slavery was protected by the Constitution and the laws of the land and was sanctioned by custom and usage; it was an integral part of the established social order; but it denied blacks individual dignity and violated the transcending moral principle that a just order must provide the freedom necessary for personal responsibility. Moreover, the South had become a misfit: its conservatism was antithetical to the order prevailing elsewhere in the country, both because of its radical agrarianism and because of its non-liberalism. From Calhoun's conservatism there was no course open to the South except the radical one of secession.

And yet there was another side to the story. The crusade against slavery was utopian in nature: the abolitionists gave no serious prudential consideration to the long-range consequences of their program. As a result, the Civil War and emancipation not only ended slavery; they also destroyed an entire society. The principal victim of that destruction was the black freedman, who fell into a peonage in which his misery was compounded many times over.

THE DECLINE OF THE OLD ORDER AND THE SEARCH FOR A NEW

Removal of the South from the mainstream of American life had another unanticipated effect: it removed a major source of restraint upon national development. The rest of the country now went racing forward, so far and so fast that it lost its bearings. During the three decades after the Civil War, technological innovation, economic growth, urbanization, new immigration, and the rise of great corporations rent the old social order asunder.

For a generation and more, conservatives floundered helplessly amid the seas of change, knowing that something was wrong and despising it, but not understanding just what it was and having no program for correcting it. The conservatives' disorientation is epitomized by the work of the great literary figures of the Gilded Age, particularly Henry Adams. A lifelong search for some kind of order in which he could believe left Adams entirely baffled. He thought that political corruption, introduced by the Jacksonians, and materialism, awesomely stimulated and symbolized by the dynamo, had dissolved America's connections with the past, and he contemplated the future with dread.

By the mid-1890's economic depression, political corruption, working-class radicalism, and

the Populist movement made it evident that bold measures of some kind were necessary for the restoration of order. In broad terms, three options presented themselves. The first, a radical movement toward socialism, ran counter to all American tradition and gained few adherents. The second, a concerted attempt to dismantle the great units of private economic power that had emerged, was nostalgic and reactionary, but it appealed strongly to many Americans, especially those of old stock and of the middle class. The weakness in that approach was, as Theodore Roosevelt put it, that "business cannot be successfully conducted in accordance with the practices and theories of sixty years ago unless we abolish steam, electricity, big cities, and, in short, not only all modern business and modern industrial conditions, but all the modern conditions of our civilization." The third option was a revitalization of Hamiltonian conservatism, a reinvigoration of the federal government's power to channel the diversity of private activity so that it would once again flow in the interests of the public.

The philosophical and historical rationale was provided by Herbert Croly in a celebrated book, *The Promise of American Life* (1909). The Jeffersonians and Jacksonians, Croly maintained, had equated democracy with state or local autonomy and equated tyranny with central government, thus making "faith in the people equivalent to a profound suspicion of responsible official leadership" on the national level. Croly believed that Theodore Roosevelt, in the presidency just ended, had "emancipated American democracy from its Jeffersonian bondage. . . . The whole tendency of his programme is to give a democratic meaning and purpose to the Hamiltonian tradition and method." It is easy to overrate Roosevelt's achievements; and it is also easy to forget that Mark Hanna, the conservative industrialist and political manager who had engineered the election of McKinley, initiated much of the new program. Nonetheless, what Croly outlined remained at the heart of the conservative agenda during the first third of the twentieth century.

There was a neo-Jeffersonian countermovement, the New Freedom of Woodrow Wilson; but Wilson's efforts at dismantling, like those of Jefferson before him, were overcome by war. To mobilize the nation for World War I, the Wilson administration tied big government and big business together as partners, on a scale never dreamed of by either Hamilton or Theodore Roosevelt. The impetus in that direction continued during the postwar decade, reaching its climax in the ill-fated presidency of Herbert Hoover.

But if Wilson was unable to derail the conservative express in domestic affairs, he introduced into foreign affairs a utopian vision that conservatives found deeply disturbing, then and later. Wilson led the nation into war not, as was traditional, out of concern for national interests but as a holy crusade to make the world safe for democracy. In the conservative view, utopian crusades always lead to tyranny, and the fruits of American participation in the war were tyranny abroad and, for three nightmarish years, repression at home. Then there was Wilson's idealistic effort to secure world peace through the League of Nations. Participation would have violated an American tradition going back to Washington's Farewell Address, and conservatives rejected it; but the episode left an uncomfortable legacy. American conservatives had always favored close relations with Europe, for practical, prudential, cultural, and historical reasons. Now that Wilson had tied internationalism to utopianism, conservatives were forced to rethink their position. That rethinking, in time, would lead many of them toward isolationism.

THE DECLINE AND REBIRTH OF CONSERVATISM, 1933–1980

Then came the New Deal and World War II: the years from 1933 to 1945 brought a revolution in America. It is true that Franklin D. Roosevelt, who presided over the revolution, believed in God and country and the American Way; that his radical rhetoric often masked traditional policies; that his administration expressly rejected extremist alternatives to capitalism and democracy; and that the revolution in America was a moderate affair in comparison with what happened during those years in much of the world. Nonetheless, in domestic affairs the Roosevelt administration laid the foundations for or brought into being redistributive taxation, the welfare state, and gigantic government essentially unchecked by the Constitution; and inter-

nationally it committed the United States to a defense of utopian human rights through an equally utopian United Nations organization. The new statism and internationalism came to be called, inappropriately enough, liberalism.

Conservatives, meanwhile, were fighting a desperate and almost entirely ineffectual rear-guard action. Herbert Hoover shrilly—and yet, postwar conservatives believed, prophetically—declared that the New Deal was leading the nation to ruin, but few listened. Conservative northern Democrats, led by Alfred E. Smith and the Du Ponts, formed the Liberty League to proclaim the same message, with similar results. A "conservative coalition" of southern Democrats and northern Republicans gained control of Congress in 1938, but its braking power was limited and short-lived. The America First Committee, a strange alliance of conservatives and old midwestern radicals, made a massive effort to prevent the United States from becoming involved in another Wilsonian international crusade, but the attack on Pearl Harbor silenced that movement. And, being patriots, conservatives were scarcely able to protest the enormous but supposedly temporary growth of the federal government during the war years. By 1945 "conservative" had become a dirty word in America, interchangeable with "old fogy" if not with "heartless reactionary" or even "fascist."

Yet a conservative renascence had already begun, and by 1955 it could be said that the new conservatism was a "movement," although a fledgling one. This renascence had three sources and took three forms: classical liberalism, traditionalism, and anticommunism. The first two were, in the early stages, essentially dissenting intellectual movements; the third swept the country politically.

The impetus for the revival of classical liberalism came in 1944 with the publication of works by two Austrians, Ludwig von Mises and his student Friedrich A. Hayek. Mises' books, *Omnipotent Government* and *Bureaucracy,* were ponderous but persuasive defenses of the proposition that freedom was possible only under a laissez-faire economic system. Hayek's *The Road to Serfdom* was a small, dramatic polemic against socialism; it contended that "central direction of all economic activity according to a single plan" inevitably necessitated "dictatorship" and "suppression of freedom." To prevent such a calamity, Hayek espoused a return to "the abandoned road" of individualism and classical liberalism. *The Road to Serfdom* elicited fierce critical opposition, but it was also a sensational popular success, especially after *Reader's Digest* produced a condensed edition that sold more than a million copies. During the next few years, a handful of American journalists, intellectuals, and economists took up the cry; and by the early 1950's, though Harry Truman's Fair Deal had moved the country further down the "road to serfdom," a sizeable body of respectable opposition literature had come into existence.

The traditionalist revival was taking place at the same time and, in considerable measure, for the same reason, namely, a reaction to the horrors of World War II. The traditionalists—the most influential being Richard M. Weaver, Russell Kirk, Eric Voegelin, Peter Viereck, Leo Strauss, and Thomas Molnar—were intellectually and spiritually preoccupied with what they perceived as the impending demise of Western civilization. Somewhere along the line, they believed, Western man had taken a fatal turn away from his rich Judeo-Christian and Greco-Roman heritage. They disagreed as to who or what was responsible for the turn, Machiavelli, the Reformation, the French Revolution, and John Stuart Mill being their favorite culprits; but they agreed as to the nature of the misstep. It was, as Voegelin put it, "Gnosticism," the "divinization" of society, the belief that mankind's perfection and fulfillment lay in this world and not in the hereafter.

The third source of the new conservatism, anticommunism, was a widespread political reaction to the Cold War and to sensational accusations of subversion in government; but it too had an intellectual side. Former isolationists suddenly became, during the five years after World War II, ardent internationalists, determined to arrest the "worldwide Communist conspiracy," and at home Senator Joseph McCarthy was only the most spectacular of many politicians who made demagogic capital out of tracking down "reds" and "fellow travelers." A more intellectual and ideological anticommunism emanated from a number of ex-Communists, among the more influential of whom were James Burnham, Whittaker Chambers, Will Herberg, Willmoore Kendall, and Max Eastman, who now embraced the Right as ardently as they had once embraced the Left.

These three strands of renascent conservatism were not entirely compatible. Many of the traditionalists objected to the materialism of the classical liberals and found anticommunism, or at least McCarthyism, distasteful. The classical liberals feared the enlarged power of the state that was inherent in a sustained global campaign against communism. The ex-Communist intellectuals, as ideologues, were by no means conservatives, and many of them rejected traditionalism or classical liberalism or both.

Reconciling these differences and fusing them into a single movement was largely the work of William F. Buckley, Jr., and a group of intellectuals he assembled to write, edit, and publish the conservative journal *National Review*. Buckley had, in 1951, published *God and Man at Yale,* a widely (and often angrily) reviewed and discussed book in which he contended that liberal atheism and collectivism dominated the curriculum as it was being taught at his alma mater. In 1955 he founded the *National Review,* which continued to be the leading voice of the conservative movement into the 1980's. In 1957 Russell Kirk founded *Modern Age* as a conservative scholarly forum, and other conservative organs were soon to follow.

In the late 1950's and early 1960's, the nascent conservative movement underwent an important change. Until then, believing themselves a small minority, most conservatives had been antimajoritarian and somewhat elitist, the most conspicuous exception being *National Review* senior editor Frank Meyer. Now, they began to share Meyer's belief that they could succeed in national politics. Because of general disgust with the Eisenhower administration's middle-of-the-road Republicanism and with what they regarded as the unconstitutional decisions emanating from the Supreme Court under Eisenhower's appointee Chief Justice Earl Warren, they could not agree to support Richard Nixon in 1960. But they cast their eyes on 1964. Their man was Arizona Senator Barry Goldwater, whose book *The Conscience of a Conservative* (ghostwritten by Buckley's brother-in-law L. Brent Bozell) was immensely popular in the early 1960's. Thanks largely to the organizational skills of F. Clifton White, a leader of the Draft Goldwater Committee, Goldwater captured the Republican presidential nomination in 1964, but the time was not ripe. Lyndon Johnson preempted the center, the mass media depicted Goldwater as representing a lunatic-fringe extreme Right, and the conservative candidate was buried under a landslide.

The later 1960's and early 1970's were phantasmic for conservatives—and, increasingly, for millions of other Americans as well. Vietnam, race riots, student confrontations, and the rise of a nihilistic New Left were only part of the story. Every branch of the federal government—the executive, the Congress, the Supreme Court, and a metastasized federal bureaucracy—seemed intent on destroying the constitutional, moral, and social order, and erecting in its place a standardless, tasteless, egalitarian utopia. Nor did things improve under Nixon's presidency, though Nixon had portrayed himself as a "Disraeli conservative" in 1968: the rioting and the demonstrations abated, but détente, price controls, and a rapid growth of welfarism alienated most conservatives even before the Watergate scandal brought about Nixon's disgrace and political demise.

Yet from all the turmoil came a dramatic development that reinvigorated the conservative movement: a massive political realignment and the emergence of neoconservatism. Leading members of the Jewish intellectual community—in particular, Norman Podhoretz, Irving Kristol, Nathan Glazer, Midge Decter, and Sidney Hook—became disenchanted with liberalism's shift away from seeking equality of opportunity to seeking equality of results, from espousing freedom to favoring bureaucratic statism, from combating communism to assuming that the worldwide drift to totalitarianism and socialism was inevitable. Infused with fresh blood and brainpower, conservatism finally overcame the negative image that had long burdened it. Liberalism had been the program "with a heart"; now conservatives and neoconservatives blasted liberals with an onslaught of studies demonstrating that liberal remedies for the problems of the poor, the dispossessed, and the racial and ethnic minorities had worsened the maladies they had sought to cure and had created monstrous new ones in the bargain.

In 1980, for the first time in a half-century, the American voters elected a bona fide conservative to the presidency. Naïvely underestimating the

barriers to change posed by entrenched power blocs in Washington, most conservatives set their expectations as high as their hopes. Many, accordingly, felt betrayed when Ronald Reagan failed to work miracles—or, for that matter, seemed unable to accomplish much of anything.

But few despaired. Conservatism was no longer, as John Stuart Mill had once sneered, "the stupid party"; that label, conservatives believed, now applied to their gnostic opponents. In the long range, they could hope, the rightward shift of America's intellectual power would prove more important than what happened in the short run in the political arena. For, as Richard Weaver had written in 1948, ideas have consequences.

BIBLIOGRAPHY

William F. Buckley, Jr., ed., *Did You Ever See a Dream Walking? American Conservative Thought in the Twentieth Century* (Indianapolis, 1970), is a useful primary source as well as an introduction to modern American conservatism. Jeffrey Hart, *The American Dissent: A Decade of Modern Conservatism* (Garden City, N.Y., 1966), is a survey of the various views of *National Review* contributors during the magazine's formative years. Russell Kirk, *The Conservative Mind, From Burke to Santayana* (Chicago, 1953), a pioneer work in the traditionalist revival, is regarded by many as the most eloquent and definitive statement on the subject. Frank S. Meyer, *In Defense of Freedom: A Conservative Credo* (Chicago, 1962), is a vital "fusionist" work advocating a middle way between the several strands of post-1945 conservatism—but one that was attacked by both traditionalists and extreme libertarians. George H. Nash, *The Conservative Intellectual Movement in America, Since 1945* (New York, 1976), is an indispensable survey, both sympathetic and critical, that is likely to become a classic. Norman Podhoretz, ed., "What Is a Liberal—Who Is a Conservative? A Symposium," in *Commentary*, 62 (September 1976), contains essays—some brilliant, some less so—by sixty-four distinguished intellectuals representing nearly the entire American political spectrum.

Clinton L. Rossiter, *Conservatism in America: The Thankless Persuasion*, 2nd ed. rev. (New York, 1962), is a survey covering the full range of American history—excellent to 1865, weaker from then until 1945, not nearly on a par with Nash's work after 1945. David L. Schaefer, Jr., "The Legacy of Leo Strauss: A Bibliographical Introduction," in *Intercollegiate Review*, 9 (Summer 1974), is a useful survey of the works of the eminent political philosopher, though one which, unfortunately, does not apprise the reader that many conservatives find the Straussian approach unsatisfactory. Peter Viereck, *Conservatism: From John Adams to Churchill* (Princeton, 1956), is broader even than its title suggests and contains a number of crucial documents. Eric Voegelin, *Science, Politics, and Gnosticism* (Chicago, 1968), one of the most influential of the seminal traditionalist studies, argues powerfully that the source of Western decadence is to be found in the Middle Ages. Richard M. Weaver, *Ideas Have Consequences* (Chicago, 1948), presents traditionalism arrived at through the agrarian perspective; it is regarded by many as the source and origin of the contemporary American conservative movement.

[*See also* HISTORIOGRAPHY OF AMERICAN POLITICAL HISTORY; AMERICAN REVOLUTION; ANTEBELLUM REFORM; CONSTITU-TION; DECLARATION OF INDEPENDENCE; EGALITARIANISM; ENGLISH AND EUROPEAN POLITICAL INHERITANCE; FEDERALISM; THE FEDERALIST PAPERS; INDIVIDUALISM AND CONFORMITY; JACKSONIAN DEMOCRACY; JEFFERSONIAN DEMOCRACY; LAISSEZ-FAIRE; LIBERALISM; NEW DEAL; NEW FREEDOM; PLURALISM; POLITICAL PARTIES; PROGRESSIVISM; RADICALISM; REPUBLICANISM; *and* SLAVERY, SECTIONALISM, AND SECESSION.]

CONSPIRACY AND CONSPIRACY THEORIES

William W. Freehling

HAS a peculiarly American style of paranoid thought been the cause of the great public events in our history? Only in recent times would important professional historians have answered yes. Earlier in the twentieth century, scholars characteristically found their political causes in clashes of great material interests rather than in delusions of cranky paranoiacs. Revolution, Constitution, Civil War, populism, progressivism, and New Dealism—all were interpreted as growing out of highly practical wars between British mercantilists and colonial merchants, between creditors and debtors, between slave-labor capitalists and free-labor entrepreneurs, between the business community and the rest of society. When early-twentieth-century historians deviated from emphasizing the clash of interests, they usually stressed some highly rational conflict-of-belief systems. Irrational roots of behavior, when emphasized, characteristically took the form of cynical political manipulators using propaganda to gull the inflamed multitude. In this propaganda version of the "interest" theory of American history, the propagandist rationally pursuing his own political interest, not the irrational propaganda he employed, became the cause of political disruption.

In the late 1940's, with the rise of Senator Joseph R. McCarthy, some frightened academics began calling the irrational the key to the peculiar history of the United States. Although McCarthy and his threat to free thought and academic liberty were the immediate cause of this new "paranoia" interpretation, a certain growing sophistication of political historians and an alienation of the sophisticated from mass popular culture were also involved. Earlier historians emphasizing "interest" politics, such as Charles Beard, Vernon Parrington, Frederick Jackson Turner, and Arthur Schlesinger, Sr., had themselves identified with an alleged great popular interest being assaulted by Englishmen, slaveholders, or plutocrats. Historians fighting the people's battles had no trouble calling the crusades holy and the enemy real.

But in the years after World War II, Richard Hofstadter, the founder of the "paranoid" school of interpretation, drew back with a shudder from mainstream "gaucheries." Through Hofstadter's cynical eyes, American popular culture became cranky, weird, dangerous—a hotbed of irrationalities worthy of a psychiatrist's couch.

Hofstadter's shudder at McCarthy's paranoid public also stemmed from his rejection of previous, historically simplistic explanations. To a thinker as subtle as Hofstadter, the old "interest" explanation seemed hopelessly superficial. American history could hardly have been a battle between rich and poor, for the rich were divided among themselves and would have been swamped by the more numerous poor. Furthermore, the rich vs. poor clash left out the most numerous body of Americans, the great middle class. The old ideological explanation of a great clash of world views also seemed naïve to Hofstadter. Could a public so gullible as to cheer McCarthy be moved by rational philosopher-statesmen?

As for the old propaganda theory, it was closest to Hofstadter's new sophistication but put the emphasis in the wrong place. If propaganda moved the multitude, then the propaganda—and the crazed capacity of the masses to be moved—was the true cause and required the deepest explanation. The propagandist, once called the cause, was only the precipitator and was himself, Hofstadter thought, often a genuine believer in the irrational stuff of his own devising.

Out of the McCarthyite moment and the Hofstadterite ascent from the vulgarities of the American public grew an influential new theory, emphasizing the irrational. To a generation of readers coming of age in the late 1940's, Hofstadter's emphasis on a peculiarly conspiratorial tradition was a fresh and exciting alternative to the tired and simplistic "interest," "rational," and "propaganda" interpretations. The tradition continues in the work of Bernard Bailyn on the American Revolution and David Brion Davis on antebellum culture. Historians now can offer a rounded explanation of every great event in American history as a deluded response to imagined danger.

The conspiratorial theory has merit. It recognizes that inflamed rhetoric is not cynical manipulation but a barometer of a culture's thought. It catches hold of the great truth that what a culture thinks is happening, not what is really happening, ultimately moves the culture to action. It emphasizes that what we perceive has much to do with our capacity to misperceive. And it seizes on that irrational fury which even the most rational causes often need to endure and overcome.

But the conspiratorial interpretation has so many problems that it seems destined to become a supplemental rather than the central element of a late-twentieth-century, sophisticated reinterpretation of the past. First, Hofstadter and his followers have not even tried to demonstrate that the conspiratorial mentality is peculiarly American. In fact, notions of conspiracies against (or by) the established order are rampant in the record of every modern nation state—and premodern, too, for that matter. That those who would subvert or crush must organize in secret and plot with stealth is simply the sense of the matter everywhere, whether in Revolutionary France or Hitlerite Germany—or the "paranoid" United States.

Second, the conspiracy theory, like all accounts of the process of perception that emphasize only the perceiver, separates the historian and his or her reader from the other half of the perceptual process, that is, what is being perceived. What there is to be seen, not just the peculiar way we perceive it, forms what we see. If Americans have often thought they saw plots against liberty, perhaps antilibertarian campaigns (at least as the perceiver defined liberty) were being deployed. "Conspiratorial" beliefs, in short, can lead the historian to real dangers, even to real conspiracies, although these are more often likely to be diffuse threats rather than tightly organized plots.

Finally, the conspiratorial interpretation tends to overlook the counterconspiratorial tradition, the resistance to believing in a plot and the inclination to draw back from unsubstantiated delusions. If Americans, like other people, have had a long history of belief in plots, especially against liberty, they have also had a long history of moving rather quickly in revulsion against conspiratorial prophets whose fancied plots were too poorly substantiated. The swift repudiation of McCarthy, the man who set Hofstadter to writing, is a classic case in point.

Let us, then, look at some of the great conspiratorial notions that have seized the imagination of part of the American public. These frenzied perceptions will lead us straight to what Americans worried most passionately about. But let us not assume that worries are necessarily delusions, or that the undeluded will not fight back, or that Americans are more deluded than other folk. Let us, in short, see where frenzied rhetoric arose, how long it lasted, and whether, when long-lasting, it had a substantial basis in fact.

As Bernard Bailyn has emphasized (1967), theories of a conspiracy against liberty were rampant at the very beginning of the American national experience. The revolutionaries struck for independence in the belief that a tight coterie in Parliament was plotting against American liberty. The series of revolutionary events—Stamp Act, sugar tax, quartering troops in American homes, suspending the New York legislature, closing Massachusetts town meetings, and all the rest—indicated an antilibertarian pattern so persistent as to "prove" that Parliament plotted to produce tyranny.

Bailyn found the origins of this "paranoia" in the mind-set that colonists brought to the controversy. Colonists had been reading English left-wing propagandists such as John Trenchard and Thomas Gordon, who taught them to see any act against the populace as part of a long-range antilibertarian plot of the establishment. Through the Trenchard-Gordon lens, Bailyn believed, British action was seen as such an antilibertarian conspiracy as to demand revolution.

The conspiratorial interpretation of the American Revolution helpfully clarifies the violence impelling the colonists forward. But were they really deluded? Was what they "saw" purely a product of the Trenchard-Gordon lens through which they suspiciously viewed the established order?

The colonists' view of a tightly organized English plot does seem off target. The pre-Revolutionary English policy—passing acts and repealing them, restricting liberty and easing the restrictions—indicated that the rulers were uncertain and divided about how to deal with fractious colonists. But the basic vision driving the parliamentary majority, whenever it came down hard on the colonists' fancied "rights," was that local self-rule in the colonies was a privilege, not a right, that had to be denied whenever it interfered with Parliament's right to rule. That parliamentary mentality produced the so-called Intolerable Acts, and those centralizing acts intolerably violated the colonists' conception of local liberty at its source. The "violations," furthermore, were indeed passed after secret planning, if not by the whole Parliament then clearly by the ministry in secret cabinet.

Englishmen passed these acts, in part, because they believed that Americans conspired. The English conspiratorial mind-set, understandably ignored by those who would make the conspiratorial mentality peculiarly American, led to the conviction that a small coterie of colonists, based in Boston and led by Samuel Adams, plotted to escape English authority. The English conspiratorial vision, like the American, overstated the organized coherence of the opponent's movements. American resistors, like English consolidators, waffled and were divided. But English authorities were perfectly right in believing that colonists plotted to escape the English definition of centralized liberty, that the campaigns of outfits such as the Sons of Liberty for local liberty were planned in private, that the planning centered in Boston, and that Samuel Adams loved to conspire.

Ultimately, revolution came because both sides learned from a stream of objective events that fears that the other side would insist on a contervailing definition of liberty were not paranoia but fact. At the root of the event was not the paranoia but the two colliding, insistent versions of what liberty entailed. Throughout the rising stream of events, the colonial opponents of revolution and the English opponents of repression kept insisting that the other side was not that bad, that conceptions of conspiracy were overblown, that rational men could arrive at a mutually acceptable conception of liberty. These doubters of conspiracy failed to defuse the confrontation because at every defusion, some new explosion reiterated the difference between "plotters" on both sides of the Atlantic. Events out there to be perceived gave the perceiver enough material to think that the "conspiratorial" threat to his conception of liberty was not wholly fanciful.

The American Revolution offers a jewel-like model of the "American" tradition of conspiratorial thought. The tradition, beginning in England with Trenchard and Gordon, is not at all "American." Conspiratorial thought is most likely to flare up at a threat to democratic liberty, especially of the local sort, for that is Americanism at its source. The conspiratorial mentality is likely to exaggerate the degree of organized coherence in the opponent. Men decrying conspiracy are likely to play on the exaggerations to bring the public scene back to quiet rationalism. These dousers of the flames may prevail unless mounting evidence of threats keeps on sustaining conspiratorial fears. But with enough proof of a campaign against everything they hold dear, Americans, like any people, will act as if a conspiracy existed.

Just as conspiratorial theories abounded when independence was established, so inflamed theories of plots against liberty flourished in the midst of the first political parties. In the 1790's, during the struggle between Jeffersonian Republicans and Hamiltonian Federalists, both sides accused each other of joining European conspiracies against the two parties. The differing accusations pointed to very real differences in conceptions of liberty in organized society. But the accusations of a difference so great as to coalesce with European scoundrels were not sufficiently accurate to be long sustained.

The Federalists' conspiratorial theory waxed with the undeclared war with France in 1798–1800 and waned shortly thereafter. The French Revolution was the great event of the era and, to the Federalists, the most frightful. Rumors of horrid conspiracies swept Jacobinic France. One of the more savage supposed plots, publicized in Great Britain by John Robison of the University of Edinburgh, involved the Order of the Illuminati. The Illuminati, preached Robison, was a secret international organization, born in Bavaria, flourishing in France, and plotting to escalate the Revolution and destroy marriage, church, school, and state throughout the Western world.

In the United States, the Reverend Jedidiah Morse of Boston was most responsible for publicizing the alleged Illuminati. Morse charged that Jeffersonians were joining in the international plot to destroy Christian society and establish freethinking, individualistic anarchy. More extreme Federalists probably believed the thesis and, at any rate, used it to urge that President John Adams wield the Alien and Sedition Acts. Adams was asked to jail Jeffersonian extremists who claimed to oppose only war with France but were actually against anything that would stand in the way of French revolutionary excesses.

The Illuminati thesis flourished far more extensively (and had a greater basis in reality) in Europe, where it originated, than in the United States, where it supposedly was part of an American conspiratorial tradition. The notion was picked up, if with less fervor, in the United States because it touched the Federalists' worse fears about Jeffersonians. The Federalists were at their strongest in New England's tight-knit towns; their ideology called for a tighter-knit national community; and they worried that Jeffersonian libertarianism would carry American individualistic liberty into an assault on all established institutions. The most holy institution in New England remained churches such as Morse's. Jeffersonians were known to be less than passionate about organized religion and, at their fringes, atheists and freethinkers. In the Jeffersonian hostility for war with France, Federalists caught a whiff of French excesses all too likely to be Illuminati-inspired.

President John Adams, alas, caught no such scent. A classic example of American resistance to conspiratorial thought, he shared the extreme Federalists' sense that Jeffersonians were tending to be overly antireligious and anarchical. But he doubted that the tendency went so far as plotting with the Illuminati, and he refused to throw the opposition leaders in prison. He allowed them to crusade against Federalism and to unseat him in what the Jedidiah Morses of the Federalist camp were afraid would be the "Revolution of 1800."

The unrevolutionary winners thanked Adams for his restraint by accusing him of joining their own version of a conspiracy against republicanism. Federalists, they claimed, plotted to make the American president an English king and to establish a quasi-English church throughout the nation. The accusation made sense to a Jeffersonian mentality strongest in the southern plantation states, in which the individual planter, not the organized church, was the essence of established rule. Jeffersonians wished to keep a national community sustained by a national state to a minimum, to avoid all established churches, and to scotch Federalists' alleged monarchical tendencies. In the Federalists' war with libertarian France and their alliance with monarchical England, Jeffersonians thought they saw the need to win the American Revolution again.

President Jefferson suspected the "disloyal" opposition but was ultimately as tolerant of it as Adams had been. No heads rolled in the Revolution of 1800. The president announced in his inaugural address that we are all Jeffersonians, all Federalists. Hard evidence of extensive Federalist monarchical plotting was lacking. Exaggerated notions of conspiracy faded away. Wild rhetoric was replaced by that very real struggle between a more communitarian and a more individualistic conception of liberty that had fed conspiratorial belief. But conspiratorial fears had not been sustained sufficiently to lead either side to violent revolutionary—or to reactionary—action.

In the late 1820's, a new theory of conspiracy spread over the American prairies. The conspirators this time were supposedly Masonic lodges, secretly plotting to take over American democracy. Masonic demons had allegedly kidnapped and murdered one William Morgan in New York in 1826. It was believed that they intended to kidnap more, kill more, and destroy everything opposing their takeover of democracy. Allegedly, their ultimate goal was to replace the open procedures of democracy with the closed caucuses of a Masonic lodge.

Anti-Masonry was the fastest growing American political idea in the late 1820's. Anti-Masons captured several state governments and held the first national political convention in 1831. The message of the convention was that political decisions, to be democratic, must be taken in the open air. That the idea of a public convention was ultimately to degenerate into the institutional setting for rubber-stamp nominations made in smoke-filled back rooms was an irony cruelly unfair to the impetus of this crusade for a wide-open democracy.

Masons had evidently conspired to murder William Morgan lest he divulge their secrets. But the deeper source of Anti-Masonic rhetoric was the burgeoning movement to take decision-making away from the elite in private caucuses and give it to the people to control. In the late 1820's, Andrew Jackson was acquiring a stranglehold on that movement. His opponents were fatally compromised by association with John Quincy Adams, who had been "undemocratically" elected in the House of Representatives' "Corrupt Bargain" election of 1824. The Anti-Masonic idea gave incipient Whigs such as William Seward and Thurlow Weed the freedom to break away from undemocratic associations. They could express an anti-Jacksonian lust for open-air politics by roasting the closed, secret Masonic lodges.

The Whig movement could begin, but could not command, on the Anti-Masonic basis. As with the Bavarian Illuminati, the countervailing national inclination to disbelieve in conspiracies was too strong for a conspiratorial notion not sufficiently proved. If Masonic lodges were indeed secret, they could not be shown to be extensive plotters against American liberty. To grow beyond its initial spurt, the Anti-Masonic movement had to be incorporated into a new anticonspiratorial libertarian movement, this time against "King Andrew's" alleged plot to crush American freedom.

The King Andrew conspiracy theory fed on the far greater use of presidential power by Andrew Jackson than by any of his predecessors. Jackson's wielding of the veto, his seizure of national bank funds, his putting the people's cash in his own pet banks all added up, so said Whigs, to executive despotism. The people had not elected Jackson to do such things. His crimes against the public had all been hatched in secret Kitchen Cabinet meetings.

Once again the Whig conspiratorial thought was based on real concerns about liberty: excessive presidential power and extensive secret meetings. But once again the basis for the charges was insufficient. Jackson had not been elected to slay the Bank of the United States, but he thought he was expressing the popular will by drawing his sword. He was right. The people triumphantly reelected their hero in 1832 and confirmed his hand-picked successor, Martin Van Buren, in 1836.

Jackson won partly by publicizing his own conspiratorial notion. Jackson accused the president of the "monster bank," Nicholas Biddle, of conspiring to control the people's money even though the public had never elected Biddle to anything. The monster-bank conspiracy thesis was remarkably close to the King Andrew conspiracy thesis and the Masonic conspiracy thesis; all of them accused plotters of taking decisions out of the public's hands. The three theories, taken together, are a window onto the United States' gravest concerns amid the hatching of the more democratic politics of the Age of Jackson.

Jackson's version of the conspiratorial mentality won hands down. The president secured such an overwhelming victory as to make the name of the era his own. But the very completeness of his victory made his conspiratorial charge a one-shot affair. The slain monster bank was not the continuing enemy to confirm a sustained plot against the people's control over their own decisions. Whigs, desperate to capture the banner of popular democracy as their own, continued to search for a new plot against the people's liberties. In the early 1850's, in the Roman Catholic church, they found the new villain.

The name of the new movement was the Know-Nothings, so called because the Know-Nothings, when asked what they advocated, denied that they knew anything. But the Know-Nothings knew very well that their central thrust was to destroy immigrant influence on American democracy. Between 1840 and 1860, the first great wave of new immigrants from non-English-speaking countries came to American shores—over four million Germans, Irish, Italians, and other Europeans. Most voted Democratic, when they voted at all.

Whiggish agitators saw in this wave of "non-Americans," unpracticed in American democracy, another possible subversion of popular traditions. The Know-Nothing solution was a long delay in enfranchising the newcomers. Their fear was that unprincipled demagogues would infect inexperienced peasants; their terror was that the pope would control where spoilsmen couldn't. Know-Nothings painted a portrait of the emperor of the Vatican, to whom American Catholics owed primary allegiance, as secretly directing and destroying the American republic.

The Know-Nothing movement was the fastest growing new political crusade since the Anti-Masons of the 1830's. Once again, the conspiratorial theory fed on Whiggish belief that demagogic Jacksonians were the real enemy of the people and were themselves the puppets of secret forces. But once again, the conspiratorial vision could go only so far. The pope obviously was not controlling; immigrants obviously were not subverting. The countervailing American capacity to disbelieve in unproved conspiracy once again dispelled a surging movement.

Custodians of the Whig consciousness again had to melt into a larger movement; but this time they seized on a conspiratorial enemy more obvious in the factual record than anything since the "antilibertarian" Englishmen of 1776. Since the 1830's, important Whigs such as John Quincy Adams had been fulminating about a slave-power conspiracy against white men's liberty. The event that set Adams off was the House of Representatives' decision in 1836 to table, without debate, antislavery petitions. This Gag Rule was passed by the national Democratic party at the insistence of its southern wing. Adams charged that this so-called Democratic party was ruled by slaveholders; that the slavocracy, to control blacks, secretly conspired against white men's right of petition; and that the conspiracy would soon take the form of plots to grab Texas and more territories for the South. When a southern president, John Tyler, and his southern secretary of state, John C. Calhoun, did in fact annex Texas in 1844–1845, and when the southern President James Polk gobbled up huge segments of Mexico in 1845–1849, Adams' prophecy was fulfilled. When Stephen A. Douglas' Kansas-Nebraska Act of 1854 opened up formerly free-soil Kansas for potential southern settlements, the slave-power-conspiracy thesis came into its own.

This thesis was the property of the old Whigs and the old Know-Nothings, now merged with free-soil Democrats in the new Republican party. Republicans noted that every piece of proslavery legislation—the Gag Rule, Texas annexation, Fugitive Slave Law, Kansas-Nebraska Act—was passed by the old Jacksonian so-called Democratic party, at the insistence of its southern wing. Southerners, a minority in the nation, were a majority in the Democratic party, which in turn had a national majority. The slave-power minority, according to the charge, used its party leverage to dominate the white majority. The slave-power strategies were hatched in secret. The slave-power minority acted as one man. The conspiracy would save tyranny over blacks by tyrannizing whites in the Union if it could, and by disunion if the plot to enslave whites failed.

Southerners hurled back their own charge of conspiracy. Slaveholders claimed that abolitionists plotted in secret to destroy slavery; that Adams, when arguing that he sought only white men's right to petition, was a fraud. Adams was secretly using this argument, they claimed, in league with his organized puritan cronies, to discredit slaveholders and wear them down.

As in the American Revolution, both cries of conspiracy exaggerated the organized planning of the other side. The Republican party was in fact no sustained abolitionist conspiracy but a motley crew of northerners united only in their distaste for the South's "undemocratic" power over them. Still, secret abolitionists in the party—John Quincy Adams had indeed been one—did plot to escalate the crusade for white men's rights into a campaign against black men's enslavement. Moreover, the Republican determination to stop any new national laws protecting slavery could by itself weaken slavery, especially where it was already weak, in the northernmost slave states. If the Republican party was not primarily an abolitionist plot, southerners were hardly paranoid in seeing a danger from the North.

Nor did slaveholders form a solid block. The South's masters were badly split on every issue, and slavery's more extreme spirits could never rally a majority. But in the South as in the North, the more moderate were stiffening. Southern white men, like American colonists, were worried about local liberty as they defined it, which meant to them liberty to use the national government to strengthen local black slavery. North and South were on a collision course on this issue, which conspiratorial theories exaggerated but also correctly indicated. With the election of Lincoln, the collision came.

The catastrophe again indicated when worries about conspiracies against liberty could and could not long prevail. Just as it had taken a long and obvious string of English acts to confirm colonial theories about antilibertarian plots, so it took a long and obvious string of southern pro-slavery legislation to confirm northern theories about slave-power maneuvers. When the string of proofs was not forthcoming—as with the Illuminati, the Masons, and the pope—the nation doubted, and the shooting star of a movement faded. The inclination toward conspiratorial theorizing was guarded and subtle and capable of being defeated by its anticonspiratorial tradition whenever the doubts were massively justified.

Since the Civil War, the same tendencies toward suspecting plots have been displayed. But the alleged plots have been less against liberty than against the nation's economic and international well-being. Repeatedly in modern American reform movements, reformers have talked about Wall Street conspiracies against the poor. An alleged railroad, banking, and mercantile plot to defraud the farmers was at the center of populist rhetoric in the 1890's. Rural demagogues sometimes went so far as to call the alleged plot to control silver an international Jewish conspiracy, although most populists avoided such anti-Semitism. This thundering against the "money power"—organized, grasping, and united to squeeze the weak—was also very powerful in the rhetoric of progressives such as Robert La Follette and could even infect Franklin Delano Roosevelt's roasting of the "economic royalists."

Entrenched capitalists have had their own conspiratorial tradition. Since the Civil War, the establishment has periodically roared against socialists or communists, secretly organized in Europe or the United States, plotting to take over labor unions. Such rhetorical flights helped inspire such horrors as the Haymarket Riot of 1886 and periodic jailing of socialists in the twentieth century.

Still, without minimizing the occasional inhumanity, it is possible to see that conspiratorial thought about the dangers to capitalism is in the earlier tradition of a roar that swiftly passes into silence. Farmers have not constantly berated Shylock's control of the system. Rather, they have characteristically learned how to control the system for themselves. And capitalists have not constantly seen communists in every labor union. Rather, they have characteristically learned how to pay higher wages and glean higher profits as well.

Nor have either reformers or establishmentarians been altogether wrong in their conspiratorial thoughts. Socialists, including some of the more violent revolutionary sort, have plotted in the United States, if not as extensively as capitalists feared. And Wall Street combinations, in secret rooms, have sought their own interests, which were not always in the people's interest. The American tradition of conspiratorial thought about economics has had some basis in fact and a large tendency to evaporate when the proof is not forthcoming.

In viewing foreign policy, Americans have also espied their share of supposed conspiracies and have occasionally reacted with unmentionable ferocity. A. Mitchell Palmer's "Red Scare" of 1919–1921 was perhaps the worst early-twentieth-century example of national hysteria about an internal, international threat. Henry Ford's fulminations about an international Jewish conspiracy in the 1920's compare noxiously with Hitler's anti-Semitism before coming to power, a record perhaps bested by Father Charles E. Coughlin in the 1930's.

The great period of such conspiratorial rhetoric was, understandably, the first years of the Cold War. In the midst of the national realization that the Soviet Union was the enemy and that its spies were after our atomic secrets, the nation fell into an awful moment of seeing reds everywhere. Out of that moment grew McCarthy's obsessive red-baiting, and out of the horror came Richard Hofstadter's search for the historical roots of American conspiratorial obsessions.

But even McCarthy deserves to be put in a calmer perspective. For all the harm he did to the reputations of individuals and the climate of academic freedom, he lasted barely as long as the crazed cries about the Bavarian Illuminati, and nothing remotely as extensive as his red-baiting has been seen since. The politician who most soared initially on McCarthyite red-baiting, Richard Nixon, quickly had to bottle it up. In his most important achievement as president, the ex-redbaiter came to rapprochement with Red China.

In the wake of McCarthy, as Nixon shrewdly sensed, the American popular mentality had taken a historic swing away from giving any credence to conspiratorial rhetoric. In recent years, Americans have had a knee-jerk tendency to doubt that any conspiracy exists, lest some McCarthy return to power proclaiming plots. In circumstances that at any other time in our history would have inspired at least an initial conviction about a conspiracy and at least a full airing of the possibility, such as the murders of John F. Kennedy, Martin Luther King, and Robert F. Kennedy and the shootings of George Wallace and Ronald Reagan, Americans have almost desperately needed to believe that no conspiracy could have existed, that one crazed man must have acted alone. Official commissions have been appointed almost with the purpose of destroying all thought of a plot.

This is not to say that the various commissions' anticonspiratorial findings were wrong. It is only to point out how striking is the sigh of belief and relief that they inspired. Joseph McCarthy, because of whom Richard Hofstadter set out to discover a historical tradition of conspiratorial thought, may have left the mainstream, ironically, with only its countervailing anticonspiratorial tradition fully intact.

BIBLIOGRAPHY

Bernard Bailyn, *The Ideological Origins of the American Revolution* (Cambridge, Mass., 1967), is a vigorous exposition of the theory that fears of conspiracy caused the American Revolution. David Brion Davis, ed., *The Fear of Conspiracy: Images of Un-American Subversion from the Revolution to the Present* (Ithaca, N.Y., and London, 1971), is an anthology of various American writings about conspiracy, with an excellent introduction. Davis, *The Slave Power Conspiracy and the Paranoid Style* (Baton Rouge, La., 1969), is the most sustained argument that fears of conspiracy caused the Civil War. Richard Hofstadter, *The Age of Reform: From Bryan to F.D.R.* (New York, 1955), contains a strong exposition of the thesis that conspiratorial fears infected modern American reform rhetoric. And Hofstadter, *The Paranoid Style in American Politics, and Other Essays* (New York and London, 1965), is a rounded effort to make paranoia *the* American style.
[*See also* AMERICAN REVOLUTION; AUTHORITY; CENSORSHIP; CIVIL DISOBEDIENCE; COLLECTIVE VIOLENCE; CONTROL, SUPPRESSION, AND INTIMIDATION; IMPEACHMENT; MACHINE POLITICS; PUBLIC OPINION; *and* SOCIALISM.]

CONSTITUTION

Paul L. Murphy

THE American Constitution has existed at a number of levels and in a variety of different conceptualizations. It constitutes a living symbol around which generations of Americans have rallied. In this regard it plays somewhat the same role as the monarchy in Britain, affording a unifying focus to national unity and commitment. The Constitution has also served as a standard of moral judgment. It has been the touchstone against which the legitimacy of governmental action has been continually measured, the higher standard by which human law has been judged. But the Constitution has not been regarded as a rigid straitjacket. John Marshall early pointed out that it was "intended to endure for ages to come, and consequently to be adapted to the various crises of human affairs." This view was restated in modern terms by Franklin D. Roosevelt: "Our Constitution is so simple and practical that it is possible always to meet extraordinary needs by changes in emphasis and arrangement without loss of essential form. That is why our constitutional system has proved itself the most superbly enduring political mechanism the modern world has produced."

This brief 7,000-word document has also established a concrete manifestation of constitutionalism in America, representing a commitment to limited government and the rule of law. Its system of sanctions implements the view that government exists only to serve specified ends and properly functions only according to specified rules. The sanctions include specific concepts of limited government and, accordingly, specific kinds and techniques of limitation. They reflect early American experience as later distilled into two major principles of the Declaration of Independence: that the Constitution is supreme and derives its authority from the will of the people—"the consent of the governed"; and that a constitution should provide the major and adequate arrangements necessary to liberty, that is, should secure the inalienable rights of the people—"to secure these rights, Governments are instituted among Men."

The American Constitution, intended to be a practical instrument, has had a particularly political dimension. Because it is viewed as the final source from which concrete public policy should evolve, there has always been controversy over whether that public policy conforms to the purposes and intent of the original document and its framers. Constitutional politics in America has inevitably taken the form of an argument over the true constitutional faith and the way it can best be put into operation. The result has been to invoke the Constitution as a rationalization for action or, more frequently, until recent times, for inaction. Such constitutional dialogue has involved classes; geographical sections; ethnic, racial, religious, and gender groups; and special-interest groups from business and labor to militarists and pacifists. One of its major consequences has been that Americans have continually and instinctively assumed that to limit and channel government properly was a constitutional responsibility in which they shared.

THE DEVELOPMENT OF CONSTITUTIONALISM IN AMERICA

The unique American constitutionalism was a product of the post-1760's crisis with England. American colonists had earlier developed local self-government for most internal affairs. Such government functioned under British authorization, generally in the form of a charter. Prized as evidence of the rights and immunities belonging to all the king's subjects in America, charters acquired transcendent sanction over the years. It was assumed that they were recognized as part of the English constitution, which was thought of by Americans prior to 1760 as that which was constituted—as the arrangement of governmental institutions, laws, and customs, together with the principles and goals that animated them. The professed objective of the unwritten English constitution had been, since the days of the Stuarts, the attainment of liberty through limiting prerogative power when it became a threat to liberty. When the use of that power began to include the corruption of Parliament by the ministry, and a resultant threat to Americans' charter rights, the colonists began to see the necessity of emphasizing principles above institutions. They further came to appreciate the necessity of redefining constitutionalism as a limitation on the power of lawmaking bodies. A constitution could and should constitute a set of fixed principles and rules, distinguishable from, antecedent to, and more fundamental than the institutions of government. Such higher law should control positive acts of government providing, especially for judges, principles of interpretation to modify gross inequities and unreasonableness. Thus, before resorting to revolution as a sanction for constitutional principles, colonial leaders explored the concept of balancing power by pitting group against group to forestall usurpation. They talked of judicial review whereby laws "against reason and the constitution were void." Such sanctions of constitutionalism were difficult to use and make effective without a formal prior document. Hence, from the early 1760's calls were heard for a unique American constitutionalism embodied in a written charter as basic law.

The process of making the sentiments concrete began at the state level, with constitution-making occurring almost simultaneously with the move for independence. The first state constitutions tended to extend, with important modifications, colonial governmental structures. Legislative supremacy was the norm, with weak executives and a dependent judiciary. And while some democratization occurred, and formal bills of rights were written, the legal rights of slaves, Indians, and women remained the same or retro-

gressed. Furthermore, an important change in emphasis occurred as privatism and individualism tended to replace communal values and an earlier sense of corporate purpose, a trend noticeable constitutionally as legal forms and procedures underwriting personal freedom gained further preference over those of the interdependent local community. Growing commerce, material advancement, and rising population were other factors requiring new governmental legal institutions and a rethinking of the constitutional dimensions of self-government.

The move for a central government and a national charter occurred initially in this setting. The Articles of Confederation, which created a federated national government, were placed before the states for ratification in November 1777 and became operational in March 1781. As a constitution the Articles proved disappointing. The state constitutions had made the people the sources of political power but had channeled that power through local government. Reflecting continued fear that the British abuse of central authority might be reenacted, the national government as conceived in the Articles was so circumscribed as to be impotent. Lacking national executive, judiciary, and military forces, the central government was unable to enforce its laws. It could not directly impose its will on its citizens and therefore could not prevent violations by a state of the rights of another, nor could it conduct effective relations with foreign powers. Furthermore, the requirement of unanimous support of thirteen states for amendment of the Articles precluded strengthening the central government through normal processes.

Critical developments in the Confederation period demonstrated the necessity for a "more perfect union," based upon a more effective and practical constitution. The inability of the central government to manage the economy meant a severe dislocation of orderly commerce as commercial rivalries grew and a chaotic currency situation was further exacerbated. Breakdowns of law and order frightened conservative, propertied elements, fearful that excessive local democracy would abrogate private property rights. James Madison well expressed a common feeling when he emphasized the need for overall constitutional restrictions against "interested and overbearing" state legislative majorities, violative of the rights of property and contracts.

Thomas Jefferson, who served as governor of Virginia under the state constitution of 1776, deplored the concentration of all powers of government in the legislature. "Such a consolidation," he argued, "is precisely the definition of despotic government. An elective despotism was not the government we fought for." Similar complaints came from other state spokesmen, who issued growing denials that legislative sovereignty was the same as popular sovereignty, and questioned whether the representatives in the state legislatures were the sole or adequate spokesmen for those they presumed to represent. To many Americans, what was needed was a new constitutional structure that would serve the growth of commerce, promote orderly economic development, restore national credit, and guarantee domestic tranquility, by protecting the rights of the people from governmental and private tyranny.

Talk of revision thus grew steadily. Alexander Hamilton had been dissatisfied with the Articles from the start. Several attempts to amend them failed, and state representatives met in Mt. Vernon in 1785 and Annapolis in 1786 to consider various alternatives. The Annapolis Convention was poorly attended, but the delegates conceded that a remedy for the evils affecting commerce and trade must be found in some broader constitutional framework. They adopted a resolution calling for a further convention to "render the Constitution of the Federal Government adequate to the exigencies of the Union." Following Annapolis, the Confederation Congress responded cautiously but favorably to a resolution for a special convention so long as the "sole and express purpose" was revising the Articles. Five states named delegates in 1786. Shays's Rebellion in Massachusetts speeded the process in others. By 1787 twelve states (all except Rhode Island) had named seventy-four delegates, fifty-five of whom came to the Philadelphia Convention and thirty-nine of whom eventually signed the Constitution.

CREATING A "MORE PERFECT UNION"

The Convention of 1787, its members, their motives, and the meaning of its work have been of perennial interest to Americans seeking the roots of their constitutional origins. Controversy has abounded and will continue. It involves dispute as to what facts are most centrally pertinent; what happened, and made it happen, is not disputed. The delegates represented activist politicians committed to an effective national structure. Most of them educated, respected men of affairs, and some with considerable wealth, they had in many cases participated prominently in the unified national effort against the British in the revolutionary years, therein sublimating their local interests to the broader national cause.

George Washington (who presided over the convention), James Madison, Alexander Hamilton, James Wilson, John Jay, Rufus King, Edmund Randolph, Gouverneur Morris, Benjamin Franklin, and others had served either in the army, or as diplomats, or key administrative officers of the Confederation government, or members of its Congress. Forty-six delegates had served in colonial or state legislatures, ten had helped draft state constitutions, seven had served as state governors, and six had signed the Articles of Confederation. Clearly, they had had ample opportunities to learn about the problems that confronted the convention. In addition to their intellectual stature and public experience, they were experienced in economic affairs. Forty owned public securities; fourteen speculated in land; twenty-four lent money at interest; eleven had mercantile, manufacturing, or shipping connections; and fifteen operated plantations. Thus most were personally involved in the economic sphere that would be affected by the convention's decisions. Also, nearly two-thirds of the delegates were lawyers. And while legal education was crude, practice necessitated a respect for precedent, procedure, and precision, all of which influenced the content and style of the final document.

The intent of the group was fairly consensual. As students of comparative government, and of America's prior experience, they aimed to create a workable republican structure strong enough to establish national supremacy and to control "the turbulence and follies of democracy," but limited enough to ensure individual self-determination within a structure of ordered liberty. Their common objectives were summarized by Madison as "the necessity of providing more effectively for the security of private rights and the steady dispensation of justice.''

What divided the delegates were their views about the best road to the achievement of those objectives. By far the largest group was intent upon the creation of a genuinely national government, with adequate power to promote security, financial stability, and commercial prosperity through a centralized governmental structure. These nationalists could, on most occasions, command the support of a group of moderates, who accepted the necessity for a strong central government but were willing to compromise substantially with the conventional states' rights bloc. That bloc, a decided minority, was firmly opposed to the creation of a sovereign national government. While recognizing the need for constitutional reform, bloc members still believed that a confederation type of government should be retained and that by granting the Congress certain additional powers—above all to tax and regulate commerce—the Articles could be converted into an adequate framework of government.

The Virginia Plan, developed in advance in private meetings by members of the larger states, was promptly proposed by Edmund Randolph and put before the convention for deliberation. The plan suggested a national executive, national judiciary, and national legislature of two branches, both elected according to population. This national government was to be virtually all-powerful and act directly upon individuals instead of the states. It would possess its own agents, courts, marshals, and tax collectors and would in essence define the extent of its authority and that of the states. It could pass any laws necessary for the whole nation and could legislate ''in all cases in which the separate States were incompetent.'' The inference seemed to be that there was no limit to the national government's authority except its good judgment. A Council of Revision, made up of the president and members of the judiciary, would review all acts of Congress; but because the council was a federal agency, the states had no way of checking congressional authority. Furthermore, the plan gave Congress the power to veto or throw out any state law challenging the federal Constitution. As to sanction, the federal government was to have the power to ''call forth the force of the Union against any member . . . failing to fulfill

its duty'' under the document. Such a proposal seemed contradictory, since it had already been provided that the federal government would act directly upon the people and bypass the states. Another provision would have made state officials take an oath supporting the federal Constitution, a stipulation, like many others, bitterly offensive to localists.

These delegates, with William Paterson of New Jersey as their spokesman, first seethed and then presented a counterplan. It contained almost every feature of the Articles of Confederation but added strengthening amendments. Representation would be by state, not population, but the federal government would now tax, regulate commerce, and coerce recalcitrant states. This New Jersey Plan still failed to solve the problem of sanction, however, for it entailed potential armed intervention, no more practical a solution than that afforded in the Virginia Plan. Generally, the whole approach assumed that the federal government acted on the states and not the people. Its success would have depended upon the states' agreement and cooperation. Yet the plan did contain one clause of far-reaching importance. Under it the Constitution and all acts of the Congress became the supreme law of the land, as did treaties. The judiciary of the states was bound to uphold these even in the face of state laws to the contrary.

This plan was quickly defeated but impasse remained. The ultimate solution was found in the Great Compromise, in which each state was conceded an equal vote in the Senate, irrespective of its size, but representation in the House was to be based on the ''federal ratio,'' the number of free inhabitants plus three-fifths of the number of slaves. It was agreed that the same ratio would apply for determining state taxation, and the House was given the prerogative of introducing all fiscal legislation. The compromise had the effect of saving the convention from dissolution and laying the basis for an independent bicameral legislature acceptable to both factions.

Other compromises further eased tensions. The mercantile North was assured federal protection of trade and commerce, while the agrarian South was guaranteed permanent relief from export taxes and assurance that the importation of slaves would not be prohibited for at least twenty years. Southern and western demands for a two-thirds Senate ratification of treaties were honored with the same ratio applied in defining the proportion of senators necessary to approve executive appointments and to override the presidential vetoes of congressional legislation.

The debate on the executive had also been protracted and difficult, and its outcome again amounted to a victory for strong central government. The nationalists were determined to have a strong, independently constituted executive, and defeated a move to have the office filled by Congress. Thus the possibility of a parliamentary-cabinet form of government was precluded at the outset. But popular election created apprehensions, and the electoral college, with electors chosen by the states, was the result. It was logical that an independent judiciary should complement the independent executive. Ultimately the powers and functions of each were defined narrowly, if somewhat ambiguously. From the New Jersey Plan, the delegates retrieved the "supremacy clause." It constituted another victory for the nationalist cause, since it made the state courts an agency for enforcing federal law. This maneuver was later converted into a further instrument for nationalism when state court actions were held subject to the surveillance of the United States Supreme Court.

The sticky question of federalism, successfully dividing authority between central and local government, was finally treated by rejecting the Virginia Plan's solution and delegating explicit powers to the federal government, while leaving the residue—with some specific exceptions—to the states. States could determine the extent and nature of the suffrage. Certain areas were to be open to concurrent authority, but even here the separateness of powers and functions was reasonably delineated.

On 7 September 1787 the rough document was entrusted to a committee on style, and on 17 September the finished Constitution was engrossed and signed. Few of the framers believed that they had created a perfect instrument, but many did feel that a majority of Americans could be persuaded to accept the new Constitution.

RATIFICATION AND ACCEPTANCE

The strengths and weaknesses of the new Constitution, as a reflection of constitutionalism, were partly appreciated at the time but stood out more clearly as political leaders set out to govern. The Constitution's Framers were convinced they had obtained a judicious balance between the effectiveness of political power exercised by a central system and the distribution of power that would prevent the system from becoming tyrannical. They were also pleased with the boldness of their extension of national principles and the widened popular participation that the document presumably would induce. They saw the Constitution as endowing a workable government with successful diffusion of governmental power through territorial federalism, functional separation of power, checks and balances, and the sublimation of military to civil authority. They were convinced that constitutionalism had been served by obliging the government to observe the fundamental law. They hoped the document would allow for desirable economic growth through a system of taxing and financial powers of the federal government; a uniform, controlled monetary system; and an effective but not repressive commercial authority that would circumscribe the states in the spheres of interstate commerce, monetary affairs, and foreign trade, delimiting the economic role of state and local government.

What the Framers did not foresee was that fear of the abuse of central authority and the potential for impinging on inalienable rights was still strong; therefore, limitations on national power over individual liberties had to be spelled out more precisely. The authority and power of the federal courts, regarding judicial review and their relations with state courts, were not well defined. The nature and extent of the implied powers of Congress produced two decades of controversy. The failure to define the precise locus of sovereignty left open a door for a vigorous states' rights movement and led ultimately to the Civil War. It took the same national emergency to clarify many of the presidential powers, especially in times of crisis.

The immediate problem was ratification. The nationalists promptly moved to bypass the provision in the Articles for ratification of constitutional amendments by unanimous action of the several state legislatures. Instead, they called for ratification by conventions in the several states, stipulating that any nine would be sufficient to put the Constitution into effect. This maneuver, stressing ratification by the people but in the states, combined features of democracy and federalism. It appealed to the political feelings of Americans of the time; yet the sweeping changes that the Constitution seemed to promise excited powerful opposition.

The advantaged economic interests feared new national fiscal and commercial policy. State-based politicians feared downgrading by the creation of a powerful national government. The old small-republic sentiment aroused popular alarm that a remote and powerful central government would crush the people's liberties by becoming an instrument for aristocratic tyranny. Generally, these self-proclaimed Antifederalist heirs of the true spirit of the Revolution were convinced that the republican principle they embraced locally could not be extended to encompass all thirteen states without the creation of a type of central authority that would suppress property rights and local interests. The lack of a Bill of Rights to check such abuse seemed particularly unjustified and suspicious to them. Thus they launched campaigns against the Constitution that were sufficiently aggressive to force its champions to produce elaborate defenses.

These defenses demonstrated the political acumen of the Constitution's advocates. They involved showcasing the fact that illustrious public figures—Washington, Franklin, Madison, Jay, Hamilton, King, Pinckney, Wilson—favored ratification. They included mustering the delegates in the state ratifying conventions, who had fortuitously been chosen by state legislatures in which people most keenly aware of the deficiencies of the Confederation government were strong. They also entailed a propaganda battle, which included publishing a series of advocacy pieces on the virtue of the Constitution later collected as *The Federalist*. These essays pointed out not only the reasons for the structure but also the benefits to all Americans from its operations and the functionalism of its explicit solutions to perennial governmental problems—"a republican remedy for the diseases incident to republican government."

In formulating this popular explication, the Federalists persuasively defended their new theory of constitutional politics against the extension and vigorous assaults of its decentralist critics. Finally, the champions proved politically and parliamentarily more astute and shrewd, playing upon, as Hamilton stated, "ambition, avarice,

personal animosity, party opposition, and many more motives not more laudable than these" to finally gain their end. The pledge to secure a Bill of Rights finally brought along the essential states of Virginia and New York, and the powerful local political opposition was obliged to channel that opposition into controlling the new government.

The completed document represented an American model of constitutionalism, a composite of fundamental principles and arrangements that gave the American polity its essential character. It was partially original, partially derivative, commendably practical, and constructively open-ended. The last quality made it possible, as new circumstances arose, to infer and develop from constitutional principles new institutions, practices, and interpretations for dealing with those circumstances. The task was to judge whether proposed innovations were consistent with the basic constitutional order. This depended upon whether the innovation conformed to the essential principles of that order.

The question of which agency of government was the proper one to do that was one to which the Framers suggested only partial answers. Clearly, the amendment process was one avenue, involving congressional enactment and state ratification. Amendment has been used successfully twenty-six times in 180 years. Congress could extend adaptability through statutory enactments. Similarly, executive action could afford new rules and mechanisms for confronting new challenges. But who was to say whether such positive law squared with constitutional provisions and principles? Was Congress to police itself? Would the executive be the judge of the constitutionality of its own action? Or would the judiciary, most particularly the Supreme Court, have this role? On this the document was silent.

However, clear inferences existed. Only laws "made in pursuance" of the Constitution were to stand with the Constitution as the "supreme law of the land," and "the judicial Power shall extend to all Cases . . . arising under this Constitution." This meant, as Hamilton argued in *The Federalist* number 78, that "the interpretation of the laws is the proper and peculiar province of the courts." From this was eventually hammered out a theory of judicial review that institutionalized the theory of constitutionalism and made the Supreme Court the major instrument for applying that theory. The acceptance of this principle was not achieved without a struggle, and the principle itself has remained a focus of controversy throughout the nation's history. For while many judges have been paragons of detachment and objectivity, many have not, and all have been subject to human bias, prejudice, and contemporary political pressure. This has made the attainment of absolute neutrality difficult and put the judiciary in the political arena almost from the outset, since its critics have generally sought not its neutrality but its beneficent partiality.

CONSTITUTIONAL GOVERNING: SEVENTY CONTENTIOUS YEARS, 1790–1860

Following ratification, Congress quickly moved to erect the strong national government that the Constitution had envisioned. It began with a Judiciary Act in 1789, which created a federal judicial system, emphasizing the principle of national supremacy, determining federal court procedure, and defining federal state jurisdiction. It went on to charter a National Bank, fund the states' Revolutionary War debts, set up a system of protective tariffs, impose excise taxes directly upon the people, pass navigation laws favoring American over foreign shipping, and create a national army and navy.

Antifederalists viewed such actions skeptically, arguing that they raised disturbing constitutional concerns over basic concepts of fundamental law, national power, popular sovereignty, local democracy, and generally over the proper meaning of republicanism. This first crucial decade of the Constitution's implementation saw bitter controversy arise over such specific issues as the nature of the Constitution's implied powers and particularly the meaning of the "necessary and proper" clause. The controversy centered on Jeffersonian contentions denying the necessity and the constitutionality of the Bank of the United States, a position refuted strongly and successfully by Alexander Hamilton. Conversely, local interests successfully challenged a Supreme Court decision (*Chisholm* v. *Georgia,* 1793) upholding the right of a citizen of one state to sue another state in a federal court. Alarmed by this judicial assertion of national power, states' rights advocates fought successfully in Congress to abrogate the decision, with the Eleventh Amendment (1798) as a result.

But in the area of foreign policy, the nationalists won the struggle. President Washington, through assertion and a broad view of the powers of the presidency, established presidential prerogative in the conduct of foreign policy. The Supreme Court, in a case involving a Virginia law in conflict with a federal treaty regarding debts owed by Virginia (*Ware* v. *Hylton,* 1797), established an important, although challenged, precedent that state laws are subordinate to treaties made by the United States. The Federalists, however, were unwilling to stop with such centralist victories and pushed their partisanship to extremes in the Alien and Sedition Acts of 1798, imposing federal criminal penalties on opponents of their policies under the guise of national security. Viewing these acts not only as a frontal assault on the Bill of Rights but also as a dangerous extension of governmental centralization, the Antifederalists replied with the Kentucky and Virginia resolutions, setting forth a classic constitutional argument on behalf of individual liberties, strict construction ("no submission to undelegated authority"), and states' rights. Although such opposition did not produce immediate legal victories, it produced political ones, rallying Americans behind Thomas Jefferson (one of the resolutions' authors) in his successful campaign for the presidency in 1800. The outcome of the election was confusing, given the lack of constitutional recognition of political parties, and led to the enactment of the Twelfth Amendment to the Constitution in 1803, implicitly integrating the two-party system into election procedures.

The cumulative result of the decade saw constitutional battle lines drawn, with nationalist victories achieved but with a professed anticentralist party in control of the government. Before that control went into effect, one further centralist act occurred that had long-range consequences. In 1801, before leaving office, President John Adams appointed a new chief justice, John Marshall, and a number of Federalist judges to the lower courts. Although Jeffersonian critics complained that the Federalists, having lost at the polls, were now retreating into the judiciary, immediate constitutional remedies for such a political retreat were not available.

During the period from the ascension of Mar-

CONSTITUTION

shall to the North's ultimate victory in the Civil War, the true nature of the Union and its relation to the Constitution formed a major bone of contention in public debate. Was the Constitution an instrument condoning central authority or encouraging local diversity and minority rights? The battle lines, while generally drawn along sectional and class lines, were nonetheless mobile. Those in power defended central authority on national grounds, and those out of power turned to states' rights or decentralist arguments. Thomas Jefferson, having earlier deplored excessive national authority, purchased Louisiana while president, thereby doubling the size of the nation. He defended on broad construction grounds the right to acquire such foreign territory and to admit it to statehood without altering the nature of the Union unconstitutionally. He went on to use federal authority to impose a destructive embargo on American shipping to forestall hostilities on the high seas. Such policies were bitterly opposed by northern Federalists, who considered them damaging to the special interest of their region and constituents.

Although periodically losing temporary skirmishes, the nationalists basically won the "war," and the nationalist character of the Union was established. In this struggle, the rhetorical role of the Constitution as a unifying symbol was substantial. Congressional debate, executive pronouncements, and the theories of influential statesmen and party leaders embodied significant constitutional doctrine. The Supreme Court, while adjudicating constitutional issues, was not accepted as the ultimate and single authority on the subject of constitutionality until the end of the period. Thus rulings of the Marshall and Taney courts were open to challenge and subjected to popular pressures regarding proper constitutionalism.

John Marshall, as the skillful leader of an activist, nationalistic Supreme Court, began his long public judicial career (1801–1835) by seeking to establish the legitimacy of judicial review. *Marbury* v. *Madison* (1803) thus constituted an effort to resolve the Framers' intent. The ruling was strongly challenged by the Jeffersonians. Indeed the only other example of the use of this claimed authority before the Civil War was the ill-fated *Dred Scott* ruling (1857); it was repudiated more vigorously than *Marbury,* although by

a nationalist constituency, which deplored its states' rights and proslavery overtones.

Probably the most controversial of the Marshall nationalist rulings was *McCulloch* v. *Maryland* (1819), dealing with the constitutionality of the Bank of the United States. Here well-known Marshallian pragmatism took the ultimate form in his oft quoted assertion regarding "implied powers": "Let the end be legitimate, let it be within the scope of the Constitution, and all means which are appropriate, which are plainly adapted to that end, which are not prohibited, but consistent with the letter and spirit of the constitution, are constitutional." Jeffersonian backlash was strong. Previously the former president had characterized the Court as "constantly working under ground to undermine the foundations of our confederated fabric." He now spoke of judicial usurpation, deploring the nationalist concept that the Constitution "is a mere thing of wax in the hands of the judiciary, which they may twist and shape into any form they please." And the 1820's saw that criticism seized upon by states' rights congressmen seeking to reverse the centralizing decisions of the Marshall Court by limiting its authority.

In *Gibbons* v. *Ogden* (1824), Marshall attempted to temper that criticism. In ruling that an unpopular state-authorized steamboat monopoly was in conflict with Congress's paramount authority over interstate commerce, he again expanded national power and freed economic enterprise, at an important stage in the development of national transportation, from unwarranted state restraints. Similarly, the Constitution's clause preventing states from passing laws impairing the obligation of contracts was turned into an instrument for federally guaranteeing property rights, by being interpreted to include everything from private contracts to state-granted charters of incorporation to private companies.

Roger B. Taney, as Marshall's successor (1836–1864), set out on a slightly different tack. While accepting much of the power that Marshall had carved out for the national government, Taney sought to shore up the concurrent power of the states. Reflecting his Jacksonian views and commitments to a new generation of entrepreneurs seeking open economic opportunity and national commercial growth, he saw proper constitutionalism as a form of dual federalism in which sovereignty over local affairs rested in the states, while sovereignty over general matters of national concern rested in the federal government. Both governments were obligated to work out the best balance possible, and the Supreme Court was the ultimate agency to settle borderline questions. Its rulings, however, were to be treated as the law of the land and adhered to without question by all parties.

Starting with this view, Taney set out to turn the Supreme Court into an instrument for pragmatic line-drawing: continuing the federal government's ultimate authority over contracts, while conceding the "community's" right to preserve the well-being of its citizens from corporate exploitation (*Charles River Bridge* v. *Warren Bridge,* 1837); finding a way constitutionally for the states to regulate banking and money practices without denying the final federal authority over currency (*Briscoe* v. *Bank of the Commonwealth of Kentucky,* 1837); condoning corporations doing business in different states but leaving the states free to regulate such "foreign" corporations (*Bank of Augusta* v. *Earle,* 1839); and embracing "selective exclusiveness" in the commerce field, whereby states had concurrent authority, unless the federal government had occupied the field or unless the subject required "uniform national control" (*Cooley* v. *Board of Wardens of Port of Philadelphia,* 1852). Had Taney continued as judiciously in his *Dred Scott* ruling, rather than blatantly siding with the South and virtually condoning slavery, he might very well have been able to use the judiciary as a gyroscope to continue sectional compromise. As it was, the partisanship of his *Dred Scott* opinion jettisoned his credibility and that of the Court for a generation.

But even Taney's pre–*Dred Scott* constitutionalism had had less impact upon his fellow southerners than had that of South Carolina's John C. Calhoun. When it came to the meaning of the Constitution, Calhoun as spokesman for the southern planter class was the more persuasive. Unlike Marshall and Taney, Calhoun felt that sovereignty—the ultimate will of the community—could not be divided. It could not be inherent in both local and central government. To Calhoun, the Constitution was not supreme law; it was an agreement between equal sovereign states. It was thus a contract, and the Union that existed was one in which the central government was the agent of the sovereign states; those states had the final authority to interpret the Constitution. Pursuing such a theory, South Carolina attempted to nullify a federal tariff law in the early 1830's, only to be forced to back down following a statement from President Jackson insisting upon the supremacy of federal law. Calhoun next moved to link proslavery policy with state sovereignty and national impotency. This view was challenged by abolitionists and ultimately by northern antislavery advocates. The former, however, early departed from constitutional arguments, feeling that the document itself condoned slavery and was "a covenant with death and an agreement with Hell."

The Calhoun vision of the Constitution engaged southern leaders, and it was to it that the South turned as its national political power and influence waned in the late 1850's. Southern secession was justified on the grounds that the South had a true understanding of the Constitution. Its leaders, ironically, wrote a Constitution for the Confederate States of America that copied the original document in virtually every detail but that broke down during the military conflict on the rock of southern states' rights and resultant central-government impotence.

MODERN GOVERNMENTAL ISSUES AND CONSTITUTIONAL REALISM

Southern collapse, plus the emphasis by Lincoln and the northern wartime Congress that saving the Union was the way to save the Constitution, contributed to its postwar restoration. Congressional leaders capitalized on that momentum to strengthen the central government vis-à-vis the states. During the war this meant creating the foundations of a new political economy with the Homestead Act (1862), the National Banking Act (1863), and a system of land grants to transcontinental railroads. Following the war, the strengthening of central authority was carried out through a congressional program of reconstruction, which included three constitutional amendments: the Thirteenth (1865), Fourteenth (1868), and Fifteenth (1870). The Thirteenth ended slavery; the Fourteenth defined national citizenship and made its prior prerogatives a national responsibility to be protected against state infringements, and private infringements by individuals acting for the states; and the Fifteenth represented an attempt to federally guarantee voting rights against unwarranted state and local interference.

In turn, the Supreme Court proclaimed, abstractly (*Texas* v. *White,* 1869), that the constitutional nature of the postwar Union was "an indestructible Union, composed of indestructible states." The ruling spoke little about the nature of the powers possessed by the central government. By the 1880's the Court had backed off sharply on this point. It now set about restricting congressional actions in behalf of the freedmen, through sharp curtailment of the thrust of the Reconstruction legislation (*Slaughterhouse* cases, 1873; *United States* v. *Reese,* 1875; *Civil Rights* cases, 1883; *Hurtado* v. *California,* 1884; *Plessy* v. *Ferguson,* 1896). Such rulings emasculated the Fourteenth Amendment's privileges and immunities clause, and curtailed its equal protection and due process clauses, making them meaningless as instruments for gaining equal rights and equal justice. Property-oriented, conservative justices also undermined much of the dual federalism carefully erected by the Taney Court, in which the "rights of the community" from private exploitation were a consideration addressed by that branch of government, state or national, which was most appropriate. Thus, the due process clause of the Fourteenth Amendment, as a legal instrument with which to ensure fair treatment of citizens in state actions, was altered so as to make it a substantive protection for property rights against state interference and regulation.

Such laissez-faire jurisprudence was extended in the 1880's as business-oriented justices came to dominate the high court, turning it into an activist body with a mission to contain the excesses of legislative democracy. By the 1890's, the majority's ideology had contributed heavily to a particular vision of proper government role under the Constitution. State regulation of commerce was suspect (*Wabash, St. Louis, and Pacific Railway* v. *Illinois,* 1886). But congressional efforts to respond to popular discontent and curtail questionable railroad and business practices (the Interstate Commerce Act, 1887; the Sherman Antitrust Act, 1890), based upon a broad Marshallian view of the commerce power, were also to be judicially curtailed (*I.C.C.* v. *Cincinnati, New Orleans, and Texas Pacific Railway,* 1896;

United States v. *E. C. Knight,* 1895). A federal income tax was ruled unconstitutional (*Pollock* v. *Farmers' Loan and Trust,* 1895). But the strong intervention of federal authority to break a national strike (the Pullman strike of 1894) was upheld (*in re Debs,* 1895).

The effect of this composite of pro–big business and antipopulist rulings, particularly given the constitutional inconsistency that they evinced, was to destroy both the vision of neutrality and the credibility of the Supreme Court. It particularly raised questions about the Court's authority to negate popular legislative judgments and to check the public's will in the interest of a minority. Coming at a time of severe national depression, these rulings also affected the Constitution. A remarkable period of economic growth and development had led many Americans to feel that the Constitution had created the system that had brought this about and was some kind of remarkable energizing document. When that economic structure collapsed, it was natural to blame the Constitution and ask a series of critical questions. These concerned the circumstances of its historical origins and its role in the conduct of public affairs, and resulted in a careful probing of its nature.

Previous perceptions of the Constitution had been simplistic, with the document admired as a stable and static code of formal legal elements. Antebellum northern statesmen had early encouraged this kind of Constitution apotheosis, in which the framers took on a certain divinity, and their inspired purpose became characterized as "the nearest approach of mortal to supreme wisdom." This view, particularly in light of Calhoun's "heresy," was blended with a northern view of the Union wherein the Constitution became the Union's embodiment. Early legal writers James Kent and Joseph Story incorporated this viewpoint into their constitutional commentaries. Maintaining that the North's aim in the Civil War was to sustain the Union, Lincoln built a tenacious devotion to the Constitution, although secession had occurred and the war that followed revealed the incapacity of the document to resolve serious antagonisms.

By the 1870's and 1880's, constitutional scholars had given up thinking that the Constitution was an ahistorical, static document. Rather, as the leading constitutional historian of the day, Hermann Eduard von Holst, argued, it was the result of actual circumstances of the past and present, a document that "ripened as the matured fruit of political experience." Woodrow Wilson, then a young political scientist, criticized undiscriminating and blind worship of the Constitution and asked whether the Constitution was still being adapted to serve the purposes for which it was intended. The historian John Franklin Jameson was convinced that the Constitution was the original document plus its judicial gloss, and that the study of the Constitution must go beyond mere formal legal elements to include impacting political and social factors. The Constitution was a record of the evolution of government in America, which proved that the laws of historical development applied to Americans. To such scholars, the Constitution's role and place had been as a part of the American political process, and it had served political demands and power both beneficial and detrimental to the general public.

Was the Constitution a democratic document? The conservative answer was "No, and rightly so." It "legalized and therefore makes possible and successful the opposition to the popular will," wrote Christopher Tiedeman in 1890, thereby enabling the United States to "prevent the development of democratic absolutism." To liberal critics, it also was not democratic, but that was its problem. It was an instrument that could be manipulated by the wealthy and powerful, with constitutionalism serving as a defense of existing property rights and economic power and preventing effective political action. The behavior of the undemocratic Supreme Court in the 1880's and 1890's was a graphic example.

As to the Founding Fathers and the Constitution's framing, the critics of the 1890's were cautious. Although they seemed to dramatize the fact that the Constitution was being manipulated for economic and class ends, scholars were reluctant to move to a conspiratorial theory about its origins. Clearly they saw the Constitution as a political instrument, much of it unwritten. But the targets of their criticism at the time were the currently wealthy and powerful, and the judiciary that served them and denied the popular will.

By the early twentieth century the Constitution was undergoing critical and refined assessment from a new generation of scholars. Absorbing the diffused ideas of Marx and later of Freud,

and the new assumptions of behaviorist psychology, these scholars sought to probe beneath the surface of events to understand judicial decisions, constitutions, and other political acts. They proceeded on the general assumption that these were the product of the political process and interacting economic and social interests. The outcome of such constitutional realism was varied, and presented a new Constitution to Americans.

Max Farrand summed up a generation of thought, emphasizing in *The Framing of the Constitution of the United States* (1913) that the Constitution was not a timeless and rational document but a "bundle of compromises," designed to meet very specific needs and defects of the Articles of Confederation. More iconoclastic were the works of James Allen Smith and Charles A. Beard. Smith, in *The Spirit of American Government* (1907), was the first to give historical legitimacy to the emerging view that the Constitution, far from being a natural expression of American democracy, was an aristocratic, reactionary document created by tight-fisted mercantile and creditor elements who were frightened by the popular agrarian tendencies of the Revolution. It was designed, by its checks and balances and the difficulty of amendment and judicial review, to thwart the popular will. Beard took the next step in *An Economic Interpretation of the Constitution of the United States* (1913), which proved to be a bombshell and has dominated scholarship on the subject ever since. For Beard, the Constitution was a class document, the result of a deep-seated conflict between a popular party based on paper money and agrarian interests, and a conservative party centered in the towns and resting on financial, mercantile, and personal property interests. People's consciousness and behavior were the products of their social and economic situation. The Founding Fathers' interest in the Constitution was stimulated by a desire to protect their own interests and class by constitutionally hamstringing the democratic masses with a new, stronger, controllable national government. This view, reflective of the political circumstances of the era, was quickly challenged by conservative scholars for its scholarship and ideological bias.

The factual backdrop against which Beard was writing was the Progressive Period (1901–1920), an era in which constitutional issues were very much a matter of public concern. Progressivism entailed a new positive approach to government, enhanced popular participation in the political process, and led to new governmental structures—bureaus and commissions—created to oversee and administer state and federal programs for dealing with multifarious social and economic problems. These ranged from factory and working conditions and child labor, to tariff, tax, and monetary reform, to protecting the nation's natural resources and raising its moral climate.

A Constitution geared to limiting governmental action hardly seemed the vehicle for such a program. For many reformers, debunking the Founding Fathers was a way to emancipate the present from the moral claims and restrictive vision of the past and open the way for positive proposals of drastic reform. The progressive Constitution, then, further shaped by the legal community's embracing of a new sociological jurisprudence, was a response generally to national reform demands and more specifically to Theodore Roosevelt's New Nationalism and Woodrow Wilson's New Freedom. It was a Constitution further augmented by legislative enactments at the state and federal level, spreading its coverage and shelter to a whole range of new subjects. Four further amendments (the Sixteenth, 1913; Seventeenth, 1913; Eighteenth, 1919; and Nineteenth, 1920) authorized a federal income tax; provided for direct election of Senators; prohibited the manufacture, sale, or transportation of intoxicating liquors; and guaranteed women's suffrage. Such change led to the expansion of government and its functions, a trend greatly accelerated by wartime crisis, but generally condoned by a judiciary that was prepared to give broad reach to the Constitution's commerce and taxing powers, and to the states' "police powers" to protect the health, safety, and welfare of their citizens.

Constitutional line-drawing did occur when labor's demands became too aggressive and public regulation seemed to threaten property rights and "freedom of contract." Even here the Court moved cautiously, since "undemocratic" judicial review was a Progressive *bête noire*, giving rise to talk of the recall of judicial decisions and of judges.

With the return of normalcy in the 1920's and the recapture of the Supreme Court by conserva-tive judicial activists, headed by Chief Justice William Howard Taft, the static ideal of conservative constitutionalism used by business interests to maintain freedom from public control gained new conservative defenders. Beard's work was maligned and attacked by scholars from Charles Warren and Edward S. Corwin to Andrew McLaughlin. Conservatives pushed this neo-constitutionalism through patriotic organizations and into the schools, only to find themselves again on the defensive when an even greater depression than that of the 1890's left the American economic structure—and by partial implication its constitutional framework—in ruins.

The 1930's thus saw constitutionalism under sharp fire, particularly by legal realist scholars. Walton Hamilton's essay in the *Encyclopedia of the Social Sciences* in 1931 referred to it as "the name given to the trust which men repose in the power of words engrossed on parchment to keep a government in order." "Such fetishism," wrote Thurman Arnold, "blocked progressive change." Max Lerner argued that the provisions of the Bill of Rights, rather than setting boundaries of arbitrary power, were a "pack of tricks to defeat the purposes of majority rule." The only valid meaning of civil liberties for Lerner was the right of the majority to organize new economic alignments. The realists and the positivist jurisprudes thus dismissed law as nothing more than command, and dismissed the idea that law, to be authoritative, must accord with reason or some conception of right higher than the state. The rule of law was inhibiting practical and pragmatic political experimentation. Prior rules and structures that imposed uniformities of behavior, such as a constitution, precluded true political freedom and open-ended actions and, more important, impeded evolving essential solutions to unprecedented social and economic problems.

THE NEW DEAL AND A NEW CONSTITUTION

The New Deal Constitution, as conceived by the New Deal's also relying upon a conception of the Constitution as the people's political law, set up the foundation of a modern welfare state through the inauguration of the Social Security system in 1935, which with its subsidiary programs expanded aid to deprived and dependent groups in American society. In two other ways, a new constitutionalism emerged. Governmental economic management grew, and federal taxation and expenditure became prime movers in the economy. Such a policy, which entailed emergency expenditures for relief of unemployment and public works in the 1930's, was turned into military support during World War II. The two were combined into a continued rise in federal expenditures for a peacetime military establishment and for civilian purposes in the postwar era. Again, the impact on traditional constitutional structures was pronounced. Centralization changed the character of the federal system, with the states expected to cooperate with federal policy to receive grants for projects from urban housing and education to broad programs of hospital construction, building, and aid to urban areas. This meant the states lost considerable discretionary powers to Washington.

President Franklin D. Roosevelt and a dutifully supporting Congress stimulated this atmosphere. Through expansive constitutional reinterpretation, federal policies and programs of a breadth exceeding progressivism at its most expansive were put in place. Initially, this involved central planning and expanded control through the National Industrial Recovery Act and the Agricultural Adjustment Act of 1933. Using industry-wide agreements given effect by the president (to whom Congress delegated authority), the modern industrial sector was to be centrally managed. So was agriculture through a federal program of acreage allotments, price supports, and general control of resources. When struck down by a hostile conservative judiciary (*Schechter* v. *United States*, 1935; *United States* v. *Butler*, 1936), these measures were reenacted in more careful and legally precise ways. The government also extended similar regulatory supervision and control to labor-management relations, securities markets, various transportation and communication agencies, housing, and eventually wages and hours. The agencies involved were given legislative, judicial, and administrative powers to reach far into traditionally private matters. The result was a changed system, in which bureaucratic units gained broad discretion regarding the activities they would conduct, the aid they would extend, and the terms on which it would be granted.

Initially, the conservative Supreme Court's Constitution was used by the justices to block these new developments. Emphasizing sharp separation of powers, liberty of contract, restrictive interpretations of the commerce and due process clause, and heavy emphasis upon the Tenth Amendment as a restriction on federal power, the justices ruled twelve acts of Congress unconstitutional between 1934 and 1937 in a display of conservative judicial activism unprecedented in American history. Under fire from New Deal leaders and some of its own members the majority backed off (in his Butler dissent, Harlan Fiske Stone maintained, "Courts are not the only agencies of government that must be assumed to have the capacity to govern"). By the early 1940's the body had condoned practically the entire New Deal program, constitutionally underwriting the plenary nature of national power over almost every aspect of the nation's public life. Harry Scheiber has written, "The ideology of 'national needs' invoked to justify the new federalism, paralleled the creation of new legal doctrines in earlier periods when social and economic imperatives demanded legal shifts."

Liberals and reform realists applauded those developments. They saw them as "a new articulation of powers, which is aimed at getting things done," and even argued that energetic national government, regulating and promoting economic development, rather than letting it drift along in the manner of laissez faire, was consistent with the outlook of the founding fathers. Traditional constitutionalists were not sure. Such an invitation to the virtually unbridled use of power on the part of national leadership, they argued, had led Europe to a type of arbitrary, coercive, totalitarian authority—the antithesis of a constitutional state. Ultimately a war was fought against such totalitarianism so the world, as the slogan went, "would be ruled by the force of law and not the law of force." By the end of World War II, and as the confrontational cold war with the Soviet Union progressed, neo-constitutionalists regained some initiative and made considerable headway in defining the latter struggle in essentially political rather than economic terms. Soviet rule, like Nazi rule, flouted the rule of law and the commitments of a constitutional state to limited government and fair and equitable procedure.

Such a posture encouraged the growth in the

late 1940's and 1950's of a new consensus regarding the American past. Internal conflicts and particularly economic class analysis were very much soft-pedaled; and the virtues of the American constitutional order, with its emphasis upon limited government and individual freedom, were again celebrated. Such cold war constitutionalism had a moral dimension as well, with a number of champions arguing that it was a healthy antidote to relativistic positivism. It could and should serve to provide the formative beliefs that shaped the character of citizens. This turn toward natural law troubled others, who pointed out that natural law had been an ideological foundation for fascism, whereas positivism had been its chief nemesis.

PROBING THE MEANING AND UTILITY OF AMERICAN CONSTITUTIONALISM

In such a climate it was natural that some historians, seeking to underwrite this conservative consensus, would again probe the historical background of the Constitution. Beard's work again proved to be the target. One group, the neo-conservatives, emerged with the 1956 study by Robert Eldon Brown, *Charles Beard and the Constitution.* Brown was determined to exorcise the economic interpretation by a head-on refutation of Beard's work. He hit hard at Beard's contention that the Founding Fathers' holdings of securities dictated their beliefs and actions. And he also challenged one of Beard's underlying assumptions: that the Constitution was an undemocratic document, because the "propertyless masses" were unable to participate in the political process. Rather, he contended, the America of the 1780's represented a middle-class democracy, with the Constitution a reflection of that middle class. Thus, rather than a product of class struggle, the Constitution was a product of class consensus. Forrest McDonald in *We the People: The Economic Origins of the Constitution* (1958) analyzed the economic interests of the delegates to the state and federal conventions to prove that Beard's asserted black-and-white economic alignment over the Constitution was simplistic and erroneous, missing the complexity of the pluralistic political and economic interests at work on local, state, and regional levels. The ef-

fect of these studies was again to emphasize that economic and class conflicts were not at the heart of the framing and that the Constitution was primarily a political document, focusing mainly on the problem of federalism.

This view was reinforced by John P. Roche, Stanley Elkins, and Eric McKitrick. Roche stressed the agreement on fundamentals that occurred during the convention in what he referred to as a "reform caucus in action" and "a classic example of the potentialities of a democratic elite." Elkins and McKitrick similarly contended that the issues of constitutional reform were not fought on economic or ideological grounds. They even downgraded the conflict as a struggle between nationalism and localism, contrasting the youthful energy, far-sightedness, and political effectiveness of the Federalists with the inertia, particularism, and political ineptness of the Antifederalists.

A second revisionist school also rejected Beard's emphasis upon economic considerations, without moving to consensus as an alternative. These "new intellectual historians" proposed an ideological or social interpretation that rested upon a careful reconstruction of the late-eighteenth-century intellectual world. This renewed interest in ideas and context led scholars like Bernard Bailyn, Caroline Robbins, and Gordon Wood to view the confederation period and the writing of the Constitution in a completely different light. Focusing upon American political thought from the Revolution to the Constitution, Robbins and Bailyn demonstrated the importance of British antiauthoritarian views and how they influenced the formulation of America's republican ideology. Thus the writing of the Constitution was placed within an Anglo-American framework. In turn, issues of representation, the relationship of rulers to ruled, the nature of human rights, and the concept of divided sovereignty were traced to earlier British traditions of republicanism. The positive expectations of the Constitution were also assessed differently. Rather than a document to serve the dominant economic class, the frame of government was seen as carefully designed to assure the preservation of an ordered polity. Abuse of power would be checked through the existence, in a large republic, of a multiplicity of factions and interests arising from its size, which in competition for self-interested ends would balance each other's excessive and overly selfish ambitions. Minority factions would thus be safe, and an open and stable order would be achieved.

Gordon Wood's *The Creation of the American Republic, 1776–1787* (1969) capped this new republican synthesis. By unraveling the emerging American conception of politics, Wood pictured the Constitution as an attempt to save the Revolution from failure by restraining some overly democratic consequences. The forward-looking Federalists, unlike their overly cautious opponents, had learned from and been sobered by the confederation experience. They sought to create an authoritative, national republican government with mechanical devices and institutional contrivances to contain excessive democracy, man's selfish nature, and the excesses of state legislative localism. To them, sovereignty rested in the people rather than in any agency of government; government should be divided into separate parts, not because each part represented a different social constituency but because it would act as a check upon the others; every part was equally representative of the people; liberty involved not merely the right of the subject to participate in government but also the protection of individual rights against all governmental encroachments. The Federalists' achievement combined diffuse and often rudimentary ideas into the federal constitution and made this new conception of constitutional politics intelligible and consistent. The ultimate objective of Wood's Federalists was not fully explored, however, possibly to keep motives ideological and to avoid qualifying the argument by injecting economic goals such as expansion and development.

A third group to reconceptualize the Constitution, its origins, meaning, and purpose, comprised "neo-Progressive" scholars, out to extend the Beardian interpretation. This school, launched by Merrill Jensen in the late 1940's and early 1950's, operated on economic assumptions and saw the Constitution as the product of a deliberate conservative counter-revolution designed to serve creditor and merchant interests. Jackson Turner Main and E. James Ferguson refined this polarized argument further to make it more persuasive. Main described two fairly consistent socioeconomic "parties" in each state during the 1780's: commercial–urban combinations led by cosmopolitan notables on one hand, and agrarian groups headed by new men with local connections and outlooks on the other. He widened the argument from an economic and political one to a broader social one in which people's whole lives were examined to explain differing motivations. A clear relationship existed between the degree to which individuals were tied into the commercial life of the region in which they lived and their stand for or against the Constitution. Ferguson reinforced the idea of social cleavage but showed that mercantile capitalists and agrarians split in complex ways over public questions of financial policy.

This "neo-Progressive" school was carried to its logical extreme in the 1960's by New Left historians eager to discredit "the establishment" and "the system" by seeing principally its flaws. Thus the Constitution was portrayed as providing the foundation for a national system of economics and politics that called for constantly expanding American imperialism. It was shown to represent primarily a triumph for the idea of mercantilism. Staughton Lynd particularly argued that contrary to Beard, property owners most supportive of the Constitution were those who held property in slaves. The document was thus seen in neo-abolitionist terms as morally reprehensible. Others have stressed the movement for a federal constitution as the conservative way of changing the rules so as to end the conditions that had enabled the radicals to triumph, and radical methods had sufficiently modified conservative institutions by 1790 to create a stable government and a "liberal bourgeois society."

But in the public climate of the prosperous 1960's and early 1970's economic considerations were not the most pressing. The rule of law was seen as a political force in the struggle for the third world and in the reconstruction of American society to eliminate alleged inequities and hypocrisies. A new liberal democratic constitutionalism arose as a response to such public demands. American commitment to the rule of law was projected in dramatic contrast to Soviet authoritarianism. It also was pushed as the best tactic for Americans in this struggle. It was essential, it was argued, to make the American system work better. This meant broadening the application of the rule of law based on a more expansive and broad-gauged extension of the principles of liberty, justice, and equality, and assuring access to educational, economic, and political opportunities for the powerless.

The Warren Court proved to be the cutting edge for achieving this democratic structural purpose, ultimately bringing Congress and Presidents Kennedy and Johnson along as partners in the movement. For Earl Warren, the Constitution was a body of ethical imperatives that, if properly followed, should produce a decent, moral, and civilized society. These imperatives were so clear, and his duty to implement them so apparent, that matters of doctrinal interpretation remained simple and institutional power became nearly irrelevant. His principal concern as a jurist was to discern that underlying ethical structure in the Constitution and rigorously apply its imperatives to current circumstances, even if such application did not necessarily achieve orthodox doctrinal consistency.

Operating from such assumptions, the Supreme Court set new directions on subjects as far-ranging as school desegregation and integration of public facilities; voting rights and legislative reapportionment; the operation of the nation's criminal justice system through a "due process revolution," which brought Constitutional imperatives heavily into law enforcement; freedom of speech and press; and church-state relations. Court decisions, laws, and executive orders were justified, constitutionally, on sweeping reinterpretations of the equal protection clause, the due process clause, the commerce clause, and federalism generally. The national government was charged with new responsibilities for protecting its citizens against violations of their rights and freedoms from the states, private citizens, and citizen groups. The impact of these policies, especially the insistence that the Fourteenth Amendment required truly equal treatment of all persons regardless of race and sex, set in motion a movement for basic changes in federal law affecting employment practices, as well as public expenditures, education, and personnel policies. Further bureaucracy and regulation were required for enforcement of these changes.

Critics from the Right and the Left challenged the trend. Conservative neo-constitutionalists, while they agreed that the essence of constitutionalism was the right of individual liberty and property against governmental interference, deplored growing nationalization as an assault upon states' rights. They charged that Warren's reliance on ethical principle rather than legal precedent or a strict reading of the constitutional language produced doctrinal inconsistency. Such "result-oriented" jurisprudence, they contended, rejected the deliberative process, involving a pluralism of views, and constituted a type of political partisanship hardly distinguishable from arbitrary authoritarianism. Manifesting a theocratic, elitist bias, many such conservatives deplored the lack of universal, classical, moral norms in a liberal constitutionalism, suggesting that a proper jurisprudence based upon "neutral principles," transcending any immediate result, would come closer to affording right order in human society.

Left-leaning, neo-realist critics, by contrast, attacked liberal neo-constitutionalism as a simple underwriting of "vital center" and mainstream pluralist politics. They did not reject the instrumentalism of using the rule of law for political reasons, but they disagreed with the reasons. The Court, they contended, had admirably protected freedom of speech, press, and religion; but this achieved little since it did not address "the other face of power," the class bias of pluralist politics that prevented the issues of real concern to the community from being brought into the political arena. Liberal constitutionalism was generally flawed by failure to contain a theory of political action that would lead to a more equitable society. Furthermore, these antipluralists indicated, it had too narrow an economic conception of people, and focused too heavily on the lack of governmental restraints upon economic pursuits. True constitutionalism to them would encourage citizen participation in their public life, stimulate the rebirth of community, and call for the application of constitutional limitations and standards of public responsibility to the public power of corporations, trade organizations, labor unions, and other voluntary associations whose leadership and operations affected people's daily lives in multifarious ways.

The Constitution's relationship to power, although viewed from widely divergent personal and ideological vantage points, remained a central and serious American concern as the country entered the 1970's. Widespread public hostility to the government's massive involvement in an unpopular war in Asia intensified the concern as critical leaders warned of the "arrogance of power." So did an executive branch armed with such prerogatives that many criticized it as "the imperial presidency." Watergate demonstrated that such fears were more than hypothetical, as the revelations of Richard Nixon's cynical lack of respect for constitutional processes and his justification of dubious actions by resort to "executive privilege" became more extensive and insistent, and as parallel, unauthorized, and questionable CIA and FBI activities were brought to light.

Some authorities have argued that the removal of a president, uncommitted to the constitutional limitations of his office, demonstrated the essential health of the constitutional system. According to others the United States was fortunate that the Watergate co-conspirators were so inept and that ineptitude saved the nation. Whether the Constitution "worked" was ultimately far less important than that the electorate seemed to want it to work and demanded that it work. Efforts in the 1970's and early 1980's by women, taxpayers, fundamentalist religionists, and anti-abortionists to amend the document seemed again a manifestation of respect for higher law. It confirmed the view that the Constitution was essentially a living political document through which people could and should continue to govern themselves. Furthermore, some subtlety of understanding seemed present, when both liberals and conservatives protested congressional attempts to curtail the power and authority of the Supreme Court over certain constitutional areas.

Thus while few Americans have fully understood the refinements and complexities of the governmental structure that the Constitution authorized, a majority have been committed to its value and importance, and to retaining the fine tuning built in by its creators and perfected by its interpreters.

BIBLIOGRAPHY

The bibliography on the Constitution is massive, running the gamut from general, abstract evaluations of constitution-

alism, such as James Roland Pennock and John W. Chapman, eds., *Constitutionalism* (New York, 1979), to extended texts on specific constitutional experiences, like Alfred H. Kelly, Winfred A. Harbison, and Herman Belz, *The American Constitution: Its Origins and Development*, 6th ed. (New York, 1983). The modern view of the Constitution as an aspect of political experience and political development was set forth by James G. Randall, "The Interrelation of Social and Constitutional History," in *American Historical Review*, 35 (1929); reiterated with a differing focus and concern in Paul L. Murphy, "Time to Reclaim: The Current Challenge of American Constitutional History," *ibid.*, 69 (1963); and updated in Harry N. Scheiber, "American Constitutional History and the New Legal History: Complementary Themes in Two Modes," in *Journal of American History*, 68 (1981).

The political role of the Constitution, changing perceptions of the proper nature of that role, and views of the Constitution as a legitimate political instrument have been carefully explored in a series of articles by Herman Belz: "The Constitution in the Gilded Age: The Beginnings of Constitutional Realism in American Scholarship," in *American Journal of Legal History*, 13 (1969); "The Realist Critique of Constitutionalism in the Era of Reform," *ibid.*, 15 (1971); "Changing Conceptions of Constitutionalism in the Era of World War II and the Cold War," in *Journal of American History*, 59 (1972); and "New Left Reverberations in the Academy: The Antipluralist Critique of Constitutionalism," in *Review of Politics*, 38 (1974). There is a useful assessment of the historiography of judicial review as political process in Charles A. Beard, *The Constitution and the Supreme Court*, Alan F. Westin, ed. (New York, 1962).

Studies of the framing, cited above, are fruitfully augmented by James Morton Smith, ed., *The Constitution* (New York, 1971). Various editions of *The Federalist* are available, and the literature on ratification has been recently enriched by Herbert J. Storing and Murray Dry, eds., *The Complete Anti-Federalist*, 7 vols. (Chicago, 1981), which analyzes Antifederalist thought and principles on the contention that they speak to the ongoing dialogue over the political life of the community. Also useful is Robert A. Goldwin and William A. Schambra, eds., *How Democratic Is the Constitution?* (Washington, D.C., 1980), a series of current essays on the point.

The most current detailed assessments of the American Constitution's history are Loren P. Beth, *The Development of the American Constitution, 1877–1917* (New York, 1971); Harold M. Hyman and William M. Wiecek, *Equal Justice Under Law: Constitutional Development, 1835–1875* (New York, 1982); and Paul L. Murphy, *The Constitution in Crisis Times, 1918–1969* (New York, 1972). All contain extensive bibliographies, which can be augmented by Kermit L. Hall, *A Comprehensive Bibliography of American Constitutional and Legal History, 1896–1979*, 5 vols. (Millwood, N.Y., 1984).

[See also ARTICLES OF CONFEDERATION; BILL OF RIGHTS; FEDERALISM; THE FEDERALIST PAPERS; JUDICIAL SYSTEM; SEPARATION OF POWERS; and STATE GOVERNMENTS.]

CONTROL, SUPPRESSION, AND INTIMIDATION

Michael Paul Rogin

A HISTORY of American political suppression must attend to the repression of active, political dissent. But it must also direct attention to prepolitical institutional settings that have excluded some Americans from politics and influenced the terms on which others enter the political arena. An account of American political suppression must acknowledge the suppression of politics itself. It must notice the relations between politics and private life. Countersubversive ideologies, psychological mechanisms, and an intrusive state apparatus all respond to the fear of subversion in America. We begin with the controls exercised over peoples of color.

PEOPLES OF COLOR: INDIANS

"History begins for us with murder and enslavement, not with discovery," wrote the American poet William Carlos Williams. He was calling attention to the historical origins of the United States in violence against peoples of color. He was pointing to America's origins during the beginning of a capitalist world system. Indian land and black labor generated a European-American-African trade in the seventeenth century and contributed to the development of commodity agriculture, industrial production, and state power in Europe and the Americas. Karl Marx wrote, "The discovery of gold and silver in America, the extirpation, enslavement, and entombment in mines of the aboriginal population, the beginning of the conquest and the looting of the East Indies, and turning of Africa into a warren for the commercial hunting of black-skins, signalized the rosy dawn of capitalist production. These idyllic pro-

ceedings are the chief momenta of primitive accumulation."

By primitive accumulation Marx meant the forcible acquisition of land and labor, by a mixture of state and private violence, to serve the accumulation of capital. Primitive accumulation made land, labor, and commodities available for the marketplace, before the free market could act on its own. The suppression, intimidation, and control of peoples of color supplies the prehistory of the American history of freedom. Moreover, people of color were important not only at the origins of America but also in its ongoing history—through westward expansion against Indians and Mexicans, chattel slavery and the exclusion of emancipated blacks from political and economic freedom, and the repressive responses to Hispanic and Asian workers. The American economy exploited peoples of color, but American racial history is not reducible to its economic roots. A distinctive American political tradition, fearful of primitivism and disorder, developed in response to peoples of color. That tradition defines itself against alien threats to the American way of life and sanctions violent and exclusionary responses to them.

Indians in early America came to embody the masterless men who appeared in Europe with the breakdown of traditional society. "Liv[ing] without government," in the words of one early report, and freed of the restraints of family, church, and village as well, the idle, wandering savages were depicted as engaging in incest, cannibalism, devil worship, and murder. Some European-Americans, to be sure, depicted them not as monstrous but as noble. Traders, promoters of commercial ventures, settlers no longer threatened by powerful tribes, and humanists drawn to a classical or Christian golden age all

392

imagined peaceful primitives enjoying a state of innocence. But the noble savage and his dark double were joined. Both images of primitivism appropriated Indians for white purposes. Both made the Indians children of nature instead of creators and inhabitants of their own cultures. Both ignored Indian agriculture and depicted a tribalism that menaced private property and the family. Neither the noble nor the devilish savage could coexist with the advancing white civilization. Both images rationalized the dispossession of the tribes.

Indians did not use the land for agriculture, explained Massachusetts Bay Governor John Winthrop. Since the wandering tribes failed to "subdue and replenish" the earth, white farmers could acquire their land. Winthrop's principle of expropriation was an accepted tenet of international law by the early eighteenth century. It did not justify individual acquisition of farming plots, however, but rather state action. First the colonies and the mother country, then the independent states, and finally the federal government expropriated land by making treaties with Indian tribes. George Washington, justifying the treaty method, defended

> . . . the propriety of purchasing their lands in preference to attempting to drive them by force of arms out of our country; which, as we have already experienced, is like driving the wild beasts of ye forests, which will return as soon as the pursuit is at an end, and fall, perhaps upon those that are left there; when the gradual extension of our settlements will as certainly cause the savage, as the wolf, to retire; both being beasts of prey tho' they differ in shape.

Indians were animals, but fortunately they were men as well. As men they could make contracts, accept money, and consent to the loss of their land. Treaties presented a fiction of Indian freedom to disguise the realities of coerced consent, bribery, deception about boundaries, agreements with one faction enforced on an entire tribe, and the encouragement of tribal debts—real and inflated—to be paid off by the cession of land.

The policy of Indian removal, conceived by Thomas Jefferson, employed in his and succeeding administrations, and forced upon the southern Indians by Andrew Jackson, offered Indians the freedom to move west if they relinquished their ancestral holdings. Southern states, encouraged by Jackson, extended their sovereignty over tribal land. Jackson gave Indians the freedom either to remain where they were (subject to state laws and settler invasions) or to give up their lands for equivalent holdings in the West. Removal, Jackson told them, offered the freedom treasured by white Americans, the freedom to move west to improve themselves. Provisions for protection against further white encroachment were, in these cases and others, not enforced. Nonetheless, the treaty method allowed Indian expropriation to proceed under the color of law. It engaged Indians in consent to their own subjugation. Alexis de Tocqueville, coming upon the removal of starving, freezing Choctaws in 1831, observed, "Nowadays the dispossession of the Indians is accomplished in a regular and, so to say, quite legal manner. . . . It is impossible to destroy men with more respect to the laws of humanity."

The federal government abrogated tribal treaty-making rights in 1871. In return for depriving Indians of their collective freedom, the government promised individual freedom. Freedom had begun to be offered to individual Indians early in the nineteenth century, to atomize tribes and subject their members to market pressures and state laws. Jackson, for example, sought to break the power of aristocratic tribal chiefs, so that the "poor Indians" could pursue their interests on their own. The most important individual freedom offered Indians was freedom from communal land ownership. Jackson's treaties with the Creek and Choctaw Indians were the first to employ individual land allotments on a large scale. Tribal leaders believed that individual allotments were the only way to preserve Indian land, but widespread fraud and intimidation quickly transferred Indian freeholds to white land companies. The Dawes Severalty Act of 1887, which Theodore Roosevelt praised as "a mighty pulverizing engine to break up the tribal mass," offered Indians the opportunity to become free Americans; the freedom that they actually acquired was the freedom to alienate their land. Railroads, mining interests, cattlemen, and land corporations acquired the land allotments granted Indians. Between 1887 and 1934 the tribes lost an estimated 60 percent of their holdings. In 1983 Secretary of the Interior James

Watt proposed to grant Indians "freedom" from their "socialistic" dependence on the federal government and on their tribes; Indian spokesmen, in response, denied they were reds. The freedom offered Indians, from Jackson to Watt, has undermined communal loyalties as sources of political resistance.

American Indian policy from the beginning combined freedom with coercion, the method of the marketplace with the method of the state. Government has shown two faces to the tribes, one of violence, the other of paternal guardianship. Consider the acquisition of land. Whites claimed Indian land not only by right of treaty or proper use but also as the fruits of a just war. Conflicts over land and living space produced a series of Indian wars, beginning with Virginia's war against the Powhatan confederacy in 1622, and with the New England Pequot War of 1636–1637. White expansion provoked most of these wars; savage atrocities were cited to justify them. Wars over living space produced civilian casualties on both sides; but whereas Indian violence was attributed to primitive ferocity, the systematic destruction of Indian crops and villages was defended as a matter of deliberate policy. White victories, it was said, proved the superiority of civilization over savagery. Indian wars were important in the colonies and during the Revolution. They also promoted American continental expansion, from the War of 1812 to the closing of the frontier. More than 200 pitched battles were fought in the West during the Gilded Age, and there was also periodic guerilla warfare in outlying regions. The history of Indian war ended at Wounded Knee, South Dakota, in 1890 with the massacre of 200 Sioux men, women, and children, including the old warrior Sitting Bull, after a ghost dance ceremony.

Indians displaced by treaty or defeated in war were offered "paternal guardianship." Indian tribes were "in a state of pupilage," ruled the Supreme Court in *Cherokee Nation* v. *Georgia* (1831); "their relation to the United States resembles that of a ward to his guardian." As the equals of whites, Indians had the freedom to lose their land; as wards of a paternal government, Indians were confined. The government adopted a reservations policy before the Civil War and enforced it on the western tribes in the late nineteenth century. Confined to reservations, tribes were dependent on government food, clothing, and shelter. Although they were held in protective custody, their land continued to be subject to encroachments from cattle, agricultural, and mineral interests.

Confinement was seen not simply as the opposite of Indian freedom but as preparation for a new kind of liberty. "Civilized and domesticated," reservation Indians were to be freed from their tribal identities and remade as free men. "Push improvement on them by education, alienation, and individuation," urged an Osage agent in the late nineteenth century. Indian agents encouraged commodity agriculture, ignoring unsuitable topographical and cultural conditions, and the presence of rapacious whites. Compulsory government boarding schools regimented children in barracks far from their parents' homes, forced them to abandon tribal dress, and punished them for using their native tongue. Reservation tribes maintained some autonomy, thanks in part to varying mixtures of accommodation and resistance, and in part to federal recognition (beginning with the New Deal) of Indian rights. Today Indian tribes remain what *Cherokee Nation* v. *Georgia* defined them to be: "domestic, dependent nations" within the United States.

The dispossession of Indians did not happen once and for all in American history. America was continually expanding west and while doing so it decimated, removed, or confined one tribe after another. That history had major consequences not only for Indian-white relations but also for American history as a whole. It defined America from the beginning as a settler society, an expanding, domestic, imperial power. Expansion guaranteed American freedom, so it was believed, protecting Americans from the crowded conditions and social class divisions of Europe. Indian wars exemplified state violence. They fed an opposite myth—the myth of the self-made man. Masterless Indians challenged European institutional restraints at the beginning of American history. By the Age of Jackson, Americans celebrated their own independence, which Indian tribalism threatened to confine. White Americans contrasted their own freedom, disciplined by self-restraint, with the subversive, idle, and violent freedom of the Indians. The self-reliant American gained his freedom, won his authority, and defined the American national identity in violent Indian combat in the West.

CONTROL, SUPPRESSION, AND INTIMIDATION

With the perceived closing of the continental frontier in the 1890's, the policy of Manifest Destiny was extended to Asia. The suppression of the Philippine independence movement after the Spanish-American War caused hundreds of thousands of deaths. America was, according to those who carried out and defended its Philippine policy, continuing its conquest over and tutelage of primitive tribes. Indian policy also set precedents for twentieth-century interventions in Latin America. The country's expansionist history against savage peoples of color culminated, rhetorically and in practice, in the war in Vietnam.

Indian policy also had domestic implications. Indians were the first people to stand in American history as emblems of disorder, of civilized breakdown, and of alien control. Differences between reds and whites made cultural adaptation seem at once dangerous and impossible. The violent conquest of Indians legitimized violence against other alien groups, making coexistence appear to be unnecessary. The paranoid style in American politics, as the historian Richard Hofstadter has labeled it, goes back to responses to Indians. The series of red scares that have swept the country since the 1870's have roots in the original red scares. Later countersubversive movements attacked aliens, but those who originally assaulted reds were themselves the aliens in the land. Responses to the Indians point to the mixture of cultural arrogance and insecurity in the American history of countersubversion. The identity of a self-making people, engaged in a national, purifying mission, may be particularly vulnerable to threats of contamination and disintegration. The need to draw rigid boundaries between the alien and the self suggests fears of too dangerous an intimacy between them.

Just as fears of subversion moved from Indians to other social groups, so also did techniques of control. The group ties of workers and immigrants were assaulted in the name of individual freedom. State violence, used to punish Indians who fought instead of working, was also employed against striking workers. A paternal model of interracial relations developed in slavery as well as Indian policy. Finally, Indians shared their status as beneficiaries of meliorist confinement with the inmates of total institutions. These arenas—of slavery, the asylum, labor relations, and the intimidation of radical dissent—form the major loci of American political suppression.

PEOPLES OF COLOR: BLACKS AND ASIAN-AMERICANS

The early repressive labor system in the colonies, with restrictive terms of indenture for both white and black workers, gave way by the eighteenth century to freedom for whites and slavery for blacks. That division had less significance in the North, which lacked a large, propertyless proletariat, than in the South. Slavery secured a labor force for southern plantations. It overcame the twin threats of, on the one hand, class war against whites by land-hungry white servant workers and, on the other, of interracial, lower-class solidarity. A slave labor system restricted to blacks could not have developed without preexisting, invidious racial distinctions. But slavery intensified racism. Racialist thinking at once justified black enslavement and forged racial bonds across class lines among whites.

Both blacks and Indians, in racialist thought, posed primitive threats to the social order. But those threats differed, in keeping with the contrasting white desires for Indian land and black labor. Indians were "on our borders," in James Madison's words; "the black race [was] within our bosom." Indians, on the margins of white settlement, posed the subversive threat of freedom; it was met by the displacement, elimination, and confinement of the tribes. Blacks, upon whose labor whites depended, posed the subversive threat of reversing the relations of dependence. Indians offered escape from political, social, and familial institutions; blacks threatened social and sexual upheaval.

Fears of black sexuality played a central role in the denial of freedom and equality to blacks. A 1662 Virginia law doubling the fine for interracial (as opposed to same-race) fornication was the first strictly racial legal discrimination in the colonies. The first statements and acts that distinguished between individuals purely on the grounds of ancestry had to do with interracial sex and with determining the status of mixed offspring. By defining children of interracial unions as black and therefore slaves, legal enactments guaranteed a slave labor force. Other slave societies, with small white settler populations, created a special caste of mulattoes; human beings in the United States had to be either white or black. Although this absolute bifurcation had practical origins, it also derived from northern European, Protestant cultural phobias.

Thomas Jefferson warned that the slave who engaged in interracial sex was "staining the blood of his master." Jefferson feared the black man's desire for the white woman, reversing the actual direction of interracial sexual exploitation under slavery. Women were identified with blacks in the seventeenth century as sources of dangerous, sexual passion. Prohibitions against sex between black men and white women helped keep the women within a patriarchal, family-centered society. As fears of female sexuality went underground, in the later eighteenth century, black men were alleged to threaten white women by what they wanted from them, not by what they shared with them. The repressive effect was the same. "Mulattoes are monsters," warned the nineteenth-century Mississippi defender of slavery Henry Hughes. "Amalgamation is incest." Hughes's association of miscegenation with incest suggests that he feared blacks not because they were so alien to whites but because they were all too close to them.

Unlike racialist thinkers such as Hughes, Jefferson did not justify slavery. But he did identify black freedom with a black sexual threat and warned against the consequences of emancipation were blacks allowed to remain in America. When the abolition of slavery was not accompanied by the removal of the slaves, lynchings and mob violence punished black assertions of freedom. Countless mutilated black bodies testified that mobs treated black claims to independence as sexual at their core. Laws against miscegenation lasted well into the twentieth century.

Slaves were excluded from the political process in antebellum America. Fears that they would enter politics in a revolutionary way, through slave uprisings, mass murder, and rape, led to harsh southern slave codes. These codes forbade teaching slaves to read or write and prohibited slaves from congregating for social or religious purposes without the presence of a white or from leaving their plantations without a pass. Southern states made manumission difficult or impossible. Slave marriages enjoyed no legal protection, and slaves had no recourse against being bought or sold. A paternalist ideology claimed that the plantation was a family and made the master entirely responsible for the welfare of his slave children. Slave codes were enforced intermittently, to be sure, and the life of southern blacks was not defined solely by them; many planters, moreover, took seriously their paternal obligations. But even on its own terms paternalism attended to slaves only by depriving them of the right to speak and act for themselves. In combination with the slave codes, planter paternalism deprived slaves of all legal protection. Slave patrols of armed white men maintained racial order. In real or imagined times of trouble, these patrols or other white mobs took racial matters into their own hands.

Free blacks did not fare much better than slaves, either in the North or in the South. Southern states tried to expel free blacks; many had no legal residency status. Northern states prohibited blacks from voting, serving on juries, or testifying in court and deprived them of civil rights as well. The 1850 fugitive slave law financially rewarded commissioners who returned alleged runaways to slavery, and deprived accused slaves of the right to a jury trial. Northern mobs rioted against free blacks, destroying neighborhoods and killing men, women, and children.

Slavery not only denied freedom to blacks; it also decisively influenced the history of freedom for whites. White freedom was built on black slavery. Americans fought a revolution in part to protect property created by slave labor, and the profits from that labor financed the revolutionary alliance with France. In addition, the vast majority of propertyless black workers in revolutionary America were in chains, racially divided from the mass of free whites. White Americans could demand the end of their enslavement (as they called it) to Britain, with less fear than in Europe that propertyless workers would demand their natural rights as well.

Slavery also guaranteed white freedom in the antebellum South. The South was a *Herrenvolk* democracy, in which political and social equality among whites rested on the subjugation of blacks, and in which the aspiration to acquire slaves made ambitious yeomen into imitators rather than adversaries of the planter class. The racial division mitigated tensions between the paternalist and premodern plantation, on which the southern elite lived, and the individualist and formally democratic order outside its gates.

The Denmark Vesey slave conspiracy of 1822, the Nat Turner rebellion a decade later, and the beginnings of abolitionist agitation in the early 1830's all fed southern fears of racial rebellion. The resulting restrictions imposed on slaves underlined the dependence of southern white freedom on black slavery. But the fear of antislavery agitation drastically curtailed political and intellectual freedom for southern whites as well. It was illegal to argue in southern states that slavery was an illegitimate form of property or to advocate its abolition. The federal government acquiesced in the censorship of southern mail to prevent the circulation of antislavery literature. Mob violence intimidated the occasional antislavery editor, and the fear of subversive ideas spread beyond antislavery to inhibit intellectual and cultural expression more broadly.

The defense of slavery also restricted political freedom in the nation as a whole. Congress adopted a gag rule in 1836 to prevent discussion of antislavery petitions. Antiabolitionist mobs, more often than not led by local gentlemen of property and standing, invaded abolitionist meetings and destroyed abolitionist newspapers. In Alton, Illinois, in 1837, a mob murdered the abolitionist editor Elijah Lovejoy.

The abolition of slavery, in spite of proslavery fears, led to neither political nor social freedom for blacks. A new, quasi-peonage system replaced slavery as the dominant form of labor in southern agriculture. Sharecropping arrangements, tenant farming, and a crop lien credit system tied black agricultural workers to planters and merchants. Black convicts, often imprisoned without due process, worked southern mines and built and repaired southern roads. The Ku Klux Klan terrorized blacks during Reconstruction, when they enjoyed a measure of political power. Jim Crow laws developed to enforce social segregation.

Black efforts to acquire political power climaxed at the end of the nineteenth century in southern Populism, an interracial alliance of black and white farmers. Physical intimidation, electoral fraud, and racial fears all played a part in its defeat. That defeat was followed by the total disenfranchisement of blacks. Suffrage restrictions excluded many poor whites as well. The specter of black power, and the political ex-

clusion of blacks, created a system of one-party politics in the South. That politics was characterized by low participation, shifting, personally based factions, demagogic appeals, and the emergence of leaders hostile not just to racial equality but to a variety of ideas that were labeled un-American.

A pseudoscientific racist ideology, justifying black subordination and stigmatizing non-Teutonic European immigrants as well, developed in postbellum America. Imperial democrats like Theodore Roosevelt and Woodrow Wilson merged tutelary visions of the white man's burden abroad with justifications of racial inequality at home. Blacks were deprived of political power and suffered from economic discrimination in the North as well as the South, but no legal, state-enforced system of segregation developed in the North. A formal commitment to racial equality was enshrined in the Fourteenth and Fifteenth Amendments to the Constitution. Courts used the Fourteenth Amendment for seventy-five years to protect corporations instead of blacks. But a series of rulings against discrimination culminated in 1954 in *Brown* v. *Board of Education of Topeka,* which outlawed legally segregated schools. It set in motion a movement for black political and civil rights, the intimidation of which belongs with a discussion of the politics of the 1960's.

The 1790 naturalization law, one of the first acts of the new federal government, prohibited nonwhite immigrants from becoming naturalized citizens. That act expressed desires for a homogeneous population the consequences of which have reached beyond racial exclusion. Peoples of color, nonetheless, have felt the legal effects of such desires with particular force. Hispanics and Asians who came to work in the United States, or who lived on land seized by the expanding nation, were denied full civil and political rights well into the twentieth century. Most worked in labor-repressive systems in the farms and mines of California and the Southwest. Anti-Chinese agitation played a central role in California politics from the 1870's through the Progressive period. In perhaps the greatest single deprivation of rights in all American history, 110,000 Japanese-Americans were rounded up and interned in "concentration camps" (as President Franklin Roosevelt called them) during World War II. The Japanese were, according to the army official who recommended their incarceration, an "enemy race." Earl Warren, then the California attorney general, explained that he knew methods to "test the loyalty" of individual Caucasians. "But [he complained] when we deal with the Japanese we are in an entirely different field, and we cannot form any opinion that we believe to be sound." The Supreme Court upheld forcible Japanese internment in *Korematsu* v. *U.S.* (1943) on national emergency grounds. President Harry Truman rewarded Dillon S. Myer for directing the War Relocation Authority by appointing him Commissioner of Indian Affairs in 1950.

American history is normally seen as a history of freedom rather than of suppression. American racial history suggests that the suppression of peoples of color outside the normal political system has supported the freedom of the people within it. But the connections—real or imagined—between Indians and masterless Europeans, black and white workers, black sexuality and white women, all call into question any simple notion that whites were granted political rights while peoples of color were denied them. A fear of subversion has converted conflicts of interest in race relations into all-encompassing, psychologically based dangers to personal and national identity. That same fear of subversion underlies the nonracial history of American political repression.

ANTEBELLUM SOURCES OF COUNTERSUBVERSION AND CONTROL

The Alien and Sedition Acts of 1798 nearly abolished freedom of speech and the press in the new nation. The Sedition Act made criminal "any false, scandalous and malicious" writings or utterances against the government that were intended to defame government officers or excite against them the hatred of the people. The Alien Acts increased the period of residency prior to citizenship to fourteen years, authorized the president to deport any alien he considered dangerous to domestic peace, and empowered him to expel citizens of a country at war with the United States. These acts were the culmination of a dominant strand of thought in eighteenth-century America hostile to political liberty.

The English common law of seditious libel, valid in the colonies, punished criticism that lowered the government in public esteem and threatened to disturb the peace. Defenders of free expression in the colonies, before and during the Revolution, never attacked this concept of seditious libel at its roots. They did oppose prior restraints on the press, which the First Amendment eventually prohibited. They also demanded jury trials in seditious libel prosecutions and that truth be allowed to stand as a defense. There is no evidence that the authors of the First Amendment intended to abolish the common law of seditious libel. The Alien and Sedition Acts themselves instituted no prior restraint, called for trial by jury, and permitted truth as a defense. Hence their supporters could well have found the acts consistent with the First Amendment.

Prior to the Revolution, popular pressure had generally protected colonists who attacked crown representatives from being tried for seditious libel. New York's prosecution of the printer John Peter Zenger, in 1735, was an exception. A jury acquitted Zenger, but his defense did not challenge the concept of seditious libel. Those attacking colonial assemblies rather than crown representatives were more likely to face seditious libel prosecutions.

Mobs attacked loyalist presses during the Revolution, and states required loyalty oaths even of those who desired to remain neutral in the conflict with England. Demands for loyalty during the Revolution had practical urgency. But such demands derived from a theory that attributed colonial factionalism to the British crown. Once that alien presence was removed from American life, it was thought, factional conflicts would disappear. No theory justified an institutionalized opposition to popularly based government. Trial by jury and truth as a defense protected Americans who attacked the crown; they offered no refuge for those critical of locally popular governments. Only one case brought under the Alien and Sedition Acts ended in acquittal.

The Alien and Sedition Acts refused to countenance the existence of a legitimate political opposition. Jeffersonian Republicans, targets of the acts, developed in response the first theory of free expression in America to repudiate seditious libel. The Jeffersonians rejected the distinction between ordered liberty and license, the distinction upon which earlier defenses of free speech had rested. The need to show the truth of an idea, they argued, inadequately protected freedom of opinion. Madison, in *The Federalist* number 10, had already insisted that factions could not be suppressed without destroying liberty. His 1800 Report to the Virginia House of Delegates argued that popular governments, unlike hereditary monarchies, could not be libeled. A system of popular rule required freedom to criticize the government, wrote Madison. A free press, "checkered as it is with abuses," could not be subject to charges of sedition. The defeat of the Federalists in 1800 established the legitimacy of political opposition in America.

Legitimate opposition was still to be distinguished from illegitimate opposition. President Jefferson himself countenanced seditious libel prosecutions in the states. Abraham Lincoln suspended the writ of habeas corpus during the Civil War and presided over the arrest and confinement, without due process, of thousands of opponents of the war. State action to suppress dissent, derived from the law of seditious libel, would come to play a major role in the twentieth century. Modern governments seeking to suppress sedition would draw on the tradition enshrined in the other half of the Alien and Sedition Acts, the belief that aliens are to blame for sedition.

Federalists had charged that agents of the French Revolution, in combination with a secret order of freemasons and Bavarian illuminati, were conspiring to destroy American independence. Although state laws were rarely passed to suppress such foreign threats in antebellum America, conspiratorial fears still dominated politics. Americans mounted a series of crusades against the "Popish Whore of Babylon," the Masons, the Mormon church, the "monster hydra" Bank of the United States, the abolitionists, the slave power conspiracy, and the demon rum. This fear of alien conspiracies led to the blaming of problems in American life on forces operating outside it. Conspiracy-hunting turned political differences into absolute struggles between good and evil. Antebellum crusades had millennial, Protestant roots. They also reflected the dark side of American individualism. Countersubversive movements blamed centers of hidden, collective power for constraints on the individual. They drew strength from suspicions of

hidden motives in a mobile society where individuals influenced others to advance themselves and hid their real identities behind confidence-inspiring facades.

Efforts to stigmatize aliens were often more than rhetorical. Mobs not only assaulted abolitionists and free blacks; they also attacked Catholic neighborhoods and destroyed Mormon communities. The mob that burned a Roman Catholic convent in Charlestown, Massachusetts, in 1834, had been stirred by the fiery sermons of the Reverend Lyman Beecher. Beecher attacked popery as the enemy of religion and republicanism, exhorting his audience to action against it. But those, like Beecher, concerned with alien dangers before the Civil War relied most heavily neither on state laws against dissent nor on mob action. They sought instead to build institutions and form characters that would domesticate American freedom.

The men and women who discovered the asylum and reformed the family proposed to work on the interior of the self. Their efforts dovetailed with the pressures to conformity, Tocqueville observed on his trip to America. The tyranny of public opinion, the ideology of domesticity, and the discovery of the asylum all limited political dissent, in scarcely measurable ways. Insofar as they have succeeded, they have inhibited the formation of political opposition, not simply intimidated opposition already formed. Our subject now is the suppression of politics at the prepolitical level, through the transformation of potentially political discontent into problems of personal life.

The removal of external, British authority created a crisis of order for elites in the new nation. "We have changed our form of government," explained the Philadelphia physician Benjamin Rush, "but it remains yet to effect a revolution in our principles, opinions, and manners to accommodate them to the forms of government we have adopted." One solution (which Rush himself favored in the Pennsylvania constitutional debates of 1776) was to maintain a restricted suffrage and keep those who might threaten property and order out of electoral politics. But suffrage was already widespread before the Revolution. By the Jacksonian period all states except Rhode Island and South Carolina had universal, white, manhood suffrage.

Suffrage restriction continued to deny a political voice to women and peoples of color. Susan B. Anthony and fifteen other women were arrested for voting in the 1872 presidential election and charged with violating a federal law. Women's Party picketers in Washington, D.C., were assaulted by mobs, arrested, and jailed during World War I for attacking the effort to make the world "safe for democracy" in a country that denied half its citizens the vote. Although women received the franchise in some states in the late nineteenth and early twentieth centuries, they were not granted voting rights in the nation as a whole until the Nineteenth Amendment was ratified in 1920.

Nineteenth-century women were denied not only the vote but also control of their own property and entrance to many professions and trade unions as well. An ideology of domesticity justified restricting women's sphere to the home. The proponents of domestic ideology (such as Lyman Beecher's daughter Catharine) offered women the power to shape their husbands and sons in the family in return for relinquishing direct claims to exercise power in society. Some women (such as Catharine Beecher's sister, Harriet Beecher Stowe) employed domestic values against antifamilial social practices; slavery and alcoholic intemperance were the most prominent targets. But women who entered public life directly were said to unsex themselves and unman men. Women who resisted confinement in the home, or who replaced with bloomers the layers of clothing that confined their bodies, were greeted with public opprobrium. Instead, domestic ideology made women the instruments of confining others, of morality and social control.

Domestic ideology offered the family as both a refuge from and solution to social disorder. Its turn to the family did not so much enrich private life, however, as socialize it. Denying the truly private character of the home, domesticity made the family less a haven for protecting eccentricity than an arena for forming and standardizing personality. Enlisting the child's desire for love, and threatening him with the loss of love, the mother would influence the child to internalize morality. Characters formed by regulated affection in the home could safely enter the world. This retreat to the family encouraged the displacement onto politics of discontents originating (but forbidden to be traced to their source) in domestic life. At

the same time, domesticity dissolved political into personal problems. By locating social troubles and their solution in the family, domestic ideology shifted attention from the public arena into the home. It thereby took its place as part of the second method (other than suffrage restriction) that Rush had proposed to domesticate political freedom, the method of internalizing authority.

The internalization of authority in antebellum America had four components: a shift away from ceremonial public places into private but standardized interiors; a redefinition of political, social, and cultural conflicts as problems of crime and disease; loving confinement as the method of punishment and reform; and the creation of a self-controlled interior, resistant to corrupting temptations from the body and the world. Benjamin Rush, friend of John Adams and other revolutionary leaders, was the founder of the new discipline. Rush was a leading prison reformer and opponent of public executions; the father of the mental hospital; a promoter of public schools; and, as the American who discovered the dangers posed to the vigilant self by liquor and masturbation, the guiding spirit behind the nineteenth-century movements against alcoholic consumption and self-abuse.

Rush proposed to convert men into "republican machines. This must be done if we expect them to perform their parts properly, in the great machine of the government of the state." Such "good citizens" would exercise their freedom in a self-controlled way. Rush preserved the distinction between liberty and license by moving it from state enforcement into the individual conscience. New institutions were to form that conscience. For the middle class, as domestic ideology signaled, the most important of these institutions was the nuclear family, and it was supplemented by the school. Those falling out of the middle class—or never in it to begin with—were to be confined and reformed in asylums: schools, prisons, hospitals, and factories. Their purpose, Rush explained, was to "render the mass of the people more homogeneous, and thereby fit them more easily for uniform and peaceable government."

Asylums responded to the perceived breakdown of a deferential order in post-revolutionary America. They housed those masterless men and women no longer ordered within the traditional structures of kin group, church, and community. Some asylums, like the mental hospital, offered protection from the pressures of a mobile, acquisitive society. Others, like the prison and the paternally organized factory, contained the threat posed by the "dangerous classes" of urban immigrants and the poor. Just as the reservation would confine and reform the "perishing classes" of savages, so the urban "dangerous classes" were offered the prison.

Rush opposed public executions because they stimulated crowds not to obedience but to disorder. Physical violence not only provoked mob violence in return but also failed to reform the criminal. Whipping offenders subdued their bodies, according to prison reformers, but failed to reach their hearts. Instead of whipping the wrongdoer and setting him loose (the normal practice in the eighteenth century), the new prisons confined criminals behind walls. Like the home, the asylum provided a place of refuge and, as in the home, replaced physical force by disciplined love. In a kind of mockery of developing domestic practices, greater privacy for the inmate was combined with surveillance over him and attention to his interior. English and American reformers advocated removing the chains from the prisoner and enlisting him in his own cure. Isolated from the bad influences of one another, regimented, observed, and subjected to a regularized authority, criminals would learn to love society. Although in practice the prison sacrificed the regeneration of the criminal to his confinement, in theory it offered a perfect marriage of the two methods that were coming to dominate the American practice of control: concentrated state coercive power and the creation through interior reform of a free man.

Tocqueville and Gustave de Beaumont, who came to America to study the new prisons, observed that "while society in the United States gives the example of a most extended liberty, the prisons of the same country offer a spectacle of the most complete despotism." That paradox reflected the rise of total institutions in response to the fears of extended liberty. But a deeper commonality lay underneath the contrast. Both the society and the prison wiped out traditional loyalties that bound people together. The spread of freedom, in such a society of extended liberty, required the formation of selves who would not

abuse that liberty. Both the mobile society and the total institution isolated the self and invaded his interior. Individuals fearful of incurring disapproval, wrote Tocqueville, and deprived of support from traditional subcultures and kin groups, would not risk isolating themselves from the democratic mass. They would not develop the freedom of opinion to entertain subversive ideas. Tocqueville explained, "Despotism, to reach the soul, clumsily struck at the body, and the soul, escaping from such blows, rose gloriously above it. Such is not the course adopted by tyranny in democratic republics. There the body is left free, and the soul is enslaved."

The task of enforcing the distinction between liberty and license, which once belonged to the state, moved in Tocqueville's analysis at once within the individual conscience and out into public opinion. Those who stepped beyond the bonds of legitimate controversy faced not so much punishment by the state as estrangement from the social mass. The institutional structures that domestic and asylum reformers favored molded characters vulnerable to the social pressures that Tocqueville described.

Reformers and institution-builders in the twentieth century reacted against the regimented isolation of inmates in the nineteenth-century prison. Progressives proposed to attend to the life history of the individual case and to turn the prison into a protocommunity. They shifted attention from the crime to the criminal, and from guilt or innocence to sickness or health. But since confinement itself remained intact, the consequence was to extend surveillance inside and outside the prison walls. The parole system tracked inmates after their release. Juvenile courts investigated offenders before they were institutionalized. The young, the welfare recipient, and the mentally ill surrendered legal rights to members of the helping professions. Those incarcerated in "moral hospitals," as Denver judge Ben Lindsay called the asylums, did not need protection from authority.

A therapeutic approach to social problems affected the treatment not only of crime, poverty, and mental disturbance but also of political conflict as well. Reform practice turned conflicts of interest into problems of personal and social adjustment. Its soft form of coercion competed, in politics as in crime, with a punitive, law-and-order methodology. Both dissolved the distinction between political and personal disturbance, the one in the name of therapy, the other in the name of punishment. The criminalization of political differences, the collapse of politics into disease, the spread of surveillance, and the stigmatization of dissenters as social pariahs have all played important roles in the suppression of radical politics. They have done so not merely, as in Tocqueville's analysis, through the pressures of public opinion, but through the armed force of the state.

RED SCARES:
CLASS CONFLICT

Antebellum politics had at its center the repression of Indians and blacks; workers took their place after the Civil War. The rhetoric of a struggle between savagery and civilization moved from the frontier West to urban America, from Indian conflict to class war. A series of red scares, one in the 1870's, one in 1886, and one in 1919, marked the half-century between 1870 and 1920. Each located subversive political ideas within an alien, immigrant working class.

The modern history of countersubversion began with the red scare of 1873–1878. It arose in response to the Paris Commune abroad and to a major depression and radical labor protest at home. "Today there is not in our language, nor in any language, a more hateful word than communism," proclaimed a professor at the Union Theological Seminary. Cities built armories to protect themselves against working-class uprisings, states revived militias, and police attacked strikers and unemployment demonstrators. Hundreds of thousands of unemployed, roaming the country in search of work, generated a "tramp" scare.

The dean of the Yale Law School, in a paper delivered at the 1877 meeting of the American Social Science Association, announced, "As we hear the word *tramp*, there arises straightaway before us the spectacle of a lazy, incorrigible, cowardly, utterly depraved savage." Tramps, like Indians before them, were wandering, masterless men. The industrial capitalist threat to homogeneous, ordered communities was located in its wandering victims. The breakdown in social order was real. It stemmed, however, not from savages and communists but from centralized

corporations and their need for a national market in labor and other commodities. Social breakdown climaxed in the nationwide railway strike of 1877, called "nothing more nor less than French Communism," by an official of President Hayes's administration, in which strikers fought with police and mobs seized and burned the Pittsburgh railway yards.

The first antired political trial with nationwide significance took place in Chicago in 1886. It was a response to mass, working-class support for the Knights of Labor, a strike against Jay Gould's railroad system, and a national movement for the eight-hour day. When mounted police ordered an anarchist demonstration in Haymarket Square to disperse, someone threw a bomb. It injured seventy policemen and killed one. Eight Chicago anarchists, some neither present at the rally nor known to one another, and none connected to the bombing, were found guilty of conspiracy to commit murder. Four were executed. (One killed himself in jail, and the remaining three were pardoned in 1893.) The Haymarket anarchists were convicted for radical ideas and violent talk. Their trial, which was conducted in an atmosphere of national hysteria, destroyed not only the Chicago anarchist movement but the Knights of Labor as well. For the next forty years industrial unions organizing unskilled workers were the targets of state and state-sanctioned violence.

The most significant state labor repression in the next half-century was the repression of the Pullman boycott and nationwide railway strike of 1894. Attorney General Richard Olney, a former corporate lawyer who sat on the board of one of the struck railways, obtained a federal injunction that effectively outlawed union activity. The injunction permitted individual workers to leave their jobs, because to force them to work would violate their freedom of contract. But, in a massive prohibition of freedom of speech and assembly, workers and union leaders were forbidden to convince others to quit work. The injunction safeguarded the same private freedom that was offered to Indians who abandoned their tribal ties. It outlawed political freedom, the freedom of a community to speak and act together. American Railway Union leaders were arrested for violating the injunction; the union's president, Eugene Victor Debs, went to jail.

States continued to suppress labor's free

speech and assembly in the twentieth century and to meet organizing efforts with violence. Western miners suffered from a particularly bloody history of state and corporate violence. When the anticapitalist Industrial Workers of the World (IWW) was formed in 1905, western miners and woodworkers provided its major support. Local officials jailed IWW organizers for making public speeches, a practice that led to free-speech fights in such western cities as Spokane, Washington; Fresno and San Diego, California; and Minot, North Dakota. Wobblies arrested for exercising their rights of free speech filled the local jails; their nonviolent civil disobedience often generated violence in return. San Diego police turned prisoners over to vigilantes who escorted them to the state line and beat them before setting them free. Wobblies were also the victims of state and state-sponsored violence during strikes of eastern immigrant workers. In the 1913 Paterson textile strike, for example, New Jersey cities relinquished their police authority to mill owners, whose agents broke up meetings and arrested strikers.

Hostility to the IWW and to subversive ideas climaxed in the red scare during and after World War I. The IWW gained organizational strength among western woodworkers and miners during World War I. States and the federal government responded with a campaign of repression that destroyed the organization. The broadest search warrants ever issued by the American judiciary resulted in the seizure of tons of IWW material around the country in September 1917. Hundreds of Wobbly activists were rounded up, and over 300 were indicted. In the second great Chicago conspiracy trial, thirty years after Haymarket, 101 Wobblies were convicted of conspiring to obstruct the war. Many were guilty simply of membership in the IWW. Others were convicted on the basis of statements made before American entry into the war. IWW fund-raising and defense materials were barred from the mails; IWW defense meetings were broken up.

Even before American entry into the war, President Woodrow Wilson had attacked "citizens of the United States . . . born under other flags . . . who have poured the poison of disloyalty into the very arteries of our national life." Wilson was stigmatizing radicals who opposed American preparations for war, not simply German-Americans sympathetic to their homeland.

The Espionage and Sedition Acts of 1917–1918 made it a crime to speak or act against the war. Aliens, even if they remained silent and inactive, were subject to summary arrest. Sedition indictments were obtained against members of the Socialist party who opposed the war. Socialist Congressman Victor Berger, appealing his conviction under the Espionage Act, was barred from taking his congressional seat by a vote of 311–1. Debs, who had become a Socialist party leader after the suppression of the Pullman strike, was sentenced to ten years in prison for making an antiwar speech. The U.S. Post Office conducted a campaign of censorship against the Socialist party and the IWW, removing their publications from the mail.

State governments also passed laws outlawing opposition to the war and forbidding expressions of revolutionary disloyalty to the American form of government. American citizens were jailed for up to twenty years for criticizing the war; those guilty in England of equivalent offenses received fines or minor jail sentences. The Supreme Court upheld convictions under state criminal syndicalism laws, ruling that states could punish revolutionary words spoken with malicious intent that might have a tendency to provoke violence in the future. These rulings revived the doctrine of seditious libel.

War intensified the hysteria over disloyalty in America, but the red scare reached its greatest heights after the war was over. America in 1919, reported a British journalist, "was hag-ridden by the spectre of Bolshevism. It was like a sleeper in a nightmare, enveloped by a thousand phantoms of destruction." One of every five workers struck during 1919, and a series of bombings culminated in an effort to dynamite the home of Attorney General A. Mitchell Palmer. In response to the Russian Revolution, the radical labor ferment, and the bombings, state and federal governments mounted an assault on subversion.

Their campaign climaxed in two events: the suppression of the 1919 steel strike and a series of Justice Department raids that rounded up thousands of allegedly subversive foreigners for deportation. State and private violence, combined with accusations of subversive influence, broke the steel strike. In the Pittsburgh area alone, 25,000 deputies, acting under legal authority, were picked and armed by the steel companies. The alien raids attacked radical political and labor organizations. On the night of 2 January 1920 federal agents seized 10,000 alleged subversives, including leaders of the Communist and Communist Labor parties, as well as thousands of immigrant citizens and aliens involved simply in socialist, union, or cooperative ventures. Attorney General Palmer described the targets of his raids as "alien filth," with "sly and crafty eyes . . . lopsided faces, sloping brows, and misshapen features." Decades of pseudoscientific racial theories, applied to immigrants as well as blacks, bore fruit in the raids. Although some of those seized were deported, most were ultimately released.

Government repression destroyed the IWW. The Socialist party survived in the industrial centers, with its base restricted to recent immigrants. Its branches in the smaller towns and rural areas could not withstand the combination of official repression and mob attacks. The red scare drove the small communist parties underground and confirmed them in their apocalyptic, conspiratorial view of American politics. In the name of destroying alien influences, the red scare assaulted the American roots of American radicalism. It helped create the alien enemy that it had imagined, even if the actual red specter was only a shadow of the fantasy. The red scare ushered in the nativist mood and the obsession with 100 percent Americanism that dominated the politics of the 1920's.

In 1927 the last and most prominent victims of the postwar hysteria, the anarchists Nicola Sacco and Bartolomeo Vanzetti, were executed by the state of Massachusetts. Sacco and Vanzetti had been convicted of a murder committed during a 1920 payroll robbery. No convincing evidence linked Vanzetti to the crime, although Sacco's guilt is still in dispute. A three-member commission headed by Harvard President A. Lawrence Lowell determined that the two had been given a fair trial. The trial record shows that they were actually convicted for their political beliefs. Sacco and Vanzetti were executed for their threat to property and the state, a threat that lay in their anarchist doctrines, not their alleged crime.

Political interventions helped destroy the Knights of Labor, the American Railway Union, the IWW, and the Steelworkers; the conservative craft unions of the American Federation of Labor survived and grew between 1886 and 1920. Nevertheless, the entire labor movement enjoyed little better than an outlaw status before 1935. The repression of labor in America was more violent and severe than that in any other Western, industrializing country. The Supreme Court, in *In Re Debs* (1894), legalized the use of court injunctions to break strikes; judges issued nearly 2,000 injunctions between 1880 and 1920. Employers enjoyed injunctive relief from strikes that damaged "probable expectancies" of future profit rather than existing real property. Unions were subject to conspiracy prosecutions for boycotting nonunion goods; for having large numbers of strikers present at plant gates; and for inducing workers to break contracts that committed them not to join unions. Courts protected the individual "freedom of contract" of workers at the expense not only of worker collective action but also of political efforts to regulate the conditions of employment. Wage, hour, and child-labor laws were all ruled unconstitutional.

State violence, which controlled peoples of color before the Civil War, repressed postbellum working-class and radical protest. State militia and federal troops were used to break strikes; strike-breaking became, with the end of the Indian wars, the most conspicuous function of the regular army. Violence, killings, and massive arrests occurred during strikes. The national state also abdicated its monopoly over legitimate force to corporations and detective agencies. These private bodies conducted surveillance and employed armed men. They punished union workers and organizers, acting sometimes on their own, sometimes in cooperation with, or under color of, legal authority. Corporations engaged in labor espionage, blacklisting, the large-scale recruitment of nonunion workers during strikes, and the use of private police. With a force of 2,000 trained active men and 30,000 reserves, the Pinkerton Detective Agency was larger in the late nineteenth century than the American army. Between 1933 and 1937 four steel companies ordered more tear gas equipment than did any law enforcement agency. The abdication of state functions to private groups, a general feature of American politics, played an important role in labor conflicts through the 1930's. Together, state and private action deprived workers before the New Deal of their right to organize.

The 1935 Wagner Act, called labor's Magna

Carta, made employer interference with the right to organize into an unfair labor practice. One historian has labeled the act "perhaps the most important civil liberties statute ever passed by Congress." Three years earlier the Norris-La Guardia Act had outlawed the use of the labor injunction. The Supreme Court, in *Thornhill* v. *Alabama* (1940), extended First Amendment protection to peaceful picketing in labor disputes. Later courts restricted the scope of *Thornhill*, and the 1947 Taft-Hartley Act removed some of the legal protections for union organizing activity. Nevertheless, since the 1930's organized labor has been accepted as a legitimate interest in American society.

The organization of industrial workers into the Congress of Industrial Organizations, and the ties of CIO unions to the welfare state and the Democratic party, began to eliminate working-class activity as the target of counter-subversion. Labor struggles remained important, however, at the origins of the post–World War II red scare. Communists and their allies controlled several CIO unions. Those unions supported the war and were allied with the Democratic party. When the beginnings of the cold war ended that alliance, the government and its union supporters moved to destroy left-wing labor. The Taft-Hartley Act deprived unions whose officers refused to sign anticommunist loyalty oaths of the protections of the National Labor Relations Board. The CIO expelled those unions in 1948. Labor-management conflict in the motion picture industry also contributed to the postwar red scare, by helping to generate the Hollywood blacklist. Once the domestic cold war was fairly launched, however, labor was not its central target.

Earlier red scares developed out of class conflicts between labor and capital, in which the state served mostly as the agent of the capitalist class. The Soviet Union replaced the immigrant working class as the source of anxiety in the decades after World War II. The combat between workers and capitalists was supplanted by one between intellectuals, government employees, students, and middle-class activists on the one hand, and a state national-security apparatus on the other.

Both the postwar Soviet Union and the radical labor movement of an earlier period posed genuine threats to dominant interests in American society, although the nature and extent of those threats are a matter of controversy. There were also real conflicts of interest between white Americans and peoples of color. But the countersubversive response transformed interest conflicts into psychologically based anxieties over national security and American identity. Exaggerated responses to the domestic Communist menace narrowed the bounds of permissible political disagreement and generated a national-security state. The rise of a security-oriented state bureaucracy is the most important new factor in the modern history of American political intimidation.

RED SCARES:
THE NATIONAL-SECURITY STATE

The cold war marks the third major moment in the history of countersubversion. The first moment was racial; it pitted whites against peoples of color. The second was class and ethnic; it pitted Americans against aliens. The third moment, in which a national-security bureaucracy confronts the invisible agents of a foreign power, revolves around mass society and the state.

Throughout American history, the subversive has threatened the family, property, and personal and national identity. But three shifts distinguish the first red scares from their cold war descendant. First, subversives were visibly alien in earlier red scares; they were The Other. They moved inside American minds and bodies in the 1950's, and one could not tell them from anyone else. No longer part of a conflict between contrasting races or classes, 1950's Communists were the invisible members of (and thereby exposed anxieties about) American mass society.

Second, as the visible differences that stigmatized subversives disappeared, the imagined danger shifted from the body to the mind. Instead of representing primitivism, loss of restraint, and disorder, the subversive threatened control by a sophisticated, alien order. That danger justified the third departure in countersubversive history, the rise of the national-security state.

In July 1919, without congressional authorization, the attorney general's office created a General Intelligence Division (GID) within the Justice Department. Its purpose was to infiltrate and collect information on radical organizations. The GID borrowed the techniques of labor espionage and surveillance employed by private corporations and detective agencies. It was headed by J. Edgar Hoover, a twenty-four-year-old former cataloguer in the Library of Congress, who had moved to a clerkship in the Justice Department's Enemy Alien Registration unit. Hoover boasted of his role in breaking the 1919 steel strike. He and Attorney General Palmer supervised the alien raids of 1919–1920. Hoover also made a series of sensational charges against alleged radicals.

Blaming subversives for the 1919 race riots (and thereby not only imagining conspiracies that did not exist but also making blacks the perpetrators rather than the victims of the outrages), Hoover attacked black leaders for being under Bolshevik influence. He charged them with being "openly, defiantly assertive" of their "own equality or even superiority." Hoover established files on alleged subversives. He investigated and tried to discredit people who opposed his actions, like the noted civil libertarians Zechariah Chafee, Jr., and Felix Frankfurter. When Assistant Secretary of Labor Louis Post began to release individuals illegally detained in the alien raids, Hoover ordered Post's subversive links investigated.

Attorney General Harlan Stone terminated the GID in 1924, the year he reorganized the Federal Bureau of Investigation. Stone placed Hoover in charge of the entire FBI and ordered the FBI to limit its investigations to actual violations of federal law. In violation of Stone's memorandum, the FBI continued to collect information on radical labor and political organizations. Hoover's appointment, moreover, united criminal detection and political surveillance in a single agency, as was the case in no other country. Stone placed in charge a man trained in political countersubversion rather than law enforcement. Hoover's rise to head the FBI confirmed the confusion between crime and radical dissent at the heart of the American fear of subversion.

Franklin Roosevelt secretly rescinded Stone's restrictions on the FBI in 1936, reactivating it as a political surveillance agency. Two years later the president placed the FBI in charge of all domestic surveillance and, in violation of federal law and Supreme Court decisions, permitted it to engage in warrantless wiretaps.

Roosevelt claimed only to want surveillance of fascist and Communist agents of the foreign, totalitarian powers, although he occasionally used Hoover for intelligence against his own political adversaries. Roosevelt was not aware of the large-scale expansion in bureau activities that began under his presidency. Hoover was creating a secret political police to infiltrate, influence, and seek to punish dissenting political speech and action.

Other branches of the federal government also developed countersubversive instruments. The House of Representatives created a committee to investigate un-American activities in 1938. In 1940 Congress passed the Smith Act, making it a crime to advocate, or conspire to advocate, the overthrow of the government by force or violence. Congress attached this prohibition to the Alien Registration Act, perpetuating the association of aliens and sedition. By American entry into World War II, the countersubversive trio of executive surveillance, legislative investigation, and court legal action was established. That trio, in relationships sometimes of cooperation and sometimes of conflict, continues to dominate subversive control.

Nazism provided the occasion for the emergence of the national-security apparatus. Communists, who were to be its major targets, actually helped develop the countersubversive ideological rationale. That is less a paradox than it seems, for countersubversive theory and practice mirror the enemy they are out to destroy. The pro-Soviet wartime film *Mission to Moscow* (1943) employed the imagery of national defense and domestic conspiracy to justify Stalin's purge trials. The film blamed a Trotskyist-Nazi alliance for weakening Russia against the imminent German invasion. The first prosecutions under the Smith Act, welcomed by the Communists, were of leaders of the Trotskyist Socialist Workers party. Within a few years the screenwriter for *Mission to Moscow* would find himself blacklisted, his demonology having turned against him, and the Communist party would be the target of Smith Act prosecutions. Since the end of World War II, as had been true for decades preceding it, Communists and their alleged sympathizers have been the major targets of the suppression of political dissent.

In March 1947, President Harry Truman announced he was sending military aid to Greece and Turkey to defend their regimes against Communist attacks. In that same month the president established a new government loyalty program. Declaring communism a domestic as well as a foreign menace, he set the stage for the red scare of 1947–1954. All present and prospective government employees were to undergo investigations of their loyalty, with each government agency establishing its own loyalty review board. How was loyalty to be established? Loyalty boards gave great weight to past beliefs and memberships. They asked questions about political views and social practices. Such questions included, "Do you ever have Negroes in your home?" "Do you read Howard Fast? Tom Paine? Upton Sinclair?" Loyalty boards relied heavily on information supplied by anonymous informers, who included former Communists, FBI infiltrators, and ordinary citizens who claimed to have derogatory knowledge of those against whom they informed. Accused employees were not entitled to hear the specific charges against them or to know the names of government informers. The burden of proof lay on the accused individual, who had to establish not only that he or she had been loyal in the past but also that there were no reasonable grounds to expect disloyalty in the future.

An estimated 13.5 million workers, 20 percent of the labor force, were subject to loyalty programs in government and sensitive private industry. Other nations facing greater political instability instituted no elaborate loyalty tests for government employment. The historic American fear of subversion was spawning a government bureaucracy, whose growth marked a sharp, institutional break with the past.

J. Robert Oppenheimer, father of the atomic bomb, was the most famous individual refused security clearance. Oppenheimer was ostensibly denied access to classified material because of the former political associations of his friends and relatives. He was actually being persecuted for his opposition to the development of the hydrogen bomb. Other government employees not as well known as Oppenheimer, particularly former Socialists or Communists, also faced political persecution. Val R. Lorwin, an anticommunist Socialist who later became a noted labor historian, was charged with perjury for denying he had been a Communist. The government case, eventually thrown out of court,

was based on the testimony of a mendacious informer.

The criteria for determining loyalty included past or present membership in any organization designated as subversive by the attorney general. The attorney general's authority to issue such a list, wrote civil libertarian Alan Barth, gave him "perhaps the most arbitrary and far-reaching power ever exercised by a single public official in the history of the United States." The attorney general's list played a major role both inside and outside the government. "Its aim," explained Attorney General Tom Clark, was "to isolate subversive movements in this country from effective interference with the body politic." The attorney general could proscribe any organization and thereby deprive individuals who had once belonged to it of government employment. The list was also used to deny employment to individuals in the private sector and to stigmatize political opponents.

The Truman and Eisenhower administrations moved against alleged subversives in society as well as in government. Communists, warned Truman's attorney general, J. Howard McGrath, "are everywhere—in factories, offices, butcher shops, on street corners, in private business, and each carries in himself the germs of death for society." Communist party leaders were arrested and convicted under the Smith Act. The government denied passports to anyone whose travel was "not in the interests" of the United States, including the black singer and actor Paul Robeson. "Foreign propaganda," such as the works of Lenin, was seized as it entered the country, and the Central Intelligence Agency began secretly to open correspondence addressed to American citizens from abroad. Hundreds of aliens were arrested for deportation in early 1948 alone, and prominent resident aliens (like Charlie Chaplin) were denied reentry. The State Department also moved to deport naturalized citizens. When Rose Chernin resisted such efforts, as head of the Los Angeles Committee for the Protection of the Foreign-Born, the government tried to deport her, too. During the years of the cold war and the Korean War, the Supreme Court excluded Communists and Communist-sympathizers from the protections of the Bill of Rights. It allowed Communists to be jailed for preaching revolution, upheld their firing from public schools, denied Communist-led unions the protections of the labor laws, upheld the deportation of former Communists with American-born children, and permitted the discretionary imprisonment of aliens, without indictment or trial, on national-security grounds. But in *Yates* v. *U.S.* (1957), the Court ruled that those convicted of conspiracy to advocate the overthrow of the government by force must be shown to have urged others "to do something rather than merely to believe in something." That decision, which freed Rose Chernin and other Communist leaders convicted with her, effectively ended prosecutions under the Smith Act.

National-security agencies of the government greatly expanded their activities under presidents Truman and Eisenhower. The FBI perfected its two major countersubversive weapons, surveillance and files. By 1960 the bureau maintained 430,000 files on individuals allegedly connected to subversive activities. Private citizens cooperated with the bureau in reporting suspicious behavior. According to Sigmund Diamond, writing in the *Nation* (1979), Harvard professor Henry Kissinger opened a letter sent to a participant in his international relations seminar and communicated its contents to the Boston FBI office. The FBI also kept an index of those who posed a danger to national security and who should be rounded up during a national emergency. The index contained the names of writer Norman Mailer and of Senator Paul Douglas, a liberal Democrat and an anticommunist.

The FBI relied heavily on wiretaps and bugs. It wiretapped the conversations between Oppenheimer and his lawyers during hearings before the Atomic Energy Commission. Eisenhower's attorney general, Herbert Brownell, authorized break-ins to install wiretaps. Brownell boasted that FBI investigations covered "the entire spectrum of the social and labor movement" in the country. Under the COMINFIL program, the bureau did not wait to act until it had evidence of Communist activity; rather it infiltrated any organization where it suspected it might find Communists.

Hoover kept files on the private lives of congressmen and other prominent Americans. He used information from those files to intimidate or discredit those critical of the FBI. Fear of reprisals helps explain Hoover's political untouchability during the half-century he headed the bureau. His mass and elite popularity also stemmed from the obsession with communism in American life and with the equation of the fight against communism with the fight against crime.

The transformation of political dissent into criminal disloyalty was fed by sensational accusations of espionage in the late 1940's against Alger Hiss, Judith Coplon, and Ethel and Julius Rosenberg. Congressman Richard Nixon, who rose to national prominence through the Hiss case, described it as "a small part of the whole shocking story of Communist espionage in the United States." Hiss, accused of transmitting confidential State Department documents, was convicted of perjury. The Rosenbergs were executed for, in Judge Irving Kaufman's words, "putting into the hands of the Russians the A-bomb." Judge Kaufman accused the Rosenbergs of responsibility for Communist aggression and American deaths in Korea. Hiss and the Rosenbergs may well have passed confidential information to the Russians; their guilt is still in dispute. But they neither gave the Soviet Union the atomic bomb nor caused the Korean War. Their highly publicized trials and unprecedented death sentence helped to justify the obsession with national security and to identify opposition to American policies in the cold war with criminal, treasonable disloyalty.

The domestic red scare was a response not just to the external Soviet threat but also to the formation of a third party by former vice-president Henry Wallace. The Wallace campaign of 1948, in which Communists were active, threatened Truman's reelection. The president insisted that the "fact that the Communists are guiding and using the third party shows that this party does not represent American ideals." The first Smith Act indictments were handed down shortly before the Progressive party convention, and the 1948 deportations concentrated on Wallace campaign activists.

Truman and his anticommunist, liberal supporters distinguished the Communist party from legitimate political oppositions. The Communist party, they argued, was an international conspiracy to overthrow American government, taking orders from a foreign power. Soviet expansion into Eastern Europe, the Berlin blockade, and the invasion of South Korea required, in their view, a firm American response. Anticommunist liberals rightly called attention to Soviet expansion, to the monstrous crimes of the Russian state against its own people, and to Moscow's direction of the American Communist party. Some members of the party were probably spies and murderers, just as were some agents of the American state. But the assault on Communists and Communist sympathizers focused not on actual crimes but on memberships, beliefs, and associations. It thereby spread by its own logic to so-called fellow travelers, those who associated with Communists, shared their beliefs, and might secretly be responsive to party direction.

The red scare joined together—as one danger—atomic spying, revelations of confidential government proceedings, Communist party membership, membership in "communist front" organizations, and subversive ideas. In that chain reaction of guilt by free association, the ideas became the source of the atomic contamination. As if to reverse the only actual use of nuclear weapons, that by the United States, the red scare made un-American ideas radioactive. Communists, to quote again from Truman's attorney general, carried "germs of death" to the American body politic.

The Truman administration initiated the postwar anticommunist obsession, but its logic turned it against those who had given it birth. Congressional Republicans found the Democratic administration itself sympathetic to communism. Senator Joseph McCarthy of Wisconsin was the most prominent Republican to accuse Truman of "coddling" Communists. Accusations by McCarthy and other Republicans intensified the pressures on government employees for political conformity. Caught between the Truman loyalty program and McCarthyite charges, countless individuals either left the government or tailored their recommendations to avoid charges of Communist sympathy.

By 1952 virtually the entire China section of the State Department had been purged, since its predictions of a Chinese Communist victory were taken as signs that its members were "soft on communism." The firings had a chilling effect on personnel who remained. Had State Department employees and elected political leaders not been committed to a military solution in Southeast Asia, to avoid charges of complicity in another Asian defeat, the United States might have avoided the war in Vietnam.

Congressional committees investigated the political associations of private citizens and government employees. Individuals were forced to name the names of their alleged Communist associates, take the Fifth Amendment against self-incrimination, or go to jail for contempt of Congress. The major function of these degradation ceremonies was neither to discover crimes nor to make new laws but, rather, to stigmatize individuals, proscribe political ideas, and turn community members against one another. Like the effort to break up Indian tribes, and like the labor injunction, the ritual of naming names atomized political association. Isolated individuals, as Tocqueville had foreseen, faced the opprobrium of public opinion. They also faced reprisals from private employers and from the state.

Senator McCarthy gave his name to the atmosphere of suspicion and political fear that dominated America from 1947 until after the end of the Korean War. McCarthy's use of the red scare against both the Truman and Eisenhower administrations led to calling the domestic red scare McCarthyism and to interpreting McCarthyism as popular hysteria against the responsible, elite policymakers. Such views ignored McCarthy's institutional support—in the Republican party, in Congress, and among local elites. Labeling the red scare McCarthyism also deflected attention from the origins and continuation of countersubversive practices within the executive branch; from the growth of a national-security bureaucracy; and from the association of red scares with liberal, Democratic presidents. Democratic chief executives, forging a strong, personal presidency and carrying out an idealist, expansionist foreign policy, have been the major presidential sources of red scares. A line runs from Andrew Jackson's presidency through the administrations of Woodrow Wilson, Harry Truman, and Lyndon Johnson.

State, local, and private agencies also sought to purify America of subversive influences during the cold war. New York City fired alleged Communists from its public schools. California made its college teachers sign loyalty oaths. The American Legion pressured communities to ban subversive speakers and movies and to remove subversive books from public libraries. The motion picture industry blacklisted those who refused to name names before HUAC.

Ronald Reagan supported the Hollywood

blacklist as president (1947–1960) of the Screen Actors Guild. Leading the fight to drive subversives out of Hollywood, he formed a political perspective that centered on the dangers of communism. As he later put it, Reagan opposed "the Communist plan . . . to take over the motion picture business. . . . Its gradual transformation into a Communist grist mill," he wrote, "would have been a major coup for our enemies." Thinking that Communists were close to controlling Hollywood was fantastic, but understanding that movies played a major role in shaping American consciousness was not. As Reagan explained, after he became president of the United States, "It is the motion picture that shows us not only how we look and sound, but—more important—how we feel." Attention to mass fears of communism, to the tyranny of public opinion and the pressures for political conformity, is essential in understanding the power of countersubversion in American political life. But cold war America suffered not from an active popular threat to political freedom but from institutions that formed a public opinion fearful of unorthodox political ideas and quiescent at their suppression. The movies, as Reagan understood, were one such institution. They at once reflected, shaped, and expressed the buried dynamics of a repressive political consciousness.

In reparation for the handful of movies made in the 1940's either sympathetic to the Soviet Union or critical of American life, Hollywood produced a series of anticommunist movies during the cold war. Some, like *Walk East on Beacon* (1952) and *I Was a Communist for the FBI* (1951), were made in cooperation with the bureau. In *I was a Communist,* Warner Brothers reversed its *Mission to Moscow.* Both films used a documentary voice-over to give fiction the sound of news, both showed factory sabotage, and both warned against an imminent foreign invasion. A conspiratorial cabal in both films threatened the national defense, played upon divisive social discontent, and undermined the nation's will. The difference was that the threat was now from Russia—not to it. Anticommunist films like this one, making Communists into gangsters, equated communism with crime. They also showed how Communists turned family members against one another and endangered private life.

But the films also expressed anxieties about the internal vulnerability of the family. They suggested that domestic ideology, far from protecting Americans against alien ideas, generated aliens from within its bosom. In *My Son John* (1952), derived from the Judith Coplon spy case, John's father fails to command respect. His sons make fun of him, and the film exposes his American Legion costume and his simple-minded slogans to ridicule. The father's old-fashioned coercive methods do not control John, just as family and prison reformers had predicted they would not. But the newer, maternal methods of loving influence only make matters worse. John has become a Communist, the film suggests, because of the liberal ideas and sexual availability of his mother. But John has betrayed his mother for a female spy, and his mother turns against him when she sees that a key he has retrieved from her fits the other woman's lock. "Mothers . . . Our Only Hope" announced J. Edgar Hoover's article enlisting domestic ideology in the fight against crime. In *My Son John,* and again in *The Manchurian Candidate* (1962), the special bond between mother and son engendered psychological and political bad influence.

The FBI tracks down John and saves his parents; weakened paternal authority required the help of the state. Anticommunist films attacked the police state; yet they glorified an FBI whose agents and electronic devices, controlled from a central source, penetrated the deepest recesses of private life. It was often difficult to tell the faceless Communists from their counterparts in the FBI. Anticommunist films also violated the sanctity of the family by justifying the informer, who betrayed subversive members of his or her own family. Both *My Son John* and *Walk East on Beacon* made informing on Communist family members into an act of moral heroism.

On the Waterfront (1954) and *Storm Warning* (1951) moved the defense of informing into other walks of life, labor racketeering and southern violence. The effort to turn the informer into a culture hero had particular resonance in Hollywood, where naming names had become a condition of employment. The Ku Klux Klan was the stand-in for the Communist party in *Storm Warning,* as it often was in justifications of FBI surveillance. Reagan, in the role of District Attorney Burt Rainey, is asked at the outset of the film if he plans to "name names" and expose the respected members of his community who secretly belong to the Klan. Rainey responds that he stands for "law and order." In the film's major action, he tries to convince a woman (played by Ginger Rogers) who has seen a Klan murder to inform on her brother-in-law. By failing to do so, she allows herself to be brutalized and her younger sister to be killed.

Aside from its anticommunist films, Hollywood avoided political themes in the 1950's. Monogram Studios dropped plans for a movie on Hiawatha, fearing that his efforts for peace among the Iroquois nations would be seen as aiding Communist peace propaganda. The actress Judy Holliday, called before HUAC for having supported Henry Wallace, insisted, "I don't say 'yes' to anything now except cancer, polio, and cerebral palsy, things like that." Listing diseases as the only safe evils to oppose, Holliday unwittingly exposed the logic of countersubversion, which equated communism with disease. She also inadvertently explained the popularity of those films in which alien invaders came not from political conspiracies but from outer space.

The advertising industry, like Hollywood, promoted the displacement of politics by private life. Advertisements encouraged personal anxieties that its products would alleviate. This attention to the consuming personality had, at the origins of advertising as a major industry, an explicitly antipolitical thrust. Advertising in the 1920's responded to the political turmoil of the postwar years. Advertisers proposed to replace workers as producers, who engaged in class conflict, with workers as consumers. Advertising executive Paul Nystrom explained that commercialized leisure and mass consumption offered the only alternatives to "class thinking" and socialism. Mass society would replace class society, since goods bound together people at antagonistic ends of the political spectrum.

Through consumer purchases, buyers were "constantly participating in . . . their industrial government," claimed department store magnate Edward Filene. Such arguments legitimated private concentrations of power and directed voter-consumers away from political challenges to the corporation. Direct public participation was dangerous; by contrast, explained market researcher Edward Bernays, the ads and surveys that determined consumer preferences marked a Declaration of Independence from traditional democratic ideas. Such arguments moved in the 1950's from advertising into the political arena itself. Political scientists who had engaged in market research or were adapting its survey techniques defined political democracy on the model of consumer democracy. Democracy, as they conceived of it, was restricted to offering the masses a choice between elite institutions.

The advertising industry, which reached its maturity in the 1950's, promised a suburban utopia of pacified private life. The red scare enforced that utopia. Both advertising and countersubversion stigmatized un-American activities. External coercion and internal influence worked together, as in Indian policy and asylum reform, to domesticate the self and make it safe for political freedom.

But the 1950's American dream contained within it the seeds of its own disintegration. The expectations about private life that Hollywood and the advertising industry had helped to create formed a generation that would turn to political action to fulfill personal desires. This generation of New Left activists entered political life as the anticommunist politics of the cold war were culminating in Vietnam. Expansion against Asian Communists generated opposition from the "new barbarians" (as their critics called them) in America. This symbolic reenactment, at home and in Asia, of the conflict between civilization and savagery coalesced with a black protest movement in which the original New Left cadres had been formed. The racial politics of American history, in a massive return of the repressed, produced in response a massive state repression of political dissent. That repression climaxed in presidential usurpations of power and in the only resignation of an American president.

The end of the Korean War, the Senate censure of Joseph McCarthy, and Supreme Court decisions in several civil liberties cases all reduced political suppression in the latter 1950's. The Court declared the attorney general's list illegal and, in *New York Times Co.* v. *Sullivan* (1964), ruled that the crime of seditious libel violated the First Amendment. The national-security surveillance bureaucracy was still firmly in place, however, and the tiny Communist and Socialist Workers parties continued to be its targets. These groups were on the fringes of American politics. The rise of the civil rights and New Left movements in the early 1960's triggered a broader campaign of intimidation.

In 1962 the FBI placed Martin Luther King,

Jr., leader of nonviolent mass protests against southern segregation, on its list of those to be arrested in a national emergency. King was, according to Hoover's assistant William C. Sullivan, "the most dangerous Negro of the future in this Nation from the standpoint of Communism, the Negro and National Security." Hoover began a campaign to discredit him. Accusing King of being under Communist influence, Hoover obtained Attorney General Robert Kennedy's permission to tap his phone. The FBI already had under surveillance the National Association for the Advancement of Colored People. It now extended that surveillance to King and to other civil rights organizations. Hoover bugged hotels where King stayed. He sent the minister a tape recording that allegedly exposed King's sexual indiscretions and threatened to make it public. At the same time, the FBI refused to protect the civil rights of those whose legal protests against segregation resulted in police and mob violence against them. Civil rights workers and southern blacks suffered in the 1960's from a campaign of intimidation, led by southern political leaders and officers of the law. By October 1964, in Mississippi alone, there had been fifteen murders, thirty-seven church bombings or burnings, and over 1,000 arrests (none for the violent crimes). Police arrested or assaulted thousands of people who were exercising their constitutional rights of speech and assembly. Civil rights workers were often the victims of mob violence and even murder with the connivance of local officials. An FBI informer was involved in the murder of the activist Viola Liuzzo. The bureau was informed of plans to beat up "freedom riders," who were trying to integrate southern public transportation, but did nothing to protect them.

Voting rights legislation, passed in response to civil rights pressure, allowed southern blacks to vote for the first time since Reconstruction. Democratic party leaders pushed that legislation, but they also worried about the civil rights movement. Lyndon Johnson used the FBI at the 1964 Democratic national convention to spy on the interracial Mississippi Freedom Democratic Party. The MFDP was demanding to be seated in place of the segregated regular Mississippi Democratic organization. Johnson also received FBI intelligence on the campaign of Barry Goldwater, his Republican opponent. The rise of a mass movement against the war in Vietnam, after

Johnson's reelection and his escalation of the war, vastly expanded the campaign of political intimidation.

The decade from 1965 to 1975, marked by antiwar and student protests, urban black ghetto uprisings, and the impeachment proceedings against Nixon, was the most turbulent period of the century. Presidents Johnson and Nixon believed that Moscow was behind the antiwar movement. Johnson's vice-president, Hubert Humphrey, charged that the "international Communist movement" had "organized and masterminded" demonstrations against the draft. In the earlier cold war period, when left-wing political opposition was weak, Communists played a major role in it. The view that the mass protests of the 1960's were Communist-inspired was sheer fantasy. Both Johnson and Nixon enlisted several government agencies to search out Communist influence in the movement. Failure to find the conspirators only intensified the investigations. Under Johnson the CIA developed an illegal domestic surveillance network; its existence was denied under oath by director Richard Helms, who had set it up (Donner, pp. 277–278). Citizens who wrote letters to the president protesting the war received acknowledgments from the Internal Security Division of the Justice Department. Johnson asked the FBI for reports on senators, journalists, and private citizens critical of his Vietnam policies. Among those investigated were the philosopher Hannah Arendt and the journalist Joseph Kraft.

Between 1967 and 1971 army intelligence collected information, as the Senate Intelligence Committee later reported, on "virtually every group seeking political change in the United States." The FBI vastly expanded its surveillance activities, including break-ins. It infiltrated the nation's campuses, planting informers and obtaining access to confidential files, often with the cooperation of university administrations. The bureau expanded its COINTELPRO program of deliberate disruption from the Communist and Socialist Workers parties to New Left and militant black groups.

COINTELPRO, according to one FBI document, would "enhance the paranoia endemic in these circles, and will further serve to get the point across that there is an FBI agent behind every mailbox." Under COINTELPRO, FBI agents forged letters, set political associates and marital partners against one another, got people fired, and instigated violence. A staff report of the Senate Intelligence Committee called COINTELPRO a "sophisticated vigilante operation aimed squarely at preventing the exercise of First Amendment rights of speech and association." Political activists could not be sure whether those with whom they worked were comrades, informers, or provocateurs.

Political repression, brutal and public in the last decades of the nineteenth century, was carried on by private as well as public bodies. It became bureaucratized and more centered in a state apparatus during the red scares following both world wars. As state surveillance intensified after World War II, violent intimidation decreased. Political repression went underground, intimidating by its invisibility. Surveillance worked by concealing the identity of its actors but letting the existence of its network be known. Like warders in Jeremy Bentham's model prison, the panopticon, the surveillants planted in subversive organizations could see without being seen. The political activist, like Bentham's or Rush's prisoner, or Tocqueville's democratic man, was always to wonder whether he or she was being observed. The state was carrying on a hidden war against the bonds of trust that make political opposition possible.

National security supplanted un-American activities during the cold war as the major justification for suppressing political dissent. At the same time that it increased political surveillance, the national-security bureaucracy expanded its system of classifying government documents. By keeping its policies and political disputes secret, the state took politics out of the public realm. To publicize confidential government proceedings was, under those circumstances, not to engage in political controversy but to endanger the national security. The Nixon administration thus prosecuted Daniel Ellsberg for making public the Pentagon papers. This classified set of materials on American involvement in Vietnam contained nothing to endanger the national security but much to endanger the justifications for the continued prosecution of the war.

Public prosecutions played an important role in the suppression of political dissent. The Johnson administration prosecuted the pediatrician Benjamin Spock, Yale chaplain William Sloane Coffin, and other antiwar leaders for

counseling opposition to the draft. Spock was proscribed from advising the young men who had been raised on his child-care book. The Nixon administration initiated the third great Chicago conspiracy trial. In an eerie reenactment of the Haymarket affair, it prosecuted eight leaders of the antiwar movement, some of whom had never met, for conspiracy to riot. The indictment made antiwar activists responsible for the police violence that had erupted against protesters at the 1968 Democratic convention. Nixon's Justice Department also used grand juries as a weapon of political intimidation. It jailed for contempt those refusing to answer questions about friends or political associates who were accused of illegal acts. Although the courts countenanced this use of grand juries, they ultimately invalidated most convictions in other political prosecutions. Nevertheless, the political trials harassed the antiwar movement and depleted its resources.

Violence, which had receded during the cold war, reemerged as a weapon of political punishment during the war in Vietnam. Chicago police assaulted peaceful protesters, including convention delegates, at the 1968 Democratic convention. The next year California police fired buckshot at Berkeley demonstrators who opposed the university's enclosure of land being used for a "people's park." Police killed one demonstrator and wounded several others. "If it's a bloodbath they want, let it be now," announced California's governor, Ronald Reagan. The Ohio National Guard fired on Kent State demonstrators protesting the invasion of Cambodia in May 1970, killing four students.

Northern law-enforcement officials were treating white students the way southern police had treated blacks. The first student killed by law-enforcement officers was shot at Jackson State in May 1967. Police at Orangeburg, South Carolina, also fired on black students. The Black Panther party, a militant, northern ghetto organization, was the target of concerted assaults by local and federal agencies of the law. Massive FBI COINTELPRO operations disrupted the Panthers and led, in at least one case, to the murder of some black militants by others. Chicago police, with FBI cooperation, raided Chicago Panthers headquarters and killed two leaders of the party. The Panthers were themselves violence-prone; but by preemptively attacking the organization instead of prosecuting it for crimes, law-enforcement officers engaged in acts of political suppression.

The merger of politics with crime, in both the origins of the asylum and the practice of countersubversion, normally depoliticized discontent. But the treatment of politics in the 1960's as crime politicized crime and punishment. Radical fringe groups emerged who confused criminal acts with political protest. Ghetto uprisings, along with the rise of a militant black power movement, focused attention on prison conditions. The New Left made heroes of such black convicts as Eldridge Cleaver (a Panthers founder) and George Jackson. Victims of state repression, turned into criminals because of their politics, sympathized with prisoners behind bars. Prisoners, in turn, demanded political and human rights; they protested against overcrowding, censorship, isolation, brutality, and the manipulation of parole. When prisoners at the state prison in Attica, New York, seized hostages in 1971 and demanded that authorities negotiate, Governor Nelson Rockefeller refused. He ordered a massive use of firepower instead; forty-three inmates and hostages died.

Although political repression helped destroy the Panthers, it broadened opposition to the government and its war in Vietnam. Repression helped split the protest movement into a violent fringe on the one hand, enraged at and isolated from American life, and a vast, more amorphous, liberal opposition on the other. The Nixon administration's public statements stigmatized opponents of its Vietnam policies as members of the violent fringe. The administration's covert operations moved against the large, respectable antiwar movement as well. Nixon also tried to intimidate long-established American political institutions. He even antagonized the traditional centers of countersubversion, the FBI and the CIA, by trying to centralize their operations in the White House. The significance of Nixon's activities, and the ultimate cause of his downfall, lay in his systematic application to mainstream politics of techniques long accepted for use against alleged subversives.

The Nixon administration kept an "enemies" list, which read like a who's who of prominent Americans. The purpose of that list, according to a memo by presidential counsellor John Dean,

was to use "available federal machinery to screw our political enemies." The president enlisted the Internal Revenue Service to investigate allegedly subversive organizations like the Americans for Democratic Action, the American Civil Liberties Union, and the *New York Review of Books.* The IRS also targeted such Nixon opponents as Senators Charles Goodell and Ernest Gruening. Nixon sought to use the Federal Communications Commission against his critics in the media, and he illegally impounded government funds appropriated by Congress for purposes that he opposed. Attorney General John Mitchell asserted the president's right to institute warrantless wiretaps in any case that he determined to fall in the area of national security. (The Supreme Court unanimously ruled against that claim in 1972.) Solicitor General (later Supreme Court Justice) William Rehnquist insisted that the president had an inherent right to maintain surveillance against anyone who might violate the law and to claim executive privilege over any area under his jurisdiction. The Nixon administration was driven to these expedients not simply because of the character of the chief executive and his entourage, but because of the administration's desire to continue and expand the Vietnam War.

J. Edgar Hoover and Henry Kissinger, Nixon's national-security adviser, initiated illegal wiretaps against newspapermen, government officials, and members of Kissinger's own staff. Their purpose was to discover who had leaked the information that America was secretly bombing Cambodia. The release of the Pentagon papers resulted in a secret White House "plumbers'" unit, to plug news leaks. The plumbers burglarized the office of Daniel Ellsberg's psychiatrist after Ellsberg had been indicted in the Pentagon papers case. To keep hidden the knowledge of that burglary, and of illegal wiretaps of Ellsberg, presidential assistant John Ehrlichman dangled the directorship of the FBI before the presiding judge in the Ellsberg trial. Although Judge Byrne did not report the attempted bribe, he ruled that illegal government actions necessitated a mistrial.

The administration also initiated a variety of COINTELPRO-type operations against the Democratic party. A White House unit disrupted Senator Edmund Muskie's campaign for the

1972 Democratic presidential nomination. The "plumbers" broke into and bugged Democratic party headquarters at the Watergate Hotel in Washington. The discovery of that operation initiated the chain of events that brought Nixon down. To prevent the Watergate investigation from exposing the administration's other illegal activities, Nixon ordered the CIA to obstruct the FBI investigation of the Watergate break-in. The revelation of Nixon's order, recorded on the secret taping system that he had installed in the White House, finally caused the president to resign. Nixon had engaged in a series of obstructions of justice, to keep secret his "national security" operations. He had confused his political security with the national security. He had resurrected the hostility to legitimate opposition that lay behind the Alien and Sedition Acts.

Nixon's resignation was followed by the end of the Vietnam War and of the political turmoil that surrounded it. The suppression of political opposition that climaxed under Nixon had, it was widely felt, endangered the constitutional fabric of the nation. Gerald Ford's attorney general, Edward Levi, promulgated rules limiting the FBI to law enforcement and bringing its actions under the law. FBI officials were convicted of authorizing illegal burglaries. Former CIA director Helms, indicted for perjury, pleaded *nolo contendere* to a lesser charge; he received a suspended sentence and a $2,000 fine. The House and Senate Internal Security Committees were abolished, and Congress established an Intelligence Oversight Committee.

Neither the national-security bureaucracy nor the rationale for countersubversion was subjected to fundamental challenge, however. The Supreme Court ruled in 1980 that former CIA agent Frank Snepp violated the terms of his employment by failing to clear his book manuscript with the agency. Snepp disclosed no classified information, and the Court's decision implied that anyone who worked in the national-security bureaucracy permanently waived his First Amendment right to publish without prior restraint.

Ronald Reagan extended the Snepp principle in his 1983 "Presidential Directive on Safeguarding National Security Information." Officials who handle sensitive, classified material, according to the executive order, must agree not to say or write anything on national-security matters, even after leaving the government, without first getting official clearance. The directive also requires employees in sixty government agencies to take lie detector tests when ordered to by officials investigating leaks of sensitive information. The Reagan administration also issued new FBI guidelines that, unlike the Levi rules, permit surveillance without evidence of crime. The new guidelines allow the infiltration of "violence-prone" groups that engage in the "advocacy of" criminal acts or have the "apparent intent" to commit crimes. The president also granted the CIA authority to conduct surveillance within the United States.

The alleged menace of international terrorism provides the rationale for these executive orders. The Soviet state is accused of directing small bands of terrorists, mostly from the Third World, to commit acts of political violence. The theory of international terrorism merges savages, revolutionaries, and Soviet agents. It thereby encapsulates and brings up to date the entire history of American countersubversion.

BIBLIOGRAPHY

Robert F. Berkhofer, Jr., *The White Man's Indian: Images of the American Indian from Columbus to the Present* (New York, 1978), is a comprehensive treatment, connecting images to policies. David Caute, *The Great Fear: The Anti-Communist Purge Under Truman and Eisenhower* (New York, 1978), offers a detailed account of the anticommunist purge and its effects on individuals. Frank J. Donner, *The Age of Surveillance: The Aims and Methods of the American Political Intelligence System* (New York, 1980), deals with the development, rationale, and practice of the national-security bureaucracy. George M. Fredrickson, *White Supremacy: A Comparative Study in American and South African History* (New York, 1981), is the best interpretive history of American race relations—compact, comprehensive, and brilliant. Robert Justin Goldstein, *Political Repression in Modern America, from 1870 to the Present* (Cambridge, Mass., 1978), the most valuable single work on the subject, is detailed and comprehensive and includes an exhaustive bibliography. Winthrop D. Jordan, *White Over Black: American Attitudes Toward the Negro, 1550–1812* (Chapel Hill, N.C., 1968), is the classic study and still indispensable.

Leonard W. Levy, *Legacy of Suppression: Freedom of Speech and Press in Early American History* (Cambridge, Mass., 1960), is controversial but persuasive; although later scholarship has not superseded this book, it should be read in conjunction with other sources. J. Anthony Lukas, *Nightmare: The Underside of the Nixon Years* (New York, 1976), is the most useful book on political intimidation during the Nixon presidency, particularly for its command of detail. Michael Paul Rogin, *Fathers and Children: Andrew Jackson and the Subjugation of the American Indians* (New York, 1975), establishes the importance of Indian relations in antebellum America and its significance in American history. David J. Rothman, *The Discovery of the Asylum: Social Order and Disorder in the New Republic* (Boston, 1971), the classic study, is still seminal but should be read in conjunction with more recent European and American studies. Ronald T. Takaki, *Iron Cages: Race and Culture in Nineteenth-Century America* (New York, 1979), offers a multiracial treatment, with attention to Asian and Hispanic Americans, as well as Indians and blacks.

[*See also* AMERICAN REVOLUTION; ANTEBELLUM REFORM; CIVIL RIGHTS MOVEMENT; CIVIL WAR; COLLECTIVE VIOLENCE; COLONIAL GOVERNMENTS; ETHNIC MOVEMENTS; INDIAN RELATIONS; JACKSONIAN DEMOCRACY; JEFFERSONIAN DEMOCRACY; LABOR MOVEMENT; MACHINE POLITICS; PACIFISM AND PEACE MOVEMENTS; PROHIBITION AND TEMPERANCE; RACE AND RACISM; RECONSTRUCTION; SOCIALISM; *and* SUFFRAGE.]

CORRUPTION IN GOVERNMENT

Edwin G. Burrows

CORRUPTION in government—the betrayal of an office or duty for some consideration—is a familiar subject among American historians, but for several reasons the history of corruption as such is not. For one thing, *corruption* has never denoted a specific kind or form of misconduct, much less a specific crime. No one has ever gone to jail for it. It is essentially only an accusation that encompasses a large and shifting ensemble of determinate abuses—bribery, fraud, graft, extortion, embezzlement, influence peddling, ticket fixing, nepotism—not all of which have always been recognized as improper; some of which continue to be regarded as more consequential than others; most of which have been defined in different ways at different times; and each of which, arguably, deserves a quite different historical treatment. For another thing, the extreme decentralization of American political life and institutions has multiplied the effective arenas within which corruption in any or all of its manifestations can be discovered and examined. Here too it is at least arguable that the history of, say, urban corruption would turn out very differently from that of corruption on the colonial and state level, neither of which, in turn, would resemble the history of corruption in national government. Nor is it clear which of these potentially variant histories would throw the most light on the changing structure and experience of American politics generally: sensational dishonesty in high places does not, after all, necessarily mean as much or reveal as much as routinized kickbacks from state highway contractors or payoffs to city health inspectors. Finally, as Walter Lippmann once remarked, the history of corruption is really the history of reform—of those occasions, that is, when corruption is alleged, found, and attacked. The evidence of its existence almost always originates with hostile, prosecutorial sources and comes tangled in controversy, conflict, and cant. This is not to say that corruption lies merely in the eye of the beholder, but that its true extent can never be known with precision and cannot serve as the sole measure of its significance.

These and related complications have always frustrated the development of a satisfactory historical literature on American corruption, and even now there is no definitive survey of the entire subject. What follows, therefore, is not a synopsis of prevailing opinion but, rather, a sketch or diagram of how a history of corruption in American government might be organized. It proposes that there have been three principal phases in the history of American corruption, each characterized by its own dominant patterns, political setting, and ideological conventions: the era of the "Old Corruption," lasting from the early eighteenth to the early nineteenth century; the era of "Transitional Corruption," which began in the early nineteenth century and continued into the early twentieth; and the era of the "New Corruption," which began around the middle of the twentieth century and does not appear likely to end anytime soon.

THE OLD CORRUPTION

Judging by a number of notorious examples from seventeenth-century Virginia and New Netherland, both of which began as profit-making enterprises and had remarkably similar organizational histories, corruption was brought over on the first ships. Captain Samuel Argall, deputy governor of Virginia from 1617 to 1619, boasted of his intention to "make hay whilst the

417

sunne doth shine, however it may fare with the generality," then systematically looted Virginia Company warehouses of grain and tobacco, sold off company servants and animals to his own account, appropriated the Indian trade for himself, extorted bribes, and even dabbled in West Indian piracy. Contemporary sources say that he got away with as much as £80,000, a fortune at the time. Wouter van Twiller, director general of New Netherland from 1633 to 1637, wheeled and dealed his way into tens of thousands of acres of prime land around New Amsterdam, diverted Dutch West India Company livestock onto his own property, and genially presided over widespread fur smuggling, illegal traffic in arms and liquor to the Indians, and the virtual collapse of law and order. When another company official criticized his rapacity and incompetence, van Twiller hounded him out of town, then had him arrested and shipped back to Holland without pay. Van Twiller's successor, Willem Kieft, was a merchant who had just left France "in a hurry" and was rumored to have absconded some years before with money raised to ransom Christians held prisoner by the Turks. During his ten years as director, some leading members of the community later charged, "his principal aim and endeavors were to provide well for himself and to leave a great name after him." What New Netherland needs, they declared wearily, are "godly, honorable and intelligent rulers who are not too indigent, or indeed not too covetous. A covetous chief makes poor subjects." None of this escaped the attention of New England Puritans, whose purpose in emigrating had been to reform the pervasive corruption of the English church and English society, and who seem to have managed their affairs with far greater probity than was shown by their neighbors to the south. As John Winthrop was once reassured after one of his frequent complaints about the high private costs of public service: better you should have remained poor in office "then if you had gayned riches as other Governours doe, both in Virginia and elsewhere."

To all appearances, the available examples of official corruption became considerably more numerous and ingenious in the last half of the seventeenth century, as the relationship between the colonies and the mother country became more clearly and strictly defined, and as the colonies themselves became more attractive for settlement and moneymaking. No doubt the single most effective stimulus to the growth of corruption was the series of Acts of Trade and Navigation passed by Parliament between the 1650's and the 1690's to regulate colonial commerce. The extent to which this legislation inhibited or distorted the economic development of the colonies remains a matter of dispute among historians, but not the fact that its burdens and restrictions were widely, even systematically, evaded by colonial merchants—often with the connivance of those responsible for enforcing it. One of the most conspicuous offenders was Governor Benjamin Fletcher of New York (1692–1698), whose greed and cunning would not be exceeded by any big-city grafter of the nineteenth century. Ordered to suppress the flourishing trade between New York City merchants and Madagascar pirates, Fletcher instead devised a kind of protection racket that allowed it to go on so long as he got a cut of the profits. He also collected bribes from licensed Indian traders, bilked the customs service, padded military payrolls, and misappropriated funds raised to pay the provincial debt. "To recount all his arts of squeezing money both out of the publick and private purses would make a volume instead of a letter," grumbled one of Fletcher's contemporaries.

Fletcher was by no means alone. Sir Lionel Copley, governor of Maryland (1691–1693), and Nehemiah Blakiston, collector of customs on the Potomac, apparently conspired to divert crown revenues into their own pockets and repeatedly used their official powers to obstruct investigations into what was going on. Then there was Captain Robert Jones of the Royal Navy, who patrolled the Virginia coast with an armed sloop and a crew of eight, collected pay for a crew of twelve, and got rich by "adviseing Tradeing with and Sheltering Severall Pyrates and unlawfull Traders. . . ." Captain John Crofts, who followed Jones, demonstrated equal zeal for personal gain and once, while shaking down an honest tobacco merchant, emphasized that he had accepted his post "to gaine an Estate, and he would gett one before he left the Country." What has been called "customs racketeering" was in fact an established practice everywhere in the colonies by the beginning of the eighteenth century, aided and abetted by defiant juries and by venal judges—one of whom is reported to have said "that in his opinion the Nicetyes of the Law ought not to be observed."

Behind such abuses lay a number of conditions and circumstances: plural officeholding, imperfect or immature standards of bureaucratic integrity, the presumption that fees and perquisites would supplement woefully inadequate salaries, the use of colonial appointments to pay off political debts and help well-connected ne'er-do-wells repair their fortunes, and the quickening tempo, on both sides of the Atlantic, of capitalist accumulation, which often indeed made short work of "the Nicetyes of the Law" when the law got in the way. It is thus virtually impossible to say what these violations of imperial trade regulations really cost. On paper, the bill looked enormous. Official estimates ranged from losses of £100,000 a year in 1676 to a staggering £700,000 a year in 1765, by which time the customs service had an annual budget of around £9,000 and took in a mere £2,000. Seen from a different point of view, corruption on so vast a scale appears to have constituted a cheap, informal alternative to worse things. Inasmuch as the main purpose of the Navigation Acts had been to drive foreign competitors out of the colonial trade—ensuring that colonial wealth would be shifted into exclusively British hands—widespread graft, extortion, and bribery probably helped things go much more smoothly on both sides of the Atlantic than might otherwise have been the case. They lubricated the division of spoils at home, drained off resentment abroad, and even ensured that some income would be derived from smuggling and piracy. State revenues suffered greatly, to be sure, but that aroused little concern outside the Treasury or Admiralty until the 1760's, when new legislation tightened enforcement and the entire system collapsed in revolution and war.

The Navigation Acts were not, in any event, the only nursery of governmental corruption in the colonial era. The reconstruction and expansion of the Royal Navy in the eighteenth century created a vast and lucrative market for naval stores, which many colonial officials found to contain opportunities for personal gain as well. Benning Wentworth, for one, governor of New Hampshire from 1742 to 1767, was required by law to reserve the best timber in his colony for the Royal Navy but instead gave the rights to his brother, who thereupon sold it back to the navy for a handsome profit. Then, too, there were the opportunities opened up by the rising demand for land. Southern planters, New England farmers, Pennsylvania traders with capital to invest, English noblemen and merchants caught up in the speculative mania—everyone wanted land in the colonies, and everyone who had something to do with handing it out had ready-made possibilities for graft, inside dealing, favoritism, fraud, and simple theft. For sheer cynicism nothing surpassed the notorious "Walking Purchase" of 1737, in which Pennsylvania authorities tricked the Delaware Indians out of most of their homeland on the west side of the Delaware River. It was in New York, however, that chicanery in the distribution of land became an exact science. Under a succession of governors —Thomas Dongan, Benjamin Fletcher, Lord Cornbury, William Cosby, and George Clarke—millions of acres of the colony's land were dealt out with flagrant disregard for law or royal policy, often to dummy patentees, and typically in exchange for lavish gifts and a kickback of one-third to one-half of the property for the governor himself. Many grants were as large as entire English counties. Cornbury's Kayoderosseras Patent ran to 800,000 acres and his Hardenbergh Patent to an amazing 2,000,000 acres, larger even than the colony of Connecticut.

But examples alone cannot adequately convey the distinctive and decisive meaning that official corruption was acquiring for colonial Americans by the middle of the eighteenth century, or indeed the lengths to which they were prepared to go to check its evident growth. For by then, just below the surface of political life, three quite unrelated streams of experience and belief had begun to converge into a single current that would sweep the colonies into revolution, independence, and republicanism. The oldest and slowest-moving of these was the conviction that America had been selected, by historical accident or by divine intent, as a refuge from the advanced corruption of European society and government—perhaps even as the very instrument by which it would be challenged and reformed. The widening suspicion that this great cause had been neglected as the work of settlement progressed—a suspicion most fully and frequently elaborated at the end of the seventeenth century in the jeremiads of New England ministers—only affirmed America's moral preeminence and the urgency of asserting it. So did, by the 1740's and 1750's, the anxious, angry warnings heard in every colony that advancing material prosperity had unleashed a contagion of self-seeking, extravagance, idleness, deceit, disobedience, irreligion, and venality. And so did the escalating fear of corruption in England itself. For corruption had become the central moral issue of the Augustan era, its causes and cures the preoccupation of essayists and novelists and pamphleteers, of educational theorists and the writers of child-rearing manuals, of architects and landscape designers. In the colonies, where metropolitan standards and styles were studied with true provincial diligence, America's comparative purity looked all the more rare, precious, and fragile. The question was how to protect it, how to check the spread of individual and collective wickedness and keep faith with the virtuous aspirations of previous generations.

A specifically political answer to that question would emerge out of a century and a half of exposure to grasping and crooked colonial governors. For it was proconsular corruption—the endless, dreary burden, from which no colony seemed certain to be exempt, of executive plotting, plunder, and patronage—that appeared to have posed the gravest threat to public happiness and well-being and done most to undermine public morality. This was exactly the complaint, no doubt self-serving, that Nathaniel Bacon had raised against Governor William Berkeley of Virginia and his entourage in Bacon's ill-fated revolt of 1676. By "Caball and mistery," Bacon declared, "many of those whom wee call great men" have like "spounges . . . suckt up the Publique Treasure" and allowed it to be "privately contrived away by unworthy Favourites and juggling Parasites whose tottering Fortunes have bin repaired and supported at the Publique charge." A dozen years later, summarizing the resentments that had led to the overthrow of Governor Edmund Andros and the collapse of the Dominion of New England, Cotton Mather described the governor's "far-fetch Instruments that were growing rich among us" and the "Crew of abject Persons fetched from New York" who extorted "extraordinary and intollerable Fees" from a hapless populace "without any Rules but those of their own insatiable Avarice and Beggary." "A small volume," he

protested, would "not contain the other Illegalities done by these Horse-leeches in the two or three years that they have been sucking of us."

So common, and essentially alike, were these outpourings of bitter exasperation from almost every colony in the years to follow that they may be said to have constituted, by the mid-eighteenth century, a native tradition of high-strung apprehension that those who exercised executive power were certain to abuse it for their own sordid purposes—and in so doing would arouse, by interest and example, greed and dishonesty in society generally.

One solution, of course, was to get men whose own fortunes, rank, and abilities would elevate them above covetousness and spoliation, but it was widely understood that this was a practical impossibility. No wonder "the View that Governours generally have is private Gain," remarked one colonial official, for "it can hardly be expected but that these Corruptions must happen when one considers that few Gentlemen will cross the Seas for a Government, whose Circumstances are not a little streight at Home, and that they know by how slight and uncertain Tenure they hold their Commissions; from whence they wisely conclude, that no Time is to be lost." The New York Assembly concurred. "What can be expected but the grossest misapplication" of public monies, it wondered, when colonial governors "are entire strangers to the People they govern," know their time in office to be short, and seek only to "raise Estates to themselves?" "They come only to make money as fast as they can," Benjamin Franklin remarked in 1768. They "are sometimes men of vicious characters and broken fortunes," and "as they intend staying in the country no longer than their government continues and purpose to leave no family behind them, they are apt to be regardless of the good of the people."

Under the circumstances, therefore, the sensible thing was to make sure that executive rapacity had as little room to maneuver as possible—if good men were not available, then bad men would have to be bridled and leashed—and it was the colonial legislatures that everywhere in the course of the eighteenth century took this as an unavoidable summons to enlarge their own powers at the expense of those of the governors sent to rule over them. One by one, often indeed in the teeth of gubernatorial opposition, the assemblies asserted and successfully defended the exclusive right to raise and spend money, to fix the compensation of all public officials, to name their own officers, to meet often and at times and places of their own choosing, to apportion themselves and be the judges of their own members, to exercise full investigative powers, and to enjoy freedom of speech in the conduct of public business. Legislative spokesmen repeatedly declared that this radical assault on executive authority and privilege followed directly upon and emulated Parliament's struggle for supremacy a century or more earlier. Its driving force, however, was the homegrown conviction, nourished by hard experience, that greedy governors with too much power had proved to be a persistent and dangerous cause of corruption throughout colonial government and society.

These two indigenous traditions—one, that America was to be the special habitat of virtue in the world; the other, that executive power could not be trusted to uphold public and private morality—were in time linked to a third, imported doubt that even strong, independent legislatures could always stem the tide of official corruption. For what if the motive behind it extended beyond the personal enrichment of penurious governors and their fawning dependents? What if there existed formidable groups or classes in society, not known to the political constitution but prepared to enlarge their power by exploiting the avarice and gullibility of magistrates? And what if the resources of the one and the ambitions of the other were then mobilized against the legislature, subverting its responsibilities to the commonweal by enlisting its members in the very schemes of oppression and extortion that they were meant to resist?

These troublesome questions had already been raised in England, over and over again, by beleaguered bands of unreconstructed Tories and old-fashioned radical Whigs who feared the rise of a new moneyed interest in English life and believed that ministerial "influence"—favors, places, contracts, pensions, offices, percentages, and the like—had during the eighteenth century made Parliament its accomplice and destroyed the delicate constitutional balance that guaranteed English liberty. Orthodox opinion held otherwise, to be sure: English public affairs seemed orderly and on track for the first time in generations, the usual explanation being that the

"mixed" constitution had at last harmonized relations between crown, lords, and commons. In the colonies, however, "opposition" ideas found a more receptive audience; and by the 1750's and 1760's ministerial corruption of Parliament—William Cobbett would call it the "Old Corruption"—had become a matter of settled conviction in the most knowledgeable and sophisticated segments of colonial society. There was nothing mysterious about this. The picture of a systematically corrupted Parliament appealed greatly to conventional American dogma about Old World decadence and institutional collapse. It explained the presence of so many hungry governors in the colonies over the years, thereby situating the obstinacy of local assemblies in the larger context of social transformation and the cause of English liberty. In at least some colonies it also suggested how certain governors had managed to organize sizable legislative factions on whose support they could always rely.

As opposition ideas and habits of mind thus embedded themselves in native political experience, they not only achieved a currency and respect denied them in England but also helped produce a distinctively American science of politics in which corruption, or rather the dread of corruption, drew together a number of quite different assumptions, expectations, and dispositions. One of these was the belief that the appearance of political parties or factions constituted tangible proof of illicit influence over a legislative body and an unmistakable symptom of indifference to the general good. Another was the heightened importance of individual willingness to subordinate private advantage to the public interest—*virtue* was the word for this—inasmuch as the best defense against corruptible legislatures was an incorruptible citizenry. And still another was an exaggerated inclination toward conspiratorial interpretations of political events. For unlike the corruption that sprang from mere greed, the corruption that managed and muzzled legislatures necessarily proceeded by stealth, indirection, and falsehood. More often than not its presence could only be inferred from the pattern of things rather than demonstrated empirically, much less proved legally. As William Livingston of New York put it, in a corrupt and corruptible world nothing could be taken at face value: "No

Man who has projected the Subversion of his Country," Livingston reasoned, "will employ *Force* and *Violence,* till he has, by sowing the Seeds of *Corruption,* ripen'd it for Servility and Acquiescence: He will *conceal* his Design, till he spies an Opportunity of accomplishing his Iniquity by a single Blow."

The final consolidation and institutionalization of such thinking was accomplished by the abrupt, disturbing shifts in British policy toward America in the 1760's and 1770's. Parliament's efforts to raise revenue in the colonies, its truculent assertions of legislative supremacy, its alarming extension of vice-admiralty court jurisdiction and the dispatching of new swarms of customs officials, its unprecedented intervention in the proceedings of local assemblies, its apparent deference to the interests of certain great trading concerns, its enthusiasm for the use of regular troops to police the colonial populations—seemed reason enough to believe that a vast, corrupt conspiracy had been formed to deprive the colonists of their liberty and so extend the regime of avarice and vice to the other side of the Atlantic. The source of our troubles, said Charles Carroll in 1774, was "the ambition of corrupt ministers intent on spreading that corruption thro' America, by which they govern absolutely in G[reat] B[ritain]."

Early in 1775, writing as "Novanglus," John Adams offered a detailed account of what was happening. The "dark intrigues and wicked machinations" against American liberty, he declared, had actually originated with a venal "junto" in his own colony whose idea was to establish parliamentary taxes as a fund for suborning unruly American assemblies. Anticipating that they would enjoy "the fingering of the money themselves," they wanted to employ it so that "governments here would be able and willing to carry into execution any acts of parliament, or measures of the ministry, for fleecing the people here, to pay debts, or support pensioners on the American establishment, or bribe electors or members of parliament, or any other purpose that a virtuous ministry could desire." Unfortunately for the conspirators, however, they laid the plan before George Grenville, who had "hungry cormorants enough about him in England" and who "thought if America could afford any revenue at all, and he could get it by authority of Parliament, he might have it for himself, to give to his friends, as well as raise it for the junto here, to spend themselves, or give to theirs."

Subsequent ministries embraced the scheme without any resistance from Parliament, Adams continued. For what security could be found in Parliament "when luxury, effeminacy, and venality are arrived at such a shocking pitch in England, when both electors and elected are become one mass of corruption, when the nation is oppressed to death with debts and taxes, owing to their own extravagance and want of wisdom . . . ?" The answer, of course, was no security at all, and so it could be expected, Adams warned, that the assault on American liberties would only become more ferocious and desperate: "Like a cancer, it eats faster and faster every hour. The revenue creates pensioners, and the pensioners urge for more revenue. The people grow less steady, spirited, and virtuous, the seekers more numerous and more corrupt and every day increases the circles of their dependents and expectants, untill virtue, integrity, public spirit, simplicity, frugality, become the objects of ridicule and scorn, and vanity, luxury, foppery, selfishness, meanness, and downright venality swallow up the whole society."

But Adams was not saying anything that had not already been said, many times over, by patriot politicians and pamphleteers in every colony; and within a year it had become clear that there was no way to stem the tide of parliamentary corruption except through the assertion of American political and moral autonomy. This meant more than independence. It meant as well a thorough reformation of American society and character—a rediscovery of the virtuous severity and selflessness ascribed to earlier generations—and that meant, in turn, the creation of original, specifically republican institutions to formalize and defend the reign of virtue. If all went according to plan, therefore, the success of the American Revolution would be immediately observable in the setting up of governments incorruptible by ministerial influence and in the happiness of a people once again uncorrupted by self-interest and material prosperity.

All did not go according to plan. Considerable energy and ingenuity were thrown into the work of drafting new state constitutions sharply limiting executive power, confirming legislative independence, and even, as in Pennsylvania, stipulating that "laws for the encouragement of virtue, and prevention of vice and immorality, shall be made and constantly kept in force. . . ." Yet to many observers, the struggle for independence seemed to have brought more, not less, corruption in its wake. Military procurements, the sale of western land, the disposition of confiscated Loyalist estates, and privateering—these and more held out fresh incentives to individual gain; and from every section of the country came complaints of rampant profiteering, speculation, embezzlement, and graft. "Notwithstanding all the publick virtue which is ascrib'd to these people," Washington said of the inhabitants of Massachusetts soon after assuming command of the Continental army, "there is no nation under the sun (that I ever came across) pay greater adoration to money than they do." "Such a dearth of public spirit, and want of virtue, such stock jobbing and fertility in all the low arts to obtain advantages of one kind and another, I never saw before, and pray God I may never be witness to again," he added later. "I tremble at the prospect. Such a dirty, mercenary spirit pervades the whole, that I should not be surprised at any disaster that may happen."

That kind of frustration and resentment, ballooning out all over in the later 1770's and early 1780's, was acutely aggravated by controversies about corruption in the Continental Congress itself. The most prolonged of these centered on the activities of Silas Deane, the commercial agent of Congress in France, who was accused of using his position to make a small fortune for himself (and who may also have passed secrets to the British for good measure). Charges of fraud and venality were also made against Robert Morris, superintendant of finance; General Benedict Arnold, military commander of Philadelphia; and Samuel Chase, delegate to Congress from Maryland. Some stout republicans began to suggest that "a joynt Combination of political and Commercial Men" was conspiring to corrupt Congress and "get the Trade, the Wealth, the Power and the Government of America into their own hands."

Fears of corruption were further intensified by the growth of public indebtedness as the Revolution progressed. For according to the English opposition, there was no more pernicious source of political or personal depravity: a national debt encouraged selfish speculations, supported idleness, promoted inequality, and provided administrations with the resources for suborning entire legislatures. No one seriously maintained that Congress or the states could wage a revolutionary war without borrowing money. The question was whether, once the war had ended, these debts should be funded—gradually discharged through the application of specific revenue to the payment of interest and principal—or retired promptly, in full. With some important exceptions, most writers who addressed this difficult subject advocated the elimination of all debts at the earliest possible moment, invariably with knowing references to the sordid fate of England. There were those, indeed, who thought that the corrupting effects of borrowed money on government and society were fully visible within a matter of years after the war was over. Richard Price, for one, saw from London the need to remind American republicans that careless and profligate public borrowing "become the worst evils, by giving to the rulers of states a command of revenue for the purposes of corruption." In England, agreed an anonymous writer in New York, the national debt had proved to be the "parent of corruption." Thus American republicans must never consent "from the impulse of temporary exigence, to the adoption of a system which experience has found to be productive of undue influence, inordinate power, national corruption, and popular ruin."

Even as the struggle against corruption forged beyond independence, however, there were signals that the distinctive alliance of ideas on which it rested was shifting and breaking up under the accumulated pressures of adverse experience and new opportunity. One of these was the willingness of some thoughtful men to consider the advantages of funded public debts and other contrivances—standing armies, excise taxes—long associated with corruption in the English opposition literature. Another was the drafting and ratification of the federal Constitution, which revealed, or summoned up, a number of striking departures from what had been received wisdom only a few years earlier—that the bulwark of liberty was a balanced constitution, not an autonomous legislature; that administrative "influence" had legitimate purposes; that rational self-interest was a more realistic and reasonable guide to personal conduct in a republic than an unattainable "virtue." Antifederalists kept the old faith, flailing away at the dangers of corruption created by the proposed Constitution, and their defeat indicated that its continued vitality would more and more depend on purely partisan exertions.

That would be amply demonstrated during the turbulent 1790's, as the emerging Democratic-Republican party, led by James Madison, Thomas Jefferson, and Albert Gallatin, monopolized the anticorruption tradition and played out an eerie reenactment of the controversies of the 1760's and 1770's. The object of their attention this time was Secretary of the Treasury Alexander Hamilton, whose proposals to assume and fund state debts, establish a bank, and encourage manufactures had all the earmarks of a sinister conspiracy against republican values and institutions: they could not be understood by honest citizens, they promoted deceitful speculations in government paper, they aroused avarice and undermined virtue, they raised up a class of wealthy public creditors and servile officeholders, and they laid the foundations for illicit ministerial influence over Congress. "These are not visionary fears," said one writer in the *National Gazette,* "but apprehensions, justified by the same effects produced from the same causes in other countries; particularly England, from whence all these schemes are imported." The Virginia General Assembly pointedly informed Congress that it had carefully studied Hamilton's financial program and discovered "a striking resemblance between this system and that which was introduced into England at the [Glorious] Revolution—a system which has perpetuated upon that nation an enormous debt, and has, moreover, insinuated into the hands of the Executive an unbounded influence, which, pervading every branch of the Government, bears down all opposition, and daily threatens the destruction of every thing that appertains to English liberty. The same causes produce the same effects."

Jefferson himself thought he had found out what Hamilton was up to as early as April 1791, when he, Hamilton, and John Adams had a conversation over dinner about the role of corruption in the British government. Adams, according to Jefferson, declared that the British constitution, purged of corruption, would be perfect. "Hamilton paused and said, 'purge it of its corruption and . . . it would become an impracticable government; as it stands at present,

with all its supposed defects, it is the most perfect government which ever existed.'" "Hamilton was not only a monarchist, but for a monarchy bottomed on corruption," Jefferson concluded sourly. He soon took the matter directly to President Washington, warning him repeatedly that because of Hamilton's policies a new brood of monarchists "have been hatched in a bed of corruption made up after the model of their beloved England. Too many of these stock jobbers and king jobbers have come into our legislature, or rather too many of our legislature have become stock jobbers and king jobbers." Hamilton had conspired to "undermine and demolish the republic, by creating an influence of his department over the members of the legislature. I saw this influence actually produced. . . ." Surely, Jefferson pleaded, the president "must know, and everybody knew, there was a considerable squadron in both houses, whose votes were devoted to the paper and stock-jobbing interest, that the names of a weighty number were known and several others suspected on good grounds."

But if Jefferson and his followers had thus managed to keep old oppositional fears of ministerial corruption in the foreground of American political life during the Federalist era, the effect, ironically, was to emphasize their oppositional, sectarian character and remove them still further from the mainstream of political discourse. Washington's refusal to abandon Hamilton or his program was a serious blow, as was the conspicuous probity of both Federalist administrations in all other matters. Despite his association with William Duer, a speculator in government paper whose dealings eventually landed him in prison, Hamilton's personal integrity never came into question. Secretary of State Edmund Randolph resigned his office when an intercepted dispatch suggested that he had solicited a bribe from the French government, although he was almost certainly innocent of the charge. And when Speaker Jonathan Dayton took too long to settle his official accounts with the Treasury, Secretary Oliver Wolcott hurried over in person to retrieve some $18,000 in unspent funds lest there be even the appearance of wrongdoing. What was more, Congress had in fact acted promptly to erect statutory safeguards against various kinds of corrupt practices—oaths of allegiance of office

CORRUPTION IN GOVERNMENT

for state as well as federal officials; penalties for neglect of or refusal to perform a duty; injunctions against the pursuit of private business while in a position of public trust; and explicit prohibitions against fraud, extortion, collusion, and bribery. Federalist opinion generally held that federal officials were also subject to common-law provisions against corruption, for as Judge Richard Peters observed in 1798, "Whenever an offense aims at the subversion of any Federal institution, or at the corruption of its public officers, it is an offense against the well-being of the *United States;* from its very nature, it is cognizable under their authority."

With Madison and Gallatin leading the Democratic-Republican forces in Congress, moreover, party strategy became increasingly narrow and legalistic by comparison with the expansive moral indignation that had carried the country into revolution two decades before. The emphasis now fell not on personal or social reformation, much less on a resurgent Antifederalism, but rather on the available constitutional remedies to excessive ministerial influence: frugality with the people's money, specific rather than general appropriations, rapid reduction of the debt, and firm resistance to large military and naval establishments. All we want, Gallatin assured the House, is to preserve "the equilibrium intended by the Constitution. . . . The chief object of our Constitution has been to divide and distribute the powers between the several branches of government. With that distribution, and with the share alloted to us [Congress], we are fully satisfied." The intention, Jefferson affirmed many years later, had been only "to preserve the legislature pure and independent of the executive, to restrain the administration to republican forms and principles, and not permit the Constitution to be construed into a monarchy and to be warped in practice into all the principles and pollutions of their favorite English model."

Jefferson's narrow triumph in the election of 1800, followed by twenty-four years of Democratic-Republican rule and the collapse of the Federalist party, confirmed the demise of the old oppositional way of thinking about corruption. Apart from minor irregularities during the War of 1812 and the rather pathetic case of General James Wilkinson, who among other things sold military secrets to the Spanish, the administrations of Jefferson, Madison, and Monroe were as free of serious misconduct as those of their Federalist predecessors: even were they inclined to do so (which plainly they were not), the defeated and divided Federalists thus had little opportunity to rehabilitate oppositional doctrine for their own purposes. More to the point, Jefferson's conciliatory policies—especially his refusal to purge all Federalist officeholders straightaway or to dismantle Hamilton's financial program—dissipated much of the old oppositional fear of party government and encouraged a new appreciation of its stabilizing effect on the political system. And then there was the Yazoo controversy. In 1795 the Georgia legislature had sold some 35 million acres of land—most of present Mississippi and Alabama—to four land companies at bargain-basement prices. When it turned out that the companies had bribed numerous members of the legislature, the legislature voided the sale. Investors and subsequent investors clamored for relief, and in 1803 three special commissioners appointed by Jefferson—Madison, Gallatin, and Levi Lincoln—proposed a compromise settlement to Congress. Outraged by this heretical concession to corruption, John Randolph mounted an old-fashioned oppositional attack on it—its proponents, he said, were "the unblushing advocates of unblushing corruption"—but succeeded chiefly in emphasizing the indifference of everyone else to a system of thought that had a generation earlier commanded widespread support. In the case of *Fletcher* v. *Peck* (1810) the Supreme Court declared that the Georgia legislature erred in overturning the Yazoo sales, despite their fraudulent basis, and Congress subsequently awarded the claimants over $4 million to settle the matter. Although Randolph and his followers fought on for years, it was clear that things would never again be the same.

TRANSITIONAL CORRUPTION

Between the 1820's and the 1920's a new capitalist social order took shape in the United States, energized and propelled by a succession of breathtaking transformations in virtually every aspect of national life—industrialization,

425

urbanization, mass political participation, rapid improvements in transportation and communication, the westward movement, foreign war and civil war, imperialism, and the continued spread of a competitive, possessive, and individualistic culture. But long before the full meaning of these developments became clear, the wildly disruptive effects of the transitional process had wrought great changes in the quantity and quality of political corruption and recast the question of reform. There were essentially two explanations for this. One was the institutionalization of organized political parties, once associated with sedition and unrepublican partiality but now gaining favor as the means to manage elections, negotiate conflicts of interest and opinion, establish the boundaries of legitimate dissent, and regulate access to power. The other was the concurrent expansion in the importance of government itself at all levels to economic growth and development, not merely as a short-run source of lucrative charters, franchises, licenses, and contracts but also now as the source of the laws of property and exchange that in the long run promoted the accumulation of capital. Each of these alone held unprecedented opportunities for corruption. Together they led to a debasement of American politics so extreme that it is difficult even at this distance to determine whether we are seeing only a passing aberration or the very basis of the entire political system.

As a matter of both fact and controversy, what might be called transitional corruption would always be quite closely identified with municipal and state government—focal points of business pressure for vital concessions and privileges, and the forcing beds of the great nineteenth-century political machines and their legendary bosses. Its characteristic form was a web of arrangements and understandings between the party leadership, the men they put in office, and those enterprisers and entrepreneurs in the community willing to cut a few corners to keep ahead of the game. The organization, or machine, in return for getting out the vote, received exclusive control of government appointments and programs within its territory (the so-called spoils system). Its placemen and dependents in turn handed back a fixed percentage of their official salaries to the organization and split with it any kickbacks, rake-offs, shares, or bribes that their ingenuity could devise with outside interests. The resulting stream of "boodle" (for a lush new vocabulary of corruption was also being created along the way) then passed down through a well-defined corporate hierarchy of county and district leaders, ward heelers, and precinct captains, who completed the cycle by distributing the gifts and favors that ensured voter loyalty and brought victory to the organization on election day. It was all, in its own way, ruthlessly efficient and disciplined. It placed the organization in a position to command virtually every aspect of local affairs, from public works to police and fire protection, the administration of justice, restaurant and tavern licensing, sanitation, transportation, tax collection, street lighting, and even gambling and prostitution. It also attracted a steady procession of European observers who had never seen anything like it before.

The earliest examples on view were Martin Van Buren's "Albany Regency," which dominated New York state politics in the 1820's and 1830's, and the notorious Tammany Society of New York City, which had already by then become the driving force of the Democratic party there, thanks in no small measure to the efforts of Aaron Burr. By the late 1820's Joel B. Sutherland's South Side machine had established him as Philadelphia's first boss, and within the next half-century or so similar machines had appeared in many cities and states under the leadership of a long and colorful cast of characters. In Philadelphia, James ("King") McManes, Israel ("Judge") Durham, Boies Penrose, and the Vare brothers, William and Edwin, kept the Republican machine in control of the city from the 1850's to the 1930's. From the 1860's to the 1920's, New York City was ruled by just four Tammany bosses: William ("Boss") Tweed, "Honest" John Kelly, Richard Croker, and Charles F. Murphy. During the same sixty-odd years, Chicago was run by the likes of "King" Mike MacDonald, Michael ("Hinky Dink") Kenna, John Joseph ("Bathhouse John") Coughlin, and William Hale ("Big Bill") Thompson. Abe Ruef and Eugene Schmitz had mastered San Francisco around the turn of the century, and Thomas J. Pendergast was just then consolidating his power in Kansas City. In the 1880's John R. McLean's Democratic machine and its Republican counterpart under Tom Campbell actually joined forces to rule Cincinnati, although this triumph of practicality was

CORRUPTION IN GOVERNMENT

soon eclipsed by the rise of George B. Cox in the Republican machine and its single-handed grip on the city in the 1890's and early 1900's. The same story could be told in dozens of other cities and more than a few states, most conspicuously New York and Ohio, where powerful Republican machines emerged toward the end of the century under the leadership of, in the former case, Roscoe Conkling and his protégé, Thomas C. ("Me Too") Platt, and in the latter, Joseph B. Foraker and Marcus A. Hanna.

By all accounts, the arrival of the political machines unleashed an epidemic of graft, bribery, and electoral fraud unimagined by the jumpiest critics of the "Old Corruption" in eighteenth-century legislatures. Writing in the 1880's, James Bryce figured that corrupt machines ran every one of the biggest cities in the United States, many of the medium-sized ones, and a considerable number of even the smallest, along with a dozen or more states. "There is no denying," he wrote in a famous passage, "that the government of cities is the one conspicuous failure of the United States."

> The faults of the State governments are insignificant compared with the extravagance, corruption, and mismanagement which mark the administrations of most of the great cities. The commonest mistake of Europeans who talk about America is to assume that the political vices of New York are found everywhere. The next most common is to suppose that they are found nowhere else. In New York they have revealed themselves on the largest scale. They are "gross as a mountain, monstrous, palpable." But there is not a city with a population exceeding 200,000 where the poison germs have not sprung into a vigorous life; and in some of the smaller ones, down to 70,000, it needs no microscope to note the results of their growth.

Investigative journalism, spurred by a fivefold increase in the number of daily newspapers in the last half of the nineteenth century and the advent of mass-market magazines, delivered study after study that more than confirmed Bryce's observations by tracing out the ligaments of interest binding the machines to business. Lincoln Steffens, whose articles for *McClure's* and other magazines were reprinted as *The Shame of the Cities* (1904), declared that he had discovered businessmen "buying boodlers in Saint Louis, de-

fending grafters in Minneapolis, originating corruption in Pittsburgh, sharing with bosses in Philadelphia, deploring reform in Chicago, and beating good government with corruption funds in New York." In Chicago, he said, party organizations were controlled by rings, which in turn were backed and used by leading business interests through which this corrupt and corrupting system reached with its ramifications far and high and low into the social organization." Cincinnati's Boss Cox, wrote Frederick C. Howe, controlled the city "by binding together and to himself the rich and powerful members of the community, for whom he secured and protects the franchises of street-railway, gas and electric lighting companies. They, in turn, become his friends and protectors, and through him, and for him, controlled the press and organized public opinion." "The extra-constitutional place of the boss in government was as the extra-constitutional guardian of business," concluded William Allen White.

> If a telephone company desired to put its poles in the street, and the city council objected, straightway went the owner of the telephone stock to the boss. He straightened matters out. If a street car company was having trouble with the city street department, the manager of the street railway went to the boss, and the street department became reasonable. If the water company was harassed by public litigation, the boss arranged a friendly suit to settle matters. Always business was considered. And in some exceptional cases, vice was considered business. . . . Money in politics was there for the purpose of protecting the rights of property under the law, as against the rights of men. . . . The greed of capital was rampant, the force of democracy was dormant.

Corruption spread somewhat more slowly and haphazardly on the national level in the nineteenth century, partly because the federal government at first commanded relatively fewer resources and was called upon to make fewer decisions bearing directly on capitalist development, and partly because effectively controlling it was for a time beyond the capacity of private interests. Some members of Congress, in the pre–Civil War era, seem to have maintained now-questionable relationships with outside firms or individuals. Daniel Webster, the best-known example, accepted sizable cash presents from Massachusetts bankers and manufacturers who did not want him to retire from the Senate for lack of an adequate income. Webster, Henry Clay, John C. Calhoun, fifty-odd members of Congress, and various other government officials, past and present, routinely accepted "personal loans" from the Second Bank of the United States. Lewis Cass, while governor of the Michigan Territory, took money from John Jacob Astor's American Fur Company for unexplained services. Jackson's postmaster general, William T. Barry, resigned in the wake of charges that he had tolerated widespread fraud and collusion in his department. Webster himself, while John Tyler's secretary of state, was accused of using an executive "secret service fund" to obstruct justice, influence newspapers, and perhaps line his own pockets as well. Zachary Taylor's secretary of war, George W. Crawford, was embarrassed by the discovery that he would receive almost half of the $235,000 that the attorney general and secretary of the treasury awarded in payment of an old pre-revolutionary debt. James Buchanan's secretary of war, John B. Floyd, quit amid a flurry of accusations that he had favored his cronies with lucrative contracts and signed millions of dollars worth of bogus bills presented to him for payment. Buchanan himself would be threatened by testimony that his administration had attempted to buy congressional votes for the Lecompton Constitution in 1858. None of these cases, however, resulted in legal proceedings against the individuals concerned.

Increasing numbers of lesser federal officials were meanwhile turning up with their hands in the till or colluding with contractors and speculators to defraud the government. In 1829, Tobias Watkins, the close personal friend of former President John Quincy Adams, was found to have embezzled over $7,000 while serving as fourth auditor of the Treasury. In 1835 and again in 1839 Congress learned of "atrocious and outrageous frauds" in many land offices around the country. In 1838, Samuel Swartwout, collector of the port of New York, fled the country with over $1.2 million, and the subsequent investigation revealed pervasive negligence and connivance in both the customhouse and treasury. Swartwout's successor, Jesse Hoyt, likewise fled after revelations that he had looted the customs revenue of some $200,000 for private stock

speculations and presided over an orgy of graft, bribery, and extortion more flagrant even than in Swartwout's day. Hoyt's successor, Edward Curtis, was not considered a significant improvement, though no one ever caught him at anything. Nor was the customhouse the only scene of concerted venality. The New York City post office had an equally poor reputation—never poorer than in 1860, when Isaac V. Fowler, the postmaster, absconded to Mexico leaving arrearages in excess of $150,000. The inevitable inquiry uncovered additional culprits and widespread indifference to minimal standards of public service. Swartwout, Hoyt, Curtis, and Fowler were all political appointees connected with local machines (Whig in Curtis' case, the others Democratic), and their various plunderings are perhaps better interpreted as early evidence of municipal corruption in the nineteenth century than as indications of its penetration into national affairs.

The same cannot be said of the claims agents and lobbyists who began converging on Washington in the 1830's and 1840's, for it was their extraconstitutional representation of private interests—the functional equivalent, as it were, of the local machine—that signaled the appearance of transitional corruption on a national level. Conventional assumptions about legislative propriety and the legislative process would be the first casualties, as the promoters of this or that special measure crowded more and more closely on the members of Congress, and as more and more members themselves became paid advocates of such measures. The claims agents, congressmen among them, soon proved so troublesome that in 1853 new rules were adopted regulating access to the Senate floor, the agency system was reformed to prevent members of either house from acting as agents of private claimants, and new penalties were provided for bribery and attempted bribery of members. But things had already gone too far to be set right so easily. In 1854 four members of the House were recommended for expulsion for improper conduct, and one observer noted that politicians in Washington were still being bought and sold "like fancy railroad stock or copper-mine shares."

Lobbyists for commercial and industrial interests presented an even greater challenge to traditional notions of legislative integrity. In 1846

CORRUPTION IN GOVERNMENT

President James Polk complained that "Capitalists who are engaged in manufactures" had launched an all-out attack on the tariff-reduction bill and that Washington was "swarming with manufacturers who are making tremendous exertions to defeat it. The truth is that such a struggle has rarely been witnessed in Congress." Yet only a few years later, as lobbyists for new steamship and railroad companies joined in the scramble for government support and protection, such struggles had become routine. James Buchanan told Franklin Pierce in 1852 that the situation already seemed almost out of control. "The hosts of contractors, speculators, stock jobbers, & lobby members which haunt the halls of Congress, all desirous per fas aut nefas and on any & every pretext to get their arms into the public Treasury, are sufficient to alarm every friend of his Country," he said. "Their progress must be arrested, or our Government will soon become as corrupt as that of Great Britain." It was no longer unusual to hear cynical conversation on the ease with which legislation could be purchased or on the vast sums laid out to do so. There was much talk of bribery in 1854, for example, when Samuel Colt and his associates tried unsuccessfully to renew the patent on the colonel's revolver, though a congressional inquiry later turned up only some suspiciously large gifts and "costly and extravagant entertainments" for willing legislators.

In practice, of course, it is often impossible to draw a neat distinction between bribery and extortion, and the pressure of outside interests on the federal government was doubtless intensified by the mounting number of cases in which political power was used to wring money out of private companies and individuals, and by the spreading belief that payoffs and kickbacks to those in power were therefore customary and necessary. The classic example in these years remains the cheerfully bipartisan "Black Horse Cavalry" of the New York state legislature, who auctioned off their votes to the highest bidder and kept the bidding brisk by introducing bills that would, if passed, do grave damage to one or another interest. During the Erie Railway war in the 1860's, they had the price up to $5,000 per vote until the game's principal victims, Cornelius Vanderbilt and Jay Gould, reached a truce and the market collapsed.

Though rarely so audacious, much the same kind of political blackmail figured prominently in the scandals that plagued the national government during and after the Civil War. It was blatant in the case of the Sanborn Contracts (1873), commingled with ordinary graft and collusion in the cases of the Collectors' Ring (1872) and the Whiskey Ring (1875), and apparent to varying degrees in the frauds and rackets that brought down so many of President Ulysses S. Grant's entourage—Minister Robert Schenck (1870), Secretary of the Interior Columbus Delano (1875), Secretary of War W. W. Belknap (1876), and Navy Secretary George M. Robeson (1876), not to mention Grant's private secretary, Orville H. Babcock, Grant's son, and Grant's brother. Congress, too, contributed to the climate of official rapacity, most obviously in the Credit Mobilier scandal (1872), which saw two members of the House expelled, one senator recommended for expulsion, two vice-presidents in disgrace, and at least eight additional congressmen, including James A. Garfield, tainted with the suspicion of wrongdoing. Small wonder, observed the *Century* magazine in 1892, that railroads, banks, and other great corporations would therefore think it justifiable to buy up as many legislators as possible: "They argue that so long as legislative bodies are constituted as they are at present, with venal elements frequently holding the balance of power, direct bribery is the only method for warding off injurious legislation, or securing desirable legislation."

The price tag on all this—the boodling of the machines and the concerted thieving in Washington—so far exceeded seventeenth- and eighteenth-century precedents that contemporary observers could be excused for thinking corruption an entirely new phenomenon. According to one estimate, the New York City customhouse alone failed to find between $12 million and $25 million every year, while another source suggested that the Grant administration lost almost $96 million every year to corrupt practices of one kind or another. Congress learned in 1874 that the cost of collecting revenue in the United States ran three, four, and five times higher than in France, Germany, and Great Britain, respectively. And from 1876 to 1881 the Post Office Department was bilked of some $4 million in the Star Route frauds. But all such calculations are deceptively precise. Typically partisan in origin, they were meant to astound and dismay, and many historians have in fact concluded that things were nowhere nearly so bad.

What no one disputes, in any case, is that corruption was reestablished as the central issue of American political life and thought during the last half of the nineteenth century. "The diminution of political corruption is the great question of our time," proclaimed E. L. Godkin's new magazine, *The Nation,* in 1867. "It is greater than the [question of Negro] suffrage, greater than reconstruction." Godkin was off to an early start, to be sure—really widespread concern about political corruption still lay two or even three decades in the future—but upper-class opinion at least was moving in the same direction behind Charles Eliot Norton, George William Curtis, Henry Adams, and other "genteel reformers" of the post–Civil War era, who, like Godkin, were already alienated from the new, chaotic capitalism of the age. Like their counterparts a century earlier, they regarded the corruption all around them as the consequence of a general moral collapse brought on by rampant individualism and self-seeking, in and out of government. "We are, at present, witnessing in the immorality which pervades the commercial world, and taints nearly every branch of business, the results of the decline of habit as a social force, before mental and moral culture has reached a sufficiently advanced stage to take its place," Godkin wrote. "Every man at present may be said literally to live by his wits; hardly anybody lives by tradition, or authority, or under the dominion of habits acquired in youth. The result is a kind of moral anarchy." Some years later, Norton explained to Godkin that he too saw "systems of individualism and competition" at the heart of the problem. "We have erected selfishness into a rule of conduct," Norton said, "and we applaud the man who 'gets on' no matter at what cost to other men." The dominant philosophy of our time, Mark Twain agreed, was: "Get money. Get it quickly. Get it in abundance. Get it in prodigious abundance. Get it dishonestly if you can, honestly if you must."

Unlike their eighteenth-century predecessors, the opponents of "moral anarchy" did not trace corruption specifically to a ministerial plot against republicanism and the legislative independence that was its bulwark; what troubled the genteel reformers of the nineteenth century,

rather, was precisely that the corruption of their era seemed to be without conscious political direction. It was, to their way of thinking, not only ubiquitous but also spontaneous, capricious, and essentially contemptuous of any purpose or authority whatever—organized but also unsystematic, opportunistic, and moronic. If anyone deserved to be blamed, most reformers would probably have blamed businessmen. "Is there any doubt about the responsibility for this kind of corruption?" asked a contributor to *The Century.* "Does it rest upon the miserable creatures who have been attracted, like flies to offal, by the bribes offered in the halls of legislation, or upon the men of character and standing in the community who as presidents, directors, and managers of corporations and institutions furnish the bribes?" The answer was plain: "There never has been any corruption in politics, in any nation, that the world has ever seen, in which the responsibility did not rest upon the man who offered the bribe rather than upon the man who took it." Walt Whitman said it even more bluntly. "The depravity of the business classes of our country is not less than has been supposed, but infinitely greater," he wrote in *Democratic Vistas* (1871). Because of it, "the official services of America, national, state, and municipal, in all their branches and departments, except the judiciary, are saturated in corruption, bribery, falsehood, maladministration; and the judiciary is tainted." Much the same conclusion would be drawn by workingmen's parties, Mugwumps, Single Taxers, Greenbackers, Prohibitionists, and Populists.

Especially among the genteel reformers there were always additional culprits to be reckoned with as well: the immigrant masses who could be driven to the polls like cattle, the grasping bosses, the unprincipled placeholders who belonged to the machines and treated public office as an opportunity to treat themselves. Each of these suggested a reform strategy of far greater scope and difficulty than anything contemplated by the critics of ministerial corruption in the seventeenth and eighteenth centuries. The business community as a whole would have to be persuaded to turn its back on corruption, to adopt a new and higher code of conduct for itself, and to encourage its best and brightest members to enter public service. Immigration restriction would be necessary to undermine the power of the bosses, as would the expansion of voter registration procedures and secret balloting. Then, too, certain fundamental changes could be made in the structure and management of state and local government—narrowing the scope of private and local legislation, for one, defining corrupt practices more clearly and fixing stricter laws against them, for another, as well as creating new regulatory agencies to root out corruption in key industries, adopting general acts of incorporation, and, another indication of how profoundly current thinking about corruption differed from that of earlier centuries, strengthening executive control over appointments at all levels of government. Perhaps the most appealing idea was the establishment of an effective, professional, and nonpartisan civil service that would place tens of thousands of government jobs beyond the reach of crooked spoilsmen.

As the end of the century approached, more had probably been accomplished along these lines than reformers had a right to expect, given their limited numbers and frankly elitist outlook. Charter reform in New York, Philadelphia, Washington, and other cities centralized executive power and shifted control of various municipal functions into the hands of impartial boards—not always, to be sure, with perfect success. In New York City, for example, one of the motives behind the consolidation of Greater New York in 1898 had been to create a government too large and efficient for Tammany to subjugate, but Tammany soon demonstrated that it was more than equal to the task. On the state level, constitutional revisions and legislation in New York, Pennsylvania, and elsewhere had begun the development of effective legal remedies for a broad range of abuses: the New York Corrupt Practices Act of 1890, modeled after the famous English Corrupt and Illegal Practices Act of 1883, enjoyed considerable influence in this respect, and within the next decade sixteen other states had closely imitated it. The so-called Granger Laws of the 1870's, though aimed chiefly at ending railroad rate discrimination, promised also to eliminate the bribery, inside dealing, and favoritism with which the major lines had dominated more than one legislature over the years. By the late 1890's, moreover, thirty-nine states had adopted the secret ballot.

On the national level, reformers could point to a few scattered but significant victories. The Covode Commission investigations of fraud in the letting of government printing contracts had led, in 1860, to the organization of the Government Printing Office. In 1870 and 1871, with an eye to ending violence and intimidation at the polls in northern cities as well as in the South, Congress adopted three force bills that prohibited interference with elections, gave federal courts jurisdiction over cases arising out of this legislation, and authorized the use of the army to enforce the decisions of the courts when necessary. In 1874 Congress eliminated the old moiety system for collecting delinquent taxes and duties, the abuse of which had become apparent that year in the Sanborn Contracts and Phelps-Dodge scandals. President Rutherford Hayes, in 1877, ordered sweeping investigations of customhouses around the country; and in the wake of disclosures that led to his removal of Chester A. Arthur as collector of customs in New York, Hayes flatly banned political activity by federal officeholders, as well as the practice of assessing them for political contributions in proportion to their salaries—measures that alarmed and outraged regulars in both parties. The long struggle for civil service reform was finally rewarded by passage in 1883 of the Pendleton Act, which provided for a bipartisan Civil Service Commission to administer competitive examinations to prospective federal appointees. Only about one in ten government jobs would be immediately affected, but the reformers had at least got a foot in the door. The Interstate Commerce Act of 1887 set up an Interstate Commerce Commission to regulate railroads passing through more than one state—the first such commission created by the national government and, despite certain obvious limitations, an important step toward the formulation of new, more stable relations between business and the major parties.

For the parties would remain. Their existence was no longer regarded as prima facie evidence of corruption in high places: it was now understood, reformers said, that parties contributed to the vitality and the effectiveness of the political system. The issue was who controlled them—and for what purposes. Like-minded people naturally want to cooperate in the expression of their political beliefs, reasoned R. R. Bowker in 1880. "This organized cooperation is party, and nothing yet has been suggested to take its place." For that reason, he continued, "no one objects to organization: it is the abuse of organization which is stigmatized as 'the machine.' When a railroad train is wrecked by reckless driving, it is not proposed to abolish steam-engines, but to discharge drunken engineers." George William Curtis, for one, did not fail to appreciate that the struggle against corruption in his time thus appeared to have ventured into new ideological territory. In an 1892 address on "Party and Patronage," he reviewed seventeenth- and eighteenth-century apprehensions about executive manipulation of legislatures and recalled Hume's argument that parliamentary corruption, stabilizing support for the crown, had been vital to the maintenance of royal power. What reformers now confronted, by contrast, was the argument that corruption is vital to the maintenance of the great political parties:

> A hundred years ago in England the king bought votes in Parliament; to-day in America party buys votes at the polls. . . . Tammany Hall defends itself as Hume defended the king. The plea of both is the same. The king must maintain the crown against the parliament, and he can do it only by corruption, said Hume. Party is necessary, says Tammany, but party organization can be made effective only by workers. Workers must be paid, and the patronage of the government, that is to say the emolument of place, is the natural fund for such payment. This is the simple plea of the spoils system. It places every party on a venal basis.

So it was really the reformers who had the greatest confidence in the party system, for they continued to believe that it did not require steady infusions of graft, bribery, and patronage to function properly: what had once been perceived as a fountainhead of corruption had become, for Curtis, its principal victim. Accordingly, modern reformers occupied very different ground from their predecessors. "Our forefathers," explained John Brooks Leavitt, "took it for granted that, pending the coming of the political millennium which republicanism would surely bring, primary gatherings of citizens inspired by the love of political liberty would suffice to supply the motive power for administering the new government." But disinterested virtue is not in fashion anymore, Leavitt added, and responsible reformers accept that "government . . . must be ad-

ministered by a party." The fight against corruption today must take place within the party system, not outside it or against it.

As with parties, so too with the capitalist order itself. For despite their loathing of the moral chaos that it brought in its wake, and despite their conviction that business must bear ultimate responsibility for political corruption, reformers recoiled from any implication that the economic system as a whole ought to be changed. Typically prosperous entrepreneurs and professionals themselves—one count of over 400 New York Mugwumps in the 1880's revealed that most were well-to-do merchants, manufacturers, lawyers, financiers, and the like—they never wavered in their loyalty to the prevailing orthodoxies of laissez-faire liberalism, free trade, balanced budgets, and sound money. If business corrupted politics, their solution was nothing more extreme than the demand that right-thinking people, the supply of whom they did not think to question and among whom they did not doubt they belonged, should get into public life and set things straight again.

Thus it would prove perhaps the most enduring legacy of the Gilded Age reformers that these two propositions—the necessity of party and the inviolability of capitalist institutions—remained the intellectual boundaries of Progressive attacks on corruption in the later 1890's and early 1900's. For the Progressives, unlike their genteel predecessors of the postwar decades, were aggressive, predominantly middle-class in outlook and background, and hugely successful at attracting a mass following. Vernon Louis Parrington likened them to "inquisitive plumbers" who found that "some hidden cesspool was fouling American life . . . not one cesspool but many, under every state capitol—dug secretly by politicians in the pay of respectable business men. . . . It was a dramatic discovery and when the corruption of American politics was laid on the threshold of business—like a bastard on the doorsteps of the father—a tremendous disturbance resulted." Ironically, of course, patrician reformers had been saying the same thing for decades without creating a "tremendous disturbance," and, on the national level at least, the Progressive era never witnessed corruption as relentless and shocking as that of the two Grant administrations. There were charges in 1894 that representatives of the sugar industry, per-

CORRUPTION IN GOVERNMENT

haps with the knowledge of Secretary of the Treasury John G. Carlisle, had bribed several senators to secure favorable treatment in the Wilson-Gorman Tariff of the same year. The Dodge Commission reported in 1899 that the War Department had mismanaged virtually every aspect of the recent war effort and that the army was riddled with corruption. Between 1902 and 1909 the administration of Theodore Roosevelt suffered through a number of scandals in the Indian Service, Post Office Department, and General Land Office—the last of which saw Oregon Senator John H. Mitchell jailed in 1905 for accepting a bribe and two members of the House tried on charges of fraud, conspiracy, and perjury. A major controversy did break out in 1904, when Democratic newspapers charged that George B. Cortelyou, Roosevelt's secretary of commerce and labor, had extorted substantial campaign contributions from big business—"Cortelyouism," the papers called it—and despite fervent denials by Cortelyou, Roosevelt, and others, the accusation was revived year after year. Finally, in 1912, Senator Moses Clapp of Minnesota launched an investigation into the entire subject of campaign financing. The Clapp Committee report of the following year revealed that giant corporations had indeed provided almost three-fourths of Republican campaign funds in 1904 but found no conclusive evidence of individual wrongdoing. The corruption that David Graham Phillips described in 1906 in his *Cosmopolitan* series entitled "The Treason of the Senate" was, from this perspective, only an elaboration on the theme developed, a generation earlier, by Godkin, Curtis, Norton, and Adams.

Even so, around the middle of the first decade of the twentieth century, there was an eruption of public indignation at the corrupting influence of business on government and politics, the likes of which genteel reformers had only dreamed about. Much of it sprang from fresh revelations of bribery, graft, and fraud in scores of cities and states across the country, and the immediate result was a burst of legislative action aimed at curbing the illicit power of special interests. Between 1903 and 1908, according to one count, a dozen states passed new laws to regulate lobbies, twenty-two prohibited corporate campaign contributions, twenty-four outlawed or regulated free transportation passes for public officials, thirty-one enacted mandatory direct

primary laws, and forty-one established or strengthened commissions to regulate transportation and utility corporations. A New York state legislative probe of the life insurance industry in 1905 produced compelling evidence that the three biggest firms—New York Life, Equitable Life, and Mutual Life—had poured money for years into Republican campaigns and maintained lobbyists all over the United States and Canada. The ensuing outcry against political contributions by corporations prompted President Roosevelt to ask for federal legislation on the subject; and in January 1907, after a good deal of maneuvering, Congress passed the Tillman Act, prohibiting federally chartered banks and corporations from making "a money contribution in connection with any election to any political office" and "any corporation whatever" from contributing to elections in which presidential electors or members of either house of Congress are to be chosen. The Hepburn Act of 1906 had meanwhile improved the ability of the ICC to deal with illegal practices on the railroads, and a series of other measures would soon follow, wholly or in part concerned with the elimination of corruption: ratification of the Seventeenth Amendment in 1913, providing for the election of United States senators by direct popular vote rather than by more easily corruptible state legislatures; creation of the Federal Trade Commission in 1914, laying the groundwork for closer federal supervision of corporations engaged in interstate commerce; and passage, also in 1914, of the Clayton Antitrust Act, greatly strengthening the ineffective Sherman Antitrust Act of 1890 and broadening the definition of illegal business practices.

There were other possible outcomes to the discovery that business corrupted politics. This was, after all, the golden age of American socialism, with Eugene Debs gathering nearly a million votes in the elections of 1912 and 1920 and socialist candidates winning office in cities and states throughout the country. But by World War I, it was already evident that the sudden accretion of new federal administrative and regulatory responsibilities had successfully drained off enough moderate energy and indignation to make a socialist solution to corruption more and more remote. For Progressives proved in the end no more eager than Gilded Age reformers to abandon the party system or stir up resentment against capitalist values and institutions. Their task, in retrospect, had been to end the moral anarchy introduced into American political and social life by the movement toward an industrial economy. Their solution, neither reactionary nor revolutionary, was the corporate state—government by commissions, bureaus, agencies, boards, and authorities, all in the hands of professional experts whose only professed loyalties were to honesty, impartiality, and efficiency. A century and a half earlier, the solution to corruption had been national independence, legislative autonomy, and republican virtue. If the first of these remained essentially uncompromised, the second had long since been rendered meaningless by the universal acceptance of organized political parties, and the third was now conclusively obsolete except for faint traces that remained in the ethical codes of the new bureaucratic classes. The disruptive, demoralizing public consequences of private self-seeking would henceforth be controlled and corrected by official edicts and rulings rather than by individual conscience or indeed by the silent movements of the marketplace.

THE NEW CORRUPTION

Since the 1920's—and especially since the burgeoning of federal administrative and regulatory bodies during the New Deal of the 1930's—the full-throated, rough-and-tumble corruption characteristic of the transition to capitalist society has slowly but surely subsided and yielded ground to newer, rather different forms. There appear to be at least two reasons for what took place. For one thing (as the growth of proscriptive statutes since 1907 will emphasize), wholesale grafting and bribery have become less and less appropriate, ideologically as well as functionally, since the advent of the corporate state. The allegiance of the political system to the process of capital accumulation has been securely established. Unimpeded expansion of monopolistic enterprises has concentrated economic power in the hands of a relatively small number of managers and financiers whose rivalries, unlike those of Vanderbilt and Gould a century ago, no longer require the purchase of entire legislatures. And as for the ebullient laissez-faire creed of the nineteenth century, it

has degenerated into a rebarbative small-town Toryism that has yet to find the political or moral footing for a sustained opposition to corporatist values and institutions. For another thing, the construction of the corporate state has been credited with certain direct changes in the organization and conduct of American politics that decisively altered the environment within which prior forms of corruption had flourished. Among these are a sharp reduction in the rate of political participation in the early decades of the twentieth century, the formalization of interest-group politics during the New Deal, and the disappearance, by midcentury, of all but one or two of the old urban machines, as their part in maintaining public order and welfare was taken over by new government programs and agencies.

The retreat of the machines figures very importantly in the story, for it also coincided with the rise of organized crime and its penetration of local law enforcement—now probably the most pervasive and familiar form of governmental corruption around the country. Whether this was more than coincidental remains tantalizingly unclear, but a succession of investigations over the last fifty years has confirmed that during Prohibition (1919–1933) mobsters supplanted bosses as the unofficial masters of American cities and surrounded themselves with unprecedented numbers of venal attorneys, police, politicians, and judges. The final report in 1931 of the Wickersham Commission (formally the National Commission on Law Observance and Enforcement) confirmed massive corruption in the federal Prohibition Enforcement Bureau and traced it to the appearance of new, sophisticated criminal "syndicates" that had reaped millions from bootlegging and speakeasies and had already begun to move aggressively into gambling, prostitution, protection, and other rackets.

Chicago provided the archetype of the new corruption. By the end of the 1920's, according to the federal Bureau of Internal Revenue, the Al Capone gang was taking in more than $100 million annually from its extensive operations and had half the Chicago police force on its payroll. "Big Bill" Thompson, one of the city's most corrupt mayors and an ally of Capone, estimated that in 1927 alone the Chicago police received some $30 million in payoffs from all sources; and during the late 1930's and early 1940's, when Frank Nitti ruled the underworld, forty police captains were said to have become millionaires.

In New York City, the Seabury Commission probe of the magistrates' court and the New York County district attorney's office, completed in 1931, revealed extensive underworld influence over the Tammany organization and prompted the resignation of Mayor James J. Walker the following year, a blow from which Tammany never fully recovered. Additional details of the increasing power of organized crime came to light during the widely publicized investigations conducted by Thomas E. Dewey between 1931 and 1942—first in the U.S. attorney's office, then as special prosecutor, and finally as district attorney of New York County—which resulted in the convictions of a dozen prominent gangsters with Tammany connections, including Charles ("Lucky") Luciano, Waxey Gordon, and Jimmy Hines. But the mob was rich and resilient, and during the 1940's and 1950's, under the aegis of Frank Costello, Thomas ("Three Finger Brown") Luchese, and Joe Adonis, it completed the capture of Tammany and soon controlled city councilmen, mayors, justices of the state supreme court, congressmen, and high-ranking police officials. The 1971 Knapp Commission report on police corruption in New York City found extortion and bribery throughout the department, none of the proceeds of which was siphoned off any longer by the moribund machine and much of which now originated with illegal traffic in narcotics.

More or less identical stories of gangland influence in Philadelphia, Kansas City, Boston, Detroit, and Las Vegas, as well as in many states, had meanwhile attracted federal attention. The 1950–1951 hearings of the Senate Special Committee to Investigate Organized Crime in Interstate Commerce, chaired by Estes Kefauver, explored corrupt relations between public officials and organized crime in a number of cities and produced evidence that a new generation of mob leaders had learned how to infiltrate and hide behind legitimate businesses. Between 1957 and 1960, a special Senate committee under John L. McClellan, with Robert F. Kennedy as counsel, heard further testimony on the political influence of the mobs in the course of its inquiry into labor racketeering; much alarmed speculation about national and even international criminal confederations was meanwhile touched off by the discovery, in Apalachin, New York, at the end of 1957, of a summit conference between top gangsters in the United States and abroad. More speculation about the political reach of organized crime followed the 1960 presidential election, in which John F. Kennedy's narrow margin of victory depended on fraudulent returns from Cook County, and then flourished in the wake of Kennedy's assassination, which according to certain fashionable but unproved theories was a mob-financed contract killing. Four years later, in 1967, the National Crime Commission (formally the President's Commission on Law Enforcement and Administration of Justice) estimated that organized crime grossed billions of dollars every year and had undermined local and state law enforcement virtually everywhere in the country. An outpouring of official reports, grand jury investigations, popular accounts, and scholarly monographs since then has amply confirmed the commission's findings.

The ability of organized crime to withstand repeated legislative and judicial assault is perhaps the most telling measure of the extent to which its immense resources now command political protection and support. According to one estimate, the illegal narcotics trade alone had mushroomed into a nearly $79-billion-a-year cash business by 1980, which, as Attorney General William French Smith observed, closely rivals "the combined profits of America's 500 largest industrial corporations." The New York City market for illegal drugs accounted for some $45 billion of this total, making it far and away the city's most lucrative enterprise—almost twice as large as the legitimate retail trade and bigger even than the garment industry, manufacturing, tourism, and entertainment combined. It was also the city's third largest employer, with a force of somewhere between 100,000 and 300,000 full- or part-time workers, while its revenues were believed to have been funneled into countless legal businesses. The scope of the problem there and elsewhere is such that, nationwide, over $11 billion was being spent every year on drug-related police, court, and prison expenses, although no one thinks this figure even remotely adequate. What most authorities do think is that there has been a virtual disintegration of local law enforcement under the crushing weight of the narcotics trade in particular and of organized crime in general. If that is so—and, as usual, both theory and research trail rather far behind events—then this constitutes corruption of a kind and on a scale for which there simply are no precedents in American historical experience. More remarkable still may be the absence thus far of anything like the broad, mass-based reform movements that attacked corruption in earlier centuries.

It is against just this background, moreover, that the apparent decline in high-level bribery and graft since World War I comes into sharper focus. Immediately after the war the Harding administration wallowed in a succession of scandals reminiscent of the Grant era. Attorney General Harry M. Daugherty's years in office (1921–1924) were marked by repeated charges that he failed to prosecute war profiteers and bootleggers and, in cahoots with a band of politicians known as the "Ohio Gang," was involved in all sorts of shady schemes. In 1922 the House Judiciary Committee found no evidence to support an impeachment motion against Daugherty; but in early 1924, only months after Harding's death, a Senate investigation implicated Daugherty in fraudulent stock transactions and the illegal sale of liquor permits from the Ohio Gang's headquarters in a "little green house on K Street." Coolidge demanded his resignation, and in 1926 Daugherty was tried but not convicted on the specific charge of having conspired with the alien-property custodian to defraud the government. Interior Secretary Albert B. Fall proved less fortunate. It was revealed in 1922 that he had approved, without competitive bidding, the lease of Naval Reserve oil fields in Teapot Dome, Wyoming, and Elk Hills, California, to two millionaire oilmen, Edward Doheny and Harry Sinclair. Fall resigned the next year, and subsequent investigation by the Senate Committee on Public Lands revealed that he had on at least one occasion received a large sum of money from Doheny. All three were later acquitted of charges that they had conspired to defraud the government, but in 1929 Fall was convicted and jailed for taking a bribe. Navy Secretary Edwin Denby had meanwhile resigned in the face of charges that he had unwisely given Fall's Interior Department jurisdiction over the oil fields in the first place. Charles R. Forbes, director of the Veterans' Bureau, was convicted and imprisoned in 1924 for fraud and conspiracy in the sale of surplus hospital supplies. As for Harding himself, rumors circulated for years about a history of payoffs, swindles, and bribery in his own affairs.

But Teapot Dome did not, as it happened, signal a fresh outbreak of corruption in high places. In 1925 Congress passed a new Federal Corrupt Practices Act, revising the Tillman Act to include subsequent legislation that had required disclosure of campaign contributions and expenditures and attempted to impose campaign spending limits. Although these restrictions proved rather easy to circumvent, their adoption was followed by a remarkable four or five decades in which the chronic, systematic venality of the late nineteenth and early twentieth centuries virtually disappeared from view. Charges that Roosevelt's Works Progress Administration (WPA) had been politicized led, in 1939, to passage of the Hatch Act, barring non–civil service federal employees below the policy-making level from taking part in political campaigns or soliciting campaign contributions. A 1940 amendment extended the ban to state and local government workers paid out of federal funds, imposed a $3 million limit on the annual expenditures of political parties, and fixed a maximum of $5,000 on individual campaign contributions. The Smith-Connally Act of 1943 and the Taft-Hartley Act of 1947 included further prohibitions against union contributions to political campaigns.

Scandal struck the Truman administration in the early 1950's when a congressional probe of the Bureau of Internal Revenue produced evidence of widespread extortion, fraud, and favoritism in offices around the country. Nine district collectors and some 160 other bureau officials were removed by the end of 1951. Commissioner Joseph D. Nunan was convicted of tax evasion. T. Lamar Caudle, head of the Justice Department's tax division, was ousted and later convicted on conspiracy charges along with Matthew J. Connelly, Truman's appointments secretary. Charles Oliphant, chief counsel of the bureau, resigned when implicated in a shakedown plot. Accusations of misconduct had meanwhile been made against Brigadier General Harry H. Vaughan, Truman's military aide, as well as the Reconstruction Finance Corporation, the Office of the Alien Property Custodian, the Federal Power Commission, the antitrust division of the Justice Department, the Maritime Commission, the Securities and Exchange Commission, the Civil Aeronautics Board, and the Department of Agriculture. Early in 1952 the Justice Department launched a special investigation of corruption in the government under the direction of Newbold Morris, but Morris was not free of suspicion himself and quickly ran into difficulty with both Congress and Attorney General J. Howard McGrath. Two months later, McGrath fired Morris, Truman fired McGrath, and the investigation collapsed.

The Truman, Eisenhower, Kennedy, and Johnson administrations also rode out a succession of lesser controversies over influence peddling, conflict of interest, gift giving, and the like. In 1949, for example, a brief uproar followed the disclosure that Vaughan had finagled a new freezer for Mrs. Truman from the manufacturer, an old friend. In 1955 Secretary of the Air Force Harold E. Talbot stepped down after the revelation that he had drummed up business for a firm in which he held a 50 percent interest. An Atomic Energy Commission agreement with the private firm organized by power company executives Edgar H. Dixon and Eugene A. Yates led, also in 1955, to a noisy but inconclusive dispute over "cronyism" in government. In 1958 Eisenhower's chief of staff, Sherman Adams, came under heavy criticism for accepting the gift of an expensive vicuna coat from industrialist Bernard Goldfine. A controversy likewise broke out in 1963 when it was revealed that a $10 billion contract for TFX fighter bombers had not gone to the firm submitting the best and cheapest design. But even taken as a whole, these and a handful of other such incidents do not suggest either widespread or systematic venality. In view of the massive growth of federal spending and the federal bureaucracy at the same time, they tend rather to confirm the increasingly adventitious and marginal nature of corruption in the executive branch since the 1920's.

Much the same can be said of the legislative branch, although the story is more complicated. Between 1941 and 1971, one member of the Senate and fifteen members of the House were charged with such crimes as bribery, racketeering, conspiracy, mail fraud, extortion, misappropriation of funds, and income tax evasion. One of the few cases that did not result in conviction involved New York Representative Adam Clayton Powell. In 1961, after a federal judge dismissed two of three counts of tax evasion against him, and after his trial on the third had ended in a hung jury, federal prosecutors asked that the

action against Powell be dropped. In 1967, however, the House excluded him on the grounds that he had falsified expense records and misappropriated public funds. Two years later, acknowledging that he had won a resounding re-election victory, the House allowed Powell to take his seat but deprived him of his seniority. Although the Supreme Court ruled shortly thereafter that Powell had been improperly excluded in the first place, it refused to overturn this punishment. The nearly simultaneous case of Connecticut Senator Thomas J. Dodd suggested to many observers that Powell's fate had less to do with any specific wrongdoing than with the abrasive personal style that made him unpopular with many of his colleagues. In 1967, in the wake of revelations that he too had diverted campaign contributions into his personal account and falsified expense records, the Senate censured Dodd but did not expel him. Nor was he prosecuted.

Twice in the 1960's it emerged that congressional aides had also taken advantage of their positions for illicit purposes. Between 1963 and 1965 the Senate investigated charges that Robert G. (Bobby) Baker, secretary to the Senate Majority, had made a small fortune for himself in private business deals by trading on his extensive political connections. In 1967 Baker was found guilty on seven counts of fraud, conspiracy, and income tax evasion. Two years later, a similar scandal struck the office of House Speaker John W. McCormack. McCormack, it was revealed, had permitted a well-known lobbyist named Nathan M. Voloshen to operate out of his office and collected a share of Voloshen's impressive fees. Voloshen pleaded guilty in 1970 to conspiracy and perjury, and Dr. Martin Sweig, one of McCormack's top aides, was shortly thereafter convicted of perjury and improper use of the speaker's office to influence government decisions.

The cumulative effect of these incidents was soon apparent. The Senate Rules Committee's probe of the Baker case produced new recommendations that senators and Senate employees be required to reveal certain categories of assets and income and that the Senate establish a standing ethics committee. A permanent Select Committee on Standards and Conduct was accordingly set up in 1964 and shortly thereafter began looking into the affairs of Senator Dodd. In 1968, with the Dodd case behind it, the select committee drafted the Senate's first comprehensive code of ethics, prohibiting members and employees from receiving compensation for any outside business or professional activity unless it is "not inconsistent nor in conflict with the conscientious performance" of their official duties, requiring members and candidates to report all political contributions and to use them only for political purposes, and obligating members and candidates to file an annual disclosure of personal income, interests, gifts, property, and debts. Meanwhile, amid the furor over the Powell case, the House was also considering a code of ethics. A new Select Committee on Standards of Official Conduct began public hearings in 1967, just weeks after Powell's exclusion, and in 1968 produced a detailed Code of Official Conduct that, like the Senate code, required annual financial disclosures and fixed rules for the receipt and use of political contributions.

The most vexing question of all was not what happened to political contributions but where they came from. The soaring cost of campaigns had dramatically enlarged the importance of wealthy individuals and organizations and led to many ingenious circumventions of the 1907 and 1925 prohibitions against contributions by corporations and banks, as well as of the 1940 limits on individual contributions and annual party expenditures. This was not the first time that concern had been expressed over the potentially corrupting influence of big money in the political process—it was of course a characteristic preoccupation of eighteenth-century oppositional thought and a principal theme of genteel reformers and Progressives a century later—but now, with the legitimacy of the party system and capitalist institutions no longer at issue, the range of solutions had been sharply narrowed. In 1970, Congress agreed to limit spending for political advertising on television and radio, only to have the measure vetoed by President Nixon on the grounds that it discriminated against the broadcasting industry. The 1971 Federal Election Campaign Act, consolidating and supplanting all previous legislation, did succeed in restricting the amount that individuals could spend on their own campaigns and placing a ceiling on expenditures for political advertising.

Just how little had been accomplished by the 1971 act would become apparent in the course of the scandal that broke the following June,

when five well-dressed burglars were arrested at Democratic national headquarters in Washington's Watergate complex. Revelations over the next six months linked them to the Committee to Re-Elect the President (CREEP) and exposed the existence of a secret slush fund out of which the committee had financed a "dirty tricks" campaign to discredit Democratic candidates. Nixon and his staff repeatedly denied any White House involvement in the affair, but in January 1973 the five burglars were convicted along with E. Howard Hunt, Jr., a White House consultant, and G. Gordon Liddy, finance counsel for CREEP. One of the burglars then informed presiding Judge John Sirica that hush money had been paid to head off a full investigation of the break-in and keep damaging evidence out of the trial. This revelation intensified official as well as public curiosity, and by late spring new evidence of a White House conspiracy and cover-up had forced the resignations of L. Patrick Gray, acting director of the FBI, Attorney General Richard Kleindienst, and two Nixon aides, H. R. Haldeman and John D. Ehrlichman. A special Senate committee chaired by Senator Sam Ervin of North Carolina heard testimony from former White House counsel John Dean that former Attorney General John Mitchell had actually approved the Watergate burglary and that Nixon himself had directed the cover-up. In May, Archibald Cox was named special prosecutor to conduct a full-scale inquiry into the entire matter. Cox's office turned up evidence of, among other things, massive illegal corporate contributions to Nixon's 1972 campaign and individual contributions on an unprecedented scale: CREEP was said to have raised almost $17 million alone from 124 donors who gave over $50,000 each. When Ervin's committee learned that all conversations in the president's office had been recorded since 1971, Cox sued Nixon for the relevant tapes. Nixon fired Cox, whereupon Attorney General Elliot Richardson resigned in protest. The House Judiciary Committee, chaired by Peter Rodino of New Jersey, then began consideration of impeachment proceedings against the president. Vice-President Spiro Agnew had meanwhile run afoul of a Justice Department probe and resigned in mid-October. In return for a plea of no contest to one count of federal income tax evasion, the Justice Department agreed not to act on indictments charging

CORRUPTION IN GOVERNMENT

Agnew with conspiracy, extortion, and bribery during his careers in both Maryland and Washington.

Public outcry against his removal of Cox compelled Nixon to name a new special prosecutor, Leon Jaworski, and to hand over the subpoenaed tapes to Judge Sirica. Nixon's position deteriorated steadily in the months that followed. A grand jury named him as an unindicted coconspirator in the Watergate break-in and cover-up, and one of the requested tapes contained mysterious erasures. In July 1974 the Supreme Court supported Jaworski's demand for additional tapes, and the House Judiciary Committee adopted articles of impeachment charging Nixon with obstruction of justice, misuse of power, and failure to comply with a proper congressional request for evidence. In early August, after the new tapes confirmed that he had been party to the cover-up all along, Nixon resigned. His successor, President Gerald Ford, subsequently pardoned him for any federal crimes that he had "committed or may have committed or taken part in" while in office. Fifty-six others were ultimately convicted of Watergate-related crimes, among them twenty former members of the cabinet, the White House staff, and CREEP.

Even before Nixon had departed, Congress was at work on changes in the 1971 Federal Election Campaign Act made necessary by the Watergate revelations. Adopted in 1974, the FECA amendments set a $1,000 maximum on individual and organizational contributions to, or independent expenditures on behalf of, candidates for federal office; prohibited cash contributions in excess of $100; provided for public financing of presidential campaigns; and established a Federal Election Commission to enforce federal election laws. Three years later, both houses of Congress also strengthened the codes of ethics that each had adopted in 1968. Financial disclosure rules were tightened, outside earned income was limited to 15 percent of a member's salary, and a ceiling of $750 was placed on honoraria. A new ethics-in-government law of the same year, revised and extended in early 1983, authorized the office of the special prosecutor, first occupied by Cox and Jaworski, to investigate all charges of corruption against federal officials. Meanwhile, on the state level, parallel efforts were underway to reform the financing of political campaigns: in 1974

alone, some twenty-six states adopted legislation similar to the FECA amendments of that year.

By the late 1970's and early 1980's the significance of these reforms had already been blunted by a series of scandals that revealed the fragility of the new ethics codes and the profound reluctance of Congress to enforce them. In 1975 the Gulf Oil Corporation was shown to have made substantial illegal contributions to the campaigns of numerous members of both houses between 1960 and 1973. Yet only one member was prosecuted—he paid a fine of $200—and the Senate Ethics Committee declined to pursue allegations that Minority Leader Hugh Scott of Pennsylvania had alone received over $100,000 from Gulf. In 1976 the House Ethics Committee refused to recommend the expulsion of a member convicted of receiving illegal gifts and campaign contributions while serving as county assessor in his home state, though it did, in the same year, reprimand another member for financial misconduct. In 1979 the House voted to censure rather than expel Representative Charles C. Diggs, Jr., of Michigan, convicted the previous year on more than two dozen felony counts for diverting staff salaries to his personal use. Also in 1979 the Senate Ethics Committee voted to "denounce" rather than censure or reprimand Senator Herman E. Talmadge of Georgia for "reprehensible" irregularities in the finances of his office.

Perhaps the most telling demonstration of congressional diffidence in the application of its new ethical codes followed what would be known as the "Koreagate" revelations. In 1976 reports had begun to circulate in the press that as many as 115 senators and representatives had received illegal cash payments from Tongsun Park, a South Korean rice dealer, Washington socialite, and crony of South Korean president Park Chung Hee. Nearly two years of investigations by Senate and House ethics committees as well as the Justice Department confirmed South Korean efforts to purchase influence in Congress and produced the names of dozens of congressmen who had in fact taken money or gifts from South Korean agents. Late in 1978 the House nonetheless managed to reprimand only three of its members; the Senate took no disciplinary action at all. Two former representatives were tried on charges of conspiracy and income tax evasion; one of them was acquitted, and the other

CORRUPTION IN GOVERNMENT

served one year of a two-year jail sentence. Late in 1979 the Justice Department dropped its case against Tongsun Park.

Meanwhile, in early 1978, the FBI's Organized Crime Strike Force for the Eastern District of New York had launched its so-called Abscam investigation, in which agents and informers, posing as Arab sheiks who would pay generously for help with immigration authorities, found numerous elected and appointed officials ready to cooperate for the right price. After the nature and scope of the investigation became public in the first months of 1980, six congressmen and one senator were brought to trial and convicted of bribery. Considerable debate occurred over the issue of entrapment and the danger that such clandestine investigations posed for civil liberties. A special Senate committee looking into the matter concluded in December 1982 that no serious improprieties had been committed. In addition, the committee observed, Abscam and other undercover operations of the Justice Department "have substantially contributed to the detection, investigation, and prosecution of criminal activity, especially organized crime and consensual crimes such as narcotics trafficking, fencing of stolen property, and political corruption. In this era of increasingly powerful and sophisticated criminals, some use of the undercover technique is indispensable to the achievement of effective law enforcement." Left unsaid was that this unprecedented use of undercover agents against members of Congress did not reflect well on congressional attempts over the previous two decades or so to prevent and punish corruption in its own ranks.

Concurrently, the Supreme Court had begun to rethink the assumption—first formulated on the federal level in the Tillman Act of 1907—that corporate campaign contributions, by their very nature, imperiled the integrity of the electoral process and the independence of elected officials. In *Buckley* v. *Valeo* (1976), a test of the constitutionality of the amended FECA limitations on campaign contributions and expenditures, the Court upheld restrictions on contributions as an appropriate means for preventing "the actuality and appearance of corruption" in elections. But it struck down the restriction on independent expenditures outside campaign organizations on the grounds that such restrictions constitute an impermissible restraint on First Amendment rights to free speech. That this applied to artificial persons as well as natural persons became clear in *First National Bank of Boston* v. *Bellotti* (1978) and *Consolidated Edison Co.* v. *Public Service Commission* (1980), where the Court argued at length that corporations as well as individuals must be protected from encroachments on their freedom of expression. This marked a radical departure from the older doctrine that corporate "speech" is, in reality, only the speech of those who manage and control the corporation—greatly amplified by the corporation's organizational power and financial resources—and that democracy works best when it responds to the diversity of opinion in the community, not to the distribution of wealth. How much further the Court would press its reinterpretation of the First Amendment remained unclear, although the relaxation of long-established corrupt-practices legislation on the state level was immediately apparent. By the early 1980's, in direct response to the Court's position, more than a dozen states had either eliminated or substantially narrowed previous limitations on corporate political expenditures.

Finally, in a development closely related to the Court's extension of First Amendment rights to corporations, the number of political action committees, or PAC's, began to grow exponentially, channeling vast sums of money into congressional campaigns. The first PAC's appeared in the 1940's but did not become conspicuous until the 1971 Federal Election Campaign Act and its amendments in 1974 expressly allowed both unions and corporations to establish and administer such committees, the money for which would come from voluntary contributions by members and employees. By 1982, according to Federal Election Commission figures, some 3,400 PAC's had poured over $70 million into that year's Senate and House races—about one-fourth of all campaign funds raised and 50 percent above the 1980 total. In the House races alone, PAC's provided one out of every three dollars raised by winners and half or more of all monies raised by 106 members. The 80 freshmen congressmen proved especially dependent on PAC money, averaging around $15,000 each, as against $5,000 for all other House members. By all accounts, the PAC's—and later such powerful trade associations of PAC's as the National As-

440

sociation of Business Political Action Committees (NABPAC)—already enjoyed so much influence over Congress because of their lavish spending that a quiet revolution may be said to have taken place in the structure and practice of American politics.

Inevitably, these events and circumstances —the ineffectiveness of congressional reform, the Supreme Court's newfound First Amendment rights for corporations, and the sudden rise of the political action committee—all might be taken as evidence that political corruption is as widespread and deeply rooted as ever, and perhaps destined to become even more so. What is "new" about the "new" corruption, from this perspective, is in large part that Congress and the Supreme Court appear unwilling or unable to do anything about it.

It bears repeating, therefore, that some things have indeed changed, and one of them is the context in which corruption occurs and the functions that it may be said to serve. Both as a matter of fact and as a matter of perception, the "new" corruption reflects neither the stresses and strains of a colonial political system nor the struggle to legitimize capitalist values and institutions. If anything, the PAC phenomenon and the effort to inject corporations into the political process emphasize the passing of older definitions of corruption and the advent of political forms and practices suitable to a mature capitalist system. It is also worth considering, once again, that in light of the awesome increases in the size and scope of government at all levels during the twentieth century, all of the cases of congressional venality together may still represent a relative decline in the frequency and severity of corruption: the "new" corruption may be "new" because there is, in proportion to the steady enlargement of government activity, simply less of it.

Then, too, as the Abscam investigation appeared to indicate, federal and state authorities have begun to adopt new stratagems for detecting and rooting out corruption. In 1969 former Illinois Governor Otto Kerner had been convicted of accepting a bribe to influence the state racing commission. Federal bribery statutes did not apply in the case, but the prosecution successfully argued that Kerner had violated federal mail-fraud statutes by defrauding the citi-

zens of Illinois of their intangible right to his honest and loyal services. This novel theory was expanded in the 1979 federal prosecution of Maryland Governor Marvin Mandel, charged and convicted under the federal mail-fraud statutes of defrauding Maryland citizens "of the right to conscientious, loyal, faithful, disinterested, and honest government through bribery and nondisclosure and concealment of material information." The government case did not contend that Mandel had in fact received a bribe—merely that he had breached a fiduciary trust by doing favors for friends (also, as it happened, in the racetrack business) and then trying to hide what had taken place. In effect, federal prosecutors were rapidly transforming the mail-fraud statute into a general anticorruption measure that reached well beyond existing legislation.

The next step came in 1981 with the federal indictment of Nassau County, New York, Republican Chairman Joseph Margiotta. Margiotta, unlike Kerner and Mandel, did not hold an elected or appointed public office, and the thrust of the charges against him was that he had negotiated an arrangement between the county and a local insurance agency, which then kicked back a percentage of its commissions to the party organization. Here the claim was that even a private citizen could, in circumstances such as Margiotta's, owe a fiduciary duty to the public that could be enforced under the federal mail-fraud statute. What was more, traditionally accepted forms of political patronage may be interpreted as fraud under the statute, even when no personal gain was realized or contemplated. Margiotta was convicted, and the U.S. Court of Appeals upheld his conviction in 1982, although one justice remarked that to use "mail fraud as a catch-all prohibition of political disingenuousness . . . subjects virtually every active participant in the political process to potential criminal investigation and prosecution." The Supreme Court's refusal in 1983 to hear Margiotta's appeal sent him to jail but left unresolved this disturbing implication of his conviction. It would make an ironic conclusion to the history of corruption in American government if, even as older standards of legislative integrity broke down, the prosecution of corruption did indeed lay the foundation for the persecution of opposition.

BIBLIOGRAPHY

Association of the Bar of the City of New York, Special Committee on Congressional Ethics, *Congress and the Public Trust* (New York, 1970), is particularly helpful on the evolution of congressional ethics committees. George C. S. Benson, *et al.,* *Political Corruption in America* (Lexington, Mass., 1978), has the advantage of devoting attention to historical as well as current experience but is lacking in conceptual sophistication. Rowland Berthoff, "Independence and Attachment, Virtue and Interest: From Republican Citizen to Free Enterpriser, 1787–1837," in Richard L. Bushman, *et al.,* eds., *Uprooted Americans: Essays to Honor Oscar Handlin* (Boston, 1979), is an elegant commentary on the demise of classical republican ideas about corruption. Richard L. Bushman, "Corruption and Power in Provincial America," in Library of Congress Symposia on the American Revolution, *The Development of a Revolutionary Mentality* (Washington, D.C., 1972), is based largely on evidence from New England colonies but brilliantly illuminates the entire subject, especially the indigenous sources of American political culture in the Revolutionary period. John Coffee, "From Tort to Crime: Some Reflections on the Criminalization of Fiduciary Breaches and the Problematic Line Between Law and Ethics," in *American Criminal Law Review,* 19 (1981), is a valuable account. Congressional Quarterly, *Congressional Ethics,* 2nd ed. (Washington, D.C., 1980), is a thorough and judicious compilation of recent cases, reform efforts, and relevant law; see also the first edition for Watergate-related material omitted from the later edition. Elizabeth Drew, *Politics and Money: The New Road to Corruption* (New York, 1983), contains brief but thoughtful observations by the Washington journalist and is especially good on the proliferation of political action committees. Abraham S. Eisenstadt, *et al.,* eds., *Before Watergate: Problems of Corruption in American Society* (New York, 1978), comprises conference papers treating social and cultural as well as political aspects of corruption since the Revolution.

Robert S. Getz, *Congressional Ethics: The Conflict of Interest Issue* (Princeton, N.J., 1966), though dated, is still an instructive introduction to an intricate subject. Arnold J. Heidenheimer, ed., *Political Corruption: Readings in Comparative Analysis* (New York, 1970), is an excellent sampler of modern research on corruption in the United States and elsewhere. Ari Hoogenboom, *Outlawing the Spoils: A History of the Civil Service Reform Movement, 1865–1883* (Urbana, Ill., 1968), the standard account, is rich in detail and insight into the nature and meaning of corruption in nineteenth-century America. Milton M. Klein, "Corruption in Colonial America," in *South At-*lantic Quarterly,* 78 (1979), is the only scholarly attempt to date to get down to cases and is an indispensable point of departure for serious thinking about the role of corruption and ideas about corruption in the Revolutionary period and after. John M. Kramer, "Political Corruption in the U.S.S.R.," in *Western Political Quarterly,* 30 (1977), marshals evidence that corruption is not unique to capitalist governments and societies. David G. Loth, *Public Plunder: A History of Graft in America* (New York, 1938), is still the most entertaining of the popular accounts of corruption in American history, though it is marred by an us-and-them simplemindedness. Richard L. McCormick, "The Discovery That Business Corrupts Politics: A Reappraisal of the Origins of Progressivism," in *American Historical Review,* 86 (1981), offers useful details. Donald A. MacPhee, "The Yazoo Controversy: The Beginning of the 'Quid' Revolt," in *Georgia Historical Quarterly,* 49 (1965), gives essential details of this important land-fraud case and the role of John Randolph. Robert E. Mutch, "Corporate Money and Elections," in *State Legislatures* (Feb. 1983), summarizes the relaxation of state restrictions against corporate political activity after the *Bellotti* decision. William Patton and Randall Bartlett, "Corporate 'Persons' and Freedom of Speech: The Political Impact of Legal Mythology," in *1981 Wisconsin Law Review,* no. 4, presents the case against First Amendment rights for corporations from a historical as well as legal point of view. John G. Peters and Susan Welch, "Political Corruption in America: A Search for Definitions and a Theory, or, If Political Corruption Is in the Mainstream of American Politics, Why Is It Not in the Mainstream of American Politics Research?" in *American Political Science Review,* 72 (1978), does not quite manage to answer that fundamental question but does, along the way, provide an excellent synopsis of post-Watergate attempts, especially by political scientists, to clarify the issues involved.

Robert A. Prentice, "*Consolidated Edison* and *Bellotti:* First Amendment Protection of Corporate Political Speech, in *Tulsa Law Journal,* 16 (1981), argues in favor of First Amendment rights for corporations. Leonard D. White's four-volume series on administrative history in the United States from 1801 to 1901, *The Federalists, The Jeffersonians, The Jacksonians,* and *The Republicans* (New York, 1948–1958), is absolutely essential for the study of political corruption on the national level. C. Vann Woodward, ed., *Responses of the President to Charges of Misconduct* (New York, 1974), is an administration-by-administration review and is very useful despite the uneven quality of its chapters and the lack of an overall perspective.

[*See also* BUSINESS AND GOVERNMENT; CONSPIRACY AND CONSPIRACY THEORIES; IMPEACHMENT; MACHINE POLITICS; *and* PRESIDENCY.]

CRIME AND PUNISHMENT

Eric H. Monkkonen

A TRADITIONAL, relatively static system of criminal justice characterized English colonies in North America. The laws, the apparatus for enforcement and punishment, and the organizations all resembled the traditional models provided by the English Middle Ages. The nineteenth and early twentieth centuries saw a dramatic transformation, and virtually all of the modern tools of crime control had been created by 1930. On the other hand, the actual offense rate, the number of criminal acts per capita, did not change so abruptly or dramatically. Rates of serious crime apparently have been gradually declining since the Middle Ages, throughout the Western world. To be sure, there have been periods of dramatically increased crime rates—the 1850's, 1960's, and 1970's, for instance—but the best evidence is somewhat encouraging, suggesting that for unknown reasons our world has witnessed continuously less criminal violence.

Historians in general act with caution when making claims about the utility of lessons from the past; few of them have the temerity to expect their work to speak to—much less change—the present (Rothman, 1981). Yet historians of crime cannot help but feel that their work does have lessons for the present. Of course, the history of crime is never studied primarily for purely utilitarian reasons. Like other forms of historical analysis, its main goals are to explain and understand the past in order to gain deeper social knowledge. But, as opposed to many other historical topics, crime and criminal justice carry an invisible policy imperative.

It is important, therefore, to make explicit the reasons for studying the history of crime and criminal justice. This ensures that the goal of our analysis will not obstruct our understanding of the subject. Thus there are two conceptual frameworks with which to structure criminal justice history. The first is purely historical, to understand the past for its own sake and to understand society. The second is more pragmatic, to achieve analytic insights into the control of crime and to use the crime rate and our handling of crime as a social barometer.

The notion that crime rates provide a social barometer with which to compare societies was challenged and rejected by Émile Durkheim at the turn of the century. Arguing that a society needs crime to define the boundaries of acceptable behavior, Durkheim maintained that the amount of crime should be constant, although the kind of crime would change as the society changed. Durkheim's notion has inspired both historical and criminological research, covering the whole span of American history. Most notable have been Kai Erikson's provocative work (1966) on crime in colonial Massachusetts and the research of Alfred Blumstein, his associates, and his critics (1979), who have analyzed long-range trends in imprisonment rates.

As used by historians and sociologists, Durkheim's argument speaks less to offense rates than to punishment rates. Thus one can assert the constancy of punishment while examining variations in the per-capita rate of offenses. We can use crime to see not only how we are doing but also how we are changing. This dualistic aspect of criminal justice history, therefore, is less contradictory than it may appear.

The purposive change of the criminal justice system has always been rife with argument and conflict. Indeed, the issues posed by "law-and-order" advocates in the late 1960's mirror only very faintly those of an earlier age. As elaborated in England in the eighteenth century, the most significant issue was centered on the apparently irreconcilable conflict between liberty and order. Those measures perceived as necessary to control public crimes of violence—the creation of a regularized police, more systematic surveillance, and a generally more intrusive criminal justice system—seemed to subtract from private liberty as they added to public order. Given this apparent trade-off, the English elite long resisted any criminal justice reforms that appeared to intrude on their liberties. The French police were always pointed to as a bad example of the consequences of greater organization in the name of crime control: they spied, they constantly trespassed on political liberties, they oppressively maintained the status quo. Thus when Sir Robert Peel created the London police in the late 1820's, he carefully avoided the word *police,* cautiously invoking notions of "public safety" instead.

That the criminal justice system underwent such great transformation in the nineteenth century suggests that the process was an aspect of modernization, of the ascent to power of the bourgeoisie, and of the evolution of Western society from agrarian to industrial. Each of these changes did indeed affect the criminal justice system, which by its very nature is political. Crime is most reasonably, if circularly, defined as behavior that violates the criminal law. And organized systems of control and a body of laws created by political systems cannot help but reflect the major socioeconomic changes of an age. Yet the political aspect of crime does not account for the criminal behavior of individuals, and here a conundrum appears. For, although the crime control system was transformed, there is little evidence of such transformation in criminal behavior. That is, there is no good reason to find any cause-and-effect in either direction between the actions of criminal offenders and change in the system designed to control them. This makes the historian's job both interesting and difficult: changes in the system cannot be analyzed simply as passively responsive, nor can the directional variations of crime rates be analyzed as responding to the system.

Recent work on the policy of criminal justice has highlighted this conundrum and its disturbing implications for modern policy makers. One might conclude from Silberman's study (1978) of crime and crime control, for instance, that "nothing works," that policy directed toward

crime is bound to fail. But a more accurate appraisal is that the relationships between crime control and crime cannot be established with any confidence. In a sense, the strength of history, working through tradition, makes us fear to deal with crime in new ways; at the same time we are not convinced that the means given to us by the past are adequate.

Yet a centuries-long, gradual decline in Western per-capita felony rates contrasts with the comparatively abrupt transformation of the criminal justice system in the nineteenth century. The contrast suggests that, at least on the grand scale, the simplest message to be drawn from the past is as unclear as that of recent criminal justice research. There is no immediately visible relationship between actual crime and the system intended to control it. How, then, can the crime control system be effectively manipulated? Are crime rates driven by causal mechanisms independent of those implemented by the control system? Is crime control merely whistling in the dark? Only a careful and tentative look at the history of criminal justice can begin to help us to understand the past for its own sake and to think with some clarity about current options.

THE CRIMINAL LAW

Most of what we call crime today would have been recognized as such by our colonial forebears, just as we would consider crime most of the offenses that they prosecuted. Unlike the civil law, which some historians argue underwent a capitalist "transformation" in the late eighteenth and early nineteenth centuries, criminal law changed slowly and imperceptibly (Horwitz, 1977; Fletcher, 1976)—so subtly as to escape most legal and historical analysts. Even if its history has not been filled with sudden or surprising developments, it is important to start with the law itself.

In a formal and important sense, crime begins with the criminal law. When criminologists define crime as behavior proscribed by the criminal law, they are expressing more than a circular argument. Before behavior can be criminal, there must be a state. The wrongful action of an individual becomes an offense against the state when it threatens the state's power. When the state has little power, or its power is limited in geographical scope, the range of criminal offenses is like-wise limited. In English law the notion of the king's peace in the Middle Ages at first applied only to the area near the king, then later to the king's highways, and finally to the country as a whole. As the scope of criminal law expanded, so did the power of the state. In a state with lim-ited power, even homicide is a private wrong; not until the state itself gains the right to take an in-dividual life does it become criminalized.

Therefore, only because it is proscribed by law is criminal behavior raised from the level of private wrong to a wrong against the state. Spe-cifically created as a behavioral category by law, crime is essentially political. Here *political* does not mean that offenders of the law act with politi-cal intentions but that the political system has given their actions conceptual significance. And this sense of *political* is far from trivial, for the in-corporation of private wrongs into the criminal law created a new sense of rights in the Western world, the right to freedom from criminal vio-lence.

By the mid-nineteenth century, American criminal justice officials had grouped all offenses into three categories for the purpose of tabula-tion: crimes against property, crimes against per-sons, and crimes against morality or statutes. As far as the first two categories are concerned, the law and perception of criminal behavior have not changed very much. In the late twentieth century most forms of theft and personal violence still look about the same, even if the technology asso-ciated with them has become more sophisticated. Most seventeenth-century crimes against moral-ity still exist, even if they go unprosecuted. And statutory crimes have expanded, but they make up a tiny proportion of all criminal behavior.

This rather surprising stability in legal and perceived definitions of serious criminal behav-ior may be epitomized in the Federal Bureau of Investigation's *Uniform Crime Reports*. In spite of criticism and the FBI's own disavowal of the sta-tistical utility of the first thirty-five years of the series, the reports have become the bench mark for definitions of crime in the United States. Since 1930 they have given monthly updates and annual indices of seven different offenses, or "index crimes," known to the police: homicide, rape, robbery, burglary, larceny, assault, and auto theft. Only the last would be incomprehen-sible to colonial Americans, although they might

perhaps have included some moral offenses —adultery, for instance—that the FBI has dropped from the statistical forefront.

Theft, which has changed only slightly on the surface, has undergone an interesting and subtle shift in the common law since the sixteenth cen-tury. Its definition has had to encompass forms of property and economic life radically different from those that the law originally protected. Yet its essence has remained trespass and the con-cept of thief-like behavior. That is, the thief has had to act like a thief, to be defined under the law as a thief. In the sixteenth century these basic principles covered most forms of theft. If the owner of a piece of portable property gave it to someone who converted it for personal gain, this action would not constitute theft under the com-mon law, for the receiver had "possessorial im-munity." Carrier's case in the late fifteenth cen-tury dealt with this problem, establishing that if the receiver broke the bulk of the other's proper-ty—that is, broke into a package removing some or all of its contents—then a felonious trespass had occurred.

The law of theft tried to accommodate in-creasingly complex forms of property relation-ships until the late eighteenth and early nine-teenth centuries, when what Fletcher has called a "metamorphosis" occurred. This metamor-phosis refocused the law away from the specific moment of the criminal act—for example, a de-livery person's breaking into a package—and away from possessorial immunity. The new ob-ject of scrutiny became the actor instead of the act. Although acting "like a thief" may seem to attend to the actor, it did so only at the instant of the offense—when the offender violently broke into a house, for instance. The new focus turned away from the instant of the action to ac-commodate planning, execution, and conse-quences.

A subtle conceptual metamorphosis with only modest consequences for the vast bulk of thefts, this shift does have a direct analogue to modes of punishment. As delineated by Foucault, the changing modes of punishment can be related to a whole new notion, the rise of the individual, and a reconception that the individual's "ca-reer," rather than particular acts, is the object of importance. In Foucault's formulation, this change came about as a consequence of growing state power and its simultaneous disappearance behind the mask of bureaucracy. In the case of larceny, this conceptual shift had little visible effect on the definition or day-to-day aspects of criminal behavior. On the other hand, the parallel change in punishment was indeed dramatic: torture declined, public executions disappeared, and penitentiaries began to dot the landscape.

A more practical problem for the criminal law arose as theft became commercialized in a mass urban setting, particularly in London in the early eighteenth century. Jonathan Wild, the self-proclaimed "thief-taker general" for London, epitomized and made famous the role of the fence, flamboyantly capitalizing on the demands of both the thief and his victim: the thief wanted to convert stolen goods to money, the victim wanted to recover the goods. In an age before personal-property insurance, the fence provided a useful function, returning the missing items to the owner—for a fee. Thus the victim recovered the goods, and the thief and fence made a small profit. Since Wild's time fences have caused legal difficulties. They do not act like thieves; they act like merchants. (For their actions to be criminal they must know that the goods they receive have been stolen.) Yet, the fence provides a critical nexus in supporting the economic enterprise of larceny. The criminal receiver legislation enacted in the mid-eighteenth century confronted but could not solve this persistent problem. Convicting a fence continues to be very difficult, often requiring perjury on the part of law enforcement officials (Hall, 1952; Klockars, 1980).

Although the history of the law of larceny is conceptually exciting, like most of our criminal law it is hardly filled with stunning reversals. Witchcraft might be considered a major and sensational exception to this generalization. Few people today believe in witches, and as a result, their trials and executions in the seventeenth century appear fanatical and wrong. One must not presume the innocence of seventeenth-century witches, however (Butler, 1979). In an age that took its religion seriously, witches could use their powers in ways as malevolent as other felons. The problem with the Salem witchcraft trials of 1692–1693 was not witchcraft itself but the admission of the "spectral evidence" of accusers. This troubled Cotton Mather; for, although the witches may have been real, there was no way to corroborate their accusers' visions.

Two other aspects of criminal law from the colonial period, which seem equally foreign today, remind us that ours is a secular world. Many criminal offenses in the colonies retained "benefit of clergy" until the end of the eighteenth century. A common-law device, the benefit of clergy had been designed to preserve the division between ecclesiastical and secular law. Many common-law offenses were stipulated as clergiable, indicating that clergymen could not be prosecuted for them. In practice, the determination of a defendant's clergiable status amounted to a literacy test, the reading aloud of a section of the Bible. Such a test, particularly given jailed defendants' powers of memorization, ensured the acquittal of many. An equally peculiar practice persisted into the seventeenth century. This was deodand, a nonhuman object, such as an animal or tool, that had been instrumental in a criminal act (resulting in death). It was not formally abolished in England until 1846, when the application of the concept to train accidents could have proven very costly. The deodand, if an animal, might be executed or, if a tool or instrument, confiscated by the state. Although interesting, these practices were only a small part of the criminal law or criminal behavior. But crimes of magic and conjuring, the benefit of clergy, and deodand serve to remind us of our tacit acceptance of a material world unsuffused with spiritual meanings.

Fornication by unmarried people is still an offense in many states. Virtually unprosecuted today, more court cases of fornication were prosecuted during the mid-eighteenth century than cases of theft or interpersonal violence (Nelson, 1975; Hindus, 1980; Greenberg, 1976). But these prosecutions had motives rooted in local economies: local courts could establish paternity to remove the women and children involved from local welfare rolls. These prosecutions served as a way to evade the local obligation to support poor residents (Jones, 1983). Thus, rather than interpreting fornication statutes as signs of intrusive colonial concern with private morality, they might instead be seen as a means of transferring nominal public obligations to private individuals.

In the nineteenth century, legal reformers struggled to rationalize state legal systems that seemed to defy Enlightenment principles of criminal law. To deter crime, the thinking went, the list of proscriptions and punishments must be public, rational, and easily understood. The existing criminal laws, built by accretion on a common-law inheritance, were exactly the opposite of such a system. In this context, it is easier to understand the passion that surrounded the codification movement, which its supporters envisioned as a rationalizing, liberal reform. Massachusetts led the way in codification. Although reformers never enacted a code, they did get a collection of revised statutes in 1835 that served as a reasonable substitute. South Carolina, ever conservative, resisted codification or even a rational compilation until forced to do so during Reconstruction (Hindus, 1980; Friedman, 1973).

By the end of the nineteenth century, the rationale behind much criminal law had become buried, as Friedman points out, in legal "inflation." In many states the number of specific offenses enumerated in the criminal code had become large and hopelessly detailed: for example, section 2121 of the 1881 Indiana code prohibiting the selling of grain seed that harbored the seeds of Canada thistle (Friedman, 1973). But the apparent irrationality of these codes actually preceded the creation of the law of regulation. To give bite to regulatory law, legislators by the end of the nineteenth century often criminalized the behavior under question, as in the grain seed example above. Thus the apparent plethora of criminal conducts represented the more detailed regulation of the economy. The control of monopolies illustrates this best. The Sherman Antitrust Act of 1890, for instance, seemed ineffectual until given a criminal bite by the Clayton Antitrust Act twenty-four years later. Fines enforced the Sherman Act; the Clayton Act added imprisonment—presumably a greater deterrent for corporate representatives.

Finally, public and legislative concern about the morality and efficacy of capital punishment increased. By the mid-nineteenth century, Wisconsin had entered the Union without any capital offenses; Maine and Michigan abolished capital punishment in the 1880's. In contrast, South Carolina reduced its capital offenses from 165 in 1813 to a mere 22 by 1850 (Friedman, 1973). In related developments, northern states reduced or ended corporal punishment, whereas southern states tended to retain it. These legal differences should not automatically be attributed to conservative southern attitudes toward crime. Most southern states had weak governments and very low levels of public services. Criminal justice reforms, such as the codification of laws or the creation of more just criminal justice systems, are costly. Southern states spent little money or legislative time on any aspect of their governmental apparatus. Under such circumstances one must not be surprised to find corporal punishment; it is not only inexpensive but also emphasizes the power of the state.

The United States now has fifty-one criminal codes, one for each state and one for the federal government; regulatory law, too, often prescribes criminal punishment for its offenders. These codes alone define crime—but they do not tell us what occurs in the outside world, to which the laws apply. For this, we must examine policing systems and the behavior of criminal offenders.

POLICE

Police are uniformed officers whose task it is to enforce local ordinances and the criminal laws of the government. As the Greek root *(polis)* suggests, the police are urban in locus, although in the early twentieth century contradictorily labeled "rural police" appeared. American cities began to create police departments in the mid-nineteenth century. The first uniformed police, in Boston and New York, were explicitly modeled on the Metropolitan Police of London, established in 1829 (Lane, 1967; Miller, 1977; Monkkonen, 1981). These organizations replaced an ancient and traditional system, the constable and night watch. The constable-and-watch system had long been criticized for its bumbling ineffectiveness and, since Shakespeare's time, had furnished material for comedies. This system and the police that followed it exemplify the dramatic transition from an organic to a rational system. Conceptually, organizationally, and behaviorally, the contrast between the two forms of crime control highlights the differences between the modern and premodern world.

In theory, the constable and the night watch represented the community. The constable served the court, his remuneration coming from fees attached to the individual services he performed. The watch, on the other hand, represented community members, who each took his turn at night patrolling the town. Their guidance came from the constable, their legal authority from the notion of posse comitatus, which required that all adult males in the community be responsible for pursuing felons. Whereas the night watch was "proactive," patrolling to prevent disturbances as well as to report anything untoward, the constable was "reactive," not actively seeking offenses or offenders but responding to complaints made either to him or to the courts.

The night watch had ceased to be composed of volunteer townsmen long before the English brought the institution to North America. By then it consisted of hired "substitutes," usually unemployable or—quite literally—moon-lighting men. Virtually every reference to the night watch pokes fun at them, citing their cowardice, drunkenness, laziness, and overall ineptness. No historian has yet tried to ascertain the accuracy of these charges but one thing is clear: the differing patrol and scheduling traditions of the constable and the watch led to great organizational inefficiency. The night watch patrolled from sunset to sunrise; the constables usually served from 8 A.M. until 5 P.M. In the summer, as a consequence, no one served for the long daylight periods in the morning and evening.

Moreover, the reactive nature of the constables, the requirement of paying them fees, and the apparent inefficiency of the watch resulted in a passive policing system that not only had little or no investigative capacity and no responsibility to seek out offenses, but also placed the burden of law enforcement on the victims. For the poor in particular, seeking the constable's assistance would be far more costly than suffering the damages. Until the introduction of non-fee-based policing, the state's power in crime control was only nominal. A passive agent, the criminal law came into action only when the seriousness of the offense outweighed the costs of calling on the state for assistance.

The creation of the uniformed urban police made the criminal law active. This did not necessarily mean that the creators had wanted an active law, for the reasons that had led to the uniforming of the police did not often portend their functions once they began to patrol. Americans traveling in England had often admired London's orderliness and apparent lack of crime,

which observers often attributed to Robert Peel's Metropolitan Police. Both in Boston and New York, a small number of wealthy, educated reformers began working to replace the antiquated constable-and-watch system with a police modeled on the bobbies or peelers. The reformers wanted polite policemen who would bring order to the streets.

The new police, they hoped, would replace the loosely organized watch with efficient, well-organized, and uniformed officers. They would follow orders, deter crime through their uniformed presence, and detect unreported crimes. The uniforms symbolized the importance of the goals and provided the means to implement them. Before the new form of policing was adopted, the constables and watch wore what they pleased and, when given stars or other badges, placed them on easily covered parts of their jackets. The plain clothes gave them freedom to be their own boss, once out of the sight of their superiors. Anonymity preserved their independence and made them virtually masterless in the streets. Like the urban artisans whose own autonomy was being eroded at the same time, the police vigorously resisted any constraint on their independence. Bringing them under tight control and making them regularly visible and available constituted the central vision of their creators. The intimidating sight of the uniformed officer, it was confidently predicted, would deter the potential criminal. The almost military command structure would swiftly direct and coordinate police actions; regular, aggressive patrolling would find and prosecute criminals who had operated undiscovered under the looser systems.

The transition from one system to another came about slowly in the first cities making the change, but by the 1860's and 1870's the rate of change began to accelerate. In Boston and New York, a separate night police, headed by a constable or captain, mirrored the day police, but each operated independently. The two forces served as a transitional form and probably provided increased resistance to the final unification of New York's police in 1853, Boston's in 1859. Although the reformation of the police was opposed in all quarters, the most vigorous protest came from the police officers themselves. They saw the change as degrading their autonomy and status, for in the antebellum United States, only servants wore nonmilitary uniforms. City governments themselves resisted the new police, for the earlier police were far less costly, because they paid themselves with the fees they collected.

England's example provided the prototype for the urban police, but Americans introduced significant modifications, perhaps unknowingly. No one considered organizing the police from the top down, at the federal or even state level. In each city the reform began locally and stayed local, and from the beginning the police acted as agents of local government. This difference accompanied another structural shift. The constable had been an agent of the courts, doing both civil and criminal work, like the sheriff at the county level. In contrast, the new police had their allegiance to the executive branch of city government, partly because the city courts had complete jurisdiction only over minor criminal offenses and partly because the new police worked around the clock. Unlike courts, which adjudicate only what comes to them, the new police did not wait to respond but were, rather, active agents in the administration of urban order.

These seemingly subtle differences signaled a profound change in the nature of criminal justice. The police made the justice system an active shaper of the social system, and their purview included a broadly defined world of public and private behavior. The criminal law contributed a significant component of their guidelines for action, of course, but local ordinances increased the scope of their charge so that arresting criminal offenders represented only a small portion of their activity.

Police looked after the welfare of indigents, inspected boilers, shot stray dogs, reported open sewers, returned lost children to their parents, and sometimes even ran soup lines, and, while doing these jobs, unintentionally expanded the role of city government in providing services. Never before had the city offered an easily identified representative on the street, and in the era of pre-electronic communication this constituted a service revolution. Whereas earlier, the parents of lost children had located them with great difficulty, with the police organization they could go to precinct or central headquarters and recover them. This centralization affected all areas of police activity; officers could more easily be on the alert for known offenders, public health threats, or other potential problems. In a sense,

the creation of the police had opened a Pandora's box.

As a formal organization of social control the police often took partisan political action, and they had an electoral role as well, as an important part of urban political machines. Their jobs provided patronage. By the end of the nineteenth century they were the final arm of urban political machines, literally standing at the ballot boxes to ensure proper voting outcomes. But when machines lost, so did the police officers. For other reasons as well, the typical police officer did not stay long on the job, and his loyalty was not, as it is today, to the organization or the job culture. The police often took sides in class conflicts, usually protecting the rights of property against the demands of labor. But sometimes they refused to side with property owners in strikes, and the reasons illustrate one of the consequences of their localism. Individually, police officers were recruited from and related to the working class. Few officers stayed on the job long, partly because they were political appointees and partly because most did not see themselves as careerists. As a result, especially in smaller cities, strikes involved their relatives and centered on issues of wages that the police themselves might soon face. Thus they could not always be relied upon to protect scabs or break strikes; sometimes they did—but sometimes they did not (Harring, 1981; Walkowitz, 1978).

Even though their organizational structure seemed to favor military-like action and control, police behavior in strikes and riots showed the hopelessness of depending on them in any kind of group action. Major riots usually ended with the arrival of the national guard or army as, most spectacularly, in the New York City Draft Riots of 1863. The individualistic, day-to-day reality of police work, although centrally organized, featured an independent or small-group working pattern that impeded the formation of an army.

The very features of policing that made it precipitate a broad range of urban functions finally led, in the early twentieth century, to a narrowing of police duties. The primary intention had been for the police to deter crime—a problematic charge, to say the least, for how does one determine if an imminent criminal offense did not occur? Nevertheless, as police lost their broader role, they fell back on their crime-control responsibility. The various national organizations of police chiefs emphasized crime fighting, and officers began to conceive of themselves as crime fighters. And the very public that had made so many kinds of demands on the police also wanted them to be the primary force against crime.

As the police's crime-fighting image grew, so did their image of corruption, violence, and politicization. In 1894 the Lexow Commission in New York created a sensation by exposing police corruption, both political and vice-related. Investigations in other cities and on the federal level, culminating in the Wickersham Commission's investigation (1929), echoed these findings (Fogelson, 1977). The nature of the corruption and its exposure varied little. But there was a clear trend toward the removal of police both from political action and from the patronage system. In large part this dissociation came about as a part of the decline of political machines, rather than as a result of change in the police departments themselves. In addition, the use of torture in forcing confessions, euphemistically referred to as the "third degree," fell into disrepute. The role of the forensic expert in investigation came to the fore as the public acceptance of a brutal police declined.

Seen in this context, the *Miranda* decision (1966), limiting the duplicitous gathering of evidence, constituted one more step in the forced decline of inquisitorial tactics. Somehow, we still expect our police to be wiser than Maigret and braver than Dick Tracy. Since 1894 at least, we have been asking the police to act as subtly as their fictional counterparts. Each outraged exposé, each failure to deter crime, has been counted as an indictment of the police. The consequence has been to cement the singular image of the police as crime-control agents. Most police historians today, and certainly the police themselves, recognize that crime-related work occupies only a small fraction of their time. But the rich and complex history of the police has been one of constant yet unrealistic narrowing of function, so that the institution has acquired both a public image and a self-image at odds with reality.

A classic social contradiction fosters another kind of police corruption, unrelated to electoral politics. For most vice offenses, for instance, those in a position to provide prosecutorial evidence have also been willing participants in the criminal behavior. Known as "victimless crimes," all of these offenses, with the exception of receiving stolen goods, require the police to place themselves in compromising positions to gather evidence (Skolnick, 1966). They must participate in drug buys, visits to prostitutes, selling stolen goods, and gambling, and must present evidence of this. Perjury almost becomes a prerequisite for conviction, and evidence on pimping and other higher levels of vice is even more difficult to get.

In these cases, the contradiction is that the criminal law creates nominal "victims" but the expectation is that a certain amount of proscribed offenses is tolerable. Police are asked to limit, not eliminate, vice. The limitation creates the opportunity for bribery, because limiting suggests that only some offenders should be arrested, that the offense is only partially criminal. Thus the police in vice control internalize the social and legislative contradiction, sometimes at personal profit if at a moral loss.

PRISONS

Since the 1833 publication of the Beaumont and Tocqueville volume on American prisons, the United States has had an international reputation for its model penitentiaries. In the twentieth century this reputation has suffered, and few international commissions come today to learn from our system. Yet early in the nineteenth century the penitentiaries were often a part of an American tour; Tocqueville came on a specific government mission to learn from the prison system. From the European perspective, the United States had invented a place to reform rather than to punish. That American penitentiaries should have institutionalized the Enlightenment vision of human perfectibility seemed to fulfill the highest European hopes, and visitors arrived prepared to find innovation, optimism, and the successful reformation of human character. Not that these penitentiaries coddled the inmates. Tocqueville observed: "They are unhappy, they deserve to be so; having become better, they will be happy in that society whose laws they have been taught to respect" (Beaumont and Tocqueville, 1964).

The notion of locking up offenders as punishment was ancient; the seemingly unique American contribution to penology was to construe the prison as a place for more than punishment. David Rothman (1980) considers this innovation an outcome of the optimistic social expectations of the Jacksonian era. Jacksonian culture, says Rothman, assumed that human nature could be changed. And the democratic Jacksonian United States, which had raised the common man, could also change the habitual criminal offender, the mentally ill, or the pauper. In the proper institutional setting these defects could be remedied, and after treatment, the miscreant could be released, ready to participate fully in normal society. Human nature itself could be changed.

In the early nineteenth century two models of penitentiaries developed, the Auburn system and the Walnut Street Jail, or Philadelphia, system. Both demanded silence, daily productive work, and heavy doses of Bible reading. The Auburn system, implemented in the 1820's at Auburn (N.Y.) prison, allowed prisoners to work in groups, whereas the Philadelphia system required complete physical isolation. Hence they were often referred to as the silent system and the separate system. Both assumed that an inherent and universal moral sense, if given the opportunity, would convince the offender of the wrongness of the criminal offense. Solitude provided the reflective opportunity; "alone, in view of his crime, he learns to hate it," and the subsequent remorse ensured that when released, the offender would never again turn to evil (Beaumont and Tocqueville, 1964).

The view of human nature informing such expectations was indeed optimistic, if not naïve. Moreover, the assumption that a criminal offense is an easily isolated social act of inherent, universal wrongfulness virtually denied the existence of conflicting social values or the power of the state against which the offense was made. Foucault's observation (1977) that the modern punishment system masks state power is appropriate here. Both the silent and the separate penal systems tried to remove the offenders from all contact with society, insisting that the wrong was solely within the individual, that crime was not even a conflict between right social norms and wrong individual actions or power and powerlessness, but that the state's side of the conflict did not exist at all. In a sense, the ideology of the new form of prison dissolved the increased organizational power of the state in a cloud of words.

The innovational and rhetorical aspects of the American penitentiary system little affected the day-to-day reality facing most incarcerated offenders in the nineteenth and early twentieth centuries. They spent their hours in the county jail, the city jail, or the work farm; were hired out as contract labor; or worked on the chain gang. In the nineteenth century jails often held witnesses, the mentally ill, and those for whom there was no other place of confinement. In the 1840's, Dorothea Dix visited hundreds of jails, valiantly trying to have the insane and debtors placed elsewhere. Conditions in these places often made them a greater punishment than anything coming later. A national scandal down until the present time, they were usually overcrowded, understaffed, and dangerous. The county paid the costs of jail maintenance and construction and for the food and guards. Because jails were theoretically only temporary places of confinement, they had (and usually still have) no places for exercise and no facilities other than cells. In a sense, the county paid the costs of enforcing state law, and the taxpayers had no interest in spending money on jail facilities.

The idea that able-bodied men were locked up at the taxpayers' expense suggested that there was potential labor to be exploited. In fact, in most nineteenth-century institutions, the inmates were always expected to pay their own way, if not turn a profit. In the North, such exploitation usually failed. Inmates in prisons and poorhouses did indeed work, but only until they threatened the interests of labor in commercial business. Thus by the last third of the nineteenth century most inmate labor was to produce items used in the institution, such as food and shoes. Contemporary prison manufacturing of license plates continues this tradition of not threatening regular commercial enterprise. The irony here is that the Jacksonian principle of teaching the inmates to value honest and useful labor was frustrated by the limited range of skills that they could be taught.

In the South, things were different. Legislators resisted building prisons by substituting capital or corporal punishment. When this began to appear too inhumane, and when slavery was abolished, states began to rent out their convicts and counties created the infamous chain gangs (Carleton, 1971; Conley, 1981). Chain gangs did road work and other activities to maintain both urban and rural infrastructures. County sheriffs often received work orders indicating the number of men needed for work projects, which usually lasted from spring through fall, and they made enough arrests to procure these work gangs. The system, when abused, amounted to little more than forced labor. Convict leasing offered employers a chance to rent men and to extract their maximum labor value. This turned a profit for the state or county, while it simply used up prisoners. Unlike slaves, prisoners had no resale value to encourage the employer to keep them alive. In Louisiana, the death rate was 20 percent annually in 1896, and the system of convict leasing persisted until 1901. Until the 1960's the sugar mill at the state penitentiary continued to be a profit-making business, where prisoners worked under brutal and degrading conditions (Carleton, 1971). No latter-day Tocqueville came to broadcast the praises of such a system.

The use of convict labor poses a continuing problem. We define useful and socially integrating work as a means of integrating people into society and deterring them from crime. For incarcerated offenders, the opportunity to learn and do useful work seems an appropriate mode of treatment. In a society where full employment is still a dream, why should prisoners be given an opportunity unavailable to law-abiding citizens? The puzzle is almost two centuries old.

In addition to providing a substitute for corporal punishment or banishment, the penitentiary also created a new problem, the socialization of released prisoners, mainly men who had often spent a formative decade in prison. Compared to their predecessors, these ex-offenders had a much more severe social-entry problem. Forms of ameliorating this new problem soon appeared, especially probation and parole. Both were aimed at reintegrating the ex-offender, a task presumably attendant on anyone who had been deliberately severed from society. Ironically, the penitentiary "solution" created a social problem that required the attention of the most humane social activists. The Boston shoemaker John Augustus, who between 1841 and 1858 aided ex-offenders in finding jobs, and to whom courts often delivered prisoners in an early form of parole, well deserves the attention he has been paid for his thankless and compassionate efforts (Hindus, 1980).

The growing mid-nineteenth-century apparatus of police and prisons represented a socially costly means of dealing with offenders. Because police officers were public servants, it was difficult to stint on their pay; after all, they could quit. But the physical conditions of prisons and jails stayed at a minimally tolerable level. Similarly, the costs associated with full court trials were kept down with a means that is still familiar, the guilty plea or plea bargain. Although much research remains to be done, the practice of pleading guilty appears to have pervaded mid- and late-nineteenth-century criminal courts (Friedman, 1981). The extent to which these pleas were exchanged for lesser sentences has not yet been systematically estimated, but preliminary work implies that the plea-bargaining "evil" so sensationalized today is well over a century old.

CRIME

Historians would like to know two very basic things about crime: how its rate has changed over time and how it has changed in kind. Both answers remain frustratingly elusive. What we can know with greatest certainty tells us least about these. The best data, available in limited range only since the federally sponsored National Crime Survey began in 1973, tell how many criminal offenses there have been. This survey regularly interviews a random sample of the general population and derives a rate of victimization. (Even in these best circumstances, we do not know how many offenders were responsible.) But if we had such estimated rates of victimization over the past centuries, we could analyze with some accuracy trends both in kind and amount of crime.

Next to victimization information is a measure called by the FBI "offenses known to the police," which includes all offenses known to and recorded as such by the police. The FBI has collected such data from local police departments with increasing coverage since 1930, publishing the statistics in the *Uniform Crime Reports*. The quality of these data has been controversial, as they depend on voluntary local collection and can be difficult to ascertain on a per-capita basis. This source comprises more than fifty years of crime information; but because most of the significant changes in crime control have occurred over a longer period, analysts still lack a sufficiently long perspective. The most useful data after offenses known are the arrest rates. These figures obviously measure police behavior and provide a murky reflection of actual crime. But these data stretch back to the earliest police departments and even to some constabulary systems, thus spanning over 150 years of change (Monkkonen, 1981; Ferdinand, 1980). Prison data begin in the 1830's of course, and court cases can be counted back into the early seventeenth century. But these latter two kinds of data tell us only about final outcomes, which bear an even more ambiguous relationship to actual crime than do arrest rates.

Just as the best data are furthest from that which we wish to understand, those crimes most completely recorded are the least common and most sensational. We can accurately count presidential assassinations and ransom kidnappings (Alix, 1978), but for theft, for instance, uncertainty prevails. Homicide is most often taken by historians as an index crime, for most homicides are "cleared" by arrest and go to trial. As a result, the newspapers, arrest data, and court cases may be combed to establish something approximating a true homicide rate (Lane, 1979). The results of various studies suggest that homicides per capita have long been declining, perhaps even since the fourteenth century.

One must be cautious in assessing such generalizations, of course, for several factors make comparison difficult. Medical care has presumably improved, thus causing fewer assaults to result in death. On the other hand, weapons have also improved, making it easier to kill with a gun than with a crossbow, for instance. To counter this, the anonymity of urban life creates opportunities for murderers to disappear and avoid arrest. Yet, in intimate communities, witnesses may be easily intimidated. Do these various factors negate each other? They appear to, and we may tentatively conclude that Anglo-American history is one with decreasing murder rates.

Similar but less reliable evidence suggests that the trend toward fewer murders parallels other crimes of violence (Gurr, 1981). Theft is more difficult to analyze. It may have increased in the eighteenth century, perhaps even until the mid-nineteenth century. With a little more assur-

ance we may say that since the mid-nineteenth century, both in England and the United States, theft appears to have been declining. Perhaps public disorders, breaches of the peace, and drunkenness have also been declining (Monkkonen, 1981). Everybody can be thankful for such apparent declines, but historians would like to understand why they have occurred.

Several arguments have been advanced to account for them. They range from that of Lane (1974), who claims that one of the consequences of urbanization has been a "civilizing effect," to that of Gatrell (1980), who argues for the actual deterrent effect of the nineteenth-century transformation of the criminal justice system. Certainly, increased real wealth has had its effects. In the Middle Ages there simply was less personal property to steal, for instance; but on the other hand, depressions and famines probably forced the poor to steal grain. Through the late eighteenth, or perhaps early nineteenth, century, subsistence crises probably did force the poor to steal but in gradually diminishing amounts. But by the Great Depression, destitution forced few people to steal for survival. Thus, amid growing opportunity for theft, the circumstances that required that the poor steal simply to survive diminished.

This analysis does not account for decreasing crimes of violence. The history of the police suggests that the service they provide, free criminal arrests, has promoted a new social right to live free from crime. Crimes of violence, whatever else they are, often represent ways of resolving disputes. In thinking of small-scale societies, we sometimes imagine that they have informal dispute-settlement mechanisms that somehow function better than the formal ones of urban society. Assaults and murders would have to be considered two such techniques. In a large-scale society, such direct, "informal," and drastic methods are no longer necessary or practical.

The long-run decline in crimes of violence may well be due to the relatively new organizational means of dealing with personal problems. In a very weak state, even murder may be a personal wrong rather than a criminal offense. In a strong state, even personal quarrels may find a resolution on an institutionalized basis. The criminal law that provides the basis for this absorption of individual action into bureaucratic solutions has not had to change, for its major outlines were established by the time the English settled North America.

It is the actual means of implementing the existing law that have changed and that have moved us from a world of personal action to one of state action. And the system of criminal justice created in the United States has proved unexpectedly costly. The police arrest too many people; court trials are too long and expensive; imprisonment requires huge capital investments; released prisoners need help; reformatories don't seem to reform people. These problems run parallel to the notion that the system, if only it were properly implemented, would work to deter crime and reform criminals. On this, the evidence is not yet in. The data, poor as they are, suggest that over the centuries crime has declined and ordinary people are less victimized. Whether or not the criminal justice apparatus has had anything to do with this remains an open question.

BIBLIOGRAPHY

Ernest K. Alix, *Ransom Kidnapping in America, 1874–1974: The Creation of a Capital Crime* (Carbondale, Ill., 1978); Gustave de Beaumont and Alexis de Tocqueville, *On the Penitentiary System in the United States and Its Application in France* (Carbondale, Ill., 1964); Alfred Blumstein and Soumyo Moitra, "An Analysis of the Time Series of the Imprisonment Rate in the States of the United States: A Further Test of the Stability of Punishment Hypothesis," in *Journal of Criminal Law and Criminology*, 70 (1979); Jon Butler, "Magic, Astrology, and the Early American Religious Heritage, 1600–1760," in *American Historical Review*, 84 (April 1979); Mark T. Carleton, *Politics and Punishment: The History of the Louisiana State Penal System* (Baton Rouge, La., 1971).

John A. Conley, "Revising Conceptions About the Origins of Prisons: The Importance of Economic Considerations," in *Social Science Quarterly*, 62 (1981); Émile Durkheim, *Division of Labor in Society* (New York, 1947), and *Rules of Sociological Method*, 8th ed. (New York, 1950); Kai Erikson, *Wayward Puritans: A Study in the Sociology of Deviance* (New York, 1966); Theodore N. Ferdinand, "Criminality, the Courts, and the Constabulary in Boston: 1702–1967," in *Journal of Research in Crime and Delinquency*, 17 (1980); George P. Fletcher, "The Metamorphosis of Larceny," in *Harvard Law Review*, 89 (1976); Robert M. Fogelson, *Big City Police* (Cambridge, Mass., 1977); Michel Foucault, *Discipline and Punish: The Birth of the Prison*, Alan Sheridan, trans. (New York, 1977); Lawrence M. Friedman, *A History of American Law* (New York, 1973), and "History, Social Policy, and Criminal Justice," in

David J. Rothman and Stanton Wheeler, eds., *Social History and Social Policy* (New York, 1981).

V. A. C. Gatrell, "The Decline of Theft and Violence in Victorian and Edwardian England," in Gatrell, Bruce P. Lenman, and Geoffrey Parker, *Crime and the Law: The Social History of Crime in Western Europe Since 1500* (London, 1980); Douglas Greenberg, *Crime and Law Enforcement in the Colony of New York, 1691–1776* (Ithaca, N.Y., 1976); Ted R. Gurr, "Historical Trends in Violent Crime: A Critical Review of the Evidence," in Michael Tonry and Norval Morris, eds., *Crime and Justice: An Annual Review of Research*, III (Chicago, 1981); Jerome Hall, *Theft, Law, and Society*, 2nd ed. (Indianapolis, 1952); Sidney L. Harring, "Policing a Class Society: The Expansion of the Urban Police in the Late Nineteenth and Early Twentieth Centuries," in David F. Greenberg, ed., *Crime and Capitalism: Essays in Marxist Criminology* (Palo Alto, Calif., 1981); Michael S. Hindus, *Prison and Plantation: Crime, Justice and Authority in Massachusetts and South Carolina, 1767–1878* (Chapel Hill, N.C., 1980).

Morton J. Horwitz, *The Transformation of American Law, 1780–1860* (Cambridge, Mass., 1977); Douglas L. Jones, "The Transformation of the Law of Poverty in Twentieth Century Massachusetts," in Daniel S. Coquillette, *et al.*, eds., *Law in Colonial Massachusetts* (Charlottesville, Mass., 1983); Carl B. Klockars, *The Professional Fence* (New York, 1974), and "Jonathan Wild and the Modern Sting," in James A. Inciardi and Charles E. Faupel, eds., *History and Crime: Implications for Criminal Justice Policy* (Beverly Hills, 1980); Roger Lane, *Policing the City: Boston, 1822–1885* (Cambridge, Mass., 1967), "Crime and the Industrial Revolution: British and American Views," in *Journal of Social History*, 7 (1974), and *Violent Death in the City: Suicide, Accident and Murder in Nineteenth-Century Philadelphia* (Cambridge, Mass., 1979).

Wilbur R. Miller, *Cops and Bobbies: Police Authority in New York and London, 1830–1870* (Chicago, 1977); Eric H. Monkkonen, *Police in Urban America, 1860–1929* (New York, 1981), and "The Organized Response to Crime in Nineteenth- and Twentieth-Century America," in *Journal of Interdisciplinary History*, 14 (1983); William E. Nelson, *The Americanization of the Common Law: The Impact of Legal Change on Massachusetts Society, 1760–1830* (Cambridge, Mass., 1975); David Rauma, "Crime and Punishment Reconsidered: Some Comments on Blumstein's Stability of Punishment Hypothesis," in *Journal of Criminal Law and Criminology*, 72 (1981); David Rothman, *Conscience and Convenience: The Asylum and Its Alternatives in Progressive America* (Boston, 1980); David J. Rothman and Stanton Wheeler, eds., *Social History and Social Policy* (New York, 1981); Charles E. Silberman, *Criminal Violence, Criminal Justice* (New York, 1978); Jerome H. Skolnick, *Justice Without Trial: Law Enforcement in Democratic Society* (New York, 1966); Daniel J. Walkowitz, *Worker City, Company Town: Iron and Cotton-Worker Protest in Troy and Cohoes, New York, 1855–84* (Urbana, Ill., 1978); and James Q. Wilson, "Crime and American Culture," in *Public Interest*, 70 (1983).

[*See also* AUTHORITY; BILL OF RIGHTS; CENSORSHIP; CIVIL DISOBEDIENCE; CIVIL SERVICE REFORM; COLLECTIVE VIOLENCE; CONTROL, SUPPRESSION, AND INTIMIDATION; ENGLISH AND EUROPEAN POLITICAL INHERITANCE; MACHINE POLITICS; *and* PROHIBITION AND TEMPERANCE.]

DECLARATION OF INDEPENDENCE

Ronald Hamowy

PRESSURE for a formal separation from Great Britain had been mounting in the American colonies since the first months of 1776. On 20 December 1775 the Massachusetts Provincial Congress replaced Thomas Cushing, a conservative, with Elbridge Gerry, a radical and follower of Samuel Adams, as a delegate to the Continental Congress, thus securing for the pro-independence forces a majority in the Massachusetts delegation. And in March, by which time Gerry had arrived in Philadelphia to take his seat, the Virginia delegation had shifted into the radical camp with the defection of Benjamin Harrison from the conservative to the independence faction and the return to Philadelphia of Richard Henry Lee. The delegations of the two most populous colonies were thus united in supporting independence by the early spring of 1776. The impetus toward separation was further accelerated by news that Parliament had enacted legislation in the final weeks of 1775 declaring the various colonies beyond the protection of the crown and prohibiting trade with them. The act further authorized the seizure and confiscation of American ships and cargoes as enemy property and the impressment of captured crews onto British ships of war. John Adams viewed this action of Parliament as a virtual declaration that the colonies were to be treated as independent of Great Britain, noting that "it may be fortunate that the Act of Independency should come from the British Parliament rather than the American Congress: But it is very odd that Americans should hesitate at accepting such a gift."

Perhaps the single most decisive factor in putting an end to such hesitation was the publication of Tom Paine's *Common Sense* in January 1776. In what must be regarded as one of the most electrifying political polemics ever written,

Paine described the ties that connected the colonies to the mother country as chains that fettered a flourishing people, depriving them of their birthright of freedom. No benefit, advantage, or profit, Paine argued, could be gained from reconciliation with the British monarch, a tyrant whose hands were already stained with the blood of American patriots. "It is repugnant to reason," he concluded,

> to the universal order of things, to all examples from the former ages, to suppose that this continent can longer remain subject to any external power. The most sanguine in Britain does not think so. The utmost stretch of human wisdom cannot, at this time, compass a plan short of separation, which can promise the continent even a year's security. Reconciliation is now a fallacious dream. Nature hath deserted the connection, and Art cannot supply her place.

The success of Paine's pamphlet was nothing short of phenomenal. It has been estimated that 120,000 copies were sold in the first three months following its appearance, almost half a million over the course of 1776. In addition, excerpts were reprinted in newspapers throughout the colonies. In the crucial days before 4 July it would have been close to impossible for any literate colonist not to have been familiar with the arguments Paine put forward nor to have been unaffected by them.

The momentum for independence had, by May 1776, reached a point where no other course was politically feasible. On 15 May the Continental Congress adopted a resolution drafted by John Adams recommending that the colonies assume full powers of government and that all exercise of authority under the crown be suppressed. And on the same day, the Virginia Convention in Williamsburg resolved to instruct the colony's delegates to Congress to propose to that body that they declare "the United Colonies free and independent states, absolved from all allegience to, or dependence on, the Crown or Parliament of Great Britain." In compliance with the instructions received from Virginia, Richard Henry Lee, seconded by John Adams, moved on 7 June "that these United Colonies are, and of right ought to be, free and independent States, that they are absolved from all allegiance to the British Crown, and that all political connection between them and the State of Great Britain is, and ought to be, totally dissolved."

The conservative opposition in Congress could, by this point, only delay passage of the Lee resolution, but the proseparatist forces were conscious that a declaration of this sort would have far greater impact if it were supported by all the colonies. Consequently, it was agreed that Congress postpone consideration of Lee's motion for three weeks; by then, they believed, the middle colonies could be brought into line. As Jefferson remarked in his notes on the proceedings of the Congress, "It appearing in the course of these debates that the colonies of N. York, New Jersey, Pennsylvania, Delaware, Maryland & South Carolina were not yet matured for falling from the parent stem, but that they were fast advancing to that state, it was thought most prudent to wait a while for them, and to postpone the final decision to July 1." There could be little doubt about the ultimate outcome of a vote on the issue, however, and on 11 June Congress appointed a committee to draft a declaration to serve as a preamble to Lee's resolution. The committee consisted of John Adams, Benjamin Franklin, Thomas Jefferson, and Roger Sherman, all of whom were outspoken supporters of independence, and Robert R. Livingston, its sole conservative member. The choice of Jefferson as the senior member of the committee—his name came first in the order of the vote—was particularly felicitous. A writer of remarkable power and great elegance, Jefferson was selected by the committee to prepare a draft of the document, which, as it was to turn out, was presented to the Congress for consideration with only minor alterations.

Jefferson's draft did not, nor was it intended to, offer an original theory of government upon which the colonists were to rely in rebelling against the crown. In formulating the political principles that underpinned the Revolution—and revolution it certainly was—Jefferson, as he was later to write, sought

> not to find out new principles, or new arguments, never before thought of, not merely to say things which had never been said before; but to place before mankind the common sense of the subject, in terms so plain and firm as to command assent, and to justify ourselves in the independent stand we are compelled to take. Neither aiming at originality of principle or sentiment, nor yet copied from any particular and previous writing, [the Declaration] was intended to be an expression of the American mind, and to give to that expression the proper tone and spirit called for by the occasion. All its authority rests then on the harmonizing sentiments of the day, whether expressed in conversation, in letters, printed essays, or in the elementary books of public right, as Aristotle, Cicero, Locke, Sidney, etc.

Indeed, absence of originality of principle can hardly be regarded as legitimate criticism of a document intended to justify to a new nation and to the world the necessity of resorting to arms against a tyrannous government. Jefferson's task was to draft a statement setting forth the justice of the American cause that would prove acceptable not only to himself but to the colonies' delegates assembled in Philadelphia and, ultimately, to the American people. In doing this, he composed a document that captured the ideological substance of American revolutionary thought, which was grounded in a theory of natural, inalienable rights. It might well be true of the Declaration, as John Adams observed some years later, that "there is not an idea in it but what had been hackneyed in Congress for two years before." But, although meant as criticism, this charge only strengthens one's admiration for Jefferson's handiwork in distilling the revolutionaries' philosophy of government and their political aspirations in so clear and compelling a manner.

The opening paragraph of the Declaration provides the reasons for its publication:

> When in the Course of human events, it becomes necessary for one people to dissolve the political bands which have connected them with another, and to assume among the powers of the

earth, the separate and equal station to which the Laws of Nature and of Nature's God entitle them, a decent respect to the opinions of mankind requires that they should declare the causes which impel them to the separation.

Jefferson then sets forth the ideological foundations, upon which the Revolution was predicated, in which he explicates his reference to "the Laws of Nature and of Nature's God":

> We hold these truths to be self-evident, that all men are created equal, that they are endowed by their Creator with certain unalienable Rights, that among these are Life, Liberty and the pursuit of Happiness. That to secure these rights, Governments are instituted among Men, deriving their just powers from the consent of the governed. That whenever any Form of Government becomes destructive of these ends, it is the Right of the People to alter or to abolish it, and to institute new Government, laying its foundation on such principles and organizing its powers in such form, as to them shall seem most likely to effect their Safety and Happiness. Prudence, indeed, will dictate that Governments long established should not be changed for light and transient causes; and accordingly all experience hath shewn, that mankind are more disposed to suffer, while evils are sufferable, than to right themselves by abolishing the forms to which they are accustomed. But when a long train of abuses and usurpations, pursuing invariably the same Object evinces a design to reduce them under absolute Despotism, it is their right, it is their duty, to throw off such Government, and to provide new Guards for their future security.

Here follows a catalog of the abuses and usurpations that the colonies had suffered at the hands of the British crown and from which no redress appeared possible. As important as was this list of grievances, however, it is the document's preamble, which contains the Declaration's political philosophy, that has occupied the close attention of political theorists and intellectual historians since its first appearance.

There is no question that the theory of government propounded in the Declaration bears the indelible imprint of Whig revolutionary thought and, particularly, of its chief exponent, John Locke. It is not surprising that the sentiments Jefferson expressed—at times even the phrasing he employed—regarding the social

contract, the nature of individual rights, and the right to rebellion echoed Locke's *Second Treatise of Government*. Examination of booksellers' lists and the catalogs of institutional, circulating, and private libraries in the period before 1776 shows Locke's works, both philosophical and political, to have been readily accessible to any colonist, as indeed were other, lesser Whig treatises, particularly Algernon Sidney's *Discourses Concerning Government* and John Trenchard and Thomas Gordon's *Cato's Letters* (Lundberg and May, 1976). Locke's political philosophy pervaded colonial thinking, both directly or through the writings of those heavily influenced by him, such as Trenchard and Gordon. Bernard Bailyn, in his definitive analysis of the sources of American revolutionary ideology (1967), has found that "in pamphlet after pamphlet the American writers cited Locke on natural rights and on the social and governmental contract," and that Locke's treatises stood with *Cato's Letters* as "the most authoritative statement of the nature of political liberty." Indeed, if any one political work could be said to have captured "the harmonizing sentiments of the day" in the period immediately prior to the Revolution, it would be Locke's *Second Treatise*.

Although not published until after James II had been successfully deposed, Locke's work on government was actually written some ten years earlier. Peter Laslett has shown that the composition of the *Second Treatise*—at least a substantial portion of it—dates from 1679–1680, a decade before the Glorious Revolution. As Laslett notes, the treatise was "a demand for a revolution to be brought about, not the rationalization of a revolution in need of defence," and, as such, its conclusions respecting the limits of authority of the civil magistrate and the right to revolt against a government that exceeded those limits were particularly apposite. Indeed, the arguments justifying rebellion against a Stuart despot, as put forward by Locke, would serve quite adequately against a Hanoverian or any other tyrant.

The main argument of Locke's philosophy, echoed in the Declaration, is easily grasped. Certain rights that all men possess are anterior to the establishment of any political authority and do not issue as a consequence of the actions of that authority. The right to govern is founded solely on the consent of the governed, and the governing magistrate is bound to act solely in the interests of his subjects. When any government violates this trust, the subjects may by right abolish it and, possessed of that ultimate power of which particular governments are mere creatures, the people may establish a new government more likely to effect those ends for which governments are instituted. The Declaration, following Locke, thus wedded the doctrine of natural rights to the notion of government founded on individual consent. In an age in which democracy has become the paradigm of good government, it is tempting to assume that the primary thrust of the Declaration—and its most compelling testament to modern American politics—is its vindication of the view that governments are bound to act in the interests of the governed. The principle that the only legitimate basis of political authority is popular consent does, of course, appear in the Declaration, just as it earlier appeared in Locke's *Second Treatise* and in much of the American revolutionary literature. But the implications that both revolutionary ideology and the Declaration had for democratic government did not in any way compromise Jefferson's views that the locus of government activity was circumscribed by the dictates of natural law. On this score, the Declaration is clear. Public authority rests on the consent of the people, but that authority is by its nature severely restricted.

The crucial test of all government, no matter how constituted, lies in whether or not it respects the inalienable rights with which all men are endowed. These rights owe their existence neither to convention nor to the presence of a sovereign who, as Hobbes had argued, both created them and made their exercise possible. They are rooted in man's very nature and are unconditional and nontransferable. Men do not, nor can they, compromise them by entering into civil society; nor can these rights be modified in some way to conform to the dictates of the magistrate. The transcendent purpose of government is the preservation of these rights. Locke wrote: "The great and *chief end* therefore, of Mens uniting into Commonwealths, and putting themselves under Government, is the *Preservation of their Property.*" And "property," Locke noted in the sentence preceding, refers to men's "Lives, Liberties and Estates." The Declaration affirms this conclusion when it asserts that all men "are endowed by their Creator with certain unalienable

Rights, that among these are Life, Liberty and the pursuit of Happiness" and "That to secure these rights, Governments are instituted among Men."

Cecelia M. Kenyon, writing on the philosophy of the Declaration, has raised some questions about the logical structure of an argument that holds that the rights enumerated in the Declaration can be secured to all men equally. With respect to the right to liberty, for example, Kenyon has inquired (1973): "If the liberty asserted by one man should come into conflict with the liberty asserted by another, how could the rights of both men be secured? What criterion could one devise to decide which assertion of natural right was the more valid?" The inconsistencies suggested by these questions are in fact specious. The liberty of which both Locke and the American revolutionary theorists, including Jefferson, wrote is negatively, not positively, conceived and has reference solely to certain limitations imposed on how men may act toward each other. One's liberty never requires that others act in certain ways but only that they refrain from acting in certain ways; that is, one's liberty entails only prohibitions on others and never positive commands. To the extent that one's liberty is not constrained, one is let alone; one is not "forced," "required," "commanded" by others to do (or not to do) something that one "can," "is able," "has the capacity" to do. The only boundaries limiting one's liberty, therefore, are those prohibitions extending around the liberty of others. Under this definition, there are no conditions under which the liberty of one man could conflict with the liberty of another, since it is perfectly consistent that neither be constrained to act (or not to act) in any noninvasive way. It follows that all voluntary arrangements are consistent with the liberty of all men.

Nor is there any substance to Kenyon's charge that "the three rights [enumerated in the Declaration] can sometimes be in conflict with each other," since each of these rights has as its basis a similar negative conception, prohibiting both public and private interference with men's actions. Thus, her claim that "happiness as an individual right was new, and it seems even more amenable to subjective interpretation than either liberty or life" misconstrues the nature of rights as Jefferson understood them. It should be emphasized that Jefferson did not claim that men had a "right to happiness" but that they had an inalienable right to pursue it. While it might well be the case that one man's happiness might conflict with the happiness of another, it by no means follows that one's right—properly understood—to pursue happiness involves trespassing upon the same right in others. To affirm an inalienable right of all men to pursue their own happiness free from the interference of others is to assert no less objective a right than the right to one's life. The right to one's life does not entail that one will be free from fatal microorganisms nor that it is incumbent on others to do all they can to prevent one from dying, but only that they not actively intervene to kill you. Even under circumstances where two people are confronted with conditions such that one man's life is contingent on the death of the other, neither may raise his hand against the other under pain of violating this right, despite the fact that both will die.

That Jefferson understood the rights he enumerated as impelling others, either individually or collectively, to positive actions, lies at the root of a whole series of misinterpretations of the meaning of the Declaration long preceding the appearance of Kenyon's article. Thus, much has been made by certain commentators of the fact that Jefferson affirmed a right to pursue happiness, rather than the more customary right to property, which Locke and the other Whig radicals had made central to their theory of inalienable rights. Gilbert Chinard, for example, viewed Jefferson's choice of language as asserting "a new principle of government," one that placed a positive obligation on the civil magistrate to ensure the happiness of his subjects. "I do not believe," Chinard wrote (1929), "that any other State paper in any nation had ever proclaimed so emphatically and with such finality that one of the essential functions of government is to make men happy." And Arthur M. Schlesinger later offered a similar interpretation of Jefferson's use of "pursuit of happiness," basing his argument on references in the revolutionary literature (particularly in John Adams' *Thoughts on Government*) to the notion that the happiness of the subjects is the end of government. "In short," Schlesinger concluded, "none of these spokesmen of the American cause thought of happiness as something a people were entitled to strive for but as some-

thing that was theirs by natural right" (1964).

In so representing the thrust of the Declaration's argument, both Chinard and Schlesinger, among others, have failed to grasp the nature of the rights to which Jefferson refers. The Declaration describes these rights as belonging to all men by virtue of their being men, and they unmistakably precede the establishment of any political authority. Therefore, the conditions under which these rights may be exercised cannot be contingent on the actions of government: they cannot be understood as imposing a set of positive commands on others. Radical natural-law theorists, and especially Locke, whose work formed the basis of the political philosophy contained in the Declaration, held that the ends of civil government limited the extent of political authority. When men consented to the creation of that authority they transferred only those original rights as were necessary to achieve those specific ends. Now a right that is inalienable cannot be so transferred, and it is among these rights that Jefferson includes the "pursuit of happiness." Not only does the right to pursue happiness, then, owe its existence to a source higher than that of any government, but its exercise must in some crucial sense be separable and distinct from any action of government.

Much confusion surrounding what Jefferson meant when he coupled the notion of happiness with his theory of rights could be avoided if careful attention were paid to the Declaration's language. The functions of government are clearly stipulated. Although the origins of civil authority lie in the welfare of its subjects, its duties are circumscribed to those consonant with the purposes for which it was created, namely, the securing of those inalienable rights that all men possess. The end of government is neither to maximize happiness nor to ensure that men attain happiness, but to provide the framework in which each person may pursue his own happiness as he individually sees fit. To endow the term "pursuit of happiness" with tortured meanings—as Schlesinger does when he suggests that it be understood to signify the "practice" of happiness, as in the "pursuit" of law—neither contravenes the Declaration's assertion that the pursuit of happiness is a personal right nor does justice to Jefferson's skill as a lucid prose stylist. It is no less a distortion of the philosophy underlying the Declaration to claim that when Jefferson stipulated a right to pursue happiness, his purpose was that of asserting a scientific law, that all men cannot help but pursue happiness. The inclusion of this phrase in the Declaration, Garry Wills has claimed, reflects Jefferson's intention "to state scientific law in the human area —natural *law* as human *right.*" Not only is this reading incompatible with Wills's erroneous conclusion that the document "makes happiness a hard political test of any reign's very legitimacy," but it totally perverts the logical structure of the Declaration.

We are still confronted with the question of why Jefferson chose to employ the term "pursuit of happiness" in his list of inalienable rights instead of the more usual "property." It appears to be beyond question that Jefferson was familiar with—and possibly had before him—a copy of George Mason's Virginia Declaration of Rights when he composed the Declaration of Independence. Julian P. Boyd notes that Mason's draft was reprinted in the *Pennsylvania Evening Post* of 6 June and again in the *Pennsylvania Gazette* of 12 June, the day following Jefferson's appointment to a congressional committee whose function was to compose a declaration justifying independence. The similarities between the two documents strongly suggest that Jefferson's formulation of the Declaration's philosophical preamble owed much to Mason's document and particularly to its opening paragraph. Mason wrote:

> All men are born equally free and independant, and have certain inherent natural Rights, of which they cannot by any Compact, deprive or divest their Posterity; among which are the Enjoyment of Life and Liberty, with the Means of acquiring and possessing Property, and pursuing and obtaining Happiness and Safety.

It seems probable that Jefferson, who was as familiar with this view of inherent rights as was Mason and who espoused it with no less fervor, decided to compress the notion of a right comprising "the Means of acquiring and possessing Property, and pursuing and obtaining Happiness and Safety" into a more concise right to pursue happiness. The right to pursue one's happiness does not, nor was it meant to, preclude the right to acquire, maintain, or transfer property, which—in any of its specific forms—is alienable

by consent. When Jefferson wrote of an inalienable right to the pursuit of happiness he was asserting a broader right that guaranteed to all men the freedom both to choose the form their own happiness would take and to seek to attain that happiness as they saw fit. The right to pursue one's happiness is inclusive of a natural right to the products of one's labor, just as the right to pursue the means to certain ends is implied by a right to pursue those ends. By substituting the words "pursuit of happiness," Jefferson was in no way disavowing a natural right to property, as Locke and the other Whig theorists understood the term.

Certain critics, antagonistic to the concept of property rights, have insisted on reading into Jefferson's words an outright rejection of the notion of private property as an indefeasible right. Thus, Vernon L. Parrington concluded (1927) that "the substitution of 'pursuit of happiness' for 'property' marks a complete break with the Whiggish doctrine of property rights that Locke bequeathed to the English middle class, and the substitution of a broader sociological conception; and it is this substitution that gave to the document the note of idealism which was to make its appeal so perennially human and vital." That Parrington did not find the concept of a right to property "human and vital," however, is not to suggest that it was not so regarded by Jefferson and the other patriots caught up in the revolutionary struggle. Jefferson's own views on the question are plainly set forth in a letter to Pierre Samuel Dupont de Nemours, dated 24 April 1816, in which he wrote that "a right to property is founded in our natural wants, in the means with which we are endowed to satisfy these wants, and the right to what we acquire by those means without violating the similar rights of other sensible beings." And, with respect to the relation between government and the individual's right to liberty and to the product of his labors, Jefferson remarked in his first inaugural address:

> Still one thing more, fellow citizens—a wise and frugal government, which shall restrain men from injuring one another, which shall leave them otherwise free to regulate their own pursuits of industry and improvement, and shall not take from the mouth of labor the bread it has

earned. This is the sum of good government, and this is necessary to close the circle of our felicities.

This sentiment, proclaimed on 4 March 1801, epitomizes the philosophy that Jefferson had affirmed in the Declaration. Although the document's preamble underwent a series of changes between the time Jefferson completed his original draft—before he submitted it to the other members of the drafting committee—and its final adoption by Congress, nothing of critical philosophical importance was altered. Carl L. Becker has succeeded in reconstructing Jefferson's basic text by comparing his Rough Draft, which contains a whole series of corrections and emendations made at all stages of the document's evolution, with copies of the Declaration as it read at several points before its final adoption. The critical portion of the preamble, as Jefferson originally wrote it, reads:

> We hold these truths to be sacred & undeniable; that all men are created equal & independant, that from that equal creation they derive rights inherent & inalienable, among which are the preservation of life, & liberty, & the pursuit of happiness; that to secure these ends, governments are instituted among men, deriving their just powers from the consent of the governed; that whenever any form of government shall become destructive of these ends, it is the right of the people to alter or abolish it, & to institute new government, laying it's foundation on such principles & organizing it's powers in such form, as to them shall seem most likely to effect their safety & happiness.

With reference to Jefferson's original wording, Morton White argued (1978) that the change from "ends" to "rights" in the document's clause respecting what it is governments are to secure ("the preservation of life, & liberty, & the pursuit of happiness") marks a fundamental philosophical shift in the Declaration's statement concerning the purpose of government. In the context here used, White contended, Jefferson could have meant only that the functions of government were more positive and far-reaching than those narrowly consistent with the preservation of natural rights. White's analysis rests on interpreting the word "secure" in "secure these ends" to mean "attain" rather than "guard." White acknowledged that the change in wording, from "ends" to "rights," was made by Jefferson himself before the document was submitted to Congress for its consideration. But in doing so, White concluded, Jefferson altered the Declaration's political philosophy "so as to give the impression that governments are instituted to *secure* in the sense of *guard* certain *rights* rather than that they are instituted to *secure* in the sense of *attain* certain *ends.*" This change, White suggests, reflected Jefferson's ambiguity respecting "whether the end of government is merely to protect certain rights or whether government was to go further and *encourage* man's exercise of those rights."

As interesting as White's analysis is, there are several problems with accepting his conclusion that when Jefferson drafted the Declaration "two warring philosophical souls dwelt within [his] breast." Jefferson himself appears to have regarded the changes made in the draft before its submission to Congress as of minor importance only; in writing of these alterations to James Madison some years later, he referred to them as "merely verbal." Indeed, there is no evidence that Jefferson perceived that there was any important philosophical difference between his original reference to "ends" and his subsequent use of "rights." Nor is there any reason to accept White's inference that when Jefferson wrote "to secure these ends" he meant this term to signify that the functions of government were to actively "aid and abet men in attaining ends proposed by God." In fact, when Jefferson asserted that governments are instituted among men to secure these ends, namely, the preservation of life and liberty, and the pursuit of happiness, he probably meant no more than did Locke, who announced in the *Second Treatise* that the great end of men's putting themselves under government is the preservation of their lives, liberties, and estates.

The change from "ends" to "rights" was not the only revision that either Jefferson or the other members of the drafting committee made to the basic text before the document was reported to Congress on 28 June. Boyd has calculated that the Rough Draft, as finally submitted, contained forty-seven alterations. Some of these were of no importance, such as the deletion of a partially written word; while others were made for what appear to be purely stylistic purposes. In addition, Jefferson supplemented his bill of indictment against the crown by appending three new charges. Of these revisions and additions, only seven are apparently in a hand other than Jefferson's; two would seem to have been made by Adams, and the others by Franklin. It appears probable that all the changes occurring in the Declaration's philosophical preamble as reported to Congress were Jefferson's.

The constraints of space do not permit detailed discussion of the list of grievances, which constitutes the major portion of the Declaration. It should be noted, however, that the charges specified in the document were leveled not against the Parliament of Great Britain, but against the crown. The American conception of the constitutional status of the colonies within the British empire viewed them as linked to Great Britain only in the sense that they acknowledged a common monarch. The Parliament of Great Britain had no more legal authority over the various provinces of British North America than the House of Burgesses of Virginia had over Great Britain or over any other dominion owing allegiance to George III. By mid-1776, this view had become a commonplace among Americans. They regarded their fealty to the king as one that had originally been assumed voluntarily, that is, by the consent of the people, and they thus felt free to retract it at their pleasure. The colonists' right to rebel against tyrannical government was predicated not on the privileges that they possessed as British subjects—for, in fact, they did not regard themselves as such—but on the natural rights that they, in company with all men at all times, possessed. And the injuries and usurpations under which the colonists suffered, as enumerated in the Declaration's indictment, were not simply trespasses on the privileges traditionally accorded Englishmen by their sovereign, but violations of the colonists' fundamental indefeasible rights as human beings. This view was adumbrated in Jefferson's *A Summary View of the Rights of British America* in 1774 and in his draft of the Declaration of the Causes and Necessity for Taking Up Arms, composed at the beginning of July 1775. In addition to assuming a theory of imperial confederation, both these documents' summaries of grievances contributed to the list of charges that were eventually to take their final form in the Declaration.

Of more immediate influence on Jefferson's bill of indictment was his draft of a proposed constitution for Virginia—probably written sometime in late May or early June 1776—the preamble to which enumerated a series of injuries suffered by the colonies at the hands of the British crown. The basic text of the Declaration contains eighteen grievances, one of which is divided into eight distinct counts, twenty-five charges in all. Of these, twenty were taken almost verbatim from the earlier document and, with two exceptions, appear in the same order. The sequence and language of the charges enumerated in the Declaration, as Boyd observed, appear to leave no question that Jefferson had the text of his Preamble to the Virginia Constitution before him when he composed the grievances incorporated in the document.

Before submitting the draft of the Declaration to Congress, Jefferson added three new charges against George III, among them a censure of the Quebec Act of 1774, which extended the boundaries of Quebec to the Mississippi in the west and southward to the Ohio River. The act further provided that legislative authority in the province be vested solely in a royally appointed council and granted to the British Parliament the power to levy all but purely local taxes. Finally, English civil law was abolished and the Anglican church disestablished. In their place, French civil law, which precluded trial of civil cases by jury, was reinstituted and Roman Catholicism was reimposed as the established communion, one section of the bill expressly guaranteeing to the clergy the "dues and rights" they had earlier received under the French regime. This pernicious act, restoring many of the laws and religious privileges earlier imposed by an openly autocratic regime on a territory that would henceforth constitute the largest area of North America, was regarded with particular loathing by the colonists, who saw in it a direct threat to their own political and civil institutions.

By far the most significant addition to Jefferson's charges was his denunciation of slavery. At some point between the completion of his original text and submission of the draft of the Declaration to Congress, Jefferson added the following indictment of George III:

He has waged cruel war against human nature itself, violating its most sacred rights of life and liberty in the persons of a distant people who never offended him, captivating and carrying them into slavery in another hemisphere, or to incur miserable death in their transportation thither. This piratical warfare, the opprobrium of *infidel* powers, is the warfare of the *Christian* king of Great Britain. Determined to keep open a market where MEN should be bought and sold, he has prostituted his negative for suppressing every legislative attempt to prohibit or to restrain this execrable commerce.

Becker suggested that there was something hypocritical in this charge, which, like the others, is couched in the form of an indictment of the crown. Certainly it is true that the subsequent history of the slave trade and of slavery itself in the United States points to more villainy on this side of the Atlantic than in Great Britain. But there is a complex of irrefragable evidence pointing to the complicity of the British government in perpetuating this satanic institution. Edward Dumbauld noted that on at least six occasions colonial acts imposing prohibitively high duties on the slave trade were disallowed by the king-in-council, thus permitting an unusually lucrative British market to flourish unhindered. Of far greater importance, however, is the fact that a document proclaiming the inalienable natural rights of all men—and this probably accounts for why "men" is capitalized in Jefferson's draft—should have vigorously condemned slavery as inimical to the principles upon which the new nation was to rest. The excision of this charge by the Congress cannot but have impoverished the document, just as the institution itself was to impoverish the republic until its bloody repudiation ninety years later.

On 28 June Jefferson and the other members of the committee reported the amended draft of the Declaration to Congress. Jefferson is known to have consulted with Adams and Franklin, both of whom had made minor revisions to the language of the document, after which the draft was submitted to the whole committee. There is, unfortunately, no way to determine whether any of the alterations and additions that appear in Jefferson's own handwriting were the result of suggestions made by the other members or were the product of Jefferson's own judgment; nor, indeed, is it possible to determine whether these changes were made before or after Sherman and Livingston were first shown Jefferson's draft. Given the style of the revisions and Jefferson's later recounting of the events of this period, it is not unlikely that at least the greater part of the emendations made in the basic text were Jefferson's alone.

On 2 July the Congress, at the outset meeting in Committee of the Whole, adopted the Lee resolution, whereby the American colonies declared themselves to be free and independent states, absolved from any allegiance to the British crown. The vote on the resolution would have been unanimous if the New York delegation had not felt compelled to abstain, having received no reply from the provincial congress to their earlier request for instructions. On 1 July a preliminary vote showed only nine colonies prepared to support independence. Both South Carolina and Pennsylvania voted against the Lee resolution, New York abstained, and the two delegates from Delaware then present in Philadelphia were divided on the issue. By the next day, however, a dramatic shift had occurred. The South Carolina delegation, led by Edward Rutledge, joined the proindependence faction for the sake of intercolonial unity, and the Delaware delegation was enlarged by the last-minute arrival of Caesar Rodney, hastily called from Dover to cast that colony's tie-breaking vote in favor of independence. Finally, Pennsylvania's delegation, which had opposed the Lee resolution by a vote of four to three on 1 July, moved into the independence camp when two opponents, John Dickinson and Robert Morris, deliberately absented themselves on the following day. Thus, on 2 July, with twelve delegations voting in favor and one abstaining, the united colonies declared their independence from Great Britain and so became free states.

Following passage of the Lee resolution, the Congress immediately turned its attention to consideration of the Declaration, whose function was to justify the decision just reached. Inasmuch as the debate on the Declaration was undertaken by Congress again meeting in Committee of the Whole, the Rough and Corrected Journals are silent on the nature of the discussion that took place. It is, of course, known that a number of alterations and deletions were made, many for purely stylistic pur-

463

poses. There appears to have been no attempt to tamper with the Declaration's theory of government, so eloquently expressed in Jefferson's preamble. Indeed, the view of government there affirmed was the product of legal and political principles embraced by all the revolutionaries, as it emerged in the writings of natural-rights theorists from Hugo Grotius and Samuel Pufendorf, through Locke and the other Whig radicals, to the continental writers inspired by Locke, particularly Jean Jacques Burlamaqui. Congress made only two minor changes in the phrasing of Jefferson's philosophical preamble: "inherent and unalienable rights" was altered to "certain unalienable rights," and the words "begun at a distinguished period, and" were deleted from Jefferson's more wordy "But when a long train of abuses & usurpations, begun at a distinguished period, & pursuing invariably the same Object evinces a design to reduce them under absolute Despotism."

The Congress did not stop at minor revisions, however. It excised two major passages from the draft as submitted, among them, as already noted, Jefferson's condemnation of slavery and of the slave trade. The second major deletion involved Jefferson's final paragraph, in which he denounced the British electorate for its complicity in the abuses perpetrated by the British government in North America. As the author of the Declaration, Jefferson was naturally disheartened that Congress should have seen fit to use so heavy a hand in editing a document that had been framed with such care. He appears to have been particularly offended at the deletion of the paragraph on slavery and his indictment of the British public. With respect to these excisions, he observed in his notes on the proceedings of Congress:

> The pusillanimous idea that we had friends in England worth keeping terms with, still haunted the minds of many. For this reason those passages which conveyed censures on the people of England were struck out, lest they should give them offence. The clause too, reprobating the enslaving the inhabitants of Africa, was struck out in complaisance to South Carolina & Georgia, who had never attempted to restrain the importation of slaves, and who on the contrary still wished to continue it. Our Northern brethren also I believe felt a little tender under those censures; for tho' their people have very few slaves

themselves yet they had been pretty considerable carriers of them to others.

Jefferson was, predictably, convinced that his final draft was superior to the Declaration as Congress amended it, and he sent copies of the text as he submitted it to several friends, both while it was being altered by Congress and soon afterward. But, with the exception of its deletion of his condemnation of the slave trade, the reader is compelled to agree with Boyd that "it is difficult to point out a passage in the Declaration, great as it was, that was not improved by [Congress's] attention. That a public body would reduce rather than increase the number of words in a political document is in itself a remarkable testimony to their sagacity and ability to express themselves. Certainly the final paragraph, considered as parliamentary practice, as political principle, and as literature was greatly improved by the changes of Congress."

On the evening of 4 July the Declaration, as amended, was reported by the Committee of the Whole and duly approved by the Congress without dissent. The document was then ordered authenticated and printed, at which point John Hancock signed the authenticated copy "by Order and in Behalf of the Congress." At that moment, it is reported, the bell atop the State House, where the Congress was then meeting, began to ring to herald the event. The bell itself is inscribed with the following words from Leviticus: "Proclaim liberty throughout all the land unto all the inhabitants thereof." No nation—no kingdom or principality—was born with greater majesty than was the United States, whose founding charter proclaimed to the world the revolutionary doctrine that all men, no matter how base their status, were endowed with God-given rights, upon which governments trespassed only at the gravest peril.

John Adams had expected that the new nation would commemorate 2 July, the date on which Lee's resolution of independence passed Congress, as its independence day; but through a curious anomaly, 4 July received the honor. The date that Americans annually celebrate is not the anniversary of the day on which independence from Great Britain was first declared but, rather, the anniversary of the day on which the Congress proclaimed a universal theory of government based on the inalienable rights of man. It is altogether fitting to the American spirit that we commemorate not merely a political act but an ideological one.

On 9 July the New York provincial congress, sitting in White Plains, voted unanimously to ratify the Declaration. On 19 July, four days after New York's acquiescence had been read to the Congress, it was ordered that the Declaration be engrossed on parchment and that its title be altered to "The Unanimous Declaration of the 13 United States of America." Finally, on 2 August, the engrossed copy was signed by the members of the Continental Congress. Immediately after its passage, copies of the Declaration had been dispatched to all the colonies, where it was read with suitable pomp and celebration before approving crowds; for this charter upon which the new republic was founded gave voice to the fact that the war in which the colonists were then engaged was in reality the most principled act of rebellion against despotism of which mankind has record.

BIBLIOGRAPHY

Bernard Bailyn, *The Ideological Origins of the American Revolution* (Cambridge, Mass., 1967), the definitive work on the subject, establishes beyond question that the Revolution was strongly motivated by a devotion to ideological principle. Carl L. Becker, *The Declaration of Independence: A Study in the History of Political Ideas* (New York, 1921; repr. 1966), a brilliant study of the political philosophy underlying the Declaration, still remains the most important treatise on the subject. Julian P. Boyd, *The Declaration of Independence: The Evolution of the Text* (Princeton, N.J., 1945), is an indispensable work for any historian studying the Declaration; Boyd's valuable introductory essay, which analyzes the development of the Declaration's text, is supplemented by reproductions of all the relevant drafts of the document. Gilbert Chinard, *Thomas Jefferson: The Apostle of Americanism* (New York, 1929), is one of the standard works on Jefferson's life and thought; Chinard's chapter on the Declaration offers some interesting insights into the document. Edward Dumbauld, *The Declaration of Independence and What It Means Today* (Norman, Okla., 1950), provides useful historical background to each of the clauses in the Declaration and is particularly useful in its analysis of the grievances against the crown.

Herbert Friedenwald, *The Declaration of Independence: An Interpretation and an Analysis* (New York, 1904), is one of the few studies devoted exclusively to the Declaration; Friedenwald's monograph concentrates on the political developments leading up to and surrounding passage of the document by Congress. John H. Hazelton, *The Declaration of Independence: Its History* (New York, 1906), remains a standard reference on the background and text of the Declaration. Cecelia M. Kenyon, "The Declaration of Independence," in *Fundamental Testaments of the American Revolution*, Library of Congress Symposia on the American Revolution, 2 (Washington, D.C., 1973), an interesting essay, is at times badly flawed by a weak grasp of eighteenth-century political theory. John Locke, *Two Treatises of Government*, Peter Laslett, ed. (Cambridge, rev. ed. 1963), is the definitive critical edition of Locke's *Treatises*, coupled with Laslett's own path-breaking essay on the history and development of Locke's classic essay on government. David Lundberg and Henry F. May, "The Enlightened Reader in America," in *American Quarterly*, 28 (1976), is a useful statistical analysis of the reception in America of the major British and continental authors, both before the Revolution and up to 1813.

Dumas Malone, Hirst Milhollen, and Milton Kaplan, *The Story of the Declaration of Independence* (New York, 1954), is a fine essay by one of the nation's leading Jefferson scholars, heavily illustrated by Milhollen and Kaplan; the monograph contains brief biographies of each of the signers. Vernon Louis Parrington, *Main Currents in American Thought*. Vol. I, *The Colonial Mind, 1620–1800* (New York, 1927), a brief discussion of the Declaration, remains of historical interest only. Arthur M. Schlesinger, "The Lost Meaning of 'The Pursuit of Happiness,'" in *William and Mary Quarterly*, 3rd ser., 21 (1964), is a slight essay, in which the author puts forward the case that the Declaration's reference to "the pursuit of happiness" is to be understood as making the crucial test of governments whether they effect the happiness of their subjects. Morton G. White, *The Philosophy of the American Revolution* (New York, 1978), contains an excellent and clearly written exposition of the political and moral philosophy that permeated the thought of Jefferson and the other leading revolutionary writers. Garry Wills, *Inventing America: Jefferson's Declaration of Independence* (Garden City, N.Y., 1978), glosses the Declaration as the product of Scottish Enlightenment influences and dismisses Locke and the other Whig writers as playing no role in structuring Jefferson's thought; in light of the evidence, the work can only be regarded as a curiosity, devoid of scholarly merit.

[*See also* AMERICAN REVOLUTION; BILL OF RIGHTS; ENGLISH AND EUROPEAN POLITICAL INHERITANCE; *and* JEFFERSONIAN DEMOCRACY.]

EDUCATION

Carl F. Kaestle

UNLIKE other industrial nations, the United States does not have a unified national system of education. Authority for curriculum, finance, attendance, professional training, and teacher selection is divided between local school districts and state governments. The political history of American education is thus both unusual and complicated. The local and voluntary nature of public school development in early nineteenth-century America contrasts with the experience of other nations, while the lack of national control has given rise in the twentieth century to a baffling array of formal and informal influences on schools. Political influences beyond the local community include not only formal state and federal control but also such forces as the textbook industry, the vocational education lobby, teacher training institutions, educational researchers, and teachers' unions. Still, no aspect of local control has been so prized and so symbolically important as community control of public schools; the formal division of authority in education thus remains a hotly debated issue in the ongoing experiment of American federalism.

Locus of control, then, has been a central issue in the political history of American education. Other issues tied intimately to the politics of education include cultural pluralism and assimilation, equality of opportunity, moral education, the place of religion in the schools, and discrimination on the basis of race, sex, or religion. Each of these issues can be traced back into the nineteenth century and is important today. They arose from the particular circumstances of educational history in America, specifically the effort to create common public schools within a federal political system that has stated ideals of freedom and equality, but a diverse and often deeply divided population.

During the colonial period, the purpose of schooling everywhere was religious as well as social. School attendance was voluntary and was governed by parents' initiative. Whether under town control or individual enterprise, schools usually charged some tuition. Only occasionally did colonial governments take a hand in education, requiring masters to teach their apprentices to read or requiring towns of a certain size to maintain schools. For the most part, education was unregulated and was shared by the family, the school, the church, and the workplace. Among the colonists of British America, schooling and literacy were on the rise by the mid-eighteenth century. Commercial development, political activity, and a growing acceptance of women's educational role as mothers and teachers spurred the establishment of district schools for both sexes. Enrollments increased. Both pre-industrial capitalism and republican political ideas predated the Revolution, and both affected education.

When the Revolution transformed the colonies into a nation, at least on paper, its leaders looked to education to play a critical role in shaping a national consciousness. Benjamin Rush, Thomas Jefferson, Noah Webster, George Clinton, and others argued the necessity of education for intelligent citizens and virtuous mothers. They urged their legislatures to establish systems of free schools to make education more practical, more uniform, and more nationalistic. Rush, displaying the influence of Enlightenment perfectionism, declared that "pupils must be taught that there can be no durable liberty but in a republic and that government, like all other sciences, is of a progressive nature." Women should be educated, he emphasized, because "there have been few great or good men who

466

have not been blessed with wise and prudent mothers." Noah Webster advocated new textbooks, better teachers, and state systems of schools to rid America of dependence upon a decadent Europe. "As soon as he opens his lips," Webster wrote, a student "should rehearse the history of his own country; he should lisp the praise of liberty and of those illustrious heroes and statesmen who have wrought a revolution in her favor." Liberty required order; freedom could be preserved only through discipline. The educational essays of this period reflect a drive toward unity and discipline as well as a drive toward enlightenment, social progress, and political liberty.

Jefferson's bills for state-regulated free common schools failed in Virginia in the 1780's and 1790's, as did Rush's attempts in Pennsylvania. Connecticut, New York, and Massachusetts passed laws for the encouragement of common schools in the decade following the ratification of the federal Constitution, but they had little impact on the prevailing arrangements based on local control and parents' initiative. While some of the Founding Fathers argued that the fate of the republic depended in large measure on republican education, their sense of urgency was not widely shared. They did not arouse sufficient support for their proposed systems, which would have meant sharp departures from tradition.

The variegated nature of America's educational arrangements was reinforced in the early national period by the proliferation of independent, local academies and the founding of dozens of diverse colleges. At the time of the Revolution there were only nine colleges, and despite their denominational affiliations, they had a recognized public status. By 1819 there were forty-five colleges, some of them competing with each other and colliding with the intentions of state legislators. In the *Dartmouth College* case of that year the Supreme Court asserted the sanctity of charters, protecting private institutions from state interference. The splintering of Protestant denominations spawned colleges in the shadows of the old colonial nine and out into the frontier. America had no tradition of central educational control, and attempts to invent mechanisms for the coordinated state control of education at all levels, such as the University of Georgia or the "Cathelopistemiad" of Michigan,

remained only legislative pipe dreams in this period.

America in the 1820's was still a country where elementary education was voluntary, unregulated, and local. Legislation of the early national period was designed chiefly to create state funds to which localities or institutions could apply for assistance in providing charity schooling for the poor, district schools for rural areas, or secondary education in academies. In most states, legislators deemed these functions to be in the public interest but not in the public domain. While there were differences in the amount of schooling provided in the North and the South, the institutional arrangements and the politics of education were similar throughout the young nation. Although the importance of education in a republic was widely acknowledged, reformers' demands for state systems of common schools were countered by traditions of localism, nonintervention, and private endeavor. The result was a patchwork of private-venture schools and neighborhood schools charging tuition.

Why did this situation change? Historians debate the question. The formal politics of education in the period from 1830 to 1860 are clear enough, but the underlying causes of educational change are open to quite different interpretations. The institutional arrangements of the late eighteenth century—district schools in rural areas and a mix of entrepreneurial and charity schools in the cities—had withstood the Founding Fathers' efforts at reform and had proved capable of handling expanding enrollments. But by the 1830's northern reformers were alarmed by the growing numbers of urban, churchless poor, and they renewed their efforts to create free common schools for moral education and political socialization. Free schools, reformers argued, would provide equal access to elementary education for all white Americans. They found allies in the early workingmen's parties of the Northeast, which agitated for public elementary schools instead of state aid to elite colleges and academies. This coalition of the early 1830's did not achieve major legislative breakthroughs in the funding or organization of education, but locally the common-school concept was gaining ground, and a gradual shift was under way from independent schools to publicly administered schools.

EDUCATION

In the 1840's systematic school reform became associated with the Whig party, in keeping with its advocacy of state intervention and moral regulation, although many Democrats joined ranks on the desirability of providing free elementary schooling. Although rural enrollments were high, and people in small towns supported elementary education, they also tended to favor strong local control, limited expenditures, and short school terms. Pressure for a more ambitious educational system emanated from larger towns—the commercial and industrial centers of the Northeast and the budding, competing crossroads of the Midwest. Although the priorities of organized labor shifted from legal and institutional reform to specific workplace issues, and school reform leadership passed in the 1840's to lawyers and ministers of middle-class backgrounds, there is little evidence that blue-collar workers opposed school reform in a class-conscious fashion. The most vocal and easily identifiable opponents of state intervention in school matters were rural localists, who opposed state regulation and the consolidation of districts; Roman Catholics, who opposed the Protestant bias of the public schools; and black integrationists, who opposed the separate and inferior schools offered to their children. Some women fought within the reform movement for equal access and fairer status. A variety of other opponents challenged the establishment of state-regulated free schooling, on either political or cultural grounds. The sum of rural, religious, and ideological opposition was sufficient to make antebellum school reform a long, contentious legislative process. After a budget-cutting Connecticut legislature had abolished the state's board of education in 1842, leaving Henry Barnard without a job, an uncomprehending school supporter complained, "The common people have in reality the greatest interest in the subject. . . . Why can they not be made to realize this?" He failed to realize that not all Americans wished to invest in a state system of schools guided by a particular set of political, economic, and religious values. Still, the values that pervaded early common schools were widely shared. Furthermore, many parents supported improved public schools even if they dissented in part from the prevailing values, or belonged to a disfavored group. One could be a Roman Catholic and yet decide on balance that a child's best entrée to American society was public schooling, as New York City's *Truth Teller* urged its immigrant readers. And one could be a factory laborer, believe that the economic system was unfair, and yet decide that children were well served by gaining literacy, even if school texts praised the economic system and attributed poverty to bad character. The common-school reform effort of the mid-nineteenth century presented a Janus-like prospect—literacy and opportunity for the resourceless, social stability for nervous Victorian Americans. School officials and pro-education legislators often tried to broaden consensus by avoiding sectarian and controversial subjects and by compromising when necessary on such issues as Bible-reading or foreign-language instruction.

By 1860 northern legislatures had accepted much of the school reform program. Most states had created public school systems featuring a state school officer, tax-supported free schools, legislation encouraging the consolidation of rural districts, and a modicum of state support for teacher training in normal schools and academies. School terms were lengthened, attendance became more regular, dilapidated schoolhouses were upgraded, and teachers were better paid. Horace Mann of Massachusetts, Henry Barnard of Connecticut, Samuel Lewis of Ohio, John Pierce of Michigan, and like-minded reform leaders elsewhere had spread the word, apparently with some success, that moral persuasion was better than corporal punishment, that graded schools were better than one-room schoolhouses, and that universal public education could alleviate a host of social ills, from crime and indolence to ignorant voting and social-class tensions.

But advocates of common schools could toast their success with only half-filled glasses. Local control was still strong, centralized control still controversial. District consolidation laws and school taxes were overturned in some states, and school officials complained of their puny powers of enforcement. Passive resistance and local indifference to the reform program were widespread. Southern legislatures, dominated by the wealthy planter class, resisted northern-style reform and clung to traditional modes of independent and charitable schooling. Meanwhile, Roman Catholic officials had embarked upon the creation of an alternative school system. Within the public schools, racial segregation, religious and ethnic bias, and discrimination against women reflected prevailing beliefs about the destiny of white Anglo-Americans and the proper role of women. Reflecting these beliefs, schools also transmitted and perpetuated them, thus performing an important didactic role in American Victorian culture. Then as now, schools could have a liberating or a constraining political effect. Public schools in nineteenth-century America simultaneously demonstrated and explained the constraints upon equality in American life. Still, by 1860 the amount of free schooling available in the United States had greatly increased. Despite much segregation and discrimination, access to education had improved for women, free blacks, and European immigrants. For better or for worse, the rudimentary structures of more inclusive, state-regulated, free school systems were visible in the North.

The period from the 1870's to the early 1890's was one of consolidation and increasing professional control of schools. Public school tuition was eliminated in the last of the northern states. Most states passed laws regulating the certification of teachers, and attendance at normal schools increased. Some large cities hired a professional superintendent, replacing the system of direct supervision by school board laymen. Rural district consolidation continued but remained controversial. The biggest failure of the public schools in this era was their inability to come to terms with the aims of Roman Catholic educators. Consequently, there were periodic "Bible wars" and the substantial expansion of the parochial schools. The depression and labor strife of the 1870's gave some critics occasion to complain that public schools had not fulfilled the utopian promises of their founders, but other writers argued all the more insistently the importance of education for stability and productivity. This view prevailed among the public, it seems. The schools weathered the depression with stable enrollments and increased financial support.

Southern common-school reformers had labored unsuccessfully to achieve the same type of systems and the same levels of support prevailing in the North. North Carolina and Kentucky had adopted some features of state public schooling in the 1850's; but in most states, despite much up-country and middle-class agita-

tion for free schools, legislatures declined to follow the northern model. In the immediate aftermath of the Civil War, northern reformers saw an opportunity to demonstrate the power of popular education by creating schools for the freed slaves. The Freedmen's Bureau, initially set up to assist wartime refugees, took up the goal of free schooling for blacks after the war. Congress granted the agency limited funds to support the independent educational efforts of such groups as the American Missionary Association, the American Freedman's Union Commission, and dozens of similar groups. Education, along with agricultural recovery, became a keystone of Reconstruction policy. Thousands of northern teachers went south in this missionary venture, carrying Webster's blue-backed *Spelling Book* and McGuffey's *Reader* to freedmen long deprived of literacy. Millions of dollars were spent on the crusade. Most of the funds came through northern philanthropy, although the financial and organizational efforts made by southern blacks on their own behalf were impressive, given the condition from which they had just escaped.

The story of the evangelical northern women teachers contains elements of heroism, naïveté, and incipient feminism. Like some of the Union soldiers and Freedmen's Bureau officials in the South, many teachers strove to improve the political and economic condition of freedmen. But they were on hostile ground, and soon they had to acquiesce in a federal policy aimed at returning black workers to their former plantations with meager contract wages. By 1870 the enthusiasm for the educational crusade had waned, and most of the northern teachers moved back north or on to new missionary ventures. The combined educational effort of southern blacks and northern whites, however, had dramatically increased the literacy rate among black Americans, as reflected in the federal censuses of 1870 and 1880. Another legacy of the period was the establishment of segregated black academies and colleges, crucial to the educational fate of black southerners after the expulsion of the northern teachers. From these institutions —Fisk, Tuskegee, Howard, and others—came the teachers of the next generation and, eventually, the leaders of the twentieth-century civil rights movement, including Thurgood Marshall and Martin Luther King, Jr.

The subsequent political history of education in the nineteenth-century South is complicated. Publicly funded, segregated school systems, erected by Reconstruction legislatures, were retained by later white "redeemer" governments; but sharp inequity of funding continued between black and white schools, along with a general hostility to local property taxation as the means to improve public education. Agricultural stagnation, rural conditions, racism, and hostility to northern institutions spelled continuing difficulties for educational reform. Around the turn of the century, northern philanthropists again made a concerted effort to change the politics and the funding of southern education. Working through such organizations as the Southern Education Board, in alliance with progressive southern politicians, wealthy businessmen financed campaigns to overcome popular resistance to property taxes and increased school expenditures. They succeeded, but only by abandoning black schools to an even smaller proportion of public funds. The improved white education systems of the South rode on the backs of blacks. In South Carolina, for example, per-pupil expenditures for whites were six times those for blacks in 1900, but twelve times as much by 1915. For whites and blacks alike, rural expenditures were lower, and most blacks lived in rural areas. Thus demography reinforced racism.

The black educational experience in the North was more mixed in the nineteenth century, but there too treatment was generally separate and unequal. In Massachusetts a number of towns voluntarily desegregated their schools in the antebellum period, partly in accordance with principles of equality, and partly because it was inefficient to run separate schools for the relatively small proportion of blacks in northern cities. The Boston School Committee balked at this innovation, and when it was challenged legally, the state supreme court declared in the *Roberts* case of 1849 that separate but equal facilities were permissible because culture and custom so clearly divided the races, a view given the sanction of the United States Supreme Court in *Plessy* v. *Ferguson* in 1896. But shortly after the *Roberts* decision, the Massachusetts legislature required desegregation by law. Boston reluctantly complied, while the *New York Tribune,* commenting on the statute, lamented the impending "mongrelization" of the races. Still, during the last three decades of the nineteenth century there was some moderate optimism among black rights activists in the North. In schooling, as in voting, marital, property, and jury rights, some localities and states moved toward formal equality. Rhode Island in 1866, Connecticut in 1868, and Illinois in 1874 forbade explicit racial segregation in schools.

But the trend was not uniform. Some midwestern states (Ohio, for example) passed Jim Crow laws that predated the wave of renewed legal segregation in the South. Other states, like New York, remained silent on the issue while their cities continued to operate separate schools. Moreover, as black migration to northern cities increased, new racial tensions and demands for formal segregation emerged. In Chicago these demands were fended off only by the staunch efforts of superintendent Ella Flagg Young. Still, school boards in Chicago and throughout the North achieved school segregation through less explicit policies: manipulation of school district lines, transfer rules, and school construction policies, all aided by residential segregation. Some black parents protested on their children's behalf, boycotted separate schools, and sought equality through the courts. These efforts were costly and dangerous to individuals and generally ended in failure. Moreover, racially segregated schools created a serious political dilemma for blacks. Some opposed integration efforts on the grounds that mixed schools would cost the jobs of black teachers and expose black children to worse racism than they encountered in segregated schools. "Shame upon their narrow souls!" Frederick Douglass had exclaimed about such prosegregation blacks in Rochester in the 1840's. But this division among blacks was common in the nineteenth century, and similar debates revived during the school desegregation movement of the 1960's.

Black parents and political leaders in the late nineteenth century faced separate and unequal schools, frequent violence, uneven and shaky civil rights, and white allies who had decided that it was now time for blacks to earn further acceptance through sobriety, thrift, and cooperativeness. In view of these conditions, some black leaders counseled pragmatic accommodation. Booker T. Washington, founder of Tuskegee Institute in Alabama, became highly influential among educators and politicians of both races when he conceded in his Atlanta Exposition address of 1896 that "no race can prosper till it learns that there is as much dignity in tilling a field as in writing a poem. It is at the bottom of life we must begin and not the top." Privately, Washington was disturbed by racism and scornful of white supremacists, but he prided himself on his political realism. Publicly, he urged blacks to support vocational education and accept the reality of social segregation.

The movement to provide manual training for children's presumed occupational roles was not limited to blacks. It was symptomatic of a general transformation of public secondary schooling. Between 1890 and 1920 the proportion of youths aged 14 to 17 attending high school rose from 7 to 32 percent, and by 1930 it exceeded 50 percent. The white-collar sector of the work force expanded, teenagers found fewer jobs in industry, more employers began to emphasize school credentials, and more people came to believe that secondary education was a good investment. Manual education had begun as an educational reform for all youth, as a way to promote the dignity of manual labor and children's understanding of craft work; but when the high school population expanded, discussions of the secondary curriculum increasingly focused upon the practicality and vocational value of subject matter. An early stage in the transition is expressed by the 1893 report of the National Education Association's Committee of Ten, chaired by Harvard's president, Charles Eliot. His committee argued the value of modern and practical subjects and advocated alternative high school courses of study, but they were intended to be equivalent and were not aimed at different occupational futures. But by 1918 an NEA report known as *Cardinal Principles of Secondary Education* added social adjustment goals to intellectual training and advocated practical, everyday education geared to different adult work roles for different children. A controversial movement for separate vocational schools faded because it undermined the ideal of common schooling; but in the comprehensive American high school, equality of opportunity was redefined.

With vocational, commercial, general, and college preparatory courses of study available, educators found themselves making predictions about their students' future occupations. Equality of opportunity came to mean that the school

should develop an array of appropriate and useful courses so that each student could realize his or her potential, as determined by the school. Educators' eagerness to live up to this new definition may be seen in the vogues of testing, of utilitarian curriculum development, and of vocational guidance, all of which flourished after World War I. Although in theory each child was evaluated as an individual, curriculum tracking often coincided with social groupings of sex, race, and class. David Snedden, soon to be commissioner of education in Massachusetts, explained the philosophy in 1908: "Equality of opportunity can be secured by recognition of differences which, theoretically individual, may nevertheless for practical purposes, be regarded as characterizing distinguishable groups of children." Classification would be based on the child's mental ability, the family's economic situation, and the child's probable occupation.

Public acceptance of the transformed high school was dramatized by the passage in 1917 of the Smith-Hughes Act for support of vocational education, the only programmatic intervention of the federal government in precollegiate education prior to the 1950's. Vocational education developed an effective lobby, centering on the National Society for the Promotion of Industrial Education (later the American Vocational Association). Its political activities, plus the appealing idea that vocational education democratized high schools, assured the support of Congress through the 1970's, despite periodic studies showing that vocational training in schools did little to prepare students for the specific jobs they later held.

Next to the expansion of secondary education and its increasing vocational emphasis, the most important change in public schooling during the Progressive Era (*ca.* 1890–1920) was administrative centralization. Influential educators like Ellwood Cubberley continued to emphasize the importance of rural consolidation because, he argued, rural education was "burdened by educational traditions, lacking in effective supervision, controlled largely by rural people, who, too often, do not realize either their own needs or the possibilities of rural education." But the most visible and contentious episodes in the centralization of control occurred in the cities.

In the nineteenth century many urban school boards were based on representation by wards and had become very large. Milwaukee's board numbered forty-two, and the largest, New York's, reached forty-six. In several cities, including St. Louis, Milwaukee, Philadelphia, Rochester, Toledo, and New York, reformers waged "school wars" in the 1890's over the issue of ward representation. In cities like Chicago and San Francisco, which had discontinued ward representation in the 1870's, reform bills sought smaller boards and stronger authority for the professional superintendent. Support for centralization came from a coalition of good-government reformers bent on eliminating the corruption and incompetence that they associated with ethnic ward politics, along with professional educators, including university presidents and public school superintendents, who advocated expert management on a business model. These forces for consolidation and professional control drew fire from ward politicians, of course, but also from many teachers and parents who believed that their system of supervision by local trustees worked well and was more democratic. Thus the opposition to centralized control ranged from middle-class New York parents, to the Chicago teachers' union, to the Irish political machine of San Francisco.

There was some basis for the reformers' charges of nepotism and corruption. In Philadelphia several administrators were dismissed for graft in 1903, and in Toledo the pro-working-class *Evening Bee* called bribery by the textbook monopoly a "slimy octopus whose tentacles wind through and around all branches of our school system." And, in the depression of the 1890's, the schools of many large systems were overcrowded and rundown, belying the claim that ward representation served the interests of ordinary people well. The interests of parents were not always the same as those of ward politicians. Nor were large school boards necessarily very democratic; much influence fell to officers or small executive committees. Even the ward-based boards of the nineteenth century were dominated by businessmen and professionals. On the other hand, the successful reorganization and streamlining of city school boards did not completely eliminate the influence of ethnic machine politics. In Chicago, Boston, and elsewhere, when machine politicians controlled city governments, they controlled school boards as effectively as they had under the ward system.

The "school wars," then, wrought more formal than real political change and did not immediately make school government less political. Although the reformers eliminated the geographical basis of representation, their reforms sparked much bitter political conflict in the Progressive Era. Editor William Taggart labeled the Philadelphia reorganization "an effort of the so-called social status people, who have no faith in the wisdom of boilermakers, carpenters, and painters," while opponents in San Francisco called the bill for a small, appointed school board a "Chamber of Commerce conspiracy."

These debates provided a dramatic chapter in the long-range story of increasing centralization and professionalization of school governance. The model that gained much publicity and popularity by the 1920's was a corporate model, featuring a small school board elected at large, with an appointed professional superintendent. Throughout the twentieth century such boards were dominated by male businessmen and professionals who increasingly delegated authority to the professional administrators. Many who wrote about education claimed that such board members were more disinterested and had a broader view of the community's good than other people. This view was labeled a "pious fraud" by Teachers College's iconoclastic George Counts; nevertheless it became an article of faith in America's educational mythology.

A second, related myth that gained currency during the Progressive period was that appointed or nonpartisan elected boards, supporting expert professional administrators, could insulate public schooling from politics. This belief has had some real effects and fostered some illusions. School board candidates are usually not formally associated with political parties; and national political party platforms, from the Civil War to the civil rights movement of the 1960's, said little about educational policy. At the same time, the real politics of education—the politics of policy, power, and participation—have been somewhat obscured by the myth. The nonpolitical commitment of the education profession has also had a dampening effect on teachers' political activities.

Educators believed that centralized, uniform public schooling would increase efficiency. They also thought that professional control and state regulation would upgrade quality and lead to

EDUCATION

equal opportunity. A crucial additional purpose of inclusive public schooling was political integration. Early national leaders like Noah Webster had believed that public schools must create a national culture and overcome regional differences. By the 1830's educational reformers had shifted the emphasis to the political socialization of immigrants. The great influx of European immigrants, said Michigan school superintendent John Pierce in 1837, made the American republic "the boldest experiment upon the stability of government ever made in the annals of time."

Only through a common school system could American democracy surmount the challenge of ethnic fragmentation, language diversity, and imported political problems, whether radicalism or passivity. Political socialization became more and more urgent as the volume of immigration increased in the closing decades of the nineteenth century and shifted dramatically to the more culturally different peoples of eastern and southern Europe. English-speaking Americans' tolerance of bilingual and foreign-language schooling had been common during the mid-nineteenth century in some places where German or Spanish speakers were concentrated, but by the closing years of the century it was waning. The new waves of immigrants, plus the anti-German sentiments generated by World War I, strengthened a nationwide resolve to have only English taught in the public schools. Fifteen states passed laws implementing an English-only policy by 1919. In the meantime educators launched an adult education effort in night schools. This "Americanization" movement aimed not only at English-language instruction and citizenship education but also at domestic science for immigrant women and industrial work discipline for men. Most immigrants, of course, were untouched by this educational program, and many immigrant groups developed alternative ways to adjust to their new situation. Immigration restriction in the 1920's rendered the adult Americanization movement less important. In the long run, a more pervasive assimilation strategy has been the public schools' portrayal of American history and culture as Anglo-American, stemming from the New England Puritans, with supplementary contributions by outstanding individuals from other groups. The reality of the melting pot has been not mixing but conversion to a mainstream norm

of white, male, Protestant leadership and values.

The central developments in education during the Progressive Era were not the introduction of child-centered pedagogy, which never spread very far beyond private middle-class schools, nor John Dewey's notion that schools should be a microcosm of democratic life, another idea that did not widely penetrate local public schools. Rather, the schools were transformed in this era by the expansion of secondary schooling and the introduction of a differentiated, vocationalized curriculum that enhanced the role of schools as arbiters between family and work force. Second, there was a gradual but unmistakable drift toward centralized, professional control and increased state regulation, accompanied by the credo that schools should be run like businesses and should be kept "out of politics." Third, educators and legislators stiffened their resolve that cultural assimilation would be based on the English language. Fourth, southern states accepted tax-based local school financing, but they increased the disparity of resources between white and black schools. Despite these elements of ethnocentricity and inequality, public schooling received support from a sufficient number of immigrants, workers, non-Protestants, blacks, and women to make it a durable, successful American institution.

Americans' faith in public education was soon to be tested again, in the depression of the 1930's. Some schools, like some sectors of the economy, were in serious financial trouble by the late 1920's. There was great local variation in the economic impact of the depression of the 1930's on public schooling. But aggregated national figures suggest that enrollments went up and per-pupil expenditures kept pace nationally, despite hard times. Nor did the average American lose faith in the value of public schooling, although there were some tense years in the mid-1930's when educators feared budget slashing by a hard-pressed and disillusioned public. The threat of weakened public support caused many professional spokesmen to question the wisdom of their corporate model of school management and their attempt to insulate schools from lay opinion. Teachers and administrators started on a publicity blitz about the needs and benefits of the schools, and they joined the public in a brief period of blaming businessmen for the nation's ills.

473

EDUCATION

A few went further. George Counts and a group of educational theorists known as "reconstructionists," centered at Teachers College, condemned capitalism as cruel and unsuccessful. They called upon the schools to be a dynamic force for political and economic change. Like his elder colleague John Dewey, Counts wanted the schools to "establish an organic relation with the community." Unlike Dewey, the reconstructionists advocated a change in the direction of socialism. Counts urged educators to "become less frightened than they are today at the bogies of imposition and indoctrination." Boyd Bode of Ohio State University explained that "partisanship is inescapable. . . . We are confronted by what William James would have called a 'forced option.'" This characterization rested on the twin judgments that schools necessarily indoctrinated children with political and economic values, and that capitalism had proved destructive. William Randolph Hearst led the journalistic assault on Counts and like-minded critics, while patriotic organizations demanded teacher loyalty oaths. Still, there was little reason to believe that many educators would become radicalized. In 1932 Agnes de Lima wrote in the *New Republic* that "to expect teachers to lead us out of our morass is fantastic indeed. . . . A class long trained to social docility and economically protected by life tenure of office—on good behavior—is unlikely to challenge unduly the status quo." Likewise, school administrators—overwhelmingly Protestant males of Anglo-Saxon parentage and rural backgrounds, beholden to boards composed of professionals and businessmen—were not ready recruits to socialism. Instead, educators' organizations repudiated the reconstructionists' position and denounced partisanship in the curriculum. The schools of Muncie, Indiana, concluded Robert and Helen Lynd, reflected the status of educational reform in the 1930's: "In the struggle between quantitative administrative efficiency and qualitative goals in an era of strain, the big guns are all on the side of the former." The Great Depression, then, did not divert the main thrust of progressive education reform.

Despite the commitment to keep education apolitical, educators of the Progressive Era had established many new professional organizations, and some of these became politically active. Although the National Education Association, founded in the 1870's, remained a small group of elites dominated by administrators who shunned politics, some state and local teachers' organizations entered more directly into politics. The Chicago Teachers Union, formed in 1897, was led by the articulate and politically progressive Margaret Haley. Her union became active in issues ranging from teachers' salaries to school board corruption to the misuse of intelligence testing. It affiliated with the American Federation of Labor, following the lead of the San Antonio teachers, who had taken that bold step in 1902. The fledgling teacher-union movement of the Progressive Era culminated in the founding of the American Federation of Teachers in 1916. But only tiny numbers of teachers belonged to any union in these early years. The central fulcrum of teachers' political influence was the state teachers' associations, which had enrolled about 35 percent of all teachers by 1916. These groups lobbied legislatures with some success for better wages, tenure protection, and fringe benefits.

Meanwhile, classroom teachers fought for a voice in the National Education Association. With Margaret Haley's help, Ella Flagg Young was elected president in 1910, and in 1913 they succeeded in creating a new Department of Classroom Teachers within the NEA. This helped the organization expand its membership dramatically in the 1920's and 1930's, but it did not end the tension between teachers and administrators. Gender remained an essential factor in the politics of teachers' organizations. In the nineteenth century, female teachers' salaries had typically equaled 40 to 60 percent of salaries for their male counterparts. In cities such as New York and Chicago, men and women teachers formed separate organizations in the Progressive Era. Women teachers fought for state legislation guaranteeing equal pay for equal work. The movement had its first successes in the West and gradually moved east. By 1880, California, Idaho, Nevada, Arizona, and Missouri had such legislation. New York legislators held out until a strenuous campaign by the New York City Female Teachers Association carried the day in 1911. These laws did not end gender inequities; for while almost all elementary teachers were women, a majority of high school teachers were men, and the salaries were higher at the secondary level. An increase in the number of female secondary teachers caused a backlash in the Progressive Era. In 1892 the U.S. commissioner of

EDUCATION

education worried about "increasing femininity" in the schools, and the New York City Men's Teachers Association argued in 1904 that boys over ten need manly examples. A 1914 article on "The Woman Peril" in the *Educational Review* wondered how the United States would ever compete with Prussia while female secondary teachers here turned out "a feminized manhood, emotional, illogical, [and] non-combative." Nonetheless, the backlash subsided, and by 1940 women held 58 percent of all secondary teaching positions.

The expansion, professionalization, and attempted political insulation of elementary and secondary schooling had analogies in higher education. The antebellum expansion of collegiate education had been fueled by denominational splintering, local boosterism, and democratic aspirations. Many small institutions failed, and some that were called colleges differed only in name from academies. But the total percentage of youth attending college, and the proportion of those from poor backgrounds, certainly increased between the Revolution and the Civil War. The expansion of access continued after the 1860's as women's colleges were established and state legislatures created or expanded public universities. The Morrill Act of 1862 granted public lands to states, the proceeds from which were to be used by collegiate institutions engaged in scientific, agricultural, and engineering training. The recipients ranged from new agricultural and metallurgical colleges, to branches of expanding state universities, to Yale's Sheffield Scientific School and the Massachusetts Institute of Technology. The Morrill Act nurtured a trend toward service and utilitarian studies, ideals that animated the large midwestern universities and led to the founding in 1868 of Ezra Cornell's institution at Ithaca, New York.

The influence of the German research ideal and the elaboration of academic disciplines soon furthered the expansion of higher education, as well as its professionalization. Johns Hopkins in 1876, then Clark University in 1889, were created explicitly to further basic research, but they were only a small part of the expansion of the late nineteenth century, which witnessed the founding of several universities (Chicago and Stanford among them) and the expansion of others into new fields. While the social scientists differentiated themselves into distinct disciplines

and joined in the enthusiasm for "pure" research, the administration of higher education also moved in more professional and bureaucratic directions. Governing boards enlarged the authority of their presidents, now called "captains of education" like their counterparts in the public schools. Indeed, some university presidents, like Nicholas Murray Butler of Columbia and William Rainey Harper of Chicago, were active in the politics of public-school centralization in their cities. Within the universities, new structures, positions, and traditions evolved: departments, chairmen, deans, and statutes proliferated. Unlike Clark and Johns Hopkins, most large universities were not devoted solely to research and graduate training; but while they tried to reconcile their traditional collegiate functions with heady new research and public service ideals, they too moved toward professionalism and its consequences. "Publish or perish" norms became more important after 1900, as did arguments for academic freedom, again bolstered by the German model. Professional autonomy in the academic world meant the freedom to pursue research to whatever conclusions seemed warranted by academic standards, however politically unpopular. This newly claimed autonomy was quickly put to the test.

Two of the most celebrated academic freedom cases were those of Richard Ely of Wisconsin and Edward A. Ross of Stanford. Ely, an economist with leftist theoretical leanings, spoke favorably in his classes about labor strikes and boycotts. Furthermore, complained one of the university's regents, his books provided "a moral justification of attack upon life and property." Wisconsin's president, Charles Kendall Adams, defended Ely, who was acquitted in 1894 after an investigation by the regents, who declared themselves in favor of "that continual and fearless sifting and winnowing by which alone the truth can be found." But not all universities found their professors' politics sacrosanct. Many were dismissed—some after great debate, some quietly and summarily, some for views more conservative than their employers', more often for prolabor and antimonopoly views. Edward Ross, a Stanford sociologist, campaigned publicly for Democrats in 1896, defying a ban on faculty political participation outside the classroom levied by Mrs. Jane Stanford, who then controlled the university. Ross soon angered Mrs. Stanford fur-

475

ther by speaking in favor of public ownership of utilities and against the importation of Asian labor, both views offensive to the Stanford family, whose wealth came from railroads and mining. Mrs. Stanford required President David Jordan to dismiss Ross, which he did in 1900, but both Ross and Stanford lost in the affair. In the aftermath of Ross's departure, seven other faculty members resigned.

Eventually university faculties achieved a system of tenure and a supportive if not invulnerable concept of academic freedom within which to operate. They achieved this autonomy partly because the credentials conferred by experts became increasingly valuable in the twentieth century and partly because the experience of two world wars dramatized the increasing complexity of a technological society and enhanced the universities' role in pursuing national interests. The very expertise that had insulated higher education from lay control at the local and amateur level brought it back within the sphere of public policy at a new level—responsiveness to national research and manpower training priorities.

Similarly, at the elementary and secondary levels, the political drama moved to the federal level after World War II. Some emergency measures undertaken during the depression and war years had affected public education marginally but had little lasting impact. By the early 1950's the schools were facing budget declines from economy-minded taxpayers, sporadic McCarthyite assaults on liberal textbooks, and a serious barrage of criticism from observers scornful of the academic vapidity of "life adjustment education," then popular with education professors and school superintendents. Public schooling was ripe for reform. First the cold war and then the civil rights movement enlisted public opinion and the national government in that cause.

By the time the Soviet Union launched *Sputnik* in 1957, James Conant had already begun work on *The American High School Today* (1959). Acting as a mediator between beleaguered educationists and academic critics, Conant urged stronger state education agencies, larger high schools, more science, mathematics, and foreign languages in the curriculum, and greater emphasis on intellectual training in general. *Sputnik* boosted this message, giving it urgency and spectacular publicity. The United States space gap did not last very long, but it helped produce

a wave of innovative curriculum development in mathematics and the sciences, and it helped persuade Congress to pass the National Defense Education Act of 1958. The NDEA continued the Smith-Hughes precedent of aid to specific curriculum areas, but it broadened and increased the national government's involvement in local school systems. Some educators worried about strings attached to federal money, and some humanists warned about the danger of unbalancing the curriculum; but hard-pressed local school boards and superintendents generally welcomed the optional federal funds for curriculum development, language laboratories, and library expansion. The themes that generated the new intervention were manpower training for international competition and the return of intellectual training as the central purpose of the schools, especially for academically talented children.

But new crises were brewing in the 1950's, crises that would shift the focus of federal intervention in education. The issues were race and poverty, and they bubbled to the top of American politics between 1955 and 1965. The U.S. Supreme Court's decision in *Brown* v. *Board of Education of Topeka* (1954), which declared statutory school segregation unconstitutional, did not come out of the blue. In the background of *Brown* were Supreme Court decisions from the 1920's to the 1940's applying the Bill of Rights to state laws on issues of religious freedom and freedom of speech. Black soldiers' participation in World War II also helped set the stage. Many Americans were repelled by Hitler's racism, the U.S. Army was partially integrated, and the G.I. Bill allowed more minority students to attend college after the war. More specifically, *Brown* flowed from Supreme Court decisions in higher-education cases of the 1950's that chipped away at the separate but equal doctrine and from two decades of lower court cases in which blacks challenged segregated elementary and secondary schooling, led by Thurgood Marshall of the National Association for the Advancement of Colored People.

The *Brown* decision demanded an end to segregation by law as practiced in the South. It did not demand integration, it did not apply to segregation in the North, it was vague about timing, and it was weak on enforcement. During the next decade the Supreme Court faced these problems, demanding integration and demanding more speed. Still, by 1964, only two southern states had more than 2 percent of their black children in integrated schools. Brutality against civil rights demonstrators turned public opinion against this inaction on the segregation issue. The enforcement problem was solved by tougher court decisions insisting upon immediate compliance and by the passage of Title VI of the Civil Rights Act of 1964, giving the federal government authority to withhold federal funds from noncomplying districts. By 1965 the administration of Lyndon B. Johnson had the tools to end formally segregated schooling. This was substantially accomplished by 1970.

The other challenges on the education agenda of Johnson's Great Society—extending integration to the North, improving the cognitive skills of poor children, and ensuring equality of opportunity for all groups—proved even more recalcitrant. These were the dramatic educational policy issues of the early 1970's. In the *Swann* v. *Charlotte-Mecklenburg* decision (1971) the Supreme Court declared that busing was required where other means of integration were insufficient. In *Keyes* v. *School District No. 1, Denver* (1973) and other cases the Court reinterpreted the distinction between *de jure* segregation (established by law) and *de facto* segregation (attributed to residential patterns). Where northern school segregation was shown to be the result of deliberate policy decisions (such as district definitions or new school siting), it was unconstitutional. In *Keyes* the Court also declared that where a pattern of intentional segregation occurred within a school district, the desegregation order could be generalized to the entire district. Progress toward integration in the North was slow in the 1970's and early 1980's, however. A somewhat weary federal judiciary began demanding more clear-cut evidence of intentional segregation, and the demography of large cities made integration difficult even with massive crosstown busing. By 1980 black and Hispanic people made up more than 50 percent of the population of Detroit, San Antonio, Baltimore, Newark, and several other large cities. The public school populations of large cities were even more heavily nonwhite, due to the inmigration of young minority families, differential birthrates, and the withdrawal of white children from the public schools. In 1974 the Court ruled in *Milliken* v. *Bradley* that white suburbs were not required to integrate with politically independent inner cities. But the Court required metropolitan solutions on other matters, such as housing, where metropolitan governmental structures were already in existence. On the eve of a 1983 federal court hearing on suburbs' liability for the segregation of St. Louis schools, that city's suburbs agreed to a comprehensive metropolitan busing plan for integration. Thus the future of court-mandated integration in the North remained in doubt. The federal government had also pressed for integration and equal access at the higher-education level, but the courts issued ambiguous decrees on such thorny matters as the existence of all-black colleges (*Adams* v. *Richardson*, 1973) and affirmative-action admissions quotas (*Bakke* v. *California Regents*, 1978).

While the federal government tried to equalize educational opportunity through integration, it also created a major program of compensatory schooling for poor children through Title I of the Elementary and Secondary Education Act of 1965. Although the evaluation efforts of educational researchers showed only mixed and modest success, Congress's instinctive belief in compensatory education rivaled its faith in vocational education, as did the political appeal of the idea. Funding targeted for basic skills training in schools with concentrations of low-income students survived even the reduced education budgets of the early Reagan administration.

These programs originated in the ferment of the civil rights movement and were strongly identified with black Americans. During the 1970's the federal government attempted through legislation and court decisions to expand civil rights protection in the education sector to women, to non-English speakers, and to handicapped people. Title IX of the Education Amendments of 1972 prohibited discrimination on the basis of sex in any educational program receiving federal funds. In *Lau* v. *Nichols* (1974) the Supreme Court declared that the promise of nondiscrimination in the Civil Rights Act of 1964 required school systems to make special provisions for students whose native language was not English. The Education for All Handicapped Children Act of 1975 required access to free, appropriate education for handicapped students. The remarkable flurry of legislation and guidelines that flowed from these mandates imposed new requirements and demanded new attitudes at the local level. Affirmative action, bilingual education, equity in sports programs, accessible buildings, and staff retraining cost money and challenged customs, resulting in widespread frustration and objections. The trend since 1980 has been toward reduced enforcement of existing guidelines and little expansion of the rights concepts elaborated in the 1970's. Nevertheless, these initiatives have become part of state law in many states and have worked their way into the procedures and goals of many local schools. The presence of handicapped children in regular classrooms, and the continued adjudication of court-regulated integration plans, aroused sensitivity about gender prejudice, and other legacies of the 1970's did not disappear in the conservative countertrend of 1980.

Of course, not all recent issues in the politics of education have been generated by the federal government. Issues of teacher unionization, taxpayers' revolts, book censorship, and competency testing have been focused at the local or state level. By 1983 most public school teachers belonged to a union, affiliated with the American Federation of Teachers or, more frequently, with the National Education Association. The rival organizations' policies on collective bargaining became more similar as public-sector wage negotiations became more common in the 1970's. But despite increased collective bargaining, teachers' real wages decreased through most of the 1970's. It was a decade when declining enrollments and taxpayers' revolts made school boards either unsympathetic to teachers' wage demands or unable to meet them. Declining birthrates and an aging population meant that a smaller proportion of voters were parents of school-age children. Pressed by inflation and angry at government programs for minorities and the poor, taxpayers in some states (California in 1978 and Massachusetts in 1979) took drastic action to limit increases in local property taxes. Local school board deliberations were therefore dominated by budget matters: school closings, teachers' wages, and declining services.

The politics of morality provided another constellation of issues that troubled school boards and educators during the mid-1970's and into the early 1980's. As a combined result of federal constitutional initiatives supporting mi-

nority cultures and curbing religion in the schools, curriculum developments in the direction of diversity and choice, and the assertive youth culture of the late 1960's and early 1970's, many adults came to look upon the public schools as permissive, relativistic, and amoral. Disaffection over the Supreme Court's religion decisions (*Engel* v. *Vitale,* 1962, banning prayer in schools, and *Abington Township* v. *Schempp,* 1963, banning Bible reading), along with a belief among traditional parents that the public schools had lost their commitment to discipline, morality, and the three R's, had three political consequences in the late 1970's: a slight increase in private school attendance, adding to the constituency favoring aid to private schooling; a stronger and more frequent traditionalist voice in local debates, whether over sex education, book censorship, or a "back-to-basics" curriculum; and a bonus to political candidates who promised to reassert traditional educational values. Although some reforms had been modestly successful in the seventeen years from the Johnson presidency through the Carter administration—integration of southern schools, increased recognition of cultural diversity in the curriculum, improved access to educational programs, and moderate equalization of educational resources—confidence in public schooling had reached another periodic low by 1980. Retrenchment and recrimination often replaced reform at the local level, and the election of Ronald Reagan signaled a retreat from federal intervention on some constitutional issues.

Schools conserve and transmit particular cultures. Education in all societies is largely conservative. At the same time, people in industrial, multicultural nations often look to schools to solve social problems. It is easier to think of transforming the ideas and behavior of malleable children than to reconstruct the fixed institutions and vested interests of adults. To say that schools have both a conserving and a reforming potential perhaps belabors the obvious, but the tension between these contrasting functions generates much of the politics of education. This has continually been the case in America, with its diverse population and its divided educational authority. When outsiders and reformers fight for change, insiders and traditionalists fear that their children's morality and cultural moorings are in danger. The tension generates specific ed-

EDUCATION

ucational issues about language, moral instruction, the structure of schools, and the goals of teaching. But in the American political system, the arguments about particular issues have also often coincided with and intensified arguments about which level of government should control educational policy. Specific issues may wax and wane over the years, or disappear altogether as peculiar products of their time, but locus of control has been a constant tension in the politics of education in America. The myth that Americans have kept education "out of politics" is a strange fiction in a country where educational decision-making has involved so many organized interest groups and where educational control has been so hotly contested.

BIBLIOGRAPHY

Bernard Bailyn, *Education in the Forming of American Society: Needs and Opportunities for Study* (Chapel Hill, N.C., 1960), includes an interpretive essay that helped reshape the historiography of American education and a bibliographical essay that surveys works about colonial America pertinent to his broad definition of education. Robert L. Church and Michael W. Sedlak, *Education in the United States: An Interpretive History* (New York, 1976), is the best textbook on the history of American education; it deals extensively with politics and has helpful bibliographies. Lawrence A. Cremin, *The Transformation of the School: Progressivism in American Education, 1876–1957* (New York, 1961), chronicles the origins and the fate of the diverse educational ideas that went under the name *Progressive*. Cremin's *American Education: The Colonial Experience, 1607–1783* (New York, 1970), is a comprehensive treatment of the educational culture and institutions of colonial America. Erudite, it leans toward intellectual history but connects with politics at several points; his *American Education: The National Experience, 1783–1876* (New York, 1980), the second volume of an ongoing three-volume work, employs a broad definition of education; both of these large, important books deal with politics from a cultural historian's point of view; both have excellent bibliographical essays. Joseph M. Cronin, *The Control of Urban Schools* (New York, 1973), is the most thorough examination of changing local school board and administrative structures from 1850 to 1970. Marshall O. Donley, Jr., *Power to the Teacher: How America's Educators Became Militant* (Bloomington, Ind., 1976), is a historical survey of teacher organization in the twentieth century. Louis R. Harlan, *Separate and Unequal: Public School Campaigns and Racism in the Southern Seaboard States, 1901–1915* (Chapel Hill, N.C., 1958), analyzes northern philanthropists' political efforts to upgrade southern education; it contains much detailed information about school systems and the politics of education in the early-twentieth-century South.

Jurgen Herbst, *From Crisis to Crisis: American College Government, 1636–1819* (Cambridge, Mass., 1982), is more than a history of college government; it is a fresh look at the relationship of colleges and society from colonial times to the *Dartmouth College* decision. Richard Hofstadter and Walter P. Metzger, *The Development of Academic Freedom in the United States* (New York, 1955), is also much broader than its title, but it does analyze in detail the development of academic freedom from colonial Harvard to the A.A.U.P. Jacqueline Jones, *Soldiers of Light and Love: Northern Teachers and Georgia Blacks, 1865–1873* (Chapel Hill, N.C., 1980), is a lively social history of the American Missionary Association teachers and their educational efforts, based on their letters. Carl F. Kaestle, *Pillars of the Republic: Common Schools and American Society, 1780–1860* (New York, 1983), reassesses the common-school reform movement, stressing the importance of native, Protestant ideology while examining sympathetically a variety of opponents of state-regulated common schools; Carl F. Kaestle and Marshall S. Smith, "The Federal Role in Elementary and Secondary Education, 1940–1980," in *Harvard Educational Review,* 52 (1982), sketches a historical interpretation of federal intervention, arguing that events of the period 1958 to 1980 are thematically and organizationally continuous with earlier trends in American educational history. Carl F. Kaestle and Maris A. Vinovskis, *Education and Social Change in Nineteenth-Century Massachusetts* (New York, 1980), is a quantitative exploration of the determinants of educational change, including a chapter analyzing the politics of reform in Horace Mann's Massachusetts.

Harvey Kantor and David B. Tyack, eds., *Work, Youth, and Schooling: Historical Perspectives on Vocationalism in American Education* (Stanford, Calif., 1982), a conference volume, provides new interpretations of vocational education but also much historical detail not available elsewhere. Michael B. Katz, *The Irony of Early School Reform: Educational Innovation in Mid-Nineteenth Century Massachusetts* (Cambridge, Mass., 1968), is the most influential of the class-based analyses of educational reform, viewing public schooling as a middle-class imposition on an ill-served and reluctant working class. Richard Kluger, *Simple Justice* (New York, 1976), is a detailed narrative history of the background, buildup, deliberation, and aftermath of the *Brown* desegregation decision. Edward A. Krug, *The Shaping of the American High School,* vol.1 (New York, 1964), and *The Shaping of the American High School,* vol. 2 (Madison, Wis., 1972), comprise a comprehensive history of the curriculum, leadership, and professional culture of American secondary education. Marvin Lazerson, *Origins of the Urban School: Public Education in Massachusetts, 1870–1915* (Cambridge, Mass., 1971), focuses on the kindergarten, vocational education, and Americanization movements in ten cities, relating educational policy to economic and cultural changes. Marvin Lazerson and W. Norton Grubb, eds., *American Education and Vocationalism: A Documentary History, 1870–1970* (New York, 1974), provides an interpretive introduction and brief documents that recapture the flavor of arguments for vocational education. August Meier and Elliott Rudwick wrote three case studies that illustrate the agonizing dilemmas of early black protests: "Early Boycotts of Segregated Schools: The Alton, Illinois, Case, 1897–1908," in *Journal of Negro Education,* 36 (1967); "Early Boycotts of Segregated Schools: The East Orange, New Jersey, Experience, 1899–1906," in *History of Education Quarterly,* 4 (1967); and "Early Boycotts of Secondary Schools: The Case of Springfield, Ohio, 1922–23," in *American Quarterly,* 20 (1968). Mi-

EDUCATION

chael R. Olneck and Marvin Lazerson, "Education," in Stephan Thernstrom, ed., *Harvard Encyclopedia of American Ethnic Groups* (Cambridge, Mass., 1980), packs a lot of information into an interpretive essay on the history of educational policies toward immigrants and non-English speakers. Robert M. O'Neil, *Classrooms in the Crossfire* (Bloomington, Ind., 1981), surveys legal and political developments of the last twenty years in the areas of religion and censorship in the schools, from a strong First Amendment perspective. Gary Orfield, *The Reconstruction of Southern Education: The Schools and the 1964 Civil Rights Act* (New York, 1969), is a narrative and a political analysis of how judicial, legislative, and administrative efforts combined to desegregate southern public schools; and his *Must We Bus?: Segregated Schools and National Policy* (Washington, D.C., 1978), charts the negative turn in the desegregation movement over the busing issue.

William J. Reese, *Progressivism and the Grass Roots* (London, 1984), uses case studies of six cities to examine the politics of urban education, from socialists to ward bosses to women's clubs. Frederick Rudolph, ed., *Essays on Education in the Early Republic* (Cambridge, Mass., 1965), reproduces essays written between 1786 and 1799 by Benjamin Rush, Noah Webster, and others, urging the importance of common schooling for the new republic. Marshall S. Smith and John W. Jenkins, "Legislation," in Harold E. Mitzel, ed., *Encyclopedia of Educational Research,* 5th ed. (New York, 1982), covers state and federal legislation from 1960 to 1980, ranging from bilingual education, to collective bargaining, to college tuition loans. It notes some of the achievements and failures of this active twenty-year period. Joel Spring, *The Sorting Machine: National Educational Policy Since 1945* (New York, 1976), the only book-length survey of federal education policy in this period, has chapters on manpower training, civil rights, the war on poverty, and career training. David B. Tyack, "Education and Social Unrest, 1873–1878," in *Harvard Educational Review,* 31 (1961), investigates the impact of the 1870's depression on the schools, concluding that public confidence and financial support persisted despite hard times. Tyack's *The One Best System: A History of American Urban Education* (Cambridge, Mass., 1974), is an influential synthesis of urban school history that centers attention on the centralization of school administration and the ideas and programs of the "administrative progressives." David Tyack and Elisabeth Hansot, *Managers of Virtue: Public School Leadership in America, 1820–1980* (New York, 1982), dissects leadership styles and goals in three periods, each of which witnessed educational reform. David Tyack and Robert Lowe, *Public Schools in Hard Times: The Depression Years* (forthcoming), the only book about public schooling in the 1930's, analyzes the difficulties and the results of the depression for public schools. Laurence R. Veysey, *The Emergence of the American University* (Chicago, 1965), analyzes the contrasting ideals of service, research, and liberal education that shaped higher education from 1865 to 1910 and then probes the problems of the turn-of-the-century university. Thomas Woody, *A History of Women's Education in the United States,* 2 vols. (New York, 1929; repr. 1966), contains much information and is the only general work on this important subject.

[*See also* ANTEBELLUM REFORM; FEDERALISM; LOCAL GOVERNMENT; PLURALISM; PROGRESSIVISM; *and* RACE AND RACISM.]